RoadMaster™
TRAVEL PLANNER

NEW & UPDATED

New England

Connecticut / Maine / Massachusetts / New Hampshire / Rhode Island / Vermont
Eastern Canada (New Brunswick / Nova Scotia / Ontario / Prince Edward Island / Quebec)

BARNES
&NOBLE
BOOKS

ACKNOWLEDGMENTS

We gratefully acknowledge the help of our representatives for their efficient and perceptive inspection of the lodging and dining establishments listed; the establishments' proprietors for their cooperation in showing their facilities and providing information about them; the many users of previous editions of these guides who have taken the time to share their experiences; and for their time and information, the thousands of chambers of commerce, convention and visitors bureaus, city, state, and provincial tourism offices, and government agencies who assisted in our research.

A BARNES & NOBLE BOOK

RRD-C

CONTENTS

Maps

Introduction

New England/Eastern Canada

MAP SYMBOLS

═══ Free limited-access highway	🛡90 🛡190 🛡80/90 Interstate highway	▓▓ Urbanized area in state maps; in city maps
--- New — under construction	🛡ALT/17 🛡183 🛡18 U.S. highway	▓▓ Separate cities within metro area
═══ Toll limited-access highway		⊕ ⊛ National capital; state capital; cities; towns
--- New — under construction	⑧ ⑱ 🛡14/83 State or provincial highway	● ○ ○ (size of type indicates relative population)
═══ Other multilane highway	④ 🛡43 🛡147 Other highway	▬▬ U.S. or Canadian National Park
—— Principal highway	Miles between arrows	▬▬ State/Provincial Park or Recreation Area
—— Other through highway	⊢—9—⊣ One mile or less not shown	National Forest or Grassland, city park
—— Other road	2 10 Interchanges and interchange	▪ ▭ Point of interest
···· Unpaved road	⊢—▭—□—⊣ numbers	▣ ▭ Hospital, medical center
------ Ferry	------ Time zone boundary	········ Continental divide

© 2003 Rand McNally & Company

Cities and Towns

Connecticut

Ansonia	H-3
Avon	F-4
Beacon Falls	H-3
Bethel	H-2
Bloomfield	F-4
Bridgeport	I-2
Bristol	G-3
Brooklyn	F-6
Canaan	E-2
Clinton	H-5
Colchester	G-5
Cromwell	G-4
Danbury	H-2
Danielson	F-7
Deep River	H-5
Derby	H-3
East Hartford	F-4
East Haven	H-3
Enfield	E-4
Fairfield	I-2
Farmington	F-4
Georgetown	H-2
Goshen	E-3
Granby	E-4
Greenwich	I-1
Groton	H-6
Guilford	H-4
Hamden	H-3
Hartford	F-4
Litchfield	F-3
Manchester	F-5
Marlborough	G-5
Meriden	G-4
Middlebury	G-3
Middletown	G-4
Milford	H-3
Moodus	G-5
Moosup	F-7
Mystic	H-6
Naugatuck	G-3
New Britain	G-4
New Canaan	I-1
New Fairfield	H-3
New Hartford	F-3
New Haven	H-3
New London	H-6
New Milford	G-2
New Preston	G-2
Newington	F-4
Northford	H-4
Norwalk	I-2
Norwich	G-6
Old Lyme	H-5
Old Saybrook	H-5
Pawcatuck	G-7
Plainfield	G-6
Plainville	G-3
Portland	G-4
Putnam	F-7
Ridgefield	H-1
Salisbury	E-2
Sandy Hook	H-2
Seymour	H-3
Shelton	H-3
Simsbury	E-4
Somers	E-5
South Windsor	F-4
Southbury	G-2
Southington	G-3
Stafford Springs	E-5
Stamford	I-1
Storrs	F-6
Stratford	I-3
Terryville	G-3
Thomaston	G-3
Torrington	F-3
Trumbull	H-2
Unionville	F-3
Vernon	F-5
Wallingford	G-4
Waterbury	G-3
Watertown	G-3
West Hartford	F-4
West Haven	H-3
Wethersfield	F-4
Willimantic	F-5
Wilton	I-2
Windsor	E-4
Windsor Locks	E-4
Winsted	E-3

Massachusetts

Adams	C-3
Agawam	E-4
Amesbury	B-9
Amherst	D-5
Andover	B-8
Athol	C-5
Attleboro	E-8
Auburn	D-7
Ayer	C-7
Barnstable	F-11
Bedford	C-8
Beverly	C-9
Billerica	C-8
Boston	D-9
Braintree	D-9
Brewster	F-12
Bridgewater	E-9
Brockton	D-9
Brookline	D-9
Buzzards Bay	F-10
Cambridge	D-9
Chatham	F-12
Chicopee	E-4
Clinton	C-7
Cohasset	D-10
Concord	C-8
Dalton	C-3
Danvers	C-9
Dedham	D-8
Deerfield	C-4
Duxbury	E-10
East Falmouth	G-10
East Longmeadow	E-5
East Pepperell	B-7
Eastham	F-12
Easthampton	D-4
Edgartown	H-11
Everett	C-9
Fairhaven	G-9
Fall River	F-8

Falmouth	G-10
Fitchburg	C-7
Foxboro	E-8
Framingham	D-8
Gardner	C-6
Gloucester	C-10
Grafton	D-7
Great Barrington	D-2
Greenfield	C-4
Harwich Port	G-12
Haverhill	B-9
Hingham	D-9
Holliston	D-8
Holyoke	D-4
Housatonic	D-2
Hudson	D-7
Hyannis	G-11
Ipswich	B-9
Lawrence	B-8
Lenox	D-2
Leominster	C-7
Lexington	C-8
Longmeadow	E-4
Lowell	C-8
Ludlow	D-5
Lynn	C-9
Lynnfield	C-9
Mansfield	E-8
Marblehead	C-9
Marion	F-10
Marlborough	D-7
Marshfield	E-10
Mattapoisett	G-10
Maynard	C-8
Methuen	B-8
Middleboro	E-9
Middleton	C-9
Milford	E-8
Nantucket	H-12
Natick	D-8
New Bedford	G-9
Newburyport	B-9
Newton	D-8
North Adams	B-3
North Andover	B-8
North Attleborough	E-8
Northampton	D-4
Northfield	B-5
Norwood	D-8
Oak Bluffs	G-10
Orange	C-5
Oxford	E-7
Palmer	E-5
Peabody	C-9
Petersham	C-5
Pittsfield	C-2
Plymouth	E-10
Princeton	C-7
Provincetown	E-12
Quincy	D-9
Randolph	D-9
Revere	C-9
Rockland	E-9
Rockport	B-10
Rutland	D-6
Salem	C-9
Salisbury	B-9
Sandwich	F-11
Saugus	C-9
Sharon	D-8
Shelburne Falls	C-4
Shrewsbury	D-7
Smith Mills	G-9
Somerset	F-9
South Hadley	D-4
South Yarmouth	G-12
Southbridge	E-6
Spencer	D-6
Springfield	E-4
Stoneham	C-9
Stoughton	D-9
Sturbridge	E-6
Sudbury Center	D-8
Swampscott	C-9
Taunton	F-9
Townsend	B-7
Truro	E-12
Uxbridge	E-7
Vineyard Haven	G-10
Wakefield	C-9
Walpole	D-8
Waltham	D-8
Ware	D-5
Wareham	F-10
Webster	E-7
Wellesley	D-8
Wellfleet	E-12
West Boylston	C-7
West Bridgewater	E-9
West Brookfield	D-6
West Springfield	E-4
Westfield	E-4
Westminster	C-6
Weymouth	D-9
Whitman	E-9
Wilmington	C-8
Winchendon	B-6
Woburn	C-9
Woods Hole	G-10
Worcester	D-7
Wrentham	E-8

Rhode Island

Anthony	F-7
Bristol	G-8
Central Falls	F-8
Cranston	F-8
East Greenwich	G-8
East Providence	G-8
Jamestown	G-8
Kingston	G-8
Middletown	H-8
Narragansett	H-8
Newport	G-8
North Kingstown	G-8
Pawtucket	F-8
Portsmouth	G-8
Providence	F-8
Slatersville	E-7
Tiverton	G-8
Wakefield	H-8
Warwick	F-8
West Warwick	F-8
Westerly	H-7
Woonsocket	E-8

Cities and Towns
Maine

03–1

© 2003 Rand McNally & Company

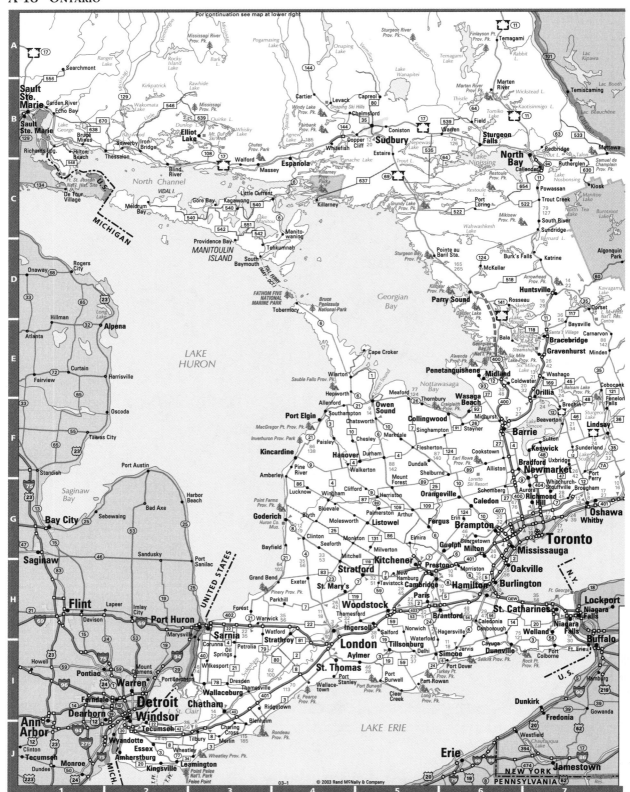

For continuation see map at lower right

© 2003 Rand McNally & Company

03-1

Cities and Towns

© 2003 Rand McNally

Cape Cod, MA

Montpelier / Barre, VT

Burlington, VT

How to Use This Book

The *RoadMaster™ Travel Planners* are designed for ease of use. Each state has its own chapter. The chapter begins with a general introduction, which provides both a general geographical and historical orientation to the state; it also covers basic statewide tourist information, from state recreation areas to seatbelt laws. The remainder of each chapter is devoted to the travel destinations within the state—cities and towns, state and national parks, and tourist areas—which, like the states, are arranged alphabetically.

The following is an explanation of the wealth of information you'll find regarding those travel destinations—information on the area, on things to see and do there, and on where to stay and eat.

Maps and Map Coordinates

Next to some destinations are a set of map coordinates. These are referenced to the appropriate state map in the front of this book. In addition, we have provided maps of selected larger cities.

Destination Information

Because many travel destinations are close to other cities and towns where visitors might find additional attractions, accommodations, and restaurants, cross-references to those places are included whenever possible. Also listed are addresses and phone numbers for travel information resources—usually the local chamber of commerce or office of tourism—as well as pertinent vital statistics and a brief introduction to the area.

What to See and Do

Almost 20,000 museums, art galleries, amusement parks, universities, historic sites and houses, plantations, churches, state parks, ski areas, and other attractions are described in the *RoadMaster™ Travel Planners*. A white star on a black background ✪ signals that the attraction is one of the best in the state. Because municipal parks, public tennis courts, swimming pools, and small educational institutions are common to most towns, they are generally not represented within the city.

Following the attraction's description, you'll find the months and days it's open, address/location and phone number, and admission costs (see the inside front cover for an explanation of the cost symbols). Note that directions are given from the center of the town under which the attraction is listed, which may not necessarily be the town in which the attraction is located. Zip codes are listed only if they differ from those given for the town.

Driving and Walking Tours

The driving tours are usually day trips—though they can be longer—that make for interesting side trips. This is a way to get off the beaten track and visit an area often overlooked. These trips frequently cover areas of natural beauty or historical significance. The walking tours focus on a particularly interesting area of a city or town. Again, these can be a break from more everyday tourist attractions. The tours often include places to stop for a meal or snack.

Special Events

Special events can either be annual events that last only a short time, such as festivals and fairs, or longer, seasonal events such as horse racing, summer theater and concerts, and professional sports. Special event listings might also include an infrequently occurring occasion that marks a certain date or event, such as a centennial or other commemorative celebration.

Major Cities

Additional information on airports and ground transportation, and suburbs may be included for large cities.

Lodging and Restaurant Listings

ORGANIZATION

For both lodgings and restaurants, when a property is in a town that does not have its own heading, the listing appears under the town nearest its location with the address and town immediately after the establishment name. In large cities, lodgings located within five miles of major commercial airports are listed under a separate "Airport" heading, following the city listings.

LODGING CLASSIFICATIONS

Each property is classified by type according to the characteristics below. Because the following features and services are found at most motels and hotels, they are not shown in those listings:

- Year-round operation with a single rate structure unless otherwise quoted
- European plan (meals not included in room rate)
- Bathroom with tub and/or shower in each room
- Air-conditioned/heated, often with individual room control
- Cots
- Daily maid service
- In-room phones
- Elevators

Motels/Motor Lodges. Accommodations are in low-rise structures with rooms easily accessible to parking (which is usually free). Properties have outdoor room entry and small, functional lobbies. Service is often limited, and dining may not be offered in lower-rated motels and lodges. Shops and businesses are found only in higher-rated properties, as are bellhops, room service, and restaurants serving three meals daily.

Hotels. To be categorized as a hotel, an establishment must have most of the following facilities and services: multiple floors, a restaurant and/or coffee shop, elevators, room service, bellhops, a spacious lobby, and recreational facilities. In addition, the following features and services not shown in listings are also found:

- Valet service (one-day laundry/cleaning service)
- Room service during hours restaurant is open
- Bellhops
- Some oversize beds

Resorts. These specialize in stays of three days or more and usually offer American plan and/or housekeeping accommodations. Their emphasis is on recreational facilities, and a social director is often available. Food services are of primary importance, and guests must be able to eat three meals a day on the premises, either in restaurants or by having access to an on-site grocery store and preparing their own meals.

All Suites. All Suites' guest rooms consist of two rooms, one bedroom and one living room. Higher rated properties offer facilities and services comparable to regular hotels.

B&Bs/Small Inns. Frequently thought of as a small hotel, a bed-and-breakfast or an inn is a place of homelike comfort and warm hospitality. It is often a structure of historic significance, with an equally interesting setting. Meals are a special occasion, and refreshments are frequently served in late afternoon. Rooms are usually individually decorated, often with antiques or furnishings representative of the locale. Phones, bathrooms, or TVs may not be available in every room.

Guest Ranches. Like resorts, guest ranches specialize in stays of three days or more. Guest ranches also offer meal plans and extensive outdoor activities. Horseback riding is usually a feature; there are stables and trails on the ranch property, and trail rides and daily instruction are part of the program. Many guest ranches are working ranches, ranging from casual to rustic, and guests are encouraged to participate in ranch life. Eating is often family style and may also include cookouts. Western saddles are assumed; phone ahead to inquire about English saddle availability.

Extended Stay. These hotels specialize in stays of three days or more and usually offer weekly room rates. Service is often limited and dining might not be offered at lower-rated extended-stay hotels.

Villas/Condos. Similar to Cottage Colonies, these establishments are usually found in recreational areas. They are often separate houses, often luxuriously furnished, and rarely offer restaurants and only a small variety of services on the premises.

Conference Centers. Conference Centers are hotels with extended meeting space facilities designed to house multiday conferences and seminars. Amenities are often geared toward groups staying for longer than one night and often include restaurants and fitness facilities. Larger Conference Center Hotels are often referred to as Convention Center Hotels.

Casinos. Casino Hotels incorporate areas that offer games of chance like Blackjack, Poker, Slot machines, etc., and are only found in states that legalize gambling. Casino Hotels offer a wide range of services and amenities, comparable to regular hotels.

Cottage Colonies. These are housekeeping cottages and cabins that are usually found in recreational areas. Any dining or recreational facilities are noted in our listing.

DINING CLASSIFICATIONS

Restaurants. Most dining establishments fall into this category. All have a full kitchen and offer table service and a complete menu. Parking on or near the premises, in a lot or garage, is assumed. When a property offers valet or other special parking features, or when only street parking is available, it is noted in the listing.

Unrated Dining Spots. These places, listed after Restaurants in many cities, are chosen for their unique atmosphere, specialized menu, or local flavor. They include delis, ice-cream parlors, cafeterias, tearooms, and pizzerias. Because they may not have a full kitchen or table service, they are not given a *RoadMaster™ Travel Planners* rating. Often they offer extraordinary value and quick service.

QUALITY RATINGS

All listed establishments were inspected by experienced field representatives or evaluated by a senior staff member. Ratings are based upon their detailed inspection reports of the individual properties, on written evaluations of staff members who stay and dine anonymously, and on an extensive review of comments from our readers.

You'll find a key to the rating categories, ★ through ★★★★★, on the inside front cover. All establishments in the book are recommended. Even a ★ clean, convenient, limited service, usually providing a basic, informal experience. Rating categories reflect both the features the property offers and its quality in relation to similar establishments.

For example, lodging ratings take into account the number and quality of facilities and services, the luxury of appointments, and the attitude and professionalism of staff and management. A ★ establishment provides a comfortable night's lodging. A ★★ property offers more than a facility that rates one star, and the decor is well planned and integrated. Establishments that rate ★★★ are well-appointed, with full services and amenities; the lodging experience is truly excellent, and the range of facilities is extensive. Properties that have been given ★★★★ not only offer many services but also have their own style and personality; they are luxurious, creatively decorated, and superbly maintained. The ★★★★★ properties are among the best in North America, superb in every respect and entirely memorable, year in and year out.

Restaurant evaluations reflect the quality of the food and the ingredients, preparation, presentation, service levels, as well as the property's decor and ambience. A restaurant that has fairly simple goals for menu and decor but that achieves those goals superbly might receive the same number of stars as a restaurant with somewhat loftier ambitions, but the execution of which falls short of the mark. In general, ★ indicates a restaurant that's a good choice in its area, usually fairly simple and perhaps catering to a clientele of locals and families; ★★ denotes restaurants that are more highly recommended in their area; ★★★ restaurants are of national caliber, with professional and attentive service and a skilled chef in the kitchen; ★★★★ reflect superb dining choices, where remarkable food is served in equally remarkable surroundings; and ★★★★★ represent that rare group of the best restaurants in the country, where in addition to near perfection in every detail, there's that special something extra that makes for an unforgettable dining experience.

A list of the four-star and five-star establishments in each region is located just before the state listings.

Each rating is reviewed annually and each establishment must work to maintain its rating (or improve it). Every effort is made to assure that ratings are fair and accurate; the designated ratings are published purely as an aid to travelers. In general, properties that are very new or have recently undergone major management changes are considered difficult to assess fairly and are often listed without ratings.

LODGINGS

Each listing gives the name, address, phone number (local and 800), fax number, number and type of rooms available, room rates, and seasons open (if not year-round). Also included are details on recreational and dining facilities on the property or nearby, the presence of a luxury level, and credit card information. A key to the symbols at the end of each listing is on the inside front cover.

All prices quoted in the *RoadMaster™ Travel Planners* publications are expected to be in effect at the time of publication and during the entire year; however, prices cannot be guaranteed. In some localities there may be short-term price variations because of special events or holidays. Whenever possible, these price charges are noted. Certain resorts have complicated rate structures that vary with the time of year; always confirm listed rates when you make your plans.

RESTAURANTS

Each listing gives the name, address, phone number, hours and days of operation (if not open daily year-round), reservation policy, cuisine (if other than American), price range for each meal served, children's menu (if offered), specialties, and credit card information. In addition, special features such as chef ownership, ambience, and entertainment are noted. By carefully reading the detailed restaurant information and comparing prices, you can easily determine whether the restaurant is formal and elegant or informal and comfortable for families.

TERMS AND ABBREVIATIONS IN LISTINGS

The following terms and abbreviations are used throughout the listings:

A la carte entrees With a price, refers to the cost of entrees/main dishes that are not accompanied by side dishes.

AP American plan (lodging plus all meals).

Bar Liquor, wine, and beer are served in a bar or cocktail lounge and usually with meals unless otherwise indicated (e.g., "wine, beer").

Business center The property has a designated area accessible to all guests with business services.

Business servs avail The property can perform/arrange at least two of the following services for a guest: audiovisual equipment rental, binding, computer rental, faxing, messenger services, modem availability, notary service, obtaining office supplies, photocopying, shipping, and typing.

Cable Standard cable service; "premium" indicates that HBO, Disney, Showtime, or similar cable services are available.

Ck-in, ck-out Check-in time, check-out time.

Coin lndry Self-service laundry.

Complete meal Soup and/or salad, entree, and dessert, plus nonalcoholic beverage.

Continental bkfst Usually coffee and a roll or doughnut.

Cr cds: A, American Express; C, Carte Blanche; D, Diners Club; DS, Discover; ER, enRoute; JCB, Japanese Credit Bureau; MC, MasterCard; V, Visa.

D Followed by a price, indicates room rate for a "double"—two people in one room in one or two beds (the charge may be higher for two double beds).

Downhill/X-country ski Downhill and/or cross-country skiing within 20 miles of property.

Each addl Extra charge for each additional person beyond the stated number of persons at a reduced price.

Early-bird dinner A meal served at specified hours, typically around 4:30-6:30 pm.

Exc Except.

Exercise equipt Two or more pieces of exercise equipment on the premises.

Exercise rm Both exercise equipment and room, with an instructor on the premises.

Fax Facsimile machines available to all guests.

Golf privileges Privileges at a course within ten miles.

Hols Holidays.

In-rm modem link Every guest room has a connection for a modem that's separate from the phone line.

Kit. or **Kits.** A kitchen or kitchenette that contains stove or microwave, sink, and refrigerator and that is either part of the room or a separate room. If the kitchen is not fully equipped, the listing will indicate "no equipt" or "some equipt."

Luxury level A special section of a lodging, covering at least an entire floor, that offers increased luxury accommodations. Management must provide no less than three of these four services: separate check-in and check-out, concierge, private lounge, and private elevator service (key access). Complimentary breakfast and snacks are commonly offered.

MAP Modified American plan (lodging plus two meals).

Movies Prerecorded videos are available for rental.

No cr cds accepted No credit cards are accepted.

No elvtr In hotels with more than two stories, it's assumed there are elevators; only their absence is noted.

No phones Phones, too, are assumed; only their absence is noted.

Parking There is a parking lot on the premises.

Private club A cocktail lounge or bar available to members and their guests. In motels and hotels where these clubs exist, registered guests can usually use the club as guests of the management; the same is frequently true of restaurants.

Prix fixe A full meal for a stated price; usually one price is quoted.

Res Reservations.

S Followed by a price, indicates room rate for a "single," i.e., one person.

Serv bar A service bar, where drinks are prepared for dining patrons only.

Serv charge Service charge is the amount added to the restaurant check in lieu of a tip.

Table d'hôte A full meal for a stated price, dependent upon entree selection; no a la carte options are available.

Tennis privileges Privileges at tennis courts within five miles.

TV Indicates color television.

Under certain age free Children under that age are not charged if staying in room with a parent.

Valet parking An attendant is available to park and retrieve a car.

VCR VCRs in all guest rooms.

VCR avail VCRs are available for hookup in guest rooms.

Special Information for Travelers with Disabilities

The *RoadMaster™ Travel Planners* [D] symbol shown in accommodation and restaurant listings indicates establishments that are at least partially accessible to people with mobility problems.

The *RoadMaster™ Travel Planners* criteria for accessibility are unique to our publication. Please do not confuse them with the universal symbol for wheelchair accessibility. When the [D] symbol appears following a listing, the establishment is equipped with facilities to accommodate people using wheelchairs or crutches or otherwise needing easy access to doorways and rest rooms. Travelers with severe mobility problems or with hearing or visual impairments may or may not find facilities they need. Always phone ahead to make sure that an establishment can meet your needs.

All lodgings bearing our [D] symbol have the following facilities:

- ISA-designated parking near access ramps
- Level or ramped entryways to building
- Swinging building entryway doors minimum 39"
- Public rest rooms on main level with space to operate a wheelchair; handrails at commode areas
- Elevators equipped with grab bars and lowered control buttons

- Restaurants with accessible doorways; rest rooms with space to operate wheelchair; handrails at commode areas
- Minimum 39" width entryway to guest rooms
- Low-pile carpet in rooms
- Telephone at bedside and in bathroom
- Bed placed at wheelchair height
- Minimum 39" width doorway to bathroom
- Bath with open sink—no cabinet; room to operate wheelchair
- Handrails at commode areas; tub handrails
- Wheelchair-accessible peephole in room entry door
- Wheelchair-accessible closet rods and shelves

All restaurants bearing our D symbol offer the following facilities:

- ISA-designated parking beside access ramps
- Level or ramped front entryways to building
- Tables to accommodate wheelchairs
- Main-floor rest rooms; minimum 39" width entryway
- Rest rooms with space to operate wheelchair; handrails at commode areas

In general, the newest properties are apt to impose the fewest barriers.

To get the kind of service you need and have a right to expect, do not hesitate when making a reservation to question the management in detail about the availability of accessible rooms, parking, entrances, restaurants, lounges, or any other facilities that are important to you, and confirm what is meant by "accessible." Some guests with mobility impairments report that lodging establishments' housekeeping and maintenance departments are most helpful in describing barriers. Also inquire about any special equipment, transportation, or services you may need.

MAKING THE MOST OF YOUR TRIP

A few hardy souls might look with fondness upon the trip where the car broke down and they were stranded for a week. Or maybe even the vacation that cost twice what it was supposed to. For most travelers, though, the best trips are those that are safe, smooth, and within their budget. To help you make your trip the best it can be, we've assembled a few tips and resources.

Saving Money

ON LODGING

After you've seen the published rates, it's time to look for discounts. Many hotels and motels offer them—for senior citizens, business travelers, families, you name it. It never hurts to ask—politely, that is. Sometimes, especially in late afternoon, desk clerks are instructed to fill beds, and you might be offered a lower rate, or a nicer room, to entice you to stay. Look for bargains on stays over multiple nights, in the off-season, and on weekdays or weekends (depending on location). Many hotels in major metropolitan areas, for example, have special weekend package plans that offer considerable savings on rooms; they may include breakfast, cocktails, and meal discounts. Prices can change frequently throughout the year, so phone ahead.

Another way to save money is to choose accommodations that give you more than just a standard room. Rooms with kitchen facilities enable you to cook some meals for yourself, reducing restaurant costs. A suite might save money for two couples traveling together. Even hotel luxury levels can provide good value, as many include breakfast or cocktails in the price of the room.

State and city sales taxes, as well as special room taxes, can increase your room rates as much as 25 percent per day. We are unable to include this specific information in the listings, but we strongly urge that you ask about these taxes when placing reservations to understand the total cost of your lodgings.

Watch out for telephone-usage charges that hotels frequently impose on long-distance calls, credit-card calls, and other phone calls—even those that go unanswered. Before phoning from your room, read the information given to you at check-in, and then be sure to read your bill carefully before checking out. You won't be expected to pay for charges that they did not spell out. (On the other hand, it's not unusual for a hotel to bill you for your calls after you return home.) Consider using your cell phone; or, if public telephones are available in the hotel lobby, your cost savings may outweigh the inconvenience.

ON DINING

There are several ways to get a less expensive meal at a more expensive restaurant. Early-bird dinners are popular in many parts of the country and offer considerable savings. If you're interested in sampling a 4- or 5-star establishment, consider going at lunchtime. While the prices then are probably relatively high, they may be half of those at dinner and come with the same ambience, service, and cuisine.

ON PARK PASSES

Although many national parks, monuments, seashores, historic sites, and recreation areas may be used free of charge, others charge an entrance fee (ranging from $1 to $6 per person to $5 to $15 per carload) and/or a "use fee" for special services and facilities. If you plan to make several visits to federal recreation areas, consider one of the following National Park Service money-saving programs:

Park Pass. This is an annual entrance permit to a specific unit in the National Park Service system that normally charges an entrance fee. The pass admits the permit holder and any accompanying passengers in a private noncommercial vehicle or, in the case of walk-in facilities, the holder's spouse, children, and parents. It is valid for entrance fees only. A Park Pass may be purchased in person or by mail from the National Park Service unit at which the pass will be honored. The cost is $15 to $20, depending upon the area.

Golden Eagle Passport. This pass, available to people who are between 17 and 61, entitles the purchaser and accompanying passengers in a private noncommercial vehicle to enter any outdoor National Park Service unit that charges an entrance fee and admits the purchaser and family to most walk-in fee-charging areas. Like the Park Pass, it is good for one year and does not cover use fees. It may be purchased from the National Park Service, Office of Public Inquiries, Room 1013, US Department of the Interior, 18th and C sts NW, Washington, D.C. 20240, phone 202/208-4747; at any of the ten regional offices throughout the country; and at any National Park Service area that charges a fee. The cost is $50.

Golden Age Passport. Available to citizens and permanent residents of the United States 62 years or older, this is a lifetime entrance permit to fee-charging recreation areas. The fee exemption extends to those accompanying the permit holder in a private noncommercial vehicle or, in the case of walk-in facilities, to the holder's spouse and children. The passport also entitles the holder to a 50 percent discount on use fees charged in park areas but not to fees charged by concessionaires. Golden Age Passports must be obtained in person. The applicant must show proof of age, i.e., a driver's license, birth certificate, or signed affidavit attesting to age (Medicare cards are not acceptable proof). These passports are available at most park service units where they're used, at National Park Service headquarters (see above), at park system regional offices, at National Forest Supervisors' offices, and at most Ranger Station offices. The cost is $10.

Golden Access Passport. Issued to citizens and permanent residents of the United States who are physically disabled or visually impaired, this passport is a free lifetime entrance permit to fee-charging recreation areas. The fee exemption extends to those accompanying the permit holder in a private noncommercial vehicle or, in the case of walk-in facilities, to the holder's spouse and children. The passport also entitles the holder to a 50 percent discount on use fees charged in park areas but not to fees charged by concessionaires. Golden Access Passports must be obtained in person. Proof of eligibility to receive federal benefits is required (under programs such as Disability Retirement, Compensation for Military Service-Connected Disability, Coal Mine Safety and Health Act, etc.), or an affidavit must be signed attesting to eligibility. These passports are available at the same outlets as Golden Age Passports.

FOR SENIOR CITIZENS

Look for the senior-citizen discount symbol in the lodging and restaurant listings. Always call ahead to confirm that the discount is being offered, and be sure to carry proof of age. At places not listed in the book, it never hurts to ask if a senior-citizen discount is offered. Additional information for mature travelers is available from the American Association of Retired Persons (AARP), 601 E St NW, Washington, D.C. 20049, phone 202/434-2277.

Tipping

Tipping is an expression of appreciation for good service, and often service workers rely on tips as a significant part of their income. However, you never need to tip if service is poor.

IN HOTELS

Door attendants in major city hotels are usually given $1 for getting you a cab. Bellhops expect $1 per bag, usually $2 if you have only one bag. Concierges are tipped according to the service they perform. It's not mandatory to tip when you've asked for suggestions on sightseeing or restaurants or help in making reservations for dining. However, when a concierge books you a table at a restaurant known to be difficult to get into, a gratuity of $5 is appropriate. For obtaining theater or sporting event tickets, $5-$10 is expected. Maids, often overlooked by guests, may be tipped $1-$2 per days of stay.

AT RESTAURANTS

Coffee shop and counter service waitstaff are usually given 8 percent–10 percent of the bill. In full-service restaurants, tip 15 percent of the bill, before sales tax. In fine restaurants, where the staff is large and shares the gratuity, 18 percent–20 percent for the waiter is appropriate. In most cases, tip the maitre d' only if service has been extraordinary and only on the way out; $20 is the minimum in upscale properties in major metropolitan areas. If there is a wine steward, tip him or her at least $6 a bottle, more if the wine was decanted or if the bottle was very expensive. If your bus person has been unusually attentive, $2 pressed into his hand on departure is a nice gesture. An increasing number of restaurants automatically add a service charge to the bill instead of a gratuity. Before tipping, carefully review your check. If you are in doubt, ask your server.

AT AIRPORTS

Curbside luggage handlers expect $1 per bag. Car-rental shuttle drivers who help with your luggage appreciate a $1 or $2 tip.

Staying Safe

The best way to deal with emergencies is to be prepared enough to avoid them. However, unforeseen situations do happen, and you can prepare for them.

IN YOUR CAR

Before your trip, make sure your car has been serviced and is in good working order. Change the oil, check the battery and belts, and make sure tires are inflated properly (this can also improve gas mileage). Other inspections recommended by the car's manufacturer should be made, too.

Next, be sure you have the tools and equipment to deal with a routine breakdown: jack, spare tire, lug wrench, repair kit, emergency tools, jumper cables, spare fan belt, auto fuses, flares and/or reflectors, flashlights, first-aid kit, and, in winter, windshield wiper fluid, a windshield scraper, and snow shovel.

Bring all appropriate and up-to-date documentation—licenses, registration, and insurance cards—and know what's covered by your insurance. Also bring an extra set of keys, just in case.

En route, always buckle up! In most states it is required by law.

If your car does break down, get out of traffic as soon as possible—pull well off the road. Raise the hood and turn on your emergency flashers or tie a white cloth to the roadside door handle or antenna. Stay near your car. Use flares or reflectors to keep your car from being hit.

IN YOUR LODGING

Chances are slim that you will encounter a hotel or motel fire. The 🔥 in a listing indicates that there were smoke detectors and/or sprinkler systems in the rooms we inspected. Once you've checked in, make sure that any smoke detector in your room is working properly. Ascertain the locations of fire extinguishers and at least two fire exits. Never use an elevator in a fire.

For personal security, use the peephole in your room's door.

PROTECTING AGAINST THEFT

To guard against theft wherever you go, don't bring anything of more value than you need. If you do bring valuables, leave them at your hotel rather than in your car, and if you have something very expensive, lock it in a safe. Many hotels have one in each room; others will store your valuables in the hotel's safe. And of course, don't carry more money than you need; use traveler's checks and credit cards, or visit cash machines.

For Travelers with Disabilities

A number of publications can provide assistance. The most complete listing of published material for travelers with disabilities is available from The Disability Bookshop, Twin Peaks Press, Box 129, Vancouver, WA 98666, phone 360/694-2462.

The Reference Section of the National Library Service for the Blind and Physically Handicapped (Library of Congress, Washington, D.C. 20542, phone 202/707-9276 or 202/707-5100) provides information and resources for persons with mobility problems and hearing and vision impairments, as well as information about the NILS talking program (or visit your local library).

IMPORTANT TOLL-FREE NUMBERS AND ONLINE INFORMATION

Hotels and Motels

Adams Mark   800-444-2326
www.adamsmark.com
Amerisuites   800-833-1516
www.amerisuites.com
AMFA Parks & Resorts   800-236-7916
www.amfac.com
Baymont Inns   800-229-6668
www.baymontinns.com
Best Western   800-780-7234
www.bestwestern.com
Budget Host Inn   800-283-4678
www.budgethost.com
Candlewood Suites   888-226-3539
www.candlewoodsuites.com
Clarion Hotels   800-252-7466
www.choicehotels.com
Clubhouse Inns   800-258-2466
www.clubhouseinn.com
Coast Hotels & Resorts   800-663-1144
www.coasthotels.com
Comfort Inns   800-252-7466
www.choicehotels.com
Concorde Hotels   800-888-4747
www.concorde-hotel.com
Country Hearth Inns   800-848-5767
www.countryhearth.com
Country Inns   800-456-4000
www.countryinns.com
Courtyard by Marriott   888-236-2437
www.courtyard.com
Crown Plaza Hotels   800-227-6963
www.crowneplaza.com
Days Inn   800-544-8313
www.daysinn.com
Delta Hotels   800-268-1133
www.deltahotels.com
Destination Hotels & Resorts   800-434-7347
www.destinationhotels.com
Doubletree   800-222-8733
www.doubletree.com
Drury Inns   800-378-7946
www.druryinn.com
Econolodge   800-553-2666
www.econolodge.com
Embassy Suites   800-362-2779
www.embassysuites.com
Fairfield Inns   800-228-2800
www.fairfieldinn.com
Fairmont Hotels   800-441-1414
www.fairmont.com
Family Inns of America   800-251-9752
www.familyinnsofamerica.com

Forte Hotels   800-300-9147
www.fortehotels.com
Four Points by Sheraton   888-625-5144
www.starwood.com
Four Seasons   800-545-4000
www.fourseasons.com
Hampton Inns   800-426-7866
www.hamptoninn.com
Hilton   800-774-1500
www.hilton.com
Holiday Inn   800-465-4329
www.holiday-inn.com
Homestead Studio Suites   888-782-9473
www.stayhsd.com
Homewood Suites   800-225-5466
www.homewoodsuites.com
Howard Johnson   800-406-1411
www.hojo.com
Hyatt   800-633-7313
www.hyatt.com
Inn Suites Hotels & Suites   800-842-4242
www.innsuites.com
Inter-Continental   888-567-8725
www.interconti.com
Jameson Inns   800-526-3766
www.jamesoninns.com
Kempinski Hotels   800-426-3135
www.kempinski.com
Kimpton Hotels   888-546-7866
www.kimptongroup.com
La Quinta   800-531-5900
www.laquinta.com
Leading Hotels of the World   800-223-6800
www.lhw.com
Loews Hotels   800-235-6397
www.loewshotels.com
Mainstay Suites   800-660-6246
www.choicehotels.com
Mandarin Oriental   800-526-6566
www.mandarin-oriental.com
Marriott   888-236-2427
www.marriott.com
Nikko Hotels   800-645-5687
www.nikkohotels.com
Omni Hotels   800-843-6664
www.omnihotels.com
Preferred Hotels & Resorts   800-323-7500
Worldwide
www.preferredhotels.com
Quality Inn   800-228-5151
www.qualityinn.com
Radisson Hotels   800-333-3333
www.radisson.com

Ramada	888-298-2054
www.ramada.com	
Red Lion Inns	800-733-5466
www.redlion.com	
Red Roof Inns	800-733-7663
www.redroof.com	
Regal Hotels	800-222-8888
www.regal-hotels.com	
Regent International	800-545-4000
www.regenthotels.com	
Renaissance Hotels	888-236-2427
www.renaissancehotels.com	
Residence Inns	888-236-2427
www.residenceinn.com	
Ritz Carlton	800-241-3333
www.ritzcarlton.com	
Rodeway Inns	800-228-2000
www.rodeway.com	
Rosewood Hotels & Resorts	888-767-3966
www.rosewood-hotels.com	
Sheraton	888-625-5144
www.sheraton.com	
Shilo Inns	800-222-2244
www.shiloinns.com	
Shoney's Inns	800-552-4667
www.shoneysinn.com	
Sleep Inns	800-453-3746
www.sleepinn.com	
Small Luxury Hotels	800-525-4800
www.slh.com	
Sofitel	800-763-4835
www.sofitel.com	
Sonesta Hotels & Resorts	800-766-3782
www.sonesta.com	
SRS Worldhotels	800-223-5652
www.srs-worldhotels.com	
Summerfield Suites	800-833-4353
www.summerfieldsuites.com	
Summit International	800-457-4000
www.summithotels.com	
Swissotel	800-637-9477
www.swissotel.com	
The Peninsula Group	
www.peninsula.com	
Travelodge	800-578-7878
www.travelodge.com	
Westin Hotels & Resorts	800-937-8461
www.westin.com	
Wingate Inns	800-228-1000
www.wingateinns.com	
Woodfin Suite Hotels	800-966-3346
www.woodfinsuitehotels.com	
Wyndham Hotels & Resorts	800-996-3426
www.wyndham.com	

Airlines

Air Canada	888-247-2262
www.aircanada.ca	
Alaska	800-252-7522
www.alaska-air.com	
American	800-433-7300
www.aa.com	
America West	800-235-9292
www.americawest.com	
British Airways	800-247-9297
www.british-airways.com	
Continental	800-523-3273
www.flycontinental.com	
Delta	800-221-1212
www.delta-air.com	
Island Air	800-323-3345
www.islandair.com	
Mesa	800-637-2247
www.mesa-air.com	
Northwest	800-225-2525
www.nwa.com	
Southwest	800-435-9792
www.southwest.com	
United	800-241-6522
www.ual.com	
US Air	800-428-4322
www.usair.com	

Car Rentals

Advantage	800-777-5500
www.arac.com	
Alamo	800-327-9633
www.goalamo.com	
Allstate	800-634-6186
www.bnm.com/as.htm	
Avis	800-831-2847
www.avis.com	
Budget	800-527-0700
www.budgetrentacar.com	
Dollar	800-800-4000
www.dollarcar.com	
Enterprise	800-325-8007
www.pickenterprise.com	
Hertz	800-654-3131
www.hertz.com	
National	800-227-7368
www.nationalcar.com	
Payless	800-729-5377
www.800-payless.com	
Rent-A-Wreck.com	800-535-1391
www.rent-a-wreck.com	
Sears	800-527-0770
www.budget.com	
Thrifty	800-847-4389
www.thrifty.com	

FOUR-STAR AND FIVE-STAR ESTABLISHMENTS IN NEW ENGLAND AND EASTERN CANADA

Connecticut

★★★★★ Lodging
The Mayflower Inn, *Washington*

★★★★ Restaurant
Thomas Henkelmann, *Greenwich*

Maine

★★★★ Lodging
The White Barn Inn, *Kennebunkport*

★★★★ Restaurant
The White Barn Restaurant, *Kennebunkport*

Massachusetts

★★★★★ Lodgings
Blantyre, *Lenox*
Four Seasons Hotel Boston, *Boston*

★★★★ Lodgings
Boston Harbor Hotel, *Boston*
The Charlotte Inn, *Martha's Vineyard*
Le Meridien Boston, *Boston*
The Ritz-Carlton, Boston, *Boston*
The Ritz-Carlton, Boston Commons, *Boston*
The Wauwinet, *Nantucket Island*
XV Beacon, *Boston*

★★★★ Restaurants
Aujourd'hui, *Boston*
Clio, *Boston*
Grill 23 & Bar, *Boston*
Hamersley's Bistro, *Boston*
L'Espalier, *Boston*
No. 9 Park, *Boston*
Radius, *Boston*
Rialto, *Cambridge*
Silks, *Lowell*

Vermont

★★★★★ Lodging
Twin Farms, *Woodstock*

★★★★ Lodgings
The Governor's Inn, *Ludlow*
The Inn At Sawmill Farm, *West Dover*
Rabbit Hill Inn, *St. Johnsbury*
Topnotch At Stowe, *Stowe*

★★★★ Restaurants
Hemingway's, *Killington*
The Inn at Sawmill Farm, *West Dover*

CANADA

New Brunswick

★★★★ Lodging
Kingsbrae Arms, *St. Andrews*

Ontario

★★★★ Lodgings
Four Seasons Hotel Toronto, *Toronto*
The Metropolitan Hotel, *Toronto*
Park Hyatt Toronto, *Toronto*
Windsor Arms Hotel, *Toronto*

★★★★ Restaurants
Canoe, *Toronto*
Chiado, *Toronto*
The Fifth, *Toronto*
Hemispheres, *Toronto*
North 44 Degrees, *Toronto*
Scaramouche, *Toronto*
Truffles, *Toronto*

Québec

★★★★ Lodging

Loews Hotel Vogue, *Montréal*

★★★★ Restaurants

Laurie Raphael, *Québec City*
L'eau a la Bouche, *Montréal*
Le Piment Rouge, *Montréal*
Mediterraneo Grill & Wine Bar, *Montréal*
Nuances, *Montréal*
Queue de Cheval, *Montréal*
Toque!, *Montréal*

CONNECTICUT

Connecticut is a state of beautiful hills and lakes and lovely old towns with white church steeples rising above green commons. It is also a state with a tradition of high technical achievement and fine machining. Old houses and buildings enchant the visitor; a re-creation of the life of the old sailing ship days at Mystic Seaport leads the traveler back to times long gone.

Adriaen Block sailed into the Connecticut River in 1614. This great river splits Massachusetts and Connecticut and separates Vermont from New Hampshire. It was the river by which Connecticut's first settlers, coming from Massachusetts in 1633, settled in Hartford, Windsor, and Wethersfield. These three towns created a practical constitution called the Fundamental Orders, through which a powerful "General Court" exercised both judicial and legislative duties. The Royal Charter of 1662 was so liberal that Sir Edmund Andros, governor of New England, tried to seize it (1687). To save it, citizens hid the charter in the Charter Oak, which once stood in Hartford.

Poultry, dairy products, and tobacco are the state's most important agricultural products; forest products, nursery stock, and fruit and vegetable produce follow in importance. Aircraft engines, helicopters, hardware, tools, nuclear submarines, and machinery are the principal manufactured products. The home offices of more than 40 insurance companies are located in the state.

Population: 3,282,031
Area: 4,872 square miles
Elevation: 0-2,380 feet
Peak: Mount Frissel (Litchfield County)
Entered Union: Fifth of original thirteen states (January 9, 1788)
Capital: Hartford
Motto: He who transplanted, still sustains
Nickname: Constitution State
Flower: Mountain Laurel
Bird: American Robin
Tree: White Oak
Time Zone: Eastern
Website: www.tourism.state.ct.us

When to Go/Climate

Connecticut's climate is the mildest of all the New England states. Coastal breezes help keep the humidity manageable, and mud season (between winter and spring, when topsoil thaws and lower earth remains frozen) is shorter here than in other New England states.

AVERAGE HIGH/LOW TEMPERATURES (°F)

BRIDGEPORT

Jan 29/22	**May** 59/50	**Sept** 66/58
Feb 31/23	**June** 68/59	**Oct** 56/47
Mar 39/31	**July** 74/66	**Nov** 46/38
Apr 49/40	**Aug** 73/65	**Dec** 35/28

HARTFORD

Jan 25/16	**May** 60/48	**Sept** 64/52
Feb 28/19	**June** 69/57	**Oct** 53/41
Mar 38/28	**July** 74/62	**Nov** 42/33
Apr 49/38	**Aug** 72/60	**Dec** 30/21

Parks and Recreation Finder

Directions to and information about the parks and recreation areas below are given under their respective town/city sections. Please refer to those sections for details.

STATE PARK AND RECREATION AREAS

Key to abbreviations. I.P. = Interstate Park; S.A.P. = State Archaeological Park; S.B. = State Beach; S.C.A. = State Conservation Area; S.C.P. = State Conservation Park; S.Cp. = State Campground; S.F. = State Forest; S.G. = State Garden; S.H.A. = State Historic Area; S.H.P. = State Historic Park; S.H.S. = State Historic Site; S.M.P. = State Marine Park; S.N.A. = State Natural Area; S.P. = State Park; S.P.C. = State Public Campground; S.R. = State Reserve; S.R.A. = State Recreation Area; S.Res. = State Reservoir; S.Res.P. = State Resort Park; S.R.P. = State Rustic Park.

Place Name	Listed Under
Campbell Falls S.P.	NORFOLK
Chatfield Hollow S.P.	CLINTON
Dennis Hill S.P.	NORFOLK
Dinosaur S.P.	WETHERSFIELD
Fort Griswold Battlefield S.P.	GROTON
Gillette Castle S.P.	EAST HADDAM
Hammonasset Beach S.P.	MADISON
Hatstack Mountain S.P.	NORFOLK
Housatonic Meadows S.P.	CORNWALL BRIDGE
Kent Falls S.P.	KENT
Kettletown S.P.	SOUTHBURY
Lake Waramaug S.P.	NEW PRESTON
Macedonia Brook S.P.	KENT
Rocky Neck S.P.	OLD LYME
Southford Falls S.P.	SOUTHBURY
Squantz Pond S.P.	DANBURY
Talcott Mountain S.P.	HARTFORD
Topsmead S.F.	LITCHFIELD
Wadsworth Falls S.P.	MIDDLETOWN

Water-related activities, hiking, riding, various other sports, picnicking and visitor centers, as well as camping, are available in some of these areas. There are 32 state forests and 92 state parks inland and on the shore. A parking fee ($4-$12) is charged at many of these. Camping, mid-April-September; shore parks $15/site/night; inland parks with swimming $13/site/night; inland parks without swimming $11/site/night; additional charge per person for groups larger than four persons. Two- to three-week limit, mid-April-September; three-day limit, October-December. No camping January-mid-April. Forms for reservations for stays of more than two days may be obtained after January 15 by writing to the address in Hartford; these reservations should then be mailed to the park itself; no reservations by phone. Parks and forests are open all year, 8 am-sunset. Most shore parks allow all-night fishing (with permit). Inland swimming areas are open 8 am-sunset. No pets allowed in state park campgrounds. For further information, reservations, and regulations contact Department of Environmental Protection, Bureau of Outdoor Recreation, 79 Elm St, Hartford 06106; 860/424-3200.

SKI AREAS

Place Name	Listed Under
Mohawk Mountain Ski Area	CORNWALL BRIDGE
Mount Southington Ski Area	MERIDEN
Powder Ridge Ski Area	MIDDLETOWN
Ski Sundown	AVON

FISHING AND HUNTING

Hunting license: nonresident, $42 (firearms). Archery permit (including big and small game): nonresident, $44. Deer permit: nonresident, $30 (firearms). Fishing license: nonresident, season, $25; 3-day, $8. Combination firearm hunting, fishing license: nonresident, $55. Further information, including the latest regulations, can be obtained from Department of Environmental Protection, Licensing and Revenue, 79 Elm St, Hartford 06106; 860/424-3105.

CALENDAR HIGHLIGHTS

APRIL

Connecticut Storytelling Festival (New London). Connecticut College. Nationally acclaimed artists; workshops, concerts. Phone 860/439-2764.

MAY

Garlicfest (Fairfield). Notre Dame Catholic High School. Vendors prepare international array of garlic-seasoned cuisine. Sales, entertainment. Phone 203/372-6521.

Lobsterfest (Mystic). Seaport. Outdoor food festival. Phone 860/57-0711.

JUNE

Taste of Hartford (Hartford). Main Street. Four-day event features specialties of more than 50 area restaurants; continuous entertainment. Phone 860/728-3089.

International Festival of Arts and Ideas (New Haven). Celebration of the arts and humanities. Phone 888/ART-IDEA.

JULY

Riverfest (Hartford). Celebration of America's independence and the Connecticut River. Family entertainment, concerts, food, fireworks display over river.

Mark Twain Days (Hartford). Celebration of Twain's legacy and Hartford's cultural heritage with more than 100 events. Concerts, riverboat rides, medieval jousting, tours of Twain House, entertainment. Phone 860/247-0998.

Barnum Festival (Bridgeport). Commemorates the life of P. T. Barnum.

AUGUST

Pilot Pen International Tennis Tournament (New Haven). Connecticut Tennis Center, near Yale Bowl. Championship Series on the ATP Tour. Phone 888-99-PILOT.

SEPTEMBER

Durham Fair (Middletown). Fairgrounds, in Durham on CT 17. State's largest agricultural fair. Phone 860/349-9495.

OCTOBER

Apple Harvest Festival (Meriden). 3 mi S on CT 120, in Southington, on Town Green. Street festival celebrating local apple harvest. Carnival, arts and crafts, parade, road race, food booths, entertainment. Phone 860/628-8036.

DECEMBER

Christmas Torchlight Parade (Old Saybrook). Over 40 fife and drum corps march down Main Street.

Driving Information

Safety belts are mandatory for all persons in front seat of vehicle. Children under four years must be in an approved passenger restraint anywhere in vehicle: ages one through three may use a regulation safety belt; under age one must use an approved safety seat.

INTERSTATE HIGHWAY SYSTEM

The following alphabetical listing of Connecticut towns in the *RoadMaster™ Drive USA Travel Guide* shows that these cities are within ten miles of the indicated interstate highways. A highway map, however, should be checked for the nearest exit.

Highway Number	Cities/Towns within ten miles
Interstate 84	Danbury, Farmington, Hartford, Manchester, Southbury, Stafford Springs, Vernon, Waterbury.
Interstate 91	Enfield, Hartford, Meriden, Middletown, New Haven, Wethersfield, Windsor, Windsor Locks.
Interstate 95	Branford, Bridgeport, Clinton, Fairfield, Greenwich, Groton, Guilford, Madison, Milford, Mystic, New Haven, New London, Norwalk, Old Saybrook, Stamford, Stonington, Stratford, Westport.
Interstate 395	Groton, New London, Norwich, Plainfield, Putnam.

Additional Visitor Information

Pamphlets, maps, and booklets, including the Connecticut Vacation Guide, are available to tourists by contacting the State of Connecticut, Department of Economic and Community Development, 505 Hudson St, Hartford 06106; 800/282-6863. In addition, *Connecticut*—a monthly magazine published by Communications International, 789 Reservoir Ave, Bridgeport 06606—gives a listing of activities around the state; available by subscription or at newsstands.

Connecticut tourism information centers also provide useful information: on I-95 southbound at North Stonington, northbound at Darien, northbound at Westbrook (seasonal); on I-84 eastbound at Danbury, eastbound at Southington (seasonal), westbound at Willington; on I-91 northbound at Middletown, southbound at Wallingford; on Merritt Parkway (CT 15) northbound at Greenwich (seasonal). Also, several privately operated tourism centers are located throughout the state.

A CLASSIC NEW ENGLAND ROAD TRIP

The town of Mystic (roughly halfway between New York and Boston on I-95) represents the state's top coastal lodgings/attractions hub. Mystic Seaport Museum, Mystic Aquarium, and a shopping mall in the shape of a New England village are popular attractions. Foxwoods Resort Casino, in nearby Ledyard, is the world's largest gambling casino; its complex includes lodging and a museum devoted to the Mashantucket Pequot, the tribe that owns the casino. From Mystic, take I-95 to Old Lyme, home of the Florence Griswold Art Museum and Rocky Neck State Park beach. Cross the bridge into Old Saybrook, and follow Route 9 to Essex, a picturesque village with shops and restaurants. The Connecticut River Museum is located here, as is the departure point for the Valley Railroad, which runs along the river. (Railroad passengers can connect with a riverboat for a one-hour Connecticut River cruise.) Follow scenic Route 154 to Chester, and take the country's oldest continuous ferry (it also carries cars) across to Gillette Castle in East Haddam. Or continue over the bridge to East Haddam for a great view of the Victorian Goodspeed Opera House, which stages American musicals and is a destination in its own right. You can return via Route 9 (limited-access highway) or take the scenic way (country roads), Route 82 to Route 156 to I-95, back along the eastern side of the river. Continue west on I-95 to Hammonasset Beach State Park in Madison (the big beach in this area). Then head down Route 1, past the town's classic historic homes, to Guilford (classic green), site of the Henry Whitfield State Museum. Get back on I-95 and follow it into New Haven. Another trip option from Mystic is to head east on I-95 to Stonington, a picturesque fishing village, and then to Watch Hill, a resort town with good beaches. From Stonington, it's a scenic 40-mile coastal drive along Route 1, which passes the Rhode Island fishing resort towns of Charlestown and Narragansett (departure point for ferries to Block Island) and crosses to Jamestown Island in Newport, RI. **(APPROX 112 MI ROUND-TRIP; APPROX 124 MI ROUND-TRIP FROM MYSTIC TO JAMESTOWN ISLAND)**

Avon

See also Bristol, Farmington, Hartford, Wethersfield

Pop 13,937 **Elev** 202 ft **Area code** 860 **Zip** 06001
Information Greater Hartford Tourism District, 234 Murphy Rd, Hartford 06114; 860/244-8181 or 800/793-4480
Web www.enjoyhartford.com

What to See and Do

Farmington Valley Arts Center. Twenty studios, located in historic stone explosives plant, occupied by artists and artisans and open to public at artist's discretion. Fisher Gallery and Shop featuring guest-curated exhibitions and a juried collection of handmade crafts, gifts, and artwork. (Jan-Oct, Wed-Sat, Sun afternoons; Nov-Dec, daily; closed hols) 25 Arts Center Ln, Avon Park N, off US 44. Phone 860/678-1867. **FREE**

Roaring Brook Nature Center. This 112-acre wildlife refuge has interpretive building with seasonal natural history exhibits, wildlife observation area; six mi of marked trails. Gift shop. (Sept-June, Tues-Sun; rest of yr, daily; closed hols) 1½ mi N of US 44 at 70 Gracey Rd in Canton. Phone 860/693-0263. ¢¢

Skiing. Ski Sundown. Three triple, double chairlift; Pomalift; snowmaking; school, patrol, rentals, half-day rate; bar, snack bar. Fifteen trails. Longest run 1 mi; vertical drop 625 ft. (Dec-Mar, daily) 6 mi W via CT 44, then 1½ mi NE on CT 219, in New Hartford. Phone 860/379-9851. ¢¢¢¢

Hotel

★★★ **AVON OLD FARMS HOTEL.** *279 Avon Mountain (06001). 860/677-1651; fax 860/677-0364; toll-free 800/836-4000. www.avonoldfarmshotel.com.* 160 rms, 3 story. S, D $139-$179; suites $160-$260; under 18 free. Crib free. Pet accepted, some restrictions. TV; cable, VCR avail. Pool. Complimentary continental bkfst. Restaurant 6:30-10 am, 11:30 am-2 pm, 5-9 pm; Sun 7 am-1 pm. Rm serv. Ck-out noon. Meeting rms. Business servs avail. Valet serv. Beauty shop. Exercise equipt; sauna. Cr cds: A, C, D, DS, MC, V.
⊡ ⬤ ⬤ ⬤ ⬤ ⬤ ⬤

Restaurants

★★★ **AVON OLD FARMS INN.** *1 Nod Rd (06001). 860/677-2818. www.avonoldfarmsinn.com.* Own baking. Hrs: noon-9:30 pm; Fri to 10 pm; Sat to 10:30 pm; Sun 5:30-8:30 pm; Sun brunch 10 am-2:30 pm. Res required. Bar. Lunch $6.95-$13.95, dinner $18.95-$26.95. Sun brunch $15.95. Child's menu. Entertainment. 1757 stagecoach stop. Cr cds: A, DS, MC, V.
⊡ ⬤

★★ **DAKOTA.** *225 W Main St (06001). 860/677-4311. www.dakotarestaurant.com.* Specializes in steak, seafood. Salad bar. Hrs: 5-10 pm; Fri to 11 pm; Sat 4-11 pm; Sun 4-9 pm. Res accepted. Bar. A la carte entrees: dinner $9.95-$23.95. Child's menu. Casual, rustic atmosphere with a touch of Southwestern decor. Cr cds: A, D, DS, MC, V.
⊡ ⬤

Branford

See also Meriden, Milford, New Haven

Settled 1644 **Pop** 27,603 **Elev** 49 ft **Area code** 203 **Zip** 06405
Information Connecticut River Valley & Shoreline Visitors Council, 393 Main St, Middletown 06457; 860/347-0028 or 800/486-3346
Web www.cttourism.org

Once a busy shipping center, Branford has become a residential and industrial suburb of New Haven. The community's bays and beaches attract many summertime vacationers. Branford's large green, dating from colonial days, is surrounded by public buildings.

What to See and Do

Harrison House. (ca 1725) Classic colonial saltbox restored by J. Frederick Kelly, an early 20th-century architect; stone chimney, herb garden, period furnishings, and farm implements. (June-Sept, Thurs-Sat mid-late afternoon; also by appt) 124 Main St. Phone 203/488-4828 or 203/488-2126. **FREE**

Thimble Islands Cruise. Legends of treasures hidden by Captain Kidd, along with picturesque shores and vegetation, have for more than 250 yrs lured people to these 20 to 30 rocky islets in Long Island Sound. Narrated tours (30-45 min) leave hrly aboard the *Volsunga III*. (May-Oct, Tues-Sun) Res required. Departs from Stony Creek Dock. Phone 203/481-3345 or 203/488-9978. ¢¢

Motel/Motor Lodge

★ **DAYS INN.** *375 E Main St (06405). 203/488-8314; fax 203/483-6885; toll-free 800/329-7466. www.daysinn.com.* 74 rms, 2 story. S $75-$80; D $90-$99; each addl $10; suites $245; under 16 free. Crib free. Pet accepted; $10. TV; cable (premium), VCR avail. Pool. Complimentary continental bkfst. Coffee in rms. Restaurant 7 am-2 pm; Sat, Sun to noon. Ck-out 11 am. Valet serv. Meeting rms. Business center. Gift shop. Barber, beauty shop. Refrigerators avail. Cr cds: A, C, D, DS, ER, JCB, MC, V.
⊡ ⬤ ⬤ ⬤ ⬤ ⬤ SC ⬤

Bridgeport

See also Fairfield, Milford, Norwalk, Stratford, Westport

Settled 1639 **Pop** 141,686 **Elev** 20 ft **Area code** 203
Information Chamber of Commerce, 10 Middle St, 14th floor, 06604; 203/335-3800
Web www.brbcnet.com

An important manufacturing city, Bridgeport is home to dozens of well-known companies that produce a highly diversified array of manufactured products. The University of Bridgeport (1927) is also located in the city.

Bridgeport's most famous resident was probably P. T. Barnum. The city's most famous son was 28-inch Charles S. Stratton, who was promoted by Barnum as General Tom Thumb. There was a time when train passengers in and out of Bridgeport occasionally saw elephants hitched to plows; the elephants, of course, were from Barnum's winter quarters. As well as running the "Greatest Show on Earth," Barnum was for a time the mayor of Bridgeport.

What to See and Do

◪ **The Barnum Museum.** Houses memorabilia from P. T. Barnum's life and circus career, including artifacts relating to Barnum's legendary discoveries, General Tom Thumb and Jenny Lind; scale model of three-ring circus; displays of Victorian Bridgeport; changing exhibits; art gallery. (Tues-Sun; closed hols) 820 Main St. Phone 203/331-1104. ¢¢

Beardsley Zoological Gardens. This 30-acre zoo, the state's only, houses more than 200 animals; Siberian tiger exhibit; farmyard; concession; gift shop. (Daily; closed Jan 1, Thanksgiving, Dec 25) Noble Ave, Beardsley Park, off I-95 exit 27A. Phone 203/394-6565. ¢¢¢

Captain's Cove Seaport. Replica of the HMS *Rose*, the British warship that triggered the founding of the American Navy during the Revolutionary War. Marina; shops, restaurant, fish market. (Schedule varies) 1 Bostwick Ave, I-95 exit 26. Phone 203/335-1433.

Discovery Museum. Planetarium; films; approx 120 hands-on science and art exhibits; children's museum; Challenger Learning Center; changing art exhibits; lectures, demonstrations, and workshops. (Tues-Sun; closed Labor Day, Thanksgiving, Dec 25) 4450 Park Ave, off Merritt Pkwy, exit 47. Phone 203/372-3521. ¢¢¢

Ferry to Port Jefferson, Long Island. Car and passenger service across Long Island Sound (1 hr, 20 min). (Daily) Union Square Dock, at foot of State St. Phone 631/473-0286.

Statue of Tom Thumb. Life-size statue on ten-ft base. Mountain Grove Cemetery, North Ave and Dewey St.

Special Event

Barnum Festival. Commemorates the life of P. T. Barnum. (Apr-July.) Phone 866/867-8495.

Motel/Motor Lodge

★★ **HOLIDAY INN.** *1070 Main St (06604). 203/334-1234; fax 203/367-1985; res 800/465-4329. www.holiday-inn.com.* 234 rms, 9 story. S $79-$119; D $89-$129; each addl $10; suites $179-$450; under 16 free; family, wkend rates. Crib free. Pet accepted, some restrictions. TV; cable. Indoor/outdoor pool. Restaurant 6 am-10 pm. Bar 4 pm-midnight. Ck-out noon. Meeting rms. Business center. In-rm modem link. Free covered parking. Free airport, RR station, bus depot transportation. Exercise equipt. Refrigerator in some suites. Atrium; waterfall. Beach 4 blks. Cr cds: A, D, DS, MC, V.

🅳 🐾 🕭 🏊 🏃 ⛷ 🔥 🏃

Hotel

★★★ **MARRIOTT MERRITT PARKWAY TRUMBULL.** *180 Hawley Ln, Trumbull (06611). 203/378-1400; fax 203/378-4958; toll-free 800/682-4095. www.marriott.com.* 320 rms, 5 story. S $144-$189; D $164-$209; each addl $20; suites $300-$400; under 18 free; wkend rates. Crib free. TV; cable (premium), VCR avail. 2 pools, 1 indoor; whirlpool, poolside serv. Coffee in rms. Restaurants 6:30 am-11 pm. Bars 11-1 am; entertainment. Ck-out noon. Convention facilities. Business center. In-rm modem link. Gift shop. Exercise equipt; sauna. Some refrigerators. Cr cds: A, C, D, DS, ER, JCB, MC, V.

🅳 🏊 🏃 ⛷ 🔥 SC 🏃

Restaurant

★ **BLACK ROCK CASTLE.** *2895 Fairfield Ave (06605). 203/336-3990.* Irish menu. Specialties: flaming Irish whiskey steak, beef. Hrs: 11:30 am-2:30 pm, 5-10 pm; Fri, Sat to 11 pm. Closed Jan 1, Dec 25. Res accepted. A la carte entrees: lunch $4.95-$6.95, dinner $9.95-$16.95. Child's menu. Entertainment Wed-Sun. Valet parking. Castle motif; dining beneath tower. Cr cds: A, D, DS, MC, V.

🅳 SC ⬅

Bristol

See also Meriden, New Britain, Waterbury

Settled 1727 **Pop** 60,640 **Elev** 289 ft **Area code** 860 **Zip** 06010

Information Greater Bristol Chamber of Commerce, 10 Main St; 860/584-4718. Litchfield Hills Visitors Bureau, PO Box 968, Litchfield 06759; 860/567-4506

Web www.bristol-chamber.org

Gideon Roberts began making and selling clocks here in 1790. Bristol has since been famous for clocks—particularly for Sessions and Ingraham. Today Bristol is also the home of Associated Spring Corporation; Dana Corporation/Warner Electric; Theis Precision Steel; and ESPN, the nation's first all-sports cable television network.

What to See and Do

American Clock and Watch Museum. More than 3,000 timepieces; exhibits and video show on history of clock and watch manufacturing located in historic house built 1801. Also award-winning sundial garden; bookshop. (Apr-Nov, daily; closed Thanksgiving) 100 Maple St. Phone 860/583-6070. ¢¢

Burlington Trout Hatchery. Hatchery building houses incubators and tanks; development of trout from egg to fish. (Daily) 10 mi N via CT 69, then approx 1 mi E on CT 4 to Belden Rd, in Burlington. Phone 860/673-2340. **FREE**

H. C. Barnes Memorial Nature Center. Self-guiding trails through 70-acre preserve. Interpretive building features ecological and animal displays. (Sat, also Wed-Fri and Sun afternoons) Trails (daily; closed hols) 175 Shrub Rd, 3 mi N on CT 69. Phone 860/589-6082. ¢

Lake Compounce Theme Park. One of the oldest continuously operating amusement parks in the nation. Over 25 wet and dry attractions including roller coasters, white water raft ride, vintage trolley, bumper cars, and 1911 carousel. Special events. (June-Aug, Mon, Wed-Sun; Sept, wkends) 822 Lake Ave. Phone 860/583-3631. All-day ride pass ¢¢¢¢

Lock Museum of America. Antique locks, displays on lock history and design. (May-Oct, Tues-Sun, limited hrs) 3½ mi NW on CT 72, then W ¾ mi on US 6 to 130 Main St in Terryville. Phone 860/589-6359. ¢¢ 2 blks W is

> **Eli Terry, Jr. Waterwheel.** Built in the early 1840s, this 20-ft diameter, rack-and-pinion, breast-type wheel is an excellent example of the type of waterwheel used to supply power to industrial buildings during this period. 160 Main St.

New England Carousel Museum. Displays more than 300 carved, wooden antique carousel figures, including two chariots. Restoration workshop on view. (Apr-Oct, daily; rest of yr, Thurs-Sat, also Sun afternoons; closed hols) 95 Riverside Ave. Phone 860/585-5411. ¢

Special Events

Balloons Over Bristol. Bristol Eastern High School. More than 60 hot-air balloons from around the country gather to participate in three-day event; carnival, crafts fair, food booths. Phone 860/584-4718. Memorial Day wkend.

Chrysanthemum Festival. Music, art, theater, hayrides, picking pumpkins, parades, and dances, Historical Society tours. Phone 860/584-4718. Late Sept.

B&B/Small Inn

★★★ **CHIMNEY CREST MANOR.** *5 Founders Dr (06010). 860/582-4219; fax 860/584-5903.* 6 units, 3 story, 4 suites. S, D $85-$150; each addl $15. Closed Dec 24-25. Crib free. TV; cable (premium), VCR avail. Complimentary full bkfst. Ck-out 11 am, ck-in 3 pm. Framed artwork, beamed ceilings in 32-rm Tudor-style mansion (1930). Library; sun rm. Totally nonsmoking. Cr cds: A, MC, V.
🖼 🔥 SC

Clinton

See also Essex, Guilford, Madison, New Haven, Old Saybrook

Settled 1663 **Pop** 12,767 **Elev** 25 ft **Area code** 860 **Zip** 06413
Information Chamber of Commerce, 50 E Main St, PO Box 334; 860/669-3889
Web www.ClintonCT.com

What to See and Do

Chamard Vinyards. A 15-acre vineyard and winery offering Chardonnay, Pinot Noir, Merlot, and other varieties. Tours and tastings (Wed-Sat). 115 Cow Hill Rd. Phone 800/371-1609. **FREE**

Chatfield Hollow State Park. Approx 550 acres situated in a heavily wooded hollow with fine fall scenery and natural caves that once provided shelter for Native Americans. Pond swimming, fishing; hiking, ice skating, picnicking. Standard hrs, fees. 7 mi NW via CT 80 and 81, on N Branford Rd in Killingworth. Phone 860/663-2030. ¢¢

Stanton House. (1789) Thirteen-room house connected to general store; original site of first classroom of Yale University. Period furnishings; antique American and Staffordshire dinnerware; weapon collection; bed used by Marquis de Lafayette during 1824 visit. (June-Sept, Tues-Sun) 63 E Main St. Phone 860/669-2132. **FREE**

Motel/Motor Lodge

★ **CLINTON MOTEL.** *163 E Main St (06413). 860/669-8850; fax 860/669-3849.* 15 rms. Mid-June-mid-Sept: S $42-$72; D $48-$89; lower rates rest of yr. Crib free. TV; cable, VCR avail. Pool. Restaurant nearby. Ck-out 11 am. Lawn games. Refrigerators. Cr cds: A, DS, MC, V.
🖼 🖼 🔥

Restaurant

★ **LOG CABIN RESTAURANT AND LOUNGE.** *232 Boston Post Rd (06413). 860/669-6253.* Italian, American menu. Specializes in seafood, steak, pasta. Hrs: 11:30 am-10 pm. Closed Dec 25. Res accepted. Bar. Lunch $4.95-$7.95, dinner $10.95-$18.95. Child's menu. Fireplace. Log cabin decor. Cr cds: A, D, MC, V.
D 🖼

Cornwall Bridge

See also Kent

Pop 450 **Elev** 445 ft **Area code** 860 **Zip** 06754
Information Litchfield Hills Visitors Bureau, PO Box 968, Litchfield 06759; 860/567-4506
Web www.litchfieldhills.com

The small central valley containing the villages of Cornwall, West Cornwall, and Cornwall Bridge was avoided by early settlers because its heavy stand of pine made the clearing of land difficult.

What to See and Do

Covered bridge. Designed by Ithiel Town, in continuous service since 1837. 4 mi N via US 7 to CT 128 near West Cornwall, at Housatonic River. **FREE**

Housatonic Meadows State Park. A 452-acre park bordering the Housatonic River. Fishing, boating, canoeing; picnicking, camping (dump station). No pets. Standard hrs, fees. 1 mi N on US 7. Phone 860/927-3238. **FREE**

Mohawk Mountain Ski Area. More than 20 trails and slopes, most with snowmaking; triple, four double chair-lifts; patrol, school, rentals; cafeteria. Longest run 1¼ mi; vertical drop 650 ft. (Late Nov-early Apr, daily; closed hols) More than 40 mi of cross-country trails. Night skiing Mon-Sat. 4 mi NE on CT 4, S on CT 128, on Great Hollow Rd in Mohawk Mountain State Park. Phone 860/672-6100.

Sharon Audubon Center. National Audubon Society wildlife sanctuary (684 acres) includes nature center, 11 mi of walking trails, self-guided tours, herb and wildflower garden, gift/bookstore. Grounds (daily). Nature center, store (Tues-Sun; closed hols) Approx 8 mi NW on CT 4 near Sharon. Phone 860/364-0520. ¢¢

B&B/Small Inn

★ **CORNWALL INN AND RESTAURANT.** *270 Kent Rd; Rte 7 (06754).* 860/672-6884; fax 860/672-0352; toll-free 800/786-6884. www.cornwallinn.com. 13 rms, 2 story, 1 suite. No rm phones. S, D $50-$110; each addl $10; suite $150; under 5 free. Crib free. Pet accepted, some restrictions. TV in some rms, also in sitting rm. Pool. Complimentary continental bkfst. Dining rm 6-9 pm Thurs-Mon; res required. Bar 5-10 pm. Ck-out 11 am, ck-in 2 pm. Bellhop. Bus depot transportation. Downhill ski 5 mi; x-country ski ¼ mi. Picnic tables. Restored 19th-century country inn; antiques. Cr cds: A, DS, MC, V.
🅳 ⬛ 🏊 🛏 🔥

Danbury

See also Southbury, Woodbury

Settled 1685 **Pop** 65,585 **Elev** 378 ft **Area code** 203
Information Housatonic Valley Tourism District, 30 Main St, PO Box 406, 06810; 203/743-0546 or 800/841-4488
Web www.housatonic.org

Danbury, originally settled by eight Norwalk families seeking fertile land, played an important role during the American Revolution as a supply depot and site of a military hospital for the Continental Army. After the war and until the 1950s, the community was the center of the hat industry. Zadoc Benedict is credited with the first factory in 1790, which made three hats a day.

What to See and Do

Candlewood Lake. Connecticut's largest lake, more than 14 mi long and with more than 60 mi of shoreline, extends one finger into Danbury. Swimming, fishing, boating; picnicking, concession. Fees for some activities. 2 mi NW on CT 37, then E on Hayestown Ave to E Hayestown Rd. On the west shore are Pootatuck State Forest and

Squantz Pond State Park. More than 170 acres. Freshwater swimming, scuba diving, fishing, boating (7½ hp limit), canoeing; hiking, biking, picnicking, concessions. No pets. Standard hrs, fees. 10 mi N on CT 37 and 39 in New Fairfield. Phone 203/797-4165. ¢¢¢

Scott-Fanton Museum. Includes Rider House (1785), period furnishings, New England memorabilia; Dodd Shop (ca 1790), historical display of hat industry; Huntington Hall, changing exhibits and research library. (Wed-Sun afternoons; closed hols) 43 Main St. Phone 203/743-5200. **Donation**

Special Events

Charles Ives Center for the Arts. At Westside campus, Western Connecticut State University, on Mill Plain Rd. Outdoor classical, country, folk, jazz, and pop concerts. Fri-Sun, July-Sept. Phone 203/837-9226.

Taste O' Danbury. Sept. Phone 203/790-6970 or 203/743-0546.

Motels/Motor Lodges

★★ **BEST WESTERN BERKSHIRE INN.** *11 Stony Hill Rd, US 6, Bethel (06801).* 203/744-3200; fax 203/744-3979; res 800/780-7234. www.bestwestern.com. 69 rms, 3 story. May-Oct: S, D $100-$110; each addl $8; under 12 free; higher rates: Special Olympics, Dec 31; lower rates rest of yr. Crib $10. TV; cable (premium). Complimentary continental bkfst. Restaurant nearby. Ck-out 11 am. Meeting rms. Business servs avail. In-rm modem link. Health club privileges. Playground. Microwaves avail. Cr cds: A, C, D, DS, MC, V.
🅳 ⬛ 🔥 **SC**

★★ **BEST WESTERN STONY HILL INN.** *46 Stoney Hill Rd US Rte 6, Bethel (06801).* 203/743-5533; fax 203/743-4958; res 800/780-7234. www.bestwestern.com. 36 rms, 4 kits. May-Oct: S, D $90-$120; each addl $8; kit. units $100; under 12 free; lower rates rest of yr. Crib $10. TV; cable (premium). Pool. Playground. Complimentary continental bkfst. Restaurant 11:30 am-2 pm, 5-9:30 pm; Fri from 5 pm; Sat to 10 pm; Sun 10:30 am-2:30 pm. Bar; pianist Fri, Sat. Ck-out 11 am. Coin lndry. Meeting rms. Golf pro, driving range. Health club privileges. Extensive grounds; pond. Cr cds: A, C, D, DS, MC, V.
🅳 🍴 🏊 ⬛ 🔥 **SC**

★★ **HOLIDAY INN.** *80 Newtown Rd (06810).* 203/792-4000; fax 203/797-0810; toll-free 800/465-4329. www.danburyholidayinn.com. 114 rms, 4 story. Apr-Dec: S, D $124; suites $109-$114; under 18 free; lower rates rest of yr. Crib free. Pet accepted. TV; cable (premium), VCR avail (movies). Pool; poolside serv. Complimentary coffee in rms. Restaurant 6 am-midnight. Rm serv 24 hrs. Bar noon-2 am. Ck-out noon. Meeting rms. Business servs avail. In-rm modem link. Bellhops. Valet serv. Shopping arcade. Free airport transportation. Health club privileges. Some refrigerators; microwaves avail. Cr cds: A, D, DS, MC, V.
🅳 ⬛ 🏊 ⬛ 🔥 **SC**

★ **RAMADA INN.** *116 Newtown Rd (06801).* 203/792-3800; fax 203/730-1899; toll-free 800/228-2828. www.ramada.com. 181 rms, 2-5 story. S $79-$145; D $79-$155; each addl $15; under 16 free; wkend rates. Pet accepted, some restrictions. TV; cable (premium). Indoor/outdoor pool. Coffee in rms. Restaurant 6:30 am-10:30 pm; Fri to 11 pm; hrs vary wkends. Rm serv. Bar 11-1 am. Ck-out 11 am. Coin lndry.

Meeting rms. Business servs avail. In-rm modem link. Valet serv. Health club privileges. Refrigerators, microwaves avail. Cr cds: A, C, D, DS, ER, JCB, MC, V.

D ◑ ⩳ ⊠ 🐾 SC

Hotels

★★ **THE INN AT ETHAN ALLEN.** *21 Lake Ave (06811). 203/744-1776; fax 203/791-9673; toll-free 800/742-1776.* 195 rms, 6 story. S $108-$115; D $123-$130; each addl $15; suites $113-$130; under 17 free; wkend rates. TV; cable (premium). Pool. Restaurant 6:30-10 am, noon-2 pm, 5-10 pm; Sat, Sun 7:30 am-2 pm. Bar 4 pm-1 am, wkends from 11:30 am. Ck-out noon. Coin lndry. Meeting rms. Business center. In-rm modem link. Free RR station, bus depot transportation. Airport transportation. Exercise equipt; sauna. Microwaves avail. Owned by Ethan Allen furniture company. Cr cds: A, DS, MC, V.

D ⩳ 🏋 🎿 🔥 ⊠

★★★ **SHERATON DANBURY AND TOWERS.** *18 Old Ridgebury Rd (06810). 203/794-0600; fax 203/798-2709; res 800/445-8667. www.sheraton.com.* 242 rms, 10 story. S, D $125-$195; each addl $15; family, wkend rates. Crib free. Pet accepted, some restrictions. TV; cable (premium), VCR (movies). Indoor pool; whirlpool, poolside serv. Restaurant 6:30 am-10 pm. Bar 11-2 am; entertainment. Ck-out noon. Meeting rms. Business center. In-rm modem link. Coin lndry. Lighted tennis. Exercise equipt; sauna. Health club privileges. Microwaves avail. Cr cds: A, DS, MC, V.

◑ 🏋 ⩳ 🏋 🎿 🔥 ⊠

B&B/Small Inn

★★ **THE HOMESTEAD INN.** *5 Elm St, New Milford (06776). 860/354-4080; fax 860/354-7046. www.homesteadct.com.* 8 rms in 2-story inn, 6 motel rms. S $86; D $96; each addl $10; family rates. Crib free. TV; cable, VCR avail. Complimentary continental bkfst. Restaurant nearby. Ck-out 11 am, ck-in 2 pm. Business servs avail. In-rm modem link. Health club privileges. Microwaves avail. Inn built 1853; many rms furnished with country antiques. Cr cds: A, C, D, DS, MC, V.

⊠ 🐾

Restaurants

★★ **CIAO CAFE AND WINE BAR.** *2B Ives St (06810). 203/791-0404.* Italian menu. Specialties: veal Christine, rigatoni with tortanella cheese. Hrs: 11 am-10 pm; Fri, Sat to 11 pm; Sun brunch to 2 pm. Closed Labor Day, Dec 25. Res accepted; required Fri, Sat. Bar. Wine list. A la carte entrees: lunch $5.95-$8.95, dinner $8.75-$16.95. Sun brunch $7.95. Outdoor dining. Contemporary decor. Cr cds: A, MC, V.

D

★ **THE HEARTH.** *US 7, Brookfield (06804). 203/775-3360.* Specializes in open-hearth steak, seafood. Hrs: noon-2:30 pm, 5-9 pm; Fri, Sat 5-9:30 pm; Sun 1-8 pm. Closed Mon; Thanksgiving, Dec 24, 25; Feb. Serv bar. Lunch $4.75-$7,

dinner $8.95-$22.95. Complete meals: dinner $11.50-$23. Child's menu. Open-hearth cooking in center of restaurant. Cr cds: A, MC, V.

◄

★★ **TWO STEPS DOWNTOWN GRILLE.** *5 Ives St (06810). 203/794-0032.* Southwestern, American menu. Specialties: fajitas, baby back ribs. Hrs: 11 am-10 pm; wkends to midnight; Sun brunch 10 am-2 pm. Closed Labor Day, Dec 25. Res accepted. Bar. Lunch $5.95-$7.95, dinner $7.95-$15.95. Sun brunch $7.95. Child's menu. Outdoor dining. Former firehouse; lower level has Western decor. Cr cds: A, D, MC, V.

D ◄

East Haddam

See also Essex, Middletown

Pop 6,676 **Elev** 35 ft **Area code** 860 **Zip** 06423

Information Connecticut River Valley & Shoreline Visitors Council, 393 Main St, Middletown 06457; 860/347-0028 or 800/486-3346

Web www.cttourism.org

The longest remaining swinging bridge in New England crosses the Connecticut River to Haddam.

What to See and Do

Amasa Day House. (1816) Period furnishings include some pieces owned by three generations of the Day family; stenciled floors and stairs. (June-Labor Day, Fri-Sun) 4 mi N on CT 149 at jct CT 151 in Moodus. Phone 860/873-8144 or 860/247-8996. ¢¢

Gillette Castle State Park. The 184-acre park surrounds a 24-room castle built by turn-of-the-century actor/playwright William Gillette; medieval German design with dramatically decorated rms. (Late May-mid-Oct, daily; mid-Oct-mid-Dec, Sat and Sun) Picnicking and hiking trails in the surrounding park. Standard hrs. 4 mi SE via local roads to 67 River Rd. Phone 860/526-2336. ¢¢

Goodspeed Opera House. Home of the American Musical Theatre (1876). Performances of American musicals (Apr-Dec, Wed-Sun eves, matinees Wed, Sat, and Sun) Guided tours (June-Sept, Mon and Sat; fee). On CT 82 at East Haddam Bridge. Phone 860/873-8668. ¢

Nathan Hale Schoolhouse. One-rm school where the American Revolutionary patriot taught during winter of 1773; period furnishings, memorabilia. Church has bell said to have been cast in Spain in A.D. 815. (Memorial Day-Labor Day, Sat, Sun, and hols, limited hrs) Main St (CT 149) at rear of St. Stephen's Church. **FREE**

Sightseeing.

Camelot Cruises, Inc. Offers Connecticut River cruises, Long Island cruises, Murder Mystery cruises, and evening music excursions. Long Island cruises (mid June-Labor Day, daily; after Labor Day-mid Oct, Sun). Murder Mystery cruises (Mar-Dec, Fri and Sat eves).W on CT 82, across river at Marine Park in Haddam. Phone 860/345-8591. ¢¢¢¢

Eagle Aviation. Scenic airplane rides over the Connecticut River Valley. (Daily; closed Dec 25-Jan 8) Goodspeed Airport and Seaplane Base, Goodspeed Landing, Lumberyard Rd. Phone 860/873-8568 or 860/873-8658. ¢¢¢¢

B&B/Small Inn

★★ **BISHOPSGATE INN.** *7 Norwich Rd (06423). 860/873-1677; fax 860/873-3898. www.bishopsgate.com.* 6 rms, 2 story. S $95-$150; D $100-$150; each addl $15; suite $150. Children over 5 yrs only. Complimentary full bkfst; afternoon refreshments. Restaurant nearby. Ck-out 11 am, ck-in 2 pm. RR station transportation. Near Connecticut River. Colonial house (1818) furnished with period pieces. Cr cds: DS, MC, V.

D ◈ 辶 觉 ⊁ ⊠ 炎

Enfield

See also Windsor Locks

Settled 1680 **Pop** 45,532 **Elev** 150 ft **Area code** 860 **Zip** 6082

Information Connecticut's Heritage Valley North Central Tourism Bureau, 111 Hazard Ave; 860/763-2578 or 800/248-8283

Web www.cnctb.org

Located on the Connecticut River, Enfield was an important embarking point for flat-bottom boats transporting wares to Springfield, Massachusetts, in the 18th century. The Enfield Society for the Detection of Horse Thieves and Robbers was founded here over a century ago. Jonathan Edwards, a famous theologian, delivered his fire and brimstone sermon "Sinners in the Hands of an Angry God" here in 1741.

What to See and Do

Martha A. Parsons House. (1782) Constructed on land put aside for use by parsons or ministers, this house holds 180 yrs' worth of antiques collected by the Parsons family; tables brought from West Indies, George Washington memorial wallpaper. (May-Oct, Sun afternoons or by appt) 1387 Enfield St. Phone 860/745-6064. **FREE**

Old Town Hall (Purple Heart Museum). Incl inventions of the Shakers, a religious sect that observed a doctrine of celibacy, common property, and community living; medals and service memorabilia, 46-star flag; local historical displays and artifacts. (May-Oct, Sun afternoons or by appt) 1294 Enfield St. Phone 860/745-1729. **FREE**

Motel/Motor Lodge

★ **RED ROOF INN.** *5 Hazard Ave (06082). 860/741-2571; fax 860/741-2576; toll-free 800/843-7663. www.redroof.com.* 109 rms, 2 story. S $34.99-$42.99; D $39.99-$46.99; under 18 free. Crib free. Pet accepted. TV; cable (premium). Restaurant adj 6:30-12:30 am. Ck-out noon. Business servs avail. In-rm modem link. X-country ski 15 mi. Cr cds: A, C, D, DS, MC, V.

D ◈ ⊁ ⊠ 炎

Hotel

★★ **RADISSON HOTEL SPRINGFIELD.** *1 Bright Meadow Blvd (06082). 860/741-2211; fax 860/741-6917; res 800/333-3333. www.radisson.com.* 181 rms, 6 story. S $104-$114; D $114-$124; each addl $10; under 18 free; wkend rates. Crib free. TV; cable (premium), VCR avail. 2 pools, 1 indoor; whirlpool, lifeguard (summer wkends). Restaurant 6:30 am-2 pm, 5:30-10 pm; Sat, Sun from 7 am. Bar 11 am-midnight; Sun to 11 pm; entertainment. Ck-out 11 am. Meeting rms. Business servs avail. In-rm modem link. Concierge. Free airport, RR station, bus depot transportation. Lighted tennis. Exercise equipt; sauna. Health club privileges. Game rm. Lawn games. Some in-rm steam baths. Picnic area. Cr cds: A, C, D, DS, ER, JCB, MC, V.

D ⊬ 辶 觉 ⊁ 炎

Essex

See also Clinton, East Haddam, Middletown, Old Lyme, Old Saybrook

Pop 5,904 **Elev** 100 ft **Area code** 860 **Zip** 06426

Information Connecticut River Valley & Shoreline Visitors Council, 393 Main St, Middletown 06457; 860/347-0028 or 800/486-3346

Web www.cttourism.org

What to See and Do

Connecticut River Museum. Housed in the last remaining steamboat dock building on the Connecticut River. Presents exhibits celebrating the rich cultural heritage and natural resources of the river valley. Incl the only full-size, operating replica of the Turtle, America's first successful submarine, built along the Connecticut River during the Revolutionary War. (Tues-Sun; closed hols) At foot of Main St at river. Phone 860/767-8269. ¢

Valley Railroad. Scenic 12-mi steam train excursion along Connecticut River to Chester; can opt to connect with a riverboat for one-hr Connecticut River cruise (addl fare). Cruise passengers are returned to Essex via later connecting trains. Turn-of-the-century equipment. (Early May-late Oct, days vary; also Christmas trips) 1 Railroad Ave. Phone 860/767-0103. Train ¢¢ Train and cruise ¢¢¢¢

THE BEST SMALL TOWN IN AMERICA

The lower reaches of the Connecticut River are so unspoiled by development that about ten years ago, the Nature Conservancy named the area to its list of "Last Great Places" in the Western Hemisphere. Then in 1996, the riverfront town of Essex won honors as "The Best Small Town in America" in a much-publicized book by Norman Crampton. The village part of the town is ideal for walking and sightseeing; a loop that takes in the whole peninsula is just about a mile in length.

Start at the top of Main Street at Essex Square (street parking is free and easy to find), then walk south along Main. You'll pass dozens of appealing shops selling everything from clothing to antiques. The town's brick post office is next to Essex Park, a lovely swath of grass and trees overlooking Middle Cove. St. John's Episcopal Church is across the street in an imposing brownstone. Built in the late 1800s in the style of H. H. Richardson, the church is decades younger than many of the white clapboard houses that line Main Street. The older houses date to the mid-1700s, when Essex was a major shipbuilding center. Ships' captains and merchants built their houses close to what is now the Town Dock at the foot of Main. Today, some of these houses have been converted to delis, coffeehouses, and shops, but others are still private homes, decked with window boxes and encircled with blooming gardens.

The Griswold Inn (locally known as The Griz) is a landmark that has been offering travelers hospitality since 1776. It's famous for its Sunday morning English-style Hunt Breakfast. The Connecticut River Museum is housed in a former steamboat warehouse next to the Town Dock; it showcases the history of the river with memorabilia and ship models. Reversing direction, head north on Main, then turn right onto Ferry Street to the Dauntless Shipyard and Essex Island Marina. Turn left onto Pratt Street to return to the starting point at Essex Square.

Special Event

Deep River Ancient Muster and Parade. 2½ mi N via CT 9, at Devitt's Field, Main St, in Deep River. Approx 60 fife and drum corps recall Revolutionary War period; displays. Third Sat July. Phone 860/526-0058.

B&Bs/Small Inns

★★★ **THE COPPER BEECH INN.** *46 Main St, Ivoryton (06442). 860/767-0330; toll-free 888/809-2056. www.copperbeechinn.com.* 13 rms, 2 story. D $105-$180. Children over 8 yrs only. Closed 1st wk Jan, Dec 24-25. TV. Complimentary buffet bkfst. Restaurant (see also COPPER BEECH INN). Ck-out 11 am. Whirlpools. Restored Victorian building (1889), once residence of prominent ivory importer; on 7 acres of wooded countryside, terraced gardens. Totally nonsmoking. Cr cds: A, C, D, MC, V.
D ⊠ 🔥

★★ **GRISWOLD INN.** *36 Main St (06426). 860/767-1776; fax 860/767-0481. www.griswoldinn.com.* 30 rms, 3 story. S, D $90-$185; each addl $10. Crib $10. TV in sitting rm. Complimentary continental bkfst. Restaurant (see also GRISWOLD INN). Ck-out 11 am, ck-in 2 pm. Business servs avail. Inn since 1776. Fireplace in spacious library. Many antiques. Near Connecticut River. Cr cds: A, MC, V.
D ⊠ 🔥

Restaurants

★★★ **COPPER BEECH INN.** *46 Main St (06426). 860/767-0330. www.copperbeechinn.com.* French country menu. Specialties: bouillabaisse, breast of duck, veal. Own baking. Hrs: 5:30-8 pm; Fri, Sat to 9 pm; Sun 1-7 pm. Closed Mon, Tues (Jan-Mar); Jan 1, Dec 24, 25. Res accepted; required Sat. Serv bar. A la carte entrees: dinner $20.75-$26.25. In restored Victorian building (1889), once residence of prominent ivory importer. Jacket. Totally nonsmoking. Cr cds: A, D, MC, V.
D

★★★ **GRISWOLD INN.** *36 Main St (06426). 860/767-1776. www.griswoldinn.com.* Specializes in prime rib, local seafood, game (winter). Own sausage. Hrs: 11:45 am-3 pm, 5:30-9 pm; Fri, Sat 11:30 am-3 pm, 5-10 pm; Sun 4:30-9 pm; Sun brunch 11 am-2:30 pm. Closed Dec 24 eve, 25. Res accepted. Bar 11-1 am; Fri, Sat to 2 am. Lunch $6.95-$12.95, dinner $12.95-$22.95. Sun brunch $12.95. Child's menu. Entertainment, banjo concerts Fri and Sun, jazz pianist Sat. 1776 inn. Family-owned. Cr cds: A, MC, V.
D

★★ **SAGE AMERICAN BAR & GRILL.** *129 W Main St, Chester (06412). 860/526-9898.* Specializes in seafood, prime rib, steak. Hrs: 5-9:30 pm; Fri to 10 pm; Sat to 10:30 pm; Sun 4-9 pm. Res accepted. Dinner $13.95-$23.95. Child's menu. Outdoor lounge. In converted 19th-century mill with wheels and belts overhead. Overlooks waterfall, brook, covered walking bridge. Cr cds: A, D, DS, MC, V.
D

★★ **STEVE CENTERBROOK CAFE.** *78 Main St, Centerbrook (06409). 860/767-1277.* European, Amer menu. Specializes in grill items, pasta. Hrs: 5:30-9 pm. Closed Mon. Res accepted. Bar. A la carte entrees: dinner $15.95-$19.50. Victorian house; country decor. Totally nonsmoking. Cr cds: A, MC, V.
D

Fairfield

See also Bridgeport, Milford, Norwalk, Stamford, Stratford

Settled 1639 **Pop** 53,418 **Elev** 15 ft **Area code** 203
Information Chamber of Commerce, 1597 Post Rd, 06430; 203/255-1011
Web www.fairfieldchamber.com

A small band of colonists led by Roger Ludlowe settled Fairfield two years after the Pequot were subdued in the Great Swamp Fight. In 1779 British troops under General Tyron marched into the area and requested that the people submit to royal authority. When this was refused, the village was put to the torch.

What to See and Do

Connecticut Audubon Society Birdcraft Museum and Sanctuary. Established in 1914, this vest-pocket, six-acre sanctuary houses natural history museum with wildlife displays, dinosaur footprints, trails, ponds. (Tues-Sun) 314 Unquowa Rd. Phone 203/259-0416. **FREE**

Connecticut Audubon Society Fairfield Nature Center and Larsen Sanctuary. Center features Connecticut wildlife and flora, solar greenhouse, natural history library, nature store. (Tues-Sat; also Sun in spring, fall; closed hols) **Donation** Adj is 160-acre sanctuary with six mi of trails through woodlands, meadows, ponds, streams. (Daily) Trail for the disabled. 2325 Burr St. Phone 203/259-6305. ¢

Fairfield Historical Society. Museum with permanent displays of furniture, paintings, maritime memorabilia, dolls, toys, farm implements, clocks; changing exhibits of history, costumes, decorative arts; genealogical and research library. (Tues-Sun; closed hols) 636 Old Post Rd. Phone 203/259-1598. ¢¢

Ogden House. (ca 1750) Maintained by the Fairfield Historical Society, this 18th-century saltbox farmhouse, with authentic furnishings, has been restored to the time of its building by David and Jane Ogden; mid-18th-century kitchen garden. (Mid-May-mid-Oct, Thurs and Sun; other times by appt) 1520 Bronson Rd. Phone 203/259-1598. ¢¢

Special Events

Dogwood Festival. At Greenfield Hill Congregational Church, 1045 Old Academy Rd. Herbs, plants; arts and crafts; walking tours, music programs; food. Phone 203/259-5596. Early or mid-May.

Garlicfest. Notre Dame Catholic High School, 220 Jefferson St. Vendors prepare intl array of garlic-seasoned cuisine. Sales, entertainment. Phone 203/372-6521 or 203/374-4053. First wkend May.

Chamber Arts & Crafts Festival. On Sherman Green. Phone 203/255-1011. Mid-June.

Motel/Motor Lodge

★★ **FAIRFIELD INN AND RESTAURANT.** *417 Post Rd (06430). 203/255-0491; fax 203/255-2073; toll-free 800/347-0414.* 80 rms, 2 story. S, D $70-$110; each addl $10; under 15 free. Crib $10. TV; cable (premium). Pool. Restaurant noon-9 pm. Bar to 1 am; entertainment. Ck-out 11 am. Meeting rms. In-rm modem link. Cr cds: A, C, D, MC, V.
🖼️ 🗦 🐾 SC

Farmington

See also Bristol, Hartford, New Britain, Wethersfield

Settled 1640 **Pop** 20,608 **Elev** 245 ft **Area code** 860 **Zip** 06032

Information Greater Hartford Tourism District, 234 Murphy Rd, Hartford 06114; 860/244-8181 or 800/793-4480

Web www.enjoyhartford.com

In 1802 and 1803, 15,000 yards of linen cloth were loomed in Farmington, and 2,500 hats were made in a shop on Hatter's Lane. There were silversmiths, tinsmiths, cabinet-makers, clockmakers, and carriage builders. Today, Farmington is a beautiful community—one of New England's museum pieces. It is also the home of Miss Porter's School (1844), a well-known private preparatory school for girls.

What to See and Do

Hill-Stead Museum. (1901) Colonial revival-style country house designed by Theodate Pope in collaboration with McKim, Mead, and White for industrialist A. A. Pope; contains Pope's collection of French impressionist paintings and decorative arts. Set on 152 acres, which incl a sunken garden. One-hr tours. (Tues-Sun) 35 Mountain Rd. Phone 860/677-9064. ¢¢¢

Stanley-Whitman House. (ca 1720) This is one of the finest early 18th-century houses in the US; period furniture, local artifacts; changing displays; living history presentations; 18th-century herb and flower gardens. (May-Oct, Wed-Sun afternoons; Nov-Apr, Sun afternoons, also by appt) 37 High St. Phone 860/677-9222. ¢¢

Special Event

Farmington Antiques Weekend. Polo Grounds. One of the largest antique events in Connecticut; approx 600 dealers. Phone 860/871-7914. Early or mid-June.

Hotels

★★ **FARMINGTON INN OF GREATER HARTFORD.** *827 Farmington Ave (06032). 860/269-2340; fax 860/677-8332; toll-free 800/648-9804. www.farmingtoninn.com.* 72 rms, 2 story. S, D $119-$149; each addl $10; suites $109-$149; under 16 free. Crib free. Pet accepted. TV; cable (premium), VCR avail. Complimentary continental bkfst. Ck-out 11 am. Meeting rms. Business servs avail. In-rm modem link. Sundries. Tennis privileges. Golf privileges. X-country ski 1½ mi. Health club privileges. Cr cds: A, C, D, DS, MC, V.
🄳 🗦 🐾 ⚡ 🗦 🎿 🏌 🗦 🐾 SC

★★★ **MARRIOTT FARMINGTON HARTFORD.** *15 Farm Springs Rd (06032). 860/678-1000; fax 860/677-8849; res 800/627-7468. www.marriott.com.* 381 rms, 4 story. S, D $79-$145; suites $250-$500; studio rms $145; under 18 free; wkend rates. TV; cable (premium), VCR avail. 2 pools, 1 indoor; whirlpool, poolside serv. Restaurant 6:30 am-midnight. Bar 11:30-1 am; Fri, Sat to 2 am; Sun to midnight;

entertainment. Ck-out noon. Coin lndry. Convention facilities. Business center. In-rm modem link. Gift shop. 2 tennis courts. Downhill ski 15 mi. Exercise equipt. Game rm. Lawn games. Some bathrm phones. Refrigerator in some suites. Private patios, balconies. Luxury level. Cr cds: A, DS, MC, V.

All Suite

★★ **CENTENNIAL INN.** *5 Spring Ln (06032). 860/677-4647; fax 860/676-0685; toll-free 800/852-2052. www.centennialinn.com.* 112 kit. suites, 2 story. S, D $119-$209; family, wkend rates. Crib free. Pet accepted. TV; cable (premium), VCR (movies $4). Pool; whirlpool. Complimentary continental bkfst. Complimentary coffee in rms. Ck-out noon. Coin lndry. Meeting rms. Business center. In-rm modem link. Downhill ski 15 mi. Exercise equipt. Fireplaces. Balconies. Grills. On 12 wooded acres. Cr cds: A, DS, MC, V.

Restaurants

★★ **APRICOT'S.** *1593 Farmington Ave (06032). 860/673-5405.* Specializes in fresh seafood. Hrs: 11:30 am-2:30 pm, 6-10 pm; Sun 5:30-9 pm; Sun brunch 11:30 am-2:30 pm. Res required. Bar to 1 am. A la carte entrees: lunch $7-$12, dinner $15-$28. Sun brunch $7-$14.95. Child's menu. Pianist Wed-Sat. Patio dining. Converted trolley house. Cr cds: A, D, DS, MC, V.

★ **STONEWELL.** *354 Colt Hwy (06032). 860/677-8855.* Specializes in seafood, steak. Hrs: 11:30 am-3 pm, 5-9 pm; Wed, Thurs to 10 pm; Fri to 11 pm; Sat 11:30 am-11 pm; Sun 3-9 pm; Sun brunch 11 am-3 pm. Closed July 4, Dec 25. Res accepted. Bar to 1 am; Fri, Sat to 2 am. Lunch $4.95-$11.95, dinner $6.25-$17.95. Sun brunch $12.95. Child's menu. Fri, Sat sing-along. Large stone fireplace. Informal atmosphere. Cr cds: A, D, MC, V.

Glastonbury

(see Hartford)

Greenwich

See also Norwalk, Stamford

Settled 1640 **Pop** 58,441 **Elev** 71 ft **Area code** 203

Information Chamber of Commerce, 21 W Putnam Ave, 06830; 203/869-3500

Web www.greenwichchamber.com

Greenwich (GREN-itch) is on the New York state line just 28 miles from Times Square. Behind the city's old New England facade, community leaders continue searching for ways to preserve 18th-century charm in the face of present-day economic, political, and social problems.

What to See and Do

Audubon Center in Greenwich. This 522-acre sanctuary incl self-guided nature trail; interpretive building with exhibits. (Daily) 613 Riversville Rd, 8 mi NW. Phone 203/869-5272. ¢¢

Bruce Museum. Arts and sciences museum features exhibits, lectures, concerts, and educational programs. (Tues-Sun) 1 Museum Dr. Phone 203/869-0376. ¢¢

Bush-Holley House. (1732) Headquarters of the Historical Society of the Town of Greenwich. Residence of a successful 18th-century farmer, it became the site of the Cos Cob art colony at the turn of the century. Exhibits incl late 18th-century Connecticut furniture; paintings by Childe Hassam, Elmer Livingston MacRae, John Henry Twachtman; sculptures by John Rogers; pottery by Leon Volkmar. (Tues-Fri and Sun, afternoons; closed hols) S off US 1, at 39 Strickland Rd in Cos Cob. Phone 203/869-6899. ¢¢

Putnam Cottage/Knapp Tavern. (ca 1690) Near this tavern, Revolutionary General Israel Putnam made a daring escape from the Redcoats in 1779; museum exhibits; rare scalloped shingles; herb garden, restored barn on grounds. (Wed, Fri, and Sun; also by appt) 243 E Putnam Ave. Phone 203/869-9697. ¢

Hotel

★★★ **HYATT REGENCY GREENWICH.** *1800 E Putnam Ave, Old Greenwich (06870). 203/637-1234; fax 203/637-2940; res 800/233-1234. www.hyatt.com.* 374 rms, 4 story. S $219-$275; D $254-$280; each addl $25; suites $325-$850; under 18 free; wkend rates. TV; cable (premium), VCR avail. Indoor pool; whirlpool. Restaurant 6:30 am-11 pm. Rm serv 6-1 am. Bar 11:30 am-midnight; Fri, Sat to 1 am. Ck-out noon. Convention facilities. Business center. In-rm modem link. Gift shop. Exercise equipt; sauna, steam rm. Health club privileges. 4-story atrium; skylights; garden paths and waterways. Luxury level. Cr cds: A, DS, MC, V.

B&Bs/Small Inns

★★ **HARBOR HOUSE INN.** *165 Shore Rd, Old Greenwich (06870). 203/637-0145; fax 203/698-0943. www.hhinn.com.* 23 rms, 6 share bath, 3 story. No elvtr. S, D $169-$279. Crib free. TV; VCR (movies). Complimentary continental bkfst. Complimentary coffee in rms. Restaurant nearby. Ck-out 11 am, ck-in 2 pm. Meeting rm. Business servs avail. In-rm modem link. Health club privileges. Refrigerators. Picnic tables. Totally nonsmoking. Cr cds: A, D, MC, V.

★★★ **HOMESTEAD INN.** *420 Field Point Rd (06830). 203/869-7500; fax 203/869-7502. www.homesteadinn.com.* 19 rms. S, D $250-$450. Children over 14 yrs only. TV; cable, VCR. Restaurant (see also THOMAS HENKELMANN).

Bar 11:30 am-midnight. Ck-out noon, ck-in 3 pm. Meeting rm. Business servs avail. Private patios, verandas. Wraparound porch. Built 1799; antiques. Extensive grounds. Cr cds: A, D, MC, V.

⬛ 🔲 🔥

★★ **STANTON HOUSE INN.** *76 Maple Ave (06830). 203/869-2110; fax 203/629-2116.* 24 rms, 2 share bath, 3 story. S, D $105; each addl $20. TV; cable. Pool. Complimentary continental bkfst. Ck-out 11 am, ck-in 2 pm. Business servs avail. Health club privileges. Some refrigerators. Built 1900; antiques. Totally nonsmoking. Cr cds: A, C, D, DS, MC, V.

⬛ 🔲 🔲 🔲 🔥

Restaurants

★★★ **JEAN-LOUIS.** *61 Lewis St (06830). 203/622-8450. www.restaurantjeanlouis.com.* French menu. Specializes in seafood, poultry. Own baking. Hrs: noon-2 pm; 6-9 pm. Closed Sun. Res accepted. Wine cellar. A la carte entrees: lunch, dinner $30-$35. Street parking. Jacket. Cr cds: A, D, MC, V.

★★ **TERRA RISTORANTE ITALIANO.** *156 Greenwich Ave (06830). 203/629-5222.* Italian menu. Specialty: wood-fired pizza. Hrs: noon-2:30 pm, 5:30-10 pm; Fri, Sat to 10:30 pm; Sun 5:30-9:30 pm. Closed some major hols. Res accepted. Wine, beer. A la carte entrees: lunch $4-$25, dinner $13-$29. Outdoor dining. Italian villa decor; arched ceiling with original frescoes. Cr cds: A, D, MC, V.

⬛ 🔲

★★★ **THOMAS HENKELMANN.** *420 Field Point Rd (06830). 203/869-7500. www.thomashenkelmann.com.* Chef Thomas Henkelmann creates dishes that combine touches of his native Germany with French techniques at this sophisticated French country restaurant. The inn and restaurant, which Henkelmann owns with his wife Theresa, reside in a charmingly renovated 1799 Victorian manor house with a relaxing and eclectic French decor. Try the baked peaches with marzipan he recalls from a favorite childhood combination. Specializes in veal, game, seafood. Own baking. Hrs: 7-9:30 am, noon-2:30 pm, 6-9:30 pm; Fri to 10 pm; Sat 8-10 am, 6-10 pm; Sun 8-10 am, 6-10 pm. Closed Jan 1, summer hols. Res accepted. Bar. Wine cellar. Bkfst $10.50-$16, lunch $15-$27, dinner $26-$38. Valet parking (dinner). Porch; overlooks garden. Fireplaces. Jacket (dinner). Cr cds: A, D, MC, V.

⬛

Groton

See also Mystic, New London, Norwich

Settled 1705 **Pop** 9,837 **Elev** 90 ft **Area code** 860 **Zip** 06340
Information Connecticut's Mystic & More, 470 Bank St, PO Box 89, New London 06320; 860/444-2206 or 800/TO-ENJOY (outside CT)
Web www.mysticmore.com

Groton is the home of a huge US naval submarine base. It is also the place where the Electric Boat Division of the General Dynamics Corporation, the world's largest private builder of submarines, built the first diesel-powered submarine (1912) and the first nuclear-powered submarine, *Nautilus* (1955). Pfizer Incorporated operates one of the largest antibiotic plants in the world and maintains a research laboratory here.

What to See and Do

Charter fishing trips. Several companies offer full- and ½-day saltwater fishing trips both for small and large groups.

Fort Griswold Battlefield State Park. Incl 135-ft monument to 88 Revolutionary soldiers slain here in 1781 by British troops under the command of Benedict Arnold. Park (daily). Monument and museum (Memorial Day-Labor Day, daily; Labor Day-Columbus Day, Sat and Sun). 1½ mi S of US 1 on Monument St and Park Ave. Phone 860/449-6877 or 860/445-1729.

Historic Ship *Nautilus* and Submarine Force Museum. Permanent home for *Nautilus*, world's first nuclear-powered submarine. Self-guided, audio tour; museum exhibits depicting history of the US Submarine Force; working periscopes; authentic submarine control rm; four mini-subs; mini-theaters. Picnicking. (Spring-fall, daily; winter, Mon, Wed-Sun; closed Jan 1, Thanksgiving, Dec 25, also first two wks May and last two wks Oct) 2 mi N on CT 12 at Crystal Lake Rd. Phone 860/694-3174 or 800/343-0079. **FREE**

Oceanographic cruise. A 2½-hr educational cruise on Long Island Sound aboard marine research vessels *Enviro-lab II* and *Enviro-lab III*. (Summer). Also board a Harbor Seal Watch on Long Island Sound (winter), or visit Ledge Lighthouse. Opportunity to use nets and scientific instruments to explore marine environment firsthand. (June-Aug) Avery Point. Phone 800/364-8472. ¢¢¢¢

Motels/Motor Lodges

★ **CLARION INN.** *156 Kings Hwy (06340). 860/446-0660; fax 860/445-4082; toll-free 800/252-7466. www.clarioninn.com.* 69 rms, 2 story, 34 kits. July-Oct: S, D, kit. units $76-$139; each addl $10; suites $89-$179; under 18 free; lower rates rest of yr. Crib free. TV; cable (premium). Indoor pool; whirlpool. Restaurant 6 am-10 pm; wkends from 7 am. Rm serv. Bar 11-1 am. Ck-out 11 am. Coin lndry. Meeting rms. Business servs avail. Valet serv. Barber, beauty shop. Exercise equipt; sauna. Game rm. Many refrigerators; some wet bars. Balconies. Picnic tables, grills. Cr cds: A, C, D, DS, MC, V.

🔲 🔲 🔲 🔲 **SC**

★ **QUALITY INN.** *404 Bridge St (06340). 860/445-8141. www.qualityinn.com.* 106 rms, 3 story. No elvtr. Late May-late Oct: S, D $90-$130; each addl $10; under 18 free; monthly rates; lower rates rest of yr. Crib free. TV; cable (premium). Pool. Restaurant hrs vary. Bar noon-midnight. Ck-out 11 am. Meeting rms. Business servs avail. Exercise equipt. Refrigerators avail. Cr cds: A, D, DS, MC, V.

⬛ 🔲 🔲 🔲 🔥

Hotel

★★★ **MARRIOTT MYSTIC HOTEL AND SPA.** *625 North Rd (06340).* 860/446-2600. www.marriott.com. 285 rms, 6 story. S, D $195-$325; under 18 free. Crib avail. TV; cable (premium). Indoor pool; whirlpool. Restaurant 6:30 am-10 pm. Bar to midnight. Ck-out 11 am. Meeting rms. Business center. In-rm modem link. Concierge. Exercise equipt. Minibars; many refrigerators in suites. Spa. Cr cds: A, C, D, DS, ER, JCB, MC, V.

Guilford

See also Branford, Clinton, Madison, New Haven

Founded 1639 **Pop** 19,848 **Elev** 20 ft **Area code** 203
Zip 06437
Information Chamber of Commerce, 63 Whitfield St; 203/453-9677
Web www.guilfordct.com

Guilford was settled by a group of Puritans who followed Reverend Henry Whitfield here from England. One of the residents, Samuel Hill, gave rise to the expression "run like Sam Hill" when he repeatedly ran for political office.

What to See and Do

Henry Whitfield State Museum. (1639) The oldest house in the state and among the oldest of stone houses in New England. Restored with 17th- and 18th-century furnishings; exhibits. Gift shop. (Apr-Dec 14, Wed-Sun; closed hols) ½ mi S on Whitfield St. Phone 203/453-2457. ¢¢

Hyland House. (1660) Restored and furnished in 17th-century period, herb garden; guided tours. (Early June-Oct, Tues-Sun) A map of historic houses in Guilford avail. 84 Boston St. Phone 203/453-9477. ¢

Thomas Griswold House Museum. (ca 1775) Fine example of a saltbox house; costumes of 1800s, changing historical exhibits, period gardens, restored working blacksmith shop. (Early June-Oct, Tues-Sun; winter by appt) 171 Boston St. Phone 203/453-5517. ¢

All Suite

★ **TOWER SUITES MOTEL.** *320 Boston Post Rd (06437).* 203/453-9069; fax 203/458-2727. 14 kit. units. May-Oct: S $55; D $69; each addl $10; under 12 free; lower rates rest of yr. Crib free. TV; cable (premium). Coffee in rms. Restaurant nearby. Ck-out 11 am. Lawn games. Cr cds: A, DS, MC, V.

Restaurant

★★ **SACHEM COUNTRY HOUSE.** *111 Goose Ln (06437).* 203/453-5261. Specializes in seafood, prime rib. Hrs: 4-9 pm; Fri to 10 pm; Sat 5-10 pm; Sun 11 am-7:30 pm; Sun brunch to 2:30 pm. Res required Fri, Sat. Dinner $10.95-$14.95. Sun brunch $12.95. Child's menu. In 18th-century house; fireplace. Family-owned. Cr cds: A, MC, V. Ⓓ

Hartford

See also Avon, Farmington, Wethersfield

Settled 1633 **Pop** 139,739 **Elev** 50 ft **Area code** 860
Information Greater Hartford Convention & Visitors Bureau, One Civic Center Plaza, Suite 300, 06103; 860/728-6789 or 800/446-7811 (outside CT)
Web www.enjoyhartford.com

The capital of Connecticut and a major industrial and cultural center on the Connecticut River, Hartford is headquarters for many of the nation's insurance companies.

Roots of American democracy are deep in Hartford's history. The city was made virtually independent in 1662 by Charles II, but an attempt was made by Sir Edmund Andros, governor of New England, to seize its charter. The document was hidden by Joseph Wadsworth in a hollow tree since known as the Charter Oak. The tree was blown down in 1856; a plaque on Charter Oak Avenue marks the spot.

Hartford has what is said to be the oldest continuously published newspaper in the United States, the *Courant*. Founded in 1764, it became a daily in 1837. Trinity College (1823), the American School for the Deaf, Connecticut Institute for the Blind, and the Institute of Living (for mental illness) are located in the city.

Transportation

Car Rental Agencies. See IMPORTANT TOLL-FREE NUMBERS.

Public Transportation. Buses (Connecticut Transit), phone 860/525-9181.

Rail Passenger Service. Amtrak 800/872-7245.

Airport Information

Hartford Bradley Intl Airport. Information 860/627-3000; lost and found 860/627-3340; cash machines, Terminal B, Concourse A.

What to See and Do

Bushnell Park. The 41-acre park contains 150 varieties of trees and a restored 1914 carousel (schedule varies; fee); concerts and special events (spring-fall). Downtown, between Jewell, Elm, and Trinity Sts. Phone 860/246-7739. FREE

Butler-McCook Homestead and Main Street History Center. (1782) Preserved house, occupied by four generations of one family (1782-1971), has possessions dating back 200 yrs; collection of Victorian toys; Japanese armor; Victorian garden. (Wed-Sun; closed hols) 396 Main St. Phone 860/522-1806 or 860/247-8996. ¢¢

Center Church and Ancient Burying Ground. Church (1807) is patterned after London's St. Martin-in-the-Fields, with Tiffany stained-glass windows. Cemetery contains markers dating back to 1640. Main and Gold Sts. Phone 860/247-4080.

Connecticut Audubon Society Holland Brook Nature Center. On 48 acres adj to Connecticut River, the center features a variety of natural history exhibits incl discovery rm. Many activities. (Tues-Sun; closed hols) 5 mi SE via CT 2 at 1361 Main St, in Glastonbury. Phone 860/633-8402. Discovery rm ¢

Connecticut Historical Society. Library contains more than three million books and manuscripts. (Tues-Sat; closed hols). Museum has nine galleries featuring permanent and changing exhibits on state history (Tues-Sun). 1 Elizabeth St. Phone 860/236-5621. ¢¢

Elizabeth Park. Public gardens feature 900 varieties of roses and more than 14,000 other plants; first municipal rose garden in country; greenhouses (all yr). Outdoor concerts in summer; ice-skating in winter. (Daily) Prospect and Asylum Aves. Phone 860/242-0017. **FREE**

Harriet Beecher Stowe House. (1871) The restored Victorian cottage of the author of *Uncle Tom's Cabin* contains original furniture, memorabilia. Tours. (Tues-Sat, also Sun afternoons; also Mon June-Columbus Day and Dec) 77 Forest St. Phone 860/522-9258. ¢¢

Mark Twain House. (1874) *Tom Sawyer, Huckleberry Finn,* and other books were published while Samuel Clemens (Mark Twain) lived in this three-story Victorian mansion featuring the decorative work of Charles Comfort Tiffany and the Associated Artists; Tiffany-glass light fixtures, windows, and Tiffany-designed stencilwork in gold and silver leaf. Tours. (May-Oct and Dec, daily; rest of yr, Mon, Wed-Sun; closed hols) 351 Farmington Ave. Phone 860/247-0998. ¢¢

Noah Webster Foundation and Historical Society. This 18th-century homestead was birthplace of America's first lexicographer, writer of the *Blue-Backed Speller* (1783) and the *American Dictionary* (1828). Period furnishings, memorabilia; costumed guides; period gardens. (Mon, Thurs-Sun; closed hols) 227 S Main St in West Hartford. Phone 860/521-5362. ¢¢

Old State House. (1796) Oldest state house in nation, designed by Charles Bulfinch; restored Senate chamber with Gilbert Stuart portrait of Washington; displays and rotating exhibitions. Tourist information center; museum shop. Guided tours by appt. (Mon-Sat; closed hols) 800 Main St. Phone 860/522-6766. **FREE**

Raymond E. Baldwin Museum of Connecticut History. Exhibits incl Colt Collection of Firearms; Connecticut artifacts, incl original 1662 Royal Charter; portraits of Connecticut's governors. Library features law, social sciences, history, genealogy collections, and official state archives. (Daily; closed hols) Connecticut State Library, 231 Capitol Ave, opp Capitol. Phone 860/737-6535. **FREE**

Science Center of Connecticut. Computer lab; UTC Wildlife Sanctuary; physical sciences discovery rm; walk-in replica of sperm whale; "KaleidoSight," a giant walk-in kaleidoscope; planetarium shows; changing exhibits.

(Tues-Sat, also Sun afternoons, also Mon during summer; closed hols) 950 Trout Brook Dr in West Hartford. Phone 860/231-2824. ¢¢

Sightseeing tours.

    Connecticut River Cruise. The *Lady Fenwick,* a reproduction of an 1850s steam yacht, makes 1- to 2 ½-hr trips on the Connecticut River. (Memorial Day-Labor Day, daily; after Labor Day-Oct, Sat-Sun) Departs from Charter Oak Landing. Phone 860/526-4954. ¢¢

    Heritage Trails Sightseeing. Guided and narrated tours of Hartford and Farmington. (Daily) Phone 860/677-8867. ¢¢¢

State Capitol. (1879) Guided tours (1 hr) of the restored, gold-domed capitol building and the contemporary legislative office building (Mon-Fri; closed hols, also Dec 25-Jan 1); incl historical displays. 210 Capitol Ave, at Trinity St. Phone 860/240-0222. **FREE**

Talcott Mountain State Park. The 557-acre park features the 165-ft Heublein Tower, on mountaintop 1,000 ft above Farmington River; considered best view in state. (Third Sat Apr-Labor Day, Thurs-Sun; after Labor Day-first wkend Nov, daily) Picnicking, shelters. 8 mi NW via US 44, off CT 185, near Simsbury. Phone 860/677-0662.

University of Hartford. (1877) 6,844 students. Independent institution on 320-acre campus. Many free concerts, operas, lectures, and art exhibits. 4 mi W, at 200 Bloomfield Ave in West Hartford. Phone 860/768-4100. Located here is

    Museum of American Political Life. Exhibits incl life-size mannequins re-creating political marches from 1830s-1960s; 70-ft wall of historical pictures and images; political television commercials since 1952. (Tues-Sun afternoons; closed hols) In the Harry Jack Gray Center. Phone 860/768-4090. **FREE**

⚔ **Wadsworth Atheneum Museum of Art.** One of nation's oldest continuously operating public art museums with more than 40,000 works of art, spanning 5,000 yrs; 15th- to 20th-century paintings, American furniture, sculpture, porcelains, English and American silver, the Amistad Collection of African-American art; changing contemporary exhibits. (Tues-Sun; closed hols) Free admission Thurs and Sat morning. 600 Main St. Phone 860/278-2670.

Special Events

Taste of Hartford. Main St, downtown. Four-day event features specialties of more than 50 area restaurants; continuous entertainment. Phone 860/920-5337. June.

Riverfest. Celebration of America's independence and the Connecticut River. Family entertainment, concerts, food, fireworks display over river. Early July. Phone 860/713-3131.

Mark Twain Days. Celebration of Twain's legacy and Hartford's cultural heritage with more than 100 events. Concerts, riverboat rides, medieval jousting, tours of Twain House, entertainment. Aug. Phone 860/247-0998.

Christmas Crafts Expo I & II. Hartford Civic Center. Exhibits and demonstrations of traditional and contemporary craft media. First and second wkends Dec. Phone 860/249-6333.

Motels/Motor Lodges

★★ **HOLIDAY INN.** *363 Roberts St, East Hartford (06108).* *860/528-9611; fax 860/289-0270; toll-free 800/465-4329.* *www.holiday-inn.com.* 130 rms, 5 story. S, D $65-$85; under 18 free; wkend rates. Crib free. Pet accepted. TV; cable (premium). Indoor pool. Complimentary coffee in rms. Restaurant 6 am-10 pm. Rm serv. Bar 4 pm-midnight. Ck-out noon. Coin lndry. Meeting rms. Business servs avail. In-rm modem link. Valet serv. Exercise equipt. Some refrigerators. Cr cds: A, DS, MC, V.

★ **RAMADA INN CAPITOL HILL.** *440 Asylum St (06103).* *860/246-6591; fax 860/728-1382; 800/228-2828.* *www. ramada.com.* 96 rms, 9 story. S $49-$65; D $55-$65; each addl $10. Crib free. Pet accepted, some restrictions. TV; cable (premium). Ck-out noon. Business servs avail. Free valet parking. Cr cds: A, D, DS, MC, V.

Hotels

★★★ **CROWNE PLAZA.** *50 Morgan St (06120).* *860/549-2400; fax 860/549-7844; toll-free 800/227-6963.* *www. crowneplaza.com.* 342 rms, 18 story. S $79.95-$119.95; D $89.95-$129.95; each addl $10; suites $225; under 18 free; wkend rates. Crib free. Pet accepted. TV; cable (premium), VCR avail. Pool; poolside serv. Restaurant 6:30 am-10 pm. Bar 4 pm-2 am. Ck-out noon. Convention facilities. Business center. In-rm modem link. Free airport transportation. Exercise equipt. Cr cds: A, C, D, DS, JCB, MC, V.

★★★ **GOODWIN HOTEL.** *1 Haynes St (06013).* *860/246-7500; fax 860/247-4576; toll-free 800/922-5006.* *www.goodwinhotel.com.* 124 rms, 6 story. S, D $119; suites $228-$786; under 18 free; wkend rates and packages. Crib free. Garage, valet parking $13. TV; cable (premium), VCR avail. Restaurant 6:30 am-10:30 pm. Rm serv 6 am-midnight. Bar 11-1 am. Ck-out noon. Meeting rms. Business servs avail. In-rm modem link. Concierge. Exercise equipt. Bathrm phones; some fireplaces. Refrigerators avail. Small, European-style luxury hotel in red-brick, Queen Anne-style building (1881) built for J.P. Morgan; 19th-century paintings and replicas of sailing ships. Cr cds: A, C, D, DS, MC, V.

★★★ **HILTON.** *315 Trumbull St (06103).* *860/728-5151; fax 860/240-7246; res 800/445-8667.* *www.hartford.hilton.com.* 388 rms, 22 story. S, D $199; each addl $15; suites $250-$600; under 17 free; wkend, hol rates. Crib free. Garage parking $10. TV; cable (premium), VCR avail. Indoor pool; whirlpool. Coffee in rms. Restaurant 6:30 am-11 pm. Bar. Ck-out noon. Convention facilities. Business servs avail. In-rm modem link. Exercise equipt; sauna. Civic Center Plaza adj; shops. Cr cds: A, C, D, DS, MC, V.

★★★ **MARRIOTT ROCKY HILL.** *100 Capital Blvd, Rocky Hill (06067).* *860/257-6000; 800/228-9290.* *www.marriott .com.* 247 rms, 4 story. S, D $255-$325; under 18 free. Crib avail. TV; cable (premium). Indoor pool; whirlpool. Restaurant 6:30 am-10 pm. Bar to midnight. Ck-out 1 pm. Meeting rms. Business center. In-rm modem link. Concierge. Exercise equipt. Minibars; many refrigerators in suites. Cr cds: A, C, D, DS, ER, JCB, MC, V.

★★★ **SHERATON HARTFORD HOTEL.** *100 E River Dr, East Hartford (06108).* *860/528-9703; fax 860/289-4728; res 800/325-3535.* *www.sheraton.com.* 199 rms, 8 story. S $219; each addl $150-$200; suites $150-$200; under 18 free; wkend rates. Crib free. Pet accepted. TV; cable (premium). Indoor pool. Playground. Restaurant 6:30 am-2 pm, 5-10 pm. Rm serv. Bar. Ck-out 11 am. Coin lndry. Meeting rms. Business servs avail. In-rm modem link. Valet serv. Health club privileges. Cr cds: A, C, D, DS, ER, JCB, MC, V.

Restaurants

★★ **BUTTERFLY.** *831 Farmington Ave, West Hartford (06119).* *860/236-2816.* Chinese menu. Specializes in Szechwan cuisine. Hrs: 11:30 am-10 pm; Fri, Sat to 11 pm; Sun brunch to 4 pm. Closed Thanksgiving. Res accepted. Bar. A la carte entrees: lunch $5.50-$6.95, dinner $5.95-$14.95. Sun brunch $12.95. Parking. Contemporary decor. Cr cds: A, DS, MC, V.

★★★ **CARBONE'S.** *588 Franklin Ave (06114).* *860/296-9646.* Italian menu. Specialties: fettucine carbonara, vitello cuscinetto. Own baking, desserts. Hrs: 11:30 am-2 pm, 5-9:30 pm; Sat from 5 pm. Closed Sun; major hols. Res accepted. Bar. Lunch $8-$11, dinner $12-$20. Parking. Tableside preparation. Family-owned. Cr cds: A, D, MC, V.

★ **HOT TOMATOES.** *1 Union Pl (06103).* *860/249-5100.* Italian menu. Specializes in pasta, veal. Hrs: 11:30 am-2:30 pm, 5:30-9:30 pm; Fri, Sat to 10:30 pm; Sun, Mon 5:30-9 pm. Res accepted. Bar. A la carte entrees: lunch $6.95-$8.95, dinner $8.95-$18.95. Outdoor dining. Cr cds: A, D, MC, V.

★★ **MAX DOWNTOWN.** *185 Asylum St (06103).* *860/522-2530.* *www.maxdowntown.com.* Specializes in black Angus beef, stone pies. Hrs: 11:30 am-2:30 pm, 5-10 pm; Fri to 11 pm; Sat 5-11 pm; Sun 5-9 pm. Closed most major hols. Res accepted. Bar. A la carte entrees: lunch $6.95-$9.95, dinner $9.95-$23. Child's menu. Intimate bistro atmosphere. Cr cds: A, D, DS, MC, V.

★★★ **PASTIS.** *201 Ann St (06103).* *860/278-8852.* *www.pastisbrasserie.com.* Specializes in steak frettes, coq au vin, cassoulet. Hrs: 11:30 am-10 pm; Fri to 11 pm; Sat 5-11 pm. Closed Sun. Res accepted. Wine list. Lunch $6.95-$16.95; dinner $15.95-$24.95. Cr cds: A, D, MC, V.

★★ **PEPPERCORN'S GRILL.** *357 Main St (06106). 860/547-1714.* Italian menu. Specialties: orange ravioli, veal chops, osso buco. Hrs: 11:30 am-2:30 pm, 5-10 pm; Thurs to 10:30 pm; Fri to 11:30 pm; Sat 5-11:30 pm. Closed Sun; major hols. Res accepted. Bar. A la carte entrees: lunch $6.95-$16.95, dinner $16.95-$45. Child's menu. Parking. Contemporary bistro atmosphere. Cr cds: A, D, MC, V.
D

Unrated Dining Spot

RESTAURANT BRICCO. *78 LaSalle Rd, West Hartford (06903). 860/233-0220.* Specializes in Australian lamb, stone pies. Own baking and desserts. Hrs: 11:30 am-3 pm, 5-10 pm; Fri, Sat to 11 pm; Sun to 9 pm. Child's menu. Lunch $11-$14, dinner $15-$25. Patio outdoor dining. Family-owned. Cr cds: MC, V.
D

Kent

See also Cornwall Bridge, New Preston

Pop 2,918 **Elev** 395 ft **Area code** 860 **Zip** 06757
Information Litchfield Hills Visitors Bureau, PO Box 968, Litchfield 06759; 860/567-4506
Web www.litchfieldhills.com

Kent, a small community near the western border of Connecticut, has become an art and antique center. Home to a large art colony, the surrounding area is characterized by massive hills that overlook the plain of the Housatonic River. The village of Kent was incorporated in 1738, after the tract of land was sold in a public auction. Although early development was based on agriculture, by the middle of the 19th century Kent was a booming industrial village with three iron furnaces operating in the area.

What to See and Do

Kent Falls State Park. This 295-acre park is beautiful in spring when the stream is high and in fall when leaves are changing; 200-ft cascading waterfall. Stream fishing; hiking, picnicking. Standard fees. (Daily) 5 mi N on US 7. Phone 860/927-4100 or 860/927-3238.

Macedonia Brook State Park. These 2,300 acres provide one of the state's finest nature study areas, as well as views of the Catskills and Taconic mountains. Trout-stocked stream fishing; hiking, picnicking, camping (late Apr-Sept) on 84 sites in open and wooded settings. Standard fees. (Daily) 2 mi E on CT 341, N on Macedonia Brook Rd. Phone 860/927-4100 or 860/927-3238. **FREE**

Sloane-Stanley Museum and Kent Furnace. New England barn houses Eric Sloane's collection of early American tools, re-creation of his studio, artifacts, works; on site of old Kent furnace (1826); video presentation. (Mid May-Oct, Wed-Sun) 1 mi N on US 7. ¢¢

Special Event

Fall Festival. Exhibits incl steam and traction engines, road roller (ca 1910), windmill; threshers; broom making, shingle sawing; antique cars, steamboats, tractors, and trucks. 1 mi N on US 7, on grounds of the Connecticut Antique Machinery Museum. Late Sept. Phone 860/927-0050.

B&B/Small Inn

★★ **FIFE N DRUM RESTAURANT & INN.** *53 N Main St (06757). 860/927-3509; fax 860/927-4595. www.fifendrum .com.* 8 rms. Apr-Oct: D $95-$110; each addl $12.50; lower rates rest of yr. TV. Complimentary coffee. Restaurant (see also FIFE 'N DRUM). Rm serv. Bar 11:30 am-11 pm; wkends to midnight; entertainment. Ck-out 11 am, ck-in 2 pm. Gift shop. Downhill/x-country ski 11 mi. Balconies. Cr cds: A, DS, MC, V.
D ⊁ ⇩ ⚲

Restaurant

★★★ **FIFE'N DRUM.** *53 N Main St (06757). 860/927-3509. www.fifendrum.com.* Continental menu. Specialties: roast duckling, filet mignon au poivre, sweetbreads. Own baking. Hrs: 11:30 am-3 pm, 5:30-9:30 pm; Fri to 10 pm; Sat to 10:30 pm; Sun brunch to 3 pm. Closed Tues; Dec 25. Res accepted. Bar; Fri, Sat to midnight. Wine cellar. Lunch $4.50-$7.95, dinner $8.95-$24.50. Sun brunch $15.95. Child's menu. Entertainment. Cr cds: A, D, DS, MC, V.
D ⇩

Lakeville

See also Cornwall Bridge, Norfolk

Settled 1740 **Pop** 1,800 **Elev** 764 ft **Area code** 860
Zip 06039
Information Litchfield Hills Visitors Bureau, PO Box 968, Litchfield 06759; 860/567-4506
Web www.litchfieldhills.com

Lakeville, located on Lake Wononscopomuc in the Litchfield Hills area, developed around a major blast furnace once owned by Ethan Allen. The furnace and nearby metals foundry cast many of the weapons used in the American Revolution as well as the guns for the USS *Constellation*. When the furnace was torn down in 1843, the first knife manufacturing factory was erected there. Nearby is the famous Hotchkiss School, a coed prep school.

What to See and Do

Holley House. Museums of 18th and 19th-century history incl 1768 iron-master's home with 1808 Classical-revival wing; Holley Manufacturing Company pocketknife exhibit from 1876; hands-on 1870s kitchen exhibit illustrating the debate over women's roles. 1876 Living History Tours (four tours daily). (Mid-June-mid-Oct, Sat, Sun, and hol afternoons; also by appt) Main St at Millerton Rd. Phone 860/435-2878. Also here is

Salisbury Cannon Museum. Hands-on exhibits illustrate contributions of local iron industry to American Revolution. Incl ice house, cutting tools, outhouse, 19th-century heritage gardens, and Nature's Medicine Cabinet exhibit. Same hrs as Holley House. Phone 860/435-2878. **FREE**

Special Events

Grand Prix at Lime Rock. Phone 800/RACE-LRP. Memorial Day wkend.

Music Mountain Summer Music Festival. On Music Mtn, 5 mi NE via US 44, 3 mi S on CT 126 to Falls Village, then 2½ mi E on CT 126 to top of Music Mtn Rd. Performances by known ensembles and guest artists; also jazz series. Sat, Sun. Phone 860/824-7126 (box office). Mid June-early Sept.

Sports car racing. Lime Rock Park, 2 mi S on CT 41, then 4 mi E on CT 112, at jct US 7. Sat and Mon hols. Phone 800/RACE-LRP.

Motels/Motor Lodges

★★ **INN AT IRON MASTERS.** *229 N Main St (06039). 860/435-9844; fax 860/435-2254. www.innatironmasters.com.* 28 rms. Apr-Nov: S $95-$135; D $105-$145; each addl $15; under 15 free; lower rates rest of yr. Crib free. Pet accepted, some restrictions. TV; cable. Heated pool. Continental bkfst. Coffee in rms. Restaurant 11 am-9 pm; Thurs-Sat to 10 pm. Bar. Ck-out 11 am. Cr cds: A, MC, V.

★ **SHARON MOTOR LODGE.** *1 Calkinstown Rd, Sharon (06069). 860/364-0036; fax 860/364-0462.* 22 rms. May-Oct: S, D $79-$135; lower rates rest of yr. Crib $10. TV; cable. Pool. Restaurant opp 7:30 am-10:30 pm. Ck-out 11 am. Business servs avail. Downhill/x-country ski 10 mi. Cr cds: A, DS, MC, V.

Resort

★★★ **INTERLAKEN INN.** *74 Interlaken Rd (06039). 860/435-9878; fax 860/435-2980; toll-free 800/222-2909. www.interlakeninn.com.* 80 rms, 2 story. May-Oct: S, D $129-$199; each addl $15; suites $265; higher rates special events; lower rates rest of yr. Crib $10. Pet accepted. TV; cable (premium), VCR (movies). Heated pool. Restaurant 7 am-9 pm; Fri, Sat to 10 pm. Rm serv. Ck-out noon, ck-in 3 pm. Meeting rms. Business servs avail. In-rm modem link. Valet serv. Tennis. 9-hole golf, pro. Rowboats, canoes, sailboats, paddleboats. Lawn games. Rec rm. Exercise equipt; sauna. Refrigerator avail. Balconies. Cr cds: A, DS, MC, V.

B&B/Small Inn

★★ **WAKE ROBIN INN.** *Rte 41 (06039). 860/435-2515; fax 860/435-2000. www.wakerobininn.com.* 39 rms, 2 story. Apr-Nov: S, D $95-$250; each addl $10; lower rates rest of yr. Crib free. Pet accepted. TV; cable (premium). Ck-out noon, ck-in 2 pm. Former girls school (1896); antiques. Library, sitting rm. On hill. Cr cds: A, MC, V.

Litchfield

See also Bristol, Cornwall Bridge

Settled 1720 **Pop** 8,365 **Elev** 1,085 ft **Area code** 860 **Zip** 06759

Information Litchfield Hills Visitors Bureau, PO Box 968; 860/567-4506

Web www.litchfieldhills.com

Litchfield, on a plateau above the Naugatuck Valley, has preserved a semblance of the 18th century through both its many early homes and its air of peace and quiet. Because the railroads laid their main lines below in the valley, industry largely bypassed Litchfield. The Reverend Henry Ward Beecher and his sister, Harriet Beecher Stowe, author of *Uncle Tom's Cabin,* grew up in Litchfield. Tapping Reeve established the first law school in the country here in the late 18th century.

What to See and Do

Haight Vineyard and Winery. First Connecticut winery; one of the few to grow vinifera grapes in New England. Tours, tastings; vineyard walk, picnic tables; gift shop. (Daily; closed hols) Chestnut Hill Rd. Phone 860/567-4045. **FREE**

Litchfield History Museum. Houses an outstanding collection of American art and artifacts from the 18th-21st centuries; research library, changing exhibits, video presentation. (Mid-Apr-Nov, Tues-Sun; closed hols) On the Green, at jct East and South Sts. Phone 860/567-4501. ¢¢

Tapping Reeve House. (1773) **And Law School** (1784). Introducing visitors to 19th century Litchfield through the lives of the students who attended the Litchfield Law School and the Litchfield Female Academy; graduates incl Aaron Burr and John C. Calhoun; garden. (Mid Apr-Nov, Tues-Sun; closed July 4, Labor Day) South St. Phone 860/567-4501. ¢

Topsmead State Forest. This 511-acre forest incl an English Tudor mansion overlooking a 40-acre wildlife preserve. Tours of mansion (Second and fourth wkends, June-Oct). Phone 860/567-5694 or 860/485-0226. **FREE**

White Memorial Foundation, Inc. The 4,000-acre conservation area is contiguous with part of Bantam Lake shoreline (largest natural lake in the state), the Bantam River, and several small streams and ponds. Rolling woodland has wide variety of trees, flowers, ferns, mosses, 35 mi of trails; woodland birds, both nesting and in migration; and other woodland animals. The Conservation Center has displays and exhibits, extensive nature library with children's rm (daily; fee). Swimming, fishing, boating; hiking trails, incl "trail of the senses," x-country skiing, camping. 2½ mi W on US 202. Phone 860/567-0857.

Special Event

Open House Tour. Tour of Litchfield's historic homes, special exhibits, tea, and luncheon. (Early July) Phone 860/567-9423. Same day ¢¢¢¢ In advance ¢¢¢

B&B/Small Inn

★★ **LITCHFIELD INN.** *432 Bantam Rd (06759). 860/567-4503; fax 860/567-5358; toll-free 800/499-3444. www. litchfieldinnct.com.* 32 rms, 2 story. Apr-Oct: S $105-$115; D $115-$125; each addl $10; under 12 free; lower rates rest of yr. Crib free. TV; cable (premium), VCR. Complimentary continental bkfst. Restaurant 6:30-10 am, noon-3 pm, 5:30-9 pm. Rm serv. Bar noon-closing. Ck-out noon. Meeting rms. Business servs avail. In-rm modem link. Downhill ski 20 mi; x-country ski 5 mi. Game rm. Lawn games. Some refrigerators. Picnic tables. Country inn with theme rms such as The Lace Room and The Presidential Quarters. Cr cds: A, D, MC, V.

[D] [>] [≈] [▲] [SC]

Restaurants

★★ **VILLAGE RESTAURANT.** *25 West St (06759). 860/567-8307.* Continental menu. Specializes in fresh seafood, steak. Hrs: 11:30 am-9 pm; Fri, Sat to 10 pm; Sun brunch 11:30 am-3:30 pm. Closed Dec 25. Res accepted. Bar. A la carte entrees: lunch $6-$10, dinner $12-$20. Sun brunch $8-$12. Child's menu. Overlooks village green. Cr cds: A, C, MC, V.

★★★ **WEST STREET GRILL.** *43 West St (06759). 860/567-3885.* Contemporary Amer menu. Hrs: 11:30 am-3 pm, 5:30-9 pm; Fri, Sat 11:30 am-4 pm, 5:30-10 pm. Closed Dec 25. Res accepted; required Fri, Sat. Bar. Wine cellar. A la carte entrees: lunch $4.95-$14.95, dinner $6.95-$25.95. Child's menu. Contemporary black and white decor. Cr cds: A, MC, V.

[D]

Madison

See also Branford, Clinton, Guilford, New Haven

Settled 1649 **Pop** 15,485 **Elev** 22 ft **Area code** 203
Zip 06443
Information Chamber of Commerce, 22 Scotland Ave, PO Box 706; 203/245-7394; Tourism Office, 22 School St; 203/245-5659
Web www.madisonct.com

What to See and Do

Allis-Bushnell House and Museum. (ca 1785) Period rms with four-corner fireplaces; doctor's office and equipment; exhibits of costumes, dolls, household implements, farming, fishing and shipbuilding tools; original paneling; herb garden. (May-Oct, Wed, Fri and Sat, limited hrs; other times by appt) 853 Boston Post Rd. Phone 203/245-4567. **Donation**

Deacon John Grave House. Frame garrison colonial house (1685). (Memorial Day-Labor Day, Tues-Sun; spring and fall, wkends only) Academy and School Sts. Phone 203/245-4798. **Donation**

Hammonasset Beach State Park. More than 900 acres with two-mi beach on Long Island Sound. Saltwater swimming, scuba diving, fishing, boating; hiking, picnicking (shelters), camping. Nature center. Standard fees. 1 mi S of I-95 exit 62. Phone 203/245-1817.

B&B/Small Inn

★★ **MADISON BEACH HOTEL.** *94 W Wharf Rd (06443). 203/245-1404; fax 203/245-0410. www.madisonbeachhotel.com.* 35 rms, 4 story. No elvtr. May-Oct: S, D $85-$125; each addl $10; suites $150-$225; under 18 free; wkly rates; lower rates Mar-mid-May, Oct-Dec. Closed Jan-Feb. TV; cable (premium). Complimentary continental bkfst. Restaurant 11:30 am-3 pm, 5:30-10 pm. Bar to 1 am; entertainment Fri, Sat. Ck-out 11 am. Meeting rms. Business servs avail. Lawn games. Some refrigerators. Many balconies. On ocean. Cr cds: A, D, DS, MC, V.

[D] [⚓] [≈] [▲]

Restaurants

★★★ **CAFE ALLEGRE.** *725 Boston Post Rd (06443). 203/245-7773.* Continental menu. Specializes in regional and international dishes. Hrs: 11:30 am-10 pm; Sun brunch to 4 pm. Closed Jan 1, Dec 25. Res accepted. Bar. Wine cellar. A la carte entrees: lunch $5.95-$9.95, dinner $13.95-$21.95. Sun brunch $14.95. Child's menu. Pianist, harpist Sun. Outdoor dining. Garden atmosphere; 3 dining rms. Cr cds: A, D, MC, V.

[D] [≈]

★★ **FRIENDS AND COMPANY.** *11 Boston Post Rd (06443). 203/245-0462.* Specializes in fresh seafood, steak, seasonal dishes. Own baking, desserts. Hrs: noon-2:30 pm, 5-10 pm; Fri to 11 pm; Sat 5-11 pm; Sun 4:30-9 pm; early-bird dinner Sun-Fri 5-6 pm; Sun brunch 11 am-2:30 pm. Closed Thanksgiving, Dec 25; also last Mon June. Bar. Lunch $5.75-$8.95, dinner $5.75-$15.50. Sun brunch $5.75-$8.75. Child's menu. Totally nonsmoking. Cr cds: A, D, DS, MC, V.

[D]

Manchester

See also Hartford, Storrs, Windsor

Settled 1672 **Pop** 51,618 **Elev** 272 ft **Area code** 860
Zip 06040
Information Greater Manchester Chamber of Commerce,
20 Hartford Rd; 860/646-2223
Web www.manchesterchamber.com

The "city of village charm" has the peaceful air of another
era, with great trees and 18th-century houses. Manchester,
once the silk capital of the Western world, is still a major
manufacturing center with more than 100 industries—
many, more than a century old.

What to See and Do

Cheney Homestead. (ca 1780) Birthplace of the brothers
that launched the state's once-promising silk industry; built
by Timothy Cheney, clockmaker. Paintings and etchings,
early 19th-century furniture; replica of schoolhouse. (Fri-
Sun) 106 Hartford Rd. Phone 860/643-5588. ¢

Connecticut Firemen's Historical Society Fire Museum.
Located in 1901 firehouse, this museum exhibits antique
firefighting equipment and memorabilia; leather fire buck-
ets, hoses, and helmets, hand-pulled engines, horse-drawn
hose wagon, old prints and lithographs. (Mid Apr-mid
Nov, Fri-Sun) 230 Pine St. Phone 860/649-9436. **Donation**

Lutz Children's Museum. Houses participatory exhibits on
natural and physical science, art, ethnology, and history;
live animal exhibit. (Tues-Sun; closed hols) 247 S Main St.
Phone 860/643-0949. ¢¢

Oak Grove Nature Center. More than 50 acres of woods,
fields, stream, pond; trails. (Daily) Oak Grove St. Phone
860/647-3321. **FREE**

Wickham Park. More than 200 acres with gardens, incl
ornamental, woods, ponds; log cabin (refreshments wkends);
playgrounds, picnic areas; nature center; aviary and small
zoo; tennis courts, softball fields (Apr-Oct, daily). 1329 W
Middle Tpke, entrance on US 44, off I-84 exit 60. Phone
860/528-0856. Parking fee ¢¢

Motels/Motor Lodges

★ **CONNECTICUT MOTOR LODGE.** *400 Tolland Tpke
(06040). 860/643-1555; fax 860/643-1881.* 31 rms. S $45-
$50; D $55-$65; each addl $5. Crib $5. TV; cable. Restaurant
adj 7 am-11 pm. Ck-out 11 am. Cr cds: A, C, D, DS, JCB,
MC, V.
⊠ 🐾 SC

★ **ECONO LODGE MANCHESTER.** *100 E Center St
(06040). 860/646-2300; fax 860/649-6499.* 44 rms, 2 story.
S, D $65-$125; each addl $10; under 18 free. Crib free.
Pet accepted. TV; cable (premium), VCR (movies).
Complimentary coffee in lobby. Restaurant opp 6:30 am-
9 pm. Ck-out 11 am. Business servs avail. Sundries.
Balconies. Picnic tables. Cr cds: A, C, D, DS, MC, V.
🐾 ⊠ 🐾 SC

All Suite

★ **CLARION SUITES INN.** *191 Spencer St
(06040). 860/643-5811; toll-free 800/992-4004.
www.clarionsuites.com.* 104 kit. suites, 2 story. S, D $99-
$139; under 16 free; wkend rates. Crib free. Pet accepted;
$250 refundable and $10/day. TV; cable, VCR. Heated pool;
whirlpool. Complimentary full bkfst. Complimentary coffee in rms. Restaurant adj 6:30 am-midnight. Ck-out noon.
Coin lndry. Meeting rms. Business servs avail. Sundries. Gift
shop. Grocery store. Drug store. Valet serv. Free airport,
railroad-station transportation. Downhill/x-country ski
20 mi. Ex-ercise equipt. Lawn games. Balconies. Cr cds:
A, DS, MC, V.
🐾 🐾 🏊 🧗 🔥 🐾

Restaurants

★★★ **CAVEY'S FRENCH RESTAURANT.** *45 E Center St
(06040). 860/643-2751.* French menu. Own baking. Hrs:
6-10 pm. Closed Sun, Mon; major hols. Res accepted;
required Sat. Bar. Wine cellar. A la carte entrees: dinner
$19-$27. Prix fixe: dinner from $55. Parts of building from
old mansions. Cr cds: A, MC, V.

★★★ **CAVEY'S ITALIAN RESTAURANT.** *45 E Center St
(06040). 860/643-2751.* Northern Italian menu. Hrs: 11:30
am-2:30 pm, 5:30-9:30 pm; Fri to 10 pm; Sat noon-2:30 pm,
5:30-10 pm. Closed Sun, Mon; major hols. Res accepted;
required Sat. Bar. A la carte entrees: lunch $8-$12, dinner
$13-$19. Entertainment Fri, Sat. Country Mediterranean
decor. Family-owned since 1933. Cr cds: A, MC, V.
D

Meriden

See also Hartford, Middletown, New Haven

Settled 1661 **Pop** 59,479 **Elev** 144 ft **Area code** 203
Zip 06450
Information Greater Meriden Chamber of Commerce,
5 Colony St, 06451; 203/235-7901
Web www.meridenchamber.com

Located in the heart of the central Connecticut Valley,
Meriden was named after Meriden Farm in Warwickshire,
England. Once called the "silver city of the world" because
its principal business was the manufacture of silver products,
Meriden now has a broad industrial base.

What to See and Do

Castle Craig Tower. Road leads to tower atop East Peak, site
of Easter sunrise services. (May-Oct) In Hubbard Park, 2 mi
W on I-691/CT 66.

Skiing. Mount Southington Ski Area. Triple, double chairlifts, two T-bars, two handle tows, J-bar; snowmaking, patrol,
school, rentals; cafeteria, lounge. Fourteen trails; longest
run approx one mi; vertical drop 425 ft. Night skiing.
(Dec-Mar, daily) Approx 10 mi W; ½ mi W of I-84 exit 30,
at Mt Vernon Rd in Southington. Phone 860/628-7669.

Solomon Goffe House. (1711) Gambrel-roofed house features period furnishings, artifacts. Costumed guides. (July-Aug, Sat and Sun; rest of yr, first Sun of month) 677 N Colony St. Phone 203/634-9088. ¢

Special Events

Daffodil Festival. Hubbard Park, W Main St. Approx 500,000 daffodils in bloom; various events. Mid-Apr. Phone 203/630-4259.

Apple Harvest Festival. Street festival celebrating local apple harvest. Carnival, arts and crafts, parade, road race, food booths, entertainment. 3 mi S on CT 120, in Southington, on Town Green. Phone 860/628-8036. Seven days early Oct.

Motels/Motor Lodges

★★ **HAMPTON INN.** *10 Bee St (06450). 203/235-5154; fax 203/235-7139; toll-free 800/426-4329. www.hamptoninn.com.* 125 rms, 4 story. S, D $75-$85; under 18 free; wkend rates. Crib free. TV; cable (premium). Complimentary continental bkfst. Coffee in rms. Restaurant nearby. Ck-out noon. Meeting rms. Business servs avail. In-rm modem link. Cr cds: A, C, D, DS, MC, V.

D ⊠ ⊠ SC

★★ **HOLIDAY INN EXPRESS.** *120 Laning St, Southington (06489). 860/276-0736; fax 860/276-9405; toll-free 800/465-4329. www.holiday-inn.com.* 122 rms, 3 story. May-Oct: S $59-$69; D $64-$74; each addl $6; under 18 free; lower rates rest of yr. Crib free. TV; cable, VCR avail. Pool. Complimentary continental bkfst. Restaurant adj 11:30 am-10 pm. Ck-out 11 am. Meeting rms. Business servs avail. In-rm modem link. Valet serv. Downhill ski 5 mi. Exercise equipt. Some refrigerators. Cr cds: A, C, D, DS, ER, JCB, MC, V.

D ⊠ ⊠ ⊼ ⊠ ⊠ SC

★ **RAMADA PLAZA INN.** *275 Research Pkwy (06450). 203/238-2380; fax 203/238-3172; res 800/228-2828. www.ramada.com.* 150 rms, 6 story. S $109-$139; D $119-$149; each addl (after 3rd person) $10; suites $150-$200; under 18 free; wkend rates; higher rates college graduation. Crib free. TV; cable (premium), VCR avail. Indoor pool; poolside serv. Complimentary coffee in rms. Restaurant 6:30 am-10 pm. Rm serv. Bar 11-1 am; entertainment. Ck-out noon. Coin lndry. Meeting rms. Business center. Bellhops. Valet serv. Free RR station transportation. Downhill ski 10 mi. Exercise equipt; sauna. Refrigerator, wet bar in suites. Cr cds: A, C, D, DS, ER, JCB, MC, V.

D ⊡ ⊠ ⊼ ⊠ ⊠ SC ⊼

Restaurant

★★ **BRANNIGAN'S.** *176 Laning St, Southington (06489). 860/621-9311. www.brannigans.com.* Specializes in barbecue ribs, seafood. Hrs: 11:30 am-midnight; Sun brunch 11 am-2:30 pm. Closed Memorial Day, Dec 25. Res accepted. Bar. Lunch $4.95-$8.95, dinner $4.95-$15.95. Sun brunch $10.95. Child's menu. Cr cds: A, MC, V.

D ⊠

Middletown

See also Hartford, Meriden

Settled 1650 **Pop** 42,762 **Elev** 51 ft **Area code** 860 **Zip** 06457
Information Connecticut River Valley & Shoreline Visitors Council, 393 Main St; 860/347-0028 or 800/486-3346
Web www.cttourism.org

On the Connecticut River between Hartford and New Haven, Middletown was once an important shipping point for trade with the West Indies. The first official pistol-maker to the US Government, Simeon North, had his factory here in 1799. Today Middletown boasts diversified industry and one of the longest and widest main streets in New England.

What to See and Do

Powder Ridge Ski Area. Quad, three double chairlifts, handletow; patrol, school, rentals; snowmaking; bar, restaurant, cafeteria; nursery. Fourteen trails; vertical drop 500 ft. (Nov-Apr, daily) 5 mi SW off CT 147, on Powder Hill Rd in Middlefield. ¢¢¢¢

Wadsworth Falls State Park. These 285 acres surround Wadsworth Falls and lookout. Pond swimming, stream fishing; hiking along wooded area with mountain laurel display, picnicking. Beautiful waterfall with overlook. Standard hrs, fees. 3 mi SW off CT 66, on CT 157. Phone 860/566-2304.

Special Event

Durham Fair. Fairgrounds, in Durham on CT 17. State's largest agricultural fair. Phone 860/349-9495. Last wkend Sept.

Motels/Motor Lodges

★ **COMFORT INN.** *111 Berlin Rd (Hwy 372), Cromwell (06416). 860/635-4100; fax 860/632-9546; toll-free 800/228-5150. www.comfortinn.com.* 77 rms, 4 story. S $54; D $61; each addl $6; under 18 free. Crib free. Pet accepted; $75 refundable. TV; VCR avail. Swimming privileges. Complimentary continental bkfst. Restaurant opp 5:30 am-10 pm. Ck-out 11 am. Health club privileges. Cr cds: A, C, D, DS, ER, JCB, MC, V.

D ⊠ ⊠ ⊠ SC

★★ **HOLIDAY INN.** *4 Sebethe Dr, Cromwell (06416). 860/635-1001; fax 860/635-0684; res 800/465-4329. www.holiday-inn.com.* 145 rms, 3 story. S $79-$139; D $89-$149; each addl $10; suites $149; under 18 free; wkend rates. Crib free. TV; cable (premium). Indoor pool. Restaurant 6 am-10 pm. Rm serv. Bar. Ck-out 11 am. Coin lndry. Meeting rms. Business servs avail. In-rm modem link. Valet serv. Sundries. Airport transportation. Exercise equipt; sauna. Health club privileges. Lawn games. Picnic tables. Cr cds: A, DS, MC, V.

⊠ ⊼ ⊠ ⊠

Hotel

★★ RADISSON HOTEL AND CONFERENCE CENTER. *100 Berlin Rd, Cromwell (06416). 860/635-2000; fax 860/635-6970; res 800/333-3333. www.radisson.com.* 211 rms, 4 story. S $69-$99; D $79-$109; suites $195-$350; under 18 free; wkend rates. Crib free. TV; cable, VCR avail. Indoor pool; whirlpool, poolside serv. Coffee in rms. Restaurants 6:30 am-10:30 pm. Rm serv. Bar noon-1 am; entertainment Sat. Ck-out noon. Meeting rms. Business servs avail. In-rm modem link. Gift shop. Exercise equipt; sauna. Some bathrm phones. Cr cds: A, DS, MC, V.

Milford

See also Bridgeport, Fairfield, New Haven, Stratford

Settled 1639 **Pop** 49,938 **Elev** 89 ft **Area code** 203 **Zip** 06460
Information Milford Chamber of Commerce, 5 Broad St; 203/878-0681
Web www.milfordct.com

What to See and Do

Milford Historical Society Wharf Lane Complex. Three historical houses incl Eells-Stow House (ca 1700), believed to be oldest house in Milford and featuring unusual "dog sled" stairway; Stockade House (ca 1780), first house built outside the city's early stockade; and Bryan-Downs House (ca 1785), two-story early American structure housing more than 400 Native American artifacts spanning more than 10,000 yrs. (Memorial Day-Columbus Day, Sun; also by appt) 34 High St. Phone 203/874-2664. ¢

Special Event

Oyster Festival. Arts and crafts exhibits, races, boat tours; games, food; entertainment. Milford Center, town green. Phone 203/878-5363. Mid-Aug.

Motel/Motor Lodge

★★ HAMPTON INN. *129 Plains Rd (06460). 203/874-4400; fax 203/874-5348; res 800/426-7866. www.hamptoninn.com.* 148 rms, 3 story. S, D $95; under 18 free. TV; cable (premium). Continental bkfst. Ck-out noon. Coin lndry. Meeting rms. Business servs avail. Valet serv. Some refrigerators. Cr cds: A, C, D, DS, MC, V.

Restaurants

★ ALDARIO'S. *240 Naugatuck Ave (06460). 203/874-6096. www.aldarios.com.* Italian menu. Specializes in seafood, veal. Salad bar (lunch). Hrs: 11:30 am-2 pm, 4:30-10 pm. Closed Mon; some major hols. Res accepted. Bar. Lunch $4.50-$9.95, dinner $8.95-$16.95. Child's menu. Family-owned. Cr cds: A, D, DS, MC, V.

★★ THE GATHERING. *989 Boston Post Rd (06460). 203/878-6537. www.thegatheringrestaurant.com.* Specializes in fresh fish, steak, prime rib. Salad bar. Hrs: 4:30-9:30 pm; Fri, Sat to 10 pm; Sun to 9 pm; Sun brunch 11 am-2:30 pm. Closed Dec 25. Res accepted. Bar 4-11:30 pm; Thurs to midnight; Fri, Sat to 2 am. Dinner $9.95-$16.95. Child's menu. Colonial decor. Family-owned. Cr cds: A, MC, V.

★★ SCRIBNER'S. *31 Village Rd (06460). 203/878-7019. www.scribnersrestaurant.com.* Specializes in exotic fish, fresh seafood, Angus beef. Hrs: 11:30 am-2:30 pm, 5 pm-closing. Closed most major hols. Res accepted. Bar. Lunch $4.95-$8.95, dinner $17.95-$26.95. Child's menu. Casual dining. Nautical decor. Cr cds: A, MC, V.

Mystic

See also Groton, New London, Norwich, Stonington

Settled 1654 **Pop** 2,618 **Elev** 16 ft **Area code** 860 **Zip** 06355
Information Tourist Information Center, Building 1D, Olde Mistick Village; 860/536-1641; or Connecticut's Mystic & More!, 470 Bank St, PO Box 89, New London 06320; 860/444-2206 or 800/TO-ENJOY (outside CT)
Web www.mysticmore.com

The community of Mystic, divided by the Mystic River, was a shipbuilding and whaling center from the 17th to the 19th centuries. It derives its name from the Pequot, "Mistuket."

What to See and Do

Denison Homestead. (1717) Restored in the style of five eras (18th to mid-20th centuries); furnished with heirlooms of 11 generations of a single family. Guided tour (Mid-May-mid-Oct, Wed-Mon afternoons; rest of yr, by appt). 2 mi E of I-95 exit 90, on Pequotsepos Rd. Phone 860/536-9248. ¢¢

Denison Pequotsepos Nature Center. An environmental education center and natural history museum active in wildlife rehabilitation. The 125-acre sanctuary has more than seven mi of trails; family nature walks, films, lectures. (Daily; closed hols) 2 mi NE of I-95 exit 90, on Pequotsepos Rd. Phone 860/536-1216. ¢¢

Mystic Marinelife Aquarium. Exhibits feature more than 6,000 live specimens from all waters of the world; demonstrations with dolphins, sea lions, and the only whales in New England; Seal Island, outdoor exhibit of seals and sea lions in natural settings; penguin pavilion. (Daily; closed Jan 1, Thanksgiving, Dec, also last full wk Jan) 55 Coogan Blvd. Phone 860/536-3323. ¢¢¢

Mystic Seaport. This 17-acre complex is the nation's largest maritime museum, dedicated to preservation of 19th-century maritime history. Visitors may board the 1841 wooden whaleship *Charles W. Morgan*, square-rigged ship *Joseph Conrad*, or fishing schooner *L.A. Dunton*. Collection also incl some 400 smaller vessels; representative seaport community with historic homes and waterfront industries, some staff in 19th-century costume; exhibits, demonstrations, working shipyard; children's museum, planetarium (fee), 1908 steamboat cruises (May-Oct, daily; fee); restaurants; shopping; special events throughout the yr. (Daily; closed Dec 25) 75 Greenmanville Ave (CT 27), 1 mi S of I-95 exit 90. Phone 860/572-5315. ¢¢¢¢

Olde Mistick Village. More than 60 shops and restaurants in 1720s-style New England village, on 22 acres; duck pond, millwheel, waterfalls; entertainment, carillon (May-Oct, Sat and Sun). Village (daily). Coogan Blvd and CT 27. Phone 860/536-4941. **FREE**

Special Event

Lobsterfest. Mystic Seaport. Outdoor food festival. Phone 860/572-5315. Late May.

Motels/Motor Lodges

★★ **BEST WESTERN SOVEREIGN HOTEL.** *Rtes 27 & I-95 (06355). 860/536-4281; toll-free 800/780-7234. www. bestwestern.com.* 150 rms, 2 story, 4 suites. June-Oct: S $109; D $139; suites $279; each addl $5; under 18 free; lower rates rest of yr. Crib avail, fee. Parking lot. Indoor pool. TV; cable. Complimentary full bkfst, coffee in rms, newspaper. Restaurant 6:30 am-9 pm. Bar. Ck-out 11 am. Meeting rms. Bellhops. Dry cleaning. Exercise equipt, sauna, steam rm. Golf. Beach access. Supervised children's activities. Hiking trail. Picnic facilities. Video games. Cr cds: A, D, DS, MC, V.

D ⬤ ⬤ ⬤ ⬤ ⬤ ⬤

★ **COMFORT INN.** *48 Whitehall Ave (06355). 860/572-8531; fax 860/572-9358; toll-free 800/572-9339. www.whghotels.com.* 120 rms, 2 story. May-Oct: S, D $49-$169; each addl $10; under 17 free; lower rates rest of yr. Crib free. TV; cable. Complimentary continental bkfst. Restaurant nearby. Ck-out 11 am. Meeting rms. Business servs avail. Valet serv. Exercise equipt. Cr cds: A, C, D, DS, ER, JCB, MC, V.

D ⬤ ⬤ ⬤ SC

★ **DAYS INN.** *55 Whitehall Ave (06355). 860/572-0574; fax 860/572-1164; res 800/329-7466. www.whghotels.com.* 122 rms, 2 story. Mid-May-mid-Oct: S, D $49-$199; each addl $10; under 18 free; lower rates rest of yr. Crib free. TV; cable. Pool. Playground. Coffee in rms. Restaurant 6 am-9 pm; Fri, Sat to 10 pm. Rm serv. Ck-out 11 am. Meeting rms. Business servs avail. In-rm modem link. Valet serv. Airport transportation. Health club privileges. Refrigerators avail. Cr cds: A, C, D, DS, ER, JCB, MC, V.

D ⬤ ⬤ ⬤ SC

★★★ **INN AT MYSTIC.** *Rtes 1 & 27 (06355). 860/536-9604; fax 860/572-1635; toll-free 800/237-2415. www.innatmystic.com.* 67 rms, 2 story. May-Oct: S, D $100-$235; each addl $10; under 18 free; lower rates rest of yr. Crib $10. TV; cable (premium), VCR avail. Heated pool; whirlpool. Complimentary afternoon tea. Restaurant

(see also FLOOD TIDE). Rm serv. Bar. Ck-out 11 am. Meeting rm. Business servs avail. Tennis. Some in-rm whirlpools, fireplaces. Some private patios, balconies. Formal gardens. Long Island Sound ¼ mi. Cr cds: A, DS, MC, V.

⬤ ⬤ ⬤ ⬤

★★★ **TWO TREES INN.** *240 Indian Tower Rd, Ledyard (06339). 860/312-3000; fax 860/312-4050; toll-free 800/369-9663. www.pequotcasino.com.* 280 rms, 3 story, 60 suites. Late June-early Sept: S, D $150; each addl $20; suites $175; under 18 free; package plans; lower rates rest of yr. Crib $10. TV; cable (premium), VCR avail. Indoor pool; whirlpool. Complimentary continental bkfst. Restaurant 11:30 am-10 pm. Ck-out noon. Business servs avail. Bellhops. Health club privileges. Refrigerators. Foxwoods Casino adj. Cr cds: A, DS, MC, V.

D ⬤ ⬤ ⬤ ⬤ SC

Hotel

★★★ **HILTON.** *20 Coogan Blvd (06355). 860/572-0731; fax 860/572-0328; toll-free 800/445-8667. www.visitmystic.com/hilton.* 184 rms, 4 story. S, D $149-$225; each addl $20; suites $295-$825; family rates. Crib free. TV; cable (premium). Indoor pool. Supervised children's activities wkends; also July, Aug. Restaurant 6:30 am-10 pm. Rm serv. Bar 11-1 am; entertainment Fri, Sat. Ck-out 11 am. Guest lndry. Meeting rms. Business servs avail. In-rm modem link. Free valet parking. Bellhops. Tennis privileges. Exercise equipt. Refrigerators avail. Cr cds: A, C, D, DS, MC, V.

D ⬤ ⬤ ⬤ ⬤ ⬤

B&Bs/Small Inns

★ **APPLEWOOD FARMS INN.** *528 Colonel Ledyard Hwy (06339). 860/536-2022; fax 860/536-6015; toll-free 800/ 717-4262. www.visitmystic.com/applewoodfarmsinn.* 5 rms, 3 with shower only, 2 story, 1 suite. No rm phones. S $109; D $125, each addl $25; suite $250; wkly rates; wkends (2-day min), hols (3-day min). Children over 8 yrs only. Pet accepted, some restrictions. Complimentary full bkfst; afternoon refreshments. Ck-out 11 am, ck-in 3 pm. Luggage handling. Picnic tables. Putting green. Whirlpool. House built 1826, once used as town hall; many fireplaces, Colonial atmosphere. Cr cds: A, DS, MC, V.

⬤ ⬤ ⬤

★★ **THE OLD MYSTIC INN.** *52 Main St, Old Mystic (06372). 860/572-9422; fax 860/572-9954. www.visitmystic.com/oldmysticinn.* 8 rms, 2 story. No rm phones. May-mid-Oct: S $95-$135; D $115-$145; each addl $30-$40; higher rates: wkends, hols (2-day min); lower rates rest of yr. TV in sitting rm; cable. Complimentary afternoon refreshments. Ck-out 11 am, ck-in 2 pm. Business servs avail. In-rm modem link. Lawn games. Picnic tables. Built 1794; early Amer decor. Cr cds: A, MC, V.

⬤ ⬤ ⬤

★★ **RED BROOK INN.** *Rte 184 & Welles Rd (06372).* *860/572-0349; toll-free 800/290-5619. www.redbrookinn.com.* 11 rms, 2 story. No rm phones. S, D $119-$189. Crib free. TV; cable. Complimentary full bkfst. Restaurants nearby. Ck-out 11 am, ck-in noon. Concierge serv. Some fireplaces. Two Colonial buildings (ca 1740 and ca 1770) furnished with period antiques. Totally nonsmoking. Cr cds: A, DS, MC, V.

★★ **WHALER'S INN.** *20 E Main St (06355). 860/536-1506; fax 860/572-1250; toll-free 800/243-2588.* 41 rms, 18 with shower only, 2 story. May-late Oct: S $99-$105; D $119-$139; suite $175-$210; each addl $10; under 18 free; lower rates rest of yr. Crib $5. TV; cable. Dining rm 11:30 am-9 pm. Ck-out 11 am, ck-in 2 pm. Business servs avail. In-rm modem link. Balconies. Built 1865; Colonial decor. Cr cds: A, DS, MC, V.

Casino

★★★ **FOXWOODS RESORT CASINO.** *Rte 2, PO Box 3777, Mashantucket (06339). 860/312-3000. www.foxwoods.com.* 312 rms, 6 story, 40 suites. July-early Sept: S, D $200; each addl $20; suites $275; under 18 free; lower rates rest of yr. Crib $10. TV; cable (premium), VCR avail. Indoor pool; whirlpool, lifeguard. Restaurants open 24 hrs. Bar 11-1:30 am; entertainment. Ck-out noon. Meeting rms. Business servs avail. In-rm modem link. Concierge. Shopping arcade. Barber, beauty shop. Free garage, valet parking. Exercise rm. Some refrigerators. Connected to casino. Cr cds: A, C, D, DS, ER, JCB, MC, V.

Restaurants

★★★ **BRAVO BRAVO.** *20 E Main St (06355). 860/536-3228.* Specializes in Maryland crab cakes with lobster sauce, pasta with seafood. Hrs: 11:30 am-9 pm; Fri, Sat to 10 pm. Closed Mon. Res accepted. Extensive wine list. Lunch $6.95-$12.95; dinner $13.95-$24.95. Entertainment. Cr cds: A, D, DS, MC, V.

★★★ **FLOOD TIDE.** *Jct US 1 and CT 27 (06355). 860/536-8140. www.innatmystic.com.* Continental menu. Specialties: beef Wellington, châteaubriand, Caesar salad. Hrs: 7-10:30 am, 11:30 am-2 pm, 5:30-9:30 pm; Fri, Sat to 10 pm; Sun 7 am-2 pm, 5:30-9 pm; Sun brunch 11 am-2 pm. Res required. Bar. Wine list. A la carte entrees: bkfst $2-$10, lunch $5.95-$19.95, dinner $13.95-$25.95. Buffet: bkfst $8.95, lunch $11.95. Sun brunch $15.95. Child's menu. Pianist evenings. Parking. Outdoor dining. Nautical decor; elegant dining with view of sea. Cr cds: A, DS, MC, V.

★★ **GO FISH.** *Olde Mistick Village (06355). 860/536-2662.* Specializes in seafood pasta, go fish crabcakes. Raw bar. Sushi bar. Hrs: 11:30 am-9:30 pm; Fri, Sat to 10:30 pm;

Sun to 9:30 pm. Res accepted. Wine, beer. Lunch $5.95-$13.50; dinner $10.95-$19.95. Child's menu. Entertainment. In Olde Mistick Village. Cr cds: A, D, DS, ER, MC, V.

★★ **J. P. DANIELS.** *CT 27 and CT 184, Old Mystic (06355). 860/572-9564.* Continental menu. Specializes in veal, seafood. Hrs: 5-9 pm; Fri, Sat to 9:30 pm; Sun brunch 11 am-2 pm. Closed Dec 24, 25. Res accepted. Bar. Wine list. Dinner $8.95-$17.95. Sun brunch $13.95. Child's menu. Parking. Elegant dining in relaxed country setting. Totally nonsmoking. Cr cds: A, DS, MC, V.

★ **MYSTIC PIZZA.** *56 W Main St (06355). 860/536-3700. www.mystic-pizza.com.* Specializes in pizza, pasta. Hrs: 10 am-midnight. Closed Easter, Thanksgiving, Dec 25. Wine, beer. A la carte entrees: lunch $2-$8.75, dinner $2-$9.25. Child's menu. Parking. Popular pizza parlor immortalized in the Julia Roberts film by the same name. Family-owned. Cr cds: C, DS, MC, V.

★★ **SEAMEN'S INNE.** *105 Greenmanville Ave (06355). 860/536-9649. www.seamensinne.com.* Specializes in prime rib, fresh Atlantic seafood. Hrs: 11:30 am-9 pm; Fri to 10 pm; Sat, Sun 11 am-10 pm; Sun brunch 10:30 am-2 pm. Closed Dec 25. Res accepted. Bar. Lunch $4.95-$9.95, dinner $10.95-$18.95. Sun brunch $9.95. Child's menu. Family entertainment Wed-Sun. 19th-century sea captain's house decor; overlooks river. Cr cds: A, D, DS, MC, V.

★ **STEAK LOFT.** *Olde Mistick Village (06355). 860/536-2661.* Specializes in steak, seafood. Salad bar. Hrs: 11:30 am-10:30 pm. Closed Thanksgiving, Dec 25. Bar to 1 am. Lunch $3-$12, dinner $11-20. Child's menu. Entertainment Wed-Sun. Parking. Casual New England atmosphere. Cr cds: A, D, DS, MC, V.

New Britain

See also Hartford, Meriden, Wethersfield

Settled 1686 **Pop** 75,491 **Elev** 179 ft **Area code** 860

Information Chamber of Commerce, 1 Court St, 06051, phone; 860/229-1665; or the Central Connecticut Tourism District, 1 Grove St, 06053, phone 860/225-3901

Web www.newbritainchamber.com

This is the "hardware city." Production of sleigh bells and farm tools began about 1800, followed by locks and saddlery hardware. Many tool, hardware, and machinery manufacturers, including The Stanley Works, organized in 1843, are headquartered in New Britain.

What to See and Do

Central Connecticut State University. (1849) 14,000 students. On campus is Copernican Planetarium and Observatory, featuring one of the largest public telescopes in the US; planetarium shows (Fri, Sat; children's shows Sat) Phone 860/827-7000. Planetarium shows ¢¢

Hungerford Outdoor Education Center. Outdoor animal areas, trails, gardens, pond, exhibits of regional and natural history, nutrition and energy; picnicking. (Apr-Oct, Tues-Sun; rest of yr, Tues-Sat) Approx 3 mi S via CT 372, at 191 Farmington Ave in Kensington. Phone 860/827-9064. ¢

New Britain Museum of American Art. Works by outstanding American artists from 1740 to the present; works by Whistler, Church, Sargent, Wyeth; Thomas Hart Benton murals; Sanford Low Collection of American illustrations; Charles and Elizabeth Buchanan Collection of American impressionists. (Tues-Sun afternoons; closed hols) 56 Lexington St. Phone 860/229-0257. **FREE**

New Britain Youth Museum. Exhibits of Americana, cultures of other nations, circus miniatures, dolls, hands-on displays. (Tues-Fri) 30 High St. Phone 860/225-3020. **FREE**

Special Events

Baseball. New Britain Rock Cats (AA team). New Britain Stadium, Willowbrook Park. Phone 860/224-8383. Mid Apr-Sept.

Main Street, USA. Street festival featuring wide variety of ethnic foods, entertainment, rides, arts and crafts. Phone 860/225-3901. Second Sat June.

Dozynki Polish Harvest Festival. Street dancing; polka bands; cultural displays; beer, singing, ethnic food; pony and hayrides; Polish arts and crafts. Phone 860/225-3901. Broad St. Third wkend Sept.

Motel/Motor Lodge

★★ **CENTRAL INN AND CONFERENCE CENTER.** *65 Columbus Blvd (06051). 860/224-9161; fax 860/224-1796; toll-free 800/272-6232.* 119 rms, 6 story. S, D $45-$95; each addl $10; suites $125; under 19 free; wkend plans. Crib free. Pet accepted, some restrictions; $10. TV; cable (premium), VCR avail. Ck-out noon. Coin lndry. Meeting rms. Business servs avail. Airport transportation. Garage parking. Downhill ski 5 mi. Cr cds: A, C, D, DS, JCB, MC, V.

[D] [icons]

Restaurant

★ **EAST SIDE.** *131 Dwight St (06051). 860/223-1188.* German, Amer menu. Specializes in German dishes, baked shrimp, steak. Hrs: 11:30 am-2:30 pm, 4:30-10 pm; Sun noon-8 pm. Closed Mon; July 4, Dec 25. Res accepted. Bar to 10 pm. Lunch $4.95-$9.95, dinner $10.95-$16.95. Child's menu. European atmosphere. Family-owned. Cr cds: MC, V.

[D] [icon]

New Canaan

See also Norwalk, Stamford

Founded 1801 **Pop** 17,864 **Elev** 300 ft **Area code** 203 **Zip** 06840
Information Chamber of Commerce, 111 Elm St; 203/966-2004
Web www.newcanaanchamber.com

New Canaan was settled in 1731 as Canaan Parish, a church society encompassing parts of Norwalk and Stamford. A quiet residential community situated on high ridges, New Canaan has retained its rural character despite its proximity to industrial areas.

What to See and Do

New Canaan Historical Society. The First Town House (original town hall) has costume museum, library, and Cody Drugstore (1845), a restoration of the town's first pharmacy; on grounds of Hanford-Silliman House Museum (ca 1765) are a tool museum, hand press, one-rm schoolhouse, and sculptor John Roger's studio and museum. (Town House, Tues-Sat; other buildings Wed, Thurs, and Sun, limited afternoon hrs; closed hols) 13 Oenoke Ridge Rd. Phone 203/966-1776. ¢¢

New Canaan Nature Center. More than 40 acres of woodland, ponds, and meadows; discovery center with hands-on exhibits; suburban ecology exhibits; solar greenhouse; cider house, and maple sugar shed; herb and wildflower gardens; trails, marsh boardwalk; animals. Grounds (daily). Buildings (Mon-Sat; closed hols). 144 Oenoke Ridge Rd. Phone 203/966-9577. **FREE**

Silvermine Guild Arts Center. Art center in rustic six-acre setting has a school of the arts and three galleries with changing exhibits by member artists and artisans; invitational and juried exhibitions; many educational events and programs. (Tues-Sun; closed Jan 1, Thanksgiving, Dec 25) 1037 Silvermine Rd. **FREE**

B&B/Small Inn

★★★ **ROGER SHERMAN INN.** *195 Oenoke Ridge Rd (06840). 203/966-4541; fax 203/966-0503. www.rogershermaninn.com.* 18 rms, 2 story. S $105; D $160; each addl $20. TV; cable. Complimentary continental bkfst. Dining rm noon-2 pm, 6-9:30 pm. Ck-out 11 am, ck-in 2-6 pm. Business servs avail. Some fireplaces. Colonial inn (ca 1740); antiques. Cr cds: A, D, MC, V.

[D] [icons]

New Haven

See also Branford, Milford

Settled 1638 **Pop** 130,474 **Elev** 25 ft **Area code** 203

Information Greater New Haven Convention & Visitors Bureau, 59 Elm St, First floor, 06510; 203/777-8550 or 800/332-STAY

Web www.newhavencvb.org or www.cityofnewhaven.com

New Haven is only 75 miles from New York City, but it is typically New England. Its colorful history is built into the stones and timbers of the area. Here Eli Whitney worked out the principle of interchangeable parts for mass production. Around the corner, Nathan Hale roomed as a student, not far from where Noah Webster compiled the first dictionary. In addition to all this, Yale University puts New Haven on any list of the world's cultural centers.

Northwest of New Haven is a 400-foot red sandstone cliff called West Rock. In 1661 three Cromwellian judges, who had ordered Charles I beheaded, took refuge here from the soldiers of Charles II.

What to See and Do

Amistad Memorial. This 14-ft bronze relief sculpture is a unique three-sided form. Each side depicts a significant episode of the life of Joseph Cinque, one of 50 Africans kidnapped from Sierra Leone and slated for sale in Cuba in 1839. After secretly rerouting the slave ship to Long Island Sound, the battle for the would-be slaves' freedom ensued in New Haven. Two yrs later, their victory was complete. Ed Hamilton sculpted this important piece. In front of City Hall. 165 Church St.

East Rock Park. City's largest park incl Pardee Rose Gardens, bird sanctuary, hiking trails, athletic fields, tennis courts, picnic grounds. Excellent view of harbor and Long Island Sound. (Apr-Nov, daily; rest of yr, Sat, Sun, and hols) 1 mi NE at foot of Orange St, on E Rock Rd. Phone 203/946-6086. **FREE**

Fort Nathan Hale Park and Black Rock Fort. Here Federal guns kept British warships out of the harbor in 1812. Old Black Rock Fort, from Revolutionary War days, has been restored, and archaeological excavations are in progress. Fort Nathan Hale, from Civil War era, also has been reconstructed. Both offer spectacular views of the harbor. Picnicking. Group guided tours (Memorial Day-Labor Day, daily). 36 Woodward Ave. Phone 203/946-8790.

The Green. In 1638 these 16 acres were laid out, making New Haven the first planned city in America. On the town common are three churches—United (1813), Trinity Episcopal (1814), and Center Congregational (1813), which is one of the masterpieces of American Georgian architecture. **FREE**

Grove Street Cemetery. First cemetery in the US divided into family plots. Buried here are Noah Webster, Charles Goodyear, Eli Whitney, and many early settlers of the area. Grove and Prospect Sts. **FREE**

Lighthouse Point Park. This 82-acre park on Long Island Sound has lighthouse built in 1840; restored antique carousel (fee); bird sanctuary. Beach, bathhouse, playfield, picnic facilities, boat ramp. (Daily) Parking fee (Memorial Day-Labor Day only). End of Lighthouse Rd, 5 mi SE off I-95, exit 50. Phone 203/946-8005. ¢¢

New Haven Colony Historical Society Museum. Museum of local history; special exhibits; also research library (fee). (Tues-Fri; closed hols) 114 Whitney Ave. Phone 203/562-4183. ¢

Pardee-Morris House. (1750) Built in 18th century, burned by the British in 1779, then rebuilt in 1780 around surviving masonry; American period furnishings; kitchen garden. (June-Aug, Sat and Sun) 325 Lighthouse Rd, S of I-95 exit 50. Phone 203/772-7060. ¢

Shore Line Trolley Museum. Collection of trolley, interurban, and rapid-transit cars from 15 states and Canada. A National Historic Site. Cars on display incl pre-1900 trolleys (1893, 1899), the first commercially produced electric locomotive (1888), and a trolley parlor car. Exhibits on electric railways. Scenic trolley ride in authentic, restored cars; operator narrates on tour of display buildings and restoration shop; trolleys depart every 30 min (inquire for schedule). Picnic grove (May-Oct); gift shop; special events. (Memorial Day-Labor Day, daily; May, Sept, Oct, Dec, wkends and hols; Apr and Nov, Sun only) 5 mi E via I-95 exit 51 or 52, at 17 River St in East Haven. Phone 203/467-6927. ¢¢

Shubert Performing Arts Center. Full-service performing arts venue opened in 1914. Known as the "Birthplace of the Nation's Greatest Hits." Home to dance, musical, comedy and dramatic performances. (Sept-June) 247 College St. Phone 888/736-2663.

West Rock Nature Center. Nature center features native Connecticut wildlife in outdoor bird and mammal sections; indoor nature house with reptiles and other displays. Hiking trails; picnic areas. (Mon-Fri; closed hols) On Wintergreen Ave, 1 mi N of Southern Connecticut State University. Phone 203/946-8016. **FREE**

✪ **Yale University.** (1701) 10,000 students. Founded by 10 Connecticut ministers and named for Elihu Yale, an early donor to the school. In Sept 1969, the undergraduate school became coeducational. Walking tours conducted daily by undergraduate students. Hear about Yale's rich 300-yr history. See the school's distinctive architecture and visit both Sterling Memorial Library and the Beinecke Rare Book Library. Tours leave from Yale Visitor Center. Wkdays 10:30 am, 2 pm; Sat, Sun 1:30 pm (free). 149 Elm St, on N side of New Haven Green. Phone 203/432-2300. Of special interest are

Beinecke Rare Book and Manuscript Library. Exhibits of famous collections, Gutenberg Bible. (Sept-July, Mon-Sat; Aug, Mon-Fri; closed hols) Best approach is from College St via Cross Campus Walk, on High St. **FREE**

Collection of Musical Instruments. Total holdings of 850 musical instruments; permanent displays and changing exhibits; lectures, concerts, special events. (Sept-June, Tues-Thurs afternoons; closed school hols) Under 14 only with adult. 15 Hillhouse Ave. Phone 203/432-0822. ¢

The Old Campus. Nathan Hale (class of 1773) roomed. One-hr guided walking tours (Mon-Fri, one tour morning, one tour afternoon; Sat, Sun, one tour afternoon). Inquire at Visitor Information Office. 149 Elm St. Phone 203/432-2300. **FREE**

Peabody Museum of Natural History. Exhibits on mammals, invertebrate life, Plains and Connecticut Native Americans, meteorites, minerals and rocks, birds of Connecticut; several life-size dinosaur exhibits incl a brontosaurus (60-ft long) reconstructed from original fossil material; dioramas of North American flora and fauna; wkend films (free). (Daily; closed hols) 170 Whitney Ave at Sachem St. ¢¢

Yale Art Gallery. Collections incl Italian Renaissance paintings, American paintings and decorative arts, ancient art, African sculpture, Near and Far Eastern art, and European paintings from the 13th-20th centuries. (Tues-Sat, also Sun afternoons; closed hols) 1111 Chapel St at York St. Phone 203/432-0600. **FREE**

Yale Bowl. An Ivy League football mecca. 2 mi W on Chapel St. Phone 203/432-4747.

Yale Center for British Art. British paintings, prints, drawings, sculpture, and rare books from Elizabethan period to present. Reference library and photo archive. Lectures, tours, films, concerts. (Tues-Sun; closed hols) 1080 Chapel St. Phone 203/432-2800. **FREE**

Special Events

International Festival of Arts and Ideas. Celebration of the arts and humanities. Phone 888/ART-IDEA. 195 Church St. Late June. Phone 888/278-4332.

Pilot Pen International Tennis Tournament. Connecticut Tennis Center, near Yale Bowl. Championship Series on the ATP tour. Mid-Aug. Phone 888-99-PILOT or 888-997-4568. Phone 888/997-4568.

Yale Repertory Theater. 1120 Chapel St. Sept-May. Phone 203/432-1234.

Long Wharf Theatre. Features new plays as well as classics. Sept-June. 222 Sargent Dr, at I-95 exit 46. Phone 203/787-4282 (box office).

New Haven Symphony Orchestra. Woolsey Hall, College and Grove Sts. Series of concerts by leading artists. Oct-May. Phone 203/776-1444.

Motel/Motor Lodge

★★ **HOLIDAY INN AT YALE UNIVERSITY.** *30 Whalley Ave (06511).* 203/777-6221; fax 203/772-1089; res 800/465-4329. www.holiday-inn.com. 160 rms, 8 story. S, D $95; under 18 free; higher rates Yale special events. Crib free. TV; cable (premium). Pool. Coffee in rms. Restaurant 6 am-2 pm, 5-10 pm. Rm serv. Bar 5 pm-midnight. Ck-out noon. Meeting rms. Business servs avail. In-rm modem link. Bellhops. Valet serv. Cr cds: A, D, DS, JCB, MC, V.

Hotels

★★   **THE COLONY.** *1157 Chapel St (06511).* 203/776-1234; fax 203/772-3929; toll-free 800/458-8810. www.colonyatyale.com. 86 rms, 4 story. May-Oct: S $89; D $99; each addl $10; suites $195; kit. units $450; under 12 free; higher rates Yale events. Crib free. Parking $4. TV; cable. Restaurant 6:30 am-10 pm. Rm serv. Ck-out noon.

Business servs avail. In-rm modem link. Concierge. Bellhops. Free airport, RR station transportation. Refrigerators avail. Within walking distance of Yale theaters. Cr cds: A, D, MC, V.

★★★ **OMNI NEW HAVEN HOTEL AT YALE.** *155 Temple St (06510).* 203/772-6664. www.omnihotels.com. 306 rms, 25 story. S, D $250-$375; under 18 free. Crib avail. TV; cable (premium). Indoor pool; whirlpool. Restaurant 6:30 am-10 pm. Bar to midnight. Ck-out noon, ck-in 3 pm. Meeting rms. Business center. In-rm modem link. Concierge. Exercise equipt. Minibars; many refrigerators in suites. Cr cds: A, D, DS, MC, V.

B&B/Small Inn

★★★ **THREE CHIMNEYS.** *1201 Chapel St (06511).* 203/789-1201; fax 203/776-7363; toll-free 800/443-1554. www.threechimneysinn.com. 10 rms, 3 story. S, D $180; each addl $20. TV; cable (premium), VCR avail. Complimentary full bkfst; afternoon refreshments. Restaurant nearby. Concierge serv. Ck-out 11 am, ck-in 3 pm. Business servs avail. Restored Victorian mansion (ca 1870). Rms individually furnished with antiques and period pieces. Cr cds: A, DS, MC, V.

Extended Stay

★★ **RESIDENCE INN BY MARRIOTT.** *3 Long Wharf Dr (06511).* 203/777-5337; fax 203/777-2808; toll-free 800/331-3131. www.residenceinn.com. 112 kit. suites, 2 story. S, D $135-$145. Crib avail. TV; cable (premium). Pool; whirlpool. Complimentary continental bkfst. Complimentary coffee in rms. Restaurant nearby. Ck-out noon. Coin lndry. Meeting rms. Business servs avail. In-rm modem link. Valet serv. Free airport transportation. Health club privileges. Stone fireplace in lobby. Cr cds: A, C, D, DS, MC, V.

Restaurants

★★ **500 BLAKE ST.** *500 Blake St., Westville (06515).* 203/387-0500. Italian, Amer menu. Specializes in fresh fish, Italian dishes. Hrs: 11:30 am-midnight; Sun to 9 pm; Sun brunch 11 am-3 pm. Res accepted. A la carte entrees: lunch $6.95-$19.95, dinner $14.95-$29.95. Sun brunch $19.95. Pianist. Turn-of-century decor, antiques. Cr cds: A, C, D, DS, MC, V.

★ **INDOCHINE PAVILLION.** *1180 Chapel St (06511).* 203/865-5033. Vietnamese menu. Specialties: spicy chicken, Saigon noodle soup, Saigon sound pancakes. Hrs: noon-2:30 pm, 5:30-9:30 pm; Sat from 5:30 pm; Sun 5-9 pm. Closed Mon; major hols. Res accepted. Serv bar. Lunch $4.95-$6.95, dinner $8.75-$17.95. Storefront restaurant; Asian paintings. Cr cds: A, DS, MC, V.

★★ **LA MIRAGE.** *111 Scrub Oak Rd, North Haven (06773).* *203/239-1961.* Specializes in baked stuffed shrimp, prime rib. Hrs: 5:30-10 pm; Sun to 7 pm. Closed Mon-Thurs; July 4, Dec 25. Res accepted. Bar. Dinner $10.95-$18.95. Family-owned. Cr cds: A, MC, V.

New London

See also Groton, Mystic, Norwich, Stonington

Settled 1646 **Pop** 28,540 **Elev** 33 ft **Area code** 860 **Zip** 06320
Information Connecticut's Mystic & More, 470 Bank St, PO Box 89; 860/444-2206 or 800/TO-ENJOY
Web www.mysticmore.com

New London is a seagoing community and always has been; it has one of the finest deep-water ports on the Atlantic coast. From the first days of the republic into the 20th century, whalers brought fortunes home to New London. Townspeople still welcome all ships—submarines, cutters, yachts, cruisers. Today the city's manufacturing industries include turbines, steel fabrication, high-tech products, medicines, electronics, and other products.

What to See and Do

Eugene O'Neill Theater Center. Complex incl O'Neill Playwrights Conference, O'Neill Critics Institute, O'Neill Music Theater Conference, O'Neill Puppetry Conference, National Theater Institute. Staged readings of new plays and musicals during summer at Barn Theater, Amphitheater, and Instant Theater (June-Aug). W via US 1, at 305 Great Neck Rd in Waterford. Phone 860/443-5378.

Ferries.

New London-Block Island, RI. Auto ferry makes two-hr crossing; one round-trip (mid-June-Labor Day). Phone 860/442-9553. Individuals, vehicles ¢¢¢¢¢

New London-Fishers Island, NY. Auto ferries *Race Point* and *Munnatawket* make crossing to Fishers Island; several departures daily. Departs from New London Pier, foot of State St. Phone 860/443-6851 or 516/788-7463. One way: pedestrian ¢¢ Vehicle and driver ¢¢¢¢¢

New London-Orient Point, NY. Five auto ferries make 90-min trip across Long Island Sound. High-speed passenger ferry makes a 40-min trip daily. (Daily; no trip Dec 25) Departs from 2 Ferry St. Advance res required for vehicles. Phone 860/443-7394. ¢¢¢¢¢

Joshua Hempsted House. (1678) Oldest house in city; restored, 17th- and 18th-century furnishings; Hempsted family diary detailing life in the house during colonial times. (Mid-May-mid-Oct, Tues-Sun afternoons) 11 Hempstead St. Phone 860/443-7949 or 860/247-8996. ¢¢ Admission incl

Nathaniel Hempsted House. (1759) One of two surviving examples of mid-18th-century cut-stone architecture in state. Stone exterior bake oven, seven rms with period furnishings. (Mid May-mid-Oct, Tues-Sun afternoons) Phone 860/443-7949 or 860/247-8996.

Lyman Allyn Art Museum. Over 15,000 works of art. The collection incl Contemporary, Modern and Early American fine arts; collection of dolls, doll houses; American and European paintings; Asian and primitive art. (Tues-Sun; closed hols) 625 Williams St. Phone 860/443-2545. ¢¢

Monte Cristo Cottage. Restored boyhood home of playwright and Nobel prize winner Eugene O'Neill; houses research library and memorabilia. Multimedia presentation. Literary readings. (Mid June-late Oct, Tues-Sun) 325 Pequot Ave. Phone 860/443-0051 or 860/443-5378. ¢¢

Ocean Beach Park. Swimming in ocean, Olympic-size pool, waterslide; sheltered pavilion, boardwalk, picnic area, concessions, miniature golf, novelty shop, amusement arcade, entertainment. (Sat before Memorial Day-Labor Day, daily) 3 mi S on Ocean Ave, on Long Island Sound. Phone 800/510-7263. Per vehicle ¢¢¢

Science Center of Eastern Connecticut. Regional science museum located on 415-acre Connecticut Arboretum with trees and shrubs native to the area (daily). Major exhibit on eastern Connecticut's natural and cultural history entitled "Time and the River: The Story of Land and People in the Thames River Basin"; workshops and courses; field trips, special programs; nature trail, herb garden; museum shop. (Tues-Sun; closed hols) 33 Gallows Ln, N of I-95 exit 83. Phone 860/442-0391. ¢¢

Shaw Perkins Mansion. (1756) Naval headquarters for state during Revolution; genealogical and historical library. Unique paneled cement fireplace walls. 305 Bank St. Phone 860/443-1209. ¢

Sunbeam Fleet Nature Cruises. Cruises to view bald eagles (Feb-Mar) and seals (Apr-May). Res suggested. Departs from dock near Niantic River bridge in Waterford, W via I-95 exit 74, S on CT 161, left on CT 156 to first dock on left past bridge. Phone 860/443-7259. ¢¢¢¢

US Coast Guard Academy. (1876) 800 cadets. Visitors' Pavilion with multimedia show (May-Oct, daily). US Coast Guard Museum (daily; closed hols). Cadet parade-reviews (fall, spring, usually Fri). Barque *Eagle,* 295 ft, open to visitors (Fri-Sun, when in port; limited hrs); photography permitted. Mohegan Ave, 1 mi N on I-95 exit 83. Phone 860/444-8270. **FREE**

Ye Antientiest Burial Ground. (1653) Huntington St. **FREE**

Ye Olde Towne Mill. (1650) Built for John Winthrop, Jr., founder of New London and Connecticut's sixth governor; restored 1981; overshot waterwheel (closed to public). Mill St and State Pier Rd, under Gold Star Bridge.

Special Events

Connecticut Storytelling Festival. Connecticut College. Nationally acclaimed artists; workshops, concerts. Late Apr. Phone 860/439-2764.

Sailfest. City Pier. Phone 860/443-1879. One wkend July.

Motels/Motor Lodges

★ **NIANTIC INN.** *345 Main St, Niantic (06357). 860/739-5451; fax 860/691-1488.* 24 suites, 3 story. Mid-May-late Oct: suites $145; each addl $30; under 12 free; lower rates rest of yr. Crib free. TV; cable. Complimentary coffee in rms. Restaurant nearby. Ck-out 11 am. Business servs avail. Refrigerators. Picnic tables. Swimming beach opp. Cr cds: A, D, DS, MC, V.

★ **RAMADA INN.** *248 Flanders Rd, Niantic (06357). 860/739-5483; fax 860/739-4877; toll-free 800/942-8466. www.ramada.com.* 50 rms, 2 story. July-Labor Day: S, D $69-$139; each addl $10; under 17 free; lower rates rest of yr. Crib free. TV; cable (premium). Pool. Complimentary bkfst. Ck-out 11 am. Meeting rms. Business servs avail. In-rm modem link. Valet serv. Game rm. Health club privileges. Beach privileges. Cr cds: A, C, D, DS, JCB, MC, V.

★ **RED ROOF INN.** *707 Colman St (06320). 860/444-0001; fax 860/443-7154; res 800/843-7663. www.redroof.com.* 108 rms, 2 story. May-Oct: S $39.99-$57; D $34.99-$77; each addl $5; under 18 free; higher rates special events; lower rates rest of yr. Crib free. Pet accepted. TV; cable (premium), VCR avail. Complimentary coffee in lobby. Restaurant nearby. Ck-out noon. Meeting rms. Business servs avail. In-rm modem link. Cr cds: A, DS, MC, V.

★ **STARLIGHT MOTOR INN.** *256 Flanders Rd, Niantic (06357). 860/739-5462; fax 860/739-0567.* 48 rms, 2 story. May-Sept: S, D $44-$99; lower rates rest of yr. TV; cable (premium), VCR avail. Pool. Restaurant nearby. Cr cds: A, C, D, DS, MC, V.

Hotel

★★ **RADISSON.** *35 Governor Winthrop Blvd (06320). 860/443-7000; fax 860/443-1239; res 800/333-3333. www.radisson.com.* 120 rms, 5 story. S, D $65-$155; each addl $20; suites $75-$165; under 18 free; wknd packages. Crib free. TV; cable (premium). Indoor pool; whirlpool. Restaurant 6:30 am-9 pm. Bar 11-1 am. Ck-out noon. Meeting rms. Business servs avail. In-rm modem link. Bellhops. Valet serv. Sundries. Free airport, railroad station, bus depot transportation. Lighted tennis privileges. Health club privileges. Refrigerator, wet bar in most suites. Cr cds: A, DS, MC, V.

B&B/Small Inn

★★ **QUEEN ANNE INN.** *265 Williams St (06320). 860/447-2600; fax 860/443-0857; toll-free 800/347-8818. www.queen-anne.com.* 10 rms, 2 share bath, 7 with shower only, 3 story, 1 kit. suite. Some rm phones. S $95; D $145; each addl $25; kit. suite $185; 2-day min wknds, May-Sept. Children over 12 yrs only. TV in some rms; cable. Complimentary full bkfst. Ck-out 11 am, ck-in 3-9 pm.

Queen Anne Victorian built in 1903. Turn-of-the-century art and antiques. Totally nonsmoking. Cr cds: A, C, D, DS, MC, V.

Restaurant

★ **CONSTANTINE'S.** *252 Main St, Niantic (06357). 860/739-2848. www.constantinesrestaurant.com.* Specializes in fresh seafood. Hrs: 11:30 am-9 pm; wkends to 10 pm; summer hrs vary. Closed Mon; Thanksgiving, Dec 25. Bar to 1 am. Lunch $2-$8.50, dinner $6.95-$20.95. Child's menu. View of Long Island Sound. Family-owned. Cr cds: A, DS, MC, V.

New Preston

See also Cornwall Bridge, Kent

Pop 1,217 **Elev** 700 ft **Area code** 860 **Zip** 06777
Information Litchfield Hills Visitors Bureau, PO Box 968, Litchfield 06759; 860/567-4506
Web www.litchfieldhills.com

What to See and Do

Historical Museum of Gunn Memorial Library. House built 1781; contains collections and exhibits on area history; paintings, furnishings, gowns, dolls, dollhouses, and tools. (Thurs-Sun afternoons) 4 mi SW via CT 47 at jct Wykeham Rd, on the green in Washington. Phone 860/868-7756.
FREE

✪ **The Institute for American Indian Studies.** A museum of Northeastern Woodland Indian artifacts with permanent exhibit hall. Exhibits incl changing Native American art displays; also a replicated indoor longhouse, outdoor replicated Algonkian village, simulated archaeological site, and nature trail. Special programs. (Daily; closed hols) 4 mi SW via CT 47 to CT 199S, then 1½ mi to Curtis Rd in Washington. Phone 860/868-0518. ¢¢

Lake Waramaug State Park. Swimming, fishing, scuba diving; field sports, hiking, ice-skating, camping, picnicking. Standard hrs, fees. 5 mi N on Lake Waramaug Rd (CT 478).

B&Bs/Small Inns

★★★ **BOULDERS INN.** *E Shore Rd (CT 45) (06777). 860/868-0541; fax 860/868-1925; toll-free 800/555-2685. www.bouldersinn.com.* 6 rms in inn, 2 story, 8 rms in cottages, 3 rms in carriage house. MAP: S $200-$300; D $250-$350; each addl $50. Restaurant (see also BOULDERS). Bar. Ck-out 11:30 am. Business servs avail. In-rm modem link. Tennis. Downhill ski 20 mi; x-country ski 5 mi. Rec rm. Refrigerators, fireplace in cottages and carriage house. Balconies. Canoes, rowboats, sailboats, paddleboats. Bicycles. Hiking. Private beach on lake. Cr cds: A, DS, MC, V.

★★ **HOPKINS INN.** *22 Hopkins Rd (06777). 860/868-7295; fax 860/868-7464. www.thehopkinsinn.com.* 11 rms, 2 share bath, 3 story. No A/C. No rm phones. Apr-Dec: S, D $67-$150; each addl $7. Closed rest of yr. Restaurant (see also HOPKINS INN). Bar. Ck-out 11 am, ck-in 1 pm. Lake Waramaug opp, private beach. Established 1847. Cr cds: A, MC, V.
⊠ ▧

Restaurants

★★★ **BOULDERS.** *E Shore Rd (06777). 860/868-0541. www.bouldersinn.com.* Own baking. Hrs: 6-8 pm; Fri, Sat to 9 pm; Sun 5-8 pm. Closed Dec 25; also Mon, Tues (winter), Tues (summer). Res accepted; required wkends. Serv bar. A la carte entrees: dinner $17.50-$24. Outdoor dining. In turn-of-the-century summer home. Cr cds: A, MC, V.
[D]

★★ **HOPKINS INN.** *22 Hopkins Rd (06777). 860/868-7295. www.thehopkinsinn.com.* Continental menu. Specialties: roast duck a l'orange, sweetbreads, Wiener schnitzel. Hrs: noon-2 pm, 6-9 pm; Fri to 10 pm; Sat noon-2 pm, 5:30-10 pm; Sun 12:30-8:30 pm; Apr, Nov, Dec 6-9 pm, wkend hrs vary. Closed Mon; also Jan-Mar. Res accepted. Bar. Lunch $10-$14, dinner $18-$21. Child's menu. Terrace dining. In old inn on hill overlooking lake. Cr cds: A, DS, MC, V.

★★★ **LE BON COIN.** *223 Witchfield Tpke (06777). 860/868-7763.* Country French menu. Specializes in sweetbreads, Dover sole. Hrs: noon-2 pm, 6-9 pm; Sat to 10 pm; Sun 5-9 pm. Closed Tues, Wed; Jan 1, Memorial Day, Dec 25. Res accepted. Bar. Wine list. A la carte entrees: lunch $4.75-$10, dinner $12.75-$19. Child's menu. Country French atmosphere. Cr cds: MC, V.
[D] ⊠

Niantic

(see New London)

Norfolk

See also Lakeville, Riverton

Founded 1758 **Pop** 2,060 **Elev** 1,230 ft **Area code** 860 **Zip** 06058
Information Litchfield Hills Visitors Bureau, PO Box 968, Litchfield 06759; 860/567-4506
Web www.litchfieldhills.com

What to See and Do

Historical Museum. Located in former Norfolk Academy (1840). Exhibits on history of Norfolk incl displays of a country store and post office as well as a children's rm with an 1879 doll house. (Late May-mid-Oct, Sat and Sun; rest of yr, by appt) On the green. Phone 860/542-5761. **FREE**

State parks. 1 mi N on CT 272.

Campbell Falls. Winding trails through woodland composed of many splashing cascades; focal point is Campbell Falls. Fishing; hiking, picnicking. 6 mi N on CT 272. Phone 860/482-1817. **FREE**

Dennis Hill. A unique summit pavilion (formerly a summer residence) is located at an elevation of 1,627 ft, providing a panoramic view of the Litchfield Hills and beyond. Picnicking, hiking, x-country skiing. 2 mi S on CT 272. Phone 860/482-1817. **FREE**

Hatstack Mountain. A 34-ft-high stone tower at the summit, 1,716 ft above sea level, provides an excellent view of Long Island Sound, the Berkshires, and peaks in New York. A ½-mi trail leads from parking lot to tower. Picnicking; hiking. 1 mi N on CT 272. Phone 860/482-1817.

Special Event

Norfolk Chamber Music Festival. Musical performances Fri, Sat eves in acoustically superb 1906 Music Shed located on grounds of 19th-century estate; also picnicking, indoor performances, and art gallery before concerts; informal chamber music recitals Thurs and Sat. E. B. Stoeckel Estate at jct US 44, CT 272. Phone 860/542-3000 (June-Oct); 203/432-1966 (rest of yr). Mid-June-mid-Sept.

B&B/Small Inn

★ **MOUNTAIN VIEW INN.** *67 Litchfield Rd (CT 272) (06058). 860/542-6991; fax 860/542-5689. www.mvinn.com.* 7 rms, 6 with bath, 2 story. No A/C. S $75-$95; D $85-$135; each addl $10; family rates. Crib free. Complimentary full bkfst. Restaurant. Bar. Ck-out noon. Downhill ski 20 mi; x-country ski 2 mi. Lawn games. Victorian building (1880s); turn-of-the-century decor, antiques; 4 fireplaces. Cr cds: DS, MC, V.
▧ ▧

Norwalk

See also Bridgeport, Fairfield, Greenwich, Stamford

Founded 1651 **Pop** 78,331 **Elev** 42 ft **Area code** 203
Information Coastal Fairfield County Convention & Visitors Bureau, 297 West Ave, 06850; 203/899-2799 or 800/866-7925
Web www.coastalct.com

Norwalk's growth was heavily influenced by Long Island Sound. The city evolved rapidly from an agriculturally based community to a major seaport, then to a manufacturing center known for high-fashion hats, corsets, and clocks. The Sound still plays an important part in Norwalk's development, providing beauty, recreation and, of course, oysters.

What to See and Do

Charter fishing trips. Several companies offer full- and ½-day saltwater fishing excursions. Contact the Coastal Fairfield County Tourism District for details. Phone 800/866-7925.

Ferry to Sheffield Island Lighthouse. Departs from Hope Dock, jct Washington and N Water St, in South Norwalk. Ferry through Norwalk Harbor to historic Sheffield lighthouse (1868) on three-acre island. Tour. Picnicking. (Memorial Day-June, wkends; July-Labor Day, daily) Phone 203/838-9444. Round trip ¢¢¢¢

Historic South Norwalk (SoNo). Nineteenth-century waterfront neighborhood on National Register featuring historical buildings, unique shops, art galleries, and restaurants. 1 mi SE via I-95 exit 14 N/15 S, bounded by Washington, Water, N and S Main Sts, in South Norwalk. Phone 800/866-7925.

Lockwood-Mathews Mansion Museum. (1864-1868) Fifty-rm Victorian mansion built by financier LeGrand Lockwood; 42-ft skylit rotunda, ornamented doors, and carved marble, inlaid woodwork throughout, period furnishings, musical boxes, and mechanical music exhibit; one-hr guided tour. Victorian Ice-Cream Social (mid-July) and Antiques Show (late Oct). (Mid-Mar-Dec, Wed-Sun; rest of yr, by appt only; closed hols) 295 West Ave. ¢¢¢

Maritime Aquarium at Norwalk. Hands-on maritime museum featuring shark touch tank and harbor seal pool; 125 species, touch tanks, films on IMAX screen; boat building exhibit. Guided harbor study tours. (Daily; closed Thanksgiving, Dec 25) 2 mi S via I-95 exit 14 N or 15 S, at 10 N Water St. Phone 203/852-0700. ¢¢¢

Mill Hill Historic Park. Complex of historic early American buildings incl the Town House Museum (ca 1835), Fitch House Law Office (ca 1740), and schoolhouse (1826); also old cemetery. (May-Oct, Sun) Wall St and East Ave. Phone 203/846-0525. **FREE**

St. Paul's-on-the-Green. This Gothic style stone church contains the Seabury Altar; medieval stained glass; exquisite needlepoint. Antique organ. Also here is colonial cemetery. (Daily by appt) 60 East Ave. Phone 203/847-2806.

WPA Murals. America's largest collection of Works Progress Administration murals depict life in southeastern Fairfield County in the 1930s. (Mon-Fri; closed hols) City Hall, 125 East Ave (parking entrance, Sunset Hill Ave). Phone 203/854-7900. **FREE**

Special Events

Norwalk Harbor Splash. South Norwalk. Regatta, harbor tours, music. Late May or early June. Phone 203/838-9444.

Round Hill Highland Games. Cranbury Park. Heritage celebration with Highland dancing, pipe bands, caber tossing, clan tents, Scottish and American food. Late June or early July. Phone 800/866-7925.

SoNo Arts Celebration. Juried crafts, kinetic sculpture race, entertainment, concessions, blk party. Washington St, in Historic South Norwalk. First wkend Aug. Phone 800/866-7925.

Oyster Festival. Veteran's Park, East Norwalk. Three-day event featuring entertainment, boat rides, concessions. Wkend after Labor Day. Phone 800/866-7925.

International In-water Boat Show. Cove Marina, Calf Pasture Beach Rd. Phone 800/866-7925. Mid-Sept.

Motel/Motor Lodge

★★ **FOUR POINTS BY SHERATON.** *426 Main Ave (06851). 203/849-9828; fax 203/846-6925; toll-free 800/329-7466. www.fourpoints.com.* 127 rms, 4 story. S, D $169; each addl $10; under 18 free; wkend rates. Crib free. TV; cable (premium). Coffee in rms. Restaurant 7 am-10 pm. Bar. Ck-out noon. Coin lndry. Meeting rms. Business servs avail. Sundries. Exercise equipt. Health club privileges. Cr cds: A, C, D, DS, MC, V.

D 🏋 🖿 🐾 **SC**

Hotel

★★ **DOUBLETREE CLUB HOTEL - NORWALK.** *789 Connecticut Ave (06854). 203/853-3477; fax 203/523-2292; toll-free 800/222-8733. www.doubletree.com.* 268 rms, 8 story. S, D $89-$149; each addl $10; under 18 free; wkend rates. Crib free. TV; cable (premium). Indoor pool. Coffee in rms. Restaurant 6 am-11 pm. Bar 5 pm-midnight. Ck-out noon. Meeting rms. Business center. In-rm modem link. Exercise equipt. Covered parking. Cr cds: A, C, D, DS, ER, JCB, MC, V.

D 🛋 🏋 🖿 🐾 🏃

B&B/Small Inn

★★ **THE SILVERMINE TAVERN.** *194 Perry Ave (06850). 203/847-4558; fax 203/847-9171. www.silverminetavern.com.* 10 rms, 2 story. No rm phones. S $80; D $145; each addl $18; higher rates wkends. Closed Dec 25; also Tues Sept-May. Complimentary continental bkfst. Restaurant (see also SILVERMINE TAVERN). Bar noon-10 pm. Ck-out 11 am. Meeting rms. Business servs avail. Some balconies. On river. Country inn (1767); antiques. Cr cds: A, C, D, MC, V.

🖿 🐾

Restaurants

★★ **MESON GALICIA.** *10 Wall St (06850). 203/866-8800.* Spanish menu. Specializes in seafood, duckling, lamb. Hrs: noon-2:30 pm, 6-9:30 pm; Fri to 10:30 pm; Sat 6-10:30 pm; Sun 6-9 pm. Closed Mon; most major hols. Res accepted; required Fri, Sat. Bar. A la carte entrees: lunch $9-$16, dinner $17.50-$25. Outdoor dining. Bldg once a trolley barn (1800s). Totally nonsmoking. Cr cds: A, C, D, DS, ER, MC, V.

D

★★★ **PASTA NOSTRA.** *116 Washington St, South Norwalk (06854). 203/854-9700. www.pastanostra.com.* Italian cuisine. Hrs: 5:30-9:30 pm; Wed from 6 pm. Closed Sun-Tues. Res required wkends. Dinner $17-$29. Cr cds: DS, MC, V.

D

★★ **SILVERMINE TAVERN.** *194 Perry Ave (06850). 203/847-4558. www.silverminetavern.com.* Specializes in New England fare, fresh seafood. Hrs: noon-3 pm, 6-9 pm; Sun 3-9 pm; Sun brunch 11 am-2:30 pm. Closed Dec 25; also Tues. Res accepted. Bar. Lunch $6.50-$11.95, dinner $15.50-$24.95. Buffet: dinner (Thurs) $17.50. Sun brunch $18.50. Child's menu. Outdoor dining. 18th-century Colonial tavern overlooking mill pond; antiques. Country store opp. Family-owned. Cr cds: A, C, D, ER, MC, V.

Norwich

See also Groton, New London

Settled 1659 **Pop** 37,391 **Elev** 52 ft **Area code** 860
Zip 06360
Information Connecticut's Mystic and More!, 470 Bank St, PO Box 89, New London 06320; 860/444-2206 or 800/863-6569 outside CT
Web www.mysticmore.com

Norwich was one of the first cities chartered in Connecticut. Since the end of the 18th century, it has been a leader in the industrial development of the state. Here the colony's first paper mill was opened in 1766, and the first cut nails in America were made in 1772. Cotton spinning began about 1790.

There are three distinct sections: NorwichTown to the northwest, a living museum of the past; the business section near the Thames docks; and a central residential section with many 19th-century homes.

What to See and Do

Indian Leap. The falls was a favorite resort and outpost of the Mohegan. Legend has it that a band of Narragansetts, during the Battle of Great Plains in 1643, fled from pursuing Mohegans. As they came upon the falls, many were forced to jump off the cliffs and into the chasm below, hence the name. Can be viewed from the Monroe St footbridge. Yantic Falls off Yantic St. Phone 860/886-4683. **FREE**

Leffingwell Inn. (1675) Scene of Revolutionary War councils. Museum; period rms. (Mid-May-Labor Day, Tues-Sun; rest of yr, by appt) 348 Washington St at CT Tpke exit 81E. Phone 860/889-9440. ¢¢

Mohegan Park and Memorial Rose Garden. Picnic and play area; swimming area (June-Labor Day, daily). Rose garden; best time to visit, June-Sept. (Daily) Entrances on Judd Rd and Rockwell St. Phone 860/823-3759. **FREE**

Native American Burial Grounds. Resting place of Uncas, chief of the Mohegans (more popularly known as Mohicans) who gave the original land for the settlement of Norwich. Sachem St, off CT 32. Phone 860/886-4683.

The Old Burying Ground. Burial place of many Revolutionary War soldiers, incl French soldiers; also Samuel Huntington, signer of the Declaration of Independence. Entrance from E Town St; brochure avail at Cemetery Ln entrance. Phone 860/886-4683.

Slater Memorial Museum & Converse Art Gallery. Roman and Greek casts; Vanderpoel Collection of Oriental Art; 17th to 20th-century American art and furnishings; changing exhibits. (Sept-June, daily; rest of yr, Tues-Sun; closed hols) Approx 1 mi N via I-395 exit 81 E, on campus of Norwich Free Academy, 108 Crescent St. Phone 860/887-2506.

Tantaquidgeon Indian Museum. Works of Mohegan and other New England tribes, past and present; also displays of Southeast, Southwest, and Northern Plains Native Americans. (May-Oct, Tues-Sun) 5 mi S on CT 32, at 1819 Norwich-New London Tpke, in Uncasville. Phone 860/848-9145. **Donation**

Special Events

Chelsea Street Festival. Chelsea district. Fine arts, entertainment, hayrides, children's events. Phone 860/887-2789. Third Sat May.

Blue Grass Festival. Strawberry Park. Phone 860/886-1944. Late May.

Rose-Arts Festival. Broadway and Washington Sts. Crowning of Rose Queen; arts and crafts shows; children's activities; entertainment; intl food festival; flower competition; golf tournament; bicycle and road races. Ten days late June-early July. Phone 860/444-2206.

Harbor Day. Brown Memorial Park, at waterfront. Raft race; boat rides; dunking booth; arts and crafts; entertainment. Late Aug. Phone 860/444-2206.

Historic Norwichtown Days. Norwichtown Green. Living history events, crafts, parade. Phone 860/444-2206. Second wkend Sept.

Motel/Motor Lodge

★ **RAMADA INN.** *10 Laura Blvd (06360). 860/889-5201; fax 860/889-1767; toll-free 800/272-6232. www.ramada.com.* 127 rms, 6 story. Mid-May-mid-Oct: S $79-$149; D $89-$159; each addl $10-$15; suites $200; under 18 free; package plans; lower rates rest of yr. TV; cable (premium). Indoor pool. Restaurant 6:30 am-10 pm. Rm serv. Bar 4 pm-midnight. Ck-out 11 am. Meeting rms. In-rm modem link. Valet serv. Sundries. Some bathrm phones. Private patios, balconies. Cr cds: A, C, D, DS, JCB, MC, V.

Resort

★★★ **THE SPA AT NORWICH INN.** *607 W Thames St (06360). 860/886-2401; fax 860/886-9483; toll-free 800/ASK-4SPA. www.thespaatnorwichinn.com.* 65 rms in inn, 3 story, 70 villas. May-Oct: S, D $130-$150; suites $165-$245; lower rates rest of yr. TV; cable, VCR avail (movies). 2 pools; whirlpool. Restaurant. Bar 4 pm-midnight; Fri, Sat to 1 am; entertainment Fri, Sat. Ck-out noon. Meeting rms. Business center. Concierge serv. RR station transportation. Lighted tennis, pro. Exercise rm; sauna. Massage. Lawn games. Built in 1929 as gathering place for prominent persons. Cr cds: A, DS, MC, V.

Restaurant

★★ **KENSINGTON.** *607 W Thames St (06360). 860/886-2401.* Specializes in classic New England cuisine. Own baking, desserts. Hrs: 7-10 am, noon-2 pm, 6:30-9 pm; Fri, Sat to 10 pm; Sun brunch 11:30 am-2:30 pm. Res accepted. Bar 4 pm-midnight. Bkfst buffet $6.95- $12.95. A la carte entrees: lunch $10.95-$14.95, dinner $19-$29. Sun brunch $15.95. Outdoor dining. Georgian Colonial decor; antiques. Totally nonsmoking. Cr cds: A, MC, V.
D

Old Lyme

See also Essex, New London, Old Saybrook

Settled 1665 **Pop** 6,535 **Elev** 17 ft **Area code** 860 **Zip** 06371
Information Connecticut's Mystic and More!, 470 Bank St, PO Box 89, New London 06320; 860/444-2206 or 800/863-6569
Web www.mysticmore.com

Once, long ago, they say a sea captain lived in every house in Old Lyme. Fortunately, a good many of the houses are still standing on the tree-lined streets of this sleepy old village. Named for Lyme Regis, England, it is a summer resort and an artists' colony, one of the first on the coast.

What to See and Do

Florence Griswold Museum. (1817) Stately late-Georgian mansion that housed America's most celebrated art colony at the turn of the century. Paintings by Willard Metcalf, Childe Hassam, and other artists of the colony; exhibits of 18th- and 19th-century New England furnishings and decorative arts. (Jan-Mar, Wed-Sun; Apr-Dec, Tues-Sun) 96 Lyme St, 1 blk W off CT Tpke exit 70. Phone 860/434-5542.

Rocky Neck State Park. Approx 560 acres with ½-mi frontage on Long Island Sound. Saltwater swimming, scuba diving, fishing; hiking, picnicking (shelters, concessions). Camping. Standard hrs, fees. 6 mi E via I-95 exit 72, on CT 156 in East Lyme. Phone 860/739-5471.

B&Bs/Small Inns

★★★ **BEE AND THISTLE INN.** *100 Lyme St (06371). 860/434-1667; fax 860/434-3407; toll-free 800/622-4046. www.beeandthistleinn.com.* 11 rms, 3 story, 1 cottage. S $75-$150; D $75-$155; each addl $15; cottage $210. Children over 12 yrs only. Closed 2 wks Jan. TV in cottage. Restaurant (see also BEE AND THISTLE INN). Rm serv 8:30-10 am. Bar noon-11 pm; guitarist Fri; harpist Sat. Ck-out 11 am, ck-in 2 pm; cottage: ck-out noon, ck-in 3 pm. Picnic tables. Colonial house (1756); antique furniture. 5 acres on river. Cr cds: A, DS, MC, V.

★★★ **OLD LYME INN.** *85 Lyme St (06371). 860/434-2600; fax 860/434-5352; toll-free 800/434-5352. www.oldlymeinn .com.* 13 rms, 2 story. S $86-$133; D $99-$160. Pet accepted. TV; VCR avail. Complimentary continental bkfst. Restaurant (see also OLD LYME INN). Bar. Ck-out noon, ck-in 3-11 pm. Business center. Built 1850, former farm; antiques, murals. Ocean ½ mi. Cr cds: A, C, D, DS, MC, V.
D

Restaurants

★★★ **BEE AND THISTLE INN.** *100 Lyme St (06371). 860/434-1667. www.beeandthistleinn.com.* Changing menu. Hrs: 8-10 am, 11:30 am-2 pm, 6-9:30 pm; Sun 8-9:30 am, 5:30-9:30 pm; Sun brunch 11 am-2 pm. Afternoon tea (Nov-Apr) Mon, Wed and Thurs 3:30-5 pm. Closed Tues; Dec 24 evening-Dec 25; also 2 wks Jan. Res accepted. Bar. A la carte entrees: bkfst $3.50-$7, lunch $8.95-$12, dinner $19-$28. Sun brunch $10.95-$15. Guitar duo Fri, harpist Sat. In Colonial house (1756); 4 fireplaces. Cr cds: A, DS, MC, V.

★★★ **OLD LYME INN.** *85 Lyme St (06371). 860/434-2600. www.oldlymeinn.com.* Own baking. Hrs: noon-2 pm, 6-9 pm; Sun 11 am-9 pm; Sun brunch to 3 pm. Res accepted. Bar. Wine list. Lunch $6.95-$10.95, dinner $19.95-$27.95. Jazz guitarist Fri, Sat. Restored 1850 home; 3 fireplaces; many antiques; murals by local artist. In historic district. Cr cds: A, DS, MC, V.
D

Old Saybrook

See also Clinton, Essex, New London, Old Lyme

Settled 1635 **Pop** 9,552 **Elev** 31 ft **Area code** 860 **Zip** 06475
Information Chamber of Commerce, 146 Main St, PO Box 625; phone 860/388-3266; or the Connecticut Valley Tourism Commission, 393 Main St, Middletown 06457; phone 860/347-0028
Web www.oldsaybrookct.com

Old Saybrook, at the mouth of the Connecticut River, is popular with summer vacationers. It is the third-oldest named community in Connecticut and is the oldest officially chartered town in the state. It was also the original site of Yale College until 1716.

What to See and Do

Fort Saybrook Monument Park. Nearly 18-acre park with remains of Fort Saybrook, first military fortification in the state; picnicking. (Daily) On College St, at Saybrook Point.

General William Hart House. (1767) Provincial Georgian-style, colonial residence of well-to-do New England merchant and politician; features incl eight corner fireplaces, one of which is decorated with Sadler and Green transfer-print tiles illustrating Aesop's Fables; original wainscotting; Federal-style pieces, several of which are Hart family items; antique furniture, costumes, artifacts; on grounds are re-created colonial gardens, incl award-winning herb garden. (Mid June-mid-Sept, Fri-Sun, limited hrs). 350 Main St. Phone 860/388-2622. **Donation**

Special Events

Arts and Crafts Show. More than 200 artists and crafts-persons exhibiting. Town Green, Main St. Last full wkend July. Phone 860/388-3266.

Christmas Torchlight Parade. More than 40 fife and drum corps march down Main St. Second Sat Dec. Phone 860/388-3266.

Motels/Motor Lodges

★★ **HERITAGE MOTOR INN.** *1500 Boston Post Rd (06475). 860/388-3743.* 12 rms. May-Nov: S, D $95-$105; each addl $7; suites $140; lower rates rest of yr. Crib free. TV; cable. Pool. Restaurant nearby. Ck-out 11 am. Some refrigerators. Beach privileges. Connected to Nathaniel Bushnell House (1755). Cr cds: A, D, DS, MC, V.
🌊 ⛵ 🔥

★ **SANDPIPER MOTOR INN.** *1750 Boston Post Rd (06475). 860/399-7973; fax 860/399-7387; toll-free 800/323-7973. www.thesandpiper.com.* 44 rms, 3 story. Mid-May-Oct: S $50-$95; D $65-$110; each addl $6; under 12 free; lower rates rest of yr. Crib free. TV; cable, VCR avail. Pool. Complimentary continental bkfst. Restaurant adj. Ck-out 11 am. Meeting rm. In-rm modem link. Some refrigerators. Picnic tables, grills. Near Long Island Sound. Cr cds: A, DS, MC, V.
🅳 🐾 🌊 ⛵ 🔥

Resorts

★★★ **SAYBROOK POINT INN AND SPA.** *2 Bridge St; Rte 154 (06475). 860/395-2000; fax 860/388-1504; toll-free 800/243-0212. www.saybrookpointinn.com.* 62 rms, 3 story, 7 suites. May-Oct: S, D $179-$259; suites $299-$495; under 12 free; lower rates rest of yr. Crib avail. TV; cable, VCR avail (movies). 2 pools, 1 indoor; whirlpool. Restaurant 8 am-9 pm. Bar noon-1 am. Ck-out noon. Coin lndry. Meeting rms. Business servs avail. In-rm modem link. Bellhops. Valet serv. Concierge. Gift shop. RR station transportation. Exercise rm; sauna. Touring bicycles. Health club privileges. Refrigerators, wet bars. Balconies. Cr cds: A, C, D, DS, MC, V.
🅳 🐾 🌊 🏋 🏃 🛇 SC

★★★ **WATER'S EDGE RESORT AND CONFERENCE CENTER.** *1525 Boston Post Rd, Westbrook (06498). 860/399-5901; fax 860/399-6172; toll-free 800/222-5901. www. watersedge-resort.com.* 32 rms in hotel, 1-3 story, 66 villas. May-Oct: S, D $170-$295; villas $200-$280; wkly rates; lower rates rest of yr. Crib free. TV; cable; VCR in villas. 2 pools, 1 indoor; whirlpool. Supervised children's activities (May-Sept); ages 4-12. Dining rm (public by res) 7-10 am, 11:30 am-2:30 pm, 5-9 pm; Sun 8 am-9 pm. Rm serv. Bar noon-1 am; Fri, Sat to 2 am; Sun to 11 pm. Ck-

out noon, ck-in 3 pm. Business servs avail. In-rm modem link. Grocery, package store ¼ mi. Bellhops. Valet serv. Tennis. Downhill ski 20 mi. Exercise equipt; sauna. Bicycles. Lawn games. Soc dir. Game rm. Fishing guides. Fireplaces. Refrigerator in villas. Balconies. Sitting rm in main lodge. On Long Island Sound. Private beach. Cr cds: A, D, DS, MC, V.
🅳 🐾 ⛵ 🎿 🏊 🏃 ✈ ⛵ 🛇

Restaurants

★★ **ALEIA'S.** *1687 Boston Post Rd, Westbrook (06475). 860/399-5050. www.aleias.com.* Mediterranean menu. Specializes in fish, pasta, steak. Hrs: 5:30-9 pm; Fri, Sat to 10 pm. Closed Mon. Res accepted. Bar. Dinner $13.50-$19.95. Child's menu. Pianist Fri, Sat. Outdoor dining. Bistro atmosphere. Cr cds: A, MC, V.
🅳

★★ **DOCK AND DINE.** *College St (06475). 860/388-4665.* Specializes in fresh seafood, steak, ribs. Hrs: 11:30 am-10 pm; Sun from noon; winter to 9 pm. Closed Mon, Tues (mid-Oct- mid-Apr); Thanksgiving, Dec 24, 25. Res accepted. Bar. Lunch $5.95-$10.95, dinner $11.95-$21.95. Child's menu. Entertainment Fri-Sun (summer). View of Sound, dock. Cr cds: A, C, D, DS, ER, MC, V.
🅳 ⬒

★ **SAYBROOK FISH HOUSE.** *99 Essex Rd (06475). 860/388-4836.* Specializes in fresh seafood. Hrs: 11:45 am-9:30 pm; Fri, Sat to 10:30 pm; Sun noon-9 pm; early-bird dinner Mon-Fri 4:30-6 pm, Sat 4-5:30 pm, Sun noon-9 pm. Closed Thanksgiving, Dec 25. Bar. Lunch $4.95-$8.95, dinner $11.95-$19.95. Child's menu. Tables covered with brown packing paper. Cr cds: A, C, D, DS, ER, MC, V.
🅳 SC ⬒

Plainfield

See also Norwich, Putnam

Settled 1689 **Pop** 14,363 **Elev** 203 ft **Area code** 860 **Zip** 06374
Information Northeast Connecticut Visitors District, 13 Canterbury Rd, Suite 3, PO Box 145, Putnam 06260; 860/779-6383 or 888/628-1228
Web www.ctquietcorner.org

What to See and Do

Plainfield Greyhound Park. Pari-mutuel betting. Concessions, bar. No minors. Races daily. (All yr) Phone 860/564-3391. ¢¢

Prudence Crandall House. Site of New England's first academy for black girls (1833-34). Restored two-story frame bldg with changing exhibits, period furnishings; research library. Gift shop. (Wed-Sun; closed Thanksgiving; also mid-Dec-mid-Jan) W on CT 14A at jct CT 169 in Canterbury. Phone 860/546-9916. ¢

Quinebaug Valley Trout Hatchery. A 1,200-acre hatchery for brook, brown, and rainbow trout. Exhibits and displays (daily). Fishing by permit only (Mar-May, wkends and hols). Trout Hatchery Rd, at end of Cady Ln, in Central Village. Phone 860/564-7542. **FREE**

Motels/Motor Lodges

★ **PLAINFIELD MOTEL.** *66 E Main St, Moosup (06354).* *860/564-2791.* 35 rms. S, D $56-$89; each addl $10. Pet accepted, some restrictions. TV; cable (premium). Pool. Restaurant adj 5:30 am-9 pm; wkends 24 hrs. Ck-out noon. Coin lndry. Business servs avail. Sundries. Picnic tables, grills. Cr cds: A, C, D, DS, MC, V.

⊡ 🔦 🌊 📶 🔥 🐾

★ **PLAINFIELD YANKEE MOTOR INN.** *55 Lathrop Rd (06354).* *860/564-4021. www.plainfieldyankeemotorinn.com.* 48 rms, 2 story. Late May-mid-Oct: S $69; D $75; each addl $10; under 18 free; wkly rates; lower rates rest of yr. Crib $10. TV; cable (premium). Ck-out 11 am. Meeting rms. Business servs avail. Health club privileges. Refrigerators avail. Picnic tables. Cr cds: A, C, D, DS, MC, V.

⊡ 📶 🔥

Putnam

See also Plainfield

Pop 9,031 **Elev** 290 ft **Area code** 860 **Zip** 06260
Information Northeast Connecticut Visitors District, 13 Cantebury Rd, Suite 3, PO Box 145; 860/779-6383 or 888/628-1228
Web www.ctquietcorner.org

Named for Revolutionary War hero Israel Putnam, this town is situated on four small hills. Because it was located at Cargill Falls on the Quinebaug River and a railroad station served as a connecting point between New York and Boston, Putnam at one time ranked eighth in New England in the volume of freight handled.

What to See and Do

⊠ **Roseland Cottage.** (1846) Influential abolitionist publisher Henry C. Bowen's summer home. One of the most important surviving examples of a Gothic-revival "cottage," complete with period furnishings. Located on Woodstock Hill with its bright pink exterior and picturesque profile, it stands in contrast to the otherwise colonial character of this New England village. Surrounded by original outbuildings, incl one of the oldest indoor bowling alleys in the country; aviary. Boasts one of the oldest parterre gardens in New England, edged by 1,800 ft of dwarf boxwood. Presidents Grant, Hayes, Harrison, and McKinley attended Bowen's celebrated Fourth of July parties here. (June-mid-Oct, Wed-Sun; closed hols) 7 mi NW via CT 171 and 169 in Woodstock. Phone 860/928-4074. ¢¢

Motel/Motor Lodge

★★ **KINGS INN.** *5 Heritage Rd (06260).* *860/928-7961; fax 860/963-2463; toll-free 800/541-7304.* 41 rms, 1-2 story. S $62-$72; D $68-$78; each addl $8; under 12 free; wkly rates. Crib free. Pet accepted. TV; cable (premium), VCR avail. Pool. Complimentary continental bkfst. Restarant 11 am-10 pm; Fri, Sat to 10:30 pm. Bar. Ck-out 11 am. Meeting rms. Business servs avail. On pond; gazebo. Cr cds: A, D, DS, MC, V.

🔦 ⚓ 🌊 📶 🐾 SC

B&B/Small Inn

★★★ **INN AT WOODSTOCK HILL.** *94 Plaine Hill Rd, South Woodstock (06267).* *860/928-0528; fax 860/928-3236. www.woodstockhill.com.* 22 rms, 3 story, 7 suites. May-Oct: S $82-$145; D $90-$155; each addl $12; suites $100-$155; lower rates rest of yr. TV; cable (premium), VCR avail. Complimentary continental bkfst. Restaurant 11 am-2 pm, 5:30-9 pm; Sun to 7:30 pm; closed Mon. Limited rm serv. Bar. Ck-out 11 am, ck-in 2 pm. Business servs avail. Concierge serv. Lawn games. Fireplaces. Library, sitting rm. Historic building (1815). Cr cds: A, D, MC, V.

⊡ 📶 🐾

Ridgefield

See also Danbury, New Canaan, Norwalk, Stamford

Settled 1709 **Pop** 20,919 **Elev** 749 ft **Area code** 203
Zip 06877
Information Chamber of Commerce, 9 Bailey Ave; 203/438-5992 or 800/FUN-1708; or Housatonic Valley Tourism Commission, Box 406, 30 Main St, Danbury 06810; 203/743-0546 or 800/841-4488 (outside CT)
Web www.ridgefieldchamber.org

Ridgefield is unusual among communities settled in the 19th century because it has a main street of boulevard width—99 feet lined with tree-shaded houses. On this street in 1777, Benedict Arnold (still a revolutionary) set up barricades and fought the Battle of Ridgefield against General Tyron.

What to See and Do

Aldrich Museum of Contemporary Art. Changing exhibits; sculpture garden (daily; free). Museum (Tues-Sun afternoons). 258 Main St. Phone 203/438-4519. ¢

Keeler Tavern. Restored 18th-century tavern, stagecoach stop, home. Once Revolutionary patriot headquarters; British cannonball still embedded in wall. Summer home of architect Cass Gilbert. Period furnishings; gardens; tours; museum shop. (Wed, Sat, and Sun afternoons; closed Jan) 132 Main St. Phone 203/438-5485. ¢¢

B&Bs/Small Inns

★★★ **THE ELMS INN.** *500 Main St (06877). 203/438-2541. www.elmsinn.com.* 20 rms, 2-3 story. No elvtr. S $110-$165; D $120-$175; each addl $15; suites $175. Crib free. TV; cable (premium). Complimentary continental bkfst. Restaurant (see also THE ELMS). Bar. Ck-out noon. X-country ski 10 mi. Built in 1760s; in 1799 became inn. Four-poster beds in some rms. Fireplaces in public rms. Cr cds: A, C, D, MC, V.
⊠ 🐾 📺

★★★ **STONEHENGE INN.** *35 Stonehenge Rd (06877). 203/438-6511; fax 203/438-2478.* 16 rms, 2 story. S, D $75-$200; each addl $10. Crib avail. TV; cable. Complimentary continental bkfst. Restaurant (see also STONEHENGE). Bar 6-11 pm. Ck-out 11 am. Pond with geese. Cr cds: A, D, DS, MC, V.
D 🐾 ⊠ 🔥

★★★ **WEST LANE INN.** *22 West Ln (06877). 203/438-7323; fax 203/438-7325. www.westlaneinn.com.* 18 rms, 3 story, 4 kits. No elvtr. S $80-$120; D $125-$185. Crib free. TV; cable, VCR avail. Complimentary continental bkfst. Restaurant. Ck-out 11 am. Meeting rm. Business servs avail. In-rm modem link. Heated towel racks; some fireplaces. Each rm individually decorated. Mid-1800s architecture. Cr cds: A, D, DS, MC, V.
⊠ 🔥

Restaurants

★★★ **THE ELMS.** *500 Main St (06877). 203/438-9206. www.elmsinn.com.* Specializes in game, lobster, seafood. Own baking. Hrs: 11:30 am-9:30 pm. Res required dinner. Closed Easter, Dec 25. Bar. Wine cellar. Lunch $7.95-$14.95, dinner $23-$27. Child's menu. Patio dining. Oldest continuously-run inn in Ridgefield; established 1799. Family-owned. Cr cds: A, D, DS, MC, V.

★★★ **STONEHENGE.** *35 Stonehenge Rd (06877). 203/438-6511.* Continental menu. Specializes in fresh brook trout, rack of lamb, game. Own baking. Hrs: 6-9 pm; Sat to 9:30 pm; Sun 4-8 pm; Sun brunch noon-2:30 pm. Closed Mon. Res accepted; required wkends. Wine cellar. Dinner $14-$28. Complete meals: dinner $46. Sun brunch $26. Valet parking. Restored home (1853) near pond. Cr cds: A, MC, V.
SC

Riverton

See also Hartford, Norfolk

Pop 500 **Elev** 505 ft **Area code** 860 **Zip** 06065
Information Litchfield Hills Visitors Bureau, PO Box 968, Litchfield 06759; 860/567-4506
Web www.litchfieldhills.com

Lambert Hitchcock, one of America's greatest chairmakers, built his original chair factory here in 1826. His famous stenciled chairs and cabinet furniture are now prized pieces. The old factory is still in operation, and some antiques are on display. Today, the grand colonial houses and tree-lined streets of this New England village are filled with emporiums and shops.

What to See and Do

Hitchcock Museum. Collection of original 18th-century furnishings by Hitchcock and others, displayed in historic church (1829). (Apr-Dec, Thurs-Sun) CT 20, center of village. Phone 860/738-4950. **Donation**

Solomon Rockwell House. (1813) Antebellum house built by early industrialist; Hitchcock chairs, antique clocks, Revolutionary and Civil War memorabilia, wedding gown collection, melodeon. (June-Oct, Thurs-Sun afternoons) 3 mi SW on CT 20, 2 mi S on CT 8, at 225 Prospect St in Winsted. Phone 860/379-8433. ¢

Special Event

Riverton Fair. 1800s country village fair, held since 1909; chopping, sawing, and pie-eating competitions; displays, art and crafts, entertainment. Second wkend Oct. Phone 860/567-4506.

Simsbury

See also Avon, Farmington, Hartford

Settled 1660 **Pop** 22,023 **Elev** 181 ft **Area code** 860
Zip 06070
Information Simsbury Chamber of Commerce, 749 Hopmeadow St, PO Box 224; 860/651-7307
Web www.simsburycoc.org

Hopmeadow Street, in this characteristic New England village, is so named because hops were grown in the area to supply early distillers. Simsbury's handsome Congregational Church was built in 1830.

After it was founded, Simsbury developed steadily until 1676, when the settlers fled in terror during King Philip's War. Scouts returning three days later found the settlement in ashes. Soon the village was reconstructed and activity was again stimulated by the discovery of copper at East Granby (then part of Simsbury).

What to See and Do

The Phelps Tavern Museum. Period rms and interactive exhibition galleries interprets the use of the historic Capt. Elisha Phelps house as an inn from 1786 to 1849. Three successive generations of the Phelps tavernkeepers are chronicled along with the social history of taverns in New England. Part of a two-acre complex, which incl a museum store, research library, and award winning period gardens. Group tours avail. (Tues-Sat) 800 Hopmeadow St. Phone 860/658-2500. ¢¢

Simsbury Farms. Recreational facility covering 300 acres; swimming; picnicking, ice-skating, tennis, golf, x-country skiing, nature and family fitness trails, volleyball, paddle tennis. (Daily; some activities seasonal) Fees for most activities. 100 Old Farms Rd.

Motel/Motor Lodge

★ **IRON HORSE INN.** *969 Hopmeadow St (06070). 860/658-2216; fax 860/651-0822; toll-free 800/245-9938. www.ironhorseofsimsbury.com.* 27 kit. units (no ovens), 2 story. S $79; D $89; under 12 free; wkly rates. Crib free. Pet accepted; $15. TV; cable. Pool; sauna. Complimentary continental bkfst. Restaurant nearby. Ck-out 11 am. Coin lndry. In-rm modem link. Bathrm phones, refrigerators. Balconies. Picnic tables. Cr cds: A, MC, V.

⬛⬛⬛⬛ SC

Hotel

★★★ **SIMSBURY INN.** *397 Hopmeadow St (06070). 860/651-5700; fax 860/651-8024; toll-free 800/634-2719. www.simsburyinn.com.* 98 rms, 4 story. S, D $159-$169; suites $200-$400; under 18 free; wkend rates. Crib free. TV; cable, VCR avail. Indoor pool; whirlpool. Complimentary continental bkfst. Restaurant 6:30 am-9:30 pm. Bar. Ck-out 11 am. Meeting rms. Business servs avail. In-rm modem link. Bellhops. Free airport, RR station transportation. Tennis. 18-hole golf privileges, pro, putting green. Downhill/x-country ski 15 mi. Exercise equipt; sauna. Lawn games. Refrigerators. Traditional New England country inn atmosphere. Cr cds: A, D, DS, MC, V.

⬛⬛⬛⬛⬛⬛⬛⬛⬛⬛

B&B/Small Inn

★★ **SIMSBURY 1820 HOUSE.** *731 Hopmeadow St (06070). 860/658-7658; fax 860/651-0724; toll-free 800/879-1820. www.simsbury1820house.com.* 32 rms, 3 story. S, D $115-$185; each addl $10. TV. Complimentary continental bkfst. Restaurant 5:30-8:30 pm. Ck-out 11 am, ck-in 3 pm. Business servs avail. Private patios, balconies. Built 1820; antiques. Veranda. Cr cds: A, DS, MC, V.

⬛⬛⬛

Restaurants

★★ **CHART HOUSE.** *4 Hartford Rd, Weatoque (06070). 860/658-0059. www.chart-house.com.* Specializes in steak, prime rib, fresh seafood. Own dressings. Hrs: 5-10 pm; Fri, Sat to 11 pm; Sun 4-9 pm; early-bird dinner 5-6:30 pm. Res accepted. Bar. Dinner $14-$32. Child's menu. Former tavern (1780); period furnishings, antiques. Cr cds: A, C, D, DS, ER, MC, V.

⬛

★ **ONE-WAY FARE.** *4 Railroad St (06070). 860/658-4477.* Specializes in chili, homemade soups, hamburgers. Hrs: 11:30 am-midnight; Fri, Sat to 1 am; Sun brunch 10:30 am-3 pm. Closed Labor Day, Thanksgiving, Dec 25. Bar. Lunch, dinner $4.50-$16.50. Sun brunch $3.95-$16.50. Outdoor dining. Old brick RR station (1874); RR memorabilia. Cr cds: A, MC, V.

⬛⬛

Southbury

See also Danbury, Waterbury, Woodbury

Settled 1673 **Pop** 15,818 **Elev** 257 ft **Area code** 203 **Zip** 06488
Information Litchfield Hills Visitors Bureau, PO Box 968, Litchfield 06759; 860/567-4506
Web www.litchfieldhills.com

What to See and Do

Bullet Hill Schoolhouse. One of the oldest school buildings in the country, estimated to have been built in 1789, in use until 1942; some experts believe it antedates the Revolutionary War; early schooling exhibits. (Apr-May, limited hours; rest of yr, by appt) ½ mi E of I-84 exit 15, on US 6. Phone 203/264-8781. **Donation**

State parks. 4 mi SE via CT 67 & 188.

Kettletown. The name of this park is derived from the time when settlers first arrived and purchased this tract of land from the Native Americans for one brass kettle. Swimming, fishing; hiking, sports field, picnicking, camping. Nature trail for the disabled. Standard hrs, fees. 5 mi S via I-84, exit 15. Phone 203/264-5169.

Southford Falls. Approx 120 acres. Former site of Diamond Match Company. Stream and pond fishing; ice-skating, bridle trail nearby, scenic hiking along Eight Mile River; picnicking. (Daily) 4 mi SE via CT 67 and 188. Phone 203/264-5169. ¢

Hotel

★★★ **HILTON SOUTHBURY HOTEL.** *1284 Strongtown Rd (06488). 203/598-7600; fax 203/598-0261; res 800/445-8667. www.hilton.com.* 198 rms, 3 story. S $95-$140; suites $125-$315; under 12 free; wkend, hol rates. Crib free. Pet accepted. TV; cable (premium), VCR avail. Indoor pool; whirlpool, poolside serv. Coffee in rms. Restaurant 6:30 am-10:30 pm. Rm serv. Bar. Ck-out noon. Convention facilities. Business servs avail. In-rm modem link. Bellhops. Valet serv. Sundries. Exercise equipt; sauna. Cr cds: A, C, D, DS, MC, V.

⬛⬛⬛⬛⬛⬛

Restaurant

★★ **TARTUFO.** *900 Main St S (06488). 203/262-8001. www.tartufos.com.* Northern Italian menu. Specialties: fettuccine with truffles, risotto alla Piemontese. Hrs: noon-2:30 pm, 5-9 pm; Thurs, Fri to 10 pm; Sat 6-10 pm; Sun 5-8 pm; Sun brunch noon-2:30 pm. Closed some major hols. Res accepted. Bar. A la carte entrees: lunch $6.50-$14, dinner $14.95-$23. Sun brunch $18.95. Child's menu. Jazz Thurs-Sat. Country setting. Cr cds: A, DS, MC, V.

⬛

Southington

(see Meriden)

Stafford Springs

See also Enfield, Storrs, Windsor

Settled 1719 **Pop** 4,100 **Elev** 591 ft **Area code** 860
Zip 06076
Information Connecticut North Central Tourism & Visitors Bureau, 111 Hazard Ave, Enfield 06082; 860/763-2578 or 800/248-8283
Web www.cnctb.org

Stafford Springs is known for its production of woolen fabrics, printed circuits, and industrial filters.

What to See and Do

Civilian Conservation Corps Museum. New Deal program devoted to state and national parks is commemorated. Video and photograph exhibits; equipment and uniforms; camp memorabilia. (Late May-Aug afternoons) 166 Chestnut Hill Rd (CT 190). Phone 860/684-3430. **Donation**

Mineral Springs. Located here are the springs that gave the town its name. In 1771, John Adams, future president of the US, came to bathe in the springs after hearing of their healing effects. Spring St, between Grace Episcopal Church and the library. **FREE**

Special Event

Stafford Motor Speedway. A ½-mi paved oval track for stock car racing. CT 140W. Apr-Sept. Phone 860/684-2783.

Stamford

(G-1) *See also Greenwich, New Canaan, Norwalk*

Settled 1641 **Pop** 108,056 **Elev** 10 ft **Area code** 203
Information Chamber of Commerce, 733 Summer St, 06901; 203/359-4761
Web www.stamfordchamber.com

Stamford is a corporate headquarters, manufacturing, and research center, as well as a residential suburb of New York City. More than 20 *Fortune* 500 corporations are located in this area. An assortment of marinas and beaches provide recreation on Long Island Sound.

What to See and Do

Bartlett Arboretum and Gardens. Collections of dwarf conifers, rhododendrons, azaleas, wildflowers, perennials, and witches brooms; ecology trails and swamp walk are within the natural woodlands surrounding the gardens. Grounds (daily). 151 Brookdale Rd, off High Ridge Rd, 1 mi N of Merritt Pkwy (CT 15) exit 35. Phone 203/322-6971. **FREE**

First Presbyterian Church. (1958) Contemporary building shaped like a fish, designed by Wallace Harrison; glass by Gabriel Loire of Chartres, France; 56-bell carillon tower (1968), summer concerts (July, Thurs night). 1101 Bedford St. Phone 203/324-9522. **FREE**

Special Event

Festival of Arts. Mill River Park. Various exhibits of performing and visual arts. Late June. Phone 203/359-4761.

Motels/Motor Lodges

★★ **HOLIDAY INN SELECT.** *700 Main St (06901). 203/358-8400; fax 203/358-8872; toll-free 800/408-7640. www.holiday-inn.com.* 385 rms, 10 story. S, D $99-$139; suites $400-$500; under 12 free; wkend rates. Crib free. TV; cable (premium), VCR avail. Indoor pool. Coffee in rms. Restaurants 6-11 am, 5-11 pm. Bar noon-midnight; wkends to 1:30 am. Ck-out noon. Coin lndry. Convention facilities. Business center. Gift shop. Garage. Free RR station transportation. Exercise equipt. Health club privileges. Some refrigerators. Microwaves avail. Luxury level. Cr cds: A, C, D, DS, JCB, MC, V.
D ⚊ 🏋 🏊 🔥 SC 🚶

★ **SUPER 8.** *32 Grenhart Rd (06902). 203/324-8887; fax 203/964-8465; res 800/800-8000. www.super8.com.* 99 rms, 4 story. S $69-$79; D $79-$89; each addl $5; under 12 free; wkly rates; higher rates special events. Crib avail. TV; cable (premium), VCR avail. Complimentary continental bkfst. Restaurant nearby. Ck-out 1 pm. Refrigerators, microwaves avail. Cr cds: A, D, DS, ER, MC, V.
🏋 🏊 🔥 SC

Hotels

★★★ **MARRIOTT STAMFORD.** *2 Stamford Forum (06901). 203/357-9555; fax 203/324-6897; res 800/732-9689. www.marriott.com.* 506 rms, 17 story. S, D $145-$164; each addl $10; suites $250-$440; wkend rates. Crib free. Covered parking $3/day. TV; cable (premium), VCR avail. Indoor/outdoor pool; whirlpool, poolside serv. Restaurant 6:30 am-2 pm, 5-10 pm; Sat, Sun 7 am-10 pm. Bars; entertainment. Ck-out noon. Coin lndry. Convention facilities. Business center. In-rm modem link. Gift shop. Beauty shop. Exercise rm; sauna, steam rm. Game rm. Luxury level. Cr cds: A, C, D, DS, MC, V.
D ⚊ 🏋 🚶

★★★ **SHERATON STAMFORD HOTEL.** *2701 Summer St (06905).* 203/359-1300; fax 203/348-7937; res 888/627-8315. *www.sheraton.com.* 445 rms, 5 story. S, D $99-$260; each addl $30; suites $179-$300; under 18 free; wkend rates. Crib free. TV; cable (premium), VCR avail. Heated pool; whirlpool. Restaurant 6:30 am-11 pm. Bar noon- midnight. Ck-out noon. Coin lndry. Convention facilities. Business center. Beauty shop. Exercise rm; sauna. Some refrigerators; microwaves avail. 5-story atrium lobby. Cr cds: A, C, D, DS, MC, V.

D ♥ ⊁ ➿ ✕ ⊠ ♨ SC

★★★ **THE WESTIN STAMFORD.** *1 1st Stamford Pl (06901).* 203/967-2222; fax 203/967-3475; 800/937-8461. *www.westin.com.* 480 rms, 10 story. S, D $145; each addl $20; suites $200-$500; wkend rates. Crib free. Garage: self-park free, valet parking $6. TV; cable (premium), VCR avail. Indoor pool; whirlpool, poolside serv. Coffee in rms. Restaurants 6 am-10:30 pm. Bar 11:30-1:00 am. Ck-out noon. Convention facilities. Business center. In-rm modem link. Concierge. Gift shop. Tennis. Exercise equipt. Health club privileges. Some bathrm phones; microwaves avail. Cr cds: A, C, D, DS, ER, JCB, MC, V.

D ⊁ ➿ ✕ ⊠ ♨ SC ⋀

All Suite

★★ **STAMFORD SUITES.** *720 Bedford St (06901).* 203/359-7300; fax 203/359-7304. *www.stamfordsuites.com.* 42 suites, 8 story. July-Oct: S $229; suites $229; each addl $15; under 12 free; wkly, wkend, hol, monthly rates. Crib free. TV; cable (premium). Complimentary continental bkfst. Restaurants nearby. Ck-out 11 am. Business center. In-rm modem link. No bellhops. Free garage parking. Health club privileges. Bathrm phones, in-rm whirlpools, refrigerators, microwaves, minibars. Cr cds: A, C, D, DS, MC, V.

D ⊠ ♨ ⋀

Restaurants

★ **CRAB SHELL.** *46 Southfield Ave (06902).* 203/967-7229. *www.crabshell.com.* Specializes in grilled seafood, Maryland blue crab, ribs. Hrs: 11:30 am-3 pm, 5-10 pm; Fri to 11 pm; Sat noon-11 pm; Sun noon-9:30 pm. Bar. Lunch $6.95-$12.95, dinner $8.95-$29.95. Child's menu. Parking. Entertainment. Waterfront dining. Cr cds: A, D, MC, V.

D ⊰

★★ **GIOVANNI'S.** *1297 Long Ridge Rd (06903).* 203/322-8870. Specializes in steak and chops, seafood. Own pasta. Hrs: 11:30 am-3 pm, 4:30-10 pm; Sat 4:30-10:30 pm; Sun noon-9 pm. Closed Thanksgiving, Dec 25. Bar. Lunch $6-$11, dinner $12-$27.95. Child's menu. Three dining rms with semi-formal atmosphere; lobster tank in lobby. Family-owned. Cr cds: A, C, D, DS, ER, MC, V.

D ⊰

★★ **IL FALCO.** *59 Broad St (06902).* 203/327-0002. *www.ilfalco.com.* Italian menu. Specializes in pasta, veal, fresh seafood. Hrs: noon-3 pm, 5:30-10:30 pm; Fri to 11 pm; Sat 5:30-11 pm. Closed Sun; some major hols. Res accepted. Bar. A la carte entrees: lunch $9.50-$15.50, dinner $11.50-$22. Parking. Pleasant atmosphere. Cr cds: A, D, MC, V.

D ⊰

★★ **LA BRETAGNE.** *2010 W Main St (US 1) (06902).* 203/324-9539. Country French menu. Specializes in seafood, veal, duck. Hrs: noon-2:30 pm, 6-9:30 pm; Fri, Sat to 10 pm. Closed Sun; most major hols. Res accepted; required Sat. Bar. Lunch $9-$18, dinner $21-$28. Child's menu. Parking. Cr cds: A, D, MC, V.

D ⊰

★★ **LA HACIENDA.** *222 Summer St (06901).* 203/324-0577. Mexican menu. Specializes in fresh fish, game. Hrs: 11:30 am-2:30 pm, 5-10 pm; Fri to 11:30 pm; Sat noon-11:30 pm; Sun 1-9:30 pm. Closed Thanksgiving, Dec 25. Res accepted. Bar. Lunch $8.95-$14.95, dinner $10.95-$17.95. Parking. Outdoor dining. Multi-level dining. Southwestern decor. Cr cds: A, D, MC, V.

D ⊰

★ **MEERA INDIAN CUISINE.** *227 Summer St (06901).* 203/975-0477. Indian menu. Specializes in tandoori chicken, chicken tikka kebab. Salad bar. Hrs: 11:45 am-2:30 pm, 5:30-10 pm; Fri to 11 pm; Sat 5-11 pm. Res accepted. Bar. A la carte entrees: lunch, dinner $5-$12.95. Lunch buffet $8.95. Indian decor. Cr cds: A, D, MC, V.

D ⊰

Stonington

See also Groton, Mystic, New London, Norwich, Old Lyme, Old Saybrook

Settled 1649 **Pop** 16,919 **Elev** 7 ft **Area code** 860 **Zip** 06378

Information Connecticut's Mystic and More!, 470 Bank St, PO Box 89, New London 06320; 860/444-2206 or 800/863-6569 outside CT

Web www.mysticmore.com

Until their defeat at Mystic Fort in 1637, the Pequot dominated the area around Stonington. In 1649, the first European settlers came here from Rehoboth, Massachusetts. Connecticut and Massachusetts both claimed ownership of the territory. In 1662, permanent control was granted to Connecticut by charter from King Charles II. Three years later the area was officially called Mystic, and in 1666 the name was changed to Stonington (which includes Stonington Borough).

The conclusion of the King Philip War in 1676 effectively ended the Native American threat in southern New England. The local economy, based on farming, shipping, and manufacturing, thrived. Prior to the Civil War, whaling and sealing expeditions left Stonington's port at regular intervals. After the war, maritime interests flourished as Stonington served as the connecting point for rail and steamer service to New York City. Today this maritime heritage is represented by a commercial fishing fleet and recreational boating.

What to See and Do

Old Lighthouse Museum. First government-operated lighthouse in Connecticut (1823); exhibits incl Stonington-made firearms, stoneware; ship models, whaling gear; China trade objects; folk art; local artifacts. Children's gallery. Visitors can climb the tower for a panoramic view of Long Island Sound. (May-June and Sept-Oct, Tues-Sun; July-Aug, daily; rest of yr, by appt) 7 Water St. ¢

B&B/Small Inn

★★ **RANDALL'S ORDINARY.** *Rte 2, North Stonington (06359). 860/599-4540; fax 860/599-3308; toll-free 877/599-4540. www.randallsordinary.com.* 15 units in 2 bldgs, 2 story, 1 suite. Many rm phones. S, D, suite $165; each addl $10. TV in most rms; cable (premium). Complimentary continental bkfst. Dining rm 7-11 am, noon-2 pm, 7-10 pm. Ck-out 11 am, ck-in 2 pm. Business servs avail. X-country ski on site. Lawn games. Picnic tables. Historic buildings (1685 and 1819); many antiques; 3 dining rms, each with fireplace. Rural setting; 200 acres with barn and some farm animals. Cr cds: A, MC, V.

⊡ ⧓ 🐾 ⧓

Storrs

See also Hartford, Manchester, Stafford Springs

Pop 12,198 **Elev** 600 ft **Area code** 860 **Zip** 06268
Information Northeast Connecticut Visitors District, 13 Cantebury Rd, Suite 3, PO Box 145, Brooklyn 06234; 860/779-6383 or 888/628-1228
Web www.ctquietcorner.org

What to See and Do

Ballard Institute and Museum of Puppetry. Features changing exhibits from collection of more than 2,000 puppets. Gives visitors appreciation of puppetry as art form. (Mid-Apr-mid-Nov, Fri and Sat) 6 Boum Pl. Phone 860/468-4605. **FREE**

Caprilands Herb Farm. More than 30 different theme gardens using herbs, spices, and wild grasses; 18th-century farm building; lunchtime lectures (Apr-Dec; fee). Tea program (Sun). Basket and bookshops. (Daily) 8 mi SW via US 44 to 534 Silver St in Coventry. Phone 860/742-7244. **FREE**

Nathan Hale Homestead. (1776) Country-Georgian-style structure built by Nathan's father, Richard. Restored; many original furnishings. (Mid-May-mid-Oct, afternoons) 8 mi SW via US 44 to 2299 South St in Coventry. Phone 860/742-6917 or 860/247-8996. ¢¢

University of Connecticut. (1881) 26,200 students. On campus are state's largest public research library, art galleries, museums, animal barns, biological and floricultural greenhouses (tours; free). (See SPECIAL EVENT) SE on I-84 exit 68, then S on CT 195. Phone 860/486-3530. Also here are

Connecticut State Museum of Natural History. Exhibits on Native Americans, mounted birds of prey, honey bees, sharks, minerals. (Mon, Thurs-Sun, afternoons) Wilbur Cross Building. Phone 860/486-4460. **FREE**

William Benton Museum of Art. Permanent collection incl American and European paintings, sculpture, prints, and drawings; changing exhibits. (Tues-Sun; closed hols and between exhibitions) 245 Glenbrook Rd. Phone 860/486-4520. **FREE**

Special Event

Connecticut Repertory Theatre. University of Connecticut, Harriet S. Jorgensen Theatre. Musicals, comedies, and dramas. Nightly. Feb-May, July, Sept-Dec. Phone 860/486-4226.

Stratford

See also Bridgeport, Fairfield, Milford, Norwalk

Settled 1639 **Pop** 49,389 **Elev** 25 ft **Area code** 203
Information Chamber of Commerce, 10 Middle St, PO Box 999, Bridgeport, 06601-0999; 203/335-3800

A fine port on the Housatonic River, Stratford has been a hub of shipbuilding and industry for more than three centuries.

What to See and Do

Boothe Memorial Park. Former Boothe homestead (1663-1949) on 30 acres; unusual, historical buildings; Boothe home and carriage house (Mid-May-late Oct, Tues-Sun), Americana Museum, blacksmith shop, architecturally eccentric "technocratic cathedral"; flower gardens, rose garden, picnicking, playgrounds. Park (daily). Other buildings (Memorial Day-late Oct, daily). Main St. Phone 203/385-4085. **FREE**

Captain David Judson House. (ca 1750) Restored and furnished Colonial house; period furnishings and crafts, slave quarters, tool display; local history exhibits. (June-Oct, Wed, Sat, Sun; closed Memorial Day, July 4) 967 Academy Hill. Phone 203/378-0630. ¢ Admission incl

Catharine B. Mitchell Museum. Changing and permanent exhibits depict history of the Stratford area 1639-1830; local memorabilia. (Same hrs as Judson House) Phone 203/378-0630.

Motels/Motor Lodges

★ **HONEYSPOT LODGE.** *360 Honeyspot Rd (06497). 203/375-5666; fax 203/378-1509.* 90 rms, 2 story. S $50; D $55; each addl $8; under 18 free. Crib avail. TV; cable (premium). Pool. Ck-out noon. Meeting rms. Business servs avail. Cr cds: A, C, D, DS, MC, V.

⧓ ⧓ 🐾 **SC**

★ **RAMADA INN STRATFORD.** *I-95 (06615). 203/375-8866; fax 203/375-2482; res 800/272-6232. www.ramada.com.* 145 rms, 6 story. S, D $85-$100; each addl $10; under 18 free; wkend rates. Crib free. TV; cable (premium). Indoor pool. Restaurant 6:30 am-2 pm, 5-10 pm; Sun 7 am-9 pm. Bar. Ck-out noon. Meeting rms. Business servs avail. Free airport, RR station, bus depot transportation. Health club privileges. Cr cds: A, DS, MC, V.

Terryville

(see Bristol)

Vernon

See also Hartford, Manchester, Windsor

Pop 29,841 **Elev** 350 ft **Area code** 860 **Zip** 06066
Information Greater Hartford Tourism District, 234 Murphy Rd, Hartford 06114; 860/244-8181 or 800/793-4480
Web www.enjoyhartford.com

Motel/Motor Lodge

★ **QUALITY INN AND CONFERENCE CENTER.**
51 Hartford Tpke (06066). 860/646-5700; fax 860/646-0202; res 800/221-2222. www.qualityinn.com. 127 rms, 2 story. S $49.95-$79; D $79-$125; under 18 free. Crib free. TV; cable (premium). Pool. Continental bkfst. Restaurant 11:30 am-10 pm; Sat, Sun, hols 7 am-11 pm. Rm serv 11:30 am-9 pm; Sun from noon. Bar 11:30 am-midnight; Fri, Sat to 1 am. Ck-out 11 am. Coin lndry. Meeting rms. Business servs avail. In-rm modem link. Valet serv. Sundries. Par-3 golf; miniature golf. Health club privileges. Game rm. Refrigerators. Cr cds: A, C, D, DS, MC, V.

B&B/Small Inn

★★ **TOLLAND INN.** *63 Tolland Green, Tolland (06084). 860/872-0800; fax 860/870-7958; toll-free 877/465-0800. www.tollandinn.com.* 7 rms, 4 with shower only, 2 story, 2 suites. No rm phones. S $85; D $95; suites $110-$130; wkly rates; wkends May and Oct (2-day min). Children over 10 yrs only. TV; VCR. Complimentary full bkfst. Ck-out 11 am, ck-in 4-9 pm. Concierge serv. Luggage handling. X-country ski 7 mi. Refrigerators. Picnic tables. New England inn built 1800; handcrafted furniture. Totally nonsmoking. Cr cds: A, C, D, DS, MC, V.

Restaurant

★ **REIN'S NEW YORK-STYLE DELI.** *435 Hartford Tpke (06066). 860/875-1344.* New York-style delicatessen. Specializes in corned beef, lox and bagels, pastrami. Hrs: 7 am-midnight. Bar. Bkfst, lunch, dinner $3.75-$8.95. Child's menu. Cr cds: A, C, MC, V.

Washington

Area code 860

B&B/Small Inn

★★★★★ **THE MAYFLOWER INN.** *118 Woodbury Rd (06793). 860/868-9466; fax 860/868-1497. www.mayflowerinn.com.* This 1920 inn reflects its name in the 25 bedrooms and suites as well as the public areas. Guests will feel like royalty with the nine acres of flowers, fully equipped fitness center, tennis courts, oil paintings, Oriental rugs, clocks, and antiques. The elegantly decorated guest rooms feature four-post beds, marble bathrooms with deep tubs, and mahogany wainscoting. 25 rms in 3 bldgs, 2-3 story, 8 suites. S, D $450; each addl $50; suites $690-$1,000; 2-3-day min wkends. Children over 12 yrs only. Valet parking wkends. TV; cable (premium), VCR avail (movies). Heated pool. Dining rm 7:30-11 am, noon-2 pm, 6-9 pm. Rm serv 24 hrs. Ck-out 1 pm, ck-in 3 pm. Meeting rms. Business servs avail. In-rm modem link. Luggage handling. Sundries. Gift shop. Tennis, pro. 9-hole golf privileges. Extensive exercise rm; sauna, steam rm. Massage. Game rm. Refrigerators, minibars. Balconies. Some fireplaces. Bathrm phones. Totally nonsmoking. Cr cds: A, MC, V.

Waterbury

See also Bristol, Meriden, New Britain

Settled 1674 **Pop** 108,961 **Elev** 290 ft **Area code** 203
Information Waterbury Region Convention & Visitors Bureau, 21 Church St, 06702-2106; 203/597-9527 or 888/588-7880 (outside CT)
Web www.wrcvb.com

Waterbury, fourth-largest city in Connecticut, was once an important manufacturing center for brass-related products. Today, high-technology manufacturing and the banking industry dominate the economy. Waterbury's location near major highways provides quick and direct access to all Eastern cities.

What to See and Do

Brass Mill Center. More than one million-sq-ft indoor mall with many shops, food court, and 12-screen movie theater. (Daily) I-84 exit 22 or 23 at 495 Union St. Phone 203/755-5003.

Mattatuck Museum. Industrial history exhibit, decorative arts, period rms, paintings and prints by Connecticut artists. (July-Aug, Tues-Sat; rest of yr, Tues-Sun; closed hols) 144 W Main St. Phone 203/753-0381. ¢¢

Quassy Amusement Park. More than 30 different rides and activities set against Lake Quassapaug; beach, swimming, boating; miniature golf, picnicking, concession. (Late May-Labor Day, daily; Apr-late May, after Labor Day-Oct, wkends) 5 mi W on I-84 exit 17, on CT 64 in Middlebury. Phone 203/758-2913. ¢¢¢¢ Parking fee ¢¢

Motel/Motor Lodge

★ **AMERICAN MOTOR LODGE.** *2636 S Main St (06706). 203/756-7961; fax 203/754-6642.* 84 rms, 2 story. S $59; D $64; each addl $8; under 18 free. Crib free. Pet accepted; $8. TV; cable (premium). Pool. Restaurant open 24 hrs. Bar. Ck-out 11 am. Meeting rms. Business center. Valet serv. Sundries. Balconies. Cr cds: A, C, D, DS, MC, V.

[D] [icons] SC [icon]

Hotel

★★★ **SHERATON WATERBURY.** *3580 E Main St (06705). 203/573-1000; fax 203/573-1349; toll-free 800/541-0469. www.sheraton.com.* 279 rms, 4 story. S, D $109-$129; under 18 free; wkend rates. Crib free. Pet accepted. TV; cable (premium). Indoor pool; whirlpool. Restaurant 6:30 am-11 pm. Rm serv. Sports bar. Ck-out noon. Convention facilities. Business servs avail. In-rm modem link. Bellhops. Sundries. Valet serv. Exercise equipt; sauna, steam rm. Some refrigerators. Balconies. Cr cds: A, C, D, DS, MC, V.

[D] [icons] SC

B&B/Small Inn

★★ **HOUSE ON THE HILL BED & BREAKFAST.** *92 Woodlawn Terrace (06710). 203/757-9901.* 4 suites, 3 story, 1 kit. unit. 1 rm with A/C. Suites $125-$175; kit. unit $100; wkly rates; wkends, hols (2-day min). TV; cable. Complimentary full bkfst. Coffee in rms. Ck-out 11 am, ck-in 3-6 pm. Concierge serv. Luggage handling. Free RR station, bus depot transportation. Lawn games. Some refrigerators. Historic mansion built in 1888; library, gardens, many fireplaces. Totally nonsmoking. Cr cds: A, C, D, DS, MC, V.

[icons]

Westport

See also Bridgeport, Fairfield, Norwalk, Stamford

Settled 1648 **Pop** 24,410 **Elev** 78 ft **Area code** 203
Information Westport/Weston Chamber of Commerce, 60 Church Ln, PO Box 30; 203/227-9234
Web www.westportchamber.com

Westport is a fashionable community on Long Island Sound 45 miles from New York City. Well-known writers and many successful actors, illustrators, and corporate and advertising executives make their homes here. Westport is surrounded by wooded hills and has three municipal beaches and a state park on the Sound.

Special Events

Westport Handcrafts Fair. Staples High School Field House. Features 100 crafts artisans. Memorial Day wkend. Phone 203/227-7844.

Westport Country Playhouse. Broadway and pre-Broadway presentations by professional companies. Nightly Mon-Sat; matinees Wed and Sat; children's shows Fri. Phone 203/227-4177. Mid-June-mid-Sept. 25 Powers Court, on Post Rd E.

Levitt Pavilion for the Performing Arts. Jesup Green, on the Saugatuck River. Nightly free outdoor performances of classical, jazz, pop, rock; dance, children's series. Late June-early Aug. Phone 203/226-7600.

Antique Dealers Outdoor Show and Sale. Early Sept. Phone 203/227-9234.

B&B/Small Inns

★★ **THE INN AT LONGSHORE.** *260 Compo Rd S (06880). 203/226-3316; fax 203/227-5344.* 10 rms, 3 story, 3 suites. Apr-Oct: S, D $125-$145; suites $165-$195; lower rates rest of yr. Crib free. TV; cable. Pool. Playground. Complimentary coffee in rms. Complimentary continental bkfst. Restaurant 11:30 am-2:30 pm, 5:30-11 pm. Ck-out noon, ck-in 3 pm. Business servs avail. Lighted tennis. 18-hole golf, greens fee $38, pro, putting green, driving range. Built as a private estate in 1890; overlooks Long Island Sound. Cr cds: A, MC, V.

[icons]

★★★ **THE INN AT NATIONAL HALL.** *2 Post Rd W (06880). 203/221-1351; fax 203/221-0276; toll-free 800/628-4255. www.innatnationalhall.com.* 8 rms, 7 suites, 3 story. S, D $300-$350; each addl $15; suites $440-$600; 2-day min wkends May-Oct. Crib free. TV; cable (premium), VCR (movies). Complimentary continental bkfst; refreshments in rms. Restaurant 5:30-10 pm. Rm serv dinner only. Ck-out 11:30 am, ck-in 3 pm. Business servs avail. Bellhops. Concierge. Health club privileges. Bathrm phones. Refrigerators. Totally nonsmoking. Walking distance to shopping, galleries, beach. Cr cds: A, C, D, MC, V.

[D] [icons]

★★ **WESTPORT INN.** *1595 Post Rd E (06880). 203/259-5236; fax 203/254-8439; toll-free 800/446-8997. www. westportinn.com.* 116 rms, 2 story. S $99-$154; D $109-$164; each addl $10; suites $210-$285; under 18 free. Crib free. TV; cable (premium), VCR avail (movies). Indoor pool; whirlpool. Coffee in rms. Restaurant 7-11 am, 6-10 pm. Rm serv. Bar. Meeting rms. Bellhops. Sundries. Exercise equipt; sauna. Game rm. Bathrm phone, wetbar, refrigerator in suites. Cr cds: A, C, D, DS, MC, V.

[D] [icons]

Restaurants

★★★ **COBB'S MILL INN.** *12 Old Mill Rd, Weston (06880). 203/227-7221. www.cobbsmillinn.com.* Specializes in steak, chops, seafood. Hrs: 11:30 am-2:30 pm, 5-9 pm; Fri, Sat 6-10 pm; early-bird dinner Mon-Thurs 5-6:30 pm. Res accepted. Bar. A la carte entrees: lunch $6-$11, dinner $19-$27. Valet parking. In 200-yr-old grist and lumber mill; Colonial decor, pewter display. Overlooks waterfall, lake. Cr cds: A, C, D, DS, ER, MC, V.

★ **CONNOLLY'S.** *221 Post Rd W (06880). 203/226-5591.* Specializes in seafood, steak. Salad bar. Hrs: 11:30 am-9:30 pm; Fri, Sat to 10 pm; Sun 5-9 pm. Closed major hols. Bar. Lunch $4.50-$10.95, dinner $5.50-$18.95. Child's menu. Outdoor dining. Cr cds: A, DS, MC, V.
D

★★★ **MIRAMAR.** *2 Post Rd W (06880). 203/222-2267. www.innatnationalhall.com.* Mediterranean rustic menu. Specializes in top sirloin. Hrs: 5:30-10 pm, Sun 5-9 pm. Closed Mon. Res required. Wine list. Dinner $19-$32. Cr cds: A, D, MC, V.
D

★★ **NISTICO'S RED BARN.** *292 Wilton Rd (06880). 203/222-9549. www.redbarnrestaurant.com.* Continental menu. Specializes in live Maine lobster, rack of lamb, prime rib. Hrs: 11:30 am-2:15 pm, 5-10 pm; Sun from 5 pm; Sun brunch sittings 11:30 am and 1:30 pm. Closed Dec 24-25. Res accepted. Serv bar. Lunch $5.95-$12.95, dinner $14.95-$29.95. Sun brunch $16.95. Child's menu. Pianist Fri, Sat. Valet parking Sat. Outdoor dining. Cr cds: A, DS, MC, V.
D

Wethersfield

See also Avon, Hartford, Windsor

Settled 1634 **Pop** 25,651 **Elev** 45 ft **Area code** 860 **Zip** 06109

Information Wethersfield Historical Society, 150 Main St; 860/529-7656

Web www.wethhist.org

Wethersfield, "the most ancient towne in Connecticut," has a rich heritage. Settled by a group of Massachusetts colonists, it became the commercial center of the Connecticut River communities and an important post in the trade between the American colonies and the West Indies. Agriculture, especially corn, rye, and, later, the famous red onion, was the source of Wethersfield's trade. During the Revolutionary War years, notable figures, such as George Washington and Count de Rochambeau, came to Wethersfield and decided upon plans that became part of US history. Many existing buildings date from the Revolutionary War.

With the birth and development of the railroad and the shift of trade to the coastal villages, Wethersfield's importance as an industrial and commercial center declined.

What to See and Do

Buttolph-Williams House. (ca 1700) Restored building contains fine collection of pewter, delft, fabrics, period furniture. (May-Oct, Wed-Mon, limited hrs) 249 Broad St, at Marsh St. Phone 860/529-0460 or 529/061-2860. ¢

⭐ **Dinosaur State Park.** While excavating the site of a new building, a stone slab bearing the three-toed tracks of dinosaurs, which roamed the area 200 million yrs ago, was discovered. Construction was halted, and a 65-acre area was designated a state park. Eventually more than 2,000 prints were unearthed. A geodesic dome was set up over parts of the trackway to protect the find. Visitors are able to examine the crisscrossing tracks and view a skeletal cast and life-size models of the area's prehistoric inhabitants. Nature trails; picnicking. Exhibit center (Tues-Sun; closed Jan 1, Thanksgiving, Dec 25). Park (daily). 3 mi S via I-91 exit 23, off West St in Rocky Hill. Phone 860/529-8423. ¢

First Church of Christ, Congregational United Church of Christ. Church established 1635; the Meetinghouse (1761; restored 1973) is the third one to stand on or near this site. (Mon-Fri; also by appt) Main and Marsh Sts. Phone 860/529-1575. **FREE**

Hurlburt-Dunham House. Georgian house updated in Italianate style. Rich in decoration, incl original Rococo Revival wallpapers, painted ceilings, and a varied collection of furniture. (Mid-Mar-mid-May, mid-Oct-Dec 25, Sat and Sun) 212 Main St. Phone 860/529-7656. ¢¢

Webb-Deane-Stevens Museum. Consists of three 18th-century houses that stand at the center of old Wethersfield: the Joseph Webb house (1752), the Silas Deane house (1766), and the Isaac Stevens house (1789). The houses have been restored and are furnished with objects to reflect the different ways of life of their owners—a merchant, a diplomat, and a tradesman; also colonial revival garden. (May-Oct, Mon, Wed-Sun; rest of yr, Sat-Sun) 211 Main St. Phone 860/529-0612. Combination ticket ¢¢¢

Wethersfield Museum. Changing exhibit galleries; permanent Wethersfield exhibit. (Tues-Sun) Keeney Memorial Cultural Center, 200 Main St. Phone 860/529-7161. ¢

Motel/Motor Lodge

★ **RAMADA INN.** *1330 Silas Deane Hwy (06109). 860/563-2311; fax 860/529-2974; toll-free 800/228-2828. www. ramada.com.* 112 rms, 4 story. S, D $42-$59; under 18 free. Crib free. Pet accepted. TV; cable (premium), VCR avail. Complimentary continental bkfst. Restaurant adj 11 am- 10 pm. Bar; entertainment Fri, Sat. Ck-out noon. Coin lndry. Meeting rms. Business servs avail. In-rm modem link. Downhill ski 20 mi. Health club privileges. Some in-rm whirlpools. Cr cds: A, C, D, DS, MC, V.
D ⮞ ⊠ ⊠ ⊠ SC

Windsor

(E-3) *See also Enfield, Hartford, Manchester*

Settled 1633 **Pop** 27,817 **Elev** 57 ft **Area code** 860 **Zip** 06095

Information Chamber of Commerce, 261 Broad St, PO Box 9, 06095-0009; 860/688-5165; or the Heritage Valley North Central Tourism Bureau, 111 Hazard Ave, Enfield 06082; 860/763-2578

Web www.windsorcc.org

Windsor was first settled by members of an expeditionary group from the original Plymouth Colony. A farming center since the 17th century, it is only nine miles north of Hartford. The village is divided by the Farmington River; there is a green and many colonial houses on each side of the river.

What to See and Do

Connecticut Trolley Museum. Unlimited three-mi ride on vintage trolleys; static displays. (Memorial Day-Labor Day, Wed-Sun; Apr-Dec, Sat-Sun) 58 North Rd. Phone 860/627-6540. ¢¢

The First Church in Windsor. (1630) United Church of Christ Congregational. Classic Georgian-style architecture (1794); cemetery (1633) adj. Request key at church office, 107 Palisado Ave. (Daily) 75 Palisado Ave. Phone 860/688-7229. **FREE**

Oliver Ellsworth Homestead. (1781) Home of one of five men who drafted the Constitution; third Chief Justice of the US and one of the first senators from Connecticut; Washington and Adams visited the house. Restored to period; many original Ellsworth furnishings. (May-Oct, Tues, Wed, Sat) 778 Palisado Ave. Phone 860/688-8717. ¢

Windsor Historical Society. Walking tours of the John and Sarah Strong House (1758) and the Dr. Hezekiah Chaffee House (1765); period costumes and furnishings; Puritan cemetery. (Tues-Sat) 96 Palisado Ave. Phone 860/688-3813. ¢¢

Motel/Motor Lodge

★★ **COURTYARD BY MARRIOTT.** *1 Day Hill Rd (06095). 860/683-0022; fax 860/683-1072. www.marriott.com.* 149 rms, 2 story. S, D $119; suites $139; wkend rates. Crib free. TV; cable (premium), VCR avail. Indoor pool; whirlpool. Complimentary coffee in rms. Restaurant 6:30-10:30 am, 5-10 pm; Sat-Sun 7-11 am, 5-10 pm. Ck-out 1 pm. Coin lndry. Meeting rms. Business servs avail. In-rm modem link. Valet serv. Sundries. Exercise equipt. Game rm. Refrigerator in suites. Balconies. Marble courtyard, gazebo. Cr cds: A, C, D, DS, MC, V.
🄳 ⇆ 🏋 ⇆ 🔥

Extended Stay

★★ **RESIDENCE INN BY MARRIOTT.** *100 Dunfey Ln (06095). 860/688-7474; fax 860/683-8457. www. residenceinn.com.* 96 kit. suites, 2 story. S, D $129-$159. Crib avail. Pet accepted; $100. TV; cable (premium), VCR avail. Pool; whirlpool. Complimentary continental bkfst. Complimentary coffee in rms. Ck-out noon. Coin lndry. Meeting rm. Business servs avail. In-rm modem link. Valet serv. Free airport transportation. Lawn games. Some fireplaces. Picnic tables, grill. Cr cds: A, C, D, DS, JCB, MC, V.
🄳 ⇆ 🐾 ⚡ ⇆ ⇆ 🔥

Windsor Locks

See also Enfield, Hartford, Windsor

Pop 12,358 **Elev** 80 ft **Area code** 860 **Zip** 06096

Information Chamber of Commerce, PO Box 257; 860/623-9319

Web www.wmch.com

What to See and Do

New England Air Museum. One of the largest and most comprehensive collections of aircraft and aeronautical memorabilia in the world. More than 80 aircraft on display incl bombers, fighters, helicopters, and gliders dating from 1909-present era; movies; jet fighter cockpit simulator. (Daily; closed Jan 1, Thanksgiving, Dec 25) Adj to Bradley International Airport, 3 mi SW via I-91 exit 40, W on CT 20 to CT 75, follow signs. Phone 860/623-3305. ¢¢

Noden-Reed House & Barn. Housed in 1840 house and 1825 barn are antique sleigh bed, 1871 taffeta evening dress, 1884 wedding dress, antique quilts, kitchen utensils, 1880s newspapers and periodicals. (May-Oct, Sun afternoons) 58 West St. Phone 860/627-9212.

Old New Gate Prison. Site of a copper mine (1707) converted to Revolutionary prison for Tories (1775-1782) and a state prison (until 1827); self-guided tour of underground caverns where prisoners lived. (Mid May-Oct, Wed-Sun) 8 mi W on US 91 to exit 40; in East Granby at jct Newgate Rd and CT 120. Phone 860/653-3563 or 860/566-3005. ¢¢

Trolley Museum. Exhibits incl more than 50 antique trolley cars from 1894-1949; operating trolleys take visitors on three-mi ride through countryside; electric passenger trains also operate some wkends. (Memorial Day-Labor Day, daily; rest of yr, Sat, Sun, and hols; closed Thanksgiving, Dec 25) In East Windsor at 58 North Rd (CT 140); from Windsor Locks proceed NE on I-91 to exit 45, then ¾ mi E on CT 140 *(for clarification of directions, phone ahead).* Phone 860/627-6540. ¢¢ On grounds is

  Connecticut Fire Museum. Collection of fire engines and antique motorcoaches from 1856-1954. (June-Aug, daily; Apr-May and Sept-Oct, Sat and Sun) Phone 860/623-4732. ¢

Hotels

★★ **DOUBLETREE HOTEL.** *16 Ella Grasso Tpke (06096). 860/627-5171; fax 860/627-7029; toll-free 800/222-8733. www.doubletreehotels.com.* 200 rms, 5 story. S, D $69-$119; each addl $10; suites $150-$195; under 18 free; wkend rates; higher rates Dec 31. Crib avail. TV; cable (premium), VCR avail. Indoor pool; whirlpool. Restaurant 6:30 am-10 pm. Rm serv. Bar 4-11 pm. Ck-out noon. Coin lndry. Meeting rms. Business servs avail. Bellhops. Valet serv. Free airport, RR station transportation. Exercise equipt; sauna. Game rm. Cr cds: A, C, D, DS, ER, JCB, MC, V.

⬛ 🏊 🏃 ✈ 🛷 🐾 SC

★★★ **SHERATON BRADLEY.** *1 Bradley International Airport (06096). 860/627-5311; fax 860/627-9348; res 800/325-3535. www.sheraton.com/bradleyairport.* 237 rms, 8 story. Sept-June: S, D $139-$205; each addl $15; suites $225-$300; under 5 free; lower rates rest of yr. Crib free. Pet accepted, some restrictions. Free garage parking. TV; cable (premium), VCR avail. Indoor pool. Complimentary coffee in rms. Restaurant 6:30 am-10 pm. Bar 11 am-midnight; entertainment Tues-Thurs. Ck-out noon. Meeting rms. Business servs avail. Concierge. Free RR station transportation. Exercise equipt; sauna. Cr cds: A, C, D, DS, JCB, MC, V.

⬛ 🐾 🏊 🏃 ✈ 🛷 🔥 SC

All Suite

★★ **HOMEWOOD SUITES BY HILTON.** *65 Ella Grasso Tpke (06096). 860/627-8463; fax 860/627-9313; res 800/225-5466. www.homewoodsuites.com.* 132 kit. suites, 2-3 story. S, D $99-$140. Crib free. Pet accepted, some restrictions; $10. TV; cable, VCR (movies). Pool. Complimentary continental bkfst. Complimentary coffee in rms. Restaurant nearby. Ck-out noon. Coin lndry. Business servs avail. In-rm modem link. Valet serv. Sundries. Gift shop. Free airport, RR station transportation. Exercise equipt. Lawn games. Picnic tables. Cr cds: A, C, D, DS, MC, V.

🐾 🏊 🏃 ✈

Woodbury

See also Bristol, Danbury, Waterbury

Pop 1,290 **Elev** 264 ft **Area code** 203 **Zip** 06798
Information Litchfield Hills Visitors Bureau, PO Box 968, Litchfield 06759; 860/567-4506
Web www.litchfieldhills.com

What to See and Do

Flanders Nature Center. Large conservation area with woodland hiking trails, wildlife marshes; wildflower trails. Self-guided tour; special events incl maple syrup demonstration (Mar). (Daily) Church Hill and Flanders Rd. Phone 203/263-3711. **FREE**

Glebe House and Gertrude Jekyll Garden. (ca 1770) Minister's farmhouse or *glebe,* where Samuel Seabury was elected America's first Episcopal bishop in 1783; restored with 18th-century furnishings, original paneling; garden designed by Gertrude Jekyll. (Apr-Nov, Wed-Sun afternoons; rest of yr, by appt) On Hollow Rd off US 6. Phone 203/263-2855. ¢¢

B&B/Small Inn

★ **CURTIS HOUSE.** *506 Main St S (06798). 203/263-2101; fax 203/263-6265. www.thecurtishouse.com.* 18 rms, 12 with bath, 12 A/C, 3 story. S $39-$112; D $67-$123; each addl $10. TV in most rms; cable (premium). Restaurant (see also CURTIS HOUSE). Bar. Ck-out 11 am, ck-in 2 pm. Downhill/x-country ski 5 mi. Oldest inn in state (1754). Cr cds: DS, MC, V.

🍽 🐾

Restaurants

★★ **CAROLE PECK'S GOOD NEWS CAFE.** *694 Main St S (06798). 203/266-4663.* Specialties: wok-seared shrimp, free-range rotisserie chicken. Hrs: 11:30 am-10 pm. Closed Tues; some major hols. Res accepted. Bar. A la carte entrees: lunch $5.95-$9.95, dinner $11.50-$20. Child's menu. Jazz Sat. Outdoor dining. Modern café with changing artwork. Cr cds: A, D, MC, V.

⬛

★ **CURTIS HOUSE.** *506 Main St S (06798). 203/263-2101. www.thecurtishouse.com.* Hrs: noon-2 pm, 5-8:30 pm; Mon from 5 pm; Sun noon-8 pm. Closed Dec 25. Res accepted; hols. Bar to 10 pm. Complete meals: lunch $7.50-$11.50, dinner $13.50-$20. Child's menu. 3 dining rms. Family-owned. Cr cds: DS, MC, V.

⬛ 🍽

MAINE

Here are the highest tides (28 feet in Passamaquoddy Bay), the tastiest potatoes, and the tartest conversation in the country. Flat Yankee twang and the patois of French Canadians make Maine's speech as salty as its sea. Hunters, anglers, canoeists, and campers appreciate its 6,000 lakes and ponds, and summer vacationers enjoy its 3,500 miles of seacoast even though the water is a bit chilly.

Downeasters brag about the state's temperature range from -46° to 105°F, as well as its famous lobsters. Paper and allied products are the chief manufactured products; machine tools, electronic components, and other metal products are important. Food canning and freezing are major industries. Potatoes, blueberries, poultry, eggs, dairy products, and apples are leading farm crops.

Maine's first settlement (1604) was on St. Croix Island; it lasted one winter. Another early settlement was established near Pemaquid Point. The short-lived Popham Colony, at the mouth of the Kennebec River, built America's first transatlantic trader, the *Virginia,* in 1607. Until 1819 Maine was a part of Massachusetts. It was admitted to the Union in 1820.

Most of Maine's 17.6 million acres of forest land is open to public recreational use including more than 580,000 acres owned by the state. For more information about recreational use of public and private forestland, contact the Maine Bureau of Public Lands, 207/287-3061, or the Maine Forest Service at 207/287-2791.

Population: 1,253,040
Area: 30,995 square miles
Elevation: 0-5,268 feet
Peak: Mount Katahdin (Piscataquis County)
Entered Union: March 15, 1820 (23rd state)
Capital: Augusta
Motto: I lead
Nickname: Pine Tree State
Flower: Pine Cone and Tassel
Bird: Chickadee
Tree: Eastern White Pine
Fair: August 7-16, 2003, in Skowhegan
Time Zone: Eastern
Website: www.visitmaine.com

When to Go/Climate

Maine is a large state affected by several different weather patterns. Coastal temperatures are more moderate than inland temperatures, and fog is common in spring and fall. In general, winters are cold and snowy. Summers are filled with warm, sunny days and cool, clear nights. Fall's famous "nor'easters" can bring high tides, gale-force winds, and huge amounts of rain to the coastal areas.

AVERAGE HIGH/LOW TEMPERATURES (°F)

CARIBOU

Jan 19/-2	**May** 62/40	**Sept** 64/43
Feb 23/7	**June** 72/49	**Oct** 52/34
Mar 34/15	**July** 77/55	**Nov** 38/24
Apr 47/29	**Aug** 74/52	**Dec** 42/6

PORTLAND

Jan 30/11	**May** 63/43	**Sept** 69/49
Feb 33/14	**June** 73/52	**Oct** 59/38
Mar 41/25	**July** 79/58	**Nov** 47/30
Apr 52/34	**Aug** 77/57	**Dec** 35/18

Parks and Recreation Finder

Directions to and information about the parks and recreation areas below are given under their respective town/city sections. Please refer to those sections for details.

NATIONAL PARK AND RECREATION AREAS

Key to abbreviations. I.H.S. = International Historic Site; I.P.M. = International Peace Memorial; N.B. = National Battlefield; N.B.P. = National Battlefield Park; N.B.C. = National Battlefield and Cemetery; N.C.A. = National Conservation Area; N.E.M. = National Expansion Memorial; N.F. = National Forest; N.G. = National Grassland; N.H.P. = National Historical Park; N.H.C. = National Heritage Corridor; N.H.S. = National Historic Site; N.L. = National Lakeshore; N.M. = National Monument; N.M.P. = National Military Park; N.Mem. = National Memorial; N.P. = National Park; N.Pres. = National Preserve; N.R.A. = National Recreational Area; N.R.R. = National Recreational River; N.Riv. = National River; N.S. = National Seashore; N.S.R. = National Scenic Riverway; N.S.T. = National Scenic Trail; N.Sc. = National Scientific Reserve; N.V.M. = National Volcanic Monument.

Place Name	Listed Under
Acadia N.P.	same
St. Croix Island I.H.S.	CALAIS
White Mountain N.F.	BETHEL

STATE PARK AND RECREATION AREAS

Key to abbreviations. I.P. = Interstate Park; S.A.P. = State Archaeological Park; S.B. = State Beach; S.C.A. = State Conservation Area; S.C.P. = State Conservation Park; S.Cp. = State Campground; S.F. = State Forest; S.G. = State Garden; S.H.A. = State Historic Area; S.H.P. = State Historic Park; S.H.S. = State Historic Site; S.M.P. = State Marine Park; S.N.A. = State Natural Area; S.P. = State Park; S.P.C. = State Public Campground; S.R. = State Reserve; S.R.A. = State Recreation Area; S.Res. = State Reservoir; S.Res.P. = State Resort Park; S.R.P. = State Rustic Park.

Place Name	Listed Under
Aroostook S.P.	PRESQUE ISLE
Baxter S.P.	same
Camden Hills S.P.	CAMDEN
Cobscook Bay S.P.	MACHIAS
Crescent Beach S.P.	PORTLAND
Ferry Beach S.P.	SACO
Fort Knox S.P.	BUCKSPORT
Fort O'Brien Memorial S.P.	MACHIAS
Fort Point S.P.	BUCKSPORT
Grafton Notch S.P.	BETHEL
Lake St. George S.P.	BELFAST
Lamoine S.P.	ELLSWORTH
Mount Blue S.P.	RUMFORD
Popham Beach S.P.	BATH
Rangeley Lake S.P.	RANGELEY
Reid S.P.	BATH
Roque Bluffs S.P.	MACHIAS
Sebago Lake S.P.	SEBAGO LAKE
Two Lights S.P.	PORTLAND

Water-related activities, hiking, biking, various other sports, picnicking and visitor centers, as well as camping, are available in many of these areas. Most state parks and historic sites are open seasonally, 9 am-sunset; Popham Beach, John Paul Jones Memorial, and Reid are open year-round. Most areas have day-use and/or parking fees, $1.50-$3/person; annual pass, $40/vehicle, $20/individual. Camping May-Oct (areas vary), nonresidents $11-$17/site, residents $9-$13/site; reservation fee $2/night. Camping reservations may be made by mail to the Bureau of Parks and Lands, Station #22, Augusta 04333, Attention Reservation Clerk; in person at the office of the Bureau of Parks and Lands in Augusta; by phone, 207/287-3824 or 800/332-1501 (ME). Maine historic sites fee $2.50-$3. Pets on leash only in most parks. No dogs on beaches (or at Sebago Lake campground). For information contact the Bureau of Parks and Lands, Maine Department of Conservation, 286 Water St, Key Bank Plaza, Augusta 04333; 207/287-3821.

CALENDAR HIGHLIGHTS

FEBRUARY

Kennebunk Winter Carnival (Kennebunk). Snow sculpture contests, snow palace moonwalk, magic show, ice-skating party, chili and chowder contests, children's events. Phone 207/985-6890.

MAY

Maine State Parade (Lewiston). Downtown Lewiston and Auburn. Maine's largest parade; over 30,000 people represent 60 communities. Phone Androscoggin County Chamber of Commerce, 207/783-2249.

JUNE

Windjammer Days (Boothbay Harbor). Old schooners that formerly sailed the trade routes and now cruise the Maine coast sail en masse into harbor. Waterfront food court, entertainment, street parade, children's activities. Phone 207/633-2353.

JULY

Great Whatever Family Festival Week (Augusta). More than 60 events including tournaments, carnival, barbecue, parade, and fireworks. Festivities culminate with the canoe and kayak regatta on the Kennebec River between Augusta and Gardiner. There are also canoe and kayak races. Phone Kennebec Valley Chamber of Commerce, 207/623-4559.

Bangor Fair (Bangor). One of the country's oldest fairs. Horse racing, exhibits, stage shows. Phone 207/942-9000.

Festival de Joie (Lewiston). Central Maine Civic Center. Celebration of Lewiston and Auburn's Franco-American heritage. Features ethnic song, dance, cultural activities, traditional foods. Phone Androscoggin County Chamber of Commerce, 207/783-2249.

Schooner Days and North Atlantic Blues Festival (Rockland). Three-day festival celebrating Maine's maritime heritage; features Parade of Schooners, arts, entertainment, concessions, fireworks; blues bands and club crawl. Phone 207/596-0376.

AUGUST

Maine Lobster Festival (Rockland). A five-day event centered around Maine's chief marine creature, with a huge tent cafeteria serving lobster and other seafood. Parade, harbor cruises, maritime displays, bands, entertainment. Phone 207/596-0376.

Skowhegan State Fair (Skowhegan). One of the oldest fairs in the country (1818). Mile-long midway, stage shows, harness racing; contests, exhibits. Phone 207/474-2947.

DECEMBER

Christmas by the Sea (Camden). Celebration of holiday season with musical entertainment, horse-drawn wagon rides, Holiday House Tour, Santa's arrival by lobsterboat. Phone 207/236-4404.

SKI AREAS

Place Name	Listed Under
Camden Snow Bowl	CAMDEN
Carter's X-C Ski Center	BETHEL
Lonesome Pine Trails	FORT KENT
Lost Valley Ski Area	AUBURN
Mountain Jefferson Ski Area	LINCOLN
Saddleback Ski & Summer Lake Preserve	RANGELEY
Shawnee Peak at Pleasant Mountain Ski Area	BRIDGTON
Sugarloaf/USA Ski Area	KINGFIELD
Sunday River Ski Resort	BETHEL

FISHING AND HUNTING

Nonresident fishing license: $51; 12-15 years, $8; 15-day license, $39; seven-day license, $35; three-day license, $22; one-day license, $10. Nonresident hunting license for birds and animals except deer, bear, turkey, moose, bobcat, and raccoon: $56; including all legal game species: $86. These fees do not include agent fees, which range from $1-$2. More detailed information on the state's regulations is available in the brochures *Maine Hunting and Trapping Laws* and *Maine Open Water Fishing Laws* from the Maine Fish and Wildlife Department, Station 41, 284 State St, Augusta 04333; 207/287-8000.

Driving Information

Every person must be in an approved passenger restraint anywhere in vehicle: children under age four must use an approved safety seat. For further information phone 207/871-7771.

INTERSTATE HIGHWAY SYSTEM

The following alphabetical listing of Maine towns in *the RoadMaster™ Drive USA Travel Guide* shows that these cities are within ten miles of the indicated interstate highway. A highway map, however, should be checked for the nearest exit.

Highway Number	Cities/Towns within ten miles
Interstate 95	Augusta, Bangor, Bath, Biddeford, Brunswick, Freeport, Houlton, Kennebunk, Kittery, Lincoln, Millinocket, Newport, Ogunquit, Old Orchard Beach, Orono, Portland, Saco, Scarborough, Waterville, Wells, Yarmouth, York.

Additional Visitor Information

The pulp and paper industry mills throughout Maine offer tours of their woodlands and manufacturing facilities at various times of the year. For further information contact the Maine Pulp and Paper Association Information Office, 104 Sewall St, PO Box 5670, Augusta 04332; 207/622-3166.

There are eight official information service centers in Maine; visitors who stop by will find information and brochures helpful in planning stops to points of interest. Their locations are as follows: in Bethel, on US 2; at Kittery, between I-95 and US 1; in Fryeburg (summer only), on US 302; in Calais, on Union St, off US 1; in Hampden, on I-95N at mile marker 169, on I-95S between mile markers 171 and 172; in Houlton, on Ludlow Rd; in Yarmouth, between I-95 exit 17 and US 1.

THE COASTAL ROUTE

Most tourists stick to coastal Route 1 when it splits from I-95 at Brunswick, home of the Bowdoin College museums, the Joshua Chamberlain Museum, and outstanding summer music and theater. Bath is worth a stop to see the Maine Maritime Museum and Shipyard. Traffic streams down a peninsula to Boothbay Harbor, a resort village with a footbridge across its harbor that is a departure point for numerous excursion boats. Rockland is the next must-see stop on Route 1. Visit the Farnsworth Art Museum and Wyeth Center, Owls Head Transportation Museum, or Shore Village Museum. Maine Windjammers and ferries to Vinalhaven and North Haven depart from here. Next on the route is Camden, a town backed by hills and filled with inns, restaurants, and shops. Camden Hills State Park offers spectacular views of the coast, as well as hiking, camping, and picnic facilities. Belfast, another interesting old port, is a departure point for excursion boats and for the Belfast & Moosehead Lake Railroad Company excursion train. Continue up coastal Route 1 to Ellsworth, then turn down Route 3 to Mount Desert Island, site of Acadia National Park. The big tourist town here is Bar Harbor (the park is the big draw, along with many excursion boats). Return the same way, perhaps taking the ferry to Yarmouth, Nova Scotia, for an interesting side trip. Another option is to continue north on Route 1 past Ellsworth (the turnoff for Bar Harbor). Here Route 1 changes, becoming far quieter, especially after the turnoff for Schoodic Point, which is part of Acadia National Park. The next stop is in Machias where the Burnham Tavern Museum tells the area's revolutionary history. Take a detour at the cliffside walking trails of Quoddy Head State Park (the easternmost point in the United States). Then continue on to Lubec and over the bridge to Campobello to see the Roosevelt Campobello International Park with Franklin D. Roosevelt's summer home as its centerpiece. The park also includes a golf course and extensive hiking trails. Return to Bar Harbor along the same route. **(APPROX 306 MI; ADD 128 MI IF CONTINUING ON TO LUBEC)**

Acadia National Park

See also Bar Harbor, Northeast Harbor, Southwest Harbor

(On Mt Desert Island, S and W of Bar Harbor; entrance off ME 3)

Waves crashing against a rocky coastline, thick woodlands abundant with wildlife, and mountains scraping the sky—this, Acadia National Park, is the Maine of storybooks. Occupying nearly half of Mount Desert Island, with smaller areas on Isle au Haut, Little Cranberry Island (see CRANBERRY ISLES), Baker Island, Little Moose Island, and part of the mainland at Schoodic Point, Acadia amazes visitors. It is a sea-lashed granite coastal area of forested valleys, lakes, and mountains, all created by the force of the glaciers. At 40,000 acres, Acadia is small compared to other national parks; however, it is one of the most visited national parks in the United States, and the only national park in the northeastern United States. A 27-mile loop road connects the park's eastern sights on Mount Desert Island, and ferry services take travelers to some of the smaller islands. Visitors can explore 1,530-foot Cadillac Mountain, the highest point on the Atlantic Coast of the United States; watch waves crash against Thunder Hole, creating a thunderous boom; or swim in the ocean at various coastal beaches. A road to the summit of Cadillac provides views of Frenchman, Blue Hill, and Penobscot bays.

Mount Desert Island was named by the French explorer Samuel de Champlain in 1604. Shortly thereafter, French Jesuit missionaries settled here until driven off by an armed vessel from Virginia. This was the first act of overt warfare between France and England for control of North America. Until 1713, the island was a part of French Acadia. It was not until after the Revolutionary War that it was extensively settled. In 1916, a portion of the area was proclaimed Sieur de Monts National Monument. It was changed to Lafayette National Park in 1919, and finally, in 1929, it was enlarged and renamed Acadia National Park.

Like all national parks, Acadia is a wildlife sanctuary. Fir, pine, spruce, many hardwoods, and hundreds of varieties of wildflowers thrive. Nature lovers will be delighted with the more than 120 miles of trails; park rangers take visitors on various walks and cruises, pointing out and explaining the natural, cultural, and historical features of the park. Forty-five miles of carriage roads offer bicyclists scenic rides through Acadia. Copies of ranger-led programs and trail maps are available at the visitor center.

There is saltwater swimming at Sand Beach and freshwater swimming at Echo Lake. Snowmobiles are allowed in some areas and cross-country skiing is available. Most facilities are open Memorial Day-September; however, portions of the park are open year-round; picnic grounds are open May-October. Limited camping is available at two park campgrounds: Blackwoods, open year-round, requires reservations from mid-June-mid-September; Seawall, open late May-late September, is on a first-come, first-served basis. The park headquarters, 2½ miles west of Bar Harbor (see) on ME 233 provides visitor information (November-April, daily; closed January 1, Thanksgiving, December 24,

25). For further information contact the Superintendent, PO Box 177, Bar Harbor 04609; phone 207/288-3338. Golden Eagle, Golden Age, and Golden Access passports accepted (see MAKING THE MOST OF YOUR TRIP). Park entrance fee (subject to change) ¢¢; Per vehicle ¢¢¢ In the park are

Visitor Center. 3 mi NW of Bar Harbor at Hulls Cove. (May-Oct, daily)

The Robert Abbe Museum. Exhibits feature Native American prehistoric and ethnographic artifacts. (Mid May-Oct, daily) At Sieur de Monts Spring. Phone 207/288-3519. ¢

Islesford Historical Museum. In Islesford, on Little Cranberry Island, 2 mi S of Seal Harbor, a 30-min boat trip from Northeast Harbor. (See CRANBERRY ISLES) **FREE**

Isle au Haut (EEL-oh-HO). Mountains rise more than 540 ft on this island of forested shores and cobblestone beaches; hiking trails; small primitive campground (advance mail reservations; phone 207/288-3338 for reservation form). A ferry from Stonington (see DEER ISLE) takes visitors on the 45-min trip to island (daily exc Sun; no hols; fee).

Ferry Service. Connects Islesford, Great Cranberry Island, and Northeast Harbor on a regular schedule all yr. Phone 207/244-3575. ¢¢

Park tours. Narrated sightseeing trips through the park. Buses leave Main St, Bar Harbor. (June-early Oct) For tickets and information on tour schedules and fees contact Testa's Cafe, 53 Main St, Bar Harbor, phone 207/288-3327. ¢¢¢

Naturalist Sea Cruises. Marine life and history of the area are explained. Cruises visit Frenchman Bay (phone 207/288-3322), Islesford (phone 207/276-5352), and Baker Island (phone 207/276-3717). (Daily during summer season, schedules vary; phone for fees)

Auto Tape Tours. A scenic, 56-mile self-guided tour gives a mile-by-mile description of points of interest, history, and geology of the park. Tape avail May-Oct at visitor center. Cassette player and tape rental, deposit required; or tape may be purchased. ¢¢¢-¢¢¢¢¢

Allagash Wilderness Waterway

See also Fort Kent

In 1970 the Allagash River was designated a national wild river. Stretching 95 miles through 200,000 acres of lakes, rivers, and timberland in Maine's northern wilderness, this waterway is a favorite of canoeists. A good put-in point is Chamberlain Thoroughfare at the junction of Chamberlain and Telos lakes. The trip ends at Allagash Village, eight miles north of Allagash Falls, near the Canadian border, where the Allagash flows into the St. John River. Some canoe experience is necessary before attempting the entire trip as high winds can be a problem on the lakes and, depending on the level of the Allagash, the rapids can be dangerous.

Registration is required upon entering and leaving the waterway; rangers are at Allagash Lake, Chamberlain Thoroughfare, Eagle Lake, Churchill Dam, Long Lake Thoroughfare, and the Michaud Farm. Supplies and canoes must be brought in; gasoline is not available. There are restrictions regarding the size of parties using the waterway, as well as watercraft permitted. Numerous primitive campsites accessible only by water are scattered along the waterway (mid-May–mid-Oct). Campsite fee per person, per night ¢¢

For further information and rules contact the Bureau of Parks & Lands, Maine Department of Conservation, Northern Regional Office, BMHI Complex, Building H, 106 Hogan Rd, Bangor, 04401; phone 207/941-4014.

Auburn

See also Lewiston

Settled 1797 **Pop** 24,309 **Elev** 188 ft **Area code** 207
Information Androscoggin County Chamber of Commerce, 179 Lisbon St, PO Box 59, Lewiston 04243-0059; 207/783-2249
Web www.androscoggincounty.com

Auburn, together with its sister city Lewiston, make up an important manufacturing center. In 1836, the first organized shoe company was started here. The Minot Shoe Company prospered, selling more than $6 million in shoes by 1900, and becoming the fifth-largest shoe company in the United States by 1920. When the depression hit, the company suffered a severe blow. The city continued to expand, however, and today Auburn is one of the largest cities in the state.

What to See and Do

Androscoggin Historical Society Library and Museum. Exhibits trace local, county and state history. (Wed-Fri; closed hols) Museum; library. County Building, 2 Turner St at Court St. Phone 207/784-0586. **FREE**

Norlands Living History Center. Life as it was lived a century ago; clothing, customs. Yr-round working farm with oxen, horses, cows, crops and seasonal activities. Features 19th-century Victorian home of Washburn family; school, library, church, farmer's cottage, barn. Tours (July-Sept, daily). Picnicking. (See SPECIAL EVENTS) 25 mi N just off ME 4, in Livermore. Phone 207/897-4366. ¢¢

Skiing. Lost Valley Ski Area. Two double chairlifts, T-bar; snowmaking; patrol, school, rentals; bar, lounge, restaurant. (Dec-mid-Mar, daily) Follow signs off ME 11. Phone 207/784-1561. ¢¢¢¢

Special Events

Maple Days. Norlands Living History Center. Mid-Mar. Phone 207/897-4366.

Autumn Celebration. Norlands Living History Center. Sept. Phone 207/897-4366.

Augusta

See also Waterville

Settled 1628 **Pop** 21,325 **Elev** 153 ft **Area code** 207
Information Kennebec Valley Chamber of Commerce, 21 University Dr, PO Box 676, 04332-0192; 207/623-4559
Web www.augustamaine.com

Augusta, the capital of Maine, began in 1628 when men from Plymouth established a trading post on the site of Cushnoc, a Native American village. From there, Fort Western was built in 1754 to protect settlers against Native American raids, and the settlement grew. Today, 39 miles from the sea, Augusta is at the head of navigation on the Kennebec River; some of the town's leading industries include steel and food processing and service-related industries.

What to See and Do

Old Fort Western. Fort complex built in 1754 by Boston merchants; main house and reproduction blockhouse, watchboxes, and palisade. Costumed staff interprets 18th-century life on the Kennebec River. (Memorial Day-Labor Day, daily; after Labor Day-Columbus Day, Sat and Sun, limited hrs) City Center Plaza, 16 Cony St. Phone 207/626-2385.

State House. (1829-1832) The original design for this impressive building was by Charles Bulfinch (architect of the Massachusetts State House). Remodeled and enlarged (1909-1910), it rises majestically above Capitol Park and the Kennebec River. On its 185-ft dome is a statue, designed by W. Clark Noble, of a classically robed woman bearing a pine bough torch. (Mon-Fri; closed hols) State and Capitol Sts. Phone 207/287-2301. **FREE** Also here are

Blaine House. (1833) House of James G. Blaine, Speaker of the US House of Representatives and 1884 presidential candidate. Since 1919, this 28-rm house has been official residence of Maine's governors. Originally built in Federal style, it was remodeled several times and today appears semicolonial. Tours (Tues-Thurs, limited hrs; closed hols). State and Capitol Sts. Phone 207/287-2301. **FREE**

Maine State Museum. Exhibits of Maine's natural environment, prehistory, social history, and manufacturing heritage. "This Land Called Maine" features five natural history scenes as well as a presentation of 40 spectacular gems and gem minerals found in Maine. "Made in Maine" presents 19th-century products and manufacturing technologies and incl a water-powered woodworking mill, a two-story textile factory, and more than 1,000 Maine-made objects. Other exhibits examine the early economic activities of agriculture, fishing, granite quarrying, ice harvesting, lumbering, and shipbuilding. Also featured are a display of military, political, and geographical artifacts relating to the formation of the state of Maine as well as an exhibition on Maine glass. Gift shop. (Daily; closed hols) Phone 207/287-2301. **FREE**

Special Event

Great Whatever Family Festival Week. Augusta/Gardiner area. More than 60 events incl tournaments, carnival, barbecue, parade, and fireworks. Festivities culminate with the canoe and kayak regatta on the Kennebec River between Augusta and Gardiner. There are also canoe and kayak races. Contact Chamber of Commerce. Ten days late June-early July. Phone 207/623-4559.

Motels/Motor Lodges

★★ **BEST INN.** 65 Whitten Rd (04330). 207/622-3776; fax 207/622-3778; res 800/237-8466. www.bestinn.com. 58 rms, 8 kit, 2 story. May-Oct: S $55.70-$61.70; D $57.70-$77.70; kit $73.70-$90.70. Crib $5. TV; cable (premium). Heated pool. Complimentary continental bkfst. Restaurant nearby. Ck-out 11 am. Coin lndry. Meeting rm. Business servs avail. Cr cds: A, D, DS, MC, V.
🖼🖼🖼

★★ **BEST WESTERN SENATOR INN.** 284 Western Ave; I-95 (04330). 207/622-5804; fax 207/622-8803; toll-free 877/772-2224. www.bestwestern.com. 125 rms, 1-2 story. July-Aug: S $79-$99; D $89-$109; each addl $9; suites $149-$189; under 18 free; lower rates rest of yr. Crib free. Pet accepted, some restrictions; $50. TV; cable (premium), VCR avail (movies). 2 heated pools, 1 indoor. Playground. Complimentary full bkfst. Complimentary coffee in rms. Restaurant 6:30 am-10 pm. Rm serv. Bar to 1 am. Ck-out noon. Coin lndry. Meeting rms. Business servs avail. In-rm modem link. Sundries. Exercise rm; sauna. Massage. Indoor putting green. Game rm. Some refrigerators, fireplaces. Picnic tables. Cr cds: A, C, D, DS, MC, V.
🖼🖼🖼🖼🖼🖼🖼

★ **COMFORT INN.** 281 Civic Center Dr (04330). 207/623-1000; fax 207/623-3505; res 800/228-5150. www.comfortinn.com. 99 rms, 3 story. Late June-mid-Oct: S, D $89-$139; each addl $10; under 18 free; higher rates camp wkends; lower rates rest of yr. Crib free. TV; cable (premium). Indoor pool; wading pool, whirlpool. Complimentary continental bkfst. Restaurant 11 am-10 pm. Bar. Ck-out 11 am. Meeting rms. Business servs avail. Valet serv. X-country ski 10 mi. Exercise equipt; sauna. Cr cds: A, D, DS, MC, V.
🖼🖼🖼🖼🖼🖼🖼🖼

★ **MOTEL 6.** 18 Edison Dr (04330). 207/622-0000; fax 207/622-1048; toll-free 800/440-6000. www.motel6.com. 68 rms, 2 story. Late June-Sept: S $32.99; D $38.99; each addl $3; under 18 free. Crib free. Pet accepted, some restrictions. TV; cable (premium). Complimentary coffee in lobby. Restaurant nearby. Ck-out noon. Coin lndry. Cr cds: A, D, DS, MC, V.
🖼🖼🖼🖼

★ **TRAVELODGE HOTEL.** 390 Western Ave (04330). 207/622-6371; fax 207/621-0349; res 800/578-7878. www.travelodge.com. 98 rms, 30 kit. suites, 2 story. Mid-June-late Oct: S, D $60-$70; each addl $10; under 18 free; lower rates rest of yr. Pet accepted. TV; cable (premium). Pool; wading pool. Complimentary continental bkfst.

Coffee in rms. Restaurant 6 am-2 pm, 4 pm-1 am. Bar. Ck-out 11 am. Coin lndry. Meeting rms. Business servs avail. Valet serv. Microwaves avail. Cr cds: A, C, DS, MC, V.
🖼🖼🖼🖼🖼🖼

B&B/Small Inn

★★ **WINGS HILL INN.** Rte 27, Belgrade Lakes (04918). 207/495-2400; fax 207/495-3400; toll-free 866/495-2400. www.wingshillinn.com. 8 rms, 2 story. No rm phones. May-Oct: S, D $110-$140; each addl $30; wkend rates (2-day min); lower rates rest of yr. TV in common rm; cable, VCR avail. Complimentary full bkfst. Restaurant nearby. Ck-out 11 am, ck-in 3-9 pm. Some balconies. Renovated farmhouse built 1800; antique quilts. Totally nonsmoking. Cr cds: DS, MC, V.
🖼🖼🖼🖼🖼

Bailey Island

See also Brunswick

Elev 20 ft **Area code** 207 **Zip** 04003
Information Chamber of Commerce of the Bath-Brunswick Region, 59 Pleasant St, Brunswick 04011; 207/725-8797
Web www.midcoastmaine.com

At the terminus of ME 24, along the northern shore of Casco Bay, lies Bailey Island, the most popular of the 365 Calendar Islands. Together with Orr's Island, to which it is connected by a cribstone bridge, Bailey is a resort and fishing center. Originally called Newwaggin by an early trader from Kittery, Bailey Island was renamed after Deacon Timothy Bailey of Massachusetts, who claimed the land for himself and banished early settlers. Bailey Island and Orr's Island partially enclose an arm of Casco Bay called Harpswell Sound—the locale of John Whittier's poem "The Dead Ship of Harpswell" and of Harriet Beecher Stowe's "Pearl of Orr's Island."

What to See and Do

Bailey Island Cribstone Bridge. Unique construction of uncemented granite blocks laid honeycomb fashion, allowing the tides to flow through. On ME 24 S, over Will Straits. **FREE**

Giant Staircase. Natural rock formation dropping 200 ft in steps to ocean. Scenic overlook area. Washington St. **FREE**

Motel/Motor Lodge

★ **COOK'S ISLAND VIEW MOTEL.** Rte 24 (04003). 207/833-7780. 18 rms, 3 kits. No A/C. July-Labor Day, hol wkends: D $80; kit. units $15 addl; under 18 free; lower rates after Memorial Day-June, after Labor Day-Oct. Closed rest of yr. Pet accepted, some restrictions. TV; cable. Pool. Restaurant nearby. Ck-out 11 am. Cr cds: A, MC, V.
🖼🖼🖼

B&Bs/Small Inns

★ **BAILEY ISLAND MOTEL.** *Rt 24 (04003). 207/833-2886; fax 207/833-7721. www.baileyislandmotel.com.* 11 rms, 2 story. 1 kit. No A/C. No rm phones. Mid-June-early Oct: D $85-$110; each addl $10; under 10 free; lower rates May-mid-June, Oct. Closed rest of yr. Crib free. TV; cable. Complimentary continental bkfst. Ck-out 11 am. Picnic tables. Balconies. On ocean. Totally nonsmoking. Cr cds: A, D, DS, MC, V.
⬛ ⬛ ⬛

★★ **LOG CABIN ISLAND INN.** *5 Log Cabin Ln (04003). 207/833-5546; fax 207/833-7858.* 8 rms, 2 with shower only, 1 suite, 4 kit. units. Memorial Day-Labor Day: S, D $109-$199; each addl $19.95; suite $199; kit. units $129-$219; wkly rates; hols 2-day min; lower rates rest of yr. Closed Nov-Mar. TV; cable, VCR (movies). Complimentary full bkfst. Complimentary coffee in rms. Restaurant 5-8 pm. Ck-out 11 am, ck-in 3 pm. Business servs avail. Gift shop. Refrigerators; some in-rm whirlpools, fireplaces. Balconies. Built in 1940s. Log cabin; panoramic view of bay, islands. Totally nonsmoking. Cr cds: A, DS, MC, V.
⬛ ⬛

Restaurant

★ **COOK'S LOBSTER HOUSE.** *Garrison Cove Rd (04003). 207/833-2818. www.cookslobsterhouse.com.* Specializes in baked stuffed lobster, shore dinners, steak. Raw bar. Hrs: 11:30 am-9 pm; mid-June-Aug to 10 pm. No A/C. Bar. Lunch $2.95-$9.95, dinner $9.25-$26.95. Child's meals. Outdoor dining. Dockage. Family-owned. Cr cds: DS, MC, V.
Ⓓ

Bangor

Settled 1769 **Pop** 33,181 **Elev** 61 ft **Area code** 207 **Zip** 04401
Information Bangor Convention and Visitors Bureau, PO Box 1938, 04402
Web www.bangorcvb.org

In 1604, Samuel de Champlain sailed up the Penobscot River to the area that was to become Bangor and reported that the country was "most pleasant and agreeable," the hunting good, and the oak trees impressive. As the area grew, these things remained true. Begun as a harbor town, as did many of Maine's coastal areas, Bangor turned to lumber when the railroads picked up much of the shipping business. In 1842, it became the second-largest lumber port in the country.

Bangor received its name by mistake. An early settler, Reverend Seth Noble, was sent to register the new town under its chosen name of Sunbury; however, when officials asked Noble for the name, he thought they were asking him for the name of a tune he was humming, and replied "Bangor" instead. Today, the city is the third-largest in Maine and a trading and distribution center.

What to See and Do

Bangor Historical Museum. (Thomas A. Hill House, 1834) Tour of first flr of Greek Revival house; second-flr gallery features changing exhibits. (Tues-Sat, June-Dec) 159 Union St at High St. Phone 207/942-5766. ¢

Cole Land Transportation Museum. Exhibits on more than 200 vehicles incl vintage cars, horse-drawn logging sleds and fire engines. Historic photographs of Maine also on display. (May-early Nov, daily) 405 Perry Rd. Phone 207/990-3600. ¢¢

Monument to Paul Bunyan. A 31-ft-tall statue commemorating the legendary lumberjack. Main St in Bass Park. **FREE**

Special Events

Kenduskeag Stream Canoe Race. Mid-Apr. Phone 207/947-1018.

Bangor Fair. One of country's oldest. Horse racing, exhibits, stage shows. Phone 207/990-4444. Late June-first wk Aug. Phone 207/947-5555.

Band concerts. Paul Bunyan Park. Phone 207/947-1018. Tues eves, July-Aug.

Motels/Motor Lodges

★ **BEST INN BANGOR.** *570 Main St (04401). 207/947-0566; res 800/237-8466. www.bestinn.com.* 50 rms, 2 story. June-Oct: S $50-$75; D $60-$80; each addl $5; under 12 free; lower rates rest of yr. Crib free. Pet accepted. TV; cable. Restaurant 7 am-10 pm; Sun to 9 pm. Bar 11-1 am. Ck-out 11 am. Business servs avail. Sundries. Cr cds: A, C, D, DS, MC, V.
Ⓓ ⬛ ⬛ ⬛

★★ **BEST WESTERN WHITE HOUSE INN.** *155 Littlefield Ave (04401). 207/862-3737; res 800/780-7234. www. bestwestern.com.* 66 rms, 3 story. May-Oct: S, D $60-$100; each addl $5; family rm $79-$99; under 12 free; lower rates rest of yr. Crib $3. Pet accepted. TV; cable, VCR avail (movies). Heated pool; sauna. Complimentary continental bkfst. Complimentary coffee in rms. Restaurant adj open 24 hrs. Bar 4 pm-1 am. Ck-out 11 am. Coin lndry. Business servs avail. In-rm modem link. Sundries. Downhill/x-country ski 4 mi. Lawn games. Refrigerators avail. Picnic tables. Cr cds: A, C, D, DS, MC, V.
⬛ ⬛ ⬛ ⬛ ⬛

★ **COMFORT INN.** *750 Hogan Rd (04401). 207/942-7899; fax 207/942-6463; res 800/228-5150. www.comfortinn.com.* 96 rms, 2 story. Mid-June-Oct: S $49-$89; D $59-$99; each addl $5; under 19 free; lower rates rest of yr. Crib free. Pet accepted; $6. TV; cable (premium). Pool. Complimentary continental bkfst. Complimentary coffee in rms. Ck-out noon. Meeting rms. Business servs avail. Sundries. Free airport transportation. Game rm. Exercise equipt. X-country ski 10 mi. Shopping mall adj. Cr cds: A, D, MC, V.
⬛ ⬛ ⬛ ⬛ ⬛ ⬛

★ **DAYS INN.** *250 Odlin Rd (04401). 207/942-8272; fax 207/942-1382; toll-free 800/329-7466. www.daysinn.com.* 101 rms, 2 story. July-Oct: S $50-$65; D $55-$85; each addl $6; under 12 free; lower rates rest of yr. Crib free. Pet accepted; $6. TV; cable (premium), VCR avail. Indoor pool; whirlpool. Complimentary continental bkfst. Restaurant adj 11-1 am. Rm serv. Ck-out 11 am. Meeting rm. Business servs avail. In-rm modem link. Sundries. Free airport transportation. Downhill/x-country ski 12 mi. Game rm. Cr cds: A, C, D, DS, JCB, MC, V.

D 🐾 ➤ ➤ ✈ 🏊 ❄ 🔥

★ **ECONO LODGE.** *327 Odlin Rd (04401). 207/945-0111; fax 207/942-8856; res 800/553-2666. www.econolodge.com.* 128 rms, 4 story. S $29.95-$65.95; D $39.95-$85.95; under 19 free. Crib free. Pet accepted; $6/day. TV; cable (premium). Complimentary coffee in lobby. Ck-out 11 am. Coin lndry. Business servs avail. In-rm modem link. Downhill/x-country ski 7 mi. Some refrigerators, microwaves. Cr cds: A, DS, MC, V.

D 🐾 ➤ ❄ 🔥 **SC**

★★ **FAIRFIELD INN.** *300 Odlin Rd (04401). 207/990-0001; fax 207/990-0917; res 800/228-2800. www.fairfieldinn.com.* 153 rms, 3 story. Mid-June-mid-Oct: S, D $49.95-$84.95; each addl $3; under 18 free; lower rates rest of yr. Crib free. TV; cable (premium). Indoor pool; whirlpool. Complimentary continental bkfst. Restaurant adj 6 am-10 pm. Ck-out noon. Coin lndry. Meeting rm. Business servs avail. In-rm modem link. Downhill ski 7 mi; x-country ski 5 mi. Exercise equipt; sauna. Cr cds: A, D, DS, MC, V.

D ➤ ➤ ❄ 🔥 🏃

★★ **FOUR POINTS BY SHERATON.** *308 Godfrey Blvd (04401). 207/947-6721; fax 207/941-9761; res 800/325-3535. www.fourpoints.com.* 101 rms, 9 story. S, D $98-$155; each addl $15; under 18 free. Crib free. Pet accepted. TV; cable (premium). Pool. Complimentary coffee in rms. Restaurant 6 am-2:30 pm, 5-11 pm. Bar 2 pm-midnight. Ck-out noon. Meeting rms. Business center. In-rm modem link. Gift shop. Validated parking. Airport transportation. Downhill/x-country ski 7 mi. Exercise equipt. Enclosed walkway to airport. Cr cds: A, DS, MC, V.

D 🐾 ❄ ✈ ❄ 🔥 **SC** ➤ 🏃 🏃

Hotels

★★ **HOLIDAY INN.** *404 Odlin Rd (04401). 207/947-0101; fax 207/947-7619; toll-free 800/914-0101. www.holiday-inn.com/bangor-odlin.* 207 rms, 3 story. July-Oct: S $89-$99; D $99-$109; each addl $10; under 19 free; lower rates rest of yr. Crib free. Pet accepted. TV; cable (premium), VCR avail. 2 pools; 1 indoor, whirlpool. Complimentary coffee in rms. Restaurant 6:30 am-1:30 pm, 5-10 pm. Rm serv. Bar noon-1 am; entertainment. Ck-out noon. Coin lndry. Meeting rms. Business servs avail. In-rm modem link. Sundries. Valet serv. Free airport transportation. Downhill ski 15 mi; x-country ski 10 mi. Health club privileges. Some refrigerators. Cr cds: A, C, D, DS, JCB, MC, V.

D 🐾 ➤ ➤ ✈ **SC**

★★ **HOLIDAY INN.** *500 Main St (04401). 207/947-8651; fax 207/942-2848; res 800/465-4329. www.holidayinn.com/bangor-civic.* 121 rms, 4 story. May-Oct: S, D $59-$99; suites $115-$200; under 19 free; lower rates rest of yr. Crib free. Pet accepted. TV; cable (premium). Pool. Complimentary coffee in rms. Restaurant 6:30 am-1:30 pm, 5-10 pm. Rm serv. Bar 3:30 pm-1 am; entertainment Tues-Sat. Ck-out noon. Coin lndry. Meeting rms. Business servs avail. In-rm modem link. Valet serv. Sundries. Free airport transportation. Downhill ski 10 mi. Health club privileges. Some bathrm phones. Opp Civic Center. Cr cds: A, C, D, DS, JCB, MC, V.

D 🐾 ➤ ➤ ✈ ❄ 🔥 **SC**

B&Bs/Small Inns

★★ **THE LUCERNE INN.** *Rte 1A Bar Harbor Rd, Holden (04429). 207/843-5123; fax 207/843-6138; toll-free 800/325-5123. www.lucerneinn.com.* 25 rms, 3 story. July-Oct: S, D $99-$159; each addl $15; package plans; lower rates rest of yr. TV; cable (premium). Pool. Complimentary continental bkfst. Dining rm 5-9 pm; Sun brunch 9 am-1 pm. Rm serv. Ck-out 11 am, ck-in 2 pm. Meeting rm. Business servs avail. Downhill/x-country ski 20 mi. Fireplaces. Colonial-style farmhouse and connecting stable, established as inn in 1814; antiques. Gazebo. On hill overlooking Phillips Lake. Cr cds: A, MC, V.

D ➤ ➤ ❄ 🔥

★★ **THE PHENIX INN AT WEST MARKET SQUARE.** *20 Broad St (04401). 207/947-0411; fax 207/947-0255. www.phenixinn.com.* 32 rms, 4 story. July-late-Oct: S, D $96-$179; lower rates rest of yr. Crib free. Pet accepted. TV; cable, VCR avail. Complimentary continental bkfst. Restaurant adj 7:15 am-10:30 pm. Ck-out noon, ck-in 1 pm. Guest lndry. Meeting rm. Business servs avail. Downhill ski 10 mi. Exercise equipt. Refrigerator avail. Restored commercial building (1873) located in West Market Square; furnished with antique reproductions. Near river. Cr cds: A, C, D, DS, MC, V.

D 🐾 🛎 🔥 ➤ 🏃 ❄ 🔥

Restaurants

★ **CAPTAIN NICK'S SEAFOOD HOUSE.** *1165 Union St (04401). 207/942-6444.* Specializes in lobster, seafood, local dishes. Hrs: 11 am-10 pm; wkends to 11 pm. Closed Thanksgiving, Dec 25. Res accepted. Bar. Lunch $3.50-$7.25, dinner $6.95-$17.95. Child's menu. Cr cds: A, C, DS, ER, MC, V.

D **SC**

★★ **MILLER'S.** *427 Main St (04401). 207/945-5663.* Specializes in prime rib, fresh seafood, rotisserie chicken. Extensive salad bar. Dessert bar. Own baking. Hrs: 11 am-10 pm; Sun 10:30 am-9 pm; Sun brunch to noon. Closed Dec 25. Res accepted. Lunch $3.95-$7.50, dinner $8.95-$21.95. Sun brunch $6.95. Child's menu. 2 separate dining areas. Family-owned. Cr cds: A, DS, MC, V.

D **SC**

★★ **PILOTS GRILL.** *1528 Hammond St (04401). 207/942-6325.* Specialties: baked stuffed lobster, baked haddock, prime rib. Own desserts. Hrs: 11:30 am-2 pm, 5-9 pm; Sun 11:30 am-9 pm. Closed July 4, Dec 25. Res accepted. Bar. Lunch $5.95-$9.95, dinner $8.95-$19.95. Child's menu. Family-owned since 1940. Cr cds: A, C, D, DS, ER, MC, V.

Bar Harbor

See also Cranberry Isles, Northeast Harbor, Southwest Harbor

Pop 2,768 **Elev** 20 ft **Area code** 207 **Zip** 04609
Information Chamber of Commerce, 93 Cottage St, PO Box 158; 207/288-5103
Web www.barharborinfo.com

Bar Harbor, the largest village on Mount Desert Island, has a summer population of as many as 20,000 and is headquarters for the surrounding summer resort area. The island, which includes most of Acadia National Park, is mainly rugged granite, forested and flowered, with many bays and inlets where sailing is popular. In the mid-1800s, socially prominent figures, including publisher Joseph Pulitzer, had elaborate summer cottages built on the island. The era of elegance ebbed, however, with the Great Depression, World War II, and the "Great Fire of 1947," which destroyed many of the estates and scorched more than 17,000 acres. As a result, the forests in the area now have younger, more varied trees bearing red, yellow, and orange leaves instead of just evergreens.

What to See and Do

The Abbe Museum. Collection of Native American artifacts. (May-Oct) ME 3 S to Sieur de Monts exit. ¢¢

Acadia National Park. (see). Borders town on west and south. Headquarters 2½ mi W on ME 233.

Bar Harbor Historical Society Museum. Collection of early photographs of hotels, summer cottages, and Green Mtn cog railroad; hotel registers from the early to late 1800s; maps, scrapbook of the 1947 fire. (Mid-June-Oct, Mon-Sat; closed hols) 34 Mt Desert St, Jesup Memorial Library. Phone 207/288-0000. **FREE**

Bar Harbor Whale Watch Company. Offers variety of cruises aboard catamarans *Friendship V* or *Helen H* to view whales, seal, puffin, osprey, and more. Also nature cruises and lobster and seal watching. Cruises vary in length and destination. (May-Oct, daily) Depart from Bluenose Ferry Terminal, 1 mi N on ME 3. Phone 207/288-2386.

Ferry service to Yarmouth, Nova Scotia. Passenger and car carrier *Cat Ferry* makes 3-hr trips. Phone 888/249-7245. ¢¢¢¢

Fishing. Fresh water in many lakes and streams (check regulations, obtain license). Salt water off coast; commercial boat operators will arrange trips.

The Jackson Laboratory. An internationally known mammalian genetics laboratory conducting research relevant to cancer, diabetes, AIDS, heart disease, blood disorders, birth defects, aging, and normal growth and development.

Audiovisual and lecture programs (Early-June-late Aug, Wed afternoons; closed one wk late July and one wk mid-Aug). 2 mi S on ME 3. Phone 207/288-6049. **FREE**

Natural History Museum. More than 50 exhibits depicting animals in their natural settings; 22-ft Minke whale skeleton. Interpretive programs; eve lectures in summer (Wed). (June-Labor Day, Mon-Sat; rest of yr, Thurs-Sat or by appt) Eden St. In historic Turrets Building on College of the Atlantic waterfront campus. Phone 207/288-5015. ¢¢

Oceanarium-Bar Harbor. An extension of the Mt Desert Oceanarium in Southwest Harbor (see); features incl lobster hatchery, salt-marsh walks, viewing tower; also lobster museum with hands-on exhibits. (Mid May-mid Oct, Mon-Sat) 9 mi N on ME 3. Phone 207/288-5005. ¢¢ Also incl is the

  Lobster Hatchery. Young lobsters are hatched from eggs to ½ inch in length, then returned to ocean to supplement supply; guides narrate process. (Mid-May-mid-Oct, Mon-Sat) Phone 207/288-2334.

Special Events

Celebrate Bar Harbor. Mid-June. Phone 207/288-5103.

Art Exhibit. Village Green. Third wkend in July and Aug. Phone 207/288-5103.

Motels/Motor Lodges

★★ **ATLANTIC EYRIE LODGE.** *6 Norman Rd (04609). 207/288-9786; fax 207/288-8500; toll-free 800/422-2883.* 58 rms, 5 story. July-Labor Day: S, D $139-$195; each addl $10; suites, kit. units $184; under 7 free; lower rates late May-June, after Labor Day-mid-Oct. Closed rest of yr. Crib free. TV; cable. Pool. Complimentary continental bkfst. Restaurant nearby. Ck-out 11 am. Coin lndry. Meeting rms. Business servs avail. Refrigerators avail. Private patios, balconies. Picnic tables. Cr cds: A, MC, V.

[icons]

★★ **BAR HARBOR MOTEL.** *100 Eden St, Rte 3 (04609). 207/288-3453; fax 207/288-3598; toll-free 800/388-3453. www.barharbormotel.com.* 70 rms, 16 suites. July-Aug: S, D $89-$152; each addl $8; suites $137; under 13 free; lower rates mid-May-June, Sept-mid-Oct. Closed rest of yr. Crib free. TV; cable. Heated pool. Playground. Complimentary coffee in lobby. Restaurant adj 11:30 am-11 pm. Ck-out 11 am. Business servs avail. Refrigerators. Picnic tables. Cr cds: DS, MC, V.

[icons]

★ **BAR HARBOR QUALITY INN.** *40 Kebo St (04609). 207/288-5403; fax 207/288-5473; res 800/228-5151. www.acadia.net/quality.* 77 rms, 2 story, 10 kits. Late June-Aug: S, D $69-$169; each addl $10; kits. (3-day min) $149; under 19 free; lower rates late Apr-late June, Sept-late Oct. Closed rest of yr. Crib free. TV; cable. Heated pool; whirlpool. Complimentary coffee in rms. Restaurant opp 7-10:30 am, 4:30-9 pm. Ck-out 11 am. Coin lndry. Business servs avail. Sundries. Gift shop. Refrigerators avail. Balconies. Picnic tables, grill. 4 blks to ocean. Totally nonsmoking. Cr cds: A, C, D, DS, ER, JCB, MC, V.

[icons]

★★ **BEST WESTERN INN.** *Rte 3 (04609). 207/288-5823; fax 207/288-9827; res800/528-1234.www.bestwesterninn. com.* 70 rms. July-mid-Sept: S, D $67-$105; each addl $10; under 12 free; lower rates May-June, Sept-Oct. Closed Nov-Apr. Crib $5. TV; cable (premium). Heated pool. Complimentary continental bkfst. Ck-out 11 am. Coin lndry. Some refrigerators. Cr cds: A, C, D, DS, MC, V.

⌨ ⌨ ⌨ SC

★ **CADILLAC MOTOR INN.** *336 Main St (04609). 207/288-3831; fax 207/288-9370; toll-free 888/207-2593. cadillacmotorinn.com.* 49 rms, 1-2 story, 5 suites, 18 kits. 22 A/C. July-Labor Day: S, D $54-$99; each addl $10; suites $125-$150; kit. units $69-$150; under 13 free; lower rates May-June, after Labor Day-Oct. Closed rest of yr. Crib $10. TV; cable (premium). Complimentary coffee in lobby. Restaurant nearby. Ck-out 11 am. Coin lndry. Some fireplaces. Balconies. Picnic tables. Cr cds: A, DS, MC, V.

⌨ ⌨ ⌨

★★ **CROMWELL HARBOR MOTEL.** *359 Main St (04609). 207/288-3201; toll-free 800/544-3201. www.cromwellharbor.com.* 25 rms, 9 A/C. Mid-July-Aug: S $58-$98; D $88-$115; each addl $10; lower rates rest of yr. TV; cable (premium). Heated pool. Restaurant nearby. Ck-out 11 am. Some refrigerators, microwaves. Picnic tables. Cr cds: A, MC, V.

⌨ ⌨ ⌨ ⌨

★★ **DREAMWOOD PINES MOTEL.** *RR 3, Box 1100 (04609). 207/288-9717; fax 207/288-4194. www. dreamwoodpines.com.* 22 rms, 5 kit. units. July-Aug: S, D $88-$184; each addl $8; kit. units $98-$158; lower rates May-June, Sept-late Oct. Closed rest of yr. Crib $6. TV; cable (premium). Heated pool. Complimentary coffee in rms. Restaurant adj 6 am-8 pm. Ck-out 11 am. Picnic tables, grills. Wooded grounds. Cr cds: DS, MC, V.

⌨ ⌨

★ **EDENBROOK MOTEL.** *96 Eden St (04609). 207/288-4975; toll-free 800/323-7819. www.acadia.net/edenbrook/office.html.* 47 rms in 4 bldgs, 1-2 story, July-Aug: S, D $36-$90; each addl $5; lower rates late May-June, Sept-late Oct. Closed rest of yr. Crib $5. TV; cable. Complimentary coffee in rms. Ck-out 11 am. Some refrigerators. Some balconies. Cr cds: A, DS, MC, V.

⌨ ⌨

★ **EDGEWATER COTTAGES AND MOTEL.** *Old Barharbor Rd, Salisbury Cove (04672). 207/288-3491; res 888/310-9920. www.edgewaterbarharbor.com.* 23 units, 1-2 story, 8 motel rms, 4 kits. 11 kit. cottages, 4 apts (2-bedrm). July-Labor Day: S, D $97; kits. $107; each addl $10; kit. cottages, apts $78-$130; wkly rates; lower rates mid-Apr-June, early Sept-Oct. Closed rest of yr. TV; cable (premium). Complimentary coffee in lobby. Ck-out 11 am. Coin lndry. Refrigerators; some fireplaces. Patios, balconies. Picnic tables, grills. On Frenchman Bay; swimming beach. Cr cds: MC, V.

⌨

★★ **GOLDEN ANCHOR INN.** *55 West St (04609). 207/288-5033; fax 207/288-4577; toll-free 800/328-5033. www.goldenanchorinn.com.* 88 rms, 4 kit. units, 2 story. July-early Sept: S, D $110-$185; each addl $10; under 5 free, 5-12 $2.50; lower rates Apr-June, early Sept-Oct. Closed rest of yr. Crib free. TV; cable. Heated pool; whirlpool.

Complimentary bkfst buffet in season. Restaurant 7 am-10 pm. Rm serv 1-9 pm. Bar from noon. Ck-out 11 am. Business servs avail. In-rm modem link. Balconies. On ocean. Private pier, dockage; whale watching cruises in season. Cr cds: D, DS, MC, V.

⌨ ⌨ ⌨ ⌨ ⌨

★ **HIGGINS HOLIDAY HOTEL.** *43 Holland Ave (04609). 207/288-3829; fax 207/288-4982; toll-free 800/345-0305.* 25 rms, 7 kit. units, 1-2 story. Some A/C. July-Labor Day: S, D $43-$89; each addl $5; kit. units $96-$150; wkly rates kit. units; lower rates mid-May-June, Labor Day-Oct. Closed rest of yr. Crib $5. TV; cable. Complimentary coffee in rms. Restaurant nearby. Ck-out 11 am. Cr cds: DS, MC, V.

⌨ ⌨ ⌨

★ **HIGH SEAS.** *RR 1, Box 1085 (04609). 207/288-5836; toll-free 800/959-5836. www.highseasmotel.com.* 34 rms. July-Aug: S, D $68-$98; under 12 free; lower rates May-June, Sept-mid Oct. Closed rest of yr. Crib $2. TV; cable. Heated pool. Restaurant 6 am-9 pm. Ck-out 11 am. Refrigerators avail. Cr cds: DS, MC, V.

⌨ ⌨ ⌨ SC

★ **MAINE STREET MOTEL.** *315 Main St (04609). 207/288-3188; toll-free 800/333-3188. www.mainestreetmotel.com.* 44 rms, 1-2 story. July-Aug: S, D $99-$125; each addl $10; under 16 free; lower rates Apr-June, Sept-Oct. Closed rest of yr. Crib $10. TV; cable (premium). Restaurant adj from 11 am. Ck-out 11 am. Business servs avail. Cr cds: A, DS, MC, V.

⌨ ⌨ ⌨

★★ **PARK ENTRANCE OCEANFRONT MOTEL.** *15 Ocean Dr (04609). 207/288-9703; res 800/288-9703. www.parkentrance.com.* 58 rms, 24 A/C, 2 story, 6 kits. (5 no ovens). Aug: S, D $125-$229; kit. units $199-$299; under 18 free; lower rates early May-July, Sept-late Oct. Closed rest of yr. Crib $6. TV; cable (premium). Heated pool; whirlpool. Complimentary coffee in rms. Restaurant nearby. Ck-out 11 am. Business servs avail. Lawn games. Refrigerators avail. Private patios, balconies. Picnic tables, grills. Overlooks bay, beach. Mooring, dock; fishing pier. Cr cds: A, DS, MC, V.

⌨ ⌨ ⌨ ⌨ ⌨

★ **VILLAGER MOTEL.** *207 Main St (04609). 207/288-3211; fax 207/288-2270. www.acadia.net/villager.* 52 rms, 2 story. July-Aug: S, D $89-$128; each addl $10; under 5 free; lower rates May-June, Sept-late Oct. Closed rest of yr. Crib $5. TV; cable. Heated pool. Complimentary coffee in lobby. Restaurant nearby. Ck-out 11 am. Cr cds: A, MC, V.

⌨ ⌨ ⌨

★★ **WONDER VIEW INN.** *50 Eden St (10801). 207/288-3358; fax 207/288-2005; toll-free 888/439-8439. www. wonderviewinn.com.* 79 rms, 10 with shower only, 26 A/C, 1-2 story. July-Labor Day: S, D $119-$179; each addl $10; under 12 free; lower rates early May-June, Labor Day-Oct. Closed rest of yr. Crib $10. TV; cable. Pool. Complimentary coffee in lobby. Restaurant 7-10 am, 5-9 pm. Bar from 5 pm. Ck-out 11 am. Business servs avail. Refrigerator avail. Balconies. Picnic tables. Cr cds: A, DS, MC, V.

⌨ ⌨ ⌨

Hotels

★★ **ACADIA INN.** *98 Eden St (04609). 207/288-3500; fax 207/288-8424; res 800/638-3636. www.acadiainn.com.* 95 rms, 3 story. Late June-Aug: S, D $109-$175; under 10 free; lower rates early Apr-late June, Sept-mid-Nov. Closed rest of yr. Crib free. TV; cable (premium). Heated pool; whirlpool. Playground. Complimentary continental bkfst. Restaurant nearby. Ck-out 11 am. Coin lndry. Meeting rms. Business servs avail. In-rm modem link. Gift shop. Refrigerators avail. Picnic tables. Cr cds: A, DS, MC, V.
D ⊠ ⊠ ⊠ SC

★★★ **BAR HARBOR HOTEL - BLUENOSE INN.** *90 Eden St (04609). 207/288-3348; fax 207/288-2183; toll-free 800/445-4077. www.bluenoseinn.com.* 49 rms, 48 suites. 3-4 story. July-Aug: S, D $189-$385; suites $385-$425; each addl $25; lower rates Apr-June, Sept-Oct. Closed rest of yr. TV; cable (premium), VCR avail. 2 heated pools, 1 indoor; whirlpool. Complimentary coffee in rms. Restaurant 7-10:30 am, 5:30-9:30 pm. Rm serv. Bar 5-11 pm. Ck-out 11 am, ck-in 3 pm. Coin lndry. Meeting rm. Business servs avail. Bellhops. Gift shop. Whale watching, sailing, kayaking, hiking, bicycle riding nearby. Exercise equipt. Refrigerators; fireplaces, bathrm phones in suites only. Balconies. Ocean view. Totally nonsmoking. Cr cds: A, DS, MC, V.
D ⊠ ⊠ ⊠ ⊠

★★★ **BAR HARBOR INN.** *Newport Dr (04609). 207/288-3351; fax 207/288-5296; res 800/248-3351. barharborinn .com.* 153 rms, 2 story. July-Aug: S, D $175-$319; each addl $20; suites (to 4 persons) $319-$415; under 16 free; lower rates Apr-June, Sept-Nov. Crib $15. TV; cable (premium), VCR avail (movies). Heated pool. Complimentary continental bkfst. Coffee in rms. Restaurant (see READING ROOM). Rm serv. Bar 11:30 am-closing. Ck-out 11 am. Meeting rms. Business servs avail. Bellhops. Valet parking. Sundries. Gift shop. Exercise equipt. Health club privileges. Some refrigerators. Some balconies. On beach. Pier; sailing cruises on 19th-century replica schooner. Cr cds: A, D, DS, MC, V.
D ⊠ ⊠ ⊠ ⊠ ⊠

★★★ **THE BAYVIEW.** *111 Eden St (04609). 207/288-5861; fax 207/288-3173; toll-free 800/356-3585. www. thebarharbor.com/bayview.* 33 rms, 2-3 story, 6 kit. town homes. No elvtr. Mid-May-mid-Oct: S, D $135-$260; each addl $20; ages 12-18 $10; under 12 free; town homes $185-$450; lower rates mid-May-late June, Labor Day-late Oct. Closed rest of yr. TV; cable (premium), VCR avail. Heated pool; poolside serv. Complimentary bkfst buffet; afternoon refreshments. Restaurant 7-10 am; 5-8:30 pm. Bar 11-1 am. Ck-out 11 am. Meeting rms. Business servs avail. Airport transportation. Lighted tennis privileges. Exercise equipt. Massage. Lawn games. Whirlpool in town homes. Private patios, balconies. Situated on 8 wooded acres with water frontage on Frenchmen Bay. Former estate; Georgian country house furnished with antiques. Fireplaces. Library. Gardens. Cr cds: A, DS, MC, V.
D ⊠ ⊠ ⊠ ⊠ ⊠ ⊠

Resort

★★★ **BAR HARBOR REGENCY.** *123 Eden St (04609). 207/288-9723; fax 207/288-3089; res 800/465-4329. barharborholidayinn.com.* 221 rms, 4 story. Late June-late Aug: S, D $165-$205; suites, kit. units $250-$500; under 19 free; lower rates May-late June, late Aug-Oct. Closed rest of yr. Crib avail. TV; cable. Heated pool; poolside serv. Supervised children's activities (July-Aug). Coffee in rms. Restaurant 6:30 am-10 pm; hrs vary off season. Rm serv. Bar 11 am-midnight. Ck-out noon. Meeting rms. Business servs avail. Bellhops. Gift shop. Lighted tennis. Putting green. Lawn games. Exercise equipt; sauna. Refrigerators. Balconies. On ocean; marina, dockage. Whale watch tours. Cr cds: A, D, DS, MC, V.
D ⊠ ⊠ ⊠ ⊠ ⊠ ⊠ ⊠

B&Bs/Small Inns

★★ **BLACK FRIAR INN.** *10 Summer St (04609). 207/288-5091; fax 207/288-4197. www.blackfriar.com.* 7 rms, 3 story. No rm phones. Mid-June-Columbus Day: S, D $105-$150; lower rates May-mid-June, Columbus Day-Nov. Children over 12 yrs only. TV in sun rm; VCR avail (free movies). Complimentary full bkfst; afternoon refreshments. Ck-out 11 am, ck-in after 4 pm. Victorian decor; antiques. Totally nonsmoking. Cr cds: DS, MC, V.
⊠ ⊠ SC

★★ **CANTERBURY COTTAGE.** *12 Roberts Ave (04609). 207/288-2112; fax 207/288-5681. www.canterburycottage.com.* 4 rms, 3 with shower only, 2 story. No A/C. No rm phones. Mid-June-mid-Oct: S, D $95-$115; each addl $15; hols 2-day min (in season); lower rates rest of yr. Children over 8 yrs only. Cable TV in common rm; VCR. Complimentary full bkfst; afternoon refreshments. Restaurant nearby. Ck-out 11 am, ck-in 2 pm. Built in 1900. Totally nonsmoking. Cr cds: MC, V.
⊠ ⊠

★★★ **CASTELMAINE.** *39 Holland Ave (04609). 207/288-4563; fax 207/288-4525; toll-free 800/338-4563. www. castlemaineinn.com.* 17 rms, 3 story, 4 suites. No rm phones. July-Aug: S, D $98-$250; each addl $25; suites $155-$175; lower rates May-June, Sept-Oct. Closed rest of yr. TV; cable, VCR (movies $2). Complimentary continental bkfst. Restaurant nearby. Ck-out 11 am, ck-in 2 pm. Some refrigerators, whirlpools; many fireplaces. Many balconies. Rambling, Victorian-style house (1886), once the summer residence of Austro-Hungarian ambassador; parlor, antiques. Totally nonsmoking. Cr cds: MC, V.
⊠ ⊠ ⊠

★★★ **CLEFTSTONE MANOR.** *92 Eden St (04609). 207/288-4951; fax 207/288-2089; toll-free 888/288-4951. www.cleftstone.com.* 16 rms, 3 story. No rm phones. Mid-June-Oct: S, D $100-$200; lower rates May-mid-June. Closed rest of yr. Children over 8 yrs only. Complimentary full bkfst; afternoon, evening refreshments. Ck-out 11 am, ck-in 3 pm. Some fireplaces, balconies. Victorian mansion (1894) once owned by Blair family of Washington, DC. Antiques. Victorian gardens. Totally nonsmoking. Cr cds: MC, V.

★★ **GRAYCOTE INN.** *40 Holland Ave (04609). 207/288-3044; fax 207/288-2719. www.graycoteinn.com.* 12 rms, 3 story, 2 suites. Some A/C. No rm phones. Mid-June-Columbus Day: S $75-$125; D $83-$130; suites $200; each addl $20; lower rates rest of yr. Children over 9 yrs only. TV in suites. Complimentary full bkfst; afternoon refreshments. Ck-out 10:30 am, ck-in 3 pm. Some balconies. Near ocean. Restored 19th-century Victorian cottage; 5 fireplaces, antiques, parlor. Totally nonsmoking. Cr cds: A, DS, MC, V.

★★ **HATFIELD BED & BREAKFAST.** *20 Roberts Ave (04609). 207/288-9655. www.hatfieldinn.com.* 6 rms, 3 story. A/C. No elvtr. No rm phones. S, D $65-$125 (2-night min, hol wkends 3-night min). Children over 10 yrs only. Complimentary full bkfst; afternoon refreshments. Restaurant nearby. Ck-out 11 am, ck-in 2 pm. Luggage handling. X-country ski 1 mi. Built in 1895; antiques. Totally nonsmoking. Cr cds: DS, MC, V.

★★ **HEARTHSIDE BED & BREAKFAST.** *7 High St (04609). 207/288-4533; fax 207/288-9818. www.hearthsideinn.com.* 9 rms, 4 with shower only, 3 story. No rm phones. Mid-June-mid-Oct: S $85-$120; D $90-$135; lower rates rest of yr. Children over 10 yrs only. Complimentary full bkfst. Restaurant nearby. Ck-out 11 am, ck-in 1 pm. X-country ski 5 mi. Some in-rm whirlpools, fireplaces. Former doctor's house (1907); antiques. Parlor. Totally nonsmoking. Cr cds: DS, MC, V.

★★★ **INN AT BAY LEDGE.** *1385 Sand Point Rd (04609). 207/288-4204; fax 207/288-5573. www.innatbayledge.com.* 10 rms, 2 story. No A/C. No rm phones. Mid-June-mid-Oct: S $135-$250; D $200-$325; each addl $25; lower rates May-mid-June, Oct. Closed rest of yr. Children over 15 yrs only. TV in sitting rm; cable, VCR (free movies). Heated pool. Complimentary full bkfst; afternoon refreshments. Ck-out 11 am, ck-in 3 pm. Sauna, steam rm. Some in-rm whirlpools. Built 1907; antiques, country decor. Atop rocky hill overlooking Frenchman Bay; surrounded by pine forest. Near Acadia National Park. Totally nonsmoking. Cr cds: MC, V.

★★★ **MANOR HOUSE INN.** *106 West St (04609). 207/288-3759; fax 207/288-2974; toll-free 800/437-0088. www.barharbormanorhouse.com.* 14 rms, 7 A/C, 3 story, 5 suites, 2 cottages. No rm phones. July-Columbus Day: S, D $75-$155; each addl $20; suites $105-$175; lower rates mid-Apr-June, after Columbus Day-mid-Nov. Closed rest of yr. Children over 10 yrs only. TV in sitting rm, cottages; cable. Complimentary full bkfst; afternoon refreshments.

Restaurant nearby. Ck-out 10:30 am, ck-in 3 pm. Lawn games. Picnic tables. Near ocean. Restored historic Victorian mansion (1887); period antiques, library. Some fireplaces. Totally nonsmoking. Cr cds: A, DS, MC, V.

★★ **MAPLES INN.** *16 Roberts Ave (04609). 207/288-3443; fax 207/288-0356. www.maplesinn.com.* 6 rms, 3 story, 1 suite. 1 A/C. No rm phones. Mid-June-mid-Oct: S $70-$115; D $90-$120; each addl $15; suite $150; higher rates Memorial Day wkend; lower rates mid-Apr-mid-June, mid-Oct-early Dec. Closed rest of yr. Children over 8 yrs only. Complimentary full bkfst. Restaurant nearby. Ck-out 11 am, ck-in 2 pm. X-country ski 5 mi. Some fireplaces. Balconies. Restored, turn-of-the-century Victorian inn. Totally nonsmoking. Cr cds: DS, MC, V.

★★★ **MIRA MONTE INN & SUITES.** *69 Mt Desert St (04609). 207/288-4263; fax 207/288-3115; toll-free 800/553-5109. www.miramonte.com.* 16 rms in 2 bldgs, 2 story, 2 suites. Mid-June-mid-Oct: S, D $105-$175; each addl $15; suites $205; lower rates May-mid-June. Closed rest of yr. TV; cable. Complimentary full bkfst buffet; afternoon refreshments. Restaurant nearby. Ck-out 11 am, ck-in 2 pm. Business servs avail. Lawn games. Many fireplaces. Balconies. Restored Victorian home (1864) on 2½ acres; wrap-around porch, two formal gardens, library, period furnishings. Totally nonsoking. Cr cds: A, D, DS, MC, V.

★★ **THE RIDGEWAY INN.** *11 High St (04609). 207/288-9682; toll-free 800/360-5226. theridewayinn .com.* 5 rms, 1 with shower only, 3 story. No rm phones. Mid-June-Columbus Day: S, D $70-$150; each addl $15; suites $125-$150; lower rates May-mid-June, Columbus Day-late Oct. Closed rest of yr. Children over 8 yrs only. Complimentary full bkfst; afternoon refreshments. Restaurant nearby. Ck-out 11 am, ck-in 3 pm. 2 blks from ocean. Built 1884; many antiques. Fireplace in parlor and dining rm. Totally nonsmoking. Cr cds: MC, V.

★★ **STRATFORD HOUSE INN.** *45 Mt Desert St (04609). 207/288-5189; fax 207/288-4184. www.stratfordhouseinn.com.* 10 rms, 2 share bath, 3 story. July-mid-Sept: S, D $75-$150; each addl $15; under 5 free; lower rates mid May-June, mid-Sept-mid-Oct. Closed rest of yr. TV. Complimentary continental bkfst 8-10 am. Ck-out 11 am, ck-in 1 pm. Fireplaces. Music rm. Built by publisher of Louisa May Alcott's "Little Women" (1900); English Tudor design modeled after Shakespeare's house in Stratford-on-Avon, original Jacobean furniture. Totally nonsmoking. Cr cds: DS, MC, V.

★★★ **THORNHEDGE INN.** *47 Mt Desert St (04609).* *207/288-5398; res 877/288-5398.* 13 rms, 3 story. 1 A/C. Mid-June-mid-Oct: S, D $80-$140; lower rates mid-May-mid-June. Closed rest of yr. TV; cable. Continental bkfst; evening refreshments. Ck-out 11 am, ck-in noon. Some fireplaces. Queen Anne-style structure built by publisher of Louisa May Alcott's "Little Women" as a summer cottage (1900). Totally nonsmoking. Cr cds: MC, V.
🖼️ 🔥

Cottage Colony

★ **EMERY'S COTTAGES ON THE SHORE.** *181 Sand Point Rd (04609). 207/288-3432. www.emeryscottages.com.* 21 cottages, 13 kits. (oven in 6). No A/C. No rm phones. Late June-Labor Day: S, D $36-$114; kit. units $90-$110; wkly rates; lower rates early May-late June, Labor Day-Oct. Closed rest of yr. Crib free. TV; cable (premium). Complimentary coffee. Ck-out 10 am, ck-in 2 pm. Coin lndry. Refrigerators. Picnic tables, grills. On Frenchman Bay. Cr cds: A, DS, MC, V.
🔥 🔥

Restaurants

★★ **124 COTTAGE STREET.** *124 Cottage St (04609). 207/288-4383.* Continental menu. Specializes in fresh fish, desserts. Salad bar. Hrs: 5-10 pm; early-bird dinner 5-6 pm. Closed Nov-May. Res accepted. Bar. Dinner $8.95-$18.95. Child's menu. Outdoor dining. In restored, turn-of-the-century cottage. Cr cds: A, C, MC, V.

★ **FREDDIE'S ROUTE 66.** *21 Cottage St (04609). 207/288-3708.* Specializes in prime rib, lobster, roast pork. Hrs: 4:30-10 pm; early-bird dinner 4:30-6 pm. Closed mid Oct-mid-May. Res accepted. Bar. Dinner $7.95-$15.95. Child's menu. 1950s-theme decor. Family-owned. Cr cds: A, C, D, DS, ER, MC, V.
D

★★★ **GEORGE'S.** *7 Stephens Ln (04609). 207/288-4505. www.georgesbarharbor.com.* Mediterranean menu. Specializes in grilled fish, lobster, lamb. Own baking. Hrs: 5:30-10 pm; hrs vary after Labor Day. Closed Nov-Memorial Day. Res accepted. No A/C. Bar. Wine list. Dinner $12-$24. Prix fixe: dinner $33-$36. Child's menu. Pianist or guitarist Wed-Sat. Outdoor dining. In restored mid-1800s home; near ocean. Totally nonsmoking. Cr cds: A, C, D, DS, MC, V.

★ **ISLAND CHOWDER HOUSE.** *38 Cottage St (04609). 207/288-4905.* Specializes in lobster, chowder. Own desserts. Hrs: 11 am-10 pm; early-bird dinner 11 am-6 pm. Closed Nov-Apr. Res accepted. Bar. Lunch $4.29-$9.99, dinner $8.99-$19.99. Child's menu. Pub decor with model train operating in dining rm. Cr cds: A, DS, MC, V.
D

★★ **MAGGIE'S CLASSIC SCALES.** *6 Summer St (04609). 207/288-9007.* Specializes in fresh local seafood. Own desserts. Hrs: 5-10 pm. Closed Oct 16-3rd wk in June. Res accepted. Bar. Dinner $12-$21. Totally nonsmoking. Cr cds: C, DS, MC, V.

★ **MIGUEL'S MEXICAN.** *51 Rodick St (04609). 207/288-5117.* Mexican menu. Specializes in tostadas, enchiladas, fajitas. Hrs: 5-10 pm. Closed mid-Nov-Mar. Bar. Complete meals: dinner $5.95-$13.95. Child's menu. Outdoor dining. Mexican atmosphere; artifacts, tiled floors. Braille menu. Cr cds: MC, V.
D

★★ **QUARTER DECK.** *1 Main St (04609). 207/288-5292.* Specialties: lobster crepe a la Reine, sole Marguery hollandaise au supreme. Hrs: 11 am-10 pm; early-bird dinner 4-6 pm. Closed Nov-Apr. Serv bar. Lunch $3.95-$10.95, dinner $10.95-$19.95. Outdoor dining. Totally nonsmoking. Cr cds: A, D, DS, MC, V.
D

★★★ **READING ROOM.** *Newport Dr (04609). 207/288-3351. www.barharborinn.com.* Specializes in fresh local seafood. Own baking. Hrs: 7-10:30 am, 5:30-9:30 pm; Sun brunch 11:30 am-2:30 pm. Closed mid-Nov-Easter. Res accepted. Bar from 4:30 pm. Wine list. A la carte entrees: bkfst $1.50-$9.50. Buffet: bkfst $7.50-9.50. Dinner $15.95-$24.95. Sun brunch $17.95. Child's menu. Pianist or harpist. Valet parking. Panoramic view of harbor and docks. Cr cds: A, C, D, DS, ER, MC, V.
D

★★ **RINEHART DINING PAVILLION.** *Highbrook Rd (04609). 207/288-5663.* Specializes in prime rib, seafood. Hrs: 7-10 am, 5-9 pm. Closed Nov-Apr. Bar. Buffet: bkfst $7. Dinner $10.95-$19.95. Child's menu. Parking. Octagonal building on hill; overlooks harbor. Cr cds: DS, V.
D

Unrated Dining Spot

FISHERMAN'S LANDING. *35 West St (04609). 207/288-4632.* Specializes in lobster, seafood. Hrs: noon-9 pm. Closed Oct-May. No A/C. Bar. Lunch, dinner $1.50-$9. Outdoor deck dining. Built over water. Lobster tanks; select own lobster. Blackboard menu. Family-owned. Cr cds: MC, V.
D

Bath

See also Boothbay Harbor, Brunswick, Freeport

Pop 9,799 **Elev** 13 ft **Area code** 207 **Zip** 04530
Information Chamber of Commerce of the Bath-Brunswick Region, 45 Front St; 207/443-9751
Web www.midcoastmaine.com

For more than two centuries Bath has been a shipbuilding center on the west bank of the Kennebec River. The Bath Iron Works, which dates back to 1833, began building ships in 1889. It has produced destroyers, cruisers, a battleship, pleasure craft, and steamers, and now also produces patrol frigates. Altogether, Bath has launched more than 4,000 ships from its shores, and launching a ship today is still a great event.

Many fine old mansions, built when Bath was a great seaport, still stand. A restored 19th-century business district, waterfront park, and public landing are also part of the city.

What to See and Do

Fort Popham Memorial. Construction of the fort began in 1861. Never finished, it was garrisoned in 1865-1866 and remains an impressive masonry structure with gun emplacements. Picnic tables (no garbage receptacles). (May-Sept, daily) 16 mi S on ME 209 in Popham Beach. Phone 207/389-1335.

Maine Maritime Museum. Maritime History Building has exhibits of maritime art and artifacts, shipmodels and paintings. Tours of original shipyard buildings, demonstrations of seafaring techniques (seasonal); waterfront picnic area and playground. Museum store. (Daily; closed Jan 1, Thanksgiving, Dec 25) 243 Washington St, 2 mi S of US 1, located on Kennebec River. Phone 207/443-1316. ¢¢

Popham Colony. A picturesque drive. In 1607 the first American vessel, the *Virginia*, was built here by colonists who shortly thereafter returned to England, many of them in the ship they had built. On the hilltop nearby is Fort Baldwin, built during WWI. A 70-ft tower offers a panoramic view of the coast and the Kennebec River. 16 mi S on ME 209 on Sabino Head. **FREE**

State parks.

Popham Beach. Swimming, tidal pools (Mid-Apr-Nov), surfing; fishing; picnicking. (Daily) Standard fees. 12 mi S on ME 209. Phone 207/389-1335. ¢

Reid. Swimming, saltwater lagoon, bathhouse, fishing; picnic facilities, concession. (Daily) Standard fees. 1 mi E on US 1 to Woolwich, then 13 mi SE on ME 127 to Georgetown, then SE. Phone 207/371-2303. ¢¢

Motel/Motor Lodge

★★ **HOLIDAY INN BATH.** *139 Richardson St (04530). 207/443-9741; fax 207/442-8281. www.holiday-inn.com.* 141 rms, 4 story. Late June-early Oct: S, D $85-$119; each addl $10; under 19 free; lower rates rest of yr. Crib free. Pet accepted. TV; cable, premium. Heated pool; whirlpool. Complimentary coffee in rms. Restaurant 6 am-2 pm, 5-10 pm. Bar 11-1 am; Sun from noon; entertainment Wed-Sun. Ck-out noon. Meeting rm. Business servs avail. In-rm modem link. Valet serv. Sundries. Coin lndry. Exercise equipt; sauna. Refrigerators. Cr cds: A, DS, MC, V.

[D] [🛂] [≈] [🏃] [⇲] [🐾] [SC]

B&Bs/Small Inns

★★ **FAIRHAVEN INN.** *118 N Bath Rd (04530). 207/443-4391; fax 207/443-6412; toll-free 888/443-4391. www. mainecoast.com/fairhaveninn.* 8 rms, 2 share bath, 2 story. No A/C. No rm phones. Mid-May-Oct: S, D $80-$140; each addl $15; wkly rates; lower rates rest of yr. Crib free. Complimentary full bkfst. Ck-out 11 am, ck-in 4-6 pm. Meeting rms. X-country ski on site. Picnic tables. Federalist house (1790) with tavern rm, library, antique and country furnishings; on 16 acres on Kennebec River. Cr cds: DS, MC, V.

[⇲] [≈] [🐾]

★★★ **GALEN C. MOSES HOUSE.** *1009 Washington St (04530). 207/442-8771; fax 207/442-0808; toll-free 888/442-8771. www.galenmoses.com.* 4 rms, 2 shower only. No rm phones. Mid-May-Oct: S, D $119-$149; wkends 2-day min (in season); lower rates rest of yr. Children over 12 yrs only. Cable TV in common rm, VCR avail (movies). Complimentary full bkfst; afternoon refreshments. Ck-out 11 am, ck-in 3-8 pm. Picnic tables, grills. Built in 1874; antiques. Italian bldg with Victorian interior; stained glass windows. Totally nonsmoking. Cr cds: A, DS, MC, V.

[♿] [⚡] [⇲] [🐾]

Restaurants

★★ **KRISTINA'S.** *160 Centre St (04530). 207/442-8577.* Hrs: 8 am-9 pm (July-Labor Day); Sat, Sun brunch 9 am-2 pm. Varied hrs off season. Closed Thanksgiving, Dec 25; also Jan, Mon off season. Res accepted. Bar. Bkfst $3.25-$7.50, lunch $4.95-$8.95, dinner $10.95-$15.95. Sat, Sun brunch $3.50-$9.25. Child's menu. Patio dining. Bakery on premises. Cr cds: DS, MC, V.

[D]

★ **TASTE OF MAINE.** *US 1, Woolwich (04579). 207/443-4554. www.tasteofmaine.com.* Specializes in lobster, seafood, steak. Hrs: 11 am-9 pm. Serv bar. Lunch, dinner $2.95-$24.95. Child's menu. Gift shop. Outdoor dining. Overlooks fork of Kennebec River. Cr cds: A, D, DS, MC, V.

[D]

Baxter State Park

See also Millinocket

(18 mi NW of Millinocket via park roads)

While serving as a legislator and as governor of Maine, Percival P. Baxter urged creation of a wilderness park around Mount Katahdin—Maine's highest peak (5,267 feet). Rebuffed but not defeated, Baxter bought the land with his own money and deeded to the state of Maine a 201,018-acre park "to be forever left in its natural, wild state." The park can be reached from Greenville via paper company roads, from Millinocket via ME 157, or from Patten via ME 159.

The Park Authority operates the following campgrounds: Katahdin Stream, Abol and Nesowadnehunk, Roaring Brook (Roaring Brook Road), Chimney Pond (by trail 3.3 miles beyond Roaring Brook), Russell Pond (Wassataquoik Valley, seven miles by trail beyond Roaring Brook), South Branch Pond (at outlet of Lower South Branch Pond), Trout Brook Farm (Trout Brook Crossing). There are cabins ($17/person/night) at Daicey Pond off Nesowadnehunk Road and at Kidney Pond. All areas except Chimney, Kidney, and Daicey ponds have tent space, and all areas except Trout Brook Farm, Kidney, and Daicey ponds have lean-tos ($6/person/night), water (unprotected, should be purified), and primitive facilities (no indoor plumbing, no running water; some springs); bunkhouses ($7/night) at some campgrounds. Under age seven free throughout the park.

Reservations should be made by mail (and paid in full) in advance. For detailed information contact the Reservation Clerk, Baxter State Park, 64 Balsam Dr, Millinocket 04462. Swimming, fishing, canoes for rent at Russell Pond, South Branch Pond, Daicey Pond, Kidney Pond, and Trout Brook farm.

The park is open for camping mid-May–mid-October. No pets or motorcycles are permitted. Vehicles exceeding seven feet wide, nine feet high, or 22 feet long will not be admitted. For further information contact Park Manager, 64 Balsam Dr, Millinocket 04462; phone 207/723-5140. Nonresident vehicle fee ¢¢¢

Belfast

See also Bucksport, Camden, Searsport

Settled 1770 **Pop** 6,355 **Elev** 103 ft **Area code** 207
Zip 04915
Information Chamber of Commerce, 17 Main St, PO Box 58; 207/338-5900
Web www.belfastmaine.org

Belfast, named for the city in Northern Ireland, was settled in 1770 by Irish and Scottish immigrants. An old seaport on the west shore of Penobscot Bay, Belfast is also a hub of small boat traffic to the bay islands. It is the seat of Waldo County, with sardine canneries, potato processing, window making, and printing as its major industries.

What to See and Do

Lake St. George State Park. More than 360 acres. Swimming, bathhouse, lifeguard, fishing, boating (ramp, rentals); snow-mobiling permitted, picnicking, camping. (Mid-May-mid-Oct) Standard fees. 19 mi W on ME 3, near Montville. Phone 207/589-4255.

Special Event

Belfast Bay Festival. City Park. Parade, concerts, carnival. July. Phone 207/338-5719.

Motels/Motor Lodges

★★ **BELFAST HARBOR INN.** *RR5 Box 5230, Rte 1 (04915).* 207/338-2740; fax 207/338-5205; toll-free 800/545-8576. *belfastharborinn.com.* 61 rms, 2 story. July-Aug: S, D $79-$139; each addl $10; under 12 free; wkly rates; lower rates rest of yr. Crib free. Pet accepted; $5. TV; cable (premium). Pool. Complimentary continental bkfst. Restaurant 11 am-9 pm. Ck-out 11 am. Meeting rm. Business servs avail. Downhill/x-country ski 15 mi. Balconies. Picnic tables. Overlooks Penobscot Bay. Cr cds: A, DS, MC, V.
D 🐾 🖾 🛥 🔥

★ **GULL MOTEL.** *US Rte 1, Searsport Ave (04915).* 207/338-4030. 14 rms, 2 story. July-Labor Day: S, D $39-$79; each addl $5, under 12 $3; lower rates rest of yr. Crib $5. Pet accepted, some restrictions. TV; cable. Restaurant nearby. Ck-out 11 am. Overlooks bay. Cr cds: MC, V.
🐾

★ **WONDERVIEW COTTAGES.** *RR 5 Box 5339 (04915). 207/338-1455. www.maineguide.com/belfast/wonderview.* 20 kit. cottages, 1 condo. No A/C. July-Labor Day, wkly: kit. cottages for 2-6, $475-$850; lower rates Apr-June, Sept-late Oct. Closed rest of yr. Crib free. Pet accepted. TV; cable. Playground. Restaurant nearby. Ck-out 10:30 am. Lawn games. Fireplaces. Screened porches. Picnic tables, grills. Private beach on Penobscot Bay. Cr cds: DS, MC, V.
D 🐾 🔥 🛥

B&B/Small Inn

★★ **BELFAST BAY MEADOWS INN.** *192 Northport Ave (04915).* 207/338-5715; res 800/335-2370. *www. baymeadowsinn.com.* 19 rms, 1-3 story. July-Aug: S, D $85-$165; each addl $15; lower rates rest of yr. Crib free. Pet accepted. TV in some rms, sitting rm; cable, VCR avail (free movies). Playground. Complimentary full bkfst. Ck-out 11 am, ck-in 3:30-6:30 pm. Meeting rm. ≠Business servs avail. Refrigerators avail. Turn-of-the-century country inn; antiques. Overlooks bay. Totally nonsmoking. Cr cds: A, DS, MC, V.
🐾 🖾 🔥

Restaurant

★★ **DARBY'S.** *155 High St (04915).* 207/338-2339. Eclectic menu. Specialties: pad Thai, mahogany duck. Own desserts. Hrs: 11 am-3:30 pm, 5-9:30 pm. Closed Easter, Dec 25. Res accepted. Bar. Lu nch $3.95-$10.95, dinner $6.95-$16.95. Child's menu. Street parking. Cr cds: DS, MC, V.
D

Bethel

Settled 1774 **Pop** 2,329 **Elev** 700 ft **Area code** 207
Zip 04217
Information Chamber of Commerce, PO Box 1247; 207/824-2282 or 800/442-5826
Web www.bethelmaine.com

Bethel, on both banks of the winding Androscoggin River, is built on the rolling Oxford Hills and is backed by the rough foothills of the White Mountains. In addition to being a year-round resort, it's an educational and wood products center. One of Maine's leading preparatory schools, Gould Academy (founded 1836), is located here.

What to See and Do

Dr. Moses Mason House Museum. (1813) Restored home of prominent congressman who served during administration of Andrew Jackson. Antique furnishings, early American murals. (July-Labor Day, Sat and Sun afternoons; rest of yr, Mon-Fri, also by appt) Broad St, in National Historic District. Phone 207/824-2908. ¢

Grafton Notch State Park. The Appalachian Trail passes through the notch; interpretive displays, scenic view, picnicking; fishing. (Mid-May-mid-Oct) Approx 9 mi NW via US 2, ME 26. Phone 207/824-2912. ¢

Ski areas.

Carter's X-C Ski Center. 1,000 acres with 65 km of groomed x-country trails. Rentals, lessons; lounge, shop; two lodges. (Nov-Mar, daily) Middle Intervale Rd. Phone 207/539-4848. ¢¢

Sunday River Ski Resort. Nine quad, four triple, two double chairlifts (incl four high-speed detachables, one surface lift); patrol, school, rentals, ski shop; snowmaking; cafeterias, restaurants; bars. 127 runs; longest run three mi; vertical drop 2,340 ft. (Early Oct-mid-May, daily) 100 x-country trails adj. Mountain biking (May-Labor Day, daily; Labor Day-late Oct, wkends). 6 mi NE on US 2. Phone 207/824-3000. ¢¢¢¢

Swimming, picnicking, camping, boating, fishing. Songo Lake in Bethel; Christopher Lake in Bryant Pond; North and South ponds in Locke Mills; Littlefield beaches and Stony Brook campgrounds. E on ME 26.

White Mountain National Forest. (see under NEW HAMPSHIRE). More than 49,000 acres of this forest extend into Maine southwest of here. Birches and sugar maples turn fall into a season of breathtaking color. Fishing; hiking, rock hounding, camping (fee). For information contact the Supervisor, 719 Main St, PO Box 638, Laconia, NH 03247. Phone 603/528-8721.

Motels/Motor Lodges

★ **INN AT THE ROSTAY.** *186 Mayville Rd; US 2 (04217). 207/824-3111; fax 207/824-0482; toll-free 888/754-0072. www.rostay.com.* 18 rms, 10 with shower only. No A/C. No rm phones. Mid-Dec-mid-Apr: S $40-$98; D $45-$110; each addl $5; under 12 free; lower rates rest of yr. TV; cable. Restaurant opp open 24 hrs. Ck-out 11 am. Downhill ski 5 mi; x-country ski 4 mi. Some refrigerators, microwaves. Some balconies. Cr cds: A, DS, MC, V.

📅 🐾 ⚡ 🎿 ➤ 🔁 🔥

★★ **NORSEMAN INN.** *134 Mayville Rd (04217). 207/824-2002; fax 207/824-0640. www.norsemaninn.com.* 31 rms, 22 A/C, 2 story. No rm phones. S $45-$98; D $52-$118; each addl $10; higher rates: hol wkends, fall foliage, winter. Crib free. TV; cable. Complimentary continental bkfst. Restaurant opp 7 am-9 pm. Ck-out 10:30 am. Coin lndry. Downhill ski 5 mi; x-country ski on site. Game rm. Lawn games. Some balconies. Picnic tables. Cr cds: DS, MC, V.

📅 🐾 ➤ ✈ 🔁 🔥

★★ **RIVER VIEW.** *357 Mayville Rd (04217). 207/824-2808; fax 207/824-6808. www.riverviewresort.com.* 32 kit. units (2-bedrm). Mid-Dec-mid-Apr: D $89-$139; each addl $20; suites $150-$250; 2-day min; higher rates hols; lower rates rest of yr. TV; cable (premium). Indoor pool; whirlpool. Playground. Ck-out 10 am. Tennis. Downhill ski 4 mi; x-country ski 3 mi. Sauna. Game rm. Lawn games. Picnic tables, grills. On river. Cr cds: A, DS, MC, V.

🐾 🐾 ➤ 🎿 ➤ 🔁 🔥

Resorts

★★ **BETHEL INN AND COUNTRY CLUB.** *On the Common (04217). 207/824-2175; fax 207/824-2233; toll-free 800/654-0125. www.bethelinn.com.* 60 rms in 5-bldg complex, 40 2-bedrm townhouses. No A/C. May-Oct, Dec-Mar: S $99-$149; D $200-$300; each addl $55; MAP: suites $90-$175; EP: townhouses $79-$129/person; lower rates rest of yr. Pet accepted. TV; cable, VCR avail. Heated pool; whirlpool, poolside serv. Supervised child's activities (July 7-Labor Day); ages 5-12. Dining rm 7:30-9:30 am, 11:30 am-3 pm, 5:30-9 pm. Bars; entertainment. Ck-out 11 am, ck-in 2 pm. Meeting rms. Business servs avail. Gift shop. Tennis. 18-hole golf, greens fee $35-$40, pro, putting green, driving range. Canoes, sailboats. Downhill ski 7 mi; x-country ski on site. Exercise equipt; saunas. Massage. Lawn games. Cr cds: A, C, D, DS, MC, V.

📅 🐾 🐾 🎿 ➤ 🔁 ⛷ 🏃 🚶

★★★ **GRAND SUMMIT.** *Sunday River Access Rd (04217). 207/824-3500; fax 207/824-3993; toll-free 800/543-2754. www.grandsummitresorts.com.* 230 rms, 4 story, 150 kit. units. Mid-Dec-mid-Apr: S, D $80-$285; each addl $10; kits. $95-$440; family, wkend, hol, wkly rates; ski plan; lower rates rest of yr. Crib $10. TV; cable, VCR avail. Heated pool; whirlpool, poolside serv. Supervised children's activities (mid-Dec-Apr); ages 6 wks-12 yrs. Restaurant 7-11 am, noon-3 pm, 5-10 pm. Bar; entertainment (in season). Ck-out 10:30 am. Coin lndry. Meeting rms. Business servs avail. Valet serv. Concierge. Gift shop. Lighted tennis. 18-hole golf privileges. Downhill/x-country ski on site. Exercise equipt; sauna. Game rm. Microwaves avail. Lawn games. Some balconies. Cr cds: A, C, D, DS, MC, V.

📅 🐾 🎿 🍴 🏃 ➤ 🔁 🔁 🔥

B&B/Small Inn

★★ **BRIAR LEA INN & RESTAURANT.** *150 Mayville Rd (04217). 207/824-4717; fax 207/824-7121; toll-free 877/311-1299. briarleainnrestaurant.com.* 6 rms, 3 with shower only. No A/C. No rm phones. Jan-Apr, mid-Sept-mid-Oct: S $79; D $89-$99; each addl $15; ski plans; wkends, hols (2-day min); higher rates major hols; lower rates rest of yr. Crib $15. Pet accepted, some restrictions. TV in common rm; cable, VCR avail. Complimentary full bkfst. Restaurant 6:30-11 am, 5-9:30 pm; Sun to noon. Serv bar. Ck-out 11 am, ck-in 4 pm. Downhill ski 5 mi; x-country ski on site. Built in 1850s; farmhouse atmosphere; antiques. Cr cds: A, DS, MC, V.

🐾 🐾 🎿 ✈ 🔥 🔁

Restaurant

★ **MOTHER'S.** *43 Main St (04217). 207/824-2589.* Specializes in seafood, chicken, pasta. Own soups. Hrs: 11:30 am-9:30 pm; hrs vary off season. Closed Thanksgiving, Dec 24, 25. Serv bar. Lunch $4.50-$14.50, dinner $6.50-$19. Child's menu. Parking. Outdoor dining. Gothic gingerbread-style house (late 1800s); antiques. Cr cds: C, DS, ER, MC, V.

Bingham

See also Skowhegan

Settled 1785 **Pop** 1,071 **Elev** 371 ft **Area code** 207
Zip 04920

What to See and Do

Wilderness Expeditions. Guided raft trips on the Kennebec, Penobscot, and Dead rivers; also canoe outfitting, guided kayaking and ski tours. (May-Sept, daily) Phone 207/534-7305. ¢¢¢¢

Motel/Motor Lodge

★ **BINGHAM MOTOR INN & SPORTS COMPLEX.** *Rte 201 (04920). 207/672-4135; fax 207/672-4138. www.binghammotorinn.com.* 20 rms, 4 kits. July-Labor Day, hunting season: S $44.86-$48; D $52.34-$58; each addl $5; kit. units $5 addl; wkly; lower rates rest of yr. Crib $5. Pet accepted, some restrictions. TV; cable. Pool. Restaurant nearby. Ck-out 10 am. Downhill ski 3 mi. Lawn games. Some refrigerators. Picnic tables. Cr cds: A, DS, MC, V.

☐ 🐾 🛉 🏖 🏊 ✈ 🏊

Blue Hill

See also Bar Harbor, Ellsworth

Settled 1722 **Pop** 1,941 **Elev** 40 ft **Area code** 207 **Zip** 04614
Information Blue Hill Peninsula Chamber of Commerce, PO Box 520; 207/374-3242
Web www.bluehillme.com

Named for a nearby hill that gives a beautiful view of Mount Desert Island, Blue Hill changed from a thriving seaport to a summer colony known for its crafts and antiques. Mary Ellen Chase, born here in 1887, wrote about Blue Hill in *A Goodly Heritage* and *Mary Peters*.

What to See and Do

Holt House. One of the oldest houses in Blue Hill; now home of the Blue Hill Historical Society. Memorabilia. (Tues, Thurs, Sat afternoons; closed hols) For further information contact the town clerk. Phone 207/326-8250. ¢

Jonathan Fisher House. (1814) House designed and built by town's first minister, who also made most of his own furniture and household articles; paintings and woodcuts by the minister; memorabilia. (June-Oct, Mon-Sat afternoons) On ME 15. Phone 207/374-2844. ¢¢

Rackliffe Pottery. Family manufactures wheel-thrown dinnerware from native red-firing clay. Open workshop. (July-Aug, daily; rest of yr, Mon-Sat; closed hols) Ellsworth Rd. Phone 207/374-2297. **FREE**

Rowantrees Pottery. Manufactures functional pottery and wheel-thrown handcrafted dinnerware. (June-Sept, daily; rest of yr, Mon-Fri; closed hols) Union St. Phone 207/374-5535. **FREE**

Wooden Boat School. (Daily) Naskeag Rd and Brooklyn. Phone 207/359-4651.

Special Event

Blue Hill Fair. Sheep dog trials, agriculture and livestock exhibits; midway, harness racing, crafts. Five days Labor Day wkend. Phone 207/374-3701.

Motel/Motor Lodge

★★ **HERITAGE INN.** *Ellsworth Rd (04614). 207/374-5646. www.bhheritagemotorinn.com.* 23 rms, 2 story. July-Labor Day: S, D $85; each addl $8; kit. unit $115; lower rates rest of yr. Crib $5. TV; cable. Complimentary coffee in rms. Restaurant nearby. Ck-out 11 am. On hillside, overlooking bay. Cr cds: MC, V.

🏊 🔥

B&B/Small Inn

★★★ **BLUE HILL INN.** *Union St (04614). 207/374-2844; fax 207/374-2829; toll-free 800/826-7415. bluehillinn.com.* 12 rms, 3 story. 3 A/C. MAP, July-mid-Oct: S $138; D $185; each addl $50; lower rates rest of yr. Closed mid-May-June, Nov. Closed rest of yr. Complimentary coffee; afternoon refreshments. Dining rm 8-9:30 am, dinner sitting 7 pm (public by res only); closed Mon, Tues. Ck-out 10:30 am, ck-in 2-5 pm. Airport transportation. Fireplaces. Inn since 1840. Antiques. Flower garden. Totally nonsmoking. Cr cds: A, MC, V.

☐ 🛉 🏊 🔥

Restaurant

★★ **JONATHAN'S.** *Main St (04614). 207/374-5226.* Specialties: braised lamb shank, poached Atlantic salmon. Hrs: 5-9:30 pm; off-season hrs vary. Closed Mon (off-season); also most major hols. Res accepted. Liquor, wine, beer. A la carte entrees: dinner $16-$19.50. Street parking. Totally nonsmoking. Cr cds: MC, V.

Boothbay Harbor

See also Damariscotta, Wiscasset

Pop 1,267 **Elev** 16 ft **Area code** 207 **Zip** 04538
Information Boothbay Harbor Region Chamber of Commerce, PO Box 356; 207/633-2353 or 800/266-8422
Web www.boothbayharbor.com

Native Americans were paid 20 beaver pelts for the area encompassing Boothbay Harbor. Today, its protected harbor, a haven for boatmen, is the scene of well-attended regattas several times a summer. Boothbay Harbor, on the peninsula between the Sheepscot and Damariscotta rivers, shares the peninsula and adjacent islands with a dozen other communities, including Boothbay (settled 1630), of which it was once a part.

What to See and Do

Boat trips.

Balmy Days. Makes trips to Monhegan Island (see) with four-hr stopover. (June-Sept, daily) Pier 8, Commercial St. Phone 207/633-2284.

Cap'n Fish's Boat Trips and Deep Sea Fishing. Boats make varied excursions: 1¼- to three-hr trips; puffin, seal, and whale watches; scenic, sunset, and cruises; fall foliage and Kennebec River trips; charters. (Mid-May-Oct; days vary) Pier 1. Phone 207/633-3244. ¢¢¢¢

Novelty. One-hr harbor cruises with stop at Squirrel Island; Night Lights cruises (July-Aug, Tues-Sat). Harbor cruises (Apr-Oct, Daily). Pier 8, Commercial St. Phone 207/633-2284.

Boothbay Railway Village. Historical Maine exhibits of rural life, railroads, and antique autos and trucks. Rides on a coal-fired, narrow-gauge steam train to an antique vehicle display. Also on exhibit on eight acres are displays of early fire equipt, a general store, a one-rm schoolhouse, and two restored railroad stations. (Mid-June-mid-Oct, daily) 1 mi N of Boothbay Center on ME 27. Phone 207/633-4727. ¢

Boothbay Region Historical Society Museum. Artifacts of Boothbay Region. (July-Labor Day, Wed, Fri, Sat; rest of yr, Sat only) 70 Oak St **Donation**

Fishing. In inland waters, Golf Course Brook, Adams, West Harbor and Knickerbocker ponds in Boothbay; Meadow Brook in East Boothbay. Ocean fishing from harbor docks. Boat rentals, deep-sea fishing.

Picnicking. Boothbay Region Lobstermen's Cooperative, Atlantic Ave. Lobsterman's Wharf, East Boothbay. Robinson's Wharf, ME 27 at bridge, Southport. Boiled lobsters and steamed clams, snacks avail. Phone 207/633-5160.

Special Events

Fisherman's Festival. Phone 207/633-2353. Mid-Apr.

Windjammer Days. Old schooners that formerly sailed the trade routes and now cruise the Maine coast sail en masse into harbor. Waterfront food court, entertainment, street parade, children's activities. Phone 207/633-2353. Late June.

Antique Auto Days. Phone 207/633-4727. Third wkend July.

Fall Foliage Festival. Foliage drives, harvest suppers, boat trips, country fair. Phone 207/633-4743 or 207/633-4727. Columbus Day wkend.

Harbor Lights Festival. Craft fair, lighted boat parade. Phone 207/633-2353. First Sat Dec.

Motels/Motor Lodges

★★★ **BROWN'S WHARF MOTEL.** *105 Atlantic Ave (04538). 207/633-5440; toll-free 800/334-8110. brownswharfinn.com.* 70 rms, 3 story. No elvtr. Late June-

Labor Day: S, D $129-$159; each addl $15; kit. unit $30 addl; kit. apts $50 addl; lower rates May-mid-June, Labor Day-Oct. Closed rest of yr. Crib free. TV; cable. Restaurant 8-10 am, 5:30-8:30 pm. Bar to 9:30 pm in season. Ck-out 11 am. Coin lndry. Meeting rm. Business servs avail. Balconies. All rms with harbor view. Dockage; marina; trolley stop (in season). Cr cds: A, MC, V.
D ⬛ 🛠 ✈ ⬛ ⬛ SC

★★ **CAP'N FISH'S MOTEL & MARINA.** *65 Atlantic Ave (04538). 207/633-6605; fax 207/633-6239; toll-free 800/633-0860. www.capnfishmotel.com.* 54 rms, 2 story. Mid-June-Sept: S, D $50-$120; each addl $8; kit. unit $110; lower rates mid-May-mid-June and Oct. Closed rest of yr. Crib free. TV; cable. Restaurant 7-9 am. Ck-out 11 am. Business servs avail. Some refrigerators. Picnic tables. On harbor, dockage. Cruises, whale-watching avail. Cr cds: A, MC, V.
D ⬛ ⬛

★★ **FLAGSHIP MOTOR INN.** *200 Townsend Ave; ME 27 (04538). 207/633-5094; fax 207/633-7055. www.boothbaylodging.com.* 84 rms, 2 story. Mid-July-Labor Day: S, D $75-$95; each addl $10; under 13 free; lower rates rest of yr. Crib $5. TV; cable. Pool. Restaurant 6 am-9 pm. Bar 4-11 pm. Ck-out 11 am. Balconies. Cr cds: A, DS, MC, V.
D ⬛ ⬛ ⬛

★★ **LAWNMEER INN.** *65 Hendrix Hill Rd, West Boothbay Harbor (04575). 207/633-2544; fax 207/633-0762; toll-free 800/633-7645. www.lawnmeerinn.com.* 32 rms, 1-2 story. Some A/C. July-Labor Day: D $88-$140; each addl $25; lower rates: mid-May-June, wkdays after Labor Day-mid-Oct. Closed rest of yr. Pet accepted; $10. TV; cable. Restaurant 7:30-10 am, 6-9 pm. Bar 5:30-9 pm. Ck-out 11 am. Lawn games. Balconies. Built 1898. On inlet; dock. Cr cds: MC, V.
D ⬛ ⬛ ⬛

★★★ **OCEAN GATE INN.** *Rte 27, Southport (04576). 207/633-3321; fax 207/633-2900; toll-free 800/221-5924. www.oceangateinn.com.* 67 rms, 1-2 story. 15 A/C. July-Aug: S, D, kit. units $125-$165; each addl $15; suites for 2-4 $175-$325; kit. cottages for 2-8, $2,000/wk; under 12 free; lower rates mid-May-June, Sept-mid-Oct. Closed rest of yr. Crib $5. TV; cable. Heated pool; whirlpool. Playground. Complimentary full bkfst. Complimentary coffee in rms. Ck-out 11 am. Coin lndry. Tennis. Exercise equipt. Refrigerators avail. Lawn games. Private porch on most rms. On 85 wooded-acres. On ocean; dock, boats avail. View of harbor. Cr cds: DS, MC, V.
D ⬛ ⬛ ⬛ ⬛ ⬛ ⬛

★ **PINES MOTEL.** *Sunset Rd (04538). 207/633-4555. www.gwi.net/~pinesmo.* 29 rms. July-Aug: S $70; D $85; each addl $8; lower rates May-June, after Sept-mid-Oct. Closed rest of yr. Crib free. Pet accepted. TV; cable. Heated pool. Playground. Ck-out 11 am. Tennis. Lawn games. Refrigerators. Balconies, decks. In wooded area; view of harbor. Cr cds: DS, MC, V.
⬛ ⬛ ⬛ ⬛

★ **SEAGATE.** *138 Townsend Ave (04538).*
207/633-3900; fax 207/633-3998; toll-free 800/633-1707.
www.seagatemotel.com. 25 rms, 4 kit. units. Mid-June-
mid-Oct: S, D $65-$90; each addl $5; under 13 free; lower
rates Apr-mid-June. Closed rest of yr. Crib $5. TV; cable.
Continental bkfst. Restaurant nearby. Ck-out 11 am.
Refrigerators. Picnic tables. Cr cds: A, DS, MC, V.

★★ **SMUGGLER'S COVE MOTOR INN.** *Rte 96, East
Boothbay (04544). 207/633-2800; fax 207/633-5926; toll-
free 800/633-3008. www.smugglerscovemotel.com.* 60 units,
2 story, 6 kit. units (most without ovens). Late June-Labor
Day: S, D $69-$169; each addl $10; kit. units $85-$140;
under 12 free; wkly rates; lower rates after Labor Day-
mid-Oct. Closed rest of yr. Crib $10. Pet accepted, some
restrictions; $50 deposit, refundable. TV; cable. Heated
pool. Restaurant 8-10 am, 6-9 pm. Bar from 5:30 pm.
Ck-out 11 am. Business servs avail. Balconies. On ocean;
swimming beach. Cr cds: A, DS, MC, V.

★ **TOPSIDE MOTEL.** *60 McKown St (04538). 207/633-
5404; fax 207/633-2206. www.gwi.net/topside.* 7 rms, 17
motel rms, 2-3 story, kit. suite. No A/C. No elvtr. July-Aug:
D $90-$150; each addl $10; under 8 free; lower rates late
May-June, after Labor Day-mid-Oct. Closed rest of yr. Crib
free. TV in motel rms; cable. Complimentary continental
bkfst. Coffee in rms. Restaurant nearby. Ck-out 11 am.
Lawn games. Refrigerator in motel rms. View of bay, harbor.
Cr cds: DS, MC, V.

★ **THE WATER'S EDGE MOTEL.** *549 Ocean Point Rd,
East Boothbay (04544). 207/633-2505.*
www.watersedge-linekinbay.com. 16 units, 1-2 story, 20 kit.
units, 7 cottages. No A/C. No rm phones. Late June-late
Aug: S, D $85-$120; kit; lower rates mid-May-late June, late
Aug-mid-Oct. Closed rest of yr. Crib $5. Pet accepted, some
restrictions; $10. TV; cable. Playground. Ck-out 10 am. Coin
lndry. Lawn games. Refrigerators. Balconies. Picnic tables,
grills. On ocean; dockage; swimming beach. Cr cds: MC, V.

Hotels

★★ **FISHERMAN'S WHARF INN.** *22 Commercial St
(04538). 207/633-5090; fax 207/633-5092; toll-free 800/
628-6872. www.fishermanswharfinn.com.* 54 rms, 2-3 story.
No elvtr. Mid-July-mid-Aug: S, D $105-$190; each addl
$10; suites $120-$170; lower rates mid-May-mid-July,
Mid-Aug-Oct. Closed rest of yr. Crib $5. TV; cable (pre-
mium). Complimentary continental bkfst. Restaurant
(see FISHERMAN'S WHARF INN). Bar 11 am-11 pm. Ck-
out 11 am. Business servs avail. Gift shop. Valet parking.
Balconies. On wharf overlooking harbor; pickup point for
boat tour, whale watch. Cr cds: A, C, D, DS, MC, V.

★★★ **TUGBOAT INN.** *80 Commercial St (04538).
207/633-4434; toll-free 800/248-2628. www.tugboatinn.com.*
64 rms, 1-2 story, 2 kit. Late June-early Sept: D $75-$165;
each addl $15; suites $160-$195; under 12 free; lower rates

late Mar-late June, early Sept-Nov. Closed rest of yr. Crib $10.
TV; cable (premium). Restaurant 7:30-10 am, 11:30 am-
2:30 pm, 5:30-9 pm. Bar noon-11:30 pm; entertainment
(seasonal). Ck-out 11 am. Coin lndry. Meeting rm. Business
servs avail. Valet parking in season. Refrigerators avail.
Balconies. On pier overlooking harbor; marina; dockage,
mooring avail. Cr cds: A, DS, MC, V.

Resorts

★★★ **SPRUCE POINT INN.** *Atlantic Ave (04538).
207/633-4152; fax 207/633-7138; toll-free 800/553-0289.
www.sprucepointinn.com.* 93 units, 1-3 story, 9 rms in inn,
27 suites, 45 rms in cottages (1-3 bedrm), 4 rms in condos
(2-3 bedrm). A/C in suites. July-Aug, MAP: cottage units
$132-$174/person; each addl (exc cottages) $59; suites
$184-$198; MAP: condo units $365-$532; family rates;
lower rates late May-June, Sept-mid-Oct. Closed rest of
yr. TV; cable, VCR avail. 2 pools, 1 saltwater; whirlpool.
Playground. Dining rm 7:30-9:30 am, 6-9 pm. Box lunches,
lobster cookouts. Bar 5 pm-midnight. Ck-out 11 am, ck-in
3 pm. Meeting rms. Business servs avail. Tennis. Putting
green. Exercise equipt. Massage. Dock, yacht moorings;
sunset cruise sail. Lawn games. Entertainment; movies. Rec
rm. Library. Some in-rm whirlpools. Located on 100-acre
wooded peninsula; ocean view. Cr cds: A, C, D, DS, MC, V.

B&Bs/Small Inns

★★ **1830 ADMIRAL'S QUARTERS INN.**
*71 Commercial St. (04538). 207/633-2474; fax 207/633-
5904. www.admiral squartersinn.com.* 6 rms, 2 with shower
only, 4 suites. Late June-Columbus Day: S, D $165-$195;
each addl $20; suites $105-$135; lower rates rest of yr.
Closed mid-Dec-mid-Feb. Children over 12 yrs only. TV;
cable. Complimentary full bkfst; afternoon refreshments.
Restaurant opp 7 am-9 pm. Ck-out 11 am, ck-in 2-6 pm.
Luggage handling. Gift shop. Coin lndry. Balconies. Picnic
tables. Opp ocean; overlooks harbor. Built in 1830; antiques.
Totally nonsmoking. Cr cds: DS, MC, V.

★★ **ANCHOR WATCH BED & BREAKFAST.**
*9 Eames Rd (04538). 207/633-7565; fax 207/633-5319.
www.anchor watch.com.* 5 rms, 3 with shower only, some
A/C, 3 story. No rm phones. Mid-June-Oct: S, D $90-$140;
each addl $20; lower rates rest of yr. Children over 9 yrs only.
TV in sitting rm; cable, VCR (movies). Complimentary
full bkfst. Restaurant nearby. Ck-out 11 am, ck-in 2 pm.
Whirlpool in 1 rm. Ocean views. Cruises avail. Totally
nonsmoking. Cr cds: DS, MC, V.

★★ **FIVE GABLES INN.** *107 Murray Hill Rd,
East Boothbay (04544). 207/633-4551; toll-free 800/451-
5048. www. fivegablesinn.com.* 15 rms, 10 with shower only,
3 story. No A/C. No elvtr. Mid-May-Oct: S, D $100-$165;
each addl $25; lower rates rest of yr. Children over 11 yrs
only. Complimentary full bkfst; afternoon refreshments.
Restaurant nearby. Ck-out 11 am, ck-in 2 pm. Some fire-

places. Opp ocean. Built in 1890; Victorian decor, antiques. Totally nonsmoking. Cr cds: MC, V.

⚓ ⚡ 🖅 🔥

★★ HARBOUR TOWNE INN ON WATERFRONT.
71 Townsend Ave (04538). 207/633-4300. *www.harbourtowneinn.com.* 12 rms, 3 story, 7 kits. Memorial Day-Oct: S, D $99-$175; suite $275; each addl $25; kits. $129-$175; lower rates rest of yr. Crib $25. TV; cable. Complimentary continental bkfst; afternoon refreshments. Restaurant nearby. Ck-out 10 am, ck-in 3:30 pm. Balconies. On harbor. Totally nonsmoking. Cr cds: A, MC, V.

D 🖅 🔥

★★ HOWARD HOUSE LODGE. *347 Townsend Ave*
(04538). 207/633-3933; fax 207/633-6244; toll-free 800/466-6697. www.howardhouselodge.com. 14 rms, 2 story. No A/C. No rm phones. Late June-Labor Day: D $87; each addl $15; lower rates rest of yr. TV; cable. Complimentary bkfst buffet (Memorial Day-Oct). Restaurant nearby. Ck-out 11 am. Balconies. Country, chalet-style building in wooded area. Cr cds: A, MC, V.

D 🖅 🐾 SC

★★ KENNISTON HILL INN. *Wiscasset Ed; Rte 27,*
Boothbay (04537). 207/633-2159; toll-free 800/992-2915. www.maine.com/innkeeper/. 10 rms, 7 with shower only, 1-2 story. No A/C. No rm phones. Mid-June-Oct: D $69-$110; each addl $25; lower rates rest of yr. Children over 10 yrs only. Complimentary full bkfst; afternoon refreshments. Ck-out 11 am, ck-in 3 pm. Some fireplaces. Restored Colonial-style farmhouse (1786); antiques. Totally nonsmoking. Cr cds: DS, MC, V.

🖅 🔥

★★ OCEAN POINT INN. *Shore Rd, East Boothbay*
(04544). 207/633-4200; toll-free 800/552-5554. www.oceanpointinn .com. 61 units, 1-2 story, 50 rms in 5 bldgs, 6 cottage units; 5 kit. units. Some A/C. Late June-early Sept: S, D $96-$160; each addl $10; cottage units $91-$136; kit. units $925-$1,020/wk; under 13, $5 (cottages only); hol wkends (3-day min); lower rates late May-late June, early Sept-mid-Oct. Closed rest of yr. Crib $5. TV; cable. Heated pool. Dining rm (in season) 7:30-10 am, 6-9 pm; closed Sun, early Sept-mid-Oct. Bar 5-10 pm. Ck-out 11 am, ck-in 3 pm. Refrigerators. Some balconies; porch on cottages. On peninsula at entrance to Linekin Bay. Cr cds: A, DS, MC, V.

D 🖾 🔥

Cottage Colony

★ HILLSIDE ACRES CABINS & MOTEL. *Adams Pond Rd,*
Boothbay (04537). 207/633-3411; fax 207/633-2295. www.gwi.net/~hillside/. 14 units, 2 share bath, 1-2 story, 7 kit. units, 7 cottages. No A/C. No rm phones. July-Aug: S, D $40-$75; kit. cottages $63-$75; cottages $57; wkly rates; lower rates rest of yr. Crib free. Pet accepted. TV; cable. Pool. Complimentary continental bkfst (mid-June-Labor Day). Ck-out 10:30 am. Picnic tables, grills. Cr cds: MC, V.

🐾 🖾 🖅 🐾 SC

Restaurants

★ ANDREW'S HARBORSIDE. *12 Bridge St (04538).*
207/633-4074. Specializes in seafood, cinnamon rolls. Own soups, desserts. Hrs: 7:30-11 am, 11:30 am-3 pm, 5:30-9 pm; wkends to 9:30 pm. Closed mid-Oct-Apr. Serv bar. Bkfst $2.25-$6.25, lunch $3.95-$10.95, dinner $9.95-$16.95. Child's menu. Overlooks harbor. Cr cds: DS, MC, V.

D

★ CHINA BY THE SEA. *96 Townsend Ave (04538).*
207/633-4449. www.chinabythesea.com. Chinese menu. Hrs: 11 am-10 pm. Closed Thanksgiving, Dec 25. Res accepted. Serv bar. Lunch, dinner $4.50-$14.95. Outdoor dining. Overlooks harbor. Cr cds: A, C, D, DS, ER, MC, V.

D

★ EBB TIDE. *43 Commercial St (04538). 207/633-5692.*
Specializes in seafood, omelettes. Own desserts. Hrs: 6:30 am-9 pm; Fri, Sat to 9:30 pm; hrs vary off season. Closed Dec 25. Bkfst $3-$5.50, lunch $3-$12.95, dinner $7-$12.95. Child's menu. Totally nonsmoking. Cr cds: A, MC, V.

★★ FISHERMAN'S WHARF INN. *22 Commercial St*
(04538). 207/633-5090. www.fishermanswharfinn.com. Specializes in seafood. Hrs: 11:30 am-9 pm; wkends to 9:30 pm. Closed mid-Oct-mid-May. Bar 11 am-11 pm. Lunch, dinner $6-$27. Valet parking. Outdoor dining. Scenic murals. Waterfront view. Family-owned. Cr cds: A, C, D, DS, MC, V.

D 🖾

Bridgton

See also Poland Spring, Sebago Lake

Pop 2,195 **Elev** 494 ft **Area code** 207 **Zip** 04009
Information Bridgton Lakes Region Chamber of Commerce, PO Box 236; 207/647-3472
Web www.mainelakeschamber.com

Primarily a resort, this community between Long and Highland lakes is within easy reach of Pleasant Mountain (2,007 feet), a recreational area that offers skiing as well as a magnificent view of 50 lakes. Bridgton also has many unique craft and antique shops located within a two-mile radius of the town center.

What to See and Do

Gibbs Avenue Museum. Headquarters of Bridgton Historical Society. Permanent exhibits incl narrow-gauge railroad memorabilia; Civil War artifacts; Sears "horseless carriage" (1911). Special summer exhibits. Genealogy research facility incl Bridgton and Saw River railroad documents. (Sept-June, Tues and Thurs; rest of yr, Tues-Fri; closed hols) Gibbs Ave. Phone 207/647-3699. ¢

Skiing. Shawnee Peak Ski Area. Quad, two triple, double chairlift; snowmaking, school, rentals, patrol; nursery; restaurant, cafeteria, bar. Longest run 1½ mi; vertical drop 1,350 ft. Night skiing. (Dec-Mar, daily) 6 mi W, off US 302. Phone 207/647-8444.

Special Event

Quilt Show. Town hall. New and old quilts; demonstrations. Contact Chamber of Commerce. Mid-July. Phone 207/647-3472.

B&B/Small Inn

★ ★ ★ **THE INN AT LONG LAKE.** *Lakhouse Rd & Rte 302, Naples (04055). 207/693-6226; toll-free 800/437-0328. www.innatlonglake.com.* 16 rms, 4 story. No elvtr. July-Labor Day: S, D $99-$150; suites $115-$180; mid-wk rates; lower rates Apr-June, Labor Day-Dec. Closed rest of yr. TV. Complimentary continental bkfst. Restaurant opp 8 am-8 pm (summer). Ck-out 11 am, ck-in 3 pm. Built 1906; stone fireplace. Near lake. Totally nonsmoking. Cr cds: DS, MC, V.

⬛🔲🔲🔲 **SC**

Restaurant

★ **BLACK HORSE TAVERN.** *8 Portland St (04099). 207/647-5300.* Specializes in ribs, steak, fresh seafood. Hrs: 11 am-10 pm; Sun 9 am-9 pm; Sun brunch 9 am-3 pm; hrs may vary off season. Closed Thanksgiving, Dec 25. Bar. Lunch $3.95-$7.95, dinner $5.95-$19.95. Sun brunch $1.50-$5.95. Child's menu. In restored homestead. Equestrian motif; saddles, bridles, harnesses on display. Cr cds: DS, MC, V.

D

Brunswick

See also Bailey Island

Settled 1628 **Pop** 20,906 **Elev** 67 ft **Area code** 207 **Zip** 04011
Information Chamber of Commerce of the Bath-Brunswick Region, 59 Pleasant St; 207/725-8797
Web www.midcoastmaine.com

Once a lumbering center and later a mill town, Brunswick is now mainly concerned with trade, health care, and education; it is the home of Bowdoin College and Brunswick Naval Air Station. The city lies northeast of a summer resort area on the shores and islands of Casco Bay. Magnificent Federalist mansions along Federal Street and Park Row remind visitors of Brunswick's past.

What to See and Do

Bowdoin College. (1794) 1,500 students. Nathaniel Hawthorne, Henry Wadsworth Longfellow, Robert Peary, Franklin Pierce, and Joan Benoit Samuelson graduated from here. Tours. Maine St. Phone 207/725-3000.

Museum of Art. Portraits by Stuart, Feke and Copley; paintings by Homer and Eakins; Greek and Roman vases and sculpture. (Tues-Sun; closed hols) Walker Art Building. Phone 207/725-3275. **FREE**

Peary-MacMillan Arctic Museum. Exhibits relating to Arctic exploration, ecology, and Inuit (Eskimo) culture. (Tues-Sun; closed hols) Hubbard Hall. Phone 207/725-3416. **FREE**

Pejepscot Historical Society Museum. Regional historical museum housed in an 1858 sea captain's home; changing exhibits, research facilities. (Tues-Sat; closed hols) 159 Park Row. Phone 207/729-6606. **FREE** The Society also operates

Joshua L. Chamberlain Museum. Former residence of Maine's greatest Civil War hero, four-term Governor of Maine, and president of Bowdoin College. Guided tours. (June-mid-Oct, Tues-Sat; closed hols) 226 Maine St.

Skolfield-Whittier House. An 18-rm Victorian structure last occupied in 1925; furnishings and housewares of three generations. Guided tours. (June-mid-Oct, Tues-Sat; closed hols) 161 Park Row. ¢¢¢

Thomas Point Beach. Swimming, lifeguard. Picnicking, tables, fireplaces. Snack bar; gift shop, arcade, playground; camping (fee). (Memorial Day-Labor Day, daily) Off ME 24, at Cook's Corner. Phone 207/725-6009.

Special Events

Maine State Music Theater. Pickard Theater, Bowdoin College campus. Broadway musicals by professional cast. Tues-Sat eves; Wed, Fri, Sun matinees. Phone 207/725-8769. Mid-June-Aug.

Bowdoin Summer Music Festival and School. Brunswick High School and Bowdoin College campus. Chamber music, concert series. Phone 207/373-1400. Fri eves, late June-Aug.

Music on the Mall. Downtown. Free outdoor family concert series. Phone 207/725-8797. Wed eves, July and Aug.

Topsham Fair. N via ME 24 in Topsham. Entertainment, arts and crafts. Seven days early Aug. Phone 207/725-8797.

Bluegrass Festival. At Thomas Point Beach. Labor Day wkend. Phone 207/725-8797.

Motels/Motor Lodges

★ **ATRIUM TRAVELODGE.** *21 Gurnet Rd, Cooks Corner (04011). 207/729-5555; fax 207/729-5149. www.travelodge .com.* 184 rms, 3 story. July-Aug: S, D $74-$86; each addl $10; suites $125; under 19 free; lower rates rest of yr. Crib free. Pet accepted. TV; cable, VCR (movies $2.95). Indoor pool; wading pool, whirlpool. Complimentary coffee in lobby. Restaurant 6 am-10 pm. Rm serv. Bar to midnight. Ck-out noon. Meeting rms. Business servs avail. Sundries. Coin lndry. Exercise equipt; sauna. Game rm. Lawn games. Refrigerators. Cr cds: A, D, DS, MC, V.

🔲🔲🔲🔲🔲

★ **COMFORT INN.** *199 Pleasant St (04011). 207/729-1129; fax 207/725-8310. www.comfortinn.com.* 80 rms, 2 story. May-Oct: S, D $80-$89; each addl $7; under 18 free; lower rates rest of yr. Crib free. TV; cable (premium). Complimentary continental bkfst. Restaurant nearby. Ck-out 11 am. Business servs avail. Valet serv Mon-Fri. Cr cds: A, D, DS, MC, V.

[icons]

★ **ECONO LODGE.** *215 Pleasant St; Rte 1 and I-95 (04011). 207/729-9991; fax 207/721-0413; toll-free 800/654-9991. www.econolodge.com.* 29 rms, 1-2 story. July-Labor Day: D $76-$83; each addl $7; lower rates rest of yr. Crib $3. TV; cable. Pool. Complimentary coffee in lobby. Restaurant nearby. Ck-out 11 am. Coin lndry. Business servs avail. Sundries. Cr cds: A, C, D, DS, MC, V.

[icons]

★ **SUPER 8 MOTEL.** *224 Bath Rd (04011). 207/725-8883; fax 207/729-8766; res 800/800-8000. www.super8.com.* 71 rms. June-Oct: S $35-$57; D $40-$85; each addl $5; suite $92.82; under 16 free; higher rates: graduation, local festivals; lower rates rest of yr. Crib free. TV; cable, VCR avail (movies). Complimentary continental bkfst. Restaurant opp 10 am-10 pm. Ck-out 11 am. Picnic tables. Cr cds: A, DS, MC, V.

[icons] SC

★ **VIKING MOTOR INN.** *287 Bath Rd (04011). 207/729-6661; toll-free 800/429-6661. www.vikingmotorinn.com.* 28 rms, 10 kit. units. July-Oct: S $39-$69; D $49-$79; each addl $5; under 12 free; wkly rates off season; lower rates rest of yr. Pet accepted, some restrictions; fee. TV; cable. Pool. Playground. Ck-out 10 am. Lawn games. Refrigerators, microwaves avail. Picnic tables, grill. Cr cds: A, D, DS, MC, V.

[icons]

B&B/Small Inn

★★★ **CAPTAIN DANIEL STONE INN.** *10 Water St (04011). 207/725-9898; fax 207/725-9898; res 800/267-0525. www.netquarters.net/cdsi.* 34 rms, 3 story, 4 suites. Mid-July-mid-Sept: S, D $125-$145; each addl $10; suites $175-$210; lower rates rest of yr. Crib free. TV; cable, VCR (movies). Complimentary continental bkfst. Dining rm 11:30 am-2 pm, 5-9 pm. Bar 4-10 pm. Ck-out 11 am, ck-in 4 pm. Business servs avail. Bathrm phones; some in-rm whirlpools. Balconies. Antiques. Screened veranda. Former sea captain's house (1819). Cr cds: A, D, MC, V.

[icons] SC

Restaurant

★★ **GREAT IMPASTA.** *42 Maine St (04011). 207/729-5858.* Specializes in pasta, veal. Hrs: 11 am-9 pm; Fri, Sat to 10 pm; Sun 5-9 pm. Closed Thanksgiving, Dec 25. Italian menu. Serv bar. Lunch $3.95-$6.95, dinner $7.95-$12.95. Totally nonsmoking. Cr cds: A, DS, MC, V.

[icon]

Bucksport

See also Bangor, Belfast, Ellsworth

Settled 1762 **Pop** 4,825 **Elev** 43 ft **Area code** 207 **Zip** 04416
Information Bucksport Chamber of Commerce, PO Box 1880; 207/469-6818
Web www.allmaine.com/bucksport

Although originally settled in 1762, the Penobscot valley town of Bucksport was so thoroughly burned by the British in 1779 that it was not resettled until 1812. On the east bank of the Penobscot River, Bucksport is a shopping center for the area, but is primarily an industrial town with an emphasis on paper manufacturing. The Waldo Hancock Bridge crosses the Penobscot to Verona Island.

What to See and Do

Accursed Tombstone. Granite obelisk over grave of founder Jonathan Buck bears an indelible mark in the shape of a woman's leg—said to have been put there by a witch whom he had hanged. Buck Cemetery, Main and Hinks Sts, near Verona Island Bridge. **FREE**

Fort Knox State Park. Consists of 124 acres around huge granite fort started in 1844 and used as a defense in the Aroostook War. Structure incl spiral staircases. Hiking. Picnicking. Interpretive displays. Tours (Aug, Sept). (May-Oct) Standard fees. S on US 1 across Waldo Hancock Bridge. Phone 207/469-7719.

Fort Point State Park. Ocean view. Fishing; picnicking. (Memorial Day-Labor Day) Standard fees. 8 mi S on US 1. Phone 207/469-6818.

Northeast Historic Film. The Alamo Theatre (1916) houses museum, theater, store and archives of northern New England film and video. Exhibits present 100 yrs of movie-going, from nickelodeons to mall cinemas. Video and film presentations interpret regional culture. (Mon-Fri) 379 Main St. Phone 207/469-0924. **FREE**

Wilson Museum. Prehistoric, historic, geologic and art exhibits (Late May-Sept, Tues-Sun, also hols). On grounds are John Perkins House (1763-1783), Hearse House, Blacksmith Shop (July-Aug, Wed and Sun). 18 mi S via ME 175, 166 in Castine. Phone 207/326-9247. ¢¢

Motels/Motor Lodges

★★ **BEST WESTERN JED PROUTY MOTOR INN.** *52 Main St (04416). 207/469-3113; toll-free 800/528-1234. www.bestwestern.com.* 40 rms, 2-4 story. July-Oct: S $89; D $99; each addl $10; suites $125; under 12 free; lower rates rest of yr. Pet accepted, some restrictions. TV; cable. Restaurant opp 5:30-9:30 pm. Ck-out 11 am. Business servs avail. In-rm modem link. On Penobscot River. Cr cds: A, C, D, DS, MC, V.

[icons] SC

★ **BUCKSPORT MOTOR INN.** *Rte 1 (04416). 207/469-3111; fax 207/469-1045; res 800/626-9734.* 24 rms, some A/C. Aug: S $40-$72; D $45-$72; each addl $5; lower rates rest of yr. Pet accepted. TV; cable. Complimentary coffee in rms. Restaurant nearby. Ck-out 11 am. Cr cds: A, DS, MC, V.
◧ ⊠ ⊠ **SC**

B&Bs/Small Inns

★★ **CASTINE INN.** *Main St, Castine (04421). 207/326-4365; fax 207/326-4570. www.castineinn.com.* 19 rms, 4 suites, 3 story. No A/C. No rm phones. Memorial Day-Columbus Day: D $85-$130; each addl $20; suites $135-$210; lower rates May, Columbus Day-mid-Dec. Closed rest of yr. Children over 8 yrs only. Complimentary full bkfst. Dining rm 8-9:30 am, 5:30-8:30 pm. Bar 5-10 pm. Ck-out 11 am, ck-in 3 pm. Business servs avail. Built 1898; sitting rm with wood-burning fireplace. Many rms with harbor view; perennial and rose gardens. Totally nonsmoking. Cr cds: MC, V.
⊠

★★ **PENTAGOET INN.** *26 Main St, Castine (04421). 207/326-8616; fax 207/326-9382. www.pentagoet.com.* 16 rms in 2 bldgs, 3 story. No A/C. No rm phones. Late-May-mid-Oct: S $80; D $130. Closed rest of yr. Complimentary full bkfst; afternoon refreshments. Ck-out 10:30 am, ck-in 2-6 pm. Street parking. Victorian main building (1894) with smaller, Colonial annex (ca 1770); library/sitting rm, antiques, period furnishings. Landscaped gardens. Totally nonsmoking. Cr cds: MC, V.
⊠ ⊠ ⊠

Restaurant

★★ **L'ERMITAGE.** *219 Main St (04416). 207/469-3361.* Continental menu. Specialties: steak au poivre, steak chasseur, shrimp Arlesienne. Own desserts. Hrs: 5:30-9 pm. Closed Mon, Tues; also 1st 2 wks Apr. Res accepted. No A/C. Serv Bar. Wine list. Dinner $12.95-$19.95. Guest rms avail. Cr cds: A, C, DS, MC, V.
⊠

Calais

Settled 1770 **Pop** 3,963 **Elev** 19 ft **Area code** 207 **Zip** 04619
Information Calais Regional Chamber of Commerce, 16 Swan St, PO Box 368; 207/454-2308 or 888/422-3112
Web www.visitcalais.com

International cooperation is rarely as warm and helpful as it is between Calais (KAL-iss) and St. Stephen, New Brunswick, just across the St. Croix River in Canada. Because of an early closing law in St. Stephen, Canadians stroll over to the United States for a nightcap, and fire engines and ambulances cross the International Bridge in both directions as needed. (For Border Crossing Regulations, see MAKING THE MOST OF YOUR TRIP.) **Note:** New Brunswick is on Atlantic Time, one hour ahead of Eastern Standard Time.

Calais has a unique distinction—it is located exactly halfway between the North Pole and the equator. The 45th Parallel passes a few miles south of town; a marker on US 1 near Perry indicates the spot. Bass, togue, trout, and salmon fishing is available in many lakes and streams in Calais, and there is swimming at Meddybemps Lake, 13 miles north on ME 191.

What to See and Do

Moosehorn National Wildlife Refuge. Glacial terrain with forests, valleys, lakes, bogs, and marshes. Abundant wildlife. Fishing; hiking, hunting, x-country skiing, bird-watching. (Daily) 4 mi N via US 1, on Charlotte Rd. Contact Refuge Manager, PO Box 1077. Phone 207/454-7161. **FREE**

St. Croix Island International Historic Site. In 1604 French explorers Pierre Duguaf and Samuel de Champlain, leading a group of approx 75 men, selected this as the site of the first attempted European settlement on the Atlantic Coast north of Florida. Information shelter; no facilities. (Daily) 8 mi S via US 1, opp Red Beach in St. Croix River; accessible only by boat. Phone 207/288-3338.

Special Event

International Festival Week. Celebration of friendship between Calais and St. Stephen, New Brunswick; entertainment, concessions, contests, fireworks, parade. Early Aug. Phone 888/422-3112.

Motels/Motor Lodges

★ **HESLIN'S MOTEL DINIG ROOM.** *Rte 1, Box 111 (04619). 207/454-3762; fax 207/454-0148.* 11 motel rms, 9 cottages. No cottage phones. S $55; D $70; each addl $5; cottages $48-$80; kit. cottages $80-$100; under 12 free; wkly rates. Closed Dec-Apr. Crib $5. TV; cable. Heated pool; wading pool. Complimentary coffee in rms. Restaurant 5-9 pm. Bar. Ck-out 10 am. Meeting rm. View of St. Croix River and Canada. Cr cds: DS, MC, V.
⊠ ⊠ ⊠

★ **INTERNATIONAL MOTEL.** *276 Main St (04619). 207/454-7515; fax 207/454-3396.* 61 rms. June-Sept: S $39-$60; D $45-$60; each addl $5; studio rms $80; suites $90; lower rates rest of yr. TV; cable. Complimentary coffee in rms. Restaurant adj 6 am-10 pm. Ck-out 11 am. Business servs avail. Cr cds: A, C, D, DS, MC, V.
D ⊠ ⊠ **SC**

★★ **REDCLYFFE SHORE MOTOR INN.** *ME 1, Robbinston (04671). 207/454-3270; fax 207/454-8723. www.redclyffe motorinn.com.* 17 rms. S, D $62-$73; each addl $5. Closed Dec-Apr. TV; cable (premium). Complimentary coffee in rms. Restaurant 5-9 pm. Ck-out 10 am. Victorian Gothic building (1863); on bluff overlooking St. Croix River, Passamaquoddy Bay. Cr cds: A, MC, V.
D ⊠ ⊠ ⊠ **SC**

Restaurant

★ **WICKACHEE.** *282 Main St (04619). 207/454-3400.* Specializes in steak, seafood. Salad bar. Hrs: 6 am-10 pm. Closed Dec 25. Res accepted. Beer, wine. bkfst $1.75-$4, lunch $2.50-$8.95, dinner $6.95-$13.95. Child's menu. Cr cds: MC, V.

D

Camden

See also Belfast, Rockland

Pop 5,060 **Elev** 33 ft **Area code** 207 **Zip** 04843
Information Camden-Rockport-Lincolnville Chamber of Commerce, Public Landing, PO Box 919; 207/236-4404
Web www.camdenme.org

Camden's unique setting—where the mountains meet the sea—makes it a popular four-season resort area. Recreational activities include boat cruises and boat rentals, swimming, fishing, camping, hiking, and picnicking, as well as winter activities. The poet Edna St. Vincent Millay began her career in Camden.

What to See and Do

Bay Chamber Concerts. Classical music performances by Vermeer Quartet and guest artists (July and Aug, Thurs and Fri eves). Jazz musicians perform Sept-June (one show each month). Rockport Opera House, Central St in Rockport. Phone 207/236-2823.

Camden Hills State Park. Maine's third-largest state park, surrounding 1,380-ft Mt Megunticook. Road leads to Mt Battie (800 ft). Spectacular view of coast. Hiking, picnic facilities, camping (dump station). (Memorial Day-Columbus Day) Standard fees. 2 mi NE on US 1. Phone 207/236-3109.

Conway Homestead-Cramer Museum. Authentically restored 18th-century farmhouse. Collection of carriages, sleighs and farm implements in old barn; blacksmith shop, privy, and herb garden. Mary Meeker Cramer Museum contains paintings, ship models, quilts; costumes, documents, and other memorabilia; changing exhibits. (July-Aug, Tues-Fri) On US 1, near city limits. Phone 207/236-2257. ¢

Kelmscott Farm. Working farm established to conserve rare and endangered breeds of farm livestock, incl Cotswold sheep, Ancient White Park cattle, American Cream Draft horse, Suffolk Punch horse, Kerry cattle, and Gloucestershire Old Spots pigs. Educational demonstrations. Farm tours (Labor Day-Memorial Day, by appt). Museum and gift shop. Picnic area. Special events throughout the yr. (Tues-Sun) N on ME 52, in Lincolnville. Phone 207/763-4088. ¢¢

Maine State Ferry Service. 20-min trip to Islesboro (Dark Harbor) on *Margaret Chase Smith*. (Mid-May-late Oct, wkdays, nine trips; Sun, eight trips; rest of yr, six trips daily) 6 mi N on US 1 in Lincolnville Beach. Phone 207/789-5611. ¢¢

Sailing trips. Old-time schooners leave from Camden and Rockport Harbors for ½- to six-day trips along the coast of Maine. (May-Oct) For further information, rates, schedules, or res, contact the individual companies.

Angelique. PO Box 736. Phone 800/282-9989.
Appledore. Lily Pond Dr. Phone 207/236-8353.
Maine Windjammer Cruises. PO Box 617. Phone 207/236-2938.
Olad and *Northwind.* PO Box 432. Phone 207/236-2323.
Schooner *Lewis R. French.* PO Box 992. Phone 800/469-4635.
Schooner *Mary Day.* PO Box 798M. Phone 800/992-2218.
Schooner *Roseway.* PO Box 696X. Phone 800/255-4449.
Schooner *Surprise.* PO Box 450. Phone 207/236-4687.
Schooner *Timberwind.* PO Box 247, Rockport 04856. Phone 207/236-3639.
Schooner Yacht *Wendameen.* PO Box 252. Phone 207/594-1751.

Sightseeing cruises on Penobscot Bay. Cruises (one to four hrs) leave from public landing. Contact Chamber of Commerce. Phone 207/236-4404.

Skiing. Camden Snow Bowl. Double chairlift, two T-bars; patrol, school, rentals; toboggan chute and rentals; snowboarding; snowmaking; snack bar, lodge. (Mid-Dec-mid-Mar, daily) S on US 1 to John St to Hosmer Pond Rd. Phone 207/236-3438.

Special Events

Camden Opera House. Elm St. Theater with musical and theatrical performances and concerts. July-Aug. Phone 207/236-7963.

Garden Club Open House Day. Tour of homes and gardens (fee). Third Thurs July. Phone 207/236-6375.

Windjammer Weekend. Celebration of windjammer industry; fireworks. Phone 207/236-4404. Labor Day wkend.

Christmas by the Sea. Celebration of holiday season with musical entertainment, horse-drawn wagon rides, Holiday House Tour, Santa's arrival by lobster boat. Phone 207/236-4404. First wkend Dec.

Motels/Motor Lodges

★★ **BEST WESTERN.** *11 Tannery Ln (04843). 207/236-0500; fax 207/236-4711; res 800/755-7483. www.camdenmaine.com.* 35 rms, 3 story. Mid-July-Labor Day: S, D $149-$199; under 17 free; lower rates rest of yr. Crib free. TV; cable (premium), VCR avail. Indoor pool; whirlpool. Complimentary continental bkfst. Restaurant nearby. Ck-out 11 am. Meeting rms. Business servs avail. In-rm modem link. Sundries. Downhill/x-country ski 5 mi. Exercise equipt. Some refrigerators; many microwaves. Cr cds: A, C, D, DS, JCB, MC, V.

D ⚡ ≋ 🏋 ⊠ 🐾 SC

★★★ **BLACK HORSE INN.** *Rte 1 N, Lincolnville (04849). 207/236-6800; fax 207/236-6509; res 800/374-9085. www.midcoast.com/~blkhorse.* 21 rms, 2 story. Mid-June-mid-Oct: S, D $89-$150; under 13 free; lower rates rest of yr. Crib $5. TV; cable. Restaurant 7-10 am, 5-9 pm; Sun to 10 am; closed Mon-Wed. Ck-out 11 am. Business servs avail. Downhill ski 6 mi, x-country ski 2 mi. Some refrigerators. Borders Camden Hills State Park. Totally nonsmoking. Cr cds: A, DS, MC, V.

D ⚡ ⊠ 🐾

★★ **CEDAR CREST MOTEL.** *115 Elm St (04845). 207/236-4859; toll-free 800/422-4964. www.cedarcrestmotel.com.* 37 rms, 1-2 story. July-Labor Day: D $99-$125; each addl $10; lower rates May-June, Labor Day-Oct. Closed Nov-Apr. Crib free. TV; cable. Heated pool. Playground. Restaurant 6 am-noon; closed Mon. Ck-out 11 am. Coin lndry. Some refrigerators. Balconies. Cr cds: A, MC, V.

★★ **GLENMOOR BY THE SEA.** *RR 1, Box 3291 (04843). 207/236-3466; fax 207/236-7043; toll-free 800/439-3541. www.glenmoorbythesea.com.* 35 units, 7 cottages, 1 kit. unit. Early July-Aug: D $109-$169; each addl $10; cottages $169-$295; under 19 free; lower rates mid-May-early July, Sept-early Nov. Closed rest of yr. Crib $5. TV; cable, VCR avail. Heated pool. Complimentary continental bkfst. Ck-out 11 am. Tennis. Refrigerators avail. Balconies. Sun deck. On ocean. Totally nonsmoking. Cr cds: A, MC, V.

★★ **MOUNT BATTIE MOTEL.** *US Rte 1, RR 3 Box 570, Lincolnville (04849). 207/236-3870; fax 207/230-0068; res 800/224-3870. www.acadia.net/mtbattie.* 21 rms. July-mid-Oct: S, D $65-$115; each addl $15; lower rates May-June and mid-Oct-early Nov. Closed rest of yr. Crib $5. TV; cable. Complimentary continental bkfst. Complimentary coffee in rms. Ck-out 11 am. Business servs avail. Refrigerators. Picnic tables, sundeck, gazebo, grill. Totally nonsmoking. Cr cds: A, MC, V.

★★ **SNOW HILL LODGE.** *Atlantic Hwy; US 1, Lincolnville Beach (04849). 207/236-3452; fax 207/236-8052; toll-free 800/476-4775. www.midcoast.com/~theview.* 30 rms, 1-2 story. No A/C. Mid-June-late-Oct: S, D $50-$80; each addl $10; lower rates rest of yr. Crib $6. TV; cable. Restaurant 7-10 am. Ck-out 10:30 am. Downhill/x-country ski 4 mi. Lawn games. Picnic tables, grills. Tree-shaded grounds. View of bay. Cr cds: A, DS, MC, V.

Hotel

★★★ **INN AT OCEAN'S EDGE.** *US 1 (PO Box 704) (04843). 207/236-0945; fax 207/236-0609. www.innatoceansedge.com.* 15 rms, 3 story, 1 suite. June-Oct: D $220; suites $250; each addl $35; lower rates rest of yr. TV; cable, VCR avail. Complimentary full bkfst, newspaper. Restaurant nearby. Ck-out 11 am. Meeting rm. Bellhops. Exercise equipt. Golf. Tennis, 5 courts. Downhill skiing. Beach access. Bike rentals. Hiking trail. Cr cds: MC, V.

B&Bs/Small Inns

★★★ **BLUE HARBOR HOUSE, A VILLAGE INN.** *67 Elm St (04843). 207/236-3196; fax 207/236-6523; toll-free 800/248-3196. www.blueharborhouse.com.* 10 units, 2 story, 2 suites, 2 kits. Some A/C. S, D $145; each addl $30; suites, kit. units $145; MAP avail. Crib free. TV in some rms; cable, VCR. Complimentary full bkfst. Restaurant

nearby. Ck-out 11 am, ck-in 2-6 pm. Downhill/x-country ski 4 mi. Restored New England Cape (1810); country antiques, hand-fashioned quilts, sun porch. Totally nonsmoking. Cr cds: A, DS, MC, V.

★★★ **CAMDEN WINDWARD HOUSE.** *6 High St (04843). 207/236-9656; fax 207/230-0433; toll-free 877/492-9656. www.windwardhouse.com.* 8 rms, 5 with shower only, 3 story. No A/C. No rm phones. Memorial Day-mid-Oct: S, D $169-$235; lower rates rest of yr. Children over 12 yrs only. Complimentary full bkfst; afternoon refreshments. Restaurant nearby. Ck-out 11 am, ck-in 3 pm. Downhill/x-country ski 5 mi. Some fireplaces. Picnic tables. Built in 1854; some antiques. Totally nonsmoking. Cr cds: A, MC, V.

★★★ **DARK HARBOR HOUSE.** *117 Getty Rd, Islesboro (04848). 207/734-6669; fax 207/734-6938. www.darkharborhouse.com.* 11 rms, 2-3 story, 3 suites. Some A/C. No rm phones. May-Oct: D, suites $160; each addl $15. Closed rest of yr. Adults only. Complimentary full bkfst. Dining rm (by res only) 5:30-8:30 pm. Serv bar. Ck-out 11 am, ck-in 1:30 pm. Some fireplaces. Many private porches, balconies. Georgian Revival summer mansion (1896) with double staircase, wide veranda, library/sitting rm, antiques. Bicycles. Totally nonsmoking. Cr cds: MC, V.

★★ **ELMS BED & BREAKFAST.** *84 Elm St (04843). 207/236-6250; fax 207/236-7330; toll-free 800/755-3567. www.elmsinn.net.* 6 rms, 1 with A/C, 3 with shower only, 3 story. No elvtr. Mid-June-mid-Oct: S, D $105-$125; each addl $30; package plans; lower rates rest of yr. Children over 9 yrs only. Complimentary full bkfst; afternoon refreshments. Restaurant nearby. Ck-out 10:30 am, ck-in 3-6 pm. In-rm modem link. Downhill/x-country ski 3 mi. Lawn games. Built in 1806; lighthouse theme. Federal-style home; fireplace in parlor, sun deck. Totally nonsmoking. Cr cds: DS, MC, V.

★★★ **HAWTHORN INN.** *9 High St (04843). 207/236-8842; fax 207/236-6181. www.camdeninn.com.* 9 units in 2 bldgs, 2 story. No A/C. Mid-June-mid-Oct: S, D $175-$240; each addl $30; lower rates rest of yr. Closed Jan. Children over 12 yrs only. TV; cable, VCR avail (free movies). Complimentary full bkfst; afternoon refreshments. Restaurant nearby. Ck-out 11 am, ck-in 3 pm. Downhill/x-country ski 5 mi. Some fireplaces. Balconies. Victorian mansion (1894) built by wealthy coal merchant; turret, original stained-glass panels. Carriage house adj. View of harbor. Totally nonsmoking. Cr cds: A, MC, V.

★★★ **INN AT SUNRISE POINT.** *Rte 1, Fireroad 9 (04849). 207/236-7716; fax 207/236-0820; res 800/435-6278. www.sunrisepoint.com.* 7 rms, 2 story. No A/C. July, Aug, Oct: D $160-$375; lower rates Memorial Day-June, Sept. Closed rest of yr. Children over 16 yrs only. TV; cable, VCR (free movies). Complimentary full bkfst; afternoon refreshments. Ck-out 11 am, ck-in 3 pm. In-rm modem link. Sundries. Refrigerators, fireplaces. Whirlpools in cottages. Four-acre estate situated along Penobscot Bay; glass conservatory. Totally nonsmoking. Cr cds: A, MC, V.

★★ **THE LODGE AT CAMDEN HILLS.** *US 1 (04843). 207/236-8478; fax 207/236-7163; toll-free 800/832-7058. www.thelodgeatcamdenhills.com.* 23 units. S, D $125-$249; each addl $15; suites, kit. units $159-$199; under 16 free; wkly rates. Crib free. TV; cable, VCR avail. Complimentary coffee in rms. Restaurant nearby. Ck-out 11 am, ck-in 3 pm. Business servs avail. In-rm modem link. Downhill/x-country ski 5 mi. Refrigerators; some in-rm whirlpools, fireplaces, microwaves. Quiet, wooded setting. View of bay. Totally nonsmoking. Cr cds: A, DS, MC, V.

★★ **MAINE STAY BED & BREAKFAST.** *22 High St (04843). 207/236-9636; fax 207/236-0621. www.mainestay.com.* 8 rms, 5 with shower only, 3 story. No A/C. Rm phones avail. June-late Oct: D $80-$100; lower rates rest of yr. Children over 10 yrs only. TV in sitting rm, some rms; cable, VCR (free movies). Complimentary full bkfst. Coffee and tea in library. Restaurant nearby. Ck-out 11 am, ck-in 2 pm. Business servs avail. Luggage handling. Downhill/x-country ski 4 mi. Some fireplaces. Picnic tables. Farm house built 1802; barn and carriage house. Antiques include a 17th-century samurai chest. Totally nonsmoking. Cr cds: A, MC, V.

★★★ **NORUMBEGA INN.** *61 High St (04843). 207/236-4646; fax 207/236-0824. www.norumbegainn.com.* 13 rms, 1 A/C, 4 story, 2 suites. No elvtr. July-mid-Oct: D $155-$325; each addl $35; suites $375-$450; lower rates rest of yr. Children over 7 yrs only. TV in some rms; cable, VCR in suites. Complimentary full bkfst; afternoon refreshments. Restaurant nearby. Ck-out 11 am, ck-in 3 pm. Business servs avail. In-rm modem link. Downhill/x-country ski 4 mi. Lawn games. Some fireplaces. Balconies. Stone castle (1886); hand-carved oak woodwork, baby grand piano, antique billiard table, library within turret. Built by inventor of duplex telegraphy. Murder mystery wkends. Totally nonsmoking. Cr cds: A, DS, MC, V.

★★ **THE VICTORIAN BY THE SEA.** *Sea View Dr, Lincolnville (04849). 207/236-3785; fax 207/236-0017; toll-free 800/382-9817. www.victorianbythesea.com.* 7 rms, 2 with shower only, 1 A/C, 3 story. Mid-June-mid-Oct: S, D $160-$215; each addl $20; suites $205; wkly rates; 2-day min wkends in season; lower rates rest of yr. Children over 12 yrs only. Complimentary full bkfst; afternoon refreshments. Ck-out 11 am, ck-in 3 pm. Luggage handling. Downhill/x-country ski 7 mi. Lawn games. Many fireplaces. Some balconies. Antiques. Victorian summer cottage built in 1881. Totally nonsmoking. Cr cds: A, MC, V.

★★ **WHITEHALL INN.** *52 High St (04843). 207/236-3391; fax 207/236-4427; toll-free 800/789-6565. www.whitehall-inn.com.* 50 rms in 3 bldgs, most with bath, 2-3 story. No A/C. MAP, July-mid-Oct: S $85-$100; D $140-$180; each addl $45; under 14, $35; EP avail; lower rates Memorial Day-June. Closed rest of yr. Serv charge 15%. Crib $10. TV; cable in lobby. Afternoon refreshments. Restaurant (see WHITEHALL DINING ROOM). Bar. Ck-out 11 am, ck-in after 3 pm. Meeting rm. Business servs avail. Tennis. Health club privileges. Lawn games. Spacious old resort inn (1834); poet Edna St Vincent Millay gave a reading here in 1912. Garden with patio. Cr cds: A, MC, V.

Restaurants

★★ **CORK RESTAURANT.** *51 Bayview St (04843). 207/230-0533. www.corkrestaurant.com.* Specializes in prime meats, seafood, and game. Menu changes weekly. Hrs: 5:30-9:30 pm; winter hrs vary. Closed Sun, Mon. Res accepted. Extensive wine list. Dinner $16-$40. Cr cds: A, DS, MC, V.

★★ **THE HELM.** *RR 1, Camden Rd, Rockport (04856). 207/236-4337.* French, Amer menu. Specialties: French onion soup, steak au poivre, fresh seafood. Salad bar. Own desserts. Hrs: 11:30 am-8:30 pm; July-Labor Day to 9 pm. Closed mid-Dec-early Apr. Res accepted. Bar. Lunch, dinner $7-$17. Child's menu. Parking. Cr cds: DS, MC, V.

★★ **LOBSTER POUND.** *US 1, Lincolnville (04849). 207/789-5550.* Specializes in seafood, turkey, steak. Own desserts. Hrs: 11:30 am-9 pm. Closed Nov-Apr. Res accepted. Serv bar. Lunch, dinner $4.95-$13.95. Complete meals: dinner $9.95-$34.95. Child's menu. Parking. Lobster tanks. Outdoor dining. Fireplace. Gift shop. Overlooks Penobscot Bay. Family-owned. Cr cds: A, C, D, DS, ER, MC, V.

★★ **PETER OTT'S.** *16 Bayview St (04843). 207/236-4032.* Specializes in local seafood, black Angus beef. Own desserts. Salad bar. Hrs: 5:30-9:30 pm; July-Aug to 10 pm. Closed Jan 1, Dec 25; also Mon mid-Sept-mid-May. Bar 5-11 pm. Dinner $7.95-$22.95. Child's menu. Harbor view. Totally nonsmoking. Cr cds: MC, V.

★★ **WATERFRONT.** *40 Bayview St (04843). 207/236-3747.* Specializes in seafood. Own desserts. Hrs: 11:30 am-9:30 pm; June-Aug to 10 pm. Closed Thanksgiving, Dec 25. No A/C. Bar. Lunch $5.95-$13.95, dinner $12.95-$21.95. Child's menu. Parking. Outdoor dining. On harbor. Cr cds: A, MC, V.

★★★ **WHITEHALL DINING ROOM.** *52 High St (US 1) (04843). 207/236-3391. www.whitehall-inn.com.* Regional menu. Specializes in seafood, beef, vegetarian specials. Own baking, desserts. Hrs: 8-9:30 am, 6-8:30 pm. Closed mid-Oct-mid-June. No A/C. Bar. Wine list. Bkfst $7.95, dinner $15-$18. Child's menu. Cr cds: A, MC, V.

Caribou

See also Presque Isle

Pop 9,415 **Elev** 442 ft **Area code** 207 **Zip** 04736
Information Chamber of Commerce, 24 Sweden St, Suite 101
Web www.cariboumaine.net

Caribou, the nation's northeasternmost city, is primarily an agricultural area but has become diversified in manufacturing. Located here are a food processing plant, a paper bag manufacturing plant, and an electronics manufacturing plant. Swimming, fishing, boating, camping, and hunting are available in the many lakes located 20 miles northwest on ME 161.

What to See and Do

Caribou Historical Center. Museum housing history of northern Maine. (June-Aug, Thurs-Sat; rest of yr, by appt) 3 mi S on US 1. Phone 207/498-2556. **Donation**

Nylander Museum. Fossils, rocks, minerals, butterflies, and shells collected by Olof Nylander, Swedish-born geologist and naturalist; early man artifacts; changing exhibits. Gift shop. (Memorial Day-Labor Day, Wed-Sun; rest of yr, wkends and by appt) 393 Main St, ¼ mi S on ME 161. Phone 207/493-4209.

Rosie O'Grady's Balloon of Peace Monument. Honoring Colonel Joe W. Kittinger, Jr., who in 1984 was the first balloonist to fly solo across the Atlantic Ocean, breaking distance record set earlier by the *Double Eagle II* flight. 2 mi S on S Main St.

Special Event

Winter Carnival. Phone 800/722-7648. Feb.

Motels/Motor Lodges

★★★ **CARIBOU INN & CONVENTION CENTER.** *19 Main St (04736).* 207/498-3733; *res* 800/235-0466. *www.caribouinn.com.* 73 rms, 3 story. No elvtr. S, D $56-$80; suites $98-$106; each addl $8; under 12 free. Crib free. TV; cable (premium), VCR avail. Indoor pool; whirlpool. Restaurant 6 am-2 pm, 5-9 pm; Sat 7 am-2 pm, 5-9 pm; Sun 7 am-2 pm, 4-8 pm. Rm serv. Bar 5 pm-midnight; entertainment Fri, Sat. Ck-out 11 am. Coin lndry. Meeting rms. Business servs avail. Free airport transportation. X-country ski ½ mi. Exercise rm; sauna. Health club privileges. Game rm. Rec rm. Refrigerators, minibars. Some balconies. Cr cds: A, C, D, DS, MC, V.
🅓 ⬥ ≈ 🏋 ⊠ 🐾

★★ **CROWN PARK INN.** *Access Hwy (04736).* 207/493-3311; *fax* 207/498-3990; *toll-free* 888/493-3311. 60 rms, 2 story. S, D $50-$58; each addl $10; under 18 free. Crib $7. TV; cable, VCR avail (movies). Complimentary continental bkfst. Restaurant nearby. Bar 4 pm-1 am. Ck-out 11 am. Coin lndry. Meeting rm. Business servs avail. In-rm modem link. Exercise equipt. Some refrigerators. Cr cds: A, D, DS, MC, V.
🛇 ⛷ 🏋 🐾

Restaurants

★ **JADE PALACE.** *Skyway Plz (04736).* 207/498-3648. Chinese, Amer menu. Specialties: sizzling imperial steak, flaming Hawaiian duck, seafood. Hrs: 11 am-10 pm; wkends to 11 pm. Closed Thanksgiving. Res accepted. Bar. Lunch $1.95-$5.55, dinner $4.55-$12.95. Buffet: lunch $5.95, Sun $7.95. Cr cds: A, DS, MC, V.
🅓 ⓢⓒ

★ **RENO'S.** *117 Sweden St (04736).* 207/496-5331. Italian, Amer menu. Specializes in pizza, sandwiches, fish. Salad bar. Hrs: 5 am-11 pm; Sun 6 am-10 pm. Closed Memorial Day, Thanksgiving, Dec 25. Bkfst 95¢-$5, lunch $2.50-$7.95, dinner $2.50-$9. Child's menu. Cr cds: DS, MC, V.
🅓 ⓢⓒ

Center Lovell

Pop 100 **Elev** 532 ft **Area code** 207 **Zip** 04016

This community on Kezar Lake is close to the New Hampshire border and the recreational opportunities of the White Mountain National Forest (see BETHEL). The surrounding region is rich in gems and minerals.

Resort

★★ **QUISISANA LODGE.** *Pleasant Point Rd (04016).* 207/925-3500; *fax* 207/925-1004. *quisisanaresort.com.* 16 rms in 2 lodges, 38 cottages (1-3 bedrm). No A/C. AP, mid-June-Aug: S $280; D $330; each addl $80; July-Aug (1-wk min). Closed rest of yr. Crib free. TV rm. Dining rm. Box lunches. Ck-out 11 am, ck-in 2 pm. Tennis. Private sand beaches. Waterskiing. Boats, motors; rowboats, canoes. Fishing guides. Windsurfing. Lawn games. Musicals, operas, concerts performed by staff (music students). Game rm. Rec rms. Dancing. Units vary. Refrigerators, fireplaces. Porch in cottages. Lake sightseeing tours. On Lake Kezar in foothills of White Mts. Cr cds: A, MC, V.
⛵ ⛷ ✈ ⊠ 🔥 🐾

B&Bs/Small Inns

★★★ **ADMIRAL PEARY HOUSE.** *9 Elm St, Fryeburg (04037).* 207/935-3365; *toll-free* 800/237-8080. *www.admiralpearyhouse.com.* 6 rms, 3 story. No rm phones. S, D $80-$148; ski package; higher rates fall foliage; lower rates winter. TV in sitting rm; cable. Complimentary full bkfst. Restaurant nearby. Ck-out 11 am, ck-in 3 pm. Free airport transportation. Tennis. Bicycles. Downhill ski 8 mi; x-country ski on site. Billiard rm. Whirlpool. Bicycles. Home of Arctic explorer Robert E. Peary (1865). Extensive library. Totally nonsmoking. Cr cds: A, MC, V.
⛵ ⛷ 🐾 ⊠ 🐾

★★ **OXFORD HOUSE INN.** *105 Main St, Fryeburg (04037).* 207/935-3442; *fax* 207/935-7046; *toll-free* 800/261-7206. *www.oxfordhouseinn.com.* 4 rms, 3 story. No rm phones. D $80-$125; each addl $15. TV in some rms, sitting rm;

cable. Complimentary full bkfst. Restaurant (see OXFORD HOUSE INN). Ck-out 11 am, ck-in 1 pm. Downhill ski 8 mi; x-country ski on site. Historic house (1913); antiques, verandah. Totally nonsmoking. Cr cds: A, D, DS, MC, V.

Restaurant

★★ **OXFORD HOUSE INN.** *105 Main St, Fryeburg (04037). 207/935-3442. www.oxfordhouseinn.com.* Specializes in fresh seafood, sauteed dishes. Hrs: 6-9 pm. Closed Dec 24-25; also Mon-Wed winter and spring. Res required. Bar. Dinner $17-$22. Child's menu. Outdoor dining on screened porch. Fireplace. View of mountains. Totally nonsmoking. Cr cds: A, C, D, DS, MC, V.

Chebeague Islands

Pop 300 **Elev** 40 ft **Area code** 207 **Zip** 04017

Little Chebeague (sha-BEEG) and Great Chebeague islands, off the coast of Portland in Casco Bay, were at one time a favorite camping spot of various tribes. The Native Americans had a penchant for clams; the first European settlers thus found heaps of clamshells scattered across the land. Those shells were later used to pave many of the islands' roads, some of which still exist today.

Great Chebeague, six miles long and approximately three miles wide, is connected to Little Chebeague at low tide by a sandbar. There are various locations for swimming. Additionally, both islands lend themselves well to exploring on foot or bicycle. At one time, Great Chebeague was home to a bustling fishing and shipbuilding community, and it was a quarrying center in the late 1700s. Today, it welcomes hundreds of visitors every summer.

What to See and Do

Ferry service from mainland.

Casco Bay Lines. From Portland, Commercial, and Franklin Sts; one-hr crossing. (Daily) Phone 207/774-7871. ¢¢¢

Chebeague Transportation. From Cousins Island, near Yarmouth; 15-min crossing. (Daily) Off-site parking with shuttle to ferry. Phone 207/846-3700. ¢¢

Cranberry Isles

See also Bar Harbor, Northeast Harbor, Southwest Harbor

Pop 189 **Elev** 20 ft **Area code** 207 **Zip** 04625

The Cranberry Isles, named because of the rich, red cranberry bogs that once covered Great Cranberry Isle, lie off the southeast coast of Mount Desert Island. There are five islands in the group: Little and Great Cranberry, Sutton,

Bear, and Baker. Great Cranberry, the largest, covers about 900 acres. Baker Island is part of Acadia National Park, and Sutton is privately owned. In 1830, the islands petitioned the state to separate from Mount Desert Island. In the late 1800s, the area was a thriving fishing community.

What to See and Do

Acadia National Park. (see). N on Mt Desert Island.

Ferry service. Ferry connects Little Cranberry and Great Cranberry with Northeast Harbor (see) on Mt Desert Island; three-mi, 30-min crossing. (Summer, daily; rest of yr, varied schedule) Phone 207/244-3575. ¢¢

Islesford Historical Museum. Exhibits on local island history from 1604. (July-Aug, daily; Sept, by appt) Islesford, on Little Cranberry Island. Phone 207/244-9224. **FREE**

Damariscotta

See also Boothbay Harbor, Wiscasset

Settled 1730 **Pop** 1,811 **Elev** 69 ft **Area code** 207 **Zip** 04543
Information Chamber of Commerce, PO Box 13; 207/563-8340
Web www.damariscottaregion.com

Damariscotta, whose name is an Abenaki word meaning "river of many fishes," has a number of colonial, Greek Revival, and pre-Civil War houses. With the neighboring city of Newcastle across the Damariscotta River, this is a trading center for a seaside resort region extending to Pemaquid Point and Christmas Cove.

What to See and Do

Chapman-Hall House. (1754) Restored house with original whitewash kitchen, period furniture; local shipbuilding exhibition. (July-early Sept, Mon-Sat) Main and Church Sts. ¢

Colonial Pemaquid State Memorial. Excavations have uncovered foundations of jail, tavern, private homes. Fishing, boat ramp; picnicking; free parking. (Memorial Day-Labor Day, daily) Standard fees. 14 mi S via ME 130, in New Harbor. Phone 207/677-2423. Also here is

Fort William Henry State Memorial. Reconstructed 1692 fort tower; museum contains relics, portraits, maps, and copies of Native American deeds (fee).

☆ **Pemaquid Point Lighthouse Park.** Incl 1827 lighthouse that towers above the pounding surf (not open to public); Fishermen's Museum housed in old lightkeeper's dwelling (donation); art gallery; some recreational facilities. Fishermen's Museum (Memorial Day-Columbus Day, daily; rest of yr by appt). 15 mi S at end of ME 130 on Pemaquid Point. Phone 207/677-2494. ¢

St. Patrick's Church. (1808) Early Federal architecture; Revere bell in steeple; one of the oldest surviving Catholic churches in New England. W to Newcastle, then 2 mi N off US 1. Phone 207/563-3240.

Swimming. Pemaquid Beach, N of lighthouse.

Motel/Motor Lodge

★★ **OYSTER SHELL MOTEL.** *3063 Bristol Rd (04543). 207/563-3747; toll-free 800/874-3747. www.lincoln.midcoast.com/~oystrshl/.* 19 kit. suites, 4 story. No elvtr. July-Labor Day: S, D $125-$149; under 12 free; lower rates rest of yr. Crib free. TV; cable (premium). Heated pool. Complimentary coffee in rms. Restaurant nearby. Ck-out 11 am. X-country ski 2 mi. Microwaves. Balconies. Overlooks saltwater bay. Totally nonsmoking. Cr cds: A, MC, V.

⬛⬛⬛⬛

B&Bs/Small Inns

★★★ **THE BRADLEY INN.** *3063 Bristol Rd, New Harbor (04554). 207/677-2105; fax 207/677-3367; res 800/942-5560. www.bradleyinn.com.* 16 rms, 5 with shower only, 3 story. No A/C. June-Oct: S, D $105-$135; each addl $25; suites $140-$185; lower rates rest of yr. Crib avail. TV in parlor; cable. Complimentary full bkfst; afternoon refreshments. Restaurant 6-9 pm. Ck-out 11 am, ck-in 2-6 pm. Luggage handling. Bicycles. Lawn games. Some fireplaces. Built by a sea captain for his new bride in 1880. Near Pemaquid Lighthouse. Cr cds: A, MC, V.

⬛⬛⬛⬛

★★ **BRANNON-BUNKER INN.** *349 Rte 129, Walpole (04573). 207/563-5941.* 8 rms, 2 share bath, 2 story, 3 kits. No A/C. No rm phones. S $70; D $75; kit. units $70-$120. TV in sitting rm; VCR avail (free movies). Complimentary continental bkfst. Ck-out 11 am, ck-in 2 pm. Former barn and carriage house (1820s); antiques. WWI memorabilia. On river. Totally nonsmoking. Cr cds: A, C, D, DS, MC, V.

⬛⬛⬛

★★ **DOWN EASTER INN.** *218 Bristol Rd (04543). 207/563-5332.* 22 rms, 2 story. No A/C. No rm phones. Memorial Day-Oct: S $63.50; D $70-$80; each addl $10; under 16 free. Closed rest of yr. TV. Complimentary continental bkfst. Restaurant 6:30-10 am, 11 am-3 pm, 5-9 pm. Ck-out 11 am, ck-in 2 pm. Antiques. Lawn games. Greek Revival farmhouse (1785); built by a ship chandler whose ancestors were among the first settlers of Bristol. Cr cds: MC, V.

⬛⬛⬛ SC

★★★ **NEWCASTLE INN.** *60 River Rd, Newcastle (04553). 207/563-5685; fax 207/563-6877; toll-free 800/832-8669. www.newcastleinn.com.* 15 rms, some A/C, 3 story. No rm phones. S, D $250-$295; lower rates rest of yr. Children over 12 yrs only. TV in sitting rm; cable. Dining rm 8-9 am, 5:30-7:30 pm. Bar. Ck-out 11 am, ck-in 3 pm. X-country ski 3 mi. Some fireplaces, in-rm whirlpools. Dormered, clapboard, Federal-style inn (1850); library, antiques. Overlooks Damariscotta River. Totally nonsmoking. Cr cds: A, MC, V.

⬛⬛⬛

Restaurant

★★ **BACKSTREET LANDING.** *Elm St Plz (04543). 207/563-5666.* Specializes in seafood, vegetarian dishes. Own desserts. Hrs: 11:30 am-9 pm; July-Aug to 9:30 pm. Closed Jan 1, Thanksgiving, Dec 25; Wed Nov-Apr. Bar. Lunch $3.95-$13.95, dinner $8.95-$20.95. Child's menu. On river; scenic view. Cr cds: C, D, DS, ER, MC, V.

Ⓓ

Deer Isle

Settled 1762 **Pop** 1,829 **Elev** 23 ft **Area code** 207 **Zip** 04627
Information Deer Isle/Stonington Chamber of Commerce, PO Box 459, Stonington 04681; 207/348-6124 in season
Web www.deerisle.com

A bridge over Eggemoggin Reach connects these islands with the mainland. There are two major villages here—Deer Isle (the older) and Stonington. Lobster fishing and tourism are the backbone of the economy, and Stonington also cans sardines. Fishing, sailing, tennis, and golf are available in the area.

What to See and Do

Isle au Haut. (EEL-oh-HO) Reached by ferry from Stonington. Much of this island—with hills more than 500 ft tall, forested shores and cobblestone beaches—is in Acadia National Park (see). Phone 207/367-5193.

Isle au Haut Ferry Service. Service to the island and excursion trips avail. Phone 207/367-5193.

Resort

★★ **GOOSE COVE LODGE.** *Goose Cove Rd, Sunset (04683). 207/348-2508; fax 207/348-2624; toll-free 800/728-1963. www.goosecovelodge.com.* 22 units in cabins and lodge, 2 suites, 10 kit. units. No A/C. MAP, late June-Labor Day (2-day min): S $102-$140; D $120-$180; lower rates May-late June, Labor Day-mid-Oct. Closed rest of yr. Serv charge 15%. Crib avail. Playground. Free supervised children's activities. Sitting (public by res): lunch 11:30-3:30; dinner 5:30, 6:30, 7:30 pm. Box lunches, lobster cookouts. Ck-out 10:30 am, ck-in 3 pm. Business servs avail. Gift shop. Grocery, coin lndry 2 mi. Tennis privileges. Golf privileges. Private beach. Boats, sailboats, canoes, kayaks. Bicycles. Nature trails. Lawn games. Rec rm. Entertainment. Refrigerators; many fireplaces. Sun decks. Library with over 1,000 volumes. Rustic atmosphere. View of cove; on 21 acres. Cr cds: A, DS, MC, V.

⬛⬛⬛⬛⬛

B&B/Small Inn

★ ★ ★ **PILGRIMS INN.** *Main St on ME15 (04627). 207/348-6615; fax 207/348-6615. www.pilgrimsinn.com.* 15 rms, 3 share bath, 4 story. No A/C. MAP, July-Aug: D $160-$180; each addl $65; kit. cottage $215; wkly rates; lower rates mid-May-June and Sept-late Oct. Serv charge 15%. Closed rest of yr. Dining rm 8-9 am, 7 pm (one sitting; by res only). Honor bar. Ck-out 11 am, ck-in 1-5 pm. Gift shop. Fireplaces in library/sitting rm. Antiques. On ocean. Built 1793. Cr cds: A, DS, MC, V.
🔥

Eastport

See also Lubec

Settled 1780 **Pop** 1,965 **Elev** 60 ft **Area code** 207 **Zip** 04631
Information Chamber of Commerce, PO Box 254; 207/853-4644
Web www.eastport.net

At the southern end of Passamaquoddy Bay, Eastport is a community with 150-year-old houses and ancient elms. The average tide at Eastport is approximately 18 feet, but tides up to 25 feet have been recorded here. Eastport was the site of one of the country's first tide-powered electric generating projects, and though never completed, it resulted in the construction of two tidal dams. The city also boasts of being the nation's salmonid aquaculture capital, where millions of salmon and trout are raised in pens in the chilly off shore waters.

What to See and Do

Barracks Museum. This 1822 building once served as the officers' barracks for a nearby fort, which was held by British troops during the War of 1812. Museum. (Memorial Day-Labor Day, Tues-Sat afternoons) 74 Washington St. **FREE**

Ferry to Deer Island, New Brunswick. A 20-min trip; camping, picnicking on Deer Island. (June-Sept, daily) For schedules, fees inquire locally. (For Border Crossing Regulations, see MAKING THE MOST OF YOUR TRIP.) ¢¢

Fishing. Pollock, cod, flounder, and others caught from wharves. Charter boats avail for deep-sea fishing in sheltered waters.

Old Sow Whirlpool. One of largest in Western Hemisphere; most active three hrs before high tide. Between Dog and Deer islands.

Passamaquoddy Indian Reservation. Champlain, in 1604, was the first European to encounter members of this Algonquin tribe. Festivals and ceremonies throughout the yr (see SPECIAL EVENTS). About 5 mi N on ME 190 at Pleasant Point. Phone 207/853-2551. **FREE**

Whale-watching trips. Boat excursions during the summer to view whales in the bay.

Special Events

Indian Festival. At Passamaquoddy Indian Reservation. Ceremonies, fireworks, traditional celebrations. Second wkend Aug. Phone 207/853-4644.

Salmon Festival. Tours of aquaculture pens; music, crafts, educational displays; farm-raised Atlantic salmon dinners. Phone 207/853-4644. Sun after Labor Day.

Motel/Motor Lodge

★ ★ **THE MOTEL EAST.** *23A Water St (04631). 207/853-4747.* 14 rms, 2 story. No A/C. No elvtr. S $80; D $85; each addl $10; under 18 free. TV; cable. Complimentary coffee in rms. Restaurant adj. Ck-out 11 am. Business servs avail. Many refrigerators, microwaves. Many balconies. Picnic tables. On ocean. Cr cds: A, C, D, DS, ER, MC, V.
🄳 🛥 🖼 🔥

B&Bs/Small Inns

★ ★ **TODD HOUSE.** *1 Capen Ave (04631). 207/853-2328.* 8 rms, 6 share bath, 2 story, 2 kits. No A/C. No rm phones. S $45; D $50-$80; each addl $5-$10; under 5 free; wkly rates. Pet accepted. TV in most rms; cable. Complimentary continental bkfst. Restaurant nearby. Ck-out 11 am, ck-in 2 pm. Picnic tables, grill. This authentic New England Cape once housed soldiers during the War of 1812. Period antiques; original chimney. Near ocean; view of bay. Cr cds: MC, V.
🄳 🐾 🖼 🔥

★ ★ **WESTON HOUSE BED & BREAKFAST.** *26 Boyton St (04631). 207/853-2907; fax 207/853-0981; toll-free 800/853-2907.* 5 rms, 2 share baths. No A/C. S, D $50-$75; each addl $15. Complimentary full bkfst; afternoon refreshments. Restaurant nearby. Ck-out 11 am, ck-in 1 pm. Lawn games. Picnic tables. Restored 19th-century residence; sitting rm with tin ceiling. Cr cds: A, MC, V.
🖼 🔥

Cottage Colony

★ **SEAVIEW CAMPGROUND.** *16 Norwood Rd (04631). 207/853-4471. www.eastportmaine.com.* 13 units, 12 with shower only, 9 kit. cottages. No A/C. No rm phones. Mid-May-mid-Oct: S, D $50-$75; cottages $45-$55; wkly, monthly rates. Closed rest of yr. Crib free. TV; cable. Playground. Restaurant 6:30-10:30 am. Ck-out 10:30 am. Coin lndry. Gift shop. Rec rm. Lawn games. Picnic tables. On ocean, overlooking bay. Cr cds: DS, MC, V.
🛥 🖼 🖼

Ellsworth

See also Bar Harbor

Settled 1763 **Pop** 5,975 **Elev** 100 ft **Area code** 207 **Zip** 04605

Information Chamber of Commerce, 163 High St, PO Box 267; 207/667-5584 or 207/667-5584
Web www.ellsworthchamber.org

This is the shire town and trading center for Hancock County—which includes some of the country's choicest resort territory, including Bar Harbor. In the beginning of the 19th century, Ellsworth was the second biggest lumber shipping port in the world. Its business district was destroyed by fire in 1933, but was handsomely rebuilt, contrasting with the old residential streets.

What to See and Do

Lamoine State Park. A 55-acre recreation area around beach on Frenchman Bay. Fishing; boating (ramp); picnicking, camping. (Memorial Day-mid-Oct, daily) Standard fees. 8 mi SE on ME 184. Phone 207/667-4778. ¢

Stanwood Sanctuary (Birdsacre) and Homestead Museum. Trails, ponds, and picnic areas on 130-acre site. Collections incl mounted birds, nests and eggs. Wildlife rehabilitation center with shelters for injured birds, incl hawks and owls. Museum was home of pioneer ornithologist, photographer and writer Cordelia Stanwood (1865-1958). Sanctuary and rehabilitation center (daily; free); museum (mid-June-mid-Oct, daily). Gift shop. On Bar Harbor Rd (ME 3). Phone 207/667-8460. ¢¢

Woodlawn Museum (The Black House). (ca 1820) Federal house built by a local landowner; antiques. Garden; carriage house with old carriages and sleighs. (June-Sept, Tues-Sun) W Main St. Phone 207/667-8671. ¢¢

Motels/Motor Lodges

★ **COLONIAL TRAVELODGE.** *321 High St (04605). 207/667-5548; fax 207/667-5549; res 800/578-7878. www.acadia.net/colonial.* 68 rms, 2 story, 18 kit. units. July-Aug: S $78-$110; D $88-$120; each addl $6; suites $125; kit. units $78-$94; under 17 free; wkly rates; lower rates rest of yr. Crib $6. Pet accepted. TV. Indoor pool; whirlpool. Complimentary continental bkfst (June-Sept). Complimentary coffee in rms. Restaurant 11 am-9 pm. Ck-out 11 am. Business servs avail. X-country ski 15 mi. Health club privileges. Refrigerator avail. Balconies. Picnic tables. Cr cds: A, DS, MC, V.
🄳 🔌 🐾 ⛷ ≈ 🔌 🐾 SC

★ **ELLSWORTH MOTEL.** *24 High St (04605). 207/667-4424; fax 207/667-6942.* 16 rms, many with shower only, 1-2 story. Some A/C. July-Labor Day: S $34-$48; D $38-$64; each addl $8; lower rates rest of yr. Crib $4. TV; cable. Pool. Restaurant nearby. Ck-out 10 am. Cr cds: MC, V.
≈ 🔌 🐾

★★ **HOLIDAY INN.** *215 High St (04605). 207/667-9341; fax 207/667-7294; res 800/401-9341. www.holidayinn ellsworth.com.* 103 rms, 2 story. July-Aug: S $109-$119; D $119-$129; each addl $10; under 19 free; lower rates rest of yr. Crib free. Pet accepted. TV; cable, premium. Indoor pool; whirlpool, poolside serv. Complimentary coffee in rms. Restaurant 7-11 am, 5-10 pm. Rm serv. Bar 4 pm-1 am.

Ck-out noon. Coin lndry. Meeting rms. Business servs avail. In-rm modem link. Sundries. Indoor tennis. X-country ski 15 mi. Exercise equipt; sauna. Near river. Cr cds: A, C, D, DS, MC, V.
🄳 🔌 🐾 🛐 ≈ 🕇 🔌 🐾 SC

★ **HOMESTEAD MOTEL.** *RR 3 (04605). 207/667-8193.* 14 rms, some A/C. July-Aug: S $47-$52; D $48-$62; each addl $5; under 12 free; lower rates mid-May-June, Sept-mid-Oct. Closed rest of yr. TV; cable. Complimentary coffee in lobby. Ck-out 11 am. Some refrigerators. Totally nonsmoking. Cr cds: A, DS, MC, V.
🔌 🐾

★★ **TWILITE MOTEL.** *147 Bucksport Rd (04605). 207/667-8165; fax 207/667-0289; toll-free 800/395-5097. www. twilitemotel.com.* 22 rms, some A/C. July-Labor Day: S, D $50-$86; each addl $5; lower rates rest of yr. Crib free. Pet accepted; $5. TV; cable, VCR avail. Complimentary continental bkfst. Ck-out 10 am. Some refrigerators. Picnic table, grill. Cr cds: A, D, DS, MC, V.
🐾 🔌 🐾 SC

Restaurants

★★ **ARMANDO'S.** *ME 1, Hancock (04640). 207/422-3151.* Specializes in pasta, seafood. Hrs: 5-9 pm. Closed Jan 1, Easter, Dec 25; also Sun-Mon in summer, Sun-Thurs in winter. Res accepted. Italian menu. No A/C. Bar. Dinner $8.95-$16.95. Two-sided, stone fireplaces. Cr cds: MC, V.

★ **HILLTOP HOUSE.** *Bar Harbor Rd (04605). 207/667-9368.* Specializes in steak, seafood, pizza. Own baking. Hrs: 11 am-9:30 pm. Closed Jan 1, Thanksgiving, Dec 25. Bar. Lunch $2.25-$9.95, dinner $4.25-$16.95. Child's menu. Cr cds: A, C, D, DS, ER, MC, V.
🄳

Fort Kent

Settled 1829 **Pop** 4,268 **Area code** 207 **Zip** 04743
Information Chamber of Commerce, PO Box 430; 207/834-5354 or 800/733-3563

Fort Kent, at the northern end of famous US 1 (the other end is at Key West, Florida), is the chief community of Maine's "far north." A bridge across the St. John River leads to Clair, New Brunswick. (For Border Crossing Regulations, see MAKING THE MOST OF YOUR TRIP.) The town is a lumbering, farming, hunting, and fishing center, and canoeing, downhill and cross-country skiing, and snowmobiling are popular here. A campus of the University of Maine is located here.

What to See and Do

Canoeing. Fort Kent is the downstream terminus of the St. John-Allagash canoe trip, which starts at East Seboomook on Moosehead Lake, 156 mi and six portages away. (See ALLAGASH WILDERNESS WATERWAY)

Cross-country skiing. Fort Kent has 11½ mi of scenic intermediate and advanced trails. **FREE**

Fishing. Guides, boats, and gear avail for short or long expeditions up the Fish River chain of lakes for salmon or trout; St. John or Allagash rivers for trout.

Fort Kent Block House. Built in 1839, during the Aroostook Bloodless War with Britain, used for training exercises and as a guard post. Restored; antique hand tools in museum; interpretive displays. Picnicking. (Memorial Day-Labor Day, daily) N edge of town. Phone 207/834-3866.

Fort Kent Historical Society Museum and Gardens. Former Bangor and Aroostook railroad station, built in early 1900s, now houses historical museum. (Usually last two wks June-first wk Aug, Tues-Sat) 54 W Main St. For further information contact the Chamber of Commerce.

Skiing. Lonesome Pine Trails. Thirteen trails, 2,300-ft slope with 500-ft drop; beginners slope and tow; rope tow, T-bar; school, patrol, rentals; lodge, concession. (Dec-Apr, Wed and Fri-Sun, also hols) Forest Ave. Phone 207/834-5202. ¢¢¢¢

Special Event

Can Am Crown Sled Dog Races. Late Feb-early Mar. Phone 800/733-3563.

Freeport

See also Bath, Brunswick, Yarmouth

Pop 6,905 **Elev** 130 ft **Area code** 207 **Zip** 04032
Information Freeport Merchants Association, Hose Tower Information Center, 23 Depot St, PO Box 452; 207/865-1212 or 800/865-1994
Web www.freeportusa.com

It was in Freeport that legislators signed papers granting Maine independence from Massachusetts and, eventually, its statehood. The town is home to the renowned L. L. Bean clothing and sporting goods store; its major industries include retail, tourism, crabbing, and crabmeat packing.

What to See and Do

Atlantic Seal **Cruises.** Cruises aboard 40-ft, 28-passenger vessel on Casco Bay to Eagle Island and Robert E. Peary house museum; also seal- and bird-watching trips, fall foliage sightseeing cruises. (Schedules vary) Tickets must be purchased at Main St office, South Freeport. Depart from Town Wharf, foot of Main St in South Freeport, 2 mi S on S Freeport Rd. Phone 207/865-6112.

⚒ **Factory outlet stores.** Freeport is home to more than 120 outlet stores and centers that offer brand-name merchandise at discounted prices, incl the famous L. L. Bean clothing and sporting goods store, which stays open 24 hrs a day. For a list of outlet stores contact the Freeport Merchants Association. Phone 800/865-1994.

Mast Landing Sanctuary. A 140-acre area maintained by the Maine Audubon Society. Hiking, x-country skiing. (Daily) Upper Mast Landing Rd, 1½ mi E. Phone 207/781-2330. **FREE**

Winslow Memorial Park. Campground with swimming, boating (fee), x-country skiing; picnicking. (Schedule varies) Staples Point, 5 mi S off US 1, I-95. Phone 207/865-4198. ¢

Motels/Motor Lodges

★ **CASCO BAY INN.** *107 US 1 (04032).* 207/865-4925; fax 207/865-0696; toll-free 800/570-4970. www.cascobayinn.com. 30 rms, 2 story. July-mid-Oct: S, D $89-$109; each addl $7; lower rates mid-Apr-June, mid-Oct-mid-Dec. Closed rest of yr. TV; cable. Continental bkfst. Restaurant nearby. Ck-out 11 am. Totally nonsmoking. Cr cds: DS, MC, V.
🅳 🐾 🖼

★★ **COASTLINE INN.** *209 US 1 (04032).* 207/865-3777; fax 207/865-4678; toll-free 800/470-9494. coastlineinnmaine.com. 108 rms in 3 bldgs, 2 story. July-Oct: S $49-$89; D $59-$99; under 12 free; wkly rates (off season); lower rates rest of yr. TV; cable (premium), VCR avail. Pet accepted, some restrictions. Complimentary continental bkfst. Coffee in rms. Restaurant nearby. Ck-out 11 am. Coin lndry. Balconies. Picnic tables, grills. Cr cds: A, DS, JCB, MC, V.
🅳 🐾 🖼 🔥 🖼

Hotel

★★ **FREEPORT INN.** *31 US Rte 1 (04032).* 207/865-3106; fax 207/865-6364; toll-free 800/998-2583. www.freeportinn .com. 80 rms, 3 story. No elvtr. May-Oct: S, D $60-$100; each addl $10; lower rates rest of yr. Crib $10. Pet accepted, some restrictions. TV; cable. Pool. Restaurant 6 am-9 pm; to 8 pm off season. Ck-out 11 am. Meeting rms. Business servs avail. In-rm modem links. Valet serv. Lawn games. Balconies. Picnic tables. On 25 acres; river; canoe. Some refrigerators. Cr cds: A, D, DS, MC, V.
🅳 🐾 🖼 🖼 🔥 🖼

B&Bs/Small Inns

★★ **181 MAIN STREET BED & BREAKFAST.** *181 Main St. (04032).* 207/865-1226; toll-free 800/235-9750. 7 rms, 2 story. 4 A/C. No rm phones. Memorial Day-Oct: S $85; D $110; lower rates rest of yr. Children over 14 yrs only. TV in sitting rm; cable, VCR. Pool. Complimentary full bkfst. Restaurant nearby. Ck-out 11 am, ck-in 3-7 pm. X-country ski 2 mi. Antiques. Library. Restored Greek Revival Cape (ca 1840); Colonial furnishings. Totally nonsmoking. Cr cds: MC, V.
🖼 🖼 🖼 🔥

★★ **THE BAGLEY HOUSE.** *1290 Royalsborough Rd, Durham (04222).* 207/865-6566; fax 207/353-5878; toll-free 800/765-1772. www.bagleyhouse.com. 8 rms, 2 story. No A/C. No rm phones. Early July-Oct: S $75-$90; D $90-$150; each addl $25; lower rates rest of yr. Complimentary full bkfst; afternoon refreshments. Ck-out 11 am, ck-in 3 pm. Meeting rm. X-country ski on site. Some fireplaces. Picnic tables. Antiques. Library. Restored country inn (1772); hand-hewn wood beams, wide pine floors, original beehive oven. Totally nonsmoking. Cr cds: A, D, DS, JCB, MC, V.
🅳 🖼 🖼 🔥 🆂🅲

★ ★ BREWSTER HOUSE BED & BREAKFAST.
180 Main St (04032). 207/865-4121; fax 207/865-4221; toll-free 800/865-0822. www.brewsterhouse.com. 7 rms, 1 with shower only, 3 story. No rm phones. Memorial Day-Oct: S $80-$115; D $90-$125; each addl $15; suites $125; lower rates rest of yr. Children over 7 yrs only. TV in sitting rm; cable. Complimentary full bkfst. Restaurant nearby. Ck-out 11 am, ck-in 3 pm. Built in 1888; antiques. Totally non-smoking. Cr cds: A, DS, MC, V.
🖼 🖼

★ ★ ★ HARRASEEKET INN. *162 Main St (04032). 207/865-9377; fax 207/865-1684; toll-free 800/342-6423. www.harraseeketinn.com.* 84 rms, 3 story. Late May-Oct: S, D $100-$205; each addl $20; suites $225; under 6 free; lower rates rest of yr. Crib $5. TV; cable, VCR avail. Indoor pool. Complimentary full bkfst. Dining rm (see THE MAINE DINING ROOM). Rm serv. Bar. Ck-out 11 am, ck-in 3 pm. Meeting rms. Business servs avail. In-rm modem link. Luggage handling. Gift shop. Airport transportation. X-country ski 8 mi. Exercise equipt. Some in-rm whirlpools, fireplaces. Consists of 3 structures: Federalist house (1798), early Victorian house (1850) modern, Colonial-style inn; drawing rm, antiques. On 5 acres. Cr cds: A, C, D, DS, MC, V.
🖼 🖼 🖼 🖼 🖼 🖼 🖼 🖼

★ ★ KENDALL TAVERN B&B. *213 Main St (04032). 207/865-1338; fax 207/865-3544; toll-free 800/341-9572. www.bedandbreakfast.com.* 7 rms, 3 story. No A/C. No rm phones. Memorial Day-Oct: S $75-$105; D $85-$120; each addl $20; lower rates rest of yr. TV in sitting rm; cable. Complimentary full bkfst. Restaurant nearby. Ck-out 11 am, ck-in 3 pm. Whirlpool. X-country ski 2 mi. Restored New England farmhouse (ca 1850); antiques. Totally nonsmoking. Cr cds: A, C, D, DS, MC, V.
🖼 🖼 🖼

★ ★ WHITE CEDAR INN. *178 Main St (04032). 207/865-9099; toll-free 800/853-1269. www.whitecedarinn.com.* 7 rms, 6 with shower only, 2 story. No rm phones. July-Oct, wkends in June, Nov, Dec: S, D $95-$130; each addl $15; lower rates rest of yr. Children over 11 yrs only. TV in sitting rm; cable. Complimentary full bkfst. Restaurant adj 11 am-10 pm. Ck-out 11 am, ck-in 3 pm. Luggage handling. Former home of Arctic explorer Donald MacMillan. Totally nonsmoking. Cr cds: A, DS, MC, V.
🖼 🖼

Restaurants

★ CORSICAN. *9 Mechanic St (04032). 207/865-9421.* Italian, Amer menu. Specialties: pesto and tomato pizza, vegetable lasagne, calzones. Hrs: 11 am-9 pm. Closed Jan 1, Thanksgiving, Dec 25. Beer, wine. Lunch $4-$9.95, dinner $4-$14.95. Totally nonsmoking. Cr cds: D, DS, MC, V.

★ GRITTY MCDUFF'S. *183 Lower Main St (US 1) (04032). 207/865-4321. www.grittys.com.* Specializes in seafood, pizza. Hrs: 11:30-1 am. Res accepted. Bar. Lunch, dinner $4.25-$12.50. Child's menu. Outdoor dining. Casual decor. Cr cds: A, MC, V.
🖼 🖼 🖼

★ ★ JAMESON TAVERN. *115 Main St (US 1) (04032). 207/865-4196.* Specializes in seafood, steak. Hrs: 11 am-2:30 pm, 5-10 pm. Closed Dec 25. Res accepted. Bar to 11 pm. Lunch $4.95-$9.50, dinner $10.25-$21.95. Child's menu. Parking. Patio dining. Historic tavern (1779); final papers separating Maine from the Commonwealth of Massachusetts were signed here. Cr cds: A, D, DS, MC, V.
🖼

★ LOBSTER COOKER. *39 Main St (US 1) (04032). 207/865-4349. www.lobstercooker.com.* Specializes in fresh crab and lobster rolls, chowder. Hrs: 11 am-9 pm. No A/C. Wine, beer. A la carte entrees: lunch, dinner $2.95-$12.95. Parking. Outdoor dining. Lobster tank. Historic building (1816). Cr cds: A, MC, V.
🖼

★ ★ ★ THE MAINE DINING ROOM. *162 Main St (04032). 207/865-1085. www.harraseeketinn.com.* Regional menu with organically raised ingredients. Hrs: 6-9:30 pm. Res accepted. Bar to 10 pm. Wine cellar. Dinner $18-$32. Complete meals for 2: dinner $60. Child's menu. Parking. Own baking. Outdoor dining. Colonial decor; some antiques. Totally nonsmoking. Cr cds: A, C, D, DS, ER, MC, V.
🖼

Greenville

Settled 1824 **Pop** 1,884 **Elev** 1,038 ft **Area code** 207 **Zip** 04441

Information Moosehead Lake Region Chamber of Commerce, PO Box 581; 207/695-2702 or 888/876-2778

Web www.mooseheadlake.org

Greenville is a starting point for trips into the Moosehead Lake region (see). Until it was incorporated in 1836, it was known as Haskell, in honor of its founder Nathaniel Haskell.

What to See and Do

Baxter State Park. (see). Approx 45 mi NE via private paper company roads.

Lily Bay State Park. A 924-acre park on Moosehead Lake. Swimming, fishing, boating (ramp); picnicking, camping (dump station). (Mid-May-mid-Oct) Snowmobiling permitted. Standard fees. 8 mi N via local roads, near Beaver Cove. Phone 207/695-2700.

Moosehead Marine Museum. On steamboat *Katahdin*, berthed in East Cove. Exhibits of the steamboat era and the Kineo Hotel; cruises avail. (July-Columbus Day, daily; June, Sat and Sun) Phone 207/695-2716. ¢¢¢¢

Skiing. Moosehead Resort on Big Squaw Mountain. Double, triple chairlifts, T-bar, pony lift; novice-to-expert trails; rentals, school, patrol, snowmaking; cafeteria, restaurant, bar; nursery; lodge. Longest run 2½ mi; vertical drop 1,750 ft. (Late Nov-Apr, daily) X-country trails. Chairlift rides (June-mid-Oct; fee). 5 mi NW on ME 6/15, then 2 mi W on access road. For further information contact the Chamber of Commerce. Phone 800/940-2112.

Special Event

MooseMainea. Various locations around Greenville. Celebration honoring the moose. Canoe race, rowing regatta, fly-fishing championship, Tour de Moose bike race. Family Fun Day with parade, crafts, entertainment. Moose-sighting tours. Phone 207/695-2702. Mid-May-mid-June.

Motels/Motor Lodges

★ **CHALET MOOSEHEAD LAKEFRONT MOTEL.** *Rte 15, Greenville Jct (04442). 207/695-2950; toll-free 800/290-3645. www.mooseheadlodging.com.* 15 rms, 8 kit. units (no ovens); 2-story motel unit, 2 kit. cottages. No A/C. Late June-early Sept, also Memorial Day, Columbus Day wkends: S, D $45-$75; each addl $10; cottages $80-$100; kit. units $72; under 5 free; lower rates rest of yr. Pet accepted; $10. TV; cable (premium). Complimentary coffee in lobby. Restaurant nearby. Ck-out 10 am. Boat rentals. Seaplane rides nearby. Lawn games. Picnic tables, grills. On Moosehead Lake; dockage, canoes, paddleboats. Cr cds: A, DS, MC, V.

⌨ 🐾 🎣 ✈ 🖼 🔥

★ **INDIAN HILL.** *S Main St (04441). 207/695-2623; fax 207/695-2950; toll-free 800/771-4620. www.mooseheadlodging.com.* 15 rms. No A/C. May-Oct: S $45-$65; D $50-$65; each addl $10; lower rates rest of yr. TV; cable (premium). Complimentary coffee in lobby. Restaurant nearby. Ck-out 10:30 am. Gift shop. View of Moosehead Lake, mountains. Cr cds: A, DS, MC, V.

⌨ ✈ 🖼 🔥

★ **KINEO VIEW MOTOR LODGE.** *Rte 15 (04441). 207/695-4470; fax 207/695-4656; toll-free 800/659-8439. www.kineoview.com.* 12 rms, 2 story. No A/C. Memorial Day-mid-Oct: D $65-$75; each addl $5; under 13 free; wkly rates; lower rates rest of yr. Pet accepted; $5. TV. Whirlpool. Complimentary continental bkfst in season. Ck-out 10:30 am. Downhill ski 9 mi; x-country ski on site. Game rm. Lawn games. Balconies. Picnic tables. Lake views. Cr cds: A, DS, MC, V.

🐾 🖼 🖼 🔥 SC

Hotel

★ **GREENWOOD.** *Rte 15; Rockwood Rd, Greenvlle Jct (04442). 207/695-3321; fax 207/695-2122; toll-free 800/477-4386. www.greenwoodmotel.com.* 16 rms, 2 story. Mid-May-mid-Sept: S $39.95-$59; D $44.95-$64; each addl $5; hunting plans; lower rates rest of yr. Crib free. Pet accepted; $5. TV; cable (premium). Pool. Complimentary continental bkfst. Complimentary coffee in rms. Restaurant nearby. Ck-out 10:30 am. Meeting rm. Business servs avail. 9-hole golf privileges. Downhill/x-country ski 3 mi. Hiking trails. Lawn games. Refrigerators. Picnic tables, grills. Cr cds: A, C, D, DS, MC, V.

⌨ 🐾 ⌨ 🖼 🍴 🖼 ✈ 🖼 🔥

B&Bs/Small Inns

★★ **GREENVILLE INN.** *Norris St (04441). 207/695-2206; fax 207/695-0335; toll-free 888/695-6000. www.greenvilleinn.com.* 5 rms, 3 story, 1 suite, 6 cottages. No rm phones. Late June-mid Oct: S, D $155-$165; each addl $20; suite $195; lower rates rest of yr. Complimentary continental bkfst. Dining rm May-Oct 6-9 pm. Bar 5-11 pm. Ck-out 11 am, ck-in 3 pm. TV in some rms, cottages; cable. Downhill/x-country ski 8 mi. Some refrigerators, fireplaces. Former lumber baron residence (1895); cherrywood, mahogany antiques. Porches with view of mountains, lake; flower gardens. Cr cds: DS, MC, V.

🖼 ✈ 🖼 🔥

★★★ **THE LODGE AT MOOSEHEAD LAKE.** *Lily Bay Rd (04441). 207/695-4400; fax 207/695-2281. www.lodgeat mooseheadlake.com.* 5 rms, 3 suites, 2 story. No rm phones. Jan-late Mar, mid-May-late Oct: S, D $175-$395; 2-night min. Children over 14 yrs only. TV; cable, VCR. Complimentary full bkfst. Complimentary coffee in rms. Ck-out 11 am, ck-in 3 pm. Concierge. Business servs avail. Downhill ski 10 mi; x-country ski 2 mi; Totally non-smoking. Cr cds: A, DS, MC, V.

🦽 🖼 🖼 🖼 🔥

Houlton

Settled 1805 **Pop** 6,613 **Elev** 366 ft **Area code** 207 **Zip** 04730

Information Greater Houlton Chamber of Commerce, 109 Main St; 207/532-4216

Web www.greaterhoulton.com

Houlton prospered first from lumber, then from the famous Maine potatoes. It is young by New England standards, but was the first town settled in Aroostook County. Industries include woodworking and wood chip and waferboard factories. It is two miles from the Canadian border and a major port of entry. Swimming is available at Nickerson Lake. Fishing is available in several nearby lakes. (For Border Crossing Regulations, see MAKING THE MOST OF YOUR TRIP.)

What to See and Do

Aroostook Historical and Art Museum. Pioneer exhibits, local historical items incl model and artifacts from Hancock Barracks, memorabilia from the now closed Ricker College. (Memorial Day-Labor Day, Mon-Fri) 109 Main St. Phone 207/532-4216. **FREE**

Hancock Barracks. Second northernmost Federal outpost in the country; manned by troops from 1828-1846. Garrison Hill, 1 mi E on US 2. **FREE**

Market Square Historic District. These historic 1890s buildings show a high degree of design artistry. Contact Chamber of Commerce for walking tour maps. Main St between Kendall and Broadway. **FREE**

Museum of Vintage Fashions. Contains 17 rms of men's, women's, and children's vintage fashions. Dress-makers shop, hat boutique, bridal rm, haberdashery. (June-early Oct, Mon-Thurs, also Fri-Sun by appt only) 25 mi SW via US 2 to Island Falls, on Sherman St. Phone 207/463-2404. **Donation**

Special Events

Meduxnekeag River Canoe Race. Late Apr. Phone 207/532-4216.

Houlton Fair. Entertainment, concessions, rides. Early July. Phone 207/532-4216.

Houlton Potato Feast Days. Last full wkend Aug. Phone 207/532-4216.

Motels/Motor Lodges

★★ **IVEYS MOTOR LODGE.** *Hwy 1 & I-95 (04730). 207/532-4206; toll-free 800/244-4206. www.mainerec.com/ivey.html.* 24 rms. June-mid-Oct: S $48-$64; D $64-$68; each addl $8; lower rates rest of yr. Crib $8. TV; cable (premium). Complimentary coffee in rms. Restaurant adj open 24 hrs. Bar 4 pm-midnight. Ck-out 11 am. Meeting rms. Business servs avail. Health club privileges. Refrigerators. Cr cds: A, C, D, DS, MC, V.
🅳 🔄 🐾

★ **SCOTTISH INN.** *239 Bangor St (04730). 207/532-2236; fax 207/532-9893.* 43 rms. May-mid-Nov: S, D $44-$48; each addl $6; lower rates rest of yr. Crib $6. Pet accepted; $6. TV; cable (premium). Complimentary coffee in lobby. Restaurant nearby. Ck-out 11 am. Business servs avail. Refrigerators. Cr cds: A, MC, V.
🐾 🔄 🔥 SC

★★ **SHIRETOWN MOTOR INN.** *282 North St at I-95 (04730). 207/532-9421; fax 207/532-3390; toll-free 800/441-9421. www.shiretownmotorairport.com.* 51 rms. June-mid Oct: S, D $60-$62; each addl $10; suites $72; kit. units $72. Crib $7. TV; cable (premium). Indoor pool. Complimentary coffee in lobby. Restaurant 5-10 pm. Bar to 1 am. Ck-out 11 am. Coin lndry. Meeting rms. Business servs avail. Tennis. Exercise equipt. Refrigerators. Cr cds: A, MC, V.
🎾 🔄 🏋 🔥

★ **STARDUST.** *672 North St (04730). 207/532-6538; fax 207/532-4143; toll-free 800/437-8406.* 11 rms. May-Sept: S $35; D $45; each addl $5; lower rates rest of yr. TV; cable (premium). Ck-out 11 am. Cr cds: A, DS, MC, V.
🐾 🔄 🔥

Kennebunk

See also Kennebunkport, Old Orchard Beach, Portland, Saco

Settled 1650 **Pop** 8,004 **Elev** 50 ft **Area code** 207 **Zip** 04043
Information Chamber of Commerce, 17 Western Ave, ME 9-Lower Village, PO Box 740; 207/967-0857
Web www.kkcc.maine.org

The original settlement that was to become Kennebunk was at one time a part of Wells. When Maine separated from Massachusetts in 1820, Kennebunk separated from Wells. Once a shipbuilding community on the Mousam and Kennebunk rivers, Kennebunk today is the principal business center of a summer resort area that includes Kennebunkport (see) and Kennebunk Beach.

What to See and Do

Brick Store Museum. A blk of restored 19th-century buildings incl William Lord's Brick Store (1825); exhibits of fine and decorative arts, historical and maritime collections. (Wed-Fri; closed hols) 117 Main St, US 1, opp library. Phone 207/985-4802. ¢¢

Taylor-Barry House. (ca 1803) Sea captain's Federal period house with furniture, stenciled hallway; 20th-century artist's studio. (June-Sept, Tues-Fri afternoons) 24 Summer St. Phone 207/985-4802. ¢¢

Special Event

Winter Carnival. Snow sculpture contests, snow palace moonwalk, magic show, ice-skating party, chili and chowder contests, children's events. Phone 800/982-4421. Feb.

Motels/Motor Lodges

★ **THE SEASONS INN OF THE KENNEBUNK.** *55 York St (04043). 207/985-6100; fax 207/985-4031; toll-free 800/336-5634.* 44 rms, 2 story. July-mid Oct: S, D $99-$149; each addl $10; under 18 free; lower rates rest of yr. Crib $10. TV; cable. Pool. Complimentary continental bkfst. Complimentary coffee in rms. Ck-out 11 am. Balconies. Some refrigerators; microwaves avail.
🅳 🔄 🐾 SC

★ **TURNPIKE MOTEL.** *77 Old Alewive Rd (04043). 207/985-4404.* 25 rms, 2 story. Mid-June-early Sept: S, D $45-$70; each addl $5; lower rates rest of yr. Crib $5. TV; cable. Complimentary coffee in rms. Ck-out 11 am. Refrigerators. Picnic tables. Cr cds: MC, V.
🔄 🔥

B&Bs/Small Inns

★★ **ARUNDEL MEADOWS INN.** *1024 Portland Rd, Rundel (04046). 207/985-3770. www.arundelsmeadowsinn.com.* 7 rms, 2 story, 2 suites. No rm phones. June-Oct: S, D $75-$95; each addl $20; suites $100-$125; wkly rates; lower rates rest of yr. Children over 11 yrs only. TV in some rms; cable. Complimentary full bkfst. Ck-out 11 am, ck-in 2 pm. Some fireplaces. Picnic tables, grills. Sitting rm. Restored farmhouse (1827); artwork, antiques, garden. Totally nonsmoking. Cr cds: MC, V.
🔄 🔥

★★★ **THE BEACH HOUSE.** *211 Beach Ave, Kennebunk Beach (04043). 207/967-3850; fax 207/967-4719. www.beachhseinn.com.* 34 rms, 2-4 story. Late June-early Sept: S $115-$195; D $145-$210; each addl $25; 3-day min high-season, hols; lower rates rest of yr. TV; cable.

Complimentary continental bkfst. Ck-out 11 am, ck-in 2 pm. Built circa 1890; period antiques, gardens. Overlooks ocean, swimming beach. Totally nonsmoking. Cr cds: A, MC, V.

★★ **THE KENNEBUNK INN.** *45 Main St (04043). 207/985-3351; fax 207/985-8865. www.thekennebunkinn.com.* 28 rms, 3 story, 4 suites. Some rm phones. Mid-June-late Oct: S, D $55-$95; each addl $10; suites $160; under 5 free; lower rates rest of yr. Crib $10. Pet accepted. TV in some rms, sitting rm; cable. Complimentary continental bkfst. Dining rm (see THE KENNEBUNK INN). Ck-out 11 am, ck-in 3 pm. Business servs avail. Built 1799; turn-of-the-century decor, antiques, library. Cr cds: A, DS, MC, V.

Restaurants

★★★ **GRISSINI.** *27 Western Ave (04043). 207/967-2211.* Specializes in fresh pasta, wood-oven pizza. Hrs: 5:30-9:30 pm; Sat from 5 pm; off-season hrs vary. Closed Thanksgiving. Res accepted. Northern Italian menu. Bar. Wine list. Dinner $10.95-$17.95. Child's menu. Parking. Outdoor dining. Totally nonsmoking. Cr cds: A, DS, MC, V.

★★ **THE KENNEBUNK INN.** *45 Main St (04043). 207/985-3351. www.thekennebunkinn.com.* Contemporary Amer menu. Specialties: grilled loin of lamb, flaming creme brulee. Hrs: 5-9:30 pm. Closed Dec 25. Res accepted. Bar from 4 pm. Dinner $11-$19. Child's menu. Parking. Outdoor dining. Inn built 1799; stained-glass windows. Totally nonsmoking. Cr cds: A, C, DS, MC, V.

★★★ **WINDOWS ON THE WATER.** *12 Chase Hill Rd (04043). 207/967-3313. www.windowsonthewater.com.* Regional Amer menu. Specializes in lobster. Hrs: 11:45 am-2:30 pm, 5:30-9:30 pm. Closed Dec 25. Res accepted. Serv bar. Wine list. Lunch $6.90-$12.90, dinner $12.90-$25.90. Child's menu. Outdoor dining. Contemporary decor with views of river and marina; open kitchen. Totally nonsmoking. Cr cds: A, C, D, DS, ER, MC, V.

Kennebunkport

See also Kennebunk, Old Orchard Beach, Portland, Saco

Settled 1629 **Pop** 3,356 **Elev** 20 ft **Area code** 207 **Zip** 04046
Information Chamber of Commerce, 17 Western Ave, ME 9-Lower Village, PO Box 740, Kennebunk 04043; 207/967-0857
Web www.kkcc.maine.org

At the mouth of the Kennebunk River, this coastal town is a summer and winter resort, as well as an art and literary colony. It was the home of author Kenneth Roberts and the scene of his novel *Arundel*. During the Bush administration, the town achieved fame as the summer residence of the 41st President.

What to See and Do

Architectural Walking Tour. Tours of historic district (June-Sept, Wed, Fri). Phone 207/985-4802. ¢¢

The Nott House. (1853) Greek Revival house with original wallpaper and furnishings from the Perkins-Nott family. Tours. (June-mid-Oct, Tues-Fri afternoons) 8 Maine St. Phone 207/967-2751. ¢¢

School House. (1899) Headquarters of the Kennebunkport Historical Society. Houses collections of genealogy, photographs, maritime history, and many artifacts and documents on Kennebunkport's history. (Wed-Fri afternoons) 135 North St. Phone 207/967-2751. **FREE**

Seashore Trolley Museum. Approx 200 antique streetcars from US and abroad; special events. (Late May-mid-Oct, daily) 3½ mi N on Log Cabin Rd (North St). Phone 207/967-2800. ¢¢¢

Swimming. Colony Beach and Goose Rocks Beach.

Motels/Motor Lodges

★★ **CAPE ARUNDEL INN.** *208 Ocean Ave (04046). 207/967-2125; fax 207/967-1199. www.capearundelinn.com.* 7 inn rms, 6 motel rms. No A/C. Mid-June-late-Oct: inn rms $235-$350; motel rms $175; each addl $20; lower rates late-Apr-mid-June, late-Oct-mid-Dec. Closed rest of yr. TV in motel rms; cable. Complimentary continental bkfst. Restaurant 6-9 pm. Ck-out 11 am. Balconies on motel rms. Victorian-style inn (1890); turn-of-the-century decor. Overlooks seacoast. Totally nonsmoking. Cr cds: A, DS, MC, V.

★★ **RHUMB LINE MOTOR LODGE.** *Ocean Ave (04046). 207/967-5457; fax 207/967-4418; toll-free 800/337-4862. www.rhumblinemaine.com.* 59 units, 1-3 story. No elvtr. July-Aug: S $69-$149; D $79-$159; suites $125-$145; under 12 free; wkly rates; lower rates rest of yr. Crib free. TV; cable. 2 pools, 1 indoor; whirlpool. Complimentary continental bkfst. Bar to 8 pm (in season). Ck-out 11 am. Meeting rms. Business servs avail. Exercise equipt; sauna. Refrigerators. Balconies. Picnic tables. Secluded woodland location. On trolley route. Cr cds: A, DS, MC, V.

★★ **VILLAGE COVE INN.** *29 S Maine St (04046). 207/967-3993; fax 207/967-3164; toll-free 800/879-5778. www.villagecoveinn.com.* 32 rms, 1-2 story. July-Aug: S, D $149-$239; each addl $25; under 12 free; lower rates rest of yr. Crib $20. TV; cable. 2 pools, 1 indoor; poolside serv in season. Complimentary full bkfst. Restaurant 7:30-10 am, 5:30-9:30 pm; varied hrs off season. Bar 11:30 am-closing, off-season from 4:30 pm; entertainment wkends. Ck-out 11 am. Meeting rms. Business servs avail. Refrigerators. Totally nonsmoking. Cr cds: A, DS, MC, V.

★★ **YACHTSMAN LODGE & MARINA.**
Ocean Ave (04046). 207/967-2511; fax 207/967-5056.
www.yachtsmanlodge.com. 30 rms. Some A/C. July-early
Sept: D $139-$175; each addl $15; lower rates May-June,
early Sept-Oct. Closed rest of yr. TV; cable (premium).
Complimentary continental bkfst. Restaurant opp 8 am-
8 pm. Ck-out 11 am. Business servs avail. Refrigerators.
Patios. Picnic tables, grill. On river; marina, dockage.
Cr cds: A, MC, V.

Hotels

★ **AUSTINS INN TOWN HOTEL.** *28 Dock Sq (04046).*
207/967-4241; toll-free 888/228-0548. 14 rms, 3 story, 2
suites, 2 kits. No rm phones. Mid-June-mid-Oct: S, D $54-
$69; each addl $15; suites $99-$198; kit. units $99-$198;
mid-wk rates; lower rates Apr-mid-June, mid-late Oct.
Closed rest of yr. Crib free. TV; cable (premium). Restaurant
nearby. Ck-out 11 am. Gift shop. In historic district on
Kennebunk River. Cr cds: DS, MC, V.

★★★ **KENNEBUNKPORT INN.** *1 Dock Sq (04046).*
207/967-2621; fax 207/967-3705; toll-free 800/248-2621.
www.kennebunkportinn.com. 34 rms, 2-3 story. Late June-
Oct: S $80-$239; D $89-$310; each addl $12; MAP avail;
summer and hol wkends (3-day min), spring, fall wkends
(2-day min); lower rates rest of yr. Crib $12. TV; cable.
Pool. Outdoor lunch noon-2:30 pm; Dining rm 8-10 am,
6-9 pm (May-Oct). Bar 5 pm-1 am; pianist in season. Ck-
out 11 am. Business servs avail. Victorian mansion (1899)
built by wealthy tea and coffee merchant, renovated to an
inn (1926); lounge/sitting rm, antiques. Cr cds: A, MC, V.

★★ **THE SCHOONERS INN.** *127 Ocean Ave (04046).*
207/967-5333; fax 207/967-2040. www.schoonersinn.com.
17 rms, 3 story. Mid-June-mid-Oct: S, D $295-$525; each
addl $10; suite $250; under 12 free; wkends (2-day min);
higher rates hols; lower rates rest of yr. Crib $10. TV; cable
(premium), VCR avail. Complimentary continental bkfst.
Restaurant 7 am-2 pm. Rm serv. Ck-out 11 am. Business
servs avail. Luggage handling. Concierge serv. Gift shop.
Refrigerators. Some balconies. On river with views of
Atlantic Ocean. Cr cds: A, MC, V.

★★ **SEASIDE HOUSE & COTTAGES.** *Goochs Beach,*
Kennebunkport Beach (04046). 207/967-4461; fax 207/967-
1135. www.kennebunkbeach.com. 22 rms, 1-2 story, 10 kit.
cottages (1-wk min). No A/C. July-late Aug: S $79-$189; D
$89-$199; lower rates rest of yr. Cottages closed Nov-Apr.
Crib avail. Pet accepted, some restrictions; $50 refundable.
TV; cable. Playground. Ck-out 11 am. Coin lndry. Lawn
games. Refrigerators. Private patios, balconies. Private beach;
boat ramps. Cr cds: A, MC, V.

Resorts

★★★ **COLONY HOTEL.** *140 Ocean Ave, PO Box 511*
(04046). 207/967-3331; fax 207/967-8738; toll-free 800/
552-2363. www.thecolonyhotel.com/maine. 125 rms in hotel,
annex and motel, 2-4 story. No A/C. July-early Sept (wkends
2-day min in hotel), MAP: D $175-$375; each addl $30;
EP avail off season; lower rates mid-May-June, Sept-late
Oct. Closed rest of yr. Crib free. Pet accepted; $22. TV in
some rms. Heated saltwater pool. Dining rm 7:30-9:30 am,
6:30-8:30 pm; Sun brunch 11 am-2 pm; poolside lunches in
season. Rm serv. Bar. Ck-out 11 am. Meeting rms. Business
servs avail. In-rm modem link. Bellhops. Gift shop. Tennis
privileges. Golf privileges. Putting green. Private beach.
Bicycles. Lawn games. Soc dir in summer; entertainment;
movies. On trolley route. Spacious grounds; on ocean
peninsula. Family-operated since 1948. Totally nonsmoking.
Cr cds: A, MC, V.

★★★ **NONANTUM RESORT.** *95 Ocean Ave (04046).*
207/967-4050; fax 207/967-8451; toll-free 800/552-5651.
www.nonantumresort.com. 116 rms, 26 kit units, 3-4 story.
Late May-early Sept: S, D $129-$229; each addl $10; lower
rates Apr-late May, early Sept-Nov. Closed rest of yr. TV;
cable. Heated pool; poolside serv. Restaurant 7:30-10:30
am, 6-9 pm. Bar; entertainment (in season). Ck-out 11 am.
Meeting rm. Business servs avail. Bellhops. Lawn games.
Some refrigerators, microwaves. Picnic tables. One of oldest operating inns in state. On Kennebunk River; dockage.
Lighthouse. Cr cds: A, MC, V.

B&Bs/Small Inns

★★ **BREAKWATER INN AND RESTAURANT.** *133 Ocean*
Ave (04046). 207/967-3118. www.breakwaterinn.com. 20 rms
in 2 houses, 2 with shower only, 3-4 story, 2 suites. No
elvtr. No rm phones. Late June-Labor Day: S $65-$165;
D $75-$175; suites $115; wkly rates; lower rates Labor Day-
late Oct and May-late June. Closed rest of yr. Crib free. TV;
cable. Complimentary continental bkfst. Restaurant (see
BREAKWATER INN). Ck-out 11 am, ck-in 2 pm. Many
refrigerators; some balconies. Built 1883. Located at mouth
of Kennebunkport Harbor; views of Atlantic, harbor. Cr cds:
A, MC, V.

★★★ **BUFFLEHEAD COVE.** *Bufflehead Cove Rd (04046).*
207/967-3879. www.buffleheadcove.com. 5 rms, 3 with
shower only, 2 story. Late June-late Oct:
S, D $155-$310; 2-day min in season; open wkends only
Jan-Mar. Children over 11 yrs only. Complimentary full
bkfst; afternoon refreshments. Ck-out 11 am, ck-in 3 pm.
Concierge serv. Many fireplaces. Balconies. Picnic tables.
On river, swimming. Secluded late 19th-century shingle
cottage on Kennebunk River. Riverboats avail. Totally
nonsmoking. Cr cds: DS, MC, V.

★★★ **CAPTAIN FAIRFIELD INN.** *8 Pleasant St (04046). 207/967-4454; fax 207/967-8537; toll-free 800/322-1928. www.captainfairfield.com.* 9 rms, 2 story. 6 A/C. No rm phones. Mid-June-mid-Oct: S, D $150-$200; each addl $25; lower rates rest of yr. Children over 6 yrs only. TV in sitting rm; cable, VCR avail. Complimentary full bkfst; afternoon refreshments. Restaurant nearby. Ck-out 11 am, ck-in 3 pm. Business servs avail. Some fireplaces.Federal-style mansion (1813); former sea captain's residence. Overlooks Village Green. Totally nonsmoking. Cr cds: A, D, DS, MC, V.

★★★ **THE CAPTAIN JEFFERDS INN.** *5 Pearl St (04046). 207/967-2311; fax 207/964-0721; toll-free 800/839-6844. www.captainjeffersinn.com.* 16 rms, 3 story, 1 kit. suite in attached carriage house. Most A/C. No rm phones. Memorial Day-Oct: S $90; D $105-$240; each addl $20; lower rates rest of yr. Closed last 2 wks Dec. Children over 7 yrs only. Pet accepted; $20. TV in sitting rm; VCR avail. Complimentary full bkfst; afternoon refreshments. Restaurant nearby. Ck-out 11 am, ck-in 3 pm. Some fireplaces. Federal-style house (1804) built by a merchant sea captain. Solarium; antique furnishings. Near harbor. Totally nonsmoking. Cr cds: A, MC, V.

★★★ **THE CAPTAIN LORD MANSION.** *6 Pleasant St (04046). 207/967-3141; fax 207/967-3172. www.captainlord.com.* 16 rms, 3 story; 4 rms in main inn. May-Dec: D $159-$299; each addl $25; suite $399; 2-day min wkends, 3-day min hol wkends; lower rates rest of yr. Children over 12 yrs only. Complimentary full bkfst; afternoon refreshments. Restaurants nearby. Ck-out 11 am, ck-in after 3 pm. Meeting rms. Business servs avail. Gift shop. Totally nonsmoking. Cr cds: A, MC, V.

★★ **ENGLISH MEADOWS INN.** *141 Port Rd (04043). 207/967-5766; fax 207/967-3868; toll-free 800/272-0698. www.englishmeadowsinn.com.* 12 rms, 2 share bath, 3 story, 2 kit. units. 3 A/C. No rm phones. Mid-June-Oct: S $110-$120; D $115-$130; each addl $20; kit. units $145; wkly rates; lower rates rest of yr. Closed Jan. TV in living rm and kit. units; cable. Complimentary full bkfst; afternoon refreshments. Restaurant nearby. Ck-out 11 am, ck-in 3 pm. Victorian farmhouse (1860) and attached carriage house; library/sitting rm, antiques. Totally nonsmoking. Cr cds: A, MC, V.

★★★ **THE INN AT HARBOR HEAD.** *41 Pier Rd (04046). 207/967-5564; fax 207/967-1294. www.harborhead.com.* 4 rms, 2 story, 2 suites. Rm phones avail. Late May-mid-Oct: S, D $190-$315; suites $290-$315; lower rates Feb-May, Oct-Mid Dec. Children over 12 yrs only. Complimentary full bkfst; afternoon refreshments. Ck-out 11 am, ck-in 3 pm. Some balconies. Private beach. Totally nonsmoking. Cr cds: A, MC, V.

★★★ **MAINE STAY INN & COTTAGES.** *34 Maine St (04046). 207/967-2117; fax 207/967-8757; toll-free 800/950-2117. www.mainestayinn.com.* 17 rms, 1-2 story, 11 cottages, some kits. No rm phones. Late June-mid-Oct: S, D, cottages $115-$180; each addl $10-$20; suites $195-$215; higher rates Christmas, prelude wkends; lower rates rest of yr. Crib $15. TV; cable, some VCRs. Complimentary full bkfst; afternoon refreshments. Ck-out 11 am, ck-in 3 pm. Meeting rm. Business servs avail. Some refrigerators, fireplaces. Picnic tables, grills. Playground. Near harbor, beach. In historic preservation district. Built 1860. Antique furnishings. Totally nonsmoking. Cr cds: A, MC, V.

★★★ **OLD FORT INN.** *8 Old Fort Ave (04046). 207/967-5353; fax 207/967-4547; toll-free 800/828-3678. www.oldfortinn.com.* 16 rms, 2 story. Mid-June-Oct: S, D $160-$350; each addl $25; wkends, July-Labor Day (2-day min); hol wkends (3-day min); lower rates mid-Apr-mid-June and Nov-mid-Dec. Closed rest of yr. TV; cable. Heated pool. Complimentary full bkfst. Coffee in rms. Restaurant nearby. Ck-out 11 am, ck-in 2 pm. Coin lndry. Meeting rm. Business servs avail. Tennis. Lawn games. Refrigerators, microwaves. Some fireplaces. Antique shop. 1880 carriage house converted to inn; early Amer decor. Extensive grounds. Totally nonsmoking. Cr cds: A, C, D, DS, MC, V.

★★ **TIDES INN BY THE SEA.** *252 Kings Hwy Goose Rocks Beach (04046). 207/967-3757; fax 207/967-5183. www.tidesinnbythesea.com.* 24 rms, 4 share bath, 3 with shower only, 3 story, 3 kits. No A/C. No rm phones. Mid-June-Labor Day (3-day min wkends): D $195-$295; kit. units $2,400-$2,900/wk; lower rates mid-May-mid-June and Labor Day-Columbus Day. Closed rest of yr. Crib $20. TV in lobby, some rms. Dining rm (see also THE BELVIDERE ROOM). Ck-out 10:30 am, ck-in 3 pm. Swimming beach. Built as inn 1899; antiques. Original guest book on display; signatures incl T. Roosevelt and Arthur Conan Doyle. Cr cds: A, MC, V.

★★★★ **THE WHITE BARN INN.** *37 Beach Ave (04046). 207/967-2321; fax 207/967-1100. www.whitebarninn.com.* Twenty-five rooms are tucked away amidst this inn's lush greenery and gardens and all include continental breakfast, afternoon tea, and luxurious touches of fresh flowers and fruit, CD players, and terry robes. The unique pool is sunk into a natural stone patio complete with private poolside cabanas for massage appointments. Finish the day at the inn's nationally recognized New England restaurant. 25 rms, 1-3 story, 9 suites. May-Oct: S, D $255-$425; suites $435-$675; 2-day min wkends, 3-day min hols; lower rates rest of yr. Children over 12 yrs only. TV avail; cable. Heated pool. Complimentary continental bkfst; afternoon refreshments. Restaurant (see also THE WHITE BARN RESTAURANT). Ck-out 11 am, ck-in 3 pm. Concierge serv. Luggage handling. Golf privileges. Bicycles, canoes. Some fireplaces, in-rm whirlpools. Restored 1820s farmhouse with barn and carriage house; many antiques. Perennial, herb, and vegetable gardens. Cr cds: A, MC, V.

Restaurants

★ **ALISSON'S.** *5 Dock Sq (04046). 207/967-4841. www.alissons.com.* Specialty: extra-long lobster roll. Hrs: 11 am-11 pm; to 10 pm off season. Closed Thanksgiving, Dec 25. Seafood menu. Bar to 1 am. Lunch $5-$8, dinner $11-$16. Child's menu. Two store-front rms; 2nd flr overlooks Dock Sq. Family-owned. Cr cds: A, DS, MC, V.
D

★★ **ARUNDEL WHARF.** *43 Ocean Ave (04046). 207/967-3444. www.arundelwharf.com.* Specializes in seafood. Hrs: 11:30 am-10 pm. Closed Nov-Mar. Res accepted. Bar. Lunch $4-$15, dinner $13-$25. Outdoor dining overlooking Kennebunkport River, marina. Fireplace. Cr cds: A, C, D, DS, ER, MC, V.
D

★ **BARTLEY'S DOCKSIDE DINING.** *Western Ave (04046). 207/967-5050. www.int-usa.net/bartley/.* Specialties: seafood-stuffed haddock, bouillabaisse, blueberry pie. Hrs: 11 am-10 pm. Closed mid Dec-Apr. Res accepted. Serv bar. Lunch $2.95-$14.95, dinner $6.50-$23.95. Child's menu. Parking. Outdoor dining. View of water. Family owned. Cr cds: A, MC, V.
D

★★ **THE BELVIDERE ROOM.** *252 Kings Hwy (04046). 207/967-3757. www.tidesinnbythesea.com.* Regional Amer menu. Specialties: lobster burrito, wild game, shellfish ragout. Own baking, ice cream. Hrs: 8-10:30 am, 5-9:30 pm. Closed mid-Oct-mid-May. Res accepted (dinner). Bar 5 pm-midnight. Wine list. Bkfst $4.95-$7.95, dinner $16.95-$30.95. Child's menu. In historic inn. View of beach and ocean; antique china; player piano. Family-owned. Totally nonsmoking. Cr cds: A, MC, V.

★★ **BREAKWATER INN.** *133 Ocean Ave (04046). 207/967-3118.* Specializes in lobster, fresh seafood. Own desserts. Hrs: 5:30-9 pm early May-late Oct. Closed rest of yr. Res accepted. No A/C. Bar. Dinner $13.95. Child's menu. Parking. Built 1883 as guest house; view of river, ocean. Cr cds: A, MC, V.

★ **MABEL'S LOBSTER CLAW.** *124 Ocean Ave (04046). 207/967-2562.* Specialties: lobster Savannah, baked stuffed lobster. Own desserts. Hrs: 11:30 am-3 pm, 5-10 pm. Closed early Nov-Apr. Res accepted. Serv bar. Lunch $5-$9, dinner $12.95-$24. Child's menu. Outdoor dining. Family-owned. Totally nonsmoking. Cr cds: A, MC, V.
D

★★★ **SEASCAPES.** *77 Pier Rd, Cape Porpoise (04046). 207/967-8500. www.seascapesrestaurant.com.* Mediterranean, Pacific Rim cuisine. Specialties: medallions of roasted lobster, Christina's shrimp, sugar cane-planked seafood grille. Hrs: 11:30 am-9 pm; Fri, Sat to 10 pm. Closed Nov-mid-Apr. Res accepted. Serv bar. Wine list. Lunch $7.95-$14.95, dinner $19.95-$26.95. Pianist Wed-Sun in season. Parking. Situated over tidal harbor. Cr cds: A, C, D, DS, ER, MC, V.

★★★★ **THE WHITE BARN RESTAURANT.** *37 Beach St (04046). 207/967-2321. www.whitebarninn.com.* This restaurant, which dates back to 1820, is housed in two restored barns. The menu changes weekly and offers prix-fixe dinners of contemporary New England cuisine. Wine tastings, cigar dinners, and receptions are held in the "Wine Room,"

which is located in the wine cellar and can accommodate up to 14 guests. Menu changes wkly. Specializes in fresh Maine seafood, seasonal game. Hrs: 6-9 pm. Closed 2 wks in Jan. Res required. Bar. Wine cellar. Prix fixe: 4-course dinner $81. Pianist. Cr cds: A, MC, V.
D

Kingfield

Pop 1,114 **Elev** 560 ft **Area code** 207 **Zip** 04947

On a narrow intervale in the valley of the Carrabassett River, Kingfield once had several lumber mills. The town was named after William King, Maine's first governor, and was the birthplace of F. E. and F. O. Stanley, the twins who developed the Stanley Steamer. There is good canoeing, hiking, trout fishing, and hunting in nearby areas.

What to See and Do

Carrabassett Valley Ski Touring Center. Approx 50 mi of ski touring trails. Center offers lunch (daily); school, rentals; skating rink (fee), rentals; trail information area; shop. (Early Dec-late Apr, daily) Half-day rates. 15 mi N via ME 16/27. Phone 207/237-2000. ¢¢¢¢

Sugarloaf/USA Ski Area. Two quad, triple, eight double chairlifts; T-bar; school, patrol, rentals; snowmaking; lodge; restaurants, coffee shop, cafeteria, bars; nursery; bank, health club, shops. Six Olympic runs, 45 mi of trails; longest run 3½ mi; vertical drop 2,820 ft. (Early Nov-May, daily) 65 mi of cross-country trails. 15 mi N on ME 16/27. Phone 207/237-2000. ¢¢¢¢

Hotels

★★ **THE HERBERT HOTEL.** *Main St (04947). 207/265-2000; fax 207/265-4597.* 33 rms, 3 story, 4 suites. No A/C. No rm phones. Dec 25-Mar: S $45-$59; D $69-$79; each addl $10; suites $90-$150; under 12 free; MAP avail; wkly rates; package plans; lower rates rest of yr. Crib free. Pet accepted. TV in sitting rm. Complimentary continental bkfst. Dining rm (public by res) 5:30-9 pm. Rm serv. Ck-out 11 am, ck-in noon. Gift shop. Downhill/x-country ski 14 mi. Massage. In-rm whirlpools. Built 1917; antiques, elaborate fumed oak woodwork. On river. Cr cds: A, C, D, DS, JCB, MC, V.

★★ **SUGARLOAF INN.** *ME 27 (04947). 207/237-3768. www.sugarloaf.com.* 42 rms, 325 condos, 2-5 bedrm, 3-4 story. A/C in inn, some condos. EP, Dec 25-Mar: D $89-$185; studio $110-$208; 2-5 bedrm $158-$526; under 12 free; higher rates hols; lower rates rest of yr. Crib $11. TV; cable. 2 pools, 1 indoor; whirlpool. Dining rm 7-10 am, 6-9 pm; hrs vary summer. Bar. Ck-out 11 am, ck-in 4 pm. Meeting rms. Tennis. Golf. Downhill ski on site; x-country ski adj. Exercise rm; sauna, steam rm. Massage. Fishing, hiking, whitewater rafting. Mountain bike rentals, guides. Lawn games. Cr cds: A, D, MC, V.

Resort

★★★ **GRAND SUMMIT HOTEL.** *Sugarloaf/USA (04947). 207/237-2222; fax 207/237-2874; toll-free 800/527-9879. www.sugarloaf.com.* 120 rms, 6 story. No A/C. Late Dec-Mar: S $85-$235; D $95-$235; suites, kit. units (1-2-bedrm) $130-$300; family rates; tennis, golf, ski, rafting packages; lower rates rest of yr. Crib free. TV; cable (premium), VCR (movies $3). Restaurant 7-10 am, 6-9 pm. Bar 4 pm-1 am. Ck-out 10 am. Coin lndry. Meeting rms. Business servs avail. Bellhops. Valet serv. Concierge (in season). Sundries. Gift shop. Tennis. 18-hole golf, greens fee $76, pro, putting green. Downhill/x-country ski on site. Exercise rm; sauna. Massage. Whirlpool. Game rm. Refrigerators, wet bars. At base of slopes. Cr cds: A, C, D, DS, ER, MC.

D ⛷ 🏊 🎿 🏋 🏃 ☀ SC

Restaurant

★★ **LONGFELLOW'S.** *Main and Kingfield Sts (04947). 207/265-4394.* Continental menu. Specializes in prime rib, seafood, chicken, beef. Hrs: 11 am-9 pm; wkends to 9:30 pm. Res accepted. Lunch $2.95-$6.75, dinner $5.50-$13.50. Child's menu. Outdoor dining overlooking river. One of town's oldest buildings (1860s). Cr cds: MC, V.

D

Kittery

See also York

Settled 1623 **Pop** 9,372 **Elev** 22 ft **Area code** 207 **Zip** 03904
Information Greater York Region Chamber of Commerce, 1 Stonewall Ln; 207/363-4422
Web www.yorkme.org

This old sea community has built ships since its early days. Kittery men built the *Ranger,* which sailed to France under John Paul Jones with the news of Burgoyne's surrender. Across the Piscataqua River from Portsmouth, New Hampshire, Kittery is the home of the Portsmouth Naval Shipyard, which sprawls over islands on the Maine side of the river.

What to See and Do

Factory Outlet Stores. Approx 120 outlet stores can be found throughout Kittery. For a complete listing, contact the Chamber of Commerce.

Fort Foster Park. A 92-acre park with picnicking, pavilion; beach; baseball field; fishing pier. X-country skiing in winter. (June-Aug, daily; May and Sept, Sat and Sun) Entrance fee per individual and per vehicle. NE via ME 103 to Gerrish Island. Phone 207/439-3800.

Fort McClary Memorial. Restored hexagonal blockhouse on site of 1809 fort. Interpretive displays; picnicking. (Memorial Day-Labor Day, daily) For further information contact the Chamber of Commerce. 3½ mi E of US 1 in Kittery Point.

Hamilton House. (ca 1785) This Georgian house, situated overlooking the Salmon Falls River, was redecorated at the turn of the century with a mixture of antiques, painted murals and country furnishings to create an interpretation of America's Colonial past. Perennial garden, flowering trees and shrubs, and garden cottage. Tours. (June-mid-Oct, Tues, Thurs, Sat and Sun afternoons) N on I-95 to ME 236, then approx 10 mi NW to Vaughan Ln in South Berwick. Phone 207/384-5269. ¢¢

John Paul Jones State Memorial. Memorial to the sailors and soldiers of Maine. (Daily) River bank, E side of US 1 at entrance to Kittery. Phone 207/384-5160. **FREE**

Kittery Historical and Naval Museum. Exhibits portray history of US Navy and Kittery—Maine's oldest incorporated town—as well as southern Maine's maritime heritage. (June-Oct, Tues-Sat; rest of yr, Fri and by appt) Rogers Rd, off US 1 by Rotary at ME 236. Phone 207/439-3080. ¢¢

Sarah Orne Jewett House. (1774) Novelist Sarah Orne Jewett spent most of her life in this fine Georgian residence. Interior restored to recreate the appearance of the house during her time (1849-1909). Contains some original 18th- and 19th-century wallpaper; fine paneling. Her own bedrm-study has been left as she arranged it. (June-mid-Oct, Wed-Sun) N on I-95 to ME 236, then approx 10 mi NW to 5 Portland St in South Berwick. Phone 207/384-2454. ¢¢

Motel/Motor Lodge

★ **DAYS INN.** *2 Gorges Rd (03904). 207/439-5555; toll-free 800/329-7466. www.daysinn.com.* 108 rms, 1-3 story. Late June-early Sept: S $89.90; D $94.90; each addl $6; under 18 free; package plans off-season; lower rates rest of yr. Crib free. TV; cable (premium); VCR avail (movies). Indoor pool; sauna. Restaurant 7-11 am, 5-9 pm; off-season hrs vary. Bar 5 pm-midnight. Ck-out 11 am. Coin lndry. Meeting rms. Business servs avail. Valet serv. Sundries. Refrigerators, microwaves avail. Cr cds: A, D, DS, MC, V.

D 🏊 🔽 ☀ SC

B&B/Small Inn

★★ **COACHMAN INN.** *380 US Rte 1 (03904). 207/439-4434; fax 207/439-6757; toll-free 800/824-6183. www.visit-maine.com/coachman.* 43 rms, 2 story. July-Aug: S $66-$110; D $72-$115; each addl $10; package plans off-season; lower rates rest of yr. Crib free. TV; cable (premium). Pool. Complimentary continental bkfst. Restaurant nearby. Ck-out 11 am. Business servs avail. Sundries. Cr cds: A, DS, MC, V.

D 🏊 🔽 ☀ SC

Restaurants

★ **CAPTAIN SIMON'S GALLEY.** *90 Pepperell Rd (ME 103), Kittery Point (03905). 207/439-3655.* Specializes in fresh seafood, steak, chicken. Hrs: 11 am-10 pm; Sun brunch 10 am-2 pm; off-season hrs vary. Closed Thanksgiving, Dec 25; also Tues (off season). Res accepted. Bar Thurs-Sat 4 pm-midnight. Lunch $2.95-$8.95, dinner $6.95-$14.25. Sun brunch $1.99-$5.95. Nautical decor. Original hand-hewn beams from 17th-century boathouse; views of pier, lighthouses. Cr cds: A, DS, MC, V.

D

★★ **WARREN'S LOBSTER HOUSE.** *11 Water St (03904).* *207/439-1630. www.lobsterhouse.com.* Specializes in lobster Thermidor, fresh seafood. Salad bar. Own baking. Hrs: 11:30 am-9 pm; Fri, Sat to 10 pm; Sun brunch 11 am-2 pm. Hrs vary off season. Closed Jan 1, Dec 24-25. Bar. Lunch $4.50-$9.95, dinner $9.95-$15.95. Sun brunch $10.95. Child's menu. Nautical decor. Outdoor dining. View of waterfront. Cr cds: A, C, D, ER, MC, V.
D

Lewiston

See also Auburn

Settled 1770 **Pop** 39,757 **Elev** 210 ft **Area code** 207
Information Androscoggin County Chamber of Commerce, 179 Lisbon St, PO Box 59, 04243-0059; 207/783-2249
Web www.androscoggincounty.com

Maine's second-largest city is 30 miles up the Androscoggin River from the sea, directly across the river from its sister city of Auburn (see). Known as the Twin Cities, both are strong manufacturing and service-oriented communities. Lewiston was the first of the two cities to harness the water power of the Androscoggin Falls; however, both cities have benefitted from the river.

What to See and Do

Bates College. (1855) 1,600 students. New England's oldest and the nation's second-oldest coeducational institution of higher learning; originally the Maine State Seminary, it was renamed after a prominent Boston investor. Liberal arts and sciences. On its well-landscaped campus are the Edmund S. Muskie Archives (1936 alumnus and former Senator and US Secretary of State) and a beautiful chapel containing a hand-crafted tracker-action organ. College St and Campus Ave. Phone 207/786-6255. Also on campus are

  Mount David. A 340-ft rocky hill offering a view of Lewiston, the Androscoggin Valley, and the Presidential Range of the White Mtns to the west.

  Olin Arts Center. Multilevel facility overlooking campus lake houses a concert hall and a Museum of Art that contains a variety of changing and permanent exhibits (Tues-Sun; closed hols; free). Phone 207/786-6158. **FREE**

Special Events

Maine State Parade. Downtown Lewiston and Auburn. Maine's largest parade; over 30,000 people representing 60 communities. Televised statewide. Phone 207/784-0599. First wkend May.

Lewiston-Auburn Garden Tour. Tour of six gardens in the area. Ticket purchase required. Phone 207/782-1403. July.

Festival de Joie. Central Maine Civic Center. Celebration of Lewiston and Auburn's Franco-American heritage. Features ethnic song, dance, cultural activities, traditional foods. Late July-early Aug. Phone 207/782-6231.

Motels/Motor Lodges

★ **CHALET.** *1243 Lisbon St (04240).* *207/784-0600; fax 207/786-4214; toll-free 800/733-7787.* 74 units, 2-3 story, 8 suites, 7 kit. units (some equipt). No elvtr. Mid-May-mid-Nov: S $36; D $40-$45; each addl $5; suites $60-$85; kit. units $5 addl; under 13 free; lower rates rest of yr. Crib $5. TV; cable (premium). Indoor pool; whirlpool. Restaurant 6-11 am. Bar 4 pm-midnight. Ck-out 11 am. Coin lndry. Downhill/x-country ski 15 mi. Exercise equipt; sauna. Refrigerators avail. Picnic tables, grills. Cr cds: A, D, DS, MC, V.
D ▧ ▧ ▧ ▧ ▧ ▧

★ **RAMADA INN CONFERENCE CENTER.** *490 Pleasant St (04240).* *207/784-2331; fax 207/784-2332; res 800/272-6232. www.ramadamaine.com.* 117 rms, 2 story. Mid-May-mid-Oct: S $74.90; D $89-$99; each addl $10; suites $149; studio rms $79-$99; under 18 free. Crib free. TV; cable. Indoor pool; whirlpool. Complimentary bkfst buffet. Coffee in rms. Restaurant 7 am-1:30 pm, 5-10 pm. Bar 11-1 am; entertainment. Ck-out 11 am. Coin lndry. Meeting rms. Business center. In-rm modem link. Gift shop. Downhill ski 10 mi. Exercise equipt; sauna. Cr cds: A, D, DS, MC, V.
D ▧ ▧ ▧ ▧ ▧

★ **SUPER 8.** *1440 Lisbon St (04240).* *207/784-8882; fax 207/784-1778; toll-free 800/800-8000. www.super8.com.* 49 rms. July-Sept: S $40.88-$43.88; D $55.88; each addl $6; under 12 free; lower rates rest of yr. Crib free. TV; cable, VCR avail (movies). Complimentary continental bkfst. Restaurant nearby. Ck-out 11 am. Downhill/x-country ski 15 mi. Cr cds: A, C, D, DS, MC, V.
D ▧ ▧ ▧ ▧

Lincoln

Pop 5,587 **Elev** 180 ft **Area code** 207 **Zip** 04457
Information Lincoln Lakes Region Chamber of Commerce, 75 Main St, PO Box 164; 207/794-8065 or 800/794-8065
Web www.lincolnmechamber.org

What to See and Do

Skiing. Mount Jefferson Ski Area. Novice, intermediate, and expert trails; two T-bar, rope tow; patrol, school, rentals; lodge, concession. Longest run 0.7 mi, vertical drop 432 ft. (Jan-Mar, Tues-Thurs, Sat and Sun; daily during school vacations) 12 mi NE via ME 6 in Lee. Phone 207/738-2377.

Motel/Motor Lodge

★ **BRIARWOOD MOTOR INN.** *Outer West Broadway (04457). 207/794-6731. www.angelfire.com/me4/briarwood.* 24 rms, 2 story. July-Aug: S $45; D $50; each addl $5; lower rates rest of yr. Crib $5. Pet accepted. TV; cable (premium). Complimentary coffee in lobby. Restaurant nearby. Ck-out 11 am. Downhill ski 11 mi; x-country ski 2 mi. Refrigerators avail. Cr cds: A, MC, V.

⊡ ☜ 🛉 🏊 ✕ 🖼 🔥

Lubec

See also Eastport

Pop 1,853 **Elev** 20 ft **Area code** 207 **Zip** 04652

Quoddy Head State Park, the easternmost point in the United States, is located in Lubec. There is a lighthouse here, as well as the Franklin D. Roosevelt Memorial Bridge, which stretches over Lubec Narrows to Campobello Island. Herring smoking and sardine packing are local industries.

What to See and Do

Roosevelt Campobello International Park. Canadian property jointly maintained by Canada and US. Approx 2,800 acres incl the 11-acre estate where Franklin D. Roosevelt had his summer home and was stricken with poliomyelitis. Self-guided tours of 34-rm house, interpretive guides avail; films shown in visitor center; picnic sites in natural area; observation platforms and interpretive panels at Friar's Head; vistas. No camping. (Sat before Memorial Day-Oct 31st, daily) 1½ mi E off ME 189 on Campobello Island. Phone 506/752-2922. **FREE**

Motel/Motor Lodge

★ **EASTLAND.** *Rte 189 (04652). 207/733-5501; fax 207/733-2932.* 20 rms. Some A/C. Mid-June-Oct: S $38-$45; D $52-$62; each addl $4; under 17, $2; lower rates rest of yr. Crib free. Pet accepted; $3. TV; cable (premium). Ck-out 10 am. Complimentary coffee in lobby. Airport for small planes adj. Cr cds: A, DS, MC, V.

⊡ ☜ 🛉 🖼 🔥

B&Bs/Small Inns

★★ **HOME PORT INN.** *45 Main St (04652). 207/733-2077; fax 207/733-2950; toll-free 800/457-2077. www.homeportinn.com.* 7 rms, 2 story. No rm phones. Memorial Day-mid-Oct: S, D $60-$80; each addl $10. Closed rest of yr. TV in sitting rm; VCR avail. Complimentary continental bkfst. Restaurant (see HOME PORT INN). Ck-out 10 am, ck-in 2 pm. Gift shop. Picnic tables. Built 1880; antiques, library. Totally nonsmoking. Cr cds: A, DS, MC, V.

⊡ 🛉 🖼 🔥

★★ **OWEN HOUSE.** *11 Welshpool Rd, Campobello Island (E0G 3H0). 506/752-2977.* 9 rms, 4 share bath, 3 story. No rm phones. Memorial Day-mid-Oct: S, D $60-$83; each addl $15. Closed rest of yr. TV in sitting rm. Complimentary full bkfst. Restaurant nearby. Ck-out 11 am, ck-in noon. Built by son of first settler of Campobello Island. On ocean. Totally nonsmoking. Cr cds: V.

🛉 🖼 🔥

Restaurant

★★ **HOME PORT INN.** *45 Main St (04652). 207/733-2077. www.homeportinn.com.* Specializes in seafood, beef, chicken. Hrs: 5-8 pm. Open June-Columbus Day. Res accepted. No A/C. Wine, beer. Dinner $9.99-$18.99. Dining rm of inn; antiques displayed. Totally nonsmoking. Cr cds: DS, MC, V.

⊡

Machias

See also Lubec

Settled 1763 **Pop** 2,569 **Elev** 70 ft **Area code** 207 **Zip** 04654
Information Machias Bay Area Chamber of Commerce, PO Box 606; 207/255-4402
Web www.nemaine.com/mbacc

For almost a hundred years before 1750, Machias (muh-CHY-as) was the headquarters for a number of pirates including Samuel Bellamy, called the Robin Hood of Atlantic pirates. After pirating abated, Machias became a hotbed of Revolutionary fervor. Off Machiasport, downriver, the British schooner *Margaretta* was captured (June 1775) in the first naval engagement of the war. Today the area is noted particularly for hunting, fishing, and nature trails. Bear, deer, puffin, salmon, and striped bass abound nearby. The University of Maine has a branch in Machias.

What to See and Do

Burnham Tavern Museum. (1770) Memorabilia from 1770-1830. (June-Sept, Mon-Fri; rest of yr, by appt) Main St, just off US 1 on ME 192. Phone 207/255-4432. ¢

Ruggles House. (1820) This home exhibits Adam-style architecture and unusual "flying" staircase. Intricate wood carving; period furnishings. (June-mid-Oct, daily) 20 mi S on US 1, then ¼ mi off US 1 in Columbia Falls. Phone 207/483-4637. ¢

State parks.

Cobscook Bay. Fishing, boating (ramp); hiking, picnicking, snowmobiling permitted, camping (dump station). (Mid-May-mid-Oct, daily) Standard fees. 20 mi NE on US 1 near Whiting. Phone 207/726-4412. ¢

Fort O'Brien State Historic Site. Remains of a fort commanding the harbor, commissioned by Washington in 1775. Hiking, picnicking. (Memorial Day-Labor Day, daily) 5 mi E on ME 92. Phone 207/941-4014. **FREE**

Roque Bluffs. Oceanfront pebble beach; freshwater pond. Swimming, fishing; picnicking. (Mid-May-mid-Oct, daily) 7 mi S, off US 1. Phone 207/255-3475. ¢

Special Event

Wild Blueberry Festival. Third wkend Aug. Phone 207/255-4402.

Motel/Motor Lodge

★ **BLUEBIRD MOTEL.** *RR 1, Box 45 (04654)* . *207/255-3332.* 40 rms. Mid-June-mid-Sept: S $48-$54; D $52-$60; each addl $4; lower rates rest of yr. Crib free. Pet accepted. TV; cable. Ck-out 11 am. Cr cds: A, MC, V.

Millinocket

Pop 6,956 **Elev** 350 ft **Area code** 207 **Zip** 04462
Information Katahdin Area Chamber of Commerce, 1029 Central St; 207/723-4443
Web www.katahdinmaine.com

What to See and Do

Baxter State Park. (see). 18 mi NW via state park road.

Motels/Motor Lodges

★★ **BEST WESTERN HERITAGE MOTOR INN.** *935 Central St (04462). 207/723-9777; fax 207/723-9777; toll-free 800/528-1234. www.bestwestern.com.* 49 rms, 2 story. June-Aug: S $69; D$79; each addl $10; under 12 free; lower rates rest of yr. Crib free. Pet accepted, some restrictions. TV; cable. Complimentary continental bkfst. Restaurant 4-10 pm. Bar. Ck-out 11 am. Meeting rm. Business servs avail. Sundries. Exercise equipt. Whirlpools. Refrigerators avail. Cr cds: A, D, DS, MC, V.

★★ **KATAHDIN INN.** *740 Central St (04462). 207/723-4555; fax 207/723-6480; toll-free 877/902-4555. www.katahdininn.com.* 82 rms, 3 story, 10 suites. June-Oct: S $65-$75; D $70-$80; each addl $5; suites $90; under 18 free; ski plans; lower rates rest of yr. Crib free. Pet accepted. TV; cable, VCR avail. Indoor pool; wading pool, whirlpool. Playground. Complimentary bkfst buffet. Restaurant nearby. Bar 4 pm-midnight. Ck-out noon. Coin lndry. Meeting rms. Sundries. X-country ski 10 mi. Exercise equipt. Rec rm. Some refrigerators; microwaves avail; bathrm phone, wet bar in suites. Cr cds: A, MC, V.

★ **PAMOLA MOTOR LODGE.** *973 Central St (04462). 207/723-9746; fax 207/723-9746. www.millinocketmaine.com.* 29 rms, 1-2 story, 3 kits. Mid-May-mid-Oct: S $39; D $54; each addl $6; under 18 free; lower rates rest of yr. Crib free. TV; cable. Pool; whirlpool. Complimentary continental bkfst.

Restaurant 11 am-9 pm. Bar 4 pm-1 am; entertainment Fri, Sat. Ck-out 11 am. Business servs avail. Game rm. Some balconies. Cr cds: A, C, D, DS, MC, V.

Monhegan Island

See also Boothbay Harbor, Damariscotta, Rockland

Settled 1720 **Pop** 88 **Elev** 50 ft **Area code** 207 **Zip** 04852

Monhegan Plantation, nine miles out to sea, approximately two miles long and one mile wide, is profitably devoted to lobsters and summer visitors. Rockwell Kent and Milton Burns were among the first of many artists to summer here. Today, the warm-weather population is about 20 times the year-round number. There is more work in winter: by special law, lobsters may be trapped in Monhegan waters only from January to June. This gives them the other six months to fatten. Monhegan lobsters thus command the highest prices.

Leif Ericson may have landed on Monhegan Island in A.D. 1000. In its early years, Monhegan Island was a landmark for sailors, and by 1611 it was well known as a general headquarters for European fishermen, traders, and explorers. For a time, the island was a pirate den. Small compared to other Maine islands, Monhegan is a land of contrasts. On one side of the island sheer cliffs drop 150 feet to the ocean below, while on the other side, Cathedral Woods offers visitors a serene haven.

What to See and Do

Boat and ferry service.

Ferry from Port Clyde. *Laura B* makes 11-mi journey (1 hr, 10 min) from Muscongus Bay. (Memorial Day-Columbus Day, three trips daily; no trips hols) No cars permitted; res required. Foot of ME 131. Phone 207/372-8848. ¢¢¢¢

Trips from Boothbay Harbor. *Balmy Days* makes trips from mainland (see BOOTHBAY HARBOR). (June-Sept, daily) Phone 207/633-2284. ¢¢¢¢

Monhegan Lighthouse. Historic lighthouse has been in operation since 1824; automated since 1959. Magnificent views. **FREE**

Moosehead Lake

See also Greenville, Rockwood

(N of Greenville; approx 32 mi E of Jackman)

The largest of Maine's countless lakes, Moosehead is also the center for the state's wilderness sports. The source of the Kennebec River, Moosehead Lake is 40 miles long and 20 miles wide, with many bays, islands, ponds, rivers, and brooks surrounding it. Its waters are good for ice-fishing in

THE FRAGILE BEAUTY OF MONHEGAN ISLAND

Just one square mile in area, Monhegan is one of Maine's best known islands because it is spectacularly beautiful. No roads are paved, and there are 17 miles of walking trails. They lead through woods and over rocky ledges, along some of the highest ocean cliffs along the coast of Maine. Less than 20 percent of the island is inhabited.

Ideally visitors should spend at least a night or two on Monhegan but most come for just a few hours. The following loop offers a sense of the island's variety with time to still make the boat. (Note: Wear sensible shoes and appropriate weather gear. Respect the fragile beauty of the island and do not litter or pick flowers.)

The Lupine Gallery near the ferry wharf is the logical first stop because it showcases the work of the many artists who work on the island and hold open studios. Turn right on the single village street and follow it past Swim Beach and Fish Beach to the first and only intersection. Turn left here at Monhegan House and walk up Horn Hill. Note the island's only public rest rooms (behind the hotel) and the small signs indicating open artists' studios. At a Y follow the main path to the left as it climbs steeply up to Burnt Head, a cliff that rises a sheer 140 feet above the open ocean. It's the obvious spot for a picnic or at least to catch your breath and take in the beauty of the rocks, fir trees, and flowers. The narrow path continues along the cliffs, dipping between unusual rock formations at Gull Cove, and on to more cliffs at White Head and Little White Head. Turn on to the Whitehead Trail and follow it across the island to Monhegan Island Light, built in 1850, automated in 1959. The former keeper's cottage is now the Monhegan Museum, with a spellbinding display on local flora and fauna, art, and history. A separate art museum offers special exhibits. The view of the village from the lighthouse is one of the most memorable along the entire coast and itself appears in numerous art museums. Walk back down to the main road and turn left toward the dock.

the winter, and trout, landlocked salmon, and togue can be caught in the summer. The lake is located in the heart of Maine's North Woods. Here is the largest moose population in the continental United States. Moose can best be seen in the early morning or at dusk. Being placid creatures, the moose allow watchers plenty of time to snap pictures. It is possible to hunt moose in northern Maine in season, but only by permit granted through a lottery.

Greenville (see), at the southern tip of the lake, is headquarters for moose-watching, hunting, fishing, camping, whitewater rafting, canoeing, hiking, snowmobiling, and cross-country and alpine skiing. The town has an airport with two runways, one 3,000 feet long. Other communities around Moosehead Lake include Rockwood, Kokadjo, and Greenville Junction.

Newport

See also Skowhegan

Pop 3,036 **Elev** 202 ft **Area code** 207 **Zip** 04953

Motel/Motor Lodge

★★ **LOVLEY'S MOTEL.** *Rfd 2, Box 147 (04953). 207/ 368-4311; toll-free 800/666-6760.* 63 rms, 1-2 story, 3 kits. (no ovens, equipt). June-Nov: S $29.70-$49.90; D $39.90- $89.90; each addl $5; kit. units $8 addl; lower rates rest of yr. Crib $8. Pet accepted. TV; cable (premium). Heated pool; whirlpool. Complimentary coffee in rms. Restaurant nearby. Ck-out 11 am. Coin lndry. Business servs avail. Lawn games, gliders. Picnic tables. Cr cds: A, DS, MC, V.

D 🐾 ⛇ ⋈ 🔥

B&B/Small Inn

★★ **BREWSTER INN.** *37 Zions Hill Rd, Dexter (04930). 207/924-3130; fax 207/924-9768. www.bbonline.com/me/brewsterinn.* 7 rms, 3 with shower only, 2 story, 2 suites. No rm phones. S, D $59-$69; each addl $10; suites $79-$89; wkly rates. Crib free. TV; cable, VCR avail. Complimentary full bkfst; afternoon refreshments. Restaurant nearby. Ck-out 11 am, ck-in 3 pm. Luggage handling. Downhill ski 15 mi. Some fireplaces; refrigerators avail. Built in 1935; original fixtures. Totally nonsmoking. Cr cds: A, DS, MC, V.

D ⛇ ⋈ 🔥 SC

Restaurant

★ **LOG CABIN DINER.** *ME 2, East Newport (04953). 207/368-4551.* Specializes in steak, seafood. Own desserts. Hrs: 6 am-9 pm; Sun 7 am-8 pm. Closed Dec-Mar. Bkfst, lunch, dinner $1.95-$14.95. Child's menu. Family-owned. Cr cds: MC, V.

D SC

Northeast Harbor

See also Bar Harbor

Pop 650 **Elev** 80 ft **Area code** 207 **Zip** 04662

This coastal village is located on Mount Desert Island, a land of rocky coastlines, forests, and lakes. The island is reached from the mainland by a short bridge.

What to See and Do

Acadia National Park. (see). N via ME 3.

Ferry Service. Connects Northeast Harbor with the Cranberry Isles (see); three-mi, 30-min crossing. (Summer, daily; rest of yr, schedule varies) Phone 207/244-3575. ¢¢

Motel/Motor Lodge

★★ **KIMBALL TERRACE INN.** *Huntington Rd (04662). 207/276-3383; fax 207/276-4102; toll-free 800/454-6225. kimballterraceinn.com.* 70 rms, 2-3 story. No A/C. July-Labor Day: S, D $64-$145; each addl $10; under 6 free; lower rates Apr-June, Labor Day-Oct; closed rest of yr. Crib $5. TV; cable (premium). Pool. Restaurant 7 am-9 pm. Rm serv. Ck-out 11 am. Meeting rms. Business servs avail. Gift shop. Tennis adj. Balconies. Overlooks harbor. Cr cds: A, DS, MC, V.

D ⚡ 🏊 📶 🔥

B&Bs/Small Inns

★★ **ASTICOU INN.** *Asticou Way (04662). 207/276-3344; fax 207/276-3373; toll-free 800/258-3373. www.asticou.com.* 33 rms in inn, 14 rms in 5 cottages, 7 kits. (no ovens). No A/C. Mid-June-mid-Sept, MAP: S $125-$250; D $125-$250; each addl $66.50; suites $299-$364; EP avail. Closed rest of yr. TV in game rm. Heated pool. Dining rm 7:30-9:30 am, 11:30 am-10 pm. Rm serv. Bar noon-11 pm; entertainment. Ck-out 11 am, ck-in 3 pm. Business servs avail. Luggage handling. Valet serv. Concierge serv. Tennis. Massage. Renovated country inn (1883). At head of harbor, public dock adj. Cr cds: MC, V.

🛶 ⚡ ⚡ 🏊 📶 🔥

★★ **MAISON SUISSE INN.** *144 Main St (04662). 207/276-5223; toll-free 800/624-7668. www.maisonsuisse.com.* 10 rms, 2 story, 4 suites. No A/C. Mid-July-Aug: S, D $115-$135; each addl $10-$15; suites $195-$245; under 2 free; lower rates May-mid-July and Sept-Oct. Closed rest of yr. Crib $5. TV; cable. Complimentary full bkfst. Restaurant opp 6:30 am-9 pm. Ck-out 11 am, ck-in 3-7 pm. Near ocean. Restored, shingle-style summer cottage (1892); once a speakeasy during Prohibition; library, antiques, gardens. Totally nonsmoking. Cr cds: A, MC, V.

✈ 📶 🔥

Restaurants

★ **DOCKSIDER.** *14 Sea St (04662). 207/276-3965.* Specializes in seafood. Hrs: 11 am-9 pm; hrs vary spring and fall. Closed mid-Oct-mid-May. No A/C. Beer, wine. Lunch, dinner $1.95-$16.95. Child's menu. Outdoor dining. Rustic nautical decor. Cr cds: MC, V.

D

★★ **JORDAN POND HOUSE.** *Park Loop Rd, Seal Harbor (04675). 207/276-3316. www.jordanpond.com.* Hrs: 11:30 am-9 pm; hrs vary off season. Closed Nov-late May. Res accepted. No A/C. Serv bar. Lunch, dinner $6.50-$16. Child's menu. Specializes in homemade ice cream, popovers. Outdoor dining. Cr cds: A, DS, MC, V.

D

Norway

See also Poland Spring

Pop 4,754 **Elev** 383 ft **Area code** 207 **Zip** 04268
Information Oxford Hills Chamber of Commerce, 213 Main St, South Paris 04281; 207/743-2281
Web www.oxfordhillsmaine.com

What to See and Do

Pennesseewasee Lake. This seven-mi-long lake, covering 922 acres, received its name from the Native American words meaning "sweet water." Swimming, beaches, waterskiing; fishing for brown trout, bass, and perch; boating (marina, rentals, launch). Ice skating. Contact Chamber of Commerce. W of town. **FREE**

Motel/Motor Lodge

★ **GOODWIN'S MOTOR INN.** *191 Main St, South Paris (04281). 207/743-5121; toll-free 800/424-8803.* 24 rms. S $40; D $48; under 12 free; higher rates special events. Pet accepted. TV; cable. Restaurant nearby. Ck-out 11 am. Downhill/x-country ski 6 mi. Some refrigerators. Two family units. Cr cds: A, C, D, DS, MC, V.

🐾 📶 📶 🔥

B&B/Small Inn

★★★ **WATERFORD INN.** *258 Chadbourne Rd, Waterford (04088). 207/583-4037. www.waterfordinn.com.* 9 rms, 2 share bath, 2 story. No rm phones. S, D $90-$135; each addl $29. Closed Apr. Pet accepted; $10. Complimentary full bkfst. Dining rm 8-9:30 am, 5-9 pm. Ck-out 11 am, ck-in 2 pm. Downhill ski 20 mi; x-country ski on site. Lawn games. Private patios, balconies. Built 1825; antiques. Parlor, library. Extensive grounds; flower gardens. Cr cds: A.

D 🐾 🛶 ⚡ 📶 📶 🔥

Restaurants

★ **BARJO.** *210 Main St (04268). 207/743-5784.* Specialties: marinated sirloin tips, homemade chicken pie. Salad bar. Hrs: 11 am-2 pm, 4-7 pm; Fri, Sat to 8 pm. Lunch $3.50-$8.95, dinner $4.95-$8.95. Cr cds: DS, MC, V.

D SC

★★ **MAURICE RESTAURANT FRANCAIS.** *109 Main St, South Paris (04281). 207/743-2532.* French menu. Specialties: escalope de veau flambe, roast duck a l' orange. Own desserts. Hrs: 11:30 am-1:30 pm, 4:30-9 pm; Sat from 4:30 pm; Sun brunch 11 am-2 pm. Closed Thanksgiving, Dec 24, 25. Res accepted. Serv bar. Lunch $3-$9.95, dinner $10.95-$16.95. Sun brunch $3-$9.95. Cr cds: A, C, D, DS, ER, MC, V.

D

Ogunquit

See also Kennebunk, Kittery, Wells, York

Pop 974 **Elev** 40 ft **Area code** 207 **Zip** 03907
Information Chamber of Commerce, PO Box 2289; 207/646-2939
Web www.ogunquit.org

Here Maine's "stern and rockbound coast" becomes a sunny strand—a great white beach stretching three miles, with gentle (though sometimes chilly) surf. The Ogunquit public beach is one of the finest on the Atlantic. Marine views, with the picturesque little harbor of Perkins Cove, have attracted a substantial art colony.

What to See and Do

Marginal Way. A beautiful and unusual walk along the cliffs overlooking the ocean, with tidepools at the water's edge.

Ogunquit Museum of American Art. Twentieth-century American sculpture and painting. Museum overlooks the ocean and sculpture gardens. (July-mid-Sept, daily) 183 Shore Rd, at Narrow Cove. Phone 207/646-4909. ¢¢

Special Event

Ogunquit Playhouse. One mi S on US 1. Established in the early 1930s. Top plays and musicals with professional actors. Phone 207/646-5511 (seasonal). Late June-Labor Day wkend. Phone 207/646-2402.

Motels/Motor Lodges

★★ **THE BEACHMERE INN.** *12 Beachmere Pl (03907). 207/646-2021; fax 207/646-2231; toll-free 800/336-3983. www.beachmereinn.com.* 54 units in inn, motel and cottages, 52 with bath, 2-3 story, 51 kits. Mid-June-Labor Day: D $160-$215; each addl $10; spring, fall plans; lower rates late Mar-mid-June, after Labor Day-mid-Dec. Closed rest of yr. Crib $5. TV; cable, VCR (free movies). Playground. Complimentary continental bkfst. Restaurant nearby. Ck-out 11 am. Business servs avail. 9-hole golf privileges. Many microwaves; some fireplaces. Private patios, balconies. Picnic tables, grills. Victorian-style inn (1889). On ocean, swimming beach. Cr cds: A, MC, V.

★★ **JUNIPER HILL INN.** *336 Main St (03907). 207/646-4501; fax 207/646-4595; toll-free 800/646-4544. www.ogunquit.com.* 100 rms, 2 story. July-Aug: S, D $49-$164; each addl $10-$12; higher rates hol wkends; lower rates rest of yr. Crib free. TV; cable (premium). 3 heated pools, 1 indoor; whirlpool. Complimentary coffee in lobby. Restaurant opp 11 am-9 pm. Ck-out 11 am. Coin lndry. Business servs avail. Golf privileges. Exercise equipt; sauna. Refrigerators. Balconies. Garden. Cr cds: A, D, DS, MC, V.

★★ **MEADOWMERE.** *US 1 (03907). 207/646-9661; fax 207/646-6952; toll-free 800/633-8718. www.meadowmere.com.* 145 rms, 1-2 story. Some rm phones. Late June-Labor Day: S, D $165-$395; each addl $10; under 12, $5; higher rates hols; lower rates late Apr-late June, after Labor Day-mid-Oct. Closed rest of yr. TV; cable. Pool. Complimentary continental bkfst. Restaurant adj 7 am-9 pm. Ck-out 11 am. Refrigerators. Balconies. On trolley route. Cr cds: A, DS, MC, V.

★★ **THE MILESTONE.** *687 Main St (03907). 207/646-4562; fax 207/646-1739; toll-free 800/646-6453. www.ogunquit.com.* 70 rms, 1-3 story. No elvtr. Mid-July-Aug: S, D $117-$169; each addl $12; higher rates hols; lower rates rest of yr. Closed Nov-Mar. Crib free. TV; cable (premium). Complimentary coffee in lobby. Restaurant opp 6 am-10 pm. Exercise equipt. Heated pool. Refrigerators. Many balconies. Cr cds: A, D, DS, MC, V.

★★ **NORSEMAN MOTOR INN.** *41 Beach St (03907). 207/646-7024; fax 207/646-0655; toll-free 800/822-7024. www.ogunquitbeach.com.* 94 rms, 1-3 story. No elvtr. Early July-late Aug: S, D $140-$290; each addl $15; lower rates early Apr-early June, late Aug-Oct. Closed rest of yr. Crib free. TV; cable. Restaurant 6:30 am-11 pm; off-season to 9 pm. Ck-out 11 am. Bellhops. Sundries. Many refrigerators. Private patios, balconies, decks. Rms vary. On beach Cr cds: A, DS, MC, V.

★★ **RIVERSIDE.** *159 Shore Rd (03907). 207/646-2741; fax 207/646-0216. www.riversidemotel.com.* 38 rms, 2 story. Late June-Labor Day (3-day min): S, D $60-$160; each addl $10; lower rates late Apr-late June, after Labor Day-late Oct. Closed rest of yr. Crib $10. TV; cable. Complimentary continental bkfst. Ck-out 11 am. Lawn games. Refrigerators. Balconies. Overlooks Perkins Cove. Cr cds: MC, V.

★★ **SEA CHAMBERS MOTOR LODGE.** *53 Shore Rd (03907). 207/646-9311; fax 207/646-0938. seachambers.com.* 43 rms, 2-3 story. No elvtr. Mid-June-Aug (4-day min July-Aug; 3-day min some hol wkends): S, D $118-$174; each addl $15; lower rates Apr-mid-June, Sept-mid-Dec. Closed mid-Dec-Mar. Crib free. TV; cable. Heated pool. Complimentary continental bkfst. Ck-out 11 am. Business servs avail. Bellhops. Tennis. Golf privileges. Health club privileges. Refrigerators. Most rms with ocean view. Sun decks. Cr cds: A, DS, MC, V.

★★ **SEA VIEW MOTEL.** *225 US Rte 1 (03907). 207/646-7064. www.seaviewmotel.com.* 40 rms, 2-3 story. No elvtr. July-Aug: S, D $59-$169; each addl $10; higher rates major hols; lower rates rest of yr. Crib free. TV; cable (premium). Heated pool; whirlpool. Complimentary coffee. Restaurant nearby. Ck-out 11 am. Meeting rm. Exercise equipt. Refrigerators. Cr cds: A, MC, V.

★ ★ ★ **SPARHAWK RESORT MOTEL.** *85 Shore Rd (03907).* 207/646-5562. 82 rms, 2-3 story. No elvtr. Late June-mid Aug (1-wk min): D $150-$160; each addl $15; suites $160-$180; kit. units $170-$225; lower rates mid-Apr-late June, late Aug-late Oct; hol wknds (3-day min). Closed rest of yr. Crib $5. TV; cable (premium). Heated pool. Complimentary continental bkfst. Restaurant nearby. Ck-out 11 am. Luggage handling. Tennis. Golf privileges. Lawn games. Health club privileges. Refrigerators. Balconies. Ocean view. On trolley route. Cr cds: MC, V.

⊡ 👫 🏌 ➳ ⊠ 🔥

★ **STAGE RUN MOTEL.** *238 Rte 1 (03907).* 207/646-4823; fax 207/641-2884. www.stagerunmotel.com. 24 rms, 2 story. July-Labor Day: S, D $89-$129; lower rates early Apr-June, early Sept-Oct. Closed rest of yr. Crib $10. TV; cable; VCR avail. Heated pool. Restaurant opp 6 am-9 pm. Ck-out 11 am. Refrigerators. Balconies. Near ocean, swimming beach. Cr cds: A, MC, V.

⊡ ➳ ⊠ 🔥

★ ★ **TOWNE LYNE MOTEL.** *747 Maine St (03907).* 207/646-2955; fax 207/646-1812. www.townelynemotel.com. 20 rms. Late June-Labor Day (2-day min hol wknds): D $65-$125; each addl $10; kit. unit $90-$120; lower rates Apr-late June, after Labor Day-mid Nov. Closed rest of yr. TV; cable. Complimentary coffee in rms. Restaurant nearby. Ck-out 11 am. Refrigerators avail. Some rms with screened porch overlook river. Cr cds: A, DS, MC, V.

⊠ 🔥

Hotels

★ ★ ★ **GORGES GRANT HOTEL.** *449 Main St (03907).* 207/646-7003; fax 207/646-0660; toll-free 800/646-5001. www.ogunquit.com. 81 rms. Mid-July-Aug: S, D $122-$189; each addl $12; lower rates early-Apr-mid July, Sept-mid-Dec. Closed rest of yr. Crib free. TV; cable (premium). 2 heated pools, 1 indoor; whirlpool, poolside serv. Complimentary coffee in lobby. Restaurant 6:30-11 am, 5-9 pm in season. Ck-out 11 am. Meeting rms. Business servs avail. Golf privileges. Exercise equipt. Refrigerators; some wet bars. Cr cds: A, D, DS, MC, V.

⊡ 👫 ➳ 🕴 ⊠ 🔥

★ ★ **THE GRAND HOTEL.** *108 Shore Rd (03907).* 207/646-1231; toll-free 800/806-1231. www.thegrandhotel.com. 28 suites, 3 story. Late June-early Sept (2-day min wkdays, 3-day min wknds): S, D $95-$225; lower rates mid-Apr-late June, early Sept-mid-Nov. Closed rest of yr. Crib $10. TV; cable, VCR (movies $4.50). Indoor pool. Complimentary continental bkfst. No rm serv. Restaurant adj 7 am-10 pm. Ck-out 11 am. Refrigerators. Balconies. Cr cds: A, DS, MC, V.

⊡ ➳ ⊠ 🔥

Resorts

★ ★ ★ **ANCHORAGE BY THE SEA.** *133 Shore Rd (03907).* 207/646-9384; fax 207/646-6256. www.anchoragebythesea.com. 212 rms, 2-3 story. July-Aug: S, D $59-$215; each addl $15; kit. units $175-$250; July, Aug (3-7 day min); higher rates July 4 wkend; lower rates

rest of yr. Crib $15. TV; cable. 2 pools, 1 indoor; wading pool, whirlpool, sauna. Complimentary continental bkfst Nov-Apr. Restaurant 7 am-7 pm; Oct-late May hrs vary. Ck-out 11 am. Meeting rm. Business servs avail. Bellhops. Sundries. Golf privileges. Health club privileges. Refrigerators; some fireplaces. Balconies. Gazebos. Overlooking ocean. On trolley route. Cr cds: DS, MC, V.

⊡ 🏊 🏄 🏌 ➳ ⊠ 🔥

★ ★ **COLONIAL VILLAGE RESORT.** *548 Hwy Rte 1 (03907).* 207/646-2794; fax 207/646-2463; toll-free 800/422-3341. www.colonialvillageresort.com. 67 rms, 1-2 story, 29 suites, 24 kit. units (no ovens), 4 kit. cottages (2-bedrm). July-Aug, motel (3-day min in season): D, kit. units $109-$140; each addl $15; suites $135-$173; kit. cottages for 2-4, (1-wk min July-Labor Day) $950/wk; lower rates early Apr-June, Sept-mid-Dec. Closed rest of yr. Crib $10. No maid serv in cottages. TV; cable, VCR avail (movies). 2 pools, 1 indoor; whirlpools. Complimentary continental bkfst. Restaurant nearby. Ck-out 11 am. Coin lndry. Tennis. Game rm. Private deck on cottages. Rowboats. Picnic tables, grills. On Tidal River. Cr cds: A, MC, V.

🏌 ➳ ⊠ 🔥

★ ★ **PINK BLOSSOMS FAMILY RESORT.** *66 Shore Rd (03907).* 207/646-7397; fax 207/646-2549; toll-free 800/228-7465. www.pinkb.com. 37 kit. units, 8 with shower only, 2 story. July-Aug (5-7-day min): S $145-$230; kit. units $295-$425; under 6 free; lower rates May-June, Sept-late-Oct. Closed rest of yr. Crib free. TV; cable. Heated pool. Restaurant nearby. Ck-out 11 am. Tennis. Golf privileges. Lawn games. Refrigerators, microwaves. Balconies. Picnic tables, grills. Cr cds: MC, V.

⊡ 👫 🏌 ➳ 🔥

★ ★ **THE TERRACE BY THE SEA.** *23 Wharf Ln (03907).* 207/646-3232. www.terracebythesea.com. 36 rms, 1-2 story, 7 kits. Mid-June-Labor Day: S, D $80-$210; each addl $20; spring, fall packages; lower rates May-mid-June, after Labor Day-Oct. Closed rest of yr. Crib free. TV; cable. Heated pool. Complimentary continental bkfst. Restaurant nearby. Ck-out 11 am. Refrigerators. Balconies. On ocean. Cr cds: A, MC, V.

🏊 ➳ ⊠ 🔥

B&Bs/Small Inns

★ **ABOVE TIDE INN.** *66 Beach St. (03907).* 207/646-7454. www.abovetideinn.com. 9 rms, 7 with shower only, 2 story. No rm phones. Mid-June-mid-Sept (3-day min): S, D $135-$195; each addl $30; lower rates mid-Sept-mid, mid-May-mid-June. Closed rest of yr. TV; cable. Complimentary continental bkfst. Restaurant nearby. Ck-out 11 am, ck-in 2 pm. Massage. Refrigerators. Balconies. Sun deck. Situated on pilings over river; ocean, dune views. Cr cds: MC, V.

🏊 🔥

★ ★ ★ **HARTWELL HOUSE.** *118 Shore Rd (03907).* 207/646-7210; fax 207/646-6032. www.hartwellhouseinn.com. 16 rms, 2 story, 3 suites, 2 kits. June-mid-Sept: S, D $150; kits $750-$850; spring, fall packages; lower rates rest of yr. Children over 14 yrs only. TV in parlor; cable.

Complimentary full bkfst; afternoon refreshments. Ck-out 11 am, ck-in 3 pm. Meeting rms. Restaurant nearby. Golf privileges. Private patios, balconies. Antiques. Cr cds: A, DS, MC, V.

⊡ 🏊 ✈ ⅙ ⊠ 🔥

★★ **THE PINE HILL INN.** *14 Pine Hill Rd S, PO Box 2336 (03907).* 207/361-1004; fax 207/361-1815. www.pinehill inn.com. 6 units, 4 with shower only, 1-2 story, 2-bdrm kit. cottage. No rm phones. Late June-Labor Day: S, D $120-$175; kit. cottage $100; wkly rates cottage; 3-day min cottage; lower rates rest of yr. Children over 12 yrs only in inn rms. TV in cottage, sitting rm; cable. Complimentary full bkfst (inn rms only). Ck-out 11 am, ck-in 4-6 pm. Turn-of-the-century cottage with sun porch. Short walk to ocean. Totally nonsmoking. Cr cds: A, MC, V.

⊠ 🔥

Restaurants

★★★ **ARROW'S.** *Berwick Rd (03907).* 207/361-1100. www.arrowsrestaurant.com. Contemporary Amer menu. Specialty: house-cured prosciutto. Own baking, pastas. Hrs: 6-9 pm. Closed Mon; also late Nov-late Apr. Res accepted. Bar. Wine cellar. Dinner $29.95-$35.95. Valet parking. Renovated 1765 farmhouse; original plank floors, antiques, fresh flowers. Expansive windows overlook more than 3 acres of perennial, herb and vegetable gardens. Cr cds: MC, V.

★ **BARNACLE BILLY'S.** *Perkins Cove (03907).* 207/646-5575. www.barnbilly.com. Specializes in boiled lobster, steamed clams, barbecued chicken. Hrs: 11 am-10 pm; hrs vary mid-Apr-mid-June, mid-Sept-mid-Oct. Closed mid-Oct-mid-Apr; also Mon-Thurs mid-Apr-early-May. Serv bar. Lunch from $5, dinner $7.50-$20. Valet parking in season. Outdoor dining on decks over water. Lobster tank. Fireplaces; nautical decor. Family-owned. Cr cds: A, MC, V.

⊡

★★ **BILLY'S ETC.** *Oarweed Cove Rd (03907).* 207/646-4711. www.barnbilly.com. Specializes in fresh seafood, lobster, steak. Hrs: noon-9 pm. Closed Nov-early May. Bar. Lunch, dinner $4.95-$19.95. Child's menu. Valet parking. Outdoor dining. Views of river and gardens. Totally nonsmoking. Cr cds: A, MC, V.

⊡

★★★ **CLAY HILL FARM.** *226 Clay Hill Rd, Cape Neddick (03907).* 207/361-2272. www.clayhillfarm.com. Specializes in prime rib, fresh seafood. Own pastries. Hrs: 5:30-9 pm. Closed Mon-Wed Nov-Apr. Res accepted. Bar to 9 pm. Wine cellar. Dinner $12-$24. Pianist Wed-Sat (in season), Fri-Sat (off season). Valet parking. Fireplace. Historic farmhouse (1780) in country setting; antiques, herb garden, bird sanctuary. Cr cds: A, C, DS, MC, V.

⊡

★★ **GYPSY SWEETHEARTS.** *10 Shore Rd (03907).* 207/646-7021. www.gypsysweethearts.com. Contemporary Amer menu. Specialties: shrimp margarita, almond-crusted haddock, East Coast crab cakes. Own desserts. Hrs: 5:30-

close; Sat, Sun also 7:30 am-noon; early-bird dinner to 6 pm. Closed Nov-early Apr. Res accepted. Bar to 1 am. Dinner $13.95-$22.95. Child's menu. Converted early-1800s home with original decor, perennial gardens, enclosed sunporch. Family-owned. Totally nonsmoking. Cr cds: A, DS, MC, V.

⊡

★★ **HURRICANE.** *52 Oarweed Cove Rd (03907).* 207/646-6348. www.perkinscove.com. Contemporary Amer menu. Specialties: rack of lamb, baked stuffed lobster, roasted vegetable lasagna. Own desserts. Hrs: 11:30 am-4 pm, 5:30-10:30 pm; Sun brunch Oct-May to 4 pm; winter hrs vary. Closed Thanksgiving, Dec 25. Res accepted; required dinner (May-Sept). Bar. Lunch $7-$15, dinner $14-$26. Sun brunch $7-$15. Jazz Sun brunch. Limited parking. Panoramic views of ocean. Cr cds: A, C, D, DS, ER, MC, V.

★★★ **JONATHAN'S.** *2 Bourne Ln (03907).* 207/646-4777. www.jonathansrestaurant.com. Continental menu. Specializes in seafood, beef, chicken. Own baking. Hrs: 5-11 pm; Oct-June 5:30-9 pm. Res accepted. Bar 5-11 pm. Wine cellar. Dinner $14.50-$21.95. Child's menu. Pianist Wed-Sat. Parking. Aquarium; tropical fish. Doll collection. Herb and country rock gardens. Cr cds: A, D, DS, MC, V.

⊡

★ **OARWEED COVE.** *Oarweed Rd Perkins Cove (03907).* 207/646-4022. www.oarweed.com. Specializes in lobster, lobster rolls, chowder. Hrs: 11 am-9 pm. Closed mid-Oct-Apr. No A/C. Serv bar. Lunch, dinner $3.95-$19.95. Child's menu. Parking. Outdoor dining. View of ocean. Cr cds: A, DS, MC, V.

⊡

★ **OGUNQUIT LOBSTER POUND.** *504 Main St (03907).* 207/646-2516. Specializes in boiled lobster; select your own. Hrs: May-Columbus Day: 4:30-9:30 pm. Closed rest of yr. Bar. Dinner $5.95-$25. Parking. New England decor; fireplaces. Outdoor pine grove dining. Family-owned. Cr cds: A, DS, MC, V.

⊡

★★★ **OLD VILLAGE INN.** *30 Main St (03907).* 207/646-7088. www.oldvillageinn.com. Specializes in local seafood, duckling, beef. Hrs: 5:30-9:30 pm; wkends, hols also 8-11:30 am (Sept-June only). Closed Dec 25. Bar. Wine list. Bkfst $3.95-$6.95, dinner $12.95-$22.95. Child's menu. Town's oldest commercial building (1833). Guest rms avail. Cr cds: A, DS, MC, V.

★★ **POOR RICHARD'S TAVERN.** *125 Shore Rd (03907).* 207/646-4722. www.poorrichardstavern.com. Regional Amer menu. Specialties: Yankee pot roast, lobster-stuffed filet of sole. Hrs: 5:30-9 pm. Closed Sun; also Dec-Mar. Res accepted. Bar. Dinner $12-$24. Valet parking. Outdoor dining. 1780 inn with orginal hand-hewn beams, brick fireplace, antiques. Cr cds: A, DS, MC, V.

⊡

★★★ **PROVENCE.** *104 Shore Rd (03907).* 207/646-9898. www.98provence.com. French Provençale menu. Specializes in fresh local seafood, venison, lamb. Own desserts, ice cream. Hrs: 5:30-9:30 pm. Closed Tues; also mid-Dec-

mid-Apr. Res accepted. Bar. Wine list. Dinner $20-$40. Intimate dining in country-French atmosphere; antiques and china displayed. Totally nonsmoking. Cr cds: A, MC, V.
D

Old Orchard Beach

See also Portland, Saco

Settled 1630 **Pop** 7,789 **Elev** 40 ft **Area code** 207 **Zip** 04064
Information Chamber of Commerce, PO Box 600; 207/934-2500 or 800/365-9386
Web www.oldorchardbeachmaine.com

This popular beach resort, 12 miles south of Portland, is one of the long-time favorites on the Maine Coast. It has a crescent beach seven miles long and about 700 feet wide—which in rocky Maine is a good deal of beach. In summer it is the vacation destination of thousands.

What to See and Do

Palace Playland. Amusement park featuring restored 1906 carousel, arcade, games, rides, water slide; concessions. (Late June-Labor Day, daily; Memorial Day-late June, wkends) Fee for individual attractions or one-price daily pass. Off ME 5, on beachfront. Phone 207/934-2001. ¢¢¢¢

The Pier. Extends 475 ft into the harbor; features shops, boutiques, restaurant. (May-Sept, daily)

Motels/Motor Lodges

★ **CAROLINA MOTEL.** *1 Roussin St (04064). 207/934-4476.* 34 kit. units (no ovens), 2 story. No A/C. Late June-early Sept: S, D $115-$150; each addl $8; lower rates May-late June, early Sept-Oct. Closed rest of yr. Crib free. TV; cable. Heated pool. Restaurant 8 am-8 pm. Ck-out 10 am. Some private balconies. On ocean. Cr cds: A, DS, MC, V.
⌂ 🔥

★★ **THE EDGEWATER.** *57 W Grand Ave (04064). 207/934-2221; fax 207/934-3731; toll-free 800/203-2034. www.janelle.com.* 35 rms, 2 story, 5 kits. (no ovens). Late June-mid-Aug, Labor Day wkend: S, D $69-$189; each addl $8; under 12 free; lower rates mid-Mar-late June, after Labor Day-mid-Nov. Closed rest of yr. TV; cable. Heated pool. Complimentary coffee in lobby. Restaurant adj 7:30 am-noon, 5-10 pm. Ck-out 11 am. Meeting rm. In-rm modem link. Refrigerators, microwaves. Sun deck. On ocean. Cr cds: A, DS, MC, V.
⌂ 🔥

★ **FLAGSHIP MOTEL.** *54 W Grand Ave (04064). 207/934-4866; toll-free 800/486-1681. www.flagshipmotel.com.* 27 rms, 24 A/C, 2 story, 8 suites, 1 cottage. July-Labor Day: D $79-$105; suites $89-$110; each addl $8; under 12 free; lower rates mid-May-June, after Labor Day-mid-Oct. Closed

rest of yr. Crib free. Pet accepted, some restrictions. TV; cable. Pool. Complimentary coffee in lobby. Restaurant opp 7-11 am, 5-10 pm. Ck-out 11 am. Refrigerators. Balconies. Picnic tables. Opp ocean; beach. Cr cds: A, MC, V.
🐾 ⌂ 🔥

★★ **FRIENDSHIP MOTOR INN.** *167 E Grand Ave (04064). 207/934-4644; fax 207/934-7592; toll-free 800/969-7100. www.friendshipmotorinn.com.* 71 suites (2-rm), 6 kit. units, some A/C, 2 story. Mid-June-Labor Day: S, D $59-$179; each addl $8; lower rates Apr-mid-June, after Labor Day-Nov. Closed rest of yr. Crib free. TV; cable (premium), VCR avail. Heated pool. Complimentary coffee in lobby. Restaurant nearby. Ck-out 10 am. Coin lndry. Sundries. Refrigerators, microwaves. Balconies. On ocean. Cr cds: A, DS, MC, V.
⌂ 🔥

★ **GRAND BEACH INN.** *198 E Grand Ave (04064). 207/934-4621; fax 207/934-3435; toll-free 800/834-9696. www.oobme.com.* 87 units, 2-3 story, 37 kits. No elvtr. July-early Sept: S, D $89-$139; suites, kit. units $149-$179; under 13 free; lower rates rest of yr. Closed rest of yr. Crib $10. Pet accepted, some restrictions. TV; cable. Heated pool. Playground. Restaurant 7-11 am. Ck-out 10 am. Coin lndry. Balconies. Picnic tables, grills. Cr cds: A, DS, MC, V.
🐾 ⌂ 🔥

★ **THE GULL MOTEL INN & COTTAGES.** *89 W Grand Ave (04064). 207/934-4321; fax 207/934-1742; toll-free 877/662-4855. www.gullmotel.com.* 21 kit. units, 2 story, 4 kit. cottages. Late-June-Labor Day: D $75-$115; each addl $10; kit. cottages (2-bedrm) June-Sept $750/wk; lower rates May-late-June, Labor Day-early Oct. Closed rest of yr. Crib $5. TV; cable. Heated pool. Restaurant nearby. Ck-out 10 am. Private patios, balconies. Picnic tables, grills. Cr cds: A, MC, V.
D 🐾 🔥 ⌂ ✈ 🔥

★ **ISLAND VIEW MOTEL.** *174 E Grand Ave (04064). 207/934-4262.* 15 rms, 1-3 story. No elvtr. Late June-mid-Aug: S, D $50-$95; under 12 free; each addl $5; lower rates rest of yr. Crib free. TV; cable, VCR avail (movies). Pool. Complimentary coffee in rms. Restaurant nearby. Ck-out 10 am. Refrigerators. Balconies. Opp beach. Cr cds: A, DS, MC, V.
🐾 🔥 ⌂ 🔥

★ **NEPTUNE MOTEL.** *82 E Grand Ave (04064). 207/934-5753; toll-free 800/624-6786. www.seene.com/neptune.* 16 kit. units, A/C in suites, 3 story, 12 suites. July-late Aug: S $50-$98; D $65-$135; each addl $10; suites $95; under 16 free; wkly rates; lower rates rest of yr. Crib free. TV; cable. Complimentary coffee in lobby. Restaurant nearby. Ck-out 10 am. Balconies. Picnic tables, grills. Cr cds: A, DS, MC, V.
🐾 🔥 ⌂ 🔥

★★ **ROYAL ANCHOR RESORT.** *203 E Grand Ave (04064). 207/934-4521; toll-free 800/934-4521. www.royalanchor.com.* 40 rms, 3 story. No A/C. No elvtr. Late June-late Aug: S, D $129-$179; each addl $10-$15; lower rates May-late June and late Aug-mid-Oct. Closed rest of yr. Crib free. TV; cable,

VCR avail. Heated pool. Complimentary continental bkfst. Ck-out 10:30 am. Coin lndry. Tennis. Refrigerators, microwaves. Many private patios, balconies. On ocean. Cr cds: A, DS, MC, V.

⬛⬛⬛⬛⬛⬛

★ **SAND PIPER BEACHFRONT MOTEL.**
2 Cleaves (04064). 207/934-2733; toll-free 800/611-9921. www. sandpiperbeachfrontmotel.com. 22 rms, 2 story, 10 kits. Early July-Aug: S $40-$85; D $60-$105; each addl $5; lower rates rest of yr. Crib $5. TV; cable. Complimentary continental bkfst. Restaurant nearby. Ck-out 10 am. Refrigerators. Picnic tables, grills. On beach; sun terrace. Cr cds: A, DS, MC, V.

⬛⬛⬛⬛⬛⬛

★ **SEA CLIFF HOUSE & MOTEL.** *2 Sea Cliff Ave (04064). 207/934-4874; fax 207/934-1445; toll-free 800/326-4589. www.seacliffhouse.com.* 35 rms, 2-3 story, 22 kit. suites (2-rm). July-Aug: D $89-$125; each addl $10; lower rates rest of yr. Crib $5. TV; cable, VCR avail. Heated pool. Complimentary coffee in rms. Restaurant nearby. Ck-out 10 am. Refrigerators. Balconies. On ocean, beach. Cr cds: A, DS, MC, V.

⬛⬛⬛⬛

★ **SKYLARK MOTEL.** *2 Brown St (04064). 207/934-4235. www.theskylark.com.* 22 rms, 3 story, 3 kit. suites (2-bedrm), 19 kit. units (no ovens). Mid-July-mid-Aug: S, D, kit. units $104-$120; kit. suites $160-$180; wkly rates late June-late Aug; lower rates Apr-mid-July, mid-Aug-Oct. Closed rest of yr. Crib free. TV; cable (premium). Complimentary coffee in lobby. Restaurant nearby. Ck-out 11 am. Coin lndry. Picnic tables, grill. On ocean. Cr cds: A, DS, MC, V.

⬛

B&B/Small Inn

★★ **ATLANTIC BIRCHES INN.** *20 Portland Ave (04064). 207/934-5295; fax 207/934-3781; toll-free 888/934-5295. www.atlanticbirches.com.* 10 rms, 3 A/C, 2 kit. units (no oven), 2-3 story. No rm phones. Early July-Labor Day: S, D $79-$135; each addl $10; family rates; lower rates rest of yr. Crib free. TV in sitting rm; cable, VCR avail (movies free). Pool. Playground. Complimentary continental bkfst. Restaurant nearby. Ck-out 11 am, ck-in 3-7 pm. Picnic tables, grills. Restored Victorian house. Swimming beach nearby. Totally nonsmoking. Cr cds: A, MC, V.

⬛⬛⬛

All Suite

★★ **HORIZON.** *2 Atlantic Ave (04064). 207/934-2323; fax 207/934-3215; toll-free 888/550-1745. www.horizonmotel .com.* 14 kit. suites (2-rm), 3 story. Late June-mid-Aug: S, D $90-$110; each addl $5; lower rates rest of yr. Closed Nov-Mar. Crib free. TV; cable. Restaurant nearby. Ck-out 10 am. Coin lndry. On ocean. Cr cds: A, MC, V.

⬛⬛⬛

Orono

Settled 1774 **Pop** 10,573 **Elev** 80 ft **Area code** 207 **Zip** 04473
Information Bangor Region Chamber of Commerce, 519 Main St, PO Box 1443, Bangor 04401; 207/947-0307
Web www.bangorregion.com

The Penobscot River flows through this valley town, which was named for a Native American chief called Joseph Orono (OR-a-no). The "Maine Stein Song" was popularized here in the 1930s by Rudy Vallee.

What to See and Do

University of Maine-Orono. (1865) 11,500 students. This is the largest of seven campuses of the University of Maine system. On campus is Jordan Planetarium (shows; Phone 207/581-1341. Also on campus is

Hudson Museum. Exhibits relating to history and anthropology. (Tues-Sun) At Maine Center for the Arts. Phone 207/581-1901. **FREE**

Motels/Motor Lodges

★★ **BEST WESTERN BLACK BEAR INN.** *4 Godfrey Dr (04473). 207/866-7120; fax 207/866-7433; res 800/528-1234. www.bestwestern.com.* 68 rms, 3 story. July-Oct: S $75; D $80; each addl $5; suites $109-$119; under 12 free; lower rates rest of yr. Pet accepted. TV; cable (premium), VCR avail. Complimentary continental bkfst. Complimentary coffee in rms. Restaurant 5-8 pm; closed Sun. Ck-out 11 am. Meeting rms. Business center. Exercise equipt; sauna. Microwaves avail. Cr cds: A, D, DS, MC, V.

⬛⬛⬛⬛⬛ SC ⬛

★ **MILFORD MOTEL ON THE RIVER.** *154 Main St, Milford (04461). 207/827-3200; toll-free 800/282-3330. www.mint .net/milford.motel.* 22 rms, 2 with shower only, 2 story, 8 suites. Mid-June-Aug: S, D $64-$89; suites $84; under 18 free; wkly rates; lower rates rest of yr. Crib free. Pet accepted. TV; cable (premium). Complimentary coffee in rms. Restaurant nearby. Ck-out 10 am. Coin lndry. Refrigerators. Some balconies. Picnic tables. On river. Cr cds: A, DS, MC, V.

⬛⬛⬛⬛

★★ **UNIVERSITY MOTOR INN.** *5 College Ave (04473). 207/866-4921; fax 207/866-4550; toll-free 800/321-4921. www.universitymotorinn.com.* 48 rms, 2 story. June-Sept: S $59; D $69; each addl $4-$6; under 13 free; higher rates: Univ ME graduation, homecoming; lower rates rest of yr. Crib free. Pet accepted. TV; cable. Pool. Complimentary continental bkfst. Ck-out 11 am. Private patios, balconies. Cr cds: A, D, DS, MC, V.

⬛⬛⬛⬛⬛⬛

Restaurant

★★ **MARGARITA'S.** *15 Mill St (04473). 207/866-4863.* Mexican menu. Hrs: 4-10 pm; Fri-Sun noon-10:30 pm. Bar to 12:30 am. A la carte entrees: dinner $3.25-$12.95. Child's menu. Cr cds: A, DS, MC, V.
D SC

Poland Spring

See also Auburn, Bridgton, Norway, Sebago Lake

Settled 1768 **Pop** 200 **Elev** 500 ft **Area code** 207 **Zip** 04274

The Poland Spring Inn, once New England's largest private resort (5,000 acres), stands on a rise near the mineral spring that has made it famous since 1844. Actually, the hotel had even earlier beginnings with the Mansion House built in 1794 by the Ricker brothers. In 1974 the original inn burned and was replaced by a smaller hotel.

What to See and Do

✪ **Shaker Museum.** Shaker furniture, folk and decorative arts, textiles, tin and woodenware; early American tools and farm implements displayed. Guided tours of buildings in this last active Shaker community incl Meetinghouse (1794), Ministry Shop (1839), Boys' Shop (1850), Sisters' Shop (1821), and Spin House (1816). Workshops, demonstrations, concerts, and other special events. Extensive research library (Tues-Thurs, by appt only). (Memorial Day-Columbus Day, Mon-Sat) 1 mi S on ME 26. Phone 207/926-4597. ¢¢

Portland

See also Old Orchard Beach, Scarborough, Yarmouth

Settled 1632 **Pop** 64,358 **Elev** 50 ft **Area code** 207
Information Convention & Visitors Bureau of Greater Portland, 305 Commercial St, 04101; 207/772-5800
Web www.visitportland.com

Maine's largest city is on beautiful Casco Bay, dotted with islands popular with summer visitors. Not far from the North Atlantic fishing waters, it leads Maine in this industry. Shipping is also important. It is a city of fine elms, stately old homes, historic churches, and charming streets.

Portland was raided by Native Americans several times before the Revolution. In 1775 it was bombarded by the British, who afterward burned the town. Another fire, in 1866, wiped out large sections of the city. Longfellow remarked that the ruins reminded him of Pompeii.

What to See and Do

Boat trips. Cruises along Casco Bay, some with stops at individual islands or other locations; special charters also avail. Most cruises (May-Oct). For further information, rates, schedules, or fees, contact the individual companies.

Bay View Cruises. Fisherman's Wharf, 184 Commercial St, 04101. Phone 207/761-0496.

Casco Bay Lines. PO Box 4656 DTS, 04112. Phone 207/774-7871.

Eagle Tours Inc. 19 Raybon Rd Extension, York 03909. Phone 207/774-6498.

M/S *Scotia Prince*. A 1,500-passenger cruise ferry leaves nightly for 11-hr crossing to Yarmouth, Nova Scotia. (May-Oct) Staterms avail. Phone 207/775-5616.

Olde Port Mariner Fleet, Inc. A 1,500-passenger cruise ferry leaves nightly for 11-hr crossing to Yarmouth, Nova Scotia. (May-Oct) Staterms avail. PO Box 1084, 04104. Phone 207/775-0727.

The Center for Maine History.

Research Library. World's most complete collection of Maine history materials. Incl 125,000 books and newspapers, 3,500 maps, 70,000 photos, 500 pamphlets, over 2,000,000 manuscripts, and 100,000 architectural and engineering drawings. Also Fogg collection of autographs and rare original copy of Dunlap version of the Declaration of Independence. (Tues-Sat; closed hols) Phone 207/774-1822. ¢¢¢¢

Maine History Gallery. Features Museums Collection with more than 2,000 paintings, prints, and other original works of art, and approx 8,000 artifacts. Collection incl costume and textiles, decorative arts, Native American artifacts and archeological material, political items, and military artifacts. Changing programs and exhibits trace the history of life in Maine. Gallery talks and hands-on workshops also offered. (June-Oct, daily; Dec-May, Tues-Sat) Phone 207/774-1822. ¢¢

Wadsworth-Longfellow House. (1785) Boyhood home of Henry Wadsworth Longfellow. Built by the poet's grandfather, General Peleg Wadsworth, it is maintained by the Maine Historical Society. Contains furnishings, portraits, and personal possessions of the family. (June-mid-Oct, Tues-Sat; closed July 4, Labor Day) 487 Congress St. Phone 207/772-1807.

Children's Museum of Maine. Hands-on museum where interactive exhibits allow children to become a Maine lobsterman, storekeeper, computer expert, or astronaut. (Daily) 142 Free St. Phone 207/828-1234. ¢¢

Maine Historical Society. Research library for Maine history and genealogy. (Tues-Sat; closed hols) 485 Congress St. Phone 207/774-1822.

The Museum at Portland Headlight. (1791) Said to be first lighthouse authorized by the US and oldest lighthouse in continuous use; erected on orders from George Washington. (June-Oct, daily; Nov-Dec and Apr-May, wkends) 1000 Shore Rd, in Fort Williams Park, Cape Elizabeth. Phone 207/799-2661. ¢

Old Port Exchange. A charming collection of shops and restaurants located in 19th-century, brick buildings built after the fire of 1866. Between Exchange and Pearl Sts, extending five blks from waterfront to Congress St.

Portland Museum of Art. Collections of American and European painting, sculpture, prints, and decorative art; State of Maine Collection with works by artists from and associated with Maine; John Whitney Payson Collection (Renoir, Monet, Picasso, and others). Free admission Fri evenings. (Apr-Oct, Tues-Sun; Nov-Mar, Wed-Sun; closed hols) 7 Congress Sq. Phone 207/775-6148. ¢¢

Portland Observatory. (1807) This octagonal, shingled landmark is the last surviving 19th-century signal tower on the Atlantic. Newly renovated, with 102 steps to the top. (June-Oct, daily) 138 Congress St. Phone 207/772-5561.

Southworth Planetarium. Astronomy programs, laser light concerts, children's shows. (Fri and Sat; addl shows summer months) 96 Falmouth St. Phone 207/780-4249. ¢¢

State parks.

Crescent Beach. Swimming, sand beach, bathhouse, fishing; picnicking, playground, concession. (Memorial Day–mid-Oct) Standard fees. 10 mi SE on ME 77 in Cape Elizabeth. Phone 207/799-5871.

Two Lights. Approx 40 acres along Atlantic Ocean. Fishing; picnicking. (Mid-Apr–Nov) Standard fees. 9 mi SE off ME 77 in Cape Elizabeth. Phone 207/799-5871.

Tate House. (1755) Georgian structure built by George Tate, mast agent for the British Navy. Furnished and decorated in the period of Tate's residence, 1755-1800; 18th-century herb gardens. (July-mid-Sept, Tues-Sun; mid-May-June and mid-Sept-mid-Oct, by appt only; closed July 4, Labor Day) 1270 Westbrook St. Phone 207/774-9781. ¢

University of Southern Maine. (1878) 11,000 students. One of the seven units of the University of Maine system. Special shows are held periodically in the university planetarium and in the art gallery. Also theatrical and musical events. Portland campus, off I-295 exit 6; Gorham campus, jct ME 25 and College Ave. Phone 207/780-4500.

Victoria Mansion. (1858) One of the finest examples of 19th-century architecture surviving in the US. Opulent Victorian interior incl frescoes, carved woodwork, and stained and etched glass. (May-Oct, Tues-Sun; closed most major hols) 109 Danforth St at Park St. Phone 207/772-4841. ¢¢

Special Events

Old Port Festival. Exchange St. Phone 207/772-6828. Early June.

Outdoor summer concerts. Deering Oaks Park. Phone 207/874-8793. Tues afternoons-Thurs eves, late June-Aug.

Sidewalk Art Show. Exhibits extend along Congress St from Congress Sq to Monument Sq. Phone 207/772-5800. Third Sat Aug.

New Year's Eve Portland. Fifteen indoor and many outdoor locations. More than 90 performances, mid-afternoon to midnight; a citywide, nonalcoholic celebration with parade and fireworks. Phone 207/772-5800. Dec 31.

Motels/Motor Lodges

★★ **BEST WESTERN MERRY MANOR INN.** *700 Main St, South Portland (04106). 207/774-6151; fax 207/871-0537. www.bestwestern.com.* 151 rms, 1-3 story. No elvtr. June-late Oct: S $109.95; D $119.95; each addl $10; under 12 free; lower rates rest of yr. Crib $3. Pet accepted. TV; cable (premium), VCR avail (movies). Heated pool. Coffee in rms. Restaurant 6 am-10 pm. Ck-out 11 am. Coin lndry. Meeting rms. Business servs avail. In-rm modem link. Valet serv. Health club privileges. Some refrigerators; microwaves avail. Cr cds: A, D, DS, MC, V.

★ **COMFORT INN.** *90 Maine Mall Rd, South Portland (04106). 207/775-0409; fax 207/775-1755; toll-free 800/368-6485. www.comfortinn.com.* 128 rms, 3 story. Mid-June-Oct: S, D $119-$149.95; each addl $5; under 19 free; lower rates rest of yr. Crib free. TV; cable (premium). Heated pool. Complimentary continental bkfst. Coffee in rms. Restaurant nearby. Ck-out 11 am. Coin lndry. Business servs avail. In-rm modem link. Valet serv. Free airport transportation. Health club privileges. Some refrigerators. Cr cds: A, C, D, DS, MC, V.

★★ **HAMPTON INN.** *171 Philbrook Ave, South Portland (04106). 207/773-4400; fax 207/773-6786; res 800/426-7866. www.portlandhamptoninn.com.* 118 rms, 4 story. Mid-June-late Oct: S $79-$119; D $89-$129; under 19 free; wkly rates; lower rates rest of yr. Crib free. TV; cable (premium). Complimentary continental bkfst. Restaurant nearby. Ck-out noon. Business servs avail. Sundries. Free airport transportation. Refrigerators, microwaves avail. Maine Mall opp. Cr cds: A, C, D, DS, MC, V.

★★ **HOLIDAY INN.** *81 Riverside St (04103). 207/774-5601; fax 207/774-2103; toll-free 800/465-4329. www.portlandholidayinn.com.* 200 rms, 2 story. July-Oct: S, D $108-$129; under 20 free; lower rates rest of yr. Crib free. TV; cable (premium). Heated pool; whirlpool, poolside serv. Complimentary coffee in rms. Restaurant 6 am-2 pm, 5-10 pm. Rm serv. Bar 11:30-1 am; Sun from noon. Ck-out noon. Coin lndry. Meeting rms. Business servs avail. In-rm modem link. Bellhops. Sundries. Free airport transportation. Exercise equipt; sauna. Refrigerators avail. Picnic tables. Cr cds: A, D, DS, JCB, MC, V.

★★ **HOLIDAY INN BY THE BAY.** *88 Spring St (04101). 207/775-2311; fax 207/761-8224; res 800/465-4329. www.innbythebay.com.* 239 rms, 12-14 story. Mid-June-Oct: S $105-$138; D $115-$148; each addl $10; under 20 free; lower rates rest of yr. Crib free. TV; cable (premium). Indoor pool; poolside serv. Complimentary coffee in rms. Restaurant 6:30 am-2:30 pm, 5:30-10 pm. Rm serv. Bar 11-1 am; entertainment Fri, Sat. Ck-out noon. Coin lndry. Meeting rms. Business servs avail. In-rm modem link. Bellhops. Valet serv. Gift shop. Free garage parking. Free airport transportation. Tennis privileges. Golf privileges. Exercise equipt; sauna. Some rms overlook harbor. Cr cds: A, C, D, DS, JCB, MC, V.

★ **HOWARD JOHNSON HOTEL.** *155 Riverside St (04103). 207/774-5861; fax 207/774-5861; res 800/446-4656. www.hojoportland.com.* 119 rms, 3 story. July-mid-Oct: S $75-$110; D $80-$120; each addl $10; under 18 free; lower rates rest of yr. Crib free. Pet accepted; $50 deposit. TV; cable (premium). Indoor pool; whirlpool. Coffee in rms. Restaurant 7 am-10 pm. Rm serv. Bar noon-1 am; entertainment Fri, Sat. Ck-out noon. Coin lndry. Meeting rms. Business servs avail. Bellhops. Valet serv. Sundries. Free airport transportation. Exercise equipt. Some in-rm whirlpools, microwaves. Some private patios, balconies. Cr cds: A, C, D, DS, JCB, MC, V.

★ **SUSSE CHALET LODGE.** *1200 Brighton Ave (04102). 207/774-6101; fax 207/772-8697; toll-free 800/258-1980.* 132 rms, 2 story. July-Oct: S $59.70; D $69.70-$79.70; under 19 free; lower rates rest of yr. Crib free. TV; cable (premium). Pool. Complimentary continental bkfst. Restaurant adj open 24 hrs. Ck-out 11 am. In-rm modem link. Cr cds: A, C, D, DS, MC, V.

D ⊠ ⊠ 🐾 SC

Hotels

★★ **EASTLAND PARK HOTEL.** *157 High St (04101). 207/775-5411; fax 207/775-2872. eastlandparkhotel.com.* 204 rms, 12 story. June-Oct: S, D $119-$139; each addl $15; suites $275-$350; under 18 free; lower rates rest of yr. Crib free. Garage parking, fee. TV; VCR, cable (premium). Complimentary coffee in rms. Restaurant 6:30 am-2 pm, 5:30-9 pm; Fri, Sat to 10 pm. Bar 5 pm-1 am; entertainment wkends. Ck-out noon. Meeting rms. Business center. Concierge. Gift shop. Free airport transportation. Exercise equipt; sauna. Refrigerator avail. Cr cds: A, MC, V.

D 🐾 ✈ 🐾 🚶

★★★ **MARRIOTT SABLE OAKS PORTLAND.** *200 Sable Oaks Dr, South Portland (04106). 207/871-8000; fax 207/871-7971; res 800/228-9290. www.marriott.com.* 227 rms, 6 story. Late May-early Nov: S, D $129-$159; suites $125-$300; lower rates rest of yr. Crib free. Pet accepted, some restrictions. TV; cable (premium), VCR avail. Indoor pool; whirlpool, poolside serv. Complimentary coffee in rms. Restaurant 6:30 am-11 pm. Rm serv. Bar noon-1 am. Ck-out noon. Meeting rms. Business servs avail. In-rm modem link. Bellhops. Valet serv. Gift shop. Exercise equipt; sauna. Cr cds: A, D, DS, MC, V.

D 🐾 ⊠ 🐾 🐾 🐾

★★★ **PORTLAND REGENCY HOTEL.** *20 Milk St (04101). 207/774-4200; fax 207/775-2150; toll-free 800/727-3436. www.theregency.com.* 95 rms, 4 story, 10 suites. Early July-late Oct: S, D $169-$199; each addl $10; suites $209-$249; wkend rates off-season; lower rates rest of yr. Crib free. Valet parking $5. TV; cable (premium), VCR avail. Complimentary coffee in rms. Restaurant 6:30 am-9:30 pm; Sat, Sun from 7 am. Bar 11:30 am-midnight. Ck-out noon. Meeting rms. Business servs avail. In-rm modem link. Concierge. Free airport transportation. Exercise rm; sauna. Massage. Whirlpool. Bathrm phones, minibars. Small, European-style hotel in refurbished, brick armory building (1895). Cr cds: A, MC, V.

D 🐾 🐾 🐾

★★★ **SHERATON SOUTH PORTLAND HOTEL.** *363 Maine Mall Rd, South Portland (04106). 207/775-6161; fax 207/775-0196; res 800/325-3535. sheraton.com.* 220 rms, 7-9 story. Late June-Oct: S, D $79-$259; each addl $10; under 18 free; lower rates rest of yr. Crib free. TV; cable (premium). Indoor pool. Complimentary coffee in rms. Restaurant 6:30 am-11 pm. Bar 11:30 am-midnight. Ck-out noon. Meeting rms. Business servs avail. In-rm modem link. Free airport transportation. Exercise rm; sauna. Refrigerators, microwaves avail. Cr cds: A, C, D, DS, MC, V.

D ⊠ 🐾 ✈ 🐾 🐾 SC

Resorts

★★★ **BLACK POINT INN.** *510 Black Point Rd, Prouts Neck (04074). 207/883-2500; fax 207/883-9976; toll-free 800/258-0003. www.blackpointinn.com.* 65 rms in inn, 25 units in 4 cottages. MAP, July-Aug: S $220-$260; D $300-$450; each addl $75; suites $400-$450; lower rates May-mid-June, late Oct-Nov. Closed rest of yr. Children over 8 yrs only mid-July-mid-Aug. Serv charge 15%. Crib free. TV; cable (premium), VCR avail (movies). 2 pools, 1 indoor, 1 heated; whirlpools, poolside serv, lifeguard in season. Dining rm (public by res) 8-11 am, noon-5 pm, 6-9 pm. Rm serv. Bar noon-1 am. Ck-out noon, ck-in 3 pm. Meeting rms. Business servs avail. In-rm modem link. Bellhops. Valet serv. Concierge. Gift shop. Barber, beauty shop. Airport transportation. Tennis privileges. 18-hole golf privileges. Bicycles. Exercise rm; sauna. Massage. Lawn games. Many bathrm phones; some balconies. Private beach. 1878 inn; antiques. Secluded grounds on ocean; rose garden. Cr cds: A, DS, MC, V.

D 🐾 🐾 🐾 ⊠ 🐾 🐾 🐾

★★★ **INN BY THE SEA.** *40 Bowery Beach Rd, Cape Elizabeth (04107). 207/799-3134; fax 207/799-4779; toll-free 800/888-4287. www.innbythesea.com.* 43 kit. suites, 3 story. No A/C. July-Aug: S, D $180-$549; package plans off-season; lower rates rest of yr. Pet accepted. TV; cable (premium), VCR (movies). Heated pool; poolside serv. Coffee in rms. Restaurant 7:30 am-9:30 pm. Rm serv. Ck-out noon. Meeting rms. Business servs avail. In-rm modem link. Bellhops. Concierge. Lighted tennis. Lawn games. Bicycles. Health club privileges. Bathrm phones. Balconies, decks. Picnic tables. On ocean; access to swimming beach. Totally nonsmoking. Cr cds: A, DS, MC, V.

D 🐾 🐾 🐾 🐾 🐾 ⊠ 🐾

B&Bs/Small Inns

★★ **INN AT ST. JOHN.** *939 Congress St (04102). 207/773-6481; fax 207/756-7629; res 800/636-9127. www.innat stjohn.com.* 32 rms, 16 share bath, 4 with shower only, 4 story. Some A/C. No elvtr. July-Oct: S, D $49-$134; each addl $6; under 13 free; lower rates rest of yr. Crib free. Pet accepted. TV; cable (premium). Complimentary continental bkfst. Complimentary coffee in rms. Restaurant nearby. Ck-out 11 am, ck-in varies. Business servs avail. Coin lndry. Free airport, bus depot transportation. Refrigerators, microwaves avail. Built in 1896; European motif, antiques. Cr cds: A, MC, V.

🐾 ✈ 🐾

★★ **INN ON CARLETON.** *46 Carleton St (04102). 207/775-1910; toll-free 800/639-1779. www.innoncarleton.com.* 7 rms, 3 share bath, 2 with shower only, 3 story, 1 suite. No rm phones. June-Oct: S, D $179-$199; each addl $25; suite $225; hols (2-day min); lower rates rest of yr. Children over 8 yrs only. Complimentary full bkfst. Restaurant nearby. Ck-out 10 am, ck-in 4-6:30 pm. Business servs avail. Brick townhouse built 1869; Victorian antiques. Totally nonsmoking. Cr cds: A, MC, V.

⊠ 🐾

★★★ **POMEGRANATE INN.** *49 Neal St (04102). 207/772-1006; fax 207/773-4426; toll-free 800/356-0408. www.innbook.com/pome.html.* 8 rms, 4 with shower only, 3 story. Memorial Day-Oct: S, D $95-$205; wkends and hols (2-day min); lower rates rest of yr. Children over 16 yrs only. TV; cable. Complimentary full bkfst. Ck-out 11 am, ck-in 4-6 pm. Street parking. Some in-rm fireplaces. Colonial Revival house built 1884; antiques, art collection. Totally nonsmoking. Cr cds: A, DS, MC, V.

D ⊠ 🖾

All Suite

★★ **EMBASSY SUITES.** *1050 Westbrook St (04102). 207/775-2200; fax 207/775-4052; toll-free 800/362-2779. www.embassysuitesportland.com.* 119 suites, 6 story. June-Oct: suites $159-$299; each addl $10; under 18 free; off-season packages; lower rates rest of yr. Crib free. TV; cable (premium), VCR (movies $8). Indoor pool. Complimentary full bkfst. Coffee in rms. Restaurant 6:30 am-9:30 pm. Bar noon-11 pm. Ck-out noon. Coin lndry. Meeting rms. Business servs avail. In-rm modem link. Free airport transportation. Tennis privileges. Exercise equipt; sauna. Refrigerators, microwaves. Cr cds: A, D, DS, MC, V.

D ⊠ 🖈 ✕ ⊠ 🖾 🖾

Restaurants

★★★ **BACK BAY GRILL.** *65 Portland St (04101). 207/772-8833. www.backbaygrill.com.* Specializes in fresh seafood, grilled dishes, creme brulee. Own baking. Hrs: 5:30-9:30 pm; Fri, Sat to 10 pm. Closed Sun; some major hols. Res accepted. Serv bar. Wine cellar. Dinner $14.95-$24.95. In restored pharmacy (1888). Totally nonsmoking. Cr cds: A, C, D, DS, MC, V.

D

★★ **BOONE'S.** *6 Custom House Wharf (04112). 207/774-5725.* Specializes in shore dinners, seafood, steak. Hrs: 11 am-9 pm. Closed Thanksgiving, Dec 25. Bar. Lunch $4.50-$8.95, dinner $9.95-$19.95. Child's menu. Parking. Outdoor dining. Fishing port atmosphere; built on wharf. Established in 1898. Cr cds: A, MC, V.

D

★★ **DI MILLO'S FLOATING RESTAURANT.** *25 Long Wharf (04101). 207/772-2216. www.dimillos.com.* Specializes in seafood, steak, lobster. Hrs: 11 am-11 pm. Closed Thanksgiving, Dec 25. Bar to 1 am. Lunch $3.75-$11.95, dinner $9.95-$24.95. Child's menu. Parking. Outdoor dining. Nautical decor; located on waterfront in a converted ferry boat. Family-owned. Cr cds: A, D, DS, MC, V.

D SC

★★ **FORE STREET.** *288 Fore St (04101). 207/775-2717.* Specialties: spit-roasted pork, applewood-grilled steaks, wood-baked seafood. Own desserts. Hrs: 5:30-10 pm; Fri, Sat to 10:30 pm; Sun to 9:30 pm. Closed some major hols. Res accepted. Bar to midnight. Wine list. Dinner $10.95-$21.95. Child's menu. Converted 1930s oil tank garage;

unique decor with copper and steel tables, poured-concrete bar; view of harbor and ferry terminal. Totally nonsmoking. Cr cds: A, MC, V.

D

★★ **F. PARKER REIDY'S.** *83 Exchange St (04101). 207/773-4731.* Specializes in fresh fish, seafood, steak. Hrs: 11:30 am-11 pm; Fri, Sat to 12:30 am; Sun 4:30-11 pm. Closed July 4, Thanksgiving, Dec 25. Res accepted. Bar. Lunch $3-$9, dinner $7.95-$16. Child's menu. Originally Portland Savings Bank (1866). Cr cds: A, D, DS, MC, V.

★ **NEWICK'S SEAFOOD.** *740 Broadway, South Portland (04106). 207/799-3090. www.newicks.com.* Specializes in fresh seafood. Hrs: 11:30 am-8 pm; Fri, Sat to 9 pm. Closed Mon; Thanksgiving, Dec 25. Bar. Lunch, dinner $5.25-$19.95. Child's menu. Parking. Seafood market on premises. Casual dining. Cr cds: A, DS, MC, V.

D

★★ **RIBOLITA.** *41 Middle St (04101). 207/774-2972.* Northern Italian and Tuscan menu. Specialty: risotto. Hrs: from 5 pm. Closed Sun; also most major hols. Res accepted. Dinner $9.50-$16.50. Child's menu. Street parking. Outdoor dining. Totally nonsmoking. Cr cds: MC, V.

★★★ **THE ROMA.** *769 Congress St (04102). 207/773-9873.* Continental menu. Specializes in lobster, fresh seafood, Northern Italian dishes. Own desserts. Hrs: 11:30 am-2 pm, 5-9 pm; Sat from 5 pm; Sun 5-8 pm. Closed Memorial Day, Labor Day, Dec 25; also Sun Dec-May. Res accepted. Bar to 1 am. Lunch $4.95-$9.95, dinner $9.95-$16.95. Child's menu. Parking. Fireplaces. Victorian mansion (ca 1885). Cr cds: A, DS, MC, V.

★★ **STREET & CO.** *33 Wharf St (04101). 207/775-0887.* Mediterranean seafood menu. Specialties: lobster diavolo, scallops in Pernod and cream, shrimp over linguini with tomato caper sauce. Hrs: 5:30-9:30 pm; Fri, Sat to 10 pm. Closed Jan 1, Dec 24, 25. Res accepted. Bar. Dinner $12.95-$19.95. Street parking. Outdoor dining. 19th century commercial bldg with original floor woodwork. Open kitchen. Cr cds: A, MC, V.

D

★★ **VILLAGE CAFE.** *112 Newbury St (04101). 207/772-5320. www.villagecafe.baweb.com.* Italian, Amer menu. Specializes in fried clams, lobster, veal, steak. Hrs: 11 am-10 pm; Fri, Sat to 11 pm; Sun 11:30 am-9:30 pm. Closed Thanksgiving, Dec 25. Bar. Lunch $4.25-$8.75, dinner $6.75-$24.95. Child's menu. Parking. Family-owned. Cr cds: A, DS, MC, V.

D SC

★★ **WALTER'S CAFE.** *15 Exchange St (04101). 207/871-9258. www.walterscafe.com.* Contemporary Amer menu. Specialties: lobster with angel hair pasta, crazy chicken. Own baking. Hrs: 11 am-3 pm, 5-9 pm; Sun from 5 pm. Closed Jan 1, Dec 25; also 1st Sat in May. Bar. Lunch $6.95-$12.95, dinner $11.95-$17.95. Street parking. Mid-1800s commercial bldg with much original interior; 3 dining areas on 2 levels. Totally nonsmoking. Cr cds: A, MC, V.

D

Presque Isle

See also Caribou

Settled 1820 **Pop** 10,550 **Elev** 446 ft **Area code** 207
Zip 04769
Information Presque Isle Area Chamber of Commerce,
PO Box 672; 207/764-6561 or 800/764-7420
Web www.pichamber.com

Commercial and industrial center of Aroostook County,
this city is famous for its potatoes. A deactivated air base
nearby is now a vocational school and industrial park.

What to See and Do

Aroostook Farm—Maine Agricultural Experiment Station.
Approx 375 acres operated by University of Maine; experiments to improve growing and marketing of potatoes and
grain. (Mon-Fri; closed hols) Houlton Rd, 2 mi S on US 1.
Phone 207/762-8281. **FREE**

Aroostook State Park. 577 acres. Swimming, bathhouse,
fishing, boating (rentals, ramp on Echo Lake); hiking,
x-country trails, picnicking, camping. (Mid-May-mid-Oct,
daily) Snowmobiling permitted. Standard fees. 4 mi S on
US 1, then W. Phone 207/768-8341.

Double Eagle II **Launch Site Monument.** *Double Eagle II*,
the first balloon to travel across the Atlantic Ocean, was
launched from this site in 1978. Spragueville Rd, 4 mi S
on US 1, then W. **FREE**

University of Maine at Presque Isle. (1903) 1,500 students.
During the summer there is the Pioneer Playhouse and an
Elderhostel program. In winter, the business bkfst program,
theater productions and a number of other cultural and
educational events are open to the public. US 1. Phone
207/768-9400.

Special Events

Spudland Open Amateur Golf Tournament. Presque Isle
Country Club. Mid-July. Phone 207/769-7431.

Northern Maine Fair. Midway, harness racing, entertainment.
Late July-early Aug. Phone 207/764-6561.

Motels/Motor Lodges

★ **BUDGET TRAVELER MOTOR LODGE.** *71 Main St
(04769). 207/769-0111; fax 207/764-6836; toll-free 800/958-
0111.* 53 rms, 6 kit, 2 story. S $29.95; D $35.95-$49.95;
each addl $5; under 12 free. Crib $6. TV; cable, VCR avail
(movies). Complimentary continental bkfst. Restaurant
nearby. Ck-out 11 am. Coin lndry. Business servs avail.
Free airport transportation. Refrigerators; microwaves avail.
Cr cds: A, MC, V.
🄳 ⊗ 🔥 🆂🅲

★ **NORTHERN LIGHTS.** *72 Houlton Rd (04769). 207/764-
4441; fax 207/769-6931. www.northernlightsmotel.com.* 13
rms. S $38.95; D $64.95; each addl $5; under 12 free. Crib
$5. Pet accepted; $10. TV; cable. Morning coffee. Ck-out
11 am. Cr cds: A, DS, MC, V.
🐾 🐦 🔥 ⊗ 🅰

Rangeley

Settled 1825 **Pop** 1,063 **Elev** 1,545 ft **Area code** 207
Zip 04970
Information Rangeley Lakes Chamber of Commerce,
PO Box 317; 207/864-5364 or 800/MT-LAKES (reservations)
Web www.rangeleymaine.com

Within ten miles of Rangeley there are 40 lakes and ponds.
The six lakes that form the Rangeley chain—Rangeley,
Cupsuptic, Mooselookmeguntic, Aziscoos, Upper Richardson,
and Lower Richardson—spread over a wide area and give
rise to the Androscoggin River. Some of Maine's highest
mountains rise beside the lakes. The development of ski
and snowmobiling areas has turned this summer vacation
spot into a year-round resort.

What to See and Do

Camping. Several designated public camp and picnic sites;
wilderness sites on islands.

Fishing. Boats for rent; licensed guides. The lakes are
stocked with square-tailed trout and landlocked salmon.

Rangeley Lake State Park. More than 690 acres on Rangeley
Lake. Swimming, fishing, boating (ramp, floating docks);
snowmobiling permitted, picnicking, camping (dump
station). (May-Oct) Standard fees. 4 mi S on ME 4, then
5 mi W via local road. Phone 207/864-3858.

Skiing. Saddleback Ski & Summer Lake Preserve. Two
double chairlifts, 3 T-bars; rentals, school, patrol; snowmaking; cafeteria, bar; nursery, lodge. Longest run 2.5 mi;
vertical drop 1,830 ft. (Late Nov-mid-Apr, daily) X-country
trails. 7 mi E off ME 4. Phone 207/864-5671.

Swimming, boating. Several public beaches and docks on
lakefront. Rangeley Lakeside Park on lakeshore has public
swimming, picnicking areas.

Wilhelm Reich Museum. Unusual stone building housing
scientific equipment, paintings, and other memorabilia
of this physician-scientist; slide presentation, nature trail,
discovery rm. (July-Aug, Tues-Sun; Sept, Sun only) Dodge
Pond Rd, 4 mi W off ME 4. Phone 207/864-3443. ¢¢

Special Events

Sled Dog Race. Teams from eastern US and Canada compete
in 20-mi race. Phone 207/864-5364. First wkend Mar.

Logging Museum Field Days. Logging competitions, Miss
Woodchip contest, parade, logging demonstrations. Phone
207/864-5595. Last wkend July.

Motel/Motor Lodge

★★ **COUNTRY CLUB INN.** *1 Country Club Dr (04970).
207/864-3831. www.countryclubinnrangeley.com.* 10 rms in
2 story inn; 9 rms in motel. No A/C. Late May-mid-Oct,
late Dec-Mar, MAP: S, D $160; golf plans; EP avail. Closed
Apr, Nov. Serv charge 15%. Crib $5. TV in lobby. Pool.
Dining rm 7:30-9 am, 6:30-8 pm. Box lunches. Bar.
Ck-out 10:30 am. Grocery, coin lndry 2½ mi. Free airport

transportation. Boat; waterskiing 1½ mi. Downhill/x-country ski 7 mi. Lawn games. Scenic view of mountains, lake. Cr cds: A, DS, MC, V.

Resort

★★★ **RANGELEY INN.** *51 Main St (Rt 4) (04970). 207/864-3341; fax 207/864-3634; toll-free 800/666-3687. www.rangeleyinn.com.* 50 units, 15 motel rms, 3 kits. No A/C. July-mid-Oct, hol wks, winter wkends: S, D $84-$140; each addl $6; kit. units for 2-6, $89-$109; lower rates rest of yr. Crib $6. TV; cable in motel rms, sitting rm, VCR in sitting rm (movies). Restaurant (see RANGELEY INN). Bar 4 pm-1 am; entertainment wkends. Ck-out 11 am. Meeting rms. Downhill/x-country ski 7 mi. Snowmobile trail. Some in-rm whirlpools, fireplaces. On pond. Cr cds: A, DS, MC, V.

Restaurants

★ **PEOPLE'S CHOICE.** *Main St (ME 4) (04970). 207/864-5220.* Specializes in fresh seafood. Own baking. Salad bar. Hrs: 6 am-9 pm. Closed Thanksgiving, Dec 25. Res accepted. Bar 11 am-midnight. Bkfst $2-$7, lunch $3-$9, dinner $7-$15. Child's menu. Entertainment wkends. Chainsaw-carved lumberjack on display. Cr cds: A, DS, MC, V.

★★★ **RANGELEY INN.** *51 Main St (04970). 207/864-3341. www.rangeleyinn.com.* Continental menu. Specializes in fresh seafood, rack of lamb, filet mignon. Own baking. Hrs: 7:30-10 am, 6-9 pm. Closed Dec 25; also Apr-May. Res accepted. Bar. Wine list. Bkfst $3-$7, dinner $12.95-$28.95. Child's menu. Elegant decor; oak woodwork, brass chandeliers, tin ceiling. Outdoor dining. Totally nonsmoking. Cr cds: A, DS, MC, V.

Rockland

Settled 1770 **Pop** 7,972 **Elev** 35 ft **Area code** 207 **Zip** 04841
Information Rockland-Thomaston Area Chamber of Commerce, PO Box 508; 207/596-0376 or 800/562-2529
Web www.midcoast.com/~rtacc

This town on Penobscot Bay is the banking and commercial center of the region and seat of Knox County. It is also the birthplace of the poet Edna St. Vincent Millay. Its economy is geared to the resort trade, but there is commercial fishing and light industry. It is the railhead for the whole bay. Supplies for boats, public landing, and guest moorings are here.

What to See and Do

Farnsworth Art Museum and Wyeth Center. Cultural and educational center for the region. Collection of over 10,000 works of 18th- to 20th-century American art. Center houses personal collection of Wyeth family art and archival material. (June-Sept, daily; rest of yr, Tues-Sun) 325 Main St. Phone 207/596-6457. ¢¢ Incl in admission and adj is

Farnsworth Homestead. A 19th-century Victorian mansion with period furniture. (June-Sept, daily) Phone 207/596-6457.

Fisherman's Memorial Pier and Chamber of Commerce. Public landing, Harbor Park.

Maine State Ferry Service. Ferries make 15-mi (1 hr, 15 min) trip to Vinalhaven and 12½-mi (1 hr, 10 min) trip to North Haven. (All-yr, two to three trips daily) Also 23-mi (2 hr, 15 min) trip to Matinicus Island once a month. 517A Main St. Phone 207/596-2202.

Owls Head Transportation Museum. Working display of antique cars, airplanes and 100-ton steam engine. (Daily) 2 mi S via ME 73, in Owls Head. Phone 207/594-4418. ¢¢

Sailing trips.

Coasting schooners *Isaac H. Evans, American Eagle & Heritage.* Four- and six-day cruises (Late May-mid-Oct). Phone 207/594-8007.

Schooner *J. & E. Riggin.* Three-, four-, five-, six-day cruises (May-Oct). Phone 207/594-1875.

Schooner *Stephen Taber* **& Motor Yacht** *Pauline.* Three- and six-day cruises through Penebscot, Casco, Blue Hill, and Frenchman Bay. (Late May-mid-Oct) Phone 207/236-3520.

Shore Village Museum. (Maine's Lighthouse Museum) A large collection of lighthouse lenses and artifacts; Civil War collection. Museum shop. (June-mid-Oct, daily; rest of yr, by appt) 104 Limerock St. Phone 207/594-0311.

Windjammers. Old-time schooners sail out for three to six days following the same basic route through Penobscot Bay, into Blue Hill and Frenchman's Bay, stopping at small villages and islands along the way. Each ship carries an average of 30 passengers. (Memorial Day-Columbus Day) For further information, rates, schedules, or res, contact the individual companies.

Nathaniel Bowditch. Phone 800/288-4098.

Victory Chimes. Phone 800/745-5651.

Special Events

Schooner Days & North Atlantic Blues Festival. Three-day festival celebrating Maine's maritime heritage, featuring Parade of Schooners, arts, entertainment, concessions, fireworks; blues bands and club crawl. Phone 207/596-0376. Wkend after July 4.

Maine Lobster Festival. A five-day event centered on Maine's chief marine creature, with a huge tent cafeteria serving lobster and other seafood. Parade, harbor cruises, maritime displays, bands, entertainment. First wkend Aug. Phone 800/LOB-CLAW or 207/596-0376.

Motels/Motor Lodges

★★ **GLEN COVE MOTEL.** *US 1, Glen Cove (04846). 207/594-4062; toll-free 800/453-6268. www.glencovemotel.com.* 34 rms, 1-2 story. July-Aug: S, D $129-$200; each addl $10; lower rates rest of yr. Closed Feb. Crib free. TV; cable. Heated pool. Complimentary coffee in lobby. Restaurant nearby. Ck-out 11 am. Refrigerators. Overlooks Penobscot Bay. Cr cds: A, DS, MC, V.

⬛ 🛍 🖼 🐚 🔥

★ **NAVIGATOR MOTOR INN.** *520 Main St (04841). 207/594-2131; fax 207/594-7763; toll-free 888/246-4595. www.navigatorinn.com.* 81 rms, 4-5 story, 6 kits. Mid-June-Aug: D $80-$149; each addl $10; under 16 free; lower rates rest of yr. Pet accepted, some restrictions. TV; cable. Restaurant 6:30 am-2 pm, 5:30-9:30 pm. Rm serv. Bar 11-1 am. Ck-out 11 am. Coin lndry. Meeting rms. Business servs avail. Downhill ski 10 mi; x-country ski 2 mi. Refrigerators; microwaves avail. Balconies. Near ocean. Cr cds: A, DS, MC, V.

⬛ 🐾 🖼 🐚 🔥 🖼

★ **WHITE GATES INN.** *700 Commercial St, Rockport (04856). 207/594-4625; fax 207/594-5993. www.whitegatesinn.com.* 15 rms. Early July-Sept: S $54-$69; D $64-$79; each addl $4; lower rates May-early July and Oct. Closed rest of yr. Crib $4. TV; cable. Complimentary continental bkfst. Restaurant nearby. Ck-out 11 am. Some refrigerators. Cr cds: A, DS, MC, V.

🖼 🔥

Resort

★★★ **SAMOSET RESORT.** *220 Warrenton St, Rockport (04856). 207/594-2511; fax 207/594-0722; toll-free 800/341-1650. www.samoset.com.* 178 rms, 4 story. Early July-early Sept: S $195-$230; D $217-$265; each addl $20; suites from $290; under 16 free; ski, golf, tennis plans; lower rates rest of yr. Crib free. TV; cable (premium). 2 pools, 1 indoor; whirlpool, poolside serv. Playground. Supervised children's activities. Coffee in rms. Dining rm 7 am-9 pm. Bar 11:30-1 am; entertainment. Ck-out noon, ck-in after 3 pm. Meeting rms. Business servs avail. In-rm modem link. Valet serv. Concierge. Gift shop. Sports dir. Tennis. Racquetball. 18-hole golf, putting green, driving range, pro, pro shop. Sailing. Dockage in season. Downhill ski 10 mi; x-country ski on site. Fitness trails. Lawn games. Movies. Game rm. Exercise rm; saunas. Massage. Private patios, balconies. Clambakes. On bay. Cr cds: A, MC, V.

⬛ 🖼 🎿 🏌 🏊 🏃 🖼 🐚 🆂🅲

B&Bs/Small Inns

★★★ **CAPTAIN LINDSEY HOUSE INN.** *5 Lindsey St (04841). 207/596-7950; fax 207/596-2758; toll-free 800/523-2145. www.lindseyhouse.com.* 9 rms, 3 story. No elvtr. Mid-June-early Sept: S, D $120-$175; each addl $45; wkends

2-day min (in season); lower rates rest of yr. Children over 10 yrs only. TV; cable. Complimentary continental bkfst; afternoon refreshments. Restaurant 11 am-10 pm. Ck-out 11 am, ck-in 3 pm. In-rm modem link. Luggage handling. Street parking. Downhill/x-country ski 10 mi. Built in 1830. Antiques; 1920s walk-in safe. Totally nonsmoking. Cr cds: A, DS, MC, V.

⬛ 🛍 🖼 🏊 🐚 🖼

★★ **CRAIGNAIR INN.** *533 Clark Island Rd, Spruce Head (04859). 207/594-7644; fax 207/596-7124; toll-free 800/320-9997. www.craignair.com.* 24 rms, 16 share bath, 2-3 story. No A/C. June-Sept: S $48-$62; D $65-$120; each addl $17; under 6 free; wkly rates; hols, wkends (2-day min); lower rates rest of yr. Crib $5. Pet accepted, some restrictions; $3.50/day. Cable TV in common rm, VCR avail (movies). Complimentary full bkfst; afternoon refreshments. Restaurant 8-9 am, 11 am-1:30 pm, 5:30-9 pm. Rm serv. Ck-out 11 am, ck-in 2 pm. Business servs avail. Luggage handling. Downhill/x-country ski 15 mi. On ocean. Built in 1930; boarding house converted to an inn in 1947. Antiques. Totally nonsmoking. Cr cds: DS, MC, V.

🐾 🛍 🖼 🐚 🔥

★★ **THE LAKESHORE INN BED & BREAKFAST.** *184 Lakeview Dr (04841). 207/594-4209; fax 207/596-6407. www.midcoast.com/~lakshore.* 4 rms, 1 with shower only, 2 story. S, D $135; each addl $20; wkends July-Aug (2-day min); special events (3-day min). Children over 9 yrs only. TV; VCR (movies) in sunrm. Complimentary full bkfst. Whirlpool. Ck-out 11 am, ck-in 3 pm. Downhill ski 6 mi; x-country ski 3 mi. Balconies. Colonial New England farmhouse built in 1767. Totally nonsmoking. Cr cds: MC, V.

🛍 🖼 ✈

Restaurants

★ **HARBOR VIEW.** *Thomaston Landing, Thomaston (04861). 207/354-8173.* Specializes in pasta, seafood. Hrs: 11:30 am-10 pm. Closed Thanksgiving, Dec 25; also Sun and Mon Nov-Apr. No A/C. Bar. Lunch $6.75-$12.95, dinner $9.95-$17.95. Parking. Antiques. Outdoor dining. View of harbor. Cr cds: A, D, DS, MC, V.

⬛ 🖼

★★★ **PRIMO.** *2 S Main St (04841). 207/596-0770. www.primorestaurant.com.* Italian with seafood menu. Hrs: 5:30-9:30 pm. Closed Tues. Res accepted. Wine list. Dinner $15-$18. Cr cds: A, D, DS, MC, V.

🆂🅲

Rockwood

Pop 190 **Elev** 1,050 ft **Area code** 207 **Zip** 04478

What to See and Do

Raft trips.

Northern Outdoors, Inc. Specializes in outdoor adventures incl whitewater rafting on Maine's Kennebec, Penobscot, and Dead rivers (May-Oct). Also snowmobiling (rentals), hunting, and resort facilities. Rock climbing, freshwater kayak touring. Phone 207/663-4466. ¢¢¢¢

Wilderness Expeditions, Inc. Whitewater rafting on the Kennebec, Penobscot, and Dead rivers; also canoe trips and ski tours. (May-Sept, daily) Phone 207/534-2242. ¢¢¢¢

Motel/Motor Lodge

★ **MOOSEHEAD MOTEL.** *State Rte 15 (04478). 207/534-7787. www.maineguide.com/moosehead/motel.* 27 rms, 11 A/C, 4 kit. units, 2 story. No rm phones. S, D $47-$56; kit. units $60-$75; each addl $5; family units $60-$75; hunters' plan. TV, some B/W. Restaurant 7-10 am, 5-8 pm; closed Apr, Dec. Ck-out 11 am. Private docks; canoes, boats, motorboats; fishing, hunting guides. Picnic tables, grill. Plane rides avail. Moosehead Lake opp, boat tour. Cr cds: A, DS, MC, V.

Cottage Colony

★ **THE BIRCHES & CATERING.** *Birches Rd (04478). 207/534-7305; fax 207/534-8835; res 800/825-9453. www.birches.com.* 3 rms in main lodge, shared baths; 17 kit. cottages, shower only. No A/C. AP, May-Nov: S $105; D $65/person; wkly rates; housekeeping plan (no maid serv) $550-$750/wk (4 people); lower rates rest of yr. Pet accepted; $5. Dining rm 7-10 am, 6-9 pm; also 11 am-3 pm in season. Box lunches. Bar. Ck-out 10 am, ck-in 3 pm. Business servs avail. Gift shop. Grocery, package store 2 mi. Private beach. Marina, dockage. Boats, motors; canoes, sailboats. Canoe, rafting trips. Moose-watching cruises. Downhill ski 15 mi; x-country ski on site. Ski, kayak, snowmobile rentals. Bicycles. Sauna. Whirlpool. Fishing guides; clean/store area. Rustic log cabins. On Moosehead Lake. Cr cds: A, MC, V.

Rumford

See also Bethel

Settled 1774 **Pop** 7,078 **Elev** 505 ft **Area code** 207 **Zip** 04276
Information River Valley Chamber of Commerce, 34 River St; 207/364-3241
Web www.rivervalleychamber.com

This papermill town is located in the valley of the Oxford Hills, where the Ellis, Swift, and Concord rivers flow into the Androscoggin. The spectacular Penacook Falls of the Androscoggin are right in town. Rumford serves as a year-round resort area.

What to See and Do

Mount Blue State Park. Recreation areas on Lake Webb incl swimming, bathhouse, lifeguard, fishing, boating (ramp, rentals); hiking trail to Mt Blue, x-country skiing, snowmobiling permitted, picnicking, camping (dump station). (Memorial Day-Labor Day) Standard fees. 4 mi E on US 2 to Dixfield, then 14 mi N on ME 142 in Weld. Phone 207/585-2347.

Motels/Motor Lodges

★★ **BLUE IRIS MOTOR INN.** *US Rte 2, Rumford Center (04278). 207/364-4495; toll-free 800/601-1515. www.sundayriveronline.com.* 14 rms, 5 kit. units. S $40; D $48; each addl $7; kit. units $45-$70; family, wkly rates; ski plans. TV; cable. Pool. Restaurant nearby. Ck-out 10 am. Downhill/x-country ski 5 mi. Balconies. Picnic tables. On river. Cr cds: A, DS, MC, V.

★ **LINNELL MOTEL & RESTINN CONFERENCE CENTER.** *986 Prospect Ave (04276). 207/364-4511; fax 207/369-0800; toll-free 800/446-9038. www.linnellmotel.com.* 50 rms, 1-2 story. S $50; D $60; each addl $5; kit. units $55-$60; under 12 free. Crib free. Pet accepted; $5. TV; cable. Complimentary continental bkfst. Ck-out 11 am. Coin lndry. Meeting rms. Business servs avail. Downhill/x-country ski 3 mi. Many refrigerators. Some balconies. Picnic tables. Cr cds: A, D, DS, MC, V.

★★ **MADISON RESORT INN.** *US Rte 2 (04276). 207/364-7973; fax 207/369-0341; toll-free 800/258-6234. www. madisoninn.com.* 60 rms, 38 A/C, 2 story. S, D $89-$135; each addl $15; kit. units $95-$125; under 12 free. Crib free. Pet accepted. TV; cable, VCR avail (movies). Pool; whirlpool. Restaurant 6-10 am, 5-9 pm. Bar 4-10 pm. Ck-out 11 am. Meeting rms. Business servs avail. Downhill/x-country ski 10 mi. Exercise rm; sauna. Lawn games. Refrigerators. Balconies. On river; boats, canoes. Cr cds: A, MC, V.

Saco

See also Old Orchard Beach, Portland

Settled 1631 **Pop** 15,181 **Elev** 60 ft **Area code** 207 **Zip** 04072
Information Biddeford/Saco Chamber of Commerce, 110 Main St, Suite 1202; 207/282-1567
Web www.biddefordsacochamber.com

Saco, on the east bank of the Saco River, facing its twin city Biddeford, was originally called Pepperellboro, until its name was changed in 1805. The city has diversified industry, including a machine and metalworking plant. Saco is home to the University of Maine system and is only four miles from the ocean.

What to See and Do

Aquaboggan Water Park. More than 40 acres of water and land attractions, incl five water slides, wave pool, children's pool, "aquasaucer," games, miniature golf, bumper boats, race cars. Picnicking. (May-Sept, daily) 4 mi N on US 1. Phone 207/282-3112. ¢¢¢¢

Dyer Library & York Institute Museum. Public library has arts and cultural programs. Museum features local history, decorative and fine art; American paintings, ceramics, glass, clocks, and furniture; changing exhibits. (Mon-Sat) 371 Main St, on US 1. Phone 207/283-3861.

Ferry Beach State Park. Beach, swimming, picnicking, nature and x-country trails. (Memorial Day-Labor Day, daily) Standard fees. 3½ mi N via ME 9. Phone 207/283-0067.

Funtown USA. Theme park featuring adult and kiddie rides; log flume ride; Excalibur wooden roller coaster; Grand Prix Racers; games. Picnicking. (Mid-June-Sept, daily; early May-mid-June, wkends) 2 mi NE on US 1. Phone 207/284-5139. ¢¢¢

Motels/Motor Lodges

★ **CLASSIC.** 21 Ocean Park Rd (04072). 207/282-5569; toll-free 800/290-3909. www.classicmotel.com. 17 rms, 2 story, 15 kits. (no ovens). Mid-June-Labor Day: S $50-$80; D $55-$85; each addl $10; under 13 $5; lower rates rest of yr. TV; cable. Indoor pool; whirlpool. Complimentary continental bkfst. Restaurant nearby. Ck-out 11 am. In-rm modem link. Many refrigerators. Balconies. Picnic tables. Cr cds: A, DS, MC, V.

⌨ 🏊 📶 🔥

★★ **EASTVIEW.** 924 Portland Rd (04072). 207/282-2362. www.eastviewmotel.com. 22 rms. Late June-Labor Day: S $65; D $70; each addl $5; under 12 free; lower rates May-late June, after Labor Day-late Oct. Closed rest of yr. TV; cable. Pool. Restaurant opp 8 am-10 pm. Ck-out 10 am. Lawn games. Some refrigerators. Cr cds: A, MC, V.

⌨ 🏊 📶 🔥

★ **SUNRISE MOTEL.** 962 US Rte 1 (04072). 207/283-3883; fax 207/284-8888. www.sunrisemotel.com. 30 rms, 1-2 story, 6 kit. cottages. July-Aug: S, D $40-$85; each addl $8; suites, cottages $50-$75; wkly rates; lower rates rest of yr. Crib free. TV; cable (premium). Heated pool. Playground. Complimentary continental bkfst. Ck-out 10 am. Coin lndry. Business servs avail. Sundries. Lawn games. Refrigerators, microwaves avail. Balconies. Picnic tables, grills. Cr cds: A, DS, MC, V.

D ⌨ 📶 🐾 SC

Restaurant

★★ **CASCADE INN.** 941 Portland Rd (US 1) (04072). 207/283-3271. Specializes in steak, seafood. Hrs: 8 am-10 pm; off-season 11 am-9 pm; Sun brunch 9 am-1 pm. Bar. Bkfst buffet $4.95-$5.95, lunch $3.99-$9.95, dinner $5.25-$14.95. Sun brunch $3.95-$5.95. Child's menu. Fireplaces. Cr cds: DS, MC, V.

D

Scarborough

See also Portland

Pop 12,518 **Elev** 17 ft **Area code** 207 **Zip** 04074

Information Convention & Visitors Bureau of Greater Portland, 305 Commercial St, Portland 04101; 207/772-5800

Web www.visitportland.com

Scarborough contains some industry, but it is primarily a farming community and has been for more than 300 years. It is also a bustling tourist town during the summer months as vacationers flock to nearby beaches and resorts. The first Anglican church in Maine is here, as is painter Winslow Homer's studio, now a national landmark.

What to See and Do

Scarborough Marsh Nature Center. Mi of nature and waterway trails through marshland area; canoe tours, special programs (fee). (Mid-June-Labor Day, daily) Phone 207/883-5100. **FREE**

Special Event

Harness racing. On US 1, ME Tpke exit 6. Scarborough Downs. Eves and matinees. Phone 207/883-4331. Apr-Nov.

Motels/Motor Lodges

★★ **FAIRFIELD INN.** 2 Cummings Rd (04074). 207/883-0300; fax 207/883-0572; res 800/228-2800. www.fairfieldinn.com. 120 rms, 3 story. Mid-July-Sept: S $99; D $119; under 18 free; lower rates rest of yr. Crib free. TV; cable (premium). Heated pool. Complimentary continental bkfst. Ck-out noon. Meeting rms. Business servs avail. In-rm modem link. Sundries. Refrigerators. Cr cds: DS, MC, V.

D ⌨ ✈ 📶

★★ **HOLIDAY HOUSE INN & MOTEL.** 106 E Grand Ave (04074). 207/883-4417; fax 207/883-6987. 16 rms in motel, 8 rms in inn, 1 A/C. Late June-Labor Day: D $100-$130; each addl $10; lower rates mid-May-mid-June, after Labor Day-Oct. Closed rest of yr. Crib $10. Adults only in inn. TV; cable. Restaurant nearby. Ck-out 10:30 am. Refrigerators. Picnic tables. Ceiling fans. On ocean; sun deck. Cr cds: A, MC, V.

🐾 📶 🔥

★ **LIGHTHOUSE MOTOR INN.** 366 Pine Point Rd (04074). 207/883-3213; toll-free 800/780-3213. 22 units, 1-2 story. No A/C. July-Aug: S, D $85-$150; each addl $10-$20; lower rates mid-May-June, Sept-mid-Oct. Closed rest of yr. Crib free. TV; cable. Restaurant opp 7:30-11:30 am, 5-9 pm. Ck-out 10 am. Balconies. Picnic tables. On ocean; swimming beach. Cr cds: A, DS, MC, V.

🐾 📶 🐾

★ **MILLBROOK.** *321 US 1 (04074). 207/883-6004. www.millbrookmotel.com.* 15 rms, 2 story. Early July-late Aug: S $80; D $85-$95; each addl $7.50; lower rates rest of yr. Crib $3. TV; cable (premium). Ck-out 11 am. Some balconies. Picnic tables. Cr cds: DS, MC, V.

Searsport

See also Belfast, Bucksport

Settled 1770 **Pop** 2,603 **Elev** 60 ft **Area code** 207 **Zip** 04974
Information Chamber of Commerce, Main St, PO Box 139; 207/548-6510

On the quiet upper reaches of Penobscot Bay, this is an old seafaring town. In the 1870s at least ten percent of the captains of the US Merchant Marines lived here. Sea terminal of the Bangor and Aroostook Railway, Searsport ships potatoes and newsprint. This village abounds with antique shops and is sometimes referred to as the "antique capital of Maine."

What to See and Do

Fishing, boating on bay. Town maintains wharf and boat landing, beachside park.

Penobscot Marine Museum. Old Town Hall (1845), Merithew House (ca 1860), Fowler-True-Ross House (1825), Phillips Library, and Carver Memorial Gallery. Ship models, marine paintings, American and Asian furnishings. (Memorial Day wkend-mid-Oct, daily) Church St, off US 1. Phone 207/548-2529. ¢¢

Motel/Motor Lodge

★ **YARDARM MOTEL.** *172 E Main PO Box 246 (04974). 207/548-2404; toll-free 888/676-8006. www.searsportmaine.com.* 18 rms. No A/C. Late June-late Sept: S $38-$55; D $50-$75; each addl $5-$7; under 13 free; lower rates May-late June, late Sept-Oct. Closed rest of yr. Crib $4. TV; cable. Complimentary continental bkfst. Ck-out 11 am. Refrigerators avail. Cr cds: DS, MC, V.

B&B/Small Inn

★★ **BRASS LANTERN INN BED & BREAKFAST.** *81 W Main St (04974). 207/548-0150; fax 207/548-0304; toll-free 800/691-0150. www.brasslanternmaine.com.* 5 rms, 4 with shower only, 2 story. No A/C. No rm phones. Mid-May-Oct: S $80-$90; D $85-$95; each addl $25; lower rates rest of yr. Children over 11 yrs only. TV in sitting rm; cable, VCR. Complimentary full bkfst; afternoon refreshments. Restaurant nearby. Ck-out 11 am, ck-in 4 pm. Downhill/x-country ski 20 mi. Captain's house built 1850. Totally nonsmoking. Cr cds: DS, MC, V.

Sebago Lake

See also Bridgton, Poland Spring

Second-largest of Maine's lakes, this is perhaps the most popular, partly because of its proximity to Portland. About 12 miles long and eight miles wide, it lies among wooded hills. Boats can run a total of more than 40 miles from the south end of Sebago Lake, through the Songo River to the north end of Long Lake. Numerous resort communities are hidden in the trees along the shores. Sebago, home of the landlocked salmon *(Salmo sebago),* is also stocked with lake trout.

What to See and Do

The Jones Museum of Glass and Ceramics. A decorative arts museum significant for its collection of both glass and ceramics. More than 7,000 pieces from early times to present. Changing exhibits; gallery tours, library, museum shop. (Mid-May-mid-Nov, daily) 5 mi NW via ME 114 and 107 on Douglas Hill in Sebago. Phone 207/787-3370. ¢¢

Marrett House and Garden. (1789) Built in Georgian style, but later enlarged and remodeled in the Greek Revival fashion; period furnishings; farm implements. Coin from Portland banks was stored here during the War of 1812, when it was thought that the British would take Portland. Perennial and herb garden. Tours (Mid-June-Aug, Tues, Thurs, Sat, and Sun). Approx 2 mi S on ME 25 to center of Standish. Phone 207/642-3032. ¢¢

Sebago Lake State Park. A 1,300-acre area. Extensive sand beaches, bathhouse, lifeguards; fishing, boating (rentals, ramps); picnicking, concession, camping (dump station). No pets. (May-mid-Oct, daily) Standard fees. 2 mi S of Naples off ME 11/114. Phone 207/693-6231.

Motel/Motor Lodge

★ **SUBURBAN PINES.** *322 Roosevelt Trl, Windham (04062). 207/892-4834; fax 207/892-3015.* 25 rms, 11 kits, 1-3 story. June-Oct: S, D $50-$60; suites $75-$85; under 12 free; lower rates rest of yr. Pet accepted; $50 deposit. TV; cable. Complimentary coffee. Ck-out 11 am. Coin lndry. Picnic table, grill. Maine state picnic area opp. Cr cds: DS, MC, V.

Resort

★★★ **MIGIS LODGE.** *Rte 302, South Casco (04077). 207/655-4524; fax 207/655-2054. www.migis.com.* 6 rms in lodge, 2 story, 52 units in 30 cottages. AP, late-June-mid-Sept: S $190-$215; D $300-$500; lower rates June and mid-Sept-Columbus Day wkend. Closed rest of yr. TV; cable. Playground. Supervised children's activities. Dining rm 8-9:30 am, 12:30-1:30 pm, 6:30-8 pm; jacket (dinner). Rm serv. Box lunches, island cookouts, lakeside Sat buffet, outdoor Sun bkfst, lobster bakes. Serv bar. Ck-out noon. Meeting rms. Sundries. Valet serv. Airport, bus depot transportation. Tennis. Golf privileges. Exercise rm. Private sand beaches. Waterskiing, instruction. Motorboats, sailboats, canoes, rowboats, pedalboats, boat trips; dockage. Lawn games. Hiking trails. Rec rm. Entertainment evenings. Refrigerators, wet bars; fireplaces. Porches. Library. On 97 acres; 3,500 ft of lakefront. Cr cds: A, MC, V.

🄳 ⚓ 🛠 🍴 🎿 🕴 🏊

Restaurants

★★ **BARNHOUSE TAVERN RESTAURANT.** *61 ME 35, Windham (04062).* 207/892-2221. Specialties: seafood casserole, baked stuffed haddock, steak. Hrs: 11 am-10 pm. Closed Dec 25. Res accepted. Bar to 12:30 am. Lunch $3.95-$8.95, dinner $7.95-$18.95. Entertainment Thurs-Sat. Outdoor dining. Authentically restored post-and-beam barn and farmhouse (1872); country atmosphere, loft dining. Cr cds: A, C, D, DS, ER, MC, V.

🄳 **SC**

★★★ **OLDE HOUSE.** *Rte 85, Raymond (04071).* 207/655-7841. Specialties: beef Wellington, lemon chicken, duck. Own baking. Hrs: 5-10 pm. Res accepted; required hols. Serv bar. Wine list. Dinner $15.95-$22.95. Child's menu. Historic (1790) home; Victorian decor, antiques. Cr cds: DS, MC, V.

🄳

Skowhegan

See also Newport, Waterville

Settled 1771 **Pop** 8,725 **Elev** 175 ft **Area code** 207 **Zip** 04976
Information Chamber of Commerce, 23 Commercial St; 207/474-3621 or 888/772-4392
Web www.skowheganchamber.com

Skowhegan, on the Kennebec River, is surrounded by beautiful lakes. Shoes, paper pulp, and other wood products are made here. In the village's center stands a 12-ton, 62-foot-high Native American carved of native pine by Bernard Langlais. Skowhegan is the birthplace of Margaret Chase Smith, who served three terms in the US House of Representatives and four terms in the Senate.

What to See and Do

History House. (1839) Old household furnishings; museum contains books, china, dolls, and documents. (Mid-June-mid-Sept, Tues-Fri afternoons) Elm St, on the Kennebec River. Phone 207/474-6632. ¢

Special Events

Skowhegan State Fair. One of oldest in country (1818). One-mi-long midway, stage shows, harness racing; contests, exhibits. Phone 207/474-2947. Aug 10-19.
Skowhegan Log Days. Parade, fireworks, pig roast, lobster bake, golf tournament, amateur and professional competitions, bean dinner. Commemorates last log drive on Kennebec River. Phone 207/474-3621. Last full wk Aug.

Motels/Motor Lodges

★★ **BELMONT MOTEL.** *273 Madison Ave (04976).* 207/474-8315; toll-free 800/235-6669. www.belmontmotel.com. 36 rms. July-Oct: S $50; D $65; each addl $5; suites $110-$130; higher rates State Fair, special events; lower rates rest of yr. TV; cable (premium). Pool. Restaurants nearby. Ck-out 11 am. Sundries. Downhill ski 5 mi; x-country ski 1 mi. Lawn games. Refrigerators avail. Picnic tables. Cr cds: A, D, DS, MC, V.

🄳 ⚡ 🏊 ⛵ 🗻

★★ **THE TOWNE MOTEL.** *248 Madison Ave (00497).* 207/474-5151; fax 207/474-6407; toll-free 800/843-4405. 33 rms, 1-2 story, 7 kits. July-Oct: S, D $60-$68; each addl $6; kit. units $72-$78; higher rates: state fair, racing; lower rates rest of yr. TV; cable (premium). Pool. Complimentary continental bkfst. Restaurant nearby. Ck-out 11 am. Coin lndry. Downhill/x-country ski 6 mi. Cr cds: A, MC, V.

🏊 ⛵ 🗻 🔥 **SC**

Restaurants

★★ **CANDLELIGHT.** *1 Madison Ave (04976).* 207/474-2978. Specializes in beef, seafood. Own baking. Hrs: 11 am-9 pm; Fri, Sat to 10 pm; Sun brunch 11 am-2 pm. Closed Dec 25. Res accepted. Bar. Lunch $1.50-$7.25, dinner $7.95-$14.95. Child's menu. Salad bar. Parking. Cr cds: A, DS, MC, V.

🄳

★★ **HERITAGE HOUSE.** *260 Madison Ave (04976).* 207/474-5100. Specializes in fresh seafood, steak, vegetables. Hrs: 11:30 am-2 pm, 5-9 pm; Fri, Sat 5-10 pm. Closed July 4, Dec 25. Res accepted. Bar. Lunch $3.95-$6.95, dinner $7.95-$15. Child's menu. Restored home; oak staircase. Cr cds: A, DS, MC, V.

🄳

Southwest Harbor

See also Bar Harbor, Cranberry Isles

Pop 1,952 **Elev** 50 ft **Area code** 207 **Zip** 04679
Information Chamber of Commerce, PO Box 1143; 207/244-9264 or 800/423-9264
Web www.acadia.net/swhtrcoc

This is a prosperous, working seacoast village on Mount Desert Island. There are lobster wharves, where visitors can watch about 70 fishermen bring their catch, and many shops where boats are constructed. Visitors may rent sail and power boats in Southwest Harbor to explore the coves and islands; hiking trails and quiet harbors offer relaxation.

What to See and Do

Acadia National Park. (see). West, north, and east of village.
Cranberry Cove Boating Company. Cruise to Cranberry Islands. See native wildlife and learn island history. Six departures daily. (Mid-June-mid-Sept, daily) Departs Upper Town Dock. Phone 207/244-5882. ¢¢

Maine State Ferry Service. Ferry makes six-mi (40 min) trip to Swans Island and 8¼-mi (50 min) trip to Frenchboro (limited schedule). Swans Island (all-yr, one to six trips daily). 4 mi S on ME 102 and ME 102A, in Bass Harbor. Phone 207/244-3254.

Mount Desert Oceanarium. More than 20 tanks with Gulf of Maine marine creatures. Touch tank permits animals to be picked up. Exhibits on tides, seawater, plankton, fishing gear, weather. Inquire for information on special events. (Mid-May-mid-Oct, Mon-Sat) Clark Point Rd. Phone 207/244-7330.

Wendell Gilley Museum. Art and natural history museum featuring collection of bird carvings by local artist Wendell Gilley; changing exhibits of local and historical art; films. (June-Oct, Tues-Sun; May and Nov-Dec, Fri-Sun) Main St and Herrick Rd. Phone 207/244-7555. ¢¢

B&Bs/Small Inns

★★ **THE CLARK POINT INN.** *109 Clark Point Rd (04679). 207/244-9828; fax 207/244-9924. www.clarkpointinn.com.* 5 rms, 2 with shower only, 2 story. No A/C. No rm phones. Mid-June-mid-Oct: S, D $85-$165; each addl $25; lower rates May-mid-June. Closed rest of yr. Children over 8 yrs only. TV in some rms; cable. Complimentary bkfst buffet; afternoon refreshments. Restaurant nearby. Ck-out 10:30 am, ck-in 2-6 pm. Captain's house (1857); deck with harbor view. Some in-rm whirlpools, fireplaces. Totally nonsmoking. Cr cds: MC, V.

★★ **KINGSLEIGH INN 1904.** *373 Main St (04679). 207/244-5302; fax 207/244-7691. www.kingsleighinn.com.* 8 rms, 3 story. No rm phones. July-mid-Oct: D $75-$125; each addl $20; suite $220; lower rates rest of yr. Children over 11 yrs only. TV in suite; cable. Complimentary full bkfst. Restaurant nearby. Ck-out 11 am, ck-in 3 pm. Built 1904; library, antiques, wrap-around porch. Near ocean; overlooks harbor. Totally nonsmoking. Cr cds: MC, V.

★★ **THE MOORINGS INN.** *Shore Rd Manset (04679). 207/244-5523; toll-free 800/596-5523. mooringsinn.com.* 10 rms in inn, 3 motel rms, 9 kits., 3 kit. cottages. No A/C. July-mid-Sept: S $60-$65; D $70-$75; each addl $10; suites $85; kit. cottages $100; lower rates May-June, mid-Sept-Oct. Closed rest of yr. Crib free. TV in sitting rm; VCR avail. Complimentary continental bkfst. Restaurant nearby. Ck-out 11 am, ck-in 3 pm. Fireplace in cottages. Balconies, private screened decks. Picnic tables, grills. Bicycles, canoes, kayaks avail. Sections of inn date to 1784; nautical motif. On waterfront; private beach, dock, launching ramp.

Cottage Colony

★★ **ACADIA CABINS.** *410 Main St (04679). 207/244-5388. www.acadiacabins.com.* 14 rms, 11 with shower only, 1-2 story, 9 kit. units. No A/C. Some rm phones. July-Aug: S, D $59-$79; each addl $15; kit. units $79-$95; wkly rates;

July-Aug (2-3 day min); lower rates rest of yr. TV; cable, VCR avail (movies). Complimentary continental bkfst (inn). Restaurant nearby. Ck-out 10 am, ck-in 3-6 pm. Coin lndry. X-country ski 5 mi. Pool. Many refrigerators. Picnic tables. Opp harbor. Built in 1840; 19th century farmhouse. Totally nonsmoking. Cr cds: DS, MC, V.

Restaurant

★ **SEAWALL DINING ROOM.** *566 Seawall Rd (04679). 207/244-9250. www.seawallmotel.com.* Specializes in seafood, baked stuffed lobster. Own desserts. Hrs: 11:30 am-9 pm; July-Labor Day to 10 pm. Closed Dec-Apr. Res accepted. No A/C. Lunch, dinner $3.25-$18. Child's menu. Family-owned. Cr cds: A, D, MC, V.

D

Unrated Dining Spot

BEAL'S LOBSTER PIER. *Clark Point Rd (04679). 207/244-3202.* Specializes in fresh seafood, steamed lobster. Hrs: 9 am-8 pm; hrs vary off-season. Closed July 4. No A/C. Wine, beer. A la carte entrees: lunch, dinner $10-$20. All dining outdoors on working wharf overlooking Southwest Harbor. Lobsters boiled to order; self-service. Menu boards. Family-owned since 1930. Cr cds: A, DS, MC, V.

D

Waterville

See also Augusta

Settled 1754 **Pop** 17,173 **Elev** 113 ft **Area code** 207
Information Mid-Maine Chamber of Commerce, One Post Office Sq, PO Box 142, 04903; 207/873-3315
Web www.mid-mainechamber.com

A large Native American village once occupied the west bank of the Kennebec River where many of Waterville's factories now stand. An important industrial town, Waterville is the center of the Belgrade and China lakes resort area. Manufactured goods include men's and women's shirts, paper and molded pulp products, and woolens.

What to See and Do

Colby College. (1813) 1,700 students. This 714-acre campus incl an art museum in the Bixler Art and Music Center (daily; closed hols; free), a Walcker organ designed by Albert Schweitzer in Lorimer Chapel and books, manuscripts, and letters of Maine authors Edwin Arlington Robinson and Sarah Jewett in the Miller Library (Mon-Fri; closed hols; free). Mayflower Hill Dr, 2 mi W, ½ mi E of I-95. Phone 207/872-3000.

Old Fort Halifax. (1754) Blockhouse. Bridge over Kennebec gives view of Ticonic Falls. (Memorial Day-Labor Day, daily) 1 mi E on US 201, on Bay St in Winslow, on E bank of Kennebec River.

Redington Museum. (1814) Waterville Historical Society collection incl 18th- and 19th-century furnishings, manuscripts, Civil War and Native American relics; historical library; children's rm; apothecary museum. (Mid-May-Sept, Tues-Sat) 64 Silver St. Phone 207/872-9439. ¢¢

Two-Cent Footbridge. One of the few remaining former toll footbridges in the US. Front St. **FREE**

Special Event

New England Music Camp. Five mi W on ME 137 to Oakland, then 4 mi S on ME 23; on Pond Rd. Faculty and student concerts, Sun; faculty concerts, Wed; student recitals, Fri. Phone 207/465-3025. Late June-late Aug.

Motels/Motor Lodges

★ ★ **BEST WESTERN WATERVILLE.** *356 Main St (04901). 207/873-3335. www.bestwestern.com.* 86 rms, 2 story. July-Oct: S $69-$94; D $79-$104; each addl $10; under 18 free; higher rates Colby graduation wknd; lower rates rest of yr. Crib $3. Pet accepted. TV; cable, VCR avail (movies). Pool. Coffee in rms. Restaurant 6 am-10 pm. Bar. Ck-out noon. Meeting rms. Business servs avail. Valet serv. Health club privileges. Sundries. Refrigerators, microwaves avail. Cr cds: A, C, D, DS, MC, V.

D ⬛ ⬛ ⬛ ⬛

★ ★ **HOLIDAY INN.** *375 Main St (04901). 207/873-0111; fax 207/872-2310; toll-free 800/785-0111. www.acadia.net/hiwat-cm.* 138 rms, 3 story. May-Oct: S $85; D $95; each addl $10; suite $150; under 19 free; lower rates rest of yr. Crib free. Pet accepted. TV; cable (premium), VCR avail. Indoor pool; whirlpool. Complimentary coffee in rms. Restaurant 6 am-2 pm, 5-10 pm. Rm serv. Bar 11-1 am. Ck-out noon. Coin lndry. Meeting rms. Business servs avail. In-rm modem link. Sundries. Exercise equipt; sauna. Refrigerators, microwaves avail. Cr cds: A, C, D, DS, JCB, MC, V.

D ⬛ ⬛ ⬛ ⬛ ⬛ SC

Restaurants

★ ★ **JOHN MARTIN'S MANOR.** *54 College Ave (04901). 207/873-5676.* Specializes in prime rib, popovers, seafood. Salad bar. Hrs: 11 am-9 pm; Sun 11:30 am-8 pm; early-bird dinner Mon-Fri 4-5:30 pm. Closed Dec 25. Res accepted. Bar 4:30 pm-1 am. Lunch $3.95-$7.45, dinner $6.95-$15.95. Child's menu. Cr cds: A, D, DS, MC, V.

D SC

★ **WEATHERVANE.** *470 Kennedy Memorial Dr (04901). 207/873-4522.* Specializes in seafood. Raw bar. Hrs: 11 am-9:30 pm. Closed Thanksgiving, Dec 24, 25. Serv bar. A la carte entrees: lunch $1.99-$10.95, dinner $6-$19.95. Child's menu. Fireplaces. Cr cds: MC, V.

D

Unrated Dining Spot

BIG G'S DELI. *Outer Benton Ave, Winslow (04901). 207/873-7808.* Specializes in sandwiches, bkfst dishes. Deli with self serv. Hrs: 6 am-8 pm. Bkfst $3-$5, lunch, dinner $5-$9. Child's menu. Paintings of entertainers. Cr cds: A, MC, V.

D

Wells

See also Kennebunk, Ogunquit, York

Settled 1640 **Pop** 7,778 **Elev** 70 ft **Area code** 207 **Zip** 04090
Information Chamber of Commerce, PO Box 356; 207/646-2451
Web www.wellschamber.org

One of the oldest English settlements in Maine, Wells includes Moody, Wells Beach, and Drake's Island. It was largely a farming center, with some commercial fishing, until the resort trade began in the 20th century. Charter boats, surfcasting, and pier fishing attract anglers; seven miles of beaches entice swimmers.

What to See and Do

⬛ **Rachel Carson National Wildlife Refuge.** Approx 5,000 acres of salt marsh and coastal edge habitat; more than 250 species of birds may be observed during the yr. Visitor center; one-mi interpretive nature trail. (All yr, sunrise-sunset) 3 mi NE on ME 9. Phone 207/646-9226.

Wells Auto Museum. Approx 80 antique cars dating from 1900 trace progress of the automotive industry. Also displayed is a collection of nickelodeons, picture machines, and antique arcade games to play. (Memorial Day-Columbus Day, daily) US 1. Phone 207/646-9064. ¢¢

Wells Natural Estuarine Research Reserve. Approx 1,600 acres of fields, forest, wetlands and beach. Laudholm Farm serves as visitor center. Programs on coastal ecology and stewardship, exhibits and tours. Reserve (daily). Visitor center (May-Oct, daily; rest of yr, Mon-Fri). 1½ mi N of Wells Corner on ME 1. Phone 207/646-1555. **FREE**

Motels/Motor Lodges

★ ★ **ATLANTIC MOTOR INN.** *37 Atlantic Ave (04090). 207/646-7061; fax 207/641-0607; res 800/727-7061. www.atlanticmotorinn.com.* 35 rms, 3 story. No elvtr. Early July-late Aug: S, D $49-$179; each addl $15; suites $149; higher rates hol wknds; lower rates Apr-early July, late Aug-Oct. Closed rest of yr. Crib $10. TV; cable. Heated pool. Restaurant nearby. Ck-out 11 am. Refrigerators, microwaves avail. Balconies. On beach. Cr cds: A, DS, MC, V.

⬛ ⬛ ⬛ ⬛

★ **LAFAYETTES OCEANFRONT RESORT.** *393 Mile Rd, Wells Beach (04090).* 207/646-2831; fax 207/646-6770. *www.wellsbeachmaine.com.* 128 rms, 15 with shower only, 2-3 story. Early July-Labor Day: S, D $80-$150; kit. units $115-$150; family rates; in-season and hols (2-5 day min); lower rates rest of yr. Crib $10. TV; cable. Restaurant adj 7 am-10 pm. Ck-out 11 am. Meeting rms. Business servs avail. Sundries. Coin lndry. Indoor pool; whirlpool. Refrigerators. Many balconies. On beach. Cr cds: A, MC, V.

[icons]

★ **NER BEACH MOTEL.** *395 Post Rd Rte (04054).* 207/646-2636; fax 207/641-0968. 47 rms, 1-2 story, 21 kits. (some ovens). Late June-Aug: S $49-$99; D $34-109; kit. units $89-$139; wkly rates for kit. units; lower rates Apr-late June, after Labor Day-mid-Nov. Closed rest of yr. Crib $7. Pet accepted. TV; cable. Heated pool. Playground. Restaurant nearby. Ck-out 11 am. Lawn games. Refrigerators avail. Picnic tables. Cr cds: DS, MC, V.

[icons]

★★ **SEAGULL MOTOR INN.** *1413 Post Rd (US Rt 1) PO Box 338 (04090).* 207/646-5164; fax 207/641-8301; toll-free 800/573-2485. *www.seagullvacations.com.* 24 motel rms, 24 cottages, 21 kits. (oven in 9). No A/C in cottages. July-Aug: S, D $46-$92 each addl $12; kit. cottages for 2-4, $475-$750/wk; lower rates mid-Apr-June, Sept-mid-Oct. Closed rest of yr. Crib $3. TV; cable. Heated pool; whirlpool. Playground. Ck-out 11 am. 9-hole par 3 golf. Lawn games. Refrigerators; some microwaves in cottages. Screened porch on cottages. Picnic tables. Spacious grounds. Ocean view. Cr cds: A, D, DS, ER, MC, V.

[icons]

★ **SEA MIST RESORT MOTEL.** *1524 Post Rd (04090).* 207/646-6044; fax 207/641-2199; toll-free 800/448-0925. *www.seamistmotel.com.* 68 rms, 2 story. July-Labor Day: D $85-$95; wkly rates; lower rates Apr-June, Labor Day-early Dec. Closed rest of yr. Crib $5. TV; cable. Indoor pool; whirlpool. Playground. Restaurant nearby. Ck-out 10 am. Lawn games. Refrigerators, microwaves. Balconies. Picnic tables, grills. Cr cds: DS, MC, V.

[icons]

★ **SUPER 8.** *1892 Main St, Sanford (04073).* 207/324-8823; fax 207/324-8782. *www.super8.com.* 49 rms, 2 story. Apr-Sept: S, D $50-$95; each addl $5; under 13 free; lower rates rest of yr. Crib free. TV; cable, VCR avail (movies). Complimentary coffee in lobby. Ck-out 11 am. Business servs avail. Refrigerator, microwave avail. Cr cds: A, D, DS, MC, V.

[icons]

★ **VILLAGE GREEN MOTEL & COTTAGES.** *773 Post Rd (04090).* 207/646-3285; fax 207/646-4889. *www.villagegreenmotel.com.* 18 units, 10 rms in motel, 1-2 story, 8 kit. cottages; 11 A/C. No rm phones. July-Aug: S $45-$72; D $52-$95; each addl $10; cottages $485-$720/wk; lower rates mid-Apr-June, Sept-mid-Oct. Closed rest of yr. Crib $5. TV; cable. Heated pool. Restaurant nearby. Lawn games. Refrigerators. Screened porch on cottages. Picnic tables. Cr cds: A, DS, MC, V.

[icons]

★ **WELLS-MOODY MOTEL.** *119 Post Rd; US 1, PO Box 371, Moody (04054).* 207/646-5601. *wellsmoodymotel.com.* 24 rms. Memorial Day-Labor Day: S $39-$99; D $39-$109; each addl $10; 2-day min; lower rates mid-Apr-Memorial Day, Labor Day-mid-Oct. Closed rest of yr. TV; cable. Pool. Restaurant opp 6 am-11 pm. Ck-out 11 am. Refrigerators. Picnic tables. Cr cds: A, DS, MC, V.

[icons]

Resort

★★ **GARRISON SUITES.** *1099 Post Rd; US 1 (04090).* 207/646-3497; toll-free 800/646-3497. *www.garrisonsuites .com.* 47 units, 13 cottages (shower only in 10 cottages). July-Aug (2-day min): S, D $99-$120; kits. (3-day min) $89; suites $115; kit. cottages $495-$825 wkly; lower rates May-June, Sept-Oct; off season packages. Closed rest of yr. Crib $10, $30/wk. TV; cable, VCR avail. Heated pool; whirlpool. Playground. Complimentary coffee in rms. Restaurant opp 7 am-11 pm. Ck-out 11 am. Lawn games. Refrigerators, microwaves. Picnic tables. Grills. Cr cds: MC, V.

[icons]

Cottage Colony

★ **WATERCREST COTTAGES & MOTEL.** *1277 Post Rd; Rt 1 (04090).* 207/646-2202; fax 207/646-7067; toll-free 800/847-4693. *www.watercrestcottages.com.* 9 motel rms, 4 kits., 50 kit. cottages. July-late Aug, hol wkends: S $64-$74; D $45-$79; each addl $25; cottages for 2-8 (late June-Labor Day, 1-wk min) $435-$735/wk; lower rates May-June, late Aug-mid-Oct. Closed rest of yr. Crib free. Pet accepted, some restrictions. TV; cable, VCR avail (free movies). Heated pool; whirlpool. Playground. Restaurant nearby. Ck-out 11 am; cottages 10 am. Coin lndry. Lawn games. Exercise equipt. Microwaves in cottages. Picnic tables, grills. Screened porch on cottages. Cr cds: MC, V.

[icons]

All Suite

★★★ **VILLAGE BY THE SEA.** *Rte 1 S (04090).* 207/646-1100; fax 207/646-1401; toll-free 800/444-8862. *vbts.com.* 73 kit. units, 3-4 story. No elvtr. Early July-early Sept (2-day min): kit. units (up to 4) $140-$165; each addl $10; under 12 free; wkly rates; higher rates hols; lower rates rest of yr. Crib $10. TV; cable, VCR avail (movies $3.50). 2 heated pools, 1 indoor. Restaurant nearby. Ck-out 10 am. Coin lndry. Meeting rms. Sundries. Health club privileges. Balconies. Picnic tables, grills. Wildlife refuge adj. On trolley route. Cr cds: A, DS, MC, V.

[icons] SC

Restaurants

★★ **GREY GULL.** *475 Webhannet Dr (04090).* 207/646-7501. *www.thegreygullinn.com.* Specializes in seafood, beef. Hrs: 5-9 pm; Sun brunch (mid-Sept-mid-June) 9 am-1 pm. Closed Mon-Wed mid-Dec-mid Mar. Res accepted. Bar. Dinner $10.95-$22.95. Sun brunch $4-$13. Child's menu. Classical guitarist Sun, Irish entertainment Tues. Valet parking (in season). A 19th-century inn located on ocean. Guest rms avail. Cr cds: A, DS, MC, V.

★ **HAYLOFT.** *US 1, Moody (04054). 207/646-4400.* Specializes in broasted chicken, Maine seafood, Angus beef. Hrs: 11 am-9:30 pm. Closed wk before Dec 25. Serv bar. Lunch $3.95-$7.95, dinner $6.95-$19.95. Child's menu. Country farm decor. Cr cds: A, DS, MC, V.
D

★★ **LITCHFIELD'S.** *2135 Post Rd (US 1) (04090). 207/646-5711.* Specializes in seafood, steak, pasta. Raw bar. Own desserts. Hrs: 11:30 am-3 pm, 5-9:30 pm; winter months to 9 pm; Sunday brunch 11 am-3 pm. Closed Dec 25. Res accepted. Bar to 11:30 pm. Lunch $4.95-$10.95, dinner $4-$35. Child's menu. Pianist. Parking. Cr cds: A, D, DS, MC, V.
D

★★ **LORD'S HARBORSIDE.** *352 Harbor Rd (04090). 207/646-2651.* Specializes in fresh seafood, chowders, lobster. Hrs: noon-9 pm; varied hrs off season. Closed Tues; also mid-Oct-Apr. No A/C. Serv bar. Lunch, dinner $4.95-$19.95. Child's menu. Parking. Nautical dining rm overlooking harbor. Family-owned. Cr cds: MC, V.
D

★ **MAINE DINER.** *2265 Post Rd (04090). 207/646-4441. www.mainediner.com.* Specializes in homemade chowders, lobster pie. Own desserts. Hrs: 7 am-9:30 pm; Columbus Day-Memorial Day to 8 pm. Closed Thanksgiving, Dec 25. Wine, beer. Bkfst $1.35-$7.95, lunch $2.50-$9.95, dinner $5.95-$13.95. Child's menu. Traditional diner decor; bkfst avail all day. Totally nonsmoking. Cr cds: DS, MC, V.
D

★★ **STEAKHOUSE.** *1205 Post Rd (US 1) (04090). 207/646-4200.* Specializes in steak, seafood. Hrs: 4:30-9 pm. Closed Mon; also mid-Dec-Mar. Serv bar. Dinner $7.95-$18.95. Child's menu. Parking. Antique farm implements and ship models displayed. Cr cds: D, MC, V.
D

Wiscasset

See also Bath, Boothbay Harbor, Damariscotta

Settled 1653 **Pop** 3,339 **Elev** 50 ft **Area code** 207 **Zip** 04578

Many artists and writers live here in beautiful old houses put up in the golden days of clipper ship barons and sea captains. Chiefly a summer resort area centered around its harbor, Wiscasset is half as populous as it was in 1850. Its pictorial charm is extraordinary even on the picturesque Maine coast. A noted sight in Wiscasset are the remains of two ancient wooden schooners, which were hauled into the harbor in 1932.

What to See and Do

Lincoln County Museum and Old Jail. First penitentiary built in the District of Maine (1809-1811). Jailer's house has changing exhibits, relics of Lincoln County. (July and Aug, Tues-Sun) Federal St, ME 218. Phone 207/882-6817.

Maine Art Gallery. Exhibits by Maine artists. (Mid-May-early-Oct, Tues-Sun; rest of yr Thurs-Sun) Warren St, in Old Academy Building (1807). Phone 207/882-7511. **Donation**

Musical Wonder House-Music Museum. (1852) Talking machines, antique musical boxes, player pianos shown and played in historical settings; antique furnishings; gift shop. (Late May-mid-Oct, daily) 18 High St. Phone 207/882-7163. ¢¢¢¢

Nickels-Sortwell House. (1807) Classic Federal-style elegance. Built for a shipmaster in the lumber trade, William Nickels, it was used as a hotel between 1820 and 1900. The mansion was then bought by Mayor Alvin Sortwell of Cambridge, Massachusetts, as a private home. Graceful elliptical stairway; many Sortwell family furnishings; restored garden. (June-mid-Oct, Wed-Sun) 121 Main St at Federal St, US 1. Phone 207/882-6218. ¢¢

Pownalborough Courthouse. (1761) Oldest pre-Revolutionary courthouse in Maine. Three-story building houses furnished courtrm, judges' chambers, spinning rm, tavern, bedrms, parlor, and kitchen. Nature trails along river; picnic areas; Revolutionary cemetery. (Wed-Sat; July and Aug also Sun afternoon) 8 mi N on ME 27, then 3 mi S on ME 128 in Dresden, bordering Kennebec River. Phone 207/882-6817. ¢¢

Motels/Motor Lodges

★★★ **COD COVE INN.** *22 Crossroads, Edgecomb (04556). 207/882-9586; fax 207/882-9294; toll-free 800/882-9586. www.codcoveinn.com.* 30 rms, 2 story, 1 cottage. July-Labor Day: S, D $115-$175; suite $175; each addl $10; higher rates Columbus Day wknd; lower rates mid-Apr-June, Labor Day-late Oct. TV; cable. Heated pool; whirlpool. Complimentary continental bkfst. Restaurant opp 6-9 am. Ck-out 11:30 am. Meeting rms. Business servs avail. In-rm modem link. Refrigerators; some fireplaces. Balconies. Colonial-style building. Overlooks bay. Cr cds: A, MC, V.
D ❧ ✈ ⛵ ⊠ 🔥

★ **WISCASSET MOTOR LODGE.** *596 Bath Rd (04578). 207/882-7137; toll-free 800/732-8168. www.wiscassetmotorlodge.com.* 22 rms, 2 story, 6 cabins. Some A/C. July-Labor Day: S, D $39-$68; each addl $8; lower rates Apr-June and after Labor Day-Oct. Closed rest of yr. Crib $5. TV; cable. Complimentary continental bkfst (July-Labor Day). Ck-out 11 am. Cr cds: DS, MC, V.
D ❧ 🔥

B&B/Small Inn

★★ **SQUIRE TARBOX INN.** *1181 Main Rd, Westport (04578). 207/882-7693; fax 207/882-7107. www.squiretarboxinn.com.* 11 rms, 6 A/C, 2 story. No rm phones. Mid-July-Oct: S $102; D $185; each addl $30; MAP avail; lower rates mid-May-mid-July. Closed rest of yr. Complimentary full bkfst. Dining rm (public by res): sitting 6 pm. Ck-out 11 am, ck-in 2 pm. Dock, rowboat, bicycles. Restored 18th-century farmhouse situated on working dairy goat farm; antiques; library; some fireplaces. Some rms in former stable area. Guests may view dairy operations. Totally nonsmoking. Cr cds: A, DS, MC, V.
⊠ 🔥

Cottage Colony

★ **BAY VIEW INN & COTTAGES.** *179 US 1, PO Box 117, Edgecomb (04556). 207/882-6911; toll-free 800/530-2445. www.mainesunshine.com/bayview.* 14 rms, 11 with shower only. No A/C. No rm phones. July-Labor Day: cottages S $45-$65; D $75-$95; kit. cottages $75-$85; each addl $10; wkly rates; lower rates rest of yr. Crib free. Pet accepted; $5. TV; cable. Complimentary coffee in lobby. Restaurant nearby. Ck-out 11 am. Pool. Refrigerators avail. Picnic tables, grills. Cr cds: A, DS, MC, V.

Restaurant

★★ **LE GARAGE.** *Water St (04578). 207/882-5409.* Specialties: char-broiled marinated lamb, broiled seafood platter, chicken pie. Own baking. Hrs: 11:30 am-3 pm, 5-9:30 pm; Sun 11 am-9 pm. Closed Jan; major hols. Res accepted. No A/C. Bar. Lunch $3.95-$18.95, dinner $7.95-$18.25. View of bay. Cr cds: MC, V.

Yarmouth

See also Brunswick, Freeport, Portland

Settled 1636 **Pop** 7,862 **Elev** 100 ft **Area code** 207 **Zip** 04096

Information Chamber of Commerce, 158 Main St; 207/846-3984

Web www.yarmouthmaine.org

Yarmouth is a quaint New England village ten miles north of Portland (see) on US 1. There are many well-maintained older homes and specialty shops. It is linked by a bridge to Cousins Island in the bay.

What to See and Do

Eartha. World's largest globe. Three stories high, Eartha is the largest printed image of the Earth ever created and spins in the lobby of the DeLorme Map Company. (Daily) I-95, exit 17 Phone 207/846-7000. **FREE**

Yarmouth Historical Society Museum. Two galleries with changing exhibits of local and maritime history, fine and decorative arts. Local history research rm; historical lecture series. (July-Aug, Mon-Fri afternoons; rest of yr, Tues-Sat) Third floor, Merrill Memorial Library, Main St. Phone 207/846-6259. **FREE**

    Old Ledge School. (1738) Restored one-rm schoolhouse. (By appt) W Main St. Phone 207/846-6259. **FREE**

Special Event

Clam Festival. Celebration of soft-shelled clam. Arts and crafts, entertainment, parade, fireworks. Third wkend July. Phone 207/846-3984.

Restaurant

★★ **CANNERY.** *106 Lafayette St (04096). 207/846-1226.* Specializes in fresh local seafood. Hrs: 11:30 am-9 pm; Fri, Sat to 9:30 pm. Closed Thanksgiving, Dec 25. Bar. Lunch $6.95-$12.95, dinner $10.95-$17.95. Child's menu. Outdoor dining. View of river, marina. Nautical decor. Cr cds: A, MC, V.

York

See also Kittery, Ogunquit, Wells

Settled 1624 **Pop** 9,818 **Elev** 60 ft **Area code** 207 **Zip** 03909

Information Greater York Region Chamber of Commerce, 1 Stonewall Ln, PO Box 417; 207/363-4422

Web www.yorkme.org

Originally named Agamenticus by the Plymouth Company, which settled the area in 1624, the settlement was chartered as a city—the first in America—in 1641 and renamed Gorgeanna. Following a reorganization in 1652, the "city" in the wilderness took the name York. The present-day York area includes York Village, York Harbor, York Beach, and Cape Neddick.

What to See and Do

Old York Historical Society. Tours of seven buildings dating from the early 1700s. (Mid-June-Sept, Tues-Sun) Visitor orientation and tickets at Jefferds Tavern. Administration Office houses museum offices (Mon-Fri) and historical and research library. Phone 207/363-4974. ¢

    Elizabeth Perkins House. Turn-of-the-century summer house on the banks of the York River, at Sewall's Bridge. Former home of a prominent York preservationist. The furnishings reflect the Colonial Revival period.

    Emerson-Wilcox House. Built in 1742, with later additions. Served at various times as a general store, tavern, and post office, as well as the home of two of the town's prominent early families. Now contains a series of period rms dating from 1750; antique furnishings. Phone 207/363-4422.

    George Marshall Store. Mid-19th-century general store houses local art exhibits. On Lindsay Rd at the York River.

    Jefferds Tavern and Schoolhouse. Built by Captain Samuel Jefferds in 1750 and furnished as a tavern in coastal Maine in the late 18th century; used as an orientation center and educational facility. Schoolhouse adj is probably the state's oldest surviving one-rm schoolhouse; contains exhibit on one-rm schooling in Maine.

    John Hancock Warehouse. Owned by John Hancock until 1794, this is one of the earliest surviving customs houses in Maine. Used now to interpret the maritime history of this coastal village. Lindsay Rd at York River. Phone 207/363-4974.

Old Gaol. Built in 1719 with 18th-century additions. One of the oldest English public buildings in the US, it was used as a jail until 1860. Has dungeons and cells for felons and debtors, as well as galleries of local historical artifacts, late 1800s photography exhibit. On US 1A. On Lindsay Rd at the York River.

Sayward-Wheeler House. (1718) Home of the 18th-century merchant and civic leader Tory Jonathan Sayward. Tours. (June-mid-Oct, Sat and Sun) 79 Barrell Ln, 2 mi S in York Harbor. Phone 207/436-3205. ¢¢

Special Event

Harvest Fest. Juried crafts, ox-roast, colonial theme. Mid-Oct. Phone 207/363-4422.

Motel/Motor Lodge

★★ **YORK COMMONS INN.** *362 US 1 (03909). 207/363-8903; fax 207/363-1130; toll-free 800/537-5515. www.yorkcommonsinn.com.* 90 rms. Mid-June-mid-Oct: S, D $89-$99; each addl $5; under 18 free; lower rates rest of yr. Crib free. Pet accepted, some restrictions. TV; cable. Indoor pool. Complimentary bkfst. Complimentary coffee in rms. Restaurant opp 11 am-8 pm. Business servs avail. Sundries. Refrigerators, microwaves avail. Cr cds: A, DS, MC, V.

[icons]

Resorts

★★ **ANCHORAGE MOTOR INN.** *265 Long Beach Ave, York Beach (03910). 207/363-5112; fax 207/363-6753. www.anchorageinn.com.* 179 rms, 3 story. Late June-Aug: S, D $119-$154; suites $195-$245; lower rates rest of yr. Crib $10. TV; cable. 3 pools; 2 indoor; whirlpool, poolside serv. Restaurant adj 7 am-9 pm. Bar. Ck-out 11 am. Meeting rms. Business servs avail. Golf privileges. Exercise equipt. Lawn game. Balconies. Refrigerators. Opp ocean. Cr cds: A, MC, V.

[icons]

★★★ **STAGE NECK INN.** *22 Stage Neck Rd, York Harbor (03911). 207/363-3850; fax 207/363-2221; toll-free 800/340-1130. www.stageneck.com.* 60 rms, 2-3 story. Mid-June-early Sept: S $160-$280; D $165-$285; each addl $10; under 13 free; wkends (3-day min); lower rates rest of yr; MAP avail off season. Crib $10. TV; cable, VCR avail (free movies). 2 pools, 1 indoor; whirlpool, poolside serv. Restaurant 7:30-10 am, noon-9 pm. Rm serv. Bar noon-midnight; pianist Fri, Sat. Ck-out 11 am. Coin lndry. Meeting rms. Business servs avail. Bellhops. Sundries. Tennis. 18-hole golf privileges. Exercise equipt; sauna. Game rm. Refrigerators. Balconies. On ocean; beach. Totally nonsmoking. Cr cds: A, DS, MC, V.

[icons]

B&Bs/Small Inns

★★ **DOCKSIDE GUEST QUARTERS.** *Harris Island Rd (03909). 207/363-2868; fax 207/363-1977; toll-free 888/860-7428. www.docksidegq.com.* 21 rms, 4 with shower only, 2 share bath, 6 bldgs, 6 kits., 6 suites. No A/C. No rm phones. Mid-June-late-Sept: D $105-$175; each addl $10; kits. and suites $215-$225; under 12 free; July-Oct (2-day min); lower rates rest of yr. Open wkends only Nov-Apr. Crib free. TV; cable. Playground. Restaurant (see also DOCKSIDE). Ck-out 11 am, ck-in 3 pm. Concierge serv. Luggage handling. Lawn games. Balconies. Picnic tables, grills. On wooded island with views of harbor and ocean. Power boats, rowboats, bicycles. Totally nonsmoking. Cr cds: A, DS, MC, V.

[icons]

★★ **EDWARDS HARBORSIDE INN.** *Stage Neck Rd, York Harbor (03911). 207/363-3037; fax 207/363-1544; res 800/273-2686. www.edwardsharborside.com.* 10 rms, 8 with shower only, 2 share bath, 3 story, 2 suites. July-Aug: D $90-$170; each addl $20; suites $210-$240; higher rates wkends; lower rates rest of yr. TV; cable. Complimentary continental bkfst; afternoon refreshments. Restaurant opp noon-9:30 pm. Ck-out 11 am, ck-in 3 pm. Luggage handling. Lawn games. Picnic tables. On ocean; swimming beach, dockage. Turn-of-century house with period furnishings. Totally nonsmoking. Cr cds: MC, V.

[icons]

★ **HOMESTEAD INN BED AND BREAKFAST.** *5 Longbeach Ave, York Beach (03910). 207/363-8952. hometown.aol.com/homstedBB.* 4 rms, 2 share bath, shower only, 3 story. No A/C. No elvtr. No rm phones. S, D $65; each addl $10; wkly rates. Closed Nov-Mar. Children over 12 yrs only. Complimentary continental bkfst. Restaurant nearby. Ck-out 11 am, ck-in 2 pm. Business servs avail. Opp beach. Built in 1905; former boarding house. Totally nonsmoking. Cr cds: A, MC, V.

[icons]

★★ **YORK HARBOR INN.** *Coastal Rte 1A, York Harbor (03911). 207/363-5119; fax 207/363-7151; res 800/343-3869. www.yorkharborinn.com.* 47 rms, 23 with shower only, 2 story. Apr-Oct: D $129-$319; 2-day min most wkends; higher rates New Years Eve; lower rates rest of yr. Crib $10. TV; cable, VCR avail. Complimentary continental bkfst. Restaurant (see YORK HARBOR INN). Ck-out 11 am, ck-in 2:30 pm. Business servs avail. Golf privileges. Whirlpool. Balconies. Some fireplaces, bathrm phones. Ocean opp. Original section from 1637 is now sitting rm. Cr cds: A, MC, V.

[icons]

Restaurants

★★★ **CAPE NEDDICK INN.** *1233 US 1, Cape Neddick (03902). 207/363-2899.* Contemporary Amer menu. Specializes in seafood, beef. Own baking. Hrs: 5:30-9:30 pm. Closed Dec 25. Res accepted. Bar. Wine list. Dinner $16-$27. Upscale country inn atmosphere; original artwork. Cr cds: DS, MC, V.

[icons]

★★ **DOCKSIDE.** *Harris Island Rd (03909). 207/363-2722. www.docksidegq.com.* Specializes in Maine seafood, roast duckling. Salad bar. Hrs: 11:30 am-2 pm, 5:30-9 pm; hrs vary off season. Closed Mon; also Nov-Memorial Day. Res accepted. Bar. Lunch $5.50-$9.50, dinner $9.95-$19.95. Child's menu. Outdoor dining. Nautical decor; overlooks harbor and marina. Family-owned. Cr cds: DS, MC, V.
[D]

★★ **FAZIO'S ITALIAN.** *38 Woodbridge Rd (03909). 207/363-7019. www.fazios.com.* Italian menu. Specializes in fresh pasta. Hrs: 4-9 pm; Fri, Sat to 10 pm; early-bird dinner to 5:30 pm. Closed major hols. Bar. Dinner $6.50-$14.95. Child's menu. Outdoor dining. Mural of Italian street market; photos from '30s and '40s. Cr cds: A, C, D, DS, ER, MC, V.
[D]

★★★ **YORK HARBOR INN.** *US 1A, York Harbor (03911). 207/363-5119. www.yorkharborinn.com.* Hrs: 11:30 am-2:30 pm, 5:30-9:30 pm; Fri, Sat to 10 pm; Sun brunch 8:30 am-2:30 pm. Closed Mon-Thurs in Jan-mid-May. Res accepted Fri, Sat and Sun brunch. Continental menu. Bar 3:30 pm-12:30 am. Wine cellar. Lunch $4.95-$11.95, dinner $16.95-$24.95. Sun brunch $4.95-$11.95. Child's menu. Specializes in seafood, lobster. Ocean and harbor views. Totally non-smoking. Cr cds: A, D, MC, V.

MASSACHUSETTS

Leif Ericson—or even a French or Spanish angler—may have originally discovered the Cape Cod coast. However, the first recorded visit of a European to Massachusetts was that of John Cabot in 1497. Not until the Pilgrims landed at Provincetown and settled at Plymouth was there a permanent settlement north of Virginia. Ten years later, Boston was founded with the arrival of John Winthrop and his group of Puritans.

Native American wars plagued Massachusetts until the 1680s, after which the people experienced a relatively peaceful period combined with a fast-growing, mostly agricultural economy. In the 1760s, opposition to British taxation without representation exploded into the American Revolution. It began in Massachusetts, and from here, the American tradition of freedom and justice spread around the world. The Constitution of Massachusetts is the oldest written constitution still in effect. The New England town meeting, a basic democratic institution, still governs most of its towns. The state had a child labor law in 1836, a law legalizing trade unions in 1842, and the first minimum wage law for women and children.

Massachusetts proved to be fertile ground for intellectual ideas and activities. In the early 19th century, Emerson, Thoreau, and their followers expounded the Transcendentalist theory of the innate nobilty of man and the doctrine of individual expression, which exerted a major influence on American thought, then and now. Social improvement was sought through colonies of idealists, many of which hoped to prove that sharing labor and the fruits of labor were the means to a just society. Dorothea Dix crusaded on behalf of the mentally disturbed, and Horace Mann promoted universal education. In 1831, William Lloyd Garrison, an ardent abolitionist, founded his weekly, *The Liberator*. Massachusetts was the heartland of the Abolitionist movement and her soldiers fought in the Civil War because they were convinced it was a war against slavery.

Massachusetts was also an important center during the Industrial Revolution. After the Civil War the earlier success of the textile mills, like those in Lowell, generated scores of drab, hastily built industrial towns. Now these towns are being replaced by modern plants with landscaped grounds. Modern industry is as much a part of Massachusetts as the quiet sandy beaches of Cape Cod, with their bayberry and beach plum bushes.

Massachusetts has also been home to several generations of the politically prominent Kennedy family. John F. Kennedy, 35th president of the United States, was born in the Boston suburb of Brookline, as were his younger brothers, Senators Robert and Edward.

The Bay State offers mountains, ocean swimming, camping, summer resorts, freshwater and saltwater fishing, and a variety of metropolitan cultural advantages. No other state in the Union can claim so much history in so small an area, for in Massachusetts each town or city has a part in the American story.

Population: 6,016,425
Area: 7,826 square miles
Elevation: 0–3,491 feet
Peak: Mount Greylock (Berkshire County)
Entered Union: Sixth of original thirteen states (February 6, 1788)
Capital: Boston
Motto: By the sword we seek peace, but peace only under liberty
Nickname: Bay State
Flower: Mayflower
Bird: Chickadee
Tree: American Elm
Time Zone: Eastern
Website: www.mass-vacation.com

When to Go/Climate

Massachusetts enjoys a moderate climate with four distinct seasons. Cape Cod and the Islands offer milder temperatures than other parts of the state and rarely have snow, while windchill in Boston (the windiest city in the United States) can make temperatures feel well below zero and snow is not uncommon.

AVERAGE HIGH/LOW TEMPERATURES (°F)

BOSTON

Jan 36/22	**May** 67/50	**Sept** 73/57
Feb 38/23	**June** 76/60	**Oct** 63/47
Mar 46/31	**July** 82/65	**Nov** 52/38
Apr 56/40	**Aug** 80/64	**Dec** 40/27

WORCESTER

Jan 31/15	**May** 66/45	**Sept** 70/51
Feb 33/17	**June** 75/54	**Oct** 60/41
Mar 42/25	**July** 80/60	**Nov** 47/31
Apr 54/35	**Aug** 77/59	**Dec** 35/20

Parks and Recreation Finder

Directions to and information about the parks and recreation areas below are given under their respective town/city sections. Please refer to those sections for details.

NATIONAL PARK AND RECREATION AREAS

Key to abbreviations. I.H.S. = International Historic Site; I.P.M. = International Peace Memorial; N.B. = National Battlefield; N.B.P. = National Battlefield Park; N.B.C. = National Battlefield and Cemetery; N.C.A. = National Conservation Area; N.E.M. = National Expansion Memorial; N.F. = National Forest; N.G. = National Grassland; N.H.P. = National Historical Park; N.H.C. = National Heritage Corridor; N.H.S. = National Historic Site; N.L. = National Lakeshore; N.M. = National Monument; N.M.P. = National Military Park; N.Mem. = National Memorial; N.P. = National Park; N.Pres. = National Preserve; N.R.A. = National Recreational Area; N.R.R. = National Recreational River; N.Riv. = National River; N.S. = National Seashore; N.S.R. = National Scenic Riverway; N.S.T. = National Scenic Trail; N.Sc. = National Scientific Reserve; N.V.M. = National Volcanic Monument.

Place Name	Listed Under
Adams N.H.S.	QUINCY
Blackstone River Valley N.H.C.	WORCESTER
Boston African American N.H.S.	BOSTON
Cape Cod N.S.	same
Frederick Law Olmsted N.H.S.	BOSTON
John F. Kennedy N.H.S.	BOSTON
Longfellow N.H.S.	CAMBRIDGE
Lowell N.H.P.	LOWELL
Minute Man N.H.P.	CONCORD
Salem Maritime N.H.S.	SALEM
Saugus Iron Works N.H.S.	SAUGUS
Springfield Armory N.H.S.	SPRINGFIELD

STATE PARK AND RECREATION AREAS

Key to abbreviations. I.P. = Interstate Park; S.A.P. = State Archaeological Park; S.B. = State Beach; S.C.A. = State Conservation Area; S.C.P. = State Conservation Park; S.Cp. = State Campground; S.F. = State Forest; S.G. = State Garden; S.H.A. = State Historic Area; S.H.P. = State Historic Park; S.H.S. = State Historic Site; S.M.P. = State Marine Park; S.N.A. = State Natural Area; S.P. = State Park; S.P.C. = State Public Campground; S.R. = State Reserve; S.R.A. = State Recreation Area; S.Res. = State Reservoir; S.Res.P. = State Resort Park; S.R.P. = State Rustic Park.

Place Name	Listed Under
Beartown S.F.	GREAT BARRINGTON
Brimfield S.F.	SPRINGFIELD
Fall River Heritage S.P.	FALL RIVER
Fort Phoenix Beach S.R.	NEW BEDFORD
Granville S.F.	SPRINGFIELD
Holyoke Heritage S.P.	HOLYOKE
Lawrence Heritage S.P.	LAWRENCE
Lowell Heritage S.P.	LOWELL
Lynn Heritage S.P.	LYNN
Mohawk Trail S.F.	NORTH ADAMS
Mount Greylock S.R.	NORTH ADAMS
Myles Standish S.F.	PLYMOUTH
Natural Bridge S.P.	NORTH ADAMS
Nickerson S.P.	BREWSTER
October Mountain S.F.	LEE
Savoy Mountain S.F.	NORTH ADAMS
Scusset Beach S.P.	SANDWICH
Shawme-Crowell S.F.	SANDWICH
Walden Pond S.R.	CONCORD
Western Gateway Heritage S.P.	NORTH ADAMS

Water-related activities, hiking, riding, various other sports, picnicking, and visitor centers, as well as camping, are available in many of these areas. Day-use areas (approximately Memorial Day-Labor Day, some areas all year): $5/car. Camping (approximately mid-Apr-Oct, schedule may vary, phone ahead; two-week max, last Saturday May-Saturday before Labor Day at many parks): campsites $10-$15/day; electricity $5/day. Pets on leash only in S.P.; no pets in bathing areas. Information available from Department of Environmental Management, Division of Forests and Parks, 617/727-3180.

SKI AREAS

Place Name	Listed Under
Bousquet Ski Area	PITTSFIELD
Brodie Mountain Ski Area	PITTSFIELD
Butternut Basin Ski Area	GREAT BARRINGTON
Jiminy Peak Ski Area	GREAT BARRINGTON
Mount Tom Ski Area	HOLYOKE
Otis Ridge Ski Area	GREAT BARRINGTON

FISHING AND HUNTING

Deep-sea and surf fishing are good; boats are available in most coastal towns. For information on saltwater fishing, contact Division of Marine Fisheries, phone 617/727-3193. Inland fishing is excellent in more than 500 streams and 3,000 ponds. Nonresident fishing license $40.50; three-consecutive-day nonresident license $25.50. Nonresident hunting license: small game $75.50; big game $110.50. Inquire for trapping licenses. Fees subject to change. Licenses issued by town clerks, selected sporting good stores, or from Division of Fisheries and Wildlife, phone 617/727-3151 or 800/ASK-FISH. Information on freshwater fishing, regulations, and a guide to stocked trout waters and best bass ponds are also available from Division of Fisheries and Wildlife.

CALENDAR HIGHLIGHTS

APRIL

Boston Marathon (Boston). Famous 26-mile footrace from Hopkinton to Boston. Phone 617/236-1652.

Reenactment of Battle of Lexington and Concord (Lexington). Massachusetts Ave. Reenactment of opening battle of American Revolution; parade. Phone Lexington Historical Society, 781/862-1703.

Daffodil Festival (Nantucket Island). Festival is marked by over a million blooming daffodils. Parade of antique cars, prize for best tailgate picnic. Phone Chamber of Commerce, 508/228-1700.

JUNE

La Festa (North Adams). Ethnic festival, food, entertainment, events. Phone 413/66-FESTA.

JULY

Harborfest (Boston). Hatch Shell on the Esplanade. Concerts, chowder fest, children's activities, Boston Pops Orchestra, fireworks. Phone 617/227-1528.

Green River Music and Balloon Festival (Greenfield). Hot-air balloon launches, craft show, musical entertainment, food. Phone 413/733-5463.

SEPTEMBER

The "Big E" (Springfield). Largest fair in the Northeast; entertainment, exhibits, historic Avenue of States, Storrowton Village; horse show, agricultural events, "Better Living Center" exhibit. Phone 413/737-2443.

OCTOBER

Haunted Happenings (Salem). Various sites. Psychic festival, historical exhibits, haunted house, costume parade, contests, dances. Phone Salem Halloween Office, 978/744-0013.

NOVEMBER

Thanksgiving Week (Plymouth). Programs for various events may be obtained by contacting Destination Plymouth. Phone 508/747-7525 or 800/USA-1620.

DECEMBER

Stockbridge Main Street at Christmas (Stockbridge and West Stockbridge). Events include a re-creation of Norman Rockwell's painting. Holiday marketplace, concerts, house tour, silent auction, sleigh/hay rides, caroling. Phone 413/298-5200.

Driving Information

Safety belts are mandatory for all persons. Children under 13 years must be in a federally approved child safety seat or safety belt anywhere in vehicle: it is recommended that children 40 pounds and under use a federally approved child safety seat and be placed in the back seat. For further information, phone 617/624-5070 or 800/CAR-SAFE (MA).

INTERSTATE HIGHWAY SYSTEM

The following alphabetical listing of Massachusetts towns in the *RoadMaster™ Drive USA Travel Guide* shows that these cities are within ten miles of the indicated Interstate highways. A highway map, however, should be checked for the nearest exit.

Highway Number	Cities/Towns within ten miles
Interstate 90	Boston, Cambridge, Framingham, Great Barrington, Holyoke, Lee, Lenox, Natick, Newton, Pittsfield, Springfield, Stockbridge and West Stockbridge, Sturbridge, Sudbury Center, Waltham, Wellesley, Worcester.
Interstate 91	Amherst, Deerfield, Greenfield, Holyoke, Northampton, Springfield.
Interstate 93	Andover, Boston, Lawrence, Lowell.
Interstate 95	Bedford, Boston, Burlington, Concord, Danvers, Dedham, Foxboro, Framingham, Lexington, Lynn, Lynnfield, Natick, Newton, Saugus, Sudbury Center, Waltham, Wellesley.

Additional Visitor Information

The Massachusetts Office of Travel and Tourism, 617/727-3201, has travel information. For a free *Massachusetts Getaway Guide* phone 800/447-MASS.

Many properties of the Society for the Preservation of New England Antiquities (SPNEA) are located in Massachusetts and neighboring states. For complete information on these properties contact the SPNEA Headquarters, 141 Cambridge St, Boston 02114; 617/227-3956. For information regarding the 71 properties owned and managed by The Trustees of Reservations, contact 527 Essex St, Beverly, MA 01905; 508/921-1944.

Massachusetts has many statewide fairs, though none is considered the official state fair; contact the Massachusetts Department of Agriculture, Division of Fairs, 617/727-3037.

There are several visitor centers located in Massachusetts; they are located on the Massachusetts Turnpike (daily, 9 am-6 pm) at Charlton (eastbound and westbound), Lee (eastbound), and Natick (eastbound); also I-95 at Mansfield, between exits 5 and 6 (northbound); and on MA 3 at Plymouth (southbound).

TO THE BERKSHIRES!

Two major limited-access highways link Boston with the Berkshires, traversing the width of Massachusetts. The older, slower, more scenic Route 2 runs across the state's hilly northern tier; the Massachusetts Turnpike (I-90) is the quicker way home. Begin on Route 2 in Cambridge. To explore Revolutionary War battle sites take exit 56 (Waltham Street) into the center of Lexington and turn left on Route 2A for Battle Green. Continue west on Route 2A, stopping at the Battle Road Visitors Center and moving on to Concord's Minuteman National Historical Park sites. Pick up Route 2 west again in Concord. In Harvard, take exit 38A to the hilltop Fruitlands Museums with its paintings, Shaker furnishings and local Indian artifacts. This is the Nashoba Valley, known for its orchards, served by the Johnny Appleseed information center just west of exit 35. Wachusett Mountain in Princeton (exit 25) is a popular ski area; there is also a state reservation with a road to its summit. Templeton (exit 21), just off the highway, is a classic old village with interesting shops and a local historical museum.

For a sense of Central Massachusetts countryside, detour south on Route 32 (exit 17) to the handsome old ridge town of Petersham. South of the village turn west on Route 122, skirting the Quabbin Fervor, said to be one of the largest reservoirs in the world. Rejoin the highway in the town of Orange. Here Route 2 officially becomes "The Mohawk Trail" because it is said to shadow an old Indian trail through the hills. (Note the information center at the junction of Reservoir 2, I-91, and Route 5.) Take a detour to Old Deerfield and its many historic house museums, located 12 miles south on Route 5. Or continue on Route 2 as it climbs steeply from Greenfield out of the Connecticut River valley and into the Berkshire Hills. The vintage 1930s lookout towers and Indian trading posts along this stretch are relics from when this was the state's first scenic "auto touring" route.

The village of Shelburne Falls, just off Route 2, is known for its Bridge of Flowers, shops, and restaurants. The "Trail" continues through the Deerfield River valley, threads the heavily wooded Mohawk Trail Forest (camping, swimming), and finally plunges down a series of hairpin turns into the Hoosac Valley and through the town of North Adams, site of MASS MoCA, the country's largest center for contemporary art. The Western Gateway Heritage State Park here tells the story of Hoosac Railroad Tunnel construction beneath the mountains you have just crossed.

Williamstown, 126 miles from Boston, marks the state's northwest corner. It's home to Williams College and two outstanding art museums, the Clark Art Institute and the Williams College Museum of Art. Food and lodging. are available here.

If you have more than one day, continue south on Route 7 from Williamstown. In Lanesborough note the main access road to Mount Greylock, the highest mountain in the state. Pittsfield, site of the Berkshire Museum, is also the turnoff point for the Hancock Shaker Village (five miles west on Route 20). Continue down Route 7 to Lenox, site of Tanglewood summer music festival, summer Shakespeare productions, several museums, and ample lodging. Take Route 7A south to Stockbridge and through the village to the Norman Rockwell Museum. Return on Route 102 to the entrance to the Massachusetts Turnpike (Route 90) at Lee, the quick way back to Boston. Stop at Sturbridge (exit 9) to tour Old Sturbridge Village. (**APPROX 290 MI**)

Amesbury

See also Haverhill, Newburyport

Settled 1654 **Pop** 16,450 **Elev** 50 ft **Area code** 978
Zip 01913
Information Alliance for Amesbury, 5 Market Sq,
01913-2440; 978/388-3178
Web www.amesburymass.com

In 1853, Jacob R. Huntington, "the Henry Ford of carriage-making," began a low-cost, high-quality carriage industry that became the economic backbone of Amesbury.

What to See and Do

Amesbury Sports Park. Winter snow tubing, summer go-carts, golf range, miniature golf, bumper boats, volleyball park. Restaurant; lounge. (Daily; closed Easter, Thanksgiving, Dec 25) 12 Hunt Rd. ¢¢¢

Bartlett Museum. (1870) Houses memorabilia of Amesbury's history dating from prehistoric days to the settlement and beyond. The Native American artifact collection, consisting of relics of local tribes, is considered one of the finest collections in the state. (Memorial Day-Labor Day, Wed-Sun afternoons; Labor Day-Columbus Day, Sat and Sun) 270 Main St. Phone 978/388-4528. ¢

John Greenleaf Whittier Home. John Greenleaf Whittier lived here from 1836 until his death in 1892; six rms contain books, manuscripts, pictures, and furniture; the Garden Room, where he wrote *Snow-Bound* and many other works, remains unchanged. (May-Oct, Tues-Sat) 86 Friend St. Phone 978/388-1337. ¢¢

Motel/Motor Lodge

★ **FAIRFIELD INN.** *35 Clarks Rd (01913).*
978/388-3400; fax 978/388-9850; toll-free 800/228-2800.
www.fairfield inn.com. 105 rms, 4 story. S, D $69-$89; each addl $6; under 18 free; wknd rates. TV; cable (premium). Complimentary continental bkfst. Ck-out noon. Meeting rms. Business servs avail. Health club privileges. Pool.
Cr cds: A, C, D, DS, MC, V.

⊡ ⇌ ⇥ 🔥

Amherst

Founded 1759 **Pop** 34,874 **Elev** 320 ft **Area code** 413
Zip 01002
Information Chamber of Commerce, 409 Main St;
413/253-0700
Web www.amherstchamber.com

Amherst College, founded in 1821 to educate "promising but needy youths who wished to enter the Ministry," has educated several of the nation's leaders, including Calvin Coolidge and Henry Ward Beecher. Amherst is also the seat of the University of Massachusetts and of Hampshire College. This attractive, academic town was the home of three celebrated American poets: Emily Dickinson, Eugene Field, and Robert Frost; Noah Webster also lived here.

What to See and Do

Amherst College. (1821) 1,550 students. On the tree-shaded green in the middle of town. The Robert Frost Library owns approx half of Emily Dickinson's poems in manuscript and has a Robert Frost collection, as well as materials of Wordsworth, Eugene O'Neill, and others. Phone 413/542-2000. Also on campus are

    Mead Art Museum. A notable art collection is housed here. (Sept-July, daily; Aug, by appt) **FREE**

    Pratt Museum of Geology. (1884) Some of the finest collections of dinosaur tracks, meteorites, minerals, and fossils; also the world's largest mastodon skeleton. (Academic yr, daily; closed school hols) **FREE**

Amherst History Museum. In 18th-century Strong House. House reflects changing tastes in local architecture and interior decoration; extensive collection of 18th- and 19th-century textiles and artifacts; gallery. (Mid-May-mid-Oct, Wed and Sat afternoons) 18th-century herb and flower garden open to the public (spring-summer). 67 Amity St. Phone 413/256-0678. ¢¢

Emily Dickinson Homestead. (1813) Birthplace and home of Emily Dickinson. Selected rms open for tours by appt (Afternoons: May-Oct, Wed-Sat; Mar-Apr and Nov-mid-Dec, Wed and Sat). 280 Main St. Phone 413/542-8161. ¢¢

Hadley Farm Museum. Restored 1782 barn houses agricultural implements, tools, and domestic items dating from 1700s; broom-making machines. (May-mid-Oct, Tues-Sun) 5 mi SW at jct MA 9, 47, at 147 Russell St in Hadley. **FREE**

Jones Library. Building houses collections of the Amherst authors; including an Emily Dickinson rm with some of Dickinson's personal articles, manuscripts, and a model of her bedrm. Historical collection (Mon-Sat); library (Sept-May, daily; rest of yr, Mon-Sat; closed hols). 43 Amity St. Phone 413/256-4090. **FREE**

National Yiddish Book Center. This 37,000-sq-ft nonprofit facility was founded by Aaron Lansky to preserve Yiddish literature and its history and to ensure its lasting legacy. Book Repository houses a core collection of 120,000 Yiddish books—the largest in the world—and 150,000 folios of rare Yiddish and Hebrew sheet music. Book Processing Center, shipping and receiving area, and Bibliography Center are all open for viewing as rare books are catalogued and shipped to libraries across the country. Vistor Center includes three exhibit halls, a kosher dairy kitchen, and educational story rails that introduce visitors to the books and the Center's important work. Reading Room, Yiddish Resource Center, Yiddish Writers Garden. Also galleries for print, spoken, and performing arts. Bookstore; gift store. (Mon-Fri, Sun). MA 116, on campus of Hampshire College. Phone 800/535-3595. **FREE**

University of Massachusetts. (1863) 24,000 students. State's major facility of public higher education. More than 150 buildings on 1,450-acre campus. Tours (daily), N edge of town on MA 116. Phone 413/545-4237. Also here is

    Fine Arts Center and Gallery. A variety of nationally and internationally known performances in theater, music, and dance. Art gallery (daily). Performances (Sept-May). Phone 413/545-3670.

Special Event

Maple sugaring. Visitors are welcome at maple camps, daily. Mount Toby Sugar House. (Late Feb-Mar.) NW via MA 116 to Sunderland, then 2 mi N on MA 47. Phone 413/253-0700.

Motel/Motor Lodge

★ **HOWARD JOHNSON INN.** *401 Russell St, Rte 9, Hadley (01035).* 413/586-0114; *fax* 413/584-7163; *res* 800/446-4656. *www.hojo.com.* 100 rms, 3 story. S $59-$109; D $69-$109; each addl $10; suites $79-$152; under 18 free; higher rates special events. Crib free. Pet accepted. TV; cable (premium). Pool. Complimentary bkfst. Ck-out noon. Meeting rm. Business servs avail. In-rm modem link. Downhill ski 16 mi; x-country ski 12 mi. Exercise equipt. Health club privileges. Private patios, balconies. Cr cds: A, C, D, DS, MC, V.

⊡ 🐾 🖼 🛶 SC ⛵ 🏊 🏃

B&Bs/Small Inns

★★ **ALLEN HOUSE VICTORIAN INN.** *599 Main St (01002).* 413/253-5000. *www.allenhouse.com.* 7 rms, 5 with shower only, 2 story. Rm phones avail. Apr-Nov: S $55-$105; D $65-$135; each addl $10-$20; higher rates college events; lower rates rest of yr. Children over 8 yrs only. TV in sitting rm. Complimentary full bkfst; afternoon refreshments. Restaurant nearby. Ck-out 11 am, ck-in mid-afternoon. Queen Anne-style house built 1886; many antiques. Totally nonsmoking. Cr cds: DS, MC, V.

🖼 🔥

★★ **LORD JEFFREY INN.** *30 Boltwood Ave (01002).* 413/253-2576; *fax* 413/256-6152; *toll-free* 800/742-0358. *www.lordjeffreyinn.com.* 50 rms, 4 story. S $79-$109; D $99-$119; suites $109-$163. Crib $15. TV; cable. Bar. Ck-out 11 am, ck-in 3 pm. Downhill ski 18 mi; x-country ski 12 mi. Private patios, balconies. Cr cds: A, D, DS, MC, V.

⊡ ⛵ 🖼 🔥 🐾

Andover and North Andover

Settled ca 1643 **Pop** 31,247 **Elev** 164 ft **Area code** 978
Zip Andover: 01810; North Andover: 01845
Information Merrimack Valley Chamber of Commerce, 264 Essex St, Lawrence 01840-1496; 978/686-0900
Web www.merrimackvalleychamber.com

An attempt was made in Andover in the 19th century to surpass Japan's silk industry by growing mulberry trees on which silkworms feed. But Andover has had to be content with making electronic parts and woolen and rubber goods instead. Its true fame rests on Phillips Academy, the oldest incorporated school in the United States, founded in 1778 by Samuel Phillips.

What to See and Do

Amos Blanchard House. (1819) **Barn Museum** (1818) Also **Research Library** (1978). House features period rms; special local history exhibits; 17th- to-20th-century themes. Barn Museum features early farm equipment; household items; hand-pumped fire wagon. Library houses local history, genealogy, and special collections. Guided tours (by appt). (Tues-Fri, also by appt; closed hols) 97 Main St. Phone 978/475-2236. ¢¢

Phillips Academy. (1778) 1,065 students. A coed residential school for grades 9-12. On 450 acres with 170 buildings, many of historical interest. The Cochran Sanctuary, a 65-acre landscaped area, has walking trails, a brook, and two ponds. (Daily) Main St, MA 28. Phone 978/749-4000. Also on grounds are

Addison Gallery of American Art. More than 12,000 works, including paintings, sculpture, and photographs. Changing exhibits. Ship model collection tracing era of sail through steam engine. (Sept-July, Tues-Sun; closed hols) Phone 978/749-4016. **FREE**

Peabody Museum. Exhibits on physical, cultural evolution of man; prehistoric archaeology of New England, New Mexico, Mexico, Canada. (Open by appt only) Phillips and Main Sts. Phone 978/749-4490.

Stevens-Coolidge Place. House, interior, and extensive gardens are maintained as they were in the early 20th century by diplomat John Gardener Coolidge and his wife, Helen Stevens Coolidge. Collection of Chinese porcelain, Irish and English cut glass, linens, and clothing. Early American furnishings. House (Late Apr-Oct, Sun afternoons). Gardens (daily; free). 137 Andover St, in North Andover. Phone 978/682-3580. ¢¢

Motels/Motor Lodges

★★ **HOLIDAY INN.** *4 Highwood Dr, Tewksbury (01876).* 978/640-9000; *fax* 978/640-0623; *res* 800/465-4329. *www.holiday-inn.com.* 237 rms, 11 suites, 5 story. S, D $119; under 18 free; wkend rates. TV; cable (premium). Indoor pool; whirlpool. Complimentary coffee in rms. Restaurant 6:30 am-2 pm, 5-10 pm. Rm serv. Bar; entertainment Wed. Ck-out noon. Meeting rms. Business servs avail. In-rm modem link. Sundries. Exercise equipt; sauna. Some refrigerators. Cr cds: A, C, D, DS, MC, V.

⊡ 🏊 🏃 🖼 🔥

★ **RAMADA HOTEL.** *311 Lowell St, Andover (01810).* 978/475-5400; *fax* 978/470-1108; *res* 888/298-2054. *www.ramada.com.* 179 rms, 2 story. S $99-$129; D $109-$139; each addl $12; suites $125-$250; under 18 free; group, wkend rates. Crib free. Pet accepted. TV; cable. 2 pools, 1 indoor; whirlpool. Restaurant 6:30 am-2 pm, 5-10 pm. Rm serv. Bar 11:30-1 am. Ck-out noon. Meeting rms. Business servs avail. Valet serv. Airport transportation. Indoor tennis, pro. 9-hole par 3 golf, greens fee $12-$14. Exercise equipt; sauna. Microwaves avail. Cr cds: A, C, D, DS, MC, V.

⊡ 🐾 🏊 🎾 🏃 🏌 🔥 🖼 🐾 SC

Hotels

★★ **TAGE INN-ANDOVER.** *131 River Rd, Andover (01810). 978/685-6200; fax 978/794-9626; res 800/322-8243. www.tageinn.com.* 181 rms, 3 story. S, D $84.95; suites $115.95; each addl $8; under 12 free. Crib free. TV; cable. Indoor pool; whirlpool. Complimentary continental bkfst. Restaurant 6:30-10 am, 5 pm-midnight; 7-11 am wkends. Ck-out noon. Meeting rms. Business servs avail. In-rm modem link. Valet serv. Lighted tennis. Exercise equipt. Some bathrm phones. Refrigerators avail. Cr cds: A, D, DS, MC, V.

[D] [⛵] [≈] [🏋] [≈] [♨] [SC]

★★ **WYNDHAM.** *123 Old River Rd, Andover (01810). 978/975-3600; fax 978/975-2664. www.wyndham.com.* 293 rms, 9 suites, 5 story. S, D $175; under 18 free; family rates; package plans. Crib free. Pet accepted, some restrictions. TV; cable (premium), VCR avail (movies). Indoor pool; whirlpool. Complimentary coffee in lobby. Restaurant 6:30 am-10 pm. Rm serv to 11 pm. Bar 5 pm-12:30 am; entertainment wkends. Convention facilities. Business servs avail. In-rm modem link. Bellhops. Valet serv. Sundries. Gift shop. Airport, RR station transportation. Exercise equipt; sauna. Lawn games. Some refrigerators. Many balconies. Cr cds: A, C, D, DS, JCB, MC, V.

[D] [🐾] [≈] [🏋] [≈] [♨]

B&B/Small Inn

★★★ **ANDOVER INN.** *10 Chapel Ave, Andover (01810). 978/475-5903; fax 978/475-1053; toll-free 800/242-5903. www.andoverinn.com.* 23 rms, 3 story. S $95; D $110; each addl $10; suites $140; under 12 free. Pet accepted, some restrictions. TV; VCR avail. Dining rm 7:30 am-9:45 pm. Rm serv. Bar 11:30 am-midnight. Ck-out noon. Meeting rms. Business center. In-rm modem link. Valet serv. Beauty shop. On campus of Phillips Academy. Cr cds: A, C, D, DS, MC, V.

[D] [≈] [♨] [🐾] [🏋]

Restaurant

★ **CHINA BLOSSOM.** *946 Osgood St, North Andover (01845). 978/682-2242.* Chinese menu. Daily buffet. Hrs: 11:30 am-9:30 pm; Fri, Sat to midnight; Sun noon-9:30 pm. Closed Thanksgiving. Bar. A la carte: lunch, dinner $6.95-$26. Family-owned. Cr cds: A, C, D, DS, MC, V.

[D]

Barnstable (Cape Cod)

See also Hyannis (Cape Cod), South Yarmouth (Cape Cod)

Settled 1637 **Pop** 47,821 **Elev** 37 ft **Area code** 508 **Zip** 02630

Information Cape Cod Chamber of Commerce, US 6 and MA 132, PO Box 790, Hyannis 02601-0790; 508/362-3225 or 888/33-CAPECOD

Web www.capecodchamber.org

Farmers first settled Barnstable because the marshes provided salt hay for cattle. Later the town prospered as a whaling and trading center, and when these industries declined, land development made it the political hub of the Cape. It is the seat of Barnstable County, which includes the entire Cape. Like other Cape communities, it does a thriving resort business.

What to See and Do

Cape Cod Art Association Gallery. Changing exhibits, exhibitions by New England artists; demonstrations, lectures, classes. (Apr-Nov, daily, limited hrs; rest of yr, inquire for schedule) On MA 6A. Phone 508/362-2909. **FREE**

Donald G. Trayser Memorial Museum. Marine exhibits, scrimshaw, Barnstable silver, historic documents. (July-mid-Oct, Tues-Sat afternoons) In Old Custom House and Post Office, Main St on Cobb's Hill, MA 6A. Phone 508/362-2092.

Hyannis Whale Watcher Cruises. View whales aboard the *Whale Watcher,* a 297-passenger super-cruiser, custom designed and built specifically for whale watching. Naturalist on board will narrate. Cafe on board. (Apr-Oct, daily) Res necessary. Barnstable Harbor. Contact PO Box 254. Phone 508/362-6088. ¢¢¢¢

Sturgis Library. Oldest library building (1644) in US has material on the Cape, including maritime history; genealogical records of Cape Cod families. Research fee for nonresidents. (Mon-Sat; closed hols; limited hrs) On Main St, MA 6A. Phone 508/362-6636. ¢¢

West Parish Meetinghouse. (1717) Said to be the oldest Congregational church in country; restored. Congregation established in London, 1616. Regular Sun services are held here all yr. Jct US 6, MA 149 in West Barnstable. Phone 508/362-4385. **FREE**

B&Bs/Small Inns

★★★ **ACWORTH INN.** *4352 Old Kings Hwy, Rte 64, Barnstable (02637). 508/362-3330; fax 508/375-0304; toll-free 800/362-6363. www.acworthinn.com.* 4 rms, 2 with shower only, 2 story, 1 suite. Some A/C. No rm phones. Late May-Oct: S, D $100-$125; each addl $20; suite $185; wkends, hols (2-day min); lower rates rest of yr. Children over 12 yrs only. TV in common rm; cable. Complimentary full bkfst. Restaurant nearby. Ck-out 11 am, ck-in 3-10 pm. Luggage handling. Concierge serv. Farmhouse built in 1860. Totally nonsmoking. Cr cds: A, DS, MC, V.
🖼🔥

★★★ **ASHLEY MANOR.** *3660 Main St, Barnstable (02630). 508/362-8044; fax 508/362-9927; toll-free 888/535-2246. www.ashleymanor.net.* 6 rms, 2 story, 1 cottage. Phone avail. S, D $135-$195; suites $165-$180. Children over 14 yrs only. Complimentary full bkfst; afternoon refreshments. Complimentary coffee in rms. Ck-out 11 am, ck-in 2 pm. Tennis. Lawn games. Many fireplaces; some in-rm whirlpools. Library. Antiques. Restored early 18th-century inn on 2-acre estate. Cr cds: A, DS, JCB, MC, V.
🏸🖼🔥

★★★ **BEECHWOOD INN.** *2839 Main St, Barnstable (02630). 508/362-6618; fax 508/362-0298; toll-free 800/609-6618. www.beechwoodinn.com.* 6 rms, 3 story. No rm phones. May-Oct: S, D $130-$180; each addl $20; lower rates rest of yr. Complimentary full bkfst; afternoon refreshments. Ck-out 11 am, ck-in 2 pm. Lawn games. Refrigerators; some fireplaces. Restored Victorian house (1853); veranda with rocking chairs, glider. Antique furnishings. Totally nonsmoking. Cr cds: A, DS, MC, V.
🖼🔥

★★ **HONEYSUCKLE HILL B&B.** *591 Old King's Hwy, Rte 6A, West Barnstable (02668). 508/362-8418; fax 508/362-8386; toll-free 800/444-5522. www.honeysucklehill.com.* 5 rms, 2 share bath, 2 with shower only, 2 story, 2 suites. S $100-$120; D $120-$140; suite $175; wkends, hols (2-day min). Children over 12 yrs only. Complimentary full bkfst. Restaurants nearby. Ck-out 11 am, ck-in 3 pm. Built in 1810; restored Victorian decor. Cr cds: A, DS, MC, V.
🖼🔥

Restaurants

★★ **BARNSTABLE TAVERN AND GRILLE.** *3176 Main St, Barnstable (02630). 508/362-2355.* Specializes in black Angus beef, fresh native seafood, desserts. Hrs: 11:30 am-11:30 pm. Closed Dec 24, 25. Bar. Lunch $3.95-$10.95, dinner $10.95-$21.95. Child's menu. Entertainment. Outdoor dining. Inn and tavern since 1799. Cr cds: A, MC, V.
🅳

★★ **HARBOR POINT.** *Harbor Point Rd, Cummaquid (02630). 508/362-2231.* Specializes in fresh seafood, steak. Hrs: 11:30 am-10:30 pm; wkends to midnight; Sun brunch 11 am-3 pm. Closed Feb-Mar. Res accepted. Bar. Lunch $2.95-$10.95, dinner $15.95-$22.95. Sun brunch $10.95. Child's menu. Entertainment. Overlooking bay, marsh abundant with wildlife. Fountain. Cr cds: A, C, DS, MC, V.
🅳🔲

★★ **MATTAKEESE WHARF.** *271 Mill Way, Barnstable (02630). 508/362-4511.* Specialties: bouillabaisse, baked stuffed shrimp, lobster. Own pasta. Hrs: 11:30 am-10 pm; Sun 11:30 am-9 pm; early-bird dinner Sun-Fri 4:30-6 pm; Sun brunch to 2:30 pm. Closed late Oct-early May. Res accepted. No A/C. Bar to 1 am. Lunch $5.25-$12, dinner $10.95-$19.95. Sun brunch $8.95. Child's menu. Entertainment wkends. Valet parking. View of boats in harbor; nautical motif. Family-owned. Cr cds: A, DS, MC, V.

Bedford

Pop 12,595 **Elev** 135 ft **Area code** 781 **Zip** 01730

Motels/Motor Lodges

★ **RAMADA INN.** *340 Great Rd (01730). 781/275-6700; fax 781/275-3011; res 888/298-2054. www.ramada.com.* 100 rms, 3 story. Apr-Oct: S, D $69-$119; each addl $10; under 18 free; wkend, hol rates. Crib free. TV; cable (premium). Indoor pool. Complimentary continental bkfst, coffee in rms. Restaurant 6:30-10:30 am, 5-9 pm; Sat 7-11 am, 5-9 pm; Sun 7 am-noon. Bar. Ck-out noon. Meeting rms. Business servs avail. Valet serv. Exercise equipt. Cr cds: A, C, D, DS, MC, V.
🅳🖼🔥 SC 🔲🏃

★ **TRAVELODGE.** *285 Great Rd (01730). 781/275-6120; res 888/515-6375. www.travelodge.com.* 42 rms, 2 story. S $59-$79; D $69-$89; each addl $6; under 14 free. Crib $6. TV; cable. Pool. Complimentary coffee. Restaurant nearby. Ck-out 11 am. In-rm modem link. Cr cds: A, D, DS, MC, V.
🔲🖼🔥 SC

Hotels

★★★ **RENAISSANCE BEDFORD HOTEL.** *44 Middlesex Tpke (01730). 781/275-5500; fax 781/275-3042; res 800/468-3571. www.renaissancehotels.com.* 284 rms, 8 suites, 2-3 story. S, D $170-$210; suites $200-$225; wkend rates; under 18 free. Crib free. Pet accepted, some restrictions. TV; cable (premium). VCR avail. Indoor pool; whirlpool, poolside serv. Restaurant (see also BISTRO 44). Rm serv 24 hrs. Complimentary coffee delivered to rms. Bar 11:30-1 am; entertainment. Ck-out 1 pm. Convention facilities. Business center. In-rm modem link. Concierge. Indoor and outdoor tennis, pro. Exercise rm; sauna. Health club privileges. Refrigerators, minibars. On 24 wooded acres. Cr cds: A, D, DS, JCB, MC, V.
🅳🍸🏸🔲🏃🖼🔥🏃

★★★ **WYNDHAM BILLERICA.** *270 Concord Rd (01821). 978/670-7500; fax 978/670-8898. www.wyndham.com.* 210 rms, 8 story. S, D $125-$225; under 18 free. Crib avail. TV; cable (premium). Indoor pool; whirlpool. Restaurant 6:30 am-10 pm. Bar to midnight. Ck-out noon, ck-in 4 pm. Meeting rms. Business center. In-rm modem link. Concierge. Exercise equipt. Minibars; many refrigerators in suites. Cr cds: A, C, D, DS, MC, V.
🔲🏃🏃

Berkshire Hills

This western Massachusetts resort area is just south of Vermont's Green Mountains, but has neither the ruggedness nor the lonesomeness of the range to its north. The highest peak, Mt. Greylock (elevation: 3,491 feet), is cragless and serene. Farms and villages dot the landscape. The area is famous for its variety of accommodations, culture, and recreation. There are also countless summer homes and camps for children by the lakes, ponds, and brooks.

Berkshire County is about 45 miles long from north to south, and half that from east to west. It has 90 lakes and ponds, 90,000 acres of state forest, golf courses, ski areas, ski touring centers, numerous tennis facilities, and campsites. The area first became famous when Nathaniel Hawthorne wrote *Tanglewood Tales,* and it has since become distinguished for its many summer cultural activities, including the Tanglewood Music Festival at Tanglewood (see LENOX) and the Berkshire Theatre Festival (see STOCKBRIDGE & WEST STOCKBRIDGE).

Beverly

See also Danvers

Settled 1626 **Pop** 39,862 **Elev** 26 ft **Area code** 978
Zip 01915
Information North Shore Chamber of Commerce, 5 Cherry Hill Dr, Danvers 01923; 978/774-8565
Web www.northshorechamber.org

When George Washington commissioned the first US naval vessel, the schooner *Hannah,* on September 5, 1775, at Glover's Wharf in Beverly, the town was already well established. In 1693, the local Puritan minister's wife, Mistress Hale, was accused of witchcraft. She was so far above reproach that the charge—and the hysteria—collapsed. Today, Beverly is a popular summer resort area. Saltwater fishing, boating, and scuba diving are available near Glover's Wharf.

What to See and Do

Balch House. (17th century) One of the two oldest wood-frame houses in America. Born in 1579, John Balch came to America in 1623 as one of the first permanent settlers of Massachusetts Bay. (Mid-May-mid-Oct, Wed-Sun; closed hols) Inquire about combination ticket (includes Hale and Cabot houses). 448 Cabot St. Phone 978/922-1186. ¢¢

Cabot House. (1781) Headquarters of Beverly Historical Society. Brick mansion of Revolutionary War privateer John Cabot, built a yr after it was written that "the Cabots of Beverly are now said to be by far the most wealthy in New England." Changing exhibits. (Wed-Sat) Inquire about combination ticket (includes Hale and Balch houses). 117 Cabot St. Phone 978/922-1186. ¢¢

Hale House. (1694) Built by the Reverend John Hale, who was active in the witchcraft trials and whose own wife was accused of witchcraft. Rare wallpaper and furnishings show changes through the 18th and 19th centuries. (July-Aug, Sat afternoons; closed hols) Inquire about combination ticket (includes Cabot and Balch houses). 39 Hale St. Phone 978/922-1186. ¢¢

"Le Grand David and His Own Spectacular Magic Company.". Resident stage magic company, New England's longest running theatrical attraction. This 2¼-hr stage magic production features magic, music, comedy, and dance. Five hundred costumes, two dozen sets and backdrops; 50 magic illusions. (Sun) Addl performances at Larcom Theatre (1912), 13 Wallis St. Advance tickets recommended. Cabot Street Cinema Theatre (1920), 286 Cabot St. Phone 978/927-3677. ¢¢¢¢

Wenham Museum. Doll collection representing cultures from 1500 B.C. to present; toy room, dollhouses; changing arts, crafts, and antique exhibits. Claflin-Richards House (ca 1660) containing collections of quilts, costumes, fans; period furniture. Winslow Shoe Shop displays history of shoemaking; early ice-cutting tools; research library. (Tues-Sun; closed hols) 2½ mi N on MA 1A, at 132 Main St in Wenham. Phone 978/468-2377. ¢¢

Special Events

North Shore Music Theatre. 62 Dunham Rd, at MA 128N Exit 19. Broadway musicals and plays; children's musicals; celebrity concerts. (Late Apr-late Dec). For schedule phone 978/922-8500.

Band Concerts. Lynch Park Bandshell Sun eve; downtown Ellis Square, Thurs eve. (Late June-mid-Aug.) Phone 978/774-8565.

Restaurant

★ **BEVERLY DEPOT.** *10 Park St (01915). 978/927-5402. www.barnsiderrestaurants.com.* Specializes in fresh seafood, steak, prime rib. Salad bar. Hrs: 5-10 pm; Fri, Sat to 11 pm; Sun 4-9 pm. Bar. Dinner $9-$22. Child's menu. In 1800s train depot. Cr cds: A, D, DS, MC, V.
D ⌧

Boston

Founded 1630 **Pop** 589,141 **Elev** 0-330 ft **Area code** 617
Information Greater Boston Convention & Visitors Bureau, 2 Copley Pl, Suite 105, 02116; 617/536-4100 or 888/733-2678
Web www.bostonusa.com

Suburbs Braintree, Burlington, Cambridge, Dedham, Framingham, Lexington, Lynn, Newton, Quincy, Saugus, Waltham, Wellesley. (See individual alphabetical listings.)

Greater Boston is a fascinating combination of the old and the new. It consists of 83 cities and towns in an area of 1,057 square miles with a total population of more than three million people. Boston proper is the hub of this busy complex, which many Bostonians still believe is the hub of the universe.

Boston is a haven for walkers; in fact, strolling along its streets is advised to get a true sense of this most European of all American cities. If you drive, a map is invaluable. Traffic is heavy. The streets (many of them narrow and one-way) run at odd angles and expressway traffic speeds.

Boston's wealth of historic sights makes it a must for all who are interested in America's past. John Winthrop and 800 colonists first settled in Charlestown, just north of the Charles River, and moved to Boston in 1630. Arriving too late to plant crops, 200 colonists died during the first winter, mostly of starvation. In the spring, a ship arrived with provisions, and the new Puritan commonwealth began to thrive and grow. Fisheries, fur trapping, lumbering, and trading with Native Americans were the foundation of Boston's commerce. The port is still viable, with 250 wharves along 30 miles of berthing space.

The Revolutionary War began here in 1770. British troops fired on an angry mob, killing five in what has since been called the "Boston Massacre." In 1773, the Boston Tea Party dumped East Indian tea into the bay in a dramatic protest against restriction of colonial trade by British governors. Great Britain closed the port in retaliation. The course of history was set.

In April 1775, British General Thomas Gage decided to march on Concord to capture military supplies and over-whelm the countryside. During the night of April 18-19, Paul Revere, William Dawes, and Samuel Prescott spread the news to Lexington and Concord in a ride immortalized, somewhat inaccurately, by Henry Wadsworth Longfellow. The Revolutionary War had begun in earnest; the Battle of Bunker Hill followed the battles of Lexington and Concord. On March 17, 1776, General William Howe, commander of the British forces, evacuated the city.

Boston's list of distinguished native sons includes John Hancock, Samuel Adams, Paul Revere, Henry Ward Beecher, Edward Everett Hale, Ralph Waldo Emerson, William Lloyd Garrison, Oliver Wendell Holmes (father and son), and hundreds of others.

Mention Boston and many people will automatically think of the gentry of Beacon Hill, with their elegant homes and rigid social code. However, the Irish have long had a powerful influence in Boston's politics and personality, while a stroll through an Italian neighborhood in the North End will be like stepping back to the old country.

Boston today has managed to retain its heritage and charm while thriving in the modern age. Urban renewal and increased construction have reversed an almost 40-year slump that plagued Boston earlier in the 20th century. With more than 100 universities, colleges, and trade and vocational schools in the area, Boston is a city as full of vigor and promise for the future as it is rich with the past.

Additional Visitor Information

Literature and information are available at the Greater Boston Convention & Visitors Bureau, Prudential Tower, PO Box 990468, 02199; 617/536-4100, the Prudential Visitor Center and at the visitor information center on Tremont St, Boston Common (daily; closed Jan 1, Thanksgiving, Dec 25). The National Park Visitor Center (daily) at 15 State St also has helpful information. All have informative brochures with maps of the Freedom Trail and Black History Trail. Bostix, located in Faneuil Hall Marketplace, offers half-price tickets for music, theater, and dance performances on the day of performance; also provides cultural information and calendar of events. (Tues-Sun; closed Thanksgiving, Dec 25) Phone 617/723-5181 (recording).

Transportation

Car Rental Agencies. See IMPORTANT TOLL-FREE NUMBERS.

Public Transportation. Buses, subway, and elevated trains (Massachusetts Bay Transportation Authority), visitor pass available, phone 617/722-3200.

Rail Passenger Service. Amtrak 800/872-7245.

Airport Information

Logan Intl Airport. Information 617/561-1800 or 800/235-6426; lost and found 617/561-1714; weather 617/936-1234; cash machines, Terminals A, B, C.

What to See and Do

The Bible Exhibit. Nondenominational exhibit; audiovisual activities; rare Biblical treasures; historical timeline; large Plexiglass™ wall-map with lighted journeys of six Biblical figures; historic editions; children's story corner; exploring center for reference; film and slide program on the hr. (Wed-Sun; closed Jan 1, Thanksgiving, Dec 25) Belvidere St, opp Prudential Center, in Back Bay. Phone 617/450-3732.

Blue Hills Trailside Museum. Visitor center for the 7,000-acre Blue Hills Reservation. Deer, turkey, otter, snakes, owls, and honeybees. Exhibit hall with natural science/history displays, including Native American wigwam; viewing tower. Activities include hikes, films, animal programs. Special events include maple sugaring (Mar), Hawks Weekend (Sept), and Honey Harvest (Oct). Visitor center and buildings (Wed-Sun; schedule may vary) Phone 617/333-0690. ¢¢

Boston African American National Historic Site. Includes **African Meeting House.** Part of the Museum of Afro-American History. Built by free black Bostonians in 1806, building was an educational and religious center and site of founding of New England Anti-Slavery Society in 1832. (May-Sept, daily; rest of yr, Mon-Sat) Thirty-min tour (Memorial Day-Labor Day, daily; rest of yr, by appt) of Meeting House by museum staff. Smith Ct, off Joy St on Beacon Hill. Phone 617/725-0022. **FREE** Meeting House is starting point for the

Black Heritage Trail. Marked walking tour conducted by National Park Service, past sites in the Beacon Hill section that relate the history of 19th-century black Boston. Brochure and maps are at National Park Visitor Center, 46 Joy St, second floor. Two-hr guided tours by National Park Service (by appt). Phone 617/742-5415. **FREE**

Boston College. (1863) 14,500 students. 140 Commonwealth Ave, Chestnut Hill. On campus is

Bapst Library. English Collegiate Gothic building with fine stained glass. Rare books display; changing exhibits. (Summer, Mon-Fri; rest of yr, daily) Phone 617/552-3200.

Boston Common. A 48-acre tract set aside in 1634 for a cow pasture and training field, and, by law, still available for these purposes. Free speech is honored here, and you may find groups discussing anything from atheism to zoology.

Central Burying Ground. The grave of Gilbert Stuart, the painter, is here; technically not a part of the Common, although in it.

Public Garden. Formal gardens, rare trees carefully labeled. Pond with the famous swan boats in summer and skating in winter (fee).

Boston Harbor Islands National Park Area. Includes 34 islands in Boston Harbor; visitors have access only to ten. Of these, George's Island is the hub, providing water shuttles to other undeveloped islands. George's Island is also popular due to Civil War-era Fort Warren, a National Historic Landmark (guided tours avail). Boston Light, the country's oldest and last manned lighthouse, is on Little Brewster Island, which is reachable by excursion boat. George's Island is open daily; Little Brewster is open to the public on Sat by res only. Camping permitted on selected islands. Phone 617/223-8666.

Boston Massacre Monument. Commemorates this 1770 event, which has been called the origin of the Revolution.

Boston Public Library. (1895) Italian Renaissance building by Charles McKim includes central courtyard and fountain. Mural decorations, bronze doors, sculpture. Contemporary addition (1972), by Philip Johnson, houses large circulating library, recordings, and films. Film and author programs; exhibits. Central Library (Daily; schedule may vary) Phone 617/536-5400.

Boston Tea Party Ship and Museum. Atmosphere of the Boston Tea Party (1773) is re-created. Visitors may board the full-size working replica of the Tea Party Ship and throw tea chests overboard. Exhibits, artifacts, audiovisual presentations place the event in historical perspective; costumed tour guides. Complimentary tea served. (Daily; closed Dec, Jan, and Feb) Congress St Bridge, on Harborwalk. Phone 617/338-1773. ¢¢

Boston University. (1839) 28,000 students. Information center located at 771 Commonwealth Ave in the George Sherman Union. Also located here is the George Sherman Union Gallery. Mugar Memorial Library houses papers of Dr. Martin Luther King, Jr., as well as those of Robert Frost, Isaac Asimov, and other writers and artists. Boston University Art Gallery exhibits at the School for the Arts, 855 Commonwealth Ave. Commonwealth Ave near Kenmore Sq. Campus tours from the Admissions Office, 121 Bay State Rd.

Children's Museum of Boston. Participatory exhibits on science, disabilities; cultural diversity; computers, and games; play activities. (Daily; closed Thanksgiving, Dec 25) 300 Congress St, near South Station, a short walk from Faneuil Hall. Phone 617/426-8855.

Franklin Park Zoo. "Bird's World" indoor/outdoor aviary complex with natural habitats; African tropical forest; hilltop range with camels, antelopes, zebras, mouflon; children's zoo. (Daily; closed Jan 1, Thanksgiving, Dec 25) S on Jamaicaway, E on MA 203 in Dorchester. Phone 617/541-LION. ¢¢

Frederick Law Olmsted National Historic Site. Former home and office of the founder of landscape architecture in America. Site archives contain documentation of firm's work. Site also includes landscaped grounds designed by Olmsted. Guided tours of historic offices. (Fri-Sun) 99 Warren St, in Brookline. Phone 617/566-1689.

⭐ **The Freedom Trail.** A walking tour through downtown Boston that passes 16 points of interest, plus other exhibits, monuments, and shrines just off the trail, some of which are part of **Boston National Historical Park.** The trail is marked by signs and a red sidewalk line. Brochures are at the Greater Boston Convention & Visitors Bureau information centers at the Prudential Plaza (phone 617/536-4100) and on the Boston Common. The Boston National Park Visitor Center (daily) dispenses an excellent free map and offers seasonal guided tours. Phone 617/242-5642.

State House. (1795) Designed by Charles Bulfinch, the nation's first professional architect, it has since had wings added to both sides. Inside are statues, paintings, and other interesting materials. Hall of Flags on second floor; House and Senate Chambers, State Library on third floor. Tours (Mon-Fri; closed hols). Beacon St at head of Park St. Phone 617/727-3676.

Park Street Church. (1809) Often called "Brimstone Corner" because brimstone for gunpowder was stored here during the War of 1812. William Lloyd Garrison delivered his first antislavery address here in 1829. Tours. (July and Aug, limited hrs; Sun services all yr) 1 Park St. Phone 617/523-3383.

Granary Burying Ground. Once the site of the town granary. The graves of John Hancock, Samuel Adams, Paul Revere, Benjamin Franklin's parents, many governors, another signer of the Declaration of Independence, and the martyrs of the Boston Massacre are here. (Daily) Tremont St opp end of Bromfield St.

King's Chapel. (1754) The first Anglican church in Boston (1686) became in 1786 the first Unitarian church in America. Adj is the King's Chapel Burying Ground. Tremont St at School St.

Site of the first US free public school. (1635) It was the Boston Public Latin School. School St opp Old City Hall. Across the street is

Statue of Benjamin Franklin. (1856) by Richard S. Greenough. Continue W on School St to Parker House, a hotel where Ho Chi Minh and Malcolm X once worked as waiters.

Old South Meeting House. (1729) This was the site of many important town meetings about the British, including those that sparked the Boston Tea Party. Multimedia exhibition depicts its 300-yr history. (Daily; closed hols) 310 Washington St. Phone 617/482-6439. ¢¢

Old State House. (1713) Boston's oldest public building, the Old State House served as the seat of the Royal Governor and Colonial Legislature until the Revolution. The Boston Massacre took place outside the building on Mar 5, 1770. From the balcony, the Declaration of Independence was first proclaimed to the citizens of Boston. Houses permanent and changing exhibits related to Boston history (daily; closed Jan 1, Thanksgiving, Dec 25). Reference and photograph library at 15 State St (Tues-Thurs; fee). 206 Washington St, at State St. Phone 617/720-3290. ¢¢¢

Site of the Boston Massacre. Marked by a circle of cobblestones in the pavement. 30 State St.

Faneuil Hall Marketplace. Bostonian Peter Faneuil bequeathed this two-story, bronze-domed building to the city in 1742 as a public meeting hall and marketplace. Called the "Cradle of Liberty" because it was the scene of mass meetings during the pre-Revolutionary period, the building and two other restored structures today house a bustling marketplace of more than 100 specialty shops, 20 restaurants and pubs, and a variety of pushcarts and food stalls. Marketplace (Daily). Adj is a military museum—the Ancient and Honorable Artillery Company Museum, chartered in 1638 as a school for officers. (Daily; closed hols) Merchants Row. Phone 617/242-5675 or 617/242-5642.

Paul Revere House. (ca 1680) The only 17th-century structure that is left in downtown Boston. It was from this house that the silversmith left for his historic ride on Apr 18, 1775. The interior features 17th- and 18th-century decorative arts and contains Revere artifacts and memorabilia. (Apr-Dec, daily; rest of yr, Tues-Sun; closed Jan 1,Thanksgiving, Dec 25) 19 North Sq. Phone 617/523-2338.

Old North Church. (1723) The oldest church building in Boston. From the steeple's highest window were hung two lanterns, to warn the militia in Lexington. (Daily; closed Thanksgiving, Dec 25) Also Sun services. 193 Salem St at foot of Hull St. Phone 617/523-6676.

Copp's Hill Burying Ground. First burials date from 1660. During the Revolution, British cannon here were trained on Charlestown and Bunker Hill, across the Charles River. Reverend Cotton Mather and Edmund Hart, builder of the US frigate *Constitution,* are buried here. (Daily) Hull and Snow Hill Sts.

Bunker Hill Monument. A 221-ft granite obelisk commemorates the Battle of Bunker Hill, which took place on June 17, 1775. Ranger-conducted battle talks (June-Oct, on the hr); musket firing demonstrations (late-June-Labor Day, Fri-Sun). Spiral staircase (294 steps) to top of monument, no elevator. Four sides viewing Boston area. (Daily; closed Jan 1, Thanksgiving, Dec 25) Monument Sq, Charlestown, a few blks from the *Constitution.* Phone 617/242-5641.

USS Constitution. "Old Ironsides," launched in 1797, was engaged in more than 40 battles without defeat. Oldest commissioned Navy ship afloat in world. Twenty-min tours. Museum with ship artifacts is adj. (Daily) Located in Charlestown Navy Yard, Boston National Historical Park. I-93: northbound, exit 25 and follow signs across Charlestown bridge; southbound, exit 28 to Sullivan Sq and follow signs. Phone 617/426-1812.

Gibson House Museum. Victorian townhouse with period furnishings. Tours (May-Oct, Wed-Sun afternoons; Nov-Apr, Sat and Sun; closed hols). 137 Beacon St. Phone 617/267-6338.

Guided Walking Tours. Boston by Foot. Ninety-min architectural walking tours includes the heart of Freedom Trail (daily); Beacon Hill (daily, departures vary); Victorian

Back Bay Tour (Fri-Sun); North End (Fri and Sat); children's tour (daily); downtown Boston (Sun). All tours (May-Oct). Tour of the month each fourth Sun; custom tours. Contact 77 N Washington St, 02114. Hull and Snow Hill Sts. ¢¢¢

Guild of Boston Artists. Changing exhibits of paintings, graphics, and sculpture by New England artists. (Sept-July, Tues-Sat; closed Jan 1, Thanksgiving, Dec 25) 162 Newbury St. Phone 617/536-7660. **FREE**

Harborwalk. Blue line guides visitors from Old State House to New England Aquarium, ending at the Boston Tea Party Ship and Museum, forming a walking tour with many stops in between.

Harrison Gray Otis House. (1796) Otis, a lawyer and statesman, built this first of three houses designed for him by Charles Bulfinch. A later move to Beacon Hill left this house as a rooming house for 100 yrs. Restored to reflect Boston taste and decoration of 1796-1820. Some family furnishings. Reflects the proportion and delicate detail Bulfinch introduced to Boston, strongly influencing the Federal style in New England. Museum. Headquarters for the Society for the Preservation of New England Antiquities; send stamped, self-addressed legal-size envelope to Society for guide to 22 historic homes (02114). Tours (Wed-Sun). 141 Cambridge St, enter from Lynde St. Phone 617/227-3956. ¢

Harvard Medical Area. One of the world's great centers of medicine. Huntington and Longwood Aves. Phone 617/432-1000.

Institute of Contemporary Art. Occupies a 19th-century Richardsonian-style building once used as a police station. Exhibits of contemporary art: painting, sculpture, video, and photography. Gallery talk (selected Thurs eves). Also film, video, music, dance, poetry, lectures, and performance art in the ICA Theater. Gallery (Wed-Sun). Bookstore (daily). Free admission Thurs eve. 955 Boylston St opp Prudential Center. Phone 617/266-5152. ¢¢¢

Isaac Royall House. (1637) Originally built as a four-rm farmhouse by John Winthrop, first governor of Bay State Colony; enlarged in 1732 by Isaac Royall. Example of early Georgian architecture; examples of Queen Anne, Chippendale, and Hepplewhite furnishings. (May-Sept, Wed-Sun) ¾ mi S off I-93, at 15 George St in Medford. Phone 781/396-9032. ¢

Isabella Stewart Gardner Museum. The home of this patron of the arts from 1902 until her death in 1924. Paintings, sculpture, and a flower display are in the enormous Venetian-style central courtyard, surrounded by three floors of galleries (Tues-Sun; closed hols). Concerts (late Sept-May, Sat and Sun afternoons; fees). 280 The Fenway. Phone 617/734-1359. ¢¢¢

John F. Kennedy National Historic Site. The birthplace and early childhood home of the nation's 35th president is restored in appearance to 1917, the yr of his birth. Ranger-guided tours. (Apr-Nov, Wed-Sun; closed Jan 1, Thanksgiving, Dec 25) Golden Eagle Passport accepted (see MAKING THE MOST OF YOUR TRIP). 83 Beals St, in Brookline. Phone 617/566-7937. ¢¢

John Hancock Observatory. The observatory, considered the best place to see Boston, is located on the 60th floor of the John Hancock Tower. It offers a panoramic view of Boston and eastern Massachusetts and exciting multimedia exhibits of Boston, past and present. They include "Boston 1775," a sound and light show about Boston since revolutionary days; a taped narration by the late Walter Muir Whitehill, architectural historian; and a lighted display of New England scenes. In addition, "Aviation Radio" allows visitors to tune in on the cross-talk between planes at Logan International's tower while viewing the action at the airport. (Daily; closed Thanksgiving, Dec 25) At Copley Sq. Phone 617/572-6429. ¢¢

Louisburg Square. This lovely little residential square with its central park is the ultimate in traditional Boston charm. Louisa May Alcott, William Dean Howells, and other famous Bostonians have lived here. It is one of the most treasured spots in Boston. Christmas caroling is traditional here.

The Mother Church, the First Church of Christ, Scientist. Tours. (Daily; closed hols) Christian Science Center, Huntington and Massachusetts Aves. Phone 617/450-3793. Adj is

> **Christian Science Publishing Society.** *(The Christian Science Monitor)* Inquire about tours. Mapparium, a walk-through stained-glass globe, is here. Call ahead. Massachusetts Ave at Clearway St. Phone 617/450-3793.

☒ **Museum at the John Fitzgerald Kennedy Library.** Designed by I. M. Pei, the library is considered one of the most beautiful contemporary works of architecture in the country. The library tower houses a collection of documents from the Kennedy administration as well as audiovisual programs designed to re-create the era. (Daily, closed Jan 1, Thanksgiving, Dec 25) Picnic facilities on oceanfront. 5 mi SE on I-93, off exit 15, at University of Massachusetts Columbia Point campus. Phone 617/929-4500. ¢¢

Museum of Fine Arts. Chinese, Japanese, Indian, Egyptian, Greek, Roman, European, and American collections; also silver, period rms, and musical instruments. Gallery lectures, films; library; children's programs; changing exhibits; restaurants; auditorium. (Daily; closed Thanksgiving, Dec 25) Free admission late afternoon-eve. 465 Huntington Ave. Phone 617/267-9300. ¢¢¢

Museum of Science. One of the finest and most modern science museums in the world, with many hands-on exhibits. "Seeing the Unseen," giant dinosaur model; "Human Body Discovery Space," health and environment displays; live animal, physical science, and special effects demonstrations. Children's Discovery Room. Omnimax Theatre (fee). (Daily; closed Thanksgiving, Dec 25) Science Park, on Charles River Dam Bridge between Storrow Dr and Memorial Dr. Advance tickets recommended. Phone 617/723-2500. Also here is

> **Charles Hayden Planetarium.** Shows approx 50 min. (Same hrs as museum) Children under four yrs not admitted. Phone 617/523-6664. ¢¢

New England Aquarium. One of the largest cylindrical saltwater tanks in the world, stocked with hundreds of specimens of marine life. Permanent exhibits include marine mammals, birds, and reptiles. Freshwater gallery, marine life in American rivers, including exotic animals

from the Amazon Basin area. Electric eel, turtles, and a 4,000-gallon replica of an Amazon rain forest. Adj is *The Discovery,* a barge where sea lion demonstrations are presented. (Daily; closed morning of Jan 1, Thanksgiving, Dec 25) Whale watches (mid-Apr-mid-Oct; fee; phone 973/520-0617. ¢¢¢

Nichols House Museum. (1804) Typical domestic architecture of Beacon Hill from its era; one of two homes on Beacon Hill open to the public. Attributed to Charles Bulfinch; antique furnishings and art from America, Europe, and the Orient from the 17th to early 19th centuries. Collection of Rose Standish Nichols, landscape designer and writer. (Tues-Sat afternoons) 55 Mt Vernon St. Phone 617/227-6993. ¢

Professional Sports. 4 Yawkey Way.

> **Boston Bruins (NHL).** Fleet Center, One Fleet Center Pl. Phone 617/624-1750.

> **Boston Celtics (NBA).** Fleet Center, 1 Fleet Center Pl. Phone 617/523-6050.

> **Boston Red Sox (MLB).** Fenway Park, 4 Yawkey Way. Phone 617/267-9440.

Prudential Center. Complex of retail, civic, business, residential buildings on 32-acre site in Back Bay. Prudential Tower rises 52 stories (750 ft); restaurant. The Skywalk, an observation deck on the 50th floor, provides a 360° panoramic view and has temporary exhibits and displays. (Daily) 800 Boylston St, off MA Tpke. Phone 617/859-0648.

Shirley-Eustis House. (1747) Built for royal governor William Shirley, restored to Federal-style of period when Governor William Eustis lived here (1818-1825). (June-Sept, Thurs-Sun afternoons) 33 Shirley St. Phone 617/442-2275.

Shopping. Boston has many good department and specialty stores, grouped on downtown Washington and Tremont Sts and connecting streets. Wm Filene's Sons Company and Jordan Marsh are both excellent. Filene's Basement is famous and particularly fascinating for bargain-hunters. The Back Bay area, particularly on Newbury St, is also a shopper's haven, with numerous boutiques, art galleries, and antique shops. Haymarket Sq in the North End is an open-air farmers market good for shopping and photographing (Fri, Sat). Copley Place offers shoppers more than 100 stores among its retail, office, hotel, and residential complex. Many wharves in the waterfront area now house shops and galleries.

Sightseeing Tours.

> **Bay State Cruise Company.** All-day sail to Provincetown and Cape Cod from Commonwealth Pier. 2½- and 3½-hr harbor and island cruises aboard *Spirit of Boston,* highlighting adventure and history. (Mid-June-Labor Day, daily; May-mid-June and after Labor Day-Columbus Day, Sat and Sun only) Contact Bay State Cruise Company, Commonwealth Pier, World Trade Center. Phone 617/748-1428. ¢¢¢¢

> **Boston Tours from Suburban Hotels.** Escorted bus tours departing from suburban hotels and motels along I-95/MA 128. Also departures from metrowest suburban hotels in Natick/Framingham area. Tours follow Freedom Trail and include stops at Old North Church,

"Old Ironsides," Faneuil Hall Marketplace and Cambridge. 6-hr tour (daily). 56 Williams St, in Waltham. For reservations, schedule and fee information Phone 781/899-1454. ¢¢¢¢

Brush Hill Tours. Fully lectured three-hr bus tours of Boston/Cambridge (Late Mar-mid-Nov); ½-day tours of Lexington/Concord, Salem/Marblehead (mid-June-Oct), and Plymouth (May-Oct); full-day tours of Cape Cod (includes Provincetown) and Newport, RI (June-Sept). Also 1½-hr tours along Freedom Trail aboard the Beantown Trolleys. Departures from major downtown hotels, Copley Sq, and Boston Common (daily). ¢¢¢¢

Symphony Hall. Home of Boston Symphony (late Sept-early May) and Boston Pops (May-mid-July, Tues-Sun). Huntington and Massachusetts Aves. Phone 617/266-1492.

Trinity Church. (1877) Episcopal. This Henry Hobson Richardson building, the inspiration of Phillips Brooks, was the noblest work of the architect. The interior was decorated by John LaFarge and has five of his windows as well as two by William Morris of England. Phillips Brooks, the ninth rector of Trinity Church, is known for his beautiful Christmas carol, "O Little Town of Bethlehem." His statue, by Augustus Saint Gaudens, stands outside the North Transept of the Church. Daniel Chester French created Brooks bust in the Baptistry. Phillips Brooks preached at Trinity Church for 22 yrs. Theodore Parker Ferris, one of the outstanding preachers of the 20th century, was the 15th rector of Trinity Church and preached here for 30 yrs. Phone 617/536-0944. ¢¢

"Whites of Their Eyes". Specially designed pavilion houses multimedia reenactment of the Battle of Bunker Hill using life-size figures and eyewitness narratives. Audience "viewpoint" from atop Breed's Hill. Continuous 30-min shows. (Apr-Nov, daily; closed Thanksgiving) Bunker Hill Pavilion, 55 Constitution Rd, just W of the USS *Constitution* in Charlestown. Phone 617/241-7575.

Special Events

Boston Marathon. Famous 26-mi footrace from Hopkinton to Boston. Apr. Phone 508/435-6905.

Patriots Day Celebration. Third Mon Apr. Phone 617/536-4100.

Bunker Hill Day. Mid-June. Phone 617/536-4100.

Harborfest. Hatch Shell on the Esplanade. Boston Pops Orchestra, fireworks. Jun 28-July 4. Phone 617/227-1528.

Esplanade Concerts. Musical programs by the Boston Pops in the Hatch Shell on the Esplanade. Two wks July. Phone 888/733-2678.

Charles River Regatta. Third Sun Oct. Phone 888/733-2678.

First Night Celebration. Boston Common. Dec 31. Phone 617/536-4100.

Motels/Motor Lodges

★★ **BEST WESTERN.** *342 Longwood Ave (02115). 617/731-4700; fax 617/731-6273; res 800/780-7234. www.bestwestern.com.* 160 rms, 8 story. S $139-$209; D $139-$219; each addl $15; kits. $249; under 18 free. Crib free. Covered parking $14. TV; cable (premium). Restaurant 6:30-1 am. Bar. Ck-out noon. Meeting rms. In-rm modem link. Shopping arcade. Health club privileges. Cr cds: A, C, D, DS, ER, JCB, MC, V.

D ⊠ 🔥

★★ **HOLIDAY INN AT LOGAN.** *225 McClellan Hwy (02128). 617/569-5250; fax 617/569-5159; toll-free 800/798-5849. www.holiday-inn.com.* 356 rms, 12 story. S $119-$209; D $129-$219; each addl $10; under 18 free; lower rates off season. Crib free. TV; cable (premium). Pool. Coffee in rms. Restaurant 6-11:30 am, 5-10 pm. Bar 11-2 am. Ck-out 11 am. Meeting rms. Business servs avail. In-rm modem link. Gift shop. Free airport transportation. Exercise equipt. Microwaves avail. Cr cds: A, C, D, DS, JCB, MC, V.

D ⊷ 🛪 ✈ ⊠ 🔥 SC

★★ **HOLIDAY INN SELECT BOSTON.** *5 Blossom St (02114). 617/742-7630; fax 617/742-4192; res 800/465-4329. www.holiday-inn.com.* 303 rms, 2 suites, 14 story. Apr-Nov: S, D $199-$259; each addl $20; under 19 free; wkend rates; higher rates graduation wkends; lower rates rest of yr. Crib free. Garage $20. TV; cable (premium). Pool. Restaurant 6 am-11 pm. Bar. Ck-out noon. Coin lndry. Meeting rms. Business servs avail. In-rm modem link. Valet serv. Exercise equipt. Health club privileges. Overlooks Charles River. Luxury level. Cr cds: A, D, DS, MC, V.

D ⊷ 🛪 ⊠ 🔥

★★ **RAMADA INN.** *800 Morrissey Blvd (02122). 617/287-9100; fax 617/265-9287; toll-free 800/886-0056. www.ramada.com.* 177 rms, 2-5 story. S, D $105-$159; each addl $5; under 18 free. Crib $3. TV; cable (premium). Pool; lifeguard. Restaurant adj 6:30 am-10:30 pm. Ck-out 11 am. Coin lndry. Meeting rms. Business servs avail. In-rm modem link. Gift shop. Health club privileges. Game rm. Refrigerators, microwaves avail. Cr cds: A, C, D, DS, MC, V.

D ⊷ ⊠ 🔥

Hotels

★★★★ **BOSTON HARBOR HOTEL.** *Rowes Wharf (02110). 617/439-7000; fax 617/345-6799; toll-free 800/752-7077. www.bhh.com.* This hotel affords lovely views of the harbor. All 230 rooms housed behind the well-recognized "grand arch" facade are elegantly furnished to reflect historic Boston with interesting artwork and marble bathrooms. An exceptional antique chart collection is displayed off the lobby, which also hosts the fine Rowes Wharf restaurant. 230 rms, 16 story, 26 suites. S, D $275-$425; each addl $50; suites $475-$1,800; under 18 free; wkend rates. Crib free. Pet accepted. Garage parking, valet $20 wkend, $28 wkday; self-park $15 wkend, $24 wkday. TV; cable (premium), VCR avail. Indoor pool; whirlpool, poolside serv. Restaurants (see also ROWES WHARF). Rm serv 24 hrs. Bar 11:30-1 am. Ck-out 1 pm. Meeting rms. Business center. In-rm modem link. Concierge. Exercise rm; sauna, steam rm. Extensive spa. Bathrm phones; minibars; microwaves avail. Some rooms recently renovated. Cancel 24 hrs in advance. Cr cds: A, C, D, DS, MC, V.

D ⟲ 🏋 ⊷ 🛪 ⊠ 🔥 🏃

★★ **THE BOSTON PARK PLAZA HOTEL.** *64 Arlington St (02116). 617/426-2000; fax 617/426-5545; toll-free 800/225-2008. www.bostonparkplaza.com.* 950 rms, 15 story. S $189-$269; D $209-$289; each addl $20; suites $375-$1,500. Crib $10. Garage $23; valet. TV; cable (premium). Pool privileges. Restaurant 6:30 am-midnight. Bar 11-1:30 am. Ck-out noon. Convention facilities. Business center. In-rm modem link. Concierge. Shopping arcade. Barber, beauty shop. Exercise equipt. Health club privileges. Refrigerators. Cr cds: A, D, DS, MC, V.

★★★ **THE COLONNADE HOTEL.** *120 Huntington Ave (02116). 617/424-7000; fax 617/424-1717; toll-free 800/962-3030. www.colonnadehotel.com.* 285 rms, 11 story. Sept-mid-Nov: S, D $199-$425; suites $700-$1,400; under 12 free; wkly, wkend and hol rates; higher rates: marathon, graduation; lower rates rest of yr. Crib free. Pet accepted, some restrictions. Parking $22. TV; cable (premium), VCR avail. Pool (in season); poolside serv. Supervised children's activities (May-Sept); ages 8-13. Restaurant 6:30-1 am. Rm serv 24 hrs. Bar. Ck-out noon. Convention facilities. Business center. In-rm modem link. Concierge. Exercise equipt. Minibars; refrigerators avail. Cr cds: C, D, DS, MC, V.

★★ **COPLEY INN.** *19 Garrison St (02116). 617/236-0300; fax 617/536-0816; toll-free 800/232-0306. www.copleyinn.com.* 21 kit. units, 4 with shower only, 4 story. May-Dec: S, D $85-$135; each addl $10; wkly rates; lower rates rest of yr. Crib free. TV; cable. Restaurant nearby. Ck-out 11 am, ck-in 9 am-8 pm. Brownstone built in 1880s. Cr cds: A, MC, V.

★★ **COPLEY SQUARE.** *47 Huntington Ave (02116). 617/536-9000; fax 617/267-3547; toll-free 800/225-7062. www.copleysquarehotel.com.* 143 rms, 7 story. S, D $195-$285; each addl $20; suites $299-$345; under 17 free. Crib free. Garage $20. TV; cable (premium). Complimentary coffee in rms. Restaurants 7 am-11 pm. Bar 11:30-2 am. Ck-out noon. Meeting rms. Business servs avail. In-rm modem link. Concierge. Family-owned hotel; established 1891. Cr cds: A, C, D, DS, ER, MC, V.

★★★ **THE ELIOT HOTEL.** *370 Commonwealth Ave (02215). 617/267-1607; fax 617/536-9114. www.eliothotel.com.* 95 suites, 9 story. S $255-$395; D $275-$415; 2 bedrm $550-$670; each addl $20; under 18 free. Crib free. Pet accepted, some restrictions. Valet parking $22. TV; cable (premium), VCR avail (movies). Restaurant (see also CLIO). Ck-out noon, ck-in 3 pm. Private dining rms. Business center. In-rm modem link; fax machines. Concierge. Health club privileges. Private pantry with minibars. Some balconies. Cr cds: A, D, MC, V.

★★★ **THE FAIRMONT COPLEY PLAZA BOSTON.** *138 St. James Ave (02116). 617/267-5300; fax 617/247-6681; toll-free 800/527-4727. www.fairmont.com.* 379 rms, 7 story, 54 suites. S, D $259-$479; each addl $30; suites $379-$1,500; under 18 free; package plans. Crib free. Pet accepted, some restrictions. Valet parking $29. TV; cable (premium), VCR avail. Restaurants (see also THE OAK ROOM). Rm serv 24 hrs. Bars 11:30-2 am; pianist. Ck-out noon. Meeting rms. Business center. In-rm modem link. Concierge. Shopping arcade. Barber, beauty shop. Exercise equipt. Cr cds: A, C, D, DS, MC.

★★★★★ **FOUR SEASONS HOTEL BOSTON.** *200 Boylston St (02116). 617/338-4400; fax 617/423-0154; res 800/332-3442.* There are 274 guestrooms and 72 suites in this luxurious hotel overlooking the Public Garden and Beacon Hill; even the 45-foot indoor pool has a spectacular view. Dine on renowned cuisine at Aujourd'hui or listen to evening jazz in the Bristol Lounge. For special events, guests can book one of eight function rooms, including a magnificent ballroom perched above the garden. 274 rms, 15 story. S, D $465-$605; each addl $40; suites $605-$3,500; under 18 free; wkend rates. Crib free. Pet accepted, some restrictions. Valet, garage parking $27. TV; cable (premium), VCR avail (movies). Indoor pool; whirlpool, poolside serv. Restaurants 6:30-11:30 pm; Sat to 12:30 am (see also AUJOURD'HUI and BRISTOL LOUNGE). Rm serv 24 hrs. Bar 11-2 am; entertainment. Ck-out 1 pm. Ck-in 3 pm. Convention facilities. Business center. In-rm modem link; 2-line phones. Concierge. Gift shop. Exercise rm; sauna. Massage. Overnight valet lndry, 1-hr pressing. Bathrm phones. Minibars. Cr cds: A, D, DS, MC, V.

★★ **HARBORSIDE INN.** *185 State St (02109). 617/723-7500; fax 617/670-2010. www.hagopianhotels.com.* 54 rms, 8 story, 2 suites. Mar-Oct: S, D $200; suites $330; each addl $15; under 18 free; lower rates rest of yr. Parking garage. TV; cable (premium). Complimentary continental bkfst. Restaurant 6 am-1 pm. Bar. Ck-out noon, ck-in 3 pm. Concierge serv. Valet serv. Exercise equipt. Golf, 18 holes. Cr cds: A, D, DS, MC, V.

★★★ **HILTON BACK BAY.** *40 Dalton St (02115). 617/236-1100; fax 617/867-6104; res 800/774-1500. www.hilton.com.* 385 rms, 26 story. S, D $109-$429; each addl $20; suites $450-$1,000; family rates; package plans. Pet accepted, some restrictions. Garage $17. TV; cable (premium). Indoor pool. Restaurant 7 am-midnight. Bar 5:30 pm-12:30 am. Ck-out noon. Convention facilities. Business center. In-rm modem link. Gift shop. Exercise equipt. Some balconies. Cr cds: A, C, D, DS, ER, JCB, MC, V.

★★★ **HILTON LOGAN AIRPORT.** *85 Terminal Rd (02128). 617/569-9300; fax 617/568-6800; res 800/445-8667. www.hilton.com.* 599 rms, 4 suites, 14 story. S $129-$195; D $149-$245; each addl $20; suites $400; family, wkend rates. Crib free. Pet accepted, some restrictions. TV; cable (premium). Pool; poolside serv, lifeguard. Coffee in rms. Restaurant 5:30 am-10:30 pm. Bar 11-2 am. Ck-out 11 am. Convention facilities. Business center. In-rm modem link. Concierge. Free airport transportation. Exercise equipt. Many minibars. Cr cds: A, C, D, DS, ER, MC, V.

★★★ **HYATT HARBORSIDE CONFERENCE CENTER AND HOTEL.** *101 Harborside Dr (02128). 617/568-1234; fax 617/567-8856; toll-free 800/233-1234. www.hyatt.com.* 270 rms, 11 suites, 14 story. S $230-$410; D $255-$435; suites $895. Crib free. TV; cable, VCR avail. Indoor pool; whirlpool. Coffee in rms. Restaurant 6 am-11 pm. Bar. Ck-out noon. Conference facilities. Business center. In-rm modem link. Free airport transportation. Exercise equipt; sauna. Refrigerator in suites. Adj to water shuttle. Cr cds: A, C, D, DS, ER, JCB, MC, V.

★★★★ **LE MERIDIEN BOSTON.** *250 Franklin St (02110). 617/451-1900; fax 617/423-2844; res 800/791-7781. www.lemeridienboston.com.* This sophisticated downtown business hotel feels like an elegant Boston home. The beautiful public spaces (the ceiling in the bar is spectacular) and the fine antiques and reproductions speak to a Boston of another time. Although the rooms are small, they are nicely appointed. An indoor pool and fitness center is outfitted with aerobics equipment. The main restaurant, Julien, is a gem of a place, and the more casual Fleurie, in the atrium, is light and airy, perfect for lunch. 326 rms, 9 story. S, D $310-$395; each addl $25; suites $400-$790; under 12 free; wkend rates. Crib free. Pet accepted, some restrictions. Valet parking $30. TV; cable (premium), VCR avail. Pool. Restaurants 7 am-10 pm (see also CAFE FLEURI and JULIEN). Rm serv 24 hrs. Bar 5 pm-1 am; pianist. Ck-out 1 pm. Meeting rms. Business center. In-rm modem link. Concierge. Exercise rm; sauna. Massage. Bathrm phones, minibars, refrigerators. Renaissance Revival bldg. Cr cds: A, C, D, DS, MC, V.

★★★ **LENOX.** *710 Boylston St (02116). 617/536-5300; fax 617/267-1237; toll-free 800/225-7676. www.lenoxhotel.com.* 212 rms, 11 story. S, D $308; each addl $20; suites $500; under 18 free. Crib free. TV; cable, VCR avail. Restaurant (see also ANAGO). Bars 11:30-1:30 am. Ck-out noon. Meeting rms. Business servs avail. In-rm modem link. Valet serv. Concierge. Airport transportation. Exercise equipt. Many decorative and wood-burning fireplaces. Cr cds: A, C, D, DS, ER, JCB, MC, V.

★★★ **MARRIOTT COPLEY PLACE BOSTON.** *110 Huntington Ave (02116). 617/236-5800; fax 617/236-5885; toll-free 800/228-9290. www.marriott.com/marriott/bosco.* 1,147 rms, 38 story. S, D $149-$349; suites $400-$1,200; under 18 free; wkend rates. Crib free. Valet parking $24. TV; cable (premium), VCR avail (movies). Pool; whirlpool. Restaurant 6:30-1 am. Rm serv 24 hrs. Bar 11:30-2 am; entertainment. Ck-out noon. Convention facilities. Business center. In-rm modem link. Concierge. Shopping arcade. Exercise rm; sauna. Massage therapy. Game rm. Luxury level. Cr cds: A, C, D, DS, JCB, M C , V.

★★ **MARRIOTT LONG WHARF BOSTON.** *296 State St (02109). 617/227-0800; fax 617/227-2867; toll-free 800/228-9290. www.marriott.com.* 400 rms, 7 story, 8 suites. S, D $249-$365; suites $375-$1,200; under 18 free; wkend rates. Crib free. Valet parking $27. TV; cable (premium), VCR avail (movies). Indoor pool; whirlpool; poolside serv. Coffee in rms. Restaurant 6:30-2 am. Ck-out noon. Coin lndry. Convention facilities. Business center. In-rm modem link. Gift shop. Exercise equipt; sauna. Luxury level. Cr cds: A, D, DS, MC, V.

★★★ **MARRIOTT PEABODY BOSTON.** *8A Centennial Dr, Peabody (01960). 978/977-9700; toll-free 800/228-9290. www.marriott.com.* 256 rms, 6 story. S, D $175-$275; under 18 free. Crib avail. TV; cable (premium). Indoor pool; whirlpool. Restaurant 6:30 am-10 pm. Bar to midnight. Ck-out noon, ck-in 4 pm. Meeting rms. Business center. In-rm modem link. Concierge. Exercise equipt. Minibars; many refrigerators in suites. Cr cds: A, C, D, DS, ER, JCB, MC, V.

★★★ **MILLENNIUM BOSTONIAN HOTEL.** *Faneuil Hall Marketplace (02109). 617/523-3600; fax 617/523-2454; res 800/222-8888. www.millennium-hotels.com/boston.* 201 rms, 7 story. S, D $245-$345; each addl $20; suites $450-$625; under 18 free; wkend rates. Crib free. Valet parking $24. TV; cable (premium), VCR avail. Complimentary coffee in lobby. Restaurant (see also SEASONS). Rm serv 24 hrs. Bar 2 pm-1 am; entertainment Tues-Sat. Ck-out 3 pm. Meeting rms. Business center. In-rm modem link. Concierge. Tennis privileges. Exercise equipt. Health club privileges. Bathrm phones, minibars; some in-rm whirlpools, fireplaces. Many balconies. 1 blk to harbor. Cr cds: A, DS, MC, V.

★★★ **OMNI PARKER HOUSE.** *60 School St (02108). 617/227-8600; fax 617/742-5729; toll-free 800/843-6664. www.omnihotels.com.* 551 rms, 14 story. June, early Sept-mid-Nov: S, D $109-$205; suites $199-$225; under 18 free; wkend rates; lower rates rest of yr. Crib free. Garage $24. TV; cable (premium), VCR avail. Restaurant (see also PARKER'S) Bar 6:30 am-midnight; entertainment exc Sun. Ck-out noon. Convention facilities. Business servs avail. In-rm modem link. Concierge. Gift shop. Health club privileges. Oldest continuously-operating hotel in the US. Cr cds: A, D, DS, MC, V.

★★ **RADISSON.** *200 Stuart St (02116). 617/482-1800; fax 617/451-2750; res 800/333-3333. www.radisson.com/ bostonma.* 356 rms, 24 story. S, D $128-$325; each addl $20; suites $230-$350; under 18 free. Crib free. Valet parking $5. TV; cable (premium). Indoor pool. Restaurant 6:30 am-10 pm; dining rm 11:30 am-11 pm, Sun noon-10 pm. Bar. Ck-out noon. Business servs avail. In-rm modem link. Gift shop. Exercise equipt. Cr cds: A, C, D, DS, ER, JCB, MC, V.

★★★★ **THE RITZ-CARLTON, BOSTON.** *15 Arlington St (02117). 617/536-5700; fax 617/536-9340; res 800/241-3333. www.ritzcarlton.com.* Boasting a great location in the heart of old Boston, this hotel's rooms have pristine views of the Public Garden, Beacon Hill, or the Charles River and are within walking distance of historic sites, shopping, and the Financial District. French Provincial furnishings and evening piano music are good examples of the property's old-style grandeur. Service is genuine and continually attentive. 275 rms, 42 suites, 17 story. S, D, suites $435-$725; presidential suite $2,500; each addl $20; under 12 free. Crib free. Pet accepted, some restrictions, $30. TV; cable. Restaurants 6:30 am-midnight. Rm serv 24 hrs. Concierge. Barber. Airport transportation avail. Exercise equipt; sauna. Bathrm phones. Cr cds: A, DS, MC, V.

★★★★ **THE RITZ-CARLTON, BOSTON COMMON.** *10 Avery St (02111). 617/574-7100; fax 617/574-7200; toll-free 800/241-3333. www.ritzcarlton.com.* Located between the Financial and Theatre districts, this contemporary destination overlooks Boston Common, the oldest park in the US, and is adjacent to The Sports Club/LA, the ultimate urban country club. If fine art is more your speed, set aside time to view the property's $1 million original art collection. 193 rms, 4 floors, 63 suites. S, D $495-$695; suites $695-$4,000; package plans. Valet parking. Pet accepted. TV; cable (premium). Restaurant Sun-Thurs 7 am-3 pm, 5:30-10 pm; Fri, Sat 7 am-3 pm, 5:30-11 pm. Rm serv 24 hrs. Bar 3 pm-1 am; Sat 11-1 am; Sun noon-midnight. Ck-out noon. Meeting rms. Business center. In-rm modem link. Valet serv. Health club privileges. Massage avail. Concierge. $1 million original art collection. City views. Luxury level. Cr crds: A, D, DS, JCB, MC, V.

★★★ **SEAPORT HOTEL.** *1 Seaport Ln (02210). 617/385-4500; fax 617/385-4001; toll-free 877/732-7678.* 426 rms, 1 suite, 18 story. S $240-$315; D $265-$340; each addl $25; suites $500-$1,500; under 12 free; package plans. Pet accepted, some restrictions. Valet parking $22; garage parking $18. TV; cable (premium), VCR avail. Complimentary coffee in rms. Restaurant 6:30-11 am, 11:30 am-2 pm, 5:30-11 pm. Bar 11-1 am. Ck-out 1 pm. Convention facilities. Business center. In-rm modem link. Concierge. Gift shop. Exercise rm; sauna. Massage. Indoor pool. Bathrm phones, minibars; refrigerators, microwaves, wet bars avail. On harbor. Luxury level. Totally nonsmoking. Cr cds: A, C, D, DS, MC, V.

★★★ **SHERATON BOSTON HOTEL.** *39 Dalton St (02199). 617/236-2000; fax 617/236-1702; res 800/325-3535. www.sheraton.com.* 1,215 rms, 29 story. S, D $189-$479; each addl $20; suites from $260; under 18 free; wkend rates. Crib free. Pet accepted. Garage $23; valet $24. TV; cable (premium). Indoor/outdoor pool; whirlpool. Coffee in rms. Restaurant 6:30-1:30 am. Bars 11:30-2 am; entertainment. Rm serv 24 hrs. Ck-out noon. Convention facilities. Business center. In-rm modem link. Gift shop. Exercise equipt. Luxury level. Cr cds: A, DS, JCB, MC, V.

★★★ **SWISSOTEL BOSTON.** *1 Ave de Lafayette (02111). 617/451-2600; fax 617/451-0054; toll-free 800/621-9200. www.swissotel.com.* 500 rms, 26 suites, 22 story. S, D $329-$379; each addl $25; under 16 free; wkend rates. Crib free. Pet accepted, some restrictions. Garage $24, valet parking $28. TV; cable (premium), VCR avail (movies). Indoor pool. Restaurant 7 am-11 pm. Rm serv 24 hrs. Bar 4 pm-1 am; entertainment. Ck-out noon. Convention facilities. Business center. In-rm modem link. Concierge. Gift shop. Exercise equipt; sauna. Health club privileges. Luxury level. Cr cds: A, C, D, DS, MC, V.

★★★ **THE TREMONT BOSTON- A WYNDHAM HISTORIC HOTEL.** *275 Tremont St (02116). 617/426-1400; fax 617/482-6730; res 800/996-3426. www.wyndham.com.* 322 rms, 15 story. S, D $144-$250; each addl $10; under 18 free; wkend rates. Crib free. Valet parking $24. TV; cable (premium), VCR. Coffee in rms. Restaurant 6:30 am-11:30 pm. Bar noon-midnight; entertainment Thurs-Sun. Ck-out noon. Convention facilities. Business center. In-rm modem link. Concierge. Gift shop. Exercise equipt. Luxury level. Cr cds: A, MC, V.

★★★ **WESTIN COPLEY PLACE HOTEL.** *10 Huntington Ave (02116). 617/262-9600; fax 617/424-7483; res 888/625-5144. www.westin.com.* 800 rms, 36 story. S $189-$280; D $219-$310; each addl $25; suites $400-$1,500; under 18 free. Crib free. Pet accepted, some restrictions. TV; cable (premium). Indoor pool; whirlpool. Coffee in rms. Restaurants (see also PALM and TURNER FISHERIES). Rm serv 24 hrs. Entertainment. Ck-out noon. Convention facilities. Business center. In-rm modem link. Concierge. Barber. Valet parking $24. Airport transportation. Exercise equipt; sauna. Health club privileges. Minibars. Copley Place shopping gallery across skybridge. Luxury level. Cr cds: A, D, DS, MC, V.

★★★ **WYNDHAM CHELSEA.** *201 Everett Ave (02150). 617/884-2900; fax 617/884-7888.* 180 rms, 7 story. S, D $250-$375; under 18 free. Crib avail. TV; cable (premium). Indoor pool; whirlpool. Restaurant 6:30 am-10 pm. Bar to midnight. Ck-out noon, ck-in 4 pm. Meeting rms. Business center. In-rm modem link. Concierge. Exercise equipt. Minibars; many refrigerators in suites. Cr cds: A, C, D, DS, MC, V.

★★★★ **XV BEACON.** *15 Beacon St (02108). 617/670-1500; fax 617/670-2525; res 877/982-3226. www.xvbeacon.com.* This elegant boutique hotel features a young and enthusiastic staff. Guest rooms offer highly stylized decor with a mix of contemporary and classic furnishings. The unparalleled services available to guests include cellular phones, personalized business cards, and complimentary in-town chauffeured Mercedes car service. 61 rms, 10 story. Apr-Dec: S $395-$795; lower rates rest of yr. Crib avail. Valet parking avail. TV; cable (premium), VCR avail, CD avail. Complimentary full bkfst, newspaper. Restaurant. 24-hr rm serv. Bar. Ck-out noon, ck-in 3 pm. Meeting rm. Business servs avail. Bellhops. Concierge. Valet serv. Health club privileges. Cr cds: A, C, D, DS, MC, V.

B&Bs/Small Inns

★★★ **CHARLES STREET INN.** *94 Charles St (02114). 617/314-8900; fax 617/371-0009; toll-free 877/772-8900. www.charlesstreetinn.com.* 9 rms, 5 story. May-Oct: S, D $220-$340; each addl $50; lower rates rest of yr. Parking garage. TV; cable, VCR avail, CD avail. Complimentary continental bkfst, coffee in rms. Restaurant nearby. Ck-out 11 am, ck-in 3 pm. Business servs avail. Concierge. Valet serv. Health club privileges. Golf, 18 holes. Tennis, 2 courts. Cr cds: A, D, DS, MC, V.

★★ **NEWBURY GUEST HOUSE.** *261 Newbury St (02116). 617/437-7666; fax 617/262-4243. www.hagopianhotels.com.* 32 rms, 4 story. Mar-Dec: S $85-$130; D $95-$140; each addl $10; under 3 free; higher rates: marathon, graduations. Parking $15. TV; cable. Complimentary continental bkfst. Ck-out noon, ck-in 3 pm. Sitting rm. Built 1882. Cr cds: A, DS, MC, V.

All Suite

★★★ **DOUBLETREE SUITES.** *400 Soldiers Field Rd (02134). 617/783-0090; fax 617/783-0897; res 800/222-8733. www.doubletree.com.* 308 suites, 16 story. S, D $149-$289; each addl $20; under 18 free; wkend packages. Crib free. TV; cable (premium). Indoor pool; whirlpool. Complimentary coffee in rms. Restaurant 6:30 am-10 pm. Bar 11:30-12:45 am; entertainment Wed-Sat. Ck-out noon. Coin lndry. Convention facilities. Business center. In-rm modem link. Concierge. Exercise equipt; sauna. Game rm. Bathrm phones, refrigerators, minibars; some microwaves. Some private patios, balconies. On river. Cr cds: A, C, D, DS, ER, JCB, MC, V.

Restaurants

★★★ **AMBROSIA ON HUNTINGTON.** *116 Huntington Ave (02116). 617/247-2400. www.ambrosiaonhuntington.com.* French menu with Asian influence. Specialties: St. Pierre fish imported from France, grilled meats, sushi. Hrs: 11:30 am-2 pm, 5:30-10 pm; Fri to 10:30 pm; Sat 5-11 pm; Sun 5-9 pm. Closed some major hols. Lunch $8-$17, dinner $16-$37. Valet parking $7 (dinner). Spacious and elegant atmosphere. Cr cds: A, D, DS, MC, V.

★★ **ANTHONY'S PIER 4.** *140 Northern Ave (02210). 617/482-6262. www.pier4.com.* Specializes in smoked salmon, lobster, bouillabaisse. Hrs: noon-11 pm; Sun to 10 pm. Closed Dec 25. Res accepted. Bar. Lunch $9.95-$26.95, dinner $13.95-$26.95. Parking. Outdoor dining. Nautical decor; view of city and Boston Harbor. Jacket in main dining rm. Family-owned. Cr cds: A, D, DS, MC, V.

★★★ **AQUITAINE.** *569 Tremont St (02118). 617/424-8577. www.aquitaineboston.com.* Specializes in steak frittes, duck ravioli. Hrs: 5:30-10 pm; Thurs, Fri to 11 pm; Sat, Sun 10 am-11 pm. Closed major hols. Res accepted. Wine, beer. Dinner $18-$29. Brunch $8.95-$12.95. Cr cds: A, D, MC, V.

★★★★ **AUJOURD'HUI.** *200 Boylston St (02116). 617/338-4400. www.fourseasons.com.* Although nominally a French restaurant, this landmark in the Four Seasons Hotel serves New American cuisine with French and Asian highlights. Appetizers include Beluga caviar, veal sweetbreads, and duck prosciutto. For the main course, diners can either order a la carte (lobster, grouper, lamb, beef tenderloin, etc.) or opt for one of several awe-inspiring tasting menus. Menu changes seasonally. Own baking. Hrs: 6:30 am-2:30 pm, 5:30-10:30 pm; Sat 7 am-noon, 5:30-10:30 pm; Sun 7-11 am, 6-10:30 pm; Sun brunch 11:30 am-2 pm. Res accepted. Bar. Wine cellar. A la carte entrees: bkfst $15-$20, lunch $27-$32, dinner $60-$100. Cr cds: A, C, D, DS, ER, MC, V.

★★★ **BAY TOWER.** *60 State St (02109). 617/723-1666. www.baytower.com.* Specializes in rack of lamb, sauteed Maine lobster, creative French cuisine with a touch of global fusion. Hrs: 5:30-9:45 pm; Fri to 10:30 pm; Sat to 10:15 pm. Closed Sun; Dec 25. Res accepted. Bar 4:30 pm-1 am; Fri, Sat to 2 am. Dinner $28-$36. Entertainment. Valet parking Fri, Sat. Harbor view. Parking. Cr cds: A, D, DS, MC, V.

★★ **BOB THE CHEF'S.** *604 Columbus Ave (02118). 617/536-6204. www.bobthechefs.com.* Creole/Cajun menu. Specialties: chicken and ribs combo, Creole jambalaya, mustard-fried catfish. Hrs: 11:30 am-10 pm; Wed-Fri to midnight; Sat 11 am-midnight; Sun 11 am-10 pm; Sun brunch to 3:30 pm. Closed Mon; some major hols. Bar. Dinner $8.95-$13.95. Sun brunch $12.95. Jazz Thurs, Fri evening, Sun brunch. Bistro decor; intimate dining. Totally nonsmoking. Cr cds: A, DS, MC, V.

★★★ **BRASSERIE JO.** *120 Huntington Ave (02116). 617/425-3240. www.colonnadehotel.com.* Specializes in parisian steak frites, lobster bouillabaisse. Hrs: 6:30 am-11 pm, Sat 7 am-11 pm. Res accepted. Wine list. Lunch $8-$15, dinner $16-$25. Child's menu. Casual, lively atmosphere. Cr cds: A, C, D, DS, MC, V.

★★★ **BRISTOL LOUNGE.** *200 Boylston St (02116). 617/338-4400. www.fourseasons.com.* Contemporary Amer menu. Specializes in tapas, seasonal dishes. Own baking. Hrs: 11-1 am; Fri, Sat to 2 am; Sun 10 am-midnight; Sun brunch to 2 pm. Res accepted. Bar. Lunch $16-$26, dinner $26-$39. Sun brunch $35. Pianist, jazz duo. Valet parking. Art Deco decor with large windows overlooking Boston Gardens and flowered terrace. Cr cds: A, D, DS, MC, V.

★★ **BROWN SUGAR CAFE.** *129 Jersey St (02215). 617/266-2928. www.brownsugarcafe.com.* Thai menu. Specialties: fisherman madness, mango curry, pad Thai country-style. Hrs: 11 am-3 pm, 4-10 pm; Fri, Sat to 11 pm. Closed Jan 1, July 4, Thanksgiving. Res accepted. Bar. Lunch $5.50-$7, dinner $8-$13. Parking. Outdoor dining. Thai decor. Totally nonsmoking. Cr cds: D, DS, MC, V.
D

★★★ **CAFE FLEURI.** *250 Franklin St (02110). 617/451-1900. www.lemeridienboston.com.* French, Amer menu. Specialties: roasted Cornish hen, swordfish stir-fry, Boston clam chowder. Hrs: 7 am-10 pm; Sat, Sun from 7:30 am; Sun brunch 11 am-4 pm. Res accepted. Bar 11 am-10 pm. Bkfst $10.25-$17.95, lunch $15-$22, dinner $20-$25. Sun brunch $42. Child's menu. Jazz Sun. Valet parking. Totally nonsmoking. Cr cds: A, D, MC, V.
D

★★★ **CAFE LOUIS.** *234 Berkley St (02116). 617/266-4680. www.louisboston.com.* Traditionally influenced Italian menu. Specializes in local seafood. Hrs: 11:30 am-3 pm, 5-10 pm. Closed Sun; most major hols. Beer. Wine cellar. A la carte entrees: lunch $9-$17, dinner $16-$32. Complete meals: dinner $59. Jazz in summer. Free valet parking. Outdoor dining. Contemporary café. Totally nonsmoking. Cr cds: A, MC, V.
D

★ **CAFE MARLIAVE.** *10 Bosworth St (02108). 617/423-6340.* Italian menu. Specializes in fresh seafood, beef. Hrs: 11 am-10 pm. Closed some major hols. Res accepted. Bar. Lunch $5-$10.50, dinner $9-$22. Parking. Original artwork. Cr cds: A, D, DS, MC, V.

★★★ **THE CAPITAL GRILLE.** *359 Newbury St (02115). 617/262-8900. www.thecapitalgrille.com.* Steakhouse menu. Specialties: dry-aged 24-oz Porterhouse steak, broiled lobster, shrimp scampi. Hrs: 5-10 pm; Thurs-Sat to 11 pm. Closed July 4. Res accepted. Bar from 4 pm. Wine cellar. A la carte entrees: dinner $18-$32. Valet parking. Cr cds: A, D, DS, MC, V.
D

★★ **CASA ROMERO.** *30 Gloucester St (02115). 617/536-4341. www.casaromero.com.* Mexican menu. Specialties: marinated pork tenderloin, giant shrimp in cilantro and tomatillos. Hrs: 5-10 pm; Fri, Sat to 11 pm. Closed Jan 1, July 4, Dec 25. Res accepted. Serv bar. Dinner $12-$19.50. Outdoor dining. Authentic Mexican decor. Family-owned. Totally nonsmoking. Cr cds: DS, MC, V.
D

★ **CHARLEY'S.** *284 Newbury St (02115). 617/266-3000. www.great-food.com.* Specializes in fresh seafood, baby-back ribs, steaks. Hrs: 11:30 am-11 pm; Fri, Sat 11 am-midnight. Res accepted. Bar 11:30-2 am. Lunch $5.99-$10.99, dinner $8.99-$22.95. Child's menu. Outdoor dining. Renovated Victorian school. Cr cds: A, D, DS, MC, V.
D

★★ **CIAO BELLA.** *240A Newbury St (02116). 617/536-2626. www.ciaobella.com.* Hrs: 11:30 am-11 pm; Thurs-Sat to 11:45 pm; Sun brunch to 3:30 pm. Closed Thanksgiving, Dec 25. Res accepted. Italian menu. Bar. A la carte entrees: lunch $6.50-$14.95, dinner $8.95-$33.95. Sun brunch $4.95-$11.50. Specializes in veal chops, swordfish chops, seafood. Valet parking (Tues-Sat evening). Outdoor dining. European decor. Cr cds: A, D, DS, MC, V.

★ **CLAREMONT CAFE.** *535 Columbus Ave (02118). 617/247-9001. www.claremontcafe.com.* Continental menu. Specializes in herb-roasted chicken, seafood, tapas. Hrs: 7:30 am-3 pm, 5:30-10 pm; Fri to 10:30 pm; Sat 8 am-10:30 pm; Sun 9 am-3 pm (brunch). Closed Mon; major hols. Bkfst $3.50-$9.95, lunch $4.95-$9.95, dinner $12.95-$21.95. Sun brunch $6.50-$10.95. Valet parking. Outdoor dining. Corner café with artwork by local artists. Totally nonsmoking. Cr cds: A, MC, V.
D

★★★★ **CLIO.** *370A Commonwealth Ave (02215). 617/536-7200. www.cliorestaurant.com.* Housed in Back Bay's Eliot Hotel, this clubby, intimate dining room offers dramatically prepared French-American cuisine in an atmosphere of leopard carpets, chocolate walls, and plush sofa seating. Although portions are tiny, flavors are ultra-creative, and the tasting menu provides a convenient way to sample chef Ken Oringer's over-the-top dishes. Morning hours are making the restaurant a popular power-breakfast hangout. Specialties: seared dayboat scallops, carmelized swordfish au poivre, aromatic glazed short ribs. Hrs: 6:30-10:30 am, 5:30-10 pm; Fri 5:30-10:30 pm; Sat 7-11 am; Sun 7 am-2 pm, 5:30-10 pm; Sun extended bkfst 11:30 am-2 pm. Res accepted. Bar to 1 am. Full wine list and liquor shelf. A la carte entrees: bkfst $3-$16, dinner $22-$34. Sun brunch $8-$16. Valet parking. Parisian-style supper club. Cr cds: A, C, D, DS, MC, V.

★★ **DAVIDE.** *326 Commercial St (02109). 617/227-5745. www.davideristorante.com.* Northern Italian menu. Specialties: potato gnocchi, veal chop with fontina and prosciutto. Own pasta, ice cream. Hrs: 5-10 pm; Fri, Sat to 11 pm. Bar. A la carte entrees: dinner $14-$28. Valet parking. Cr cds: A, DS, MC, V.

★★ **DAVIO'S.** *269 Newbury St (02116). 617/262-4810. www.davios.com.* Northern Italian menu. Specializes in veal chops, homemade pasta, pizza. Hrs: 11:30 am-10:30 pm; Fri, Sat to 11 pm; Sun to 10 pm. Closed Thanksgiving, Dec 25. Res accepted. Bar. Lunch $3.95-$12.95, dinner $3.95-$26.95. Child's menu. Valet parking (dinner). Outdoor dining. Cr cds: A, D, DS, MC, V.

★★★ **THE DINING ROOM.** *15 Arlington St (02117). 617/536-5700. www.ritzcarlton.com.* Regional menu. Hrs: 5:30-10 pm; Fri, Sat to 10 pm; Sun brunch 10:45 am-2:30 pm. Closed Mon. Res accepted; required wkends. Wine cellar. Complete meals: 3-course dinner $61, 4-course dinner $69, 5-course dinner $75. A la carte entrees. Sun brunch $46. Child's menu. Pianist. Valet parking. Jacket. Cr cds: A, C, D, DS, MC, V.
D

★ **DURGIN PARK.** *340 Faneuil Hall Marketplace (02109). 617/227-2038.* Specializes in prime rib, Indian pudding, strawberry shortcake. Own soups. Hrs: 11:30 am-10 pm; Sun to 9 pm. Closed Dec 25. Bar to 2 am; entertainment. A la carte entrees: lunch $4.95-$16.95, dinner $5.95-$16.95. Near Faneuil Hall. Established 1826. Cr cds: A, D, DS, MC, V.

D ⊟

★★★ **THE FEDERALIST.** *15 Beacon St (02108). 617/670-2515. www.xvbeacon.com.* Seafood menu. Specializes in red abolone, sirloin steak. Hrs: 7 am-10 pm; Fri, Sat to 10:30 pm. Res accepted. Wine list. Bkfst, lunch $9-$13; dinner $34-$45. 18th century decor. Cr cds: A, C, D, DS, ER, JCB, MC, V.

D ⊟

★★ **FILIPPO.** *283 Causeway St (02114). 617/742-4143.* Italian menu. Specialty: cappello del Contadino. Hrs: 11:30 am-10:30 pm; Sun from noon. Closed Thanksgiving, Dec 25. Res accepted. Bar. Wine list. Lunch $5.50-$8.50, dinner $12.95-$28.50. Child's menu. Valet parking (dinner). Italian decor with large murals. Cr cds: A, MC, V.

D ⊟

★★ **GINZA.** *16 Hudson St (02111). 617/338-2261. www.bostondine.com.* Japanese menu. Specializes in maki special, sushi. Hrs: 11:30 am-2:30 pm; 5 pm-4 am; Sat 11:30 am-4 pm, 5 pm-4 am; Mon, Sun 11:30 am-4 pm, 5 pm-2 am. Res accepted. Wine, beer. Lunch $7.50-$11.75, dinner $12.50-$38.50. Upscale Japanese dining with sushi bar. Cr cds: A, D, MC, V.

D

★ **GRAND CHAU-CHOWS.** *45 Beach St (02111). 617/292-5166.* Hrs: 10-3 am; Fri, Sat to 4 am. Res accepted. Wine, beer. Lunch $4.25-$4.95; dinner $4.95-$19.95. Entertainment. Cr cds: A, DS, MC, V.

D

★★★★ **GRILL 23 & BAR.** *161 Berkeley St (02116). 617/542-2255. www.grill23.com.* The grand space of this 5,000-square-foot restaurant alone will thrill visitors with its Corinthian columns, sensual lighting, rich mahogany, and vaulted ceilings. The food is also engaging, focusing on prime dry-aged beef and creatively prepared seafood incorporating fresh fruits and vegetables. The restaurant is housed in the historic 75-year-old Salada Tea Building. Specializes in aged beef, New England seafood. Menu changes wkly. Hrs: 5:30-10:30 pm; Fri, Sat to 11 pm; Sun to 10:30 pm. Closed hols. Res accepted. Bar from 4:30 pm. A la carte entrees: $22-$40. Valet parking. Open kitchen. 1920s decor. New York-style steakhouse, fast-paced atmosphere. Cr cds: A, D, DS, MC, V.

D ⊟

★★★★ **HAMERSLEY'S BISTRO.** *553 Tremont St (02116). 617/423-2700. www.hamersleysbistro.com.* Nationally recognized chef Gordon Hamersley creates a seasonally changing menu and a pleasant blending of France and New England at his namesake bistro. The dining room is at once classy and comfortable with cozy banquettes, soft yellow walls, and an open kitchen. The menu manages this same great balance with the deliciously simple specialty roast chicken with garlic, lemon, and parsley. French, American menu. Specialties: crispy duck confit, imported Dover sole, pan-roasted lobster. Hrs: 6-10 pm; Sat, Sun 5:30-10:30 pm. Closed hols. Bar. A la carte entrees: dinner $23-$36. Valet parking. Outdoor dining. Totally nonsmoking. Cr cds: A, D, DS, MC, V.

D

★★ **THE HUNGRY I.** *71-1/2 Charles St (02114). 617/227-3524.* French country menu. Specialties: pate maison, venison au poivre. Hrs: 6-9:30 pm; Fri, Sat to 10 pm; Sat, Sun brunch 11 am-2 pm. Closed July 4, Thanksgiving, Dec 25. Res accepted. Serv bar. A la carte entrees: dinner $20-$30. Sun brunch $30. Patio dining Sun brunch only. 1840s house in historic district. Fireplaces. Cr cds: A, C, D, MC, V.

★★★ **ICARUS.** *3 Appleton St (02116). 617/426-1790. www.icarusrestaurant.com.* Specialties: grilled shrimp with mango and jalapeño sorbet, seared duck breast, game. Hrs: 6-10 pm; Fri, Sat to 11 pm. Closed most major hols. Res accepted; required wkends. Bar from 5:30 pm. Dinner $21-$34. Prix fixe: $39. Sun brunch $7-$12. Valet parking. Jazz Fri evening. Converted 1860s building. Cr cds: A, D, DS, MC, V.

★★ **JAE'S CAFE AND GRILL.** *212 Stuart St (02116). 617/451-7722.* Hrs: 11:30 am-4 pm, 5-10:30 pm; Fri, Sat to 1 am; Sun noon-10 pm. Pan-Asian menu. Bar. Lunch $8.95-$9.95, dinner $7.95-$15.95. Specialties: sushi, pad Thai, okdol bibim bab. Street parking. Totally nonsmoking. Cr cds: A, D, DS, MC, V.

D

★★ **JIMMY'S HARBORSIDE.** *242 Northern Ave (02210). 617/423-1000. www.jimmysharborside.com.* Specializes in shrimp, lobster, broiled fish. Hrs: noon-9:30 pm; Fri, Sat to 10 pm; Sun 4-9 pm. Closed Dec 25. Res accepted. Bar. A la carte entrees: lunch $9-$22, dinner $10-$32. Child's menu. Valet parking. Nautical decor. Family-owned. Cr cds: A, D, DS, MC, V.

D

★★★ **JULIEN.** *250 Franklin St (02110). 617/451-1900. www.lemeridienboston.com.* French, English menu. Specializes in seafood, lamb, breast of duck. Own baking. Hrs: noon-2 pm, 6-10 pm; Sat 6-10:30 pm; hrs vary July-Aug. Closed Sun; wk of July 4. Res accepted. Bar 5 pm-midnight. Wine list. A la carte entrees: lunch $14.50-$18.50, dinner $26-$40. Complete meals: lunch $25. Prix fixe: dinner $62. Pianist. Valet parking. Elegant surroundings; high carved-wood ceilings, crystal chandeliers. Former Federal Reserve Bank Bldg. Jacket. Cr cds: A, D, DS, MC, V.

★★ **KASHMIR.** *279 Newbury St (02116). 617/536-1695. www.kashmir.com.* Indian menu. Specialties: tandoori tikki dal, tandoori duck kadahi, tandoori seafood masala. Hrs: 11 am-11 pm; Sun to 3 pm. Res accepted. Beer, wine. Buffet: lunch $8.95. A la carte entrees: dinner $12.95-$19.95. Complete meals: dinner $14.95-$39.95. Child's menu. Valet parking. Outdoor dining. Indian artifacts and decor. Jacket evenings. Cr cds: A, D, MC, V.

★★ **LALA ROKH.** *97 Mt Vernon St (02108). 617/720-5511. www.lalarokh.com.* Persian menu. Specializes in authentic Persian dishes. Own baking. Hrs: 5:30-10 pm. Closed some major hols. Res accepted. Wine. Dinner $14-$17. Several dining areas with authentic decor; Iranian art. Cr cds: A, D, DS, MC, V.
Ⓓ

★★★★ **L'ESPALIER.** *30 Gloucester St (02115). 617/262-3023. www.lespalier.com.* Ingredients from local farms and the sea are expertly prepared at this New England-French restaurant housed in an 1886 Back Bay townhouse. The restaurant opened in 1978 and current chef/owner Frank McClelland and his wife, Catherine, took over ten years later. An excellent prix fixe, or more extensive degustation menu, is offered in the main room, salon, or wood-wrapped library. Contemporary French menu. Specialties: grilled beef short ribs with black bean mango salsa, ragout of day-boat wolf fish, pan-roasted free-range chicken in tamarind orange glaze with radishes. Own baking. Hrs: 6-10 pm. Closed Sun; most major hols. Res accepted. Cr cds: A, C, D, DS, MC, V.
Ⓓ

★★★ **LES ZYGOMATES.** *129 South St (02111). 617/542-5108. www.winebar.com.* French Bistro menu. Specializes in steak au poive, scallops. Hrs: 11:30 am-10:30 pm; Fri, Sat to 11:30 pm. Closed Sun. Res accepted. Wine, beer. Lunch $9-$14; dinner $14-$22. Entertainment: jazz. In Old Leather District. Cr cds: A, D, DS, MC, V.
⊟

★★★ **LOCKE OBER.** *3 Winter Pl (02108). 617/542-1340. www.lockeobercom.* Continental menu. Specializes in Wiener schnitzel, baked lobster Savannah. Hrs: 11:30 am-2:30 pm; Fri, Sat 5:30-10:30 pm. Closed Sun; major hols. Bar. Lunch $11.50-$20, dinner $22.75-$55. Built in 1875. Old World atmosphere. Jacket. Cr cds: A, D, DS, MC, V.
⊟

★★★ **LUCIA.** *415 Hanover St (02113). 617/523-9148.* Hrs: 4-11 pm; Fri-Sun from 11:30 am. Closed Thanksgiving, Dec 25. Res accepted. Regional Italian menu. Bar. Wine list. Lunch $4-$10, dinner $8.95-$17. Child's menu. Specializes in linguini with seafood, homemade pasta, grilled veal chops. Valet parking (dinner). Painted frescoes on walls and ceilings. Cr cds: A, MC, V.

★★★ **MAISON ROBERT.** *45 School St (02108). 617/227-3370. www.maisonrobert.com.* French menu. Specializes in rack of lamb, fresh seafood. Hrs: 11:30 am-2:30 pm, 5:30-10 pm; wkend hrs vary. Closed some major hols. Res accepted. Bar. Lunch $9-$22, dinner $17-$32. Valet parking. Outdoor dining in courtyard of former city hall. Jacket. Cr cds: A, D, MC, V.
Ⓓ

★★★ **MAMMA MARIA.** *3 North Sq (02113). 617/523-0077. www.mammamaria.com.* Italian menu. Menu changes seasonally. Hrs: 5-10 pm; Fri, Sat to 11 pm. Closed most major hols. Res accepted. Bar. A la carte entrees: dinner $18-$28. Valet parking. Private dining rms. Overlooks historic area; Paul Revere house across square. Cr cds: A, D, DS, MC, V.
Ⓓ

★★ **MARCUCCIO'S.** *125 Salem St (02113). 617/723-1807.* Italian menu. Specialties: sea bass with parsley sauce, calamari with black olive-balsamic sauce, seared scallops with marjoram-walnut pesto. Hrs: 5-10 pm; Fri, Sat to 11 pm. Closed some major hols. Res accepted. Wine list. Dinner $16-$22. Complete meals: dinner $55-$65. Child's menu. Street parking. Totally nonsmoking. Cr cds: MC, V.
Ⓓ

★★ **METROPOLIS CAFE.** *584 Tremont St (02118). 617/247-2931.* Eclectic Amer menu. Specialties: corn soup, sage and lavender roasted lamb, warm chocolate pudding cake with vanilla ice cream. Own pasta. Hrs: 5:30-10 pm; Thurs-Sat to 11 pm; Sat, Sun brunch 9 am-3 pm. Closed Jan 1, Thanksgiving, Dec 25. Res accepted. Bar. Wine list. Dinner $12.95-$18.95. Sat, Sun brunch $3.95-$6.95. Valet parking. Bistro decor with high ceilings, brass tables. Totally nonsmoking. Cr cds: A, MC, V.
Ⓓ

★★★ **MISTRAL.** *223 Columbus Ave (02116). 617/867-9300. www.mistralbistro.com.* Hrs: 5:30-10:45 pm; Thurs-Sat to 11:30 pm. Closed Thanksgiving, Dec 25. Res accepted. French, Mediterranean menu. Bar to midnight. Dinner $13-$42. Specialties: grilled portobello mushrooms, steamed black mussels, confit of duck and foie gras in brioche. Valet parking. Mediterranean garden atmosphere. Cr cds: A, D, DS, MC, V.
Ⓓ

★★ **MORTON'S OF CHICAGO.** *1 Exeter Plz (02116). 617/266-5858. www.mortons.com.* Hrs: 5:30-11 pm; Sun 5-10 pm. Closed major hols. Res accepted. Bar. A la carte entrees: dinner $18.95-$29.95. Specializes in prime dry-aged beef, fresh seafood. Valet parking. Menu recited. Cr cds: A, D, MC, V.
Ⓓ

★★★★ **NO. 9 PARK.** *9 Park St (02108). 617/742-9991.* Chef Barbara Lynch creates French- and Italian-influenced American fusion cuisine at this "in-crowd" hot spot on the Boston Common. Flavors are intense and assertive, and the cafe and two dining rooms have a noise level to match, heightened by the hard-surfaced terrazzo flooring and dark wood. Beaded lamps and black and white historical photos of the area decorate the otherwise minimalist space. French, Italian cuisine. Hrs: 11:30 am-2:30 pm; 5:30-11 pm. Closed Sun; hols. Dinner $26-$35. Cr cds: D, DS, MC, V.
Ⓓ

★★★ **THE OAK ROOM.** *138 St James Ave (02116). 617/267-5300. www.fairmont.com.* Specializes in steak, seafood. Own baking. Hrs: 5:30-10 pm; Fri, Sat to 11 pm. Res accepted. Bar 4:30 pm-1 am. A la carte entrees: dinner $18.95-$39.95. Complete meals: dinner $38-$68. Valet parking. Turn-of-the-century decor with carved moldings, crystal chandeliers. Cr cds: A, D, DS, MC, V.
Ⓓ

★★★ **OLIVES.** *10 City Sq, Charlestown (02129). 617/242-1999.* Hrs: 5:30-10:15 pm; Sat 5-10:30 pm. Closed Sun; major hols. Country Mediterranean menu. Bar. Wine list. Dinner $15.95-$28.95. Specialty: spit-roasted herb and garlic chicken. Own baking, pasta. Valet parking. Rustic European decor; large windows overlook square. Cr cds: A, C, D, MC, V.

D

★★ **PALM.** *200 Dartmouth St (02116). 617/867-9292. www.thepalm.com.* Hrs: 11:30 am-10:30 pm; Sat 5-11 pm; Sun 5-9:30 pm. Closed some major hols. Res accepted. Bar. A la carte entrees: lunch $8-$16, dinner $14-$32. Complete meals: lunch $10-$30, dinner $30-$50. Specializes in steak, lobster, Italian dishes. Own baking. Valet parking. Caricatures of regular clientele on walls. Family-owned since 1926. Cr cds: A, D, DS, MC, V.

D

★★★ **PARKER'S.** *60 School St (02108). 617/227-8600.* Hrs: 6:30 am-2 pm, 5:30-11 pm; Sat, Sun from 7 am. Res accepted. Eclectic, continental menu. Bar 11-1 am. Bkfst $8-$10, lunch $10-$15, dinner $20-$30. Child's menu. Specialties: Boston scrod, Boston cream pie. Salad bar. Piano (night). Valet parking. Cr cds: A, D, DS, MC, V.

D

★★ **PLAZA III KANSAS CITY STEAK.** *101 S Market Bldg (02109). 617/720-5570. www.plazathree.com.* Hrs: 11 am-10 pm; Thurs-Sat to 11 pm; Sun from 10 am. Res accepted. Serv bar. A la carte entrees: lunch, dinner $7.50-$28.50. Specializes in steaks, prime rib, fresh seafood. Outdoor dining. Cr cds: A, D, DS, MC, V.

D

★★★★ **RADIUS.** *8 High St (02108). 617/426-1234.* Chef Michael Schlow's Financial District haunt presents contemporary French fare that most people have a difficult time criticizing, although they certainly pay for that privilege. Foie gras, gnocchi, and scallops are among the delicious options. The sleek modern design matches the creative food. Specialties: seared Maine scallops, Australian farm-raised loin of lamb, saffron-scented New Zealand langoustines. Hrs: 11 am-2:30 pm, 5:30-10 pm, Fri to 11 pm; Sat 5:30-11 pm. Lunch $8-$19, dinner $21-$37. Res accepted. Bar. Private dining room; semi-private dining, tasting table. Valet parking (dinner). Cr cds: D, MC, V.

D

★★ **RISTORANTE TOSCANO.** *47 Charles St (02114). 617/723-4090.* Northern Italian menu. Specializes in veal, fish, pasta. Hrs: 11:30 am-2:30 pm, 5:30-10 pm; Fri, Sat to 10:30 pm; Sun 11:30 am-3 pm, 5-9 pm. Closed some major hols. Res accepted. Bar. A la carte entrees: lunch $9-$20, dinner $18-$30. Valet parking (dinner). Authentic Italian decor. Cr cds: A, MC, V.

D

★★★ **SAGE.** *69 Prince St. (02113). 617/248-8814. www.northendboston.com/sage.* Menu changes monthly. Hrs: 5:30-10:30 pm. Closed Sun. Dinner $16-$25. Cr cds: A, D, DS, MC, V.

D

★★★ **SEASONS.** *Faneuil Hall Market Place (02109). 617/523-3600.* Hrs: 6:30-10:30 am, 11:30 am-2 pm, 6-10 pm; Sat 7 am-noon, 6-11 pm; Sun 7 am-noon. Res accepted. Contemporary Amer menu. Bar. Extensive wine list. Bkfst $8-$16, lunch $10-$24, dinner $26-$37. Child's menu. Specializes in roast duckling, seasonal dishes. Own baking, pasta. Valet parking. Rooftop restaurant overlooks Faneuil Hall and city. Cr cds: A, D, DS, MC, V.

D

★★ **TAPEO.** *266 Newbury St (02116). 617/267-4799. www.tapeo.com.* Hrs: 5:30-10:30 pm; Thurs-Sat to 11 pm; Sun noon-10:30 pm. Closed Thanksgiving, Dec 24, 25. Res accepted. Spanish menu. Bar from 5 pm. A la carte entrees: lunch $2.50-$7.50, dinner $17-$22. Specializes in tapas, paellas. Valet parking. Outdoor dining. Spanish decor; handpainted tile tapas bar, fireplaces. Cr cds: A, D, MC, V.

D

★★ **TERRAMIA.** *98 Salem St (02113). 617/523-3112.* Hrs: 5-10 pm; Fri to 10:30 pm; Sat 4-10:30 pm; Sun 1-10 pm. Closed some major hols. Res accepted. Italian menu. Wine, beer. Dinner $10.50-$27. Child's menu. Specialties: Maine lobster fritter, open-face seafood ravioli, roasted pork tenderloin in spicy prune sauce. Street parking. Totally nonsmoking. Cr cds: A, D, DS, MC, V.

D

★★★ **TOP OF THE HUB.** *800 Boylston St (02199). 617/536-1775.* Hrs: 11:30 am-2:30 pm, 5:30-10 pm; Fri, Sat to 11 pm; Sun brunch 10 am-2:30 pm. Closed Dec 25. Res accepted. Bar. Wine list. A la carte entrees: lunch $6-$15, dinner $18-$30. Various jazz groups daily. Panoramic view of Charles River and downtown Boston. Cr cds: A, C, D, DS, MC, V.

D

★★★ **TORCH.** *26 Charles St (02114). 617/723-5939. www.bostontorch.com.* Specializes in hanger seared steak, seared foie gras with green apple and juniper. Hrs: Tues-Sun 5-10 pm. Brunch Sat-Sun 10 am-3 pm. Closed Mon. Res recommended. Beer, wine. Dinner $17-$26. Casual. Chef-owned. Cr cds: A, D, DS, ER, JCB, MC, V.

D

★ **TRATTORIA IL PANINO.** *120 S Market (02109). 617/573-9700. www.ilpanino.citysearch.com.* Hrs: 11 am-11 pm. Closed Dec 25. Res accepted. Italian menu. Bar. Lunch $7.95-$13.95, dinner $10.95-$23.95. Specialties: zuppe de pesce, il panino sandwich, lobster ravioli. Jazz, blues Thurs-Sat. Street parking. Outdoor dining. Cr cds: A, D, DS, MC, V.

D

★★ **TRUC.** *560 Tremont (02118). 617/338-8070.* Hrs: 6-10 pm; Fri, Sat to 10:30 pm; Sun (brunch) 11 am-2 pm, 6-9 pm. Closed Mon; some major hols. Res accepted. French menu. Wine, beer. Dinner $21-$26. Sun brunch $8-$12. Specializes in country French cuisine. Valet parking. Totally nonsmoking. Cr cds: DS, MC, V.

★★ **TURNER FISHERIES.** *10 Huntington Ave (02116). 617/424-7425. www.westin.com.* Hrs: 11 am-10:30 pm; Sun brunch 10:30 am-2 pm. Res accepted. Seafood menu. Bar.

Lunch $9-$15, dinner $17-$27. Sun brunch $28.50. Child's menu. Specialties: clam chowder, crab cakes, Oriental bamboo steamer basket. Jazz Tues-Sat. Valet parking. Cr cds: A, D, DS, MC, V.

D

★★ **THE VAULT.** *105 Water St (02109). 617/292-9966.* Hrs: 11:30 am-2:30 pm, 5:30-11:30 pm; Sat 5:30-11:30 pm. Closed Sun; also July 4, Thanksgiving, Dec 25. Res accepted. Contemporary Amer menu. Bar. A la carte entrees: dinner $15-$29. Street parking. Totally nonsmoking. Cr cds: A, D, DS, MC, V.

D

★★ **WHITE STAR TAVERN.** *565 Boylston St (02116). 617/536-4477.* Hrs: 11:30 am-midnight; Sun from 5 pm; Sun brunch 11 am-3 pm. Closed Thanksgiving, Dec 25. Bar. A la carte entrees: lunch $4.95-$9.95, dinner $8.95-$15.95. Colorful interior. Outdoor dining on Copley Square. Cr cds: A, C, D, DS, MC, V.

D

★★ **YE OLDE UNION OYSTER HOUSE.** *41 Union St (02108). 617/227-2750. www.unionoysterhouse.com.* Hrs: 11 am-9:30 pm; Fri, Sat to 10 pm. Closed Thanksgiving, Dec 25. Res accepted. Bar. Lunch $7-$16, dinner $14.95-$25. Sun brunch $9.95. Child's menu. Specializes in shore dinners, seafood platters. Valet parking (dinner). Historic oyster bar established 1826; originally a silk and dry goods shop (1742). Family-owned. Cr cds: A, D, DS, MC, V.

D

★ **ZUMA'S TEX-MEX CAFE.** *7 N Market St (02109). 617/367-9114.* Hrs: 11:30 am-11 pm; Fri, Sat to midnight; Sun noon-10 pm. Closed Dec 25. Tex-Mex menu. Bar. Lunch, dinner $5-$12. Specializes in fajitas, enchiladas, neon margaritas. Cr cds: A, D, DS, MC, V.

D

Unrated Dining Spot

RUBIN'S KOSHER DELICATESSEN. *500 Harvard St, Brookline (02446). 617/731-8787. www.rubinskosher.com.* Kosher deli menu. Hrs: 9 am-8:30 pm; Fri to 3 pm; Sun 8 am-8 pm. Closed Sat; Jewish hols. Lunch $3.50-$12, dinner $6.50-$15. Parking. Family-owned. Totally nonsmoking. Cr cds: A, C, DS, MC, V.

D

Bourne (Cape Cod)

See also Buzzards Bay (Cape Cod), Sandwich (Cape Cod)

Settled 1627 **Pop** 18,721 **Elev** 19 ft **Area code** 508 **Zip** 02532

Information Cape Cod Chamber of Commerce, US 6 and MA 132, PO Box 790, Hyannis 02601-0790; 508/362-3225 or 888/33-CAPECOD

Web www.capecodchamber.org

Named for Jonathan Bourne, a successful whaling merchant, this town has had a variety of industries since its founding. Originally a center for herring fishing, the town turned to manufacturing stoves, kettles, and later, freight cars. Bourne's current prosperity is derived from cranberries and tourism.

What to See and Do

Aptucxet Trading Post. A replica of a 1627 trading post, that may have been the first of its kind in America. Native American artifacts; rune stone believed to be proof of visits to the area by the Phoenicians in 400 B.C.; artifacts in two rms. On grounds are herb garden, site of original spring, saltworks; railroad station built for President Grover Cleveland for use at his Gray Gables home, his summer White House; Dutch-style windmill; picnic area adj to Cape Cod Canal. (July-Aug, daily; last two wkends May and June and Sept-mid-Oct, Tues-Sun) 24 Aptucxet Rd, off Shore Rd, ½ mi W of Bourne Bridge. Phone 508/759-9487. ¢

Bourne Scenic Park. Playground, picnicking; bike trails; swimming pool, bathhouse; recreation building; camping (fee); store. (Apr-May, wkends; June-Oct, daily) North bank of Cape Cod Canal. Phone 508/759-7873. ¢¢

Industrial Tour. Pairpoint Crystal Company. (est 1837) Handmade lead crystal ware, glassblowing demonstrations. Viewing (Mon-Fri). Store (Daily). 851 Sandwich Rd (MA 6A), in Sagamore. Phone 508/888-2344. **FREE**

Braintree

Settled 1634 **Pop** 33,828 **Elev** 90 ft **Area code** 781 **Zip** 02184

Information South Shore Chamber of Commerce, 36 Miller Stile Rd, Quincy 02169; 781/479-1111

Web www.southshorechamber.org

What to See and Do

Abigail Adams House. Birthplace of Abigail Smith Adams (1744), daughter of a local clerygyman, wife of President John Adams, mother of President John Quincy Adams. Period furnishings. (July-Labor Day, Tues-Sun) North and Norton Sts, 2 mi E in Weymouth. Phone 781/335-1849. ¢¢

Gilbert Bean Museum. (1720) Thayer, a soldier and educator, served as fifth Superintendent of West Point, 1817-1833. House contains 17th- and 18th-century furnishings, military exhibits, and local historical displays. (Tues-Wed, Sat-Sun) 786 Washington St. Phone 781/848-1640. ¢ Adj is a

Reconstructed 18th-Century Barn. Houses farm equipment, ice cutting and wood tools; costumes; research library and genealogical records. (Tues-Wed, Sat-Sun) **FREE**

Motels/Motor Lodges

★ ★ **HOLIDAY INN EXPRESS.** *909 Hingham St, Rockland (02370). 781/871-5660; fax 781/871-7255; res 800/465-4329. www.hiexpress.com/rocklandma.* 76 rms, 2 story. S, D $90-$114; each addl $5; under 18 free. Pet accepted. TV. Continental bkfst. Coffee in rms. Ck-out 11 am. Free guest lndry. Meeting rm. Business servs avail. Health club privileges. Microwaves avail. Cr cds: A, C, D, DS, MC, V.

D 🐾 🖼 🔥 SC

★ ★ **HOLIDAY INN RANDOLPH.** *1374 N Main St, Randolph (02368). 781/961-1000; fax 781/963-0089; res 800/465-4329. www.holiday-inn.com.* 158 rms, 4 story. S, D $85-$125; each addl $10; under 18 free; wkend rates. Crib free. TV; cable (premium). Pool; lifeguard. Restaurant 6:30 am-10 pm. Rm serv. Bar 11:30-2 am. Ck-out noon. Coin lndry. Meeting rms. Business servs avail. In-rm modem link. Bellhops. Valet serv. Sundries. Complimentary bus depot, RR, transportation. Microwaves avail. Cr cds: A, D, DS, MC, V.

D 🖼 🖼 🔥

Hotel

★ ★ ★ **SHERATON BRAINTREE HOTEL.** *37 Forbes Rd (02184). 781/848-0600; fax 781/843-9492; res 800/325-3535. www.sheraton.com/braintree.* 376 rms, 2-6 story. S, D $149-$209; each addl $15; suites $189-$395; under 18 free; wkend rates. Crib free. TV; cable (premium). 2 pools, 1 indoor. Restaurant 6:30 am-11 pm. Rm serv. Bar; entertainment Tues-Sat. Ck-out noon. Meeting rms. In-rm modem link. Bellhops. Concierge. Sundries. Gift shop. Exercise rm; steam rm, sauna. Some bathrm phones. Cr cds: A, D, DS, MC, V.

D 🖼 🏋 🖼 🔥 SC

Restaurant

★ ★ **CAFFE BELLA.** *19 Warren St (MA 139), Randolph (02368). 781/961-7729.* Italian menu. Specializes in grilled meats and seafood. Own baking, pasta. Menu changes seasonally. Hrs: 5-10 pm. Closed Sun; July 4, Thanksgiving, Dec 25. Bar. Dinner $12.50-$27.50. Mediterranean decor. Cr cds: A, C, D, ER, MC, V.

D

Brewster (Cape Cod)

Settled 1656 **Pop** 10,094 **Elev** 39 ft **Area code** 508 **Zip** 02631

Information Cape Cod Chamber of Commerce, US 6 and MA 132, PO Box 790, Hyannis 02601-0790; 508/362-3225 or 888/33-CAPECOD

Web www.capecodchamber.org

What to See and Do

Cape Cod Museum of Natural History. Exhibits on wildlife and ecology of the area; art exhibits; library; lectures; nature trails; field walks; trips to Monomoy Island. Gift shop. (Daily; closed hols) MA 6A, Brewster. Phone 508/896-3867. ¢¢

🗷 **New England Fire & History Museum.** This six-building complex houses an extensive collection of fire-fighting equipment and includes the Arthur Fiedler Memorial Fire Collection; diorama of Chicago fire of 1871; engines dating from the Revolution to the 1930s; world's only 1929 Mercedes Benz fire engine; life-size reproduction of Ben Franklin's firehouse; 19th-century blacksmith shop; largest apothecary shop in the country contains 664 gold-leaf bottles of medicine; medicinal herb gardens; library; films; theater performances. Guided tours. (Memorial Day wkend-mid-Sept, daily; mid-Sept-Columbus Day, wkends) ½ mi W of MA 137 on MA 6A. Phone 508/896-5711. ¢¢

Nickerson State Park. Swimming, fishing, boating (ramp); bicycling (Cape Cod Rail Trail), picnicking, camping (dump station). Standard fees. 3 mi E, off MA 6A. Phone 508/896-3491. **FREE**

Stoney Brook Mill. Museum upstairs includes historical exhibits, weaving. Corn grinding (July and Aug, Thurs-Sat afternoons). Old Grist Mill in West Brewster, on site of one of first gristmills in America. **FREE**

Resort

★ ★ ★ **OCEAN EDGE RESORT AND GOLF CLUB.** *2907 Main St, Brewster (02631). 508/896-9000; fax 508/896-9123; toll-free 800/343-6074. www.oceanedge.com.* 406 units, 2 story, 32 kit. villas. Apr-Oct: S, D $140-$315; suites $395-$500; cottages $475-$900; under 12 free; AP, MAP avail; wkly rates; golf, tennis plans; lower rates rest of yr. Crib $10. TV; cable, VCR avail (movies). 6 pools, 2 indoor; whirlpool; poolside serv, lifeguard. Playground. Supervised children's activities (June-Sept); ages 4-12. Dining rm 6 am-10 pm. Box lunches, snacks, picnics. Rm serv to midnight. Bar noon-1 am; entertainment. Ck-out 11 am, ck-in 3 pm. Grocery, package store 1 blk. Convention facilities. Business center. In-rm modem link. Bellhops. Valet serv. Airport transportation. Concierge. Gift shop. Sports dir. Tennis, pro. 18-hole golf, greens fee $68, pro, putting green, driving range. Swimming beach. Hiking. Bicycle rentals. Lawn games. Soc dir. Exercise equipt; sauna. Microwaves, bathrm phones. Balconies. On grounds of turn-of-the-century 380-acre estate fronting Cape Cod Bay; meeting rms in English manor house (1912) with elaborate plasterwork, woodwork and paneling, fireplaces. Cr cds: A, C, D, DS, MC, V.

D 🏋 🚶 🖼 🏋 ✈ 🖼 🔥 🚶

B&Bs/Small Inns

★ ★ **BRAMBLE INN.** *2019 Main St, Brewster (02631). 508/896-7644; fax 508/896-9332. www.brambleinn.com.* 8 rms, 2 story. No rm phones. Late May-mid-Oct: D $95-$125. Closed Jan-Apr. Children over 8 yrs only. TV in some rms; cable (premium). Complimentary full bkfst. Restaurant (see also BRAMBLE INN). Ck-out 11 am, ck-in 2 pm. Two buildings (1849-1861); many antiques. Intimate, country atmosphere. Cr cds: A, MC, V.

🖼 🔥

★★★ **BREWSTER FARMHOUSE INN.** *716 Main St, Brewster (02631).* 508/896-3910; fax 508/896-4232; toll-free 800/892-3910. 8 rms, some rms with shower only, some share bath, 2 story, 1 suite. No rm phones. Late May-Oct: D $110-$175; suite $220; lower rates rest of yr. Children over 16 only. TV; cable (premium). Heated pool; whirlpool. Complimentary full bkfst; afternoon refreshments. Ck-out 11 am, ck-in 3 pm. Business servs avail. Lawn games. Refrigerators. Balconies. Picnic tables. Built 1850; antiques and reproductions. Totally nonsmoking. Cr cds: A, C, D, DS, MC, V.

★★ **CAPTAIN FREEMAN INN.** *15 Breakwater Rd, Brewster (02631).* 508/896-7481; fax 508/896-5618; toll-free 800/843-4664. www.captainfreemaninn.com. 12 rms, 6 A/C, 3 story. Some rm phones. Late-May-Oct: S $120-$145; D $130-$165; wkly rates; lower rates rest of yr. Children over 10 yrs only. TV in some rms; VCR (free movies). Pool. Complimentary full bkfst. Restaurant nearby. Ck-out 11 am, ck-in 2 pm. Concierge serv. Free airport, bus depot transportation. Game rm. Lawn games. Some fireplaces. Balconies. Antiques. Sitting rm. House built 1866. Totally nonsmoking. Cr cds: A, MC, V.

★★ **ISAIAH CLARK HOUSE.** *1187 Main St, Brewster (02631).* 508/896-2223; fax 508/896-2138; res 800/822-4001. www.isaiahclark.com. 7 rms, 2 story. Many rm phones. Late May-mid-Oct: S $95-$135; D $120-$150; each addl $25; lower rates rest of yr. Children over 10 yrs only. TV in most rms; cable. Complimentary full bkfst; afternoon refreshments. Ck-out 11 am, ck-in 2 pm. Business servs avail. Concierge serv. Picnic tables. Antiques. Former sea captain's house (1780). Totally nonsmoking. Cr cds: A, DS, MC, V.

★★ **OLD SEA PINES INN.** *2553 Main St, Brewster (02631).* 508/896-6114; fax 508/896-7387. www.oldseapinesinn.com. 23 rms, 18 with bath, 18 A/C, 3 story. No rm phones. June-Oct: S, D $55-$115; suite $155; each addl $20; lower rates rest of yr. Children over 8 yrs only exc in family suites. Complimentary full bkfst. Rm serv. Bkfst in bed avail. Serv bar 2-10 pm. Ck-out 11 am, ck-in 2 pm. Business servs avail. Some fireplaces. Antiques. Founded 1907 as School of Charm and Personality for Young Women. On 3½ acres. Totally nonsmoking. Cr cds: A, D, MC, V.

★★ **POORE HOUSE INN.** *2311 Main St, Brewster (02631).* 508/896-0004; fax 508/896-0005; toll-free 800/233-6662. www.capecodtravel.com/poore. 5 rms, 2 story. June-Sept: S $65-$85; D $85-$125; family, wkly rates; lower rates rest of yr. Children over 8 yrs only. Pet accepted. Complimentary full bkfst. Restaurant nearby. Ck-out 11 am, ck-in 2 pm. Refrigerators. Picnic tables. Antiques. Library/sitting rm. Built 1837. Totally nonsmoking. Cr cds: DS, MC, V.

★★ **RUDDY TURNSTONE.** *463 Main St, Brewster (02631).* 508/385-9871; fax 508/385-5696; toll-free 800/654-1995. www.sunsol.com/ruddyturnstone. 5 rms, 1 with shower only, 2 story, 1 suite. No rm phones. Mid-June-mid-Oct: S, D $95-$120; suite $150; wkends, hols (2-3-day min); lower rates rest of yr. Children over 10 yrs only. Complimentary full bkfst. Ck-out 11 am, ck-in 1 pm. Luggage handling. Concierge serv. Lawn games. Picnic tables. Early 19th-century Cape Cod house; antique furnishings. Totally nonsmoking. Cr cds: DS, MC, V.

Restaurants

★★★ **BRAMBLE INN.** *2019 Main St, Brewster (02631).* 508/896-7644. www.brambleinn.com. Specialties: tenderloin of beef, rack of lamb, assorted seafood curry. Own baking. Hrs: 6-9 pm. Closed Mon-Wed off season; also Jan-Apr. Res accepted. Serv bar. Complete meals: dinner $42-$52. Parking. Built in 1861; 4 dining areas, including enclosed porch. Totally nonsmoking. Cr cds: A, DS, MC, V.

★★★ **CHILLINGSWORTH.** *2449 Main St, Brewster (02631).* 508/896-3640. www.chillingsworth.com. Modern French cuisine. Menu changes daily, emphasizing fresh native seafood, veal, pheasant. Own baking, pasta. Grows own herbs. Hrs: mid-June-mid-Sept, 2 dinner sittings: 6-7:30 pm and 8-9:30 pm; mid-May-mid-June and mid-Sept-Nov, shortened week. Cr cds: A, D, DS, MC, V.

★★★ **OLD MANSE INN AND RESTAURANT.** *1861 Main St, Brewster (02631).* 508/896-3149. www.oldmanseinn.com. Specialties: steamed lobster, braised lamb shank, lemon buttermilk pudding cake. Hrs: 5:30-10 pm. Closed Mon; Jan-Apr. Wine list. Dinner $14-$19. Parking. Two dining rms in early 19th-century inn; antiques. Romantic setting. Guest rms avail. Totally nonsmoking. Cr cds: A, DS, MC, V.

Brockton

Settled 1700 **Pop** 94,304 **Elev** 112 ft **Area code** 508
Information Metro South Chamber of Commerce, 60 School St, 02301; 508/586-0500
Web www.metrosouthchamber.com

Half of the Union Army in the Civil War marched in Brockton-made shoes. Known as the nation's shoe capital until the 20th century, diverse manufacturing and service industries contribute to the city's economic base today. Brockton was home of boxing champions Rocky Marciano and "Marvelous" Marvin Hagler.

What to See and Do

Brockton Historical Society Museums. The Heritage Center, the main building of the complex, consists of Shoe Museum, Fire Museum, and "The Homestead," an early Brockton shoemaker's home. "The Homestead" features exhibits on Thomas Edison, who electrified the first shoe factory in the world in Brockton in 1883, and former local shoemaker and undefeated world champion boxer, Rocky Marciano. (First and third Sun afternoon of each month or by appt) 216 N Pearl St. Phone 508/583-1039. ¢

Fuller Museum of Art. Permanent exhibits of 19th- and 20th-century American art; children's gallery; changing exhibits; lectures, gallery talks, and tours. Museum (Tues-Sun afternoons; closed hols). 455 Oak St, on Porter's Pond. Phone 508/588-6000. ¢¢

Special Event

Brockton Fair. Fairgrounds. Midway, agricultural exhibits, entertainment. (Early July). Phone 508/586-8000.

Motel/Motor Lodge

★★ **BEST WESTERN.** 1005 Belmont St (02301). 508/588-3333; res 800/780-7234. www.bestwestern.com. 69 rms, 2 story. S, D $49-$69; each addl $5; under 12 free. Crib free. TV; cable (premium). Pool. Restaurant 7 am-10 pm; Mon-Wed to 9 pm; Sun to noon. Rm serv. Bar 11-1 am; entertainment Thurs-Sat. Ck-out 11 am. Meeting rms. Business servs avail. In-rm modem link. Sundries. Downhill ski 11 mi. Health club privileges. Cr cds: A, D, DS, MC, V.
⬛ ⬛ ⬛ ⬛ ⬛ ⬛

Hotel

★★ **HOLIDAY INN BOSTON METRO SOUTH.** 195 Westgate Dr (02301). 508/588-6300; fax 508/580-4384; res 800/361-2116. www.holiday-inn.com. 186 rms, 3 story. S, D $109; each addl $10; under 12 free. Crib free. TV; cable (premium). Indoor pool; whirlpool. Restaurant 6:30 am-2 pm, 5-10 pm. Rm serv. Bar 4 pm-midnight. Ck-out noon. Coin lndry. Meeting rms. Business servs avail. In-rm modem link. Bellhops. Exercise equipt; sauna. Cr cds: A, D, DS, JCB, MC, V.
⬛ ⬛ ⬛ ⬛ ⬛

Restaurant

★ **CHRISTOS.** 782 Crescent St (02402). 508/588-4200. Specializes in steak, Greek salads. Hrs: 11 am-midnight. Closed Thanksgiving, Dec 25. Bar. Lunch $2.75-$6.95, dinner $5.95-$10.50. Family-owned. Cr cds: D, DS, MC, V.
⬛ ⬛

Burlington

Settled 1641 **Pop** 22,876 **Elev** 218 ft **Area code** 781 **Zip** 01803

Motels/Motor Lodges

★★ **COURTYARD BY MARRIOTT.** 240 Mishawum Rd, Woburn (01801). 781/932-3200; fax 781/935-6163; toll-free 800/321-2211. www.marriott.com. 118 rms, 2 suites, 3 story. S, D $139-$169; each addl $5; suites $159-$189; family rates; package plans. Crib avail. TV; cable (premium). Complimentary coffee in rms. Restaurant adj 11:30 am-11:30 pm. Bar 5-11 pm. Ck-out 1 pm. Meeting rms. Business servs avail. In-rm modem link. Valet serv. Sundries. Coin

lndry. Airport, RR station transportation. Exercise equipt. Health club privileges. Pool. Cr cds: A, C, D, DS, MC, V.
⬛ ⬛ ⬛ ⬛ ⬛ ⬛

★★ **HAMPTON INN.** 315 Mishawum Rd, Woburn (01801). 781/935-7666; fax 781/933-6899. www.hamptoninn.com. 99 rms, 5 story. S, D $79-$149; under 18 free; wkend rates. Crib free. Pet accepted. TV; cable (premium). Complimentary continental bkfst. Coffee in rms. Restaurant 10 am-11 pm. Rm serv noon-10 pm. Bar. Ck-out noon. Business servs avail. In-rm modem link. Valet serv. Sundries. Health club privileges. Some refrigerators. Cr cds: A, C, D, DS, MC, V.
⬛ ⬛ ⬛ ⬛

Hotel

★★★ **MARRIOTT BURLINGTON BOSTON.** 1 Mall Rd (01803). 781/229-6565; fax 781/229-7973; toll-free 800/371-3625. www.marriott.com. 419 rms, 4 suites, 9 story. S, D $159-$189; suites $250-$400; family rates wkends. TV; cable (premium). 2 pools, 1 indoor; whirlpool, poolside serv, lifeguard. Restaurant 6 am-10 pm; wkends from 7 am. Rm serv to midnight. Bar 4 pm-1 am; entertainment. Ck-out noon. Coin lndry. Convention facilities. Business servs avail. In-rm modem link. Concierge. Gift shop. Beauty shop. Exercise equipt; sauna. Massage. Game rm. Refrigerators avail. Luxury level. Cr cds: A, C, D, DS, ER, JCB, MC, V.
⬛ ⬛ ⬛ ⬛ ⬛ ⬛

Restaurant

★ **DANDELION INN.** 90 Burlington Mall Rd (01803). 781/273-1616. www.barnsiderestaurants.com. Continental menu. Specializes in fresh seafood, steak. Salad bar. Hrs: 11:30 am-midnight. Closed some major hols. Res accepted. Bar. Lunch $5.95-$12.95, dinner $7.95-$29.95. Child's menu. Greenhouse decor. Cr cds: A, C, D, DS, MC, V.
⬛

Buzzards Bay (Cape Cod)

Pop 3,549 **Elev** 10 ft **Area code** 508 **Zip** 02532

Information Cape Cod Chamber of Commerce, US 6 and MA 132, PO Box 790, Hyannis 02601-0790; 508/362-3225 or 888/33-CAPECOD

Web www.capecodchamber.org

Cape Cod is said to face "four seas": Buzzards Bay, Nantucket Sound, the Atlantic Ocean, and Cape Cod Bay. The shore is jagged and irregular, dotted with hundreds of summer resorts, public and private beaches, yacht clubs, and fishing piers. The area of Buzzards Bay is at the west entrance to the Cape Cod Canal. Among the better-known towns on the mainland shore are Nonquit and South Yarmouth (see), west of New Bedford, and Fairhaven, Crescent Beach, Mattapoisett, Wareham, and Onset, to the east. On the Cape side are Monument Beach, Pocasset, Silver Beach, West Falmouth, Woods Hole (see), and the string of Elizabeth Islands, which ends with Cuttyhunk.

What to See and Do

Cape Cod Canal Cruises. Cruises with historical narration. Also evening cocktail and entertainment cruises. (June-Oct, daily; May, Sat and Sun) 3 mi W via MA 6, 28, Onset Town Pier. Phone 508/295-3883. ¢¢¢

Porter Thermometer Museum. The world's only thermometer museum houses an enormous collection of more than 4,000 of these instruments. (Daily) 49 Zarahemla Rd, just E of jct I-495 and I-195, in Onset. Phone 508/295-5504. **FREE**

Motel/Motor Lodge

★ **BAY MOTOR INN.** *223 Main St, Buzzards Bay (02532).* 508/759-3989; fax 508/759-3199. *www.capecodtravel.com/ baymotorinn.* 17 rms, 1-2 story, 3 kits. Mid-June-Labor Day: S, D $72-$120; each addl $10; lower rates Apr-mid-June, Labor Day-mid-Nov. Closed rest of yr. Crib $7. Pet accepted. TV; cable (premium). Pool. Complimentary coffee in lobby. Restaurant adj. Ck-out 11 am. Free bus depot transportation. Picnic tables, grills. Cr cds: A, DS, MC, V.

Cambridge

See also Boston

Settled 1630 **Pop** 101,355 **Elev** 40 ft **Area code** 617
Information Chamber of Commerce, 859 Massachusetts Ave, 02139; 617/876-4100
Web www.cambcc.org

Across the Charles River from Boston, Cambridge is world-famous for its educational institutions but for the most part it is an industrial city. It is also known as a research center. It was named for Cambridge, England's famous university town.

What to See and Do

Christ Church. (1759) Episcopal. The oldest church building in Cambridge. A fine Georgian Colonial building designed by Peter Harrison that was used as a colonial barracks during the Revolution. (Daily) Garden St at the Common. Phone 617/876-0200. **FREE**

✪ **Harvard University.** 18,179 students. This magnificent university, America's oldest, was founded in 1636. Two yrs later, when a minister named John Harvard died and left half his estate and his considerable personal library, it was named for him. Includes Harvard and Radcliffe colleges as well as ten graduate and professional schools. Harvard Yard, as the original campus is called, is tree-shaded and occupied by stately red-brick buildings. Harvard Sq. In and around the yard are

Fogg Art Museum. European and American paintings, sculpture, and decorative arts; drawings, prints, photographs; changing exhibits. (Daily; closed hols) Free admission Sat mornings. 32 Quincy St. Phone 617/495-9400. ¢¢

Harvard Museum of Natural History. Contains three museums in one building, including Museum of Comparative Zoology, Botanical Museum, and Mineralogical and Geological Museum. Exhibits range from pre-Columbian art to dinosaurs, rare gems, and the famous Blaschka glass flowers. Extensive research collections. (Daily; closed major hols) 26 Oxford St. Phone 617/495-3045. ¢¢

The Houses of Harvard-Radcliffe. Between Harvard Sq and the Charles River, and NE of Harvard Yard between Shepard and Linnaean Sts.

Information Center. Provides maps, brochures. (June-Aug, daily; rest of yr, Mon-Sat) Student-guided tours begin here. 1350 Massachusetts Ave. Phone 617/495-1573.

John F. Kennedy School of Government. (1978) Contains library, classrms, public affairs forum for lectures. 79 JFK. St, on the banks of the Charles River.

Massachusetts Hall. Oldest building (1720) and architectural inspiration for the campus. **FREE**

University Hall. (1813-1815) Designed by Charles Bulfinch, made of Chelmsford granite in contrast to the surrounding brick, and one of the Yard's most handsome buildings. **FREE**

Widener Library. (1915) Has an enormous Corinthian portico; more than 3,000,000 books. Near it are Houghton, with a fine collection of rare books, and Lamont, the first undergraduate library in America. South side of Harvard Yard. Phone 617/495-4166. **FREE**

Longfellow National Historic Site. Georgian-style house built in 1759 was Washington's headquarters during the 1775-1776 siege of Boston, and Henry Wadsworth Longfellow's home from 1837 until his death in 1882. Longfellow taught at Harvard and his books are located here. (Daily; closed Jan 1, Thanksgiving, Dec 25) 105 Brattle St, ½ mi from Harvard. Phone 617/876-4491. ¢

Massachusetts Institute of Technology. (1861) 9,500 students. One of the greatest science and engineering schools in the world. On the Charles River, the campus includes 135 acres of impressive neoclassic and modern buildings. Information center in the lobby of the main building, 77 Massachusetts Ave; guided tours, two departures (Mon-Fri). 77 Massachusetts Ave. Phone 617/253-4795. On campus are

Hart Nautical Galleries. Shows ship and marine engineering development through displays of rigged merchant and naval ship models; changing exhibits. (Daily) 55 Massachusetts Ave. **FREE**

List Visual Arts Center at MIT. Changing exhibits of contemporary art. (Oct-June, daily; closed hols; free) The MIT campus also has an outstanding permanent collection of outdoor sculpture, including works by Calder, Moore, and Picasso, and significant architecture, including buildings by Aalto, Pei, and Saarinen. Walking tour map at information center. Wiesner Building, 20 Ames St.

MIT Museum. Collections and exhibits that interpret the Institute's social and educational history, developments in science and technology, and the interplay of technology and art. (Tues-Sun; closed Mon, hols) 265 Massachusetts Ave. Phone 617/253-4444. ¢¢

The Radcliffe Institute for Advanced Study. (1879) 2,700 women. Coordinate institution with Harvard. Unique women's educational and scholarly resources including the Arthur and Elizabeth Schlesinger Library on the History of Women in America (at 3 James St). More than 850 major collections of history of women from 1800 to present. Admissions office at 8 Garden St. Phone 617/495-8601.

Motels/Motor Lodges

★★ **BEST WESTERN.** 220 Alewife Brook Pkwy (02138). 617/491-8000; fax 617/491-4932; res 800/491-4914. www.bestwestern.com. 69 rms, 4 story. S $99-$199; D $109-$209; under 17 free. Crib $15. TV; cable (premium). Indoor pool; whirlpool. Complimentary continental bkfst. Restaurant adj 11:30 am-11:30 pm; Sun, Mon to 10:30 pm. Bar to 12:30 am. Ck-out noon. Meeting rm. Business servs avail. In-rm modem link. Health club privileges. Refrigerators avail. Cr cds: A, C, D, DS, MC, V.
⊠ 🔥 SC ⊠

★ **HARVARD SQUARE HOTEL.** 110 Mount Auburn St (02138). 617/864-5200; fax 617/864-2409; res 800/458-5886. 73 rms, 4 story. S, D $99-$199; under 17 free. Crib free. Garage parking $16. TV; cable (premium). Restaurant 7 am-9 pm. Ck-out 11 am. Business servs avail. In-rm modem link. Cr cds: A, C, D, DS, MC, V.
D ⊠ 🔥 SC

★★★ **THE INN AT HARVARD.** 1201 Massachusetts Ave (02138). 617/491-2222; fax 617/520-3711; res 800/222-8733. www.theinnatharvard.com. 113 rms, 4 story. S, D $169-$299; suites $250-$550; under 17 free; higher rates commencement. Crib free. Valet parking $20. TV; cable (premium). Complimentary coffee in lobby. Restaurant 6:30 am-11 pm; Sat, Sun from 7 am. Rm serv. Bar. Ck-out noon. Meeting rms. Business servs avail. In-rm modem link. Bellhops. Concierge. Valet serv. Health club privileges. Cr cds: A, DS, MC, V.
D ⊠ 🔥 SC

★ **RADISSON HOTEL CAMBRIDGE.** 777 Memorial Dr (02139). 617/492-7777; fax 617/492-6038; toll-free 800/333-3333. www.radisson.com. 205 rms, 15 story. S $90-$185; D $110-$225; each addl $10; under 18 free. Crib free. Pet accepted. TV; cable (premium). 5th-floor indoor pool. Restaurant 7-11 am, 5-10 pm. Bar 4 pm-2 am. Ck-out noon. Meeting rms. Business servs avail. In-rm modem link. Some refrigerators; microwaves avail. Some balconies. On river. Cr cds: A, C, D, DS, ER, JCB, MC, V.
🔥 ⊠ ⊠ 🔥 SC

Hotels

★★★ **THE CHARLES.** 1 Bennett St (02138). 617/864-1200; fax 617/864-5715; toll-free 800/882-1818. www.charleshotel.com. 296 rms, 10 story. S, D $250-$500; each addl $20; suites $429-$1,500; under 18 free; wkend rates. Crib free. Pet accepted, some restrictions. Valet parking $16. TV; cable (premium), VCR avail (free movies). Indoor pool; whirlpool. Restaurants (see also HENRIETTA'S TABLE and RIALTO). Rm serv 24 hrs. Bar noon-1 am; jazz. Ck-out 1 pm. Meeting rms. Business servs avail. In-rm modem link. Concierge. Beauty shop. Exercise rm; steam rm. Massage. Spa. Bathrm phones, minibars. On Charles River. Cr cds: A, C, D, JCB, MC, V.
D 🔥 ⊠ 👤 ⊠ 🔥 SC

★★ **HOLIDAY INN.** 30 Washington St, Somerville (02143). 617/628-1000; fax 617/628-0143; toll-free 800/465-4329. www.holiday-inn.com. 184 rms, 8 suites, 9 story. S $145-$185; D $155-$205; each addl $10; under 19 free; wkend rates. Crib free. TV; cable (premium). Indoor pool; whirlpool, lifeguard. Restaurant 6:30 am-noon, 5-10 pm. Bar 11:30-1 am; Fri, Sat to 2 am. Ck-out noon. Coin lndry. Meeting rms. Business servs avail. In-rm modem link. Sundries. Free parking. Exercise rm; sauna. Refrigerators avail. Cr cds: A, C, D, DS, ER, JCB, MC, V.
D ⊠ 👤 ⊠ 🔥 SC

★★★ **HYATT REGENCY.** 575 Memorial Dr (02139). 617/492-1234; fax 617/441-6489; toll-free 800/233-1234. www.hyatt.com. 469 rms, 10 suites, 16 story. S, D $159-$270; each addl $25; suites from $450; under 18 free; seasonal, wkend rates. Crib free. Garage $16. TV; cable (premium), VCR avail. Indoor pool; whirlpool. Restaurant 6:30 am-11 pm. Bar 11-1:30 am. Ck-out noon. Convention facilities. Business center. In-rm modem link. Concierge. Shopping arcade. Exercise equipt; sauna, steam rm. Refrigerators avail. Private patios, balconies. On river. Luxury level. Cr cds: A, D, DS, JCB, MC, V.
D ⊠ 👤 ⊠ 🔥 👤

★★★ **MARRIOTT CAMBRIDGE BOSTON.** 2 Cambridge Ctr (02142). 617/494-6600; fax 617/494-0036; res 800/228-9290. www.marriott.com. 431 rms, 13 suites, 26 story. Mar-Aug: S, D $229-$259; suites $400; under 18 free. Crib free. Covered valet parking $18. TV; cable (premium), VCR avail. Pool; whirlpool, poolside serv. Coffee in rms. Restaurant 6:30 am-11 pm. Bar noon-1 am; entertainment. Ck-out noon. Convention facilities. Business center. In-rm modem link. Coin lndry. Shopping arcade. Exercise equipt; sauna. Massage. Health club privileges. Some refrigerators; microwaves avail. Luxury level. Cr cds: A, D, DS, JCB, MC, V.
D ⊠ 👤 ⊠ 🔥 👤

★★★ **ROYAL SONESTA.** 5 Cambridge Pkwy (02142). 617/806-4200; fax 617/806-4232; toll-free 800/766-3782. www.sonesta.com/boston. 400 rms, 21 suites, 10 story. S, D $239-$279; each addl $25; suites $400-$850; under 18 free; wkend rates. Crib free. TV; cable (premium). Pool. Restaurant 6:30 am-11 pm. Rm serv to 1 am; Fri, Sat to 2 am. Bar 11-1 am. Ck-out noon. Convention facilities. Business servs avail. In-rm modem link. Concierge. Gift shop. Garage parking. Exercise rm. Massage. Health club privileges. Minibars; some bathrm phones. Most rms have view of Charles River and Boston. Cr cds: A, C, D, DS, ER, JCB, MC, V.
D ⊠ 👤 ⊠ 🔥 SC

★★★ **SHERATON COMMANDER HOTEL.** *16 Garden St (02138). 617/547-4800; fax 617/868-8322; toll-free 800/535-5007. www.sheraton.com.* 175 rms, 7 story. S $165-$279; D $185-$299; each addl $20; kit. suites $249-$770; under 17 free. Crib free. TV; cable (premium). Coffee in rms. Restaurant 6:30 am-10:30 pm. Bar noon-1 am. Ck-out noon. Meeting rms. Business servs avail. In-rm modem link. Concierge. Free parking. Exercise equipt. Some in-rm whirlpools, refrigerators. Cr cds: A, C, D, DS, JCB, MC, V.

D 🏋 ⌧ 🛱 SC

B&B/Small Inn

★★★ **A CAMBRIDGE HOUSE BED AND BREAKFAST INN.** *2218 Massachusetts Ave (02140). 617/491-6300; fax 617/868-2848; res 800/232-9989. www.acambridgehouse.com.* 16 rms, 3 share bath. S $129-$189; D $149-$275; each addl $40. TV; cable. Complimentary full bkfst; afternoon refreshments. Restaurant nearby. Ck-out noon, ck-in 3 pm. Business servs avail. In-rm modem link. Victorian house (1892) lavishly decorated in period style. Cr cds: A, D, DS, MC, V.

D ⌧ 🛱

Restaurants

★★ **BLUE ROOM.** *1 Kendall Sq (02139). 617/494-9034.* Specializes in multi-ethnic dishes. Hrs: 5:30-10 pm; Fri, Sat to 11 pm; Sun brunch 11 am-2:30 pm. Closed July 4, Thanksgiving, Dec 24, 25. Res accepted. Bar. Dinner $16-$22. Sun brunch $16.95. Pianist Sun. Outdoor dining. Original artwork from local artists. Cr cds: A, C, D, DS, MC, V.

★ **BOMBAY CLUB.** *57 JFK St (02138). 617/661-8100. www.bombayclub.com.* Indian menu. Specializes in kebabs, breads. Hrs: 11:30 am-11 pm. Closed Thanksgiving, Dec 25. Res accepted. Bar. Buffet: lunch $7.95-$11.95. Lunch, dinner $6.95-$13.95. Sat, Sun brunch $11.95. Indian art. Totally nonsmoking. Cr cds: A, C, D, MC, V.

D

★★ **CHEZ HENRI.** *1 Shepard St (02138). 617/354-8980.* French menu with Cuban influence. Specializes in chicken with tarragon vinegar. Hrs: 6-10 pm; Fri, Sat 5:30-11 pm; Sun to 9 pm; Sun brunch 11 am-2 pm (Sept-June), 6-9 pm. Closed Memorial Day, July 4. Bar to 1 am; Sun to 10 pm. A la carte entrees: dinner $14.95-$21.95. Complete meals: dinner $30. Sun brunch $5-$12. Cr cds: A, D, DS, MC, V.

D ⌧

★★ **DALI.** *415 Washington St, Somerville (02143). 617/661-3254. www.dalirestaurant.com.* Spanish menu. Specializes in tapas, piedra. Hrs: 5:30-11 pm. Closed most major hols; also Dec 31. Bar. A la carte entrees: lunch $2.50-$7.50, dinner $14-$22. Street parking. Spanish decor. Cr cds: A, D, MC, V.

D

★★ **EAST COAST GRILL.** *1271 Cambridge St (02139). 617/491-6568.* Specializes in grilled fish, barbecued beef and pork. Hrs: 5:30-10 pm; Fri, Sat to 10:30 pm. Closed Dec 25. A la carte entrees: dinner $12-$16. Cr cds: A, DS, MC, V.

D ⌧

★ **GRENDEL'S DEN.** *89 Winthrop St (02138). 617/491-1160.* International menu. Specializes in fresh fish, vegetarian dishes, cheese fondue. Salad bar. Hrs: 11 am-11 pm; Fri, Sat to midnight. Closed Thanksgiving, Dec 24, 25. Bar. A la carte entrees: lunch, dinner $5-$12. Outdoor dining. Casual dining; busy atmosphere. Family-owned since 1971. Cr cds: A, C, D, DS, MC, V.

D ⌧

★★★ **HARVEST.** *44 Brattle St (02138). 617/868-2255.* Specializes in mustard seed-crusted monkfish with crab cakes, grilled porterhouse lamb chops with eggplant and feta cheese custard. Hrs: noon-10:30 pm; Fri, Sat to 11 pm; Sun 11:30 am-10 pm. Res accepted. Wine list. Lunch $10-$15; dinner $19-$29. Child's menu. Outdoor garden terrace. Cr cds: A, D, DS, MC, V.

D ⌧

★★ **HELMAND.** *143 1st St (02142). 617/492-4646. www.helmandrestaurant.sbweb.switchboard.com.* Afghani menu. Specializes in authentic Afghani dishes. Own baking. Hrs: 5-10 pm; Fri, Sat to 11 pm. Closed Jan 1, Thanksgiving, Dec 25. Res accepted. Serv bar. Dinner $9.95-$16.95. Afghani decor with high ceilings. Totally nonsmoking. Cr cds: A, MC, V.

D

★★ **HENRIETTA'S TABLE.** *1 Bennett St (02138). 617/661-5005. www.charleshotel.com.* Regional Amer menu. Specialties: New England pot roast, chicken pot pie, fresh fish. Own baking, pasta. Hrs: 6:30-11 am, noon-3 pm, 5:30-10 pm; Fri to 11 pm; Sat 7 am-3 pm, 5:30-11 pm; Sun 7-10:30 am, noon-3 pm (brunch), 5:30-10 pm. Res accepted (exc Sat, Sun bkfst). Bar. Bkfst $6.50-$12, lunch $6.50-$12.50, dinner $10.50-$18.50. Sun brunch $32. Child's menu. Outdoor dining. Windows face courtyard; open kitchen; market on site. Cr cds: A, D, MC, V.

D

★ **LA GROCERIA.** *853 Main St (02139). 617/876-4162.* Italian menu. Specializes in antipasto. Own pasta. Hrs: 11:30 am-10 pm; Fri to 11 pm; Sat 4-11 pm; Sun 1-10 pm; early-bird dinner 4-6:30 pm. Closed Jan 1, Thanksgiving, Dec 25. Res accepted. Bar. Lunch $4.95-$8.95, dinner $9.95-$16.95. Child's menu. Valet parking wkends. Family-owned. Cr cds: A, DS, MC, V.

D ⌧

★ **REDBONES.** *55 Chester St, Somerville (02144). 617/628-2200. www.redbonesbbq.com.* Barbecue menu. Specializes in ribs. Hrs: 11:30-12:30 am. Closed Thanksgiving, Dec 25. Bar. Lunch $3.95-7.95, dinner $5.95-$14.95. Street parking. Southwestern decor. Cr cds: A, D, MC, V.

D

★★★★ **RIALTO.** *1 Bennett St (02138). 617/661-5050. www.rialto-restaurant.com.* Chef/owner Jody Adams has established this French Mediterranean restaurant in the Charles Hotel as one of Cambridge's favorites. The soft lighting and comfortable banquettes provide an elegant setting to enjoy her savory cuisine, and the sizeable wine list features wines from four different countries—Spain, Italy, France and the United States. The desserts are a scrumptious ending to an unforgettable meal. Continental menu. Specializes in grilled sirloin, seasonal game, fresh seafood. Own baking, pasta. Hrs: 5:30-10 pm; Fri, Sat to 11 pm. Closed most major hols. Res accepted. Bar to 11 pm; Fri, Sat to midnight. Wine list. Dinner $19-$29. Validated parking. 1940s supper club atmosphere; original artwork. Cr cds: A, D, MC, V.

D ⬛

★★★ **SALTS.** *798 Main St (02139). 617/876-8444.* Specialties: roast rabbit, duck with lavender, halibut. Hours: Tues-Sat 5:30-10 pm, Sun 5:30-9 pm. Closed Mon. Prices: $15-$25. Cr cds: D, MC, V.

★★ **SANDRINE'S.** *8 Holyoke St (02138). 617/497-5300. www.sandrines.com.* French menu. Specialties: choucroute, frog legs, tarte flambe. Hrs: 11:30 am-2:30 pm, 5:30-10 pm; Mon 5:30-10 pm; Fri, Sat to 10:30 pm; Sun 5:30-10 pm. Res accepted. Bar. Wine list. Lunch $6-$16, dinner $15-$30. Child's menu. Street parking. Classic bistro decor; casual dining. Totally nonsmoking. Cr cds: A, MC, V.

D

Cape Cod

The popularity of the automobile changed Cape Cod from a group of isolated fishing villages, big estates, and cranberry bogs into one of the world's prime resort areas. The Cape's permanent population of about 201,000 witness this change each year with the arrival of nearly 500,000 summer people.

A great many motels have sprung up since World War II, and cottages line the beaches in some areas. Yet the villages have remained virtually unchanged. The long main streets of villages like Yarmouthport and Brewster are still lined with old houses, some dating from the 17th century. The sea wind still blows across the moors below Truro and the woods of the Sandwich Hills.

The Cape is about 70 miles long and bent like an arm with its fist upraised. Buzzards Bay and the Cape Cod Canal are at the shoulder, Chatham and Nauset beach are at the elbow, and Provincetown is the fist. Because the Cape extends so far out toward the warm Gulf Stream (about 30 miles), its climate is notably gentler than that of the mainland; summers are cooler and winters are milder. It has almost 560 miles of coastline, most of which is gleaming beach—the Cape being composed of sand rather than bedrock. As if to please every taste, many towns on the Cape have two coasts—the Nantucket Sound beaches

with warm, calm waters; the Atlantic Ocean beaches with colder water and high breakers; or Cape Cod Bay with cool, calm waters. Inland woods are dotted with 365 clear freshwater ponds, known as kettle ponds.

Surf casting (day and night) and small-boat and deep-sea fishing are major sports along the entire Cape coastline. At least a dozen varieties of game fish are found, including giant tuna.

The current summer gaiety belies the Cape's hardy pioneer history. It was in Provincetown harbor that the *Mayflower* first set anchor for the winter and the first party of Pilgrims went ashore. Eighteen years earlier, in 1602, Cape Cod was named by the English explorer Bartholomew Gosnold after the great schools of fish he saw in the bay.

The following towns, villages and special areas on Cape Cod are included in the *Mobil Travel Guide*. For full information on any one of them, see the individual alphabetical listing: Barnstable, Bourne, Brewster, Buzzards Bay, Cape Cod National Seashore, Centerville, Chatham, Dennis, Eastham, Falmouth, Harwich, Hyannis, Orleans, Provincetown, Sandwich, South Yarmouth, Truro & North Truro, Wellfleet, and Woods Hole.

Cape Cod National Seashore

This recreation area consists of 44,600 acres, including submerged lands located offshore along the eastern part of Barnstable County. Headquarters are at South Wellfleet. Exhibits, interpretive programs at the Salt Pond Visitor Center in Eastham (Mid-Feb-Dec, daily; Jan-mid-Feb wkends only), phone 508/255-3421; Province Lands Visitor Center on Race Point Rd in Provincetown (mid-Apr-Nov, daily), phone 508/487-1256. Numerous private homes are within park boundaries. Swimming, lifeguards at designated areas (late June-Labor Day), fishing; hunting, bicycle trails, self-guided nature trails, guided walks, and evening programs in summer. Parking at beaches (fee); free after Labor Day. Buttonbush Trail has Braille trail markers. For further information, contact the Superintendent, 99 Marconi Site, Wellfleet 02667; phone 508/349-3785.

Centerville (Cape Cod)

See also Hyannis (Cape Cod)

Pop 9,190 **Elev** 40 ft **Area code** 508 **Zip** 02632

Information Cape Cod Chamber of Commerce, US 6 and MA 132, PO Box 790, Hyannis 02601-0790; 508/362-3225 or 888/33-CAPECOD

Web www.capecodchamber.org

What to See and Do

Centerville Historical Society Museum. Houses 14 exhibition rms interpreting Cape Cod's history, art, industry, and domestic life. Displays include early American furniture, housewares, quilts; dolls, costumes; Crowell carved birds, Sandwich glass collection, marine rm, tool rm, research library. (June-mid-Sept, Wed-Sun; winter by appt) 513 Main St. Phone 508/775-0331. ¢¢

Osterville Historical Society Museum. Sea captain's house with 18th- and 19th-century furnishings; Sandwich glass, Chinese porcelain, majolica and Staffordshire pottery; doll collection. Special events throughout the summer. Boat-building museum, ship models; catboat *Cayugha* is on display. Restored Cammett House (ca 1730) is on grounds. (Mid-June-Sept, Thurs-Sun afternoons; other times by appt) 3 mi SW, at jct West Bay and Parker Rds in Osterville. Phone 508/428-5861. ¢¢

Motels/Motor Lodges

★ **CENTERVILLE CORNERS MOTOR LODGE.** *1338 Craigville Beach Rd, Centerville (02632). 508/775-7223; fax 508/775-4147; toll-free 800/242-1137. www.centervillecorners.com.* 48 rms, 2 story. July-Labor Day: S, D $48-$130; each addl $10; kit. unit $95-$125; under 14 free; wkly rates; golf plan; lower rates rest of yr. Closed Dec-Apr. Crib $5. Pet accepted; $5. TV; cable. Indoor pool; sauna. Complimentary continental bkfst (in season). Complimentary coffee in rms. Ck-out 11 am. Lawn games. Picnic tables, grills. Cr cds: A, DS, MC, V.

★★ **TRADE WINDS INN.** *780 Craigville Beach Rd, Centerville (02632). 508/775-0365; toll-free 877/444-7966. www.twicapecod.com.* 35 rms, 2 story, 4 kits. Mid-June-Labor Day: S, D $70-$179; each addl $10; suites $190-$215; lower rates Apr-mid-June, after Labor Day-Oct. Closed rest of yr. TV; cable. Complimentary continental bkfst in season. Ck-out 11 am. Meeting rms. Putting green. Private patios, balconies. Private beach opp. Cr cds: A, MC, V.

B&B/Small Inn

★★ **ADAM'S TERRACE GARDENS INN.** *539 Main St, Centerville (02632). 508/775-4707. www.adamsterrace.com.* 7 rms, 5 with bath, 2 story. No A/C. No rm phones. Late-May-mid-Sept: S $45-$55; D $90-$110; each addl $20; lower rates rest of yr. TV; cable. Complimentary full bkfst. Restaurant nearby. Ck-out 11 am, ck-in 3 pm. Patio. Built circa 1830. Antiques. Sitting rm. Totally nonsmoking. Cr cds: MC, V.

Restaurant

★★★ **REGATTA OF COTUIT.** *4631 Falmouth Rd, Cotuit (02635). 508/428-5715.* Specialties: swordfish with scallion and lemon, lacquered duck, chocolate seduction cake. Menu changes frequently. Hrs: 5-10 pm. Res accepted. A la carte entrees: dinner $18-$26. 1790 Federal-style mansion with 8 dining rms; Early Amer decor; fireplaces; many antiques. Own herb garden. Cr cds: A, MC, V.
D

Chatham (Cape Cod)

Settled 1656 **Pop** 6,625 **Elev** 46 ft **Area code** 508 **Zip** 02633
Information Chamber of Commerce, PO Box 793; 800/715-5567; or the Cape Cod Chamber of Commerce, US 6 and MA 132, PO Box 790, Hyannis 02601-0790; 508/362-3225 or 888/CAPECOD
Web www.capecodchamber.org

Chatham is among the Cape's fashionable shopping centers. Comfortable estates in the hilly country nearby look out on Pleasant Bay and Nantucket Sound. Monomoy Island, an unattached sand bar, stretches ten miles south into the sea. It was once a haunt of "moon-cussers"—beach pirates who lured vessels aground with false lights and then looted the wrecks.

What to See and Do

Gristmill. (1797) (Daily) Shattuck Place, off Cross St, W shore of Mill Pond in Chase Park. Phone 508/945-5158. **FREE**

Monomoy National Wildlife Refuge. Wilderness area reached from Chatham (access by boat only, special regulations apply). Main St past Chatham Lighthouse, turn left onto Morris Island Rd, follow signs to headquarters on Morris Island. Vista of Pleasant Bay, Monomoy Island, and Atlantic Ocean. Surf fishing; more than 250 species of birds. No camping. (Daily) Contact Refuge Manager, Great Meadows NWR, Weir Hill Rd, Sudbury 01776. Phone 508/945-0594. **FREE**

Old Atwood House. (1752) Chatham Historical Society. Memorabilia of Joseph C. Lincoln, Cape Cod novelist. Shell collection, murals by Alice Stallknecht, "Portrait of a New England Town." China trade collection. Maritime collection. Stage Harbor Rd, ½ mi off MA 28. (Mid-June-Sept, Tues-Fri afternoons; Sat mornings; schedule may vary) Phone 508/945-2493. ¢¢

Railroad Museum. Restored "country railroad depot" houses scale models, photographs, railroad memorabilia, and relics; restored 1910 New York Central caboose. (Mid-June-mid-Sept, Tues-Sat) Depot Rd, off Main St, MA 28 **Donation**

Special Events

Band Concerts. Kate Gould Park. Fri eve. Late June-early Sept. Phone 506/362-3225.

Monomoy Theatre. 776 Main St. Ohio University Players in comedies, musicals, dramas, classics. Tues-Sat. Late June-late Aug. Phone 508/945-1589.

Motels/Motor Lodges

★ **CHATHAM HIGHLANDER.** *946 Main St, Chatham (02633). 508/945-9038; fax 508/945-5731. www. realmass.com/highlander.* 28 rms. Late-June-early Sept: S, D $96; wkends (2-day min); hols (3-day min); lower rates rest of yr. Closed Dec-Apr. TV; cable. Complimentary coffee in rms. Restaurant nearby. Ck-out 10:30 am. 2 pools. Refrigerators. Picnic tables. Cr cds: DS, MC, V.

★ **THE CHATHAM MOTEL.** *1487 Main St, Chatham (02633). 508/945-2630; toll-free 800/770-5545. www.chathammotel.com.* 32 rms. July-mid-Sept: S, D $90-$130; each addl $5; lower rates May-June, mid-Sept-Oct. Closed rest of yr. TV; cable (premium). Pool. Playground. Coffee in lobby. Restaurant nearby. Ck-out 11 am. Lawn games. Refrigerators. Picnic tables. In pine grove. Cr cds: MC, V.

★ **CHATHAM SEAFARER.** *2079 Main St, Chatham (02633). 508/432-1739; fax 508/432-8969; toll-free 800/ 786-2772. www.chathamseafarer.com.* 20 rms, 7 kit. units. Mid-July-Aug: S, D $85-$155; each addl $15; kit. units $135-$155; wkends (2-, 4-day min); higher rates Memorial Day, July 4th; lower rates rest of yr. TV; cable. Complimentary coffee in rms. Ck-out 11 am. Lawn games. Picnic tables. Cr cds: A, MC, V.

★★ **CHATHAM TIDES WATERFRONT MOTEL.** *394 Pleasant St, South Chatham (02659). 508/432-0379. www.allcapecod.com/chathamtides.* 24 kit. units in motel and townhouses, suites avail. Some A/C. July-Aug: S, D $135-$155; each addl $20; kit. suites, townhouses $1,200-$1,650/wk; lower rates Sept-May. TV; cable. Ck-out 11 am. Some microwaves. Sun decks. On private beach. Cr cds: MC, V.

★★★ **DOLPHIN OF CHATHAM INN AND MOTEL.** *352 Main St, Chatham (02633). 508/945-0070; fax 508/945-5945; toll-free 800/688-5900. www.dolphininn.com.* 38 rms, 3 kits. Late June-early Sept: S, D $144-$219; each addl $15; suites $199-$229; kit. units $154; 2-bedrm kit. cottages $1,500/wk; lower rates rest of yr. TV; cable. Heated pool; whirlpool. Coffee in rms. Restaurant 8-11 am. Ck-out 10 am. Business servs avail. Some refrigerators, in-rm whirlpools; microwaves avail. Some private patios. Picnic tables, grills. Cr cds: A, D, DS, MC, V.

★★ **THE HAWTHORNE.** *196 Shore Rd, Chatham (02633). 508/945-0372. www.thehawthorne.com.* 26 rms, 10 kits. Mid-May-mid-Oct: S, D $100-$165; kit. units $140; cottage $275; each addl $15. Closed rest of yr. TV; cable. Restaurant nearby. Ck-out 11 am. Refrigerators; some microwaves. On private beach. Cr cds: A, MC, V.

Resorts

★★★ **CHATHAM BARS INN.** *297 Shore Rd, Chatham (02633). 508/945-0096; fax 508/945-6785; toll-free 800/527-4884. www.chathambarsinn.com.* 205 rms in inn, 1-3 story, no elvtr, 29 cottages, 1-12 bedrm. Some A/C. Mid-June-mid-Sept: S, D $375-$410; suites $375-$1,000; lower rates rest of yr. Crib avail. TV; cable, VCR avail (free movies). Heated pool. Free supervised children's activities (Mid-June-Labor Day); ages 4-12. Dining rm 8 am-9 pm. Box lunches, clambakes in season. Rm serv. Bar noon-1 am, entertainment (in season). Ck-out 11 am, ck-in 3 pm. Meeting rms. Business servs avail. In-rm modem link. Bellhops. Valet serv. Concierge. Tennis, pro. Putting green. Exercise equipt. Complimentary boat shuttle. Lawn games. Rec rm. Many balconies. Spacious cottages. On 22 acres; private beach. Cr cds: A, MC, V.

★★★ **PLEASANT BAY VILLAGE RESORT.** *1191 Orleans Rd, Chatham (02633). 508/945-1133; fax 508/945-9701; toll-free 800/547-1011. www.pleasantbayvillage.com.* 58 rms, 20 kits., 10 suites (1-2 bedrm). Early June-Aug: S, D, kit. units $215-$245; each addl $15-$20; 1-bedrm suites $355; 2-bedrm suites (2-day min) $395-$415; lower rates mid-May-early June, Sept-mid-Oct. Closed rest of yr. Crib avail. TV; cable. Heated pool; poolside serv. Playground. Restaurant 8-11 am. Rm serv. Ck-out 11 am. Business servs avail. In-rm modem link. Sundries. Lawn games. Refrigerators, microwaves avail. On 6 landscaped acres. Extensive Chinese gardens; waterfall; ornamental pond. Cr cds: A, MC, V.

★★★ **WEQUASSETT INN.** *On Pleasant Bay, Chatham (02633). 508/432-5400; fax 508/432-5032; toll-free 800/225-7125. www.wequassett.com.* 98 rms, 6 suites, 1 and 2 story. Mid-Apr-mid-Nov: S, D $210-$450; suites $450-$800. Closed rest of yr. Crib free. TV; cable (premium), VCR avail. Heated pool; poolside serv. Supervised children's activities (in season); ages 3-12 yrs. Complimentary coffee in rms. Dining rm 7 am-10 pm. Rm serv 7 am-11 pm. Ck-out 11 am, ck-in 3 pm. Business center. Valet serv. Gift shop. Airport, bus depot transportation avail. Tennis, pro. Golf privileges. Exercise rm. Massage. Minibars. Some fireplaces. Many private patios, balconies. Private beach. Lawn games: bocce, croquet, shuffleboard. Basketball court, volleyball. Sailboats, windsurfing, deep-sea fishing charters, whale-watching cruises. Cr cds: A, DS, MC, V.

B&Bs/Small Inns

★★★ **CAPTAIN'S HOUSE INN.** *369-377 Old Harbor Rd, Chatham (02633). 508/945-0127; fax 508/945-0866; toll-free 800/315-0728. www.captainshouseinn.com.* 16 rms, 3 with shower only, 2 story, 6 suites. Mid-May-Oct: S, D $175-$425; suites $200-$325; wkends (3-day min); lower rates rest of yr. TV in some rms; VCR. Complimentary full bkfst; afternoon refreshments. Restaurant nearby. Ck-out 11 am, ck-in 2 pm. Luggage handling. Concierge service. Bicycles. Lawn games. Health club p\rivileges. Many in-rm whirlpools, fireplaces. Picnic tables. Greek Revival house built 1839; Williamsburg-style antiques and period pieces. Totally nonsmoking. Cr cds: A, DS, MC, V.

★★★ **CHATHAM TOWN HOUSE INN.** *11 Library Ln, Chatham (02633). 508/945-2180; fax 508/945-3990; toll-free 800/242-2180. www.chathamtownhouse.com.* 29 rms, 2½ story, 2 cottages. Late June-Sept, Columbus Day, Memorial Day: S, D $135-$350; each addl $25; cottages for 4 persons, $400; lower rates rest of yr. Crib free. TV; cable (premium). Heated pool; whirlpool, poolside serv (lunch). Complimentary full bkfst; afternoon refreshments. Ck-out noon, ck-in 3 pm. Refrigerators. Fireplace in cottages. Picnic tables. In Chatham historical district. Totally nonsmoking. Cr cds: A, C, D, DS, JCB, MC, V.

D ⌷ ⌷ ⌷

★★★ **CRANBERRY INN.** *359 Main St, Chatham (02633). 508/945-9232; fax 508/945-3769; toll-free 800/332-4667. www.cranberryinn.com.* 18 rms, 2 story. Late June-early-Sept: S, D $137-$230; each addl $30; suites $220-$260; lower rates rest of yr. Children over 8 yrs only. TV; cable. Complimentary bkfst buffet; afternoon refreshments. Restaurant nearby. Ck-out 11 am, ck-in 2 pm. Library/sitting rm; antiques and reproduction furnishings. Some fireplaces, wet bars. Some balconies. Built in 1830. Inn has been in continuous operation for more than 150 yrs. Totally nonsmoking. Cr cds: A, MC, V.

⌷ ⌷

★★★ **MOSES NICKERSON HOUSE INN.** *364 Old Harbor Rd, Chatham (02633). 508/945-5859; fax 508/945-7087; toll-free 800/628-6972. www.capecodtravel.com/mosesnickersonhouse.* 7 rms, 2 story. Late May-mid-Oct: S, D $129-$179; lower rates rest of yr. Children over 14 yrs only. TV avail. Complimentary full bkfst. Restaurant nearby. Ck-out 10:30 am, ck-in 2:30 pm. Lawn games. Antiques. Library/sitting rm. Built 1839. Totally nonsmoking. Cr cds: A, MC, V.

⌷ ⌷

★★ **OLD HARBOR INN.** *22 Old Harbor Rd, Chatham (02633). 508/945-4434; fax 508/945-7665; toll-free 800/942-4434. www.chathamoldharborinn.com.* 8 rms, 2 story. No rm phones. July-mid-Oct: S, D $139-$259; season special plans; lower rates rest of yr. Children over 14 yrs only. Complimentary bkfst buffet; afternoon refreshments. Restaurant nearby. Ck-out 11 am, ck-in 3 pm. Concierge serv. Gift shop. Built 1933; former residence of prominent doctor. Renovated and furnished with a blend of antiques and modern conveniences. Fireplace in parlor. Outside deck. Totally nonsmoking. Cr cds: MC, V.

⌷ ⌷

★★ **PORT FORTUNE INN.** *201 Main St, Chatham (02633). 508/945-0792; res 800/750-0792. www.portfortuneinn.com.* 12 rms, 2 with shower only, 2 story. Mid-June-mid-Sept: S, D $160; wkend, hols (2-3-day min); lower rates rest of yr. Children over 8 yrs only. TV in some rms; cable. Complimentary continental bkfst. Restaurant nearby. Ck-out 11 am, ck-in 2 pm. Opp beach. Built in 1910; antiques. Totally nonsmoking. Cr cds: A, MC, V.

⌷ ⌷

★★★ **QUEEN ANNE INN.** *70 Queen Anne Rd, Chatham (02633). 508/945-0394; fax 508/945-4884; toll-free 800/545-4667. www.queenanneinn.com.* 31 rms, 3 story. S, D $104-$189; each addl $25. Closed Jan. Crib free. TV; VCR avail. Heated pool; whirlpool. Complimentary continental bkfst. Restaurant (dinner only). Ck-out 11 am, ck-in 2 pm. Business servs avail. Tennis, pro. Lawn games. Antiques, handmade quilts. Many fireplaces; some in-rm whirlpools. Balconies. Built in 1840 for sea captain's daughter. Boats for excursions. Totally nonsmoking. Cr cds: A, DS, MC, V.

⌷ ⌷ ⌷ ⌷

Restaurants

★★ **CHATHAM SQUIRE.** *487 Main St, Chatham (02633). 508/945-0945. www.thesquire.com.* Specializes in local seafood. Raw bar. Hrs: 11:30 am-10:30 pm. Bar to 1 am. Lunch $4.95-$11.95, dinner $9.95-$21.95. Child's menu. Nautical decor. Cr cds: A, DS, MC, V.

D

★★ **CHRISTIAN'S.** *443 Main St, Chatham (02633). 508/945-3362. www.christiansrestaurant.com.* Specializes in fresh local seafood, homemade meatloaf, oysters. Hrs: 5-10 pm. Bar to 1 am. Dinner $8-$20. Pianist. Outdoor dining. Two-level dining. Built 1819. Cr cds: A, C, DS, MC, V.

D

★★ **IMPUDENT OYSTER.** *15 Chatham Bars Ave, Chatham (02633). 508/945-3545.* Specializes in seafood. Hrs: 11:30 am-10 pm; Sun from noon. Res required. Bar to 1 am. Lunch $6.95-$12.95, dinner $14-$23. Child's menu. Cathedral ceilings, stained-glass windows. Cr cds: A, MC, V.

D

Chicopee

(see Springfield)

Concord

See also Lexington, Sudbury Center

Settled 1635 **Pop** 16,993 **Elev** 141 ft **Area code** 978 **Zip** 01742

Information Concord Chamber of Commerce, 105 Everett St, 978/369-3120

Web www.ultranet.com/~conchamb/

This town shares with Lexington the title of Birthplace of the Republic. But it was Ralph Waldo Emerson who saw to it that the shot fired "by the rude bridge" was indeed heard 'round the world.

The town's name arose because of the "peace and concord" between the settlers and the Native Americans in the 17th century. The famous Concord grape was developed here in 1849 by Ephraim Bull.

The town of Lincoln, adjoining Concord on the east, was the scene of a running battle with the Redcoats on their withdrawal toward Boston. Here the harassing fire of the Minutemen was perhaps most effective.

What to See and Do

Codman House. (ca 1740) Originally a two-story, L-shaped Georgian mansion. In 1797-1798 it was more than doubled in size by Federal merchant John Codman to imitate an English country residence. Family furnishings. Grounds have many unusual trees and plants; formal Italian garden. (June-mid-Oct, Wed-Sun afternoons) Codman Rd, 5 mi S of MA 2 via Bedford Rd in Lincoln. Phone 781/259-8843. ¢¢

Concord Free Public Library. Modern public library, historical collections of famous Concord authors. On display is a mantelpiece from the US Capitol (ca 1815). Also statues of Emerson and others by Daniel Chester French. (Nov-May, daily, limited hrs Sun; rest of yr, Mon-Sat) Main St at Sudbury Rd. Phone 978/318-3300. **FREE**

Concord Museum. Period rms and galleries of domestic artifacts and decorative arts chronicling history of Concord from Native American habitation to present. Exhibits include Ralph Waldo Emerson's study, Henry David Thoreau's belongings used at Walden Pond, and Revolutionary War relics, including Paul Revere's signal lantern. Self-guided tours. (Daily; closed Easter, Thanksgiving, Dec 25) 200 Lexington Rd. Phone 978/369-9609. ¢¢¢

DeCordova Museum & Sculpture Park. Contemporary art museum on 35 acres of parkland overlooking Flint's Pond; changing exhibits, lectures, films, special events. (Tues-Sun) Concerts in summer (Sun). SE on Sandy Pond Rd in Lincoln. Phone 781/259-8355. ¢¢

Drumlin Farm Education Center. Demonstration farm with domestic and native wild animals and birds; gardens; hayrides; special events. (Tues-Sun and Mon hols; closed Jan 1, Thanksgiving, Dec 25) 2½ mi S on MA 126, then E on MA 117 (S Great Rd) in Lincoln. Phone 781/259-9807. ¢¢¢

Fruitlands Museums. Four museums, including the Fruitlands Farmhouse, the scene of Bronson Alcott's experiment in community life, which contains furniture, books, and memorabilia of the Alcott family and the Transcendentalists; Shaker Museum, formerly in the Harvard Shaker Village, with furniture and handicrafts; Picture Gallery, with American primitive portraits and paintings by Hudson River School artists; American Indian Museum, with prehistoric artifacts and Native American art. Hiking trails with views west to Mt Wachusett and north to Mt Monadnock. Tearoom; gift shop. (Mid-May-mid-Oct, Tues-Sun and Mon hols) 102 Prospect Hill Rd. 15 mi W via MA 2, exit 38A, in Harvard. Phone 978/456-9028. ¢¢¢

Great Meadows National Wildlife Refuge. Nature trails through wetland and upland woodland (daily). More than 200 bird species frequent this diverse habitat area. Canoeing and boating on Sudbury and Concord rivers (no rentals); nature trails, hiking, x-country skiing, snowshoeing; Concord Unit, Dike Trail; Monsen Rd off MA 62, 1 mi E from Concord Center. Contact Refuge Manager, Weir Hill Rd, Sudbury 01776. Phone 978/443-4661. **FREE**

Gropius House. (1937-1938) Family home of architect Walter Gropius. First building he designed upon arrival in the US in 1937; blends New England traditions and Bauhaus principles of function and simplicity with New England's building materials and environment. Original furniture, artwork. (June-mid-Oct, Fri-Sun afternoons; rest of yr, Sat and Sun first full wkend of each month) 68 Baker Bridge Rd, SE in Lincoln. For information, phone 781/259-8843. ¢¢

Minuteman National Historical Park. North Bridge Unit, Monument St, contains famous Minuteman statue by Daniel Chester French and reconstructed North Bridge over Concord River. Interpretive talks are given. North Bridge Visitor Center at 174 Liberty St has exhibits, information, restrms. (Daily; closed Jan 1, Thanksgiving, Dec 25) Battle Rd Visitor Center, off MA 2A in Lexington, has exhibit rm, movie, and orientation program. (Mid-May-Oct, daily) Contact Superintendent, 174 Liberty St. Phone 978/369-6993. **FREE**

The Old Manse. (1770) Parsonage of Concord's early ministers, including Reverend William Emerson, Ralph Waldo Emerson's grandfather. Nathaniel Hawthorne lived here for a time and made it the setting for *Mosses from an Old Manse*. Original furnishings. (Mid-Apr-Oct, Mon-Sat, also Sun afternoons) Monument St at the North Bridge. Phone 978/369-3909. ¢¢¢

Orchard House. Here Louisa May Alcott wrote *Little Women*. Alcott memorabilia. Guided tours. (Open yr round, hrs vary seasonally) 399 Lexington Rd. Phone 978/369-4118. ¢¢¢

Ralph Waldo Emerson House. Ralph Waldo Emerson's home from 1835 to 1882. Original furnishings and family memorabilia; 30-min guided tours. (Mid-Apr-late Oct, Thurs-Sun, limited hrs Sun) 28 Cambridge Tpke, at Lexington Rd (MA 2A). Phone 978/369-2236. ¢¢¢

Sleepy Hollow Cemetery. The Alcotts, Ralph Waldo Emerson, Nathaniel Hawthorne, Margaret Sidney, Daniel Chester French, and Henry David Thoreau are buried here. Bedford St, NE of square.

✪Walden Pond State Reservation. Located in this 304-acre park is a replica of Thoreau's cabin; also trail to cairn that marks site of original cabin. Swimming, fishing; hiking trails, interpretive programs. (All yr, daylight hrs) Standard fees. ½ mi S of MA 2 on MA 126. Phone 978/369-3254. ¢

The Wayside. 19th-century authors Nathaniel Hawthorne, the Alcotts, and Margaret Sidney, author of the *Five Little Peppers* books, lived here. Orientation program; 45-min tours (May-Oct) 455 Lexington Rd (MA 2A). Phone 978/369-6975.

Special Event

Patriots Day Parade. Events, reenactments. Mon nearest Apr 19 (or Sat if the 19th). Phone 978/369-3042.

Motels/Motor Lodges

★★ **BEST WESTERN.** *740 Elm St (01742). 978/369-6100; fax 978/371-1656; res 800/780-1234. www.bestwestern.com.* 106 rms, 2 story. S $109-$129; D $119-$139; each addl $10; under 17 free. Crib free. TV; cable (premium). Pool; whirlpool. Complimentary continental bkfst. Ck-out noon. Coin lndry. Meeting rms. Business servs avail. Valet serv. Downhill/x-country ski 3½ mi. Exercise equipt. Balconies. Cr cds: A, C, D, DS, ER, JCB, MC, V.

⬛ 🏊 🏖 🏃 🈁 🐾

★★ **HOLIDAY INN BOXBOROUGH WOODS.** *242 Adams Pl, Boxborough (01719). 978/263-8701; fax 978/263-0518. www.holiday-inn.com.* 143 rms, 3 story. S, D $119-$139; each addl $10; suites $199; under 18 free. Crib free. TV; cable (premium), VCR avail. Indoor pool. Coffee in rms. Restaurant 6:30 am-11 pm; Sat, Sun from 7 am. Rm serv. Bar 11 am-midnight. Ck-out noon. Meeting rms. Business servs avail. In-rm modem link. Valet serv. Sundries. Downhill/x-country ski 10 mi. Exercise equipt; sauna. Coin lndry. Lawn games. Refrigerators, microwaves avail. Private patios, balconies. Picnic tables. Cr cds: A, D, DS, MC, V.

⬛ 🏊 🏖 🏃 🈁 🐾 SC

B&Bs/Small Inns

★★ **COLONIAL INN.** *48 Monument Sq (01742). 978/369-9200; fax 978/371-1533; toll-free 800/370-9200. www.concordscolonialinn.com.* 49 rms, 15 in main bldg (1716), 32 in Prescott wing (1960), 2 cottages. S, D $149-$185; each addl $10; cottages $250-$285; Crib $10. TV; cable (premium). Complimentary coffee. Restaurant (see also COLONIAL INN). Bar; entertainment exc Mon. Ck-out 11 am, ck-in 2:30 pm. Meeting rms. Business servs avail. Luggage handling. Microwaves avail. Walden Pond 2 mi. Historically prominent guests noted. Cr cds: A, D, DS, MC, V.

⬛ 🈁 🐾

★★ **HAWTHORNE INN.** *462 Lexington Rd (01742). 978/369-5610; fax 978/287-4949.* 7 rms, 2 story. No rm phones. S $110-$150; D $125-$210. Complimentary continental bkfst; afternoon refreshments. Ck-out 11 am, ck-in 3 pm. RR station transportation. X-country ski 2 mi. Microwaves avail. Antiques; original artwork. Library/sitting rm with fireplace. Totally nonsmoking. Cr cds: A, DS, MC, V.

🏖 🈁 🐾

Restaurant

★★ **COLONIAL INN.** *48 Monument Sq (01742). 978/369-2373. www.concordscolonialinn.com.* Continental menu. Specializes in fresh seafood, roast prime rib, regional specialties. Hrs: 7 am-10:30 pm. Sun brunch 10:30 am-2:30 pm. Bar noon-11 pm. Bkfst $1.85-$9, lunch $3.75-$12, dinner $14.95-$25.95. Sun brunch $20.95. Entertainment. Outdoor dining. Built in 1716; Henry David Thoreau's house. Cr cds: A, C, D, DS, MC, V.

⬛

Danvers

See also Beverly

Settled 1636 **Pop** 25,212 **Elev** 48 ft **Area code** 978 **Zip** 01923

Information North Shore Chamber of Commerce, 5 Cherry Hill Dr; 978/774-8565

Web www.northshorechamber.org

This small industrial town was once Salem Village—a community started by settlers from Salem looking for more farmland. In 1692, Danvers was the scene of some of the most severe witchcraft hysteria; 20 persons were put to death.

What to See and Do

Glen Magna Farms. A 20-rm mansion; 1790-1890 furnishings; Chamberlain gardens. Derby summer house was built by Samuel McIntire (1794); on the roof are two life-size carvings (reaper and milkmaid) by the Skillin brothers; reproduction of 1844 gazebo. Various special events and programs. (June-Sept, Tues and Thurs; closed hols; also by appt) 2 mi N on US 1, then ¼ mi E via Centre St to Ingersoll St. Phone 978/774-9165. ¢¢

Rebecca Nurse Homestead. The house (ca 1680), an excellent example of the New England saltbox, was the homestead of Rebecca Nurse, a saintly woman accused of and executed for witchcraft during the hysteria of 1692. House includes restored rms with furnishings from 17th and 18th centuries; outbuildings, a reproduction of the 1672 Salem Village Meetinghouse and exhibit areas. (Mid-June-mid-Sept, Tues-Sun; mid-Sept-Oct, wkends; rest of yr, by appt; closed hols) 149 Pine St. Phone 978/774-8799. ¢¢

Witchcraft Victims Memorial. Memorial includes names of those who died, as well as quotes from eight victims. 176 Hobart St.

Special Event

Danvers Family Festival. Exhibits, fireworks, races, music. (Late June-early July.) Phone 978/774-8565.

Motels/Motor Lodges

★★ **COURTYARD BY MARRIOTT.** *275 Independence Way (01923). 978/777-8630; fax 978/777-7341; toll-free 800/321-2211. www.courtyard.com.* 120 rms, 2 suites, 3 story. Mid-Apr-mid-Nov: S, D $109-$129; suites $129-$149. Crib free. TV; cable (premium). Heated pool. Complimentary coffee in rms. Restaurant 6:30 am-10 pm; wkends from 7 am. Bar 5-10 pm. Ck-out 1 pm. Coin lndry. Meeting rms. Business servs avail. In-rm modem link. Valet serv. Sundries. Exercise equipt. Refrigerator in suites; microwaves avail. Cr cds: A, C, D, DS, MC, V.

⬛ 🏊 🏃 🈁 🐾

★ **DAYS INN.** *152 Endicott St (01923). 978/777-1030; fax 978/777-0264; res 800/329-7466. www.daysinn.com.* 129 rms, 2 story. May-Oct: S, D $69.95-$99.95; each addl $8; under 18 free; wkly, hol rates; lower rates rest of yr. Crib free. TV; cable (premium). Pool. Complimentary continental bkfst. Restaurant adj open 24 hrs. Ck-out 11 am. Coin lndry. Business servs avail. In-rm modem link. Sundries. Picnic tables. Cr cds: A, DS, MC, V.

D ⊠ ≈ ⊠ 🔥

★ **QUALITY INN.** *Trask Ln (01923). 978/774-6800; fax 978/774-6502; toll-free 800/228-5151. www.qualityinn.com.* 125 rms, 2 story. S, D $99-$130; each addl $10; suite $250; under 18 free. Crib free. TV; cable (premium), VCR avail (movies). Indoor pool; whirlpool, poolside serv. Restaurant 7 am-10 pm. Rm serv. Bar; pianist Tues-Thurs, combo Fri-Sat. Ck-out 11 am. Meeting rms. Business servs avail. In-rm modem link. Sundries. Airport transportation. Health club privileges. Microwaves avail. Private patios, balconies. Indoor tropical garden. Cr cds: A, C, D, DS, ER, JCB, MC, V.

D ≈ ⊠ 🐾 SC

★ **SUPER 8.** *225 Newbury St (01923). 978/774-6500; fax 978/762-6491; res 800/800-8000. www.super8.com.* 78 rms, 2 story, 11 kit. units. Mid-June-mid-Oct: S, D $56-$66; each addl $5; kit. units $79; under 16 free; lower rates rest of yr. Crib free. Pet accepted. TV. Pool. Complimentary continental bkfst. Restaurant 11:30 am-10 pm. Bar to 12:30 am; entertainment Thurs-Sat. Ck-out 11 am. Meeting rms. Business servs avail. Microwaves avail. Cr cds: A, D, DS, MC, V.

D 🐾 ≈ ⊠ 🐾

Hotel

★★★ **SHERATON FERNCROFT RESORT.** *50 Ferncroft Rd (01923). 978/777-2500; fax 978/750-7959; res 800/325-2525. www.sheraton.com.* 367 rms, 8 story. S, D $169-$260; each addl $15; suites $250-$800; under 18 free. Crib free. TV; cable (premium), VCR avail. 2 pools, 1 indoor; whirlpool, poolside serv, lifeguard. Coffee in rms. Restaurant 6:30 am-11 pm. Bar 11-1 am. Ck-out 11 am. Meeting rms. Business center. In-rm modem link. Airport transportation. Gift shop. Lighted tennis, pro. 27-hole golf, pro, putting green, driving range. X-country ski on site. Exercise equipt. Lawn games. Refrigerators, microwaves avail. Private patios. Cr cds: A, DS, MC, V.

D ⊁ 🏌 🎿 ≈ 🎾 ⊠ 🔥 SC 🚶

Extended Stay

★★ **RESIDENCE INN BY MARRIOTT.** *51 Newbury St (01923). 978/777-7171; fax 978/774-7195; toll-free 800/331-3131. www.residenceinn.com.* 96 suites, 2 story. Suites $89-$189; wkly, wkend rates. Crib avail. Pet accepted, some restrictions. TV; cable. Pool. Complimentary continental bkst. Restaurant nearby. Ck-out noon. Coin lndry. Business servs avail. In-rm modem link. Valet serv. Lighted tennis. Exercise equipt. Sport court. Refrigerators, microwaves. Balconies. Picnic tables. Cr cds: A, C, D, DS, JCB, MC, V.

D 🐾 🎿 ≈ 🎾 ⊠ 🔥 SC

Restaurants

★★ **THE HARDCOVER.** *15-A Newbury St (01923). 978/774-1223. www.barnsiderrestaurants.com.* Specializes in seafood, steak, prime rib. Salad bar. Hrs: 5-10 pm; Fri, Sat to 11 pm; Sun 4-9 pm. Bar. Dinner $13.95-$29.95. Child's menu. Walls lined with books, rare prints, paintings. Fireplaces. Cr cds: A, C, D, DS, ER, MC, V.

D ⊣

★★ **LEGAL SEAFOODS.** *210 Andover St, Peabody (01960). 978/532-4500.* Specializes in seafood. Hrs: 11:30 am-10 pm; Fri, Sat to 10:30 pm; Sun to 9 pm. Closed Thanksgiving, Dec 25. Res accepted. Bar. Wine list. A la carte entrees: lunch $5.25-$11.95, dinner $10.95-$19.95. Child's menu. Totally nonsmoking. Cr cds: A, DS, MC, V.

D

Dedham

Settled 1635 **Pop** 23,464 **Elev** 120 ft **Area code** 781 **Zip** 02026

Information Neponset Valley Chamber of Commerce, 190 Vanderbilt Ave, Suite 1, Norwood 02062-5047; 781/769-1126
Web www.nvcc.com

What to See and Do

Dedham Historical Society. Small but important collection of 16th- to 19th-century furniture; collection of work by silversmith Katharine Pratt; world's largest public collection of Dedham and Chelsea pottery; changing exhibits. Also 10,000-volume historical and genealogical library. (Tues-Fri, some Sat; closed hols) 612 High St. Phone 781/326-1385. ¢

Fairbanks House. (1636) One of the oldest frame houses still standing in the US. Fine example of 17th-century architecture, furnished with Fairbanks family heirlooms; guided tours. (May-Oct, Tues-Sat, also Sun afternoons) 511 East St, at Eastern Ave, off US 1. Phone 781/326-1170. ¢¢

Motel/Motor Lodge

★★ **HOLIDAY INN BOSTON-DEDHAM.** *55 Ariadne Rd (02026). 781/329-1000; fax 781/329-0903; toll-free 800/465-4329. www.holiday-inn.com.* 203 rms, 8 story. S, D $139; each addl $5; under 19 free. Crib free. TV; cable (premium). Heated pool; poolside serv, lifeguard. Restaurant 6:30 am-10 pm. Rm serv. Ck-out noon. Meeting rms. Business servs avail. In-rm modem link. Bellhops. Valet serv. Sundries. Exercise equipt. Microwaves avail. Cr cds: A, D, DS, JCB, MC, V.

D ≈ 🎾 ⊠ 🐾 SC

Hotel

★★★ **HILTON AT DEDHAM PLACE.** *25 Allied Dr (02026). 781/329-7900; fax 781/329-5552; toll-free 800/345-6565. www.dedhamplace.hilton.com.* 249 rms, 4 story. S

$119-$245; D $134-$260; each addl $15; suites $400-$600; under 18 free; wkend rates. Crib free. Pet accepted. TV; cable (premium). Indoor pool; whirlpool, poolside serv (in season). Coffee in rms. Restaurant 6:30 am-10 pm. Bar 11-1 am; pianist. Ck-out noon. Meeting rms. Business center. In-rm modem link. Garage, valet parking. Lighted tennis. Exercise rm; sauna. Bathrm phones; refrigerators avail. Cr cds: A, C, D, DS, ER, JCB, MC, V.

[D] [icons]

Deerfield

Settled 1669 **Pop** 4,750 **Elev** 150 ft **Area code** 413
Zip 01342
Information Historic Deerfield, Inc, PO Box 321; 413/774-5581
Web www.historic-deerfield.org

Twice destroyed by French and Native American attacks when it was the northwest frontier of New England, and almost forgotten by industry, Deerfield is noted for its unspoiled meadowland, beautiful houses, and nationally famous boarding schools (Deerfield Academy, 1797, a coeducational preparatory school; the Bement School, a coeducational school; and Eaglebrook School for boys).

In 1675, the Bloody Brook Massacre (King Philip's War) crippled the settlement, which was then a struggling frontier outpost. In 1704 (Queen Anne's War), half of the resettled town was burned. Forty-nine inhabitants were killed and more than 100 were captured and taken to Canada.

The village boasts that it has one of the most beautiful streets in America, known just as The Street, a mile-long stretch of 80 houses, many dating from the 18th and early 19th centuries.

What to See and Do

Historic Deerfield, Inc. Maintains 14 historic house museums (fee) furnished with collections of antique furniture, silver, ceramics, textiles. A 28,000-sq-ft Collections Study Center features changing exhibits and study-storage displays of portions of the museum's collections. Daily walking tours, meadow walk, antique forums and workshops, special events wkends. Information Center is located at Hall Tavern, The Street. (Daily; closed Thanksgiving, Dec 24, 25) Phone 413/774-5581. ¢¢¢¢

Memorial Hall Museum. (1798) The first building of Deerfield Academy; contains colonial furnishings, Native American relics. (May-Oct, daily) Memorial St. Phone 413/774-7476. ¢¢

B&B/Small Inn

★★★ **DEERFIELD INN.** 81 Old Main St (01342). 413/774-5587; fax 413/775-7221; toll-free 800/926-3865. www.deerfieldinn.com. 23 rms, 2 story. S $142-$216; D $181-$255. Crib $10. TV; cable. Complimentary afternoon refreshments. Restaurant (see also DEERFIELD INN). Bar. Ck-out noon, ck-in 2 pm. Downhill ski 18 mi; x-country ski 11 mi. Antiques. Library. Built 1884. Totally nonsmoking. Cr cds: A, D, MC, V.

[D] [icons]

Restaurants

★★★ **DEERFIELD INN.** 81 Old Main St (01342). 413/774-5587. www.deerfield.com. Specialties: fresh seafood, rack of lamb, veal dishes. Hrs: 7:30-9 am, noon-2 pm, 6-9 pm; Sat, Sun 7:30 am-10 am, noon-2 pm, 6-9 pm. Closed Dec 25. Res accepted. Bar. Bkfst $7.50-$10.50, lunch $6-$12, dinner $20-$23. Afternoon tea 4-5 pm. Child's menu. Colonial decor. Built 1884. 14 museum houses nearby. Cr cds: A, D, MC, V.

[D]

★★★ **SIENNA.** 6B Elm St (01373). 413/665-0215. www.siennarest.com. Specializes in soft shell crabs, roasted duck breast. Hrs: 5:30-9:30 pm. Closed Mon, Tues. Res accepted. Wine list. Dinner $20-$23. Chef owned. Cr cds: MC, V.

Dennis (Cape Cod)

Settled 1639 **Pop** 15,973 **Elev** 24 ft **Area code** 508
Zip 02638
Information Chamber of Commerce, 242 Swan River Rd, 508/398-3568
Web www.dennischamber.com

Dennis heads a group, often called "The Dennises," that includes Dennisport, East Dennis, South Dennis, West Dennis, and Dennis. It was here, in 1816, that Henry Hall developed the commercial cultivation of cranberries. Swimming beaches are located throughout the area.

What to See and Do

Jericho House and Historical Center. (1801) Period furniture. Barn museum contains old tools, household articles, model of salt works, photographs. (July-Aug, Wed and Fri) At jct Old Main St and Trotting Park Rd in West Dennis. Phone 508/394-6114. **Donation**

Josiah Dennis Manse. (1736) and **Old West School House** (1770). Restored home of minister for whom town was named; antiques, Pilgrim chest, children's rm, spinning and weaving exhibit, maritime wing. (July-Aug, Tues and Thurs) 77 Nobscusset Rd. Phone 508/385-3528. **Donation**

Special Events

Cape Playhouse. On MA 6A. Summer theater, Mon-Sat. Children's Theater (Fri mornings). (Late June-Labor Day). Phone 508/385-3911 (box office) or 508/385-3838.

Festival Week. Canoe and road races, antique car parade, craft fair, antique show. (Late Aug) Phone 508/398-3568.

Motels/Motor Lodges

★★ **BREAKERS MOTEL.** *61 Chase Ave, Dennisport (02639). 508/398-6905; fax 508/398-7360; toll-free 800/ 540-6905. www.capecodtravel.com/breakers.* 36 rms, 2 story, 4 kits. Late June-Labor Day: S, D $100-$190; each addl $10; suites, kit. units $200-$350; lower rates May-late June, after Labor Day-mid-Oct. Closed rest of yr. Crib $10. TV; cable (premium). Heated pool. Continental bkfst. Restaurant nearby. Ck-out 11 am. Refrigerators; some microwaves. On beach. Cr cds: A, MC, V.

★★ **COLONIAL VILLAGE RESORT.** *426 Lower County Rd, Dennisport (02639). 508/398-2071; fax 508/398-2071; toll-free 800/287-2071. www.sunsol.com/colonial village.* 49 rms, 1-2 story, 29 kits., 10 kit. cottages (4-rm, no A/C). July-Labor Day: S, D $94-$120; each addl $10; kit. units $105; kit. cottages $750/wk; each addl $60; lower rates mid-May-June, after Labor Day-mid-Oct. Closed rest of yr. TV; cable. 2 pools, 1 indoor; whirlpool, sauna. Restaurant nearby. Ck-out 11 am. Meeting rms. Fireplace, oven in cottages. Private beach. Cr cds: DS, MC, V.

★★ **CORSAIR OCEANFRONT MOTEL.** *41 Chase Ave, Dennisport (02639). 508/398-2279; fax 508/760-6681; toll-free 800/889-8037. www.corsaircrossrip.com.* 25 kit. units, 2 story. July-Aug: S, D $145-$225; each addl $10; suite $275; packages avail; higher rates hols; lower rates Apr-June, Sept-Nov. Closed rest of yr. TV; cable (premium), VCR avail. 2 pools, 1 indoor; whirlpool. Supervised children's activities (in season); ages 5-14. Complimentary continental bkfst (off season). Restaurant adj 8 am-9 pm (in season). Ck-out 11 am. Coin lndry. Lawn games. Microwaves avail. Enclosed sun deck. On private beach. Cr cds: A, MC, V.

★ **THE GARLANDS.** *117 Old Wharf Rd, Dennisport (02639). 508/398-6987.* 20 air-cooled kit. units, 2 story. July, Aug: S, D $75-$120; each addl $11; off-season package plans; lower rates mid-Apr-June, mid-Aug-mid-Oct. Closed rest of yr. Children over 5 yrs only. TV; cable. Restaurant nearby. Ck-out 10 am. Balconies. On ocean, beach.

★ **HUNTSMAN MOTOR LODGE.** *829 Main St Rt 28, West Dennis (02670). 508/394-5415; toll-free 800/628-0498. www.thehuntsman.com.* 27 rms, 2 story, 9 kits. Mid-June-early Sept: S $52-$59; D $61-$79; each addl $6-$10; kit. units $79; wkly rates; lower rates mid-Apr-mid-June, early Sept-Oct. Closed rest of yr. Crib $4. TV; cable. Pool. Complimentary coffee in lobby. Restaurant adj 7 am-2 pm. Ck-out 11 am. Lawn games. Refrigerators avail. Picnic tables, grills. Cr cds: A, MC, V.

★ **SEA LORD RESORT MOTEL.** *56 Chase Ave, Dennisport (02639). 508/398-6900. www.sunsol.com/sealord.* 27 rms, 1-3 story. July-Aug: S $49-$95; D $59-$119; kit units $75-$95; each addl $5; lower rates May-late-June, Sept-Oct. Closed rest of yr. Crib $3. TV; cable. Complimentary coffee. Ck-out 11 am. Some refrigerators. Balconies. Beach opp. Cr cds: DS, MC, V.

★ **SEA SHELL MOTEL.** *45 Chase Ave, Dennisport (02639). 508/398-8965; fax 508/394-1237; toll-free 800/698-8965. www.virtualcapecod.com/market/seashellmotel.* 17 rms, 4 in guest house, 1-2 story, 5 kits. Some A/C. July-Labor Day: S $55-$120; D $70-$195; each addl $15; kit. units $88-$190; lower rates rest of yr. Crib free. TV; cable. Complimentary continental bkfst in season. Restaurant adj 7 am-9:30 pm. Ck-out 11 am. Refrigerators, microwaves avail. Balconies. Private beach. Sun deck. Cr cds: A, DS, MC, V.

★★ **SESUIT HARBOR.** *1421 Main St, East Dennis (02641). 508/385-3326; fax 508/385-3326; toll-free 800/359-0097. www.capecod.net/sesuit.* 20 rms, 1-2 story, 2 apts, 3 kits. Mid-June-mid-Sept: S $72-$98; D $78-$99; each addl $12; children under 12 $6; apts $585-$765/wk; kits. $105; wkly rates; lower rates rest of yr. Crib free. TV; cable. Pool. Complimentary continental bkfst. Restaurant opp 6 am-2 pm. Ck-out 10:30 am. Business servs avail. In-rm modem link. Refrigerators avail. Some balconies. Picnic tables, grills. Cr cds: MC, V.

★★ **SOUDINGS SEASIDE RESORT.** *79 Chase Ave, Dennisport (02639). 505/394-6561; fax 508/374-7537. www.thesoundings.com.* 100 rms, 1-2 story, 15 kits. Late June-Labor Day: S, D $110-$230; each addl $16; package plans; lower rates late Apr-late June, after Labor Day-mid-Oct. Closed rest of yr. TV; cable (premium). 2 pools, 1 indoor; poolside serv, sauna. Restaurant 7-11 am. Ck-out 11 am. Meeting rms. Business servs avail. In-rm modem link. Gift shop. Putting green. Refrigerators. Balconies. Sun decks. On 350-ft private beach. Cr cds: A, MC, V.

★★ **SPOUTER WHALE MOTOR INN.** *405 Old Wharf Rd, Dennisport (02639). 508/398-8010; fax 508/760-3214. www.capecod.net/spouter.* 38 rms in 2 bldgs, 2 story, 6 kits. Early July-late Aug: S, D $48-$140; each addl $10; lower rates Apr-early July, late Aug-late Oct. Closed rest of yr. TV; cable. Heated pool; whirlpool. Ck-out 11 am. Health club privileges. Refrigerators. Some private balconies. On ocean; private beach, beachside bkfst bar. Patio overlooking ocean. Totally nonsmoking.

★★ **THREE SEASONS MOTOR LODGE.** *421 Old Wharf Rd, Dennisport (02639). 508/398-6091; fax 508/398-3762. www.threeseasonsmotel.com.* 61 rms, 2 story. Late June-Labor Day: D $115-$160; each addl $15; lower rates late May-late June, after Labor Day-Oct. Closed rest of yr. TV; cable. Restaurant 8 am-3 pm; 5-10 pm. Ck-out 11 am. Balconies. On private beach. Cr cds: A, MC, V.

★ **WEST DENNIS MOTOR LODGE.** *691 Main St Rte 28, West Dennis (02670). 508/394-7434; fax 508/394-1672. www.sunsol.com/westdennis.* 22 rms, 2 story. July-Labor Day: S $49-$56; D $55-$69; each addl $6-$10; lower rates rest of yr. Crib $7. TV; cable, VCR avail. Pool. Restaurant adj 7 am-2 pm. Ck-out 11 am. Refrigerators; microwaves avail. Cr cds: A, MC, V.

Resorts

★★ **EDGEWATER BEACH RESORT.** *95 Chase Ave, Dennisport (02639). 508/398-6922; fax 508/760-3447. www.edgewatercapecod.com.* 86 rms, 1-2 story, 68 kits. July-Aug: S, D, kits. $90-$205; each addl $15; lower rates mid-Mar-June, Sept-mid-Nov. Closed rest of yr. TV; cable, VCR (movies). Indoor/outdoor pool; whirlpool. Restaurant adj 7-11 am. Ck-out 11 am. Meeting rm. Sundries. Putting green. Exercise equipt; sauna. Lawn games. Refrigerators, microwaves avail. Private patios, balconies. Ocean views from most rms. Cr cds: A, DS, MC, V.

★★ **LIGHTHOUSE INN.** *1 Lighthouse Rd, West Dennis (02670). 508/398-2244; fax 508/398-5658. www.lighthouseinn.com.* 63 rms in inn, motel, cottages, 15 A/C. MAP, late-May-mid-Oct: S $80-$110; D $146-$206; each addl $35-$60; cottages to 6, $117-$140/person. Closed rest of yr. Crib free. TV; cable, VCR avail. Heated pool. Playground. Supervised children's activities (July-Aug); ages 3-10. Restaurant 8-9:15 am, noon-2 pm, 6-9 pm. Rm serv. Box lunches. Bar 11 am-1 am; entertainment. Ck-out 11 am. Meeting rms. Business center. Bellhops. Tennis. Miniature golf. Lawn games. Refrigerators. Large private beach. On ocean. Cr cds: MC, V.

B&Bs/Small Inns

★★ **BY THE SEA GUESTS.** *57 Chase Ave, Dennisport (02639). 508/398-8685; fax 508/398-0334; toll-free 800/447-9202. www.bytheseaguests.com.* 12 rms, 3 story. 1 A/C. No rm phones. July-Aug: S, D $95-$140; each addl $15; lower rates May-June, Sept-Nov. Closed rest of yr. Crib $5. TV. Complimentary continental bkfst; afternoon refreshments. Restaurant adj 7 am-3 pm. Ck-out 11 am, ck-in 2 pm. Business servs avail. Concierge. Lawn games. Refrigerators. Picnic tables, grills. On private beach. Cr cds: A, C, D, MC, V.

★★ **CAPTAIN NICKERSON INN.** *333 Main St, South Dennis (02660). 508/398-5966; fax 508/398-5966; toll-free 800/282-1619. www.bbonline.com/ma/captnick/.* 7 rms, 2 share bath, 4 with shower only, 2 story. No rm phones. June-mid-Oct: S $85-$112; D $90-$117; each addl $10; under 10 free; wkly rates; lower rates rest of yr. Crib $10-$15. TV in living rm; cable. Playground. Complimentary full bkfst. Ck-out 11 am, ck-in 3 pm. Luggage handling. Concierge serv. Bicycles. Lawn games. Picnic tables. Queen Anne-style house built in 1828. Totally nonsmoking. Cr cds: DS, MC, V.

★★ **FOUR CHIMNEYS INN.** *946 Main St, Dennis (02638). 508/385-6317; fax 508/385-6285; toll-free 800/874-5502. www.fourchimneysinn.com.* 8 air-cooled rms, 3 story. No rm phones. June-Sept: D $95-$140; wkly rates; lower rates Oct-May. Closed late Dec-mid-Feb. TV in sitting rm; cable (premium). Complimentary continental bkfst. Restaurant nearby. Ck-out 11 am, ck-in 3 pm. Lawn games. Balconies. Picnic tables. Opp lake. Former summer residence (1875); antiques. Cr cds: A, MC, V.

★★ **ISAIAH HALL BED AND BREAKFAST INN.** *152 Whig St, Dennis (02638). 508/385-9928; fax 508/385-5879; toll-free 800/736-0160. www.isaiahhallinn.com.* 10 rms, 2 story. No rm phones. Mid-June-Labor Day: S $118-$124; D $128-$134; each addl $15; suite $153; wkly rates; lower rates mid-Apr-mid-June, after Labor Day-mid-Oct. Closed rest of yr. Children over 7 yrs only. TV; VCR. Complimentary continental bkfst; afternoon refreshments. Restaurant nearby. Ck-out 11 am, ck-in 2 pm. Rec rm. Lawn games. Balconies. Picnic tables. Antiques. Library. Farmhouse built 1857. Totally nonsmoking. Cr cds: A, DS, MC, V.

Restaurants

★★ **CAPTAIN WILLIAM'S HOUSE.** *106 Depot St, Dennisport (02639). 508/398-3910.* Specializes in lobster, prime rib, fresh seafood, homemade pasta. Hrs: 4:30-10 pm; early-bird dinner 4:30-5:45 pm. Closed Jan-Mar. Res accepted. Bar. Dinner $12.95-$19.95. Child's menu. Sea captain's house (1820); Colonial decor. Cr cds: A, D, DS, MC, V.

★★ **CHRISTINE'S.** *581 Main St (MA 28), West Dennis (02638). 508/394-7333.* Lebanese Amer menu. Specialties: chicken Christine, local seafood, Lebanese dishes. Hrs: 11:30 am-10 pm; Fri, Sat to 11 pm; early-bird dinner 4-6 pm; Sun brunch 10 am-2 pm. Res accepted. Bar to 1 am. Lunch $4.95-$6.95, dinner $8.95-$17.95. Sun brunch 9.95. Child's menu. Entertainment nightly in season; off season, wkends. Parking. Contemporary decor. Cr cds: A, DS, MC, V.

★ **MARSHSIDE.** *28 Bridge St, East Dennis (02641). 508/385-4010.* Specializes in fresh seafood, lobster salad, homemade pies. Hrs: 7 am-9 pm; Sun brunch 8 am-3 pm. Closed Thanksgiving, Dec 25. Serv bar. Bkfst $2.95-$5.95, lunch $4.95-$7.95, dinner $6.95-$13.95. Sun brunch $2.95-$5.95. Child's menu. Cozy atmosphere; knick-knacks, artificial flowers. Cr cds: A, C, D, DS, MC, V.

★★★ **RED PHEASANT INN.** *905 Main St, Dennis (02638). 508/385-2133. www.redpheasantinn.com.* Specializes in salmon, rack of lamb, roast lobster. Hrs: 5-10 pm. Res accepted. Bar. A la carte entrees: dinner $15-$25. Valet parking. Once a barn (ca 1795); many antiques. Family-owned. Totally nonsmoking. Cr cds: DS, MC, V.

★ **ROYAL PALACE.** *369 Main St, West Dennis (02638). 508/398-6145.* Chinese, Polynesian menu. Specializes in Cantonese and Mandarin dishes. Hrs: 4 pm-1 am. Res accepted. Bar. Dinner $6.50-$14.95. Parking. Cr cds: A, DS, MC.

★★ **SCARGO CAFE.** *799 MA 6A, Dennis (02638). 508/385-8200. www.scargocafe.com.* Continental menu. Specialties: chicken wildcat, mussels Ferdinand, grapenut custard. Hrs: 11 am-3 pm, 4:30-10 pm; early-bird dinner 4:30-5:30 pm. Closed Thanksgiving, Dec 25. Bar. Lunch $3.95-$10.95, dinner $9.95-$17.95. Child's menu. Parking. Former residence (1865); opp nation's oldest stock company theater. Totally nonsmoking. Cr cds: A, C, DS, MC, V.

D

★ **SWAN RIVER.** *5 Lower County Rd, Dennisport (02639). 508/394-4466. www.swanriverseafoods.com.* Specialties: fried clams, fresh lobster. Hrs: noon-3 pm, 5-9:30 pm. Closed mid-Sept-late May. Res accepted. Bar to 11 pm. Lunch $5-$10, dinner $12.95-$18.95. Child's menu. Parking. Nautical decor; overlooks Swan River. Family-owned. Cr cds: A, DS, MC, V.

D

Eastham (Cape Cod)

See also Orleans (Cape Cod)

Settled 1644 **Pop** 5,453 **Elev** 48 ft **Area code** 508 **Zip** 02642
Information Chamber of Commerce, PO Box 1329; 508/240-7211 or 508/255-3444 (summer only); or visit the Information Booth at MA 6 and Fort Hill
Web www.easthamchamber.com

On the bay side of the Cape, in what is now Eastham town, the *Mayflower* shore party met their first Native Americans. Also in the town is a magnificent stretch of Nauset Beach, which was once a graveyard of ships. Nauset Light is an old friend of mariners.

What to See and Do

Eastham Historical Society. 1869 schoolhouse museum; Native American artifacts; farming and nautical implements. (July-Aug, Mon-Fri afternoons) Just off US 6. For hrs phone 508/255-0788. **Donation** The society also maintains the

Swift-Daley House. (1741) Cape Cod house contains period furniture, clothing, original hardware. (July-Aug, Mon-Fri afternoons or by appt) On US 6. Phone 508/255-1766. **FREE**

Eastham Windmill. Oldest windmill on the Cape (1680); restored in 1936. (Late June-Labor Day, daily) Windmill Green, in town center. Phone 508/240-7211. **Donation**

Motels/Motor Lodges

★ **BLUE DOLPHIN INN.** *5950 Rte 6, North Eastham (02651). 508/255-1159; fax 508/240-3676; toll-free 800/654-0504. www.capecod.net/bluedolphin.* 49 rms. Mid-June-early Sept: S, D $59-$109; each addl $10; under 16 free; lower rates Apr-mid-June, early Sept-late Oct. Closed rest of yr. Crib $10. Pet accepted. TV; cable (premium). Pool; poolside

serv. Restaurant 6:30 am-1 pm. Ck-out 11 am. Lawn games. Refrigerators. Private patios. On 7 wooded acres. Cr cds: A, MC, V.

D ⬛ ⬛ ⬛ ⬛

★★ **CAPTAIN'S QUARTERS.** *Rte 6, North Eastham (02651). 508/255-5686; fax 508/240-0280; toll-free 800/327-7769. www.captains-quarters.com.* 75 rms. Late-June-Labor Day: S, D $84-$135; each addl $8; lower rates mid-Apr-late-June, after Labor Day-mid-Nov. Closed rest of yr. Crib free. TV; cable. Heated pool. Complimentary continental bkfst. Restaurant nearby. Ck-out 11 am. Meeting rms. Tennis. Lawn games. Bicycles. Health club privileges. Refrigerators. Picnic tables, grill. Near beach. Cr cds: A, C, D, DS, MC, V.

D ⬛ ⬛ ⬛ ⬛ ⬛

★ **EAGLE WING GUEST MOTEL.** *960 Rte 6, Eastham (02642). 508/240-5656; fax 508/240-5657; toll-free 800/278-5656. www.eaglewingmotel.com.* 19 rms. Late June-early Sept: D $99-$109; wkly rates; wkends (2-day min); hols (3-day min); higher rates July 4; lower rates rest of yr. Closed Nov-May. TV; cable (premium). Complimentary coffee in lobby. Pool. Refrigerators. Totally nonsmoking. Cr cds: DS, MC, V.

⬛ ⬛ ⬛ SC

★★ **EASTHAM OCEAN VIEW MOTEL.** *Rte 6 Box 428, Eastham (02642). 508/255-1600; fax 508/240-7104; toll-free 800/742-4133. www.easthamoceanviewmotel.com.* 31 rms, 2 story. Mid-June-Labor Day: S $47-$85; D $54-$89; each addl $10; under 12 free; lower rates mid-Feb-mid-June and after Labor Day-Oct. Closed rest of yr. Crib $5. TV; cable. Heated pool. Complimentary coffee in rms. Restaurant nearby. Ck-out 11 am. Health club privileges. Refrigerators; microwaves avail. Ocean view. Cr cds: A, C, D, DS, MC, V.

⬛ ⬛ ⬛

★★ **FOUR POINTS BY SHERATON.** *3800 Rte 6, Eastham (02642). 508/255-5000; fax 508/240-1870; toll-free 800/533-3986. www.fourpoints.com.* 107 rms, 2 story. July-Aug: S, D $147.90-$174; each addl $10; suites $225; under 18 free; MAP avail; lower rates rest of yr. Crib $5-$10. TV; cable (premium). 2 pools, 1 indoor; whirlpool, poolside serv. Restaurant 7-11 am, 6-9 pm. Rm serv. Bar to 11 pm. Ck-out 11 am. Meeting rms. Business servs avail. In-rm modem link. Tennis. Exercise equipt; sauna. Health club privileges. Game rm. Some refrigerators. Cr cds: A, C, D, DS, MC, V.

D ⬛ ⬛ ⬛ ⬛ ⬛ SC

★★ **MIDWAY MOTEL & COTTAGES.** *5460 US 6, North Eastham (02651). 508/255-3117; fax 508/255-4235; toll-free 800/755-3117. www.midwaymotel.com.* 11 rms, 3 kits. Late June-Labor Day: S $56-$90; D $56-$117; studio rms $90; 1-bedrm cottage $650/wk; 3-bedrm cottage $775/wk; lower rates Mar-late June, after Labor Day-Oct. Closed rest of yr. TV; cable (premium), VCR avail. Playground. Complimentary coffee. Restaurant nearby. Ck-out 11 am. Rec rm. Lawn games. Bicycle rentals. Refrigerators, microwaves. Picnic tables, grills. Cr cds: A, DS, MC, V.

⬛

★ **TOWN CRIER MOTEL.** *3620 US 6, Eastham (02642). 508/255-4000; fax 508/255-7491; toll-free 800/932-1434. www.towncriermotel.com.* 36 rms. July-Labor Day: S, D $59-$139; each addl $12; lower rates rest of yr. TV; cable (premium). Indoor pool. Restaurant 7-11 am. Ck-out 11 am. Rec rm. Refrigerators. Cr cds: A, D, DS, MC, V.
🏊 ⛵ 🔥 **SC**

★★ **VIKING SHORES RESORT.** *Rte 6, North Eastham (02651). 508/255-3200; fax 508/240-0205; toll-free 800/242-2131. www.vsp.cape.com/~viking.* 40 rms. Mid-June-Labor Day: S, D $89-$125; each addl $8; lower rates; lower rates mid-Apr-mid-June, after Labor Day-early Nov. Closed rest of yr. Crib free. TV; cable (premium). Heated pool. Complimentary continental bkfst. Restaurant adj. Ck-out 11 am. Meeting rm. Tennis. Lawn games. Refrigerators. Picnic tables, grills. Cr cds: A, DS, MC, V.
D ⛳ 🏊 ⛵ 🔥

B&Bs/Small Inns

★★ **OVERLOOK INN OF CAPE COD.** *3085 County Rd, Rte 6, Eastham (02642). 508/255-1886; fax 508/240-0545.* 10 rms, 4 A/C, 3 story. Late June-mid-Sept: D $95-$165; lower rates rest of yr. Complimentary full bkfst; afternoon refreshments. Restaurant nearby. Ck-out 11 am, ck-in 2 pm. Rec rm. Lawn games. Picnic tables. Health club privileges. 1869 sea captain's house; many antiques. Cr cds: A, MC, V.
⛵ 🔥 **SC**

★★ **PENNY HOUSE INN.** *4885 County Rd (Route 6), Eastham (02651). 508/255-6632; fax 508/255-4893; toll-free 800/554-1751. www.pennyhouseinn.com.* 11 rms, 2 story. July-Aug: S, D $120-$145; lower rates rest of yr. Children over 8 yrs only. TV in parlor; cable (premium), VCR (free movies). Complimentary full bkfst; afternoon refreshments. Ck-out 11 am, ck-in 2 pm. Business servs avail. Lawn games. Former sea captain's house (1700); antiques. Audubon Society bird sanctuary, bicycle trails nearby. Totally non-smoking. Cr cds: A, DS, MC, V.
⛵ 🔥

Cottage Colony

★ **CRANBERRY COTTAGES.** *RR 1; 785 MA 6, Eastham (02642). 508/255-0602; toll-free 800/292-6631. www.sunsol .com/cranberrycottages.* 14 cottages, 7 kits. Some A/C. Late June-Labor Day: S, D $45-$89; each addl $10; 2-bedrm kit. cottages for 1-6, $650-$750/wk; lower rates rest of yr. Crib free. TV; cable (premium). Ck-out 10 am, ck-in 3 pm. Refrigerators; microwaves avail. Grill. Cape Cod cottages in shady grove. Cr cds: DS, MC, V.
⛵ 🔥

Fall River

See also New Bedford, also see Providence, RI

Settled 1656 **Pop** 91,938 **Elev** 200 ft **Area code** 508
Information Fall River Area Chamber of Commerce, 200 Pocasset St, 02721; 508/676-8226
Web www.fallriverchamber.com

The city's name, adopted in 1834, was translated from the Native American "quequechan." In 1892, Fall River was the scene of one of the most famous murder trials in American history—that of Lizzie Borden, who was acquitted of the ax murders of her father and stepmother. Water power and cotton textiles built Fall River into one of the largest cotton manufacturers in the world, but its industry is now greatly diversified.

What to See and Do

✪ **Battleship Cove.** Five historic naval ships of the WWII period. The submarine *Lionfish,* a WWII attack sub with all her equipment intact, and the battleship USS *Massachusetts* are open to visitors. The *Massachusetts,* commissioned in 1942, was active in the European and Pacific theaters of operation in the Second World War and now houses the state's official World War II and Gulf War Memorial; on board is a full-scale model of a Patriot missile. Also here are *PT Boat 796, PT Boat 617,* and the destroyer USS *Joseph P. Kennedy, Jr.,* which saw action in both the Korean and Vietnam conflicts and the Cuban missile blockade. The PT boats may be viewed from walkways. A landing craft (LCM) exhibit is located on the grounds. Gift shop; snack bar. (Daily; closed Jan 1, Thanksgiving, Dec 25) At jct MA 138, I-195. Phone 508/678-1100. ¢¢

Factory Outlet District. Fall River is an extensive factory outlet area. 638 Quequechan St. Phone 508/677-4949.

Fall River Heritage State Park. Nine acres on the riverfront; sailing. Visitor center (daily) has multimedia presentation on how Fall River developed into the greatest textile producer in the country; tourist information. (Daily; closed Jan 1, Dec 25) Davol St. Phone 508/675-5759. **FREE**

Fall River Historical Society. Historical displays in 16-rm Victorian mansion. Exhibits of Fall River Steamship Line, dolls, fine art, glassware, costumes; artifacts relating to the Lizzie Borden trial. Gift shop. (Apr-May, Oct-Nov, Tues-Fri; June-Sept, Tues-Sun; Dec, Mon) 451 Rock St. Phone 508/679-1071. ¢

Marine Museum. More than 100 ship models on display, including a 28-ft, one-ton model of the *Titanic,* trace the growth of maritime steam power from the early 1800s to 1937; paintings, photographs, artifacts. (Daily; closed Jan 1, Thanksgiving, Dec 25) 70 Water St. Phone 508/674-3533. ¢¢

St. Anne's Church and Shrine. (1906) Designed by Canadian architect Napoleon Bourassa, the upper church is constructed of Vermont blue marble; the lower church is of solid granite. In the upper church are stained-glass windows produced by E. Rault in Rennes, France, a "Casavant Freres" organ, and exceptional oak wood ornamentation in the vault of the ceiling. The shrine is in the lower church. S Main St, facing Kennedy Park. Phone 508/674-5651.

Motels/Motor Lodges

★★ **HAMPTON INN WESTPORT.** *53 Old Bedford Rd, Westport (02790). 508/675-8500; fax 508/675-0075; res 800/426-7866. www.hamptoninn.com.* 133 rms, 4 story. Apr-Aug: S, D $69-$99; under 18 free; lower rates rest of yr. Crib free. TV; cable (premium), VCR avail (movies). Complimentary continental bkfst, coffee in rms. Restaurant adj 11 am-10 pm. Ck-out noon. Meeting rms. Business servs avail. In-rm modem link. Sundries. Valet serv. Airport, RR station transportation. Lighted tennis. Exercise equipt; sauna. Whirlpool. Some refrigerators. Cr cds: A, MC, V.

D ✦ ✕ ⊟ SC

★★ **QUALITY INN FALL.** *1878 Wilbur Ave, Somerset (02725). 508/678-4545; fax 508/678-9352; toll-free 800/228-5151. www.qualityinn.com.* 107 rms, 2 story. Late May-Aug: S, D $69-$179; each addl $10; lower rates rest of yr; under 18 free. Crib free. Pet accepted, some restrictions. TV; cable (premium), VCR avail. Indoor/outdoor pool. Complimentary continental bkfst. Restaurant adj 6 am-10 pm. Ck-out noon. Coin lndry. Meeting rm. Business servs avail. In-rm modem link. Private patios, balconies. Cr cds: A, C, D, DS, JCB, MC, V.

D 🐾 ≈ ⊠ 🔥

Restaurant

★★ **WHITE'S OF WESTPORT.** *66 MA 6, Westport (02790). 508/675-7185. www.lafrancehospitality.com.* Specializes in steak, ribs, seafood. Hrs: 11:30 am-9 pm; Fri, Sat to 10 pm; Sun from 9 am. Closed Dec 25. Res accepted. Bar to midnight. Lunch $4.95-$8.50, dinner $8.25-$14.95. Child's menu. Nautical decor; artifacts. Family-owned. Cr cds: A, DS, MC, V.

D ⊟

Falmouth (Cape Cod)

Settled ca 1660 **Pop** 32,660 **Elev** 10 ft **Area code** 508 **Zip** 02540

Information Cape Cod Chamber of Commerce, US 6 and MA 132, PO Box 790, Hyannis 02601-0790; 508/362-3225 or 888/CAPECOD

Web www.capecodchamber.org

What to See and Do

Ashumet Holly & Wildlife Sanctuary. (Massachusetts Audubon Society) A 45-acre wildlife preserve with holly trail; herb garden; observation beehive. Trails open dawn to dusk. (Tues-Sun) Ashumet Rd, off Currier Rd; just N of MA 151. Phone 508/362-1426. ¢¢

Falmouth Historical Society Museums. Julia Wood House. (1790) and **Conant House** (ca 1740). Whaling collection; period furniture; 19th-century paintings; glassware; silver; tools; costumes; widow's walk; memorial park; Colonial garden. (Mid-June-mid-Sept, Mon-Thurs; rest of yr, by appt) Katharine Lee Bates exhibit in Conant House honors author of "America the Beautiful." (Mid-June-mid-Sept, Mon-Thurs) On village green. Phone 508/548-4857. ¢¢

Island Queen. Passenger boat trips to Martha's Vineyard; 600-passenger vessel. (Late May-mid-Oct) Phone 508/548-4800.

Special Events

College Light Opera Company at Highfield Theatre. Off Depot Ave, MA 28. Nine-wk season of musicals and operettas with full orchestra. Phone 508/548-0668 (after June 15). Mon-Sat. Late June-Labor Day. Phone 508/548-2211.

Barnstable County Fair. Horse and dog shows, horse-pulling contest; exhibits. Last wk July. 8 mi N on MA 151. Phone 508/563-3200.

Motels/Motor Lodges

★★ **ADMIRALTY INN.** *51 Teaticket Hwy, Rte 28, Falmouth (02541). 508/548-4240; fax 508/457-0535; res 800/341-5700. www.vacationinnproperties.com.* 98 rms, 3 story. 28 suites. Mid July-mid Aug: S, D $50-$170; under 12 free; hol rates; golf plans; higher rates: road race, hols; lower rates rest of yr. TV; cable (premium), VCR. 2 pools, 1 indoor; whirlpool, poolside serv. Supervised children's activities (seasonal); ages 5-12. Coffee in rms. Restaurant 4:30-10 pm; also Sat 6-10 am; Sun 8 am-1 pm. Bar 4:30 pm-1 am. Ck-out 11 am. Meeting rms. Business servs avail. Refrigerators, minibars. Cr cds: A, C, D, DS, MC, V.

D ≈ 🔥

★★ **BEST WESTERN FALMOUTH MARINA TRADEWINDS.** *26 Robbins Rd, Falmouth (02541). 508/548-4300; fax 508/548-6787; toll-free 800/341-5700. www.bestwestern.com.* 63 rms, 2 story, 18 suites, 11 kits. July-Aug: S, D $65-$165; each addl $10; kit. units $150-$205; wkly rates; lower rates Mar-June and Sept-Oct. Closed rest of yr. TV; cable (premium). Pool. Complimentary coffee in rms. Restaurant opp. Ck-out 11 am. Business servs avail. Refrigerators, wet bars. Balconies. Overlooks Falmouth Harbor. Cr cds: A, C, D, DS, MC, V.

≈ ⊠ 🔥

★ **MARINER MOTEL.** *555 Main St, Falmouth (02540). 508/548-1331; fax 508/457-9470; toll-free 800/233-2939. www.marinermotel.com.* 30 rms. Late June-Labor Day: S, D $59-$99; each addl $4-$10; lower rates rest of yr. TV; cable, VCR avail. Pool. Complimentary coffee. Restaurant nearby. Ck-out 11 am. Refrigerators. Picnic tables. Walking distance to island ferry, village shopping. Cr cds: A, C, D, DS, MC, V.

≈ ⊠ 🔥

★★ **RAMADA ON THE SQUARE.** *40 N Main St, Falmouth (02540). 508/457-0606; fax 508/457-9694; res 888/298-2054. www.ramada.com.* 72 rms, 2 story. July-Aug: S, D $139-$199; each addl $10; suites $179-$249; under 18 free; hol rates; higher rates some special events; lower rates rest of yr. Crib free. TV; cable, VCR (movies). Indoor pool. Restaurant 7 am-10 pm. Bar 11 am-10 pm. Ck-out 11 am. Meeting rms. Business center. In-rm modem link. Cr cds: A, C, D, DS, MC, V.

D ≈ 🔥 ✦

★★ **RED HORSE INN.** *28 Falmouth Hts Rd, Falmouth (02540). 508/548-0053; fax 508/540-6563; toll-free 800/628-3811. www.redhorseinn.com.* 22 rms, 2 story. Last wkend June-Labor Day: S, D $120-$180; each addl $10; under 12, $5; lower rates May-last wkend June, after Labor Day-Nov. Closed rest of yr. TV; cable (premium). Pool. Restaurant opp open 24 hrs. Ck-out 11 am. In-rm modem link. Refrigerators. Cr cds: A, MC, V.

⊡ ⇌ ⇲ 🔥

Resort

★★ **SEA CREST RESORT AND CONFERENCE CENTER.** *350 Quaker Rd, North Falmouth (02556). 508/540-9400; fax 508/548-0556; toll-free 800/225-3110. www.seacrest-resort.com.* 266 rms, 1-3 story. Mid-June-mid-Sept: S, D $160-$240; under 17 free; MAP avail; higher rates hols; lower rates rest of yr. Crib $12.50. TV; cable. 2 pools, 1 indoor; whirlpool; poolside serv, lifeguard. Playground. Free supervised children's activities (in season); ages over 3. Restaurant 7-10:30 am, 5:30-11 pm. Snack bar, deli. Rm serv. Bar 11:30-1 am; entertainment. Ck-out 11 am, ck-in 3 pm. Grocery, coin lndry, pkg store 1 mi. Convention facilities. Business center. In-rm modem link. Bellhops. Valet serv. Concierge. Gift shop. Sports dir. Tennis. Putting green. Swimming beach. Windsurfing. Lawn games. Soc dir. Game rm. Exercise equipt; sauna. Refrigerators. Balconies. Picnic tables. On ocean. Cr cds: A, D, DS, MC, V.

⊡ 🎿 ⇌ 🏊 🎾 ⇲ SC 🏃

B&Bs/Small Inns

★★ **BEACH HOUSE AT FALMOUTH HEIGHTS.** *10 Worcester Ct, Falmouth (02540). 508/457-0310; fax 508/548-7895; toll-free 800/351-3426. www.capecodbeachhouse.com.* 8 rms, 6 with shower only, 2 story. No rm phones. S $115-$125; D $129-$169; kit. units $135-$150; (2, 3-day min) wkends, hols. Closed Nov-May. Children over 12 yrs only. Pool. Complimentary continental bkfst. Restaurant nearby. Ck-out 11 am, ck-in 3-6 pm. Picnic tables. Hand-painted murals and furniture; unique theme rms. Totally nonsmoking. Cr cds: MC, V.

⇌ 🎾 ⇲ 🔥

★★★ **CAPT. TOM LAWRENCE HOUSE.** *75 Locust St, Falmouth (02540). 508/540-1445; fax 508/457-1790; toll-free 800/266-8139. www.sunsol.com/captaintom.* 7 units, 2 story, 1 apt. No rm phones. Mid-June-mid-Oct: S, D $95-$165; each addl $30; apt $125-$200; Closed Jan. TV; cable. Complimentary full bkfst. Ck-out 11 am, ck-in 3 pm. Free bus depot transportation. Island ferry tickets avail. Antiques. Whaling captain's home (1861). Totally nonsmoking. Cr cds: A, MC, V.

🔥 ⇲

★★ **ELM ARCH INN.** *26 Elm Arch Way, Falmouth (02540). 508/548-0133.* 24 rms, 8 A/C, 12 baths, 2 story. No rm phones. Mid-June-mid-Oct: D $70-$90; each addl $8-$10; lower rates rest of yr. TV in some rms; cable (premium). Pool. Complimentary morning coffee in season. Restaurant nearby. Ck-out 11 am, ck-in after noon. Screened terrace.

Built 1810; private residence of whaling captain. Bombarded by British in 1814; dining rm wall features cannonball hole. Cr cds: A, MC, V.

⇌ 🖐

★★★ **GRAFTON INN.** *261 Grand Ave S, Falmouth (02540). 508/540-8688; fax 508/540-1861; toll-free 800/642-4069. www.graftoninn.com.* 11 air-cooled rms, 3 story. No rm phones. Mid-June-mid-Oct: D $170-$210; lower rates rest of yr. Children over 16 yrs only. TV; cable (premium). Complimentary full bkfst. Restaurant nearby. Ck-out 11 am, ck-in 2 pm. Free bus depot, ferry terminal transportation. Picnic tables. Former home of sea captain; built 1850. On Nantucket Sound. Totally nonsmoking. Cr cds: A, MC, V.

⇲ 🖐

★★ **INN ON THE SOUND.** *313 Grand Ave (02540). 508/457-9666; fax 508/457-9631; toll-free 800/564-9668. www.innonthesound.com.* 10 air-cooled rms, 2 story. No rm phones. Late May-mid-Oct: S, D $140-$225; wkly rates; lower rates rest of yr. Children over 16 yrs only. TV; cable. Complimentary full bkfst. Restaurant nearby. Ck-out 11 am, ck-in 3-6 pm. Built 1880; antiques. Overlooking Vineyard Sound. Totally nonsmoking. Cr cds: A, DS, MC, V.

🖐 ⇲

★★★ **LA MAISON CAPPELLARI AT MOSTLY HALL.** *27 Main St, Falmouth (02540). 508/548-3786; fax 508/548-5778.* 6 rms, shower only, 3 story. No rm phones. May-Oct: S, D $125-$135; wkends, hols (2-, 3-day min); lower rates rest of yr. Closed Jan. Children over 16 yrs only. TV in sitting rm. Complimentary full bkfst; afternoon refreshments. Restaurant nearby. Ck-out 11 am, ck-in 3 pm. Concierge serv. Bicycles. Greek Rival house built 1849; wrap-around porch, garden gazebo. Totally nonsmoking. Cr cds: A, D, DS, MC, V.

⇲ 🖐

★★★ **THE PALMER HOUSE INN.** *81 Palmer Ave, Falmouth (02540). 508/548-1230; fax 508/540-1878; toll-free 800/472-2632. www.palmerhouseinn.com.* 13 rms, 7 with shower only, 3 story, 1 suite. Mid-June-mid-Oct: S $85-$140; D $95-$150; suite $165; higher rates wkends and hols (2-day min); lower rates rest of yr. Some TVs. Complimentary full bkfst. Restaurant nearby. Ck-out 11 am, ck-in 3 pm. Business servs avail. Luggage handling. Concierge serv. Refrigerators; some in-rm whirlpools. Queen Anne-style inn built 1901; antiques. Totally nonsmoking. Cr cds: A, C, D, DS, MC, V.

⊡ ⇲ 🖐 SC

★★★ **WILDFLOWER INN.** *167 Palmer Ave, Falmouth (02540). 508/548-9524; fax 508/548-9524; toll-free 800/294-5459. www.wildflower-inn.com.* 6 rms, 3 story. No rm phones. S $120-$175; D $95-$195; kit. units $150; wkly rates; 2-day min wkends, hols; lower rates rest of yr. TV; cable (premium). Complimentary full bkfst. Restaurant nearby. Ck-out 11 am, ck-in 3 pm. Luggage handling. Concierge serv. Game rm. Lawn games. Picnic tables. Built in 1898; wraparound porch. Totally nonsmoking. Cr cds: A, MC, V.

🖐 ⇲

Conference Center

★ ★ ★ **NEW SEABURY RESORT AND CONFERENCE CENTER.** *Rock Landing Rd, New Seabury (02649). 508/477-9111; fax 508/477-9790; res 508/477-9400. www.new seabury.com.* 160 rms, some A/C, kits. Mid-June-Aug: S $100-$215; D $130-$405; patio and pool villas $275-$380; lower rates rest of yr. Crib $10. TV; cable (premium), VCR (movies). Seaside freshwater pool; wading pool. Supervised children's activities (July-Aug). Dining rm 7 am-10 pm. Bar noon-1 am; entertainment in season. Ck-out 10 am, ck-in 4 pm. Grocery. Coin lndry. Convention facilities. Business center. In-rm modem link. Airport transportation. Sports dir. 16 all-weather tennis courts, pro. Two 18-hole golf courses, pro, putting green, driving range. Miniature golf. Sailboats, wind surfing. Bike trails. Exercise rm. Trips to islands, whale watching, deep sea fishing avail. Private patios, balconies. On 2,300 acres. Cr cds: A, C, D, MC, V.

[icons]

Restaurants

★ **COONAMESSETT INN.** *311 Gifford St, Falmouth (02540). 508/548-2300. www.capecodrestaurants.org.* Specializes in New England seafood. Hrs: 11:30 am-10 pm; Sun brunch 11 am-2 pm. Res accepted. Bar to 1 am. Lunch $6-$16, dinner $16-$27. Sun brunch $9-$18. Entertainment in season. Valet parking. Built 1796. Cathedral ceiling. Large windows with view of pond. Tranquil setting. Family-owned. Cr cds: A, MC, V.

[icon]

★ **FLYING BRIGE.** *220 Scranton Ave (02540). 508/548-2700. www.capecodrestaurants.org.* Specializes in seafood. Hrs: 11:30 am-10 pm. Bar to 1 am. Lunch, dinner $5.95-$15.95. Child's menu. Entertainment Fri. Valet parking. Outdoor dining overlooking harbor. Cr cds: A, MC, V.

[icon]

★ **GOLDEN SAILS CHINESE.** *143-145 Main St (02536). 508/548-3526.* Chinese menu. Specializes in Szechwan, Cantonese, Mandarin dishes. Hrs: 11:30-1 am; Fri, Sat noon-2 am; Sun noon-midnight. Closed Thanksgiving. Bar. A la carte entrees: lunch $4.25-$5.25, dinner $3.25-$13.50. Parking. Cr cds: A, C, D, DS, ER, MC, V.

[icons]

Foxboro

Settled 1704 **Pop** 16,246 **Elev** 280 ft **Area code** 508
Zip 02035
Information Neponset Valley Chamber of Commerce, 190 Vanderbilt Ave, Suite 1, Norwood 02062; 781/769-1126
Web www.nvcc.com

What to See and Do

Professional Sports.
  New England Patriots (NFL). Foxboro Stadium, 60 Washington St. Foxboro, MA. Phone 800/543-1776.
  New England Revolution (MLS). Foxboro Stadium. 60 Washington St. Foxboro, MA. Phone 877/GET-REVS.

Motels/Motor Lodges

★ ★ **COURTYARD BY MARRIOTT.** *35 Foxborough Blvd, Foxborough (02035). 508/543-5222; fax 508/543-0445; toll-free 800/321-2211. www.courtyard.com.* 149 rms, 3 story. S, D $139; under 18 free. Crib avail. TV; cable (premium). Indoor pool; whirlpool. Complimentary coffee in rms. Restaurant 6:30-10 am. Bar 5-11 pm. Ck-out noon. Coin lndry. Meeting rms. Business servs avail. In-rm modem link. Valet serv. Exercise equipt. Balconies. Cr cds: A, D, DS, MC, V.

[icons]

★ ★ **HOLIDAY INN.** *31 Hampshire St, Mansfield (02048). 508/339-2200; fax 508/337-8677; res 800/465-4329. www.holiday-inn.com/bos-mansfield.* 202 rms, 12 suites, 3 story. S $99-$159; D $109-$169; each addl $10; suites $300; under 18 free; wkend rates. Crib free. TV; cable (premium), VCR avail. Indoor pool. Complimentary coffee in rms. Restaurant 6:30 am-10 pm. Rm serv. Bars 11:30-1 am; entertainment. Ck-out 11 am. Coin lndry. Meeting rms. Business servs avail. In-rm modem link. Bellhops. Lighted tennis. Exercise rm. Some in-rm whirlpools. Private patios, balconies. Cr cds: A, MC, V.

[icons]

Restaurant

★ ★ **LAFAYETTE HOUSE.** *109 Washington St (US 1) (02035). 508/543-5344. www.lafayettehouse.com.* Continental menu. Specializes in roast beef, seafood. Hrs: 11:45 am-9 pm; Fri, Sat to 10 pm. Bar to midnight. Lunch$5.95- $8.95, dinner $12.95-$19.95. Child's menu. Historic Colonial tavern built in 1784. Cr cds: A, C, D, DS, MC, V.

[icons]

Framingham

Settled 1650 **Pop** 66,910 **Elev** 165 ft **Area code** 508
Zip 01701

Framingham is an industrial, commercial, and residential community. Framingham Centre, the original town, was bypassed by the railroad in the 19th century and is two miles north of downtown.

What to See and Do

Danforth Museum of Art. Six galleries, including a children's gallery; changing exhibits, special events; art reference library. (Closed major hols) 123 Union Ave. Phone 508/620-0050. ¢¢

Garden in the Woods. A 45-acre botanical garden and sanctuary. Largest landscaped collection of wild flowers in northeast. Exceptional collection of wildflowers and other native plants; variety of gardens and habitats. Headquarters of New England Wildflower Society. (Mid-June-Oct, Tues-Sun; mid-Apr-mid-June, daily) Guided walks (Daily). Visitor center; museum shop. 180 Hemenway Rd. Phone 508/877-6574. ¢¢

Hotels

★ ★ ★ SHERATON FRAMINGHAM HOTEL.
1657 Worcester Rd (01701). 508/879-7200; fax 508/875-7593; res 800/325-3535. www.sheraton.com. 373 rms, 6 story. S, D $149-$250; each addl $15; suites $165-$274; under 18 free. Crib free. TV; cable (premium), VCR avail. 2 pools, 1 indoor; whirlpool, poolside serv, lifeguard. Restaurant 6:30 am-2 pm, 5-10 pm. Bar 11-1 am; entertainment. Ck-out noon. Convention facilities. Business center. In-rm modem link. Gift shop. Exercise rm; sauna, steam rm. Bathrm phones; some in-rm whirlpools; microwaves avail. Cr cds: A, C, D, DS, ER, JCB, MC, V.

🄳 ⊠ 🕱 ⊠ 🆂🅲 ⊠

★ ★ ★ WYNDHAM WESTBOROUGH.
5400 Computer Dr (01581). 508/366-5511; fax 508/870-5965. www.wyndham.com. 223 rms, 4 story. S, D $250-$325; under 18 free. Crib avail. TV; cable (premium). Indoor pool; whirlpool. Restaurant 6:30 am-10 pm. Bar to midnight. Ck-out noon, ck-in 4 pm. Meeting rms. Business center. In-rm modem link. Concierge. Exercise equipt. Minibars; many refrigerators in suites. Cr cds: A, C, D, DS, MC, V.

⊠ 🕱 🕱 ⊠ ⊠

Gloucester

Settled 1623 **Pop** 30,273 **Elev** 50 ft **Area code** 978
Zip 01930
Information Cape Ann Chamber of Commerce, 33 Commercial St; 978/283-1601 or 800/321-0133
Web www.capeannvacations.com

It is said that more than ten thousand Gloucester men have been lost at sea in the last three centuries, which emphasizes how closely the community has been linked with seafaring. Today it is still a leading fishing port—although the fast schooners made famous in *Captains Courageous* and countless romances have been replaced by diesel trawlers. Gloucester is also the center of an extensive summer resort area that includes the famous artists' colony of Rocky Neck.

What to See and Do

"Beauport," the Sleeper-McCann House. (1907-1934) Henry Davis Sleeper, early 20th-century interior designer, began by building a 26-rm house, continually adding rms with the help of Halfdan Hanson, a Gloucester architect, until there were 40 rms; 25 are now on view, containing extraordinary collections of antique furniture, rugs, wallpaper, ceramics, glass; American and European decorative arts. Many artists, statesmen, and businessmen were entertained here. (Mid-May-mid-Sept, Mon-Fri; mid-Sept-mid-Oct, daily) 75 Eastern Point Blvd. Phone 978/283-0800. ¢¢¢

Cape Ann Historical Museum. Paintings by Fitz Hugh Lane; decorative arts and furnishings; Federal-style house (ca 1805). Emphasis on Gloucester's fishing industry; fisheries/maritime galleries and changing exhibitions depict various aspects of Cape Ann's history. (Tues-Sat; closed hols, also Feb) 27 Pleasant St. Phone 978/283-0455. ¢¢

Gloucester Fisherman. Bronze statue by Leonard Craske, a memorial to anglers lost at sea. On Stacy Blvd on the harbor.

Hammond Castle Museum. (1926-1929) Built like a medieval castle by inventor Dr. John Hays Hammond, Jr.; contains a rare collection of art objects. Great Hall contains pipe organ with 8,200 pipes; concerts (selected days throughout the yr). (Memorial Day-Labor Day, daily; after Labor Day-Columbus Day, Thurs-Sun; rest of yr, Sat and Sun; closed Jan 1, Thanksgiving, Dec 25). 80 Hesperus Ave, off MA 127. Schedule may vary. Phone 978/283-2081. ¢¢

Sargent House Museum. Late 18th-century Georgian residence, built for Judith Sargent, an early feminist writer and sister of Governor Winthrop Sargent; also home of her second husband, John Murray, leader of Universalism. Period furniture, china, glass, silver, needlework, early American portraits, paintings by John Singer Sargent. (Memorial Day-Columbus Day, Mon, Fri-Sun; closed hols) 49 Middle St. Phone 978/281-2432. ¢

Special Events

Whale Watching. Half-day trips, mornings and afternoons. (May-Oct). Phone 978/283-1601.

St. Peter's Fiesta. A four-day celebration with sports events, fireworks; procession; Blessing of the Fleet. Last wkend June. Phone 978/283-1601.

Waterfront Festival. Arts and crafts show, entertainment, food. (Third wkend Aug). Phone 978/283-1601.

Schooner Festival. Races, parade of sail, maritime activities. (Labor Day wkend). Phone 978/283-1601.

Motels/Motor Lodges

★ ATLANTIS MOTOR INN. *125 Atlantic Rd (01930). 978/283-0014; fax 978/281-8994; toll-free 800/732-6313. www.atlantismotorinn.com.* 40 rms, 2 story. No A/C. July-Aug: S $110-$130; D $110-$150; under 12 free; lower rates Sept-Oct, Apr-June. Closed rest of yr. Crib $8. TV; cable. Heated pool. Ck-out noon. Refrigerators avail. Balconies. All rms with ocean view. Cr cds: A, MC, V.

🄳 ⊠ ⊠ ⊠

★ ★ BEST WESTERN BASS ROCKS OCEAN INN.
107 Atlantic Rd (01930). 978/283-7600; fax 978/281-6489; res 800/780-7234. www.bestwestern.com/bassrocksoceaninn. 48 rms, 2 story. Mid-June-Labor Day: S, D $175-$200; each addl $8; under 13 free; lower rates Apr-mid-June, after Labor Day-Nov. Closed rest of yr. TV; cable, VCR avail (movies $5). Heated pool. Complimentary bkfst buffet. Ck-out noon. Business servs avail. In-rm modem link. Rec rm. Balconies overlook ocean. Bicycles avail. Cr cds: A, C, D, DS, MC, V.

⊠ ⊠ ⊠

★★ **CAPTAIN'S LODGE MOTEL.** *237 Eastern Ave (01930).* 978/281-2420; fax 978/283-1608. *www.seecapeann.com.* 47 rms, 7 kits. S, D $95; each addl $7; kit. units $102; lower rates rest of yr. Crib $7. TV; cable (premium). Heated pool. Restaurant 6 am-2 pm; Sat, Sun 7 am-noon. Ck-out 11 am. Tennis. Cr cds: A, C, D, DS, MC, V.

D 🏃 ⚓ 🖼 🔥 SC

★ **THE MANOR INN.** *141 Essex Ave (01930).* 978/283-0614; fax 978/283-3154. *www.themanorinnofgloucester.com.* 10 rms in 3-story manor, 4 share bath; 16 motel rms. D $69-$79; lower rates Apr-late June, early Sept-Oct. Closed rest of yr. Crib $5. Pet accepted; $5. TV. Complimentary continental bkfst. Restaurant nearby. Ck-out 11 am, ck-in 2 pm. Victorian manor house; sitting rm. Some rms overlook river. Cr cds: A, DS, MC, V.

🐾 ✈ 🖼 🔥

★ **VISTA MOTEL.** *22 Thatcher Rd (01930).* 978/281-3410; fax 978/283-7335. *www.vistamotel.com.* 40 rms, 2 story, 20 kits. Late June-Labor Day: S, D $85-$145; each addl $5; lower rates rest of yr. TV; cable (premium). Heated pool. Continental bkfst in summer. Restaurant nearby. Ck-out 11 am. Refrigerators. Private patios, balconies. Ocean opp, beach privileges. All rms with ocean view. Cr cds: A, DS, MC, V.

D ⚓ 🖼 🔥

Resort

★★ **OCEAN VIEW INN AND RESORT.** *171 Atlantic Rd (01930).* 978/283-6200; fax 978/283-1852; toll-free 800/315-7557. *www.oceanviewinnandresort.com.* 62 rms, 3 story. May-Oct: S, D $69-$190; lower rates rest of yr. Crib $10. Pet accepted. TV; cable, VCR avail. 2 heated pools. Restaurants 7 am-9:30 pm. Ck-out 11 am, ck-in 2 pm. Meeting rms. Business servs avail. In-rm modem link. Luggage handling. Rec rm. Lawn games. Some balconies. On ocean. Several buildings have accommodations, including turn-of-the-century English manor house. Cr cds: A, MC, V.

🐾 ⚓ 🔥

Restaurants

★ **CAMERON'S.** *206 Main St, Glouster (01930).* 978/281-1331. *www.camerons-restaurant.com.* Specializes in native seafood, prime rib, Italian sauteed specialties. Hrs: 11 am-10 pm; Sat, Sun 8 am-10 pm. Closed Dec 25. Res accepted. Bar to 1 am. Lunch $3.95-$7.95, dinner $6.95-$12.95. Child's menu. Entertainment Wed-Sun. Family owned since 1936. Cr cds: A, MC, V.

D SC 🖼

★★ **GLOUCESTER HOUSE RESTAURANT.** *7 Seas Wharf (01930).* 978/283-1812. *www.lobster-express.com.* Specializes in seafood. Hrs: 11:30 am-10 pm; winter hrs vary. Closed Thanksgiving, Dec 25. Res accepted. Bar. A la carte entrees: lunch $5.95-$11.95, dinner $9.95-$21.95. Child's menu. Entertainment Thurs-Sun. Outdoor dining. Gift shop. Nautical decor; view of fishing harbor. Family-owned since 1958. Cr cds: A, D, DS, MC, V.

D

★★ **WHITE RAINBOW.** *65 Main St (01930).* 978/281-0017. Continental menu. Specialties: Maui onion soup, sauteed lobster, seafood skewer. Hrs: 5:30-9:30 pm; Sat 6-10 pm. Closed Dec 24, 25; also Mon mid-Sept-June. Res accepted. Bar. Wine list. Dinner $17.95-$22.95. A la carte entrees: dinner $8.50-$11.95. An 1830 landmark building. Cr cds: A, C, D, DS, MC, V.

D 🖼

Great Barrington

Settled 1726 **Pop** 7,527 **Elev** 721 ft **Area code** 413 **Zip** 01230

Information Southern Berkshire Chamber of Commerce, 362 Main St; 413/528-1510 or 413/528-4006

Web www.greatbarrington.org

As early as 1774, the people of Great Barrington rose up against the King, seizing the courthouse. Today Great Barrington is the shopping center of the southern Berkshire resort country. Writer, professor, and lawyer James Weldon Johnson, cofounder of the NAACP, and W.E.B. du Bois, black author and editor, lived here. Another resident, the poet William Cullen Bryant, was the town clerk for 13 years.

What to See and Do

Beartown State Forest. Swimming, fishing; hunting; boating, bridle and hiking trails, snowmobiling, picnicking, camping. Standard fees. Approx 5 mi E on MA 23. Phone 413/528-0904.

Colonel Ashley House. (1735) Elegance of home reflects Colonel Ashley's prominent place in his society. One political meeting he held here produced the Sheffield Declaration, forerunner to Declaration of Independence. Period furnishings. Adj to Bartholowmew's Cobble. (July-Aug, Wed-Sun; Memorial Day-June and Sept-Columbus Day, wkends; open Mon hols) 9 mi S via MA 7 and 7A to Ashley Falls, then ½ mi on Rannapo Rd to Cooper Hill Rd. Phone 413/229-8600. ¢¢

Ski Areas.

Catamount. 7 mi W on NY 23 (see HILLSDALE, NY).

Otis Ridge. Double chairlift, T-bar, J-bar, three rope tows; patrol, school, rentals; snowmaking; cafeteria. Night skiing (Tues-Sun). Longest run one mi; vertical drop 400 ft. (Dec-Mar, daily) 16 mi E on MA 23. Phone 413/269-4444. ¢¢¢¢

Ski Butternut. Quad, triple, four double chairlifts, Pomalift, rope tow; patrol, school, rentals, snowmaking; nursery (wkends and hols after Dec 26); cafeterias; wine rm; electronically timed slalom race course. Longest run approx 1½ mi; vertical drop 1,000 ft. (Dec-Mar, daily) Also 7 mi of x-country trails; rentals. 1.5 mi E on MA 23. Phone 413/528-2000. ¢¢¢¢

Special Event

Berkshire Craft Fair. Monument Mtn Regional High School. Juried fair with more than 100 artisans. Early Aug. Phone 413/528-3346, ext 28.

Motel/Motor Lodge

★ **MONUMENT MOUNTAIN MOTEL.**
249 Stockbridge Rd (01230). 413/528-3272; fax 413/528-3132. www. monumentmountainmotel.com. 18 rms. S, D $55-$135; each addl $5-$10; wkend rates; ski plans; lower rates rest of yr. TV; cable. Pool. Playground. Complimentary coffee in rms. Restaurant nearby. Ck-out 11 am. Business servs avail. Lighted tennis. Downhill/x-country ski 3 mi. Lawn games. Picnic tables, grills. 20 acres on river. Cr cds: A, DS, MC, V.

B&Bs/Small Inns

★★ **THE EGREMONT INN.** *10 Sheffield Rd, South Egremont (01258). 413/528-2111; fax 413/528-3284; toll-free 800/859-1780. www.egremontinn.com.* 19 rms, 4 story. July-Aug (2-day min): S $90-$400; D $90-$150; suites $125-$450; ski plans; lower rates rest of yr. Crib avail. TV in sitting rm. Pool. Complimentary continental bkfst. Dining rm 5:30-9:30 pm. Ck-out 11 am, ck-in 2 pm. Business servs avail. Tennis. Downhill/x-country ski 3 mi. Antiques. Library/sitting rm. Some in-rm whirlpools. Sun porch. Built 1780; originally a stagecoach stop. Cr cds: A, DS, MC, V.

★★ **RACE BROOK LODGE.** *864 S Undermountain Rd, Sheffield (01257). 413/229-2916; fax 413/229-6629; res 888/725-6343. www.rblodge.com.* 32 rms, some with shower only, 3 story. No rm phones. June-Aug: S, D $105-$145; each addl $15; under 5 free; min stay wkends (summer); lower rates rest of yr. Pet accepted, some restrictions. TV; cable in common rm. Complimentary full bkfst. Restaurant adj 5:30-9:30 pm. Bar. Ck-out 11 am, ck-in 2-3 pm. Meeting rm. Downhill/x-country ski 7 mi. Lawn games. Barn built in 1790s. Rustic decor. Totally nonsmoking. Cr cds: A, MC, V.

★★ **THORNEWOOD INN & RESTAURANT.**
453 Stockbridge Rd (01230). 413/528-3828; fax 413/528-3307; toll-free 800/458-1008. www.thornewoodinn.com. 12 rms, 2 story. June-Aug: S $85-$115; D $115-$195; each addl $15; hol rates; higher rates: summer, foliage season; lower rates rest of yr. Children over 12 yrs only. TV; cable. Pool. Complimentary full bkfst. Restaurant (see SPENCER'S). Ck-out 11:30 am, ck-in 3 pm. Business servs avail. Downhill/x-country ski 2 mi. Antiques. Tap room. Built 1919. Cr cds: A, DS, MC, V.

★★★ **WINDFLOWER INN.** *684 S Egremont Rd, South Egremont (01230). 413/528-2720; fax 413/528-5147; toll-free 800/992-1993. www.windflowerinn.com.* 13 rms. No rm phones. S $125; D $160. Crib avail. TV. Pool. Complimentary full bkfst. Ck-out 11 am, ck-in 2 pm. Business servs avail. Downhill ski 4 mi; x-country ski adj. Rec rm. Some fireplaces. Many antiques. Golf course adj. On 10 acres. Cr cds: A.

Restaurants

★★★ **CASTLE STREET CAFE.** *10 Castle St (01230). 413/528-5244. www.castlestreetcafe.com.* Continental menu. Specializes in grilled fresh fish, grilled steak, pasta. Hrs: 5-9:30 pm; Fri, Sat to 10:30 pm. Closed Tues; Thanksgiving, Dec 25. Bar. Wine cellar. A la carte entrees: dinner $9-$22. Intimate, sophisticated bistro atmosphere. Entertainment. Totally nonsmoking. Cr cds: A, MC, V.

★★ **JODI'S COUNTRY CAFE.** *327 Stockbridge Rd (01230). 413/528-6064.* Italian menu. Specializes in fresh fish, fresh pasta, steaks. Hrs: 8 am-10 pm. Res accepted. Bar. Bkfst $1.95-$6.95, lunch $3.95-$8.95, dinner $12.95-$20.95. Child's menu. Entertainment wkends June-Oct. Porch dining. Antique decor, original 250-yr-old bldg, hardwood floors. Cr cds: A, C, D, DS, ER, MC, V.

★★ **JOHN ANDREW'S RESTAURANT.** *MA 23, South Egremont (01258). 413/528-3469.* Specialties: Napoleon of grilled shrimp, crisp duck confit. Hrs: 5-10 pm. Closed Wed Sept-June. Bar. Wine list. Dinner $13-$22. Child's menu. Outdoor dining. View of gardens. Cr cds: MC, V.

★★ **THE OLD MILL.** *53 Main St (Rte 23), South Egremont (01258). 413/528-1421.* Continental, Amer menu. Specialties: fresh filet of salmon, baby rack of lamb, sauteed calf liver with smoked bacon. Hrs: 5-9:30 pm; Fri, Sat to 10:30 pm; Sun brunch 11 am-2 pm. Closed Mon; Thanksgiving, Dec 25. Bar. Dinner $16-$24. Sun brunch $7.50-$14. Child's menu. Parking. In grist mill. Built in 1978. Cr cds: A, D, MC, V.

★★ **PAINTED LADY.** *785 S Main St (01230). 413/528-1662.* Continental menu. Specializes in fresh seafood, pasta, veal. Hrs: 5 pm-closing; Sun from 4 pm. Closed Dec 24, 25. Res accepted. Bar. Dinner $12.95-$22.95. Child's menu. Formal, intimate dining in Victorian house. Cr cds: DS, MC, V.

★★★ **SPENCER'S.** *453 Stockbridge Rd (01230). 413/528-3828. www.thornewood.com.* Continental, Amer menu. Specializes in fresh seafood, salads. Own desserts. Hrs: from 5 pm; Sun brunch 10:30 am-2 pm. Closed Tues; Jan 1; also Mon, Wed (Sept-mid-June). Res accepted. Bar. Wine cellar. A la carte entrees: dinner $15-$20. Sun brunch $14.95. Jazz Sat, Sun brunch. Parking. Outdoor dining. Family-owned since 1977. Totally nonsmoking. Cr cds: A, DS, MC, V.

Greenfield

Settled 1686 **Pop** 18,168 **Elev** 250 ft **Area code** 413
Zip 01301
Information Franklin County Chamber of Commerce,
395 Main St, PO Box 898; 413/773-5463
Web www.co.franklin.ma.us

The center of a prosperous agricultural area, Greenfield is
also the home of many factories and a center for winter
and summer sports, hunting, and fishing. The first cutlery
factory in America was established in Greenfield in the
early 19th century.

What to See and Do

Northfield Mountain Recreation and Environmental Center.
On site of Northeast Utilities Hydro Electric Pump storage
plant. Hiking, camping, riverboat ride and picnicking.
(Dec-Mar, Mon-Fri; May-Oct, Wed-Sun) Fee for some
activities. MA 63 in Northfield. Phone 413/659-3714.

Special Events

Green River Music & Balloon Festival. Hot-air balloon
launches, craft show, musical entertainment, food. (July).
Phone 413/773-5463.

Franklin County Fair. Four days starting first Thurs after
Labor Day. Phone 413/774-4282.

Motel/Motor Lodge

★ **HOWARD JOHNSON LODGE.** *125 Mohawk Tr (01301).*
413/774-2211; fax 413/772-2637; toll-free 888/244-2211.
www.hojo.com. 100 rms, 2 story. S $54-$84; D $58-$94;
each addl $10; under 18 free; higher rates: special events,
some wkends; lower rates rest of yr. Crib free. TV. Pool.
Coffee in rms. Restaurant 6 am-10 pm; Fri, Sat to 2 am. Bar
11-1 am. Ck-out 11 am. Meeting rms. Valet serv. Sundries.
Putting green, miniature golf. Downhill ski 20 mi; x-country
ski 12 mi. Private patios, balconies. Cr cds: A, C, D, DS,
MC, V.
[D] [🐾] [SC] [≈] [✈]

Hotel

★★★ **BRANDT HOUSE.** *29 Highland Ave (01301).*
413/774-3329; fax 413/772-2908; toll-free 800/235-3329.
www.brandthouse.com. 8 rms, 1 suite, 3 story. June-Oct:
suites $205; lower rates rest of yr. Crib avail, fee. Pet
accepted, some restrictions, fee. Parking lot. TV; cable, VCR
avail. Complimentary full bkfst, coffee in rms. Restaurant
nearby. Ck-out 11 am, ck-in 2 pm. Meeting rms. Business
servs avail. Exercise privileges. Golf, 18 holes. Tennis.
Downhill skiing. Bike rentals. Hiking trail. Picnic facilities.
Cr cds: A, DS, MC, V.
[➤] [≈] [🏌] [🎿] [≈] [🐾]

Restaurants

★★ **ANDIAMO.** *199 Huckle Hill Rd, Bernardston (01337).*
413/648-9107. Northern Italian menu. Specializes in veal,
pasta, steaks. Hrs: 5-9 pm. Closed Dec 24, 25. Res accepted.
Bar. Dinner $12.95-$22.95. Entertainment Fri, Sat. Dining
in greenhouse-style rm. Cr cds: A, D, DS, MC, V.
[D] [≈]

★★ **FAMOUS BILL'S.** *30 Federal St (01301). 413/773-9230.*
Specializes in lobster, prime rib, seafood. Own desserts.
Hrs: 11 am-close; Mon from 4 pm. Res accepted. Bar.
Lunch $3.75-$11.95, dinner $6.95-$17.95. Child's menu.
Family-owned. Cr cds: MC, V.
[D] [SC] [≈]

★★ **HERM'S.** *91 Main St (01301). 413/772-6300.* Specializes
in seafood, chicken, steak. Hrs: 11 am-9:30 pm; Fri, Sat to
10:30 pm. Closed Sun; Thanksgiving, Dec 25. Res accepted.
Bar. Lunch, dinner $6.95-$15.95. Child's menu. Cr cds:
A, DS, MC, V.
[D] [SC] [≈]

Harwich (Cape Cod)

Settled ca 1670 **Pop** 12,386 **Elev** 55 ft **Area code** 508
Zip 02646
Information Harwich Chamber of Commerce, PO Box 34;
508/432-1600; or the Cape Cod Chamber of Commerce,
US 6 and MA 132, PO Box 790, Hyannis 02601-0790,
508/362-3225 or 888/CAPECOD
Web www.capecodchamber.org

Harwich, whose namesake in England was dubbed
"Happy-Go-Lucky Harwich" by Queen Elizabeth, is one
of those towns made famous in New England literature.
It is "Harniss" in the Joseph C. Lincoln novels of Cape Cod.
A local citizen, Jonathan Walker, was immortalized as "the
man with the branded hand" in Whittier's poem about
helping escaped slaves; Enoch Crosby of Harwich was the
Harvey Birch of James Fenimore Cooper's novel *The Spy.*
Today, summer people own three-quarters of the land.

What to See and Do

Brooks Free Library. Houses 24 John Rogers' figurines.
(Mon-Sat; closed hols) 739 Main St, Harwich Center.
Phone 508/430-7562. **FREE**

Harwich Historical Society. Includes Brooks Academy
Building and Revolutionary War Powder House. Native
American artifacts, marine exhibit, cranberry industry arti-
cles, early newspapers and photographs. Site of one of the
first schools of navigation in US. (Usually mid-June-mid-
Sept, Tues-Fri; schedule may vary) 80 Parallel St, at Sisson
Rd, in Harwich Center. Phone 508/432-8089. **Donation**

Red River Beach. A fine Nantucket Sound swimming
beach (water 68° to 72°F in summer). Off MA 28, S on
Uncle Venies Rd in South Harwich. Sticker fee per wkday.

Saquatucket Municipal Marina. Boat ramp for launching small craft. (May-mid-Nov) Off MA 28 at 715 Main St. Phone 508/432-2562. ¢¢¢

Special Events

Harwich Junior Theatre. Plays for the family and children through high school age. Res required. (July-Aug, daily; Sept-June, monthly) Willow and Division Sts, West Harwich. For schedule phone 508/432-2002.

Cranberry Harvest Festival. Family Day, antique car show, music, arts and crafts, fireworks, carnival, parade. (One wkend mid-Sept.)

Motels/Motor Lodges

★ **COACHMAN MOTOR LODGE.** *774 Main St, Harwich Port (02646). 508/432-0707; fax 508/432-7951; toll-free 800/524-4265. www.coachmanmotorinn.com.* 28 rms. July-Aug: D $75-$199 (2-day min); each addl $15; apt for 4-5, $770; package plans off-season; lower rates Sept-mid Nov, May-July. Closed rest of yr. Crib $5. TV; cable (premium). Pool. Restaurant 7 am-midnight. Ck-out 11 am. Refrigerators avail. Cr cds: A, MC, V.
🏊 🛏 🔥

★★ **SEADAR INN.** *Bank St Beach, Harwich Port (02646). 508/432-0264; fax 508/430-1916; res 800/888-5250. www.seadarinn.com.* 20 rms, 1-2 story. No A/C. Late June-Labor Day: D $95-$275; each addl $20; lower rates late May-late June, after Labor Day-mid-Oct. Closed rest of yr. TV; cable, VCR. Complimentary continental bkfst. Restaurant nearby. Ck-out 11 am. Business servs avail. In-rm modem link. Bellhops. Lawn games. Some refrigerators. Picnic tables, grill. Near beach. Main bldg old Colonial house (1789). Early Amer decor; some rms with bay windows, ocean view. Cr cds: A, C, D, DS, MC, V.
✈ 🛏 🔥

★★ **WYCHMERE VILLAGE.** *767 Main St - Rte 28, Harwich Port (02646). 508/432-1434; fax 508/432-8904; toll-free 800/432-1434. www.wychmere.com.* 25 units, 2 A/C, 11 kits. Mid-June-mid-Sept: D $65-$129; each addl $10; under 14 free; kit. units $90-$130; cottage with kit. for 4, $1,050/wk; lower rates rest of yr. Crib $10. TV; cable. Heated pool. Playground. Coffee in lobby. Restaurant opp 7 am-noon. Ck-out 11 am. Lawn games. Refrigerators. Picnic tables, grill. Cr cds: A, DS, MC, V.
🛏 🔥 🏊

B&Bs/Small Inns

★★ **AUGUSTUS SNOW HOUSE.** *528 Main St, Harwich Port (02646). 508/430-0528; fax 508/432-6638; toll-free 800/320-0528.* 5 rms, some A/C, 2 story. Late May-mid-Oct: S, D $145-$160; wkends (2-day min); lower rates rest of yr. Children over 12 yrs only. TV; cable. Complimentary full bkfst; afternoon refreshments. Restaurant nearby. Ck-out 11 am, ck-in 2 pm. Luggage handling. Concierge serv. Free airport transportation. Some in-rm whirlpools. Built in 1901; Victorian decor. Totally nonsmoking. Cr cds: A, DS, MC, V.
🛏 🔥

★★ **CAPE COD CLADDAGH INN.** *77 Main St, West Harwich (02671). 508/432-9628; fax 508/432-6039; toll-free 800/356-9628. www.capecodcladdaghinn.com.* 8 rms, 6 with shower only, 3 story, 4 suites. No rm phones. Memorial Day-mid-Oct: S, D $85-$150; each addl $25; suites $110; wkly rates. Closed Jan-Mar. TV; cable (premium). Pool. Complimentary full bkfst. Dining rm 11:30-1 am. Ck-out 10:30 am, ck-in 2 pm. Coin lndry. Parking. Refrigerators. Picnic tables. Former Baptist parsonage (ca 1900). Antiques. Cr cds: A, MC, V.
🏊 🛏 🔥

★★ **COUNTRY INN.** *86 Sisson Rd, Harwich Port (02646). 508/432-2769; fax 508/430-1455; toll-free 800/231-1722. www.countryinncapecod.com.* 6 rms, 2 story. No rm phones. Memorial Day-Columbus Day: S, D $70-$110; each addl $15; lower rates rest of yr. TV. Pool. Complimentary continental bkfst. Dining rm (by res) 5-9 pm. Ck-out 11 am, ck-in 2 pm. Built in 1780; Colonial decor; antiques. On 6 acres. Use of private beach. Cr cds: A, MC, V.
🛏 🏊 🔥

★★★ **DUNSCROFT BY THE SEA.** *24 Pilgrim Rd, Harwich Port (02646). 508/432-0810; fax 508/432-5134; toll-free 800/432-4345. www.dunscroftbythesea.com.* 8 rms, 2 story, 1 cottage. Late May-Oct: S, D $105-$225; each addl $25; kit. unit $165-$225; lower rates rest of yr. Children over 12 yrs only. Complimentary full bkfst. Restaurants nearby. Ck-out 11 am, ck-in 2 pm. Whirlpool. Library/sitting rm; antiques. Near mile-long beach on Nantucket Sound. Cr cds: A, MC, V.
🄳 🛏 🔥

★ **SEA HEATHER INN.** *28 Sea St, Harwich Port (02646). 508/432-1275; toll-free 800/789-7809. www.seaheather.com.* 20 rms, 1-2 story. Mid-June-mid-Sept: S, D $95-$175; each addl $15; lower rates rest of yr. Children over 10 yrs only. TV; cable. Complimentary continental bkfst. Restaurant nearby. Ck-out 11 am. Lawn games. Some refrigerators, microwaves. Early Amer decor; porches, ocean view. Near beach. Totally nonsmoking. Cr cds: A, MC, V.
🔥 🛏

Restaurants

★★ **BISHOP'S TERRACE.** *MA 28, West Harwich (02671). 508/432-0253.* Specializes in swordfish, prime rib, lobster. Hrs: 4:30-9:30 pm; Sun brunch 11:30 am-2 pm. Res accepted. Bar 4:30 pm-1 am. Dinner $5.95-$25. Sun brunch $11.95. Child's menu. Entertainment (in-season, Sat only off-season). Glass-enclosed terrace dining. Restored Colonial house. Antiques. Cr cds: MC, V.
🄳 🍽

★★ **L'ALOUETTE.** *787 Main St, Harwich Port (02646). 508/430-0405. www.capecodmenu.com.* French menu. Own baking. Menu changes frequently. Hrs: 5-10 pm. Closed Mon; Dec 25; also Feb. Res required. Serv bar. A la carte entrees: dinner $15-$22. Intimate French atmosphere. Cr cds: A, DS, MC, V.
🄳

Haverhill

Settled 1640 **Pop** 58,969 **Elev** 27 ft **Area code** 978
Information Chamber of Commerce, 87 Winter St, 01830;
978/373-5663
Web www.haverhillchamber.com

Haverhill is a thriving manufacturing and commercial center located along the Merrimack River. Long known for its role in the manufacturing of women's shoes, Haverhill now boasts a highly diversified high-tech industrial base. The city features fine neighborhoods of early 19th-century homes. The Quaker poet John Greenleaf Whittier was born here.

A statue at Winter and Main Streets commemorates the remarkable Hannah Dustin, who, according to legend, was kidnapped by Native Americans in March 1697, and escaped with the scalps of ten of her captors.

What to See and Do

Haverhill Historical Society. Located in The Buttonwoods, an early 19th-century house. Period furnishings, china, glass, Hannah Dustin relics, memorabilia from turn-of-the-century theaters, Civil War artifacts, and archaeological collection. Also on grounds is the John Ward House (1641), furnished with colonial items; and an 1850s shoe factory with displays. Guided tours. (Wed, Thurs, also Sat and Sun afternoons) 240 Water St, MA 97. Phone 978/374-4626. ¢¢

John Greenleaf Whittier Birthplace. Whittier family homestead since the 17th century, this is the setting of his best-known poems, including "Snow-Bound," and "Barefoot Boy." His writing desk and mother's bedrm, built over a rock too large to move, are here. The house is furnished with original pieces and arranged as it would have appeared in his childhood. Grounds (69 acres) still actively farmed. (Tues-Sun; closed Jan 1, Thanksgiving, Dec 25) 305 Whittier Rd, I-495 exit 52, 1 mi E on MA 110. Limited hrs in winter. Phone 978/373-3979. ¢

Motel/Motor Lodge

★ ★ **BEST WESTERN.** *401 Lowell Ave (01832). 978/373-1511; fax 978/373-1517; toll-free 888/645-2025. www.bestwestern.com.* 127 rms, 3 story. Apr-Oct: S, D $79-$159; under 18 free; higher rates special events. Crib free. Pet accepted, some restrictions. TV; cable (premium). Indoor pool; whirlpool. Complimentary continental bkfst. Coffee in rms. Restaurant adj. Ck-out noon. Meeting rms. Business servs avail. In-rm modem link. Valet serv. Coin lndry. Airport transportation. Some refrigerators; microwaves avail. Some private patios. Cr cds: A, C, D, DS, MC, V.

⊡ ⇌ ⊠ ⚐ ⇱

All Suite

★ ★ **COMFORT SUITES.** *106 Bank Rd (01832). 978/374-7755; fax 978/521-1894; res 800/517-4000. www..hotelchoice .com/hotel/ma063/.* 131 rms, 4 story. S $89-$125; D $119-$139; each addl $10; under 18 free. Crib free. TV; cable (premium). Complimentary continental bkfst, coffee in rms. Restaurant nearby. Ck-out noon. Coin lndry. Meeting rms. Business servs avail. In-rm modem link. Valet serv. Exercise equipt. Whirlpool. Refrigerators. Cr cds: A, C, D, DS, ER, JCB, MC, V.

⊡ ⊼ ⇌ ⚐ SC

Holyoke

See also South Hadley, Springfield

Settled 1745 **Pop** 39,838 **Elev** 270 ft **Area code** 413
Zip 01040
Information Greater Holyoke Chamber of Commerce, 177 High St; 413/534-3376
Web www.holycham.com

Captain Elizur Holyoke explored the Connecticut Valley as early as 1633. His name is preserved in the industrial city made possible with the development of the great river by an unusual set of power canals.

What to See and Do

Holyoke Heritage State Park. Canalside park; visitor center features cultural, environmental and recreational programs, slide show and exhibits on the region and on Holyoke's history as a planned city, its canals, industries and people. Mt Park Merry-Go-Round also here (Sat and Sun afternoons; expanded summer hrs).(Wed-Sun afternoons; schedule may vary) Phone 413/534-1723. **FREE** Also on the site and adj is

    Children's Museum. Participatory museum. Exhibits include paper-making, sand pendulum, bubble making, TV studio, 2-story climbing structure, tot lot, "Cityscape," and other changing exhibits. (Daily exc Mon) 444 Dwight St. ¢

Wistariahurst Museum. Victorian mansion, family home of noted silk manufacturer William Skinner. House highlights include interior architectural detail unique to late 19th and early 20th centuries, including a leather-paneled room, conservatory and music hall; period furniture, decorative arts. Textile and archival collections available for research scholars. Changing exhibits. (Wed, Sat, Sun afternoons; schedule may vary) 238 Cabot St. Phone 413/534-2216. **Donation**

Motel/Motor Lodge

★★ **HOLIDAY INN.** *245 Whiting Farms Rd (01040). 413/534-3311; fax 413/533-8443; res 800/465-4329. www.holiday-inn.com.* 216 rms, 4 story. S $76-$80; D $86-$90; each addl $10; family rates; higher rates some college events. Crib free. Pet accepted; $25. TV; cable. Indoor pool; whirlpool, poolside serv. Restaurant 6:30 am-10 pm. Rm serv. Bar 11:30-2 am; entertainment Tues-Sat. Ck-out 11 am. Meeting rms. Business servs avail. Bellhops. Concierge. Downhill ski 3 mi. Exercise equipt; sauna. Game rm. Luxury level. Cr cds: A, D, DS, MC, V.

🅓 ⇌ 🏃 ⊠ 🐾 ➥ 🛇

B&B/Small Inn

★ **YANKEE PEDLAR INN.** *1866 Northampton St (01040). 413/532-9494; fax 413/536-8877. www.yankeepedlar.com.* 21 rms in 4 houses, 4 kit. units. S $79; D $89; wkly, monthly rates. Crib avail. TV; cable. Complimentary continental bkfst. Restaurant (see YANKEE PEDLAR). Bar 11:30-1 am; entertainment Thurs-Sat evenings. Ck-out 11 am, ck-in 2 pm. Health club privileges. Cr cds: A, MC, V.

🅓 ⊠ 🐾

Restaurants

★★★ **DELANY HOUSE.** *Rte 5 at Smith's Ferry (01040). 413/532-1800. www.delaney-house.com.* Specializes in fresh seafood, game. Own pastries and ice cream. Hrs: 5-9:30 pm; Fri, Sat to 10 pm; Sun 1-7 pm. Closed Jan 1, Dec 25. Res accepted. Bar 3:30-11 pm. Wine cellar. Dinner $12-$23. Children's meals. Dancing Fri, Sat. Valet parking. Patio dining. Late 18th-century furnishings. Cr cds: A, C, D, DS, ER, MC, V.

🅓 ⊡

★★ **YANKEE PEDLAR.** *1866 Northhampton St (01040). 413/532-9494. www.yankeepedlarinn.com.* Specializes in fresh fish, veal, beef. Own baking. Hrs: 7 am-9 pm; Sat, Sun to 10 pm; Sun brunch 10 am-2 pm. Closed Dec 25. Bar 11:30-1 am. Lunch $3.75-$12.50, dinner $8.95-$19.95. Sun brunch $13.95. Outdoor dining. Entertainment Thurs-Sat evenings. Cr cds: A, MC, V.

🅓

Hyannis (Cape Cod)

See also Martha's Vineyard, South Yarmouth (Cape Cod)

Settled 1639 **Pop** 14,120 **Elev** 19 ft **Area code** 508 **Zip** 02601

Information Chamber of Commerce, 1481 Rte 132; 508/362-5230 or 877/HYANNIS

Web www.hyannis.com

Hyannis is the main vacation and transportation center of Cape Cod. Recreational facilities and specialty areas abound, including tennis courts, golf courses, arts and crafts galleries, theaters, and antique shops. There are libraries, museums, and the Kennedy Memorial and Compound. Candle-making tours are available. Scheduled airliners and Amtrak stop here, and it is also a port for boat trips to Nantucket Island and Martha's Vineyard. More than six million people visit the village every year, and it is within an hour's drive of the many attractions on the Cape.

What to See and Do

Auto Ferry Service. Woods Hole, Martha's Vineyard, and Nantucket Steamship Authority conducts trips to Nantucket from Hyannis (yr-round); departs from South St dock. Phone 508/540-2022.

Hyannis-Nantucket or Martha's Vineyard Day Round Trip. (May-Oct) Also hrly sightseeing trips to Hyannis Port (Late Apr-Oct, daily); all-day or ½-day deep-sea fishing excursions (late Apr-mid-Oct, daily). Hy-Line, Pier #1, Ocean St Dock. Phone 508/778-2600.

John F. Kennedy Hyannis Museum. Photographic exhibits focusing on President Kennedy's relationship with Cape Cod; seven-min video presentation. Gift shop. (Mon-Sat, Sun afternoons) 397 Main St, in Old Town Hall. Phone 508/790-3077. ¢¢

John F. Kennedy Memorial. Circular fieldstone wall memorial 12 ft high with presidential seal, fountain, and small pool honors late president who grew up nearby. Ocean St.

Swimming. Craigville Beach. SW of town center. **Sea St Beach.** Sea St. Overlooking Hyannis Port harbor, bathhouse. **Kalmus Park.** Ocean St, bathhouse. **Veteran's Park.** Ocean St. Picnicking at Kalmus and Veteran's parks. Parking fee at all beaches. Phone 508/790-6345.

Special Events

Hyannis Harbor Festival. Waterfront at Bismore Park. Coast Guard cutter tours, sailboat races, marine displays, food, entertainment. Phone 508/362-5230 or 508/775-2201. Wkend early June.

Cape Cod Melody Tent. Summer musical theater in-the-round, daily; children's theater. 21 W Main St. Wed morning, July-early-Sept. Phone 508/775-9100.

Motels/Motor Lodges

★ **BUDGET HOST MOTEL.** *614 Rte 132, Hyannis (02601). 508/775-8910; fax 508/775-6476; res 800/283-4678. www.capecodtravel.com/hyannismotel.* 41 rms, 2 story, 8 kits. Late June-Labor Day: D $45-$125; each addl $10; under 17 free; lower rates rest of yr. Crib free. TV; cable (premium). Pool. Complimentary coffee in rms. Restaurant adj open 11:30 am-midnight. Ck-out 11 am. Refrigerators. Cr cds: A, D, DS, MC, V.

🅓 ⇌ ⊠ 🐾

★★ **CAPE CODDER.** *1225 Iyanough Rd, Hyannis (02601). 508/771-3000; fax 508/771-6564; toll-free 888/297-2200. www.capecodderresort.com.* 261 rms, 8 suites, 2 story. Memorial Day-Labor Day: S, D $139-$189; suites $401-$966; wkend rates; lower rates rest of yr. Crib free. TV; cable (premium), VCR avail. Heated pool; whirlpool, lifeguard. Coffee in rms. Restaurant 7 am-11:30 pm. Rm serv to 10 pm. Bar 11-1 am, Sun from noon; seasonal entertainment. Ck-out 11 am. Meeting rms. Business servs avail. In-rm modem link. Sundries. Gift shop. Airport transportation. Game rm. Tennis. Exercise equipt. Private patios, balconies. Cr cds: A, D, DS, MC, V.

🅓 🏃 ⇌ ⊠ 🏃 🐾 🛇

★★ **CAPTAIN GOSNOLD VILLAGE.** *230 Gosnold St, Hyannis (02601). 508/775-9111; fax 508/790-9776. www.captaingosnold.com.* 36 units, 16 kits., 18 kit. cottages. Some A/C. Many rm phones. Late June-Labor Day: D $90; each addl $10; kit. units $95; cottages (1-3 bedrm) $170-$280; under 5 free; lower rates mid-Apr-mid-June, Labor Day-Nov. Closed rest of yr. Crib free. TV; cable, VCR avail (free movies). Pool; lifeguard. Playground. Restaurant nearby. Ck-out 10:30 am. Lawn games. Refrigerators, microwaves. Picnic tables, grills. Cr cds: MC, V.

⌂ 🖼 SC

★ **COMFORT INN.** *1470 Rte 132, Hyannis (02601). 508/771-4804; fax 508/790-2336; res 800/228-5150. www.comfortinn-hyannis.com.* 104 rms, 3 story. No elvtr. June-mid-Sept: S $69-$175; under 18 free; higher rates wkends, hols; lower rates rest of yr. Crib free. TV; cable (premium). Indoor pool; whirlpool, lifeguard. Sauna. Complimentary continental bkfst. Restaurant nearby. Ck-out noon. Meeting rms. Business servs avail. Sundries. Health club privileges. Refrigerators, microwaves avail. Cr cds: A, C, D, DS, ER, JCB, MC, V.

D ⌂ ✈ 🖼 🖼 SC

★ **DAYS INN.** *867 Rte 132, Hyannis (02601). 508/771-6100; fax 508/775-3011; res 800/329-7466. www.daysinn.com.* 99 rms, 2 story. June-Sept: S, D $80-$200; each addl $8; under 17 free; lower rates rest of yr. Crib free. TV; cable. 2 pools, 1 indoor; whirlpool, lifeguard. Complimentary continental bkfst. Restaurant opp open 24 hrs in season. Ck-out 11 am. In-rm modem link. Exercise equipt. Refrigerators. Balconies. Cr cds: A, C, D, DS, JCB, MC, V.

D 🖼 🖼 SC ⌂ 🖼

★★ **HERITAGE HOUSE HOTEL.** *259 Main St, Hyannis (02601). 508/775-7000; fax 508/778-5687; toll-free 800/352-7189. www.heritagehousehotel.com.* 143 rms, 3 story. July 4-Labor Day: D $75-$125; each addl $12; under 16 free; package plans; lower rates rest of yr. Crib free. TV; cable (premium). 2 pools, 1 indoor; whirlpool, lifeguard. Sauna. Restaurant 7-10 am. Ck-out 11 am. Meeting rms. Balconies. Cr cds: A, C, D, DS, MC, V.

⌂ 🖼 🖼 SC

★ **RAMADA INN REGENCY.** *1127 Rte 132, Hyannis (02601). 508/775-1153; fax 508/775-1169; res 888/298-2054. www.ramada.com.* 196 rms, 2 story. July-Sept: S, D $99-$159; each addl $10; suites $119-$199; higher rates hols; lower rates rest of yr. Crib free. TV; cable. Indoor pool; lifeguard. Restaurant 7 am-10 pm. Rm serv. Bar noon-1 am. Ck-out 11 am. Meeting rms. Business servs avail. Concierge. Game rm. Balconies. Cr cds: A, C, D, DS, ER, MC, V.

D 🖼 🖼 🖼

Hotel

★★★ **INTERNATIONAL INN.** *662 Main St, Hyannis (02601). 508/775-5600; fax 508/775-3933; toll-free 877/588-3353. www.cuddles.com.* 141 rms, 2 story. June-Sept: S, D $90; each addl $16; suites $140-$210; lower rates rest of yr. Crib $10. TV; cable, VCR. 2 pools, 1 indoor; lifeguard. Sauna.

Restaurant 7-11 am, 5-9 pm. Bar 5-10 pm. Ck-out 11 am. Business servs avail. In-rm modem link. In-rm whirlpools; some bathrm phones. Cr cds: C, D, DS, ER, MC, V.

D ⌂ 🖼 🖼 🖼 🖼 🖼

Resort

★★★ **SHERATON HYANNIS RESORT.** *West End Cir, Hyannis (02601). 508/775-7775; fax 508/778-6039; res 800/598-4559. www.sheraton.com.* 224 rms, 2 story. June-Labor Day: S, D $79-$209; each addl $15; under 17 free; MAP avail; golf, wkend rates; lower rates rest of yr. Crib free. TV; cable. 2 pools, 1 indoor; whirlpool, lifeguard, poolside serv in season. Playground. Supervised children's activities (in season); ages 4-13. Coffee in rms. Dining rms 7-11 am, noon-3 pm, 5-10 pm. Snack bar. Rm serv. Bar 11-1 am. Ck-out 11 am, ck-in 4 pm. Meeting rms. Business center. In-rm modem link. Bellhops. Concierge. Gift shop. Spa. Airport transportation. Lighted tennis. 18-hole par 3 golf, greens fee $20-$30, pro, putting green. Lawn games. Soc dir; entertainment, movies. Game rm. Exercise rm; sauna, steam rm. Private patios, balconies. Picnic tables. Cr cds: A, C, D, DS, ER, JCB, MC, V.

D 🖼 🖼 🖼 🖼 🖼 🖼 🖼

B&Bs/Small Inns

★★ **SEA BREEZE INN.** *270 Ocean Ave, Hyannis (02601). 508/771-7213; fax 508/862-0663. www.seabreezeinn.com.* 14 rms, 2 cottages, 2 story. Mid-June-Labor Day: S $60-$80; D $65-$90; each addl $10; kit. unit $69; cottages $95-$150; wkly rates; lower rates rest of yr. TV; cable. Complimentary continental bkfst. Restaurant nearby. Ck-out 10:30 am, ck-in 2:30 pm. Concierge. Microwaves avail. Picnic tables. Antiques. Sitting rm. Near beach; some rms with ocean view. Cr cds: A, DS, MC, V.

🖼 🖼

★★ **SIMMONS HOMESTEAD INN.** *288 Scudder Ave, Hyannis Port (02647). 508/778-4999; fax 508/790-1342; toll-free 800/637-1649. www.capecodtravel.com/simmonsinn.* 14 rms, 2 story. No rm phones. May-Oct: S $80-$160; D $140-$180; each addl $20; suite $300; wkly rates; lower rates rest of yr. Crib free. Pet accepted. TV in sitting rm; cable. Complimentary full bkfst. Restaurant nearby. Ck-out 11 am, ck-in 1 pm. Business servs avail. Concierge. Lawn games. Rec rm. Bicycles. Health club privileges. Balconies. Restored sea captain's home built in 1820; some canopied beds, fireplaces. Unique decor; all rms have different animal themes. Library; antiques. Cr cds: A, DS, MC, V.

🖼 🖼 🖼

Restaurants

★ **DRAGON LITE.** *620 Main St (02601). 508/775-9494.* Chinese menu. Specialties: beef and chicken Szechuan, coconut shrimp, Mongolian beef. Hrs: 11:30-1 am. Closed Thanksgiving. Res accepted. Bar. Lunch $4-$6, dinner $5-$15. Street parking. Chinese decor. Cr cds: A, D, DS, MC, V.

D

★ **EGG & I.** *521 Main St (02601). 508/771-1596.* Specializes in crow's nest eggs, original bkfsts. Hrs: 11 am-1 pm. Closed Dec-Feb; wkends only Mar, Nov. Res accepted. Bkfst $2-$10. Children's meals. Street parking. Family dining. Cr cds: A, C, D, DS, ER, MC, V.
D **SC**

★ **ORIGINAL GOURMET BRUNCH.** *517 Main St (02601). 508/771-2558. www.capecod.com.* Hrs: 7 am-3 pm. Closed Thanksgiving, Dec 25. Wine, beer. Bkfst, lunch $2.95-$8. Street parking. Casual dining spot. Cr cds: A, MC, V.

★★ **PADDOCK.** *20 Scudder Ave (02601). 508/775-7677. www.capecodmenu.com.* Specializes in fresh local seafood, roast L.I. duckling. Hrs: 11:30 am-2:30 pm, 5-10 pm. Closed mid-Nov-Apr 1. Res accepted. Bar noon-1 am. Wine list. Lunch $4.95-$9.50, dinner $13.95-$24.95. Child's menu. Pianist. Valet parking. Victorian decor. Family-owned. Cr cds: A, D, DS, MC, V.
D

★★ **PENGUINS SEA GRILL.** *331 Main St (02601). 508/775-2023.* Specializes in seafood, wood-grilled meat, pasta. Hrs: 5-11 pm; winter to 10 pm. Closed Thanksgiving, Dec 25. Res accepted. Bar. Dinner $14-$19. Child's menu. Cr cds: A, C, D, DS, ER, MC, V.
D

★★ **RISTORANTE BAROLO.** *297 North St (02601). 508/778-2878. www.trulyitalian.com.* Italian menu. Specialties: antipasti, chicken saltinbocca. Hrs: 4 pm-midnight. Closed Jan 1, Easter, Dec 25. Res required. Bar to 1 am. Dinner $7.95-$21.95. Outdoor dining. Italian decor. Cr cds: A, D, MC, V.
D

★★ **ROADHOUSE CAFE.** *488 South St (02601). 508/775-2386. www.roadhousecafe.com.* Continental menu. Specializes in grilled veal chop, cioppino, thin-crust pizza. Hrs: 4-10 pm. Closed Dec 24, 25. Res accepted. Bar to 1 am. Dinner $5.95-$22.95. Entertainment. Valet parking. In 1903 house. Cr cds: A, D, DS, MC, V.
D

★ **SAM DIEGO'S.** *950 Hyannis Rd (MA 132) (02601). 508/771-8816. www.caperestaurantassociation.com.* Mexican menu. Specialties: fajitas, enchiladas, baby-back ribs. Own baking. Hrs: 11:30 am-midnight. Closed Easter, Thanksgiving, Dec 25. Bar to 1 am. Lunch $2.95-$5.95, dinner $6.95-$12.95. Child's menu. Outdoor dining. Mexican decor. Cr cds: A, DS, MC, V.
D

★ **STARBUCKS.** *668 Rte 132 (02601). 508/778-6767.* Specializes in hamburgers, fish, Mexican dishes. Hrs: 11:30-1 am. Closed Dec 25. Res accepted. Bar. Lunch, dinner $5.95-$12.95. Child's menu. Entertainment. Parking. Outdoor dining. Coney Island beach house decor. Cr cds: A, D, DS, MC, V.
D

Ipswich

See also Boston, Gloucester

Settled 1633 **Pop** 12,987 **Elev** 50 ft **Area code** 978 **Zip** 01938
Information Ipswich Visitors Center-Hall Haskell House, 36 S Main St, next to Town Hall; 978/356-8540

Ipswich is a summer resort town and home of the Ipswich clam; it has beaches nearby and a countryside of rolling woodland. Historically, Ipswich claims to have been the nation's first lacemaking town, the birthplace of the US hosiery industry, and of the American independence movement. In 1687, the Reverend John Wise rose in a meeting and denounced taxation without representation. His target was the hated Sir Edmund Andros, the British Colonial governor.

Andros and the lace are gone, but Ipswich retains the aura of its past. Besides a fine green, it has nearly 50 houses built before 1725, many from the 17th century.

What to See and Do

Crane Beach. Among the best on the Atlantic coast; five mi of beach; lifeguards, bathhouses, refreshment stand, trail. (Daily) End of Argilla Rd, on Ipswich Bay. Phone 978/356-4354.

The John Whipple House. (1640) Contains 17th- and 18th-century furniture; garden. (May-mid-Oct, Wed-Sat, Sun afternoons; closed hols) 53 S Main St, on MA 1A. Phone 978/356-2811. ¢¢ Opp is

  John Heard House. (1795) Bought as memorial to Thomas F. Waters, house has Chinese furnishings from the China sea trade. (Schedule same as Whipple House) 40 S Main St. Combination fee for both houses ¢¢

Special Event

Old Ipswich Days. Arts and crafts exhibits, games, clambakes, entertainment. Late July. Phone 978/356-8540.

Motel/Motor Lodge

★★ **COUNTRY GARDEN INN & MOTEL.** *101 Main St, Rowley (01969). 978/948-7773; fax 978/948-7947; toll-free 800/287-7773. www.countrygardenmotel.com.* 19 rms, 12 with shower only, 1-3 story, 4 suites. No elvtr. May-Oct: S $85; D $95; each addl $15; suites $80-$250; under 12 free; hols (2-day min); lower rates rest of yr. Children over 12 yrs only. Crib avail. TV; cable (premium), VCR avail (movies). Complimentary coffee in rms. Ck-out 10 am, ck-in after 1 pm. Business servs avail. X-country ski 2 mi. Lawn games. Some in-rm whirlpools, refrigerators, fireplaces. Picnic tables. Built in 1901. Cr cds: A, D, DS, MC, V.

B&B/Small Inn

★★★ **MILES RIVER COUNTRY INN B&B.** *823 Bay Rd, Hamilton (01936).* 978/468-7206; *fax* 978/468-3999. *www.milesriver.com.* 8 rms, 2 share bath, 2 with shower only, 1 suite, 3 story. No A/C. No elvtr. No rm phones. June-Oct: S, D $90-$165; each addl $15; suite $210; lower rates rest of yr. Crib $15. Complimentary full bkfst. Restaurant nearby. Ck-out 11 am, ck-in 3 pm. Many fireplaces. Built in 1790s; Colonial American decor, antiques. Totally nonsmoking. Cr cds: A, MC, V.

⊛ ⊠

Restaurant

★★★ **1640 HART HOUSE.** *51 Linebrook Rd (01938).* 978/356-9411. *www.1640harthouse.com.* Specialties: deep dish escargot, grilled boneless duck breast. Hrs: 11:30 am-3 pm, 4-9 pm; Fri to 10 pm; Sat 4-10 pm; early-bird dinner 4-6 pm. Closed Dec 25. Res accepted. Bar to midnight. Lunch $5-$11, dinner $10-$17. Child's menu. Entertainment Fri, Sat. Parking. Serving food since 1700s. Cr cds: A, C, D, DS, MC, V.

D ⊠

Lawrence

Founded 1847 **Pop** 72,043 **Elev** 50 ft **Area code** 978
Information Chamber of Commerce, 264 Essex St, 01840; 508/686-0900
Web www.merrimackvalleychamber.com

Lawrence was founded by a group of Boston financiers to tap the water power of the Merrimack River for the textile industry. As textiles moved out, diversified industries have been attracted to the community.

What to See and Do

Lawrence Heritage State Park. Twenty-three acres in city center includes restored Campagnone Common; canal and riverside esplanades. Visitor center in a restored workers' boardinghouse has participatory exhibits on the workers' experiences with industry in Lawrence and their contribution to the city's vitality. (Daily; closed Jan 1, Thanksgiving, Dec 25) Canal St. Phone 978/794-1655. **FREE**

Motel/Motor Lodge

★★ **HAMPTON INN.** *224 Winthrop Ave (01843).* 978/975-4050; *fax* 508/687-7122; *res* 800/426-7866. *www.hampton inn.com.* 126 rms, 5 story. Aug-Oct: S, D $99; under 18 free; lower rates rest of yr. Crib free. TV; cable. Complimentary continental bkfst. Restaurant nearby. Ck-out noon. Meeting rm. Business servs avail. In-rm modem link. Exercise equipt. Refrigerators, microwaves avail. Cr cds: A, MC, V.

D ⊼ ⊠ ⊛ SC

Restaurant

★★ **BISHOP'S.** *99 Hampshire St (01840).* 978/683-7143. Middle Eastern, Amer menu. Specializes in lobster, roast beef, Arabic dishes. Hrs: 11:30 am-9:30 pm; Fri to 10 pm; Sat 4-10:30 pm; Sun 2-9 pm (July, Aug from 4 pm). Closed Thanksgiving, Dec 25. Bar to 1 am. Lunch $4.50-$9, dinner $11-$25. Entertainment Fri, Sat. Moorish, Mediterranean decor. Family-owned. Cr cds: A, C, D, DS, MC, V.

D ⊠

Lee

Founded 1777 **Pop** 5,985 **Elev** 1,000 ft **Area code** 413
Zip 01238

Lee's major industry has been papermaking since the first years of the 19th century. Today, it is also a summer and ski resort area.

What to See and Do

October Mountain State Forest. Fine mountain scenery overlooking 16,000 acres. Hiking, hunting; snowmobiling. Camping on W side of forest. Standard fees. I-90 exit 2, US 20 westbound. Phone 413/243-1778.

Santarella Museum & Garden. Former studio of sculptor Sir Henry Kitson, creator of the "Minuteman" statue in Lexington. Built in the early 1920s, the house's major element is the roof, which was designed to look like thatching and to represent the rolling hills of the Berkshires in autumn; the fronting rock pillars and the grottoes between them are fashioned after similar edifices in Europe; Santarella Sculpture garden. Exhibits include ceramics, glass, paintings, graphics; also changing exhibits. Sculpture garden with lily pond. (Late May-Oct, daily) 4 mi SE in Tyringham. Phone 413/243-3260.

Special Event

Jacob's Pillow Dance Festival. Ted Shawn Theatre and Doris Duke Theatre, 8 mi E via US 20, on George Carter Rd in Becket. America's oldest and most prestigious dance festival includes performances by international dance companies. Performances Tues-Sat, some Sun. (Late June-Aug) Phone 413/243-0745 (box office) or 413/637-1322 (information).

Motel/Motor Lodge

★★ **BEST WESTERN BLACK SWAN INN.** *435 Laurel St; Rte 20 W (01238).* 413/243-2700; *fax* 413/637-0798; *toll-free* 800/876-7926. *www.bestwestern.com.* 52 rms, 2 story. July-Aug: D $95-$180; suites $120-$215; under 12 free; higher rates wkends (2-day min); lower rates rest of yr. TV; cable, VCR (movies $6). Pool; sauna. Restaurant 5-9 pm. Bar. Ck-out 11 am. Meeting rm. Business servs avail. In-rm modem link. Lawn games. Some refrigerators. Some balconies. Picnic tables. On lake. Cr cds: A, D, DS, MC, V.

D ⊯ ⊠

B&Bs/Small Inns

★★★ **APPLEGATE.** *279 W Park St (01238). 413/243-4451; fax 413/243-9832; toll-free 800/691-9012.* 6 rms, 2 with shower only, 2 story. No rm phones. June-Oct: S, D $115-$230; each addl $30; wkends, hols (3-day min); lower rates rest of yr. Children over 12 yrs only. TV in sitting rm. Pool. Complimentary continental bkfst. Restaurant nearby. Ck-out 11 am, ck-in 2 pm. Lawn games. Georgian Colonial built in 1920. Totally nonsmoking. Cr cds: A, MC, V.
⊠ 🔥

★★★ **CHAMBERY INN.** *199 Main St (US 20W) (01238). 413/243-2221; fax 413/243-0039; toll-free 800/537-4321.* 9 rms, 3 story. July-Aug, Oct: S, D, suites $99-$265; each addl $25; 2- or 3-day min wkends; lower rates rest of yr. Over 18 yrs only. TV; cable. Restaurant adj 11:30 am-9 pm. Rm serv. Ck-out 11 am, ck-in 2 pm. Luggage handling. Business servs avail. Downhill ski 8 mi. In-rm whirlpools. Berkshires' oldest parochial school (built 1885); recently restored with custom Amish-crafted furnishings. Totally nonsmoking. Cr cds: A, DS, MC, V.
D ⊠ 🔥 ⤢

★★★ **DEVONFIELD INN.** *85 Stockbridge Rd (01238). 413/243-3298; fax 413/243-1360; toll-free 800/664-0880.* 10 rms, 3 story. June-Oct: D $110-$195; each addl $20; suites $155-$260; lower rates rest of yr; (3-day min, July-Aug) wkends. Children over 10 yrs only. TV in some rms; cable. Heated pool. Complimentary full bkfst. Ck-out 11:30 am, ck-in 2 pm. Business servs avail. Tennis. Lawn games. Some fireplaces. Picnic tables. Built by Revolutionary War soldier; Federal-style rms with antique furnishings. Cr cds: A, D, DS, MC, V.
D ⤢ ⇌ ⊠ 🔥

★★★ **FEDERAL HOUSE INN.** *1560 Pleasant St, Rte 102, South Lee (01260). 413/243-1824; fax 413/243-1828; res 800/237-5747. www.federalhouseinn.com.* 10 rms, 2 story. No rm phones. Memorial Day-Oct: S, D $125-$180; each addl $20; lower rates rest of yr. Children over 12 yrs only. Complimentary full bkfst. Restaurant. Bar. Ck-out noon, ck-in 3 pm. Tennis, golf privileges. Built 1824. Cr cds: A, DS, MC, V.
⚡ ⤢ ⊠ 🔥

★★★ **HISTORIC MERRELL INN.** *1565 Pleasant St (Rte 102), South Lee (01260). 413/243-1794; fax 413/243-2669; toll-free 800/243-1794. www.merrell-inn.com.* 10 rms, 3 story. July-Oct: S $75-$155; D $85-$165; each addl $15; suite $135-$215; lower rates rest of yr. TV in some rms. Complimentary full bkfst. Ck-out 11 am, ck-in 2 pm. Downhill ski 10 mi; x-country ski 5 mi. Fireplaces. View of river. Historic New England inn (1794); English gardens. Cr cds: A, MC, V.
⊠ ⊠ 🔥

★★ **MORGAN HOUSE.** *33 Main St (01238). 413/243-3661; fax 413/243-3103; toll-free 877/571-0837.* 11 rms, 6 share bath, 3 story. No rm phones. July-Oct: S, D $85-$160; each addl $15; lower rates rest of yr. Crib free. Complimentary full bkfst. Restaurant. Bar 11-1 am. Ck-out 11 am, ck-in 1 pm. Built 1817. Stagecoach inn (1853); antiques; country-style decor. Cr cds: A, D, MC, V.
D ⊠ 🔥

Restaurants

★★ **CORK N' HEARTH.** *MA 20W (01238). 413/243-0535.* Specializes in fresh seafood, veal, beef. Hrs: 5-9 pm. Closed Mon; Thanksgiving, Dec 24, 25. Res accepted. Bar 5-11 pm. Dinner $13.95-$18.95. Child's menu. 3 dining rms. Scenic view of lake. Cr cds: A, MC, V.

★★ **SULLIVAN STATION RESTAURANT.** *109 Railroad St (01238). 413/243-2082. www.berkshireweb.com/dining/menus/sullivanstation.* Specializes in Boston baked scrod, steak, vegetarian dishes, homemade desserts. Hrs: noon-9 pm; winter hrs vary. Closed Thanksgiving, Dec 25; also 2 wks late Feb-early Mar. Res accepted. Bar. Lunch $4.95-$8.95, dinner $11.95-$18.95. Outdoor dining. Railroad memorabilia. Totally nonsmoking. Cr cds: A, DS, MC, V.
D ⊠

Lenox

Settled ca 1750 **Pop** 5,985 **Elev** 1,200 ft **Area code** 413 **Zip** 01240

Information Chamber of Commerce, 65 Main St, PO Box 646; 413/637-3646

Web www.lenox.org

This summer resort became world-famous for music when the Boston Symphony began its Berkshire Festival here in 1939. Nearby is Stockbridge Bowl, one of the prettiest lakes in the Berkshires.

What to See and Do

⊠ **Edith Wharton Restoration (The Mount).** Edith Wharton's summer estate; was planned from a book she coauthored in 1897, *The Decoration of Houses,* and built in 1902. This Classical Revival house is architecturally significant; on-going restoration. On 49 acres, with gardens. Tour of house and gardens (early June-early Nov daily). (See SPECIAL EVENTS) Plunkett St at S jct of US 7 and MA 7A. Phone 413/637-1899. ¢¢¢¢

Pleasant Valley Wildlife Sanctuary. Sanctuary of the Massachusetts Audubon Society. 1,500 acres with 7 mi of trails; beaver colony; office. (mid-June-Columbus day, Mon) No dogs. On West Mountain Rd, 1½ mi W of US 7/20. Phone 413/637-0320. ¢¢

⊠ **Tanglewood.** Where Nathaniel Hawthorne lived and wrote. Here he planned *Tanglewood Tales.* Many of the 526 acres, developed into a gentleman's estate by William Aspinwall Tappan, are in formal gardens. Well-known today as the summer home of the Boston Symphony Orchestra and the Tanglewood Music Center, the symphony's training academy for young musicians. (See SPECIAL EVENTS) Grounds (daily; free exc during concerts). On West St, 1½ mi SW on MA 183. Phone 413/637-1600.

Chamber Music Hall. Small chamber music ensembles, lectures, seminars, and large classes held here. Designed by Eliel Saarinen, who also designed

Formal Gardens. Manicured hemlock hedges and lawn, tall pine. Picnicking.

Hawthorne Cottage. Replica of "Little Red House" where Hawthorne lived 1850-1851, now contains music studios, Hawthorne memorabilia. (Open before each festival concert.)

Koussevitzky Music Shed. (1938) The so-called "Shed," where Boston Symphony Orchestra concerts take place; holds 5,121.

Main Gate Area. Friends of Tanglewood, box office, music and bookstore; cafeteria; gift shop.

Maron House. Original mansion, now Boston Symphony Orchestra Visitors Center and the Community Relations Office. Excellent view of Lake Mahkeenac, Monument Mtn.

Seiji Ozawa Concert Hall. (1941) Festival chamber music programs, Tanglewood Music Center activities; seats 1,200.

Special Events

Shakespeare & Company. The Mount. Professional theater company performs plays by Shakespeare and Edith Wharton, as well as other events. Four stages, one outdoor. Phone 413/637-3353 (box office) or 413/637-1199 (info). Tues-Sun, late May-early Nov.

Tanglewood Music Festival. Tanglewood Boston Symphony Orchestra. Concerts, Fri and Sat eve and Sun afternoons. Inquire for other musical events. Phone 413/637-1940 or 617/266-1492. July-Aug. Phone 617/266-1200.

Apple Squeeze Festival. Celebration of apple harvest; entertainment, food, music. Usually third wkend Sept. Phone 413/637-3646.

House Tours of Historic Lenox. Fall. Phone 413/637-3646.

Motels/Motor Lodges

★ **HOWARD JOHNSON EXPRESS INN.** *462 Pittsfield Rd (01240). 413/442-4000; fax 413/443-7954; toll-free 800/ 446-4656. www.hojo.com.* 44 rms, 2 story. July-Aug: S, D $85-$185; under 18 free; wkends (2-,3-day min); higher rates fall foliage; lower rates rest of yr. TV; cable. Pool. Complimentary continental bkfst. Restaurant adj 6 am-10 pm. Ck-out 11 am. Business servs avail. Sundries. Many microwaves; some refrigerators. Cr cds: A, C, D, DS, MC, V.

D ⊠ 🐾 SC ⤇

★★ **THE YANKEE HOME COMFORT.** *461 Pittsfield Rd (01240). 413/499-3700; fax 413/499-3634; toll-free 800/835-2364. www.yankeeinn.com.* 96 rms, 1-2 story. July-Aug, Oct: S, D $69-$169 (wkdays); S, D $149-$239 (wkends); 3-day min wkends in season; lower rates rest of yr. Crib free. TV; cable. Heated pool. Playground. Continental bkfst. Coffee in rms. Restaurant nearby. Ck-out 11 am. Business center. Sundries. Downhill/x-country ski 1 mi. Some refrigerators, fireplaces; microwaves avail. Picnic tables. On 7½ acres with a pond. Cr cds: A, C, D, DS, MC, V.

D ➤ ⤇ ⤇ 🐾 ⽊

Hotels

★★★★★ **BLANTYRE.** *16 Blantyre Rd (01240). 413/637-3556; fax 413/637-4282. www.blantyre.com.* This estate's castle-like brick facade alone will make visitors feel privileged. The wooded Berkshires are a perfect setting for the property's 100 acres of manicured lawns and gardens, main house, carriage house, and cottages. Rates include continental breakfast and on-site recreations including tennis, croquet, and swimming. Rich carved-mahogany furniture and detailing fill the accommodations, and there's a wonderful oak library to browse. 23 rms in main house, carriage house and cottages, 2 story, 6 suites. Mid May-mid Nov: S, D $350; each addl $50; suites $325-$675. Closed rest of yr. Children over 12 yrs only. TV; cable, VCR avail. Heated pool; whirlpool, poolside serv. Sauna. Complimentary continental bkfst; evening refreshments. Dining rm (see also BLANTYRE). Rm serv 7 am-10 pm. Ck-out noon, ck-in 3 pm. Meeting rms. Business servs avail. In-rm modem link. Luggage handling. Valet serv. Airport, bus depot transportation. Tennis, pro. Formal croquet lawns, pro. Massage. Some fireplaces. Cr cds: A, C, D, MC, V.

🏄 ⤇ 🐾

★★★ **CRANWELL RESORT AND GOLF CLUB.** *55 Lee Rd (01240). 413/637-1364; fax 413/637-0571; toll-free 800/272-6935. www.cranwell.com.* 105 rms in 7 bldgs, 2-3 story. Mid-June-Oct: S, D $199-$289; under 12 free; suites $289-$439; wkend rates; package plans; lower rates rest of yr. Crib free. TV; cable, VCR avail. Heated pool; poolside serv, lifeguard. Complimentary continental bkfst. Coffee in rms. Restaurant (see WYNDHURST); Bar; entertainment Fri, Sat. Ck-out 11 am. Meeting rms. Business servs avail. In-rm modem link. Tennis. 18-hole golf, greens fee $25-$85, pros, putting green, driving range, golf school. Downhill ski 7 mi; x-country ski on site. Exercise equipt. Some bathrm phones, fireplaces; microwaves avail. Balconies. Picnic tables. Heliport. Country Tudor mansion on 380 acres. Cr cds: A, D, DS, MC, V.

D ➤ ⽊ 🐾 ⤇ ⽊ ⽊ 🐾

★★★ **WHEATLEIGH HOTEL.** *Hawthorne Rd (01240). 413/637-0610; fax 413/637-4507. www.wheatleigh.com.* 19 rms, 2 story. S, D $175-$625; (3-day min) wkends (Tanglewood season and Oct). Children over 9 yrs only. TV; cable, VCR. Pool. Dining rm (see also WHEATLEIGH). Rm serv. Ck-out noon, ck-in 3 pm. Business servs avail. Luggage handling. Concierge serv. Valet parking. Tennis, pro. Downhill ski 9 mi. Exercise equipt. Massage. Many fireplaces. Many balconies. Built in 1893; antiques, abstract sculptures. On 22 acres; mountain views. Cr cds: A, C, D, MC.

D ⽊ ⽊ ⤇ ⽊ 🐾 🐾

B&Bs/Small Inns

★★ **APPLE TREE INN.** *10 Richmond Mountain Rd (01240). 413/637-1477; fax 413/637-2528. www.appletree-inn.com.* 35 rms, 2 share bath, 3 story, 2 suites. No rm phones. July-Aug: S, D $130-$210; suites $300; 3-day min wkends; some rms 5-day min; lower rates rest of yr. Crib free. TV in some rms; cable. Heated pool. Complimentary continental bkfst.

Restaurant (see APPLE TREE). Ck-out 11:30 am, ck-in 2 pm. Luggage handling. Tennis. X-country ski 1 mi. Picnic tables. Built in 1885; situated on 22 hilltop acres. Cr cds: A, C, D, DS, MC, V.

★★ **BIRCHWOOD INN.** 7 Hubbard St (01240). 413/637-2600; fax 413/637-4604; toll-free 800/524-1646. 12 rms, 8 with shower only, 2 share bath, 3 story, 2 kit. suites. July-Aug: S, D, kit. suites $75-$240; wkday rates; lower rates rest of yr. Children over 12 yrs only. TV in some rms; cable. Complimentary full bkfst. Restaurant adj 6-10 pm. Ck-out 11:30 am, ck-in 2 pm. Business servs avail. Downhill ski 5 mi; x-country ski adj. Built in 1767; many antiques, gardens. Totally nonsmoking. Cr cds: A, MC, V.

★★★ **BROOK FARM INN.** 15 Hawthorne St (01240). 413/637-3013; fax 413/637-4751; toll-free 800/285-7638. www.brookfarm.com. 12 rms, 3 story. July-Aug, hol wkends: S, D $140-$205; each addl $20; lower rates rest of yr. Children over 15 yrs only. Pool. Complimentary bkfst; afternoon refreshments. Ck-out noon, ck-in 3 pm. Business servs avail. Free bus depot transportation. Downhill ski 4 mi; x-country ski 1 mi. Picnic tables. Antiques. Library/sitting rm. Poetry readings Sat. Built 1870. Cr cds: MC, V.

★★ **CANDLELIGHT INN AND RESTAURANT.** 35 Walker St (01240). 413/637-1555; toll-free 800/428-0580. www.candlelightinn-lenox.com. 8 rms, 3 story. No rm phones. July-Oct: D $145-$175; each addl $30; wkly rates; lower rates rest of yr. Children over 10 yrs only. TV in sitting rm. Complimentary continental bkfst. Dining rm noon-9:30 pm. Bar in season. Ck-out 11 am, ck-in 2 pm. Downhill ski 5 mi; x-country ski ½ mi. Built 1885. Cr cds: A, DS, MC, V.

★★★ **THE GABLES INN.** 81 Walker St (01240). 413/637-3416; toll-free 800/382-9401. www.gableslenox.com. 18 rms, 3 story, 4 suites. No rm phones. Mid-June-Oct: S, D $90-$210; lower rates rest of yr. Children over 12 yrs only. TV; cable, VCR (free movies). Pool. Complimentary bkfst; afternoon refreshments. Restaurant nearby. Ck-out noon, ck-in 2 pm. Tennis. Downhill ski 5 mi; x-country ski ¼ mi. Some fireplaces. Balconies. Picnic tables. Antiques. Library/sitting rm. Queen Anne-style house (1885), once the home of Edith Wharton. Cr cds: DS, MC, V.

★★★ **GARDEN GABLES INN.** 135 Main St (01240). 413/637-0193; fax 413/637-4554. www.lenoxinn.com. 18 rms, 2 story. June-Oct: D $170-$200; wkly rates; lower rates rest of yr. Children over 12 yrs only. TV in some rms. Pool. Complimentary full bkfst; afternoon refreshments. Restaurant nearby. Ck-out 11 am, ck-in 2 pm. Business center. In-rm modem link. Downhill ski 4 mi; x-country ski ¼ mi. Fireplaces. Balconies. Picnic tables. Built 1780; antiques, books. Cr cds: A, DS, MC, V.

★★ **GATEWAYS INN.** 51 Walker St (01240). 413/637-2532; fax 413/637-1432; toll-free 888/492-9466. www.gatewaysinn.com. 12 rms, 2 story. July-Oct: S $70-$110; D $130-$200; suite $275-$400; lower rates rest of yr. Children over 12 yrs only. TV; cable. Continental bkfst. Restaurant (see GATEWAYS INN). Rm serv. Ck-out 11 am, ck-in 1 pm. Business servs avail. Downhill ski 5 mi; x-country ski ¼ mi. Many fireplaces. Restored mansion (1912). Cr cds: A, C, D, DS, MC, V.

★★★ **HARRISON HOUSE.** 174 Main St (02114). 413/637-1746; fax 413/637-9957. www.harrison-house.com. 6 rms, 2 story, 1 suite. June-Oct (2-,3-day min): S, D $95-$175; suite $230-$340; wkly rates; lower rates rest of yr. Children over 12 yrs only. TV; cable. Complimentary continental bkfst; afternoon refreshments. Restaurant nearby. Ck-out 11 am, ck-in 2 pm. Luggage handling. Free bus depot transportation. Downhill ski 4 mi; x-country ski adj. Victorian inn; fireplaces in every rm. Many antiques. Gardens. Totally nonsmoking. Cr cds: A, MC, V.

★★★ **KEMBLE INN.** 2 Kemble St (01240). 413/637-4113; toll-free 800/353-4113. www.kembleinn.com. 15 rms, 3 story. S $95-$145; D $215-$295; wkly rates. Children over 12 yrs only. TV; cable. Complimentary continental bkfst. Restaurant nearby. Ck-out 11 am, ck-in 2 pm. Fireplaces; some in-rm whirlpools. Panoramic mountain views; quiet, elegant atmosphere in restored mansion (1881). Totally nonsmoking. Cr cds: DS, MC, V.

★★ **ROOKWOOD INN.** 11 Old Stockbridge Rd (01240). 413/637-9750; fax 413/637-1532; toll-free 800/223-9750. 20 rms, 3 story, 5 suites. Phones in suites. Late June-Aug: D $110-$235; each addl $15; suites $250-$300; under 12 free; lower rates rest of yr. Crib free. TV in sitting rm and suites. Complimentary full bkfst; afternoon refreshments. Restaurant nearby. Ck-out 11 am, ck-in 3 pm. Bus depot transportation. Downhill ski 5 mi; x-country ski 1 mi. Fireplaces. Balconies. Victorian inn (1885) furnished with English antiques. Totally nonsmoking. Cr cds: A, D, DS, MC, V.

★★ **THE SUMMER WHITE HOUSE.** 17 Main St (01240). 413/637-4489; toll-free 800/382-9401. www.summerwhitehouse.com. 6 rms. No rm phones. S $155-$160; D $195. Closed Dec-Apr. Children over 16 yrs only. TV; cable. Pool privileges. Complimentary continental bkfst. Coffee in library. Restaurant nearby. Ck-out 11 am, ck-in 2 pm. Mansion built in 1885; original antiques. Totally nonsmoking. Cr cds: MC, V.

★★ **THE VILLAGE INN.** 16 Church St (01240). 413/637-0020; fax 413/637-9756; toll-free 800/253-0917. www.villageinn-lenox.com. 32 rms, 3 story. July-Aug, Oct: S $100-$225; D $125-$225; each addl $20; MAP avail; wkly, wkend rates; ski plans; lower rates rest of yr. TV rm. Restaurant 8-10:30 am, 5:30-9 pm. Bar 5 pm-1 am. Ck-out 11 am, ck-in 1 pm. Downhill ski 4 mi; x-country ski 1 mi. Some in-rm whirlpools, fireplaces. Inn since 1775. Cr cds: A, C, D, DS, MC, V.

★ **WALKER HOUSE.** *64 Walker St (01240).* *413/637-1271; fax 413/637-2387; toll-free 800/235-3098.* *www.walker house.com.* 8 rms, 2 story. No rm phones. Late June-early Sept: S $90-$125; D $120-$190; each addl $5-$15; ski plans; lower rates rest of yr. Children over 12 yrs only. Pet accepted, some restrictions. TV in sitting rm; VCR avail. Complimentary continental bkfst. Restaurant opp 11 am-10 pm. Ck-out noon, ck-in 2 pm. Business servs avail. Downhill ski 6 mi; x-country ski ½ mi. Antiques. Library. Rms named after composers. Built 1804. Totally nonsmoking. Cr cds: A, MC, V.

★★ **WHISTLER'S INN.** *5 Greenwood St (01240).* *413/637-0975; fax 419/637-2190.* 14 rms, 2 story, 3 suites. July-Aug, Oct: D $90-$225; each addl $25; suites $160-$225; summer (3-day min); lower rates rest of yr. TV; cable; VCR avail. Complimentary full bkfst; afternoon refreshments. Restaurant nearby. Ck-out noon, ck-in 3 pm. Business servs avail. Free bus depot transportation. Downhill ski 5 mi; x-country ski ½ blk. Lawn games. Fireplaces. Picnic tables. Tudor-style mansion built 1820. Library. Music rm with Steinway grand piano, Louis XVI furniture. Cr cds: A, DS, MC, V.

Restaurants

★★ **APPLE TREE.** *10 Richmond Mt Rd (01240).* *413/637-1477. www.appletree-inn.com.* Continental menu. Specialties: fresh fish of the day, black Angus steak. Own baking. Hrs: 5:30-9 pm; July-Aug 5-9:30 pm; Sun brunch 10:30 am-2 pm. Closed Mon-Wed off-season. Res accepted. Bar. Dinner $12-$23. Parking. Outdoor dining. Round dining rm with hillside view. Totally nonsmoking. Cr cds: A, D, DS, MC, V.

★★★ **BLANTYRE.** *16 Blantyre Rd (01240). 413/637-3556. www.blantyre.com.* Contemporary French menu. Specializes in fresh game and seafood. Own baking, ice cream. Hrs: 6-9 pm; July-Aug also 12:30-1:45 pm. Closed Mon; also Nov-Apr. Res required. Serv bar. Wine cellar. Prix fixe: lunch (July-Aug) 2-course $32, 3-course $40; dinner $75. Serv charge 18%. Harpist (dinner). Valet parking (dinner). Outdoor dining (lunch). Jacket. Cr cds: A, C, D, ER, MC, V.

★★ **CAFE LUCIA.** *80 Church St (01240). 413/637-2640.* Italian menu. Specializes in veal, seafood, pasta. Hrs: 5:30-10 pm; hrs vary mid-Sept-May. Closed Mon; Easter, Thanksgiving, Dec 25; also Sun Nov-June. Res accepted. Serv bar. Dinner $13-$28. Outdoor dining. Cr cds: A, C, D, DS, ER, MC, V.

★ **CAROL'S.** *8 Franklin St (01240). 413/637-8948.* Specializes in bkfst; served all day. Hrs: 8 am-3 pm. Closed Tues, Wed (Sept-June); Thanksgiving, Dec 25. Bkfst, lunch $1.95-$6.50. Child's menu. Cr cds: A, DS, MC, V.

★★ **CHURCH STREET CAFE.** *65 Church St (01240). 413/637-2745.* Regional Amer menu. Specializes in seafood, crab cakes, grilled meat and fish. Hrs: 11:30 am-2 pm, 5:30-9 pm; Fri, Sat to 9:15 pm. Closed Jan 1, Thanksgiving, Dec 25; also Sun, Mon Nov-May. Res accepted. Bar. Lunch $7.95-$13.95, dinner $16.95-$25.50. Outdoor dining. Bistro-style cafe; New England decor. Cr cds: MC, V.

★★★ **GATEWAYS INN.** *51 Walker St (01240). 413/637-2532. www.gatewaysinn.com.* Italian menu. Specialties: escargot with gnocchi, rack of lamb Provençal, seasonal dishes. Hrs: 5-9 pm. Closed Mon, Tues in winter. Res accepted. Wine list. Dinner $18-$26. Parking. Outdoor dining. Cr cds: A, C, D, DS, ER, MC, V.

★★★ **LENOX 218 RESTAURANT.** *218 Main St (01240). 413/637-4218. www.lenox218.com.* Northern Italian, Amer menu. Specialties: Tuscan clam soup; New England seafood cakes; boneless breast of chicken with almonds, sesame and sunflower seeds. Hrs: 11:30 am-2:30 pm, 5-10 pm; Sun 10:30 am-9 pm; Sun brunch to 1:30 pm. Res accepted. Bar. Lunch $5.95-$8.95, dinner $12.95-$20.95. Sun brunch $11.95. Child's menu. Parking. Casual elegance; vaulted ceilings and skylights. Cr cds: A, D, DS, MC, V.

★★ **LENOX HOUSE.** *55 Pittsfield-Lenox Rd (01240). 413/637-1341. www.regionnet.com/colberk/lenoxhouse.html.* Continental menu. Specializes in fresh fish, poultry, prime rib. Own baking. Hrs: 11:30 am-9:30 pm; Fri, Sat to 10 pm. Res accepted. Bar. Lunch $4.75-$9.95, dinner $10.95-$21.95. Parking. Totally nonsmoking. Cr cds: A, D, DS, MC, V.

★ **PANDA HOUSE CHINESE RESTAURANT.** *506 Pittsfield Rd (01240). 413/499-0660.* Chinese menu. Specialties: General Tso's chicken, vegetarian paradise. Hrs: 11:30 am-10 pm; Fri, Sat to 11 pm; Sun brunch to 3 pm. Closed Thanksgiving, Dec 25. Res accepted. Bar. Lunch $4.75-$6.25, dinner $7.95-$15.95. Sun brunch $7.95. Parking. Oriental decor. Cr cds: A, D, DS, MC, V.

★★★ **WHEATLEIGH.** *Hawthorne Rd (01240). 413/637-0610. www.wheatleigh.com.* Polished mahogany doors lead to this historic hotel's elegant restaurant. The dining room's design is just as regal as the building itself, which was modeled in 1893 after a 16th-century Florentine palazzo. Guests dine on contemporary French cuisine (degustation menu is available) in a beautiful sun-drenched room filled with oil paintings, hand-carved Chippendale chairs, and sparkling crystal chandeliers. French/American menu. Own baking. Hrs: 6-9 pm. Res required. Tasting menu: 4-course dinner $75 (changes every 2 weeks). 7-course degustation menu (changes every 2-3 days) $95. Valet parking. Cigar bar. Cr cds: A, D, DS, MC, V.

★★★ **THE WYNDHURST RESTAURANT.** *55 Lee Rd (01240). 413/637-1364. www.cranwell.com.* Specializes in lamb, fresh fish, daily specialties. Own desserts. Sittings: 5-6:30 pm and 8-9:30 pm. Res accepted. Bar. Wine list. Dinner $16.50-$28. Child's menu. Entertainment Fri, Sat. Formal decor in Tudor mansion; ornately carved fireplace, original artwork. Totally nonsmoking. Cr cds: A, DS, MC, V.
D

Leominster

Settled 1653 **Pop** 41,303 **Area code** 978 **Zip** 01453
Information Johnny Appleseed Visitor Center, 110 Erdman Way; 978/840-4300

Leominster (LEMMINst'r) has retained the pronunciation of the English town for which it was named. Known at one time as "Comb City," in 1845 Leominster housed 24 factories manufacturing horn combs. It is the birthplace of "Johnny Appleseed"—John Chapman (1774-1845)—a devout Swedenborgian missionary who traveled throughout America on foot, planting apple orchards and the seeds of his faith. The National Plastics Center and Museum is located here.

Motel/Motor Lodge

★★ **FOUR POINTS BY SHERATON LEOMINSTER.** *99 Erdman Way (01453). 978/534-9000; fax 978/534-0891; res 800/325-3535. www.fourpoints.com.* 187 rms, 7 story. S $119-$130; D $134-$145; each addl $15; suites $130-$145; under 18 free. Crib free. TV; cable. Indoor pool. Complimentary continental bkfst Mon-Fri. Restaurant 6:30 am-10 pm. Bar 11:30-1 am. Ck-out noon. Meeting rms. Business center. In-rm modem link. Downhill ski 5 mi. Whirlpool. Cr cds: A, MC, V.
D ⊠ ≈ 🐾 🎿

Conference Center

★★★ **WACHUSETT VILLAGE INN.** *9 Village Inn Rd, Westminster (01473). 978/874-2000; fax 978/874-1753; res 800/342-1905. www.wachusetvillageinn.com.* 74 rms, 2 story, 18 suites. S, D $89-$109; each addl $10; suites $129-$149; under 18 free; ski, golf plans. Crib free. Pet accepted. TV; cable. 2 pools, 1 indoor; poolside serv. Playground. Restaurant 6:30 am-9:30 pm. Ck-out 11 am. Meeting rms. Tennis. 18-hole golf privileges. Downhill/x-country ski 3 mi. Exercise equipt; sauna. Sitting rms with Colonial decor; extensive grounds. Cr cds: A, C, D, DS, MC, V.
D 🐾 ≈ 🎿 ⛷ 🏃 ⊠ 🎿

Lexington

See also Concord

Settled ca 1640 **Pop** 30,355 **Elev** 210 ft **Area code** 781 **Zip** 02173
Information Chamber of Commerce Visitors Center, 1875 Massachusetts Ave; 781/862-1450. The center, open daily, offers a diorama depicting the Battle of Lexington and has a walking tour map.

Lexington is called the birthplace of American liberty. On its Green, April 19, 1775, eight Minutemen were killed in what is traditionally considered the first organized fight of the War for Independence. However, in 1908, the US Senate recognized the counterclaim of Point Pleasant, West Virginia, as the first battle site. It is still possible to visualize the Battle of Lexington. Down the street came the British, 700 strong. To the right of the Green is the tavern the militia used as headquarters. It was here that 77 Minutemen lined up near the west end of the Green, facing down the Charlestown road. Nearby is a boulder with a plaque bearing the words of Captain John Parker, spoken just before the Redcoats opened fire: "Stand your ground. Don't fire unless fired upon. But if they mean to have a war, let it begin here!" It did—the fight then moved on to Concord.

What to See and Do

Battle Green. The Old Monument, the Minuteman Statue, and the Boulder mark the line of the Minutemen, seven of whom are buried under the monument. At the center of town.

Lexington Historical Society. Revolutionary period houses. Guided tours. Phone 781/862-1703. ¢¢¢

    Buckman Tavern. (1709) Minutemen assembled here before the battle. Period furnishings, portraits. (Mid-Apr-Oct, daily; Nov, wkends only) 1 Bedford St, facing the Battle Green. Phone 781/862-1703.

    Hancock-Clarke House. (1698) Here John Hancock and Samuel Adams were awakened by Paul Revere's alarm on Apr 18, 1775. Furniture, portraits, utensils; small museum. Fire engine exhibit in barn (by appt). (Mid-Apr-Oct, daily) 36 Hancock St. Phone 781/862-1703.

    Munroe Tavern. (1695) British hospital after the battle. George Washington dined here in 1789. Period furnishings, artifacts. (Mid-Apr-Oct, daily) 1332 Massachusetts Ave. Phone 781/862-1703.

National Heritage Museum. Museum features exhibits on American history and culture, from its founding to the present; also history of Lexington and the Revolutionary War. (Daily) 33 Marrett Rd (MA 2A), at jct Massachusetts Ave. Phone 781/861-6559. **FREE**

Special Event

Reenactment of the Battle of Lexington and Concord. Massachusetts Ave. Reenactment of opening battle of Revolutionary War; parade. Patriots Day (Mon nearest Apr 19). Phone 781/862-1450.

Motel/Motor Lodge

★★ **HOLIDAY INN EXPRESS.** *440 Bedford St (02420). 781/861-0852; fax 781/861-0821. www.holiday-inn.com.* 204 rms, 28 suites, 2 story. S, D $69-$169; each addl $10; under 12 free. Crib free. TV; cable (premium). Heated pool; whirlpool. Complimentary continental bkfst. Ck-out noon. Coin lndry. Business servs avail. In-rm modem link. Valet serv. Health club privileges. Microwaves avail. Cr cds: A, C, D, DS, JCB, MC, V.

`D` `⇌` `⊠` `🔥`

Hotel

★★ **SHERATON LEXINGTON INN.** *727 Marrett Rd (02421). 781/862-8700; fax 781/863-0404. www.sheraton.com.* 119 rms, 2 story. S, D $149-$199; each addl $10; under 18 free; wkend rates. Crib free. TV; cable (premium). Pool; poolside serv, lifeguard. Coffee in rms. Restaurant 6:30 am-2:30 pm, 5-10 pm; Sat, Sun 8 am-noon. Bar 11:30 am-11:30 pm. Ck-out noon. Meeting rms. Business servs avail. In-rm modem link. Exercise equipt. Health club privileges. Some private patios, balconies. Picnic tables. Cr cds: A, D, DS, MC, V.

`D` `⇌` `🖈` `⊠` `🔥`

Lowell

Settled 1655 **Pop** 105,167 **Elev** 102 ft **Area code** 978
Information Greater Lowell Chamber of Commerce, 77 Merrimack St, 01852; 978/459-8154
Web www.greaterlowellchamber.org

In the 19th century, the powerful Merrimack River and its canals transformed Lowell from a handicraft center to a textile industrial center. The Francis Floodgate, near Broadway and Clare Streets, was called "Francis's Folly" when it was built in 1848, but it saved the city from flood in 1936. Restoration of the historic canal system is currently in progress.

What to See and Do

American Textile History Museum. Permanent exhibit, "Textiles in America," features 18th- to 20th-century textiles, artifacts, and machinery in operation, showing the impact of the Industrial Revolution on labor. Collections of cloth samples, books, prints, photographs, and preindustrial tools may be seen by appt. Tours; activities. Library; education center. Restaurant; museum store. (Tues-Sun; closed Jan 1, Thanksgiving, Dec 25) 491 Dutton St. Phone 978/441-0400. ¢¢¢

Lowell Heritage State Park. Six mi of canals and associated linear parks and two mi of park on the bank of Merrimack River offers boating, boathouse; concert pavilion, interpretive programs. (Schedule varies) Phone 978/453-0592. **FREE**

Lowell National Historical Park. Established to commemorate Lowell's unique legacy as the most important planned industrial city in America. The nation's first large-scale center for the mechanized production of cotton cloth, Lowell became a model for 19th-century industrial development. Park includes mill buildings, 5½-mi canal system. Visitor center at Market Mills, 246 Market St, includes audiovisual show and exhibits (daily; closed Jan 1, Thanksgiving, Dec 25). Free walking and trolley tours (Mar-Nov). Tours by barge and trolley (May-Columbus Day wkend; fee), res suggested. Downtown. Contact Visitor Center, 01852. Phone 978/970-5000. Located here are

Boott Cotton Mills Museum. Industrial history museum with operating looms (ear plugs supplied). Interactive exhibits, video presentations. (Daily; closed Jan 1, Thanksgiving, Dec 25) At foot of John St. Phone 978/970-5000. ¢¢

Patrick J. Mogan Cultural Center. Restored 1836 boarding house of the Boott Cotton Mills including a re-created kitchen, keeper's rm, parlor, and mill girls' bedrm; exhibits on working people, immigrants, and labor history; also local history. (Daily) 40 French St.

New England Quilt Museum. Changing exhibits feature antique, traditional, and contemporary quilts. Museum shop. (Tues-Sat; closed hols) 18 Shattuck St. Phone 978/452-4207. ¢¢

University of MA-Lowell. 15,500 students. State-operated university formed by 1975 merger of Lowell Technological Institute (1895) and Lowell State College (1894). Music ensembles at Durgin Hall Performing Arts Center. 1 University Ave. Phone 978/934-4444.

Whistler House Museum of Art. Birthplace of the painter James Abbott McNeill Whistler. Exhibits include several of his etchings. Collection of 19th- and early 20th-century American art. (Wed-Sun; closed hols) 243 Worthen St. Phone 978/452-7641. ¢¢

Special Event

Lowell Folk Festival. Concerts, crafts, and demonstrations, ethnic food, street parade. Last full wkend July. Phone 978/970-5000.

Lowell Celebrates Kerouac Festival. Tours, music, poetry competition, book signings, panel discussions. First wkend Oct. Phone 877-KEROUAC.

Motels/Motor Lodges

★★ **BEST WESTERN CHELMSFORD INN.** *187 Chelmsford St, Chelmsford (01824). 978/256-7511; fax 978/250-1401; res 800/780-7234. www.bestwestern.com/chelmsfo.* 120 rms, 5 story. S, D $69-$109; suites $95; under 18 free; wkend rates. Crib free. TV; cable (premium), VCR avail (movies). Pool; whirlpool; poolside serv. Complimentary coffee in rms. Restaurant adj 6-1 am. Ck-out noon. Meeting rms. Business sevs avail. In-rm modem link. Valet serv. Exercise equipt; sauna. Some refrigerators, minibars; microwaves avail. Some balconies. Cr cds: A, C, D, DS, MC, V.

`D` `⇌` `🖈` `⊠` `🔥` `SC`

★★ **COURTYARD BY MARRIOTT.** *30 Industrial Ave E (01852). 978/458-7575; fax 978/458-1302; res 800/321-2211. www.marriott.com.* 120 rms, 2 suites, 3 story. S, D $99-$109; suites $129-$139; under 12 free; wkend rates. TV; cable (premium). Complimentary coffee in rms. Restaurant 6:30-10 am; Sat, Sun 7:30-11:30 am. Rm serv 5-10 pm. Bar Sun-Thurs 5-10 pm. Ck-out 1 pm. Meeting rms. Business servs avail. In-rm modem link. Valet serv. Sundries. Coin lndry. Airport transportation. Exercise equipt. Pool. Refrigerators avail. Cr cds: A, D, DS, MC, V.

Hotels

★★ **DOUBLETREE.** *50 Warren St (01852). 978/452-1200; fax 978/453-4674; toll-free 800/876-4586. www.doubletree.com.* 252 rms, 9 story. S, D $89-$129; suites $139-$250; under 18 free. Crib free. TV; cable (premium), VCR avail. Indoor pool; whirlpool, wading pool, poolside serv. Restaurant 6:30 am-10 pm. Bar. Ck-out 11 am. Coin lndry. Convention facilities. Business servs avail. In-rm modem link. Free garage parking. Exercise equipt; sauna. Cr cds: A, C, D, DS, MC, V.

★★★ **RADISSON HOTEL.** *10 Independence Dr, Chelmsford (01824). 978/256-0800; fax 978/256-0750; toll-free 800/333-3333. www.radisson.com.* 214 rms, 5 story, 82 suites. S, D $129; each addl $10; suites $149; under 16 free; wkend rates. Crib free. TV; cable (premium), VCR in suites. Indoor pool. Restaurant 6:30 am-2 pm, 5-10 pm. Rm serv. Bar 11 am-midnight. Ck-out noon. Meeting rms. Business servs avail. In-rm modem link. Sundries. Exercise equipt; sauna. Rec rm. Bathrm phone, refrigerator in suites. Cr cds: A, C, D, DS, ER, JCB, MC, V.

★★★ **WESTFORD REGENCY INN.** *219 Littleton Rd, Westford (01886). 978/692-8200; fax 978/692-7403; toll-free 800/543-7801. www.westfordregency.com.* 193 units, 4 story, 15 suites. S $114; D $140; each addl $8; suites $125-$235; under 18 free; wkend rates. Crib free. Pet accepted, some restrictions. TV; cable (premium). Indoor pool; whirlpool. Restaurant 7 am-10 pm. Bar 11 am-11 pm; entertainment. Ck-out noon. Convention facilities. Business servs avail. In-rm modem link. Exercise rm; sauna. Bathrm phones; some refrigerators. Atrium in lobby. Cr cds: A, C, D, DS, MC, V.

Resort

★★★ **STONEHEDGE INN.** *160 Pawtucket Blvd, Tyngsboro (01879). 978/649-4400; fax 978/649-9256; res 888/649-2474. www.stonehedgeinn.com.* 30 rms, 2 story. May-June, Sep-Oct: S, D $195; suites $255; lower rates rest of yr. Crib avail. Valet parking avail. Indoor/outdoor pools, whirlpool. TV; cable, VCR avail. Restaurant 6 am-9 pm. 24-hr rm serv. Bar. Ck-out noon, ck-in 3 pm. Business servs avail. Bellhops. Concierge serv. Valet serv. Exercise rm. Golf. Tennis. Downhill skiing. Bike rentals. Hiking trail. Cr cds: A, C, D, DS, ER, JCB, MC, V.

Restaurants

★★ **COBBLESTONES.** *91 Dutton St (01852). 978/970-2282. www.cobblestonesoflowell.com.* Eclectic menu. Specialties: chicken marsala, porterhouse steak, game specials. Hrs: 11:30 am-midnight. Closed Sun; Labor Day, Thanksgiving, Dec 25. Res accepted. Bar. Lunch $5.95-$7.95, dinner $10.95-$17.95. In restored 1859 building. Cr cds: A, DS, MC, V.

★★★ **LA BONICHE.** *143 Merrimack St (01852). 978/458-9473.* French menu. Specializes in homemade soups and pâtes, duck. Menu changes seasonally. Hrs: 11:30 am-2:30 pm, 5-9 pm; Fri to 9:30 pm; Sat 5-9:30 pm. Closed Sun, Mon; major hols. Res accepted. Bar. Lunch $6-$12, dinner $14-$21. Child's menu. Musicians Sat. French Provincial decor with natural woodwork. Cr cds: A, MC, V.

★★★★ **SILKS.** *160 Pawtucket Blvd, Tyngsboro (01879). 978/649-4400. www.stonehedgeinn.com.* An exhaustive wine list sets the tone for the enjoyment of Eric Brujan's cuisine, which reflects a combination of hearty New England ingredients prepared with classic French technique. Every dish is sure to please, and the staff is solicitous but not fawning. The restaurant's name comes from one of the owner's bent for thoroughbred horseracing. His Stonehedge Farm jockey's silks hang over the bar. Hrs: 7 am-10 pm, Sun 7 am-9:30 pm. Closed Mon. Res accepted. Wine list. Lunch $10-$14; dinner $22-$34. Brunch $28.50. Entertainment: pianist on Sat night. Cr cds: A, D, DS, ER, JCB, MC, V.

Lynn

See also Boston, Salem

Settled 1629 **Pop** 89,050 **Elev** 30 ft **Area code** 781
Information Chamber of Commerce, 100 Oxford St, Suite 416, 01901; 781/592-2900
Web www.lynnareachamber.com

Shoe manufacturing began as a home craft in Lynn as early as 1635. Today Lynn's industry is widely diversified. Founded here in 1883, General Electric is the biggest single enterprise. Lynn also has more than three miles of sandy beaches.

What to See and Do

Grand Army of the Republic Museum. Features Revolutionary War, Civil War, Spanish-American War, and WWI weapons, artifacts, and exhibits. (Mon-Fri by appt; closed hols) 58 Andrew St. Phone 781/477-7085. **Donation**

Lynn Heritage State Park. Five-acre waterfront park; marina. (Daily; closed Jan 1, Dec 25) Visitor center (590 Washington St) with museum-quality exhibits from past to present, from hand-crafted shoes to high-tech items; inquire for hrs. Lynnway. Phone 781/598-1974. **FREE**

Lynn Woods Reservation. Wooded area consisting of 2,200 acres. Features walking trails, 18-hole golf course, historic dungeon rock (pirates cave), stone tower; picnic areas, playgrounds. (Daily) Phone 781/477-7123.

Mary Baker Eddy Historical Home. Restored house where the founder of Christian Science lived 1875-1882. Call for tour days and times. 12 Broad St. Phone 781/593-5634. **FREE**

B&B/Small Inn

★ ★ ★ **DIAMOND DISTRICT BREAKFAST INN.** *142 Ocean St (01902). 781/599-4470; fax 781/599-5122; toll-free 800/666-3076. www.diamonddistrictinn.com.* 11 rms, 1 with shower only, 3 story. June-Oct: S, D $145-$260; each addl $20; under 3 free; lower rates rest of yr. Crib free. Pet accepted, some restrictions; $10. TV. Complimentary full bkfst. Restaurant nearby. Ck-out 11 am. Business servs avail. In-rm modem link. Gift shop. Health club privileges. Microwaves avail. Georgian residence built in 1911. Totally nonsmoking. Cr cds: A, C, D, DS, MC, V.

🔄 🐾 🔥 ⛶

Lynnfield

Settled 1639 **Pop** 11,542 **Elev** 98 ft **Area code** 781 **Zip** 01940

Hotel

★ ★ ★ **SHERATON COLONIAL HOTEL AND GOLF CLUB.** *1 Audubon Rd, Wakefield (01880). 781/245-9300; fax 781/245-0842. www.sheraton.com.* 280 rms, 11 story. S $89-$169; D $89-$189; each addl $15; suites $275-$495; wkend rates. Crib free. TV; cable (premium), VCR avail. Indoor pool; whirlpool. Coffee in rms. Restaurant 6:30 am-10:30 pm. Ck-out 11 am. Convention facilities. In-rm modem link. Barber shop. Lighted tennis. 18-hole golf, pro, putting green, driving range. Exercise rm; sauna, steam rm. Some refrigerators; microwaves avail. Cr cds: A, MC, V.

D 🥢 🚲 ⛱ ⌗ 🐾 🔥 SC

Restaurant

★ ★ **KERNWOOD.** *55 Salem St (01940). 781/245-4011.* New England menu. Specializes in seafood, prime beef. Hrs: 11 am-10 pm; Sun to 9 pm; early-bird dinner Mon-Fri 4:30-6:30 pm, Sat 4-6 pm. Closed July 4, Dec 25. Bar. Wine list. Lunch $4.95-$10.95, dinner $12-$19. Child's menu. Pianist exc Sun. Colonial atmosphere; open-hearth cooking. Family-owned. Cr cds: A, C, D, DS, ER, MC, V.

Marblehead

See also Boston, Salem

Settled 1629 **Pop** 20,377 **Elev** 65 ft **Area code** 781 **Zip** 01945
Information Chamber of Commerce, 62 Pleasant St, PO Box 76; 781/631-2868
Web www.marbleheadchamber.org

A unique blend of old and new, Marblehead is situated on a peninsula 17 miles north of Boston. Named Marble Harbor for a short time, the town was settled in 1629 by hardy fishermen from England's West counties. It now boasts a beautiful harbor and a number of busy boatyards. Pleasure craft anchor in this picturesque port each summer, and a record number of modern racing yachts participate in the annual Race Week. Beaches, boating, fishing, art exhibits, antique and curio shops—all combine to offer a choice of quiet relaxation or active recreation.

What to See and Do

Abbot Hall. Displays the original "Spirit of '76" painting and deed to town (1684) from the Nanepashemet. Museum, Marine Room. Gift shop. (Last wkend May-last wkend Oct, daily; rest of yr, Mon-Fri; closed winter hols) Abbot Hall, Washington Sq. Phone 781/631-0000. **Donation**

Jeremiah Lee Mansion. (1768) Marblehead Historical Society. Where Generals Glover, Lafayette, and Washington were entertained. Opulent Georgian architecture and interiors; Marblehead history; antiques of the period, rare original hand-painted wallpaper. (June-mid-Oct, daily; closed hols) 161 Washington St. Phone 781/631-1069. ¢¢

King Hooper Mansion. (1728) Restored house with garden. Art exhibits. (Tues-Sat afternoons; closed Jan 1, Dec 25) 8 Hooper St. Phone 781/631-2608. **FREE**

Special Event

Sailing races. Boston Yacht Club. Phone 781/631-3100. May-Oct, Wed eve and wkends. Race week third wk July.

B&Bs/Small Inns

★ ★ ★ **HARBOR LIGHT INN.** *58 Washington St (01945). 781/631-2186; fax 781/631-2216. www.harborlightinn.com.* 21 rms. S, D $115-$125; each addl $15; suites $160-$245. TV; cable (premium), VCR avail (free movies). Heated pool. Complimentary continental bkfst. Restaurant nearby. Ck-out 11 am, ck-in 1 pm. Business servs avail. In-rm modem link. Concierge serv. Airport transportation. Health club privileges. Antiques. Built 1712. Totally nonsmoking. Cr cds: A, MC, V.

⛱ 🐾

★★ **MARBLEHEAD INN.** *264 Pleasant St (01945). 781/639-9999; fax 781/639-9996; toll-free 800/399-5843. www.marbleheadinn.com.* 10 units, 3 story. S, D $119-$169; each addl $5. TV; cable (premium), VCR. Complimentary continental bkfst. Restaurants nearby. Ck-out 11 am, ck-in 3 pm. Coin lndry. Picnic tables. Refrigerators, microwaves. Antiques. Victorian inn (1872) near beach. Totally non-smoking. Cr cds: A, MC, V.

★★ **SEAGULL INN.** *106 Harbor Ave (01945). 781/631-1893; fax 781/631-3535. www.seagullinn.com.* 6 rms, 1 with shower only, 2 story, 4 suites, 2 kit. units. May-Oct: suites, kit. units $150; wkends (2-day min); lower rates rest of yr. Crib avail. Pet accepted. TV; cable, VCR (movies). Complimentary continental bkfst, coffee in rms. Restaurant nearby. Ck-out 11 am, ck-in 2 pm. Business servs avail. Lawn games. Opp ocean. Built in 1880; turn-of-the-century atmosphere. Totally nonsmoking. Cr cds: MC, V.

★★ **SPRAY CLIFF ON THE OCEAN.** *25 Spray Ave (01945). 781/631-6789; fax 781/639-4563; toll-free 800/626-1530. www.spraycliff.com.* 7 rms, 4 with shower only, 3 story. No elvtr, rm phones. May-Oct: S, D $180-$200; wkends (2-day min); lower rates rest of yr. Complimentary continental bkfst. Restaurant nearby. Ck-out 11 am, ck-in 3 pm. Some fireplaces. On ocean. Built in 1910. Cr cds: A, MC, V.

Restaurants

★ **KING'S ROOK.** *12 State St (01945). 781/631-9838.* Specializes in gourmet pizzas, sandwiches, salads. Hrs: noon-2:30 pm, 5:30-11:30 pm; Sat, Sun noon-11:30 pm. Closed Thanksgiving, Dec 25, Dec 31. Lunch, dinner $4.50-$7.50. Child's menu. Street parking. Family-owned since 1966. Cr cds: DS, MC, V.

★★ **MARBLEHEAD LANDING.** *81 Front St (01945). 781/631-1878. www.thelandingrestaurant.com.* Specializes in seafood. Hrs: 11:30 am-4 pm, 5-10 pm; Fri, Sat to 11 pm; Sun brunch 10:30 am-4 pm. Closed Thanksgiving, Dec 25. Bar. A la carte entrees: lunch $2.50-$19.95, dinner $9.95-$21.95. Sun brunch $2.95-$14.95. Child's menu. Entertainment Fri, Sun. Outdoor dining. Windows overlook beach and boating area. Family-owned. Cr cds: A, C, D, DS, ER, MC, V.

★★ **PELLINO'S.** *261 Washington St (01945). 781/631-3344. www.pellinos.com.* Northern Italian menu. Specializes in pasta, seafood, chicken. Hrs: 5-10 pm; Fri, Sat to 10:30 pm. Closed Jan 1, Easter, Dec 25. Res required. Bar. Dinner $10.95-$17.95. Parking. Italian decor. Totally nonsmoking. Cr cds: A, DS, MC, V.

Martha's Vineyard

See also Falmouth (Cape Cod), Hyannis (Cape Cod), Nantucket Island, Woods Hole

Settled 1642 **Pop** 12,690 **Elev** 0-311 ft **Area code** 508
Information Chamber of Commerce, Beach Rd, PO Box 1698, Vineyard Haven 02568; 508/693-0085
Web www.mvy.com

This triangular island below the arm of Cape Cod combines moors, dunes, multicolored cliffs, flower-filled ravines, farmland, and forest. It is less than 20 miles from west to east and 10 miles from north to south.

There was once a whaling fleet at the island, but Martha's Vineyard now devotes itself almost entirely to being a vacation playground, with summer houses that range from small cottages to elaborate mansions. The colonial atmosphere still survives in Vineyard Haven, the chief port; Oak Bluffs; Edgartown; West Tisbury; Gay Head; and Chilmark.

Gay Head is one of the few Massachusetts towns in which many inhabitants are of Native American descent.

What to See and Do
Car/Passenger Boat Trips.

Hyannis-Martha's Vineyard Day Round Trip. Passenger service from Hyannis (May-Oct). Phone 508/778-2600.

Steamship Authority. New Bedford-Martha's Vineyard Ferry. Daily passenger service (mid-May-mid-Sept) to New Bedford. Same-day round-trips avail. Also bus tours of the island. Schedule may vary; contact Steamship Authority, PO Box 4095, New Bedford, 02741. Phone 508/997-1688. ¢¢¢¢

Steamship Authority. Daily round-trips, Falmouth-Martha's Vineyard. (Daily) Phone 508/548-4800.

Woods Hole, Martha's Vineyard & Nantucket Steamship Authority. Conducts round-trip service to Martha's Vineyard (all yr, weather permitting). Phone 508/477-8600.

Felix Neck Sanctuary. Approx 350 acres with woods, far-reaching salt marshes, pond with large variety of waterfowl, reptile pond, six mi of trails; barn; exhibit centers; library. (Daily) 3 mi out of Edgartown on the Vineyard Haven-Edgartown Rd. Phone 508/627-4850. ¢

Historic Areas.

Edgartown. The island's first colonial settlement and county seat since 1642 is the location of stately white Greek Revival houses built by whaling captains. These have been carefully preserved, and North Water St has a row of captains' houses unequaled anywhere.

Oak Bluffs. In 1835, this Methodist community served as the site of annual summer camp meetings for church groups. As thousands attended these meetings, the communal tents gave way to family tents, which in turn became wooden cottages designed to look like tents. Today, visitors to the community may see these "Gingerbread Cottages of the Campground."

Recreation. Swimming. Many sheltered beaches, among them public beaches at Menemsha, Oak Bluffs, Edgartown, and Vineyard Haven. Surf swimming on south shore. **Tennis.** Public courts in Edgartown, Oak Bluffs, West Tisbury, and Vineyard Haven. **Boat rentals** at Vineyard Haven, Oak Bluffs, and Gay Head. **Fishing.** Good for striped bass, bonito, bluefish, weakfish. **Golf** at Farm Neck Club. Phone 508/693-3057.

❑ **Vincent House.** Oldest known house on the island, built in 1672. Carefully restored to allow visitors to see how buildings were constructed 300 yrs ago. Original brickwork, hardware, and woodwork. (June-early Oct, daily; rest of yr, by appt) Main St in Edgartown. Phone 508/627-4440. **FREE** Also on Main St is

    Old Whaling Church. Built in 1843, this is a fine example of Greek Revival architecture. Now a performing arts center with seating for 500. Phone 508/627-4442.

Special Event

Striped Bass & Bluefish Derby. Two thousand entrants compete for cash and prizes. Includes boat, shore, and flyrod divisions. Mid-Sept-mid-Oct. Phone 508/693-0085.

Hotels

★★★ **HARBOR VIEW HOTEL OF MARTHA'S VINEYARD.** *131 N Water St, Edgartown (02539). 508/627-7000; fax 508/627-8417; toll-free 800/225-6005. www.harbor-view.com.* 124 rms, 1-4 story, 14 kits. June-mid-Sept: D $100-$300; each addl $20; suites, kit. units $375-$625; under 12 free; lower rates rest of yr. TV; cable (premium). Heated pool; poolside serv. Restaurant (see COACH HOUSE). Bar 11 am-midnight. Ck-out 11 am. Meeting rms. Business servs avail. Concierge. Tennis. Refrigerators. Private patios, balconies. Beach opp. Overlooks harbor; view of lighthouse. In operation since 1891. Fieldstone fireplace in lobby. Extensive grounds and gardens. Cr cds: A, C, D, MC, V.

Ⓓ ⊠ ⊠ ⊠ ⊠

★★★ **KELLEY HOUSE.** *23 Kelly St, Edgartown (02539). 508/627-7900; fax 508/627-8142; res 800/225-6005. www.kelleyhouse.com.* 53 rms, 1-3 story. No elvtr. June-Sept: S, D $150-$275; each addl $20; suites, kit. units $285-$625; under 12 free; lower rates rest of yr. TV; cable (premium). Pool. Complimentary continental bkfst; afternoon refreshments. Ck-out 11 am. Meeting rms. Business servs avail. Bellhops. Concierge. Tennis privileges. Refrigerators. In operation since 1742. Rose gardens. Cr cds: A, MC, V.

⊠ ⊠ ⊠ ⊠

Resort

★★ **ISLAND INN.** *Beach Rd, Oak Bluffs (02557). 508/693-2002; fax 508/693-7911; toll-free 800/462-0269. www.islandinn.com.* 51 kit. units, 1-2 story. Mid-June-mid-Sept: $75-$165; lower rates rest of yr. Pet accepted. TV; cable. Pool. Restaurant 6-11 pm. Bar 4 pm-midnight. Ck-out 11 am. Coin lndry. Meeting rm. Business servs avail. In-rm modem link. Gift shop. Tennis, pro (in season). 18-hole golf adj, pro. Bicycle path adj. Near beach. Cr cds: A, C, D, DS, MC, V.

⊠ ⊠ ⊠ ⊠ ⊠ ⊠

B&Bs/Small Inns

★★ **THE ARBOR INN.** *222 Upper Main St., Edgartown (02539). 508/627-8137; toll-free 888/748-4383. www.mvy.com/arborinn.* 10 air-cooled rms, 8 with bath, 2 story. No rm phones. Mid-June-Sept: S $105-$135; D $150-$185; kit. cottage $700-$900/wk; lower rates May-mid-June, Oct. Closed rest of yr. Children over 12 yrs only. Complimentary continental bkfst; afternoon refreshments. Restaurant nearby. Ck-out 11 am, ck-in 2 pm. Concierge. Antique shop. Built 1880; antiques. Library/sitting rm. Cr cds: MC, V.

⊠

★★ **ASHLEY INN.** *129 Main St, Edgartown (02539). 508/627-9655; fax 508/627-6629; toll-free 800/477-9655.* 10 rms, 3 story, 2 suites. Late June-late Sept: S, D $135-$265; suites $265; each addl $15; honeymoon packages; lower rates rest of yr. Children over 12 yrs only. TV; cable. Complimentary continental bkfst. Restaurant adj. Ck-out 11 am, ck-in 2 pm. Some refrigerators, fireplaces. Picnic tables. 1860 sea captain's house; antiques. Totally non-smoking. Cr cds: A, DS, MC, V.

⊠ ⊠

★ **THE BEACH HOUSE.** *Pennacook and Seaview Aves, Oak Bluffs (02557). 508/693-3955. www.beachhousemv.com.* 9 rms, 3 story. No rm phones. July-Aug: S, D $135-$155; wkends, hols (3-day min); lower rates rest of yr. Children over 10 yrs only. TV. Complimentary continental bkfst. Ck-out 11 am, ck-in 1 pm. Luggage handling. Built in 1899; front porch. Opp ocean. Cr cds: A, MC, V.

⊠

★★★ **BEACH PLUM INN.** *50 Beach Plum Ln, Menemsha (81432). 508/645-9454; fax 508/645-2801; toll-free 877/645-7398. www.beachpluminn.com.* 11 rms, 2 story. Mid-June-mid-Sept: D $250-$400; each addl $25; under 12 free; higher rates hols; lower rates rest of yr. Crib avail. TV; cable (premium), VCR (movies). Playground. Supervised children's activities; ages 3-12. Complimentary full bkfst. Restaurant. Ck-out 11 am, ck-in 2 pm. Business servs avail. In-rm modem link. Luggage handling. Concierge serv. Tennis. Lawn games. Balconies. Picnic tables. Built 1890 from salvage of shipwreck. Most rms with ocean view. Gardens. Cr cds: A, D, DS, MC, V.

⊠ ⊠

★★ **CAPATAIN DEXTER HOUSE.** *35 Pease's Point Way, Edgartown (02539). 508/627-7289; fax 508/627-3328. www.mvy.com/cattdexter.* 11 rms, 10 A/C, 1 air-cooled, 2 story. No rm phones. June-Sept: S, D $135-$195; each addl $20; lower rates mid-Apr-May, Oct. Closed rest of yr. Complimentary continental bkfst; afternoon refreshments. Restaurant nearby. Ck-out 11 am, ck-in 2 pm. Traditional white clapboard house built in 1840 by a prominent merchant family; antiques; flower gardens. Totally non-smoking. Cr cds: A, MC, V.

⊠ ⊠

★★ **THE CAPTAIN DEXTER HOUSE OF VINEYARD HAVEN.** *92 Main St, Vineyard Haven (02568). 508/693-6564; fax 508/693-8448. www.captaindexter.com.* 8 rms, 3 story. 6 A/C. No rm phones. Memorial Day-Oct 1: D $115-$175; each addl $20; suite $175; lower rates rest of yr. Children over 12 yrs only. Complimentary continental bkfst; afternoon refreshments. Ck-out 11 am, ck-in 2 pm. Sitting garden. Some fireplaces. Old sea captain's home (1843); antiques. Totally nonsmoking. Cr cds: A, MC, V.
⬛ 🔥 SC

★★★★ **THE CHARLOTTE INN.** *27 S Summer St, Edgartown (02539). 508/627-4751; fax 508/627-6452.* A romantic escape whatever the season, this Victorian inn on Martha's Vineyard has true New England style with wide, wicker-filled porches, antiques, and lovely manicured grounds. The property has expanded from the original 1860 Captain's House and is tucked away off of the Main Street shopping area. 25 rms located in five historic buildings. S $295-$850; D $225-$550; 2 suites $750-$850; lower rates off-season. Children over 14 only. Parking avail. TV; cable (premium); VCR avail. Concierge. Restaurant 6:30-9:30 pm; closed Mon, Tues off season. Afternoon tea. Cr cds: A, MC, V.
⬛ 🔥

★★ **COLONIAL INN OF MARTHA'S VINEYARD.** *38 N Water St, Edgartown (02539). 508/627-4711; fax 508/627-5904; toll-free 800/627-4701. www.colonialinnmvy.com.* 43 rms, 1-4 story. No elvtr. Memorial Day-mid-Sept: S, D $100-$375; each addl $15; under 16 free; wkly, hol rates; lower rates late Sept-Dec, mid-Apr-Memorial Day. Closed rest of yr. Crib free. TV; cable (premium), VCR avail (free movies). Complimentary continental bkfst. Restaurant 5:30 am-12:30 pm. Ck-out 11 am. Meeting rms. Business servs avail. In-rm modem link. Bellhops. Sundries. Shopping arcade. Barber. Some refrigerators. Balconies. Cr cds: A, MC, V.
D ⬛ 🔥

★★ **DAGGETT HOUSE.** *59 N Water St, Edgartown (02539). 508/627-4600; fax 508/627-4611. www.mvweb.com/daggett.* 31 rms in 4 bldgs, 2 story, 10 kits. May-Oct: S, D $150-$225; each addl $20; lower rates rest of yr. Crib free. TV; cable. Restaurant 8-11 am, 5:30-9 pm; Sun brunch to 1 pm. Ck-out 11 am, ck-in 3 pm. Private pier. Gardens. Open hearth, antiques in dining rm, part of historic (1660) tavern. New England atmosphere. Totally nonsmoking. Cr cds: A, DS, MC, V.
⬛ 🔥

★★★ **DOCKSIDE INN.** *Circuit Ave Ext, Oak Bluffs (02557). 508/693-2966; fax 508/696-7293; toll-free 800/245-5979. www.vineyard.net/inns.* 22 rms, 3 story, 5 kit. suites. Mid-June-mid-Sept: S, D $80-$200; kit. suites $240-$350; family rates; 3-day min; lower rates mid-Sept-Nov, Apr-mid-June. Closed rest of yr. Crib free. TV; cable. Complimentary continental bkfst. Restaurant nearby. Ck-out 11 am, ck-in 2-7 pm. Luggage handling. Concierge serv. Business servs avail. In-rm modem link. Game rm. Refrigerators. Balconies. Colorful gingerbread-style inn opp docks. Totally nonsmoking. Cr cds: A, DS, MC, V.
D ⬛ 🔥

★★ **THE EDGARTOWN INN.** *56 N Water St, Edgartown (02539). 508/627-4794; fax 508/627-9420. www.edgartown inn.com.* 12 rms in inn, 8 rms in 2 annexes, 1-3 story. Late May-late Sept: annex D $90-$185; inn S $125-$185; D $155-$210; each addl $20; lower rates Oct, Apr-late-May. Closed rest of yr. TV in some rms, sitting rm. Dining rm 8-11 am. Ck-out 11 am, ck-in 2 pm. Historic (1798) sea captain's home. Inn since 1820; Colonial furnishings and antiques in rms. Cr cds: A, MC, V.
⬛ 🔥

★★ **GREENWOOD HOUSE.** *40 Greenwood Ave, Vineyard Haven (02568). 508/693-6150; fax 508/696-8113; toll-free 800/525-9466. www.greenwoodhouse.com.* 5 rms, 3 story. Mid-May-mid-Sept: S, D $169-$249; lower rates rest of yr. TV; cable. Complimentary full bkfst. Complimentary coffee in rms. Restaurant nearby. Ck-out 10 am, ck-in 2 pm. Business servs avail. In-rm modem link. Luggage handling. Concierge serv. Lawn games. Refrigerators. Built 1906. Totally nonsmoking. Cr cds: A, C, D, MC, V.
⬛ 🔥

★★★ **THE HANOVER HOUSE.** *28 Edgartown Rd, Vineyard Haven (02568). 508/693-1066; fax 508/696-6099; toll-free 800/339-1066. www.hanoverhouseinn.com.* 15 rms, 4 with shower only, 2 story, 3 suites, 2 kit. units. No rm phones. Early June-mid-Sept: S $130-$185; D $175-$200; suites, kit. units $185-$255; family, wkly rates; wknds (2-day min); lower rates rest of yr. TV; cable. Complimentary continental bkfst. Restaurant nearby. Ck-out 10 am, ck-in 2 pm. Business servs avail. Balconies. Built 1920; gardens, enclosed sitting porch. Totally nonsmoking. Cr cds: A, DS, MC, V.
🔥 ⬛

★★★ **HOB KNOB INN.** *128 Main St, Edgartown (02539). 508/627-9510; fax 508/627-4560; toll-free 800/696-2723. www.hobknob.com.* 16 rms, 3 story. Memorial Day-mid-Oct: S, D $185-$375; lower rates rest of yr. TV; cable. Complimentary full bkfst. Restaurant nearby. Ck-out 11 am, ck-in 2 pm. Meeting rm. Business servs avail. In-rm modem link. Concierge serv. Exercise equipt; sauna. Massage. Bicycle rental. Sun porch; garden. Inn built 1860; many antiques. Totally nonsmoking. Cr cds: A, MC, V.
D 🏋 ⬛ 🔥

★★ **LAMBERT'S COVE COUNTRY INN.** *Lamberts Cove Rd, Vineyard Haven (02568). 508/693-2298; fax 508/693-7890. www.lambertscoveinn.com.* 15 rms, 2 story. No rm phones. Late May-early Oct: D $145-$195; lower rates rest of yr. TV in sitting rm. Complimentary full bkfst. Dining rm (public by res) 6-9 pm. Ck-out 11 am, ck-in 2 pm. Tennis. Balconies. Picnic tables. Secluded farmhouse (1790); many antiques. Gardens, apple orchard. Cr cds: A, MC, V.
🎿 ⬛

★★★ **MARTHA'S PLACE B&B.** *114 Main St, Vineyard Haven (02568). 508/693-0253. www.marthasplace.com.* 7 rms, 3 with shower only, 2 story. No rm phones. June-Sept: S $175-$295; D $175-$450; package plans; wkends (2-day min); special events (3-day min); higher rates special events; lower rates rest of yr. TV in some rms.

Complimentary continental bkfst. Restaurant nearby. Ck-out 10 am, ck-in after noon. Business servs avail. Luggage handling. Valet serv. Some in-rm whirlpools. Balconies. Picnic tables, grills. Built in 1840; restored Greek Revival mansion. Totally nonsmoking. Cr cds: DS, MC, V.

★★★ **THE OAK HOUSE.** *Seaview & Pequot Aves, Oak Bluffs (02557). 508/693-4187; fax 508/696-7385; res 800/245-5979. www.vineyard.net/inns.* 10 rms, 9 with shower only, 3 story, 2 suites. No elvtr. Mid-June-mid-Sept: S, D $150-$190; suites $250-$260; lower rates rest of yr. Closed Mid-Oct-mid-May. Children over 10 yrs only. TV; cable, VCR avail. Complimentary continental bkfst; afternoon refreshments. Ck-out 11 am, ck-in 4 pm. Street parking. Some balconies. Picnic tables, grills. Opp beach. 1872 summer home for MA governor. Totally nonsmoking. Cr cds: A, DS, MC, V.

★★ **OUTERMOST INN.** *171 Lighthouse Rd, Chilmark (02535). 508/645-3511; fax 508/645-3514. www.outermost inn.com.* 7 rms, 2 story. No A/C. Mid-June-mid-Sept: S, D $240-$320; wkends (2-day min); lower rates mid-Apr-mid-June, mid-Sept-Oct. Children over 12 yrs only. TV. Complimentary full bkfst; afternoon refreshments. Dining rm 6-8 pm. Ck-out 11 am, ck-in 2 pm. Luggage handling. Concierge serv. Business servs avail. Balconies. Picnic tables. Picture windows provide excellent views of Vineyard Sound and Elizabeth Islands. Totally nonsmoking. Cr cds: A, DS, MC, V.

★★ **PEQUOT HOTEL.** *19 Pequot Ave, Oak Bluffs (02557). 508/693-5087; fax 508/696-9413; toll-free 800/947-8704. www.pequothotel.com.* 29 rms, 25 with shower only, 3 story. No elvtr. No rm phones. July-Aug: S, D $105-$195; kit. units $245-$385; wkday rates; higher rates July 4; lower rates rest of yr. Closed Nov-Apr. Crib $25. TV in some rms. Complimentary continental bkfst. Restaurant nearby. Ck-out 11 am, ck-in 3 pm. Street parking. Picnic tables. Built in 1920s. Cr cds: A, DS, MC, V.

★★ **POINT WAY INN.** *104 Main St, Edgartown (02539). 508/627-8633; fax 508/627-3338; toll-free 888/711-6633. www.pointway.com.* 14 rms, 1-3 story. Late May-Oct: S, D $175-$325; each addl $25; suites $325; lower rates rest of yr. Pet accepted, some restrictions; $25. TV. Complimentary continental bkfst; afternoon refreshments. Ck-out 11 am, ck-in 2 pm. Valet serv. Some balconies. Gardens. Totally nonsmoking. Cr cds: A, MC, V.

★★ **SHIRETOWN INN.** *44 N Water St, Edgartown (02539). 508/627-3353; fax 508/627-8478; res 800/541-0090. www.shiretowninn.com.* 35 rms in 4 bldgs, 1-3 story. Some A/C. Mid-June-mid-Sept: S, D $79-$149; each addl $20; suites $179-$289; cottage $1,200-$1,800/wk; under 2 free; lower rates May-late-June, mid-Sept-mid-Oct. Closed rest of yr. TV; cable. Complimentary continental bkfst. Dining rm 11 am-2 pm, 5-10 pm. Bar 11-12:30 am. Ck-out 11 am, ck-in 2 pm. Business servs avail. Balconies. Sun decks. 18th-century whaling house. Cr cds: A, DS, MC, V.

★★★ **THORNCROFT INN.** *460 Main St (02568). 508/693-3333; fax 508/693-5419; toll-free 800/332-1236. www.thorncroft.com.* 14 rms in 2 bldgs, 2 story. Mid-June-Labor Day: D $275-$325; lower rates rest of yr. TV; cable. Complimentary full bkfst; afternoon refreshments. Ck-out 11 am, ck-in 3-9 pm. Business servs avail. In-rm modem link. Luggage handling. Many fireplaces; some in-rm whirlpools. Some balconies. 1918 bungalow; antiques. Totally nonsmoking. Cr cds: A, C, D, DS, ER, MC, V.

Restaurants

★★★ **COACH HOUSE.** *131 N Water St, Edgartown (02539). 508/627-7000. www.harbor-view.com.* New England cuisine. Specialties: striped bass with artichokes, sea scallops, duck with sweet potatoes. Hrs: 7-11 am, noon-2 pm, 6-10 pm; Sun brunch 8 am-1:30 pm. Res accepted. Bar 11 am-midnight. Wine cellar. A la carte entrees: bkfst $5.95-$12, lunch $7.95-$15, dinner $24-$34. Sun brunch $16.95. Child's menu. View of harbor. Totally nonsmoking in restaurant. Cigar bar. Cr cds: A, D, MC, V.

★★ **HOME PORT.** *512 North Rd, Menemsha (02552). 508/645-2679.* Specializes in seafood, lobster. Outdoor clam bar. Hrs: 5-10 pm. Closed mid-Oct-mid Apr. Res required. No A/C. Setups. Complete meals: dinner $16-$32. Child's menu. Parking. On harbor; scenic view; nautical atmosphere. Cr cds: MC, V.

★★ **LE GRENIER FRENCH RESTAURANT.** *82 Main St, Vineyard Haven (02568). 508/693-4906.* French provincial menu. Specialties: lobster normande, steak au poivre, shrimp pernod. Hrs: 5:30-10 pm. Res accepted. A la carte entrees: dinner $18.95-$29.95. Street parking. Elegant bistro. Family-owned since 1979. Cr cds: A, D, DS, MC, V.

★ **LOUIS' TISBURY CAFE.** *350 State Rd, Vineyard Haven (02568). 508/693-3255.* Italian, seafood menu. Specialties: eggplant parmesan, rack of lamb, pasta tomato cream shrimp. Hrs: 5:30-9 pm; Fri, Sat to 9:30 pm. Closed most major hols. Dinner $12.75-$24.95. Child's menu. Parking. Italian cafe style. Totally nonsmoking. Cr cds: A, MC, V.

★★ **THE NAVIGATOR.** *2 Lower Main St, Edgartown (02539). 508/627-4320.* Specializes in seafood. Hrs: 11-1 am. Closed mid-Oct-mid-May. Bar. A la carte entrees: lunch $5.95-$11.95. Dinner $19.95-$29.95. Child's menu. Outdoor dining. Overlooks harbor. Family-owned. Cr cds: A, C, D, DS, MC, V.

★★ **SQUARE RIGGER.** *225 State Rd, Edgartown (02539). 508/627-9968.* Specializes in seafood, grilled entrees, lobster. Hrs: 5:30-10 pm. Res accepted. Bar. A la carte entrees: dinner $14-$26. Child's menu. Parking. Open hearth kitchen in dining rm. Totally nonsmoking. Cr cds: A, MC, V.

★★ **WHARF & WHARF PUB.** *Lower Main St, Edgartown (02539).* 508/627-9966. Specializes in fresh seafood, seafood Wellington pie, desserts. Hrs: 11:30 am-midnight. Closed Thanksgiving, Dec 24, 25. Res accepted. Bar. Lunch $5.95-$9.95, dinner $8.95-$17.95. Child's menu. Entertainment Wed-Sun. Cr cds: A, DS, MC, V.

D ⌐

Nantucket Island

See also Hyannis (Cape Cod), Martha's Vineyard

Settled 1659 **Pop** 6,012 **Elev** 0-108 ft **Area code** 508 **Zip** 02554

Information Chamber of Commerce, 48 Main St; 508/228-1700. General information may also be obtained at the Information Bureau, 25 Federal St; 508/228-1700

Web www.nantucketchamber.org

This is not just an island; it is an experience. Nantucket Island is at once a popular resort and a living museum. Siasconset (SCON-set) and Nantucket Town remain quiet and charming despite heavy tourism. Nantucket, with 49 square miles of lovely beaches and green moors inland, is south of Cape Cod, 30 miles at sea. The island was the world's greatest whaling port in the late 17th century until New Bedford became dominant in the early 1800s. Whaling prosperity built the towns; tourism maintains them.

There is regular car ferry and passenger service from Hyannis. If you plan to take your car, make advance reservation by mail with the Woods Hole, Martha's Vineyard & Nantucket Steamship Authority, PO Box 284, Woods Hole 02543; phone 508/477-8600. A great variety of beaches, among them the Jetties, north of Nantucket Town (harbor), and Surfside, on the south shore of the island (surf), offer swimming. Tennis, golf, fishing, sailing, and cycling can be arranged.

What to See and Do

Boat Trips. Hyannis-Nantucket Day Round Trip. Summer passenger service from Hyannis. Phone 508/778-2600. ¢¢¢¢

✪ **Main Street.** Paved with cobblestones, lined with elegant houses built by the whaling merchants, and shaded by great elms, this is one of New England's most beautiful streets. The Nantucket Historical Association maintains the following attractions (June-Oct, daily; spring and fall, limited hrs). Phone 508/228-1894.

1800 House. Home of sheriff, early 19th century. Period home and furnishings; large, round cellar; kitchen garden. Mill St, off Pleasant St. Phone 508/228-1894.

Folger-Franklin Seat & Memorial Boulder. Birthplace site of Abiah Folger, mother of Benjamin Franklin. Madaket Rd, 1 mi from W end of Main St.

Hadwen House. (1845) Greek Revival mansion; furnishings of whaling period; gardens. Main and Pleasant Sts. ¢¢

Jethro Coffin House. (1686) Nantucket's oldest house. N on North Water to West Chester, left to Sunset Hill. Phone 508/228-1894. ¢¢

Museum of Nantucket History (Macy Warehouse). Exhibits related to Nantucket history; diorama; craft demonstrations. Straight Wharf. Phone 508/228-1894. ¢¢

Old Fire Hose Cart House. (1886) Old-time firefighting equipment. Gardner St off Main St. **FREE**

Old Gaol. (1805) Unusual two-story construction; used until 1933. Vestal St. Phone 508/228-1894. **FREE**

Old Windmill. (1746) Built of wood from wrecked vessels, with original machinery and grinding stones. Corn ground daily during summer. On Mill Hill, off Prospect St. ¢

Research Center. Ships' logs, diaries, charts, and Nantucket photographs; library. (Mon-Fri) Broad St, next to Whaling Museum. Phone 508/228-1655.

Whaling Museum. Outstanding collection of relics from whaling days; whale skeleton, tryworks, scrimshaw, candle press. Broad St, near Steamboat Wharf. Phone 508/228-1736. ¢¢

Nantucket Maria Mitchell Association. Birthplace of first American woman astronomer; memorial observatory (1908). Scientific library has Nantucket historical documents, science journals and Mitchell family memorabilia. Natural science museum with local wildlife. Aquarium at 28 Washington St. (Mid-June-Aug, Tues-Sat; library also open rest of yr, Wed-Sat; closed July 4, Labor Day) 1 Vestal St. Phone 508/228-9198. ¢¢

Sightseeing Tours.

Barrett's Tours. Offers 1½-hr bus and van tours (Apr-Nov). Phone 508/228-0174.

Gail's Tours. Narrated van tours (approx 1¾ hrs) of area. Three tours daily. Res recommended. Depart from Information Center at Federal and Broad Sts. Phone 508/257-6557.

Special Events

Daffodil Festival. Parade of antique cars, prize for best tailgate picnic. (Last wkend in Apr.) Phone 508/228-1700.

Harborfest. Early June. Phone 508/228-1700.

Sand Castle Contest. Third Sat Aug. Phone 508/228-1700.

Christmas Stroll. First wkend Dec. Phone 508/228-1700.

Motels/Motor Lodges

★★ **HARBOR HOUSE HOTEL.** *S Beach St, Nantucket (02554).* 508/228-1500; fax 508/228-7639; toll-free 866/325-9300. www.nantucketislandresorts.com. 104 rms, 2-3 story. No elvtr. Late June-mid-Sept: D $325-$425; each addl $20; package plans; lower rates rest of yr. TV; cable (premium). Heated pool; poolside serv. Restaurant 7:30-10 am, 11:30 am-10 pm. Rm serv in season. Bar noon-1 am; entertainment. Ck-out 11 am. Meeting rms. Business servs avail. In-rm modem link. Bellhops. Concierge. Private patios, balconies. Authentic reproductions of Colonial-period furnishings; some antiques. Extensive grounds, elaborate landscaping. Most rms with garden view. Public beach opp. Cr cds: A, C, D, DS, MC, V.

D ⌐ ⌐ ⌐

★★ **WHARF COTTAGES.** *New Whale St, Nantucket (02554). 508/228-4620; fax 508/325-1173; toll-free 866/838-9253. www.wharfcottages.com.* 33 kit. cottages, 1-2 story. No A/C. Late May-Oct: kit. cottages $295-$575. Closed rest of yr. Crib free. TV; cable (premium). Restaurant nearby. Ck-out 11 am. Coin lndry. Bellhops. Tennis privileges. Balconies. Picnic tables, grills. Dockage. Cr cds: A, MC, V.
⊠ 🐾 ⛵

Hotel

★★★ **WHITE ELEPHANT RESORT.** *50 Easton St, Nantucket (02554). 508/228-2500; fax 508/325-1195; toll-free 800/475-2637. www.whiteelephantresort.com.* 80 rms, most A/C, 1-3 story (no elvtr); suites in 15 cottages. Mid-June-mid-Sept: D $340-$590; each addl $20; cottages with kit. $425-$700; lower rates late-May-late-June, mid-Sept-mid-Oct. Closed rest of yr. Crib free. TV; cable (premium). Heated pool; whirlpool, poolside serv, lifeguard. Restaurant 7:30-10:30 am, noon-10 pm in season. Bar noon-1 am; entertainment. Ck-out 11 am. Meeting rm. Business servs avail. In-rm modem link. Concierge. Some private patios. Playground. Beach nearby; boat slips for guests only. On harbor; waterfront view from most inn rms. Cr cds: A, C, D, DS, MC, V.
Ⓓ ⊷ 🐾 SC

Resort

★★ **NANTUCKET INN.** *27 Macy's Ln, Nantucket (02554). 508/228-6900; fax 508/228-9861; toll-free 800/321-8484. www.nantucket.net/lodging/nantucketinn.* 100 rms, 1-2 story. June-Sept: S, D $130-$190; each addl $12; under 18 free; lower rates rest of yr. Pet accepted; $25. TV; cable. 2 pools, 1 indoor; whirlpool, lifeguard. Restaurant 7:30-10:30 am, noon-2 pm, 5:30-9 pm. Rm serv. Bars. Ck-out 11 am. Coin lndry. Meeting rms. Business servs avail. Bellhops. Sundries. Free airport transportation. Lighted tennis. Exercise equipt. Refrigerators. Cr cds: A, MC, V.
🏊 🛰 ⊷ 🧍 ✈ 🐾

B&Bs/Small Inns

★★ **CARLISLE HOUSE INN.** *26 N Water St, Nantucket (02554). 508/228-0720; fax 781/639-1004. www.carlislehouse.com.* 14 rms, 5 share bath, 3 story. No rm phones. Mid-June-mid-Sept: S $75; D $95-$185; each addl $15; suites $250-$275; lower rates rest of yr. Children over 10 yrs only. Complimentary continental bkfst. Restaurant nearby. Ck-out 11 am, ck-in 2 pm. Street parking. Some fireplaces. Antiques. Library/sitting rm. Restored whaling captain's house (1765). Totally nonsmoking. Cr cds: A, MC, V.
⊠ 🐾

★ **THE CARRIAGE HOUSE.** *5 Ray's Ct, Nantucket (02554). 508/228-0326. www.carriagehousenantucket.com.* 7 rms, 2 story. No A/C. Apr-Dec: S, D $100-$180; lower rates rest of yr. Complimentary continental bkfst. Restaurant nearby. Ck-out 11 am, ck-in 1 pm. Converted 1865 carriage house. Victorian decor. Garden terrace. Totally nonsmoking. Center of Old Historic District; near ferries.
⊠ 🐾

★★★ **CENTERBOARD GUEST HOUSE.** *8 Chester St, Nantucket (02554). 508/228-9696. www.nantucket.net/lodging/centerboard.* 7 rms, 3 story, 1 suite, 1 kit. Mid-June-mid-Oct: S, D $110-$235; suite $325; lower rates rest of yr. TV. Complimentary continental bkfst. Restaurant nearby. Ck-out 11 am, ck-in 2 pm. In-rm modem link. Street parking. Refrigerators. Library/sitting rm, antiques. Restored Victorian residence (1885). Totally nonsmoking. Cr cds: A, MC, V.
🐾 ⊠

★★ **CENTRE STREET INN.** *78 Centre St, Nantucket (02554). 508/228-0199; fax 508/228-8676; toll-free 800/298-0199. www.centrestreetinn.com.* 13 rms, 6 share bath, 3 story. No rm phones. Late June-late Sept: S $75; D $95-$195; each addl $30; wkends, hols (3-day min); higher rates special hol events; lower rates May-late June, late Sept-mid-Dec. Closed rest of yr. Complimentary continental bkfst. Ck-out 11 am, ck-in 3 pm. Luggage handling. Concierge serv. Refrigerator avail. Picnic tables. Colonial house built in 1742; some antiques. Totally nonsmoking. Cr cds: A, DS, MC, V.
⊠ 🐾

★★ **COBBLESTONE INN.** *5 Ash St, Nantucket (02554). 508/228-1987; fax 508/228-6698.* 4 rms, 3 story, 1 suite. Mid-June-mid-Sept: S, D $85-$175; each addl $20; suite $250; higher rates Christmas Stroll; lower rates rest of yr. TV; cable. Complimentary bkfst. Restaurant nearby. Ck-out 11 am, ck-in 2 pm. Concierge. Lawn games. Picnic tables. Built 1725; antiques. Fireplace in library. Totally nonsmoking. Cr cds: MC, V.
⊠ 🐾

★ **CORNER HOUSE INN.** *49 Centre St Box 1828, Nantucket (02554). 508/228-1530. www.cornerhousenantucket.com.* 16 rms, 8 with shower only, 3 story, 2 suites. No rm phones. Mid-June-Late Sept: S $55-$235; D $75-$235; wkends (3-, 4-day min); lower rates rest of yr. Children over 8 yrs only. TV in most rms; cable (premium). Complimentary continental bkfst. Restaurant adj 6 am-11 pm. Ck-out 10:30 am, ck-in after 1 pm. Concierge serv. Street parking. Many refrigerators; microwave in suites. Built in 1790s as a father's wedding present for his daughter. Cr cds: A, MC, V.
⊠ 🐾

★★★ **JARED COFFIN HOUSE.** *29 Broad St, Nantucket (02554). ; fax 508/228-2400; res 800/248-2405. www.jaredcoffinhouse.com.* 60 rms in 6 bldgs. Some A/C. Elvtr in main bldg. Late June-Sept: S $85-$175; D $125-$375; each addl $25; lower rates rest of yr. Crib $10. TV. Restaurant (see JARED'S). Bar 11:30 am-11 pm. Ck-out 11 am, ck-in after 3 pm. Meeting rms. Business servs avail. In-rm modem link. Luggage handling. Concierge serv. Some refrigerators. Restored 1845 mansion; historical objets d'art. Cr cds: A, C, D, DS, ER, JCB, MC, V.
Ⓓ ⊠ 🐾

★★ **MARTIN HOUSE INN.** *61 Centre St, Nantucket (02554).* 508/228-0678. *www.nantucket.net/lodging/martinn.* 13 rms, 4 share bath, 3 story. No A/C. No elvtr. No rm phones. Mid-June-mid-Oct: S $70-$80; D $95-$175; each addl $25; suites $170; under 7 free; lower rates rest of yr. Children over 7 yrs only. TV in common rm; cable (premium). Complimentary continental bkfst. Restaurant opp 6-10 pm. Ck-out 11 am, ck-in 2 pm. In-rm modem link. Luggage handling. Street parking. Built in 1803; antiques. Totally nonsmoking. Cr cds: MC, V.

★★ **ROBERTS HOUSE INN.** *11 India St, Nantucket (02554).* 508/228-0600; fax 508/325-4046; toll-free 800/ 872-6830. *www.robertshouseinn.com.* 42 rms, 4 share bath, 3 story. Mid-June-mid-Oct: S $35-$65; D $60-$325; each addl $40; under 12 free; package plans; lower rates rest of yr exc hols and some wkends. Crib $10. TV. Complimentary continental bkfst. Coffee in rms. Ck-out 11 am, ck-in after 2 pm. Concierge serv. Microwaves; some fireplaces. Built 1846; established 1883. Cr cds: A, DS, MC, V.

★★ **SEVEN SEA STREET INN.** *7 Sea St, Nantucket (02554).* 508/228-3577; fax 508/228-3578. *www.sevenseastreetinn.com.* 11 rms, 2 story, 2 suites. July-Aug: S, D $155-$195; suites $235-$265; off-season package plans; higher rates Christmas stroll wkend; lower rates rest of yr. Children over 5 yrs only. TV; cable, VCR. Complimentary continental bkfst; afternoon refreshments. Restaurant nearby. Ck-out 11 am, ck-in 2 pm. Business servs avail. Whirlpool. Refrigerators. Picnic tables. Library/ sitting rm. View of Nantucket Harbor. Totally nonsmoking. Cr cds: A, MC, V.

★★★ **SHERBURNE INN.** *10 Gay St, Nantucket (02554).* 508/228-4425; fax 508/228-8114; toll-free 888/577-4425. *www.nantucket.net/lodging/sherburne.* 8 rms, 2 story. Mid-June-mid-Oct (3-day min): S, D $125-$235; each addl $25; higher rates: hols, special events; lower rates rest of yr. Children over 6 yrs only. Complimentary continental bkfst. Restaurant nearby. Ck-out 11 am, ck-in 2 pm. Concierge serv. Street parking. Built in 1835 as a silk factory; period antiques, fireplaced parlors. Totally nonsmoking. Cr cds: A, DS, MC, V.

★★ **SHIPS INN.** *13 Fair St, Nantucket (02554).* 508/228-0040; fax 508/228-6254. *www.nantucket.net/lodging/shipsinn.* 12 rms, 10 with bath. No A/C. Mid-May-mid-Oct: S $65-$90; D $145-$175; each addl $25. Closed rest of yr. Crib $10. TV. Complimentary continental bkfst; afternoon refreshments. Dining rm 5:30-9:30 pm. Bar 4:30-10 pm. Ck-out 10:30 am, ck-in 2 pm. Refrigerators. Built in 1831 by sea captain; many original furnishings. Totally nonsmoking. Cr cds: A, MC, V.

★★ **TUCKERNUCK INN.** *60 Union St, Nantucket (02554).* 508/228-4886; fax 508/228-4890; toll-free 800/228-4886. *tuckernuckinn.com.* 19 rms, 2-3 story. Mid-June-late-Sept: S, D $80-$180; each addl $20; suites $175-$240; higher rates: Memorial Day, Christmas stroll wkend; lower rates rest of yr. TV; cable (premium), VCR. Dining rm 8-11 am, 5:30-9:30 pm. Ck-out 11 am, ck-in 3 pm. Coin lndry. Business servs avail. Refrigerators avail. Lawn games. Picnic tables. Library/sitting rm. Sun deck. View of Nantucket Harbor. Totally nonsmoking. Cr cds: A, MC, V.

★★★★ **THE WAUWINET.** *120 Wauwinet Rd, Nantucket (02584).* 508/228-0145; fax 508/228-6712; toll-free 800/426-8718. *www.wauwinet.com.* This secluded inn, nine miles from the island's center, occupies a thin strip of land bordered by Nantucket Bay and the Atlantic Ocean and affords guests two private beaches. Twenty-six rooms and several individual cottages border a wildlife preserve and are uniquely decorated in a classic New England fashion. A 1988 renovation brought luxurious detail back to this mid-19th century landmark. 36 rms, 1-3 story, 4 suites. Mid-June-late Sept: S, D $520-$590; suites $610-$1,400; lower rates early May-mid-June, late Sep-Oct. Closed rest of yr. Crib free. TV; VCR (movies). Complimentary full bkfst; afternoon refreshments. Dining rm (see also TOPPER'S). Rm serv to 9 pm. Ck-out 11 am, ck-in 4 pm. Business servs avail. In-rm modem link. Tennis, pro shop. Rowboats, sailboats. Bicycles. Lawn games. Refrigerators avail. Some patios. Library. On ocean; swimming beach; complimentary harbor cruises. Totally nonsmoking. Cr cds: A, D, MC, V.

Restaurants

★★★ **21 FEDERAL.** *21 Federal St. (02554).* 508/228-2121. Specializes in seafood. Own baking, pasta. Menu changes daily. Hrs: 11:30 am-10 pm. Closed Jan-Mar. Res accepted. Bar. A la carte entrees: lunch $10-$15, dinner $19-$29. Outdoor dining. Display of old prints, drawings. Cr cds: A, MC, V.

★★ **AMERICAN SEASONS.** *80 Center St (02554).* 508/228-7111. Specialties: braised rabbit tostada, potato and thyme crusted sturgeon, homemade desserts. Hrs: 6-10 pm. Closed Jan-Apr. Res accepted. Bar. Dinner $16.50-$23.50. Outdoor dining. Popular spot features regional cuisine; decorated with country artifacts, hand-painted murals and gameboard tables. Cr cds: A, MC, V.

★★ **ATLANTIC CAFE.** *15 S Water St (02554).* 508/228-0570. *www.atlanticcafe.com.* Specializes in seafood, hamburgers, Mexican dishes. Hrs: 11:30 am-11:30 pm. Closed late Dec-early Jan. Bar. Lunch $5-$12, dinner $8-$21. Child's menu. Nautical decor; ship models. Cr cds: A, C, D, DS, ER, MC, V.

★★ **BOARDING HOUSE.** *12 Federal St (02554). 508/ 228-9622. www.nantucketrestaurants.com.* Specialties: twin lobster tails, seared yellowfin tuna, pistachio-crusted chocolate finale. Hrs: noon-2 pm, 6-10 pm. Res accepted. Bar noon-1 am. A la carte entrees: lunch $6-$14, dinner $20-$32. Outdoor dining. Original art. Cr cds: A, DS, MC, V.

★★ **CAP'N TOBEY'S CHOWDER HOUSE.** *Straight Wharf (02554).* 508/228-0836. Specialties: Cap'n Tobey's clam chowder, Nantucket Bay scallops, Indian pudding. Salad bar. Hrs: 11-1 am. Closed mid-Oct-mid-May. Res accepted. Bar. Lunch $6.95-$9.95, dinner $12.95-$19.95. Child's menu. Nautical decor. Wharf view. Family-owned. Cr cds: A, C, D, DS, ER, MC, V.
⊟

★★★ **CHANTICLEER.** *9 New St (02564).* 508/257-6231. *www.thechanticleerinn.com.* French menu. Specializes in fresh local seafood, lobster bisque, foie gras. Hrs: noon-2 pm, 6:30-9:30 pm. Closed Mon; also late Oct-mid-May. Res required. Bar. Wine cellar. A la carte entrees: lunch $15-$30, dinner $25-$60. Prix fixe: dinner $65. Parking. Garden dining. Elegant, romantic dining in four dining rms. View of flower and herb gardens, carousel. Cr cds: A, D, MC, V.
Ⓓ ⊟

★★★ **CIOPPINO'S.** *20 Broad St (02554).* 508/228-4622. *www.cioppinos.com.* Continental menu. Specialties: cioppino, tournedos of beef with lobster topping, grilled salmon fillet. Hrs: 11:30-2:30 pm, 5:30-10 pm. Closed Nov-May. Res accepted. Bar. Wine cellar. A la carte entrees: lunch $8.50-$13.50, dinner $19.50-$36. Patio dining. 3 dining rms in turn-of-the-century house. Cr cds: C, D, DS, ER, MC, V.

★★★ **CLUB CAR.** *1 Main St (02554).* 508/228-1101. Continental menu. Specializes in rack of lamb, fresh seafood, veal. Hrs: 6-10 pm. Closed mid-Dec-mid-May. Res required. Bar 11:30-1 am; pianist. A la carte entrees: dinner $26-$40. In authentic railroad car; railroad memorabilia, photos. Turn-of-the-century decor. Cr cds: MC, V.
⊟

★★ **COMPANY OF THE CAULDRON.** *7 India St, Nantucket (02554).* 508/228-4016. Continental, Amer menu. Specializes in fresh fish. Own pasta. 2 sittings: 7 and 9 pm. Closed Mon; also Mid-Dec-May. Res accepted. Wine, beer. Complete meals: $46-$50. Harpist Wed, Fri, Sun. Street parking. Candlelight setting. Totally nonsmoking. Cr cds: MC, V.
Ⓓ

★★ **INDIA HOUSE.** *37 India St (02554). 508/228-9043.* Specializes in lamb, swordfish, chocolate silk. Hrs: 6:30-9:30 pm; Sun brunch 9:30 am-12:30 pm. Closed Jan-Mar. Res accepted. Serv bar. A la carte entrees: dinner $15-$32. Sun brunch $16. Child's menu. Garden dining. 3 dining rms. Inn built 1803; overnight rms avail. Totally nonsmoking. Cr cds: A, DS, MC, V.

★★★ **JARED'S.** *29 Broad St, Nantucket (02554).* 508/228-2400. Specializes in bay scallops, regional dishes. Hrs: 7:30-11 am, 6-9 pm. Res accepted. Tap rm 11:30 am-9:30 pm. Complete meals: bkfst $5.95-$8.95, dinner $19-$32. Child's menu. Outdoor dining June-Sept. Family-owned. Totally nonsmoking. Cr cds: A, C, D, DS, MC, V.
Ⓓ ⊟

★★★ **LE LANGUEDOC.** *24 Broad St (02554).* 508/228-2552. *www.lelanguedoc.com.* Continental menu. Specializes in veal, lamb, fresh fish. Hrs: noon-2 pm (fall), 6-10 pm; Apr-early Sept from 6 pm. Closed Jan-Mar. Res accepted. Bar 6 pm-midnight. Lunch $8-$18, dinner $25-$35. Outdoor dining. Early 1800s building in heart of historic district. Cr cds: A, MC, V.
⊟

★★ **ROPE WALK.** *1 Straight Wharf, Nantucket (02554).* 508/228-8886. *www.theropewalk.com.* Specializes in fresh local seafood, homemade desserts. Hrs: 11 am-3 pm; 5:30-10 pm. Closed mid-Oct-mid-May. No A/C. Bar. Lunch $7.50-$12, dinner $16.50-$26. Child's menu. Outdoor dining. Nautical artifacts. At end of wharf; view of harbor. Cr cds: MC, V.
Ⓓ ⊟

★ **TAVERN AT HARBOR SQUARE.** *1 Harbor Sq (02554).* 508/228-1266. Specializes in New England clam chowder, lobster, fresh seafood. Hrs: 11 am-9:30 pm. Closed mid-Oct-late May. No A/C. Bar to midnight. Lunch $6.95-$15.95 dinner $7.95-$20.95. Child's menu. Patio dining. Nautical decor. Wharf view. Cr cds: A, MC, V.
Ⓓ ⊟

★★★ **TOPPER'S.** *120 Wauwinet Rd (02554).* 508/228-0145. *www.wauwinet.com.* Specialties: lobster and crab cakes with smoked corn, jalapeño olives and mustard sauce; Nantucket lobster with asparagus, mushrooms and fettuccine. Local seafood. Hrs: noon-2 pm, 6-9:30 pm; Sun brunch 8 am-2 pm. Closed Nov-mid-May. Res accepted. Bar from noon. Wine list. A la carte entrees: lunch $21-$25, dinner $34-$52. Sun brunch $36. Outdoor dining (summer). Within country inn; pickled oak floors; folk art collection. View of Nantucket Bay. Totally nonsmoking. Cr cds: A, C, D, MC, V.
Ⓓ

★★ **WEST CREEK CAFE.** *11 W Creek Rd, Nantucket (02554).* 508/228-4943. Contemporary Amer menu. Specialties: sauteed crab fritter with Georgia peanut vinaigrette; roasted tenderloin with polenta fries and red wine sauce; seared salmon over oven-roasted vegetable risotto and chive oil. Hrs: 6-9 pm; Fri, Sat to 9:30 pm. Closed Tues; also Jan 1, July 4, Dec 25. Res accepted. Bar. A la carte entrees: dinner $18-$26. Parking. Outdoor dining.Contemporary, elegant cafe. Totally nonsmoking. Cr cds: MC, V.

Natick

Pop 32,170 **Elev** 180 ft **Area code** 508 **Zip** 01760
Information MetroWest Chamber of Commerce, 1671 Worcester Rd, Suite 201, Framingham 01701; 508/879-5600
Web www.metrowest.org

This town was set aside as a plantation for the "Praying Indians" in 1650 at the request of Reverend John Eliot. A missionary, he believed that he could promote brotherhood between Native Americans and settlers by converting them. After half a century, the Native Americans were crowded out by settlers.

Motels/Motor Lodges

★★ **HAMPTON INN.** *319 Speen St (01760). 508/653-5000; fax 508/651-9733. www.hamptoninn.com.* 185 rms, 5 suites, 7 story. S, D $90-$99. Crib free. TV; cable (premium). Complimentary continental bkfst. Ck-out noon. Meeting rms. Business servs avail. Exercise equipt. Some refrigerators. Cr cds: A, D, DS, MC, V.

D 🏂 🖼 🐾

★ **TRAVELODGE.** *1350 Worcester Rd (01760). 508/655-2222; fax 508/655-7953; res 888/515-6375. www.travelodge.com.* 68 rms, 2 story. S $84-$109; D $99-$119; each addl $5; under 18 free. Crib free. TV; cable (premium). Complimentary coffee in rms. Ck-out noon. Business servs avail. In-rm modem link. Cr cds: A, DS, JCB, MC, V.

D 🏂 🖼 🐾

Hotels

★★★ **CROWNE PLAZA HOTEL BOSTON - NATICK.** *1360 Worcester St (01760). 508/653-8800; fax 508/653-1708. www.crowneplaza.com.* 251 units, 7 story. S $99-$220; D $99-$240; suites $450; under 19 free; wkend rates. Crib free. TV; cable (premium), VCR avail (movies). Pool; whirlpool. Restaurant 6 am-5 pm; dining rm 5-10 pm. Bar 11-1 am. Ck-out noon. Convention facilities. Business servs avail. In-rm modem link. Concierge. Bellhops. Valet serv. Gift shop. Exercise equipt; sauna. Cr cds: A, C, D, DS, ER, JCB, MC, V.

D 🏊 🏂 🖼 🐾 SC

★★ **SHERBORN INN.** *33 N Main St, Sherborn (01770). 508/655-9521; fax 508/655-5325. www.sherborninn.com.* 4 rms, 2 story. S $120. Crib avail. Complimentary continental bkfst. Restaurant (see SHERBORN INN). Rm serv. Ck-out 11 am, ck-in 3 pm. Cr cds: A, MC, V.

D 🖼 🐾

Restaurant

★★ **SHERBORN INN.** *33 N Main St, Sherborn (01770). 508/655-9521. www.sherborninn.com.* Contemporary Amer menu. Specializes in tenderloin of beef. Own baking. Hrs: 6-9 pm; Sun 5-9 pm. Res accepted. Bar. Dinner $13-$24. Jazz Tues. Restored tavern decor. Cr cds: A, MC, V.

D

New Bedford

Settled 1640 **Pop** 93,768 **Elev** 50 ft **Area code** 508
Information Bristol County Convention & Visitors Bureau, 70 N Second St, PO Box 976, 02741; 508/997-1250 or 800/288-6263
Web www.bristol-county.org

Herman Melville, author of *Moby Dick,* said that the brave houses and flowery gardens of New Bedford were one and all harpooned and dragged up from the bottom of the sea. Whaling did in fact build this city. When oil was discovered in Pennsylvania in 1857, the world's greatest whaling port nearly became a ghost town. New Bedford scrapped the great fleet and became a major cotton textile center. More recently, it has thrived on widely diversified industries. New Bedford remains a major Atlantic deep-sea fishing port. The whaling atmosphere is preserved in local museums and monuments, while the Whaling National Historical Park celebrates the town's whaling legacy. In the County Street historic district many of the mansions built for sea captains and merchants still stand.

What to See and Do

Boat Trips.

New Bedford-Cuttyhunk Ferry. (Mid-June-mid-Sept, daily; rest of yr, varied schedule) Res suggested. Departs from Fisherman's Wharf, Pier 3. Phone 508/992-1432. ¢¢¢¢

Steamship Authority. New Bedford-Martha's Vineyard Ferry. Bus tours, car rentals on Martha's Vineyard. (Mid-May-mid-Oct, daily) Same-day round-trip and one-way trips avail. Schedule may vary. Phone 508/997-1688. ¢¢¢¢

Buttonwood Park & Zoo. Greenhouse; ball fields, tennis courts, playground, picnic area, fitness circuit. Zoo exhibits include elephants, lions, deer, bears, buffalo; seal pool. (Daily; closed Thanksgiving, Dec 25, Jan 1) Rockdale Ave. Phone 508/991-6175. ¢¢

Fort Phoenix Beach State Reservation. Swimming; fine view of harbor. Nearby is Fort Phoenix, a pre-Revolutionary fortification (open to the public). Off US 6 and I-95, E via US 6 to Fairhaven, then 1 mi S; follow signs. Phone 508/992-4524. ¢

New Bedford Whaling Museum. Features an 89-ft half-scale model of whaleship *Lagoda.* Galleries devoted to scrimshaw, local artists; murals of whales and whale skeleton; period rms and collections of antique toys, dolls, prints, and ship models. Silent movie presentation (July and Aug). (Daily; closed Jan 1, Thanksgiving, Dec 25) 18 Johnny Cake Hill. Phone 508/997-0046. ¢¢

Rotch-Jones-Duff House and Garden Museum. Whaling era Greek-revival mansion (1834) and garden, has been maintained to reflect the lives of three families that lived in the house. (Daily) Museum sponsors concerts and programs throughout the yr. Tours avail, inquire for schedule. Museum shop. 396 County St. Phone 508/997-1401. ¢¢

Seamen's Bethel. (1832) "Whaleman's Chapel" referred to by Melville in *Moby Dick*. Prow-shaped pulpit later built to represent Melville's description. Also many cenotaphs dedicated to men lost at sea. Vespers third Sun each month. (Daily) 15 Johnny Cake Hill. Phone 508/992-3295.

Special Events

Feast of the Blessed Sacrament. Madeira Field, N end of town. Portuguese festival. Three days usually beginning first wkend Aug. Phone 508/992-6911.

Blessing of the Fleet. Waterfront. 4th of July wkend. Phone 508/999-5231.

First Night New Bedford. Historic waterfront and downtown. Celebration of arts and culture; fireworks. (Dec 31) Phone 800/508-5353.

Motels/Motor Lodges

★★ **COMFORT INN.** *171 Faunce Corner Rd, North Dartmouth (02747). 508/996-0800. www.comfortinn.com.* 85 rms, 2 story. Late May-early Sept: S $80-$90; D $119; each addl $5; under 18 free; lower rates rest of yr. Crib free. TV; cable (premium). Pool. Ck-out noon. Business servs avail. In-rm modem link. Cr cds: A, D, DS, MC, V.
D ⛵ ⬆ 🐾 SC

★ **DAYS INN.** *500 Hathaway Rd (02740). 508/997-1231; fax 508/984-7977.* 151 rms, 3 story. S $64-$75; D $69-$82; each addl $5; under 12 free. Crib free. Pet accepted, some restrictions. TV; cable (premium). Indoor pool. Coffee in rms. Restaurant 7 am-11 pm. Rm serv. Bar 4 pm-midnight. Ck-out 11 am. Meeting rm. Business servs avail. In-rm modem link. Coin lndry. Free airport transportation. Golf course opp. Cr cds: A, D, DS, MC, V.
D ⛵ ⬆ 🐾 ✈ 🎣

Restaurant

★★ **FREESTONE'S CITY GRILL.** *41 William St (02740). 508/993-7477. www.freestones.com.* Specializes in fish chowder, seafood, specialty salads. Hrs: 11 am-11 pm; Sun noon-10 pm. Closed Labor Day, Thanksgiving, Dec 25. Res accepted. Bar. Lunch $4-$7, dinner $4-$18. Child's menu. Street parking. Renovated bank bldg (1877); interesting art objects. Cr cds: A, D, DS, MC, V.
D

Newburyport

Settled 1635 **Pop** 17,189 **Elev** 37 ft **Area code** 978
Zip 01950
Information Greater Newburyport Chamber of Commerce & Industry, 29 State St; 978/462-6680
Web www.newburyport.chamber.org

Novelist John P. Marquand, who lived in Newburyport, said it "is not a museum piece although it sometimes looks it." High Street is surely a museum of American Federalist architecture. Ship owners and captains built these great houses. The birthplace of the US Coast Guard, Newburyport lies at the mouth of the Merrimack River. The city's early prosperity came from shipping and shipbuilding. It is now a thriving year-round tourist destination.

What to See and Do

Coffin House. (ca 1654) Developed in a series of enlargements, features 17th- and 18th-century kitchens, buttery, and parlor with early 19th-century wallpaper; furnishings of eight generations. Tours on the hr. (June-mid-Oct, Wed-Sun) 16 High Rd (US 1A). Phone 978/463-2057. ¢¢

Cushing House Museum. (Historical Society of Old Newbury; ca 1810) A Federalist-style mansion, once the home of Caleb Cushing, first envoy to China from US. Museum houses collections of needlework, paperweights, toys, paintings, furniture, silver, clocks, china; library. Also shed, carriage house, and 19th-century garden. (May-Oct, Tues-Sat; closed hols) 98 High St. Phone 978/462-2681. ¢

Custom House Maritime Museum. Collections of artifacts depicting maritime heritage of area; includes ship models, navigational instruments; decorative arts, library. (Apr-late Dec, Mon-Sat, also Sun afternoons) 25 Water St. Phone 978/462-8681. ¢¢

Parker River National Wildlife Refuge. Natural barrier beach formed by 6½ mi of beach and sand dunes is the home of many species of birds, mammals, reptiles, amphibians, and plants; saltwater and freshwater marshes provide resting and feeding place for migratory birds on the Atlantic Flyway. Hiking, bicycling, waterfowl hunting, nature trail. (Daily) Closed to public when parking lots are full. 3 mi E on Plum Island. Contact Refuge Manager, Northern Blvd, Plum Island 01950. Phone 978/465-5753. ¢¢

Special Events

Arts, Flowers, & All that Jazz. Downtown. Demonstrations, flower and garden show, crafts, exhibits and jazz concerts. (Sun, Mon of Memorial Day wkend.) Phone 978/462-6680.

Yankee Homecoming. Celebration includes parades, fireworks, exhibits; river cruises; sailboat and canoe races; craft show; lobster feeds. (Last Sat July-first Sun Aug) Phone 978/462-6680.

Fall Harvest Festival. Downtown. Juried crafts, music, entertainment, food, baking contest. (Sun, Mon of Columbus Day wkend) Phone 978/462-6680.

Hotel

★ **GARRISON INN.** *11 Brown Sq (01950). 978/499-8500; fax 978/499-8555. www.garrisoninn.com.* 24 rms, 4 story. June-Oct: S, D $97.50-$107.50 each addl $10; townhouse $135-$175; lower rates rest of yr. Crib avail. TV; cable (premium), VCR avail. Restaurant (see also DAVID'S). Supervised children's activities; ages 2-12. Bar; entertainment. Ck-out 11 am, ck-in 3 pm. Meeting rm. Business servs avail. In-rm modem link. Restored historic inn (1809). Cr cds: A, MC, V.
D ⬆ 🐾

B&Bs/Small Inns

★★ **CLARK CURRIER INN.** *45 Green St (01950). 978/465-8363. www.clarkcurrierinn.com.* 8 rms, 3 story. May-mid-Jan: S, D $95-$155; lower rates rest of yr. TV in sitting rm. Complimentary bkfst buffet. Restaurant nearby. Ck-out 11 am, ck-in 3 pm. Bus depot transportation. Built 1803 by a shipbuilder. Rms furnished with antiques. Garden with gazebo. Totally nonsmoking. Cr cds: A, DS, MC, V. ⊠ 🐾 SC

★★ **ESSEX STREET INN.** *7 Essex St (01950). 978/465-3148; fax 978/462-1907. www.newburyportchamber.org.* 19 rms, 3 story. June-Oct: S, D $85-$125; each addl $10; suites $155; kit. unit $175; townhouse $155; lower rates rest of yr. TV. Complimentary continental bkfst. Restaurant nearby. Ck-out 11 am, ck-in 2 pm. Some in-rm whirlpools. Built 1801; fireplace. Cr cds: A, MC, V. ⊠ 🐾

★★ 🍴 **MORRILL PLACE.** *209 High St (01950). 978/462-2808; fax 978/462-9966; res 888/594-4667.* 9 rms, 4 share bath, 3 story. No A/C. S, D $72-$95; each addl $10; EP avail; wkly rates. Pet accepted. TV rm; cable, VCR avail. Complimentary continental bkfst. Restaurant nearby. Ck-out noon, ck-in 4 pm. Tennis privileges. 18-hole golf privileges, pro. Built in 1806. Once owned by law partner of Daniel Webster; Webster was frequent visitor. Formal front parlor and library. Cr cds: A, MC, V. D 🐾 🍴 🔥 🐾

★★ **WINDSOR HOUSE.** *38 Federal St (01950). 978/462-3778; fax 978/465-3443; toll-free 888/873-5296. www.bbhost.com/windsorhouse.* 4 rms, 3 story. S $110-$145; D $135-$145; each addl $35. Crib free. Pet accepted, some restrictions. TV in sitting rm; VCR. Complimentary full bkfst. Coffee in rms. Restaurant nearby. Ck-out 11 am, ck-in 4 pm. Meeting rm. Business servs avail. Microwaves avail. Federal mansion (1786) built by lieutenant of the Continental Army for his wedding. Antiques. Totally nonsmoking. Cr cds: A, DS, MC, V. 🐾 ⊠ 🔥 🐾

Restaurants

★★★ **DAVID'S.** *11 Brown Sq (01950). 978/462-8077.* Eclectic menu. Specializes in lobster, scallops, sweet potatoes. Own baking. Hrs: 5-9 pm; Fri, Sat to 10 pm. Closed Jan 1, Dec 24, 25. Res accepted. Bar. Wine list. Dinner $6.95-$24.50. Prix fixe: dinner $40-$54.50. Child's menu. Guitarist Thurs-Sat. Two distinct dining areas: formal dining rm with high ceiling and informal basement pub; separate menus. Cr cds: A, DS, MC, V. D

★★ **GLENN'S GALLEY.** *44 Merrimas St (01950). 978/465-3811.* Seafood menu. Menu changes daily. Hrs: 5:30-10 pm; Sat, Sun from 4 pm. Closed Mon; also major hols. Res accepted. Bar. Wine list. Dinner $18-$22. Child's menu. Wed, Thurs, Sun entertainment. Street parking. Bistro decor. Cr cds: A, D, DS, MC, V. D

★ **THE GROG.** *13 Middle St (01950). 978/465-8008. www.thegrog.com.* Eclectic menu. Specializes in seafood. Hrs: 11:30-12:15 am. Closed Dec 25. Bar. Lunch, dinner $5.95-$14.95. Musicians Thurs-Sun. Tavern atmosphere. Family-owned. Cr cds: A, C, D, DS, ER, MC, V. D 🖭

★ **JACOB MARLEY'S.** *23 Pleasant St (01950). 978/465-5598.* Amer, fusion menu. Specializes in entree salads. Hrs: 11:30 am-11 pm; Sun from 10 am; Sun brunch 11 am-2 pm. Closed Dec 25. Bar to 1 am. Lunch, dinner $8.95-$13.95. Sun brunch $7.95-$10.95. Child's menu. Entertainment Tues, Sat, Sun. Restored mill; nautical objects. Cr cds: A, MC, V. D 🖭

★★ **MICHAEL'S HARBORSIDE.** *1 Tournament Wharf (01950). 978/462-7785.* Seafood menu. Specializes in fresh seafood. Hrs: 11:30 am-3 pm, 5-9 pm; Fri, Sat to 10 pm; Sun noon-9 pm; winter hrs vary. Closed Thanksgiving, Dec 25. Bar. Lunch $5.95-$11.95, dinner $6.95-$15.95. Entertainment Sun (summer). Parking. Outdoor dining. Cr cds: A, DS, MC, V. D

★★★ **SCANDIA.** *25 State St (01950). 978/462-6271. www.scandiarestaurant.com.* Contemporary Amer menu. Specializes in seafood, game, vegetarian dishes. Hrs: 11:30 am-3 pm, 5-10 pm; Thurs-Sun from 8 am. Closed Thanksgiving, Dec 25. Res accepted. Bar. Lunch $3.25-$12, dinner $12-$17.95. Child's menu. Outdoor dining. Traditional, formal decor; original oil paintings. Family-owned. Totally nonsmoking. Cr cds: A, DS, MC, V. D

★★ **TEN CENTER STREET.** *10 Center St (01950). 978/462-6652. www.restaurant.com.* Continental menu. Specializes in fresh seafood, veal, beef. Own baking. Hrs: 11:30 am-9:30 pm; Fri, Sat to 10:30 pm; Sun 11 am-10 pm; Sun brunch 11 am-3 pm. Res accepted. Bar to 1 am. A la carte entrees: lunch $5.95-$14.95, dinner $6.95-$22.95. Parking. Outdoor dining. In restored 1800s Federal-style house. Cr cds: A, D, DS, MC, V. D 🖭

Newton

See also Boston

Settled 1630 **Pop** 83,829 **Elev** 100 ft **Area code** 617
Information Chamber of Commerce, 199 Wells Ave, Suite 208, PO Box 590268, Newton 02459; 617/244-5300
Web www.nnchamber.com

Newton, the "Garden City," is actually a city of 13 suburban neighborhoods that have maintained their individual identities. Of the 13, eight have "Newton" in their names: Newton, Newtonville, Newton Centre, Newton Corner,

Newton Highlands, West Newton, Newton Upper Falls, and Newton Lower Falls. Five colleges are located here: Boston College, Lasell College, Mount Ida College, Andover-Newton Theological School, and Aquinas Junior College.

What to See and Do

Jackson Homestead Museum. (1809) Once a station on the Underground Railroad. Home of the Newton Historical Society. Changing exhibits; children's gallery; toys; textiles; and tools. (Tues-Sat and Sun afternoon) 527 Washington St. Phone 617/552-7238. ¢¢

Hotels

★★ **HOLIDAY INN NEWTON-BOSTON.** *399 Grove St (02462). 617/969-5300; fax 617/965-4280; res 800/465-4329. www.holiday-inn.com.* 191 rms, 7 story. S, D $160-$199; each addl $10; under 18 free; wkend rates. TV; cable (premium). Heated pool; poolside serv, lifeguard. Coffee in rms. Restaurant 6:30 am-2 pm, 5-10 pm. Rm serv. Bar 4 pm-midnight. Ck-out noon. Meeting rms. Business servs avail. In-rm modem link. Valet serv. Sundries. Exercise equipt. Refrigerators avail. Cr cds: A, C, D, DS, MC, V.
🄳 🏊 🔨 😖 🐾 SC

★★★ **MARRIOTT.** *2345 Commonwealth Ave (02466). 617/969-1000; fax 617/527-6914; toll-free 800/228-9290. www.marriott.com.* 430 rms, 6 suites, 7 story. Sept-Nov: S, D $169; suites $300-$500; under 18 free; wkend rates; lower rates rest of yr. Crib free. Pet accepted, some restrictions. TV; cable (premium). 2 pools, 1 indoor; whirlpool; poolside serv, lifeguard. Playground. Restaurant 6:30 am-midnight. Rm serv. Bar; entertainment. Ck-out 1 pm. Coin lndry. Convention facilities. Business servs avail. In-rm modem link. Bellhops. Sundries. Barber. X-country ski 1 mi. Exercise equipt; sauna. Canoes. Game rm. Lawn games. Some private patios, balconies. Picnic tables. On Charles River. Luxury level. Cr cds: A, MC, V.
🄳 🐾 🏊 🏊 🔨 😖 🐾 SC

★★★ **SHERATON HOTEL.** *100 Cabot St, Needham (02494). 781/444-1110; fax 617/449-3945; toll-free 800/274-3728. www.sheraton.needham.com.* 247 rms, 5 story, 48 suites. Mid-Apr-mid-Nov: S, D, suites $149-$325; each addl $15; under 18 free; wkend rates. TV; cable (premium). Indoor pool; poolside serv. Restaurant 6:30 am-10 pm. Bar 11:30-1 am, entertainment Thurs-Sat. Ck-out noon. Meeting rms. Business servs avail. Concierge. Garage parking. Gift shop. Exercise equipt; sauna. Health club privileges. Cr cds: A, C, D, DS, MC, V.
🄳 🏊 🔨 😖 🐾 SC

★★★ **SHERATON NEWTON HOTEL.** *320 Washington St (02158). 617/969-3010; fax 617/244-5894; toll-free 800/325-3535. www.sheraton.com.* 272 rms, 12 story. S, D $109-$199; each addl $15; wkend rates. Crib free. TV; cable (premium), VCR avail. Indoor pool. Coffee in rms. Restaurant 7 am-10 pm. Bar. Ck-out 11 am. Meeting rms. Business servs avail. In-rm modem link. Bellhops. Exercise rm; sauna. Refrigerators, microwaves avail. Cr cds: A, C, D, DS, ER, MC, V.
🄳 🏊 🔨 😖 🐾 SC

Restaurants

★★ **LEGAL SEAFOODS.** *43 Boylston St, Chestnut Hill (02467). 617/277-7300. www.legalseafoods.com.* Specialties: bluefish pâte, clam chowder, mussels au gratin. Hrs: 11 am-10 pm; Fri, Sat to 11 pm; Sun from noon. Closed Thanksgiving, Dec 25. Bar. Lunch $6.95-$13.95, dinner $9.95-$30.95. Child's menu. Fishmarket on premises. Family-owned. Totally nonsmoking. Cr cds: A, C, D, DS, JCB, MC, V.
🄳

★★★ **LUMIERE.** *1293 Washington St, West Newton (02465). 617/244-9199. www.lumiererestaurant.com.* Specializes in sea scallops over potato mousseline, torchon foie gras. Hrs: 5:30-9:30 pm; Fri 5:30-10:00 pm; Sat 5-10 pm, Sun 5-9 pm. Closed Mon. Res accepted. Wine, beer. Dinner $12-$30. Chef-owned. Cr cds: D, MC, V.
🄳

North Adams

See also Williamstown

Settled 1745 **Pop** 14,681 **Elev** 707 ft **Area code** 413 **Zip** 01247

Information Northern Berkshire Chamber of Commerce, 40 Main St; 413/663-3735

North Adams is an industrial community set in the beautiful four-season resort country of the northern Berkshires. Its factories make electronic components, textile machinery, wire, machine tools, paper boxes, and other products. Susan B. Anthony was born in nearby Adams in 1820.

What to See and Do

MASS MoCA. Center for visual, performing, and media arts. Features unconventional exhibits and performances by renowned artists and cultural institutions. Rehearsals and production studios are open to the public. Tours avail. (Daily) 1040 Mass MoCA Way. Phone 413/664-4481. ¢¢¢

Kidspace. Children's gallery presents contemporary art in manner that is interesting and accessible. Includes hands-on activity stations where children can create their own works of art. (June-Aug, Mon, Thurs-Sun; rest of yr, limited hrs) Phone 413/664-4481. **FREE**

Mohawk Trail State Forest. Spectacular scenery. Swimming, fishing; hiking, winter sports, picnicking, camping, log cabins. Standard fees. E on MA 2, near Charlemont. Phone 413/339-5504. ¢¢

Mount Greylock State Reservation. Mt Greylock, highest point in state (3,491 ft), is here. War memorial tower at summit. Fishing; hunting, cross-country skiing, snowmobiles allowed. Picnicking. Lodge, snacks; campsites (mid-May-mid-Oct). Visitor center on Rockwell Rd in Lanesborough, off MA 7. Standard fees. 1 mi W on MA 2, then N on Notch Rd. Phone 413/499-4262.

Natural Bridge State Park. A water-eroded marble bridge and rock formations, about 550 million yrs old, popularized by Nathaniel Hawthorne. Picnicking. (Mid-May-mid-Oct) 1¼ mi NE on MA 8. Phone 413/663-6392. ¢¢

Savoy Mountain State Forest. Brilliant fall foliage. Swimming, fishing, boating (ramp); hiking and riding trails, hunting, winter sports, picnicking, camping, log cabins. Waterfall. Standard fees. E on MA 2, near Florida, MA. Phone 413/664-9567. **FREE**

Western Gateway Heritage State Park. Restored freightyard with six buildings around a cobbled courtyard. Detailed historic exhibits on the construction of Hoosac Railroad Tunnel. (Daily; closed hols) Behind City Hall on MA 8. Phone 413/663-8059. **Donation**

Special Events

La Festa. Ethnic festival, ethnic food, entertainment, events. (16 days beginning mid-June.) Phone 413/66-FESTA.

Fall Foliage Festival. Parade, entertainment, dancing, children's activities. (Late Sept-early Oct) Phone 413/663-3735.

Northampton

Settled 1673 **Pop** 28,978 **Elev** 140 ft **Area code** 413 **Zip** 01060

Information Chamber of Commerce, 99 Pleasant St; 413/584-1900; or the Tourist Information Center, 33 King St; 413/665-0532 (June-Oct)

Web www.northamptonun common.com

When the famed concert singer Jenny Lind honeymooned in this town on the Connecticut River in 1852, she exclaimed, "Why, this is the paradise of America." But it was not always a peaceful town. Northampton was the scene of a frenzied religious revival movement in the first half of the 18th century. It stemmed from Jonathan Edwards, a Puritan divine who came to be regarded as the greatest preacher in New England. Later, the town was the home of President Calvin Coolidge. A granite memorial on the court house lawn honors Coolidge, who was once mayor. Clarke School for the Deaf is located here.

What to See and Do

Arcadia Nature Center and Wildlife Sanctuary, Massachusetts Audubon Society. Five hundred fifty acres on migratory flyway; an ancient oxbow of the Connecticut River; self-guiding nature trails; observation tower; courses and programs. Grounds (Tues-Sun). 4 mi SW on MA 10, follow signs, in Northampton and Easthampton. Phone 413/584-3009. ¢¢

Calvin Coolidge Memorial Room. Displays of the late president's papers and correspondence; also books and articles on Coolidge. Memorabilia includes Native American headdress and beadwork given to him, Mrs. Coolidge's needlework, photographs. (Mon-Wed; closed hols; schedule may vary) Phone 413/584-8399. **FREE**

Historic Northampton Museum Houses. All houses (Tues-Fri, Sat & Sun afternoons). 46-66 Bridge St. Phone 413/584-6011. ¢¢

Damon House. (1813) Permanent formal parlor exhibit (ca 1820). Phone 413/584-6011.

Parsons House. (ca 1730) Contains exhibits on local architecture.

Shepherd House. (1798) Includes the lifetime collection of one Northampton family and focuses on family lifestyle at the turn of the 19th century.

Look Park. Miniature train and Christenson Zoo; boating; tennis; picnicking; playgrounds, ball fields; also here is Pines Theater (musical entertainment, children's theater, and puppet programs, summer). Park (all yr). Fees for most facilities. 300 N Main St, NW off MA 9. Phone 413/584-5457. ¢

Smith College. (1871) 2,700 women. The largest private liberal arts college for women in the US. On campus are Paradise Pond, named by Jenny Lind; Helen Hills Hills Chapel; William Allan Neilson Library with more than one million volumes; Center for the Performing Arts; Plant House and Botanical Gardens; Japanese Garden. On Elm St (MA 9). Phone 413/584-2700. Also here is

Museum of Art. A fine collection with emphasis on American and European art of the 19th and 20th centuries. (Sept-May, Tues-Sun; rest of yr, Tues-Sat; closed hols) Elm St (MA 9).

■ **Words and Pictures Museum of Fine Sequential Art.** Displays of modern comic book art from 1970s to present. (Tues-Sun, afternoons) 140 Main St. Phone 413/586-8545.

Special Events

Maple Sugaring. Visitors are welcome at many maple camps. (Mid-Mar-early Apr.) Phone 413/584-1900.

Eastern National Morgan Horse Show. Three-County Fairgrounds. (Late July.) Phone 413/584-2237.

Three-County Fair. Agricultural exhibits, horse racing, parimutuel betting. (Labor Day wk) Phone 413/584-2237.

Springtime in Paradise. Major arts festival. Late May. Phone 413/584-1900.

Motels/Motor Lodges

★★ **AUTUMN INN.** *259 Elm St (01060). 413/584-7660; fax 413/586-4808. www.autumninn.com.* 28 rms, 2 story. Apr-Nov: S $68-$80; D $86-$106; each addl $6-$12; suites $110-$135; lower rates rest of yr. Crib free. TV; cable (premium). Pool. Restaurant 7-10 am, 11:30 am-2 pm; wkends 8-11 am. Bar. Ck-out 11 am. In-rm modem link. Downhill ski 5 mi; x-country ski 18 mi. Lawn games. Refrigerator in suites. Picnic table. Smith College opp. Cr cds: A, C, D, MC, V.
🏊 🛁 🔥

★★ **BEST WESTERN NORTHAMPTON.** *117 Conz St (01060). 413/586-1500; fax 413/586-6549; toll-free 800/941-3066. www.bestwestern.com.* 66 rms, 2 story. S $59-$69; D $62-$79; each addl $10; under 18 free; higher rates: Smith College graduation, hols. Crib free. TV; cable. Pool. Complimentary coffee in lobby. Restaurant nearby. Ck-out 11 am. Downhill ski 7 mi. Cr cds: A, D, DS, MC, V.
D 🏊 🛁 🔯 🔥 SC

Hotels

★★ **HOTEL NORTHAMPTON.** *36 King St (01060). 413/584-3100; fax 413/584-9455; toll-free 800/547-3529. www.hotelnorthhampton.com.* 99 rms, 5 story. Sept-Oct: S, D $109-$160; each addl $12; suites $138-$290; under 12 free; higher rates special events; lower rates rest of yr. Crib free. TV; cable (premium). Restaurants 7-1 am. Bar. Ck-out noon. Meeting rms. Business center. Private patios, balconies. Cr cds: A, D, DS, MC, V.

D 🏊 ⚓ 🐾 🏃

★★ **THE INN AT NORTHAMPTON.** *1 Atwood Dr (01060). 413/586-1211; fax 413/586-1723; toll-free 800/582-2929. www.hampshirehospitality.com.* 124 rms, 2 story. S, D $139; suites $130-$170. TV; cable. 2 pools, 1 indoor; wading pool, whirlpool, poolside serv. Restaurant 7-10:30 am, 5-9 pm; Mon to 10:30 am; Sat, Sun 7:30-11 am. Bar. Ck-out 11 am. Meeting rms. Valet serv. Sundries. Lighted tennis. Game rm. Balconies. Cr cds: A, D, DS, MC, V.

D 🏃 ⚓ 🏊 🔥

Restaurant

★★ **EASTSIDE GRILL.** *19 Strong Ave (01060). 413/586-3347.* Specializes in seafood, steak. Hrs: 5-10 pm; Fri, Sat to 11 pm; Sun 4-9 pm. Closed Thanksgiving, Dec 25. Bar. Dinner $8.95-$14.95. New Orleans-theme prints. Totally nonsmoking. Cr cds: A, C, D, DS, ER, MC, V.

D

North Truro

(see Truro & North Truro)

Orleans (Cape Cod)

See also Eastham (Cape Cod)

Settled 1693 **Pop** 6,341 **Elev** 60 ft **Area code** 508 **Zip** 02653
Information Cape Cod Chamber of Commerce, US 6 and MA 132, PO Box 790, Hyannis 02601-0790; 508/362-3225 or 888/CAPECOD
Web www.capecodchamber.org

Orleans supposedly was named in honor of the Duke of Orleans after the French Revolution. The settlers worked at shipping, fishing, and salt production. Its history includes the dubious distinction of being the only town in America to have been fired upon by the Germans during World War I. The town is now a commercial hub for the summer resort colonies along the great stretch of Nauset Beach and the coves behind it. A cable station, which provided direct communication between Orleans and Brest, France, from 1897 to 1959, is restored to its original appearance and open to the public.

What to See and Do

Academy of Performing Arts. Theater presents comedies, drama, musicals, dance. Workshops for all ages. 120 Main St. Box office. Phone 508/255-1963.

French Cable Station Museum. Built in 1890 as American end of transatlantic cable from Brest, France. Original equipt for submarine cable communication on display. (July-Labor Day, Tues-Sat afternoons) MA 28 and Cove Rd. Phone 508/240-1735. ¢¢

Nauset Beach. One of the most spectacular ocean beaches on the Atlantic Coast is now within the boundaries of Cape Cod National Seashore (see). Swimming, surfing, fishing; lifeguards. Parking fee. About 3 mi E of US 6 on marked roads. Phone 508/255-1386.

Motels/Motor Lodges

★★ **THE COVE.** *13 State Rte 28, Orleans (02653). 508/255-1203; fax 508/255-7736; toll-free 800/343-2233. www.thecoveorleans.com.* 47 rms, 1-2 story. July-Aug: S, D $99-$179 (2-day min); each addl $10; kit. units $159-$179; lower rates rest of yr. Crib $10. TV; cable (premium), VCR. Heated pool. Coffee in rms. Restaurant nearby. Ck-out 11 am. Meeting rm. Business center. Lawn games. Refrigerators, microwaves. Picnic tables, grill. Sun deck. On town cove. Float boat rides avail. Cr cds: A, MC, V.

⚓ 🐾 🔥 🏃

★ **NAUSET KNOLL MOTOR LODGE.** *237 Beach Rd, East Orleans (02643). 508/255-3348; fax 508/247-9184. www.capecodtravel.com.* 12 rms. No rm phones. Mid-June-early Sept: S, D $140-$160; each addl $14; under 6 free; lower rates mid-Apr-mid-June, early Sept-late Oct. Closed rest of yr. Crib free. TV; cable. Ck-out 11 am. Picnic tables. Overlooks ocean, beach. Cr cds: MC, V.

D 🔥

★★ **OLDE TAVERN MOTEL AND INN.** *151 MA 6A, Orleans (02653). 508/255-1565; toll-free 800/544-7705. www.capecodtravel.com/oldetavern.* 29 rms. Late June-early Sept: S $80-$105; D $59-$110; each addl $9; lower rates Apr-late June, early Sept-Nov. Closed rest of yr. Crib free. TV; cable (premium). Heated pool. Complimentary continental bkfst. Restaurant nearby. Ck-out 11 am. Refrigerators. 18 deck rms. Main building is restored inn and tavern visited by Thoreau in 1849, Daniel Webster and other personalities of the day. Cr cds: A, DS, MC, V.

⚓ 🐾 🔥

★ **RIDGEWOOD MOTEL AND COTTAGES.** *10 Quanset Rd, South Orleans (02662). 508/255-0473. www.ridgewoodmotel.com.* 12 units, some A/C, 6 cottages. No rm phones. Late June-Labor Day: S, D $69-$80; cottages $500-$610/wk; lower rates rest of yr. Crib $10. TV. Pool. Playground. Complimentary continental bkfst. Ck-out 10 am. Lawn games. Many refrigerators. Picnic tables, grills. Totally nonsmoking. Cr cds: MC, V.

⚓ 🐾 🔥

★★ **SEASHORE PARK MOTOR INN.** *24 Canal Rd, Orleans (02653). 508/255-2500; fax 508/255-9400; toll-free 800/772-6453. www.seashoreparkinn.com.* 62 rms, 2 story, 24 kits. Late-June-early Sept: S, D $99-$119; each addl $10; under 13 free; kit. units $109-$129; lower rates mid-Apr-late-June, early Sept-Oct. Closed rest of yr. TV; cable. 2 pools, 1 indoor; whirlpool, sauna. Complimentary continental bkfst. Restaurant adj 7 am-midnight. Ck-out 11 am. Business servs avail. Microwaves avail. Private patios, balconies. Sun deck. Totally nonsmoking. Cr cds: A, DS, MC, V.

★★ **SKAKET BEACH MOTEL.** *203 Cranberry Hwy, Orleans (02653). 508/255-1020; fax 508/255-6487; toll-free 800/835-0298. www.skaketbeachmotel.com.* 46 rms, 1-2 story, 6 kits. 3rd wk June-early Sept: S $53-$91; D $58-$99; each addl $9; lower rates Apr-mid-June, mid-Sept-Nov. Closed rest of yr. Crib free. Pet accepted, some restrictions; $9 (off season). TV; cable (premium). Heated pool. Complimentary continental bkfst. Restaurant nearby. Ck-out 11 am. Coin lndry. Lawn games. Refrigerators; microwaves avail. Picnic tables, grills. Cr cds: A, D, DS, MC, V.

B&Bs/Small Inns

★★ **THE PARSONAGE INN.** *202 Main St, East Orleans (02643). 508/255-8217; fax 508/255-8216; toll-free 888/422-8217. www.parsonageinn.com.* 8 rms, 2 story, 1 kit. unit. No rm phones. June-Labor Day: S, D $95-$135; each addl $10; kit. unit $125; lower rates rest of yr. Children over 6 yrs only. Some TV; cable. Complimentary full bkfst. Restaurants nearby. Ck-out 11 am, ck-in 2 pm. Antiques. Library/sitting rm. Originally a parsonage (1770) and cobbler's shop. Totally nonsmoking. Cr cds: A, MC, V.

★★ **SHIPS KNEES INN.** *186 Beach Rd, East Orleans (02643). 508/255-1312; fax 508/240-1351. www.capecodtravel.com/shipskneesinn.* 19 air-cooled rms, 8 with bath, 2 story, 1 suites. No rm phones. July-Aug: D $65-$120; each addl $20; suites $110; lower rates rest of yr. Children over 12 yrs only. TV in some rms and in sitting rm; cable. Pool. Complimentary continental bkfst. Ck-out 10:30 am, ck-in 1 pm. Tennis. Picnic tables, grills. Restored sea captain's house (ca 1820); near ocean, beach. Rms individually decorated in nautical style; many antiques, some 4-poster beds. Some rms with ocean view. Totally nonsmoking. Cr cds: MC, V.

Restaurants

★★ **BARLEY NECK INN.** *5 Beach Rd, East Orleans (02653). 508/255-0212. www.barleyneck.com.* Continental menu. Specialties: trio salmon medallions, local swordfish steak, braised lamb shank. Hrs: 5-10 pm. Res accepted. Dinner $12-$20. Pianist. Four separate dining rms, both formal and informal; fireplaces, artwork. Cr cds: A, MC, V.

★★★ **CAPTAIN LINNELL HOUSE.** *137 Skaket Beach Rd, Orleans (02653). 508/255-3400. www.linnell.com.* Specializes in local seafood, rack of lamb. Own baking. Hrs: from 5 pm. Res accepted. Dinner $16.50-$26. Child's menu. Parking. Outdoor dining. Sea captain's 1840s mansion; oil paintings; gardens. Totally nonsmoking. Cr cds: A, MC, V.

★ **DOUBLE DRAGON INN.** *MA 6A & MA 28, Orleans (02653). 508/255-4100.* Chinese, Polynesian menu. Specializes in Hunan and Cantonese cooking. Hrs: 11:30-2 am. Closed Thanksgiving. Serv bar. A la carte entrees: lunch $3.50-$5.95, dinner $4.25-$12.95. Parking. Chinese decor. Cr cds: A, D, DS, MC, V.

★ **LOBSTER CLAW.** *MA 6A, Orleans (02653). 508/255-1800. www.capecod.com/lobclaw.* Specializes in seafood, lobster, steak. Hrs: 11:30 am-9 pm; early-bird dinner 4-5:30 pm. Closed mid-Nov-Mar. No A/C. Bar. Lunch, dinner $4.95-$22.95. Child's menu. Parking. Nautical decor. Former cranberry packing factory. Family-owned. Cr cds: A, C, D, DS, ER, MC, V.

★★ **NAUSET BEACH CLUB.** *222 E Main St, East Orleans (02643). 508/255-8547.* Regional Italian menu. Specializes in soups, salads. Own pasta. Hrs: 5:30-9 pm. Closed Sun, Mon off-season. Bar. Dinner $12-$19. Paper tablecloths invite guests to draw; crayons provided. Totally nonsmoking. Cr cds: A, MC, V.

★★ **OLD JAILHOUSE TAVERN.** *28 West Rd, Orleans (02653). 508/255-5245.* Specialties: prime rib, veal Orleans, seafood. Hrs: 11:30 am-midnight; Sun brunch 11 am-2:30 pm. Closed Thanksgiving, Dec 25. Bar to 1 am. Lunch $5.25-$10.95, dinner $12.95-$19.75. Parking. Part of old jailhouse. Cr cds: A, DS, ER, MC, V.

Pittsfield

See also Berkshire Hills, Lenox, Stockbridge and West Stockbridge

Settled 1743 **Pop** 48,622 **Elev** 1,039 ft **Area code** 413 **Zip** 01201

Information Berkshire Visitors Bureau, Berkshire Common; 413/443-9186 or 800/237-5747

Web www.berkshires.org

Beautifully situated in the Berkshire Hills vacation area, this is also an old and important manufacturing center. It is the home of the Berkshire Life Insurance Company (chartered 1851) and of industries that make machinery, plastics, gauges, and paper products.

What to See and Do

Arrowhead. (1780) Herman Melville wrote *Moby Dick* while living here from 1850 to 1863; historical exhibits, furniture, costumes; gardens. Video presentation. Gift shop. Headquarters of Berkshire County Historical Society. (Memorial Day wkend-Oct, Daily) 780 Holmes Rd. Phone 413/442-1793. ¢¢

Berkshire Museum. Museum of art, natural science, and history, featuring American 19th- and 20th-century paintings; works by British, European masters; artifacts from ancient civilizations; exhibits on Berkshire County history; aquarium; changing exhibits; films, lectures, children's programs. (July-Aug, daily; rest of yr, Tues-Sun; closed hols) 39 South St (US 7). Phone 413/443-7171. ¢¢

Canoe Meadows Wildlife Sanctuary. Two hundred sixty-two acres with three mi of trails, woods, open fields, ponds; bordering the Housatonic River. (Tues-Sun) Holmes Rd. Phone 413/637-0320. ¢¢

Hancock Shaker Village. An original Shaker site (1790-1960); now a living history museum of Shaker life, crafts, and farming. Large collection of Shaker furniture and artifacts in 20 restored buildings, including the Round Stone Barn, set on 1,200 scenic acres in the Berkshires. Exhibits; seasonal craft demonstrations, Discovery Room activities, cafe (seasonal); farm animals, heirloom herb and vegetable gardens; museum shop; picnicking. 5 mi W on US 20, at jct MA 41. Phone 413/443-0188. ¢¢¢¢

Ski Areas.

Bousquet. Two double chairlifts, three rope tows; snowmaking, patrol, school, rentals; cafeteria, bar, daycare. Longest run one mi; vertical drop 750 ft. Night skiing. (Dec-Mar, daily) 2 mi S on US 7, then 1 mi W, on Dan Fox Dr. Phone 413/442-8316. ¢¢¢¢

Brodie Mountain. Four double chairlifts, two rope tows; patrol, school, rentals, snowmaking; bar, cafeteria, restaurant; nursery. (Nov-Mar, daily) X-country trails with rentals and instruction. Half-day rates. Tennis, racquetball, winter camping. 10 mi N on US 7 in New Ashford. Phone 413/443-4752.

Jiminy Peak. One six-passanger, three double chairlifts, J-bar, two quads, three triples; patrol, school, rentals, restaurant, two cafeterias, bar, lodge. Longest run two mi; vertical drop 1,140 ft. (Thanksgiving-Apr 1, daily) Night skiing. Half-day rates. Also trout fishing; 18-hole miniature golf; Alpine slide and tennis center (Memorial Day-Labor Day); fee for activities. 9 mi N, then W, between US 7 and MA 43 at 37 Corey Rd in Hancock. Phone 413/738-5500. ¢¢¢¢

Special Event

South Mountain Concerts. South St. 2 mi S on US 7, 20. Chamber music concerts. Sun, Sept-Oct. Phone 413/442-2106.

Motels/Motor Lodges

★ **ECONO LODGE SPRING'S INN.** *US 7, New Ashford (01237). 413/458-5945; fax 413/458-4351; toll-free 800/ 277-0001. www.econolodge.com.* 40 rms, 1-2 story. July-Oct: S $51-$100; D $61-$113; each addl $10; under 12 free; lower rates rest of yr. Crib $10. TV; cable, VCR avail (movies). Heated pool. Complimentary coffee in rms. Restaurant 7 am-10 pm. Rm serv. Bar from 11:30 am; entertainment Sat. Ck-out 11:30 am. Meeting rms. Sundries. Tennis. Downhill/ x-country ski opp. Game rm. Refrigerators avail. Some patios, balconies. Cr cds: A, DS, MC, V.
[D] [symbols]

★ **TRAVELODGE.** *16 Cheshire Rd (01201). 413/443-5661; fax 413/443-5866; toll-free 800/578-7878.* 47 rms, 2 story. July-mid-Oct: S $65-$105; D $81-$120; each addl $6; under 17 free; lower rates rest of yr. Crib free. TV; cable. Complimentary coffee in rms. Restaurant opp 6 am-10 pm. Ck-out 11 am. Coin lndry. Meeting rm. Business servs avail. Downhill ski 5 mi; x-country ski 12 mi. Refrigerators. Picnic table. Cr cds: A, D, DS, MC, V.
[symbols] [SC] [symbol]

Hotel

★★★ **CROWNE PLAZA.** *1 West St (01201). 413/499-2000; fax 413/442-0449; toll-free 800/227-6963.* 179 rms, 12 story. July-mid-Oct: S, D $120-$210; each addl $15; suites $295-$449; under 18 free; wkend rates; package plans; lower rates rest of yr. Crib free. TV; cable (premium). Indoor pool; whirlpool. Coffee in rms. Restaurant 6 am-11 pm. Bar 11:30-1 am. Ck-out noon. Meeting rms. Business servs avail. Beauty shop. Free covered parking. Shopping arcade. Exercise equipt; sauna. Health club privileges. Some refrigerators. Cr cds: A, C, D, DS, MC, V.
[symbols] [SC]

Resort

★★ **JIMINY PEAK MOUNTAIN RESORT.** *Corey Rd, Hancock (01237). 413/738-5500; fax 413/738-5513. www.jiminypeak.com.* 96 one-bedrm kit. suites, 3 story. S, D $99-$239; each addl $15; condos $275-$325; under 13 free; ski packages; wkly, monthly rates. Crib $5. TV; cable, VCR avail (movies $3). 2 pools, heated; whirlpool. Supervised children's activities (Dec-Mar). Dining rm 7:30 am-9 pm. Snack bar. Bar; entertainment wkends (seasonal). Ck-out 10:30 am, ck-in 4 pm. Coin lndry. Grocery 4 mi. Package store 5 mi. Meeting rms. Business servs avail. Sundries. Valet serv. Tennis courts. Downhill ski on site. Hiking. Game rm. Exercise equipt; sauna. Alpine slide. Cr cds: A, C, D, DS, MC, V.
[symbols]

Restaurant

★★ **DAKOTA.** *1035 South St (01201). 413/499-7900. www.dakotarestaurant.com.* Specializes in seafood, hand-cut aged prime beef. Salad bar. Hrs: 5-10 pm; Fri to 11 pm; Sat 4-11 pm; Sun 10 am-2 pm (brunch), 4-10 pm; early-bird dinner Mon-Fri 5-6 pm, Sat and Sun 4-5 pm. Closed Thanksgiving, Dec 25. Res accepted. Bar. Dinner $8.95-$19.95. Sun brunch $14.95. Child's menu. Rustic decor; Native Amer artifacts, mounted animals. Cr cds: A, DS, MC, V.
[D]

Plymouth

Settled 1620 **Pop** 51,701 **Elev** 50 ft **Area code** 508
Zip 02360
Information Destination Plymouth, 170 Water St, Suite 10C;
508/747-7525 or 800/872-1620
Web www.visit-plymouth.com

On December 21, 1620, 102 men, women, and children
arrived on the *Mayflower* to found the first permanent
European settlement north of Virginia. Although plagued
by exposure, cold, hunger, and disease during the terrible
first winter, the colony was firmly established by the next
year. Plymouth Rock lies under an imposing granite colonnade, marking the traditional place of landing.

Plymouth now combines a summer resort, beaches, a
harbor full of pleasure craft, an active fishing town, and
a remarkable series of restorations of the original town.

What to See and Do

Burial Hill. Governor Bradford is buried here. Just W of
Town Square.

Cole's Hill. Here Pilgrims who died during the first winter
were secretly buried. Across the street from Plymouth Rock.

Cranberry World. Visitor Center with exhibits of the history and cultivation of the cranberry. Half-hour self-guided
tours. 7 Eda Ave. Phone 508/866-8190. ¢¢¢¢

Harlow Old Fort House. (1677) Pilgrim household crafts;
spinning, weaving, and candle-dipping demonstrations;
herb garden. (July-Oct, Wed-Sat) 119 Sandwich St. Phone
508/746-9497. ¢¢

Hedge House. (1809) Period furnishings, special exhibits.
(June-Oct, Wed-Sat) 126 Water St, opp Town Wharf.
Phone 508/746-0012. ¢¢

Howland House. (1666) Restored Pilgrim house has
17th- and 18th-century furnishings. (Memorial Day-mid-
Oct, Mon-Sat, also Sun afternoons and Thanksgiving)
33 Sandwich St. Phone 508/746-9590. ¢¢

Mayflower Society House Museum. National headquarters of the General Society of Mayflower Descendants. House
built in 1754; nine rms with 17th- and 18th-century furnishings. Formal garden. (July-Labor Day, daily; Memorial
Day wkend-June and early Sept-Oct, Fri-Sun) 4 Winslow St,
off North St. Phone 508/746-2590. ¢¢

Myles Standish State Forest. Approx 15,000 acres.
Swimming, bathhouse, fishing; boating; hiking and
bicycle trails, riding, hunting, winter sports, picnicking
(fee), camping (fee; dump station). S on MA 3, exit 5,
Long Pond. Phone 508/866-2526.

National Monument to the Forefathers. Built between 1859
and 1889 (at a cost of $155,000) to depict the virtues of the
Pilgrims. At 81 ft, it is the tallest solid granite monument
in the US. (May-Oct, daily) Allerton St. Phone 508/746-
1790. **FREE**

Pilgrim Hall Museum. (1824) Decorative arts and possessions
of first Pilgrims and their descendants; includes furniture,
household items, ceramics; only known portrait of a
Mayflower passenger. (Daily; closed Jan, Dec 25) 75 Court
St, on MA 3A. Phone 508/746-1620. ¢¢

✪ **Plymouth Plantation.** Living history museum re-creates
day-to-day life in 17th-century Plymouth. All exhibits
(Apr-Nov, daily). 3 mi S on MA 3A. Phone 508/746-1622.
¢¢¢¢ On the plantation are

1627 Pilgrim Village. Fort-Meetinghouse and 14 houses.
Costumed people portray actual residents of Plymouth
and re-create life in an early farming community.

Hobbamock's (Wampanoag) Homesite. A large bark-
covered house representing Hobbamock's dwelling, as
well as specially crafted tools and artifacts, depict the
domestic environment of the Wampanoag culture. Staff
members explain this rich heritage from a modern-day
perspective.

Mayflower II. This 106-ft bark, a full-size reproduction
of the type of ship that carried the Pilgrims, was built in
England and sailed to America in 1957. Costumed men
and women portray crew and passengers who made the
1620 voyage. At State Pier, on Water St.

Visitor Center. Provides visitors with introduction to this
unique museum. Orientation program includes 12-min
multi-image screen presentation. Exhibits; educational
services; museum shop; restaurants, picnic area.

Plymouth Colony Winery. Working cranberry bogs. Wine
tasting. Watch cranberry harvest activities in fall. Winery
(Apr-late Dec, daily; Mar, Fri-Sun; also hols). US 44 W, left
on Pinewood Rd. Phone 508/747-3334. **FREE**

Plymouth Harbor Cruises. One-hr cruises of historic harbor
aboard *Pilgrim Belle,* a Mississippi-style paddlewheeler.
(Mid-May-Mid-Oct, daily) Departs from State Pier. Phone
508/747-2400. ¢¢

Plymouth National Wax Museum. Pilgrim story told
through narrations and animation; includes 26 life-size
scenes and more than 180 figures. (Mar-Nov, daily)
16 Carver St. Phone 508/746-6468. ¢¢

Plymouth Rock. Water St, on the harbor. Phone 508/866-
2580.

Provincetown Ferry. Round-trip passenger ferry departs
State Pier in the morning, returns in evening. (Mid-June-
Labor Day, daily; May-Mid-June and after Labor Day-Oct,
wkends) Phone 508/747-2400. ¢¢¢¢

Richard Sparrow House. (1640) Plymouth's oldest restored
home; craft gallery, pottery made on premises. (Memorial
Day wkend-Thanksgiving, Mon, Tues, Thurs-Sun; gallery
open through late Dec) 42 Summer St. Phone 508/747-
1240. ¢

Site of First Houses. Marked by tablets. On Leyden St, off
Water St.

Splashdown Amphibious Tours. One-hr tours of historic
Plymouth; half on land, half on water. Hrly departures
from Harbor Place and Village Landing. (Mid-Apr-late Oct,
daily) Phone 508/747-7658. ¢¢¢¢

Spooner House. (1747) Occupied by Spooner family
for five generations and furnished with their heirlooms.
Collections of Asian export wares, period furniture. (June-
Oct, Wed-Sat) 27 North St. Phone 508/746-0012. ¢¢

Supersports Family Fun Park. Rides, games, sports, mini-
golf, bumper boats. (Daily; call for off-season hours; closed
Dec 25) W of Plymoth historical area, 108 N Main St, jct
MA 58 and 44, in Carver. Phone 508/866-9655. ¢¢¢¢

Swimming. Six public beaches.

Village Landing Marketplace. Modeled after colonial market-place; contains a restaurant and specialty shops. Overlooks historic Plymouth Harbor. 170 Water St, near jct US 44 and MA 3A.

Whale watching. Four-hr trip to Stellwagen Bank to view world's largest mammals. (Early May-mid-Oct, daily; early Apr-early May and mid-Oct-early Nov, wkends) Phone 508/746-2643. ¢¢¢¢

Special Events

Destination Plymouth Sprint Triathlon. Myles Standish State Forest (see). National Championship qualifier includes ½-mi swim, 12-mi bike ride, and four-mi run. 800/USA-1620. July. Phone 508/866-2526.

Pilgrim's Progress. A reenactment of Pilgrims going to church, from Cole's Hill to Burial Hill. Each Fri in Aug; also Thanksgiving. Phone 800/USA-1620.

Autumnal Feasting. Plimoth Plantation's 1627 Pilgrim Village. A harvest celebration with Dutch colonists from Fort Amsterdam re-creating a 17th-century event. Activities, feasting, games. Phone 508/742-1622. Columbus Day wkend. Phone 800/USA-1620.

America's Hometown Thanksgiving Celebration. Programs for various events may be obtained by contacting Destination Plymouth. Phone 508/747-7525 or 800/USA-1620. Nov (Throughout Thanksgiving wkend).

Motels/Motor Lodges

★ **BLUE SPRUCE MOTEL & TOWNHOUSES.** *710 State Rd, Rte 3A (02360). 508/224-3990; fax 508/224-2279; toll-free 800/370-7080. www.bluespruce-motel.com.* 28 rms, 4 townhouses. May-Nov: S, D $70-$94; each addl $6; townhouses $165-$207; lower rates rest of yr. Crib free. TV. Pool. Restaurant nearby. Ck-out 11 am. Business servs avail. In-rm modem link. Lawn games. Refrigerators. Cr cds: A, MC, V.

🅳 ⛽ 🏊 🐾 SC

★ **COLD SPRING MOTEL.** *188 Court St (02360). 508/746-2222; fax 508/746-2744; toll-free 800/678-8667. www.coldspringmotel.com.* 60 rms. Apr-Dec: S, D $79-$199; each addl $5. Closed rest of yr. Crib $5. TV; cable (premium). Complimentary continental bkfst (in season). Restaurant nearby. Ck-out 11 am. Business servs avail. Cr cds: A, MC, V.

🐾

★ **GOVERNOR BRADFORD ON THE HARBOUR.** *98 Water St (02360). 508/746-6200; fax 508/747-3032; toll-free 800/332-1620. www.governorbradford.com.* 94 rms, 3 story. July-Oct: S, D $89-$138; each addl $10; under 16 free; lower rates rest of yr. Crib free. TV; cable (premium), VCR avail (movies). Heated pool. Complimentary coffee in rms. Restaurant adj 11:30 am-11:30 pm. Ck-out 11 am. Refrigerators. On waterfront. Cr cds: A, D, DS, MC, V.

🏊 🏝 🐾

★★ **PILGRIM SANDS.** *150 Warren Ave, Rte 3-A (02360). 508/747-0900; fax 508/746-8066; toll-free 800/729-7263. www.pilgrimsands.com.* 64 rms, 2 story. Mid-June-Labor Day: S, D $128-$160; each addl $8; lower rates rest of yr. Crib free. TV; cable (premium). 2 pools, 1 indoor; whirlpool. Continental bkfst. Ck-out 11 am. Many refrigerators. Private beach. Cr cds: A, C, D, DS, ER, JCB, MC, V.

🅳 🏊 🏝 🐾

Hotel

★★★ **SHERATON INN.** *180 Water St (02360). 508/747-4900; fax 508/746-2609; res 800/325-3535. www.sheraton plymouth.com.* 175 rms, 4 story. June-Oct: S, D $115-$195; each addl $15; suites $230; under 18 free; wkend rates; lower rates rest of yr. Crib free. TV; cable (premium), VCR avail. Indoor pool; poolside serv. Restaurant 6:30 am-2 pm, 5-10 pm. Bar; entertainment Fri-Sat. Ck-out 11 am. Meeting rms. Business servs avail. In-rm modem link. Exercise equipt. Some bathrm phones, balconies, rms with ocean view. Cr cds: A, C, D, DS, MC, V.

🅳 ⚓ 🏊 🏋 🏝 🐾 SC 🚶

B&Bs/Small Inns

★★ **JOHN CARVER INN.** *25 Summer St (02360). 508/746-7100; fax 508/746-8299; toll-free 800/274-1620. www.johncarverinn.com.* 79 rms, 3 story. Sept-Oct: S, D $130-$160; each addl $10; under 19 free; golf plan; MAP avail; package plans. Crib free. TV; cable. Pool. Restaurant (see also HEARTH AND KETTLE). Rm serv. Bar to midnight. Ck-out 11 am. Valet serv. Meeting rms. Business servs avail. Gift shop. Health club privileges. Cr cds: A, D, DS, MC, V.

🅳 🏊 🏝 🐾

★★ **THE MABBETT HOUSE.** *7 Cushman St (02360). 508/830-1911; fax 508/830-9775; toll-free 800/572-7829. www.mabbetthouse.comrte.* 3 rms, 2 story. No rm phones. S $90-$155; D $110-$139. Children over 12 yrs only. TV in lobby. Complimentary full bkfst. Restaurant nearby. Ck-out 11 am. Game rm. Colonial Revival house; artifacts collected from world travels. Totally nonsmoking. Cr cds: A, MC, V.

🏝 🐾

Restaurant

★ **HEARTH AND KETTLE.** *25 Summer St (02360). 508/746-7100. www.johncarverinn.com.* Specializes in fresh seafood. Hrs: Summer 7 am-10 pm; Winter 7-9 pm; early-bird dinner noon-6 pm. Closed Dec 25. Res accepted. Bar. Bkfst $3.99-$7.99, lunch $3.99-$10.99, dinner $9.99-$17.99. Child's menu. Servers dressed in Colonial attire. Cr cds: A, C, D, DS, ER, MC, V.

🅳 🍽

Provincetown (Cape Cod)

See also Cape Cod National Seashore

Settled ca 1700 **Pop** 3,431 **Elev** 40 ft **Area code** 508 **Zip** 02657
Information Chamber of Commerce, 307 Commercial St, PO Box 1017; 508/487-3424
Web www.capecodaccess.com/provincetownchamber

Provincetown is a startling mixture of heroic past and easygoing present. The Provincetown area may have been explored by Leif Ericson in AD 1004. It is certain that the *Mayflower* anchored first in Provincetown Harbor while the Mayflower Compact, setting up the colony's government, was signed aboard the ship. Provincetown was where the first party of Pilgrims came ashore. A bronze tablet at Commercial Street and Beach Highway marks the site of the Pilgrims' first landing. The city attracts many tourists who come each summer to explore the narrow streets and rows of picturesque old houses.

What to See and Do

Expedition Whydah's Sea Lab & Learning Center. Archaeological site of sunken pirate ship *Whydah,* struck by storms in 1717. Learn about recovery of the ship's pirate treasure, the lives and deaths of pirates, and the history of the ship and its passengers. (Apr-mid-Oct, daily; mid-Oct-Dec, wkends and school hols) 16 MacMillan Wharf. Phone 508/487-7955.

▣ Pilgrim Monument & Museum. A 252-ft granite tower commemorating the Pilgrims' 1620 landing in the New World; provides an excellent view. (Summer, daily) Phone 508/487-1310. ¢¢¢ Admission includes

Provincetown Museum. Exhibits include whaling equipt, scrimshaw, ship models, artifacts from shipwrecks; Pilgrim Room with scale model diorama of the merchant ship *Mayflower;* Donald MacMillan's Arctic exhibit; antique fire engine and firefighting equipment; theater history display. (Summer, daily) Phone 508/487-1310.

Provincetown Art Association & Museum. Changing exhibits; museum store. (Late May-Oct, daily; rest of yr, wkends) 460 Commercial St. Phone 508/487-1750.
Donation

Recreation. Swimming at surrounding beaches, including town beach, W of the village, Herring Cove and Race Point, on the ocean side. Tennis, cruises, beach buggy tours, and fishing avail.

Town Wharf (MacMillan Wharf). Off Commercial St at Standish St. Center of maritime activity. Also here is

Portuguese Princess Whale Watch. 100-ft boats offer 3½-hr narrated whale watching excursions. Naturalist aboard. (Apr-Oct, daily) Phone 508/487-2651.

Whale Watching. Offers 3½-4-hr trips (Mid-Apr-Oct, daily). Research scientists from the Provincetown Center for Coastal Studies are aboard each trip to lecture on the history of the whales being viewed. Dolphin Fleet of Provincetown. Phone 508/349-1900. ¢¢¢¢

Special Event

Portuguese Festival. Parades, concerts; dance, ethnic food court, children's games; fireworks. Culminates with blessing of the fleet (Sun). Last wk June. Phone 508/487-3424.

Motels/Motor Lodges

★★ BEST WESTERN CHATEAU MOTOR INN. *105 Bradford St W, Provincetown (02657). 508/487-1286; fax 508/487-3557; res 800/780-7234. www.bwprovincetown.com.* 54 rms, 1-2 story. Late June-Labor Day: S, D $89-$169; each addl $20; under 18 free; higher rates hols; lower rates May-late June, after Labor Day-Oct. Closed rest of yr. Crib $5. TV; cable (premium). Heated pool. Complimentary continental bkfst. Restaurant nearby. Ck-out 11 am. Business servs avail. In-rm modem link. Some refrigerators, balconies. Harbor view. Cr cds: A, C, D, DS, MC, V.
🏊 ◪ 🔥

★★ BLUE SEA MOTOR INN. *696 Shore Rd, Provincetown (02657). 508/487-1041; toll-free 888/768-7666. www.blueseamotorinn.com.* 43 rms, 1-2 story. July-Aug: S, D $117-$167; each addl $10; kit. units $830-$1,400/wk; lower rates Sept-Oct, May-June. Closed rest of yr. Crib $10. TV. Indoor pool; whirlpool. Coffee in lobby. Ck-out 10 am. Coin lndry. In-rm modem link. Refrigerators. Balconies. Picnic tables, grills. On ocean; swimming beach. Cr cds: MC, V.
🏊 ◪ 🔥

Resorts

★★ BEST WESTERN TIDES BEACHFRONT. *837 Commercial St, Provincetown (02657). 508/487-1045; fax 508/487-3557; res 800/780-7234. www.bwprovincetown.com.* 64 rms, 1-2 story. Mid-June-early Sept: S, D $89-$199; suites $199-$249; lower rates mid-May-mid-June, early Sept-mid-Oct. Closed rest of yr. TV; cable (premium). Heated pool. Restaurant 7 am-3 pm. Ck-out 11 am. Coin lndry. Business servs avail. In-rm modem link. Some refrigerators, balconies. On private beach. Cr cds: A, C, D, DS, MC, V.
🏊 ◪ 🔥

★★ THE MASTHEAD RESORT. *31-41 Commercial St, Provincetown (02657). 508/487-0523; fax 508/481-9251; toll-free 800/395-5095. www.capecodtravel.com/masthead.* 10 rms, 2 share bath, 4 cottages, 7 apts, 2 story. July-Labor Day, motel rms: S $63-$86; D $86-$165; each addl $20; apts $893/wk; kit. cottages (1-wk min) $1,200-$1,850/wk; under 12 free (limit 2); lower rates rest of yr. Crib free. TV; cable, VCRs in cottages. Restaurant nearby. Ck-out 11 am; cottages 10 am. Refrigerators; microwaves. 450-ft sun deck on water. Picnic tables; grills. On private beach. In-shore and deepwater moorings; launch serv. Cr cds: A, C, D, DS, ER, JCB, MC, V.
Ⅾ ◪ 🔥

★★ PROVINCETOWN INN. *1 Commericial St, Provincetown (02657). 508/487-9500; fax 508/487-2911; toll-free 800/942-5388. www.provincetowninn.com.* 100 rms, 1-2 story. July-Aug: S, D $64-$139; each addl $12.50; under 14 free; wkly rates; whale package plans; higher rates hols; lower rates rest of yr. TV; cable. Heated pool. Complimentary continental bkfst. Restaurant 6-9 pm.

Bar 4 pm-midnight. Ck-out 11 am. Meeting rms. Business servs avail. Sundries. Gift shop. Picnic tables. Ocean view. Private beach. Cr cds: A, MC, V.

B&Bs/Small Inns

★★ **FAIRBANKS INN.** *90 Bradford St, Provincetown (02657). 508/487-0386; fax 508/487-3540; toll-free 800/324-7265. www.fairbanksinn.com.* 14 rms, 11 with bath, 2 story. No rm phones. July-Aug: S, D $89-$175; higher rates hols; lower rates rest of yr. Children over 15 yrs only. TV; cable (premium). Complimentary continental bkfst. Restaurant nearby. Ck-out 11 am, ck-in 2 pm. Concierge. Balconies. Picnic tables, grills. Antiques. Built 1776; courtyard. Totally nonsmoking. Cr cds: A, MC, V.

★★★ **SNUG COTTAGE.** *178 Bradford St, Provincetown (02657). 508/487-1616; fax 508/487-5123.* 8 rms, 5 A/C, 1-2 story, 4 cottages, 5 townhouses. July: S, D $116-$138; each addl $20; cottages $115-$165; townhouses $135-$185; lower rates rest of yr. TV; cable, VCR (free movies). Complimentary full bkfst. Restaurant nearby. Ck-out 11 am, ck-in 3 pm. Fireplaces; microwaves avail. Built 1820. Cr cds: A, MC, V.

★★ **SOMERSET HOUSE.** *378 Commercial St, Provincetown (02657). 508/487-0383; fax 508/487-4746; toll-free 800/575-1850. www.somersethouseinn.com.* 13 rms, 10 with bath, 2-3 story. No A/C. Mid-June-Mid-Sept: S, D $75-$130; each addl $20; wkly rates; lower rates rest of yr. TV; cable. Complimentary continental bkfst. Restaurant nearby. Ck-out 11 am, ck-in 3 pm. Refrigerators. Opp beach. Restored 1850s house. Totally nonsmoking. Cr cds: MC, V.

★★ **WATERSHIP INN.** *7 Winthrop St, Provincetown (02657). 508/487-0094; res 800/330-9413. www.capecod.net/watershipinn.* 15 rms, 3 story. Some A/C. No rm phones. Mid-June-mid-Sept: S $44-$90; D $55-$120; each addl $20; 2-bedrm condo $1,210/wk; wkly rates. TV. Complimentary continental bkfst. Restaurant nearby. Ck-out 11:30 am, ck-in 2 pm. Lawn games. Picnic tables, grills. Antiques. Library/sitting rm. Built 1820. Cr cds: A, DS, MC, V.

★★ **WHITE WIND INN.** *174 Commercial St, Provincetown (02657). 508/487-1526; fax 508/487-4792. www.white windinn.com.* 12 rms, 8 with shower only, 3 story. No elvtr. No rm phones. Late May-mid-Sept: S, D $115-$190; wkend, wkly rates; wkends, hols (2-day min); higher rates hols; lower rates rest of yr. Pet accepted. TV; cable, VCR avail (movies). Complimentary continental bkfst. Restaurant nearby. Ck-out 11 am, ck-in 2 pm. Luggage handling. Concierge serv. Refrigerators; some fireplaces, balconies. Picnic tables. Opp harbor. Built in 1845; former shipbuilder's home. Totally nonsmoking. Cr cds: DS, MC, V.

All Suite

★★ **WATERMARK INN.** *603 Commercial St, Provincetown (02657). 508/487-0165; fax 508/487-2383. www.watermark-inn.com.* 10 suites, 2 story. S, D $120-$240; July-Aug: suites $135-$290 (1-wk min); each addl $10-$20; wkly rates; lower rates rest of yr. TV; cable. Restaurant nearby. Ck-out 11 am, ck-in 3 pm. Business servs avail. In-rm modem link. Microwaves. Private patios, balconies. On beach. Cr cds: A, MC, V.

Restaurants

★★ **CAFE EDWIGE.** *333 Commercial St, Provincetown (02657). 508/487-2008.* Specialties: stir-fry tofu, crab cakes, native Littleneck clams. Hrs: 8 am-1 pm, 6-11 pm. Closed Oct 31; also late May. Res accepted (dinner). No A/C. Serv bar. Bkfst $5-$10, dinner $10-$20. Street parking. Outdoor dining. Cathedral ceilings, skylights. Totally nonsmoking. Cr cds: A, MC, V.

★★ **DANCING LOBSTER CAFE.** *373 Commercial St, Provincetown (02657). 508/487-0900.* Mediterranean menu. Specialties: Venetian fish soup, crab ravioli, Provençal seafood stew. Hrs: 6-11 pm. Closed Mon; also Dec-May. Res accepted. Bar to 1 am. A la carte entrees: dinner $9.95-$18.95. On beach; harbor views. Cr cds: MC, V.

★★ **FRONT STREET.** *230 Commercial St, Provincetown (02657). 508/487-9715. www.capecod.net/frontstreet.* Italian, continental menu. Specialties: rack of lamb, tea-smoked duck, chocolate oblivion purse. Own desserts. Hrs: 6-10:30 pm. Closed Jan-Apr. Res accepted. Bar to 1 am. Dinner $12-$21. Street parking. Local artwork displayed. Totally nonsmoking. Cr cds: A, DS, MC, V.

★★ **LOBSTER POT.** *321 Commercial St, Provincetown (02657). 508/487-0842. www.provincetown.com/lobsterpot.* Specialties: chowder, bouillabaisse, clambake. Hrs: 11:30 am-10 pm. Closed Jan. Bar to 1 am. Lunch $7-$12, dinner $10-$17. Lobster and chowder market on premises. Overlooks Cape Cod Bay. Cr cds: A, DS, MC, V.

★★ **NAPI'S.** *7 Freeman St, Provincetown (02657). 508/487-1145. www.provincetown.com.* Continental menu. Specialties: bouillabaisse, shrimp Santa Fe, banana decadence. Extensive vegetarian selections. Hrs: 5-10 pm; early-bird dinner 5-6 pm. Res accepted. Bar to 1 am. Dinner $12.95-$22.95. Child's menu. Parking. Gathering place of artists and craftsmen. Large collection of art in various media, including paintings, sculpture, stained glass, graphics, ceramics and crafts. Cr cds: A, C, D, DS, MC, V.

★ ★ ★ **RED INN RESTAURANT.** *15 Commercial St, Provincetown (02657).* 508/487-0050. Continental menu. Specializes in fresh, local seafood and meats. Own desserts. Hrs: 11 am-10 pm; Sun brunch 10 am-3 pm; Jan-May: wkends only. Closed Dec 25. Res accepted. Serv bar. Lunch $6.95-$19.95, dinner $19-$24.95. Sun brunch $9-$15. Parking. Three dining rms in restored Colonial building. Many antiques. View of Cape Cod Bay. Cr cds: A, MC, V.
D

★ ★ **SAL'S PLACE.** *99 Commercial St, Provincetown (02657).* 508/487-1279. www.salsplace.com. Southern Italian menu. Specialties: steak pizzaiola, grilled shrimp, mousse pie. Hrs: 6-10 pm. Closed Nov-Apr. Res accepted. Serv bar. A la carte entrees: dinner $10-$19. Child's menus. Outdoor dining. Southern Italian decor; ocean view. Cr cds: MC, V.
D

Quincy

See also Boston

Settled 1625 **Pop** 88,025 **Elev** 20 ft **Area code** 617

Information Tourism and Visitors Bureau, 1250 Hancock St, Suite 802 N, 02169; 888/232-6737

Boston's neighbor to the south, Quincy (QUIN-zee) was the home of the Adamses, a great American family whose fame dates from Colonial days. Family members include the second and sixth presidents—John Adams and his son, John Quincy Adams. John Hancock, first signer of the Declaration of Independence, was born here. George Bush, the 41st president, was born in nearby Milton.

Thomas Morton, an early settler, held May Day rites at Merrymount (a section of Quincy) in 1627 and was shipped back to England for selling firearms and "firewater" to the Native Americans.

What to See and Do

⭐ **Adams National Historic Park.** Administered by the National Park Service. Tickets to sites can be purchased here *only*. (Mid-Apr-mid-Nov, daily; rest of yr, Tues-Fri) Golden Eagle Passport accepted (see MAKING THE MOST OF YOUR TRIP). 1250 Hancock St. Phone 617/770-1175. Combination ticket ¢¢ Includes

The Adams National Historic Site. The house (1731), bought in 1787 by John Adams, was given as a national site by the Adams family in 1946. Original furnishings. 135 Adams St, off Furnace Brook Pkwy.

John Adams and John Quincy Adams Birthplaces. Two 17th-century saltbox houses. The elder Adams was born and raised at 133 Franklin St; his son was born in the other house. While living here, Abigail Adams wrote many of her famous letters to her husband, John Adams, when he was serving in the Continental Congress in Philadelphia and as an arbitrator for peace with Great Britain in Paris. Guided tours. 133 and 141 Franklin St.

Josiah Quincy House. (1770) Built on 1635 land grant, this fine Georgian house originally had a view across Quincy Bay to Boston Harbor; was surrounded by outbuildings and much agricultural land. Long the home of the Quincy family; furnished with family heirlooms and memorabilia. Period wall paneling, fireplaces surrounded by English tiles. Tours on the hr. (July-Aug, Sat and Sun afternoons) 20 Muirhead St. Phone 617/227-3956. ¢¢

Quincy Historical Society. Museum of regional history; library. (Mon-Sat) Adams Academy Building, 8 Adams St. Phone 617/773-1144. ¢

Quincy Homestead. Four generations of Quincys lived here, including Dorothy Quincy, wife of John Hancock. Two rms built in 1686, rest of house dates from the 18th century; period furnishings; herb garden. (May-Oct, Wed-Sun) 1010 Hancock St, at Butler Rd. Phone 617/472-5117. ¢¢

United First Parish Church. (1828) Only church in US where two presidents—John Adams and John Quincy Adams—and their wives are entombed. Tours (late Apr-mid-Nov, Mon-Sat and Sun afternoons). 1306 Hancock St, at Washington St. Phone 617/773-1290. ¢¢

Special Events

Summerfest. Concerts on the Green, Ruth Gordon Amphitheatre. (Wed, mid-June-Aug.) Phone 888/232-6737.

Quincy Bay Race Week. Sailing regatta, marine parades, fireworks. (July.) Phone 888/232-6737.

South Shore Christmas Festival. Includes parade with floats. (Sun after Thanksgiving.) Phone 888/232-6737.

Hotel

★ ★ ★ **MARRIOTT BOSTON QUINCY.** *1000 Marriott Dr (02169).* 617/472-1000; fax 617/472-7095. www.marriott.com. 457 rms, 9 story. S, D $250-$325; under 18 free. Crib avail. TV; cable (premium). Indoor pool; whirlpool. Restaurant 6:30 am-10 pm. Bar to midnight. Ck-out noon, ck-in 4 pm. Meeting rms. Business center. In-rm modem link. Concierge. Exercise equipt. Minibars; many refrigerators in suite. Cr cds: A, C, D, DS, ER, JCB, MC, V.

Rockport

Settled 1690 **Pop** 7,767 **Elev** 77 ft **Area code** 978 **Zip** 01966

Information Chamber of Commerce, PO Box 67M; 978/546-6575 or 888/726-3922

Web www.rockportusa.com

Rockport is a year-round artists' colony. A weather-beaten shanty on one of the wharves has been the subject of so many paintings that it is called "Motif No. 1."

Studios, galleries, summer places, estates, and cottages dot the shore of Cape Ann from Eastern Point southeast of Gloucester all the way to Annisquam.

What to See and Do

Old Castle. (1715) A fine example of early 18th-century architecture and exhibits. (July-August, daily; rest of yr, by appt) Granite and Curtis Sts, Pigeon Cove. Phone 978/546-9533. ¢¢

The Paper House. Newspapers were used in the construction of the house and furniture. (April-Oct) 52 Pigeon Hill St. Phone 978/546-2629. ¢

Rockport Art Association. Changing exhibits of paintings, sculpture, and graphics by 250 artist members. Special events include concerts (see SPECIAL EVENT), lectures, artist demonstrations. (Daily; closed Thanksgiving, Dec 25-Jan 1) 12 Main St. Phone 978/546-6604. **FREE**

Sandy Bay Historical Society & Museums. Early American and 19th-century rms and objects, exhibits on fishing, granite industry, the Atlantic cable, and a children's rm in 1832 home constructed of granite. (Mid June-mid Sept, daily; rest of yr, by appt) 40 King St, near railroad station. Phone 978/546-9533.

Sightseeing Tours and Boat Cruises. Contact the Chamber of Commerce for a list of companies offering sightseeing, fishing, and boat tours.

Special Event

Rockport Chamber Music Festival. Phone 978/546-7391. (Four wkends June or July.)

Motels/Motor Lodges

★ **CAPTAIN BOUNTY MOTOR INN.** *1 Beach St (01966). 978/546-9557. www.cape-ann.com.* 24 rms, 3 story, 9 kits. No A/C. No elvtr. Mid-June-Labor Day: S $102-$117; D $83-$110; each addl $10; suites $110; lower rates Apr-mid-June, after Labor Day-late Oct. Closed rest of yr. TV; cable. Restaurant nearby. Ck-out 11 am. Microwaves avail. On beach; lifeguard. Cr cds: DS, MC, V.
🔥

★ **EAGLE HOUSE MOTEL.** *8 Cleaves St (01966). 978/546-6292; fax 978/540-1136. www.eaglehousemotel.com.* 15 rms, 2 story, 2 kit. units. Mid-June-Labor Day: S, D $60-$105; each addl $7; kit. units $89; higher rates: Memorial Day, Columbus Day; lower rates May-mid-June, after Labor Day-mid-Oct. Closed rest of yr. TV; cable (premium). Restaurant adj 6:30 am-11 pm. Ck-out 11 am. Refrigerators. Some balconies. Picnic tables. Beach opp. Cr cds: A, DS, MC, V.
🔄 🔥

★ **MOTEL PEG LEG.** *10 Beach St (01966). 978/546-6945; fax 978/546-5157. www.marina.cove.com/users/pegleg.* 15 rms, 2 story. No A/C. Late June-Labor Day: S $125-$135; D $85-$145; each addl $10; under 6 free; wkends (2-day min); hols (3-day min); lower rates rest of yr. Closed Nov-mid-Apr. TV; cable (premium). Restaurant adj 7 am-9 pm. Ck-out 11 am. Opp swimming beach. Cr cds: DS, MC, V.
🔄 🔥

★★★ **SANDY BAY MOTOR INN.** *173 Main St (01966). 978/546-7155; fax 978/546-9131; toll-free 800/437-7155. www.sandybaymotorinn.com.* 80 rms, 2 story, 23 kits. Late June-Labor Day: S, D $98-$142; each addl $10; family rates; lower rates rest of yr. Crib free. Pet accepted, some restrictions; deposit. TV; cable (premium), VCR avail.

Indoor pool; whirlpool, sauna. Restaurant 7-11 am; wkends, hols to noon. Ck-out 11 am. Coin lndry. Meeting rms. Business servs avail. In-rm modem link. Free RR station transportation. Tennis. Putting green. Refrigerators avail. Cr cds: A, MC, V.
D 🔄 🚶 🏊 🔄 🔥 🔄

★★ **TURK'S HEAD MOTOR INN.** *151 South St (01966). 978/546-3436. www.turksheadinn.com.* 28 rms, 2 story. Mid-June-Labor Day: S $80-$95; D $85-$101; each addl $6; lower rates Apr-mid-June, after Labor Day-mid-Oct. Closed rest of yr. TV; cable. Indoor pool. Restaurant 6:30-11 am; Sun to noon. Ck-out 11 am. 2 beaches nearby. Cr cds: A, DS, MC, V.
🏊 🔄 🔥

B&Bs/Small Inns

★★★ **ADDISON CHOATE INN.** *49 Broadway (01966). 978/546-7543; fax 978/546-7638; res 800/245-7543. www.cape-ann.com/addison-choate.* 8 rms, 2 with shower only, 3 story, 3 suites; 1 guest house. Some A/C. No elvtr. No rm phones. Children over 11 yrs only. Late June-late Sept: S, D $95; suites $140. TV in common rm; cable, VCR avail (movies). Complimentary continental bkfst. Restaurant nearby. Ck-out 11 am, ck-in 3 pm. Business servs avail. Free RR station transportation. Pool. Built in 1851; antiques. Totally nonsmoking. Cr cds: MC, V.
🏊 🔥

★★★ **EMERSON INN BY THE SEA.** *1 Cathedral Ave, Rockport (Pigeon Cove) (01966). 978/546-6321; fax 978/546-7043; toll-free 800/964-5550. www.emersoninnbythesea.com.* 35 rms, 4 story. July-Labor Day: S $90-$135; D $100-$145; each addl $7; suites $100-$145; lower rates Apr, Nov. Closed rest of yr. Crib $7. TV in lounge. Sauna. Heated saltwater pool; whirlpool. Dining rm 8-11 am, 6-9 pm. Rm serv. Ck-out noon, ck-in after 1 pm. Coin lndry. Meeting rms. Business servs avail. In-rm modem link. Luggage handling. Free RR station transportation. Lawn games. Spa, massage. Sun deck. Older inn; Victorian decor. Many rms with ocean view. Cr cds: DS, MC, V.
D 🏊 🔥

★★ **THE INN ON COVE HILL.** *37 Mount Pleasant St (01966). 978/546-2701; fax 978/576-1095; toll-free 888/546-2701. www.cape-ann.com/covehill.* 11 rms, 9 with bath, 3 story. No rm phones. S, D $90-$123; each addl $25. Closed mid-Oct-mid-Apr. TV; cable. Complimentary continental bkfst. Restaurant nearby. Ck-out 11 am, ck-in 2 pm. Free RR station transportation. Built 1791 from proceeds of pirates' gold found nearby. Period furnishings; antiques. Near wharf, yacht club. Totally nonsmoking. Cr cds: DS, MC, V.
🔄 🔥

★★ **LINDEN TREE INN.** *26 King St (01966). 978/546-2494; fax 978/546-3297; toll-free 800/865-2122. www.lindentreeinn.com.* 18 rms, 2 with shower only, 3 story, 4 kit. units, 10 A/C. No rm phones. Mid-June-early Sept (2-day min): S $70; D $99-$109; each addl $15; kit. units $105; under 4 free; lower rates rest of yr. Closed 2 wks Jan. TV in some rms; cable, VCR avail (movies). Complimentary continental bkfst, coffee in rms. Restaurant nearby. Ck-out

11 am, ck-in 2 pm. Business servs avail. Microwaves avail. Some balconies. Picnic tables. Cr cds: MC, V.

★★ **PEGLEG RESTAURANT AND INN.** 2 King St (01966). 978/546-2352; toll-free 800/346-2352. www.pegleginn.com. 33 rms in 5 houses. Mid-June-Labor Day: S, D $85-$140; each addl $10; hol wkends (3-day min); lower rates Apr-mid-June, wkdays after Labor Day-Oct. Closed rest of yr. TV. Complimentary continental bkfst. Restaurant. Ck-out 11 am, ck-in 2 pm. 6 sun decks. Totally nonsmoking. Cr cds: A, MC, V.

★★ **ROCKY SHORES INN & COTTAGES.** 65 Eden Rd (01966). 978/546-2823; toll-free 800/348-4003. 11 rms, 1 A/C, 3 story. Mid-Apr-mid-Oct: D $84-$121; each addl $10. Closed rest of yr. TV; cable. Complimentary full bkfst. Ck-out 11 am, ck-in 3 pm. Antiques. Mansion built 1905. Overlooks ocean. Cr cds: A, MC, V.

★★★ **SEACREST MANOR.** 99 Marmion Way (01966). 978/546-2211. www.seacrestmanor.com. 8 rms, 6 with bath, 2 story. No A/C. May-Oct (2-day min): S $138-$148; D $148-$158; lower rates Apr, Nov; hol wkends (3-day min). Closed rest of yr. TV; cable. Complimentary full bkfst; afternoon refreshments. Dining rm (inn guests only) 7:30-9:30 am. Ck-out 11 am, ck-in after 2 pm. RR station transportation. Bicycles. Lawn games. Library, living rm. Garden. View of ocean. Totally nonsmoking. Cr cds: A, MC, V.

★ **SEAFARER INN.** 50 Marmion Way (01966). 978/546-6248; res 800/394-9394. www.seafarer-inn.com. 5 rms, 2 suites. No A/C. No rm phones. Mid-June-mid-Oct: D $75-$110; suites $160; kit. units $95; lower rates rest of yr. TV. Complimentary continental bkfst. Ck-out 11 am, ck-in 3 pm. On Gap Cove; all rms overlook ocean. 100-yr-old bldg. Totally nonsmoking. Cr cds: MC, V.

★★★ **SEAWARD INN & COTTAGES.** 44 Marmion Way (01966). 978/546-3471; fax 978/546-7661; toll-free 877/473-2927. www.seawardinn.com. 39 rms, 9 cottages. No A/C. Mid-May-Oct: D $119-$225; each addl $20; under 3 free. Crib free. TV. Natural spring-fed swimming pond. Complimentary full bkfst. Dining rm 8-10 am, 5-9 pm. Ck-out 11 am, ck-in 2 pm. Business servs avail. Luggage handling. Airport transportation. Free RR station transportation. Lawn games. Refrigerators, microwaves avail. Bird sanctuary. Vegetable and herb garden. On 5 acres. Ocean opp. Cr cds: A, D, DS, MC, V.

★★ **THE TUCK INN B&B.** 17 High St (01966). 978/546-7260; toll-free 800/789-7260. www.thetuckinn.com. 13 rms, 6 with shower only, 2 story, 1 suite, 1 apt, 1 studio apt. No rm phones. July-mid-Oct: S $59-$79, D $79-$99; suite $115; family, wkly rates; lower rates rest of yr. TV; cable. Pool. Complimentary continental bkfst. Restaurant nearby. Ck-out 11 am, ck-in 2-9 pm. Colonial house built in 1790; within walking distance to downtown, beach. Cr cds: MC, V.

★★★ **YANKEE CLIPPER INN.** 127 Granite St (01966). 978/546-3407; fax 978/546-9730; toll-free 800/545-3699. www.yankeeclipperinn.com. 16 rms in 3 bldgs, 2-3 story, 3-bedrm villa. Late May-late Oct: S, D $99-$269; each addl $25; MAP avail; lower rates late Oct-Dec, Mar-late May. Closed rest of yr. TV; cable, VCR avail (movies). Saltwater pool. Complimentary bkfst. Dining rm (see VERANDA AT THE YANKEE CLIPPER). Ck-out 11 am. Business servs avail. Airport, RR station transportation. Some in-rm whirlpools. Movies, slides. Rms vary; some antiques. Sun porches. Terraced gardens overlook ocean. Totally nonsmoking. Cr cds: A, DS, MC, V.

Restaurants

★ **BRACKETT'S OCEANIEW.** 25 Main St (01966). 978/546-2797. www.bracketts.com. Specializes in seafood. Hrs: 11:30 am-2:30 pm, 5-8:30 pm. Closed Nov-mid-Mar. Lunch $5.95-$12.95, dinner $9.95-$17.95. Informal family dining. Cr cds: A, C, D, DS, MC, V.

★★★ **VERANDA AT THE YANKEE CLIPPER.** 127 Granite St (01966). 978/546-7795. www.yankeeclipperinn.com. Regional Amer menu. Specialties: grilled salmon, garlic-roasted duck. Own baking, pasta. Hrs: 7:30-10:30 am, 5:30-9 pm. Closed Jan, Feb. Res required. Bkfst $8.50, dinner $12-$22. Enclosed porch overlooks ocean. Cr cds: A, D, DS, MC, V.

Salem

See also Beverly, Danvers, Lynn, Marblehead

Settled 1626 **Pop** 40,407 **Elev** 9 ft **Area code** 978 **Zip** 01970
Information Chamber of Commerce, 63 Wharf St; 978/744-0004
Web www.salem-chamber.org

In old Salem the story of early New England life is told with bricks, clapboards, carvings, and gravestones. The town had two native geniuses to immortalize it: Samuel McIntire (1757-1811), master builder, and Nathaniel Hawthorne (1804-64), author. History is charmingly entangled with the people and events of Hawthorne's novels. Reality, however, could be far from charming. During the witchcraft panic of 1692, 19 persons were hanged on Gallows Hill, another "pressed" to death; at least two others died in jail. Gallows Hill is still here; so is the house of one of the trial judges.

Early in the 18th century, Salem shipbuilding and allied industries were thriving. Salem was a major port. The Revolution turned commerce into privateering. Then began the fabulous China trade and Salem's heyday. The captains came home, and Sam McIntire built splendid houses for them that still stand. Shipping declined after 1812. Salem turned to industry, which, together with tourism, is the present-day economic base.

What to See and Do

Chestnut Street. Architecturally, one of the most beautiful streets in America; laid out in 1796.

⊠ House of Seven Gables. (1668) Said to be the setting for Nathaniel Hawthorne's classic novel. Guided tours of the "Gables" and Hawthorne's birthplace (1750). On grounds are the Hathaway House (1682) and the Retire Becket House (1655), now the Museum Shop. Garden cafe (seasonal). (Daily; closed Thanksgiving, Dec 25; also first two wks Jan) 54 Turner St, off Derby St on Salem Harbor. Phone 978/744-0991. ¢¢

Peabody Museum & Essex Institute. Peabody Museum founded by sea captains in 1799 features five world-famous collections in 30 galleries. Large collections of marine art, Asian export art. Essex Institute features historical interpretations of area. Peabody Museum (daily; closed Jan 1, Thanksgiving, Dec 25). Essex Institute (Daily) East India Sq. Phone 978/745-9500. Admission includes

Crowninshield-Bentley House. (1727) Reverend William Bentley, minister and diarist, lived here 1791-1819. Period furnishings. (June-Oct, daily; rest of yr, Sat, Sun, and hols) Essex St and Hawthorne Blvd.

Gardner-Pingree House. (1804) Designed by McIntire; restored and handsomely furnished. (June-Oct, daily; rest of yr, Sat-Sun and hols) 128 Essex St.

John Ward House. (1684) Seventeenth-century furnishings. (June-Oct, daily; rest of yr, Sat-Sun and hols) Behind Essex Institute.

Peirce-Nichols House. (1782) One of the finest examples of McIntire's architectural genius; authentically furnished. (By appt only) 80 Federal St. Phone 978/745-9500.

Pickering Wharf. Six-acre commercial and residential village by the sea includes shops, restaurants, marina. Adj to Salem Maritime National Historic Site.

Pioneer Village: Salem in 1630. Reproduction of early Puritan settlement, includes dugouts, wigwams, thatched cottages; costumed interpreters. Guided tours. (Last wkend May-Oct, daily) Forest River Park, off West St. Phone 978/744-0991. ¢¢¢

Ropes Mansion and Garden. (Late 1720s) Gambrel-roofed, Georgian and Colonial mansion; restored and furnished with period pieces. The garden (laid out 1912) is nationally known for its beauty and variety. (June-Oct, daily; limited hrs Sun) 318 Essex St. Phone 978/745-9500. ¢

⊠ Salem Maritime National Historic Site. Nine acres of historic waterfront. Self-guided and guided tours. (Daily; Thanksgiving, closed Dec 25, Jan 1). Contact the Orientation Center, Central Wharf Warehouse, 174 Derby St. Phone 978/740-1660. ¢¢ Site includes

Custom House. (1819) Restored offices. (Daily; closed Jan 1, Thanksgiving, Dec 25) Derby St, opp wharf. Phone 978/745-0799.

Derby House. (1761-1762) Home of maritime merchant Elias Hasket Derby, one of the country's first millionaires. In back are the Derby House Gardens, featuring roses, herbs, and 19th-century flowers. Inquire at Orientation Center for tour information. Phone 978/745-0799.

Derby Wharf. Once a center of Salem shipping (1760-1810). Off Derby St. Phone 978/740-1660.

Narbonne House. A 17th-century house with archaeological exhibits. Inquire at Orientation Center for tour information. Phone 978/745-0799.

Scale House. (1829) and **Bonded Warehouse** (1819). Site of 19th-century customs operations. (Daily) Phone 978/745-0799.

Visitor Information. In Orientation Center and downtown visitor center at Museum Place, Essex St. Phone 978/744-0004.

West India Goods Store. (1800) Coffee, teas, spices, and goods for sale. (Daily; closed Jan 1, Thanksgiving, Dec 25) 164 Derby St.

Salem State College. (1854) 9,300 students. 352 Lafayette St. Phone 978/542-6200. On campus are

Chronicle of Salem. Mural, 60 ft by 30 ft, depicts Salem history from settlement to present in 50 sequences. (Mon-Fri; closed hols) Meier Hall.

Library Gallery. Art exhibits by local and national artists. (Mon-Sat) **FREE**

Main Stage Auditorium. This 750-seat theater presents musical and dramatic productions (Sept-Dec, Jan-Apr). Phone 978/744-3700.

Winfisky Art Gallery. Photographs, paintings, graphics, and sculpture by national and local artists. (Sept-May, Mon-Fri) **FREE**

Salem Witch Museum. Multimedia presentation reenacting the witch hysteria of 1692. (July & Aug, daily) Washington Sq. Phone 978/744-1692. ¢¢

Stephen Phillips Trust House. (1804) Federal-style mansion with McIntire mantels and woodwork. Furnishings, rugs, porcelains reflect the merchant and seafaring past of the Phillips family. Also carriage barn with carriages and antique automobiles. (Late May-Oct, Mon-Sat) 34 Chestnut St. Phone 978/744-0440. **FREE**

Witch Dungeon Museum. Reenactment of witch trial of Sarah Good by professional actresses; tour through re-created dungeon where accused witches awaited trial; original artifacts. (May-Nov, daily) 16 Lynde St. Phone 978/741-3570. ¢¢

Witch House. (1642) Home of witchcraft trial judge Jonathan Corwin. Some of the accused witches may have been examined here. (Mid-Mar-Nov, daily) 310½ Essex St. Phone 978/744-0180. ¢¢

Special Events

Heritage Days Celebration. Band concerts, parade, exhibits, ethnic festivals. (Mid-Aug.) Phone 978/744-0004.

Haunted Happenings. Various sites. Psychic festival, historical exhibits, haunted house, costume parade, contests, dances. Entire month of Oct. Phone 978/744-0004.

A Walk Through Salem

Salem is a fascinating old port city with a walkable downtown. Begin at the National Park Visitors Center at 2 Liberty Street across from the Museum Place garage. Just around the corner on the pedestrian stretch of Essex Street is the Peabody Essex Museum, New England's ultimate treasure chest of exotica, all of it brought from the farthest points of the globe by Salem sea captains in the decades after the Revolution. The Essex Institute part of the museum houses a collection of portraits and archives, including the actual records of the 1692 witch trials for which Salem is infamous; a short film puts the trials in their historical context. Historic homes on the grounds include the Gardner-Pingree House, showcasing the work of Samuel McIntire. Salem's famous architect, McIntire is known for creating airy Federal-era mansions with elegant carved detailing, arches, and stairways. You might want to detour to see Chestnut Street, famous because it is lined with McIntire mansions (walk west up Essex Street and south on Cambridge Street; return the same route).

West of the museums turn south off Essex Street to Derby Square, site of Salem's old Town Hall, a graceful brick building dating from 1816 that is now a hospitable visitor center for the Salem Chamber of Commerce. Continue down the square (it's really a mini-park) to Front Street and follow the red line on the sidewalk ("The Salem Heritage Trail") down Charter and Liberty streets, past the Old Burying Point Cemetery and the Salem Wax Museum.

Continue down along Derby Street to the Salem Maritime National Historic site on Salem Harbor. The "Friendship," a fully-rigged tall ship, is berthed at Central Wharf. The handsome brick Custom House (1819), where Nathaniel Hawthorne worked, is next door at the head of Derby Wharf. Here too is the Elias Hasket Derby House, built by the man who pioneered a new sailing route around the Cape of Good Hope and is said to have been America's first millionaire. The House of Seven Gables, immortalized by Hawthorne, is a few blocks east overlooking the harbor. Retrace your steps (following the red line) up Derby Street and turn up Hawthorne Boulevard to Salem Common. Look for the Salem Witch Museum (Washington Square North), which dramatizes the tale of the witch trials with computerized sound and light. This tour is slightly under two miles, but you can hop a trolley—also a good way to gain an overview of sites to begin with—if you tire along the way. Return down Brown Street to your starting point.

Hotel

★★ **HAWTHORNE HOTEL.** *18 Washington Sq W (01970). 978/744-4080; fax 978/745-9842; toll-free 800/729-7829. www.hawthornehotel.com.* 89 rms, 6 suites, 6 story. July-Oct: S $125-$154; D $125-$172; each addl $12; suites $285; under 18 free; lower rates rest of yr. Crib free. Pet accepted; $15. TV; cable (premium). Restaurant 6:30-11 pm; Sat, Sun from 7 am. Ck-out 11 am. Meeting rms. Business servs avail. In-rm modem link. Lndry serv. Exercise equipt. Health club privileges. Cr cds: A, C, D, DS, MC, V.
🔧 ⚕ 🖂 🐾 SC

B&Bs/Small Inns

★ **COACH HOUSE INN.** *284 Lafayette St (MA A1A) (01970). 978/744-4092; fax 978/745-8031; toll-free 800/688-8689. www.salemweb.com/biz/coachhouse.* 11 rms, 9 with bath, 9 A/C, 3 story. No rm phones. Apr-Nov: S, D $85-$135; each addl $20; suites $78-$105; lower rates rest of yr. Crib free. TV. Complimentary continental bkfst. Restaurant nearby. Ck-out 11 am, ck-in 3 pm. Microwaves avail. Built 1879; many antiques. Totally non-smoking. Cr cds: A, DS, MC, V.
🖂 🐾

★★★ **SALEM INN.** *7 Summer St; Rte 114 (01970). 978/741-0680; fax 978/744-8924; toll-free 800/446-2995. www.saleminnma.com.* 33 units, 4 story, 5 suites, 6 kits. No elvtr. S, D $139-$149; each addl $15; suites $169-$199. Pet accepted. TV; cable (premium). Complimentary continental bkfst. Ck-out 11 am, ck-in 3 pm. Meeting rm. Business servs avail. In-rm modem link. Many fireplaces; some in-rm whirlpools. Brick patio, rose garden. Sea captain's house (1834); on Salem's Heritage trail; many antiques. Cr cds: A, C, D, DS, MC, V.
🔧 🖂 🐾

Restaurants

★★ **GRAPE VINE.** *26 Congress St (01970). 978/745-9335. www.grapevinesalem.com.* Italian, Amer menu. Specializes in pasta, vegetarian entrees, chicken. Hrs: 5:30-10 pm; Wed-Fri 11:30 am-2:30 pm, 5:30-10 pm. Closed some major hols; also Super Bowl Sun. Res accepted. Bar to 1 am. Lunch $8-$12, dinner $13-$22. Parking. Outdoor dining. Eclectic déco dining rm. Cr cds: A, C, D, DS, ER, MC, V.
D 🔧

★★★ **LYCEUM.** *43 Church St (01970). 978/745-7665. www.lyceumsalem.com.* Specializes in grilled food. Own baking. Hrs: 11:30 am-3 pm, 5:30-10 pm; Sat from 5:30 pm; Sun brunch 11 am-3 pm. Closed Thanksgiving, Dec 25. Res accepted. Bar to 1 am. Lunch $5.95-$9.95, dinner $13.95-$18.95. Sun brunch $3.95-$8.95. Built in 1830. Alexander Graham Bell presented the first demonstrations of long distance telephone conversations here in 1877. Cr cds: A, DS, MC, V.
D 🔧

★★★ **RED RAVEN'S LIMP NOODLE.** *75 Congress Ave (01970). 978/745-8558.* Eclectic menu. Specialties: roasted mussels, smoked salmon. Hrs: 5:30-10 pm. Closed Mon, Sun; also most major hols. Res accepted. Bar to 1 am. Wine list. Dinner $14.95-$22.95. Street parking. Turn-of-the-century Victorian decor; paintings. Cr cds: A.
D

★ **VICTORIA STATION.** *86 Wharf St (01970). 978/745-3400. www.victoriastationinc.com.* Specializes in prime rib, seafood. Salad bar. Hrs: 11:30 am-10 pm; Fri, Sat to 11 pm. Closed Dec 25. Res accepted. Bar. Lunch $5.25-$9.95, dinner $8.95-$19.95. Child's menu. Outdoor dining. Overlooks harbor. Cr cds: A, C, D, DS, ER, MC, V.

D ⊟

Sandwich (Cape Cod)

Settled 1637 **Pop** 20,136 **Elev** 20 ft **Area code** 508
Zip 02563

Information Cape Cod Canal Region Chamber of Commerce, 70 Main St, Buzzards Bay 02532; 508/759-6000
Web www.capecodcanalchamber.org

The first town to be settled on Cape Cod, Sandwich made the glass that bears its name. This pressed glass was America's greatest contribution to the glass industry.

What to See and Do

◩ **Heritage Plantation.** 1899-mid-1930s autos including a restored and rebuilt 1931 Duesenberg Model J. Tourer built for Gary Cooper, a 1908 white steamer, and the first official presidential car, which was used by President Taft. The American History Museum houses the Lilly collection of miniature soldiers and antique firearms. Art Museum has Early American collections of scrimshaw and weather vanes, trade signs and primitive paintings including large Currier & Ives collection; jitney rides (free); ride on restored 1912 carousel; windmill (1800); entertainment (summer). Extensive rhododendron plantings on this 76-acre site. Changing exhibits. Cafe and garden shop. (Daily) Picnic area opp main parking lot. Grove and Pine Sts. Phone 508/888-3300. ¢¢¢

Hoxie House & Dexter Gristmill. Restored mid-17th-century buildings. House, operating mill; stone-ground corn meal sold. (Mid-June-mid-Oct, daily) Water St. Phone 508/888-1173.

Sandwich Glass Museum. Internationally renowned collection of exquisite Sandwich Glass (ca 1825-1888). (Apr-Oct, daily) Phone 508/888-0251. ¢¢

State Parks.

Scusset Beach. Swimming beach, fishing pier; camping (fee). Standard fees. 3 mi NW on MA 6A across canal, then 2 mi E at jct MA 3 and US 6. Phone 508/362-3225. ¢¢

Shawme-Crowell State Forest. Approx 2,700 acres. Primitive camping. Standard fees. 3 mi W on MA 130, off US 6. Phone 508/888-0351.

Motels/Motor Lodges

★ **COUNTRY ACRES MOTEL.** *187 Rte 6A, Sandwich (02563). 508/888-2878; fax 508/888-8511; toll-free 888/860-8650. www.sunsol.com/countryacres/.* 17 rms, 1 cottage. Late June-Labor Day: S, D $79-$99; each addl $8; lower rates rest of yr. Crib $8. TV; cable (premium). Pool. Ck-out 11 am. Lawn games. Refrigerators. Cr cds: A, MC, V.

🏊 🖼 🔥

★★ **EARL OF SANDWICH MOTEL.** *378 Rte 6A, East Sandwich (02537). 508/888-1415; fax 508/833-1039; toll-free 800/442-3275. www.earlofsandwich.com.* 24 rms. Late June-early Sept: S, D $65-$89; each addl $10; lower rates rest of yr. Crib $5. Pet accepted. TV. Complimentary continental bkfst. Restaurant nearby. Ck-out 11 am. Tudor motif. Cr cds: A, MC, V.

D ⬛ 🖼 🔥

★ **OLD COLONY MOTEL.** *436 Rte 6A, East Sandwich (02537). 508/888-9716; toll-free 800/786-9716. www.sunsol.com/oldcolony/.* 10 rms. Late June-Labor Day: S, D $79-$99; under 12 free; higher rates: hols (2-day min), mid-May-mid-June; lower rates mid-Sept-Nov, Mar-mid-May. Crib free. TV; cable. Pool. Playground. Complimentary continental bkfst. Restaurant nearby. Ck-out 11 am. Lawn games. Refrigerators. Picnic tables. Cr cds: A, C, D, DS, MC, V.

🏊 🖼 🔥

★ **SANDY NECK MOTEL.** *669 Rte 6A, East Sandwich (02537). 508/362-3992; fax 508/362-5170; toll-free 800/564-3992. www.sandyneck.com.* 12 rms. Mid-June-Labor Day: S, D $89-$125; each addl $10; lower rates Feb-mid-June and after Labor Day-Dec. Closed rest of yr. Crib free. TV; cable (premium). Complimentary coffee. Restaurant nearby. Ck-out 11 am. Refrigerators. Cr cds: A, C, D, DS, ER, JCB, MC, V.

🖼 🔥

★★ **SHADY NOOK INN & MOTEL.** *14 Old Kings Hwy, Sandwich (02563). 508/888-0409; fax 508/888-4039; toll-free 800/338-5208. www.shadynookinn.com.* 30 rms, 7 kits. Mid-June-Labor Day: S, D $95-$125; each addl $8; suites $125-$200; lower rates rest of yr. TV; cable (premium). Heated pool. Restaurant nearby. Ck-out 11 am. Coin lndry. In-rm modem link. Refrigerators. Cr cds: A, C, D, DS, MC, V.

🏊 🖼 🔥

★★ **SPRING HILL MOTOR LODGE.** *351 Rte 6A, East Sandwich (02537). 508/888-1456; fax 508/833-1556; toll-free 800/646-2514. www.sunsol.com/springhill.* 24 rms, 2 kit. units. Late June-Labor Day: S, D $95-$150; each addl $15; kit. units $155; lower rates rest of yr. Crib $10. TV; cable (premium). Heated pool. Coffee in rms. Restaurant nearby. Ck-out 11 am. Tennis. Picnic tables. Refrigerators. Cr cds: A, D, DS, MC, V.

🎿 🏊 🖼 🔥

B&Bs/Small Inns

★★★ **BAY BEACH BED & BREAKFAST.** *3 Bay Beach Ln, Sandwich (02563).* 508/888-8813; fax 508/888-5416; toll-free 800/475-6398. www.baybeach.com. 6 rms, 3 story. S $225; D $285. Closed Nov-mid-May. Children over 16 yrs only. TV; cable (premium). Complimentary full bkfst; afternoon refreshments. Restaurant nearby. Ck-out noon, ck-in 2-6 pm. Luggage handling. Concierge serv. Exercise equipt. Refrigerators. Balconies. Grey weathered clapboard houses with extensive gardens. On beach. Totally nonsmoking. Cr cds: MC, V.
⊼ ⊠ ⊠

★★ **THE BELFRY INN & BISTRO.** *6-8 Jarves St, Sandwich (02563).* 508/888-8550; fax 508/888-3922; toll-free 800/844-4542. www.belfryinn.com. 14 air-cooled rms, 3 with shower only, 3 story. No elvtr. Late May-mid-Oct: S, D $85-$165; package plans; wkends, hols (2-day min); lower rates rest of yr. Children over 10 yrs only. TV in common rm; cable (premium), VCR avail (movies). Complimentary full bkfst; afternoon refreshments. Restaurant 5-11 pm. Rm serv 24 hrs. Ck-out 11 am, ck-in 3 pm. Business center. In-rm modem link. Luggage handling. Valet serv. Concierge serv. Lawn games. Some in-rm whirlpools, fireplaces. Some balconies. Former rectory built 1882; belfrey access. Totally nonsmoking. Cr cds: A, D, MC, V.
D ⊠ ⊠ ⊼

★★ **CAPTAIN EZRA NYE HOUSE BED & BREAKFAST.** *152 Main St, Sandwich (02563).* 508/888-6142; fax 508/833-2897; toll-free 800/388-2278. www.captainezranyehouse.com. 6 rms, 2 story. No A/C. No rm phones. June-Oct: S $75-$95; D $85-$105; suite $110; wkly rates; lower rates rest of yr. Children over 10 yrs only. TV in sitting rm, suite; cable. Complimentary full bkfst. Restaurant nearby. Ck-out 11 am, ck-in 2 pm. Business servs avail. Built 1829; antiques. Totally nonsmoking. Cr cds: A, DS, JCB, MC, V.
⊠ ⊠

★★★ **DAN'L WEBSTER INN.** *149 Main St, Sandwich (02563).* 508/888-3622; fax 508/888-5156; toll-free 800/444-3566. www.danlwebsterinn.com. 54 rms, 1-3 story. Late May-Oct: S, D $149; each addl $10; suites $209-$335; under 12 free; MAP avail, addl $44/person; lower rates rest of yr. Crib free. TV; cable (premium). Pool. Dining rm (see DAN'L WEBSTER INN). Rm serv. Bar noon-1 am; entertainment. Ck-out 11 am, ck-in 3 pm. Meeting rms. Business center. In-rm modem link. Luggage handling. Health club privileges. Some fireplaces. Whirlpool in suites. Modeled on an 18th-century house. Cr cds: A, D, DS, MC, V.
⊠ ⊠ ⊠ ⊼

★★★ **ISAIAH JONES HOMESTEAD.** *165 Main St, Sandwich (02563).* 508/888-9115; fax 508/888-9648; toll-free 800/526-1625. www.isaiahjones.com. 7 rms, 2 with shower only, 2 story. No A/C. No rm phones. Mid-May-late Oct: S, D $125; wkend rates; lower rates rest of yr. Children over 12 yrs only. TV in sitting rm; cable. Complimentary full bkfst; afternoon refreshments. Restaurant nearby. Ck-out 11 am, ck-in 3-6 pm. Luggage handling. Concierge serv. Some in-rm whirlpools. Picnic tables. Restored Victorian house built 1849; many antiques. Totally nonsmoking. Cr cds: A, D, DS, MC, V.
⊠ ⊠

★★ **VILLAGE INN.** *4 Jarves St, Sandwich (02563).* 508/833-0363; fax 508/833-2063; toll-free 800/922-9989. www.capecodinn.com. 8 rms, 2 share bath, 3 story. No A/C. No rm phones. June-Oct: D $85-$115; wkends (2-day min); lower rates Nov-May. Children over 8 yrs only. Complimentary full bkfst; afternoon refreshments. Restaurant nearby. Ck-out 11 am, ck-in 3-6 pm. Federal-style house (1837) with wrap-around porch, gardens. Many antique furnishings. Totally nonsmoking. Cr cds: A, DS, MC, V.
⊠ ⊠

Restaurants

★ **BOBBY BYRNE'S PUB.** *Rte 6A & Tupper Rd, Sandwich (02563).* 508/888-6088. www.bobbybyrnes.com. Specializes in steak, seafood, pasta. Hrs: 11 am-1 am; early-bird dinner 4-6 pm. Closed Thanksgiving, Dec 25. Bar to 1 am. Lunch $4.95-$7.95, dinner $6.95-$10.50. Child's menu. Family-owned. Cr cds: A, D, DS, MC, V.
D ⊐

★★ **BRIDGE RESTAURANT.** *21 MA 6A, Sagamore (02561).* 508/888-8144. Specializes in Yankee pot roast, fresh scrod, grape nut custard pudding. Hrs: 11:30 am-9:30 pm; wkends from noon. Closed Thanksgiving, Dec 25. Res accepted. Bar. Lunch $1.95-$7.95, dinner $8.95-$16.95. Child's menu. Family-owned since 1953. Cr cds: DS, MC, V.
D ⊐

★★★ **DAN'L WEBSTER INN.** *149 Main St, Sandwich (02563).* 508/888-3623. www.danlwebsterinn.com. Specializes in seafood, chicken, veal. Own baking. Hrs: 8 am-9 pm; Sun brunch noon-2:30 pm; early-bird dinner 4:30-5:30 pm. Res accepted. Bar. Wine cellar. Bkfst $3.50-$6.95, lunch $5.25-$11.95, dinner $10.95-$23.95. Sun brunch $7-$12.95. Child's menu. Pianist. Valet parking. Conservatory dining overlooks garden. Reproduction of 1700s house. Several dining rms; some with fireplace. Cr cds: A, C, D, DS, MC, V.
D

★ **HORIZON'S.** *98 Town Neck Rd, Sandwich (02563).* 508/888-6166. Specializes in fresh seafood, clam bakes, steaks. Hrs: 11:30 am-midnight. Closed Nov-Apr. No A/C. Bar. Lunch $4.95-$7.95, dinner $6.95-$13.95. Child's menu. Entertainment Sat. Outdoor dining. Overlooks Cape Cod Bay. Cr cds: A, DS, MC, V.
D ⊐

Saugus

See also Boston

Settled 1630 **Pop** 26,078 **Elev** 21 ft **Area code** 781 **Zip** 01906

Saugus is the birthplace of the American steel industry. The first ironworks were built here in 1646.

What to See and Do

Saugus Iron Works National Historic Site. Commemorates America's first successful integrated ironworks. Reconstructed furnace, forge, mill on original foundations; furnished 17th-century house; museum; working blacksmith shop; seven working waterwheels; guided tours and demonstrations (Apr-Oct); film. (Daily; closed Jan 1, Thanksgiving, Dec 25) Contact the National Park Service, Saugus Iron Works National Historic Site, 244 Central St. Phone 781/233-0050. **FREE**

Restaurants

★ ★ ★ **DONATELLO.** *44 Broadway (01906). 781/233-9975. www.donatellos.com.* Specializes in regional Italian cuisine. Own pasta. Hrs: 11:30 am-10:30 pm; Sat to 11:30 pm; Sun from 3:30 pm. Closed July 4, Thanksgiving, Dec 24. Res accepted. Bar. Lunch $6-$10, dinner $5.50-$19.95. Valet parking. Italian decor. Totally nonsmoking. Cr cds: A, D, MC, V.
D ⬚

★ ★ **HILLTOP STEAK HOUSE.** *855 Broadway Rte 1 (01906). 781/233-7700.* Specializes in beef, seafood. Hrs: 11 am-10 pm; Fri, Sat to 11 pm. Closed Thanksgiving, Dec 25. Bar. Lunch $5.99-$9.95, dinner $7.99-$22.99. Child's menu. Cr cds: A, MC, V.
D

Seekonk

(see Providence, RI)

Sheffield

(see Great Barrington)

South Hadley

See also Amherst, Holyoke

Settled ca 1660 **Pop** 17,196 **Elev** 257 ft **Area code** 413 **Zip** 01075
Information Chamber of Commerce, 10 Harwich Place; 413/532-6451

Nestled on the banks of the Connecticut River, South Hadley was incorporated as a town in 1775. Twenty years later the first navigable canal in the United States began operation here. The town remained a busy shipping center until 1847, when the coming of the railroad made shipping by river unprofitable. Still visible in spots, the canal is being restored.

What to See and Do

Mount Holyoke College. (1837) 1,950 women. Campus tours (inquire for schedule). College St. Phone 413/538-2000. On grounds are

Joseph Allen Skinner Museum. Housed in a small Congregational church (1846). Collection of Early American furnishings, decorative arts; one-rm schoolhouse. (May-Oct, Wed and Sun, afternoons) MA 116. Phone 413/538-2085. **FREE**

Mount Holyoke College Art Museum. Small but choice permanent collection of paintings, drawings, prints, and sculpture; also special exhibitions. (Tues-Fri, also Sat and Sun afternoons; closed college hols) Phone 413/538-2245. **FREE**

Talcott Arboretum. Campus features variety of trees and plantings; Japanese meditation, wildflower, and formal perennial gardens; greenhouse complex has collections of exotic plants; flower show (Mar); tours by appt. (Mon-Fri, also Sat and Sun afternoons; closed hols) Phone 413/538-2199. **FREE**

Old Firehouse Museum. Served as a firehouse 1888-1974; features firefighting equipt, Native American artifacts, items relating to local history and South Hadley Canal. (June-Sept, Wed and Sun; schedule may vary) Phone 413/536-4970. **FREE**

Special Event

Women's Regatta. Brunelle's Marina. Oct. Phone 413/536-3132.

South Yarmouth (Cape Cod)

See also Hyannis (Cape Cod)

Pop 11,603 **Elev** 20 ft **Area code** 508 **Zip** 02664
Information Yarmouth Area Chamber of Commerce, PO Box 479; 800/732-1008 or the Cape Cod Chamber of Commerce, US 6 and MA 132, PO Box 790, Hyannis 02601-0790; 508/362-3225 or 888/CAPECOD
Web www.capecodchamber.org

Much of the area of the Yarmouths developed on the strength of seafaring and fishing in the first half of the 19th century. South Yarmouth is actually a village within the town of Yarmouth. Well-preserved old houses line Main Street to the north in Yarmouth Port, architecturally among the choicest communities in Massachusetts. Bass River, to the south, also contains many fine estates.

What to See and Do

Captain Bangs Hallet House. Early 19th-century sea captain's home. (June-Oct, Thurs-Sun afternoons; rest of yr, by appt) Botanic trails (all yr; donation). Gate house (June-mid-Sept, daily). Off MA 6A, near Yarmouth Port Post Office. Phone 508/362-3021. ¢¢

Swimming. Nantucket Sound and bayside beaches. Parking fee. Phone 508/430-7553.

Winslow Crocker House. (ca 1780) Georgian house adorned with 17th-, 18th-, and 19th-century furnishings collected in early 20th century. Includes furniture made by New England craftsmen in the Colonial and Federal periods; hooked rugs, ceramics, pewter. (June-mid-Oct, Tues, Thurs, Sat, and Sun) On Old King's Hwy, US 6A, in Yarmouth Port. Phone 508/362-4385. ¢¢

Motels/Motor Lodges

★★ **ALL SEASON MOTOR INN.** *1199 Rte 28, South Yarmouth (02664). 508/394-7600; fax 508/398-7160; toll-free 800/527-0359. www.allseasons.com.* 114 rms, 2 story. July-early Sept: S, D $115-$145; each addl $5; lower rates rest of yr. Crib $5. TV; cable (premium), VCR (movies). Indoor/outdoor pool; whirlpool. Playground. Restaurant 7:30-11 am, noon-3 pm (in season). Ck-out 11 am. Coin lndry. Business servs avail. Exercise equipt; sauna. Game rm. Refrigerators. Private patios, balconies. Picnic tables. Cr cds: A, MC, V.
🇩 ⇌ 🏋 ⇗ 🔥 🐾

★★ **AMERICANA HOLIDAY MOTEL.** *99 Main St, West Yarmouth (02673). 508/775-5511; fax 508/790-0597; toll-free 800/445-4497. www.americanaholiday.com.* 153 rms, 2 story. Late June-Labor Day: S, D $69-$85; each addl $5; suites $85-$105; lower rates Mar-late June, after Labor Day-Oct. Closed rest of yr. Crib free. TV; cable. 3 pools, 1 indoor; whirlpool. Playground. Complimentary coffee. Restaurant nearby. Ck-out 11 am. Putting green. Sauna. Game rm. Lawn games. Refrigerators. Cr cds: A, D, DS, V.
🇩 ⇌ ⇗ 🐾 SC

★ **BEACH N TOWNE MOTEL.** *1261 Rte 28, South Yarmouth (02664). 508/398-2311; toll-free 800/987-8556. www.sunsol.com/beachntowne.* 21 rms. Late June-late Aug: S, D $60-$67; each addl $5-$7; lower rates Feb-late June, late Aug-Dec. Closed rest of yr. Crib free. TV; cable. Pool. Playground. Coffee in lobby. Restaurant nearby. Ck-out 11 am. Lawn games. Refrigerators. Picnic tables, grills. Library. Cr cds: A, DS, MC, V.
⇌ ⇗ 🐾

★★ **BEST WESTERN BLUE ROCK.** *39 Todd Rd, South Yarmouth (02664). 508/398-6962; fax 508/398-1830; res 800/237-8887. www.bestwestern.com.* 44 rms, 1-2 story. Late June-Labor Day wkends (2-day min): S, D $105-$150; each addl $10; under 12 free; golf plan; lower rates Apr-late June, after Labor Day-late Oct. Closed rest of yr. Crib free. TV; cable. Heated pool; whirlpool. Restaurant 7 am-2:30 pm. Bar 11 am-7 pm. Ck-out 11 am. Meeting rm. Business servs avail. Tennis. 18-hole, par 3 golf, pro, greens fee $31, putting greens. Refrigerators. Private patios, balconies. Overlooks golf course. Cr cds: A, C, D, DS, MC, V.
🇩 🏌 🎾 ⇌ ⇗ 🐾

★★ **BEST WESTERN BLUE WATER ON THE OCEAN.** *291 S Shore Dr, South Yarmouth (02664). 508/398-2288; fax 508/398-1010; res 800/367-9393. www.bestwestern.com.* 106 rms, 1-2 story. Late June-Labor Day: S, D $168-$265; each addl $10; lower rates rest of yr. Crib $5. TV; cable. 2 pools, 1 indoor; whirlpool, poolside serv. Free supervised children's activities (July-Labor Day); ages 6-15. Restaurant 7:30-11 am, noon-2 pm; off-season wkend dinner only. Bar noon-1 am; entertainment Fri, Sat. Ck-out 11 am. Meeting rms. Business servs avail. Bellhops. Sundries. Tennis. Putting green. Sauna. Lawn games. Sun decks. Microwaves avail. On 600-ft private ocean beach. Cr cds: A, C, D, DS, MC, V.
🇩 ⇌ 🎾 🐾

★ **CAVALIER MOTOR LODGE.** *881 Main St, South Yarmouth (02664). 508/394-6575; fax 508/394-6578; res 800/545-3536. www.cavaliermotorlodge.com.* 66 rms, 46 A/C, 1-2 story. July-Aug: S, D $59-$99; each addl $7; kit. units $600-$975; golf plans off season; lower rates late Mar-mid-June, Sept-Oct. Closed rest of yr. TV; cable, VCR avail (movies). Indoor/outdoor pool; wading pool, whirlpool, sauna. Playground. Putting green. Lawn games. Game rm. Refrigerators, microwaves avail. Grills. Cr cds: A, MC, V.
⇌ ⇗ 🐾

★★ **GULL WING SUITES.** *822 Main St (Rte 28), South Yarmouth (02664). 508/394-9300; fax 508/394-1190. www.ccrh.com.* 136 suites, 2 story. July-Labor Day: suites $105-$130; package plans; lower rates rest of yr. Crib avail. TV; cable (premium). 2 pools, 1 indoor; whirlpool, saunas. Restaurant nearby. Ck-out 11 am. Meeting rms. Business servs avail. Game rm. Refrigerators, wet bars. Balconies. Cr cds: A, MC, V.
🇩 ⇌ ⇗ 🐾 SC

★ **HUNTERS GREEN MOTEL.** *553 Main St; Rt 28, West Yarmouth (02673). 508/771-1169; toll-free 800/775-5400. www.capecodmotel.com.* 74 rms, 2 story. Late June-Labor Day: S, D $54-$64; each addl $6; lower rates mid-Apr-late June, after Labor Day-Oct. Closed rest of yr. Crib $6. TV; cable (premium). Indoor/outdoor pool; whirlpool. Restaurant nearby. Ck-out 11 am. Lawn games. Picnic tables. Cr cds: A, DS, MC, V.
🇩 ⇌ 🔥

★ **LEWIS BAY LODGE.** *149 Rte 28, West Yarmouth (02673). 508/775-3825; fax 508/778-2870; toll-free 800/882-8995. www.lewisbaylodge.com.* 68 rms, 2 story. Late June-Aug: S, D $58-$78; higher rates special events; lower rates late Apr-late June, Sept-Oct. Closed rest of yr. Crib $6. TV; cable (premium). 2 pools, 1 indoor; whirlpool. Complimentary continental bkfst. Restaurant nearby. Ck-out 11 am. Exercise equipt. Rec rm. Microwaves avail. Cr cds: A, DS, MC, V.
🇩 ⇌ 🏋 ⇗ 🔥 🐾

★★ **MARINER MOTOR LODGE.** *573 Rte 28, West Yarmouth (02673). 508/771-7887; fax 508/771-2811; toll-free 800/445-4050. www.mariner-capecod.com.* 100 rms, 2 story. S, D $39-$89; under 18 free. Crib $5. TV; cable (premium). 2 heated pools, 1 indoor; whirlpool. Continental bkfst off-season. Restaurant nearby. Ck-out 11 am. Meeting rm. Business servs avail. Sauna. Game rm. Refrigerators. Cr cds: A, DS, MC, V.
🇩 ⇌ ⇗ 🐾 SC

★★★ **RED JACKET BEACH MOTOR INN.** *1 S Shore Dr, South Yarmouth (02664). 508/398-6941; fax 508/398-1214; toll-free 800/672-0500. www.redjacketbeach.com.* 150 rms, 1-2 story, 13 cottages. Late June-Labor Day: S, D $160-$250;

each addl $10; 2-4 bedrm cottages $200-$2,800/wk; lower rates Apr-late June, after Labor Day-late Oct. Closed rest of yr. Crib free. TV; cable. 2 pools, 1 indoor; whirlpool, poolside serv. Supervised children's activities (July-Labor Day); ages 4-12. Restaurant 7:30-11 am, noon-3 pm; also 6-9:30 pm in season. Rm serv. Bar noon-midnight. Ck-out 11 am. Coin lndry. Meeting rms. Business servs avail. Bellhops. Sundries. Tennis. Putting green. Exercise equipt; sauna. Sailing. Game rm. Lawn games. Refrigerators, microwaves avail. Private patios, balconies. On ocean, beach. Cr cds: MC, V.

🄳 ⛵ ➿ 🏃 📶 🔥

★★ **TIDEWATER MOTOR LODGE.** *135 Main St, West Yarmouth (02673). 508/775-6322; fax 508/778-5105; res 800/338-6322. www.tidewaterml.com.* 100 rms, 1-2 story. July-Aug: S, D $42-$105; each addl $6; under 12 free; golf plans; higher rates: Memorial Day, Labor Day, Columbus Day; lower rates rest of yr. Crib $5. TV; cable. 2 pools, 1 indoor; whirlpool. Playground. Complimentary coffee in lobby. Restaurant nearby. Ck-out 11 am. Sauna. Game rm. Lawn games. Refrigerators. Balconies. Picnic tables. On 4 acres; view of Mill Creek Bay. Cr cds: A, DS, MC, V.

➿ 📶 🔥

Resorts

★★ **RIVIERA BEACH RESORT.** *327 S Shore Dr, Bass River (02664). 508/398-2273; fax 508/398-1202. www.redjacket inns.com/riviera.* 125 rms, 2 story. July-early Sept: D $180-$280; each addl $10; lower rates mid-Apr-June, early Sept-late Oct. Closed rest of yr. Crib free. TV; cable, VCR avail (movies). 2 pools, 1 indoor; whirlpool. Free supervised children's activities (July-Labor Day); ages 4-11. Restaurant 7:30-11 am, noon-2 pm. Bar noon-8 pm. Ck-out 11 am. Bellhops. Sailing. Waterbikes, sailboards in season. Lawn games. Refrigerators. Some in-rm whirlpools. Balconies. Sun decks. On 415-ft private beach. Cr cds: A, MC, V.

🄳 ➿ 📶 🔥

★★ **YARMOUTH RESORT.** *343 Rte 28, West Yarmouth (02673). 508/775-5155; fax 508/790-8255; res 877/838-3524. www.yarmouthresort.com.* 138 rms, 2 story. July-Aug: D $65-$99; each addl $10; suites $75-$119; under 18 free; lower rates May-June, Sept-Oct. Crib free. TV; cable. 2 pools, 1 indoor; whirlpool. Playground. Ck-out 11 am. Meeting rms. Business servs avail. In-rm modem link. Sauna. Game rm. Many refrigerators. Balconies. Cr cds: DS, MC, V.

🄳 ➿ 📶 🔥

B&Bs/Small Inns

★★★ **CAPTAIN FARRIS HOUSE BED & BREAKFAST.** *308 Old Main St, Yarmouth (02664). 508/760-2818; fax 508/398-1262; toll-free 800/350-9477. www.captainfarris.com.* 8 rms, 4 suites. 6 A/C. Late May-mid-Oct: S, D $120-$160; suites $155-$185; wkends (2-day min); lower rates rest of yr. Children over 10 yrs only. TV; cable, VCR. Complimentary full bkfst; afternoon refreshments. Dining rm by res. Ck-out 11 am, ck-in 2 pm. Business servs

avail. In-rm modem link. Luggage handling. Concierge serv. Lawn games. Whirlpools. Refrigerators, fireplaces. Balconies. Two buildings (1825 and 1845). Many antiques. Near Bass River. Cr cds: A, DS, MC, V.

📶 🔥

★★ **COLONIAL HOUSE INN & RESTAURANT.** *277 Main St; Rte 6A, Yarmouth Port (02675). 508/362-8034; res 800/999-3416.* 21 rms, 3 story. July-mid-Oct, S $70-$95; D $85-$105; each addl $10; higher rates hol wkends; lower rates rest of yr. Crib $5. Pet accepted, some restrictions. TV; VCR avail. Indoor pool; whirlpool. Complimentary bkfst. Dining rm 11:30 am-2:30 pm, 4-9 pm. Bar to 1 am. Ck-out noon, ck-in 2 pm. Meeting rm. Business center. In-rm modem link. Massage. Lawn games. Old mansion (1730s); many antiques, handmade afghans. Cr cds: A, DS, MC, V.

🄳 🐾 ➿ 📶 🔥 🚶

★★★ **INN AT LEWIS BAY.** *57 Maine Ave, West Yarmouth (02673). 508/771-3433; fax 508/790-1186; toll-free 800/962-6679. www.innatlewisbay.com.* 7 rms, 2 with shower only, 2 story. No rm phones. Mid-May-Oct: S $75-$118; D $75-$128; wkly rates; wkends, hols (2-day min); lower rates rest of yr. Children over 12 yrs only. Complimentary full bkfst. Ck-out 11 am, ck-in 3-8 pm. Luggage handling. Concierge serv. Lawn games. Picnic tables. Beach house built in 1920s. Totally nonsmoking. Cr cds: A, MC, V.

📶 🔥

★★★ **LIBERTY HILL INN.** *77 Main St (MA 6A), Yarmouth Port (02675). 508/362-3976; fax 508/362-6485; toll-free 800/821-3977. www.libertyhillinn.com.* 9 rms, 3 story. No rm phones. Memorial Day-Columbus Day: D $100-$170; each addl $20; higher rates Presidents Day; lower rates rest of yr. Crib $8. TV. Complimentary full bkfst. Restaurant nearby. Ck-out 11 am, ck-in 3 pm. Concierge. Free airport transportation. Antiques. Greek-Revival mansion built 1825 for ship builder. Sitting rm furnished with early-American pieces. Totally nonsmoking. Cr cds: A, MC, V.

📶 🔥 SC

Restaurants

★★ **ABBICCI.** *43 Main St, Yarmouth (02664). 508/362-3501.* Italian menu. Specializes in authentic Italian cuisine, local seafood, desserts. Hrs: 11:30 am-2:30 pm, 5-10 pm. Res accepted. Bar. Lunch $6.95-$11.95, dinner $10.95-$23.95. Parking. Country inn atmosphere. Cr cds: A, D, MC, V.

🄳

★★ **HOWE'S COTTAGE.** *134 Rte 6A, Yarmouth Port (02675). 508/362-9866.* Specialties: free-range chicken breast grilled and spice-rubbed, quiche of the day, fresh grilled Maine salmon with spicy Thai noodles. Own baking. Hrs: 7:30 am-9 pm. Sun brunch 9 am-3 pm. Bar. Bkfst $3-$6, lunch $3-$7.50, dinner $11-$23. Sun brunch $3-$8. Parking. In old sea captain's house (1840) with gables and gingerbread ornamentation. Casual decor. Totally nonsmoking. Cr cds: A, C, D, DS, MC, V.

🄳

★★ **INAHO-JAPANESE RESTAURANT.** *157 Main St, Yarmouth Port (02675).* *508/362-5522.* Japanese menu. Specializes in tempura, teriyaki, sushi. Hrs: 5-10 pm. Closed Mon; Easter, Thanksgiving, Dec 25. Res accepted. Serv bar. Dinner $12-$22. Japanese decor; sushi bar. Totally nonsmoking. Cr cds: MC, V.

★★ **RIVERWAY LOBSTER HOUSE.** *MA 28, South Yarmouth (02664).* *508/398-2172.* Specializes in lobster, seafood. Hrs: 4:30-10 pm; Sun from noon; early-bird dinner Mon-Thurs 4:30-6:30 pm, Fri-Sat to 6 pm. Closed Dec 25. Res accepted. Bar. Dinner $8.50-$18. Child's menu. Parking. 2 fireplaces. Family-owned. Cr cds: A, D, DS, MC, V.
D

★ **SKIPPER RESTAURANT.** *152 S Shore Dr, South Yarmouth (02664).* *508/394-7406. www.skipperrestaurant.com.* Specializes in seafood, steak. Hrs: 11:30-1 am; Sun from 8 am; early-bird dinner 4:30-6 pm. Closed Oct-Mar. A/C upstairs only. Bar. Bkfst $1.99-$5.95, lunch $3.95-$9.95, dinner $8.95-$18.95. Child's menu. Parking. Nautical motif. Scenic view of Nantucket Sound. Cr cds: A, DS, MC, V.
D

★★ **YARMOUTH HOUSE.** *335 Main St, West Yarmouth (02673).* *508/771-5154.* Specializes in seafood, beef, chicken, stir-fry. Hrs: 11:30 am-11 pm; early-bird dinner 3-6 pm. Closed Dec 25. Res accepted. Bar. A la carte entrees: lunch $3.95-$11.95, dinner $8.95-$18.95. Child's menu. Parking. 3 dining rms; working water wheel. Cr cds: A, C, D, DS, ER, MC, V.
D

Springfield

See also Holyoke

Settled 1636 **Pop** 152,082 **Elev** 70 ft **Area code** 413

Information Greater Springfield Convention & Visitors Bureau, 1441 Main St, 01103; 413/787-1548 or 800/723-1548

Established under the leadership of William Pynchon of Springfield, England, this is now a major unit in the Connecticut River industrial empire. Springfield is also a cultural center with a fine library, museums, and a symphony orchestra, and is the home of Springfield College.

Transportation

Car Rental Agencies. See IMPORTANT TOLL-FREE NUMBERS.
Public Transportation. Pioneer Valley Transit Authority, phone 413/781-PVTA.
Rail Passenger Service. Amtrak 800/872-7245.

Airport Information

Hartford Bradley Intl Airport. Information 860/292-2000; weather 860/627-3440; cash machines, Terminals A and B.

What to See and Do

Basketball Hall of Fame. Exhibits on the game and its teams and players; shrine to the sport invented here in 1891 by Dr. James Naismith. Historic items on display; free movies; video highlights of great games; life-size, action blow-ups of Hall of Famers. Major features include: "Hoopla," a 22-min film; and "The Spalding Shoot-Out," the most popular participatory attraction, which allows visitors to try their skill at scoring a basket of varying heights while on a moving sidewalk. (Daily; closed Jan 1, Thanksgiving, Dec 25) 1150 W Columbus Ave, adj to I-91. Phone 413/781-6500. ¢¢¢

Forest Park. On 735 acres. Nature trails, tennis, swimming pool. Picnicking, playgrounds, ball fields. Zoo (Apr-Nov, daily; rest of yr, Sat and Sun; fee). Duck ponds. Pony rides, train rides (fee for both). Park (all yr). Rte 83 off I-91. ¢¢

Indian Motocycle Museum. Part of the vast complex where Indian motorcycles were made until 1953. On display are historical cycles and other American-made machines; photographs; extensive collection of toy motorcycles; other Native American products, including an early snowmobile and a 1928 roadster. (Daily; closed Jan 1, Thanksgiving, Dec 25) 33 Hendee St. Phone 413/737-2624. ¢¢

Laughing Brook Education Center and Wildlife Sanctuary. Woodlands and wetlands, 354 acres. Former house (1782) of children's author and storyteller Thornton W. Burgess. Live animal exhibits of wildlife native to New England. Observation areas of pond, field, and forest habitats. 4½ mi of walking trails; picnic area. (Tues-Sun; also Mon hols; closed Jan 1, Thanksgiving, Dec 25) 793 Main St, 7 mi SE in Hampden. Phone 413/566-8034. ¢¢

Municipal Group. Includes renovated Symphony Hall, which, together with the Springfield Civic Center, offers a performing arts complex presenting a variety of concerts, theater, children's productions, dance and sporting events, and industrial shows; 300-ft campanile, modeled after the bell tower in the Piazza San Marco of Venice. NW side of Court Sq.

Six Flags New England. Amusement park, rides, roller coasters; children's area; games and arcades; shows; restaurants. (June-Labor Day, daily; Apr, May, Sept, and Oct, wkends only) 5 mi W via MA 57 and MA 159S in Agawam. Phone 413/786-9300. ¢¢¢¢

Springfield Armory National Historic Site. US armory (1794-1968) contains one of the largest collections of military small arms in the world. Exhibits include "Organ of Guns," made famous by Longfellow's poem "The Arsenal at Springfield." Film, video presentations. (Tues-Sun; closed Jan 1, Thanksgiving, Dec 25) Old Armory Sq Green, Federal and State Sts. Phone 413/734-8551. **FREE**

Springfield Museums at the Quadrangle. Includes four museums and a library. **George Walter Vincent Smith Art Museum.** Houses collection of Asian armor, arms, jade, bronzes, and rugs; 19th-century American paintings, sculpture. **Connecticut River Valley Historical Museum** includes genealogy and local history library; period rms. **Museum of Fine Arts** has 20 galleries including an outstanding collection of American and European works. **Science Museum** has an exploration center, early aviation exhibit, aquarium, planetarium (fee), African hall, dinosaur hall. (All buildings Wed-Sun) 220 State St. Phone 413/263-6800. Inclusive admission ¢¢¢

State Forests.

Brimfield. Swimming, trout fishing from shore (stocked); hiking, picnicking. Standard fees. 24 mi E on US 20, then SE near Brimfield. ¢

Granville. Scenic gorge, laurel display. Swimming, fishing; hiking, picnicking, camping. Standard fees. 22 mi W off MA 57. Phone 413/357-6611.

Storrowton Village. A group of restored Early-American buildings: meeting house, schoolhouse, blacksmith shop, and homes. Old-fashioned herb garden. Dining (see RESTAURANTS). Guided tours (June-Labor Day, Mon-Sat; rest of yr, by appt; closed hols). Eastern States Exposition, 1305 Memorial Ave, on MA 147 in West Springfield. Phone 413/787-0136. ¢¢

Special Events

World's Largest Pancake Breakfast. A battle with Battle Creek, Michigan, to see who can serve the "world's largest breakfast." Features pancake bkfst served at a four-blk-long table. (Mid-May) Phone 413/733-3800.

Taste of Springfield. (Mid-June) Phone 413/733-3800.

Indian Day. Indian Motocycle Museum. Gathering of owners and those interested in Indian motorcycles and memorabilia. (Third Sun July) Phone 413/737-2624.

Eastern States Exposition (The Big E). 1305 Memorial Ave, on MA 147 in West Springfield. Largest fair in the Northeast; entertainment, exhibits; historic Avenue of States, Storrowton Village; horse show; agricultural events; "Better Living Center" exhibit. (Sept) Phone 413/737-2443.

Glendi Greek Celebration. Greek folk dances, observance of doctrine and ritual festivities, Greek foods, art exhibits, street dancing. (Early Sept) Phone 413/787-1548.

Hall of Fame Tip-off Classic. At Springfield Civic Center, 1277 Main St. Official opening game of the collegiate basketball season with two of the nation's top teams. (Mid-Nov) Phone 413/781-6500.

Motels/Motor Lodges

★ **DAYS INN.** 437 Riverdale St, West Springfield (01089). 413/785-5365; fax 413/732-7017; toll-free 800/329-7466. www.daysinn.com. 84 rms. S $38-$58; D $45-$65; each addl $10; higher rates special events. Crib free. TV. Pool. Complimentary continental bkfst. Restaurant nearby. Ck-out 11 am. Meeting rms. Downhill ski 9 mi. Cr cds: A, C, D, DS, MC, V.

★★ **HAMPTON INN.** 1011 Riverdale St (US 5), West Springfield (01089). 413/732-1300; fax 413/732-9883. www.hamptoninn.com. 125 rms, 4 story. S, D $70; under 18 free. Crib free. TV; cable (premium), VCR avail. Pool. Complimentary continental bkfst. Ck-out noon. Meeting rms. Business servs avail. In-rm modem link. Sundries.

Downhill/x-country ski 6 mi. Health club privileges. Cr cds: A, C, D, DS, MC, V.

★★ **HOLIDAY INN.** 711 Dwight St (01104). 413/781-0900; fax 413/785-1410; toll-free 800/465-4329. www.holiday-inn.com. 244 rms, 11 suites, 12 story. S $85-$110; D $95-$120; suites $130-$210; under 19 free; wkend, family rates. Pet accepted; $25. TV; cable. Indoor pool; whirlpool. Restaurant 6:30 am-2 pm, 5-10 pm. Bar from 4:30 pm; Sat, Sun from noon. Ck-out noon. Meeting rm. Downhill/x-country ski 10 mi. Exercise equipt. Game rm. Some refrigerators. Cr cds: A, C, D, DS, ER, JCB, MC, V.

Hotels

★★★ **MARRIOTT SPRINGFIELD.** 1500 Main St (01115). 413/781-7111; fax 413/731-8932; toll-free 800/228-9290. www.marriott.com. 265 rms, 4 suites, 16 story. S $99-$115; D $139-$149; each addl $10; suites $275; under 18 free; wkend package plans. Crib free. TV. Indoor pool; whirlpool, poolside serv. Complimentary coffee in lobby. Restaurant 6:30 am-11 pm. Bars 11:30-2 am; entertainment. Ck-out 1 pm. Meeting rms. Shopping arcade. Barber, beauty shop. Airport transportation. Downhill/x-country ski 15 mi. Exercise equipt; sauna. Some refrigerators. Luxury level. Cr cds: A, C, D, DS, ER, JCB, MC, V.

★★★ **SHERATON SPRINGFIELD AT MONARCH PLAZA.** 1 Monarch Plz (01144). 413/781-1010; fax 413/734-2349; toll-free 800/426-9004. www.sheraton.com. 325 rms, 12 story. S, D $89-$139; suites $149-$169; under 18 free; wkend plans. Crib free. Garage $7.95; valet. TV; cable (premium). Indoor pool; whirlpool, poolside serv. Restaurant 6:30 am-11 pm. Bar 11:30-2 am; entertainment Fri, Sat. Ck-out noon. Convention facilities. Business center. Shopping arcade. Airport transportation. Exercise rm; sauna, steam rm. Bathrm phones. Cr cds: A, D, DS, MC, V.

Restaurants

★★★ **HOFBRAUHAUS.** 1105 Main St, West Springfield (01089). 413/737-4905. www.hofbrauhaus.org. German, Amer menu. Specialties: lobster, Wiener schnitzel, rack of lamb. Hrs: 11:30 am-midnight; Mon 5:30-9 pm; Tues-Fri to 9 pm; Sat 5 pm-midnight. Closed Dec 25. Res accepted. Bar 11 am-midnight. Lunch $2.75-$13, dinner $10.25-$30. Child's menu. Parking. Tableside cooking. Bavarian atmosphere; antiques. Cr cds: A, C, D, DS, ER, MC, V.

★ **IVANHOE.** 1422 Elm St, West Springfield (01089). 413/736-4881. Continental menu. Specializes in prime rib, fresh seafood. Salad bar. Hrs: 11:30 am-10:30 pm; Mon to 9 pm; Tues to 10 pm; Sat from 4 pm; Sun 10 am-9 pm; Sun brunch to 3 pm. Closed Dec 25. Bar; Fri and Sat to 1 am. Lunch $3.95-$8.95, dinner $9.95-$15.95. Lunch buffet $5.75. Sun brunch $11.95. Child's menu. Parking. Contemporary decor. Casual atmosphere. Cr cds: A, C, D, DS, ER, MC, V.

★★ **MONTE CARLO.** *1020 Memorial Ave, West Springfield (01089). 413/734-6431.* Specialties: beef Marsala, veal Francaise, pasta. Hrs: 11:30 am-9 pm; Fri to 10 pm; Sat 4-10 pm; Sun from 4 pm. Closed Mon; Dec 25. Res accepted. Bar. Lunch $4.95-$8.95, dinner $8.95-$16.95. Child's menu. Family-owned. Cr cds: A, C, D, DS, ER, MC, V.

★★★ **OLD STORROWTON TAVERN.** *1305 Memorial Ave, West Springfield (01089). 413/732-4188.www.storrowton.com.* Continental menu. Specializes in seafood, veal and beef dishes. Own baking. Hrs: 11:30 am-2:30 pm, 5-8:30 pm; Sat 11:30 am-4 pm, 5-9 pm. Res required. Closed Sun; Jan 1, Dec 25. Bar. Lunch $5.75-$12, dinner $12-$22. Outdoor dining. Part of restored Colonial village. Cr cds: A, DS, MC, V.

★★ **STUDENT PRINCE & FORT.** *8 Fort St (01103). 413/734-7475. www.studentprince.com.* German, Amer menu. Specialties: jagerschnitzel, sauerbraten. Hrs: 11 am-11 pm; Sun noon-10 pm. Res accepted. Bar; imported draft beer. Lunch $4.50-$10, dinner $8.50-$24. Child's menu. Large collection of German beer steins. Family-owned. Cr cds: A, C, D, DS, ER, MC, V.

Stockbridge and West Stockbridge

See also Lenox, Pittsfield

Settled 1734 **Pop** 2,276 **Elev** 842 & 901 ft **Area code** 413
Zip Stockbridge, 01262; West Stockbridge, 01266
Information Stockbridge Chamber of Commerce, 6 Elm St, PO Box 224; 413/298-5200; or visit Main St Information Booth
Web www.stockbridgechamber.org

Established as a mission, Stockbridge was for many years a center for teaching the Mahican. The first preacher was John Sergeant. Jonathan Edwards also taught at Stockbridge. The town is now mainly a summer resort but still has many features and attractions open year round. West Stockbridge is a completely restored market village. Its Main Street is lined with well-kept storefronts, renovated in the style of the 1800s, featuring stained glass, antiques, and hand-crafted articles.

What to See and Do

Berkshire Botanical Garden. Fifteen-acre botanical garden; perennials, shrubs, trees, antique roses, ponds; wildflower exhibit, herb, vegetable gardens; solar, semitropical, and demonstration greenhouses. Garden shop. Herb products. Special events, lectures. Picnicking. (May-Oct, daily) 2 mi NW, at jct MA 102, 183 in Stockbridge. Phone 413/298-3926. ¢¢

Chesterwood. Early 20th-century summer residence and studio of Daniel Chester French, sculptor of the Minute Man statue in Concord and of Lincoln in the Memorial in Washington, D.C. Also museum; gardens, woodland walk; guided tours. A property of the National Trust for Historic Preservation. (May-Oct, daily) 2 mi S of jct MA 102 and MA 183, in Stockbridge. Phone 413/298-3579. ¢¢

Children's Chimes Bell Tower. (1878) Erected by David Dudley Field, prominent lawyer, as a memorial to his grandchildren. Carillon concerts (June-Aug, daily). Main St in Stockbridge.

Merwin House "Tranquility". (ca 1825) Brick house in late Federal period; enlarged with "shingle"-style wing at end of 19th century. European and American furniture and decorative arts. (June-mid-Oct, Tues, Thurs, Sat and Sun) 14 Main St, in Stockbridge. Phone 413/298-4703. ¢¢

Mission House. (1739) House built in 1739 for the missionary Reverend John Sergeant and his wife, Abigail Williams; now a museum of colonial life. Collection of colonial antiques; Native American museum; gardens and orchard. Guided tours. (Memorial Day wkend-Columbus Day wkend, daily) Main and Sergeant Sts in Stockbridge, on MA 102. Phone 413/298-3239. ¢¢

Naumkeag. Stanford White designed this Norman-style "Berkshire cottage" (1886); interior has antiques, Oriental rugs, collection of Chinese export porcelain. Gardens include terraces of tree peonies, fountains, Chinese garden and birch walk. Guided tours. (Memorial Day wkend-Columbus Day wkend, daily) Prospect Hill in Stockbridge. Phone 413/298-3239. ¢¢¢

✪ **Norman Rockwell Museum.** Maintains and exhibits the nation's largest collection of original art by Norman Rockwell. (Daily; closed Jan 1, Thanksgiving, Dec 25) MA 183, in Stockbridge. Phone 413/298-4100. ¢¢

Special Events

Berkshire Theatre Festival. Berkshire Playhouse. E Main St, in Stockbridge, entrance from US 7, MA 102. Summer theater (Mon-Sat); Unicorn Theater presents new and experimental plays (Mon-Sat in season); children's theater (July-Aug, Thurs-Sat). Phone 413/298-5536. Late June-late Aug.

Harvest Festival. Berkshire Botanical Garden. Celebrates beginning of harvest and foliage season in the Berkshire Hills. (First wkend Oct) Phone 413/298-3926.

Stockbridge Main Street at Christmas. Events include a re-creation of Norman Rockwell's painting. Holiday marketplace, concerts, house tour, silent auction, sleigh/hay rides, caroling. (First wkend Dec) Phone 413/298-5200.

B&Bs/Small Inns

★★★ **THE INN AT STOCKBRIDGE.** *Rte 7 N, Stockbridge (01262). 413/298-3337; fax 413/298-3406; toll-free 888/466-7865. www.stockbridgeinn.com.* 16 rms, 2 story. June-Oct: S $100, D $115-$255; each addl $30; wkend pkgs; lower rates rest of yr. Children over 12 yrs only. TV; VCR avail. Pool. Complimentary full bkfst; afternoon refreshments. Ck-out 11 am, ck-in 2 pm. Business servs avail. 1906 building on 12-acre estate. Totally nonsmoking. Cr cds: A, DS, MC, V.

★★ **RED LION INN.** *30 Main St, Stockbridge (01262). 413/298-5545; fax 413/298-5130. www.redlioninn.com.* 110 rms, 94 with bath. Mid-May-Oct: S, D $75-$195; each addl $20; suites $250-$400; lower rates rest of yr. TV; cable, VCR. Pool. Restaurant (see THE RED LION). Rm serv. Bars 11:30-1 am; entertainment. Ck-out noon, ck-in 3 pm. Meeting rms. Business servs avail. Luggage handling. Gift shop. Free train, bus station transportation. Tennis, golf privileges. Exercise equipt. Massage. Some refrigerators, microwaves in suites. Collection of antiques, china. Historic resort inn, established 1773. Victorian decor. Cr cds: A, D, DS.

🄳 ⛷ 🏌 ➳ ⚓ ✈ ➳ 🔥

★★★ **THE TAGGART HOUSE.** *18 W Main St, Stockbridge (01262). 413/298-4303. www.taggarthouse.com.* 4 rms. No rm phones. July-Aug: S $235-$295; D $275-$355; wkends (2-3 day min); lower rates rest of yr. Closed Jan-Apr. Children over 18 yrs only. Complimentary full bkfst. Restaurant adj 8 am-10 pm. Ck-out 11:30 am, ck-in 3 pm. In-rm modem link. Luggage handling. Tennis privileges. Game rm. Built in late 1800s; country manor house. Totally nonsmoking. Cr cds: A, C, D, DS, MC, V.

🏌 ➳ 🔥

★★★ **WILLIAMSVILLE INN.** *Rte 41, West Stockbridge (01266). 413/274-6118; fax 413/274-3539. www.williamsvilleinn.com.* 16 rms, 1-3 story. No rm phones. July-Oct: S $120-$140; D $120-$150; each addl $20; suite $185; lower rates rest of yr. Pool. Complimentary full bkfst. Restaurant (see WILLIAMSVILLE INN). Bar from 5 pm. Ck-out 11 am, ck-in 2 pm. Meeting rms. Tennis. Downhill/x-country ski 8 mi. Lawn games. Built 1797. Sculpture garden. Cr cds: A, MC, V.

➳ ⛷ 🏌 ⚓ ➳ 🔥

Restaurants

★★ **MICHAEL'S.** *5 Elm St, Stockbridge (01262). 413/298-3530.* Specializes in hamburgers, New England clam chowder, fettuccini Alfredo. Hrs: 11:30 am-midnight. Closed Dec 25. Res accepted. Continental menu. Bar. Lunch $4.95-$7.95, dinner $8.95-$16.95. Children's meals (dinner). Cr cds: A, MC, V.

🄳 ➳

★★★ **THE RED LION.** *30 Main St, Stockbridge (01262). 413/298-5545. www.redlioninn.com.* Contemporary New England menu. Specializes in fresh seafood, New England clam chowder, roast prime rib of beef. Hrs: 7:30-10:30 am, noon-2:30 pm, 5:30-9:30 pm; extended hrs in season. Res accepted. Bar noon-1 am. Bkfst $5-$12, lunch $8-$15, dinner $17.50-$24. Child's menu. Pianist wkends. Parking. Outdoor dining. Jacket. Cr cds: A, D, DS, MC, V.

🄳

★★ **TRUC ORIENT EXPRESS.** *1 Harris St, West Stockbridge (01266). 413/232-4204.* Vietnamese menu. Specializes in Banh Xeo (pancake stuffed with shrimp and pork). Hrs: 11 am-9 pm; wkends to 10 pm. Closed Thanksgiving, Dec 25; also Tues, Nov-Apr. Res accepted.

Bar. A la carte entrees: lunch $7.50-$11, dinner $11.50-$17. Parking. Outdoor dining. Cr cds: A, MC, V.

🄳

★★★ **WILLIAMSVILLE INN.** *MA 41, West Stockbridge (01266). 413/274-6118. www.williamsvilleinn.com.* Specializes in beef, fresh fish, duck, vegetarian dishes. Own baking. Hrs: 6-9 pm; Fri, Sat 5-9:30 pm. Closed Mon-Wed (Nov-mid-June). Res accepted. Bar. Dinner $16-$25. Parking. Intimate atmosphere in 1797 farmhouse. Cr cds: A, MC, V.

🆂🄲 ➳

Sturbridge

Settled ca 1730 **Pop** 7,837 **Elev** 619 ft **Area code** 508 **Zip** 01566-1057

Information Tourist Information Center, 380 Main St; 508/347-2761 or 888/788-7274

What to See and Do

⊠ **Old Sturbridge Village.** A living history museum that re-creates a rural New England town of the 1830s. The museum covers more than 200 acres with more than 40 restored buildings; costumed interpreters demonstrate the life, work, and community celebrations of early 19th-century New Englanders. Working historical farm; many special events; picnic area. (Apr-Nov, daily; closed Dec 25) On US 20 W, 1 mi W of jct I-84 exit 2 and MA Tpke (I-90) exit 9. Phone 508/347-3362. ¢¢¢¢

Special Event

New England Thanksgiving. Old Sturbridge Village. Re-creation of early 19th-century Thanksgiving celebration. Includes turkey shoot, hearth cooking and meetinghouse service. Phone 508/347-3362 or 508/347-5383 (TTY). Thanksgiving Day.

Motels/Motor Lodges

★★ **COMFORT INN & SUITES.** *Hwy 20, 215 Charlton Rd (01566). 508/347-3306; fax 508/347-3514; toll-free 800/228-5151. www.comfortinn.com.* 77 rms, 2 story. May-Nov: S, D $110-$175; each addl $10; under 18 free; lower rates rest of yr. TV; cable (premium), VCR avail. Pool. Playground. Restaurant adj 6:30 am-11 pm. Ck-out 11 am. Business servs avail. In-rm modem link. Sundries. Tennis. Spacious grounds; gardens, fountain. Cr cds: A, C, D, DS, MC, V.

🄳 ⛷ ⚓ ➳ 🔥 🆂🄲

★ **ECONO LODGE.** *682 Main St (01518). 508/347-2324; fax 508/347-7320; res 800/555-2666. www.econolodge.com.* 52 rms, 7 suites. June-Oct: S, D $60-$90; each addl $5; lower rates rest of yr. Crib avail. TV; cable. Pool. Ck-out 11 am. Coin lndry. Some refrigerators. Cr cds: A, MC, V.

🄳 ➳ 🔥 ⚓

★★ **OLD STURBRIDGE VILLAGE LODGES.** *Main St, Rte 20 (01566). 508/347-3327; fax 508/347-3018; toll-free 800/733-1830. www.osv.org.* 59 rms in 7 bldgs, 1-2 story. May-Oct: S, D $80-$115; each addl $5; suites $95-$130; under 12 free; lower rates rest of yr. Crib $5. TV; cable. Pool. Ck-out 11 am. Adj to Old Sturbridge Village. Cr cds: A, DS, MC, V.

D ⇨ ⇴ ⬥ SC

★★★ **PUBLICK HOUSE HISTORIC INN.** *295 Main St (01566). 508/347-3313; fax 508/347-1246. www.publickhouse.com.* 17 rms, 2 story. June-Oct: S, D $99-$165; each addl $5; under 16 free; lower rates rest of yr. Crib $5. TV avail; VCR (movies). Playground. Restaurant 7 am-10 pm (see also PUBLICK HOUSE). Bar noon-midnight. Ck-out 11 am, ck-in 3 pm. Meeting rms. Business servs avail. Bellhops. Tennis. X-country ski 1 mi. Lawn games. Founded in 1771; originally a tavern. Colonial decor; antiques. Located on historic Sturbridge Common. Cr cds: A, D, DS, MC, V.

⇲ ⇝ ⇴ ⬥

★ **STURBRIDGE COACH MOTOR LODGE.** *408 Main St, Rte 20 (01566). 508/347-7327; fax 508/347-2954. www.sturbridgecoach.com.* 54 rms, 2 story. May-Oct: S $45-$89; D $55-$100; each addl $5; higher rates special events; lower rates rest of yr. Crib $5. TV; cable. Pool. Coffee in lobby. Restaurant nearby. Ck-out 11 am. Old Sturbridge Village opp. Cr cds: A, MC, V.

⇨ ⇴ ⬥ SC

B&B/Small Inn

★★ **COLONEL EBENEZER CRAFTS INN.** *Fiske Hill Rd (01566). 508/347-3141; fax 508/347-5073; toll-free 800/782-5425.* 8 rms, 3 story. June-Oct: S, D $90-$155; each addl $5; under 16 free; lower rates rest of yr. Crib $5. TV in sun rm; cable, VCR avail (movies). Pool. Restaurant adj 7 am-10 pm. Ck-out 11 am, ck-in 3 pm. Meeting rm. Business servs avail. Luggage handling. Tennis. X-country ski 2 mi. Lawn games. Built 1786; overlooks woods. Cr cds: A, C, D, MC, V.

⇲ ⇝ ⇨ ⬥ SC

Conference Center

★★★ **STURBRIDGE HOST HOTEL & CONFERENCE CENTER.** *366 Main St (01566). 508/347-7393; fax 508/347-3944; toll-free 800/582-3232. www.fine-hotels.com.* 220 rms, 3 story. Apr-Oct: S, D $109-$149; each addl $15; suites $195-$290; under 18 free; package plans; lower rates rest of yr. Crib free. TV. Indoor pool; whirlpool, poolside serv. Restaurant 7 am-11 pm. Rm serv. Bar to 1 am; entertainment Fri, Sat. Ck-out 11 am. Meeting rms. Bellhops. Valet serv. Sundries. Tennis. X-country ski 3 mi. Exercise rm; sauna. Lawn games. Miniature golf. Many bathrm phones. On lake; paddleboats, rowboats; dockage for small boats. Luxury level. Cr cds: A, C, D, DS, MC, V.

D ⇲ ⇝ ⇨ 🎿 ⇴ ⬥

Restaurants

★★ **PUBLICK HOUSE.** *295 Main St (01566). 508/347-3313. www.publickhouse.com.* Specializes in turkey, prime rib, lobster pie. Hrs: 7 am-10 pm. Res accepted. Bar. Bkfst $3.95-$12.95, lunch $7.95-$11.95, dinner $14.95-$27. Sun bkfst buffet: $10.95. Child's menu. Entertainment Fri, Sat. Outdoor dining. Open hearth. In original Colonial structure built in 1771. Located on historic Sturbridge Common. Cr cds: A, D, MC, V.

SC ⇨

★★ **ROM'S RESTAURANT.** *MA 131 (01566). 508/347-3349. www.sturbridge.com.* Italian, Amer menu. Specialties: veal parmigiana, chicken cacciatore. Own pasta. Hrs: 11:30 am-9 pm; Sat to 10 pm. Closed Thanksgiving, Dec 25. Res accepted. Serv bar. Lunch $3.95-$7.95, dinner $4.95-$12.95. Child's menu. Family-owned. Cr cds: A, D, DS, MC, V.

D ⇨

★★★ **WHISTLING SWAN.** *502 Main St (01566). 508/347-2321. www.thewhistlingswan.com.* Continental, Amer menu. Specializes in seafood, steak. Own baking. Hrs: Whistling Swan 11:30 am-2:30 pm, 5:30-9:30 pm; Sat to 10 pm; Sun noon-8 pm; res accepted. Ugly Duckling Loft 11:30 am-11 pm; Fri, Sat to 11:30 pm. Closed Mon; some major hols. Bar to 1 am. Lunch $4.95-$12.95, dinner $12.95-$23.95. Sun dinner $9.50-$12. Child's menu. Pianist, guitarist. Whistling Swan, on 1st floor, has 3 intimate dining areas; offers fine dining. Ugling Duckling Loft offers casual dining in 1 large dining area; bar. 1800s Greek-Revival house with barn attached; many antiques. Cr cds: A, C, D, DS, ER, MC, V.

D

Sudbury Center

See also Boston

Settled 1638 **Pop** 16,841 **Area code** 978 **Zip** 01776

Information Board of Selectmen, Loring Parsonage, 288 Old Sudbury Rd, Sudbury; 978/443-8891

Sudbury, which has a number of 17th-century buildings, is best known for the Wayside Inn at South Sudbury, which was the scene of Longfellow's *Tales of a Wayside Inn* (1863).

What to See and Do

Great Meadows National Wildlife Refuge. Along with the Concord section (8 mi N), this refuge contains 3,400 acres of freshwater wetlands, open water and upland. More than 200 bird species have been recorded at this diverse habitat area. Visitor center/wildlife education center and head-quarters (May and Oct, daily; winter, Mon-Fri; closed hols in winter). Nature trail, hiking (daily). Office and visitor center off Lincoln Rd. Contact Refuge Manager, Weir Hill Rd. Phone 978/443-4661. **FREE**

Longfellow's Wayside Inn. (1702) A historical and literary shrine, this is America's oldest operating inn. Originally restored by Henry Ford, it was badly damaged by fire in Dec 1955, and restored again by the Ford Foundation. Period furniture. (Daily; closed July 4, Dec 25) Wayside Inn Rd, 3 mi SW, just off US 20. Phone 978/443-1776. Also on the property are

Gristmill. With waterwheel in operation; stone grinds wheat and corn used by inn's bakery. (Apr-Nov, daily)

Martha Mary Chapel. Built and dedicated by Henry Ford in 1940, a nondenominational, nonsectarian chapel. No services; used primarily for weddings. (By appt)

Redstone School. (1798) "The Little Red Schoolhouse" immortalized in "Mary Had a Little Lamb." (May-Oct, daily)

Special Events

Reenactment of March of Sudbury Minutemen to Concord on April 19, 1775. More than 200 costumed men muster on Common before proceeding to Old North Bridge in Concord. (Apr) Phone 978/443-1776.

Fife & Drum Muster and Colonial Fair. Muster takes place on field across from Longfellow's Wayside Inn. Fife and drum corps from New England and surrounding areas compete. Colonial crafts demonstrations and sales. Last Sat Sept. Phone 978/443-8891.

Motels/Motor Lodges

★★ **BEST WESTERN ROYAL PLAZA.** *181 W Boston Post Rd, Marlborough (01752). 508/460-0700; fax 508/480-8218; res 800/780-7234. www.bestwestern.com.* 431 rms, 6 story. S, D $149; each addl $15; suites $150; under 18 free. Crib $5. TV; cable (premium). Indoor pool. Restaurant 6:30 am-10 pm. Rm serv. Bar. Ck-out 11 am. Convention facilities. Business servs avail. In-rm modem link. Game rm. Exercise equipt; sauna. Many refrigerators; microwave in suites. Cr cds: A, C, D, DS, MC, V.

⌧ 🔥 ⇌ 🕇

★ **CLARION CARRIAGE HOUSE INN.** *738 Boston Post Rd, Sudbury (01776). 978/443-2223; fax 978/443-5830; toll-free 800/637-0113. www.choicehotels.com.* 39 rms, 3 story, 5 suites. No elvtr. S, D $150-$175; suites $175; under 18 free; wkends (2-day min). Crib free. TV; cable (premium), VCR avail (movies). Complimentary full bkfst, coffee in rms. Ck-out 11 am. Business servs avail. Valet serv. Free guest lndry. Exercise equipt. Microwaves avail. Cr cds: A, C, D, DS, MC, V.

D 🕇 ⇌ 🔥

Hotel

★★★ **RADISSON INN.** *75 Felton St, Marlborough (01752). 508/480-0015; fax 508/485-2242; toll-free 800/333-3333. www.radisson.com.* 206 rms, 5 story. S, D $89-$159; each addl $10; suites $195-$295; under 18 free; wkend rates. Crib free. TV; cable (premium), VCR avail (movies). Indoor

pool; whirlpool. Restaurant 6:30 am-2 pm, 5:30-10 pm; wkend hrs vary. Rm serv. Bar 11:30-1 am. Ck-out noon. Meeting rms. Business servs avail. In-rm modem link. Sundries. Gift shop. Exercise rm; sauna. Raquetball courts. Some refrigerators; microwaves avail. Bathrm phone, wet bar in suites. Balconies in suites. Cr cds: A, D, DS, ER, JCB, MC, V.

D ⇌ 🕇 ⇌ 🔥

B&Bs/Small Inns

★★ **THE ARABIAN HORSE INN.** *277 Old Sudbury Rd, Sudbury (01776). 978/443-7400; fax 978/443-0234. www.arabianhorseinn.com.* 4 rms, 1 with shower only, 3 story, 1 suite. June-Nov: S, D $149-$269; lower rates rest of yr. Pet accepted. TV; cable (premium). Complimentary full bkfst, coffee in rms. Restaurant nearby. Ck-out 11 am, ck-in 3 pm. In-rm modem link. X-country ski on site. Some balconies. Built in 1886. Arabian horses, antique cars on site. Totally nonsmoking. Cr cds: A, MC, V.

🐾 ⛷ ⇌ 🔥

★★ **LONGFELLOWS WAYSIDE INN.** *72 Wayside Inn Rd, Sudbury (01776). 978/443-1776; fax 978/443-8041; toll-free 800/339-1776. www.wayside.org.* 10 rms, 2 story. Sept-Dec: S $72-$145; D $98-$145; lower rates rest of yr. Complimentary full bkfst. Restaurant (see LONGFELLOW'S WAYSIDE INN). Bar. Ck-out 11 am, ck-in 3 pm. Gift shop. Period furnishings. Historic inn (1716); self-guided tours through restored public rooms. National historic site; on grounds are Wayside Gristmill and Redstone School, built by former owner Henry Ford. Totally nonsmoking. Cr cds: A, D, DS, MC, V.

D ⇌ 🔥

Restaurant

★★ **LONGFELLOW'S WAYSIDE INN.** *72 Wayside Inn Rd (01776). 978/443-1776. www.wayside.org.* Specializes in fresh seafood, prime rib. Hrs: 11:30 am-3 pm, 5-9 pm; Sun, hols, noon-8 pm. Closed Dec 25. Res accepted. Bar. Lunch $7.50-$10.50. Complete meals: dinner $16-$22. Child's menu. Totally nonsmoking. Cr cds: A, C, D, DS, ER, MC, V.

D

Truro and North Truro (Cape Cod)

Settled Truro: ca 1700 **Pop** 2,087 **Elev** 20 ft **Area code** 508 **Zip** Truro 02666; North Truro 02652

Information Cape Cod Chamber of Commerce, US 6 and MA 132, PO Box 790, Hyannis 02601-0790; 508/362-3225 or 888/CAPECOD

Web www.capecodchamber.org

Truro, named for one of the Channel towns of England, is today perhaps the most sparsely settled part of the Cape—with great stretches of rolling moorland dotted only occasionally with cottages. On the hill above the Pamet River marsh are two early 19th-century churches; one is now the town hall. The countryside is a favorite resort of artists and writers.

What to See and Do

Fishing. Surf casting on Atlantic beaches. Boat ramp at Pamet and Depot Rds; fee for use, harbor master on duty.

Pilgrim Heights Area. Interpretive display, self-guided nature trails, picnicking; rest rms. Cape Cod National Seashore (see). Off US 6. Phone 508/487-1256. **FREE**

Swimming. Head of the Meadow. A fine Atlantic beach (fee). N on US 6 and W of Chamber of Commerce booth. **Corn Hill Beach.** On the bay (fee). S on US 6, then E. A sticker for all beaches must be purchased from National Park Service Visitor Center or at beach entrances. No lifeguards. (Mid-June-Labor Day)

Truro Historical Society Museum. Collection of artifacts from the town's historic past, including shipwreck mementos, whaling gear, ship models, 17th-century firearms, pirate chest and period rms. (June-Sept, daily) Highland Rd in N Truro. Phone 508/487-3397. ¢¢

Motels/Motor Lodges

★ **CROW'S NEST MOTEL.** *496 Shore Rd, North Truro (02652).* 508/487-9031; toll-free 800/499-9799. *www.capecodtravel.com.* 33 kit. units, 2 story. No A/C. Late June-Labor Day: S, D $105-$112; each addl $10; wkly rates; lower rates Apr-late June, after Labor Day-Nov. Closed rest of yr. Crib free. TV; cable. Ck-out 10 am. Balconies. On beach. Cr cds: DS, MC, V.

★ **EAST HARBOUR MOTEL & COTTAGES.** *618 Shore Rd, North Truro (02652).* 508/487-0505; fax 508/487-6693. *www.eastharbour.com.* 9 rms, 7 kit. cottages, 1 suite. No A/C. Late June-Labor Day (2-day min): S, D $86-$110; cottages to 4, $825-$875/wk; lower rates mid-Apr-late June, after Labor Day-late Oct. Closed rest of yr. TV; cable. Complimentary coffee. Restaurant nearby. Ck-out 10 am. Coin lndry. Refrigerators, microwaves. Picnic tables, grills. Private beach. Cr cds: A, DS, MC, V.

★ **HARBOR VIEW VILLAGE.** *168 Shore Rd, North Truro (02652).* 508/487-1087; fax 508/487-6269. *www.harborviewvillage.com.* 17 rms, 9 kits, 3 cottages. No A/C. No rm phones. Late June-Labor Day: S, D $75-$93; each addl $10-$15; kits., cottages $700-$850/wk; wkly rates; lower rates rest of yr. Children over 7 yrs only (in season). TV. Restaurants nearby. Ck-out 10 am. Refrigerators. Overlooking private beach. Cr cds: MC, V.

Cottage Colony

★★ **KALMAR VILLAGE.** *674 Shore Rd Rte 6A, Truro (02652).* 508/487-0585; fax 508/487-5827. *ww.kalmarvillage.com.* 50 units, 46 kit. cottages. No A/C. July-Labor Day: kit. cottages $725-$1,595/wk; each addl $100-$150/wk; lower rates late May-June, after Labor Day-early Oct. Closed rest of yr. Crib free. TV; cable. Pool. Restaurant nearby. Ck-out 10 am, ck-in 3 pm. Coin lndry. Microwaves avail. Picnic tables, grills. On private beach. Cr cds: DS, MC, V.

Restaurants

★ **ADRIAN'S.** *535 MA 6, North Truro (02652).* 508/487-4360. *www.capecod.com/adrians.* Regional Italian menu. Specialties: shrimp pizza, linguine alle vongole, cayenne-crusted salmon. Hrs: 8 am-noon, 5:30-10 pm. Closed mid-Oct-mid-May. Bar. Bkfst $3.95-$7.50, dinner $6.95-$19.95. Child's menu. Outdoor dining. Overlooks Provincetown and bay. Cr cds: A, MC, V.

★★ **BLACKSMITH SHOP RESTAURANT.** *17 Truro Center Rd, Truro (02666).* 508/349-6554. Specializes in local seafood, free-range chicken, pasta. Hrs: 7 am-1 pm, 5-10 pm; Sun brunch 9 am-2 pm. Closed Dec 25; also Mon-Tues off-season. Res accepted. No A/C. Bar to midnight. Bkfst $3-$9, dinner $10-$21. Sun brunch $3-$11. Child's menu. Antiques; carousel horse. Cr cds: A, MC, V.

★ **MONTANO'S.** *481 MA 6, North Truro (02652).* 508/487-2026. *www.montanos.com.* Italian, Amer menu. Specialties: veal saltimbocca, seafood Fra Diavolo, baked stuffed lobster. Hrs: 4:30-10 pm; early-bird dinner 4:30-6 pm. Closed Dec 25. Res accepted. Serv bar. Dinner $8.95-$18.95. Child's menu. Nautical decor. Cr cds: A, DS, MC, V.

★ **PAPARAZZI.** *518 Shore Rd, North Truro (02652).* 508/487-7272. Italian, seafood menu. Specializes in local seafood, prime rib. Salad bar. Hrs: noon-10 pm; Mon, Tue from 4:30 pm. Closed Dec. Serv bar. Dinner $10-$30. Child's menu. Nautical decor. Overlooks bay. Cr cds: A, DS, MC, V.

Uxbridge

(see Worcester)

Waltham

See also Boston

Settled 1634 **Pop** 59,226 **Elev** 50 ft **Area code** 781 **Zip** 02154

Information Waltham West Suburban Chamber of Commerce, 84 South St; 781/894-4700

Web www.walthamchamber.com

The name Waltham, taken from the English town of Waltham Abbey, means "a home in the forest," and is still appropriate today, due to the town's many wooded areas. Originally an agricultural community, Waltham is now an industrial center. It is also the home of Bentley College and Regis College.

What to See and Do

Brandeis University. (1948) 3,700 students. The first Jewish-founded nonsectarian university in the US. Its 250-acre campus includes Three Chapels, Rose Art Museum (Sept-May, Tues-Sun; closed hols; free); Spingold Theater Arts Center (plays presented Oct-May; fee); and Slosberg Music Center, with classical and jazz performances (Sept-May). 415 South St. Phone 781/736-4300.

Cardinal Spellman Philatelic Museum. Exhibition gallery; library. (Tues-Thurs, Sat, Sun; closed hols) 4 mi W on US 20, in Weston, at 235 Wellesley St. Phone 781/894-6735. **FREE**

Gore Place. A living history farm, Gore Place may be New England's finest example of Federal-period residential architecture; changing exhibits; 40 acres of cultivated fields. The mansion, designed in Paris and built in 1805, has 22 rms filled with examples of early American, European, and Asian antiques. (Mid-Apr-mid-Nov, daily exc Mon) On US 20 at the Waltham-Watertown line. Phone 781/894-2798. ¢¢

Lyman Estate "The Vale". (1793) Designed by Samuel McIntire for Boston merchant Theodore Lyman. Enlarged and remodeled in the 1880s, the ballrm and parlor retain Federal design. Landscaped grounds. Five operating greenhouses contain grape vines, camellias, orchids, and herbs. House open by appt for groups only. Greenhouses (Mon-Sat, also Sun afternoons). 185 Lyman St. Phone 781/893-7232. ¢¢

Motels/Motor Lodges

★ ★ **BEST WESTERN TLC HOTEL.** *477 Totten Pond Rd (02451).* 781/890-7800; fax 781/890-4937; res 800/780-7234. www.bestwestern.com. 100 rms, 6 story. S, D $130-$195; each addl $10; under 12 free; higher rates special events. Crib free. TV; cable (premium), VCR avail. Indoor pool. Complimentary coffee in rms. Restaurant 7 am-10 pm; Sat, Sun 7-11 am, 5-11 pm. Rm serv. Bar 11 am-11 pm. Ck-out 11 am. Meeting rms. Business servs avail. In-rm modem link. Sundries. Exercise equipt; sauna. Health club privileges. Refrigerators, microwaves avail. Balconies. Cr cds: A, C, D, DS, MC, V.

⊅ ⇌ ⅄ ⊠ ⚒

★ ★ **HOME SUITES INN.** *455 Totten Pond Rd (02451).* 781/890-3000; fax 781/890-0233; toll-free 800/424-4021. www.homesuitesinn.com. 116 rms, 3 story. Sept-Oct: S $75-$115; D $75-$155; each addl $10; suites $89-$169; kit. unit $169; under 18 free; wkly, wkend, hol rates; higher rates special events; lower rates rest of yr. Crib free. TV; cable (premium), VCR (movies). Pool. Complimentary continental bkfst, coffee in rms. Restaurant 11 am-11 pm. Bar to midnight. Ck-out 11 am. Coin lndry. Business servs avail.

In-rm modem link. Valet serv. Sundries. Health club privileges. Many refrigerators, microwaves. Picnic tables. Cr cds: A, D, DS, MC, V.

⊅ ⇌ ⊠ ⚒

Hotel

★ ★ ★ **WESTIN.** *70 3rd Ave (02451).* 781/290-5600; fax 781/290-5626; res 800/937-8461. www.westin.com. 346 rms, 2-8 story. S, D $89-$275; each addl $15; family, wkly, wkend rates. Crib free. TV; cable, VCR avail. Indoor pool; whirlpool. Restaurant 6:30 am-10 pm. Rm serv 24 hrs. Bar; entertainment. Ck-out 1 pm. Convention facilities. Business center. In-rm modem link. Gift shop. Free garage parking. Airport transportation. Exercise equipt; sauna, steam rm. Cr cds: A, D, DS, MC, V.

⊅ ⇌ ⅄ ⊠ ⚒ ⚹

All Suite

★ ★ **DOUBLETREE GUEST SUITES BOSTON/ WALTHAM.** *550 Winter St (02451).* 781/890-6767; fax 781/890-9097; res 800/222-8733. www.doubletree.com. 275 suites, 8 story. Suites $175; each addl $15; under 18 free; lower rates rest of yr. Crib free. TV; cable (premium), VCR avail. Indoor pool; whirlpool. Coffee in rms. Restaurant (see GRILLE AT HOBBS BROOK). Bar 11:30 am-midnight. Ck-out noon. Coin lndry. Convention facilities. Business center. In-rm modem link. Gift shop. Exercise equipt; sauna. Health club privileges. Game rm. Wet bars; refrigerators, microwaves avail. Cr cds: A, C, D, DS, ER, JCB, MC, V.

⊅ ⇌ ⅄ ⊠ ⚒ ⚹

Restaurants

★ ★ ★ **GRILL AT HOBBS BROOK.** *550 Winter St (02451).* 781/487-4263. Specializes in grilled dishes. Hrs: 6:30 am-2 pm, 5-9:30 pm; Sat 7 am-2 pm, 5-10 pm; early-bird dinner to 6:30 pm; Sun brunch 7 am-2 pm. Res accepted. Bar 11:30 am-midnight. Wine list. Bkfst $6-$12.95, lunch $8-$20, dinner $13-$27. Sun brunch $12.95. Child's menu. Pianist evenings. Spacious, elegant rms offer views of chef's herb and vegetable gardens. Cr cds: A, D, DS, MC, V.

⊅

★ ★ ★ **IL CAPRICCIO.** *888 Main St (02451).* 781/894-2234. Italian menu. Specializes in baccala gnocchi, roast trout. Own pasta. Hrs: 5-10 pm. Closed Sun; major hols. Bar. Wine list. Dinner $17-$26. Complete meals: dinner $38. Fine dining. Totally nonsmoking. Cr cds: A, DS, MC, V.

⊅

★ ★ **R PLACE.** *312 Washington St, Wellesley Hills (02481).* 781/237-4560. www.opentable.com. Eclectic menu. Specialties: Southwestern Caesar salad, Louisiana crab cakes. Hrs: 11:30 am-2:30 pm, 5:30-10 pm. Closed Mon; Jan 1, Thanksgiving. Wine, beer. Lunch $4-$12, dinner $16-$23. Street parking. Fine dining; original artwork. Cr cds: A, C, D, DS, ER, MC, V.

⊅

★★ **TUSCAN GRILL.** *361 Moody St (02453). 781/891-5486.* Italian menu. Specializes in wood-grilled dishes, seasonal items. Own baking, pasta. Hrs: 5:30-10 pm; Sun 5-9 pm. Closed July 4, Thanksgiving, Dec 24, 25. Res accepted. Bar. A la carte entrees: dinner $13.95-$17.95. Parking. Modern Italian trattoria with open kitchen. Cr cds: DS, MC, V.
D

Wellesley

See also Boston

Settled 1661 **Pop** 26,613 **Elev** 141 ft **Area code** 781 **Zip** 02181
Information Chamber of Commerce, One Hollis St, Suite 111; 781/235-2446
Web www.wellesleyweb.com

This Boston suburb was named after an 18th-century landowner, Samuel Welles. It is an educational and cultural center. There are four widely known institutions here: Dana Hall, girls' preparatory school; Babson College, a business school; Massachusetts Bay Community College; and Wellesley College.

What to See and Do
Wellesley College. (1870) (2,200 women). Founded by Henry F. Durant. 500 wooded acres bordering Lake Waban. On campus are Davis Museum and Cultural Center and Margaret C. Ferguson Greenhouses (daily). Central & Washington Sts, on MA 16/135. Phone 781/283-1000.

Motel/Motor Lodge
★★ **WELLESLEY INN ON THE SQUARE.** *576 Washington St (02482). 781/235-0180; fax 781/239-0281; toll-free 800/233-4686. www.wellesleyinn.com.* 70 rms, 3-4 story. S $82-$90; D $92-$110; each addl $10; suites $150; under 18 free. Crib free. TV; cable (premium). Restaurant 7-11 am, 11:30 am-2:30 pm; 5:30-9:30 pm; Sun hrs vary. Rm serv. Bar 11:30 am-11:30 pm. Ck-out 11 am. Meeting rms. Business servs avail. Valet serv. Cr cds: A, C, D, DS, MC, V.
⬛ 🐾 SC

Hotel
★★★ **SHERATON NEEDHAM HOTEL.** *100 Cabot St (02062). 781/444-1110. www.sheraton.com.* 247 rms, 12 story. S, D $225-$375; under 18 free. Crib avail. TV; cable (premium). Indoor pool; whirlpool. Restaurant 6:30 am-10 pm. Bar to midnight. Ck-out noon, ck-in 4 pm. Meeting rms. Business center. In-rm modem link. Concierge. Exercise equipt. Minibars; many refrigerators in suites. Cr cds: A, C, D, DS, ER, JCB, MC, V.
⬛ 🏃 🎿 🔥 ⬛

Restaurant
★★★ **BLUE GINGER.** *583 Washington St (02482). 781/283-5790.* Specialties sea bass, calamari. Hrs: 11:30 am-2 pm; 5:30-9:30 pm; Fri, Sat 5:30-10 pm; Closed Sun. Lunch $8-$11; dinner $18-$25. Cr cds: MC, V.
D

Wellfleet

Settled ca 1725 **Pop** 2,749 **Elev** 50 ft **Area code** 508 **Zip** 02667
Information Chamber of Commerce, PO Box 571; 508/349-2510
Web www.wellfleetchamber.com

Once a fishing town, Wellfleet dominated the New England oyster business in the latter part of the 19th century. It is now a summer resort and an art gallery town, with many tourist homes and cottages. Southeast of town is the Marconi Station Area of Cape Cod National Seashore (see). Fishermen here can try their luck in the Atlantic surf or off deep-sea charter fishing boats.

What to See and Do
Historical Society Museum. Marine items, whaling tools, Marconi memorabilia, needlecraft, photograph collection, marine and primitive paintings. (Late June-mid-Sept, Tues-Sat; schedule may vary) Phone 508/349-9157. ¢

Sailing. Rentals at Wellfleet Marina; accommodates 150 boats; launching ramp, facilities.

Swimming. At numerous bayside and ocean beaches on marked roads off US 6. Freshwater ponds with swimming are scattered through woods E of US 6. (Parking sticker necessary mid-June to Labor Day.)

Wellfleet Bay Wildlife Sanctuary. Operated by the Massachusetts Audubon Society. Self-guiding nature trails. Natural history summer day camp for children. Guided nature walks, lectures, classes, Monomoy Island natural history tours. Sanctuary (Memorial Day-Columbus Day, daily; rest of yr, Tues-Sun). In South Wellfleet, on W side of US 6. Contact PO Box 236, South Wellfleet 02663. Phone 508/349-2615. ¢¢

Motels/Motor Lodges
★★ **EVEN'TIDE MOTEL & COTTAGES.** *650 Rte 6, South Wellfleet (02663). 508/349-3410; fax 508/349-7804; toll-free 800/368-0007. www.eventidemotel.com.* 31 rms, 2 story, 8 suites, 3 kits. Mid-June-mid-Sept wkends (2-day min): S, D $69-$140; each addl $7-$10; suites $89-$107; kit. units (3-day min) $87-$145; wkly rates; lower rates rest of yr. Crib $5-$15. TV; cable. Indoor pool. Playground. Complimentary coffee in rms. Ck-out 11 am. Coin lndry. Refrigerators. Picnic tables, grills. Cr cds: A, C, D, DS, MC, V.
D ⬛ ⬛ 🔥

★ **SOUTHFLEET MOTOR INN.** *Rte 6, South Wellfleet (02663).* 508/349-3580; fax 508/349-0250; toll-free 800/ 334-3715. *www.southfleetmotorinn.com.* 30 rms, 2 story. Late June-Labor Day (2-day min): S, D $125-$136; each addl $10; lower rates Apr-late June, after Labor Day-Oct. Closed rest of yr. Crib free. TV; cable (premium). 2 pools, 1 indoor; whirlpool. Complimentary morning coffee in lobby. Restaurant adj 8 am-10 pm (in season). Bar noon-1 am. Ck-out 11 am. Meeting rm. In-rm modem link. Game rm. Refrigerators. Cr cds: A, MC, V.
⊠ 🔥 SC

★★ **WELLFLEET MOTEL & LODGE.** *146 Rte 6, South Wellfleet (02663).* 508/349-3535; fax 508/349-1192; toll-free 800/852-2900. *www.wellfleetmotel.com.* 65 rms, 1-2 story. Late June-Labor Day: S, D $76-$125; each addl $8-$10; suites $109-$180; lower rates rest of yr. Crib $6. TV; cable (premium). 2 pools, 1 indoor; whirlpool. Complimentary coffee in rms. Restaurant 7 am-noon in season. Bar. Ck-out 11 am. Meeting rm. Refrigerators; microwaves avail. Picnic tables, grills. Cr cds: A, MC, V.
D ⊠ ⊠ 🔥

B&Bs/Small Inns

★ **THE HOLDEN INN.** *140 Commercial St (02667).* 508/349-3450. 27 rms, 13 with bath, 4 A/C, 2 story. No rm phones. May-mid-Oct: S $55; D $85. Closed rest of yr. Children over 14 yrs only. Restaurant nearby. Ck-out 10 am, ck-in 2 pm. Picnic tables. Built 1840. Cr cds: A, MC, V.
⊠ 🔥

★★ **INN AT DUCK CREEK.** *70 Main St (02667).* 508/349-9333; fax 508/349-0234; res 508/349-9333. 25 rms, 17 with bath, 4 A/C, 2-3 story. No rm phones. July-Aug: D $65-$95; each addl $15; lower rates mid-May-June, Sept-mid-Oct. Closed rest of yr. Crib $10. Complimentary continental bkfst. Restaurant (see DUCK CREEK TAVERN ROOM). Ck-out 11 am, ck-in 1 pm. Former sea captain's house (1815) furnished with period antiques. Sitting porch overlooks Duck Creek. Cr cds: A, MC, V.
⊠ 🔥

Restaurants

★★★ **AESOP'S TABLES.** *316 Main St, Wellfleet (Cape Cod) (02667).* 508/349-6450. Specialties: fresh pasta Neptune, uptown marinated duck, Aesop's oysters. Own baking. Hrs: noon-3 pm, 5:30 pm-1 am. Closed mid-Oct-mid-May. Res accepted. No A/C. Bar. Wine cellar. A la carte entrees: lunch $10-$15, dinner $13-$24. Outdoor dining, 6 dining rms in restored house (1805). Cr cds: A, D, MC, V.
D

★ **DUCK CREEKE TAVERN ROOM.** *70 Main St (02667).* 508/349-7369. *www.innatduckcreeke.com.* Specializes in seafood. Own coffee roaster. Hrs: 6:30-11 pm; early-bird dinner 5:30-7 pm. Closed mid-Oct-mid-May. Res accepted. Bar. Dinner $11-$17. Child's menu. Entertainment. Nautical decor; duck decoys. Colonial tavern atmosphere. Cr cds: A, MC, V.

★★ **VANRENSSELAER'S.** *1019 US 6, South Wellfleet (02667).* 508/349-2127. *www.vanrensselaers.com.* Specializes in creative pasta, fresh seafood, black Angus steaks. Salad bar. Hrs: 8 am-noon, 4:30-10 pm. Closed Dec-Mar. Res accepted. Bar 4-11 pm. Bkfst $2.75-$7.95, dinner $8-$19.95. Child's menu. Outdoor dining. Family-owned. Cr cds: A, D, DS, MC, V.
D

Williamstown

Settled 1749 **Pop** 8,424 **Elev** 638 ft **Area code** 413 **Zip** 01267

A French and Indian War hero, Colonel Ephraim Williams, Jr., left a bequest in 1755 to establish a "free school" in West Hoosuck, provided the town be renamed after him. In 1765, the town name was changed to Williamstown, and in 1793, the school became Williams College. The life of this charming Berkshire Hills town still centers around the college.

What to See and Do

Sterling and Francine Clark Art Institute. More than 30 paintings by Renoir, other French Impressionists; old-master paintings; English and American silver; American artists Homer, Sargent, Cassatt, Remington. Extensive art library (Mon-Fri). Museum shop. Picnic facilities on grounds. (July-Labor Day, daily; rest of yr, Tues-Sun; closed Jan 1, Thanksgiving, Dec 25) 225 South St. Phone 413/458-9545. ¢¢

Williams College. (1793) 1,950 students. Private liberal arts college; campus has wide variety of architectural styles, ranging from colonial to Gothic. Chapin Library of rare books is one of nation's finest, housing the four founding documents of the US. Hopkins Observatory, the nation's oldest (1836), has planetarium shows. Adams Memorial Theatre presents plays. The Paul Whiteman Collection houses Whiteman's recordings and memorabilia. 1 blk E of central green, US 7. Phone 413/597-3131. Also here is

Williams College Museum of Art. Considered one of the finest college art museums in the country. Houses approx 11,000 pieces. Exhibits emphasize contemporary, modern, American, and non-Western art. Museum shop. (Tues-Sat, also Sun afternoons and Mon hols; closed Jan 1, Thanksgiving, Dec 25) Main St. Phone 413/597-2429. FREE

Motels/Motor Lodges

★★★ **1896 HOUSE.** *910 Cold Spring Rd (01267).* 413/458-1896; toll-free 888/666-1896. *www.1896house.com.* 29 rms in 2 bldgs. Memorial Day-Columbus Day: S, D $60-$138; each addl $10; apt $109-$189; ski; golf rates; under 8 free; higher rates: college events, special wkends; lower rates rest of yr. Crib $5. TV; cable. Heated pool. Complimentary continental bkfst. Coffee in rms. Restaurant (see THE 1896 HOUSE). Ck-out 11 am. Business servs avail. Downhill/ x-country ski 10 mi. Refrigerators avail. On brook and pond. Cr cds: A, C, D, DS, MC, V.

⊡ ⛑ ⛱ ⛆ 🐾

★★ **BERKSHIRE HILLS MOTEL.** *1146 Cold Spring Rd (01267). 413/458-3950; fax 413/458-5878; toll-free 800/ 388-9677. www.berkshirehillsmotel.com.* 21 rms, 2 story. June-Oct: S, D $109-$129; each addl $10; under 3 free; lower rates rest of yr. Crib free. TV; cable. Heated pool. Complimentary buffet bkfst. Restaurant adj 5-10 pm. Ck-out 11 am. Downhill/x-country ski 5 mi. Gazebo in garden; wooded grounds bordering brook. Cr cds: A, D, DS, MC, V.

⛑ ⛱ ⛆ 🐾

★★ **FOUR ACRES MOTEL.** *213 Main St; Rte 2 (01267). 413/458-8158. www.fouracresmotel.com.* 31 rms, 1-2 story. May-Oct: S $50-$65; D $75; each addl $10; higher rates special events; lower rates rest of yr. Crib $10. TV; cable. Pool. Complimentary continental bkfst. Restaurant adj 11 am-10 pm. Ck-out 11 am. Downhill ski 15 mi. Lawn games. Refrigerators avail. Some balconies. Picnic tables. Cr cds: A, C, D, DS, MC, V.

⛑ ⛱ ⛆ 🐾 **SC**

Hotels

★★★ **THE ORCHARDS HOTEL.** *222 Adams Rd (01267). 413/458-9611; fax 413/458-3273; toll-free 800/225-1517. www.theorchardshotel.com.* 49 rms, 3 story. Mid-May-mid-Nov: S, D $165-$230; each addl $30; MAP avail; lower rates rest of yr. Crib $10. TV; cable (premium), VCR (movies). Pool; whirlpool. Dining rm (see THE ORCHARDS). Afternoon tea 3:30-4:30 pm. Rm serv. Bar noon-11:30 pm. Ck-out noon, ck-in 4 pm. Business servs avail. In-rm modem link. Luggage handling. Concierge serv. Tennis privileges. 18-hole golf privileges, pro, greens fee $55-$75. Downhill/x-country ski 6 mi. Exercise equipt; sauna, steam rm. Bathrm phones; many refrigerators; some fireplaces. Library. Cr cds: A, D, MC, V.

⊡ ⛑ 🏋 🎣 ⛱ 🎿 ⛆ 🐾

★★★ **WILLIAMS INN.** *On the Green, Rte 7 & 2 (01267). 413/458-9371; fax 413/458-2767; toll-free 800/828-0133. www.williamsinn.com.* 100 rms, 3 story. May-Oct: S $100; D $135-$160; each addl $15; under 14 free; package plan; lower rates rest of yr. Crib free. Pet accepted, some restrictions; $10. TV; cable. Indoor pool; whirlpool. Restaurant 7 am-10 pm. Rm serv. Bar 11-1 am; entertainment Fri, Sat. Ck-out 11 am. Meeting rms. Business servs avail. Valet serv. Sundries. Downhill/x-country ski 6 mi. Sauna. Refrigerators avail. Picnic tables. Cr cds: A, C, D, DS, MC, V.

⊡ 🐾 ⛱ ⛆ 🐾

Restaurants

★★ **1896 HOUSE.** *866 Cold Spring Rd (01267). 413/458-1896.* Specializes in fresh fish, roast turkey, prime rib. Hrs: 4:30 pm-close; Sun from noon; early-bird dinner to 5:30 pm. Res accepted. Bar. Dinner $6.96-$19.96. Parking. Pianist Sat. Outdoor dining. Cr cds: A, D, DS, MC, V.

★★★ **LE JARDIN.** *777 Cold Spring Rd (01267). 413/458-8032.* Continental menu. Specializes in fresh seafood, lamb chops, steak. Own baking. Hrs: 5-9 pm; Sat to 10 pm. Closed Tues Sept-June. Res accepted. Bar. Dinner $15-$25. Parking. Converted 19th-century estate overlooking trout ponds, waterfall. Guest rms avail. Cr cds: A, C, D, DS, ER, MC, V.

★★★ **THE ORCHARDS.** *222 Adams Rd (01267). 413/458-9611. www.theorchardshotel.com.* Continental menu. Menu changes daily. Own baking. Hrs: 7-10 am, noon-2 pm, 5:30-9 pm; Sun 7 am-2 pm; Sun brunch 10 am-2 pm. Res accepted. Bar noon-11:30 pm. Wine cellar. A la carte entrees: bkfst $6-$12, lunch $8-$16, dinner $17-$30. Sun brunch $7-$20. Child's menu. Parking. Outdoor dining in season. Scenic view of fountain pond with exotic fish, mountains. Totally nonsmoking. Cr cds: A, D, MC, V.

⊡ 🎣

★★ **WATER STREET GRILL.** *123 Water St (01267). 413/458-2175.* Continental menu. Specialties: fajitas, fresh seafood, pasta. Hrs: 11:30 am-11 pm. Closed Easter, Thanksgiving, Dec 25. Res accepted. Bar. A la carte entrees: lunch $4-$8, dinner $7-$14. Buffet: lunch Mon-Fri $5.95. Child's menu. Entertainment Fri, Sat. Parking. Locally popular; semi-formal atmosphere. Cr cds: A, MC, V.

⊡

Woods Hole

See also Martha's Vineyard, Nantucket Island

Pop 925 **Elev** 15 ft **Area code** 508

Information Cape Cod Chamber of Commerce, US 6 and MA 132, PO Box 790, Hyannis 02601-0790; 508/362-3225 or 888/CAPECOD

Web www.capecodchamber.org

A principal port of Cape Cod in the town of Falmouth. Ferries leave here for Martha's Vineyard. The Oceanographic Institution and Marine Biological Laboratories study tides, currents, and marine life (closed to the public).

What to See and Do

Bradley House Museum. Model of Woods Hole Village (ca 1895); audiovisual show of local history; restored spritsail sailboat; model ships. Walking tour of village. (July-Aug, Tues-Sat; June and Sept, Wed, Sat; schedule may vary) Phone 508/548-7270. **FREE**

Car/Passenger Boat Trips. Woods Hole, Martha's Vineyard Steamship Authority conducts trips to Martha's Vineyard (all yr). Schedule may vary. Phone 508/477-8600. ¢¢¢

Motel/Motor Lodge

★★ **NAUTILUS MOTOR INN.** *539 Woods Hole Rd (02543).* *508/548-1525; fax 508/457-9674; toll-free 800/654-2333. www.nautilusinn.com.* 54 rms in 3 bldgs, 2 story. Late June-late Aug: S, D $82-$170; each addl $6; package plans; lower rates mid-Apr-late June, late Aug-late Oct. Closed rest of yr. TV; cable (premium). Pool. Complimentary coffee in lobby. Restaurant adj 5:30-10 pm. Ck-out 11 am. Meeting rms. In-rm modem link. Tennis. Refrigerators avail. Balconies. Opp beach. Cr cds: A, D, DS, MC, V.

Restaurants

★★ **LANDFALL.** *2 Luscombe Ave (02543). 508/548-1758.* Specializes in lobster, swordfish, steak. Hrs: 11 am-10 pm; Sun brunch to 3 pm. Closed Dec-Apr. Res accepted. No A/C. Bar to 1 am. Lunch $6-$10, dinner $11-$21. Sun brunch $4-$10. Child's menu. Outdoor dining. Nautical atmosphere; maritime artifacts, old dory. On dock; overlooks harbor. Family-owned. Cr cds: A, MC, V.

★ **LEESIDE.** *29 Rail Rd (01267). 508/548-9744.* Specializes in seafood. Hrs: 11:30-10 pm; Sun from noon. Closed Thanksgiving, Dec 25. Bar to 1 am. Lunch, dinner $4.95-$10.95. Child's menu. Entertainment Fri, Sat. Nautical decor. Harbor view. Family-owned. Cr cds: A, MC, V.

Worcester

Settled 1673 **Pop** 172,648 **Elev** 480 ft **Area code** 508

Information Worcester County Convention & Visitors Bureau, 30 Worcester Center Blvd, 01608; 508/753-2920

Web www.worcester.org

The municipal seal of Worcester (WUS-ter) calls it the "Heart of the Commonwealth." One of the largest cities in New England, it is an important industrial center. Also a cultural center, it has some outstanding museums and twelve colleges.

What to See and Do

American Antiquarian Society. Research library is the largest collection of source materials pertaining to the first 250 yrs of American history. Specializing in the period up to 1877, the library has ⅔ of all pieces known to have been printed in this country between 1640 and 1821. (Mon-Fri; closed hols) Guided tours (Wed afternoons). 185 Salisbury St. Schedule may vary. Phone 508/755-5221. **FREE**

EcoTarium. Contains museum with environmental science exhibits; solar/lunar observatory, multimedia planetarium theater; African Hall. Indoor-outdoor wildlife, aquariums; train ride; picnicking. (Daily; closed hols) 222 Harrington Way, 1½ mi E. Phone 508/791-9211. ¢¢

Higgins Armory Museum. Large exhibit of medieval-Renaissance and feudal Japan's arms and armor; paintings, tapestries, stained glass. Armor demonstrations and try-ons. (Tues-Sat, also Sun afternoons; closed hols) 100 Barber Ave. Phone 508/853-6015. ¢¢

John H. Chaffy Blackstone River Valley National Heritage Corridor. This 250,000-acre region extends southward to Providence, RI (see) and includes myriad points of historical and cultural interest. Visitor center at Massachusetts Audubon Society's Broad Meadow Brook Wildlife Sanctuary, tours and interpretive programs. 414 Massasoit Rd. Phone 508/755-8899. ¢

Salisbury Mansion. (1772) House of leading businessman and philanthropist Stephen Salisbury. Restored to 1830s appearance. Guided tours. (Thurs-Sun afternoons; closed hols) 40 Highland St. Phone 508/753-8278. ¢

Worcester Art Museum. Fifty centuries of paintings, sculpture, decorative arts, prints, drawings, and photography from America to ancient Egypt; changing exhibits; tours, films, lectures. Cafe, gift shop. (Wed-Sun; closed hols) 55 Salisbury St. Phone 508/799-4406. ¢¢¢

Worcester Common Outlets. More than 100 outlet stores can be found at this indoor outlet mall. Food court. (Daily) I-290, exit 16, at 100 Front St. Phone 508/798-2581.

Special Event

Worcester Music Festival of the Worcester County Music Association. Mechanics Hall. The country's oldest music festival; folkdance companies; choral masterworks; symphony orchestras, guest soloists; young people's program. Seven to 12 concerts. Sept-Mar. Phone 508/752-5608 or 508/754-3231.

Motels/Motor Lodges

★★ **COMFORT INN.** *426 Southbridge St, Auburn (01501). 508/832-8300; fax 508/832-4579; toll-free 800/228-5150. www.comfortinn.com.* 72 rms, 3 story. June-Oct: S $64-$104; D $71-$114; each addl $10; under 18 free; wkly rates; lower rates rest of yr. Crib free. TV; cable. Complimentary continental bkfst. Ck-out 11 am. Coin lndry. Meeting rms. Valet serv. Some refrigerators. Cr cds: A, C, D, DS, MC, V.

★★ **HAMPTON INN.** *110 Summer St (01608). 508/757-0400; fax 508/831-9839. www.hamptoninn.com.* 99 rms, 5 story, 10 kits. (no equipt). S, D $55-$85; suites $125. Crib free. Pet accepted. TV; cable (premium), VCR avail. Complimentary bkfst buffet. Restaurant nearby. Ck-out 11 am. Meeting rms. Business servs avail. In-rm modem link. Sundries. Downhill ski 20 mi. Some refrigerators. Lake 3 blks. Cr cds: A, C, D, DS, MC, V.

Hotels

★★★ **BEECHWOOD HOTEL.** *363 Plantation St (01605). 508/754-5789; fax 508/752-2060; toll-free 800/344-2589. www.beechwoodhotel.com.* 73 rms, 5 story. S, D $89-$109; each addl $10; suites $119-$139; family rates; higher rates college graduation. Crib free. TV; cable. Restaurant 6:30 am-10 pm. Rm serv. Ck-out 11 am. Business servs avail. RR station, bus depot transportation. Downhill/x-country ski 15 mi. Lake 2 blks. Cr cds: A, MC, V.

⊠ ⊠ 🐾 **SC**

★★★ **CROWNE PLAZA WORCESTER.** *10 Lincoln Square (01608). 508/791-1600; fax 508/791-1796; res 800/628-4240. www.crowneplaza.com.* 243 rms, 7 suites, 9 story. S $135; D $155; each addl $10; studio rms $135-$155; suites $250-$350; under 18 free. Crib free. TV; cable. 2 pools, 1 indoor; whirlpool, poolside serv. Restaurant 6:30 am-11 pm. Rm serv. Bar 11-2 am. Ck-out noon. Convention facilities. Bellhops. Valet serv. Free airport transportation. Downhill/x-country ski 18 mi. Exercise equipt; sauna. Private patios, balconies. Cr cds: A, MC, V.

D ⊠ ⊇ 𝕏 🐾 **SC**

Restaurant

★★★ **CASTLE.** *1230 Main St, Leicester (01524). 508/892-9090. www.castlerestaurant.com.* Continental menu. Hrs: 11:30-9:30 pm. Closed Mon; Jan 1, Thanksgiving, Dec 25. Res accepted. Bar. Wine list. Lunch $8-$25, dinner $20-$45. Child's menu. Patio dining overlooking lake. Stone replica of 16th-century castle complete with medieval decor. Family-owned. Cr cds: A, C, D, DS, ER, MC, V.

D

NEW HAMPSHIRE

New Hampshire is a year-round vacation state, offering a variety of landscapes and recreational opportunities within its six unique regions. The lush Lakes Region, dominated by Lake Winnipesaukee, and the Seacoast Region, with its beaches, bays, and historic waterfront towns, are ideal for water sports. The rugged, forested White Mountains offer hiking, camping, dazzling autumn foliage, and excellent skiing. The "little cities" of the Merrimack Valley—Nashua, Manchester, and Concord—are centers of commerce, industry, government, and the arts. Rural 19th-century New England comes alive in the small towns of the Monadnock Region, and many features of these areas come together in the Dartmouth-Lake Sunapee Region, home of Dartmouth College.

The mountains in New Hampshire are known for their rugged "notches" (called "gaps" and "passes" elsewhere), and the old valley towns have a serene beauty. Some of the best skiing in the East can be found at several major resorts here. The state's many parks, antique shops, art and theater festivals, and county fairs are also popular attractions, and more than half of New England's covered bridges are in New Hampshire.

David Thomson and a small group of colonists settled on the New Hampshire coast near Portsmouth in 1623. These early settlements were part of Massachusetts. In 1679, they became a separate royal province under Charles the Second. In 1776, the Provincial Congress adopted a constitution making New Hampshire the first independent colony, seven months before the Declaration of Independence was signed.

Although New Hampshire was the only one of the thirteen original states not invaded by the British during the Revolution, its men fought long and hard on land and sea to bring about the victory. This strong, involved attitude continues in New Hampshire to this day. The New Hampshire presidential primary is the first in the nation, and the town meeting is still a working form of government here.

Manufacturing and tourism are the principal businesses here. Electrical and electronic products, machinery, plastics, fabricated metal products, footwear, other leather goods, and instrumentation are manufactured. Farmers sell poultry and eggs, dairy products, apples, potatoes, garden crops, maple syrup, and sugar. Nicknamed the "Granite State," about 200 types of rocks and minerals, including granite, mica, and feldspar, come from New Hampshire's mountains.

Population: 1,109,252
Area: 8,992 square miles
Elevation: 0-6,288 feet
Peak: Mount Washington (Coos County)
Entered Union: Ninth of original thirteen states (June 21, 1788)
Capital: Concord
Motto: Live free or die
Nickname: Granite State
Flower: Purple Lilac
Bird: Purple Finch
Tree: White Birch
Time Zone: Eastern
Website: www.visitnh.gov

When to Go/Climate

New Hampshire experiences typical New England weather—four distinct seasons with a muddy month or so between winter and spring. Snow in the mountains makes for great skiing in winter; summer temperatures can push up into the 90s.

AVERAGE HIGH/LOW TEMPERATURES (°F)

CONCORD

Jan 30/7	May 69/41	Sept 72/46
Feb 33/10	June 77/51	Oct 61/35
Mar 43/22	July 80/55	Nov 47/27
Apr 56/32	Aug 72/46	Dec 34/14

MOUNT WASHINGTON

Jan 12/-5	May 41/39	Sept 46/35
Feb 13/-3	June 50/38	Oct 36/24
Mar 20/5	July 54/43	Nov 27/14
Apr 29/16	Aug 52/42	Dec 17/-6

Parks and Recreation Finder

Directions to and information about the parks and recreation areas below are given under their respective town/city sections. Please refer to those sections for details.

NATIONAL PARK AND RECREATION AREAS

Key to abbreviations. I.H.S. = International Historic Site; I.P.M. = International Peace Memorial; N.B. = National Battlefield; N.B.P. = National Battlefield Park; N.B.C. = National Battlefield and Cemetery; N.C.A. = National Conservation Area; N.E.M. = National Expansion Memorial; N.F. = National Forest; N.G. = National Grassland; N.H.P. = National Historical Park; N.H.C. = National Heritage Corridor; N.H.S. = National Historic Site; N.L. = National Lakeshore; N.M. = National Monument; N.M.P. = National Military Park; N.Mem. = National Memorial; N.P. = National Park; N.Pres. = National Preserve; N.R.A. = National Recreational Area; N.R.R. = National Recreational River; N.Riv. = National River; N.S. = National Seashore; N.S.R. = National Scenic Riverway; N.S.T. = National Scenic Trail; N.Sc. = National Scientific Reserve; N.V.M. = National Volcanic Monument.

Place Name	Listed Under
Saint-Gaudens N.H.S.	HANOVER
White Mountain N.F.	same

STATE PARK AND RECREATION AREAS

Key to abbreviations. I.P. = Interstate Park; S.A.P. = State Archaeological Park; S.B. = State Beach; S.C.A. = State Conservation Area; S.C.P. = State Conservation Park; S.Cp. = State Campground; S.F. = State Forest; S.G. = State Garden; S.H.A. = State Historic Area; S.H.P. = State Historic Park; S.H.S. = State Historic Site; S.M.P. = State Marine Park; S.N.A. = State Natural Area; S.P. = State Park; S.P.C. = State Public Campground; S.R. = State Reserve; S.R.A. = State Recreation Area; S.Res. = State Reservoir; S.Res.P. = State Resort Park; S.R.P. = State Rustic Park.

Place Name	Listed Under
Coleman S.P.	COLEBROOK
Crawford Notch S.P.	BRETTON WOODS
Echo Lake S.P.	NORTH CONWAY
Fort Stark S.H.S.	PORTSMOUTH
Franconia Notch S.P.	same
Greenfield S.P.	PETERBOROUGH
Hampton Beach S.P.	HAMPTON BEACH
Miller S.P.	PETERBOROUGH
Monadnock S.P.	JAFFREY
Moose Brook S.P.	GORHAM
Mount Sunapee S.P.	SUNAPEE
Silver Lake S.P.	NASHUA
Wentworth S.P.	WOLFEBORO
White Lake S.P.	CENTER OSSIPEE

Water-related activities, hiking, riding, various other sports, picnicking, and visitor centers, as well as camping, are available in many of these areas. There is an admission charge at most state parks; children under 12 admitted free. Tent camping $12-$20/night; RV camp sites $24-$30/night. For further information contact the New Hampshire Division of Parks and Recreation, PO Box 1856, Concord 03302; 603/271-3556 or 603/271-3628 (camping reservations).

SKI AREAS

Place Name	Listed Under
Attitash Bear Peak Ski Resort	BARTLETT
Balsams/Wilderness Ski Area	DIXVILLE NOTCH
Black Mountain Ski	JACKSON
Bretton Woods Ski Area	BRETTON WOODS
Cannon Mountain Ski Area	FRANCONIA NOTCH STATE PARK
Dartmouth Skiway Ski Area	HANOVER
Gunstock Recreation Area	LACONIA
Jackson Ski Touring Foundation	JACKSON
King Pine Ski Area	CENTER OSSIPEE

Loon Mountain Recreation Area	LINCOLN/NORTH WOODSTOCK
Mount Cranmore Ski Area	NORTH CONWAY
Mount Sunapee S.P.	SUNAPEE
Pat's Peak Ski Area	CONCORD
Ragged Mountain Ski Area	NEW LONDON
Snowhill at Eastman Ski Area	SUNAPEE
Waterville Valley Ski Area	WATERVILLE VALLEY
Wildcat Ski and Recreation Area	PINKHAM NOTCH

CALENDAR HIGHLIGHTS

MAY

Lilac Time Festival (Franconia). 8 mi W on NH 117, then 4 mi S on US 302, in Lisbon. Celebration of the state flower and observance of Memorial Day. Parade, carnival, vendors, entertainment, special events. Phone 603/436-3988.

JUNE

Portsmouth Jazz Festival (Portsmouth). Two stages with continuous performances on the historical Portsmouth waterfront. Phone 603/436-3988.

Market Square Days (Portsmouth). Summer celebration with 10K road race, street fair, entertainment. Phone 603/436-3988.

JULY

The Old Homestead (Keene). Potash Bowl in Swanzey Center. Drama of life in Swanzey during 1880s based on the Biblical story of the Prodigal Son; first presented in 1886. Phone 603/352-0697.

AUGUST

Mount Washington Valley Equine Classic (North Conway). Horse jumping. Phone Chamber of Commerce, 603/356-3171 or 800/367-3364.

Lakes Region Fine Arts and Crafts Festival (Meredith). Juried show featuring more than 100 New England artists. Music, children's theater, food. Phone Chamber of Commerce 603/279-6121.

League of New Hampshire Craftsmen's Fair (Sunapee). Mount Sunapee State Park. Over 200 craftsmen and artists display and sell goods. Phone 603/224-3375.

SEPTEMBER

New Hampshire Highland Games (Lincoln). Loon Mountain. Largest Scottish gathering in Eastern US. Bands, competitions, concerts, workshops. Phone 800/358-SCOT.

Riverfest (Manchester). Outdoor festival with family entertainment, concerts, arts and crafts, food booths, fireworks. Phone 603/623-2623.

FISHING AND HUNTING

Nonresident season fishing license: $47; 15-day, $27.50; 7-day, $32; 3-day, $25. Nonresident hunting license: $92; small game, $47; small game three-day, $23; muzzleloader, $36. Combination hunting and fishing license, nonresident: $127. Fees subject to change. For further information and for the *New Hampshire Freshwater and Saltwater Fishing Digests,* pamphlets that summarize regulations, contact the New Hampshire Fish and Game Department, 2 Hazen Dr, Concord 03301; 603/271-3422 or 603/271-3211.

Driving Information

Passengers under 18 years must be in an approved passenger restraint anywhere in vehicle. Children under four years must be in an approved safety seat anywhere in vehicle. For further information phone 603/271-2131.

INTERSTATE HIGHWAY SYSTEM

The following alphabetical listing of New Hampshire towns in the *RoadMaster ™ Drive USA Travel Guides* shows that these cities are within ten miles of the indicated Interstate highways. A highway map should, however, be checked for the nearest exit.

Highway Number	Cities/Towns within ten miles
Interstate 89	Concord, Hanover, New London, Sunapee.
Interstate 93	Concord, Franconia, Franconia Notch State Park, Franklin, Holderness, Laconia, Lincoln/ North Woodstock, Littleton, Manchester, Meredith, Plymouth, Salem.
Interstate 95	Exeter, Hampton Beach, Portsmouth.

Additional Visitor Information

The *New Hampshire Guidebook,* with helpful information on lodging, dining, attractions, and events, is available from the New Hampshire Office of Travel and Tourism, 172 Pembroke Rd, PO Box 1856, Concord 03302; 603/271-2665 or 800/FUN-IN-NH. For recorded information about events, foliage, and alpine ski conditions, phone 800/258-3608.

The League of New Hampshire Craftsmen Foundation offers information on more than 100 galleries, museums, historic sites, craft shops, and craftsmen's studios. Send stamped, self-addressed, business-size envelope to 205 N Main St, Concord 03301; 603/224-3375.

There are several welcome centers in New Hampshire; visitors who stop by will find information and brochures most helpful in planning stops at points of interest. Open daily: on I-93 at Hooksett, Canterbury, Salem, and Sanborton Boulder; on I-89 at Lebanon, Springfield, and Sutton; on I-95 at Seabrook; and on NH 16 at North Conway. Open Memorial Day-Columbus Day: on NH 9 at Antrim; on US 3 at Colebrook; on US 4 at Epsom; on NH 25 at Rumney; and on US 2 at Shelburne.

THE UPPER CONNECTICUT RIVER VALLEY

The Upper Connecticut River valley forms one of New England's most beautiful and distinctive regions. The river, which now forms the boundary between New Hampshire and Vermont, was northern New England's first highway, and the towns scattered along both its banks were settled long before the interior of either state. Interstate 91 follows the river north for the entire length of this tour, but in numerous places the slower state roads along the river are more rewarding.

Begin in the Vermont village of Putney (I-91 exit 4 in Vermont), known for apples, private schools, crafts shops, and for Basketville, the original "world's largest basket store" on Route 5, just north of the village center. Santa's Land, a Christmas theme park with a petting zoo and miniature railroad, is another mile north on Route 5. Bellows Falls (I-91 exit 5), the largest natural falls on the entire Connecticut River, is the departure point for the Green Mountain Railroad (Depot Street), which offers 26-mile excursion rides aboard the Green Mountain Flyer to Chester Depot and back.

A mile west of I-91 exit 6 on VT 103 is the Old Rockingham Meeting House, built in 1787, Vermont's oldest unchanged public building. The Vermont Country Store, next door, has an antique cracker-making machine and an extensive stock of old-time products and gadgets. Head back up I-91 to exit 8 and cross the river to New Hampshire. Turn north on this particularly scenic stretch of Route 12A. In Cornish, North Star Canoes offers access to riverside campsites, as well as a shuttle service upstream so canoeists can paddle downstream through this beautiful landscape. Continue on Route 12A past the Cornish-Windsor Bridge, said to be the longest covered bridge in the country. Turn at the sign for the St. Gaudens National Historic Site. This one-time home of sculptor Augustus St.-Gaudens includes models of his most famous statues. The extensive grounds are the site of free Sunday afternoon concerts in July and August.

Backtrack to the covered bridge and cross to VT 5 in Windsor. Turn left for the American Precision Museum, showcasing early precision tools and changing exhibits. The entrance to Mount Ascutney State Park is three miles south of town on VT 44A, off VT 5. Within the park, you'll find hiking, camping, and a paved road to the 3,144-foot summit of Mount Ascutney.

In Windsor follow VT 5 north to the Old Constitution House, the tavern where delegates gathered in 1777 to draft the state's constitution. Continue north on VT 5, past Simon Pierce Glass (visitors welcome) to I-91 and follow this scenic highway 14 miles to exit 13 in Norwich.

The Montshire Museum of Science is right there by the river, marked from the exit. Incorporating both states in its name (it began on the New Hampshire side of the river), the Montshire, one of New England's most outstanding museums, is dedicated to demystifying natural phenomena in a way that's fun. Exhibits change but usually include an aquarium, a display on the physics of the bubble, and a hands-on corner geared to preschoolers. There are also extensive nature trails.

Cross the river into Hanover, NH, and up to the Dartmouth College green. Park (not always easy) and look for the Hood Museum on the green. This modern building houses an outstanding collection, ranging from Assyrian bas-reliefs to works by Picasso and Frank Stella. Cross back over the river to I-91 exit 13 and backtrack three miles to exit 20, the junction with I-89. **(APPROX 63 MI)**

Bartlett

See also Bretton Woods, Jackson, North Conway

Pop 2,290 **Elev** 681 ft **Area code** 603 **Zip** 03812
Information Mt Washington Valley Chamber of
Commerce, N Main St, PO Box 2300, North Conway
03860; 603/356-5701
Web www.mtwashingtonvalley.org

What to See and Do

Attitash Bear Peak Ski Resort. Two high-speed quad, three
quad, three triple, three double chairlifts; three surface lifts;
patrol, school, rentals; snowmaking; nursery; cafe teria; bar.
Longest run 1¾ mi; vertical drop 1,750 ft. (Mid-Nov-late
Apr, daily) **Summer recreation:** Alpine Slide, water slides,
scenic chairlift, horseback riding, mountain biking, hiking,
driving range (Mid-June-Labor Day, daily; Memorial Day-
mid-June and early Sept-mid-Oct, wkends; fees). On US 302.
Phone 603/374-2368. ¢¢¢¢

White Mountain National Forest. (see).

Resort

★★ **ATTITASH MOUNTAIN VILLAGE.** *Rte 302 (03812).*
603/374-6500; fax 603/374-6509; toll-free 800/862-1600.
www.attitashmtvillage.com. 253 rms, 3 story. S, D $49-$169;
studio rms $99-$229; 2-3 bedrm units for 2-8, $139-$499;
kit. units for 2-4, $79-$139; hol wks (3-day min). TV; cable,
VCR avail. 3 pools, 1 indoor; whirlpool, sauna. Playground.
Restaurant 11 am-10 pm. Bar 11:30-1 am. Ck-out 11 am.
Coin lndry. Meeting rms. Business servs avail. Tennis.
Downhill/x-country ski on site. Ice-skating. Hiking trails.
Game rm. Lawn games. Refrigerators. Private patios; many
balconies. Picnic tables. Cr cds: A, DS, MC, V.

[image: icons]

Bretton Woods

See also Franconia, Littleton, Twin Mountain

Settled 1791 **Pop** 10 **Elev** 1,600 ft **Area code** 603 **Zip** 03575

Bretton Woods is located in the heart of the White
Mountains, on a long glacial plain in the shadow of Mount
Washington (see) and the Presidential Range. Mount
Washington was first sighted in 1497; however, settlement
around it did not begin until 1771 when the Crawford
Notch, which opened the way through the mountains,
was discovered. In the 1770s Governor Wentworth named
the area Bretton Woods for his ancestral home in England.
This historic name was set aside in 1832 when all the tiny
settlements in the area were incorporated under the name
of Carroll. For a time, a railroad through the notch brought
as many as 57 trains a day, and the area grew as a resort
spot. A string of hotels sprang up, each more elegant and
fashionable than the last. In 1903 the post office, railroad
station, and express office reverted to the traditional name—
Bretton Woods. Today, Bretton Woods is a resort area at
the base of the mountain.

In 1944 the United Nations Monetary and Financial
Conference was held here; it established the gold standard
at $35 an ounce, organized plans for the International
Monetary Fund and World Bank, and chose the American
dollar as the unit of international exchange.

What to See and Do

Bretton Woods Ski Area. Two high-speed quad, quad,
triple, two double chairlifts, three surface lifts; patrol,
school, rentals, snowmaking; restaurant, cafeteria, bar;
child care; lodge. Longest run two mi; vertical drop 1,500
ft. (Thanksgiving-Apr, daily) Night skiing (early Dec-Mar,
Fri and Sat). 48 mi of x-country trails. 5 mi E on US 302.
Phone 603/278-3320. ¢¢¢¢

Crawford Notch State Park. One of state's most spectacular
passes. Mts Nancy and Willey rise to the west; Mts Crawford,
Webster and Jackson to the east. Park HQ is at the former
site of the Samuel Willey house. He, his family of six, and
two hired men died in a landslide in 1826 when they rushed
out of their house, which the landslide left untouched.
Fishing, trout-feeding pond. Hiking, walking trails on the
Appalachian system. Picnicking, concession. Camping
(standard fees). Interpretive center. (Late May-mid-Oct)
Approx 8 mi SE on US 302. Phone 603/374-2272.
In park are

  Arethusa Falls. Highest in state; 50-min walk from
  parking area. 1½ mi SW of US 302, 6 mi N of Bartlett.

  Flume Cascade. A 250-ft fall. 3 mi N.

  Silver Cascade. A 1,000-ft cataract. N end of Crawford
  Notch.

Resort

★★★ **MOUNT WASHINGTON HOTEL.** *Rte 302 (03575).*
603/278-1000; fax 603/278-8838; toll-free 800/258-0330.
www.mtwashington.com. 200 rms, 4 story. MAP: S $170-
$455; D $250-$300; each addl $70; suites avail; family rates;
golf plan. Crib avail. TV avail; VCR avail. 2 pools, 1 indoor;
sauna, poolside serv. Playground. Supervised children's
activities (June-Sept; also wkends spring and fall) ages
5-12. Dining rms 7-9 am, 11:30 am-4 pm, 6-9 pm (see
also FABYAN'S STATION). Bars 11:30-1 am; entertainment.
Ck-out 11 am, ck-in 3 pm. Meeting rms. Business servs avail.
Concierge. Gift shop. Bus depot transportation. Sports dir.
Tennis; pro. 27-hole golf, greens fee $25-$35, pro, putting
green. Hiking trails. Bicycle rentals. Lawn games. Rec rm.
Game rm. On river. Renovated hotel built 1902; view of
Mt Washington. Cr cds: A, DS, MC, V.

[image: icons]

B&B/Small Inn

★★★ **THE BRETTON ARMS COUNTRY INN.** *Rte 302 (03575). 603/278-1000; fax 603/278-8838; toll-free 800/258-0330. www.brettonarms.com.* 31 rms, 3 suites. No A/C. S, D $75-$189; suites $85-$209; ski plans. Crib avail. TV; VCR. 3 pools, 2 indoor. Playground. Supervised children's activities (June-Labor Day); ages 5-12. Dining rm 7-9 am, 6-9 pm. Ck-out 11 am, ck-in 3 pm. Business servs avail. Airport, bus depot transportation. Tennis privileges. Golf privileges. Downhill ski adj; x-country ski on site. Sleigh rides. Exercise equipt. Restored Victorian inn (1896); antiques. Cr cds: A, DS, MC, V.

🄳 🐾 ⛷ 🎿 🏋 🏊 🎣 🧍 ✈ 🔄 🔥

Restaurant

★ **FABYAN'S STATION.** *Rte 302 (03575). 603/278-2222. www.mtwashington.com.* Specializes in nachos, hamburgers, fresh fish. Hrs: 11:30 am-10 pm; hrs vary Apr-mid-June, Oct-late Dec. Bar to 12:30 am. A la carte entrees: lunch $5-$8, dinner $7-$14. Child's menu. Converted railway station. Railroad artifacts. Cr cds: A, DS, MC, V.

Center Ossipee

See also Wolfeboro

Pop 500 **Elev** 529 ft **Area code** 603 **Zip** 03814
Information Greater Ossipee Area Chamber of Commerce, 127 NH 28, Ossipee, 03864-7300; 603/539-6201 or 800/382-2371
Web www.ossipeevalley.org

The communities in Ossipee Area are part of a winter and summer sports region centering around Ossipee Lake and the Ossipee Mountains. The mountains also harbor a volcano (extinct for 120 million years) that is considered to be the most perfectly shaped volcanic formation in the world and is rivaled only by a similar formation in Nigeria. A hike up Mount Whittier gives an excellent view of the formation. In the winter, the area comes alive with snowmobiling, dog sledding, x-country skiing, and other activities.

What to See and Do

King Pine Ski Area. Triple, double chairlifts; two J-bars; snowmaking; patrol, school, rentals; night skiing; nursery; snack bar; bar. (Early Dec-late Mar, daily) 11 mi NE via NH 25, 153. Phone 603/367-8896. ¢¢¢¢

Swimming. Ossipee Lake, N and E of village; Duncan Lake, S of village. **Sailing.** Silver Lake, N and E of village; also Ossipee Lake. Marinas with small boat rentals.

White Lake State Park. Sandy beach on tree-studded shore. Swimming; trout fishing. Hiking. Picnicking, concessions. Tent camping. (Mid-May-mid-Oct) Snowmobile trails (Dec-Mar). Standard fees. 6 mi N on NH 16. Phone 603/323-7350. ¢¢

Colebrook

See also Dixville Notch

Settled 1770 **Pop** 2,444 **Elev** 1,033 ft **Area code** 603 **Zip** 03576
Information North Country Chamber of Commerce, PO Box 1; 603/237-8939 or 800/698-8939
Web www.northcountrychamber.org

At the west edge of the White Mountains, Colebrook is the gateway to excellent hunting and fishing in the Connecticut Lakes region. The Mohawk and Connecticut rivers join here. Vermont's Mount Monadnock adds scenic beauty.

What to See and Do

Beaver Brook Falls. A scenic glen. 2 mi N on NH 145.

Coleman State Park. On Little Diamond Pond in the heavily timbered Connecticut Lakes region. Lake and stream fishing; picnicking; primitive camping. (Mid-May-mid-Oct) Standard fees. 7 mi E on NH 26, then 5 mi N on Diamond Pond Rd. Phone 603/237-4520.

Columbia Covered Bridge. 75 ft high. 4 mi S on US 3.

Shrine of Our Lady of Grace. Oblates of Mary Immaculate. More than 50 Carrara marble and granite devotional monuments on 25 acres. Special events throughout season. Guided tours (Mother's Day-second Sun Oct, daily). 2 mi S on US 3. Phone 603/237-5511. **FREE**

Motel/Motor Lodge

★ **NORTHERN COMFORT MOTEL.** *RR 1 (03576). 603/237-4440. www.northerncomfortmotel.com.* 19 rms. S, D $56-$68; each addl $8-$10. Crib free. Pet accepted. TV; cable. Heated pool; whirlpool. Playground. Complimentary continental bkfst June-Sept. Restaurant nearby. Ck-out 11 am. Gift shop. Downhill/x-country ski 12 mi. Exercise equipt. Cr cds: A, DS, MC, V.

🐾 🏊 🧍 ⛷

Concord

See also Manchester

Settled 1727 **Pop** 36,006 **Elev** 288 ft **Area code** 603 **Zip** 03301
Information Chamber of Commerce, 40 Commercial St; 603/224-2508
Web www.concordnhchamber.com

New Hampshire, one of the original 13 colonies, entered the Union in 1788—but its capital was in dispute for another 20 years. Concord finally won the honor in 1808. The state house, begun immediately, was finished in 1819. The legislature is the largest (more than 400 seats) of any state. Concord is the financial center of the state and a center of diversified industry as well.

What to See and Do

Canterbury Shaker Village. Historic Shaker buildings; living museum of Shaker crafts, architecture and inventions. Guided tour of 6 historic buildings and museum. Restaurant. Gift shop. (May-Oct, daily; Apr and Nov-Dec, Sat-Sun) 15 mi N on I-93 to exit 18, follow signs. Phone 603/783-9511. ¢¢

Capitol Center for the Arts. Renovated historic theater (1920s) is state's largest. Presents nationally touring Broadway and popular family entertainment all yr. For schedule and tickets, contact 44 S Main St; phone 603/225-1111.

Christa McAuliffe Planetarium. Official state memorial to nation's first teacher in space. Changing programs. (Daily exc Mon; closed some major hols, also Apr 12) 2 Institute Dr, I-93 exit 15E. Phone 603/271-7827. ¢¢

☒ **Concord Arts & Crafts.** High-quality traditional and contemporary crafts by some of New Hampshire's finest craftsmen; monthly exhibits. (Daily exc Sun; closed most hols) 36 N Main St. Phone 603/228-8171.

League of New Hampshire Craftsmen. Six retail galleries throughout the state. Library and resource center for League Foundation members. (Mon-Fri; closed hols) 205 N Main St. Phone 603/224-1471. **FREE**

Museum of New Hampshire History. Historical museum (founded 1823) with permanent and changing exhibits, including excellent examples of the famed Concord Coach; museum store. (Tues-Sat, also Sun afternoons). 6 Eagle Sq. Phone 603/226-3189. ¢¢

Pat's Peak Ski Area. Triple, two double chairlifts, two T-bars, J-bar, pony lift; patrol, school, rentals, ski shop; snowmaking; cafeteria, lounge; nursery. Night skiing. (Dec-late Mar, daily; closed Dec 25) 8 mi N on I-89 to US 202, then 8 mi W to NH 114, then 3 mi S, near Henniker. Phone 603/428-3245.

Pierce Manse. Home of President Franklin Pierce from 1842-1848. Reconstructed and moved to present site; contains many original furnishings and period pieces. (Mid-June-mid-Sept, Mon-Fri; also by appt; closed July 4, Labor Day) 14 Penacook St, 1 mi N of State House. Phone 603/224-0094. ¢

State House. Hall of Flags; statues, portraits of state notables. (Mon-Fri; closed hols) Main St; entrance for disabled on Park St. Phone 603/271-2154. **FREE**

Motels/Motor Lodges

★ **BRICK TOWER MOTOR INN.** *414 S Main St (03301). 603/224-9565; fax 603/224-6027. www.bricktower.com.* 51 rms. May-Oct: S $52; D $59-$64; each addl $5; under 12 free; higher rates special events; lower rates rest of yr. Crib free. Pet accepted. TV; cable. Pool. Complimentary continental bkfst. Ck-out 11 am. Some in-rm saunas. Cr cds: A, DS, MC, V.

★★ **COMFORT INN.** *71 Hall St (03301). 603/226-4100; fax 603/228-2106; res 800/228-5150. www.comfortinn.com.* 100 rms, 3 story. S $92-$165; D $99-$165; each addl $10; suites $199-$209; under 18 free. Crib free. Pet accepted. TV; cable. Indoor pool; whirlpool. Complimentary conti-

nental bkfst. Restaurant nearby. Ck-out noon. Meeting rms. Business servs avail. In-rm modem link. Valet serv. Sauna. Game rm. Some bathrm phones, in-rm whirlpools, refrigerators. Cr cds: A, C, D, DS, MC, V.

★★ **DAYS INN.** *406 S Main St (03301). 603/224-2511; fax 603/224-6032; toll-free 800/329-7466. www.daysinn.com.* 40 rms, 2 story. July-Sept: S $85; D $98; each addl $10; higher rates: special events, Oct; lower rates rest of yr. Crib free. TV; cable (premium). Pool. Playground. Complimentary continental bkfst. Business servs avail. Ck-out 11 am. Some in-rm whirlpools. Cr cds: A, C, D, DS, MC, V.

★★ **HAMPTON INN.** *515 South St, Bow (03304). 603/224-5322; fax 603/224-4282; res 800/426-7866. www.hampton inn.com.* 145 rms, 4 story. S, D $75-$150; under 18 free; higher rates special events. Crib free. TV; cable (premium), VCR avail. Indoor pool; whirlpool. Complimentary continental bkfst. Restaurant opp 7 am-10 pm. Ck-out noon. Coin lndry. Meeting rms. Refrigerators avail. Picnic tables. Cr cds: A, C, D, DS, MC, V.

B&B/Small Inn

★★★ **COLBY HILL INN.** *The Oaks, Henniker (03242). 603/428-3281; fax 603/428-9218; toll-free 800/531-0330. www.colbyhillinn.com.* 16 rms, 11 with shower only, 2 story. S $85-$165; D $110-$200; suites $290-$325. Children over 8 yrs only. TV in library; cable. Pool. Complimentary full bkfst. Dining rm (see COLBY HILL INN). Ck-out 11 am, ck-in 2 pm. Downhill/x-country ski 1½ mi. Meeting rm. Business servs avail. In-rm modem link. Lawn games. Some fireplaces. Historic farmhouse (ca 1800) used as tavern, church, meeting house and private school; sitting rm, antiques. On 5 acres. Totally nonsmoking. Cr cds: A, D, DS, MC, V.

Restaurant

★★ **COLBY HILL INN.** *The Oaks, Henniker (03242). 603/428-3281. www.colbyhillinn.com.* Continental menu. Specialties: tournedos Oscar, chicken Colby Inn, seafood. Hrs: 5:30-8:30 pm; Sun 4:30-7:30 pm. Closed Dec 24, 25. Res accepted. Serv bar. Dinner $18-$34. View of garden. Totally nonsmoking. Cr cds: A, D, DS, MC, V.

Dixville Notch

See also Colebrook

Pop 30 **Elev** 1,990 ft **Area code** 603 **Zip** 3576

The small village of Dixville Notch shares its name with the most northerly of the White Mountain passes. The Notch cuts through the mountain range between Kidderville and Errol. At its narrowest point, east of Lake Gloriette, is one of the most impressive views in the state. Every four years Dixville Notch is invaded by the national news media, who report the nation's first presidential vote tally shortly after midnight on election day.

What to See and Do

Balsams/Wilderness Ski Area. Chairlift, two T-bars; patrol, school, rentals, snowmaking; restaurant, cafeteria, bar, nursery, resort (see). Longest run one mi; vertical drop 1,000 ft. (Dec-Mar, daily) Cross-country trails. On NH 26. Phone 603/255-3400. ¢¢¢¢

Table Rock. Views of New Hampshire, Maine, Vermont and Québec. ¾ mi S of NH 26, ½ mi E of village of Dixville Notch.

Resort

★★★ **THE BALSAMS.** *NH 26 (03576). 603/255-3400; fax 603/255-4221; tollfree 800/255-0600. www.thebalsams.com.* 204 rms, 3-6 story. No A/C. AP, July-Labor Day: S $145-$375; D $300-$470; suites $570-$630; family rates; MAP, ski plans avail late Dec-late Mar. 15% serv charge (late May-June, Sept-mid-Oct). Closed rest of yr. Crib avail. TV rm; cable, VCR avail (movies). Heated pool; attendant. Complimentary supervised children's activities (July-Aug); ages 5-13. Dining rm 8-9:30 am, 12:30-2 pm, 6:30-8 pm. Box lunches, snacks. Rm serv. Bars 11:30-12:45 am. Ck-out noon, ck-in 4 pm. Business servs avail. In-rm modem link. Bellhops. Shopping arcade. 6 tennis courts, pro. 27-hole golf, pro, 2 putting greens. Private lake, boats, paddleboats, canoes. Downhill/x-country ski on site. Snowmobile trails, ice skating. Mountain bikes. Horse-drawn hay rides. Hiking trails. Lawn games. Game rm. Rec rm. Exercise rm. Library. Soc dirs; dancing, entertainment, lectures, movies; theater. Stocked trout pond. Natural history program; naturalist on site. Cr cds: A, DS, M, V.

[D] [icons]

Dover

See also Portsmouth

Settled 1623 **Pop** 25,042 **Elev** 57 ft **Area code** 603
Zip 03820
Information Chamber of Commerce, 299 Central Ave; 603/742-2218
Web www.dovernh.org

With its historic trails and homes, Dover is the oldest permanent settlement in New Hampshire. The town contains the only known existing Colonial garrison.

What to See and Do

Woodman Institute. Garrison House (1675), only garrison in New Hampshire now visible in nearly its original form. Woodman House (1818), residence of the donor, is now a natural history museum with collections of minerals, Native American artifacts and displays of mammals, fish, amphibians, reptiles, birds, insects; war memorial rms.

Senator John P. Hale House (1813) contains articles of Dover history and antique furniture. (Apr-Jan, Wed-Sun afternoons; closed major hols) 182-190 Central Ave, ½ mi S on NH 108. Phone 603/742-1038. ¢¢

Special Event

Cocheco Arts Festival. Mid-July-late Aug.

Motels/Motor Lodges

★★ **DAYS INN.** *481 Central Ave (03820). 603/742-0400; fax 603/742-7790; toll-free 800/329-7466. www.dover-durham-daysinn.com.* 50 rms, 2 story, 13 kit. suites. June-Oct: S, D $72-$99; each addl $5-$8; kit. suites $85-$160; under 12 free; lower rates rest of yr. Crib avail. Pet accepted. TV; cable. Pool; whirlpool. Continental bkfst. Restaurant nearby. Ck-out 11 am. Coin lndry. Business servs avail. Cr cds: A, C, D, DS, MC, V.

[D] [icons] [SC]

★★★ **NEW ENGLAND CENTER HOTEL.** *15 Strafford Ave, Durham (03824). 603/862-2801; fax 603/862-4897; res 800/590-4334. www.newenglandcenter.com.* 115 rms, 8 story. July-Oct: S $70-$90; D $80-$110; suites $120-$150; lower rates rest of yr. TV; cable (premium), VCR avail. Indoor/outdoor pool privileges. Restaurant 7 am-10 pm. Bar 11 am-11 pm. Ck-out noon. Meeting rms. Business servs avail. Sundries. Tennis privileges. Health club privileges. On 10 wooded acres. Cr cds: A, DS, MC, V.

[D] [icons]

B&B/Small Inn

★★ **SILVER STREET INN.** *103 Silver St (03820). 603/743-3000; fax 603/749-5673. www.silverstreetinn.com.* 10 rms, 2 share bath, 3 story. May-mid-Oct: S $79; D $89; each addl $10; under 15 free; lower rates rest of yr. Crib free. TV; cable. Complimentary full bkfst. Restaurant nearby. Ck-out 11 am. Business servs avail. Victorian house built ca 1880 for local businessman. Cr cds: A, DS, V.

[D] [icon]

Restaurants

★★ **FIREHOUSE ONE.** *1 Orchard St (03820). 603/749-2220. www.firehouseone.com.* Specializes in seafood, prime rib, vegetarian dishes. Hrs: 11:30 am-9 pm; Sat from 5 pm; Sun 10 am-8 pm; Sun brunch 10 am-2 pm. Closed Dec 25. Res accepted; required hols. Bar to midnight. A la carte: lunch $4-$8, dinner $8-$21. Sun brunch $10.95. Child's menu. Outdoor dining. Old restored firehouse (1840), arched doors and windows, tin walls and ceilings, over-stuffed chairs. Cr cds: A, D, DS, MC, V.

[D] [icon]

★★★ **MAPLES.** *17 Newmarket Rd, Durham (03824). 603/868-7800. www.threechimneysinn.com.* Specializes in lamb, pastries. Hrs: 6-10 pm. Res accepted. Beer, wine, extensive wine list. Dinner $25-$30. Cr cds: A, D, DS, MC, V.

[D]

★ **NEWICK'S SEAFOOD.** *431 Dover Point Rd (03820). 603/742-3205. www.newicks.com.* Specializes in seafood. Hrs: 11 am-9 pm; hrs vary off-season. Closed Thanksgiving, Dec 25. Serv bar. Lunch, dinner $1.95-$16.95. Seafood market. Gift shop. Nautical accents. Overlooks Great Bay. Cr cds: A, D, MC, V.

⬛ 🔳

Exeter

See also Hampton Beach, Portsmouth

Settled 1638 **Pop** 12,481 **Elev** 40 ft **Area code** 603 **Zip** 03833
Information Exeter Area Chamber of Commerce, 120 Water St; 603/772-2411
Web www.exeterarea.org

A venerable preparatory school and Colonial houses belie Exeter's radical history. It had its beginnings in religious nonconformity, led by Reverend John Wheelwright and Anne Hutchinson, both of whom were banished from Massachusetts for heresy. There was an anti-British scuffle in 1734, and by 1774 Exeter was burning Lord North in effigy and talking of liberty. It was made the capital of the state during the Revolution, since there were too many Tories in Portsmouth. Exeter is the birthplace of Daniel Chester French and John Irving.

What to See and Do

American Independence Museum. Site of Revolutionary War-era state treasury building; grounds house Folsom Tavern (1775). (May-Oct, Wed-Sun) 1 Governors Ln. Phone 603/772-2622. ¢¢

Gilman Garrison House. (1676-1690) Built as a fortified garrison with hewn logs; pulley arrangement to raise and lower door still in place. Substantially remodeled in mid-18th century; wing added with 17th- and 18th-century furnishings. (Open by appt only) 12 Water St. Phone 603/436-3205. ¢¢

Exeter Fine Crafts. Work in all media by New Hampshire's finest artisans. (Mon-Sat) 61 Water St. Phone 603/778-8282. **FREE**

Phillips Exeter Academy. (1781) 990 students. On 400 acres with more than 100 buildings. Coed school for grades 9-12. Founded by John Phillips, who sought a school for "students from every quarter"; known for its student diversity. On campus are a contemporary library (1971), designed by Louis I. Kahn; the Frederick R. Mayer Art Center; and the Lamont Art Gallery. Phone 603/772-4311.

Franconia

See also Littleton

Pop 811 **Elev** 971 ft **Area code** 603 **Zip** 03580
Information Franconia Notch Chamber of Commerce, PO Box 780; 603/823-5661 or 800/237-9007
Web www.franconianotch.org

What to See and Do

Franconia Notch State Park. (see). Approx 7 mi SE via NH 18 & I-93 (Franconia Notch State Pkwy).

Frost Place. Two furnished rms of Robert Frost's home open to public; memorabilia; poetry trail; 25-min video. (July-Columbus Day, Wed-Mon afternoons; Memorial Day-June, Sat and Sun afternoons) 1 mi S on NH 116 to Bickford Hill Rd, right over bridge, left at fork, on to Ridge Rd. Phone 603/823-5510. ¢¢

New England Ski Museum. Details history of skiing in the east; exhibits feature skis and bindings, clothing, art, and photographs; vintage films. Gift shop. (Late May-mid-Oct, daily; Dec-late Mar, Mon, Tues, Fri-Sun; closed Dec 25) Franconia Notch Pkwy (US 3) exit 34B, near Cannon Mtn Tramway. Phone 603/823-7177. **FREE**

White Mountain National Forest. (see). SE on NH 18.

Special Event

Lilac Time Festival. 8 mi W on NH 117, then 4 mi S on US 302, in Lisbon. Celebration of the state flower and observance of Memorial Day. Parade, carnival, vendors, entertainment, special events. Phone 603/838-6673. Late May.

Motels/Motor Lodges

★ **GALE RIVER.** *1 Main St (03580). 603/823-5655; fax 603/823-5280; toll-free 800/255-7989. www.galerivermotel.com.* 10 rms, 2 kit. cottages (2 bedrm). No A/C. July-mid-Oct and hol ski wks: S $65-$95; D $75-$105; each addl $10; cottages $110-$150 (5-day min); package plans, wkly rates (cottages); higher rates: wkends, fall foliage; lower rates rest of yr. Crib free. TV; cable. Heated pool; whirlpool. Playground. Complimentary coffee in rms. Ck-out 11 am. Downhill ski 4 mi. Lawn games. Refrigerators. Picnic tables, grills. Cr cds: A, DS, MC, V.

⬛ 🐾 ✈ ⛷ 🏊 🔳 🔳 **SC**

★ **STONYBROOK MOTEL & LODGE.** *1098 Profile Rd; Rte 18 (03580). 603/823-8192; fax 603/823-8196; toll-free 800/722-3552. www.stonybrookmotel.com.* 23 rms. Some A/C. S, D $52-$85; each addl $7; under 18 free; wkly rates; ski plan; higher rates: fall foliage, hol wkends. Crib free. TV; cable. 2 pools, 1 indoor. Playground. Complimentary coffee in rms. Ck-out 11 am. Downhill/x-country ski 2 mi. Game rm. Rec rm. Lawn games. Some refrigerators. Picnic tables, grills. Pond, stream. Cr cds: DS, MC, V.

⬛ 🐾 ✈ ⛷ 🏊 🔳 🔥

B&Bs/Small Inns

★★★ **FRANCONIA INN.** *1300 Easton Rd (03580).*
603/823-5542; fax 603/823-8078; toll-free 800/473-5299.
www.franconiainn.com. 34 rms, 3 story. No A/C. No elvtr.
No rm phones. S $71-$86; D $81-$96; each addl $10;
suites $146; family, wknd rates; package plans; lower rates
off-season. Closed Apr-mid-May. Crib avail. TV rm; cable.
Heated pool; whirlpool. Restaurant (see THE FRANCONIA
INN). Bar from 4 pm. Ck-out 11 am, ck-in 3 pm. Tennis.
Downhill ski 3 mi; x-country ski on site. Game rm. Rec rm.
Lawn games. Trail rides. Sleigh rides, hayrides. Ice-skating;
rentals. Library. On river; swimming. Cr cds: A, DS, MC, V.
⊡ ⓓ ✦ ⛷ ☞ ⌸ ⊠ ⚒ **SC**

★★ **HILLTOP INN.** *1348 Main St, Sugar Hill (03585).*
603/823-5695; fax 603/823-5518; toll-free 800/770-5695.
www.hilltopinn.com. 6 rms, 2 story, 1 suite. No A/C. No rm
phones. S $60-$70; D $70-$95; each addl $15-$25; suite $90-
$130; wkly rates; higher rates fall foliage (2-day min). Pet
accepted; $10/day. TV in sitting rm; cable. Complimentary
full bkfst; afternoon refreshments. Ck-out 11 am, ck-in 2-
6 pm. Downhill ski 8 mi; x-country ski on site. Built 1895;
antiques, quilts. Cr cds: DS, MC, V.
☞ ⌸ ⚒

★ **THE HORSE & HOUND INN.** *205 Wells Rd*
(03580). 603/823-5501; toll-free 800/450-5501.
www.bestinns.net/usa/hh/horse.html. 10 rms, 2 share bath,
2 story. No A/C. S $75; D $90; under 6 free; ski plans; hols
(2-day min). Closed Apr. Crib $10. Pet accepted; $8.50. TV;
VCR in common rm. Complimentary full bkfst. Restaurant
(see also HORSE and HOUND). Ck-out 11 am, ck-in 3-6 pm.
Downhill ski 2 mi; x-country ski on site. Secluded country
inn near Cannon Mt. Cr cds: A, D, DS, MC, V.
⊡ ✦ ⓓ ⓔ ⛷ ☞ ⚒

★★ **INN AT FOREST HILLS.** *NH 142 (03580).*
603/823-9550; fax 603/823-8701; toll-free 800/280-9550.
www.innatforesthills.com. 7 rms, 2 with shower only,
3 story. No A/C. No rm phones. S, D $100-$140; each
addl $25; ski plans; hols (2-day min); higher rates fall
foliage. Children over 11 yrs only. TV; cable, VCR avail
(movies). Complimentary full bkfst. Ck-out 11 am, ck-in
3-6 pm. Tennis. Downhill ski 5 mi; x-country ski on site.
Cottage built in 1890; large front porch, solarium. Totally
nonsmoking. Cr cds: MC, V.
⊡ ⓓ ✦ ⛷ ⌸ ⊠ ⚒

★★ **LOVETTS INN.** *1474 Profile Rd, Rte 18 (03580).*
603/823-7761; fax 603/823-8802; res 603/823-7761.
www.lovettsinn.com. 6 rms, 5 with bath, 2 story; 16 guest
cottages. Some A/C. S $100-$150; D $140-$190; MAP avail;
package plans. Closed Apr. Crib avail. Pet accepted, some
restrictions. TV. Pool. Restaurant (see LOVETT'S INN BY
LAFAYETTE BROOK). Bar 6-10 pm. Box lunches. Ck-out
11 am, ck-in after 2 pm. Free bus depot transportation.
Downhill ski 3 mi; x-country ski on site. Game rm. Rec rm.
Lawn games. Fireplaces in cottages. Historic resort-type inn
(1784); on 10 acres with trout pond, streams. Cr cds: A, DS,
MC, V.
⊡ ⓓ ✦ ⊠ ⚒ ⌸ ☞

★★ **SUGAR HILL INN.** *Rte 117 (03580).*
603/823-5621; fax 603/823-5639; toll-free 800/548-4748.
www.sugarhillinn.com. 10 rms in inn; 6 cottage rms.
No A/C in rms. S, D $115-$175. Afternoon refreshments.
Dining rm (public by res). Bar. Ck-out 11 am, ck-in 3 pm.
Downhill ski 3 mi; x-country ski 2 mi. Some fireplaces.
Converted farmhouse (ca 1789). Totally nonsmoking.
Cr cds: A, MC, V.
☞ ⌸ ⚒

★★ **SUNSET HILL HOUSE — A GRAND INN.** *231 Sunset*
Hill Rd, Sugar Hill (03585). 603/823-5522; fax 603/823-
5738; toll-free 800/786-4455. www.sunsethillhouse.com.
30 rms, 2 story. No A/C. No rm phones. S $115-$230;
D $135-$250; each addl $20-$30; ski, golf plans; wknd
rates; 2-day min hols; higher rates fall foliage. Crib $20.
TV in common rm; cable. Heated pool. Complimentary
full bkfst. Dining rm 5:30-9 pm. Ck-out 11 am, ck-in 3 pm.
Business servs avail. 9-hole golf. Downhill ski 5 mi;
x-country ski on site. Lawn games. Built in 1882; beautiful
view of mountains, attractive grounds. Totally nonsmoking.
Cr cds: A, D, DS, MC, V.
⊡ ☞ ⛳ ⌸ ⊠ ⚒

Restaurants

★★★ **THE FRANCONIA INN.** *1300 Easton Rd (03580).*
603/823-5542. www.franconiainn.com. Continental menu.
Specialties: bouillabaisse, rack of lamb, seafood. Own
desserts. Hrs: 6-9 pm; hrs vary off-season. Closed Apr-mid-
May. Res accepted. No A/C. Bar. Dinner $16-$21. Child's
menu. Totally nonsmoking. Cr cds: A, MC, V.
⊡

★★ **HORSE & HOUND.** *205 Wells Rd (03580). 603/823-*
5501. www.bestinns.net/usa/hh/horse.html. Continental
menu. Specializes in roast duckling, chicken, veal. Hrs: 6-
8 pm. Sat to 9 pm Closed Sun-Wed. Special menu on Thurs.
Res accepted. No A/C. Bar 5-10 pm. Dinner $17-$25. Child's
menu. Totally nonsmoking. Cr cds: A, D, DS, MC, V.

★★ **LOVETT'S INN BY LAFAYETTE BROOK.**
1474 Profile Rd, Rte 18 (03580). 603/823-7761.
www.lovettsinn.com. Specialties: veal, roast mountain duck.
Own baking. Hrs: 6-9 pm. Closed Apr. Res required. Bar
6-10 pm. Historic bldg. Cr cds: A, DS, MC, V.
SC

★★ **POLLY'S PANCAKE PARLOR.** *672 NH 117, Sugar Hill*
(03585). 603/823-5575. www.pollyspancakeparlor.com.
Specializes in whole grain pancakes, waffles, sandwiches.
Own soups, sausage, desserts. Hrs: 7 am-3 pm; wknds
only Nov and Apr, hrs vary. Closed Dec-Mar. Res accepted.
No A/C. A la carte entrees: bkfst, lunch $6-$18. Child's
menu. In converted carriage shed (1840). Early Amer decor;
antiques. Family-owned. Totally nonsmoking. Cr cds: A, DS,
MC, V.

Franconia Notch State Park

See also Franconia, Lincoln/North Woodstock

(Approx 7 mi SE of Franconia via NH 18 & I-93/Franconia Notch State Pkwy)

This seven-mile pass and state park, a deep valley of 6,440 acres between the Franconia and Kinsman ranges of the White Mountains, has been a top tourist attraction since the mid-19th century. Mounts Liberty (4,460 feet), Lincoln (5,108 feet), and Lafayette (5,249 feet) loom on the east, and Cannon Mountain (4,200 feet) presents a sheer granite face. The Pemigewasset River follows the length of the Notch.

The park offers various recreational activities, including swimming at sandy beach; fishing and boating on Echo Lake (jct NH 18 and I-93 exit 3); hiking; eight-mile paved bike path through Notch; skiing; picnicking; camping. Fees for some activities. For further information contact Franconia Notch State Park, Franconia 03580; 603/823-5563.

What to See and Do

The Basin. Deep glacial pothole, 20 ft in diameter, at foot of a waterfall, polished smooth by sand, stones and water. W of I-93 (Franconia Notch State Pkwy), S of Profile Lake.

Cannon Mt Ski Area. Tramway, 2 quad, 3 triple, 2 double chairlifts, pony lift; patrol, school, rentals; snowmaking; cafeterias, bar (beer & wine); nursery. New England Ski Museum. Longest run 2 mi; vertical drop 2,146 ft. (Late Nov-mid-Apr, daily; closed Dec 25) Tramway rising 2,022 ft vertically over a distance of 1 mi in 6 min, also operates Memorial Day-mid-Oct, daily; rest of yr, wkends (weather permitting). 5 mi S of Franconia via NH 18 & I-93 (Franconia Notch State Pkwy), exit 34B or 34C. Phone 603/823-8800.

Flume Gorge & Park Information Center. Narrow, natural gorge and waterfall along the flank of Mt Liberty, accessible by stairs and walks; picnicking. Mountain flowers and mosses, Liberty Gorge, the Cascades, covered bridges. Information center offers 15-min movie introducing park every ½-hr. Interpretive exhibits. Gift shop, cafeteria. (Mid-May-late Oct, daily) 15 mi S of Franconia, I-93 (Franconia Notch State Pkwy), exit 34A. Phone 603/745-8391.

Lafayette Campground. Fishing. Hiking on Appalachian trail system. Picnicking. Camping. Fees for some activities. (Mid-May-mid-Oct, daily) 9 mi S of Franconia Village, off I-93 (Franconia Notch State Pkwy). Phone 603/823-9513. ¢¢¢

Old Man of the Mountains. Discovered in 1805, this craggy likeness of a man's face is formed naturally of 5 layers of granite and is 40 ft high; also known as the "Great Stone Face." 1,200 ft above Profile Lake, W of I-93 (Franconia Notch State Pkwy), exit 2.

Franklin

See also Laconia

Settled 1764 **Pop** 8,304 **Elev** 335 ft **Area code** 603 **Zip** 03235
Information Greater Franklin Chamber of Commerce, PO Box 464, 603/934-6909
Web www.franklin.nh.us/chamber

Franklin was named in 1828 for Benjamin Franklin; until then it was a part of Salisbury. It is the birthplace of Daniel Webster, lawyer, senator, and statesman. The Pemigewasset and Winnipesaukee rivers, joining to form the Merrimack, provide the city with abundant water power.

What to See and Do

Congregational Christian Church. (1820). Church that Daniel Webster attended; tracker action organ. A bust of Webster by Daniel Chester French is outside. (Wed and Thurs mornings, Sun, also by appt) 47 S Main St, on US 3. Phone 603/934-4242. **FREE**

Lakes Region Factory Stores. More than 50 outlet stores. (Daily) Approx 5 mi E on US 3, in Tilton. Phone 603/286-7880.

Motel/Motor Lodge

★ **SUPER 8.** *7 Tilton Rd, Tilton (03276). 603/286-8882; fax 603/286-8788; toll-free 800/800-8000. www.super8.com.* 63 rms, 2 story. July-mid-Oct: S, D $49-$149; under 12 free; higher rates special events; lower rates rest of yr. Crib free. TV; cable, VCR avail (movies). Complimentary coffee in lobby. Restaurant adj 6 am-11 pm. Ck-out 11 am. Business servs avail. Sundries. Downhill ski 5 mi. Cr cds: A, C, D, DS, MC, V.
🖨 🐾 🐕

B&B/Small Inn

★★ **MARIA ATWOOD INN.** *71 Hill Rd; Rte 3A (03235). 603/934-3666. www.atwoodinn.com.* 7 rms, 3 story. No rm phones. S $65; D $80-$90; each addl $25; under 12 free. TV in sitting rm; cable. Complimentary full bkfst. Restaurant nearby. Ck-out 11 am, ck-in 3 pm. Business servs avail. Downhill ski 10 mi; x-country ski on site. Fireplaces. Federal-style house built 1830; many antiques. Totally nonsmoking. Cr cds: A, DS, MC, V.
🇩 🐕 🐾 🖨

Restaurants

★ **MR D'S.** *428 N Main St, West Franklin (03235). 603/934-3142.* Specializes in seafood, steak, own soups. Hrs: 6 am-8 pm; Sun from 8 am. Closed some major hols. Serv bar. Bkfst $1.75-$5.95, lunch $3-$9, dinner $5-$12. Child's menu. Collection of old-fashioned photographs on walls. Cr cds: A, D, DS, MC, V.
🇩 🖨

★★★ **OLIVER'S RESTAURANT & PUB.** *4 Sanborn Rd, Tilton (03276). 603/286-7379. www.oliversrestaurantpub.com.* Specializes in veal, pasta, fresh seafood. Hrs: 11 am-9 pm; Fri, Sat to 10 pm; Sun 8:30 am-9 pm, brunch 11 am-2 pm. Res accepted. Bar to 12:30 am. Lunch $5.95-$8.95, dinner $9.95-$16.95. Sun brunch $5.95-$9.95. Child's menu. Entertainment Thurs. Country decor; some antiques. Cr cds: A, DS, MC, V.
D

Gorham

Settled 1805 **Pop** 3,173 **Elev** 801 ft **Area code** 603 **Zip** 03581

Information Northern White Mountains Chamber of Commerce, 164 Main St, PO Box 298, Berlin 03570; 603/752-6060 or 800/992-7480

Web www.northernwhitemountains.com

Commanding the northeast approaches to the Presidential Range of the White Mountains, at the north end of Pinkham Notch (see), Gorham has magnificent views and is the center for summer and winter sports. The Peabody River merges with the Androscoggin in a series of falls. A Ranger District office of the White Mountain National Forest (see) is located here.

What to See and Do

Dolly Copp Campground. 176 campsites; fishing, hiking, picnicking. 6 mi S on NH 16 in White Mt National Forest (see). Contact the District Ranger, USDA Forest Service, 300 Glen Rd. Phone 603/466-2713.

Libby Memorial Pool & Recreation Area. Natural pool, bathhouses; picnicking. (Summer, daily, weather permitting) ¼ mi S on NH 16.

Moose Brook State Park. Views of the Presidential Range of the White Mts; good stream fishing area. Swimming, bathhouse; picnicking; camping. Hiking to Randolph Range. (Late May-early Sept) Standard fees. 2 mi W on US 2. Phone 603/466-3860.

Moose Tours. Daily tours leave each evening from the Gorham Informational Booth on a specified route to locate moose for sighting. (Late May-mid-Oct) Main St. Phone 603/752-6060. ¢¢¢

Mt Washington. (see). 10 mi S on NH 16.

Motels/Motor Lodges

★ **GORHAM MOTOR INN.** *324 Main St (03581). 603/466-3381; fax 603/752-2604; toll-free 800/445-0913. www. gorhammotorinn.com.* 39 rms. S $58-$72; D $68-$84; each addl $6; higher rates fall foliage. Crib free. Pet accepted, some restrictions; $6. TV; cable (premium). Pool. Restaurant nearby. Ck-out 11 am. Downhill/x-country ski 8 mi. Some refrigerators. Cr cds: A, DS, MC, V.
D

★★ **MT. MADISON MOTEL.** *365 Main St (03581). 603/466-3622; fax 603/466-3664; toll-free 800/851-1136. www.mtmadisonmotel.com.* 33 rms, 2 story. May-Oct: S, D $45-$88; each addl $5; higher rates fall foliage. Closed rest of yr. Crib $5. TV; cable. Heated pool. Playground. Restaurant opp. Ck-out 11 am. Some refrigerators. Balconies. Cr cds: A, DS, MC, V.
D

★★ **ROYALTY INN.** *130 Main St (03581). 603/466-3312; fax 603/466-5802; toll-free 800/437-3529. www.royaltyinn.com.* 90 rms, 1-2 story. July-Labor Day, mid-Sept-Oct: S $66-$79; D $72-$86; each addl $6; kit. units $82; lower rates rest of yr. Crib $5. Pet accepted. TV; cable, VCR avail. 2 pools; 1 indoor. Restaurant 6-10:30 am, 5-9 pm. Bar 5-11 pm; Fri, Sat to 1 am. Ck-out 11 am. Coin lndry. Meeting rm. Business servs avail. Downhill ski 9 mi; x-country ski 7 mi. Exercise equipt. Health club privileges. Game rm. Some refrigerators. Cr cds: A, C, D, DS, MC, V.
D

B&B/Small Inn

★★★ **PHILBROOK FARM INN.** *881 North Rd, Shelburne (03581). 603/466-3831. www.philbrookfarminn.com.* 18 inn rms, 9 share bath, 3 story; 2 1-rm cottages, 5 kit. cottages. No A/C. No elvtr. No rm phones. MAP: S $85-$100; D $115-$145; cottages $600/wk; wkly rates. Closed Oct 31-Dec 25; also Apr. Crib $3. Pet accepted, some restrictions. Pool. Full bkfst. Dining rm: dinner (1 sitting). Ck-out 11 am (cottages 10 am), ck-in after noon. Downhill ski 15 mi; x-country ski on site. Rec rm. Lawn games. Antiques; sitting rm. Originally a farmhouse (1834), the inn has been in business since 1861. Cr cds: A, DS, MC, V.
D

Restaurant

★★ **YOKOHAMA.** *288 Main St (03581). 603/466-2501.* Japanese, Amer menu. Specialties: sukiyaki, oyako donburi, habachi platter. Hrs: 11:30 am-9 pm. Closed Mon; Thanksgiving, Dec 25; also 3 wks in Apr. Res accepted. Serv bar. Lunch $4.50-$6.50, dinner $5.75-$13.25. Child's menu. Family-owned. Cr cds: A, D, MC, V.
D

Hampton Beach

See also Portsmouth

Settled 1638 **Pop** 900 **Elev** 56 ft **Area code** 603 **Zip** 03842

Information Chamber of Commerce, 1 Park Ave, PO Box 790; 603/926-8717 or 800/GET-A-TAN

Web www.hamptonbeaches.com

What to See and Do

Fishing. Charter boats at Hampton Beach piers.

Fuller Gardens. Former estate of the late Governor Alvan T. Fuller featuring extensive rose gardens, annuals, perennials, Japanese garden, and conservatory. (May-Oct, daily) 10 Willow Ave, 4 mi NE via NH 1A, just N of NH 111 in North Hampton. Phone 603/964-5414. ¢¢

Hampton Beach State Park. Sandy beach on Atlantic Ocean. Swimming, bathhouse. Also here is the Sea Shell, a band shell and amphitheater. Camping (hookups). (Late May-Labor Day, daily) Standard fees. 3 mi S on NH 1A. Phone 603/926-3784.

Tuck Memorial Museum. Home of Hampton Historical Society. Antiques, documents, photographs, early postcards, tools, and toys; trolley exhibit; memorabilia of Hampton history. Restored one-rm schoolhouse; fire station. (Mid-June-mid-Sept; Tues-Fri and Sun, afternoons; rest of yr, by appt) 40 Park Ave, on Meeting House Green, 4 mi N via NH 1A in Hampton. Phone 603/929-0781. **FREE**

Special Events

Performing Arts Center of Winnacunet High School. Route 101E. Performances in 200-yr-old modernized ox barn. Nightly exc Mon; matinee Wed, Fri; children's shows Sat. Phone 603/926-3073. Mid-June-Labor Day.

Band concerts. On beach. Eves. Late June-Labor Day.

Motel/Motor Lodge

★ **REGAL INN OF HAMPTON BEACH.** *162 Ashworth Ave (03842). 603/926-7758; toll-free 800/445-6782. www.regalinn.com.* 36 rms, 3 story. No elvtr. July-Labor Day: S $85-$115; D $95-$125; kit. suites $129; each addl $20; under 13 free; family rates; lower rates rest yr. Crib $20. TV; cable. Heated pool; whirlpool. Complimentary continental bkfst. Restaurant nearby. Ck-out 11 am. Business servs avail. Game rm. Refrigerators; some in-rm whirlpools. Balconies. Cr cds: A, D, DS, MC, V.

D 🏄 😔 🛏 🏊 🔥

Hotels

★★ **ASHWORTH BY THE SEA.** *295 Ocean Blvd (03842). 603/926-6762; fax 603/926-2002; toll-free 800/345-6736. www.ashworthhotel.com.* 105 rms, 4 story. July-Sept: S, D $120-$275; each addl $20; under 18, $5; lower rates rest of yr. Crib $10. TV; cable (premium); VCR avail. Heated pool; poolside serv. Restaurant 6:30 am-11 pm; dining rm 8-11 am (summer), 11:45 am-2:30 pm, 5-10 pm. Bar; entertainment. Ck-out noon, Ck-in 3:00 pm. Meeting rms. Business servs avail. In-rm modem link. Gift shop. Beauty shop. Valet parking. Sun deck. Many balconies. Cr cds: A, D, DS, MC, V.

D 🛏 🔥

★★ **HAMPSHIRE INN.** *20 Spur Rd; Rte 107, Seabrook (03874). 603/474-5700; fax 603/474-2886; toll-free 800/932-8520. www.hampshireinn.com.* 35 rms, 3 story. June-Oct: S, D $79-$119; suites $158; each addl $10; under 6 free; lower rates rest of yr. Crib $10. TV; cable (premium). Indoor pool; whirlpool. Complimentary continental bkfst. Restaurant nearby. Ck-out 11 am. Coin lndry. Meeting rms. Business servs avail. In-rm modem link. Valet serv. Airport transportation. Exercise equipt. Refrigerators; some in-rm whirlpools. Cr cds: A, C, D, DS, MC, V.

D 🛏 🏋 🏊 🔥 SC

★★ **HAMPTON FALLS INN.** *11 Lafayette Rd, Hampton Falls (03844). 603/926-9545; fax 603/926-4155; toll-free 800/356-1729. www.hamptonfallsinn.com.* 47 rms, 3 story. Mid-June-mid-Oct: S, D $59-$169; each addl $10; suites $129; under 12 free; wkly, wkend, hol rates (2-day min wkends, hols); lower rates rest of yr. Crib free. Pet accepted, some restrictions; $25 refundable. TV; cable, VCR avail. Indoor pool; whirlpool. Complimentary coffee in lobby. Restaurant. Ck-out 11 am. Meeting rms. Business servs avail. Bellhops. Valet serv. Sundries. Health club privileges. Game rm. Refrigerators, microwaves. Balconies. Picnic tables. Cr cds: A, C, D, DS, MC, V.

D 🐾 😔 🏋 🛏 🏊 🔥 🏋

★★★ **INN OF HAMPTON.** *815 Lafayette Rd, Hampton (03842). 603/926-6771; fax 603/929-2160; toll-free 800/423-4561. www.theinnofhampton.com.* 71 rms, 2 story. June-early Sept: S $95-$129; D $115-$144; each addl $10; suites $194; under 12 free; lower rates rest of yr. Crib $10. TV; cable (premium), VCR avail. Indoor pool; whirlpool. Coffee in rms. Restaurant 6:30 am-2 pm, 5-9 pm; Mon to 2 pm; Sun 8 am-noon. Ck-out 11 am. Coin lndry. Meeting rm. Business servs avail. In-rm modem link. Exercise equipt. Refrigerators, microwaves. On 6 acres. Cr cds: A, C, D, DS, MC, V.

D 🛏 🏋 🏊

B&Bs/Small Inns

★★★ **D.W.'S OCEANSIDE INN.** *365 Ocean Blvd (03842). 603/926-3542; fax 603/926-3549. www.oceansideinn.com.* 10 rms, 2 story. No rm phones. July-Aug: D $125-$195; each addl $30; wkly rates; lower rates mid-May-June; Sept-mid-Oct. Closed rest of yr. TV; VCR (free movies) in library. Complimentary bkfst. Ck-out 11 am, ck-in 2 pm. Historic building (1880). Antiques; opp ocean beach; swimming, sun decks. Totally nonsmoking. Cr cds: A, DS, MC, V.

D 😔 🔥 🏊

★★ **LAMIE'S INN & TAVERN.** *490 Lafayette Rd, Hampton (03842). 603/926-0330; fax 603/929-0017; toll-free 800/805-5050. www.lamiesinn.com.* 32 rms, 2 story. Late June-Labor Day: S $89-$99; D $109-$129; each addl $10; under 17 free; lower rates rest of yr; golf packages. Crib free. TV; cable (premium). Restaurant. Bar 4 pm-midnight; entertainment Fri, Sat (in season). Ck-out noon, ck-in 3 pm. Meeting rms. Business servs avail. Valet serv. Airport transportation. Refrigerators avail. Golf privileges. Cr cds: A, DS, MC, V.

D 😔 🏋

Restaurant

★ **NEWICK'S FISHERMAN'S LANDING.** *845 Lafayette Rd, Hampton (03842).* 603/926-7646. www.newicks.com. Specializes in fresh seafood. Hrs: 11:30 am-9 pm. Closed Thanksgiving, Dec 25; Mon, Tues (winter). Serv bar. Lunch, dinner $2.95-$20.99. Child's menu. Nautical theme; large ship models, artwork. Cr cds: A, DS, MC, V.

[D] [symbol]

Hanover

Settled 1765 **Pop** 9,212 **Elev** 531 ft **Area code** 603 **Zip** 03755
Information Chamber of Commerce, PO Box 5105, 216 Nugget Bldg, Main St; 603/643-3115
Web www.hanoverchamber.org

Established four years after the first settlers came here, Dartmouth College is an integral part of Hanover. Named for the Earl of Dartmouth, one of its original supporters, the school was founded by the Reverend Eleazar Wheelock "for the instruction of the youth of Indian tribes . . . and others."

What to See and Do

Dartmouth College. (1769). (5,400 students) Main and Wheelock Sts. Phone 603/646-1110. On campus are

Baker Barry Memorial Library. (white spire). Two million volumes; notable frescoes by the Mexican artist José Clemente Orozco. (Academic yr, daily) Guide service during vacations (Mon-Fri). Wentworth and College Sts. Phone 603/646-2560.

Dartmouth Row. Early white brick buildings including Wentworth, Dartmouth, Thornton and Reed halls. Parts of Dartmouth Hall date from 1784. E side of Green.

Hood Museum and Hopkins Center for the Arts. Concert hall, theaters, changing art exhibits. Gallery (daily; free). Performing arts events all yr (fees). Opp S end of Green.

Enfield Shaker Museum. Museum devoted to Shaker culture on the site where the Shakers established their Chosen Vale in 1793. Incl exhibits, craft demonstrations, workshops, special programs, and extensive gardens. Phone 603/632-4346. ¢¢

League of New Hampshire Craftsmen. Work by some of New Hampshire's finest craftspeople. (Daily exc Sun; closed major hols) 13 Lebanon St. Phone 603/643-5050. **FREE**

✪ **Saint-Gaudens National Historic Site.** Former residence and studio of sculptor Augustus Saint-Gaudens (1848-1907); "Aspet," built ca 1800, was once a tavern. Saint-Gaudens' famous works *The Puritan, Adams Memorial,* and *Shaw Memorial* are among the 100 works on display. Also formal gardens and works by other artists; sculptor-in-residence; interpretive programs. (Memorial Day-Oct, daily) Approx 5 mi S on NH 10, then 12 mi S off NH 12A, in Cornish, across river from Windsor, VT. Contact Superintendent, RR 3, Box 73, Cornish 03745; phone 603/675-2175. ¢¢

Skiing.

Dartmouth Skiway. Quad, double chairlift, surface tow; patrol, school; lodge, snack bar. Longest run one mi; vertical drop 968 ft. (Mid-Dec-Mar, daily) 15 mi N on NH 10 to Lyme, then 3 mi E. Phone 603/795-2143. ¢¢¢¢

Webster Cottage. (1780). Residence of Daniel Webster during his last year as a Dartmouth College student; Colonial and Shaker furniture, Webster memorabilia. (June-mid-Oct, Wed, Sat and Sun afternoons) 32 N Main St. Phone 603/643-6529. **FREE**

Motels/Motor Lodges

★ **CHIEFTAIN MOTOR INN.** *84 Lyme Rd (03755).* 603/643-2550; fax 603/643-5265; toll-free 800/845-3557. www.chieftaininn.com. 22 rms, 2 story. June-Oct: S $100-$110; D $150; each addl $10; lower rates rest of yr. TV. Continental bkfst. Ck-out 11 am. Picnic tables. View of Connecticut River. Cr cds: A, D, DS, MC, V.

[D] [symbols]

★★★ **HANOVER INN.** *Main St & Wheelock St (03755).* 603/643-4300; fax 603/646-3744; toll-free 800/443-7024. www.hanoverinn.com. 92 rms, 5 story, 22 suites. S, D $207-$217; suites $217-$287; ski, golf plans. Crib free. Pet accepted. Covered parking $5; free valet parking. TV; cable, VCR avail. Indoor pool privileges; sauna. Restaurant 7 am-10 pm; Bar 11:30 am-midnight. Ck-out noon. Meeting rms. Business servs avail. Free airport transportation. Bellhops. Valet serv. Gift shop. Lighted tennis privileges, pro. 18-hole golf privileges, greens fee $33, pro, putting green, driving range. Downhill ski 7 mi. Exercise equipt. Health club privileges. Bathrm phones. Georgian-style brick structure owned by college; used as guest house since 1780. Cr cds: A, D, DS, MC, V.

[D] [symbols]

Resort

★ **LOCH LYME LODGE.** *70 Orford Rd, Rte 10, Lyme (03768).* 603/795-2141; fax 603/795-2141; toll-free 800/423-2141. www.lochlymelodge.com. 24 cottages, 12 kits. units, 4 rms in inn, all share bath. No A/C. No rm phones. S, D $52-$97; cottages $575-$850; under 4 free; MAP avail. Cottages closed Sept-May. Crib $6. Pet accepted, some restrictions. Playground. Ck-out 10 am, Ck-in 2 pm. Tennis privileges. Downhill ski 4 mi; x-country ski 10 mi. Lawn games. Fireplaces, some refrigerators. On Post Pond; swimming beach. Picnic tables, grills.

[D] [symbols]

B&Bs/Small Inns

★★ **ALDEN COUNTRY INN.** *1 Market St, Lyme (03768).* 603/795-2222; fax 603/795-9436; toll-free 800/794-2296. www.aldencountryinn.com. 15 rms, 4 story. No elvtr. June-Oct: S $95-$130; D $115-$145; each addl $20; lower rates rest of yr. Complimentary full bkfst. Restaurant 7:30-9:30 am, 5:30-9:30 pm; Sun 5-8 pm. Bar to 9 pm. Ck-out 11 am, ck-in 3 pm. Downhill ski 3 mi; x-country ski 15 mi. Original inn and tavern built 1809; antique furnishings. Cr cds: A, DS, MC, V.

[D] [symbols] [SC]

★★★ **DOWD'S COUNTRY INN.** *On the Common, Lyme (03768). 603/795-4712; fax 603/795-4220; toll-free 800/482-4712. www.dowdscountryinn.com.* 22 rms, 2 story. June-Oct: S $70-$125; D $80-$155; lower rates rest of yr. Crib $10. TV in common rm. Complimentary full bkfst. Ck-out 11 am, ck-in 3 pm. Business servs avail. RR station, bus depot transportation. Downhill ski 2 mi. Built 1780. Totally non-smoking. Cr cds: A, D, DS, MC, V.

★ **MOOSE MOUNTAIN LODGE.** *33 Moose Mtn Lodge Rd, Etna (03750). 603/643-3529; fax 603/643-4119. www.moose mountainlodge.com.* 12 rms, 5 share bath, 2 story. No A/C. No rm phones. Jan-mid-Mar, AP: $85-$90/person; Mid-June-late Oct, Dec 26-late Mar, MAP: $80; family rates. Closed rest of yr. Complimentary coffee in lobby. X-country ski on site. Totally nonsmoking. Cr cds: MC, V.

★★ **THE SHAKER INN AT THE GREAT STONE DWELLING.** *447 Route 4A, Enfield (03748). 603/632-7810; toll-free 888/707-4257. www.theshakerinn.com.* 24 rms, 4 story. S $105; D $155; each addl $15; under 18 free. Crib avail, fee. Parking lot. TV; cable. Complimentary full bkfst, toll-free calls. Restaurant 8 am-8:30 pm, closed Mon. Bar. Ck-out 11 am, ck-in 3 pm. Meeting rms. Business servs avail. Gift shop. Golf, 18 holes. Downhill skiing. Beach access. Supervised children's activities. Hiking trail. Cr cds: A, D, DS, MC, V.

★★ **WHITE GOOSE INN.** *Rte 10, Orford (03777). 603/353-4812; fax 603/353-4543; toll-free 800/358-4267. www.whitegooseinn.com.* 15 rms, 2 share bath, 8 A/C. No rm phones. May-Oct: S $75; D $85-$105; lower rates rest of yr. Children over 8 yrs only. TV in lobby. Complimentary full bkfst. Ck-out 11 am, ck-in 2 pm. Main building (1833) attached to original structure (ca 1770). Circular porch. Totally nonsmoking. Cr cds: A, DS, MC, V.

Restaurants

★★ **JESSE'S.** *RR 120 (03755). 603/643-4111. www.blueskyrestaurants.com.* Specializes in steak, seafood, Maine lobster. Salad bar. Hrs: 5-10 pm; Fri, Sat to 10:30 pm; Sun 4:30-9:30 pm. Bar 4:30 pm-midnight. Dinner $8.95-$19.95. Child's menu. Outdoor dining. Victorian decor. Open-hearth cooking; mesquite grill. Cr cds: A, MC, V.

★ **MOLLY'S.** *43 S Main St (03755). 603/643-2570. www.mollysrestaurant.com.* Specializes in burgers, creative sandwiches, pasta. Hrs: 11:30 am-10 pm; Fri, Sat to 11 pm. Closed Thanksgiving, Dec 25. Bar. Lunch $5.95-$8.95, dinner $6.95-$16.95. Greenhouse-type decor; brass railings, Southwestern motif. Cr cds: A, MC, V.

Holderness

See also Meredith, Plymouth

Settled 1770 **Pop** 1,694 **Elev** 584 ft **Area code** 603 **Zip** 03245

Holderness is the shopping center and post office for Squam Lake (second-largest lake in the state) and neighboring Little Squam. Fishing, boating, swimming, water sports, and winter sports are popular in this area. The movie *On Golden Pond* was filmed here. A Ranger District office of the White Mountain National Forest (see) is located here.

What to See and Do

League of New Hampshire Craftsmen—Sandwich Home Industries. Work by some of New Hampshire's finest crafts-people. (Mid-May-mid-Oct, daily) 12 mi NE via NH 113, on Main St in Center Sandwich. Phone 603/284-6831. **FREE**

Science Center of New Hampshire. A 200-acre wildlife sanctuary with animals in natural enclosures; features bears, deer, bobcat, otter, and birds of prey; nature trails; animal presentations. Picnicking. (May-Oct, daily) On NH 113. Phone 603/968-7194. ¢¢

Squam Lake Tours. Two-hr boat tours of area where *On Golden Pond* was filmed. (May-Oct, three tours daily) ½ mi S on US 3. Contact PO Box 185. Phone 603/968-7577. ¢¢

B&Bs/Small Inns

★★★ **GLYNN HOUSE INN.** *59 Highland St, Ashland (03217). 603/968-3775; fax 603/968-9415; toll-free 800/637-9599. www.glynnhouse.com.* 11 rms, 2 story, 5 suites. No rm phones. S $89-$109; each addl $25; suites $169-$209; wkly rates; (2-day min); golf packages. Children over 7 yrs only. TV; VCR (movies). Complimentary full bkfst. Ck-out 11 am, ck-in 3 pm. Tennis privileges. Downhill ski 17 mi; x-country ski 3 mi. Lawn games. Refrigerators. Picnic tables. Built in 1896; gingerbread wraparound porch. Totally nonsmoking. Cr cds: A, DS, MC, V.

★★ **INN ON GOLDEN POND.** *Rte 3 (03245). 603/968-7269; fax 603/968-9226. www.innongoldenpond.com.* 8 rms, 3 story, 1 suite. No rm phones. Mid-May-Nov: S $100; D $130; each addl $30; suite $165; lower rates rest of yr. Children over 12 yrs only. TV in sitting rm; cable. Complimentary full bkfst. Ck-out 11 am, ck-in 3 pm. Gift shop. Downhill ski 17 mi. Game rm. Lawn games. Built 1879; fireplace; rms individually decorated. On 50 wooded acres; hiking trails, nearby lake. Totally nonsmoking. Cr cds: A, DS, MC, V.

★★★ **MANOR ON GOLDEN POND.** *Manor Dr; Rte 3 and Shepard Hill Rd (03245). 603/968-3348; fax 603/968-2116; toll-free 800/545-2141. www.manorongoldenpond.com.* 17 inn rms, 3 story, 4 rms in the Annex Chambers, 4 rms in Carriage House, 4 cottages. S, D $225-$375; cottages

$1,750-$2,500/wk. Children over 12 yrs only. TV; cable, VCR avail (free movies). Pool. Complimentary full country bkfst, afternoon refreshments. Restaurant (see MANOR ON GOLDEN POND). Bar 5-11:30 pm. Ck-out 11 am, ck-in 3-6 pm. Meeting rms. Business servs avail. Luggage handling. Valet serv. Concierge serv. Gift shop. Lighted tennis. Downhill ski 18 mi. Lawn games. Some in-rm whirlpools, fireplaces. Some balconies. On lake; canoes, paddleboats, private beach. English country house (1903). Totally non-smoking. Cr cds: A, DS, MC, V.

⊱ ⊁ ⊯ ⊠ 🔥

Restaurants

★★ **COMMON MAN.** *60 Main St, Ashland (03245). 603/968-7030. www.thecman.com.* Specialties: baked stuffed shrimp, lobster bisque, roast prime rib. Hrs: 11:30 am-3 pm, 5-9 pm; Fri, Sat to 9:30 pm. Closed Thanksgiving, Dec 24, 25. Bar 4-11 pm. Lunch $3.50-$7.95, dinner $10.95-$16.95. Child's menu. Antiques; rustic decor. Family-owned. Cr cds: A, DS, MC, V.

D

★★ **CORNER HOUSE INN.** *22 Main St (03227). 603/284-6219.* Specialties: lobster and mushroom bisque, shellfish saute. Hrs: 11:30 am-2:30 pm, 5:30-9 pm; early-bird dinner 5:30-6:30 pm; pub to 10 pm. Closed Thanksgiving, Dec 25; also Mon Nov-May. Serv bar. Lunch $4.50-$11.95, dinner $10.95-$18.95. Victorian-style inn (1849), originally house and attached harness shop; guest rms avail. Totally non-smoking. Cr cds: A, DS, MC, V.

D

★★★ **MANOR ON GOLDEN POND.** *US 3 (03245). 603/968-3348. www.manorongoldenpond.com.* New American menu changes frequently. Hrs: 6-9 pm. Res required. Bar. Wine list. A la carte entrees: dinner $25-$40. Fireplace. Overlooks Squam Lake, mountains. Totally nonsmoking. Cr cds: A, DS, MC, V.

Jackson

See also Bartlett, North Conway

Settled 1790 **Pop** 678 **Elev** 971 ft **Area code** 603 **Zip** 03846
Information Chamber of Commerce, PO Box 304; 603/383-9356
Web www.jacksonnh.com

At the south end of Pinkham Notch (see), Jackson is a center for skiing and a year-round resort. The Wildcat River rushes over rock formations in the village; Wildcat Mountain is to the north. A covered bridge (ca 1870) spans the Ellis River.

What to See and Do

Heritage-New Hampshire. Path winds among theatrical sets and takes visitors on a walk through 30 events during 300 yrs of New Hampshire history. Each set has animation, sounds, and smells to re-create the past, from a stormy voyage to the New World to a train ride through autumn foliage in Crawford Notch. (Late May-early Oct, daily) 2 mi S on NH 16 in Glen. Phone 603/383-9776. ¢¢

Skiing.

Black Mountain. Triple, double chairlifts, J-bar; patrol, school, rentals; cafeteria; nursery. Longest run one mi; vertical drop 1,100 ft. 2½ mi N on NH 16B. Phone 603/383-4490.

Jackson Ski Touring Foundation. Maintains 95 mi of x-country trails, connecting inns and ski areas. Instruction, rentals, rescue service. (Dec-mid-Apr, daily; closed Dec 25) ¢¢

Story Land. Village of storybook settings; Cinderella's castle, Heidi's grandfather's house; themed rides, including raft ride, on 35 acres. (Mid-June-early Sept, daily; early Sept-early Oct, wkends) 2 mi S on NH 16 in Glen. Phone 603/383-4186. ¢¢¢¢

White Mountain National Forest. (see). N & S on NH 16.

Motels/Motor Lodges

★★ **LODGE AT JACKSON VILLAGE.** *Rte 16 (03846). 603/383-0999; fax 603/383-6104; toll-free 800/233-5634. www.lodgeatjacksonvillage.com.* 32 rms, 2 story. S $94-$255; D $99-$259; under 17 free; ski, golf plans; higher rates fall foliage. Crib $15. TV; cable. Pool. Complimentary coffee in lobby. Restaurant nearby. Ck-out 11 am. Coin lndry. Sundries. Tennis. Downhill ski 3 mi; x-country ski on site. Refrigerators. Private patios, balconies. Sitting rm with stone fireplace. On river. Cr cds: A, MC, V.

D t ⊱ ⊁ ⊯ ⊠ 🔥

★★ **RED APPLE INN.** *NH 302, Glen (03838). 603/383-9680; toll-free 800/826-3591. www.theredappleinn.com.* 16 rms. S, D $49-$155; each addl $10; under 13 free; ski plans. Closed 2 wks Apr and 3 wks Nov. Crib $10. TV; cable. Pool. Playground. Ck-out 11 am. Downhill ski 2 mi; x-country ski 2 mi. Game rm. Some refrigerators, fireplaces. Picnic tables, grills. In wooded area. Cr cds: A, DS, MC, V.

D ⊱ ⊯ ⊠ 🔥

Hotels

★★ **ELLIS RIVER HOUSE.** *Rte 16 (03846). 603/383-9339; fax 603/383-4142; toll-free 800/233-8309. www.erhinn.com.* 21 rms, 3 story, 4 suites. Feb, July-Oct: S $105-$289; each addl $25; lower rates rest of yr. Children over 12 yrs only. Parking lot. Pool, whirlpool. TV; cable. Complimentary full bkfst. Coffee in rms. Restaurant. Bar. Ck-out 11 am, ck-in 3 pm. Meeting rms. Business servs avail. Concierge. Dry cleaning, coin lndry. Gift shop. Exercise privileges, sauna. Golf, 18 holes. Downhill skiing. Hiking trail. Cr cds: A, C, D, DS, MC, V.

D t ⊁ ⊱ ⊯ ⊠ ✈ 🔥

★★★ **WENTWORTH RESORT HOTEL.** *Rte 16A and Carter Notch Rd (03846). 603/383-9700; fax 603/383-4265; toll-free 800/637-0013. www.thewentworth.com.* 60 rms, 2 story. S, D $79-$157; suites $205-$235 (MAP); under 12 free; package plans; wkly rates; higher rates: hol wks, fall foliage. TV; cable. Pool. Restaurant 7:30-11 am, 6-10 pm. Bar 5 pm-12:30 am; entertainment wkends (in season).

Ck-out 11 am. Meeting rms. Bus depot transportation. Downhill ski 2 mi; x-country ski on site. Lawn games. Some fireplaces. Private patios. Historic building (1860). View of river, mountains. Cr cds: A, C, D, DS, MC, V.

Resorts

★★ **EAGLE MOUNTAIN HOUSE.** *Carter Notch Rd (03846). 603/383-9111; fax 603/383-0854; toll-free 800/966-5779. www.eaglemt.com.* 93 rms, 5 story, 30 suites. No A/C. S, D $69-$159; each addl $15; suites $89-$189; under 18 free; wkly rates; ski, golf plans; higher rates fall foliage. Crib avail. TV; cable (premium), VCR avail. Heated pool; whirlpool, poolside serv. Playground. Dining rm 7 am-10 pm. Bar 11:30-12:30 am. Ck-out 11 am. Meeting rms. Business servs avail. Concierge. Lighted tennis. 9-hole golf, greens fee $12-$18. Downhill ski 1 mi; x-country ski on site. Exercise equipt; sauna. Game rm. Rec rm. Lawn games. Spectacular view of mountains and forest. Cr cds: A, C, D, DS, MC, V.

★★★ **STORYBOOK RESORT INN.** *Junction US 302 and Rte 16, Glen (03838). 603/383-6800; fax 603/383-4678. www.storybookresort.com.* 78 rms, 1-2 story. July-late Oct: S $79-$139; D $89-$159; each addl $8; wkly rates; ski plans; higher rates special events; lower rates rest of yr. Crib $7. TV; cable. 3 pools, 1 indoor; wading pool, whirlpools. Playground. Restaurant 8-10 am, 6-9 pm. Bar from 5 pm. Ck-out 11 am. Coin lndry. Meeting rms. Business servs avail. Bellhops. Gift shop. Tennis. Downhill/x-country ski 3 mi. Exercise equipt; sauna. Game rm. Rec rm. Lawn games. Some refrigerators, microwaves. Private patios, balconies. Picnic tables, grills. Cr cds: A, C, D, DS, MC, V.

B&Bs/Small Inns

★★★ **BERNERHOF INN & PRINCE PLACE RESTAURANT.** *Rte 302, Glen (03838). 603/383-9132; fax 603/383-0809; res 800/548-8007. www.bernerhofinn.com.* 9 rms, 3 story. S $75-$139; D $79-$139; package plans. Crib avail. TV; cable. Complimentary full bkfst. Restaurant (see PRINCE PLACE). Rm serv. Ck-out 10 am, ck-in after 2 pm. Downhill ski 1 mi; x-country ski 4 mi. Some in-rm whirlpools. Victorian-style house (1890) with European accents; sitting rm, antiques. Cr cds: A, D, DS, MC, V.

★★ **DANA PLACE INN.** *Pinkham Notch, Rte 16 (03846). 603/383-6822; fax 603/383-6022; res 800/537-9276. www.danaplace.com.* 30 rms, 2 story, 5 suites. Dec-Feb, July-Oct: D $225; suites $250; each addl $50; children $20; under 17 free; lower rates rest of yr. Crib avail. Pet accepted, some restrictions. Parking lot. Indoor pool, childrens pool, whirlpool. TV; cable (premium). Complimentary full bkfst, newspaper, toll-free calls. Restaurant. Bar. Meeting rm. Business center. Golf. Tennis, 2 courts. Downhill skiing. Hiking trail. Picnic facilities. Cr cds: A, C, D, DS, MC, V.

★★★ **INN AT THORN HILL.** *Thorn Hill Rd (03846). 603/383-4242; fax 603/383-8062; toll-free 800/289-8990. www.innatthornhill.com.* 10 rms in 3-story inn, 6 rms in carriage house, 3 cottages. Some rm phones. MAP: S $95-$145; D $105-$155/person; package plans. Children over 10 yrs only. TV in parlor of main bldg and in cottages; cable. Pool; whirlpool. Dining rm 8-9:30 am, 6-9 pm (public by res). Bar. Ck-out 11 am, ck-in after 3 pm. Business servs avail. Downhill ski 2 mi; x-country ski on site. Lawn games. Some in-rm whirlpools, wet bars, fireplaces. Antique furnishings. Totally nonsmoking. Cr cds: A, MC, V.

★★ **NESTLENOOK FARM RESORT.** *Dinsmore Rd (03846). 603/383-9443; fax 603/383-4515; toll-free 800/659-9443. www.luxurymountaingetaways.com.* 7 rms, 2 A/C, 3 story, 2 suites. S $125-$275; D $145-$429; 2-day min wknds. Children over 12 yrs only. TV in game rm; cable, VCR avail. Heated pool. Complimentary full bkfst; afternoon refreshments. Ck-out 11 am, ck-in 3 pm. Downhill ski 3 mi; x-country ski on site. Ice-skating; sleigh rides. Game rm. Lawn games. Picnic tables. Restored Victorian building, one of oldest in Jackson (1770); antiques, Tiffany lamps, 18th-century parlor stoves. Sitting rm with riverstone fireplace. 65 acres with screened gazebo, animal barn, open-air chapel, apple orchard, gardens and pond. On river. Totally nonsmoking. Cr cds: DS, MC, V.

Restaurants

★★ **CHRISTMAS FARM INN.** *Rte 16B (03846). 603/383-4313. www.christmasfarminn.com.* Specialties: vegetable-stuffed chicken breast, veal basilico, shrimp scampi. Own baking. Hrs: 8-9:30 am, 5:30-9 pm; wknd hrs vary. Bar from 4:30 pm. Bkfst $2.45-$4.50, dinner $17.95-$25.95. In historic building (1786). Cr cds: A, DS, MC, V.

★★★ **INN AT THORN HILL.** *Thorn Hill Rd, Box A (03846). 603/383-4242. www.innatthornhill.com.* New England fusion menu. Specializes in pan-fried beef tenderloin coated with spices, roast rack of lamb. Hrs: 6-9 pm. Res accepted. Extensive wine list. Dinner $21.95-$26.95. Romantic atmosphere. Cr cds: A, DS, MC, V.

★★★ **PRINCE PLACE.** *Jct Rte 16 & US 302, Glen (03838). 603/383-9484. www.princeplace.com.* Continental menu. Specialties: delices de gruyere, Wiener schnitzel. Own desserts. Hrs: 5:30-9:30 pm; July-Oct from 11:30 am. Res accepted. Wine list. Lunch $3.50-$9.95, dinner $13-$22. Child's menu. Parking. Host of "A Taste of the Mountains" cooking school. Cr cds: A, DS, MC, V.

★ **RED PARKA PUB.** *US 302, Glen (03838). 603/383-4344. www.redparkapub.com.* Specializes in barbecued pork spare ribs, prime rib. Salad bar. Hrs: 4:30-10 pm; Sat, Sun from 4 pm. Closed Thanksgiving, Dec 24, 25. Bar 3:30 pm-12:30 am. Dinner $5.95-$18.95. Child's menu. Entertainment wknds. Parking. Outdoor dining. One rm in 1914 railroad car. Cr cds: A, D, DS, MC, V.

★★ **WILDCAT TAVERN.** *NH 16A (03846). 603/383-4245. www.wildcattavern.com.* Specializes in fresh seafood, home-made desserts, veal, made-to-order meals. Hrs: 7:30-9:30 am, 11:30 am-3 pm, 6-9 pm; Fri, Sat to 10 pm; Bar 3 pm-12:30 am. Lunch $6.95-$10.95, dinner $16.95-$25. Tavern supper from $6.95. Child's menu. Parking. Outdoor dining. In historic inn (1896). Cr cds: A, MC, V.
[D]

Jaffrey

See also Keene, Peterborough

Settled 1760 **Pop** 5,361 **Elev** 1,013 ft **Area code** 603 **Zip** 03452

Information Chamber of Commerce, PO Box 2; 603/532-4549

Web www.jaffreycoc.org

Jaffrey, on the eastern slopes of Mount Monadnock, has been a summer resort community since the 1840s.

What to See and Do

Barrett House "Forest Hall". (1800) Federal mansion with third-floor ballrm. Twelve museum rms contain some of the most important examples of 18th- and 19th-century furniture and antique musical instruments in New England. Extensive grounds with Gothic Revival summer house on terraced hill behind main house. Guided tours. (June-mid-Oct, Thurs-Sun) 10 mi SE on NH 124, then ¼ mi S on NH 123A (Main St) in New Ipswich. Phone 603/878-2517. ¢

✪ **Cathedral of the Pines.** International nondenominational shrine. National memorial for all American war dead; Memorial Bell Tower dedicated to women who died in service. Outdoor altar, gardens, museum. (May-Oct, daily) 3 mi E on NH 124, then 3 mi S, in Rindge. Phone 603/899-3300.

Monadnock State Park. Hikers' mecca; 40-mi network of well-maintained trails on Mt Monadnock (3,165 ft). Summit views of all New England states. Picnicking, camping. Ski touring (Dec-Mar). No pets allowed. Standard fees. 2 mi W on NH 124, then N. Phone 603/532-8862. ¢

Jefferson

Settled 1772 **Pop** 965 **Elev** 1,384 ft **Area code** 603 **Zip** 03583

Information Northern White Mountain Chamber of Commerce, 164 Main St, PO Box 298, Berlin 03570; 603/752-6060 or 800/992-7480

Web www.northernwhitemountains.com

On the slopes of Mount Starr King in the White Mountains, this resort area is referred to locally as Jefferson Hill.

What to See and Do

Santa's Village. Santa and tame deer; unique rides; live shows, computerized animation. Playground; picnic area. (Father's Day-Labor Day, daily; after Labor Day-Columbus Day, Sat and Sun) 1 mi NW on US 2, ½ mi W of jct NH 116. Phone 603/586-4445. ¢¢¢¢

Six Gun City. Western frontier village; cowboy skits, frontier show, fort, Native American camp, homestead, carriage and sleigh museum, general store, snack bar; miniature horse show; pony and burro rides; bumper boats, water slides, and other rides; miniature golf, games, animals, and antiques. (Mid-June-Labor Day, daily; after Labor Day-Columbus Day, Sat and Sun) 4 mi E on US 2. Phone 603/586-4592. ¢¢

Special Event

Lancaster Fair. 6 mi NW in Lancaster. Agricultural exhibits, horse show, entertainment. Labor Day wkend. 603/788-2530

Motels/Motor Lodges

★ **EVERGREEN MOTEL.** *Hwy US 2 (03583). 603/586-4449.* 18 rms. July-Labor Day: S, D $50-$60; each addl $5; higher rates fall foliage; lower rates May-June and after Labor Day-Oct. Closed rest of yr. Crib free. TV; cable. Heated pool. Restaurant 8 am-8 pm; hrs vary off-season. Ck-out 11 am. Picnic area. Camping, trailer facilities. Cr cds: A, DS, MC, V.
🏊 🔥

★ **LANTERN RESORT MOTEL & CAMPGROUND.** *Rte 2 (03583). 603/586-7151; fax 603/586-7025. www.thelanternresort.com.* 30 rms. S, D $35-$69; each addl $4. Closed Nov-Apr. Crib $3. TV; cable. Pool; whirlpool. Playground. Coffee in lobby. Ck-out 11 am. Coin lndry. Gift shop. Game rm. Lawn games. On wooded grounds. Cr cds: A, D, DS, MC, V.
🏊 🔽 🔥

B&B/Small Inn

★ **JEFFERSON INN.** *US 2 (03583). 603/586-7998; fax 603/586-7808; toll-free 800/729-7908. www.jeffersoninn.com.* 11 rms, 3 story, 2 suites. No A/C. Some rm phones. S, D $85-$120; each addl $15; suites $100-$175; ski, golf plans; wkends, hols (2-day min). Crib free. TV in common rm. Complimentary full bkfst. Ck-out 11 am, ck-in 3 pm. Concierge serv. Business servs avail. 18-hole golf privileges, greens fee $20. Downhill ski 15 mi; x-country ski opp. Lawn games. Some refrigerators. Renovated Victorian house; wraparound porch. Totally nonsmoking. Cr cds: A, DS, MC, V.
[D] 🔽 🎿 🔽 🔥

Restaurant

★★ **SEASONINGS.** *RR 2 (03583). 603/586-7133.* Specializes in seafood, beef, desserts. Hrs: 7 am-9 pm. Res accepted. Bkfst $1.95-$4.95, lunch, dinner $2.95-$14.95. Child's menu. Sun rm gives view of mountains. Cr cds: C, MC, V.

Keene

See also Peterborough

Settled 1736 **Pop** 22,430 **Elev** 486 ft **Area code** 603 **Zip** 03431
Information Chamber of Commerce, 48 Central Sq; 603/352-1303
Web www.keenechamber.com

A modern commercial city, Keene is the chief community of the Monadnock region. Its industries manufacture many products including furniture, machinery, textiles, and toys.

What to See and Do

Colony Mill Marketplace. Restored 1838 textile mill now transformed into regional marketplace with dozens of specialty shops, an antique center, numerous dining options, and varied entertainment. (Daily) 222 West St. Phone 603/357-1240.

Horatio Colony House Museum. Stately Federalist home (1806) of son of prominent Keene mill owners. Features treasures collected from Colony's world travels; books, art, antique furniture. (May-mid-Oct, Tues-Sat; rest of yr by appt) 199 Main St. Phone 603/352-0460. **FREE**

Wyman Tavern. (1762). Scene of first meeting of Dartmouth College trustees in 1770; now furnished in 1820s style. (June-Sept, Thurs-Sat) 339 Main St. Phone 603/352-1895. ¢

Special Events

The Old Homestead. 4 mi S on NH 32, at Potash Bowl in Swanzey Center. Drama of life in Swanzey during 1880s based on the Biblical story of the Prodigal Son; first presented in 1886. For schedule phone 603/352-0697. Mid-July.

Cheshire Fair. Fairgrounds, S on NH 12 in North Swanzey. Exhibits; horse and ox pulling contests; entertainment. Phone 603/357-4740. 1st wk Aug.

Motel/Motor Lodge

★★ **BEST WESTERN SOVEREIGN.** *401 Winchester St (03431). 603/357-3038; fax 603/357-4776; res 800/528-1234. www.bwkeene.com.* 131 rms, 2 story. S $69-$150; D $79-$175; each addl $10; studio rms $90; under 18 free. Crib free. Pet accepted. TV; cable. Indoor pool. Complimentary full bkfst. Coffee in rms. Restaurant 6:30 am-10 pm. Bar 3 pm-12:30 am; entertainment. Ck-out noon. Meeting rms. Business servs avail. In-rm modem link. Game rm. Balconies. Picnic tables. Cr cds: A, C, D, DS, MC, V.

Restaurants

★★ **176 MAIN.** *176 Main St. (03457). 603/357-3100. www.176main.com.* Specializes in Mexican, Italian and seafood dishes. Hrs: 11:30 am-11 pm; Fri to midnight; Sat 11 am-midnight; Sun 11 am-10 pm. Closed some major hols. Bar. Lunch $4.95-$6.95, dinner $9.95-$16.95. Child's menu. Outdoor dining. Rustic decor; exposed beams. Local artwork. Cr cds: A, D, DS, MC, V.

★ **THE PUB.** *131 Winchester Rd (03431). 603/352-3135.* Continental menu. Specializes in lamb, seafood, prime rib. Hrs: 7 am-10:30 pm. Res accepted. Bar 11 am-11 pm. Bkfst $1.25-$3.95, lunch $3.95-$6.95, dinner $5.95-$12.95. Child's menu. Family-owned. Cr cds: A, DS, MC, V.

Laconia

See also Franklin, Meredith, Wolfeboro

Settled 1777 **Pop** 15,743 **Elev** 570 ft **Area code** 603 **Zip** 03246
Information Chamber of Commerce, 11 Veterans Sq; 603/524-5531
Web www.laconia-weirs.org

On four lakes (Winnisquam, Opechee, Pauqus Bay, and Winnipesaukee), Laconia is the commercial center of the area known as the "Lakes Region." Besides the resort trade, it has more than a score of factories whose products include knitting machinery, hosiery, knitted fabrics, ball bearings, and electronic components. The headquarters of the White Mountain National Forest (see) is also located here.

What to See and Do

Cruises on Lake Winnipesaukee.

M/S Mount Washington. Leaves Weirs Beach and Wolfeboro on 2½-hr cruises with stops at Center Harbor or Alton Bay. (Mid-May-late Oct, daily) US Mail boat leaves Weirs Beach on two-hr cruises (Mid-June-mid-Sept). **Moonlight Cruises,** dinner and dancing (July-Labor Day, Mon-Sat eves). Theme cruises (selected dates, June-Oct). Phone 603/366-5531.

Queen of Winnipesaukee. This 46-ft sloop sails from M/S *Mount Washington* dock in Weirs Beach. 1½-hr cruises (July-Labor Day, daily; mid-May-June and early Sept-early Oct, wkends). Two-hr eve, moonlight cruises (July-Aug, Tues-Sat). Phone 603/366-5531.

Gunstock Recreation Area. A 2,400-acre county-operated park. 7 mi E on NH 11A in Gilford. Phone 603/293-4341.

Summer. Picnic and camp sites (Memorial Day wkend-Columbus Day wkend; fee; hookups addl; includes swimming privileges); fireplaces; stocked pond, blazed trails, playground; special events.

Winter. Skiing. Quad, two triple, two double chairlifts, two handle tows; patrol, school, rentals; snowmaking; cafeteria, lounge; nursery. Longest run two mi; vertical drop 1,400 ft. X-country trails. Night skiing. (Nov-Mar, daily; closed Dec 25) ¢¢¢¢

Recreation. The Weirs. Swimming, boating, fishing, sailing, waterskiing, playground, picnic areas, lifeguards, bath houses, nature trails. Endicott Memorial Stone with initials of 1652 explorers, S end of beach. (Mid-June-Labor Day, daily) 5 mi N on US 3 at Weirs Beach on Lake Winnipesaukee. Phone 603/524-5046. ¢¢

✷ **Surf Coaster.** Family water park with wave pool, water slides, "Crazy River" inner tube ride, "Boomerang" rides inside translucent glass tubes; raft rentals, sun decks, showers, children's play areas, entertainment, games, prizes. Snack bar. (Mid-June-Labor Day, daily; Memorial Day-mid-June, wkends) 6 mi N on US 3, then E on NH 11B, in Weirs Beach. Phone 603/366-5600. ¢¢¢¢

Winnipesaukee Railroad. Scenic train rides along Lake Winnipesaukee; can board in Weirs Beach or Meredith. RR 2 at Center Harbor.

Special Event

New Hampshire Music Festival. Plymouth State College in Silver Cultural Arts Center. Symphony/pop concerts. Contact 88 Belknap Mtn Rd, Gilford, 03246. Phone 603/524-1000. Thurs, Fri; limited Sat performances. July-Aug.

Motels/Motor Lodges

★ **BARTON'S MOTEL.** *1330 Union Ave (03246). 603/524-5674. www.bartonsmotel.com.* 37 rms, 4 kit. cottages. Some rm phones. Mid-June-mid-Sept: S, D $80-$90; each addl $7-$15; kit. units, cottages $145-$150; lower rates rest of yr. Crib free. TV; cable. Heated pool. Restaurant adj 6 am-10 pm. Ck-out 11 am. On lake; row boats; dockage, private beach. Cr cds: A, MC, V.
🏊 🐾

★ **BIRCH KNOLL.** *867 Weirs Blvd, Rte 3 (03247). 603/366-4958. www.birchknollmotel.com.* 24 rms, 1-2 story. Late June-Labor Day: S, D $75-$105; each addl $8; higher rates special events; lower rates rest of yr. Closed Nov-Mar. Crib $6. TV; cable. Pool. Complimentary coffee. Ck-out 11 am. Business servs avail. Exercise equipt. Rec rm. Some refrigerators avail. Opp beach, boating and canoeing. Picnic tables, grill. Cr cds: A, DS, V.
D 🐾 🎣 🏊 🛶 🐾 🏃

★★ **B MAE'S RESORT INN & SUITES.** *17 Harris Shore Rd, Rte 11, Gilford (03246). 603/293-7526; fax 603/293-4340; toll-free 800/458-3877. www.bmaesresort.com.* 82 rms, 2 story. S, D $99-$110; each addl $12; suites $125-$165; under 12 free; ski plan. Crib free. TV; cable, VCR avail (movies). 2 pools, 1 indoor; whirlpool. Complimentary coffee in lobby. Restaurant 7-11 am, 5-10 pm; Sat 7-11 am, 5-10 pm; Sun 7-11 am, 4-9 pm. Bar from 4 pm. Ck-out 11 am. Meeting rm. Business servs avail. Sundries. Downhill/x-country ski 4 mi. Exercise equipt. Game rm. Private patios, balconies. Cr cds: A, C, D, DS, MC, V.
D 🐾 🏊 🏊 🛶 🔥 SC 🏃

Resort

★★ **LORD HAMPSHIRE MOTEL & COTTAGES.** *855 Laconia Rd, Winnisquam (03289). 603/524-4331; fax 603/524-1897. www.lordhampshire.com.* 8 rms, 12 kit. cottages. July-Labor Day: S $50-$85; D $55-$100; each addl $15; kit. units (2-day min) $12 addl; 1-2 bedrm cottages for 2-6 persons, $525-$1035/wk; family rates; lower rates Apr-June and after Labor Day-early Nov. Closed rest of yr. Crib $3. TV; cable. Ck-out 11 am; cottages 10:30 am. Business servs avail. Lawn games. Boat rentals. Some fireplaces. Picnic tables, grills. Some cottages with screened porches. On lake; private beach, sun deck. Cr cds: A, MC, V.
D 🐾 🏖

Restaurant

★★ **HICKORY STICK FARM.** *66 Bean Hill Rd, Belmont (03220). 603/524-3333. www.hickorystickfarm.com.* Specializes in roast duckling. Own baking. Hrs: 5-9 pm; Sun from noon; winter hrs vary. Closed Mon. Res accepted. Serv bar. Dinner $12.95-$21.95. Outdoor dining. Converted Colonial farmhouse, barn. Gift shop. Guest rms avail. Family-owned. Totally nonsmoking. Cr cds: A, DS, MC, V.
D

Lincoln/North Woodstock

Pop 1,229 **Elev** Lincoln, 811 ft; North Woodstock, 738 ft
Area code 603 **Zip** Lincoln, 03251; North Woodstock, 03262

Information Chamber of Commerce, NH 112, PO Box 358, Lincoln; 603/745-6621 or 800/227-4191
Web www.linwoodcc.org

In a spectacular mountain setting, the villages of Lincoln and Woodstock lie at the junction of the road through Franconia Notch State Park (see) and the Kancamagus Scenic Byway (NH 112).

What to See and Do

Clark's Trading Post. Entertainment park has trained New Hampshire black bears, haunted house, replica of 1884 firehouse; 30-min ride on White Mt Central railroad. Museum features early Americana, photo parlor, maple cabin, nickelodeons, ice cream parlor. Bumper boats. (July-Labor Day, daily; Memorial Day-June and early Sept-Columbus Day, wkends) 1 mi N of North Woodstock on US 3. Phone 603/745-8913. ¢¢

Franconia Notch State Park. (see). 2 mi N on US 3.

Hobo Railroad. Fifteen-mi scenic excursions along the Pemigewasset River. Features restored Pullman Dome dining car. (Daily) Railroad St, off Main. Phone 603/745-2135. ¢¢¢

Lost River Gorge. Natural boulder caves, largest known granite pothole in eastern US; Paradise Falls; boardwalks with 1,900-ft glacial gorge; nature garden with 300 varieties of native shrubs and flowers; geology exhibits; cafeteria, picnicking. (Mid-May-mid-Oct, daily) Appropriate outdoor clothing recommended. 6 mi W of North Woodstock on NH 112, Kinsman Notch. Phone 603/745-8031. ¢¢¢

Skiing. Loon Mountain Recreation Area. 7,100-ft gondola, two triple, four double chairlifts, one high-speed quad chairlift, pony lift; patrol, school, rentals, shops, snowmaking; restaurant, cafeterias, bar; nursery; lodge (see RESORT). Longest run 2½ mi; vertical drop 2,100 ft. (Late Nov-mid-Apr, daily) X-country trails (Dec-Mar). Summer activities incl: mountain biking (rentals), bike tours, in-line skating, horseback riding, skate park, climbing wall. Gondola also operates Memorial Day-mid-Oct (daily). (See SPECIAL EVENT) 3 mi E of Lincoln off NH 112 (Kancamagus Hwy). Phone 603/745-8111.

Whale's Tale Water Park. Wave pool, water slides, "lazy river," children's activity pool; playground; concession, gift shop. (Mid-June-Labor Day, daily; Memorial Day-mid-June, Sat and Sun) N on I-93, exit 33, then N on US 3. Phone 603/745-8810. ¢¢¢¢

White Mountain National Forest. (see).

Special Event

New Hampshire Highland Games. Loon Mtn. Largest Scottish gathering in eastern US. Bands, competitions, concerts, workshops. Phone 800/358-SCOT. Three days Sept.

Motels/Motor Lodges

★★ **BEACON RESORT.** *Rte 3, Lincoln (03251). 603/745-8118; fax 603/745-3783; toll-free 800/258-8934. www.beaconresort.com.* 132 rms, 1-2 story, 26 suites, 24 cottages, 47 kits. July-mid-Oct, ski season and hol wkends (3-day min): S, D $65-$150; each addl $10; suites $150-$195; cottages for 2-6, $65-$125; package plans; lower rates rest of yr. Crib $4. TV; cable. 4 pools, 2 indoor; wading pool, whirlpools, saunas. Restaurant 7:30-10:30 am, 5-8:30 pm; summer, wkends and hols to 9 pm. Bar from 5 pm; entertainment. Ck-out 11 am; cottages 10 am. Coin lndry. Meeting rm. Gift shop. Indoor tennis. Downhill ski 4 mi. Game rm. Lawn games. In-rm whirlpool, fireplace in suites. Screened porch on many cottages. Cr cds: A, DS, MC, V.

🄳 ⊠ ⅌ ≈ ☢ 🖾

★★ **DRUMMER BOY MOTOR INN.** *Rte 3, Lincoln (03251). 603/745-3661; fax 603/745-9829; toll-free 800/762-7275. www.drummerboymotorinn.com.* 53 rms, 8 kits., 2 kit. cottages. May-Oct: D $79-$89; each addl $5; kit. units $10 addl; suites, kit. cottages for 2-4, $99-$129; 4-bedrm house $250; ski plan; lower rates rest of yr. Crib $5. TV; cable, VCR avail. 2 heated pools, 1 indoor; whirlpool, sauna. Playground. Complimentary continental bkfst (in season). Restaurant nearby. Ck-out 11 am. Coin lndry. Meeting rm. Sundries. Downhill/x-country ski 3 mi. Game rm. Some refrigerators, in-rm whirlpools. Patios, balconies. Picnic tables, grill. Cr cds: A, DS, MC, V.

🄳 ⊠ ≈ 🖾 ⚗ SC

★★ **KANCAMAGUS MOTOR LODGE.** *Rte 112, Lincoln (03251). 603/745-3365; fax 603/745-6691; toll-free 800/346-4205. www.kancmotorlodge.com.* 34 rms, 2 story. Late June-mid-Oct, hol ski wks and wkends: S, D $74-$104; each addl $5-$10; under 12 free, $2; package plans; lower rates rest of yr. Crib free. TV; cable. Heated pool. Restaurant 7-11 am. Ck-out 11 am. Coin lndry. Downhill/x-country ski 2 mi. Lawn games. Game rm. In-rm steam baths. Balconies. Cr cds: A, DS, MC, V.

🄳 ⚓ ⅌ ⊠ ≈ 🖾 ⚗ SC

★★ **MILL HOUSE INN.** *Kancamagus Hwy, Lincoln (03251). 603/745-6261; fax 603/745-6896; toll-free 800/654-6183. www.millatloon.com.* 95 rms, 4 story. Late June-mid-Oct: S, D $109-$139; suites $129-$199; under 17 free; ski, golf plans; lower rates rest of yr. TV; cable, VCR avail. 2 pools, 1 indoor; whirlpools. Restaurant 7 am-10 pm. Ck-out 11 am. Meeting rms. Shopping arcade. Downhill ski 2 mi. Exercise equipt; sauna. Private patios, balconies. Cr cds: A, D, DS, MC, V.

🄳 ⊠ ≈ 🕴 🖾 ⚗

★ **MOUNT COOLIDGE MOTEL.** *US 3, Box 337, North Lincoln (03262). 603/745-8052. www.mtcoolidgemotel.com.* 18 rms. July-Nov: S $36-$62; D $42-$72; each addl $5; lower rates Apr-June. Closed rest of yr. Crib free. TV; cable. Heated pool. Restaurant adj 7:30 am-8:30 pm; closed mid-Oct-mid-May. Ck-out 11 am. On mountain stream. Cr cds: A, DS, MC, V.

🄳 ⚓ ≈ 🖾 ⚗

★ **RED DOORS MOTEL.** *RR 1, Box 109A Rte 3, Lincoln (03251). 603/745-2267; fax 603/745-3646; toll-free 800/527-7596. www.reddoorsmotel.com.* 30 rms. May-Oct, hol ski wks and wkends: S $55-$75; D $65-$85; each addl $5; under 18 free; lower rates rest of yr. Crib $5. TV; cable (premium). Heated pool. Playground. Complimentary coffee in rms. Restaurant opp 7:30 am-8:30 pm; closed mid-Oct-mid-June. Ck-out 10 am. Coin lndry. Downhill/x-country ski 5 mi. Game rm. Lawn games. Picnic tables, grills. Refrigerators avail. Cr cds: A, DS, MC, V.

🄳 ⊠ ≈ 🖾 ⚗

Resorts

★★ **INDIAN HEAD RESORT.** *RR1, Box 99, Lincoln (03251). 603/745-8000; fax 603/745-8414; toll-free 800/343-8000. www.indianheadresort.com.* 98 rms, 2 story. S, D $99-$155; each addl $5-$10; MAP avail; under 6 free; ski plans; higher rates hol wkends. Crib free. TV; cable (premium). 2 pools, 1 indoor; whirlpools, sauna. Restaurant 7 am-9 pm. Bar noon-1 am. Ck-out 11 am. Coin lndry. Meeting rms. Sundries. Gift shop. Exercise equipt. Lighted tennis. Downhill/x-country ski 5 mi. Game rm. Rec rm. Lawn games. Refrigerators; some in-rm whirlpools. Private patios, balconies. Stocked pond. View of mountains. Cr cds: A, DS, MC, V.

🄳 ⚓ ⊠ ⅌ ≈ 🕴 ⚗

★★ **JACK O'LANTERN RESORT.** *Rte 3, Woodstock (03293). 603/745-8121; fax 603/745-4989; toll-free 800/227-4454. www.jackolanternresort.com.* 23 motel rms, 20 condos. Mid-May-mid-Oct: S, D $80-$124; condos (all-yr) $136-$220; under 12 free; MAP avail in season; golf packages. Closed rest of yr. Crib $12. TV; cable, VCR avail. 2 pools, 1 indoor; wading pool, whirlpool, sauna, poolside serv in summer. Playground. Dining rm 7:30-11 am, 5:30-9 pm. Bar in season. Ck-out 11 am, ck-in 3 pm. Grocery 2 mi. Package store 4 mi. Gift shop. Exercise equipt. Tennis. 18-hole golf. Pro shop. Swimming beach. Lawn games. Entertainment. Game rm. Rec rm. 300 wooded acres on Pemigewasset River. Cr cds: A, DS, MC, V.

D 🛒 🐾 🏌 ⚡ 🛥 🏊 🎿

★★★ **MOUNTAIN CLUB ON LOON.** *Rte 112, Kancamagus Hwy, Lincoln (03251). 603/745-2244; fax 603/745-2317; toll-free 800/229-7829. www.mtnclubonloon.com.* 234 rms, 4-6 story, 117 kit. suites. Dec-mid-Apr: S, D $109-$230; each addl $20; kit. suites $179-$461; under 12 free; ski plans; lower rates rest of yr. Crib free. TV; cable. 2 pools, 1 indoor; whirlpool. Supervised children's activities (July-Aug); ages 5-12. Dining rm 7:30-10:30 am, 11:30 am-2 pm, 5:30-9 pm. Bar; entertainment Tues-Sat (ski season). Ck-out 11 am. Coin lndry. Meeting rms. Bellhops (ski season). Concierge. Tennis. Downhill/x-country ski on site. Exercise equipt; sauna. Game rm. Rec rm. Some in-rm whirlpools. Balconies. Picnic tables. Nature trail. Cr cds: A, DS, MC, V.

D 🛒 🐾 🎿 ⚡ 🏊 🏌 🛥

★★★ **WOODWARD RESORT.** *Rte 3, Lincoln (03251). 603/745-8141; fax 603/745-3408; toll-free 800/635-8968. ww.woodwardsresort.com.* 80 rms, 1-2 story. S, D $69-$119; each addl $5; 2-bedrm cottages for 2-6, $125-$155; MAP avail; ski plan. Crib free. TV; cable. 2 pools, 1 indoor; whirlpool. Playground. Restaurant 7:30-10:30 am, 5-8:30 pm. Bar from 4 pm. Ck-out 11 am. Coin lndry. Meeting rm. Tennis. Downhill ski 5 mi. Sauna. Game rm. Lawn games. Refrigerators. Some balconies. Duck pond. On mountain stream. Cr cds: A, DS, MC, V.

D 🏊 🛥 🏊 🎿

B&Bs/Small Inns

★ **WILDERNESS INN BED & BREAKFAST.** *Rtes 3 and 112, North Woodstock (03262). 603/745-3890; toll-free 888/777-7813. www.thewildernessinn.com.* 7 rms in house, 2 story, 1 cottage. No rm phones. S $55-$145; D $65-$150; each addl $10; under 6 free; ski plan; higher rates: hols (2-day min), fall foliage. Crib free. TV in sitting rm; cable. Complimentary full bkfst; afternoon refreshments. Restaurant nearby. Rm serv. Ck-out 11 am, ck-in 3 pm. Downhill/x-country ski 3 mi. Croquet. Built 1912; view of Lost River and mountains. Totally nonsmoking. Cr cds: A, MC, V.

D 🛒 🐾 🎿 🏊 🛥 🐾

★★ **WOODSTOCK INN.** *135 Main St, North Woodstock (03262). 603/745-3951; fax 603/745-3701; toll-free 800/321-3985. www.woodstockinnnh.com.* 19 rms, 11 with bath, 8 share bath, 3 story. June-Oct: S, D $89-$169; under 12 free (up to 2), each addl child $8; MAP avail; ski packages; higher rates fall foliage, some wkends; lower rates rest of yr. TV; cable, VCR avail. Complimentary full bkfst. Dining rm 7 am-10 pm. Bar 11:30 am-midnight. Ck-out 11 am, ck-in 2 pm. Gift shop. Downhill/x-country ski 3 mi. Some in-rm whirlpools, refrigerators, gas fireplaces. Balconies. Victorian house (1890); antique furnishings. Some rms with view of river. Cr cds: A, D, DS, MC, V.

D 🛒 🐾 🎿 🛥 🐾

Restaurants

★★ **COMMON MAN.** *Pollard Rd, Lincoln (03217). 603/745-3463. www.thecman.com.* Specializes in prime rib, fresh seafood, pasta. Hrs: 5-9 pm; Fri, Sat to 9:30 pm. Closed Dec 24, 25. Bar. Dinner $9.95-$16.95. Child's menu. Parking. Converted farmhouse; one of oldest structures in city. Rustic decor; fireplace, antiques. Cr cds: A, DS, MC, V.

D

★★ **GORDI'S FISH & STEAK HOUSE.** *Kancamagus Hwy, Lincoln (03251). 603/745-6635.* Specializes in Maine lobster, prime rib, seafood. Salad bar. Hrs: 5-9 pm; Fri, Sat 4:30-9:30 pm; June-Oct noon-9 pm. Closed Thanksgiving, Dec 25. Res accepted. Bar. Lunch $4-$8, dinner $6.95-$18.95. Child's menu. Parking. Contemporary building with Victorian accents. Olympic ski motif. Cr cds: A, DS, MC, V.

D

★★ **GOVONI'S ITALIAN.** *Lost River Rd, North Woodstock (03262). 603/745-8042.* Italian menu. Specialties: scallop-stuffed scampi, veal parmigiana, homemade desserts. Hrs: 4:30-9 pm. Closed Labor Day-Memorial Day; also Mon-Wed in June. Bar. Dinner $6.95-$15.95. Child's menu. Parking. White clapboard building, formerly a schoolhouse, constructed over mountain stream. Cr cds: MC, V.

★★ **OLD TIMBERMILL PUB & RESTAURANT.** *Rte 112; Main St, Lincoln (03251). 603/745-3603.* Specializes in seafood, steak. Hrs: 5-9 pm; Sun from 11:30 am; Fri to 10 pm; Sat 11:30 am-10 pm. Bar to 1 am. Lunch, dinner $10-$19. Outdoor dining. Entertainment wkends. Converted mill drying shed (1926). Cr cds: A, DS, MC, V.

★ **TRUANTS TAVERNE.** *96 Main St, North Woodstock (03262). 603/745-2239. www.truantstaverne.com.* Specializes in seafood, steak. Hrs: 11:30 am-10 pm; Fri, Sat to 11 pm. Closed Thanksgiving, Dec 25. Bar. Lunch $4.95-$10.25, dinner $4.95-$15.50. Child's menu. Parking. Rustic decor with old schoolhouse motif. Cr cds: A, DS, MC, V.

D 🛥

Littleton

See also Franconia

Chartered 1784 **Pop** 5,827 **Elev** 822 ft **Area code** 603 **Zip** 03561

Information Chamber of Commerce, 120 Main St, PO Box 105; 603/444-6561

Web www.littletonareachamber.com

Littleton is a resort area a few miles northwest of the White Mountain National Forest (see), which maintains a Ranger District office in nearby Bethlehem. Littleton is also a regional commercial center; its industries produce abrasives and electrical component parts. The Ammonoosuc River falls 235 feet on its way through the community.

What to See and Do

Littleton Historical Museum. Photographs, stereographs, local memorabilia. (Apr-Dec, Wed afternoons, July-Oct, Wed, Sat afternoons) 1 Cottage St. Phone 603/444-6435. **FREE**

Samuel C. Moore Station. Largest conventional hydro-electric plant in New England; 2,920-ft dam across Connecticut River forms Moore Reservoir, which extends nearly 11 mi and covers an area of 3,490 acres. Visitor center has exhibits (daily). Recreation areas offer hunting, fishing, boat launching, waterskiing, picnicking and nature studies. (Memorial Day-Columbus Day, daily) 8 mi W on NH 18, 135. Phone 603/653-9232.

Motel/Motor Lodge

★★ **EASTGATE MOTOR INN.** 335 Cottage St (03561). 603/444-3971; toll-free 866/640-3561. www.eastgatemotorinn.com. 55 rms. S $44-$74; D $50-$80; each addl $7; under 6 free. Pet accepted. TV; cable (premium). Heated pool; wading pool. Playground. Complimentary continental bkfst. Restaurant (see EASTGATE). Bar. Ck-out 11 am. Meeting rms. Business servs avail. Downhill ski 7 mi; x-country ski 6 mi. Lawn games. Cr cds: A, C, D, DS, MC, V.

B&Bs/Small Inns

★★★ **ADAIR COUNTRY INN.** 80 Guider Ln, Bethlehem (03574). 603/444-2600; fax 603/444-4823; toll-free 888/444-2600. www.adairinn.com. 10 rms, some A/C, 3 story, 1 suite. No rm phones. S, D $150-$355; wkends, foliage (2-day min), major hols wkends (3-day min); each addl $32. TV in lounge; VCR. Complimentary full bkfst; afternoon refreshments. Dining rm 5:30-9 pm. Ck-out 11 am, ck-in 3 pm. Luggage handling. Tennis. Downhill ski 5 mi; x-country ski 2 blks. Billiards. Some gas fireplaces. Built 1927. 200 landscaped acres designed by Olmsted Brothers. Totally nonsmoking. Cr cds: A, DS, MC, V.

★ **MULBURN.** 2370 Main St, Bethlehem (03570). 603/869-3389; fax 603/869-5633. www.mulburninn.com. 7 rms, 2 story. No A/C. No rm phones. S, D $85-$175; each addl $10; wkly rates; ski, golf plans; higher rates fall foliage. Closed Dec 24, 25. Crib $10. TV in lobby. Playground. Complimentary full bkfst. Restaurant nearby. Ck-out 10 am, ck-in 3 pm. Downhill/x-country ski 10 mi. Exercise equipt. Lawn games. Built 1913 by F.W. Woolworth as summer home. Antiques. Sitting rm. Totally nonsmoking. Cr cds: A, MC, V.

★★ **THAYER'S INN.** 111 Main St (03561). 603/444-6469; toll-free 800/634-8179. www.thayersinn.com. 39 rms, 24 with bath, 4 story, 6 suites (2-bedrm). No elvtr. Some rm phones. S, D $45-$89; suites $85-$125; under 6 free; ski, spring break plans. Crib free. TV; cable (premium). Pool privileges. Ck-out 11 am, ck-in 2 pm. Downhill/x-country ski 10 mi. Some refrigerators. Historic inn (1843); antiques, library, sitting rm. Cupola open to public. Cr cds: A, C, D, DS, MC, V.

★★ **WAYSIDE.** 3738 Main St, Bethlehem (03574). 603/869-3364; fax 603/869-5765; toll-free 800/448-9557. www.thewaysideinn.com. 14 rms in inn, 2 story; 12 rms in motel, 2 story. Mid-May-late Oct, Dec-late Mar: S, D $88-$118; each addl $8-$18; MAP avail; golf, ski plans; lower rates rest of yr. Crib avail. TV in motel rms, living rm of inn; cable. Dining rm 7:30-9:30 am, 6-9 pm. Bar. Ck-out 11 am, ck-in 3 pm. 18-hole golf privileges. Downhill ski 8 mi; x-country ski on site. Lawn games. Some in-rm whirlpools, refrigerators. Balconies in motel. Originally 4-rm homestead (1825) for the family of President Franklin Pierce. On Ammonoosuc River; natural sand beach. Cr cds: A, DS, MC, V.

Restaurants

★★ **CLAM SHELL.** 274 Dells Rd (03561). 603/444-6445. Specializes in fresh seafood, prime rib. Salad bar. Own desserts. Hrs: 11:30 am-4 pm, 5-9:30 pm; Fri, Sat to 10 pm; Sun noon-9 pm. Closed Dec 24 (eve), 25. Bar to midnight. Lunch $4-$8.50, dinner $6.95-$15.95. Child's menu. Cr cds: A, DS, MC, V.

★ **EASTGATE.** 335 Cottage St (03561). 603/444-3971. www.eastgatemotorinn.com. Amer, continental menu. Specializes in seafood, chicken, prime rib au jus. Hrs: 5-9 pm; Fri, Sat to 5-9:30 pm. Closed Dec 24. Res accepted. Bar to midnight. Dinner $5.95-$19.95. Gazebo with fountain; view of Mt Eustis. Cr cds: A, D, DS, MC, V.

★★ **ITALIAN OASIS.** 106 Main St (03561). 603/444-6995. Specializes in Italian dishes, steak, seafood. Hrs: 11:30 am-10 pm; Fri, Sat to 11 pm. Closed Easter, Thanksgiving, Dec 25. Res accepted. Bar. A la carte entrees: lunch $2.95-$6.95, dinner $4.95-$14.95. Outdoor dining. Converted Victorian home (ca 1890). Cr cds: A, DS, MC, V.

★★ **ROSA FLAMINGOS.** Main St, Bethlehem (03574). 603/869-3111. Italian menu. Specialties: tortellini carbonara, fettucine Rosa. Hrs: 11:30 am-11 pm. Closed Easter, Thanksgiving, Dec 25. Res accepted. Bar to 1 am. Lunch $3.95-$7.50, dinner $5.75-$16.75. Child's menu. Outdoor dining. Cr cds: A, MC, V.

Lyme

(see Hanover)

Manchester

See also Concord, Nashua

Settled 1722 **Pop** 99,567 **Elev** 225 ft **Area code** 603
Information Chamber of Commerce, 889 Elm St, 03101-2000; 603/666-6600
Web www.manchester-chamber.org

Manchester is a city that has refused to bow to economic adversity. When the Amoskeag Manufacturing Company (cotton textiles), which had dominated Manchester's economy, failed in 1935, it left the city poverty-stricken. With determination worthy of New Englanders, a group of citizens bought the plant for $5,000,000 and revived the city. Now Manchester is northern New England's premier financial center.

What to See and Do

Currier Gallery of Art. One of New England's leading small museums; 13th- to 20th-century European and American paintings and sculpture; New England decorative art; furniture, glass, silver, and pewter; changing exhibitions, concerts, films, other programs. Tours of Zimmerman House, designed by Frank Lloyd Wright (call for res and times, fee). (Mon, Wed-Sun; closed hols) 201 Myrtle Way. Phone 603/669-6144. ¢¢

Manchester Historic Association Millyard Museum. Museum and library with collections illustrating life in Manchester from pre-colonial times to present. Permanent and changing exhibits; firefighting equipment; decorative arts, costumes, paintings; changing exhibits. (Tues-Sat; closed hols) 129 Amherst St, 2 blks E of Elm St. Phone 603/622-7531. ¢¢

McIntyre Ski Area. Two double chairlifts, pony lift; patrol, school, rentals, snowmaking; snack bar. Vertical drop 169 ft. (Dec-Mar, daily) Kennard Rd. Phone 603/624-6571.

Palace Theatre. Productions in vintage vaudeville/opera house. 80 Hanover St. For schedule phone 603/668-5588.

Science Enrichment Encounters Museum. More than 60 interactive, hands-on exhibits demonstrate basic science principles. (Daily; closed hols) 200 Bedford St. Phone 603/669-0400. ¢¢

Special Event

Riverfest. Outdoor festival with family entertainment, concerts, arts and crafts, food booths, fireworks. Phone 603/623-2623. Labor Day wkend.

Motels/Motor Lodges

★★ **COMFORT INN.** *298 Queen City Ave (03102). 603/668-2600; res 800/228-5150. www.comfortinn.com.* 100 rms, 5 story. S, D $79-$159; each addl $5; suites $135-$250; under 18 free; higher rates some wknds. Crib free. Pet accepted. TV; cable (premium). Indoor pool. Complimentary continental bkfst. Ck-out 11 am. Coin lndry. Meeting rms. Business servs avail. In-rm modem link. Bellhops. Free airport, bus depot transportation. Exercise equipt; sauna. Some refrigerators, microwaves. Cr cds: A, C, D, DS, MC, V.
🅳 ⬤ ⇌ 🏋 ✈ ⇟ 🔥 SC

★ **ECONO LODGE.** *75 W Hancock St (03102). 603/624-0111; fax 603/623-0268; toll-free 800/553-2666. www.econolodge.com.* 120 rms, 5 story. S, D $65-$105; each addl $5; under 18 free; wkly, monthly rates. Crib free. Pet accepted. TV; cable. Complimentary continental bkfst. Restaurant opp 6:30 am-9 pm. Ck-out 11 am. Coin lndry. Business servs avail. Some refrigerators. Cr cds: A, C, D, DS, MC, V.
🅳 ⬤ ⇟ 🔥 SC

★ **FAIRFIELD INN.** *860 S Porter St (03103). 603/625-2020; fax 603/623-7562; toll-free 800/228-2800. www.fairfieldinn.com.* 102 rms, 4 story. S, D $99-$139; each addl $7. Cribs avail. TV; cable (premium). Pool. Complimentary continental bkfst. Restaurant opp 6 am-11 pm. Ck-out noon. Coin lndry. Business servs avail. In-rm modem link. Sundries. Valet serv. Refrigerators avail. Cr cds: A, C, D, DS, MC, V.
🅳 ⇌ ⇟ 🔥 SC

★★ **FOUR POINTS BY SHERATON.** *55 John E Devine Dr (03103). 603/668-6110; fax 603/668-0408; toll-free 800/325-3535. www.fourpoints.com/manchester.* 120 rms, 4 story. S, D $109-$149; each addl $10; under 18 free; higher rates fall foliage. Crib free. TV; cable (premium). Indoor pool; whirlpool. Coffee in rms. Restaurant 6-10 am, 5-10 pm. Rm serv. Bar. Ck-out noon. Meeting rms. Business servs avail. Valet serv. Sundries. Airport transportation. Health club privileges. Mall of New Hampshire opp. Refrigerator, microwave avail. Cr cds: A, C, D, DS, ER, JCB, MC, V.
🅳 ⇌ ✈ ⇟ 🔥 SC

★ **SUPER 8.** *2301 Brown Ave (03103). 603/623-0883; fax 603/624-9303; res 800/800-8000. www.super8.com.* 93 rms, 4 story. June-Labor Day: S $69-$95; D $75-$119; each addl $5; suites $109-$129; higher rates fall foliage; lower rates rest of yr. Crib free. TV; cable, VCR avail (movies). Complimentary coffee. Restaurant nearby. Ck-out 11 am. Meeting rms. Business servs avail. Valet serv. Free airport transportation. Refrigerator, whirlpool in some suites. Cr cds: A, C, D, DS, MC, V.
🅳 ✈ ⇟ 🔥

★★★ **WAYFARER INN.** *121 S River Rd, Bedford (03110). 603/622-3766; fax 603/623-5796; toll-free 877/489-3658. www.wayfarerinn.com.* 194 rms, 2-3 story. No elvtr. S, D $89-$150; each addl $10; suites $175; under 18 free; package plans. Crib free. TV; cable (premium). 2 pools, 1 indoor; whirlpool, poolside serv, lifeguard. Coffee in rms. Restaurant 6:30 am-10 pm; Sat, Sun 7 am-10:30 pm;

Bar 11:30-12:30 am; entertainment Thurs-Sat. Ck-out noon. Meeting rms. Business servs avail. In-rm modem link. Valet serv. Sundries. Free airport transportation. Exercise equipt; sauna, steam rm. Some refrigerators. Balconies. Country-inn decor. Cr cds: A, C, D, DS, ER, MC, V.

D ⬮ ⚡ ⇌ 🏃 ⊠ 🐾 SC

Hotel

★★ **CENTER OF NH HOLIDAY INN.** *700 Elm St (03101). 603/625-1000; fax 603/625-4595; res 800/465-4329. www.holiday-inn.com.* 250 rms, 12 story. S $98-$129; D $103-$150; suites $195-$495; under 19 free; wkend rates. Crib free. TV; cable (premium). Indoor pool; whirlpool. Coffee in rms. Restaurant 6:30 am-10 pm. Bar from noon; entertainment Fri, Sat. Ck-out 11 am. Convention facilities. Business servs avail. In-rm modem link. Gift shop. Validated indoor parking. Airport transportation. Exercise equipt; sauna. Bathrm phone in suites. Cr cds: A, DS, MC, V.

⇌ 🏃 ✈ ⊠ 🐾

B&B/Small Inn

★★★ **BEDFORD VILLAGE INN.** *2 Village Inn Ln, Bedford (03110). 603/472-2001; fax 603/472-2379; toll-free 800/852-1166. www.bedfordvillageinn.com.* 14 suites, 3 story, 2 kits. Suites $195-$230; kits. $210-$335. TV; cable (premium). Afternoon refreshments. Restaurant (see BEDFORD VILLAGE INN). Ck-out 11 am, ck-in 3 pm. Meeting rms. Business servs avail. In-rm modem link. Gift shop. In-rm whirlpools; some wet bars. Some balconies. Converted barn built early 1800s; antique furnishings, rms individually decorated. Cr cds: A, DS, MC, V.

⊠ 🐾

Restaurants

★★★ **BEDFORD VILLAGE INN.** *2 Village Inn Ln, Bedford (03110). 603/472-2001. www.bedfordvillageinn.com.* Specializes in New England-style dishes. Own baking. Hrs: 7-10:30 am, 11:30 am-2 pm, 5:30-9:30 pm; Sat 8 am-2 pm, 5:30-9:30 pm; Sun 8 am-2 pm, 5:30-9:30 pm; Sun brunch 11 am-2 pm. Closed Dec 25. Res accepted. Bar from 11:30 am. Wine list. Bkfst $6.95-$10.50, lunch $6-$18, dinner $17.50-$31. Sun brunch $23. Gift shop. Yellow clapboard structure originally part of homestead (1790). Cr cds: A, D, MC, V.

D

★ **PURITAN BACKROOM.** *245 Daniel Webster Hwy N (03104). 603/669-6890. www.puritanbackroom.com.* Specializes in chicken tenders, barbecued lamb. Own ice cream. Hrs: 11 am-11:30 pm; Wed, Thurs to midnight; Fri, Sat to 12:30 am. Closed Thanksgiving, Dec 25. Bar. Lunch, dinner $3.95-$21.95. Child's menu. Stained-glass windows; many paintings. Cr cds: A, DS, MC, V.

D

HIKING THE WHITE MOUNTAINS HIGH HUTS SYSTEM

New England's highest mountains are webbed with hiking trails, thanks largely to the Appalachian Mountain Club (AMC), founded in 1876. The Club blazed and mapped trails and eventually established an extensive base camp for hikers in Pinkham Notch at the eastern base of Mount Washington; a hostel in Crawford Notch, at the western base; and a chain of eight full-service "high huts" spaced over 56 miles of mountain trails, each a day's hike apart.

The huts are so much a part of the heritage and character of the White Mountains that it would be a shame to hike "The Whites" without staying at one. Seven offer three full meals in season (mid-June to mid-September) as well as bunks, pillows, and blankets (no sheets). Each hut has its resident naturalist who offers talks and walks. An AMC shuttle van circles trailheads leading to each of the huts so that hikers can begin in one place and emerge at another. It's wise to begin at Pinkham Notch Camp on NH 16 in the White Mountain National Forest, source of gear, maps, and weather information. Reservations for all AMC facilities are a must.

One of the most spectacular hikes that utilizes either one or two of the high huts is on Mount Washington itself. Begin with the Crawford Path, dating back to 1819, said to be the oldest continually used footpath in America. The trailhead is on NH 302 across from the AMC Crawford Notch Visitors Center. It follows Gibbs Brook (note the cutoff for Gibbs Falls), then angles off and up. To spend the night at Mizpah Hut Spring Hut (strongly advised), take the Mizpah cut-off. Just two miles from NH 302, this is a good base from which to explore several trails above tree line.

It's also possible, weather permitting, to continue on the Crawford Path, ascending in moderate grades, with spectacular open views alternating with patches of scrub and woods. The trail ascends steadily via Mount Pierce, Mount Eisenhower, and Mount Monroe, reaching the Lake of the Clouds Hut at seven miles. Spend the night.

Descend back to NH 302 via the Ammonoosuc Ravine Trail, which begins just south of the Lake of the Clouds and follows the Ammonoosuc River steeply for the first two miles of the total three-mile descent. There are numerous cascades and spectacular views, but many people prefer to do this hike in reverse, ascending rather than descending such a steep trail. It's also possible to cheat by taking the White Mountain Cog Railway from its base off NH 302 (near the trailhead for this trail) to the summit of Mount Washington, hiking down to the Lake of the Clouds, and then either down the Ammonoosuc Ravine or Crawford Path. Check with the AMC before hiking anywhere in The Whites (www.outdoors.org; phone 603/466-2721).

Meredith

See also Holderness, Laconia, Plymouth

Founded 1768 **Pop** 4,837 **Elev** 552 ft **Area code** 603
Zip 03253
Information Chamber of Commerce, 272 Daniel Webster Hwy, PO Box 732; 603/279-6121 or 877/279-6121
Web www.meredithcc.org

Between Lakes Winnipesaukee and Waukewan in the Lakes Region, Meredith is a year-round recreation area.

What to See and Do

League of New Hampshire Craftsmen—Meredith/Laconia Arts & Crafts. Work by some of New Hampshire's finest craftspeople. (Daily) On US 3. Phone 603/279-7920.

☒ **Winnipesaukee Scenic Railroad.** Scenic train rides along shore of Lake Winnipesaukee. Board in Meredith or Weirs Beach. (Memorial Day-Columbus Day) Fall foliage trains to Plymouth. Phone 603/279-5253.

Special Events

Great Rotary Fishing Derby. 2nd wkend Feb.

Lakes Region Fine Arts and Crafts Festival. Juried show featuring more than 100 New England artists. Music, children's theater, food. Last wkend Aug.

Altrusa Annual Antique Show and Sale. Third Sat Sept.

Motels/Motor Lodges

★ **MATTERHORN MOTOR LODGE.** *Rte 25 at Moultonboro Neck Rd, Moultonboro (03254). 603/253-4314.* 28 rms, 2 story. No rm phones. Memorial Day-Columbus Day: S, D $135; each addl $25; children up to 12 yrs $10; higher rates special events; lower rates rest of yr. Crib $5. TV; cable. Heated pool. Restaurant adj 6 am-10 pm. Ck-out 11 am. Picnic tables, grill. Beach nearby. Cr cds: A, C, D, DS, MC, V.
🐾 ⚡ 🏊 🎿 🔥

★ **MEADOWS LAKESIDE LODGING.** *Rte 25, Center Harbor (03226). 603/253-4347; fax 603/253-6171.* 35 rms, 4 story. Some rm phones. June-Sept: S, D $89-$155; each addl $20; kit. units $120; under 4 free; wkly rates; lower rates May, Oct. Closed rest of yr. Pet accepted; $7/day. TV; VCR avail (movies). Complimentary coffee in lobby. Restaurant nearby. Ck-out 11 am. Private patios, balconies. Picnic tables. On lake; beach, dockage. Cr cds: A, DS, MC, V.
🄳 🐾 🐾 🎿 🔥

B&Bs/Small Inns

★★★ **THE INN AT BAY POINT.** *312 Daniel Webster Hwy (03253). 603/279-7006; fax 603/279-6797; toll-free 800/622-6455. www.millfalls.com.* 24 rms, 4 story. June-Oct: S, D $179-$279; each addl $15; under 12 free; wkly, wkend rates; ski plans; wkends, hols (2-3-day min); lower rates rest of yr. Crib free. TV; cable, VCR avail (movies). Pool privileges. Whirlpool. Complimentary continental bkfst. Coffee in rms. Restaurant 11:30 am-9 pm. Bar. Ck-out 11 am. Meeting

rms. Business servs avail. Gift shop. Downhill ski 12 mi; x-country ski on nearby lake. Exercise equipt; sauna. Some refrigerators. Balconies. Picnic tables. On lake; private dock, beach. Cr cds: A, DS, MC, V.
🄳 🐾 🧍 🎿 🔥

★★★ **THE INN AT MILL FALLS.** *312 Daniel Webster Hwy #28 (03253). 603/279-7006; fax 603/279-6797; toll-free 800/622-6455. www.millfalls.com.* 54 rms, 5 story. June-Oct: D $149-$229; each addl $15; ski plans; lower rates rest of yr. Crib free. TV; cable, VCR avail (movies). Indoor pool; whirlpool. Complimentary coffee in lobby. Restaurant nearby. Ck-out 11 am, ck-in 3 pm. Meeting rms. Business servs avail. Sauna. Some fireplaces; refrigerators avail. Balconies. On lake. Antique furnishings; some rms with lake view. Adj to historic Mill Falls Marketplace. Cr cds: A, DS, MC, V.
🄳 🏊 🎿 🔥 🏊

★★★ **OLDE ORCHARD INN.** *108 Lee Rd, Moultonborough (03254). 603/476-5004; fax 603/476-5419; toll-free 800/598-5845. www.oldeorchardinn.com.* 9 rms. No rm phones. S, D $90-$175; each addl $25; wkends (2-day min); higher rates: summer, fall foliage. Crib $5. 1 TV; cable, VCR avail (movies). Complimentary full bkfst. Complimentary coffee in rms. Restaurant opp 5-9:30 pm. Ck-out 11 am, ck-in 3 pm. Luggage handling. Downhill ski 15 mi; x-country ski on site. Lawn games. Refrigerators. Picnic tables. Built in 1812. Totally nonsmoking. Cr cds: DS, MC, V.
🄳 🐾 ⚡ 🐾 🎿 🔥

Restaurants

★★ **HART'S TURKEY FARM.** *NH 3 and 104 (03253). 603/279-6212. www.hartsturkeyfarm.com.* Specializes in turkey, seafood, prime rib. Hrs: 11:15 am-9:30 pm. Lunch $3.95-$9.75, dinner $7.95-$16.95. Child's menu. Gift shop. Cr cds: A, D, DS, MC, V.
🄳 ➡

★★ **MAME'S.** *8 Plymouth St (03253). 603/279-4631. www.mamesrestaurant.com.* Specializes in prime rib, seafood, chicken. Hrs: 11:30 am-9 pm; wkends to 9:30 pm. Bar. Wine list. Lunch $4.95-$11.95, dinner $10.95-$21.95. Child's menu. Converted brick house and barn (1825). Cr cds: A, DS, MC, V.
🄳

Mount Washington

See also Bretton Woods, Gorham, Jackson

(10 mi S of Gorham on NH 16)

Mt Washington is the central peak of the White Mts and the highest point in the northeastern United States (6,288 feet). At the summit is a 54-acre state park with an information center, first aid station, restaurant, and gift shop. The mountain has the world's first cog railway, completed in 1869; a road to the top dates from 1861. P.T. Barnum called the view from the summit "the second-greatest show on earth."

The weather on Mount Washington is so violent that the timberline is at about 4,000 feet; in the Rockies it is nearer 10,000 feet. In the treeless zone are alpine plants and insects, some unique to the region. The weather station here recorded a wind speed of 231 miles per hour in April, 1934—a world record. The lowest temperature recorded was −49° F; the year-round average is below freezing. The peak gets nearly 15 feet of snow each year.

What to See and Do

Auto road. Trip takes approx 30 min each way. *Note:* Make sure your car is in good condition; check brakes before starting. (Mid-May-mid-Oct, daily, weather permitting) Guided tour service avail (Daily). Approaches from the E side, in Pinkham Notch, 8 mi S of Gorham on NH 16. Phone 603/466-3988. ¢¢¢¢ Opp is

Great Glen Trails. All-season, non-motorized recreational trails park featuring biking programs (rentals), hiking programs (guide or unguided), kayak and canoe tours and workshops in summer; x-country skiing, snowshoeing and snow tubing in winter. (Daily; closed Apr) For detailed brochure with schedule and fees, contact NH 16, Pinkham Notch, Gorham 03581. Phone 603/466-2333. ¢¢¢

🔲 **Cog railway.** Allow at least three hrs for round-trip. (May-Memorial Day wkend, wkends; after Memorial Day wkend-Nov, daily) Base station road, off US 302, 4 mi E of jct US 3, 302; on W slope of mountain. Phone 603/846-5404. ¢¢¢¢

Hiking trails. Many crisscross the mountain; some reach the top. Hikers should check weather conditions at Pinkham Notch headquarters before climbing. Phone 603/466-2725. **FREE**

Mount Washington Summit Museum. Displays on life in the extreme climate of the summit; rare flora and fauna; geology, history. (Memorial Day-Columbus Day, daily) Top of Mt Washington. Phone 603/466-3388.

Nashua

See also Manchester, Salem

Settled 1656 **Pop** 79,662 **Elev** 169 ft **Area code** 603
Information Greater Nashua Chamber of Commerce, 146 Main St, 2nd flr, 03060; 603/881-8333
Web www.nashuachamber.com

Originally a fur-trading post, Nashua's manufacturing began with the development of Merrimack River water power early in the 19th century. The city, second-largest in New Hampshire, has more than 100 diversified industries ranging from computers and tools to beer.

What to See and Do

Anheuser-Busch, Inc. Guided tours of brewery; sampling rm; gift shop. Children only with adult; no pets. 221 Daniel Webster Hwy (US 3) in Merrimack, Everett Tpke exit 10. Phone 603/595-1202. **FREE** Adj is

Clydesdale Hamlet. Buildings modeled after a 19th-century European-style farm are the living quarters for the famous Clydesdales (at least 15 are here at all times); carriage house contains vintage wagons. Phone 603/595-1202. **FREE**

Silver Lake State Park. 1,000-ft sand beach on a 34-acre lake; swimming, bathhouse; picnicking. (Late June-Labor Day) Standard fees. 8 mi W on NH 130 to Hollis, then 1 mi N off NH 122. Phone 603/465-2342.

Special Event

American Stage Festival. 5 mi NW off NH 101 in Milford. Five plays; music events, children's series. For schedule phone 603/886-7000. June-Sept.

Motels/Motor Lodges

★★ **COMFORT INN.** *10 St. Laurent St (03060).* *603/883-7700; fax 603/595-2107; toll-free 800/228-5150.* *www.comfortinn.com.* 103 rms, 2 story. S $69-$109; D $74-$109; under 18 free. Crib free. TV; cable (premium), VCR avail (movies). Pool. Complimentary continental bkfst. Restaurant adj 11:30 am-10:30 pm; Sun from noon. Bar. Ck-out noon. Meeting rm. Business servs avail. Valet serv. Health club privileges. Refrigerators avail. Cr cds: A, DS, MC, V.
🄳 ⊠ ⊠

★★ **FAIRFIELD INN.** *4 Amherst Rd, Merrimack (03054).* *603/424-7500; toll-free 800/228-2800. www.fairfieldinn.com.* 116 rms, 3 story. June-Labor Day: S, D $79-$109; each addl $7; under 18 free; higher rates: wkends, fall foliage; lower rates rest of yr. TV; cable (premium). Pool. Complimentary continental bkfst. Restaurant nearby. Ck-out noon. Meeting rm. Business servs avail. In-rm modem link. Valet serv. Sundries. Cr cds: A, C, D, DS, MC, V.
🄳 ⊠ ⊠ ⊠ ⊠ SC

★★ **HOLIDAY INN.** *9 Northeastern Blvd (03062).* *603/888-1551; fax 603/888-7193; toll-free 888/801-5661.* *www.holiday-inn.com.* 208 rms, 3-4 story, 24 suites. May-Nov: S, D $69-$99; each addl $4; suites $99-$129; under 19 free; package plans; lower rates rest of yr. Crib free. Pet accepted. TV; cable (premium), VCR avail. Heated pool. Restaurant 6:30 am-10 pm. Rm serv. Bar 11:30-12:30 am; entertainment. Ck-out noon. Coin lndry. Meeting rms. Business servs avail. Valet serv. Exercise equipt. Some refrigerators. Private patios, balconies. Cr cds: A, D, DS, MC, V.
🄳 ⊠ ⊠ ⊠ ⊠ ⊠

★★ **RED ROOF INN.** *77 Spitbrook Rd (03060).* *603/888-1893; fax 603/888-5889; res 800/733-7663.* *www.redroof.com.* 115 rms, 3 story. S $50-$68; D $53-$77; under 19 free. Crib free. Pet accepted. TV; cable (premium). Complimentary coffee in lobby. Ck-out noon. Business servs avail. Picnic table. Cr cds: A, C, D, DS, MC, V.
🄳 ⊠ ⊠ ⊠ SC

Hotels

★★★ **CROWNE PLAZA HOTEL.** *2 Somerset Pkwy (03063). 603/886-1200; fax 603/595-4199; toll-free 800/ 962-7482. www.crowneplaza.com.* 213 rms, 8 story. S, D $89-$129; each addl $10; suites $150-$250; under 18 free; wkend package plans. Crib free. TV; cable. Indoor pool; whirlpool. Complimentary coffee in rms. Restaurant 6 am-10 pm; dining rm from 5:30 pm. Bar 11:30-12:30 am. Ck-out noon. Meeting rms. Business servs avail. In-rm modem link. Gift shop. Beauty shop. Garage parking. Free airport transportation. Exercise rm; saunas. Massage. Some in-rm whirlpools; refrigerators avail. 48-seat amphitheater. Luxury level. Cr cds: A, C, D, DS, ER, JCB, MC, V.

⌨ ≋ 🔥 SC ✱ 🕺

★★★ **MARRIOTT NASHUA.** *2200 Southwood Dr (03063). 603/880-9100; fax 603/886-9489; toll-free 800/362-0962. www.marriott.com.* 241 rms, 4 story. Mar-mid-Sept: S, D $79-$139; wkend rates; higher rates mid-Sept-Nov; lower rates rest of yr. Crib free. Pet accepted. TV; cable (premium). Indoor pool; whirlpool. Playground. Coffee in rms. Restaurant 6:30 am-10 pm. Bar from noon; pianist Sat. Ck-out 1 pm. Convention facilities. Business center. In-rm modem link. Concierge. Gift shop. Airport transportation. Exercise equipt. Lawn games. Refrigerators avail. Czechoslovakian chandeliers and Oriental objets d'art accent lobby. Luxury level. Cr cds: A, C, D, DS, ER, JCB, MC, V.

🐾 ≋ ⊠ ⌨ 🕺 ✱

★★★ **SHERATON NASHUA HOTEL.** *11 Tara Blvd (03062). 603/888-9970; fax 603/888-4112; toll-free 800/325-3535. www.sheraton.com.* 336 rms, 7 story. S, D $100-$220; each addl $10; under 18 free; wkend rates. Crib free. TV; cable (premium), VCR avail. 2 pools, 1 indoor; whirlpool, poolside serv, lifeguard. Supervised children's activities. Coffee in rms. Restaurant 6:30 am-10 pm. Bars 11:30-1 am; entertainment Fri, Sat. Ck-out noon. Convention facilities. Business center. In-rm modem link. Gift shop. Exercise rm; sauna, steam rm. Lawn games. Some bathrm phones, in-rm whirlpools; refrigerators avail. Luxury level. Cr cds: A, C, D, DS, ER, JCB, MC, V.

⌨ ≋ ✱ ⊠ 🔥 SC ✱

Extended Stay

★★ **RESIDENCE INN BY MARRIOTT.** *246 Daniel Webster Hwy, Merrimack (03054). 603/424-8100; fax 603/424-3128; res 800/331-3131. www.residenceinn.com.* 129 kit. suites, 2 story. Kit. suites $102-$160. Crib free. Pet accepted; $50 and $5/day. TV; cable (premium). Pool; whirlpool. Complimentary continental bkfst. Ck-out noon. Coin lndry. Meeting rms. Business servs avail. In-rm modem link. Valet serv. Health club privileges. Sport court. Many fireplaces. Grills. Cr cds: A, DS, MC, V.

🐾 ⊠ 🔥 ≋

Restaurants

★★ **COUNTRY GOURMET.** *438 Daniel Webster Hwy, Merrimack (03054). 603/424-2755. www.countrygourmet.com.* French, continental menu. Specializes in seafood, beef, lamb. Hrs: 5:30-9 pm; Sun 4-8:30 pm. Closed some major hols. Res accepted. Bar to 11 pm. Dinner $15-$22. Child's menu. Entertainment Thurs-Mon. Originally built 1700s as a tavern; unique pumpkin-pine wainscoting, original fireplaces and mantels, beamed ceilings. Cr cds: A, D, DS, MC, V.
⊐

★ **HANNAH JACK TAVERN.** *Greeley St & Daniel Webster Hwy, Merrimack (03054). 603/424-4171.* Specialties: prime rib, Alaskan king crab legs. Hrs: 11:30 am-2 pm, 5-9:30 pm; Sat from 4:30 pm; Sun from 4 pm. Closed July 4, Dec 25. Res accepted. Bar. Lunch $5.50-$8.50, dinner $12-$22. Child's menu. Parking. In Colonial building over 200 yrs old. Cr cds: A, MC, V.
⊐

★ **MODERN.** *116 W Pearl St (03060). 603/883-8422.* Specializes in steak, seafood, chicken. Hrs: 11 am-8:30 pm; Fri, Sat to 9 pm. Lunch $2.99-$6.99, dinner $4.99-$17.99. Child's menu. Cr cds: A, C, D, MC, V.
SC ⊐

★ **NEWICK'S.** *696 Daniel Webster Hwy, Merrimack (03054). 603/429-0262. www.newicks.com.* Specializes in fresh seafood. Hrs: 11:30 am-8:30 pm; Fri, Sat to 9 pm. Closed Thanksgiving, Dec 25. Bar. Lunch, dinner $5.95-$20.95. Child's menu. Nautical decor. Cr cds: A, DS, MC, V.
⌨ SC ⊐

New London

See also Sunapee

Pop 3,180 **Elev** 825 ft **Area code** 603 **Zip** 03257
Information Chamber of Commerce, Main St, PO Box 532; 603/526-6575 or 877/526-6575
Web www.newlondonareanh.com

What to See and Do

Skiing.
    Ragged Mountain. Two triple, three double chairlifts, three surface tows; patrol, school, rentals, snowmaking; cafeteria, bar. Longest run 1¾ mi; vertical drop 1,250 ft. (Mid-Nov-Mar, daily) Cross-country skiing. 10 mi E on NH 11, then 7 mi N on US 4 to Danbury, then 1½ mi E on NH 104 to access road. Phone 603/768-3475 or 603/356-3042. ¢¢¢¢

Special Event

Barn Playhouse. Main St, off NH 11. Live theater presentations nightly; Wed matinees. Also Mon children's attractions. Phone 603/526-4631 or 603/526-6710. Mid-June-Labor Day.

Motels/Motor Lodges

★ **FAIRWAY MOTEL.** *Country Club Ln (03257).* 603/526-6040; fax 603/526-9622. 12 rms. S, D $55-$70; each addl $8.50; under 13 free (with 2 adults). Crib free. TV; cable. Pool. Ck-out 11 am. Tennis privileges. Downhill ski 12 mi; x-country ski on site. Cr cds: A, DS, MC, V.
🐾 🎐 ⌦

★ **LAMPLIGHTER MOTOR INN.** *6 Newport Rd (03257).* 603/526-6484; fax 603/526-9678. www.lamplightermotorinn.com. 14 rms, 2 story. S, D $55-$65; kit. units $65-$75; each addl $5. TV; cable, VCR avail. Complimentary continental bkfst. Restaurant nearby. Ck-out 11 am. Business servs avail. Downhill/x-country ski 10 mi. Refrigerators avail. Cr cds: A, DS, MC, V.
D 🏌 🎐 ⌦ 🔥

B&Bs/Small Inns

★★★ **FOLLANSBEE INN.** *Rte 114, North Sutton (03260).* 603/927-4221; fax 603/927-6307; toll-free 800/626-4221. www.follansbeeinn.com. 20 rms, 12 share bath, 3 story. No rm phones. S, D $90-$130; each addl $25. Closed 2 wks Nov and Apr. Children over 8 yrs only. Complimentary full bkfst. Serv bar. Ck-out 11 am, ck-in 3-10 pm. Downhill ski 14 mi; x-country ski on site. Restored 1840 New England farmhouse. On Kezar Lake; boats; private beach, pier. Bikes. Sitting rms with fireplaces. Totally nonsmoking. Cr cds: MC, V.
🏌 🔥 🎐 ⌦ 🔥

★★★ **INN AT PLEASANT LAKE.** *125 N Pleasant St (03257).* 603/526-6271; fax 603/526-4111; toll-free 800/626-4907. www.innatpleasantlake.com. 12 rms, some A/C, 3 story. No rm phones. S, D $110-$145; each addl $25; suite $175; wkly rates. Complimentary full bkfst. Dining rm dinner sitting 6:30 pm. Ck-out 11 am, ck-in 3 pm. Meeting rm. Downhill ski 12 mi; x-country ski 3 mi. Exercise equipt. Some fireplaces. Original Cape farmhouse (1790) converted to summer resort in late 1800s; country antique decor. On Pleasant Lake; private sand beach. Cr cds: A, DS, MC, V.
🏌 🎐 🍴 ⌦ 🔥

★★ **NEW LONDON INN.** *140 Main St (03257).* 603/526-2791; fax 603/526-2749; toll-free 800/526-2791. 23 rms, 10 with shower only, 3 story. May-Oct: S, D $100-$140; each addl $20; lower rates rest of yr. TV in sitting rm; VCR (free movies). Complimentary continental bkfst. Restaurant (see NEW LONDON INN). Bar from 5 pm. Ck-out 11 am, ck-in 3 pm. Meeting rm. Business servs avail. Downhill/x-country ski 3 mi. Health club privileges. Lawn games. Built 1792. Cr cds: A, MC, V.
D 🎐 ⌦ 🔥

Restaurants

★★ **MILLSTONE.** *Newport Rd (NH 11W) (03257).* 603/526-4201. www.millstonerestaurant.com. Specializes in veal, seafood, pasta. Own desserts. Hrs: 11:30 am-2:30 pm, 5-9 pm; Sun brunch 11 am-2:30 pm. Closed Dec 25. Res accepted. Lunch $6.50-$11.95, dinner $9.95-$19.95. Child's menu. Casual, garden-view dining. Cr cds: A, DS, MC, V.
D

★★ **NEW LONDON INN.** *140 Main St (03257).* 603/526-2791. www.newlondoninn.net. Specialties: garlic-scented New York strip steak, grilled vegetables and shiitake mushroom sampler, herb-crusted Atlantic salmon. Hrs: 5-9 pm. Res accepted; required Fri, Sat. Dinner $13-$22. Child's menu. Colonial decor. Overlooks village green, flower gardens. Totally nonsmoking. Cr cds: A, MC, V.
D

★★ **POTTER PLACE INN.** *88 Depot St, Andover (03216).* 603/735-5141. www.potterplaceinn.com. Specializes in veal, roast duckling, fresh seafood and game. Hrs: 5:30-9 pm. Closed Mon Nov-Apr. Res accepted. Serv bar. Dinner $12-$18. House built 1790s; country atmosphere. Cr cds: A, DS, MC, V.
D

Newport

See also Sunapee

Settled 1765 **Pop** 6,110 **Elev** 797 ft **Area code** 603 **Zip** 3773
Information Chamber of Commerce, 2 N Main St; 603/863-1510

Newport is the commercial headquarters for the Lake Sunapee area. Its industries include machine tools, woolens, clothing, and firearms. The Town Common Historic District has many churches and Colonial and Victorian houses.

What to See and Do

Fort at No. 4. Reconstructed French and Indian War log fort, complete with stockade, Great Hall, cow barns, and living quarters furnished to reflect 18th-century pioneer living. Exhibits incl Native American artifacts, demonstrations of colonial crafts and an audiovisual program. (Memorial Day-late Oct, daily) 10 mi W on NH 11/103, then 11 mi S on NH 11/12, near Charlestown. Phone 603/826-5700. ¢¢

B&B/Small Inn

★ **NEWPORT MOTEL.** *467 Sunapee St (03773).* 603/863-1440; fax 603/526-9678; toll-free 800/741-2619. www.newportmotelnh.com. 18 rms. June-Oct: S, D $66-$88; each addl $10; lower rates rest of yr. TV; cable. Pool. Complimentary continental bkfst. Ck-out 11 am. Downhill ski 5 mi; x-country ski 14 mi. Refrigerators avail. Cr cds: A, C, D, MC, V.
D 🎐 ⌦ 🔥

North Conway

See also Bartlett, Jackson

Settled 1764 **Pop** 2,100 **Elev** 531 ft **Area code** 603
Zip 03860
Information Mount Washington Valley Chamber of
Commerce, 1267 Main St, PO Box 2300; 603/356-5701
or 800/367-3364
Web www.mtwashingtonvalley.org

Heart of the famous Mount Washington Valley region
of the White Mountains, the area also includes Bartlett,
Glen, Jackson, Conway, Redstone, Kearsarge, and Intervale.
Mount Washington, seen from the middle of Main Street,
is one of the great views in the East.

What to See and Do

Conway Scenic Railroad. Steam and diesel trains depart
from restored Victorian station (1874) for 11-mi (55-min)
round trip. Valley Train explores the Saco River valley
(mid-May-Oct, daily; mid-Apr-mid-May, Nov and Dec,
wkends); Notch Train travels through Crawford Notch
(mid-Sept-mid-Oct, daily; late June-mid-Sept, Thurs, Sat).
Railroad museum. Depot on Main St. Phone 603/356-5251.
¢¢

Covered bridges. In Conway, Jackson, and Bartlett.

Sacobound. Specializes in rafting, canoeing, kayak touring,
and paddling school. Programs incl guided whitewater
rafting trips, whitewater canoe and kayak school, calm
water and whitewater canoe rentals. (May-Oct) US 302,
2 mi E of Center Conway. Phone 603/447-3002. ¢¢¢

Echo Lake State Park. Mountain lake in the shadow of
White Horse Ledge. Scenic road to 700-ft Cathedral Ledge,
dramatic rock formation; panoramic views of the White
Mts and the Saco River Valley. Swimming, picnicking.
(Late June-Labor Day) Standard fees. 2 mi W, off NH 302.
Phone 603/356-2672.

Factory outlet stores. Many outlet malls and stores can be
found along NH 16. Contact Chamber of Commerce for
more information. Phone 603/356-2225.

League of New Hampshire Craftsmen. Work by some of
New Hampshire's finest craftspeople. (Daily) On NH 16
(Main St). Phone 603/356-2441. **FREE**

Skiing. Mount Cranmore. Express quad, triple, double
chairlift to summit, three double chairlifts to N, S, and E
slopes, four surface lifts; patrol, school, rentals; snowmaking; restaurant, bar, cafeterias; day care. Longest run
1¾ mi; vertical drop 1,200 ft. (Nov-Apr, daily) 1 mi E off
US 302 (NH 16). Phone 603/356-7070.

White Mountain National Forest. (see). N & S on NH 16;
W on US 302.

Special Events

Eastern Slope Playhouse. Main St, on grounds of Eastern
Slope Inn Resort (see MOTELS). Mt Washington Valley
Theatre Co presents four Broadway musicals. Tues-Sun.
Phone 603/356-5776. Late June-early Sept.

Mt Washington Valley Equine Classic. Horse jumping.
Mid-Aug.

Mud Bowl. (Football) Hog Coliseum. Sept.

Motels/Motor Lodges

★★ **EASTERN SLOPE INN RESORT.** *2760 Main St
(03860).* 603/356-6847; fax 603/356-8732; toll-free 800/
862-1600. www.easternslopeinn.com. 146 rms, 3 story. S, D
$89-$279; each addl $15; townhouse suites $199-$399;
under 12 free; ski plans; higher rates fall foliage, hols.
TV; cable, VCR avail. Indoor pool; whirlpool. Restaurant
noon-midnight; entertainment Fri, Sat. Ck-out 10 am. Coin
lndry. Meeting rms. Tennis. Downhill ski 1 mi; x-country
ski on site. Sauna. Rec rm. Lawn games. Trout pond. Picnic
tables, grills. Golf course adj. Cr cds: A, DS, MC, V.
🄳 🐾 🏊 🎿 🏊 🕊

★ **GOLDEN GABLES INN.** *Rte 16 and US 302 (03860).*
603/356-2878; fax 603/356-9094; toll-free 888/422-5346.
www.goldengablesinn.com. 39 rms, 1-2 story. Late June-mid-
Oct: S, D $88-$102; each addl $5; lower rates rest of yr.
TV; cable (premium). Heated pool. Complimentary coffee.
Restaurant nearby. Ck-out 11 am. Downhill/x-country ski
2 mi. Patios, balconies. Cr cds: A, DS, MC, V.
🄳 🐾 🏊 🏊 🕊

★★ **JUNGE'S MOTEL.** *1858 White Mt. Hwy (03860).*
603/356-2886. www.jungesmotel.com. 28 rms, 1-2 story.
Mid-June-Oct: S, D $65-$90; each addl $5-$10; higher rates
special events; lower rates rest of yr. Crib $2-$5. TV; cable.
Heated pool. Playground. Restaurant nearby. Ck-out 11 am.
Downhill/x-country ski 2 mi. Rec rm. Lawn games. Picnic
tables, grills. Cr cds: A, DS, MC, V.
🄳 🎿 🏊 🏊 🕊

★ **SWISS CHALETS VILLAGE INN.** *Rte 16A, Intervale
(03845).* 603/356-2232; fax 603/356-7331; toll-free 800/
831-2727. www.swisschaletsvillage.com. 42 rms, 1-3 story.
No elvtr. S $69-$139; D $79-$169; each addl $10; suites
$109-$179; under 13 free; ski plans; higher rates fall foliage.
Crib free. Pet accepted; $15/day. TV; cable. Heated pool.
Complimentary continental bkfst. Ck-out 11 am. Downhill
ski 4 mi; x-country ski on site. Game rm. Refrigerators;
some in-rm whirlpools, fireplaces. Some balconies. Picnic
tables. Rms in Swiss chalet-style buildings; on 12 acres.
Cr cds: A, DS, MC, V.
🐾 🏊 🏊 🎿

★ **WHITE TRELLIS MOTEL.** *3245 White Mountain Hwy;
Rte 16 (03860).* 603/356-2492. www.whitetrellismotel.com.
22 rms. June-mid-Oct and hol ski wks: S, D $40-$145; each
addl $5; some lower rates rest of yr. Crib free. TV; cable.
Complimentary coffee in lobby. Restaurant nearby. Ck-out
10 am. Downhill/x-country ski 3 mi. Cr cds: DS, MC, V.
🄳 🐾 🎿 🏊 🕊

Hotels

★★★ **NORTH CONWAY GRAND HOTEL.** *72 Common
Ct (03860).* 603/356-9300; fax 603/356-6028; toll-free
800/648-4397. www.northconwaygrand.com. 200 rms,
4 story. S, D $79-$165; suites $155-$215; under 18 free;

MAP avail; ski plans. Crib $10. TV; cable (premium). Indoor pool; whirlpool. Restaurant 7 am-10:30 pm. Bar 11-1 am; entertainment wkends. Ck-out 11 am. Coin lndry. Meeting rms. Business servs avail. In-rm modem link. Downhill ski 3 mi; x-country ski 5 mi. Exercise equipt; sauna. Game rm. Bathrm phone, refrigerator, minibar in suites. Cr cds: A, C, D, DS, ER, MC, V.

★★ **NORTH CONWAY MOUNTAIN INN.** *Main St (03860).* 603/356-2803; toll-free 800/319-4405. *www.northconwaymountaininn.com.* 32 rms, 2 story. S, D $79-$159; higher rates fall foliage; lower rates off-season. Crib free. TV; cable. Restaurant opp 6 am-9 pm. Ck-out 10 am. Downhill/x-country ski 2 mi. Balconies. Totally nonsmoking. Cr cds: A, DS, MC, V.

Resorts

★★ **THE FOX RIDGE.** *White Mountain Hwy; Rte 16 (03860).* 603/356-3151; fax 603/356-0096; toll-free 800/343-1804. *www.foxridgeresort.com.* 136 rms, 2 story. July-late Oct: S, D $100-$175; each addl $10; under 16 free; package plans; higher rates hol wkends; lower rates rest of yr. Closed late Oct-mid-May. Crib free. TV; cable. 2 pools, 1 indoor; poolside serv. Playground. Supervised child's activities (July-Aug); ages 4-12. Restaurant 7:30-11 am. Ck-out 11 am. Tennis. Game rm. Lawn games. Refrigerators. Private patios, balconies. Picnic tables. Cr cds: A, MC, V.

★★ **GREEN GRANITE INN.** *Rte 16 & 302 (03860).* 603/356-6901; fax 603/356-6980; res 800/468-3666. *www.greengranite.com.* 91 rms, 2 story. S, D $75-$149; each addl $10; suites $150-$220; kit. units $79-$149; condos $129-$229; under 16 free; family rates; package plans. Crib $5. TV; cable, VCR avail. Pools, 1 indoor; whirlpool. Playground. Complimentary continental bkfst. Ck-out 11 am, ck-in 3 pm. Meeting rms. Sundries. Exercise equipt. Downhill/x-country ski 4 mi. Refrigerator, whirlpool in suites. Private patios, balconies. Picnic tables, grill. Cr cds: A, DS, MC, V.

★★★ **PURITY SPRING RESORT.** *HC 63 Box 40 Rte 153, East Madison (03849).* 603/367-8896; fax 603/367-8664; toll-free 800/373-3754. *www.purityspring.com.* 48 rms, 4 share bath; 3 cottages (2-bedrm). AP: S $79-$129; D $66-$226/person; each addl $48; EP, MAP avail; wkly rates; ski plans. TV in common areas. Indoor pool; whirlpool. Playground. Supervised children's activities (late June-Labor Day); ages infant-6 yrs. Dining rm 7:30-9:30 am, noon-1:30 pm, 5:30-7:30 pm; Apr and Nov 8-9:30 am only. Bar 5-11 pm. Ck-out 11 am, ck-in 3 pm. Coin lndry. Business servs avail. Grocery, package store 9 mi. Sports dir. Tennis, pro. Private beach; waterskiing, rowboats, canoes, sailboats. Downhill ski on site. Sledding. Ice-skating. Exercise equipt. Lawn games. Rec rm. Game rm. Fish clean and store. Picnic tables. Cr cds: A, D, DS, MC, V.

★★ **RED JACKET MOUNTAIN VIEW.** *Rte 16 (03860).* 603/356-5411; fax 603/356-3842; toll-free 800/752-2538. *www.redjacketmountainview.com.* 152 rms, 3 story, 12 kit. apts (2-bedrm). Mid-Dec-mid-Mar and Memorial Day-late Oct: S, D $109-$229; suites, 2-bedrm apts $229-$349; family rates; package plans; higher rates hols; lower rates rest of yr. Crib free. TV; cable, VCR avail. 2 heated pools, 1 indoor; poolside serv in summer. Playground. Free supervised children's activities (late-June-Labor Day); ages 4-12. Dining rms 7:30-10 am, noon-9 pm. Rm serv. Bars noon-1 am; entertainment. Ck-out 11 am. Coin lndry. Meeting rms. Business servs avail. Bellhops. Sundries. Gift shop. Valet parking. Lighted tennis. Downhill ski 2 mi; x-country ski on site. Exercise equipt. Game rm. Lawn games. Refrigerators, some in-rm whirlpools. Many private patios, balconies. Cr cds: A, C, D, DS, MC, V.

★★★ **WHITE MOUNTAIN HOTEL & RESORT.** *W Side Rd (03860).* 603/356-7100; toll-free 800/533-6301. *www.whitemountainhotel.com.* 80 rms, 3 story, 13 suites. July-Oct: S, D $109-$179; suites $149-$239; under 18 free; wkly rates; ski, golf plans; lower rates rest of yr. Crib avail. TV; cable. Heated pool; whirlpool, poolside serv. Dining rm 7-10 am, 11:30 am-9 pm. Bar 11:30-1 am; entertainment, wkends (nightly in season). Ck-out 11 am, ck-in 3 pm. Coin lndry. Meeting rms. Business servs avail. Bellhops. Tennis. 9-hole golf, pro, putting green. Downhill ski 2½ mi. Exercise equipt; sauna. Game rm. Surrounded by White Mt National Forest and Echo Lake State Park. Cr cds: A, DS, MC, V.

B&Bs/Small Inns

★★ **1785 INN.** *3582 N White Mountain Hwy (03860).* 603/356-9025; fax 603/356-6081; toll-free 800/421-1785. *www.the1785inn.com.* 17 rms, 5 share bath, 12 A/C, 3 story. No rm phones. S $49-$109; D $69-$169; each addl $10-$20; MAP avail; family rates; ski plans; higher rates fall foliage. Crib free. TV in some rms, sitting rm; cable, VCR avail. Pool; poolside serv. Playground. Complimentary full bkfst. Restaurant Downhill ski 2 mi; x-country ski on site. Lawn games. Picnic tables, grills. Colonial-style building (1785); original fireplaces, Victorian antiques. On 6 acres; river, view of Mt Washington. Totally nonsmoking. Cr cds: A, DS, MC, V.

★★ **BUTTONWOOD INN.** *Mt Surprise Rd (03860).* 603/356-2625; fax 603/356-3140; toll-free 800/258-2625. *www.buttonwoodinn.com.* 10 rms, 2 story. No A/C. S $85-$200; D $120-$250; each addl $25. TV in sitting rm; cable. Pool. Complimentary full bkfst. Ck-out 11 am, ck-in 3 pm. Downhill ski 1 mi; x-country ski on site. Cape Cod-style building (1820s); antiques, library. Seventeen wooded acres on mountainside. Totally nonsmoking. Cr cds: A, DS, MC, V.

★ **CRANMORE INN.** *80 Kearsarge St (03860).* *603/356-5502; fax 603/356-6052; toll-free 800/526-5502.* *www.cranmoreinn.com.* 18 rms, 3 story. No A/C. Late June-mid-Sept: S $52-$75; D $62-$85; suites $104-$125; wkly, family rates; package plans; higher rates fall foliage; lower rates rest of yr. Crib free. TV rm; cable. Pool. Complimentary full bkfst. Dining rm 8-9 am. Ck-out 11 am, ck-in 3 pm. Downhill ski ⅓ mi; x-country ski on site. Health club privileges. Lawn games. In operation since 1863. Cr cds: A, MC, V.

🅳 ▣ ▣ ▣ ▣

★★ **CRANMORE MOUNTAIN LODGE.** *Kearsarge St, off NH 16 (03860).* *603/356-2044; fax 603/356-4498; toll-free 800/356-3596. www.cml1.com.* 16 rms, 6 A/C, 2-3 story; 40 units in bunkhouse. No rm phones. S, D $95-$165; each addl $10-$15; bunkhouse units $20; suite $225-$305; 2-bedrm townhouse $220; MAP avail winter; wkly rates; ski plans; some lower rates off-season. Crib free. TV in some rms; cable. Pool; whirlpool. Playground. Complimentary full bkfst. Dining rm hrs vary. Ck-out 11 am, ck-in 3 pm. Coin lndry. Tennis. Downhill ski 1 mi; x-country ski on site. Ice-skating. Game rm. Lawn games. Picnic tables, grills. Historic guest house (1860); once owned by Babe Ruth's daughter. Library, sitting rm, antiques. Located on 12 acres; pond. Farm animals. Cr cds: A, DS, MC, V.

▣ ▣ ▣ ▣ ▣

★★ **DARBY FIELD COUNTRY INN.** *185 Chase Hill Rd, Albany (03818).* *603/447-2181; fax 603/447-5726; toll-free 800/426-4147. www.darbyfield.com.* 16 rms, 2 share bath, 4 A/C, 3 story. No rm phones. MAP: S $140-$195; D $160-$260; each addl $45; ski, canoeing plans; higher rates fall foliage. Children over 2 yrs only. TV in lobby; cable, VCR. Pool. Complimentary full bkfst. Dining rm 6-9 pm. Ck-out 9-11 am, ck-in 2-6 pm. Downhill ski 10 mi; x-country ski on site. Lawn games. Originally a farmhouse (1826); library, sitting rm; large fieldstone fireplace, rustic decor. View of Presidential Mts. Cr cds: A, MC, V.

🅳 ▣ ▣ ▣ ▣

★★ **EASTMAN INN.** *2331 White Mountain Hwy (03846).* *603/356-6707; fax 603/356-7708; toll-free 800/626-5855. www.eastmaninn.com.* 34 rms, some A/C, 3 story. S, D $80-$260; lower rates off-season. TV; cable. Complimentary full bkfst. Restaurant nearby. Ck-out 11 am, ck-in 3 pm. Downhill/x-country ski 1 mi. Built 1777. Antiques. Sitting rm with fireplace. Wraparound porch. Totally nonsmoking. Cr cds: A, DS, MC, V.

▣ ▣ ▣ ▣

★★ **THE FOREST, A COUNTRY INN.** *Rt 16A, Intervale (03845).* *603/356-9772; fax 603/356-5652; toll-free 877/854-6535. www.forest-inn.com.* 11 rms, 1-3 story. July-mid-Oct, Dec-mid-Apr: S $70-$125; D $80-$160; package plans; lower rates rest of yr. TV rm; cable. Heated pool. Complimentary full bkfst; afternoon refreshments. Ck-out 11 am, ck-in 3 pm. Downhill ski 4 mi; x-country ski on site. Lawn games. Tennis adj. Some fireplaces. Picnic table, grill. Operating as an inn since 1890. Totally nonsmoking. Cr cds: A, DS, MC, V.

🅳 ▣ ▣ ▣ ▣ ▣ ▣

★★ **MERRILL FARM RESORT.** *428 White Mountain Hwy (03860).* *603/447-3866; toll-free 800/445-1017. www.merrillfarm.com.* 33 rms, 2 story, 17 suites; 11 cottages, 7 with kits. S, D $49-$110; each addl $12; suites $79-$159; cottages $69-$139; under 18 free; wkend rates; package plans; higher rates fall foliage. Crib free. TV; cable. Heated pool; whirlpool, sauna. Complimentary bkfst. Restaurant adj 6:30 am-10 pm. Ck-out 11 am. Coin lndry. Meeting rms. Downhill ski 3 mi; x-country ski 4 mi. Lawn games. Many refrigerators, in-rm whirlpools; some fireplaces. Picnic tables, grills. Converted farmhouse (1885) and cottages on Saco River. Dock. Cr cds: A, DS, MC, V.

🅳 ▣ ▣ ▣ ▣

★★ **SNOWVILLAGE INN.** *Stewart Rd, Snowville (03849).* *603/447-2818; fax 603/447-5268; toll-free 800/447-4345. www.snowvillageinn.com.* 18 rms. No A/C. S $79-$125; D $99-$249, each addl $25; MAP avail; extended stay rates. Dining rm 6-9 pm (public by res). Serv bar. Business servs avail. Downhill ski 6 mi; x-country ski on site. Hiking trails. Sauna. Lawn games. Some fireplaces. Secluded, on 10 acres. Panoramic view of mountains. Totally nonsmoking. Cr cds: A, D, DS, MC, V.

🅳 ▣ ▣ ▣ ▣ ▣

Restaurants

★★★ **1785 INN.** *3582 White Mountain Hwy (03860).* *603/356-9025. www.the1785inn.com.* French, American menu. Specialties: rack of lamb, raspberry duckling, veal chop morel. Own baking. Hrs: 5-9 pm; wkends to 10 pm. Closed Dec 25. Dinner $15.85-$23.85. Res accepted. Cr cds: D, DS, MC, V.

★ **BELLINI'S.** *33 Seavey St (03860). 603/356-7000. www.bellinis.com.* Italian menu. Specialties: rigatoni broccoli chicken, veal Marsala, fresh grilled seafood. Hrs: 5-10 pm; Fri, Sat to 11 pm. Closed Tues. Bar. Dinner $7.95-$17.95. Child's menu. Tuscan country atmosphere. Cr cds: A, D, DS, MC, V.

★ **HORSEFEATHERS.** *Main St (03860). 603/356-2687. www.horsefeathers.com.* Specializes in wood-grilled foods. Hrs: 11:30 am-11:45 pm. Closed Thanksgiving, Dec 25. Bar. Lunch, dinner $6.50-$17.95. Neighborhood nostalgia; landmark restaurant. Cr cds: A, MC, V.

🅳

Unrated Dining Spot

PEACH'S. *Main St (03860). 603/356-5860.* Specializes in homemade soups, desserts, salad dressings. Hrs: 6 am-2:30 pm. Closed Thanksgiving, Dec 25. Bkfst $1.25-$5.95, lunch $2-$5.95. Totally nonsmoking. Cr cds: A, MC, V.

North Woodstock

(see Lincoln/North Woodstock Area)

Peterborough

See also Jaffrey, Keene, Nashua

Settled 1749 **Pop** 5,239 **Elev** 723 ft **Area code** 603
Zip 03458
Information Greater Peterborough Chamber of Commerce, PO Box 401; 603/924-7234
Web www.peterboroughchamber.com

This was the home of composer Edward MacDowell (1861-1908). Edward Arlington Robinson, Stephen Vincent Benét, Willa Cather, and Thornton Wilder, among others, worked at the MacDowell Colony, a thriving artists' retreat, which made Peterborough famous.

What to See and Do

Greenfield State Park. 401 acres. Swimming, bathhouse; fishing. Picnicking, concessions. Camping (dump station) with separate beach. (Mid-May-mid-Oct) Standard fees. 9 mi N on NH 136, then W on unnumbered road, near Greenfield. Phone 603/547-3497.

Miller State Park. First of the New Hampshire parks. Atop 2,288-ft Pack Monadnock Mtn; walking trails on summit; scenic drive; picnicking. (June-Labor Day, daily; May and Labor Day-Nov, Sat, Sun, and hols) Standard fees. 4 mi E on NH 101. Phone 603/924-3672.

New England Marionette Opera. Largest marionette facility in country devoted to opera. (Mid-May-late Dec, Sat eves, also Sun matinee; closed July 4, Thanksgiving) Main St. Phone 603/924-4333.

Peterborough Historical Society. Exhibits on the history of the area; historical and genealogical library. (Mon-Fri) 19 Grove St. Phone 603/924-3235. ¢¢

Sharon Arts Center. Gallery and crafts center. (Daily) School of arts and crafts located 5 mi SE on NH 123, in Depot Sq. Phone 603/924-7256. **FREE**

Motel/Motor Lodge

★ **JACK DANIELS MOTOR INN.** *Rte 202 N (03458). 603/924-7548; fax 603/924-7700. www.jackdanielsmotorinn.com.* 17 rms, shower only, 2 story. S $73-$88; D $88-$98; each addl $10; under 12 free; higher rates fall foliage. TV; cable. Complimentary coffee in lobby. Ck-out 11 am. Business servs avail. Downhill ski 10 mi. On river. Cr cds: A, DS, MC, V.

[D] [⟡] [⟲] [♨]

B&Bs/Small Inns

★★ **GREENFIELD INN.** *Rtes 31 N & 136, Greenfield (03047). 603/547-6327; fax 603/547-2418; toll-free 800/678-4144. www.greenfieldinn.com.* 13 rms, 9 with bath, 2 story. D $49-$89; each addl $20; suite $119-$169, cottage $219; wkly rates. TV; cable, VCR (free movies). Complimentary full bkfst. Restaurants nearby. Ck-out 11 am, ck-in 4 pm. Business servs avail. Downhill/x-country ski 6 mi. Cr cds: A, DS, MC, V.

[⟡] [⟲] [♨] [SC]

★★★ **HANCOCK INN.** *33 Main St, Hancock (03449). 603/525-3318; fax 603/525-9301; toll-free 800/525-1789. www.hancockinn.com.* 11 rms, 3 story. S $120; D $175-$195. Children over 12 yrs only. TV; cable. Complimentary full bkfst; afternoon refreshments. Restaurant (see HANCOCK INN). Ck-out 11 am, ck-in 2 pm. Business servs avail. In-rm modem link. Luggage handling. Built 1789. Original art by Moses Eaton and Rufus Porter; antiques. Totally nonsmoking. Cr cds: A, D, DS, MC, V.

[D] [⟡] [⟲] [♨]

Restaurant

★★★ **HANCOCK INN.** *33 Main St, Hancock (03449). 603/525-3318. www.hancockinn.com.* Specialties: Shaker cranberry pot roast, roast duckling, apple braised salmon. Hrs: 6-9 pm. Closed Dec 25. Res required. Serv bar. Dinner $20-$29. Country decor; antiques. Totally nonsmoking. Cr cds: A, D, DS, MC, V.

[D]

Pinkham Notch

See also Gorham, Jackson, North Conway

(Approx 7 mi N on NH 16)

Named for Joseph Pinkham, a 1790 settler, this easternmost White Mountain pass is closest to Mount Washington (see). Headquarters for the Appalachian Mountain Club Hut System is here.

What to See and Do

Glen Ellis Falls Scenic Area. E of NH 16, 12 mi N of Glen in White Mtn National Forest (see).

Skiing.

Wildcat Ski & Recreation Area. Detachable quad, three triple chairlifts, patrol, school, rentals; snowmaking; cafeteria, nursery. Longest run two mi; vertical drop 2,100 ft. Gondola. (Mid-Nov-late Apr, daily; closed Thanksgiving, Dec 25) Gondola also operates Memorial Day-late Oct (Daily); picnicking. 10 mi N of Jackson on NH 16 in White Mt National Forest (see). ¢¢¢¢

Plymouth

See also Holderness, Meredith, Waterville Valley

Settled 1764 **Pop** 5,811 **Elev** 660 ft **Area code** 603
Zip 03264
Information Chamber of Commerce, PO Box 65; 603/536-1001 or 800/386-3678
Web www.plymouthnh.org

Since 1795, Plymouth's varied industries have included lumber, pig iron, mattresses, gloves, and sporting goods. It has been a resort center since the mid-19th century.

What to See and Do

Mary Baker Eddy Historic House. Residence of Mary Baker Eddy from 1860-1862, prior to the founding of the Christian Science Church. (May-Oct, daily exc Mon; closed hols) Approx 7 mi W via NH 25 to Stinson Lake Rd, then approx 1 mi N to N side of the Village of Rumney. Phone 603/786-9943. ¢

Plymouth State College. (1871) 3,500 students, 1,000 part-time and graduate students. A member of the University System of New Hampshire. Art exhibits in galleries and Lamson Library. Music, theater, and dance performances in Silver Cultural Arts Center (some fees). Planetarium shows. Tours. 1 blk W of business center. Phone 603/535-5000.

Polar Caves Park. Glacial caves; animal exhibits; local minerals; scenic rock formations; maple sugar museum; gift shops, picnicking. (Early May-late Oct, daily) 5 mi W on Tenney Mt Hwy (NH 25). Phone 603/536-1888. ¢¢

Motel/Motor Lodge

★ **BEST INN.** 304 Main St (03264). 603/536-2330; fax 603/536-2686; toll-free 800/237-8466. www.bestinn.com. 38 rms, 2 story. S $58-$79; D $68-$89; each addl $10; suite $90; family rates; ski, golf, bicycle plans. Crib free. Pet accepted. TV; cable, VCR avail. Pool. Complimentary continental bkfst. Restaurant opp 6 am-11 pm. Ck-out 11 am. Coin lndry. Meeting rm. Business servs avail. In-rm modem link. Downhill/x-country ski 15 mi. Some refrigerators. Picnic tables. Cr cds: A, D, DS, MC, V.
🐾 🏊 🍴 ⚓ 🛶 🐾 SC

Restaurants

★ **JIGGER JOHNSON'S.** 75 Main St (03264). 603/536-4386. www.jiggers.com. Specialties: chicken dijon, steak Diane. Hrs: noon-10 pm; Thurs-Sat to midnight. Closed Dec 25. Bar. Lunch $2.95-$5.95, dinner $6.95-$11.95. Child's menu. Some street parking. Lively, informal atmosphere. Eclectic decor. Cr cds: A, D, DS, MC, V.
D 🍸

★ **TREE HOUSE.** 3 S Main St (03264). 603/536-4084. www.thetreehouserestaurant.com. Specializes in chicken, steak, seafood. Hrs: 11:30 am-2:30 pm, 4:30-9 pm. Closed Thanksgiving, Dec 25. Res accepted. Bar. Lunch $3.95-$8.95, dinner $8.95-$14.95. Child's menu. Musicians Fri, Sat. Rustic atmosphere; large stone fireplace, vintage items decorate rm. Cr cds: A, D, DS, MC, V.
D

Portsmouth

See also Dover, Exeter, Hampton Beach

Settled 1630 **Pop** 25,925 **Elev** 21 ft **Area code** 603

Information Greater Portsmouth Chamber of Commerce, 500 Market St, PO Box 239, 03802-0239; 603/436-3988 or 603/436-1118

Web www.portsmouthchamber.org

A tour of Portsmouth's famous houses is like a tour through time, with Colonial and Federal architecture from 1684 into the 19th century. One-time capital of New Hampshire, Portsmouth was also the home port of a dynasty of merchant seamen who grew rich and built accordingly. The old atmosphere still exists in the narrow streets near Market Square.

The US Navy Yard, located in Kittery, Maine (see), on the Piscataqua River, has long been Portsmouth's major "industry." The peace treaty ending the Russo-Japanese War was signed at the Portsmouth Navy Yard in 1905.

What to See and Do

Children's Museum of Portsmouth. Arts and science museum featuring mock submarine, space shuttle, lobster boat, exhibits, and gallery. (Summer and school vacations, daily; rest of yr, Tues-Sat, also Sun afternoons) 280 Marcy St. Phone 603/436-3853. ¢¢

Fort Constitution. (1808) The first cannon was placed on this site in 1632; in 1694 it was known as Fort William and Mary. Information about a British order to stop gunpowder from coming into the colonies, brought by Paul Revere on Dec 13, 1774, caused the Sons of Liberty from Portsmouth, New Castle, and Rye to attack and capture, the next day, a fort that held five tons of gunpowder. Much of this powder was used at Bunker Hill by the patriots. This uprising against the King's authority was one of the first overt acts of the Revolution. Little remains of the original fort except the base of its walls. Fort Constitution had been built on the same site by 1808; granite walls were added during the Civil War. (Mid-June-early Sept, daily; late May-mid-June, late Sept-mid-Oct, wkends, hols only) 4 mi E on NH 1B in New Castle.

⭐ **Fort Stark State Historic Site.** A former portion of the coastal defense system dating back to 1746, exhibiting many of the changes in military technology from the Revolutionary War through WW II. The fort is situated on Jerry's Point, overlooking the Piscataqua River, Little Harbor, and Atlantic Ocean. (Late May-mid-Oct; Sat and Sun) Wild Rose Ln, approx 5 mi E off NH 1B in New Castle. Phone 603/436-7406.

InSight Tours. Specialized tours of Historic Portsmouth and the New Hampshire coastline incl garden, history, nature, and antique tours. 24-hr advanced res requested. ¢¢¢¢

Old Harbour Area. Features craftsmen, unique shops, bookstores, restaurants. Located on Historic Waterfront; NH 95 exit 7.

Portsmouth Harbor Cruises. Narrated historical tours aboard the 49-passenger M/V *Heritage*. Ninety-min harbor, 2½-hr Isles of Shoals, one-hr cocktail, 90-min sunset cruises, 2½-hr inland river cruise, fall foliage cruise. (Mid-June-Oct) 64 Ceres St, Old Harbor District. Phone 603/436-8084.

★ **Portsmouth Historic Homes.** The Historic Associates, part of the Greater Portsmouth Chamber of Commerce, has walking tour maps for six historic houses; maps are avail free at the Chamber of Commerce, 500 Market St. Phone 603/436-1118. The houses include

Governor John Langdon House. (1784) John Langdon served three terms as governor of New Hampshire and was the first president *pro tempore* of the US Senate. House's exterior proportions are monumental; interior embellished with excellent woodcarving and fine Portsmouth-area furniture. George Washington was entertained here in 1789. Architect Stanford White was commissioned to add the large wing at the rear with dining rm in the Colonial Revival style. Surrounded by landscaped grounds with gazebo, rose and grape arbor, and restored perennial garden beds. Tours (June-mid-Oct, Wed-Sun; closed hols). Grounds avail for rental. 143 Pleasant St. Phone 603/436-3205. ¢¢

John Paul Jones House. (1758). Where the famous naval commander twice boarded; now a museum containing period furniture, collections of costumes, china, glass, documents, weapons. Guided tours (June-mid-Oct, Thurs-Mon; closed Tues, Wed). 43 Middle St, at State St. Phone 603/436-8420. ¢

Moffatt-Ladd House. (1763). Built by Capt John Moffatt; later the home of Gen William Whipple, his son-in-law, a signer of the Declaration of Independence. Many original 18th- and 19th-century furnishings. Formal gardens. (Mid-June-mid-Oct, daily) 154 Market St. Phone 603/436-8221. ¢¢

Rundlet-May House. (1807). Federalist, three-story mansion. House sits on terraces and retains its original 1812 courtyard and garden layout; landscaped grounds. House contains family furnishings and accessories, including many fine examples of Federalist craftsmanship and the latest technologies of its time. (June-mid-Oct, Wed-Sun afternoons) Guided tours Mon-Sat, Sun afternoons. Grounds avail for rental. 364 Middle St. Phone 603/436-3205. ¢¢

Warner House. (1716). One of New England's finest Georgian houses, with scagliola in the dining rm, restored mural paintings on the staircase walls, beautiful paneling, a lightning rod on the west wall said to have been installed by Benjamin Franklin in 1762, five portraits by Joseph Blackburn, appropriate furnishings. (June-mid-Oct, Mon-Sat, Sun afternoons) Guided tours. 150 Daniel St, at Chapel St. Phone 603/436-5909. ¢¢

Wentworth-Gardner House. (1760). Excellent example of Georgian architecture. Elaborate woodwork, scenic wallpaper, magnificent main staircase. (Mid-June-mid-Oct, Tues-Sun afternoons) 50 Mechanic St. Phone 603/436-4406. ¢¢

★ **Star Island and Isles of Shoals.** The M/V *Thomas Laighton* makes cruises to historic Isles of Shoals, Star Island walkabouts, lobster clambake river cruises, fall foliage excursion, and others. Party ship. (Mid-June-Labor Day, daily) Depart from Barker's Wharf, 315 Market St. Phone 603/431-5500. ¢¢¢¢

★ **Strawbery Banke Museum.** Restoration of ten-acre historic waterfront neighborhood; site of original Portsmouth settlement. 42 buildings dating from 1695-1950. Nine houses: Captain Keyran Walsh House (1796), Governor Goodwin Mansion (1811), Chase House (1762), Captain John Wheelwright House (1780), Thomas Bailey Aldrich House (1790), Drisco House (1790s), Rider-Wood House (1840s), Abbott Grocery Store (1943), and the William Pitt Tavern (1766) are restored with period furnishings. Shops, architectural exhibits, pottery shop, and demonstrations; tool, photo, archaeological and house construction exhibits; family programs and activities, special events, tours; picnicking, coffee shop. (May-Oct, Mon-Sat, Sun afternoons) Guided tours Nov-Dec; Feb-Mar, Thurs-Sun. Hancock and Marcy Sts, Downtown, follow signs. Phone 603/433-1100. ¢¢¢

Special Events

Market Square Days. Summer celebration with 10K road race, street fair, entertainment. Phone 603/431-5388. June.

Portsmouth Jazz Festival. Two stages with continuous performances on the historical Portsmouth waterfront. For schedule phone 603/436-7678. Last Sun June.

Motels/Motor Lodges

★★ **COMFORT INN.** *1390 Lafayette Rd (03801). 603/433-3338; fax 603/431-1639; res 800/228-5150. www.yokens.com.* 121 rms, 6 story. June-Labor Day: S $69-$119; D $79-$129; under 18 free; lower rates rest of yr. Crib free. TV; cable (premium). Indoor pool; whirlpool. Complimentary continental bkfst. Restaurant adj 11 am-8 pm. Ck-out 11 am. Coin lndry. Meeting rms. Business servs avail. In-rm modem link. Sundries. Gift shop. Exercise equipt. Refrigerators avail. Cr cds: A, C, D, DS, ER, JCB, MC, V.

D 🏊 🏋 🖊 🐾

★ **FAIRFIELD INN.** *650 Borthwick Ave (03801). 603/436-6363; fax 603/436-1621; res 800/228-2800. www.fairfieldinn.com.* 105 rms, 4 story. June-Labor Day: S, D $70-$120; under 18 free; lower rates rest of yr. Crib free. TV; cable (premium). Pool. Complimentary continental bkfst. Complimentary coffee. Restaurant nearby. Ck-out 11 am. Coin lndry. Business servs avail. Refrigerators avail. Cr cds: A, D, DS, MC, V.

D 🏊 🖊 🐾

★★ **HOLIDAY INN.** *300 Woodbury Ave (03801). 603/431-8000; fax 603/431-2065; toll-free 800/465-4329. www.holiday-inn.com.* 130 rms, 6 story. July-Labor Day: S, D $105.95-$150; suites $190; under 20 free; lower rates rest of yr. Crib free. TV; cable (premium). Indoor pool. Restaurant 6:30 am-9:30 pm. Bar 11:30-1 am; entertainment Tues-Sat. Ck-out 11 am. Meeting rms. Valet serv. Sundries. Exercise equipt. Game rm. Refrigerators avail. Cr cds: A, D, DS, MC, V.

D 🐾 🏊 🏋 🖊 🐾

★ **PINE HAVEN MOTEL.** *183 Lafayette Rd, North Hampton (03862). 603/964-8187; fax 603/964-5485.* 19 rms, 4 kits. (no oven). Mid-June-Labor Day (2-day min hols and wkends): S $59; D $65-$75; each addl $5; kit. units $78; lower rates rest of yr. Crib $3. TV; cable. Complimentary coffee in rms. Restaurant nearby. Ck-out 11 am. Refrigerators. Cr cds: A, DS, MC, V.

★★ **PORT MOTOR INN.** *505 Rte 1 Bypass S (03801). 603/436-4378; toll-free 800/282-7678. www.theportinn.com.* 57 rms, 1-2 story, 20 studios. July-early Sept: S $70-$125; D $80-$159; each addl $6; studios $89-$149; under 13 free; lower rates rest of yr. Crib free. Pet accepted. TV; cable (premium). Pool. Complimentary continental bkfst. Ck-out 11 am. Refrigerator in studios. Picnic tables. Cr cds: A, C, D, DS, MC, V.

Hotels

★★★ **SHERATON.** *250 Market St (03801). 603/431-2300; fax 603/431-7805; toll-free 800/325-3535. www.sheraton.com.* 200 rms, 5 story, 24 suites. Mid-Apr-late Oct: S, D $135-$185; each addl $10; suites $275-$450; under 18 free; lower rates rest of yr. Crib avail. Garage parking $6. TV; cable (premium). Indoor pool. Complimentary coffee in rms. Restaurant 6:30 am-2:30 pm, 5:30-10 pm. Bar; entertainment. Ck-out noon. Meeting rms. Business center. Bellhops. Sundries. Valet serv. Free airport transportation. Exercise equipt; sauna. Minibars; refrigerator in suites. On Piscataqua River. Cr cds: A, C, D, DS, MC, V.

★★★ **SISE INN.** *40 Court St (03801). 603/433-1200; fax 603/433-0200; toll-free 877/747-3466. www.someplacesdifferent.com.* 34 rms, 3 story, 9 suites. May-Oct: S, D $179; each addl $15; suites $209-$259; under 11 free; lower rates rest of yr. Crib avail. TV; cable, VCR avail. CD avail. Complimentary continental bkfst. Restaurant nearby. Ck-out 11 am. Meeting rms. Business servs avail. Some in-rm whirlpools. Picnic tables, grills. Built 1881; antiques. Cr cds: A, D, MC, V.

B&B/Small Inn

★ **THE INN AT CHRISTIAN SHORE.** *335 Maplewood Ave (03801). 603/431-6770; fax 603/481-7743.* 5 rms, 2 story. No rm phones. June-Labor Day: S $57-$75; D $85-$100; each addl $15; lower rates rest of yr. TV; cable (premium). Complimentary full bkfst. Restaurant nearby. Ck-out 11 am, ck-in 2 pm. Free bus depot transportation. Fireplace. Restored Federal-style house (ca 1800); antiques, oil paintings. Totally nonsmoking. Cr cds: MC, V.

Restaurants

★★★ **METRO.** *20 High St (03801). 603/436-0521. www.themetrorestaurant.com.* Specializes in clam chowder, fresh seafood, veal Metro. Hrs: 11:30 am-2:30 pm, 5:30-10 pm. Closed Sun; Thanksgiving, Dec 25. Bar. Lunch $8-$12, dinner $12-$24. Entertainment Fri, Sat. Cr cds: A, D, MC, V.

★ **PIER II.** *10 State St (03801). 603/436-8100.* Specializes in lobster, steak, seafood. Salad bar. Hrs: 11:30 am-11 pm. Closed Thanksgiving, Dec 25; also Jan. Res accepted. Bar to 1 am. Lunch $3-$6.50, dinner $8-$15. Child's menu. Entertainment Sun-Fri. Valet parking. Outdoor dining. Overlooks harbor; dockage. Cr cds: A, D, DS, MC, V.

★ **YOKEN'S THAR SHE BLOWS.** *1390 Lafayette Rd (03801). 603/436-8224. www.yokens.com.* Specializes in steak, native seafood. Hrs: 11 am-8 pm; July-Aug to 9 pm. Res accepted. Serv bar. Lunch $4.95-$6.95, dinner $8.95-$13.95. Complete meals: lunch $6.50-$9.95. Child's menu. Nautical decor. Cr cds: A, D, DS, MC, V.

Salem

Pop 25,746 **Elev** 131 ft **Area code** 603 **Zip** 3079

Information Greater Salem Chamber of Commerce, 224 N Broadway, PO Box 304; 603/893-3177

Web www.salemnhchamber.org

What to See and Do

✪ **America's Stonehenge.** A megalithic calendar site dated to 2000 B.C., with 22 stone buildings on more than 30 acres. The main site features a number of stone-constructed chambers and is surrounded by miles of stone walls containing large, shaped monoliths that indicate the rising and setting of the sun at solstice and equinox, as well as other astronomical alignments, including lunar. (Daily; closed Thanksgiving, Dec 25.) 5 mi E of I-93, just off NH 111 in North Salem. Phone 603/893-8300. ¢¢

Canobie Lake Park. Family amusement park; giant roller coaster, log flume, pirate ship, giant Ferris wheel, haunted mine ride; entertainment; lake cruise, fireworks; games, pool; concessions, restaurant. (Memorial Day-Labor Day, daily; Apr-late May, wkends) 1 mi E of I-93, exit 2. Phone 603/893-3506. ¢¢¢¢

Robert Frost Farm. Home of poet Robert Frost from 1900-1911; period furnishings; audiovisual display; poetry-nature trail. (June-Labor Day, daily; after Labor Day-mid-Oct, wkends only) 1 mi SW on NH 38, then NW on NH 28 in Derry. Phone 603/432-3091. ¢¢

Rockingham Park. Thoroughbred horse racing. Live and simulcast racing (daily). Exit 1 off I-93. Phone 603/898-2311.

Motels/Motor Lodges

★ **FAIRFIELD INN.** *8 Keewaydin Dr (03079).* *603/893-4722; fax 603/893-2898; toll-free 800/228-2800.* *www.fairfieldinn.com.* 105 rms, 4 story. S, D $75-$120; under 18 free; seasonal rates. Crib free. TV; cable (premium). Pool. Complimentary continental bkfst. Restaurant opp 6 am-11 pm. Ck-out noon. Coin lndry. Meeting rm. Business servs avail. In-rm modem link. Cr cds: A, C, D, DS, MC, V.

D 🏊 📶 🔥

★★ **HOLIDAY INN.** *1 Keewaydin Dr (03079).* *603/893-5511; fax 603/894-6728; res 800/465-4329.* *www.holiday-inn.com.* 85 rms, 6 story. May-Oct: S, D $99-$130; lower rates rest of yr. Pet accepted. TV; cable (premium). Pool; poolside serv. Complimentary continental bkfst. Complimentary coffee in rms. Restaurant 6:30 am-10 pm. Ck-out 11 am. No bellhops. Meeting rms. Business servs avail. In-rm modem link. Exercise equipt. Health club privileges. Refrigerator avail. Cr cds: A, DS, MC, V.

D 🐕 🏊 🎿 📶 🔥

★ **PARKVIEW INN.** *109 S Broadway (03079).* 603/898-5632; fax 603/894-6579. www.parkviewinn.com. 58 rms, 28 kits. May-Dec: S $55-$65; D $64-$74, kit. units (4-day min) $74; each addl $6; under 12 free; wkly rates; lower rates rest of yr. Crib free. TV; cable (premium). Complimentary continental bkfst. Restaurant nearby. Ck-out 11 am. Coin lndry. In-rm modem link. Refrigerators. Cr cds: A, D, DS, MC, V.

D 📶 🔥

Sunapee

See also New London, Newport

Pop 2,559 **Elev** 1,008 ft **Area code** 603 **Zip** 03782

Information New London - Lake Sunapee Region Chamber of Commerce, PO Box 532; 603/526-6575 or 877/526-6575

Web www.lakesunapeenh.org

This is a year-round resort community on beautiful Lake Sunapee.

What to See and Do

Lake cruises.

M/V *Kearsarge* Restaurant Ship. Buffet dinner while cruising around Lake Sunapee. Phone 603/763-4030.

M/V *Mt Sunapee II* Excursion Boat. 1½-hr narrated tours of Lake Sunapee. Boat rentals, kayaks, canoes, gift shop, restaurants, concerts. (Mid-June-Labor Day, daily; mid-May-mid-June and after Labor Day-mid-Oct, Sat and Sun) Lake Ave, Sunapee Harbor, off NH 11. Phone 603/763-4030.

Mt Sunapee State Park. 2,714 acres. 1 mi S off NH 103. Phone 603/763-2356.

Summer. Swimming beach, bathhouse (fee); trout pool; picnicking, playground, concession; chairlift rides (fee). Displays by artists and craftsmen (see SPECIAL EVENT). (Memorial Day wkend; mid-June-early Sept, daily; early Sept-Columbus Day, wkends)

Winter. Skiing. One high-speed detachable quad, two fix grip quads, three quad, two triple, double chairlift, four surface lifts; patrol, school, rentals; cafeteria; snowmaking; nursery. 60 slopes and trails. Snowboarding. (Dec-Apr, daily) ¢¢¢¢

Snowhill at Eastman Ski Area. Ski Touring Center has 30 km of x-country trails; patrol, school, rentals; bar, restaurant. Summer facilities include Eastman Lake (swimming, boating, fishing); 18-hole golf, tennis; indoor pool; hiking. (Dec-Mar, daily; closed Dec 25) 4 mi N on NH 11, then 6 mi N on I-89, exit 13. Phone 603/863-4500.

Special Event

League of New Hampshire Craftsmen's Fair. Mt Sunapee Resort (see). More than 300 craftspeople and artists display and sell goods. Phone 603/224-3375. Aug.

Motel/Motor Lodge

★ **BURKEHAVEN AT SUNAPEE.** *179 Burkehaven Hill Rd (03782).* *603/763-2788; fax 603/763-9065; toll-free 800/567-2788.* *www.burkehavenatsunapee.com.* 10 air-cooled rms, shower only, 5 kits. S, D $89-$129; each addl $15; under 6 free; kit. units $85; wkly rates; ski packages. Crib free. TV. Pool. Complimentary coffee in rms. Restaurant nearby. Ck-out 11 am. Business servs avail. Tennis. Some refrigerators. Totally nonsmoking. Cr cds: A, DS, MC, V.

🛗 🎿 🏊 📶 🔥

B&Bs/Small Inns

★★ **CANDLELITE INN.** *5 Greenhouse Ln, Bradford (03221).* 603/938-5571; fax 603/938-2564; toll-free 888/812-5571. www.candleliteinn.com. 6 rms, 2 with shower only, 3 story. No rm phones. S, D $90-$125; wkends (2-day min); higher rates fall foliage, graduation. Complimentary full bkfst. Ck-out 11 am, ck-in 3 pm. Downhill ski 7 mi. Lawn games. Built in 1897; gazebo porch. Totally nonsmoking. Cr cds: A, D, DS, MC, V.

🛗 🎿 🏊 📶

★★ **DEXTERS INN & TENNIS CLUB.** *258 Stagecoach Rd (03782).* 603/763-5571; toll-free 800/232-5571. *www.bbhost.com/dexterinn.* 10 rms in lodge, 7 rms in annex, 2 story. No rm phones. May-Nov (2-day min wkends): S $105-$150; D $130-$175; each addl $45; kit. cottage (up to 4) $390; golf, tennis plans. Closed rest of yr. Pet accepted; $10. TV in lobby. Pool. Complimentary full bkfst. Ck-out 11 am, ck-in 3 pm. Meeting rms. Business servs avail. Tennis, pro. Lawn games. On 20-acre estate. Cr cds: DS, MC, V.

D 🐕 🎿 🏊 📶 🔥

Twin Mountain

See also Bretton Woods, Franconia, Littleton

Pop 760 **Elev** 1,442 ft **Area code** 603 **Zip** 03595
Information Chamber of Commerce, PO Box 194;
800/245-8946
Web www.twinmountain.org

What to See and Do

Mt Washington. (see). E off US 302.
White Mountain National Forest. (see). E on US 302;
SW on US 3.

Motels/Motor Lodges

★★ **FOUR SEASONS MOTOR INN.** *Birch Rd and
Rte 3 (03595). 603/846-5708; toll-free 800/228-5708.
www.4seasonsmotorinn.com.* 24 rms, 2 story. No rm phones.
S $55-$62; D $65-$72; each addl $7; under 13 free; ski plans.
Crib free. TV; cable. Pool. Playground. Restaurant nearby.
Ck-out 11 am. Sundries. Downhill/x-country ski 4 mi. Game
rm. Lawn games. Some refrigerators. Balconies. Picnic tables,
grills. Totally nonsmoking. Cr cds: DS, MC, V.
🆔 🏃 ✈ ➖ 🐾 ➖ &

★ **PROFILE DELUXE MOTEL.** *Rte 3 (03595). 603/846-
5522; toll-free 800/682-7222. profiledelux.qpg.com.* 13 rms,
12 A/C. S $50-$65; D $55-$80; suites $60-$95; each addl
$5; under 13 free; wkly rates. Crib $5. TV; cable. Heated
pool. Playground. Restaurant opp 6 am-10 pm. Ck-out
11 am. Downhill ski 5 mi; x-country ski on site. Some
refrigerators. Cr cds: A, DS, MC, V.
🆔 🏃 ✈ ➖ 🐾 ➖ &️ SC

★★ **SHAKESPEARE'S INN.** *675 Rte 3 (03595). 603/846-
5562; fax 603/846-5782. www.shakespearesinn.com.* 33 rms,
2 story. S $55-$70; D $60-$80; each addl $15; wkly rates.
Closed Apr-May, Nov-Dec. Crib $10. TV; cable. Pool.
Restaurant 4:30-9 pm. Ck-out 10:30 am. Tennis. Golf
privileges. Downhill/x-country ski 5 mi. Balconies.
At base of White Mts. Cr cds: A, MC, V.
🆔 ➤ 🎿 ✈ ➖ 🐾 &

B&B/Small Inn

★★ **NORTHERN ZERMATT INN & MOTEL.** *529 Rte 3N
(03595). 603/846-5533; fax 603/846-5664; toll-free 800/535-
3214. www.zermattinn.com.* 17 rms, 9 A/C, 2-3 story. No rm
phones. S $49; D $49-$69; each addl $6; kit. units $79-$98;
under 16 free; wkly rates. TV in some rms; cable. Pool.
Playground. Complimentary continental bkfst. Restaurant
nearby. Ck-out 11 am, ck-in after 3 pm. 18-hole golf privileges. Lawn games. Picnic tables, grills. Former boarding
house (ca 1900) for loggers and railroad workers. Cr cds:
A, DS, MC, V.
&️ ✈ 🎿 ➖ 🐾 SC

Waterville Valley

See also Lincoln/North Woodstock, Plymouth

Founded 1829 **Pop** 151 **Elev** 1,519 ft **Area code** 603
Zip 03215
Information Waterville Valley Region Chamber of
Commerce, RFD 1, Box 1067, Campton 03223;
603/726-3804 or 800/237-2307
Web www.watervillevalleyregion.com

Although the resort village of Waterville Valley was
developed in the late 1960s, the surrounding area has
been attracting tourists since the mid-19th century,
when summer vacationers stayed at the Waterville Inn.
Completely encircled by the White Mountain National
Forest, the resort, which is approximately 11 miles northeast of Campton, offers a variety of winter and summer
activities, as well as spectacular views of the surrounding
mountain peaks.

What to See and Do

Waterville Valley Ski Area. Three double, two triple chairlifts, two quad chairlift, T-bar, J-bar, four platter pulls;
patrol, school; retail, rental and repair shops; snowmaking;
restaurants, cafeterias, lounge; nursery. 52 ski trails; longest
run three mi; vertical drop 2,020 ft. Limited lift tickets;
Half-day rates. (Mid-Nov-mid-Apr, daily) Ski Touring
Center with 46 mi of cross-country trails; rentals, school,
restaurants. Summer facilities include nine-hole golf, 18
clay tennis courts, small boating, hiking, fishing, bicycling;
entertainment. Indoor sports center (daily). 11 mi NE of
Campton on NH 49. Contact Waterville Valley Resort,
Town Square. Phone 800/468-2553. ¢¢¢¢

Hotel

★★ **BLACK BEAR LODGE.** *3 Village Rd (03215).
603/236-4501; fax 603/236-4114; toll-free 800/349-2327.
www.black-bear-lodge.com.* 107 kit. suites, 78 A/C, 6 story.
Suites $89-$249; ski plans; higher rates hol wkends; lower
rates off-season. Crib free. TV; cable (premium). Indoor/
outdoor pool; whirlpool. Complimentary coffee in lobby.
Restaurant opp 8 am-9 pm. No rm serv. Ck-out 11 am.
Coin lndry. Meeting rms. Business servs avail. Downhill
ski 2 mi; x-country ski ½ mi. Sauna. Health club privileges. Game rm. Fieldstone fireplace in lobby. Near pond.
Cr cds: A, C, D, DS, JCB, MC, V.
🆔 ➤ 🐾 🔥 SC ➖

Resorts

★★★ **SNOWY OWL INN.** *4 Village Rd (03215).
603/236-8383; fax 603/236-4890; toll-free 800/766-9969.
www.snowyowlinn.com.* 83 rms, 4 story. No A/C. Dec-Mar:
S, D $75-$209; each addl $10; ski, golf, tennis plans; higher
rates hol ski wk; lower rates rest of yr. Crib free. TV; cable
(premium), VCR avail. Pool. Complimentary continental

bkfst; afternoon refreshments. Restaurant nearby. Ck-out 11 am. Coin lndry. Meeting rms. Business servs avail. Exercise rm. 9-hole golf privileges, greens fee $12-$18. Downhill ski 1 mi; x-country ski on site. Whirlpool. Rec rm. Health club privileges. Some in-rm whirlpools, mini-bars. Shopping arcade adj. Cr cds: A, D, DS, MC, V.

D 🐾 🖼 🍴 🎿 🏊 ➡ 🔥 🏃

★★ **VALLEY INN & TAVERN.** *1 Tecumseh Rd (03215). 603/236-8336; fax 603/236-4294; toll-free 800/343-0969. www.valleyinn.com.* 52 rms, 5 story (enter on 2nd level). Mid-Dec-Mar: S, D $100-$250; under 12 free; package plans; lower rates summer and fall. Crib $5. TV; cable. Indoor/outdoor pool; whirlpool. Complimentary continental bkfst. Dining rm 8-11 am, 6-10 pm. Rm serv. Bar 4 pm- 1 am; entertainment Fri, Sat (in season). Ck-out 11 am, ck-in 4 pm. Coin lndry. Meeting rms. Business servs avail. In-rm modem link. Tennis privileges, pro. 9-hole golf privileges, greens fee $8-$15, pro. Downhill/x-country ski 1 mi. Rec rm. Exercise equipt; sauna. Refrigerators, wet bars, in-rm whirlpools. Cr cds: A, C, D, DS, MC, V.

D 🐾 🖼 🍴 🎿 🏊 ➡ 🔥 🏃

Restaurants

★ **CHILE PEPPERS.** *Town Sq (03215). 603/236-4646.* Mexican, Amer menu. Specialties: barbecued ribs, chile rellenos, fajitas. Hrs: noon-9 pm; Fri, Sat noon-9:30 pm. No A/C. Bar. Lunch $3.95-$7.95, dinner $6.95-$13.95. Outdoor dining. View of mountains, Snows Brook waterfall. Cr cds: A, DS, MC, V.

D 🍽

★★ **WILLIAM TELL.** *Rte 49, Thornton (03223). 603/726-3618.* Swiss, Amer menu. Specializes in fresh seafood, venison, veal. Hrs: 5-10 pm; Sun brunch noon-3 pm. Closed Wed. Res accepted. Bar. Dinner $10.50-$20. Sun brunch $6.25-$9.50. Child's menu. Patio dining overlooking duck pond. Swiss atmosphere. Family-owned. Cr cds: A, DS, MC, V.

D

White Mountain National Forest

This national forest and major New Hampshire recreation area includes the Presidential Range and a major part of the White Mts. There are more than 100 miles of roads and 1,128 miles of foot trails. The Appalachian Trail, with eight hostels, winds over some spectacular peaks. Eight peaks tower more than a mile above sea level; the highest is Mount Washington (6,288 feet). 22 mountains rise more than 4,000 feet. There are several well-defined ranges, divided by deep "notches" and broader valleys. Clear streams rush through the notches; mountain lakes and ponds dot the landscape. Deer, bear, moose, and bobcat roam the wilds; trout fishing is good.

The US Forest Service administers 23 campgrounds with more than 700 sites ($12-$16/site/night), also picnicking sites for public use. There is lodging within the forest; for information, reservations contact the Appalachian Mountain Club, Pinkham Notch, Gorham 03581; 603/466-2727. There are also many resorts, campsites, picnicking, and recreational spots in private and state-owned areas. A visitor center (daily) is at the Saco Ranger Station, 33 Kancamagus Hwy, Conway 03818; 603/447-5448. Information stations are also located at exits 28 and 32 off I-93 and at Franconia Notch State Park Visitor Center. For further information contact the Supervisor, White Mountain National Forest, 719 N Main St, Laconia 03246; 603/528-8721.

The following cities and villages in and near the forest are included in the *Guide*: Bartlett, Bretton Woods, Franconia, Franconia Notch State Park, Gorham, Jackson, Lincoln/North Woodstock Area, Mount Washington, North Conway, Pinkham Notch, Twin Mountain, and Waterville Valley. For information on any of them, see the individual alphabetical listing.

Wolfeboro

See also Center Ossipee, Laconia

Settled 1760 **Pop** 4,807 **Elev** 573 ft **Area code** 603 **Zip** 03894

Information Chamber of Commerce, 312 Central Ave, PO Box 547; 603/569-2200 or 800/516-5324

Web www.wolfeboro.com-chamber

Wolfeboro has been a resort area for more than two centuries; it is the oldest summer resort in America. In the winter, it is a ski-touring center with 40 miles of groomed trails.

What to See and Do

Clark House. Wolfeboro Historical Society is housed in Clark family homestead (1778), a one-rm schoolhouse (ca 1820), and a firehouse museum. Clark House has period furnishings, memorabilia; firehouse museum contains restored firefighting equipment dating from 1842. (July-Aug, Mon-Sat) S Main St. Phone 603/569-4997. **Donation**

Lake Winnipesaukee cruises. (See LACONIA)

Wentworth State Park. On Lake Wentworth. Swimming; bathhouse. Picnicking. (Late June-Labor Day) Standard fees. 6 mi E on NH 109. Phone 603/569-3699.

Wright Museum. Showcases American enterprise during WWII. Collection of tanks, jeeps, and other military vehicles, period memorabilia. (Daily) 77 Center St. Phone 603/569-1212. ¢¢¢

Motels/Motor Lodges

★★ **LAKE MOTEL.** *280 S Main St (03894). 603/569-1100; fax 603/569-1620; toll-free 888/569-1110. www.thelakemotel.com.* 30 rms, 5 kit. units. July-Labor Day: S, D $89-$98; each addl $6; kit. units for 2, $630/wk; each addl $8; lower rates mid-May-June and after Labor Day-mid-Oct. Closed rest of yr. Pet accepted, some restrictions. TV; cable. Playground. Coffee in lobby. Restaurant adj 7:30 am-10 pm in summer. Ck-out 11 am. Business servs avail. Sundries. Tennis. Lawn games. On Crescent Lake; private beach, dockage. Cr cds: DS, MC, V.

[D] 🐾 🧆 🛏 🦞 🎿

★★ **LAKEVIEW INN & MOTOR LODGE.** *200 N Main St (03894). 603/569-1335; fax 603/569-9426. www.lakeviewinn.net.* 14 motel rms, 3 rms in inn, 2 story, 4 kits. July-Oct: S $80; D $90; each addl $5; kit. units $5 addl; lower rates rest of yr. Crib free. TV; cable. Complimentary continental bkfst. Complimentary coffee in rms. Restaurant 5-9 pm. Bar; entertainment Fri in season. Ck-out 11 am. Business servs avail. Some private patios, balconies. Inn built 1768 on king's land grant. Cr cds: A, MC, V.

[D] 🧆 🛏 🦞

★ **PINE VIEW LODGE.** *427 GWH Rte 109, Melvin Village (03850). 603/544-3800. www.newhampshirelodging.com.* 1 1 rms, showers only. No rm phones. July-Aug: S, D $49-$85; lower rates rest of yr. TV. Complimentary coffee in lobby. Restaurant (June-Sept) 7-11 am, 5-9 pm. Bar 5 pm-1 am. Ck-out 11 am. Downhill ski 10 mi; x-country ski 2 mi. Picnic tables. Overlooks lake. Cr cds: DS, MC, V.

[D] 🧆 🎿 🛏 🦞

B&B/Small Inn

★★★ **THE WOLFEBORO INN.** *90 N Main St (03894). 603/569-3016; fax 603/569-5375; res 800/451-2389. www.wolfeboroinn.com.* 44 rms, 3 story, 3 suites, 1 kit. unit. S, D $119-$129; suites $169-$219; kit. $200; under 8 free; wkly rates; higher rates hols. Crib $10. TV; cable, VCR avail. Complimentary continental bkfst. Dining rm 7 am-11:30 pm. Ck-out 11 am, ck-in 3 pm. Business servs avail. Valet serv. Sundries. Downhill ski 20 mi; x-country ski on site. Balconies. On Lake Winnipesaukee. Original bldg from 1812. Gardens. Cr cds: A, DS, MC, V.

[D] 🦞 🛏 🦞 **SC**

Cottage Colony

★★ **CLEARWATER LODGES.** *704 N Main St (03894). 603/569-2370; fax 603/569-4608.* 14 kit. cottages (1-2 bedrm). No A/C. No rm phones. July-Labor Day: cottages up to 2, $695/wk; cottages up to 4, $910/wk; each addl $85; daily rates; lower rates late May-late June and after Labor Day-late Sept. Closed rest of yr. Crib free. TV in rec rm. Ck-out 10 am, ck-in 3 pm. Business servs avail. Grocery, package store 3 mi. Private waterfront; boats, motors. Rec rm. Barbecue, picnic areas. Rustic cottages with fireplaces and porches in tall pines on Lake Winnipesaukee.

🧆 🦞

RHODE ISLAND

Giovanni da Verrazano, a Florentine navigator in the service of France, visited the Narragansett Bay of Rhode Island in 1524; however, it wasn't until 1636 that the first permanent white settlement was founded. Roger Williams, a religious refugee from Massachusetts, bought land at Providence from the Narragansetts. Williams fled what he considered puritanical tyranny and established a policy of religious and political freedom in his new settlement. Soon others began similar communities, and in 1663 King Charles II granted them a royal charter, officially creating the "State of Rhode Island and Providence Plantations."

Although the smallest state in the nation and smaller than many of the counties in the United States, Rhode Island is rich in American tradition. It is a state of firsts. Rhode Islanders were among the first colonists to take action against the British, attacking British vessels in its waters. On May 4, 1776, the state was the first to proclaim independence from Great Britain, two months before the Declaration of Independence was signed. In 1790 Samuel Slater's mill in Pawtucket became America's first successful water-powered cotton mill, and in 1876 polo was played for the first time in the United States in Newport.

Rhode Island has a tradition of manufacturing skill. The state produces machine tools, electronic equipment, plastics, textiles, jewelry, toys, and boats. The famous Rhode Island Red Hen was developed by farmers in Little Compton. Rhode Island is also for those who follow the sea. With more than 400 miles of coastline, visitors can swim, sail, fish, or relax in the many resort areas.

Population: 1,003,464
Area: 1,054 square miles
Elevation: 0-812 feet
Peak: Jerimoth Hill
  (Providence County)
Entered Union: Thirteenth
  of original thirteen states
  (May 29, 1790)
Capital: Providence
Motto: Hope
Nickname: Ocean State
Flower: Violet
Bird: Rhode Island Red Hen
Tree: Red Maple
Time Zone: Eastern
Website: www.visitrhodeisland.com

When to Go/Climate

The weather in Rhode Island is more moderate than in other parts of New England. Breezes off Narraganset Bay make summer humidity bearable and winter temperatures less bitter than elsewhere in the region.

AVERAGE HIGH/LOW TEMPERATURES (°F)
PROVIDENCE

Jan 37/19	**May** 67/47	**Sept** 74/54
Feb 38/21	**June** 77/57	**Oct** 64/43
Mar 46/29	**July** 82/63	**Nov** 53/35
Apr 57/38	**Aug** 81/62	**Dec** 41/24

Parks and Recreation Finder

Directions to and information about the parks and recreation areas below are given under their respective town/city sections. Please refer to those sections for details.

NATIONAL PARK AND RECREATION AREAS

Key to abbreviations. I.H.S. = International Historic Site; I.P.M. = International Peace Memorial; N.B. = National Battlefield; N.B.P. = National Battlefield Park; N.B.C. = National Battlefield and Cemetery; N.C.A. = National Conservation Area; N.E.M. = National Expansion Memorial; N.F. = National Forest; N.G. = National Grassland; N.H.P. = National Historical Park; N.H.C. = National Heritage Corridor; N.H.S. = National Historic Site; N.L. = National Lakeshore; N.M. = National Monument; N.M.P. = National Military Park; N.Mem. = National Memorial; N.P. = National Park; N.Pres. = National Preserve; N.R.A. = National Recreational Area; N.R.R. = National Recreational River; N.Riv. = National River; N.S. = National Seashore; N.S.R. = National Scenic Riverway; N.S.T. = National Scenic Trail; N.Sc. = National Scientific Reserve; N.V.M. = National Volcanic Monument.

CALENDAR HIGHLIGHTS

FEBRUARY

Newport Winter Festival (Newport). Ten days of food, festivities, music. More than 200 cultural and recreational events and activities. Phone 401/849-8048, 800/326-6030, or 401/847-7666.

Mid-winter New England Surfing Championship (Narragansett). Narragansett Town Beach. Phone the Eastern Surfing Association, 401/789-1954.

MAY

Gaspee Days (Warwick). Celebration of the capture and burning of British revenue schooner Gaspee by Rhode Island patriots; arts and crafts, concert, foot races, battle reenactment, muster of fife and drum corps, parade, contests. Phone Gaspee Days Committee, 401/781-1772.

JUNE

Spring Festival of Historic Houses (Providence). Sponsored by the Providence Preservation Society. Tours of selected private houses and gardens. Phone 401/831-7440.

JUNE-JULY

Newport Music Festival (Newport). Chamber and Romantic music, held in Newport's fabled mansions. Phone 401/847-7090.

JULY

Hot-Air Balloon Festival (Kingston). University of Rhode Island. Two-day event features hot-air balloon rides, parachute demonstrations, arts and crafts, music. Phone 401/783-1770.

Place Name	Listed Under
Roger Williams N. Mem.	PROVIDENCE

STATE PARK AND RECREATION AREAS

Key to abbreviations. I.P. = Interstate Park; S.A.P. = State Archaeological Park; S.B. = State Beach; S.C.A. = State Conservation Area; S.C.P. = State Conservation Park; S.Cp. = State Campground; S.F. = State Forest; S.G. = State Garden; S.H.A. = State Historic Area; S.H.P. = State Historic Park; S.H.S. = State Historic Site; S.M.P. = State Marine Park; S.N.A. = State Natural Area; S.P. = State Park; S.P.C. = State Public Campground; S.R. = State Reserve; S.R.A. = State Recreation Area; S.Res. = State Reservoir; S.Res.P. = State Resort Park; S.R.P. = State Rustic Park.

Place Name	Listed Under
Burlingame S.P.	CHARLESTOWN
Casimir Pulaski S.P.	GLOCESTER
Colt S.P.	BRISTOL
Fort Adams S.P.	NEWPORT
Goddard Memorial S.P.	EAST GREENWICH
Lincoln Woods S.P.	PROVIDENCE
Misquamicut S.B.	WESTERLY
Salty Brine Beach, Roger Wheeler Beach, and Scarborough Beach S.P.	NARRAGANSETT

Water-related activities, hiking, riding, various other sports, picnicking, and visitor centers, as well as camping, are available in many of these areas. State parks are open sunrise to sunset. Parking fee at beaches: weekdays, $6-$12/car; weekends, holidays, $7-$14/car. Camping $14-$20/night; with electric and water $18-$25; sewer $20-$25. No pets allowed. A map is available at the Division of Parks and Recreation, Department of Environmental Management, 2321 Hartford Avenue, Johnston 02919. Phone 401/222-2632.

FISHING AND HUNTING

No license is necessary for recreational saltwater game fishing. Freshwater fishing license: nonresident, $31; three-day tourists' fee, $16. Both largemouth bass and northern pike can be found in Worden Pond; trout can be found in Wood River.

Hunting license: nonresident, $41. Resident licenses and regulations may be obtained at city and town clerks' offices and at most sporting goods shops. Nonresident licenses may be obtained by contacting DEM-Licensing, 235 Promenade St, Providence 02908; 401/222-3576. For further information write Division of Fish and Wildlife, Department of Environment Management, Government Center, Wakefield 02879. Phone 401/789-3094.

Driving Information

Children ages 4-12 must be in an approved passenger restraint anywhere in vehicle; age three and under must use an approved safety seat. For further information phone Governor's Office of Highway Safety 401/222-3024.

INTERSTATE HIGHWAY SYSTEM

The following alphabetical listing of Rhode Island towns in *RoadMaster™ Drive USA Travel Guide* shows that these cities are within ten miles of the indicated Interstate highway. A highway map, however, should be checked for the nearest exit.

Highway Number	Cities/Towns within ten miles
Interstate 95	East Greenwich, Pawtucket, Providence, Warwick, Westerly.

Additional Visitor Information

Contact the Rhode Island Economic Development Corporation Division of Marketing and Communications, 1 W Exchange St, Providence 02903; 401/222-2601 or 800/556-2484. The *Providence Journal-Bulletin Almanac* is an excellent state reference book and may be obtained from the Providence *Journal*, 75 Fountain St, Providence 02902.

There are several information centers in Rhode Island; visitors will find information and brochures most helpful in planning stops at points of interest. Visitor centers are located off I-95 in Richmond (daily) and seven miles south of Providence in Warwick, at T. F. Green Airport.

THE ROAD LESS TRAVELED

Newport and South County are the shoreline destinations that most people head for when they visit Rhode Island. As a result, both areas become clogged with traffic and tourists during the summer. But Rhode Island has a quiet, eastern coast along its border with Massachusetts that is an ideal area for a daytrip. The drive to the coastal towns of Tiverton and Little Compton takes about 50 minutes from Providence and passes through the attractive harbor town of Bristol, which is on Narragansett Bay. From downtown Providence, take Route 195 east to exit 7, Route 114 south. Stay on this highway through Barrington, Warren, and Bristol. (In Warren, you may want to stop for the dozens of antique and second-hand shops that line Main and Water streets.) Route 114 (Main Street in Warren) becomes Hope Street in Bristol, and here you'll be charmed by the many elegant Federal-era houses (some of them bed-and-breakfast inns) that show how wealthy this town was in the period before the Civil War. South of the town, a turn-of-the-century mansion and estate called Blithewold is open to the public for tours.

Drive over the Mount Hope Bridge into the Aquidneck Island town of Portsmouth. You won't see much of this town, however, as you turn left onto Route 24 to cross the Sakonnet River Bridge into Tiverton. Turn right onto Route 77 south, and stay on this road through Tiverton and Little Compton. (Route 77 ends rather ignominiously in a parking lot with a view of the ocean at Sakonnet Point in Little Compton.) There's only one traffic light along the length of Route 77, at the intersection with Route 179, an area known as Tiverton Four Corners. In this vicinity, you'll find some delightful shops, including a gourmet take-out place where you can pick up food for a picnic and Gray's Ice Cream, which has been making dozens of homemade flavors at this spot since the 1920s. Continuing south on Route 77, you'll pass open farmland with lovely vistas of Narragansett Bay. Little Compton is a wealthy summer community, so there's very little commerce in town, and you'll see old farmhouses that are now used as summer homes.

You can return by the same route, or turn right onto Route 24 north in Tiverton to drive into Fall River, MA, then head west back to Providence on Route 195. **(APPROX 40 MI)**

Block Island

See also Newport, Westerly

(By ferry from Providence, Newport, and Point Judith; by air from Westerly. Also by ferry from New London, CT, and Montauk, Long Island.)

Settled 1661 **Pop** 620 **Elev** 9 ft **Area code** 401 **Zip** 02807
Information Chamber of Commerce, Water St PO Drawer D; 401/466-2982 or 800/383-2474
Web www.blockislandchamber.com

Block Island, Rhode Island's "air-conditioned" summer resort, covers 21 square miles. Lying 12 miles out to sea from Point Judith, it received its nickname because it is 10 to15 degrees cooler than the mainland in summer and consistently milder in winter. Although Verrazano saw the island in 1524, it was named for the Dutch explorer Adriaen Block, who landed here in 1614. Until the resort trade developed, this island community was devoted to fishing and farming. Settler's Rock on Corn Neck Road displays plaques on the boulder listing the first settlers.

In recent years Block Island has become a favorite "nature retreat" for people seeking to escape fast-paced city living. More than 40 rare and endangered species of plants and animals can be found on the island, of which ¼ is in public trust. The Nature Conservancy has designated Block Island as "one of the 12 last great places in the Western Hemisphere."

What to See and Do

Ferry service. Phone 401/783-4613.
  Block Island/Montauk, Long Island. (Mid-June-Labor Day, one trip daily) Phone 516/668-5009.
  Block Island/New London, CT. Two-hr trip. (Mid-June-Labor Day, one trip daily, extra trips Fri)
  Block Island/Point Judith. Advance res for vehicles; all vehicles must be on pier 45 min before sailing. (Mid-June-mid-Sept, eight round trips daily; early May-mid-June, mid-Sept-Oct, four round trips daily; rest of yr, one round trip daily)
  Block Island/Providence, RI/Newport, RI. Departs from either Providence or Newport. (Late June-Labor Day, one trip daily) Nonvehicular ferry.

Fishing. Surf casting from most beaches; freshwater ponds for bass, pickerel, perch; deep-sea boat trips for tuna, swordfish, etc, from Old Harbor.

Fred Benson Town Beach. Swimming, bathhouse, lifeguards; picnicking, concession. Parking. ½ mi N to Crescent Beach.

Natural formations. Mohegan Bluffs. West of Southeast Light lighthouse off Mohegan Trail, are 185-ft clay cliffs that offer a fine sea view. **New Harbor,** 1 mi W on Ocean Ave, is a huge marina made by cutting through sand bar into Great Salt Pond.

New England Airlines. Twelve-min scheduled flights between Westerly State Airport and Block Island State Airport; also air taxi and charter service to all points. (Daily) Phone 401/466-5881, 401/596-2460, or 800/243-2460.

North Light. Lighthouse built 1867 at tip of island near Settler's Rock, now houses maritime museum. Bordering dunes are seagull rookery and wildlife sanctuary.

Motel/Motor Lodge

★★ **SURF MOTEL.** *Dodge St PO Box C (02807). 401/466-2241.* 47 rms, 44 share bath, 4 story. No A/C. No rm phones. Late June-early Sept: S $55-$77; D $70-$99; each addl $15; wkly, wkend rates; wkends, hols (2-day min); lower rates early Sept-Oct, May-late June. Closed rest of yr. Crib $10-$15. TV in lobby. Complimentary continental bkfst. Restaurant nearby. Ck-out 11 am. Free airport transportation. Lawn games. Refrigerators avail. Grills. On ocean. Wrap-around porch. Cr cds: DS, MC, V.
⬛⬛⬛⬛

Hotel

★★ **SPRING HOUSE.** *52 Spring St (02807). 401/466-5844; fax 401/466-2633; toll-free 800/234-9263. www.springhousehotel.com.* 49 rms, most with shower only, 3 story, 14 suites. No A/C. Mid-June-early Sept: S $149-$250; D $200-$255; each addl $20; suites $175-$250; under 12 free; wkly, wkend rates; 2-day min wkends, 3-day min hols; lower rates early Sept-Oct, May-mid-June. Closed rest of yr. Crib free. Playground. Complimentary continental bkfst. Restaurant noon-4 pm, 6-10 pm. Bar 6 pm-12:30 am. Ck-out 11 am. Meeting rms. Free airport transportation. Lawn games. On ocean. Cr cds: A, MC, V.
⬛⬛⬛

B&B/Small Inn

★★★ **THE 1661 INN & GUEST HOUSE.** *1 Spring St (02807). 401/466-2421; fax 401/466-3162; toll-free 800/626-4773. www.blockisland.com/biresorts.* 21 units, 17 with shower only, 4 share bath, 2 story, 2 suites, 2 kit. units. No A/C. Many rm phones. July-Sept: S, D $115-$248; suites $229-$325; kit. units $250; wkend rates; 3-day min wkends and hols; lower rates rest of yr. Crib free. Some cable TVs; VCR avail. Playground, petting zoo. Complimentary coffee in rms. Complimentary full bkfst; afternoon refreshments. Restaurant nearby. Ck-out 11 am, ck-in 1 pm. Luggage handling. Free airport transportation. Tennis. Lawn games. Refrigerators. Sun decks. Picnic tables. On ocean. Built 1890; restored Colonial with Early American art and antiques. Cr cds: MC, V.
⬛⬛⬛⬛⬛⬛

Restaurants

★★ **FINN'S SEAFOOD.** *Water St (02807). 401/466-2473.* Specializes in seafood, lobster. Hrs: 11:30 am-10 pm; Fri, Sat to 11 pm. Closed Nov-Apr. No A/C. Bar. A la carte entrees: lunch, dinner $4.80-$34.50. Outdoor dining. View of town and harbor. Cr cds: A, MC, V.
⬛⬛

★★★ **HOTEL MANISSES DINING ROOM.** *One Spring St (02807).* 401/466-2836. *www.blockisland.com/biresorts.* Continental menu. Hrs: 5:30-10 pm; Sat, Sun from 11:30 am. Closed Mon-Fri mid-Feb-Apr; also Dec-mid-Feb. No A/C. Bar. Wine cellar. Lunch $9-$21, dinner $15-$25. Prix fixe: dinner $29-$39. Child's menu. Outdoor dining. Stone-walled dining rm and glass-enclosed garden rm. Totally nonsmoking. Cr cds: A, MC, V.

D ⊟

★★ **MOHEGAN CAFE.** *Water St (02807).* 401/466-5911. Specializes in seafood. Hrs: 11 am-10:30 pm; Jan-Mar Sat and Sun 11 am-9 pm; Oct-Dec, Apr hrs vary. Closed Thanksgiving, Dec 25. Bar. Lunch $3.95-$9.95, dinner $8.95-$18.95. Child's menu. Panoramic view of Old Harbor. Cr cds: A, DS, MC, V.

⊟

Bristol

See also Portsmouth, Providence

Settled 1669 **Pop** 21,625 **Elev** 50 ft **Area code** 401 **Zip** 02809

Information East Bay County Chamber of Commerce, 654 Metacom Ave, PO Box 250, Warren 02885-0250; 401/245-0750

Web www.eastbaychamber.org

King Philip's War (1675-1676) began and ended on the Bristol peninsula between Mount Hope and Narragansett bays; King Philip, the Native American rebel leader, head-quartered the Wampanoag tribe in the area. After the war ended, Bristol grew into an important port, and by the turn of the 18th century the town was the fourth busiest port in the United States. Bristol was the home of General Ambrose Burnside, Civil War officer and sometime governor and senator. The town was the site of the famous Herreshoff Boatyard, where many America's Cup winners were built. Roger Williams University (1948) is located in Bristol.

What to See and Do

Blithewold Mansion and Gardens. Former turn-of-the-century summer estate; 45-rm mansion surrounded by 33 acres of landscaped grounds; many exotic trees and shrubs incl a giant sequoia. Grounds (open all yr; fee). Mansion and grounds tour (Apr-Oct, Tues-Sun; closed hols). 2 mi S on RI 114 (Ferry Rd); on Bristol Harbor overlooking Narragansett Bay. Phone 401/253-2707. ¢¢¢

Colt State Park. Three-mi scenic drive around shoreline of former Colt family estate on east side of Narragansett Bay. Fishing, boating; hiking and bridle trails, picnicking. 2½ mi NW off RI 114. ¢ In park is

Coggeshall Farm Museum. Working farm from 18th-19th century; vegetables, herbs, animals; Colonial craft demonstrations. (Tues-Sun; closed Jan) (See SPECIAL EVENTS) Phone 401/253-9062. ¢¢

Haffenreffer Museum of Anthropology. Brown University museum features Native American objects from North, Central, and South America; Eskimo collections; African and Pacific tribal arts. (June-Aug, Tues-Sun; rest of yr, Sat and Sun) 1 mi E of Metacom Ave, RI 136, follow signs; overlooks Mt Hope Bay. Phone 401/253-8388. ¢

Herreshoff Marine Museum. Herreshoff Manufacturing Company produced some of America's greatest yachts, incl eight winners of the America's Cup. Exhibits incl yachts manufactured by Herreshoff, steam engines, fittings; photographs and memorabilia from "golden age of yachting." (May-Oct, Mon-Fri afternoons; also Sat and Sun, limited hrs) 7 Burnside St. Phone 401/253-5000. ¢¢

Hope Street. Famous row of Colonial houses. On RI 114.

Prudence Island. Ferry from Church St dock.

Special Events

Blithewold Mansion and Gardens. Concerts. Phone 401/253-2707. June-Aug.

Colt State Park. Concerts in Stone Barn. Sun and Wed, early July-Aug. Phone 401/253-7482.

Harvest Fair. Coggeshall Farm Museum. Wkend mid-Sept. Phone 401/253-9062.

Motel/Motor Lodge

★ **KING PHILIP INN.** *400 Metacom Ave (02809).* 401/253-7600; fax 401/253-1857; toll-free 800/253-7610. 33 rms. Mid-May-mid-Oct: S, D $60-$79; each addl $5; under 12 free; higher rates special events; lower rates rest of yr. Crib free. TV; VCR avail. Restaurant 6-11 am, Sat-Sun 7 am-1 pm. Ck-out 11 am. Meeting rms. Business servs avail. Refrigerators. Cr cds: A, DS, MC, V.

D ⊡ ⧉ �’ ➦

B&Bs/Small Inns

★★★ **ROCKWELL HOUSE INN.** *610 Hope St (02809).* 401/253-0040; fax 401/253-1811. *www.rockwellhouseinn.com.* 4 rms, 1 with shower only, 2 story. No A/C. No rm phones. May-Oct: S $100-$135; D $125-$145; each addl $25; wkday rates; wkends, hols (2-day min); higher rates July 4th; lower rates rest of yr. Children over 12 yrs only. TV in parlor; VCR. Complimentary full bkfst. Restaurant nearby. Ck-out 11 am, ck-in noon-8 pm. Concierge serv. Luggage handling. Business servs avail. Lawn games. Refrigerator avail. Picnic tables. Federal-style house (circa 1809); fireplaces, hand stenciling in many rms. Cr cds: A, DS, MC, V.

⧉ ➥ �’ ➦

★ **WILLIAMS GRANT INN.** *154 High St (02809).* 401/253-4222; fax 401/254-0986; toll-free 800/596-4222. 5 rms, 2 share bath, 2 story. No A/C. No rm phones. May-Oct: S, D $85-$125; wkly rates; wkends, hols (2-day min); lower rates rest of yr. Children over 12 yrs only. Complimentary coffee in rms. Complimentary full bkfst. Restaurant nearby. Ck-out 11 am, ck-in noon-10 pm. Luggage handling. House built 1808; original fireplaces, artwork, many antiques. Totally nonsmoking. Cr cds: A, DS, MC, V.

⧉ �’ ➦

Restaurants

★★ **LOBSTER POT.** *119-121 Hope St (02809). 401/253-9100.* Specializes in lobster, seafood. Hrs: noon-9 pm. Closed Mon. Bar. Lunch $4.75-$12.95, dinner $7.75-$23.95. Child's menu. Pianist wkends. On waterfront; view of harbor. Family-owned. Cr cds: A, MC, V.

D ⊷

★★ **NATHANIEL PORTER INN.** *125 Water St, Warren (02885). 401/245-6622. www.nathanielporterinn.com.* Specialties: filet with bernaise sauce, seafood. Hrs: 5-9 pm; Sun 4-8 pm; Sun brunch 10:30 am-2 pm. Res accepted. Bar. Dinner $12.95-$21.95. Child's menu. House built 1795; Colonial decor, antiques. Guest rms avail. Cr cds: A, D, DS, MC, V.

⊷

Charlestown

See also Narragansett, Westerly

Pop 6,478 **Elev** 20 ft **Area code** 401 **Zip** 02813
Information Chamber of Commerce, 4945 Old Post Rd; 401/364-3878
Web www.cshell.com/ccc

Charlestown, named for King Charles II of England, was originally called Cross Mills for two gristmills that once stood here. Charlestown was first settled along the coast by summer residents and by permanent residents after World War II. The town's past can be seen in Fort Ninigret, the historic Native American church, and the Royal Indian Burial Ground.

What to See and Do

Burlingame State Park. More than 2,000 acres with wooded area. Swimming, lifeguard, fishing, boating; picnicking, concession. Tent and trailer camping (mid-Apr-Oct). Standard fees. 2 mi SW via US 1, Kings Factory Rd. Phone 401/322-7337.

Kimball Wildlife Refuge. Thirty-acre refuge on south shore of Watchaug Pond has nature trails and programs. 2½ mi SW on US 1, Windswept Farm exit, left onto Montauk Rd.

Swimming, fishing. At several Block Island Sound beaches; S of US 1 on Charlestown Beach Rd; Green Hill Rd; Moonstone Rd.

Special Events

Theatre-by-the-Sea. Historic barn theater (1933) presents professionally staged musicals. Restaurant, bar, cabaret. Tues-Sun eves; matinees Thurs; children's shows July-Aug, Fri only. 7 mi NE via US 1, then S off Matunuck Beach Rd exit to Cards Pond Rd in Matunuck. Contact 364 Cards Pond Rd, Matunuck 02879; phone 401/782-8587. June-Sept.

Seafood Festival. Seafood vendors, amateur seafood cook-off, helicopter rides, antique car show. Phone 401/364-3878. First Sat and Sun Aug.

August Meeting of the Narragansett Indian Tribe. Narragansett Indian church grounds. Dancing, music, storytelling. Said to be oldest continuous meeting in the country. Phone 401/364-1101. Second wk in Aug.

East Greenwich

See also Warwick

Pop 11,865 **Elev** 64 ft **Area code** 401 **Zip** 02818
Information Chamber of Commerce, 591 Main St; 401/885-0020
Web www.eastgreenwichchamber.com

Sometimes referred to as "the town on four hills," East Greenwich, on Narragansett Bay, is a sports and yachting center. Nathanael Greene and James M. Varnum organized the Kentish Guards, who protected the town during the Revolution, here in 1774. The Guards are still active today.

What to See and Do

Goddard Memorial State Park. Approx 490 acres with swimming at Greenwich Bay Beach (bathhouse), fishing, boating; bridle trails, nine-hole golf (fee), ice-skating, picnicking, concessions, playing fields. and fireplaces (fee). East side of Greenwich Cove, east of town via Forge Rd and Ives Rd. Phone 401/884-2010. ¢

Kentish Guards Armory. (1843) Headquarters of the Kentish Guards, local militia chartered in 1774 and still active; General Nathanael Greene was a charter member. (By appt only) 92 Pierce St. Phone 401/821-1628. ¢

Old Kent County Court House. (1750) Remodeled in 1909 and 1995. 125 Main St. Phone 401/886-8606.

Varnum House Museum. (1773) Mansion of Revolutionary War officer and lawyer; period furnishings, Colonial items, gardens. (June-Sept, by appt) 57 Pierce St. Phone 401/884-4110. ¢

Varnum Memorial Armory and Military Museum. (1913) Museum displays uniforms and armaments from the Revolutionary through the Vietnam Wars. (By appt) 6 Main St. Phone 401/884-4110. **Donation**

Glocester

Pop 5,011 **Elev** 422 ft **Area code** 401 **Zip** 02859
Information Blackstone Valley Tourism Council, 171 Main St, Pawtucket 02860; 401/724-2200 or 800/454-2882 (outside RI)

What to See and Do

Brown & Hopkins Country Store. (1799) Nation's oldest continuously operating country store; inside are antiques, gourmet food, penny candy, and a cafe. (Wed-Sun; closed hols) 3 mi SE on RI 100 to US 44 (Main St) in Chepachet. Phone 401/568-4830.

Casimir Pulaski State Park. Park has 100 acres with lake. Swimming beach; x-country skiing, picnicking. Pavilion (res). (Late May-early Sept) 3 mi SE on RI 100, 6 mi W on US 44. Phone 401/568-2085.

George Washington State Campground. Swimming beach, fishing, boating; hiking trail, picnicking, camping (no fires). Standard fees. (Mid-Apr-mid-Oct) 3 mi SE on RI 100, 4 mi W on US 44. Phone 401/568-2013. ¢

Jamestown

See also Newport

Settled ca 1670 **Pop** 4,999 **Elev** 8 ft **Area code** 401 **Zip** 02835
Information Jamestown Chamber of Commerce, PO Box 35; 401/423-3650
Web www.jamestownri.com

Jamestown is centered around the Jamestown Ferry landing, but technically the town also includes all of Conanicut—one of three main islands in Narragansett Bay. The island is connected by bridges to Newport on the east (toll) and to the mainland on the west (free). While much of Jamestown was burned by the British in 1775, some old houses do remain.

The restored Conanicut Battery, a Revolutionary redoubt two miles south on Beavertail Road, is open to the public and is the second-highest point on the island.

What to See and Do

Fishing. Striped bass, tuna, flounder, bluefish. For boat charter inquire at East Ferry slip.

Jamestown Museum. Photos and displays pertain to town and old Jamestown ferries. (Late June-Labor Day, Tues-Sat afternoons) 92 Narragansett Ave. Phone 401/423-3771. **Donation** The Jamestown Historical Society also maintains the

Old Windmill. (1787) Restored to working order. (Mid-June-mid-Sept, Sat and Sun afternoons) 1½ mi N on North Rd. Phone 401/423-1798. **Donation**

Sydney L. Wright Museum. Exhibits of Native American and early Colonial artifacts from Conanicut Island. (Mon-Sat) 26 North Rd, located in the library. Phone 401/423-7280.

Watson Farm. (1796) This 280-acre farm on Conanicut Island is being worked as a typical New England farm. Self-guided tour of farm and pastures with focus on land-use history. (June-mid-Oct, Tues, Thurs, and Sun, afternoons) North Rd, S of RI 138. Phone 401/423-0005. ¢¢

B&B/Small Inn

★★ **THE BAY VOYAGE.** *150 Conanicus Ave (02835). 401/423-2100; fax 401/423-3209; res 800/225-3522. www.equivest.com.* 32 kit. suites, 3 story. May-Sept: S, D $165-$235; wkly rates; lower rates rest of yr. Crib $15. TV; cable (premium). Pool; whirlpool. Complimentary coffee. Dining rm 6-10 pm; closed Sun, Mon off-season. Ck-out 11 am, ck-in 4 pm. Sauna. Balconies. On Narragansett Bay. Cr cds: A, DS, MC, V.
🏊 🔥

Kingston

See also Narragansett, Newport, North Kingstown

Pop 6,504 **Elev** 242 ft **Area code** 401 **Zip** 02881
Information Chamber of Commerce, 328 Main St, PO Box 289, Wakefield 02880; 401/783-2801; or the South County Tourism Council, Stedman Government Center, 4808 Tower Hill Rd, Wakefield 02879; 401/789-4422 or 800/548-4662
Web www.southcountyri.com

Known as Little Rest until 1825, Kingston was once forestland bought from the Narragansett. Early settlers were farmers who built a water-powered mill in an area still known as Biscuit City. Here, the state constitution was ratified, and a law was passed abolishing slavery in the state. Kingston overlooks a fertile flood plain, which geologists believe was an ancient river. Kingston is also the home of the University of Rhode Island.

What to See and Do

Helme House. (1802) Gallery of the South County Art Association. (Wed-Sun) Kingstown Rd. Phone 401/783-2195. **FREE**

Kingston Library. (1776) Visited by George Washington and Benjamin Franklin, this building housed the Rhode Island General Assembly at the time the British occupied Newport. (Mon-Sat) Kingstown Rd. Phone 401/783-8254.

Museum of Primitive Art and Culture. In 1856 post office building; prehistoric artifacts from New England, North America, South Seas, Africa, Europe, and Asia. (Tues-Thurs; limited hrs; also by appt) 2 mi S via RI 108 in Peace Dale at 1058 Kingstown Rd. Phone 401/783-5711. **Donation**

***Night Heron* Nature Cruises.** Offers snorkeling, nature, sunrise, sunset, and undersea nightlife cruises. Each cruise offers two or more departures daily. Phone 401/783-9977.

Special Event

Hot-Air Balloon Festival. University of Rhode Island. Two-day event features hot-air balloon rides, parachute demonstrations, arts and crafts, music. Phone 401/783-1770. Late July or early Aug.

Motel/Motor Lodge

★★ **HOLIDAY INN.** *3009 Tower Hill Rd, Saunderstown (02874). 401/789-1051; fax 401/789-0080. www.holiday-inn.com.* 105 rms, 4 story. May-Oct: S, D $75-$150; each addl $10; under 18 free; lower rates rest of yr. Crib free. TV; cable (premium). Pool; lifeguard. Bar 4 pm-1 am. Ck-out 11 am. Meeting rms. Business servs avail. In-rm modem link. Cr cds: A, C, D, DS, MC, V.

B&B/Small Inn

★★ **LARCHWOOD INN.** *521 Main St, Wakefield (02879). 401/783-5454; fax 401/783-1800; toll-free 800/275-5450. www.xpos.com/larchwoodinn.* 18 rms, 12 with bath, 3 story. Some A/C. Some rm phones. S, D $90-$140; each addl $10. Crib $10. Pet accepted; $5. TV in sitting rm. Restaurant (see LARCHWOOD INN). Bar 11-1 am; entertainment. Ck-out, ck-in noon. Meeting rms. Business servs avail. Private patio. Built 1831. Cr cds: A, C, D, DS, MC, V.

Restaurant

★★ **LARCHWOOD INN.** *521 Main St, Wakefield (02879). 401/783-5454. www.xpos.com/larchwoodinn.* Specializes in prime rib, seafood. Hrs: 7:30 am-2:30 pm, 5:30-9 pm; wkends to 10 pm; early-bird dinner Mon-Fri 5:30-6:30 pm. Res accepted. Bar 11-1 am. A la carte entrees: bkfst $1.50-$7, lunch $4-$9, dinner $8.95-$13.95. Complete meals: bkfst $2.95-$6.95, lunch $3.95-$6.75, dinner $4.50-$13.95. Country inn. Scottish decor. Family-owned. Cr cds: A, D, DS, MC, V.

Little Compton

See also Portsmouth

Pop 3,339 **Area code** 401 **Zip** 02837
Information Town Hall, PO Box 523, phone; 401/635-4400; or the Newport County Convention and Visitors Bureau, 23 America's Cup Ave, Newport 02840, phone 401/849-8048 or 800/976-5122
Web www.gonewport.com

In Little Compton's old burial ground lie the remains of the first white woman born in New England, Elizabeth Alden Pabodie, the daughter of John and Priscilla Alden.

What to See and Do

Gray's Store (1788). First post office in area (1804) features antique soda fountain, wheeled cheese, candy and tobacco cases. (Daily; closed Sun and hols in winter) 4 Main St in Adamsville, 7 mi NE on local road. Phone 401/635-4566.

Sakonnet Point. Swimming beaches, fishing. Harbor with lighthouse. W Main Rd.

Sakonnet Vineyards. Tour of winery and vineyard. Wine tasting (daily). 162 W Main Rd. Phone 401/635-8486. **FREE**

Wilbor House. (1680) Seventeenth-century house with 18th- and 19th-century additions was restored in 1956 by local historical society; period furnishings, antique farm and household implements. Display of carriages and sleighs in 1860 barn. Also one-rm schoolhouse, artist's studio. (Mid-June-mid-Sept, Wed-Sun, also by appt) 1 mi S on RI 77 at West Rd. Phone 401/635-4035. ¢¢

Narragansett

See also Block Island, Kingston, Newport

Settled 1675 **Pop** 14,985 **Elev** 20 ft **Area code** 401
Zip 02882
Information Narragansett Chamber of Commerce, The Towers Narragansett Visitors Center Ocean Rd; 401/783-7121
Web www.narragansettri.com/chamber

Part of the township of South Kingstown until 1901, Narragansett was named after the indigenous people who sold their land to the first area settlers. Once a center for shipbuilding, the town's center is still referred to as Narragansett Pier. Between 1878-1920 Narragansett was a well-known, elegant summer resort with many fine "cottages" and hotels. The most prominent landmark of that time was the Narragansett Casino. The casino's main entrance and covered promenade, "the Towers" on Ocean Road, is the only surviving element of that complex; the rest was lost in a devastating fire in 1900. Today Narragansett's most important industries are commercial fishing and tourism. It is also the home of the University of Rhode Island's renowned Graduate School of Oceanography, located at the Bay Campus on South Ferry Road.

What to See and Do

Block Island Ferry. Automobile ferries to Block Island from Point Judith and New London, CT. (Summer, daily) 5 mi S on Ocean Rd, 1 mi W on Sand Hill Cove Rd. Phone 401/783-4613.

Fishing. Wide variety of liveries at Narragansett Pier and the waterfront villages of Jerusalem, opp side of the Point Judith Pond entrance, and Jerusalem, west of Point Judith. Fishing tournaments are held throughout summer.

Point Judith. Fine sea view. 6 mi S of center on Ocean Ave, to Coast Guard Station and Lighthouse. Phone 401/789-0444.

South County Museum. Antiques representing rural life in 19th-century Rhode Island; costumes, vehicles, and nautical equipment. Farm and blacksmithing displays; toys. Country kitchen, general store, cobbler's shop. Also complete turn-of-the-century letterpress print shop. (May-Oct, Wed-Sun) Located on Canonchet Farm, Boston Neck Rd (RI 1A). Phone 401/783-5400. ¢¢

Swimming. Public beaches at **Narragansett Pier,** pavilion, fees; **Scarborough State Beach,** 1½ mi S on Ocean Ave. **Salty Brine Beach,** Ocean Ave, protected by seawall, fishing; **Roger Wheeler State Beach,** west of Point Judith, playground, picnic tables, concession; parking (fee). Similar facilities at other beaches.

❌ **The Towers.** This Romanesque entrance arch flanked by rounded, conical-topped towers is a grandiose and sad reminder of McKim, Mead, and White's 19th-century casino, destroyed by fire in 1900, and Narragansett's own past as summer mecca for the rich and fashionable. Today the Tourist and Information Center is located here. ¼ mi S on US 1.

Special Event

Mid-winter New England Surfing Championship. Narragansett Town Beach. For information contact the Eastern Surfing Association, 126 Sayles Ave, Pawtucket, 02860. Phone 401/789-1954. Third Sat Feb.

Motel/Motor Lodge

★★ **VILLAGE INN.** *1 Beach St (02882). 401/783-6767; fax 401/782-2220.* 62 rms, 3 story. Mid-June-Labor Day: S $100-$120; D $115-$168; each addl $10; under 12 free; higher rates some hols; lower rates rest of yr. TV; cable, VCR. Indoor pool; whirlpool, lifeguard. Restaurant 6 am-10 pm; Sat to 11 pm. Bar noon-1 am. Ck-out 11 am. Meeting rms. Business servs avail. Some balconies. Opp ocean; beach. Cr cds: A, DS, MC, V.

🄳 ⊶ ⊠ 🖐

Restaurant

★★ **COAST GUARD HOUSE.** *40 Ocean Rd (02882). 401/789-0700. www.thecoastguardhouse.com.* Continental menu. Specializes in seafood, prime rib, swordfish. Hrs: 11:30 am-3 pm, 5-9 pm; Fri-Sun to 11 pm; Sun brunch 10 am-2 pm, 4-9 pm. Closed Dec 24, 25. Bar 11:30-1 am; Sun from noon. Lunch $6-$10, dinner $13-$20. Sun brunch $13.95. Child's menu. Outdoor dining. Former Coast Guard station (1888); ocean view. Cr cds: A, D, DS, MC, V.

🄳 ⊷

Newport

See also Jamestown, Portsmouth

Founded 1639 **Pop** 28,227 **Elev** 96 ft **Area code** 401 **Zip** 02840

Information Newport County Convention & Visitors Bureau, 23 America's Cup Ave; 401/849-8048 or 800/976-5122

Web www.gonewport.com

Few cities in the country have a history as rich and colorful as that of Newport, and fewer still retain as much evidence of their great past. The town was founded by a group of men and women who fled the religious intolerance of Massachusetts. They established the first school in Rhode Island the following year. Shipbuilding, for which Newport is still famous, began in 1646. The first Quakers to come to the New World settled in Newport in 1657. They were followed in 1658 by 15 Jewish families who came here from Holland. Newport produced the state's first newspaper, the *Rhode Island Gazette.*

Newport took an active part in the Revolution; local residents set fire to one British ship and continued to fire on others until the British landed 9,000 men and took possession. The city was occupied for two years; it was not until the French fleet entered the harbor that the British withdrew their forces.

Newport's fame as a summer resort began after the Civil War when many wealthy families, including the August Belmonts, Ward McAllister, Harry Lehr, Mrs William Astor, and Mrs Stuyvesant Fish, made the town a center for lavish and sometimes outrageous social events. Parties for dogs and one for a monkey were among the more bizarre occasions. Hostesses spent as much as $300,000 a season entertaining their guests. Although less flamboyant than it was before World War I, the summer colony is still socially prominent.

Today Newport is famous for its boating and yachting, with boats for hire at many wharves. A bridge (toll) connects the city with Jamestown to the west.

Additional Visitor Information

The Newport County Convention and Visitor's Bureau maintains an information center at 23 America's Cup Avenue (daily). Tickets to most tourist attractions are offered for sale. An eight-minute video, maps, general tourist information and group tours and convention information are available. For further information phone 401/849-8048 or 800/976-5122.

The Preservation Society of Newport County publishes material on all Society properties. It sells combination tickets at all buildings under its administration and provides sightseeing information. Phone 401/847-1000.

What to See and Do

Artillery Company of Newport Military Museum. Military dress of many nations and periods. (June-Sept, Wed-Sat, also Sun afternoons; rest of yr, by appt) 23 Clarke St. Phone 401/846-8488. ¢¢

Brick Market. Home of the Newport Historical Society. Built by Peter Harrison, architect of Touro Synagogue, in 1762 as a market and granary. The restored building and surrounding area house boutiques and restaurants. (Daily) Long Wharf and Thames St. Phone 401/846-0813.

CCInc Auto Tape Tours. This 90-min cassette offers a mi-by-mi self-guided tour of Newport. Avail at Paper Lion, Long Wharf Mall, and Gateway Visitor Information Center (next to Marriott Hotel). Incl tape and recorder rental. Tape also may be purchased directly from CCInc, PO Box 227, 2 Elbrook Dr, Allendale, NJ 07401. Phone 201/236-1666. ¢¢¢

✪ **Cliff Walk.** Scenic walk overlooking Atlantic Ocean adjoins many Newport "cottages." Designated a National Recreational Trail in 1975. Begins at Memorial Blvd. **FREE**

Fort Adams State Park. Park surrounds Fort Adams, the second-largest bastioned fort in the US between 1799 and 1945. The rambling 21-acre fort, constructed of stone over a 33-yr period, is closed due to unsafe conditions; park remains open. Beach swimming, fishing, boating (launch, ramps, hoist); soccer and rugby fields, picnicking. Standard fees. (Memorial Day-Labor Day, daily) Harrison Ave and Ocean Dr. Phone 401/847-2400.

Friends Meeting House. (1699) Site of New England Yearly Meeting of the Society of Friends until 1905; meeting house, expanded in 1729 and 1807, spans three centuries of architecture and construction. Guided tours through Newport Historical Society. (By appt) Farewell and Marlborough Sts. Phone 401/846-0813. **FREE**

✪ **Historic Mansions and Houses.** Combination tickets to the Elms, the Breakers, Rosecliff, Marble House, Hunter House, Chateau-sur-Mer, Kingscote, and Green Animals topiary gardens (see PORTSMOUTH) are avail at any of these houses. (See ADDITIONAL VISITOR INFORMATION.)

Astors' Beechwood. Italianate summer residence of Mrs. Caroline Astor, *the* Mrs. Astor. Theatrical tour of house incl actors portraying Mrs. Astor's servants and society guests. (Mid-May-mid-Dec, daily; rest of yr, wkends only) Phone 401/846-3772. ¢¢

Belcourt Castle. (1891) Designed by Richard Morris Hunt in French château style, 62-rm house was residence of Oliver Hazard Perry Belmont and his wife, Alva Vanderbilt Belmont, who built Marble House when married to William K. Vanderbilt. Belcourt is unique for inclusion of stables within main structure; Belmont loved horses. Contains largest collection of antiques and *objets d'art* in Newport; gold coronation coach; large collection of stained-glass windows. Tea served. Special events scheduled throughout yr. (Daily; closed Thanksgiving, Dec 25, also Jan) Bellevue Ave, 2 mi S on RI 138A. Phone 401/846-0669. ¢¢

The Breakers. (1895) Seventy-rm, Northern Italian palazzo designed by Richard Morris Hunt is the largest of all Newport cottages and is impressive by its sheer size; contains original furnishings. Children's playhouse cottage has scale-size kitchen, fireplace, playrm. Built for Mr and Mrs Cornelius Vanderbilt. (Apr-Oct, daily) Ochre Point Ave. Phone 401/847-1000. ¢¢¢ Also here is **The Breakers Stable and Carriage House.** Houses several carriages, incl Vanderbilts' famous coach *Venture.* (July-Labor Day, wkends & hols) ¢

Chateau-sur-Mer. (1852) Victorian mansion remodeled in 1872 by Richard Morris Hunt has landscaped grounds with Chinese moon gate. Built for William S. Wetmore, who made his fortune in the China trade. (May-Oct, daily; rest of yr, wkends) Bellevue Ave. Phone 401/847-1000. ¢¢

Edward King House. (1846) Villa by Richard Upjohn is considered one of the finest Italianate houses in the country. Used as senior citizens' center. Tours. (Mon-Fri) 35 King St, Aquidneck Park. Phone 401/846-7426.

The Elms. (1901) Modeled after 18th-century Chateau d'Asnieres near Paris, this restored "cottage" from Newport's gilded age boasts elaborate interiors and formal, sunken gardens that are among the city's most beautiful. Built for Edward J. Berwind, Philadelphia coal magnate. (May-Oct, daily; Nov-Mar, Sat and Sun) Bellevue Ave. Phone 401/847-1000. ¢¢

Hammersmith Farm. The unofficial summer White House during Kennedy Administration, farm dates back to 1640; 28-rm, shingle-style summer house was added in 1887 by John Auchincloss; descendant Hugh D. Auchincloss married Janet Lee Bouvier, mother of Jacqueline Bouvier Kennedy; rambling cottage was site of wedding reception of John and Jacqueline Kennedy. Gardens designed by Frederick Law Olmsted. Gift shop in children's playhouse. Guided tours. (May-Oct, daily) Ocean Dr. Phone 401/846-0420. ¢¢

Hunter House. (1748) Outstanding example of Colonial architecture features gambrel roof, 12-on-12 panel windows, broken pediment doorway. Furnished with pieces by Townsend and Goddard, famous 18th-century cabinet makers. (May-Oct, daily; Apr, wkends) 54 Washington St. Phone 401/847-6543. ¢¢

Kingscote. (1839) Gothic Revival cottage designed by Richard Upjohn; in 1881 McKim, Mead, and White added the "aesthetic" dining rm, which features Tiffany-glass wall and fixtures. Outstanding Chinese export paintings and porcelains. Built for George Noble Jones of Savannah, GA, Kingscote is considered the nation's first true summer "cottage." (May-Sept, daily; Apr and Oct, wkends) Bellevue Ave. Phone 401/847-1000. ¢¢

Marble House. (1892) French-style palace designed by Richard Morris Hunt is the most sumptuous of Newport cottages. Front gates, entrance, central hall are modeled after Versailles. House is named for the many kinds of marble used on interior, which also features lavish use of gold and bronze. Original furnishings incl dining rm chairs made of gilded bronze. Built for Mrs William K. Vanderbilt. On display are yachting memorabilia and restored Chinese teahouse where Mrs Vanderbilt held suffragette meetings. (Apr-Oct, daily; rest of yr, wkends) Bellevue Ave. Phone 401/847-1000. ¢¢

Rosecliff. (1902) Designed by Stanford White after the Grand Trianon at Versailles, Rosecliff boasts largest private ballrm in Newport and famous heart-shaped staircase. Built for socialite Mrs Hermann Oelrichs. (Apr-Oct, daily) Bellevue Ave. Phone 401/847-6543. ¢¢

Samuel Whitehorne House. (1811) Features exquisite furniture, silver, and pewter made by 18th-century artisans; Chinese porcelain, Irish crystal, and Pilgrim-era furniture; garden. (May-Oct, Mon, Fri-Sun and hols; or by appt, 24-hr advance notice necessary) 416 Thames St. Phone 401/849-7300. ¢¢

Wanton-Lyman-Hazard House. (ca 1675) Oldest house in Newport, one of the finest Jacobean houses in New England, was site of 1765 Stamp Act riot; restored; 18th-century garden; guided tours. (Mid-June-late Aug, Tues-Sat; closed hols) 17 Broadway. Phone 401/846-0813. ¢

Whitehall Museum House. (1729) Restored, hip-roofed country house built by Bishop George Berkeley, British philosopher and educator; garden. (July-Aug, daily; June, by appt only) 3 mi NE on Berkeley Ave in Middletown. Phone 401/846-3116. ¢¢

⬛ International Tennis Hall of Fame & Museum. World's largest tennis museum features interactive and dynamic exhibits detailing the history of the sport. Tennis equipt, fashions, trophies, and memorabilia on display in the famous Newport Casino, built in 1880 and designed by McKim, Mead, and White. (Daily; closed Thanksgiving, Dec 25) Grass courts avail (May-Oct). Easton's Beach. Phone 401/849-3990. ¢¢¢

Newport Art Museum and Art Association. Changing exhibitions of contemporary and historical art are housed in 1864 mansion designed by Richard Morris Hunt in the "stick style" and in 1920 Beaux Arts building. Lectures, performing arts events, evening musical picnics; tours. (Tues-Sun), afternoons; closed hols) 76 Bellevue Ave, opp Touro Park. Phone 401/848-8200. ¢¢

Newport Historical Society Museum. Colonial art; Newport silver and pewter, china, early American glass, furniture. (Tues-Sat; closed hols) Walking tours of Colonial Newport (mid-June-Sept, Fri and Sat; fee). 82 Touro St, adj to Seventh Day Baptist Meeting House. Phone 401/846-0813. **FREE**

Newport Jai Alai. Pari-mutuel betting. (Daily) Fronton and Civic Center, 150 Admiral Kalbfus Rd, at base of Newport Bridge. Phone 401/849-5000.

Old Colony and Newport Railroad. Vintage one-hr train ride along scenic route to Narragansett Bay. (July-early Sept, Sat and Sun; May-June and mid-Sept-Nov, Sun; also Christmas season) Terminal, America's Cup Ave. Phone 401/624-6951. ¢¢¢

Old Stone Mill. Origin of circular stone tower supported by arches is unknown. Although excavations (1948-1949) have disproved it, some people still believe structure was built by Norsemen. Touro Park, Mill St off Bellevue Ave. **FREE**

Redwood Library and Athenaeum. Designed by master Colonial architect Peter Harrison; thought to be oldest library building (1750) in continuous use in US; used by English officers as a club during Revolution. Collections incl part of original selection of books and early portraits. (Mon-Sat; closed hols) 50 Bellevue Ave. Phone 401/847-0292. **FREE**

Seventh Day Baptist Meeting House. (1729) Historical church built by master builder Richard Munday. 82 Touro St, adj to Newport Historical Society. Phone 401/846-0813.

Swimming.

Easton's Beach. Well-developed public beach has bathhouse, snack bar, antique carousel, picnic area, designated surfing area. (Mid-June-Labor Day, daily; early June, wkends) Memorial Blvd, RI 138. ¢¢¢

Touro Synagogue National Historic Site. Oldest synagogue (1763) in America, a Georgian masterpiece by country's first architect, Peter Harrison, contains oldest Torah in North America, examples of 18th-century crafts, letter from George Washington; worship services follow Sephardic Orthodox ritual of founders. 72 Touro St. Phone 401/847-4794.

Tours.

Newport Navigation. One-hr narrated cruise of Narragansett Bay and Newport Harbor aboard the *Spirit of Newport*. (May-Oct, daily) Newport Harbor Hotel & Marina. Phone 401/849-3575. ¢¢¢

Oldport Marine Harbor Tours. One-hr cruise of Newport Harbor aboard the *Amazing Grace*. (May-mid-Oct, daily) America's Cup Ave. Phone 401/847-9109. ¢¢¢

Viking Boat Tour. One-hr narrated trip incl historic Newport, yachts, waterfront mansions; also avail is extended trip with tour of Hammersmith Farm (see). (May-Oct) *The Viking Queen* leaves Goat Island Marina off Washington St. Phone 401/847-6921.

Viking Bus Tour. Two-, three-, and four-hr narrated trips cover 150 points of interest, incl mansions and restored areas. (Schedules vary) Three-hr trips incl admission to one mansion; four-hr trip incl admission to two mansions. Leaves from Gateway Tourist Center, America's Cup Ave. Phone 401/847-6921. ¢¢¢¢

Trinity Church. (1726) First Anglican parish in state (1698), Trinity has been in continuous use since it was built. George Washington and philosopher George Berkeley were communicants. Interior features Tiffany windows and an organ tested by Handel before being shipped from London. Tours. Queen Anne Sq. Phone 401/846-0660. **FREE**

White Horse Tavern. (1673) Oldest operating tavern in the nation. (Daily) 42 Marlborough St. Phone 401/849-3600.

Special Events

Newport Winter Festival. 23 America's Cup Ave. Ten days of food, festivities, music. More than 200 cultural and recreational events and activities. Phone 401/849-8048 or 800/326-6030. Late Jan-early Feb.

Newport Irish Heritage Month. Throughout the town. A variety of Irish heritage and theme events; films, concerts, plays, arts and crafts, exhibits; food and drink; parade, road race. Phone 401/849-8048 or 401/845-9123. Mar.

Newport Music Festival. Chamber music held in Newport's fabled mansions. Three concerts daily. Phone 401/847-7090. Mid-July.

JVC Jazz Festival. Fort Adams. Phone 401/847-3700. Mid-Aug.

Christmas in Newport. A month-long series of activities incl concerts, tree lighting, and craft fairs. Phone 401/849-6454. Dec.

Motels/Motor Lodges

★★ **BEST WESTERN MAINSTAY INN.** *151 Admiral Kalbfus Rd (02840).* 401/849-9880; fax 401/849-4391; toll-free 877/545-5550. www.bestwestern.com. 165 rms, 2 story. July-Aug: S, D $95-$169; each addl $7.50; suites $125-$295; under 12 free; lower rates rest of yr. Crib avail. TV; cable. Pool; poolside serv. Restaurant 6:30 am-10 pm. Rm serv. Bar 11:30-1 am. Ck-out 11 am. Meeting rms. Business servs avail. Some refrigerators. Balconies. Cr cds: A, C, D, DS, MC, V.

⬛ ⬛ ⬛ ⬛ ⬛ ⬛

★★ **COURTYARD BY MARRIOTT.** *9 Commerce Dr, Middletown (02842). 401/849-8000; fax 401/849-8313; toll-free 888/686-5067. www.courtyard.com.* 148 rms, 3 story. May-Oct: S, D $59-$219; suites $119-225; lower rates rest of yr. Crib free. TV; cable (premium). Indoor/outdoor pool; whirlpool. Complimentary coffee in rms. Restaurant 6:30-11 am. Ck-out noon. Coin lndry. Meeting rms. Business center. In-rm modem link. Exercise equipt. Refrigerator in suites. Balconies. Cr cds: A, C, D, DS, MC, V.

D ⚒ 🏊 ⊠ ☒ SC 🏃

★ **HOWARD JOHNSON INN NEWPORT.** *351 W Main Rd, Middletown (02842). 401/849-2000; fax 401/849-6047; res 800/446-4656. www.hojo.com.* 155 rms, 2 story. Late May-mid-Oct: S $59-$144; D $69-$159; each addl $5; suites $138-$318; studio rms $84-$164; under 18 free; some wkend rates; lower rates rest of yr. Crib free. Pet accepted. TV; cable (premium) VCR avail. Heated pool; whirlpool, lifeguard. Restaurant. Bar 5 pm-1 am. Ck-out 11 am. Meeting rms. Business servs avail. Valet serv. Sundries. Tennis. Sauna. Some refrigerators. Private patios, balconies. Cr cds: A, DS, MC, V.

🏃 ☒

★★ **INN ON LONG WHARF.** *142 Long Wharf (02840). 401/847-7800; fax 401/845-0127; toll-free 800/225-3522.* 40 kit. suites, 5 story. May-Sept: S, D $180-$225; higher rates Jazz Festival; lower rates rest of yr. Crib $15. TV; cable (premium). Restaurant 5-11 pm. Bar 4 pm-1 am. Ck-out 11 am. Valet serv. Concierge. Gift shop. Some covered, valet parking. In-rm whirlpools, wet bars. Overlooks harbor. Cr cds: A, DS, MC, V.

D ⚒ ☒ ☒

★★ **INN ON THE HARBOR.** *359 Thames St (02840). 401/849-6789; fax 401/849-2680; res 800/225-3522. www.equivest.com.* 58 kit. suites, 6 story. May-Sept: S, D $140-$250; wkly rates; higher rates: Jazz Festival, major hols; lower rates rest of yr. Crib $15. TV; cable (premium). Restaurant, hrs vary. Bar; entertainment Fri-Sun. Ck-out 11 am. Valet serv. Concierge. Gift shop. Some covered parking; valet. Exercise equipt; sauna. Whirlpool. Overlooks harbor. Cr cds: A, C, D, DS, ER, JCB, MC, V.

D ⚒ ☒ ☒ ☒

★★ **NEWPORT RAMADA INN & CONFERENCE CENTER.** *936 W Main Rd, Middletown (02842). 401/846-7600; fax 401/849-6919; toll-free 800/836-8322. www.ramada.com.* 155 rms, 2 story. Mid-June-Sept: S, D $89; under 18 free; lower rates rest of yr. Crib free. Pet accepted; $10. TV; cable (premium). Indoor pool. Complimentary continental bkfst. Bar 2-11 pm. Ck-out noon. Coin lndry. Meeting rms. Business servs avail. In-rm modem link. Gift shop. Cr cds: A, C, D, DS, ER, JCB, MC.

D ⚒ 🏊 ☒ ☒

★★ **ROYAL PLAZA HOTEL.** *425 E Main Rd, Middletown (02842). 401/846-3555; fax 401/846-3666; toll-free 800/825-7072. www.royalplazahotel.net.* 125 rms, 2 story, 15 suites. May-Sept: S, D, suites $119-$189; under 14 free; lower rates rest of yr. Crib avail. TV; cable (premium), VCR avail. Complimentary continental bkfst. Ck-out 11 am. Meeting rm. Airport transportation. Cr cds: A, D, DS, MC, V.

D ☒ ☒ SC

★★ **WEST MAIN LODGE.** *1359 W Main Rd, Middletown (02842). 401/849-2718; fax 401/849-2798; toll-free 877/849-2718. www.westmainlodge.com.* 55 rms, 2 story. Mar-Dec: S, D $39-$139; each addl $15; under 12 free; higher rates hols; lower rates rest of yr. TV; cable. Restaurant nearby. Ck-out 11 am. Refrigerators avail. Some balconies. Cr cds: A, DS, MC, V.

Hotels

★★ **THE HOTEL VIKING.** *One Bellevue Ave (02840). 401/847-3300; fax 401/849-0749; toll-free 800/556-7126. www.hotelviking.com.* 184 rms, 5 story. S, D $99-$389; suites $249-$999. Crib free. TV; cable. Indoor pool; whirlpool. Restaurant 7-11 am, 5-9 pm. Bar 11-1 am. Ck-out 11 am. Meeting rms. In-rm modem link. Bellhops. Concierge. Sundries. Exercise equipt; sauna. Rooftop bar overlooks harbor. Cr cds: A, D, DS, MC, V.

D ⚒ 🏊 ☒ ☒ ☒

★★★ **HYATT REGENCY NEWPORT.** *1 Goat Island (02840). 401/849-2600; fax 401/846-7210; toll-free 800/222-8733. www.hyatt.com.* 247 rms, 17 suites, 9 story. Late May-early Sept: S, D $159-$254; each addl $15; suites $275-$550; under 17 free; lower rates rest of yr. Crib free. TV. 2 pools, 1 indoor; poolside serv. Restaurant 6:30 am-10 pm. Rm serv. Bar 10-1 am; entertainment. Ck-out noon. Convention facilities. Business center. In-rm modem link. Airport transportation. Bellhops. Valet serv. Sundries. Gift shop. Beauty shop. Tennis. Exercise equipt; sauna. Some bathrm phones. Some private patios, balconies. Heliport for guests. Marina adj. Cr cds: A, C, D, DS, MC, V.

D 🏌 🏊 ☒ ☒ ☒ 🏃 🏃

★★★ **MARRIOTT NEWPORT.** *25 America's Cup Ave (02840). 401/849-1000; fax 401/849-3422; res 800/288-2662. www.marriotthotels.com/pvdlw.* 317 rms, 7 story. Mid-June-Sept: S, D $145-$285; suites $300-$600; under 18 free; wkly rates; wkend packages (Nov-Mar); lower rates rest of yr. Crib free. Garage parking, valet $12. TV; cable, VCR avail. Indoor pool; whirlpool, poolside serv. Restaurant 6:30 am-11 pm. Bar 11-1 am. Ck-out noon. Coin lndry. Convention facilities. Business servs avail. Concierge. Gift shop. Exercise equipt; sauna. Racquetball. On harbor. Cr cds: A, C, D, DS, ER, JCB, MC, V.

D 🏊 ☒ ☒ ☒

★★★ **NEWPORT HARBOR HOTEL & MARINA.** *49 America's Cup Ave (02840). 401/847-9000; fax 401/849-6380; toll-free 800/955-2558. www.newporthotel.com.* 133 rms, 4 story. May-Oct: S, D $129-$259; each addl $15; suites $219-$679; under 17 free; lower rates rest of yr. Crib free. TV; cable, VCR avail. Indoor pool. Sauna. Coffee in rms. Ck-out 11 am. Meeting rms. Business servs avail. Cr cds: A, DS, MC, V.

🏊 ☒ ☒ SC

B&Bs/Small Inns

★ **BRINLEY VICTORIAN INN.** *23 Brinley St (02840).*
401/849-7645; fax 401/845-9634; toll-free 800/999-8523.
17 rms, 4 with shower only, 3 story. No rm phones. May-
Oct: S, D $115-$199; each addl $15; lower rates rest of yr.
Children over 8 yrs only. Complimentary continental bkfst.
Restaurant nearby. Ck-out 11 am, ck-in 2 pm. Courtyard
with tables. Victorian inn built 1860. Library; antiques;
several fireplaces. Rms individually decorated. Cr cds: A,
MC, V.
🖼️🔥

★★★ **CLIFFSIDE INN.** *2 Seaview Ave (02840).*
401/874-1811; fax 401/848-5850; toll-free 800/845-1811.
www.cliffsideinn.com. 15 rms, 2 with shower only, 3 story.
S, D $225; each addl $30; 2-day min wkends. Children over
13 yrs only. TV; cable (premium), VCR. Complimentary full
bkfst; afternoon refreshments. Ck-out 11 am, ck-in 3 pm.
Antiques; some in-rm fireplaces, whirlpools. Victorian
atmosphere. Built 1880 for Maryland Governor Thomas
Swann and later the home of artist Beatrice Turner. Totally
nonsmoking. Cr cds: A, DS, ER, JCB, MC, V.
🛁🔥🖼️🔥

★★★ **FRANCIS MALBONE HOUSE.** *392 Thames St*
(02840). 401/846-0392; fax 401/848-5956; toll-free 800/
846-0392. www.malbone.com. 18 rms, 6 with shower
only, 3 story. 1 rm phone. May-Oct: S, D $155-$295; July-Oct
(3-day min); lower rates rest of yr. TV; cable. Complimentary
full bkfst; afternoon refreshments. Restaurant nearby. Ck-out
11 am, ck-in 2 pm. Concierge serv. Luggage handling.
Business servs avail. In-rm modem link. Beautifully restored
early American house built in 1760; many fireplaces. Cr cds:
A, MC, V.
D🖼️🔥

★★ **HAMMETT HOUSE INN.** *505 Thames St (02840).*
401/846-0400; fax 401/274-2690; res 800/548-9417.
www.hammetthouseinn.com. 5 rms, 3 story. May-Oct: S, D
$99-$165; each addl $15; under 5 free; higher rates Jazz,
Folk Festivals; lower rates rest of yr. TV; cable (premium).
Complimentary continental bkfst. Dining rm 6-10 pm.
Rm serv. Ck-out 11 am, ck-in 2 pm. Luggage handling.
Georgian-style inn (1785) furnished with antique reproductions. Totally nonsmoking. Cr cds: A, DS, MC, V.
🖼️🔥

★★★ **THE INN AT CASTLE HILL.** *590 Ocean Dr (02840).*
401/849-3800; fax 401/849-3838; toll-free 888/466-1355.
www.innatcastlehill.com. 21 rms, 10 rms in 3 story inn,
11 rms adj, some share bath. S, D $95-$325; each addl $25.
Children over 12 yrs only. Complimentary continental
bkfst. Dining rm noon-3 pm, 6-9 pm. Ck-out 11 am, ck-in
3 pm. Victorian house (1874) was summer residence of
naturalist Alexander Agassiz; antique furnishings. On ocean;
swimming beach. Cr cds: A, DS, MC, V.
D🛁🖼️🔥🖼️

★★★ **IVY LODGE.** *12 Clay St (02840). 401/849-6865;*
fax 401/849-2919. www.ivylodge.com. 8 rms, 3 story. No rm
phones. May-Oct: S, D $125-$205; each addl $15; under 16
free; higher rates wkends and hols (2-, 3-day min); lower
rates rest of yr. Crib free. Complimentary full bkfst. Ck-out

11 am, ck-in 2 pm. Balconies. Built 1886; Victorian decor.
Totally nonsmoking. Cr cds: A, DS, MC, V.
🖼️🔥

★★★ **MELVILLE HOUSE.** *39 Clarke St (02840). 401/847-*
0640; fax 401/847-0956. www.melvillehouse.com. 7 rms,
2 share bath, 2 story. No rm phones. Early May-early Nov:
S, D $115-$145; lower rates rest of yr. Children over 12 yrs
only. Complimentary full bkfst; afternoon refreshments.
Restaurant nearby. Ck-out 11 am, ck-in after 2 pm.
Concierge serv. Sitting rm. Colonial inn (ca 1750); antiques.
Cr cds: A, DS, MC, V.
🖼️🔥

★★ **MILL STREET INN.** *75 Mill St (02840).*
401/849-9500; fax 401/848-5131; toll-free 888/645-5784.
www.millstreetinn.com. 23 suites, 3 story. June-Sept: suites
$125-$253; under 16 free; wkend, wkly, hol rates; higher
rates: Jazz Festival, Folk Festival; lower rates rest of yr. Crib
free. TV; cable (premium). Complimentary continental
bkfst; afternoon refreshments. Restaurant nearby. Ck-out
11 am, ck-in 3 pm. Bellhops. Concierge serv. Guest lndry.
Business servs avail. Tennis privileges. Health club privileges.
Minibars; some refrigerators. Some balconies. Contemporary
restoration of historic mill building (1890). Cr cds: A, C, D,
MC, V.
D🖼️🖼️🖼️SC

★★ **PILGRIM HOUSE.** *123 Spring St (02840).*
401/846-0040; fax 401/848-0357; toll-free 800/525-8373.
www.pilgrimhouseinn.com. 11 rms, 2 share bath, 3 story. No
rm phones. May-Oct: S, D $65-$155; each addl $25; higher
rates Jazz Fest, some hols; lower rates rest of yr. Children
over 12 yrs only. TV in sitting rm. Complimentary continental bkfst; afternoon refreshments. Restaurant nearby.
Ck-out 11 am, ck-in after 3 pm. Concierge serv. Victorian
inn (ca 1810) near harbor. Rooftop deck. Cr cds: MC, V.
🛁

★★ **VICTORIAN LADIES INN.** *63 Memorial Blvd (02840).*
401/849-9960. www.victorianladies.com. 11 rms, 3 story.
Some rm phones. S, D $85-$185. Closed Jan. Children over
10 yrs only. TV. Complimentary full bkfst. Restaurant nearby.
Ck-out 11 am, ck-in 2 pm. Built 1841; antiques, library,
sitting rm. Near ocean. Cr cds: A, DS, MC, V.
🖼️🔥

★★★ **THE WILLOW OF NEWPORT ROMANTIC INN.**
8 Willow St; Historic Point (02840). 401/846-5486; fax
401/849-8215. www.newportri.com. 5 rms in 2 bldgs, 3 with
shower only, 3 story. No rm phones. Apr-Jan: S, D $225-
$278 (2-, 3-day min); closed rest of yr. Complimentary
continental bkfst in rm. Restaurant nearby. Ck-out 11 am,
ck-in 3 pm. Concierge serv. Lawn games. Minibars. Sitting
rm. Townhouses built 1740 and 1840; antiques. Cr cds: A,
DS, MC, V.
🔥

Restaurants

★★★ **CANFIELD HOUSE.** *5 Memorial Blvd (02840). 401/*
847-0416. www.canfieldhouse.com. Specialty: châteaubriand.
Hrs: 5-10 pm. Closed Mon; Thanksgiving, Dec 25. Res

accepted. Bar 4 pm-closing. Dinner $14-$23. Parking. Cr cds: A, C, D, DS, MC, V.

D⊟

★★ **CHRISTIE'S OF NEWPORT.** *351 Thames St (02840). 401/847-5400.* Specialties: swordfish, fresh lobster, châteaubriand. Hrs: 11:30 am-10 pm; Sat to 11 pm; winter to 9 pm, Sat to 10 pm. Closed Dec 25. Res accepted. Bar to 1 am. Lunch $5.50-$12, dinner $13-$28. Child's menu. Parking. Outdoor dining. View of the water. Dockside bar; entertainment. Family-owned. Cr cds: A, DS, MC, V.

D⊟

★★ **LA FORGE CASINO.** *186 Bellevue Ave (02840). 401/847-0418.* French, Amer menu. Specializes in fresh native seafood dishes. Hrs: 11 am-10 pm; Sun brunch 10 am-3 pm. Closed Thanksgiving, Dec 25. Res accepted. Bar noon-1 am. Lunch $5.50-$13.50, dinner $14.50-$24. Sun brunch $5.25-$11.95. Child's menu. Pianist Fri, Sat evenings. Sidewalk café. Built in 1880. Adj to International Tennis Hall of Fame and Tennis Museum. Family-owned. Cr cds: A, MC, V.

D⊟

★★★ **LA PETITE AUBERGE.** *19 Charles St (02840). 401/849-6669. www.mswebpros.com/auberge.* French menu. Specializes in seafood. Hrs: 6-10 pm; Sun 5-9 pm. Closed Jan 1, Thanksgiving, Dec 25. Res accepted. Bar. Wine list. A la carte entrees: dinner $20-$38. Outdoor dining. House (1714) of naval hero Stephen Decatur; Colonial decor, fireplaces. Cr cds: A, MC, V.

★★★ **LE BISTRO.** *41 Bowen's Wharf (02840). 401/849-7778.* French menu. Specializes in seafood, Angus beef, fine pastry. Own baking. Hrs: 11:30 am-11 pm. Res accepted. Bar to 1 am. Wine cellar. Lunch $5.50-$12.95, dinner $9.95-$26.95. Parking. Cr cds: A, DS, MC, V.

★★ **THE MOORING.** *Sayer's Wharf (02840). 401/846-2260. www.mooringrestaurant.com.* Specializes in seafood. Hrs: 11:30 am-10 pm; Sat, Sun from noon. Closed Mon, Tues Nov-Mar; also Thanksgiving, Dec 25. Bar. A la carte entrees: lunch $6-$15, dinner $8.50-$21. Child's menu. Outdoor dining. View of harbor, marina. Cr cds: A, D, DS, MC, V.

D⊟

★★ **PIER.** *W Howard Wharf (02840). 401/847-3645.* Specialties: prime rib, baked stuffed lobster shipyard-style, Pier clambake. Hrs: 11:30 am-10 pm; wkends to 10:30 pm. Closed Dec 25. Res accepted. Bar noon-1 am. Lunch $5.25-$11.95, dinner $9.75-$29.95. Child's menu. Entertainment Fri, Sat. Patio dining. On Narragansett Bay, overlooking Newport Harbor. Family-owned. Cr cds: A, C, D, DS, MC, V.

D⊟

★ **RHODE ISLAND QUAHOG COMPANY.** *250 Thames St (02840). 401/848-2330.* Southwestern menu. Specializes in barbecue ribs, grilled meats, seafood. Hrs: noon-2:30 pm, from 5:30 pm. Closed Dec 25. Res accepted. Bar. A la carte entrees: lunch $4.75-$9.75, dinner $10.25-$19.75. Child's menu. Outdoor dining. Mexican decor in 1894 music hall. Cr cds: A, DS, MC, V.

⊟

★★★ **WHITE HORSE TAVERN.** *26 Marlborough St (02840). 401/849-3600. www.whitehorsetavern.com.* Specialties: rack of lamb, beef Wellington. Own baking. Hrs: noon-3 pm, 6-10 pm. Closed Jan 1, Dec 25. Res accepted. Bar to 1 am. Wine cellar. A la carte entrees: lunch $8-$14, dinner $18-$32. Sun brunch $14-$19. Parking. Oldest operating tavern in America; building (est 1673) originally constructed as a residence. Jacket (dinner). Cr cds: A, C, D, DS, MC, V.

⊟

North Kingstown

See also Providence, Warwick

Settled 1641 **Pop** 23,786 **Elev** 51 ft **Area code** 401 **Zip** 02852

Information North Kingstown Chamber of Commerce, 8045 Post Rd; 401/295-5566

Web www.northkingstown.com

North Kingstown was originally part of a much larger area named for King Charles II. The settlement was divided in 1722, creating North Kingstown and South Kingstown, as well as other townships.

What to See and Do

Casey Farm. (ca 1750) Once the site of Revolutionary War activities, this farm was built and continuously occupied by the Casey family for 200 yrs. Views of Narragansett Bay and Conanicut Island. Restored and operating farm with animals, organic gardens; 18th-century farmhouse with family paintings, furnishings; outbuildings. (June-Oct, Tues, Thurs, and Sat afternoons) 3½ mi S on RI 1A (past Jamestown Bridge approach), on Boston Neck Rd in Saunderstown. Phone 401/295-1030. ¢¢

Gilbert Stuart Birthplace. Birthplace of portraitist Gilbert Stuart (1755-1828). Antique furnishings; snuffmill powered by wooden waterwheel; partially restored gristmill. Guided tours (½ hr). (Apr-Oct, Mon-Thurs, Sat-Sun) 5 mi S off RI 1A, 815 Gilbert Stuart Rd, NW of Saunderstown. Phone 401/294-3001. ¢¢

Main Street, Wickford Village. There are 20 houses built before 1804; on side streets are 40 more. East from center.

Old Narragansett Church. (1707) Episcopal. Tours. (Mid-June-Labor Day, Fri-Sun) St. Paul's Church. Church Ln. Phone 401/294-4357.

Smith's Castle. (1678) Blockhouse (ca 1638), destroyed by fire in 1676 and rebuilt in 1678, is one of the oldest plantation houses in the country and the only known existing house where Roger Williams preached; 17th- and 18th-century furnishings; 18th-century garden. (June-Aug, Mon, Thurs-Sun, afternoons; May and Sept, Fri-Sun, afternoons; also by appt) 1½ mi N on US 1. Phone 401/294-3521. ¢¢

Special Events

Wickford Art Festival. In Wickford Village. Approx 250 artists and artisans from around the country. Phone 401/294-6840. Second wkend July.

Festival of Lights. House tours, hayrides. First wkend Dec.

Pawtucket

See also Providence

Settled 1671 **Pop** 72,644 **Elev** 73 ft **Area code** 401
Information Blackstone Valley Tourism Council, 175 Main St, 02860; 401/724-2200 or 800/454-2882 (outside RI)
Web www.tourblackstone.com

This highly concentrated industrial center, first settled by an ironworker who set up a forge at the falls on the Blackstone River, is recognized by historians as the birthplace of the Industrial Revolution in America. It was here in Pawtucket, named for the Native American phrase "falls of the water," that Samuel Slater founded the nation's first water-powered cotton mill. The town has since become one of the largest cities in the state and a major producer of textiles, machinery, wire, glass, and plastics.

What to See and Do

Slater Memorial Park. Within 200-acre park are sunken gardens; Rhode Island Watercolor Association Gallery (Tues-Sun); historical Daggett House (fee); carousel (July-Aug, daily; May-June and Sept-Oct, wkends only; fee). Tennis, playing fields, picnicking. Newport Ave off US 1A. Phone 401/728-0500. **FREE**

Slater Mill National Historic Site. Nation's first water-powered cotton mill (1793) was built by Samuel Slater; on site are also Wilkinson Mill (1810) and Sylvanus Brown House (1758). Mill features restored water-power system, incl raceways and eight-ton wheel; operating machines; spinning and weaving demonstrations; slide show. (June-Labor Day, Tues-Sun; Mar-May and after Labor Day-mid-Dec, wkends; closed hols) Roosevelt Ave at Main St. Phone 401/725-8638. ¢¢

Special Events

St. Patrick's Day Parade. First wkend Mar.

Pawtucket Red Sox. McCoy Stadium. AAA farm team of the Boston Red Sox. For schedule contact PO Box 2365, 02861. Phone 401/724-7303 or 401/724-7300. Apr-Sept.

Arts in the Park Performance Series. Slater Memorial Park. Tues-Thurs and Sun, July-Aug.

Octoberfest Parade and Craft Fair. First wkend Oct.

Motel/Motor Lodge

★★ **COMFORT INN.** *2 George St (02860). 401/723-6700; fax 401/726-6380; toll-free 800/228-5150. www.comfortinn.com.* 135 rms, 5 story. S $68-$100; D $72-$100; under 18 free; wkend rates. Crib free. TV; cable

(premium). Pool. Restaurant 6:30-12:30 am. Bar. Ck-out noon. Meeting rms. Business servs avail. Health club privileges. Sundries. Balconies. Cr cds: A, C, D, DS, MC, V.
D 🖾 🖾 🐾 SC

Portsmouth

See also Bristol, Newport

Founded 1638 **Pop** 16,857 **Elev** 122 ft **Area code** 401
Zip 02871
Information Newport County Convention and Visitor's Bureau, 23 America's Cup Ave, Newport 02840; 401/849-8048 or 800/976-5122
Web www.gonewport.com

Originally called Pocasset, Portsmouth was settled by a group led by John Clarke and William Coddington, who were sympathizers of Anne Hutchinson of Massachusetts. Soon after the town was first begun Anne Hutchinson herself, with a number of fellow religious exiles, settled here and forced Clarke and Coddington to relinquish control. Coddington then went south and founded Newport, with which Portsmouth temporarily united in 1640. Fishing, shipbuilding, and coal mining were the earliest sources of revenue. Today, Portsmouth is a summer resort area.

What to See and Do

The Butterfly Zoo. The only New England operation that breeds, raises, releases, and sells butterflies. View a wide variety of butterflies, incl a preserved specimen of one believed to be the world's largest. (Tues-Sun) 594 Aquidneck Ave, in Middletown. Phone 401/849-9519. ¢¢

⭐ **Green Animals.** Topiary gardens planted in 1880 with California privet, golden boxwood, and American boxwood sculpted into animal forms, geometric figures, and ornamental designs; also rose garden, formal flower beds. Children's toy collection in main house. (May-Oct, daily) Off RI 114. Phone 401/847-6543. ¢¢

Prescott Farm and Windmill. Restored buildings incl an operating windmill (ca 1810), General Prescott's guard house, and a country store stocked with items grown on the farm. (Apr-Nov, daily) Tours (Mon-Fri). 2009 W Main Rd (RI 114), Middletown. Phone 401/847-6230. ¢

Motel/Motor Lodge

★ **FOUNDER'S BROOK MOTEL & SUITES.** *314 Boyd's Ln (02871). 401/683-1244; fax 401/683-9129; toll-free 800/334-8765.* 32 units, 24 kit. suites. Early July-early Sept: S $39-$129; D $49-$139; kit. suites $80-$129; under 18 free; wkly rates; lower rates rest of yr. Crib $10. Pet accepted. TV; cable, VCR avail. Complimentary continental bkfst (wkends). Ck-out 11 am. Coin lndry. Picnic tables, grills. Cr cds: A, C, D, DS, MC, V.
D 🐾 🖾 🐾

Restaurant

★★★ **SEAFARE INN.** *3352 E Main Rd (02871). 401/683-0577. www.seafareinn.com.* Specializes in seafood, regional Amer cuisine. Hrs: 5-9 pm. Closed Sun, Mon; Jan 1, Dec 24, 25. Res accepted. Dinner $13.95-$22.95. In renovated 1887 Victorian mansion furnished with period pieces. Jacket. Cr cds: A, D, MC, V.

D

Providence

See also Pawtucket, Warwick

Settled 1636 **Pop** 160,728 **Elev** 24 ft **Area code** 401
Information Providence Warwick Convention & Visitors Bureau, One W Exchange St, 02903; 401/274-1636 or 800/233-1636
Web www.providencevb.com

Grateful that God's providence had led him to this spot, Roger Williams founded a town and named it accordingly. More than three-and-one-half centuries later, Providence is the capital and largest city of the State of Rhode Island and Providence Plantations, the state's official title.

In its early years Providence was a farm center. Through the great maritime epoch of the late 18th century and first half of the 19th century, clipper ships sailed from Providence to China and the West Indies. During the 19th century the city became a great industrial center which today still produces widely known Providence jewelry and silverware. Providence is also an important port of entry.

Providence's long history has created a blend of old and new: modern hotels and office buildings share the streets with historic houses. Benefit Street, overlooking Providence's modern financial district, has one of the largest concentrations of Colonial houses in America. The city's location along the upper Narragansett Bay and numerous cultural opportunities each provide many varied attractions for the visitor. In addition, Providence is the southern point of the Blackstone River Valley National Heritage Corridor, a 250,000-acre region that extends to Worcester, Massachusetts (see).

What to See and Do

The Arcade. (1828) First indoor shopping mall with national landmark status. More than 35 specialty shops; restaurants. Westminster St. Phone 401/598-1049.

Brown University. (1764) 7,500 students. Founded as Rhode Island College; school was renamed for Nicholas Brown, major benefactor and son of a founder, in 1804. Brown is the seventh-oldest college in the US. Pembroke College for Women (1891), named for the Cambridge, England *alma mater* of Roger Williams, merged with the men's college in 1971. Head of College St on Prospect. Phone 401/863-1000. Here are

Annmary Brown Memorial. (1907) Paintings; Brown family memorabilia. (Mon-Fri afternoons, by appt) 21 Brown St, N of Charlesfield St. Phone 401/863-1994.

David Winton Bell Gallery. (1971) Historical and contemporary exhibitions. (Late Aug-May, Tues-Sun; closed hols) 64 College St, in List Art Center. Phone 401/863-2932.

John Carter Brown Library. (1904) Library houses exhibits, books, and maps relating to exploration, settlement of America. (Mon-Sat; closed school vacations) S side of campus green on George St. Phone 401/863-2725. **FREE**

John Hay Library. (1910) Named for Lincoln's secretary John Hay (Brown,1858), library houses extensive special collections incl Lincoln manuscripts, Harris collection of American poetry and plays, university archives. (Mon-Fri) 20 Prospect St, across from Van Wickle gates. Phone 401/863-3723. **FREE**

Rockefeller Library. (1964) Named for John D. Rockefeller, Jr. (Brown, 1897), library houses collections in the social sciences, humanities, and fine arts. (Daily; closed school vacations) College and Prospect. Phone 401/863-2167. **FREE**

University Hall. (1770) The original "college edifice" serves as main administration building.

Wriston Quadrangle. (1952) Square named for president-emeritus Henry M. Wriston. On Brown St near John Carter Brown Library.

Cathedral of St. John. (1810) This Georgian structure with Gothic detail was built on the site of King's Church (1722). (Daily) 271 N Main St, at Church St. Phone 401/331-4622. **FREE**

First Baptist Church in America. Oldest Baptist congregation in America, established 1638, erected present building by Joseph Brown in 1775. Sun morning serv. (Mon-Fri; closed hols) 75 N Main St, at Waterman St. Phone 401/454-3418.

First Unitarian Church. (1816) Organized as First Congregational Church in 1720, the church was designed by John Holden Greene and has the largest bell ever cast by Paul Revere. Benefit and Benevolent Sts. Phone 401/421-7970. **FREE**

Governor Stephen Hopkins House. (1707) House of signer of Declaration of Independence and ten-time governor of Rhode Island; 18th-century garden; period furnishings. (Apr-Dec, Wed and Sat afternoons, also by appt) Children only with adult. Benefit and Hopkins Sts, opp courthouse. Phone 401/421-0694. **Donation**

Johnson & Wales University. (1914) 8,000 students. Two- and four-yr degree programs offered in business, hospitality, food service and technology. Tours avail by appt (free). 8 Abbott Park Pl. Phone 401/598-1000. On campus is the

Culinary Archives & Museum. Dubbed the "Smithsonian of the food service industry," this museum contains over 200,000 items related to the fields of culinary arts and hospitality collected and donated by Chicago's Chef Louis Szathmary. Incl rare US Presidential culinary autographs; tools of the trade from the third millennium B.C.; Egyptian, Roman, and Asian spoons over 1,000 yrs old;

gallery of chefs; original artwork; hotel and restaurant silver; and periodicals related to the field. Guided tours. (Tues-Sat by appt; closed hols) Trade Center at Harborside Campus, 315 Harborside Blvd. Phone 491/598-2805. ¢¢

Lincoln Woods State Park. More than 600 acres. Swimming, bathhouse, freshwater ponds, fishing, boating; hiking and bridle trails, ice-skating, picnicking, concession. Fees for some activities. 5 mi N via RI 146, S of Breakneck Hill Rd. Phone 401/723-7892. ¢

Museum of Rhode Island History at Aldrich House. Exhibits on Rhode Island's history. Headquarters for Rhode Island Historical Society. (Tues-Fri; closed Jan 1, Thanksgiving, Dec 25) 110 Benevolent St. Phone 401/331-8575. ¢¢¢

John Brown House. (1786) Georgian masterpiece by Joseph Brown, brother of John. George Washington was among the guests entertained in house. Museum of 18th-century china, glass, Rhode Island antiques, paintings; John Brown's chariot (1782), perhaps the oldest American-made vehicle extant. Guided tours. (Jan, Feb, Fri-Sun; rest of yr, Tues-Sun; closed hols) 52 Power St, at Benefit St. Phone 401/331-8575. ¢¢ The Historical Society also maintains a

Library. One of the largest genealogical collections in New England; Rhode Island imprints dating from 1727; newspapers, manuscripts, photographs, films. (Tues-Sat) 121 Hope St, at Power St.

North Burial Ground. Graves of Roger Williams and other settlers. 1 mi N of Market Sq on N Main (US 1).

Old State House. Where General Assembly of Rhode Island met between 1762 and 1900. Independence was proclaimed in Old State House two months before declaration signed in Philadelphia. (Mon-Fri; closed hols) 150 Benefit St. Phone 401/222-2678. **FREE**

Providence Athenaeum Library. (1753) One of the oldest subscription libraries in the US; housed in Greek Revival building designed by William Strickland in 1836. Rare book rm incl original Audubon elephant folios; small art collection. (Daily; summer, Mon-Fri; closed hols, also two wks early Aug) Tours. 251 Benefit St. Phone 401/421-6970. **FREE**

Providence Children's Museum. Many hands-on exhibits, incl a time-travel adventure through Rhode Island's multi-cultural history, wet-and-wild exploration of water, and hands-on geometry lab. Traveling exhibits. Wkly programs. Gift shop. (Sept-June, Tues-Sun; rest of yr, daily) 100 South St. ¢¢

Providence Preservation Society. The Providence Preservation Society offers brochures and tour booklets for several historic Providence neighborhoods. (Mon-Fri) 21 Meeting St. Phone 401/831-7440. ¢¢

Rhode Island School of Design. (1877) 1,960 students. One of the country's leading art and design schools. Tours. 2 College St. Phone 401/454-6100. On campus are

RISD Museum. Collections range from ancient to contemporary. (Tues-Sun; closed hols) 224 Benefit St. Phone 401/454-6500. ¢¢

Woods-Gerry Gallery. Mansion built 1860-1863 has special exhibits by students, faculty, and alumni. Call for schedule. 62 Prospect St. Phone 401/454-6141.

Rhode Island State House. Capitol by McKim, Mead, and White was completed in 1901. Building contains a Gilbert Stuart full-length portrait of George Washington and the original parchment charter granted to Rhode Island by Charles II in 1663. *Independent Man* statue on dome. Guided tours. Building (Mon-Fri; closed hols and second Mon Aug). Smith St. Phone 401/222-2357. **FREE**

Roger Williams National Memorial. This 4 1/2-acre park, at site of old town spring, commemorates founding of Providence and contributions made by Roger Williams to civil and religious liberty; slide presentation, exhibit. Visitor information. (Daily; closed Jan 1, Dec 25) 282 N Main St. Phone 401/521-7266. **FREE**

Roger Williams Park. Park has 430 acres of woodlands, waterways, and winding drives. Japanese garden, Betsy Williams' cottage, greenhouses. (Daily; closed Jan 1, Thanksgiving, Dec 25) 3 mi S on Elmwood Ave. Phone 401/785-9450. **FREE** Also in the park are

Museum of Natural History and Cormack Planetarium. Anthropology, geology, astronomy, and biology displays; educational and performing arts programs. (Daily; closed Jan 1, Thanksgiving, Dec 25) Elmwood Ave. Phone 401/785-9450. ¢

Zoo. Children's nature center, tropical building, African plains exhibit; Marco Polo exhibits; over 600 animals. Educational programs; tours. (Daily; closed Dec 25) Phone 401/785-3510. ¢¢

Special Events

Spring Festival of Historic Houses. Sponsored by the Providence Preservation Society, 21 Meeting St, 02903. Tours of selected private houses and gardens. Phone 401/831-7440. Second wkend June.

WaterFire. Waterplace Park. Floating bonfires in the Providence River accompanied by music. Phone 401/272-3111. Call for schedule.

Motel/Motor Lodge

★★ **RAMADA INN.** *940 Fall River Ave, Seekonk (02771). 508/336-7300; fax 508/336-2107; toll-free 800/272-6232. www.ramada.com.* 128 rms, 2 story. S $61-$82; D $66-$85; each addl $10; suites $107-$134; under 18 free; wkend rates. Crib free. TV; cable (premium). Indoor pool; whirlpool. Sauna. Playground. Restaurant 7 am-10 pm. Rm serv. Bar noon-1 am; entertainment. Ck-out noon. Meeting rms. Business center. Tennis. Putting green. Lawn games. Cr cds: A, D, DS, MC, V.

D 🏌 ⚓ 🍽 🐾 SC 🛐

Hotels

★★ **JOHNSON & WALES INN.** *213 Taunton Ave, Seekonk (02771). 508/336-8700; fax 508/336-3414; toll-free 800/232-1772. www.jwu.edu/jwinn.* 86 rms, 21 suites, 5 story. S, D $125-$135; suites $149. TV; cable (premium), VCR avail. Restaurant 6:30 am-10 pm. Rm serv. Bar. Ck-out 11 am. Meeting rms. Business center. Bellhops. Valet serv. Sundries. Health club privileges. Wet bar, whirlpool in suites. Cr cds: A, C, D, DS, MC, V.

D 🛐 ✈ 🍽 🐾 🛐

★★★ **MARRIOTT PROVIDENCE.** *1 Orms St (02904).* *401/272-2400; fax 401/273-2686; toll-free 800/937-7768.* *www.marriott.com.* 345 rms, 6 story. S, D $99-$179; suites $250; family, wkend rates; higher rates special events. Crib free. Pet accepted. TV; cable (premium), VCR avail. Indoor/outdoor pool; whirlpool, poolside serv, lifeguard. Coffee in rms. Restaurant 6:30 am-11 pm. Rm serv. Bar; entertainment. Ck-out noon. Convention facilities. Business center. In-rm modem link. Bellhops. Sundries. Gift shop. Airport transportation. Exercise equipt; sauna. Game rm. Balconies; some private patios. Cr cds: A, C, D, DS, ER, JCB, MC, V.

★★★ **THE PROVIDENCE BILTMORE.** *Kennedy Plaza (02903).* *401/421-0700; fax 401/455-3050; res 800/448-8355.* *www.providencebiltmore.com.* 244 rms, 18 story. S $120-$190; D $140-$220; each addl $20; suites $199-$750; under 18 free; wkend rates. Crib free. Pet accepted. TV; cable (premium), VCR avail. Restaurant 6:30 am-midnight. Bar noon-1 am; wkends to 2 am. Ck-out noon. Convention facilities. Business center. In-rm modem link. Beauty shop. Garage parking; valet. Exercise equipt. Refrigerators, microwaves avail. Cr cds: A, DS, MC, V.

★★ **RADISSON HOTEL PROVIDENCE HARBOR.** *220 India St (02903).* *401/272-5577; fax 401/272-0251;* *800/333-3333.* *www.radisson.com.* 136 rms, 6 story. Apr-Oct: S $89-$149; D $99-$159; each addl $10; under 12 free; lower rates rest of yr. Crib avail. TV; cable (premium). Restaurant 6:30 am-2 pm, 5-10 pm. Bar 11-1 am. Ck-out 11 am. Meeting rms. Business center. In-rm modem link. Free airport, RR station, bus depot transportation. Exercise equipt. Overlooks harbor. Cr cds: A, C, D, DS, MC, V.

★★★ **WESTIN.** *1 W Exchange St (02903).* *401/598-8000;* *fax 401/598-8200; res 800/301-1111.* *www.westin.com.* 363 rms, 25 story. 22 suites. S, D $189-$260; each addl $25; suites $260-$1200; under 18 free. TV; cable (premium), VCR avail (movies). Restaurant 6 am-10 pm. Bar to midnight. Ck-out noon. Convention facilities. Business center. In-rm modem link. Concierge. Exercise equipt; sauna. Indoor pool; whirlpool. Minibars; some bathrm phones, refrigerators. Cr cds: A, C, D, DS, ER, JCB, MC, V.

B&Bs/Small Inns

★★ **OLD COURT BED & BREAKFAST.** *144 Benefit St (02903).* *401/751-2002; fax 401/272-4830.* *www.oldcourt.com.* 10 rms, 3 story, 1 suite. May and Sept-Oct: S $120-$140; D $145-$165; suites $250; wkly rates; lower rates rest of yr. TV; cable, VCR avail. Complimentary full bkfst. Restaurant nearby. Ck-out 11:30 am, ck-in 2-11 pm. Built 1863 as a rectory. Overlooks Old State House. Sitting rms. Antique furnishings, chandeliers and memorabilia from 19th century. Cr cds: A, DS, MC, V.

★ **STATE HOUSE INN.** *43 Jewett St (02908).* *401/351-6111; fax 401/351-4261.* *www.providence-inn.com.* 10 rms, 3 story. S, D $79-$119; each addl $10; family rates. Crib avail. TV; cable, VCR avail. Complimentary full bkfst. Restaurant nearby. Ck-out 11 am, ck-in 3 pm. Built 1890. Sitting rm. Antiques, fireplaces. Totally nonsmoking. Cr cds: A, DS, MC, V.

Restaurants

★★ **ADESSO.** *161 Cushing St. (02906).* *401/521-0770.* Contemporary Italian menu. Specializes in pasta dishes, duck, California style wood-oven pizzas. Hrs: 11:45 am-10:30 pm; Fri, Sat to 11:30 pm. Closed July 4, Thanksgiving, Dec 25. Bar. A la carte entrees: lunch $6.95-$15.95, dinner $9.95-$23.95. Parking. Modern decor; open kitchen. Cr cds: A, MC, V.

★★ **HEMENWAY'S SEAFOOD GRILL.** *1 Providence-Washington Plz (02903).* *401/351-8570.* *www.oso.com.* Specializes in fresh seafood from around the world. Hrs: 11:30 am-3 pm, 5-10 pm; Fri, Sat to 11 pm; Sun noon-9 pm. Closed Thanksgiving, Dec 25. Bar to midnight. Lunch $5.45-$11.95, dinner $11.95-$21.95. Child's menu. Valet parking. Outdoor dining. Cr cds: A, D, DS, MC, V.

★★ **OLD GRIST MILL TAVERN.** *390 Fall River Ave, Seekonkma (02771).* *508/336-8460.* Specializes in prime rib, sirloin, seafood. Salad bar. Hrs: 11:30 am-2:30 pm, 4:30-10 pm; Sun noon-9 pm. Closed Thanksgiving, Dec 25. Bar 11:30 am-11 pm. Lunch $5.95-$9.95, dinner $7.95-$18.95. Child's menu. Parking. In restored mill (1745); antiques; fireplace. Gardens, pond, wooden bridge over waterfall. Cr cds: A, C, D, DS, MC, V.

★★★ **POT AU FEU.** *44 Custom House St (02903).* *401/273-8953.* French menu. Specializes in classic and regional French dishes. Hrs: 11:30 am-2 pm, 5:30-9 pm; Fri to 11 pm; Sat 5:30-11 pm; Sun 4-9 pm. Closed most major hols; also Sun June-Aug. Res accepted. Bar. A la carte entrees: lunch $4-$12, dinner $12-$29. Prix fixe: dinner $26-$39. Two tiers; bistro atmosphere on lower level, formal dining on upper level. Cr cds: A, C, D, DS, MC, V.

Wakefield

(see Kingston)

Warwick

See also East Greenwich, Providence

Chartered 1647 **Pop** 85,427 **Elev** 64 ft **Area code** 401
Information Dept of Economic Development, City Hall, 3275 Post Rd, 02886; 401/738-2000 or 800/4-WARWICK
Web www.warwickri.com

Warwick, the second-largest city in Rhode Island, is the location of T. F. Green Airport, the state's largest commercial airport. With 39 miles of coastline on Narragansett Bay, the city has more than 15 marinas. Warwick is a major retail and industrial center. The geographic diversity of Warwick promoted a decentralized pattern of settlement, which gave rise to a number of small villages including Pawtuxet, Cowesett, and Conimicut.

What to See and Do

Shopping.

Cadillac Shopping Outlet. Discounted brand-name clothing for men, women, and children. (Daily) 1689 Post Rd. Phone 401/738-5145.

Historic Pontiac Mills. Portions of 1863 mill complex have been restored and now house approx 80 small businesses, artisans, and shops. Also open-air market (Sat and Sun). (Daily) 334 Knight St. Phone 401/737-2700.

Warwick Mall. Renovated and expanded; largest mall in the state. Over 80 specialty shops and four department stores. Outdoor patio, video wall, topiary gardens. Wkly special events. (Daily) 400 Baldhill Hill Rd. Phone 401/739-7500.

Walking Tour of Historic Apponaug Village. More than 30 structures of historic and/or architectural interest are noted on walking tour brochure available through Department of Economic Development, Warwick City Hall, 3275 Post Rd, Apponaug 02886. Along Post Rd between Greenwich Ave and W Shore Rd. **FREE**

Special Events

Gaspee Days. Celebration of the capture and burning of British revenue schooner *Gaspee* by Rhode Island patriots; arts and crafts, concert, footraces, battle reenactment, fife and drum corps muster, parade, contests. Phone 800/4-WARWICK. May-June.

Warwick Heritage Festival. Warwick City Park. Revisit history with this wkend reenactment. Phone 800/4-WARWICK. Nov, Veterans Day wkend.

Motels/Motor Lodges

★★ **COMFORT INN.** *1940 Post Rd (02886). 401/732-0470; fax 401/732-4247; toll-free 877/805-8997. www.comfortinn.com.* 196 rms, 4 story. May-Oct: S, D $119-$159; each addl $10; under 18 free; lower rates rest of yr. Pet accepted, some restrictions; $50. TV; cable (premium). Complimentary continental bkfst. Restaurant nearby. Ck-out noon. Bellhops. Business servs avail. In-rm modem link. Free airport transportation. Health club privileges. Game rm. Cr cds: A, D, DS, JCB, MC, V.

★ **FAIRFIELD INN.** *36 Jefferson Blvd (02888). 401/941-6600; fax 401/785-1260. www.fairfieldinn.com.* 115 rms, 5 story. July-Oct: S $74.70; D $84.70; each addl $4-$7; under 18 free; lower rates rest of yr. Crib free. TV; cable (premium). Pool; lifeguard. Complimentary continental bkfst. Restaurant adj open 24 hrs. Ck-out 11 am. Coin lndry. Valet serv. Airport transportation. Cr cds: A, C, D, DS, MC, V.

Hotels

★★★ **CROWNE PLAZA AT THE CROSSING.** *801 Greenwich Ave (02886). 401/732-6000; fax 401/732-4839; res 800/227-6963. www.crowneplazari.com.* 266 rms, 6 story. S $179-$239; D $189-$249; suites $275-$525; under 18 free. Crib free. TV; cable. Indoor pool; whirlpool; poolside serv. Coffee in rms. Restaurant 6 am-11 pm. Rm serv. Bar 4 pm-1 am. Ck-out 11 am. Coin lndry. Convention facilities. Business center. In-rm modem link. Bellhops. Sundries. Gift shop. Free airport transportation. Exercise equipt; sauna. Many refrigerators, wet bars; bathrm phones avail. Cr cds: A, C, D, DS, MC, V.

★★★ **RADISSON AIRPORT HOTEL.** *2081 Post Rd (02886). 401/739-3000; fax 401/732-9309; toll-free 800/333-3333. www.radisson.com.* 111 units, 2 story, 39 suites. S, D $89-$150; each addl $15; suites $125-$170; under 18 free; wknd rates. Crib free. TV; cable (premium), VCR avail. Complimentary continental bkfst (Mon-Fri). Restaurant 6:30 am-11 pm. Rm serv. Bar noon-1 am. Ck-out noon. Business servs avail. Bellhops. Valet serv. Concierge. Sundries. Free airport transportation. Wet bar in suites. Cr cds: A, C, D, DS, JCB, MC, V.

★★★ **SHERATON.** *1850 Post Rd; US 1 (02886). 401/738-4000; fax 401/738-8206; res 800/325-3535. www.sheraton.com.* 207 rms, 5 story. S $199-$219; D $209-$229; each addl $15; suites $195; under 18 free; wknd rates. Crib free. Pet accepted. TV; cable (premium), VCR avail. Heated pool; lifeguard. Coffee in rms. Restaurant 6:30 am-11 pm. Bar noon-1 am. Ck-out noon. Meeting rms. Business servs avail. In-rm modem link. Bellhops. Valet serv. Free airport transportation. Exercise equipt; sauna. Cr cds: A, C, D, DS, ER, JCB, MC, V.

Extended Stay

★★ **RESIDENCE INN BY MARRIOTT.** *500 Kilvert St (02886). 401/737-7100; fax 401/739-2909; res 800/331-3131. www.residenceinn.com.* 96 kit. suites, 2 story. Kit. suites $140-$190. TV; cable (premium). Indoor pool; whirlpool. Playground. Complimentary continental bkfst. Ck-out noon. Business center. Lawn games. Balconies. Cr cds: A, D, DS, MC, V.

Restaurant

★★ **LEGAL SEAFOODS.** *2099 Post Rd (02886). 401/732-3663. www.legalseafoods.com.* Specializes in fresh seafood. Hrs: 11:30 am-10 pm; Sat 5-11 pm; Sun noon-8 pm. Closed Thanksgiving, Dec 25. Bar. Lunch $5.95-$9.95, dinner $9.95-$16.95. Child's menu. Cr cds: A, C, D, DS, MC, V.
D

Westerly

See also Charlestown

Founded 1669 **Pop** 21,605 **Elev** 50 ft **Area code** 401 **Zip** 02891

Information Westerly-Pawcatuck Area Chamber of Commerce, 1 Chamber Way; 401/596-7761 or 800/SEA-7636; or the South County Tourism Council, Stedman Government Center, 4808 Tower Hill Rd, Wakefield 02879; 401/789-4422 or 800/548-4662

Web www.westerlychamber.org

Westerly, one of the oldest towns in the state, was at one time known for its nearby granite quarries. Today local industries include textiles, the manufacture of fishing line, and tourism.

What to See and Do

Babcock-Smith House. (ca 1732) This two-story, gambrel-roofed Georgian mansion was residence of Dr. Joshua Babcock, Westerly's first physician and friend of Benjamin Franklin. Later it was home to Orlando Smith, who discovered granite on the grounds. Furniture collection covers 200 yrs; toys date from 1890s; Colonial garden and culinary herb garden. (July-mid-Sept, Wed and Sun; May-June and mid-Sept-mid-Oct, Sun only) 124 Granite St. Phone 401/596-4424. ¢

Misquamicut State Beach. Swimming, bathhouse (fee), fishing nearby; picnicking, concession. (Mid-June-early Sept, daily) Parking fee. 5 mi S off US 1A. Phone 401/596-9097. ¢¢¢

Watch Hill. Historical community of handsome summer houses, many dating from the 1870s; picturesque sea views. 6 mi S on Beach St, via Avondale. Located here are

    Flying Horse Carousel. Original amusement ride built in 1867. Watch Hill Beach.

    Lighthouse. (1856) Granite lighthouse built to replace wooden one built in 1807; lit by oil lamp until 1933, when replaced by electric. Museum exhibit (Tues and Thurs, afternoons).

Resorts

★★ **BREEZEWAY RESORT.** *70 Winnapaug Rd, Misquamicut Beach (02891). 401/348-8953; fax 401/596-3207; toll-free 800/462-8872. www.breezewayresort.com.* 50 rms, 2 story14 suites, 3 kit. units, 2 villas. Mid-June-Aug: S, D $89-$135; each addl $10-$25; suites $144-$189; kit. units $144; villas $1,540/wk; under 2 free; wkly, wkend rates; wkends, hols (3-day min); lower rates April-mid June,

Sept-Oct. Closed rest of yr. Crib $10. TV; cable. Heated pool. Playground. Complimentary continental bkfst. Bar 11:30 am-10 pm. Ck-out 11 am. Meeting rms. Business servs avail. Refrigerators. Balconies. Picnic tables. Cr cds: A, C, D, DS, MC, V.
≈ ✕ ⊠ 🔥

★★ **WINNAPAUG INN.** *169 Shore Rd (02891). 401/348-8350; fax 401/596-8654; res 800/288-9906. www.winnapauginn.com.* 49 units. July-Labor Day: S, D $79-$179; villas $1,043-$1,393/wk; lower rates Mar-June and after Labor Day. Crib free. TV; cable (premium). Heated pool. Playground. Complimentary continental bkfst. Restaurant nearby. Ck-out 11 am. Game rm. Refrigerators. Winnapaug Pond adj. Cr cds: A, C, D, DS, MC, V.
D ⏇ ≈ ⊠ 🔥

B&Bs/Small Inns

★★ **SHELTER HARBOR INN.** *10 Wagner Rd (02891). 401/322-8883; fax 401/322-7907; toll-free 800/468-8883.* 23 rms, 3 with shower only, 2 story. May-Oct: S, D $92-$136; each addl $15-$25; lower rates rest of yr. Crib $15. TV; cable. Playground. Complimentary full bkfst. Restaurant 7:30-10:30 am, 11:30 am-3 pm, 5-10 pm. Bar. Ck-out 11 am, ck-in 2 pm. Meeting rms. Business servs avail. Lawn games. Some balconies. Picnic tables. Originally a farm built early 1800s; guest house and converted barn. Cr cds: A, C, D, DS, MC, V.
D ⏇ ⊠ 🔥

★★★ **VILLA BED & BREAKFAST.** *190 Shore Rd (02891). 401/596-1054; fax 401/596-6268; toll-free 800/722-9240. www.thevillaatwesterly.com.* 6 suites, 3 story. Some rm phones. Memorial Day-Columbus Day: S $115-$175; D $120-$200; each addl $25; wkly rates; higher rates wkends, hols (2-day min); lower rates rest of yr. TV; cable (premium), VCR avail. Pool; whirlpool. Complimentary continental bkfst. Complimentary coffee in rms. Restaurant adj 6 am-midnight. Ck-out 11 am, ck-in 1 pm. Business servs avail. Luggage handling. RR station transportation. Some in-rm whirlpools, refrigerators, fireplaces. Some antiques. Mediterranean-style grounds. Cr cds: A, DS, MC, V.
⏇ ≈ ⊠ 🔥

Cottage Colony

★★ **THE PINE LODGE.** *92 Old Post Rd (02891). 401/322-0333; fax 401/322-2010.* 11 rms, 19 cottages, 30 kits. Mid-June-mid-Sept: S $72-$80; D $60-$100; each addl $8; kit. cottages $70-$91; under 16 free; wkly rates; lower rates rest of yr. Crib free. TV. Playground. Restaurant nearby. Ck-out 11 am. Lawn games. Refrigerators. Picnic tables, grills. In wooded area. Cr cds: MC, V.
🔥

Restaurant

★★ **VILLA TROMBINO.** *112 Ashway Rd (02891). 401/596-3444.* Italian, Amer menu. Specializes in pasta, fresh veal, seafood. Hrs: 4-9 pm; Sun to 9 pm; early-bird dinner 4-6 pm. Closed Mon; Thanksgiving, Dec 24, 25. Res accepted. Bar to 1 am. A la carte entrees: dinner $3.95-$19.95. Child's menu. Cr cds: A, D, DS, MC, V.
D SC ⊟

VERMONT

Vermont was the last New England state to be settled. The earliest permanent settlement date is believed to be 1724. Ethan Allen and his Green Mountain Boys made Vermont famous when they took Fort Ticonderoga from the British in 1775. Claimed by both New York and New Hampshire, Vermont framed a constitution in 1777. It was the first state to prohibit slavery and the first to provide universal male suffrage, regardless of property or income. For 14 years, Vermont was an independent republic, running its own postal service, coining its own money, naturalizing citizens of other states and countries, and negotiating with other states and nations. Vermont became the 14th state in 1791.

Although Vermont is usually thought of as a farm state, more than 17 percent of the labor force is in manufacturing. Machinery, food, wood, plastic, rubber, paper, and electrical and electronic products are made here. Dairy products lead the farm list, with sheep, maple sugar and syrup, apples, and potatoes following. Vermont leads the nation in its yield of marble and granite; limestone, slate, and talc are also quarried and mined.

Tall steeples dominate the towns, forests, mountains, and countryside where one can walk the 260-mile Long Trail along the Green Mountain crests. Vermont has one of the highest concentrations of alpine ski areas and cross-country ski touring centers in the nation. Fishing and hunting are excellent; resorts range from rustic to elegant.

Population: 562,758
Area: 9,273 square miles
Elevation: 95-4,393 feet
Peak: Mount Mansfield
  (Lamoille County)
Entered Union: March 4, 1791
  (14th state)
Capital: Montpelier
Motto: Freedom and Unity
Nickname: Green Mountain State
Flower: Red Clover
Bird: Hermit Thrush
Tree: Sugar Maple
Fair: Early September 2003,
  in Rutland
Time Zone: Eastern
Website: www.travelvermont.com

When to Go/Climate

Vermont enjoys four distinct seasons. Comfortable summers are followed by brilliantly colored falls and typically cold New England winters. Heavy snowfall makes for good skiing in winter, while spring thaws bring on the inevitable muddy months. Summer and fall are popular times to visit.

AVERAGE HIGH/LOW TEMPERATURES (°F)

BURLINGTON

Jan 25/8	**May** 67/45	**Sept** 69/49
Feb 28/9	**June** 76/55	**Oct** 57/39
Mar 39/22	**July** 81/60	**Nov** 44/30
Apr 54/34	**Aug** 78/58	**Dec** 30/16

Parks and Recreation Finder

Directions to and information about the parks and recreation areas below are given under their respective town/city sections. Please refer to those sections for details.

NATIONAL PARK AND RECREATION AREAS

Key to abbreviations. I.H.S. = International Historic Site; I.P.M. = International Peace Memorial; N.B. = National Battlefield; N.B.P. = National Battlefield Park; N.B.C. = National Battlefield and Cemetery; N.C.A. = National Conservation Area; N.E.M. = National Expansion Memorial; N.F. = National Forest; N.G. = National Grassland; N.H.P. = National Historical Park; N.H.C. = National Heritage Corridor; N.H.S. = National Historic Site; N.L. = National Lakeshore; N.M. = National Monument; N.M.P. = National Military Park; N.Mem. = National Memorial; N.P. = National Park; N.Pres. = National Preserve; N.R.A. = National Recreational Area; N.R.R. = National Recreational River; N.Riv. = National River; N.S. = National Seashore; N.S.R. = National Scenic Riverway; N.S.T. = National Scenic Trail; N.Sc. = National Scientific Reserve; N.V.M. = National Volcanic Monument.

Place Name	Listed Under
Green Mountain N.F.	same

CALENDAR HIGHLIGHTS

FEBRUARY

Winter Carnival (Brattleboro). Week-long festival includes ski races, parade, ice show, sleigh rides, road races.

APRIL

Maple Sugar Festival (St. Albans). A number of producers welcome visitors who join sugarhouse parties for sugar-on-snow, sour pickles, and raised doughnuts. Continuing events; arts and crafts; antiques; wood-chopping contests. Phone 802/524-5800 or 802/524-2444.

JUNE

Mountain Bike World Cup Race (West Dover). Mount Snow. More than 1,500 cyclists from throughout the world compete in downhill, dual slalom, and circuit racing events. Phone 800/245-7669.

JULY

Festival on the Green (Middlebury). Village green. Classical, modern, and traditional dance; chamber and folk music; theater and comedy presentations. Phone 802/388-0216.

SEPTEMBER

Vermont State Fair (Rutland). Exhibits of arts and crafts, flowers, produce, home arts, pets, animals, maple sugaring. Entertainment, agricultural displays, hot-air ballooning. Daily special events. Phone 802/775-5200.

STATE PARK AND RECREATION AREAS

Key to abbreviations. I.P. = Interstate Park; S.A.P. = State Archaeological Park; S.B. = State Beach; S.C.A. = State Conservation Area; S.C.P. = State Conservation Park; S.Cp. = State Campground; S.F. = State Forest; S.G. = State Garden; S.H.A. = State Historic Area; S.H.P. = State Historic Park; S.H.S. = State Historic Site; S.M.P. = State Marine Park; S.N.A. = State Natural Area; S.P. = State Park; S.P.C. = State Public Campground; S.R. = State Reserve; S.R.A. = State Recreation Area; S.Res. = State Reservoir; S.Res.P. = State Resort Park; S.R.P. = State Rustic Park.

Place Name	Listed Under
Branbury S.P.	BRANDON
Burton Island S.P.	ST. ALBANS
Button Bay S.P.	VERGENNES
Calvin Coolidge S.F.	PLYMOUTH
Elmore S.P.	STOWE
Emerald Lake S.P.	MANCHESTER
Gifford Woods S.P.	KILLINGTON
Groton S.F.	BARRE
Jamaica S.P.	NEWFANE
Lake Carmi S.P.	ST. ALBANS
Little River S.P.	WATERBURY
Molly Stark S.P.	WILMINGTON
Mount Ascutney S.P.	WINDSOR
Mount Mansfield S.F.	STOWE
Mount Philo S.P.	SHELBURNE
North Hero S.P.	NORTH HERO
Okemo S.F.	same
Shaftsbury S.P.	BENNINGTON
Silver Lake S.P.	WOODSTOCK
Townshend S.F.	NEWFANE
Wilgus S.P.	WINDSOR
Woodford S.P.	BENNINGTON

Water-related activities, hiking, riding, various other sports, picnicking, camping, and visitor centers are available in many of these areas. Day use areas (Memorial Day wkend-Labor Day, daily): over age 14, $2.50/person; ages 4-13, $2; under four free. Boat rentals, $5/hr. Paddleboats, $5/half-hr. Canoe rentals, $5/hr.

Camping: $15/night, lean-to $22 at areas with swimming beaches; $13/night, lean-to $20 at areas without swimming beaches. Reservations of at least two days (three days mid-May-October) and maximum of 21 days may be made by contacting park or Department of Forests, Parks, and Recreation, 103 S Main St, Waterbury 05671-0603, with full payment. Pets are allowed on leash only. Phone 802/241-3655.

SKI AREAS

Place Name	Listed Under
Bolton Valley Holiday Resort	BURLINGTON
Bromley Mountain Ski Area	PERU
Burke Mountain Ski Area	LYNDONVILLE
Grafton Ponds Cross-Country Ski Cent	GRAFTON
Haystack Ski Area	WILMINGTON
Killington Resort	KILLINGTON
Mad River Glen Ski Area	WAITSFIELD
Middlebury College Snow Bowl	MIDDLEBURY
Mount Snow Ski Area	WEST DOVER
Mountain Top Cross Country Ski Resort	KILLINGTON
Okemo Mountain Ski Area	OKEMO STATE FOREST
Smugglers' Notch Ski Area	JEFFERSONVILLE
Stowe Mountain Resort	STOWE
Stratton Mountain Ski Area	STRATTON MOUNTAIN
Sugarbush Resort	WARREN
Suicide Six Ski Area	WOODSTOCK
Wild Wings Ski Touring Center	PERU

For brochures on skiing in Vermont contact the Vermont Department of Tourism and Marketing, 6 Baldwin St, Drawer 33, Montpelier 05633-1301; 802/828-3676 or 1-800/VERMONT.

FISHING AND HUNTING

Nonresident fishing license: season $41; seven-day $30; three-day $20; one-day $15. Nonresident hunting license: $85; $25 for those under 18 years. Nonresident small game license: $40. In order for a nonresident to obtain a hunting license, he/she must prove that he/she holds a license in his/her home state. Bow and arrow license (hunting or combination license also required): nonresident $25. Combination hunting and fishing license: nonresident $110. For *Vermont Guide to Fishing* contact the Fish and Wildlife Department, 103 S Main St, Waterbury 05671-0501; 802/241-3700.

Driving Information

All vehicle occupants must be secured in federally approved safety belts. Children four years and younger must be secured in an approved child safety device. When the number of occupants exceeds the number of safety belts, children take priority and must be secured. Under one year must use an approved safety seat. For further information phone 802/828-2665.

INTERSTATE HIGHWAY SYSTEM

The following alphabetical listing of Vermont towns in the *Roadmaster™ Drive USA Travel Guide* shows that these cities are within ten miles of the indicated Interstate highways. A highway map should, however, be checked for the nearest exit.

Highway Number	Cities/Towns within ten miles
Interstate 89	Barre, Burlington, Montpelier, St. Albans, Swanton, Waterbury, White River Junction.
Interstate 91	Bellows Falls, Brattleboro, Fairlee, Grafton, Lyndonville, Newfane, Newport, St. Johnsbury, Springfield, White River Junction, Windsor, Woodstock.

Additional Visitor Information

Vermont is very well documented. The Vermont Official Transportation Map, as well as numerous descriptive folders, are distributed free by the Vermont Department of Tourism and Marketing, 6 Baldwin St, Drawer 33, 05633-1301; 802/828-3237 or 800/VERMONT. Visitor centers are located off I-89 in Guilford (daily); off I-89 in Highgate Springs (daily); off US 4 in Fair Haven (daily); and off I-93 in Waterford (daily).

The Vermont Chamber of Commerce, PO Box 37, Montpelier 05601, distributes *Vermont Traveler's Guidebook* of accommodations, restaurants, and attractions; phone 802/223-3443. *Vermont Life,* one of the nation's best known and respected regional quarterlies, presents photo essays on various aspects of life in the state; available by writing *Vermont Life,* 6 Baldwin St, Montpelier 05602. Another excellent source of information on the state is *Vermont: An Explorer's Guide* (The Countryman Press, Woodstock, VT, 1994) by Christina Tree and Peter Jennison; a comprehensive book covering attractions, events, recreational facilities, accommodations, restaurants, and places to shop. Available in bookstores.

Various books on Vermont are also available from the Vermont Historical Society, Vermont Museum, Pavilion Building, 109 State St, Montpelier 05609.

For information regarding Vermont's Long Trail, along with other hiking trails in the state, contact the Green Mountain Club, 4711 Waterbury Stowe Rd, Waterbury Center 05677; phone 802/244-7037. The Department of Agriculture, 116 State St, Drawer 20, Montpelier 05602-2901, has information on farms offering vacations and maple sugarhouses open to visitors.

Several Vermont-based companies offer inn-to-inn bicycle tours from May through October (months vary). Tours range in length from two days to several weeks; most are designed to accommodate all levels of cyclists. Bicycling enthusiasts can obtain a brochure entitled *Bicycle Touring in Vermont* from the Vermont Department of Tourism and Marketing, 6 Baldwin St, Drawer 33, Montpelier 05633-1301; 802/828-3237.

THE BEST OF VERMONT

From Montpelier, take I-89 to exit 10, then head up Route 100 to the Ben & Jerry's ice cream factory. This is the state's top tourist attraction—and for good reason. The thirty-minute factory tour begins with a short movie about the company's founders, Ben Cohen and Jerry Greenfield. From there, tour groups head to the production facilities, where the ice-cream production process is explained. The last stop on the tour—and the most popular!—is the FlavoRoom, where visitors can enjoy delicious samples of Ben and Jerry's most popular flavors. Don't forget to stop in at the gift shop for the perfect Vermont souvenirs!

Continue on Route 100 to the village of Stowe. Depending on the season, you can spend your time here biking, hiking, or cross-country skiing. Take the gondola to the top of Mount Mansfield (Vermont's highest peak at 4,393 feet) for dramatic views of the area. Enjoy a walk along the riverside Stowe Recreation Path. Or simply relax at one of the many inns, shops, and restaurants. From Stowe, continue on to Smugglers Notch (Route 108), a high, scenic pass that runs from Stowe (open summer only), through the scenic Mount Mansfield State Forest, and on to the village of Jeffersonville. Most tourists return by the same route, but there is an interesting loop return through Johnson and Morristown. Once back at I-89, continue on to Burlington, Vermont's largest city and a departure point for ferries. Visitors will enjoy biking or rollerblading along Lake Champlain, shopping, or stopping at the restaurants along the Church Street Marketplace. Be sure to take time for a guided tour of Ethan Allen Homestead, one of the top attractions in Vermont. South of Burlington on Route 7 is the town of Shelburne, also a departure point for ferries. The big draw here is the Shelburne Museum, which is located on 45 acres and includes such items as a working carousel, a 5,000-piece hand-carved miniature traveling circus, a lighthouse, an authentic country store, farm equipment, and *Ticonderoga,* a 200-foot sidewheel steamboat. From the eclectic and bizarre to the historic and educational, the Shelburne Museum is bound to have something of interest to everyone in your group—don't miss it! You'll also want to make time for trips to Shelburne Farms and the Vermont Teddy Bear Company. **(APPROX 436 MI ROUND-TRIP FROM BOSTON)**

Arlington

See also Bennington, Dorset, Manchester & Manchester Center

Settled 1763 **Pop** 2,299 **Elev** 690 ft **Area code** 802
Zip 05250

What to See and Do

Candle Mill Village. Three buildings, incl a gristmill built in 1764 by Remember Baker of the Green Mountain Boys; many music boxes, candles, cookbook and teddy bear displays. (Daily; closed Jan 1, Easter, Thanksgiving, Dec 25) 1½ mi E on Old Mill Rd. Phone 802/375-6068. **FREE**

Fishing. Trout and fly fishing on the Battenkill River. Phone 802/241-3700.

Norman Rockwell Exhibition. Hundreds of magazine covers, illustrations, advertisements, calendars and other printed works displayed in historic 1875 church in the illustrator's hometown. Hosts are Rockwell's former models. Twenty-min film. (Daily; closed Easter, Thanksgiving, Dec 25) On VT Historic Rte 7A. Phone 802/375-6423. ¢

Motel/Motor Lodge

★ **CANDLELIGHT MOTEL.** *4893 Vt Rte 7A (05250).* *802/375-6647; fax 802/375-2566; toll-free 800/348-5294.* *www.candlelightmotel.com.* 17 rms. Early Sept-mid-Oct: S $48-$60; D $59-$95; each addl $10; lower rates rest of yr. TV; cable. Pool. Complimentary continental bkfst. Ck-out 11 am. Refrigerators. Cr cds: A, MC, V.

B&Bs/Small Inns

★★★ **ARLINGTON INN.** *3904 Historic Rte 7A (05250).* *802/375-6532; fax 802/375-6534; toll-free 800/443-9442.* *www.arlingtoninn.com.* 19 rms, 2 story. Some rm phones. S, D $70-$160; each addl $20; wkly rates. TV in game rm, some rms; cable, VCR avail. Complimentary full bkfst. Restaurant (see ARLINGTON INN). Bar 4-11 pm. Ck-out 11 am, ck-in 2 pm. Meeting rms. Business servs avail. Tennis. Downhill ski 14 mi; x-country ski 1 mi. Game rm. Some private patios. Picnic tables. Greek Revival mansion built in 1848 by railroad magnate, restored to capture charm of the mid-19th century. Cr cds: A, DS, MC, V.

★★★ **ARLINGTONS WEST MOUNTAIN INN.** *River Rd and Rte 313 (05250).* *802/375-6516; fax 802/375-6553.* *www.westmountaininn.com.* 18 rms, 3 story, 4 kit. MAP: S $115-$151; D $155-$285; each addl $75; each addl child $10-$45. Serv charge 15%. Crib free. TV in library; cable. Playground. Dining rm (public by res) 8-10 am, 6-8:30 pm. Bar noon-11 pm. Ck-out, ck-in noon. Free bus depot transportation. X-country ski on site. Hiking. Game rm. Some refrigerators, fireplaces. Located on Battenkill River. Totally nonsmoking. Cr cds: A, DS, MC, V.

★★ **HILL FARM INN.** *458 Hill Farm Rd (05250).* *802/375-2269; fax 802/375-9918; toll-free 800/882-2545.* *www.hillfarminn.com.* 13 rms, 5 share bath, 2 story, 2 suites, 4 cabins. No rm phones. S $55-$140; D $95-$125; each addl $10-$25; suites $110; cabins $70-$90; wkly rates. Cabins closed late Oct-late May. Crib $5. TV in sitting rm; cable. Playground. Complimentary full bkfst; afternoon refreshments. Beer, wine. Ck-out 11 am, ck-in 2 pm. Gift shop. Free bus depot transportation. Downhill ski 15 mi; x-country ski 5 mi. Lawn games. Inn buildings consist of historic guesthouse (1790) and farmhouse (1830); antiques. Library, sitting rm. On 50 acres, on Battenkill River. Cr cds: DS, MC, V.

Restaurant

★★★ **ARLINGTON INN.** *VT 7A (05250).* *800/443-9442.* *www.arlingtoninn.com.* Specialties: pan-fried Maine crab cakes, roast duckling with apple calvados sauce, fresh seafood. Hrs: 5:30-9 pm. Closed Mon; Dec 24, 25. Res accepted. Bar from 4:30 pm. Wine cellar. A la carte entrees: dinner $16-$23. Child's menu. View of flower gardens. Totally nonsmoking. Cr cds: A, D, DS, MC, V.

Barre

See also Montpelier, Waitsfield, Warren, Waterbury

Settled 1788 **Pop** 9,482 **Elev** 609 ft **Area code** 802
Zip 05641
Information Central Vermont Chamber of Commerce, PO Box 336; 802/229-4619 or 802/229-5711
Web www.central-vt.com

Barre (BA-rie) has a busy, industrial air. It is home to the world's largest granite quarries and a granite finishing plant. Many highly skilled European stonecutters have settled here. A popular summer area, Barre serves as an overflow area for nearby ski resorts in winter.

What to See and Do

Goddard College. 400 students. Several buildings designed by students; formal gardens. Theater, concerts. 5 mi N on VT 14, then 4 mi NE on US 2, in Plainfield. Phone 802/454-8311.

Granite sculptures.

Hope Cemetery. "Museum" of granite sculpture. Headstones rival finest granite carvings anywhere. Carved by craftsmen as final tribute to themselves and their families. On VT 14 at N edge of town. Phone 802/229-5711.

Robert Burns. Figure of poet stands near city park in downtown. Erected in 1899 by admirers of the poet; regarded as one of the world's finest granite sculptures. Phone 802/229-4619.

Youth Triumphant. Erected Armistice Day, 1924. Benches around the memorial create a whisper gallery; whispers on one side of oval can be easily heard on other side. City park.

Groton State Forest. This 25,625-acre area incl three-mi-long Lake Groton (elevation 1,078 ft) and six other ponds. Miles of trails have been established to more remote sections of the forest. Nine developed recreation areas. Swimming, bathhouse, fishing, boating (rentals); nature trail, snow-mobiling, picnicking, concession. Four campgrounds (dump station), lean-tos. (Memorial Day-Columbus Day) Standard fees. 19 mi E on US 302, then N on VT 232, near Groton. Phone 802/584-3822.

Rock of Ages Quarry and Manufacturing Division. Skilled artisans creating monuments; picnic area. Visitor center (May-Oct, daily). Manufacturing Divison (all yr, Mon-Fri). 30-min quarry shuttle tour (June-Oct, Mon-Fri; fee). Exit 6 from I-89 or 2 mi S on VT 14, then 3½ mi SE on Main St, in Graniteville. Phone 802/476-3119. **FREE**

Special Event

Old Time Fiddlers' Contest. Barre Auditorium. Phone 802/476-0256. Usually last wkend Sept.

Motels/Motor Lodges

★ **DAYS INN OF BARRE.** *173-175 S Main St (05641). 802/476-6678; toll-free 800/329-7466. www.daysinn.com.* 42 rms, 1-2 story. S $39-$70; D $49-$85; each addl $6; MAP avail; higher rates special events. Crib free. TV; cable (premium). Indoor pool; whirlpool. Restaurant 7-10 am, 5-9 pm. Bar 4:30 pm-midnight. Ck-out 11 am. Meeting rms. Business servs avail. X-country ski 8 mi. Refrigerators. Cr cds: A, C, D, DS, JCB, MC, V.

★★★ **HOLLOW INN AND HOTEL.** *278 S Main St (05641). 802/479-9313; fax 802/476-5242; toll-free 800/998-9444. www.hollowinn.com.* 26 motel rms, 15 inn rms, 2 story, 9 kits. Mid-Sept-late Oct: S, D (motel) $80-$85; S, D (inn) $91-$99; each addl $10; kit. units $80-$96; family, wkly rates; lower rates rest of yr. Crib free. Pet accepted. TV; cable (premium), VCR (movies $2.50). Heated pool; whirlpools. Coffee in rms. Complimentary continental bkfst. Ck-out 11 am. Meeting rm. Business servs avail. X-country ski 8 mi. Exercise equipt; sauna. Refrigerators. Some balconies. Picnic tables, grills. Cr cds: A, DS, MC, V.

B&Bs/Small Inns

★★ **GREEN TRAILS INN.** *Stone Rd, Brookfield (05036). 802/276-3412; toll-free 800/243-3412. www.greentrailsinn.com.* 14 rms, 6 share bath, 2-3 story. No A/C. S, D $79-$161; ski plan. Children over 10 yrs only. TV in sitting rm; VCR (free movies). Complimentary coffee. Dining rm 8-9 am. Beer, wine. Ck-out 11 am. Airport, RR station, bus depot transportation. X-country ski on site; rentals, instruction. Canoe. Lawn games. Buildings date from 1790 and 1830. On site of famed "Floating Bridge." Cr cds: DS, MC, V.

★★ **SHIRE INN.** *Main St, Chelsea (05038). 802/685-3031; fax 802/685-3871; toll-free 800/441-6908. www.shireinn.com.* 6 rms, 4 with shower only, 2 story. No A/C. No rm phones. S $140; D $145; each addl $25; hols (2-day min). Children over 7 yrs only. Crib avail. Complimentary full bkfst. Ck-out 11 am, ck-in 3 pm. Business servs avail. X-country ski 20 mi. Federal-style house built in 1832. Totally nonsmoking. Cr cds: A, DS, MC, V.

Restaurant

★ **LOBSTER POT.** *1028 US 302 (05641). 802/476-9900.* Specializes in seafood, steak. Salad bar in converted row-boat. Hrs: 11 am-9 pm; Sun brunch 10 am-2 pm. Closed Mon; major hols; also 4th wk Oct. Res accepted. Bar to 9 pm. Lunch $3.95-$7.25, dinner $8.50-$18. Sun brunch $7.47. Child's menu. Family-owned. Cr cds: A, D, MC, V.

Bellows Falls

See also Brattleboro, Springfield

Settled 1753 **Pop** 3,313 **Elev** 299 ft **Area code** 802 **Zip** 05101
Information Great Falls Regional Chamber of Commerce, 55 Village Square, PO Box 554; 802/463-4280
Web www.gfrcc.org

The first construction work on a US canal was started here in 1792. Later, nine locks raised barges, rafts, and small steamers over the falls. In 1983, a series of fish ladders extending 1,024 feet was constructed to restore Atlantic salmon and American shad to their migratory route up the Connecticut River. Power from the river helps make this an industrial town; wood products, paper, and wire cord are among the chief products. Ben & Jerry's ice cream has a nationwide distribution center here.

What to See and Do

Adams Gristmill. (1831) Former mill; museum contains early electrical equipment, implements used in paper manufacturing and farming. (By appt) End of Mill St. Phone 802/463-3734.

Green Mountain Railroad. Green Mountain Flyer offers scenic train rides through three river valleys. (Late June-Labor Day, Tues-Sun; mid-Sept-Columbus Day, daily) Depot St (at Amtrak station), ¼ mi N. Phone 802/463-3069. ¢¢

Native American Petroglyphs. Carvings on rocks, unique among Native American works, by members of an early American people; as early as A.D. 1000. On riverbanks near Vilas Bridge. Phone 802/463-4280.

Rockingham Meetinghouse. (1787) Restored in 1907; Colonial architecture, antique glass windows; old burying ground with quaint epitaphs. (Mid-June-Labor Day, daily) 5 mi N on VT 103; 1 mi W of I-91 exit 6 on Old Rockingham Rd in Rockingham. Phone 802/463-3964. ¢

Special Event

Rockingham Old Home Days. Rockingham Meetinghouse. Celebrates founding of meetinghouse. Dancing, outdoor cafes, sidewalk sales, entertainment, fireworks; pilgrimage to meetinghouse last day. First wkend Aug.

Bennington

See also Arlington, Manchester & Manchester Center, Wilmington

Settled 1761 **Pop** 16,451 **Elev** 681 ft **Area code** 802
Zip 05201
Information Information Booth, 100 Veterans Memorial Dr; 802/447-3311 or 800/229-0252
Web www.bennington.com

Bennington was headquarters for Ethan Allen's Green Mountain Boys, known to New Yorkers as the "Bennington Mob," in Vermont's long struggle with New York. On August 16, 1777, this same "mob" won a decisive battle of the Revolutionary War. Bennington has three separate areas of historic significance: the Victorian and turn-of-the-century buildings downtown; the Colonial houses, church, and commons in Old Bennington (one mile west); and the three covered bridges in North Bennington.

What to See and Do

Bennington Battle Monument. A 306-ft monolith commemorates a Revolutionary War victory. Elevator to observation platform (mid-Apr-Oct, daily). Gift shop. 15 Monument Cir, in Old Bennington. Phone 802/447-0550. ¢

Bennington College. (1932) 524 students. Introduced progressive methods of education; became coeducational in 1969. The Visual and Performing Arts Center has special exhibits. Summer programs and performances. On VT 67A. Phone 802/442-5401.

Bennington Museum. Early Vermont and New England historical artifacts, incl American glass, paintings, sculpture, silver, furniture; Bennington pottery, Grandma Moses paintings, 1925 "Wasp" luxury touring car. Schoolhouse Museum contains Moses family memorabilia; Bennington flag; other Revolutionary War collections. (Daily; closed Thanksgiving, Dec 25) Genealogical library (by appt). 1 mi W on W Main St. Phone 802/447-1571. ¢¢

Long Trail. A path for hikers leading over the Green Mtns to the Canadian border, crosses VT 9 approx 5 mi E of Bennington. A section of the trail is part of the Appalachian Trail. Phone 802/447-3311.

Old First Church. (1805) Example of early Colonial architecture; original box pews; Asher Benjamin steeple. Guided tours. (Memorial Day-mid-Oct, daily) Monument Ave, in Old Bennington. Phone 802/447-1223. Adj is

    Old Burying Ground. Buried here are poet Robert Frost and those who died in the Battle of Bennington. Phone 802/447-3311.

Park-McCullough House Museum. (1865) A 35-rm Victorian mansion with period furnishings; stable with carriages; costume collection; Victorian gardens; child's playhouse. (Early May-Oct, daily) Special events held throughout the yr. N via VT 67A, in North Bennington. Phone 802/442-5441. ¢¢

Shaftsbury State Park. The 26-acre Lake Shaftsbury, a former millpond, is surrounded by 101 acres of forests and wetlands. Swimming, fishing, boating (rentals); nature and hiking trails, picnicking. (Memorial Day-Labor Day) Standard fees. 10½ mi N on US 7A, in Shaftsbury. Phone 802/375-9978. ¢

Valley View Horses & Tack Shop, Inc. Full-service equestrian facility offers guided trail rides and horse rentals (by the hr). Also "Pony Express" pony rides at the stables for young riders. Western tack shop. (Daily) 9 mi S on US 7 at Northwest Hill Rd in Pownal. Phone 802/823-4649.

Woodford State Park. At 2,400 ft, this 400-acre park has the highest elevation of any park in the state. Swimming, fishing, boating (no motors; rentals); nature and hiking trails, picnicking, tent and trailer sites (dump station), lean-tos. (Memorial Day-Columbus Day) Standard fees. Approx 10 mi E on VT 9. Phone 802/447-7169. ¢

Special Events

Mayfest. Sat of Memorial Day wkend.

Antique and Classic Car Show. Second wkend after Labor Day.

Motels/Motor Lodges

★ **BENNINGTON MOTOR INN.** *143 W Main St (05201).* 802/442-5479; toll-free 800/359-9900. *www.coolcruisers.net/benningtonmotorinn.htm.* 16 rms, 1-2 story. May-Oct: S $56-$80; D $58-$80; each addl $7; suites $68-$115; family rates; lower rates rest of yr. Crib $10. TV; cable. Restaurant adj 11 am-10 pm. Ck-out 11 am. Sundries. Downhill/x-country ski 10 mi. Some refrigerators. Balconies. Cr cds: A, DS, MC, V.
⊠ ⊠ 🔥

★★ **BEST WESTERN NEW ENGLANDER MOTOR INN.** *220 Northside Dr (05201).* 802/442-6311; res 800/780-7234. *www.bestwestern.com.* 58 rms, 1-2 story. Mid-June-late Oct: S $60-$110; D $65-$120; each addl $7; suites $75-$120; under 12 free; lower rates rest of yr. Crib free. TV; cable (premium). Heated pool. Playground. Complimentary continental bkfst. Complimentary coffee in rms. Ck-out 11 am. Meeting rm. Business servs avail. Downhill/x-country ski 9 mi. Some in-rm whirlpools, refrigerators, microwaves. Picnic tables. Near Bennington College. Cr cds: A, C, D, DS, MC, V.
D ⊷ 🖥 ⊠ ⊠ ⊠ 🔥

★ **CATAMOUNT MOTEL.** *500 South St (05201).* 802/442-5977; fax 802/447-8765; toll-free 800/213-3608. 17 rms. S $42-$79; D $62-$92; each addl $5. Crib free. TV; cable. Pool. Complimentary coffee in rms. Restaurant nearby. Ck-out 11 am. Lawn games. Picnic tables, grills. Cr cds: A, D, DS, MC, V.
⊠ ⊠ 🔥

★★ **FIFE 'N DRUM.** *693 US Rte 7 S (05201). 802/442-4074; fax 802/442-8471.* 18 rms, 1-2 story, 4 kits. May-Oct: S $42-$92; D $46-$98; each addl $7-$8; kit. units $49-$89; wkly rates off-season; lower rates rest of yr. Crib free. Pet accepted, some restrictions; $5. TV; cable (premium). Heated pool; whirlpool. Playground. Complimentary coffee in rms. Ck-out 11 am. Sundries. Gift shop. Free bus depot transportation. Downhill ski 20 mi; x-country ski 6 mi. Lawn games. Refrigerators. Picnic tables; some grills. Cr cds: A, DS, MC, V.

★ **GOVERNORS ROCK.** *4325 VT Rte 7A, Shaftsbury (05262). 802/442-4734; fax 802/719-0703. www.sover.net/~govrock1.* 9 rms, shower only. No rm phones. S $59; D $84; each addl $7; under 12 free. Closed Nov-Apr. TV; cable. Complimentary continental bkfst. Ck-out 10 am. Refrigerators. Picnic tables. Cr cds: MC, V.

★ **IRON KETTLE.** *1838 Rte 7A, Shaftsbury (05262). 802/442-4316; fax 802/447-4316.* 20 rms. Aug-Oct: S, D $55-$65; each addl $5; lower rates rest of yr. Crib $5. TV. Pool. Complimentary coffee in rms. Ck-out 11 am. Coin lndry. Picnic tables. Cr cds: A, DS, MC, V.

★ **KNOTTY PINE.** *130 Northside Dr (05201). 802/442-5487; fax 802/442-2231. bennington.com/knottypine.* 21 rms, 4 kits. May-Oct: S $46-$66; D $48-$76; each addl $6; kit. units $56-$66; wkly rates off-season; lower rates rest of yr. Crib free. TV; cable; VCR avail. Pool. Complimentary coffee in rms. Restaurant nearby. Ck-out 11 am. Business servs avail. X-country ski 9 mi. Lawn games. Refrigerators. Picnic tables, grills. Cr cds: A, C, D, DS, MC, V.

★★ **VERMONTER MOTOR LODGE.** *2964 West Rd (05201). 802/442-2529; fax 802/442-0879. www.sugarmapleinne.com.* 31 air-cooled units, 18 motel rms, 13 cottages. June-Oct: S $53-$65; D $60-$72; each addl $10; cottages $50-$55; under 12 free; wkly rates; lower rates rest of yr. Crib $5. Pet accepted. TV; cable. Restaurant 7:30-11 am, 5-9 pm. Ck-out 11 am. Business servs avail. X-country ski 20 mi. Lawn games. Refrigerators avail. Picnic tables, grills. Swimming pond. Cr cds: A, DS, MC, V.

B&Bs/Small Inns

★★★ **FOUR CHIMNEYS INN.** *21 West Rd (05201). 802/447-3500; fax 802/447-3692; toll-free 800/649-3503. www.fourchimneys.com.* 11 rms, 3 story. S $105-$115; D $125-$155; each addl $15. TV. Complimentary continental bkfst. Restaurant (see also FOUR CHIMNEYS). Ck-out 11 am, ck-in 2 pm. Business servs avail. Bus depot transportation. Tennis privileges, pro. Many in-rm whirlpools, fireplaces. Restored Georgian Revival mansion; antiques. Cr cds: A, C, D, DS, MC, V.

★★★ **SOUTH SHIRE INN.** *124 Elm St (05201). 802/447-3839; fax 802/442-3547. www.southshire.com.* 9 rms, 2 story. July-mid-Oct: S, D $105-$180; each addl $15; lower rates rest of yr. Children over 12 yrs only. TV in carriage house. Complimentary full bkfst. Ck-out 11 am, ck-in 3 pm. Business servs avail. X-country ski 8 mi. Many fireplaces; some in-rm whirlpools. Built 1850; mahogany-paneled library. Totally nonsmoking. Cr cds: A, DS, MC, V.

Cottage Colony

★ **SERENITY MOTEL.** *4379 VT Rte 7A, Shaftsbury (05262). 802/442-6490; fax 802/442-5493; toll-free 800/644-6490. www.thisisvermont.com/pages/serenity.html.* 8 units, shower only. S, D $50-$60; each addl $5; under 18 free; wkly rates. Closed Nov-Apr. Crib free. Pet accepted. TV; cable. Complimentary coffee in rms. Ck-out 11 am. Picnic tables, grills. Cr cds: A, DS, MC, V.

Restaurants

★★ **BENNINGTON STATION.** *150 Depot St (05201). 802/447-1080.* Specializes in seafood, prime rib, turkey. Hrs: 11:30 am-4 pm, 4:30-9 pm; Fri, Sat to 10 pm; Sun 4-8 pm; early-bird dinner 4:30-6 pm; Sun brunch 11 am-2:30 pm. Res accepted. Bar. Lunch $4.95-$7, dinner $9.95-$16.95. Sun brunch $9.95. Child's menu. Old RR station (1898). Totally nonsmoking. Cr cds: A, C, D, DS, MC, V.

★★★ **FOUR CHIMNEYS.** *21 West Rd (05201). 802/447-3500. www.fourchimneys.com.* Continental menu. Specializes in salmon with herbs, chicken florentine. Own pastries. Hrs: 6-8:30 pm; Sat from 5:30 pm; Sun 3:30-8 pm. Res accepted. Bar. Wine list. Dinner $20.95-$29.95. Totally nonsmoking. Cr cds: A, C, D, DS, MC, V.

★★ **PUBLYK HOUSE.** *782 Harwood Hill (05201). 802/442-8301.* Specializes in steak, fresh seafood. Salad bar. Hrs: 5-9 pm; Fri, Sat to 10 pm; Sun 4-9 pm. Closed Thanksgiving, Dec 24, 25. Bar from 4 pm. Dinner $9.95-$18.95. Child's menu. Outdoor dining. In converted barn; fireplace. Cr cds: A, D, MC, V.

Brandon

See also Middlebury, Rutland

Settled 1761 **Pop** 4,223 **Elev** 431 ft **Area code** 802
Zip 05733
Information Brandon Area Chamber of Commerce, PO Box 267; 802/247-6401
Web www.brandon.org

Brandon is a resort and residential town located at the western edge of the Green Mountains. The first US electric motor was made in nearby Forestdale by Thomas Davenport.

What to See and Do

Branbury State Park. This 76-acre park has swimming, 1,000-ft sand beach, fishing, boating, sailing; nature and hiking trails, picnicking, concession, camping (dump station), lean-tos. (Memorial Day-Columbus Day) Standard fees. 3 mi NE on VT 73, then N on VT 53, E shore of Lake Dunmore. Phone 802/247-5925.

Green Mountain National Forest. (see). E on VT 73.

Mount Independence. Wooded bluff on shore of Lake Champlain, part of Revolutionary War defense complex. Fort built in 1776 across from Fort Ticonderoga to house 12,000 troops and to protect colonies from northern invasion; evacuated in 1777. Least disturbed major Revolutionary War site in the country; four marked trails show ruins of fort complex. (Late May-early Oct, daily) 16 mi W via VT 73 and 73A, in the town of Orwell. Phone 802/759-2412. ¢¢

Stephen A. Douglas Birthplace. Cottage where the "Little Giant" was born in 1813. Douglas attended Brandon Academy before moving to Illinois in 1833. (By appt) 2 Grove St on US 7. Phone 802/247-6401. **FREE**

B&Bs/Small Inns

★★ **THE BRANDON INN.** 20 Park St (05733). 802/247-5766; fax 802/247-5768; toll-free 800/639-8685. www.historicbrandoninn.com. 37 rms, 25 A/C, 3 story. S $85-$100; D $125-$200; suites $115-$190; midwk rates; ski plans; MAP avail; higher rates fall foliage. Pool. Dining rm 8-9:30 am, 11:30 am-2 pm, 6-9 pm. Bar noon-midnight. Ck-out 11 am. Business servs avail. Downhill ski 20 mi; x-country ski 8 mi. Fireplace in lobby. Built in 1786. Cr cds: A, DS, MC, V.

D ⚹ ⚹ ⚹ ⚹

★★★ **LILAC INN.** 53 Park St (05733). 802/247-5463; fax 802/247-5499; toll-free 800/221-0720. www.lilacinn.com. 9 rms, 2 story. Rm phones avail. S $80-$100; D $150-$200; each addl $25; wkend rates; higher rates: fall foliage, hols. TV; cable, VCR avail. Complimentary afternoon refreshments. Restaurant (see also LILAC INN). Ck-out 11 am, ck-in 3 pm. Business servs avail. In-rm modem link. Putting green. Downhill ski 20 mi; x-country ski 5 mi. Library. Greek Revival inn built 1909. Totally nonsmoking. Cr cds: A, D, DS, MC, V.

D ⚹ ⚹ ⚹ ⚹ SC

★★ **MOFFETT HOUSE B & B.** 69 Park St (05733). 802/247-3843; toll-free 800/394-7239. 6 rms, 3 with shower only, 2 story. No A/C. No rm phones. S $65-$70; D $80; each addl $15; under 2 free; ski plans; hols (2-day min); higher rates fall foliage. Closed Apr. Crib free. Pet accepted. TV; cable in some rms. Complimentary full bkfst. Restaurant nearby. Ck-out 11 am, ck-in 2 pm. Downhill ski 20 mi; x-country ski 5 mi. Built in 1856. Totally nonsmoking. Cr cds: MC, V.

⚹ ⚹ ⚹ ⚹

Cottage Colony

★ **THE ADAMS MOTEL AND RESTAURANT.** 1246 Franklin St. (05733). 802/247-6644; res 800/759-6537. www.theadamsmotorinn@aol.com. 20 cottages, no kit. (1-2 rm). No A/C. Mid-May-mid-Sept: S $60-$75; D $65-$80; each addl $5; MAP avail; wkly rates; higher rates fall foliage. Closed rest of yr. TV. Pool. Restaurant 7:30-9 am, 5:30-8:30 pm. Bar from 5 pm. Ck-out 10:30 am. Miniature golf. Lawn games. Pond; trout fishing. Fireplace in some rms, lobby. Cr cds: A, DS, MC, V.

D ⚹ ⚹ ⚹ ⚹

Restaurant

★★ **LILAC INN.** 53 Park St (05733). 802/247-5463. www.lilacinn.com. Continental menu. Menu changes wkly. Hrs: 5:30-9 pm; Sun brunch 10 am-2 pm. Closed Mon, Tues. Res accepted. Bar. Dinner $10.95-$21. Sun brunch $13.95. Outdoor dining. Totally nonsmoking. Cr cds: A, D, MC, V.

D

Brattleboro

See also Bellows Falls, Marlboro, Newfane, Wilmington; also see Greenfield, MA and Keene, NH

Settled 1724 **Pop** 12,241 **Elev** 240 ft **Area code** 802 **Zip** 05301

Information Brattleboro Area Chamber of Commerce, 180 Main St; 802/254-4565

Web www.brattleboro.com

The first settlement in Vermont was at Fort Dummer (two miles south) in 1724. Rudyard Kipling married a Brattleboro woman and lived here in the 1890s. Brattleboro is a resort area and an industrial town.

What to See and Do

Brattleboro Museum & Art Center. Exhibits change periodically and feature works by New England artists; history exhibits; permanent display of Estey organ collection; frequent performances and lecture programs. (Mid-May-Nov, Tues-Sun; closed hols) Canal and Bridge Sts. Union Railroad Station. Phone 802/257-0124. ¢

Creamery Bridge. (1879) One of Vermont's best-preserved covered bridges. Approx 2 mi W on VT 9. Phone 802/254-4565.

Harlow's Sugar House. Observe working sugarhouse (Mar-mid-Apr). Maple exhibit and products. Pick your own fruit in season: strawberries, blueberries, raspberries, apples; also cider in fall. (Daily; closed Dec 25, also Jan-mid-Feb) 3 mi N via I-91, exit 4; on US 5 in Putney. Phone 802/387-5852. **FREE**

Living Memorial Park. Swimming pool (mid-June-Labor Day). Ball fields, lawn games, tennis courts, skiing (T-bar; Dec-early Mar), ice-skating (mid Nov-early-Mar). Picnicking, playground. Special events during summer. Fee for some activities. 2 mi W, just off VT 9. Phone 802/254-5808.

Santa's Land. Christmas theme village; visit with Santa, railroad ride, carousel. Petting Zoo; gardens. Concessions. (Memorial Day wkend-Dec 24, daily; closed Thanksgiving) 12 mi N on US 5 or I-91, exits 4 or 5 in Putney. Phone 802/387-5550. ¢¢¢

Special Events

Winter Carnival. Wk-long festival incl ski races, parade, ice show, sleigh rides, road races. Feb.

Yellow Barn Music Festival. 10 mi N via I-91 or US 5 in Putney, behind the Public Library. Five-wk chamber music festival. Students and well-known guest artists perform concerts. Also Special Performance Series, children's concerts. Phone 802/387-6637 or 800/639-3819. Tues, Fri, Sat eves, some Thurs, Sun, July-Aug.

Motels/Motor Lodges

★ **QUALITY INN AND SUITES.** *1380 Putney Rd (05301). 802/254-8701; fax 802/257-4727; toll-free 800/228-5151. www.qualityinnbrattleboro.com.* 92 rms, 2 story. June-Oct: S, D $89-$109; each addl $10; under 18 free; lower rates rest of yr. Crib free. TV; cable. 2 pools, 1 indoor; whirlpool, sauna. Restaurant 6:30-10:30 am, 5-9:30 pm. Rm serv. Bar 4:30-11:30 pm. Ck-out 11 am. Meeting rms. Business servs avail. In-rm modem link. Game rm. Cr cds: A, DS, MC, V.
D 🗷 🐾 SC ⚊

★ **SUPER 8.** *1043 Putney Rd (05301). 802/254-8889; fax 802/254-8323; res 800/800-8000. www.super8.com.* 64 rms, 2 story. S $65-$70; D $71-$90; each addl $5-$7; under 12 free. Crib free. TV; cable, VCR avail (movies). Complimentary coffee in lobby. Restaurant adj. Ck-out 11 am. Cr cds: A, D, DS, MC, V.
D 🐾 🗷 🐾

Hotel

★★ **LATCHIS HOTEL.** *50 Main St (05301). 802/254-6300; fax 802/254-6304. www.brattleboro.com/latchis.* 30 rms, 4 story, 3 suites. June-Oct: S $75; D $152; suites $175; each addl $10; under 12 free; lower rates rest of yr. Crib avail. Parking lot. TV; cable. Complimentary continental bkfst. Coffee in rms. Restaurant noon-5:30 pm. Bar. Ck-out 11 am, ck-in 2 pm. Business servs avail. Golf, 18 holes. Tennis, 8 courts. Downhill skiing. Bike rentals. Hiking trail. Cr cds: A, MC, V.
D 🐾 🏌 🏊 🎿 🚴 🗷

Restaurants

★ **JOLLY BUTCHER'S.** *254 Marlboro Rd, West Brattleboro (05303). 802-254-6043.* Specializes in steak, fresh seafood. Salad bar. Hrs: 11:30 am-2:30 pm, 5-10 pm; Sun noon-9 pm. Closed Thanksgiving, Dec 25. Bar from 11:30 am. Lunch $3.25-$7.95, dinner $7.95-$18.95. Child's menu. Open hearth. Lobster tank. Cr cds: A, DS, MC, V.
D

★ **MARINA.** *28 Spring Tree Rd (05301). 802/257-7563.* Specializes in fresh seafood. Hrs: 11:30 am-11 pm; Mon, Tues from 4 pm. Closed Mon, Tues in winter. Bar. Lunch $3.50-$6.75, dinner $6.75-$16.50. Child's menu. Entertainment Sun. Patio dining. Overlooks West River. Totally nonsmoking. Cr cds: A, MC, V.
D

★★ **THE PUTNEY INN.** *57 Putney Landing, Putney (05346). 802/387-5517. www.putneyinn.com.* Specializes in New England dishes. Hrs: 8 am-8:30 pm. Res accepted. Wine, beer. Lunch $9-$14; dinner $18-$24. Child's menu. Entertainment. Cr cds: A, DS, MC, V.
D SC

Burlington

See also Shelburne

Settled 1773 **Pop** 39,127 **Elev** 113 ft **Area code** 802 **Zip** 05401

Information Lake Champlain Regional Chamber of Commerce, 60 Main St, Suite 100; 802/863-3489 or 877/686-5253

Web www.vermont.org

Burlington, on Lake Champlain, is the largest city in Vermont. It is the site of the oldest university and the oldest daily newspaper (1848) in the state, the burial place of Ethan Allen, and the birthplace of philosopher John Dewey. It has a diversity of industries. The lakefront area offers a park, dock, and restaurants.

What to See and Do

Battery Park. View of Lake Champlain and Adirondacks. Guns here drove back British warships in War of 1812. VT 127 and Pearl St. Phone 802/863-3489.

Bolton Valley Ski/Summer Resort. Resort has quad, four double chairlifts; one surface lift; school, patrol, rentals; snowmaking; cafeteria, restaurants, bar; nursery. Forty-three runs, longest run over 3 mi; vertical drop 1,600 ft. (Nov-Apr, daily) Sixty-two mi of x-country trails. Also summer activities. 20 mi E at 4302 Bolton Valley Access Rd, off US 2 in Bolton; I-89 exits 10, 11.

Burlington Ferry. Makes one-hr trips across Lake Champlain to Port Kent, NY (mid-May-mid-Oct, daily). Refreshments. Leaves King St Dock. Phone 802/864-9804. ¢¢¢¢

Church Street Marketplace. Four traffic-free blks, from the Unitarian Church, designed in 1815 by Peter Banner, to City Hall at the corner of Main St. Buildings are a mix of Art Deco and 19th-century architectural styles and house more than 100 shops, restaurants, galleries, and cafes. The bricked promenade is spotted with vendors and street entertainers. Phone 802/863-1648.

Discovery Museum. "Hands-on" children's museum offers participatory exhibits in the physical and natural sciences, history, art. (Tues-Sun; closed major hols) 51 Park St, on VT 2A in Essex Junction. Phone 802/878-8687.

✖ **Ethan Allen Homestead.** Allen's preserved pioneer homestead; re-created hayfield and kitchen gardens, 1787 farmhouse. One-hr guided tours; museum exhibits; audio-visual presentation. (Early May-late Oct, daily; Nov-Apr, Sat, Sun) 2 mi N off VT 127. Phone 802/865-4556.

Ethan Allen Park. Part of Ethan Allen's farm. Ethan Allen Tower (Memorial Day-Labor Day, Wed-Sun afternoons and eves) with view of Adirondacks and Lake Champlain to the west, Green Mtns to the east. Picnicking. 2½ mi N on North Ave to Ethan Allen Pkwy. Phone 802/863-3489. **FREE**

Excursion Cruises. *Spirit of Ethan Allen III,* replica of a vintage sternwheeler and Lake Champlain's largest excursion vessel, offers sightseeing sunset, moonlight, brunch, and dinner cruises on Lake Champlain; both decks enclosed and heated. Res required for dinner cruises. (June-Oct) Burlington Boathouse, College St. Phone 802/862-8300.

Green Mountain Audubon Center. Center has 230 acres with trails through many Vermont habitats, incl beaver ponds, hemlock swamp, brook, river, marsh, old farm fields, woodland, and sugar orchard. Educational nature center with classes, interpretive programs, and special projects. Open all yr for hiking, snowshoeing, and x-country skiing. Grounds, office (hrs vary). Fee for some activities. 20 mi SE via I-89, Richmond exit, in Huntington near the Huntington-Richmond line. Phone 802/434-3068. Adj is

 The Birds of Vermont Museum. Displays carvings of 200 species of local birds; also offers nature trails, recorded bird songs. (May-Oct, Mon, Wed-Sun) Phone 802/434-2167. ¢¢

Lake Champlain Chocolates. Large glass windows allow view of chocolate-making process. Gift shop. (Mon-Sat; closed hols) 750 Pine St. Phone 802/864-1807.

St. Michael's College. (1904) 1,700 students. Chapel of St. Michael the Archangel (daily). Also professional summer theater at St. Michael's Playhouse. N via I-89 to exit 15, then ¼ mi NE on VT 15, in Winooski-Colchester. Phone 802/654-2000.

Sherman Hollow Cross-Country Skiing Center. Area has 25 mi of groomed, one-way, double-tracked cross-country ski trails; more than three mi of lighted trails for night skiing; warming hut; rentals; restaurant. (Dec-Apr) 10 mi SE on I-89 to exit 11, then E on US 2, then S on Huntington Rd to Sherman Hollow Rd, then W. Phone 802/434-4553. ¢¢

University of Vermont. (1791) 10,000 students. Fifth-oldest university in New England. Graduate and undergraduate programs. On campus are the **Billings Center,** of architectural significance; **Bailey-Howe Library,** largest in the state; Georgian-designed **Ira Allen Chapel,** named for the founder; and the **Old Mill,** classroom building with cornerstone laid by General Lafayette in 1825. Waterman Building, S Prospect St. Phone 802/656-3480. Also here is

Robert Hull Fleming Museum. American, European, African, pre-Columbian and Oriental art; changing exhibits. (Limited hrs) Colchester Ave. Phone 802/656-0750. **Donation**

Special Events

Discover Jazz Festival. A jazz extravaganza with over 150 live performances taking place in city parks, clubs, and restaurants. Phone 802/863-7992. Ten days early June.

St. Michael's Playhouse. McCarthy Arts Center, St. Michael's College. Summer theater. Professional actors perform four plays (two wks each). Phone 802/654-2535. Tues-Sat, late June-late Aug.

Vermont Mozart Festival. Features 26 chamber concerts in picturesque Vermont settings, incl the Trapp Family Meadow, Basin Harbor Club in Vergennes, and Shelburne Farms on Lake Champlain. Phone 802/862-7352. Mid-July-early Aug.

Motels/Motor Lodges

★★ **BEST WESTERN WINDJAMMER INN.** *1076 Williston Rd, South Burlington (05403). 802/863-1125; fax 802/658-1296; res 800/780-7234. www.bestwestern.com/windjammerinn.* 177 rms, 2 story. Late-June-mid-Sept: S $70-$110; D $80-$110; each addl $5; suites $80-$109; under 18 free; higher rates fall foliage; lower rates rest of yr. Crib free. Pet accepted; $5. TV; cable (premium). Pool; whirlpool. Complimentary continental bkfst. Restaurant 11:30 am-2:30 pm, 5-10 pm; Sun 10 am-2:30, 4-9 pm. Ck-out 11 am. Coin lndry. Meeting rms. Business servs avail. Free airport transportation. Exercise equipt; sauna. Nature trail. Cr cds: A, C, D, DS, MC, V.
🔲🐾🏊🧍🏊

★ **COMFORT INN.** *1285 Williston Rd, South Burlington (05403). 802/865-3400; toll-free 800/228-5150. www.comfortinn.com.* 105 rms, 3 story. May-Labor Day: S, D $79-$109; suites $89-$119; each addl $10; under 18 free; wkend rates; ski plans; higher rates fall foliage. Crib free. TV; cable (premium). Pool. Complimentary continental bkfst. Restaurant adj 11 am-10 pm. Ck-out noon. Meeting rms. Business servs avail. In-rm modem link. Valet serv. Downhill ski 15 mi; x-country ski 5 mi. Exercise equipt. Some refrigerators. Cr cds: A, DS, MC, V.
🔲🏊🧍✈

★★ **DAYS INN.** *23 College Pkwy, Colchester (05446). 802/655-0900; fax 802/655-6851; res 800/329-7466. www.daysinn.com.* 73 rms, 4 story. July-mid Oct: S $45-$95; D $50-$100; under 16 free; suites $75-$120; higher rates special events; lower rates rest of yr. Crib free. Pet accepted; $50 deposit. TV; cable (premium). Indoor pool. Complimentary continental bkfst. Ck-out 11 am. Meeting rm. Business servs avail. Sundries. X-country ski 5 mi. Refrigerators; some in-rm whirlpools. Some balconies. Cr cds: A, C, D, DS, ER, JCB, MC, V.
🔲🐾🏊🏊🧍🔥

★★ **HAMPTON INN.** *42 Lower Mountain View Dr, Colchester (05446). 802/655-6177; fax 802/655-4962; toll-free 800/426-7866. www.hampton-inn.com.* 188 rms, 5 story. Aug-Oct: S $84-$99; D $94-$109; suites $125-$135; under 18 free; lower rates rest of yr. Crib free. Pet accepted. TV; cable (premium), VCR avail. Indoor pool; whirlpool.

Complimentary continental bkfst. Coffee in rms. Restaurant 11:30 am-10 pm. Ck-out 11 am. Coin lndry. Meeting rms. Business center. In-rm modem link. Free airport transportation. Downhill ski 20 mi; x-country ski 5 mi. Exercise equipt. Refrigerators avail. Cr cds: A, C, D, DS, ER, JCB, MC, V.

★ **HO-HUM MOTEL.** *1660 Williston Rd, South Burlington (05403). 802/863-4551; fax 802/878-8119; toll-free 800/228-7031.* 36 rms. Early June-late Oct: S $50-$70; D $65-$80; lower rates rest of yr. Crib free. TV; cable. Pool. Restaurant opp 7 am-11 pm. Ck-out 11 am. Free airport transportation. Cr cds: A, DS, MC, V.

★★ **HOLIDAY INN.** *1068 Williston Rd, South Burlington (05403). 802/863-6363; fax 802/863-3061; res 800/465-4329. www.holiday-inn.com.* 174 rms, 4 story. May-Oct: S, D $85-$139; under 19 free; lower rates rest of yr. Crib free. Pet accepted. TV; cable. 2 pools, 1 indoor; whirlpool. Coffee in rms. Restaurant 6 am-10 pm. Rm serv. Bar noon-2 am, Sat to 1 am, Sun to 10 pm; entertainment Thurs-Sat. Ck-out noon. Meeting rm. Business servs avail. In-rm modem link. Bellhops. Sundries. Free airport transportation. Exercise equipt. Cr cds: A, C, DS, JCB, MC, V.

★ **HOWARD JOHNSON HOTEL.** *1720 Shelburne Rd, South Burlington (05403). 802/860-6000; fax 802/864-9919; res 800/874-1554. www.hojo.com.* 121 rms, 3 story. Mid-June-Labor Day: S, D $80-$120; each addl $10; under 18 free; wkend rates; ski plans; higher rates: college graduation, fall foliage; lower rates rest of yr. Crib free. TV. Indoor pool; whirlpool. Restaurant 6:30-9:30 am, 4:30-9:30 pm. Bar 4 pm-1 am. Ck-out noon. Coin lndry. Meeting rms. Business servs avail. In-rm modem link. Free airport transportation. Downhill ski 20 mi; x-country ski 8 mi. Exercise equipt; sauna. Cr cds: A, C, D, DS, MC, V.

Hotels

★ **CLARION HOTEL & CONFERENCE CENTER.** *1117 Williston Rd, South Burlington (05403). 802/658-0250; fax 802/660-7516; toll-free 800/272-6232. www.clarionvermont.com.* 130 rms, 2 story. S $60-$110; D $70-$115; each addl $5; under 18 free; higher rates fall foliage. Crib free. Pet accepted. TV; cable, VCR avail (movies). Pool; wading pool. Coffee in rms. Restaurant 6:30 am-10 pm. Rm serv to 9:30 pm. Bar 11-1 am; Sun to 11 pm. Ck-out noon. Meeting rms. Business servs avail. In-rm modem link. Sundries. Free airport transportation. Downhill ski 20 mi; x-country ski 6 mi. Exercise equipt. Cr cds: A, MC, V.

★★★ **INN AT ESSEX.** *70 Essex Way, Essex (05452). 802/878-1100; fax 802/878-0063; toll-free 800/727-4295. www.innatessex.com.* 97 rms, 3 story. S, D $175; each addl $10; under 12 free. Crib free. TV; cable (premium). Restaurant 5:30-10:30 pm. Rm serv 6 am-11 pm. Ck-out 11 am. Business servs avail. In-rm modem link. Concierge. Free airport, RR station, bus depot transportation. X-country ski 15 mi. Health club privileges. Some in-rm whirlpools, fireplaces.

Each rm individually decorated with 18th-century, period-style furniture. Features food preparation by the New England Culinary Institute. Cr cds: A, C, D, DS,MC, V.

★★ **RADISSON.** *60 Battery St (05401). 802/658-6500; fax 802/658-4659; res 800/333-3333. www.radisson.com.* 255 rms. S, D $110-$179; each addl $10; suites $150-$450; under 18 free; higher rates: fall foliage, special events. Crib free. TV; cable (premium). Indoor pool; whirlpool. Coffee in rms. Restaurants 6:30 am-10 pm. Bar; comedy show Fri, Sat. Ck-out noon. Meeting rms. Business servs avail. Concierge. Gift shop. Free garage parking. Free airport transportation. Exercise equipt. View of lake. Luxury level. Cr cds: A, D, DS, MC, V.

★★★ **SHERATON HOTEL AND CONFERENCE CENTER.** *870 Williston Rd, South Burlington (05403). 802/865-6600; fax 802/865-6670; toll-free 800/677-6576. www.sheraton.com.* 309 rms, 2-4 story. May-Oct: S, D $99-$155; each addl $10; suites $250; under 17 free; wkend rates; ski plan; lower rates rest of yr. Crib free. Pet accepted. TV; cable (premium); VCR avail. Indoor pool; whirlpool. Coffee in rms. Restaurant 6:30 am-2:30 pm, 5-10:30 pm. Rm serv. Bar 11 am-midnight; entertainment Fri, Sat. Ck-out noon. Meeting rms. Business center. In-rm modem link. Bellhops. Gift shop. Free airport transportation. X-country ski 6 mi. Exercise rm. Game rm. Some refrigerators. Luxury level. Cr cds: A, C, D, DS, ER, JCB, MC, V.

All Suites

★★ **HOLIDAY INN EXPRESS HOTEL & SUITES.** *1712 Shelburne Rd, South Burlington (05403). 802/860-1112; fax 802/846-1926; res 800/465-4329. innvermont.com.* 78 suites, 3 story, 6 rms. Mid-June-mid-Sept: S, D $99-$195; under 18 free; higher rates: fall foliage, special events; lower rates rest of yr. Crib free. TV; cable. Pool privileges. Complimentary continental bkfst. Complimentary coffee in rms. Restaurant adj 7 am-11 pm. Ck-out noon. Coin lndry. Meeting rms. Business servs avail. Free airport, RR station, bus depot transportation. Downhill ski 20 mi; x-country ski 12 mi. Health club privileges. Refrigerators, microwaves. Near airport. Cr cds: A, C, D, DS, MC, V.

★★ **WILSON INN.** *10 Kellogg Rd, Essex Junction (05452). 802/879-1515; fax 802/764-5149; toll-free 800/521-2334. www.wilsoninn.com.* 32 kit. suites, 3 story. No elvtr. S, D $74-$94, higher rates some wkends. Crib free. Pet accepted, some restrictions. TV; cable (premium), VCR avail. Heated pool. Playground. Complimentary bkfst buffet. Complimentary coffee in rms. Ck-out 11 am. Coin lndry. Meeting rm. Business servs avail. In-rm modem link. Downhill ski 15 mi; x-country ski 8 mi. Health club privileges. Game rm. Lawn games. Microwaves. Cr cds: A, D, DS, MC, V.

Extended Stay

★★ **RESIDENCE INN BY MARRIOTT.** *1 Hurricane Ln, Williston (05495). 802/878-2001; fax 802/878-0025; res 800/331-3131. www.residenceinn.com.* 96 kit. suites, 2 story. S, D $89-$149; wkly rates; higher rates: graduation, fall foliage. Crib free. Pet accepted. TV; cable (premium). Indoor pool; whirlpool. Playground. Complimentary continental bkfst. Ck-out noon. Coin lndry. Meeting rms. Business servs avail. In-rm modem link. Valet serv. Free airport transportation. Downhill/x-country ski 15 mi. Exercise equipt. Many fireplaces. Balconies. Cr cds: A, D, DS, MC, V.

Restaurants

★ **CARBUR'S.** *115 St. Paul St (05401). 802/862-4106.* Specializes in sandwiches. Hrs: 11:30 am-10:30 pm; Fri, Sat to 11:30 pm. Closed Thanksgiving, Dec 25. Bar. Lunch $5-$10, dinner $7-$15. Child's menu. Outdoor dining. Rustic decor, many antiques. Cr cds: A, DS, MC, V.

★ **DAILY PLANET.** *15 Center St (05401). 802/862-9647.* Continental menu. Specializes in rack of lamb, potato-crusted salmon, Thai pork loin chop. Hrs: 11:30 am-11 pm; Sat, Sun brunch 11 am-3 pm; May-Sept hrs vary. Closed some major hols. Res accepted. Bar to 2 am. Lunch $4.75-$7, dinner $6.75-$14.95. European-style cafe. Frequent art exhibits. Cr cds: A, D, MC, V.

★★ **ICE HOUSE.** *171 Battery St (05401). 802/864-1800.* Specializes in fresh seafood, steak. Own desserts. Hrs: 11:30 am-10 pm; early-bird dinner 5-6 pm; Sun brunch 10:30 am-2:30 pm. Res accepted. Lunch $4.95-$9.95, dinner $12.95-$20.95. Sun brunch $5.75-$8.95. Child's menu. Parking. Covered outdoor dining. Converted icehouse. Waterfront view. Cr cds: A, D, DS, MC, V.

★★★ **PAULINE'S.** *1834 Shelburne Rd, South Burlington (05401). 802/862-1081.* Continental menu. Specializes in fresh seafood, local products. Own baking. Hrs: 11:30 am-2:30 pm; 5-10 pm; Sun to 2:30 pm, winter to 2 pm; early-bird dinner 5-6:30 pm. Closed Dec 24 evening, 25. Res accepted. Bar. Wine list. Lunch $6.95-$8.95, dinner $14.95-$22.95. Sun brunch $5.95-$9.95. Child's menu. Parking. Outdoor dining. Cherry, oak paneling; lace curtains; some antiques. Totally nonsmoking. Cr cds: A, D, DS, MC, V.

★★ **PERRY'S FISH HOUSE.** *1080 Shelburne Rd, South Burlington (05403). 802/862-1300. www.perrysfishhouse.com.* Hrs: 5-10 pm; Fri, Sat 4:30-11 pm; Sun 4-10 pm; early-bird dinner 5-6 pm. Closed Thanksgiving, Dec 25. Res accepted. Bar 4-11 pm. Dinner $9.95-$19.95. Child's menu. Specializes in fresh seafood, prime rib. Salad bar. Parking. Outdoor dining. Nautical decor; lobster tank. Cr cds: A, D, DS, MC, V.

★★ **SWEETWATERS.** *120 Church St (05401). 802/864-9800. www.sweetwatersbistro.com.* Specializes in salads, bison burgers, char-grilled fish. Own desserts. Hrs: 11:30 am-10 pm; Fri, Sat to 11 pm; Sun brunch 10:30 am-2:30 pm. Closed Thanksgiving, Dec 25. Res accepted. Bar to 2 am. A la carte: lunch $4.95-$9.95, dinner $7.95-$19.95. Sun brunch $7.95-$9.95. Child's menu. Entertainment Thurs, Fri. Outdoor dining. Converted bank building (1882). Cr cds: A, D, DS, MC, V.

Charlotte

(see Shelburne)

Chester

(see Springfield)

Dorset

See also Manchester & Manchester Center, Peru

Settled 1768 **Pop** 1,918 **Elev** 962 ft **Area code** 802 **Zip** 05251

Information Dorset Chamber of Commerce, PO Box 121; 802/867-2450

Web www.dorsetvt.com

This charming village is surrounded by hills 3,000 feet high. In 1776 the Green Mountain Boys voted for Vermont's independence here. The first marble quarry in the country was opened in 1785 on nearby Mount Aeolus.

Special Event

Dorset Theatre Festival. Cheney Rd. Professional theater company presents five productions. Phone 802/867-5777. May-Labor Day.

B&Bs/Small Inns

★★ **BARROWS HOUSE INN.** *3156 VT 30 (05251). 802/867-4455; fax 802/867-0132; toll-free 800/639-1620. www.barrowshouse.com.* 28 rms in 9 houses, inn, 3 kits. No rm phones. June-Oct, MAP: S $125-$190; D $185-$235; each addl $30-$50; EP avail; lower rates rest of yr. Crib free. Pet accepted. TV in some rms; VCR avail. Heated pool; sauna, poolside serv. Restaurant (see also BARROWS HOUSE INN). Bar 5-11 pm. Ck-out 11 am, ck-in early afternoon. Bus depot transportation. Meeting rm. Business servs avail. Tennis. Downhill ski 12 mi; x-country ski 6 mi. Bicycles. Lawn games. Game rm. Some refrigerators, fireplaces. Private patios. Picnic tables. Library. Antiques. Gardens. Built in 1804. Cr cds: A, DS, MC, V.

★★★ **DORSET INN.** *Church and Main Sts (05251). 802/867-5500; fax 802/867-5542; toll-free 877/367-7389. www.dorsetinn.com.* 31 rms, 29 A/C, 3 story. No rm phones. S, D $75-$100. Adults only. TV in lounge. Restaurant (see also DORSET INN). Bar 4 pm-midnight. Ck-out 11 am, ck-in 2 pm. Antique furnishings. Established in 1796; oldest continuously operating inn in Vermont. Totally nonsmoking. Cr cds: A, DS, MC, V.

★★★ **INN AT WEST VIEW FARM.** *2928 Rte 30 (05251). 802/867-5715; fax 802/867-0468; toll-free 800/769-4903. www.innatwestviewfarm.com.* 10 rms, 2 story. S $100-$150; D $110-$160; each addl $25; MAP avail. TV in some rms; cable. Complimentary full bkfst. Restaurant (see also INN AT WESTVIEW FARM). Bar 5-9 pm. Ck-out 11 am, ck-in after 2 pm. 18-hole golf privileges. Downhill ski 12 mi; x-country ski 5 mi. Antiques. Cr cds: A, MC, V.

Restaurants

★★★ **BARROWS HOUSE INN.** *VT 30 (05251). 802/867-4455. www.barrowshouse.com.* Regional Amer menu. Specializes in crab cakes, fresh fish, fresh vegetables. Own desserts. Hrs: 8-9:30 am, 6-9 pm; Sat, Sun 8-10 am, 6-9 pm. Res accepted. Bar 5-11:30 pm. A la carte entrees: bkfst $8.50, dinner $10.95-$25.95. Child's menu. Parking. Greenhouse dining. Totally nonsmoking. Cr cds: A, D, DS, MC, V.

★★★ **DORSET INN.** *Church St and Rte 30 (05251). 802/867-5500. www.dorsetinn.com.* Specialties: rack of lamb, fresh fish, crispy duck confit. Own baking. Hrs: 7:30-10 am, 5-9 pm. Res accepted. Bar 4 pm-midnight. Wine list. Bkfst $7.50, dinner $12.50-$22 Parking. Historic building (1796); Colonial decor. Cr cds: A, MC, V.

★★ **INN AT WESTVIEW FARM.** *2928 VT 30 (05251). 802/867-5715. www.vtweb.com/innatwestviewfarm.* Continental menu. Specialties: rack of lamb a l'auberge, breast of duck. Own desserts. Hrs: 6-9 pm. Closed Sun-Tues; also Apr; 1st 2 wks Nov. Bar from 5 pm. A la carte entrees: dinner $21-$28. In converted 1850 farmhouse. Cr cds: MC, V.

Fairlee

See also White River Junction

Pop 883 **Elev** 436 ft **Area code** 802 **Zip** 05045
Information Town Offices, Main St, PO Box 95; 802/333-4363

Special Events

Vermont State Open Golf Tournament. Lake Morey Inn Country Club (see RESORT). Mid-June. Phone 802/333-4311.

Chicken Barbecue. On the Common, Main St. Phone 802/333-4363. July 4.

Resort

★★ **LAKE MOREY RESORT.** *Club House Rd (05045). 802/333-4311; fax 802/333-4553; toll-free 800/423-1211. www.lakemoreyresort.com.* 144 rms, 3 story. MAP, mid-May-Oct: S, D $87-$141/person; golf, ski packages; lower rates rest of yr. Crib $10. TV. Indoor/outdoor pool; whirlpool. Supervised children's activities; ages 3-12. Dining rm (public by res) 7:30-9:30 am, 6:30-9:30 pm. Bar 4-11 pm. Ck-out 11 am, ck-in 2 pm. Business servs avail. In-rm modem link. Bellhops. Two tennis courts. 18-hole golf, greens fee, pro, putting green, driving range. Beach; swimming. Canoes, rowboats. Waterskiing. Windsurfing. Downhill ski 15 mi; x-country ski on site, rentals. Snowmobile trails, sleigh rides, tobogganing. Hiking. Lawn games. Rec rm. Game rm. Exercise equipt; sauna. Refrigerators avail. Balconies. Cr cds: A, MC, V.

B&B/Small Inn

★ **SILVER MAPLE LODGE & COTTAGES.** *520 US 5 S (05045). 802/333-4326; toll-free 800/666-1946. www.silvermaplelodge.com.* 8 lodge rms, 2 share bath; 8 cottages. No A/C. No rm phones. S $69; D $79; each addl $6; cottages $69-$82; kit. cottages $75-$85. Pet accepted in cottages. TV in cottages. Complimentary continental bkfst. Restaurant nearby. Ck-out 11 am. Lodge built as farmhouse in 1790s. Wraparound porch. Cr cds: A, DS, MC, V.

Grafton

See also Bellows Falls, Londonderry, Newfane

Pop 602 **Elev** 841 ft **Area code** 802 **Zip** 05146
Information Great Falls Regional Chamber of Commerce, 55 Village Square, PO Box 554, Bellows Falls 05101; 802/463-4280
Web www.gfrcc.org

This picturesque New England village is a blend of houses, churches, galleries, antique shops, and other small shops—all circa 1800. Founded in pre-Revolutionary times under the patronage of George III, Grafton became a thriving mill town and modest industrial center after the damming of the nearby Saxton River. When water power gave way to steam, the town began to decline. Rescued, revived, and restored by the Windham Foundation, it has been returned to its former attractiveness. A creek curling through town and the peaceful air of a gentler era contribute to the charm of this village, considered a paradise for photographers.

What to See and Do

Grafton Ponds Cross-Country Ski Center. Featuring over 16 mi of groomed trails; school, rentals; concession, warming hut. (Dec-Mar, daily; closed Dec 25) In summer, walking and fitness trails (no fee). Townshend Rd. ¢¢¢¢

The Old Tavern at Grafton. (1801) Centerpiece of village. Visited by many famous guests over the yrs, incl several presidents and authors; names inscribed over the desk. Furnished with antiques, Colonial decor. Former barn converted to lounge; annex is restored from two houses; dining by res. (May-Mar, daily) (See INNS) Main St and Townshend Rd. Phone 802/843-2231.

B&Bs/Small Inns

★★ **INN AT WOODCHUCK HILL FARM.** *Woodchuck Hill Rd (05146). 802/843-2398. www.woodchuckhill.com.* 10 air-cooled rms, 8 with bath, 3 story. Rm phones in suites. S, D $120; each addl $20; suites $210-$260. TV in sitting rm. Complimentary full bkfst; afternoon refreshments. Ck-out 11 am, ck-in 1 pm. Tennis privileges. Sauna. Canoes. Lawn games. Library, sitting rm; antiques. First farmhouse in town (1790). On 200 acres; pond, gazebo. Totally nonsmoking. Cr cds: A, DS, MC, V.

⊠ ☖ ☒ ⚒

★★★ **OLD TAVERN AT GRAFTON.** *92 Main St (05146). 802/843-2231; fax 802/843-2245; toll-free 800/843-1801. www.old-tavern.com.* 65 rms, 3 story, 7 houses. S, D $135-$195; each addl $30; kit. houses $620-$850. Closed Apr. Children over 7 yrs only (exc 3 houses). TV in sitting rm; cable. Complimentary full bkfst; afternoon refreshments. Dining rm 8-10 am, noon-2 pm, 6-9 pm. Bar. Ck-out 11 am, ck-in 4 pm. Coin lndry. Meeting rms. Tennis. Downhill ski 12 mi; x-country ski on site. Game rm. Porches, balconies. Restored inn (1801); Chippendale and Windsor furnishings. Many famous authors have stayed here. Natural swimming pond. Totally nonsmoking. Cr cds: A, MC, V.

Ⓓ ☖ ☒ ⋈ ☒ ☒ ⚒

Green Mountain National Forest

See also Bennington, Manchester & Manchester Center, Rutland, Warren

This 360,000-acre tract lies along the backbone of the Green Mountains, beginning at the Massachusetts line. Its high point is Mount Ellen (4,083 ft). The 260-mile Long Trail, a celebrated hiking route, extends the length of the state; about 80 miles of it are within the forest.

Well-maintained gravel roads wind through the forests of white pine, hemlock, spruce, yellow birch, and sugar maple; there are many recreation areas and privately owned resorts. Hunting and fishing are permitted in the forest under Vermont regulations. There are whitetail deer, black bear, ruffed grouse, and other game, plus brook, rainbow, and brown trout.

Developed and primitive camping, swimming, and picnicking are found throughout the forest, as are privately operated alpine ski areas and ski touring centers. Fees charged at some recreation sites and at developed campsites. Phone 802/747-6700.

What to See and Do

Moosalamoo Recreation Area. 20,000 acres feature trails from which all the forest's diverse natural beauty can be viewed. Winter activities include x-country skiing on groomed, specially marked trails; also alpine skiing. The nation's oldest long-distance hiking trail, the Long Trail, runs the Moosalamoo border for nearly 15 mi. Biking allowed on roads and some trails. Camping facilities abound in the area. (Daily) Within Green Mtn National Forest. Phone 802/747-6700.

Highgate Springs

(see Swanton)

Jeffersonville

See also Stowe

Pop 462 **Elev** 459 ft **Area code** 802 **Zip** 05464
Information Smugglers' Notch Area Chamber of Commerce, PO Box 364
Web www.smugnotch.com

What to See and Do

Smugglers' Notch. Resort has five double chairlifts, three surface lifts; school, rentals; snowmaking; concession area, cafeteria, restaurants; nursery, lodge (see RESORT). 60 runs, longest run over 3 mi; vertical drop 2,610 ft. (Thanksgiving-mid-Apr, daily) More than 25 mi of x-country trails (Dec-Apr, daily; rentals), ice-skating. Summer activities incl ten swimming pools, three water slides; tennis, miniature golf, driving range. 5 mi S on VT 108. Phone 802/644-8851. ¢¢¢¢

Motel/Motor Lodge

★ **HIGHLANDER MOTEL.** *995 Vt Rt 108S (05464). 802/644-2725; toll-free 800/367-6471.* 15 rms. No A/C. Late Dec-Apr and late June-Oct: S $58-$64; D $64-$72; each addl $5; dorm rates; higher rates some hols; lower rates rest of yr. Crib free. Pet accepted. TV; cable. Pool; sauna. Playground. Restaurant 7:30-9 am. Ck-out 11 am. Downhill/x-country ski 3 mi. Lawn games. Rec rm. Refrigerators avail. Picnic tables, grill. View of mountains. Cr cds: MC, V.

☜ ☒ ⋈ ☒ ⚒

Resort

★★★ **SMUGGLER'S NOTCH RESORT.** *4323 VT 108 S (05464). 802/644-8851; fax 802/644-1230; res 800/451-8752. www.smuggs.com.* 525 rms, 113 A/C, 1-3 story, 400 kits. Mid-Dec-Mar: S $99-$225; D $109-$249; kit. units $109-$159; 1-5 bedrm apts avail; under 7 free; wkly rates; tennis, ski, golf plans; higher rates hols; lower rates rest of yr. Crib $20. TV; cable (premium), VCR avail (movies). Heated pool; whirlpool, lifeguard. Playgrounds. Supervised children's activities (summer, winter); ages 6 wks-17. Dining rm 7:30 am-10 pm. Bar 11-1 am; entertainment. Ck-out 10 am, 11 am in summer; ck-in 5 pm. Free lndry facilities. Convention facilities. Business servs avail. Grocery, sport shop. Airport, RR station, bus depot transportation. 12 tennis courts, 2 indoor. Downhill/x-country ski on site. Outdoor ice-skating, sleighing. Water slides. Miniature golf; driving range. Lawn games. Bicycles. Hiking. Soc dir; entertainment, movies. Teen rec rm. Exercise equipt; sauna. Massage. Washers in most rms; some fireplaces; microwaves avail. Some balconies. Cr cds: A, D, MC, V.

B&Bs/Small Inns

★★ **SINCLAIR INN BED & BREAKFAST.** *389 Vt 15, Jericho (05465). 802/899-2234; fax 802/899-2007; toll-free 800/433-4658. www.sinclairinnbb.com.* 6 rms, 4 with shower only, 3 story. No rm phones. Apr-Nov: S $95-$140; D $100-$145; each addl $10; ski plans; wkends, hols, fall foliage (2-day min); higher rates special events; lower rates rest of yr. Children over 12 yrs only. Complimentary full bkfst. Ck-out 11 am, ck-in 3 pm. Downhill ski 18 mi; x-country ski 5 mi. Exercise equipt. Lawn games. Grills. Built in 1890; restored Queen Anne Victorian inn. Totally nonsmoking. Cr cds: A, DS, MC, V.

★ **SMUGGLER'S NOTCH INN AND RESTAURANT.** *55 Church St (05464). 802/644-2412; fax 802/644-2881; toll-free 800/845-3101. www.smugglers-notch-inn.com.* 11 rms, 2 story. No A/C. S $50; D $60-$125; each addl $10-$15; MAP avail. TV in sitting rm; cable. Pool; whirlpool. Complimentary full bkfst. Dining rm 5-9 pm. Ck-out 11 am, ck-in 2 pm. Downhill ski 4 mi; x-country ski 2 mi. Picnic tables. Old country inn (1789) with large porch. Library; many handmade quilts; antiques. Cr cds: A, DS, MC, V.

Cottage Colony

★ **STERLING RIDGE INN & CABINS.** *1073 Junction Hill Rd (05464). 802/644-8265; fax 802/644-5153; toll-free 800/347-8266. www.vermont-cabins.com.* 13 rms, 4 share bath, 5 kit. cabins. No A/C. No rm phones. Dec-mid-Apr, June-Labor Day: S $45-$55; D $62-$139; kit. cabins $90-$125; under 2 free; ski plans; hols (2-day min); higher rates special events; lower rates rest of yr. Crib free. TV in cabins; cable (premium), VCR avail. Complimentary full bkfst. Ck-out 11 am, ck-in 3 pm. Downhill ski 3 mi; x-country

ski on site. Heated pool. Microwave, fireplace in cabins. Picnic tables, grills. On mountain. Totally nonsmoking. Cr cds: MC, V.

Unrated Dining Spot

WINDRIDGE INN. *Main St (05464). 802/644-5556.* Specialties: rack of lamb, red beans and wild rice, duck with Dijon sauce. French menu. Hrs: 5-9 pm. Closed Mon; Dec 25. Res accepted. Bar from 5 pm. A la carte entrees: dinner $10.95-$29.95. Elegant, formal dining in Early Amer atmosphere. Totally nonsmoking. Cr cds: MC, V.

Killington

See also Plymouth, Rutland, Woodstock

Pop 50 **Elev** 1,229 ft **Area code** 802 **Zip** 05751
Information Killington Chamber of Commerce, PO Box 114; 802/773-4181 or 800/337-1928
Web www.killingtonchamber.com

What to See and Do

Gifford Woods State Park. This 114-acre park has fishing at nearby pond, boat access to Kent Pond. Foot trails (Appalachian Trail passes through park). Virgin forest with picnic facilities. Tent and trailer sites (dump station), lean-tos. (Memorial Day-Columbus Day) Standard fees. On VT 100, 1 mi N of jct US 4. Phone 802/775-5354.

Skiing. Killington Resort. Comprises 1,200 acres with seven mountains (highest elev 4,241 ft). Two gondolas, six high-speed quad, six quad, six triple, four double chairlifts, eight surface lifts; patrol, school, rentals; snowmaking; mountaintop restaurant (with observation decks), six cafeterias, bars; children's center, nursery; lodging. More than 200 runs; longest run 10 mi, vertical drop 3,150 ft. Snowboarding; snow tubing. (Oct-June, daily) 5 mi SW of jct US 4 and VT 100, N at 4763 Killington Rd. Phone 800/621-6867.

Summer activities. Resort activities incl a tennis school (Memorial Day-Sept), 18-hole golf, mountain biking (rentals), in-line skating/skateboarding park; gondola rides to view foliage; two water slides (July 4-Sept) Also **Pico Alpine Slide and Scenic Chairlift.** Chairlift to top of mountain slope; control speed of own sled on the way down. Sports center and restaurant below. (Late May-mid-Oct) Phone 802/621-6867.

Motels/Motor Lodges

★★ **GREY BONNET INN.** *831 Rte 100 (05751). 802/775-2537; fax 802/775-3371; toll-free 800/342-2086. www.greybonnetinn.com.* 40 rms, 3 story. No elvtr. MAP, Dec-Mar: S, D $99-$149; each addl $30; EP avail; family, wkly rates, golf plans; lower rates mid-June-mid-Sept. Closed Apr-May, late-Oct-late Nov. Crib $3. TV. 2 pools,

1 indoor; whirlpool. Playground. Restaurant 7:30-9:30 am, 6-9 pm. Bar. Ck-out 11 am. Meeting rm. Tennis. Downhill ski 2 mi; x-country ski adj. Exercise equipt; sauna. Game rm. Rec rm. Lawn games. Balconies. Cr cds: A, DS, MC, V.

★★ **KILLINGTON PICO MOTOR INN.** *64 US 4 (05751). 802/773-4088; fax 802/775-9705; toll-free 800/548-4713. www.killingtonpico.com.* 29 rms. Mid-Dec-mid-Mar: S $49-$135; D $53-$150; each addl $10-$15; wkly rates; higher rates hol wks; lower rates mid-Apr-Aug. Crib avail. TV; cable. Pool; whirlpool. Complimentary full bkfst (winter), continental bkfst (summer). Dining rm mid June-Columbus Day 7-9:30 am. Bar. Ck-out 11 am. Business servs avail. Downhill/x-country ski 1 mi. Game rm. Lawn games. Refrigerators. Cr cds: A, C, D, DS, ER, JCB, MC, V.

★★ **SHERBURNE-KILLINGTON MOTEL.** *1946 US 4 (05751). 802/773-9535; fax 802/773-0011; toll-free 800/366-0493. www.lodgingkillington.com.* 20 rms. Oct-Apr: S, D $55-$115; each addl $16; under 12 free; ski plan; higher rates winter hol wks; lower rates rest of yr. Crib free. TV; cable, VCR (free movies). Heated pool. Complimentary continental bkfst. Playground. Ck-out 11 am. Downhill/x-country ski ½ mi. Lawn games. Refrigerators. Picnic tables, grills. View of mountains. Cr cds: A, DS, MC, V.

★★ **VAL ROC MOTEL.** *8006 US 4 (05751). 802/422-3881; fax 802/422-3236; toll-free 800/238-8762. www.valroc.com.* 24 rms, 16 A/C, 1-2 story, 2 kits. Mid-Dec-mid-Apr: S $49-$98; D $54-$100; each addl $12-$14; kit. units $74-$98; under 12 free; family, wkly rates; higher rates wk of Dec 25; lower rates rest of yr. Crib free. Pet accepted. TV; cable (premium), VCR avail. Heated pool; whirlpool. Complimentary continental bkfst. Complimentary coffee in rms. Ck-out 11 am. Tennis. Downhill ski ¼ mi; x-country ski 3 mi. Game rm. Lawn games. Refrigerators. Some balconies. Picnic tables. Cr cds: A, C, D, DS, MC, V.

Hotels

★★ **CASCADES LODGE.** *58 Old Mill Rd, Killington Village (05751). 802/422-3731; fax 802/422-3351; toll-free 800/345-0113. www.cascadeslodge.com.* 46 rms, 3 story. No A/C. No elvtr. S $60-$153; D $69-$189; each addl $5-$35; suites $118-$267; family rates; golf, package plans; higher rates: winter hols, wkends. Crib free. TV; cable, VCR avail (movies $2.95). Indoor pool; whirlpool. Complimentary full bkfst. Dining rm (see also CASCADES LODGE). Rm serv. Bar from noon; entertainment. Ck-out 11 am. Meeting rms. Business servs avail. In-rm modem link. Downhill/x-country ski on site. Exercise equipt; sauna. Game rm. Lawn games. Balconies. Cr cds: A, DS, JCB, MC, V.

★★ **SUMMIT LODGE.** *Killington Mountain Rd (05751). 802/422-3535; fax 802/422-3536; toll-free 800/635-6343. www.summitlodgevermont.com.* 45 rms, 2-33 story. No A/C. No elvtr. S $63-$128; D $88-$146; each addl $15; family rates; MAP avail; package plans; higher rates some hols. Serv charge 15% (MAP). Crib free. TV; VCR avail (movies $6).

2 pools, 1 heated; whirlpool, poolside serv. Playground. Dining rm 7:30-9:30 am, 6-9 pm; summer 8-10 am, 6-9 pm. Bar from noon; winter from 4 pm. Ck-out 11 am. Business servs avail. Grocery, package store 2 mi. Tennis, pro. Airport transportation. Downhill ski 1 mi; x-country ski 1 mi. Ice-skating. Lawn games. Sauna, steam rm. Massage. Entertainment. Game rm. Rec rm. Racquetball courts. Fireplaces. Balconies. Library. Cr cds: A, DS, MC, V.

Resorts

★★★ **CORTINA INN AND RESORT.** *103 US 4 (05751). 802/773-3333; fax 802/775-6948; toll-free 800/451-6108. www.cortinainn.com.* 91 rms, 6 suites. S $99-$120; D $124-$189; each addl $19-$35; suites $179-$259; under 14 free (exc Dec 25, Presidents wk); wkly, wkend rates; ski, golf, tennis plans; higher rates some hols. Crib $5. TV; cable, VCR avail. Indoor pool; whirlpool. Playground. Complimentary full bkfst. Restaurant (see also ZOLA'S GRILLE). Rm serv. Bar 4 pm-1 am; entertainment. Ck-out 11 am. Meeting rms. Business servs avail. In-rm modem link. Bellhops. Gift shop. Free airport, bus depot transportation. Tennis, pro. Downhill ski 2 mi; x-country ski 4 mi. Ice-skating, sleigh rides, snowmobiling. Exercise equipt; sauna. Massage. Hiking trail. Rec rm. Lawn games. Bicycle rentals. Some bathrm phones, refrigerators, wet bars, fireplaces. Private patios, balconies. Picnic tables, grills. Art gallery. Cr cds: A, C, D, DS, ER, JCB, MC, V.

★★★ **INN OF THE SIX MOUNTAINS.** *2617 Killington Rd (05751). 802/422-4302; fax 802/422-4321; res 800/228-4676. www.sixmountains.com.* 103 air-cooled rms, 3 story. Jan-mid-Mar: S, D $109-$189; suites $199-$309; under 12 free; MAP avail; wkly, wkend rates; higher rates hols; lower rates rest of yr. TV; cable (premium). Indoor/outdoor pool; whirlpool. Complimentary full bkfst (winter). Coffee in rms. Dining rm (public by res) 7-10 am, 6-9 pm. Bar 4 pm-closing. Ck-out noon, ck-in 4 pm. Grocery ¼ mi. Package store 4 mi. Convention facilities. Business servs avail. In-rm modem link. Gift shop. Ski area transportation. Tennis. Downhill ski ½ mi; x-country ski 3 mi. Hiking. Game rm. Exercise equipt; sauna. Massage. Refrigerators. Balconies. Fireplace in lobby. 18-hole golf adj. Cr cds: A, C, D, DS, MC, V.

B&Bs/Small Inns

★★★ **RED CLOVER INN.** *7 Woodward Rd, Mendon (05701). 802/775-2290; fax 802/773-0594; toll-free 800/752-0571. www.redcloverinn.com.* 14 rms, 2 story. MAP, Dec-Mar: S $140-$250; D $200-$545; each addl $70; higher rates hols; lower rates rest of yr. Children over 12 yrs only. Pet accepted. TV; VCR in parlor (movies). Pool. Complimentary coffee. Dining rm (see also RED CLOVER). Ck-out 11 am, ck-in 2 pm. Downhill/x-country ski 6 mi. Antiques. Some in-rm whirlpools. Library/sitting rm. Built 1840; former general's residence. Totally nonsmoking. Cr cds: A, DS, MC, V.

★★ **VERMONT INN.** *Box 37K Rte 4 (05751). 802/775-0708; fax 802/773-2440; toll-free 800/541-7795. www.vermontinn.com.* 18 rms, 2 story. Some A/C. Mid-Dec-mid-Apr, MAP: D $120-$200; each addl $30-$40; EP avail; family, wkly rates; ski plan; higher rates hols; lower rates Memorial Day-mid-Dec. Closed mid-Apr-late May. Children over 6 yrs only. TV in sitting rm. Pool; whirlpool. Restaurant (see also VERMONT INN). Bar from 5 pm. Ck-out 11 am, ck-in 2 pm. Exercise equipt; sauna. Tennis. Downhill ski 2 mi; x-country ski 6 mi. Game rm. Rec rm. Lawn games. Some fireplaces. Picnic tables. Built 1840. Totally nonsmoking. Cr cds: A, D, MC, V.

D ⯈ ⊠ ⊠ ⩕

Restaurants

★★ **CASCADES LODGE.** *58 Old Mill Rd (05751). 802/422-3731. www.cascadeslodge.com.* Continental menu. Specialties: roast duck with sauce du jour, Caribbean-style crab cakes, paella. Own desserts. Hrs: 7-10 am, 5-9 pm. Closed May. Res accepted (dinner). Bar. Bkfst $2.95-$6.95, dinner $10.95-$22.95. Child's menu. Greenhouse-style decor; large picture window offers views of mountains. Cr cds: A, DS, MC, V.

D

★★★ **HEMINGWAY'S.** *US 4 (05751). 802/422-3886. www.hemingwaysrestaurant.com.* Chef/owner Ted Fondulas and his wife, Linda, have presided over their New American restaurant since 1982. The prix-fixe menu, which can be matched with wines, may include seared scallops with truffled potatoes and caramelized onion. Humble service stands out in all three unique dining spaces: the intimate stone-wrapped wine cellar, the brick-walled garden room, or the elegant, peach-colored vaulted room. European, American menu. Specializes in Vermont lamb and game birds, lobster ravioli, pan-roasted striped bass. Own pasta, pastries, bread. Hrs: from 6 pm. Closed Mon, Tues; also mid-Apr-mid-May, first 2 wks Nov. Res accepted. Wine cellar. Prix fixe: dinner $40. Tasting menu: dinner $72, incl wine. Chef-owned. Cr cds: A, C, D, MC, V.

★★★ **RED CLOVER.** *7 Woodward Rd, Mendon (05702). 802/775-2290.* Specializes in fresh Vermont game, rack of lamb, garlic-basil millefiore pasta. Own baking. Menu changes daily. Hrs: 6-9 pm. Closed Sun (inn guests only); also day after Easter-day after Memorial Day. Res accepted. Bar. Wine cellar. Dinner $17-$26. Country decor. Totally nonsmoking. Cr cds: C, DS, MC, V.

★★ **VERMONT INN.** *US 4 (05751). 802/775-0708. www.vermontinn.com.* Specializes in fresh seafood, veal, lamb. Hrs: 5:30-9:30 pm. Closed mid-Apr-Memorial Day. Res accepted. Bar from 5 pm. Dinner $12.95-$20.95. Child's menu. Parking. Fireside dining. View of Green Mts. Totally nonsmoking. Cr cds: A, DS, MC, V.

D

★★ **ZOLA'S GRILLE.** *103 US 4 (05751). 802/773-3331. www.cortinainn.com.* Specializes in fresh seafood. Hrs: 7-10 am, 5:30-9:30 pm; Sun brunch 10:45 am-1:30 pm. Res accepted; required hols. Bar. Bkfst buffet $9. Dinner $9.95-$21.95. Sun brunch $13.95. Child's menu. Parking. Totally nonsmoking. Cr cds: D, DS, MC, V.

D SC

Londonderry

See also Grafton, Peru, Stratton Mt, Weston

Founded 1770 **Pop** 1,506 **Elev** 1,151 ft **Area code** 802 **Zip** 05148
Information Londonderry Area Chamber of Commerce Mountain Marketplace, PO Box 58; 802/824-8178
Web www.londonderryvt.com

Motel/Motor Lodge

★★ **DOSTAL'S RESORT LODGE.** *441 Magic Mt Access Rd (05148). 802/824-6700; fax 802/824-6701; toll-free 800/255-5373. www.dostals.com.* 50 rms, 2 story. A/C in dining rm, main bldg. Mid-Dec-Mar, MAP: S $52-$139; D $62-$139; each addl $34-$44; under 6 free in summer and fall; EP avail; ski plan; some wkend rates; lower rates mid-June-Oct. Closed rest of yr. Serv charge 15%. Crib $12. TV; cable. 2 pools, 1 indoor; 2 whirlpools. Restaurant 8-10 am, 6:30-8:30 pm. Bar from 4 pm. Ck-out 11 am. Tennis. Downhill ski 8 mi; x-country ski 1 mi. Game rm. Cr cds: A, DS, MC, V.

⩕ ⿻ ⊠ ⊠ ♿ ⛷

B&Bs/Small Inns

★ **BLUE GENTIAN LODGE.** *Magic Mountain Rd (05148). 802/824-5908; fax 802/824-3531; toll-free 800/456-2405. www.bluegentian.com.* 13 rms, 3 with shower only, 2 story. No A/C. No rm phones. S $40-$65; D $50-$85; each addl $20; under 5 free; ski plans; higher rates: fall foliage, ski season; lower rates rest of yr. Crib free. TV; cable. Pool. Complimentary full bkfst. Complimentary coffee in lobby. Ck-out 11 am. Business servs avail. Downhill/x-country ski 1 mi. Rec rm. Picnic tables. Totally nonsmoking. Cr cds: MC, V.

D ⯈ ⊠ ⊠ ⩕

★★ **FROG'S LEAP INN.** *RR 1 Box 107 (05148). 802/824-3019; fax 802/824-3657; toll-free 877/376-4753. www.frogsleapinn.com.* 17 rms, 15 with bath, 1-2 story, 4 suites. No A/C. No rm phones. S $85-$110; D $125-$135; each addl $10; suites $93-$103; wkly rates; ski plans. Closed 3 wks Apr and 1 wk Nov. TV in sitting rm; cable. Heated pool. Complimentary continental bkfst. Dining rm (public by res), 4 dinner sittings: 6, 6:30, 8 and 8:30 pm. Ck-out 11 am, ck-in 2 pm. Tennis. Downhill ski 15 mi; x-country ski on site, rentals avail. Game rm. Lawn games. In historic building (1842); antiques. Situated on 32 wooded acres. Cr cds: A, DS, MC, V.

D ⯈ ⿻ ⊠ ⊠ ⩕ SC

★★ **LONDONDERRY INN.** *Rte 100 (05155). 802/824-5226; fax 802/824-3146. www.londonderryinn.com.* 25 air-cooled rms, 20 baths, some share bath, 3 story. No rm phones. Mid-Dec-Mar: S $49-$69; D $59-$79; each addl $30; higher rates: hols, fall foliage, winter wkends, Dec 25-31; lower rates rest of yr. Crib $5. TV in sitting rm; cable. Pool. Complimentary continental bkfst. Dining rm 5:30-8:30 pm; wkends/hols in-season. Ck-out 11 am, ck-in 2 pm. Business servs avail. Downhill ski 10 mi; x-country ski 4 mi. Lawn games. Game rm. Former farmhouse (1826). Cr cds: A, DS, MC, V.

★★ **SNOWDON MOTEL BED & BREAKFAST.** *Rte 11 (05148). 802/824-6047; toll-free 800/419-7600. www.virtualcities.com.* 12 air-cooled rms, 1-2 story. Mid-Dec-mid-Apr: S $40-$45; D $50-$75; each addl $15; family, wkly rates; ski plan; higher rates fall foliage season; lower rates rest of yr. TV; cable (premium). Restaurant 8-9 am. Ck-out 11 am, ck-in 2 pm. Business servs avail. Golf privileges. X-country ski 1 mi. Balconies. Picnic tables, grills. Cr cds: MC, V.

★★ **SWISS INN.** *249 Rte 11 (05148). 802/824-3442; fax 802/824-6313; toll-free 800/847-9477. www.swissinn.com.* 19 rms, 2 story. June-Oct, Dec-Mar: S, D $50-$99; each addl $15; lower rates rest or yr. Crib free. TV; cable. Pool. Complimentary full bkfst. Restaurant 5:30-8:30 pm. Bar. Ck-out 11 am. Meeting rms. Tennis. Downhill ski 6 mi; x-country ski 1½ mi. Lawn games. Totally nonsmoking. Cr cds: MC, V.

Ludlow

See also Plymouth, Springfield, Weston

Chartered 1761 **Pop** 2,302 **Area code** 802 **Zip** 05149
Information Ludlow Area Chamber of Commerce, Okemo Market Pl, PO Box 333; 802/228-5830

What to See and Do

Crowley Cheese Factory. (1882) Oldest cheese factory in US; still makes cheese by hand as in 19th century. Display of tools used in early cheese factories and in home cheese-making. Watch process and sample product. (Mon-Fri) Phone 802/259-2340. **FREE**

Green Mountain Sugar House. Working maple sugar producer on shore of Lake Pauline. Shop offers syrup, candies, crafts, and gifts. (Daily) 4 mi N on VT 100 N. Phone 802/228-7151. **FREE**

Okemo Mountain Ski Area. (See OKEMO STATE FOREST)

B&Bs/Small Inns

★★★ **ANDRIE ROSE INN.** *13 Pleasant St (05149). 802/228-4846; fax 802/228-7910; toll-free 800/223-4846. www.andrieroseinn.com.* 23 rms, 6 A/C, 2 story, 9 suites. Some rm phones. Sept-Mar: S, D $110-$160; suites $215-$290; package plans; lower rates rest of yr. TV; cable

(premium), VCR avail (free movies). Complimentary full bkfst. Ck-out 11 am, ck-in 3 pm. Business servs avail. Gift shop. Downhill ski ½ mi; x-country ski 1 mi. Some in-rm whirlpools, refrigerators; fireplace in suites. Picnic tables. Grills. Elegant country inn (1829); furnished with antiques. Totally nonsmoking. Cr cds: A, MC, V.

★★ **COMBES FAMILY INN.** *953 E Lake Rd (05149). 802/228-8799; fax 802/228-8704; toll-free 800/822-8799. www.combesfamilyinn.com.* 11 units, 2 story. No rm phones. Mid-Sept-mid-Apr: S $59-$153; D $65-$160; each addl $8-$27; MAP avail; family, wkly rates; golf, ski, theater package plans; higher rates last wk of Dec 25, hols; lower rates mid-May-mid-Sept. Closed rest of yr. Pet accepted. Dining rm (public by res) 8-9:30 am, 7 pm sitting. Rm serv 8-9:30 am. Ck-out 11 am, ck-in 2 pm. Bus depot transportation. Downhill ski 4 mi; x-country ski 3 mi. Game rm. Rec rm. Lawn games. Picnic tables, grills. Restored farmhouse (1891) on 50 acres; near Lake Rescue. Cr cds: A, DS, MC, V.

★ **ECHO LAKE INN.** *VT 100 N (05149). 802/228-8602; fax 802/228-3075; toll-free 800/356-6844. www.echolakeinn .com.* 24 air-cooled rms, 17 baths, some share bath, 4 suites, 7 condos, 3 story. July-mid-Oct: S $129-$229; D $139-$239; suites $150-$170; kit. units $100-$170 (2-day min); MAP avail; family, wkly rates; ski plan; wkends fall foliage season (2-day min); lower rates rest of yr. Serv charge 15%. Closed Apr. TV in sitting rm; cable. Pool; wading pool, whirlpool, poolside serv. Steam rm. Dining rm 8-10 am, 6-9 pm; outdoor porch dining (dinner). Rm serv to 9:30 am. Bar from 4 pm. Ck-out 11 am, ck-in 2 pm. Business servs avail. Bus depot transportation. Lighted tennis. Downhill ski 6 mi; x-country ski 5 mi. Lawn games. Whirlpool in suites. Picnic tables. Private dock, canoes. 1840 Victorian building. Cr cds: A, MC, V.

★★ **GOLDEN STAGE INN.** *399 Depot St, Proctorsville (05153). 802/226-7744; fax 802/226-7882; toll-free 800/253-8226. www.goldenstageinn.com.* 9 rms, 2 share bath. No A/C. July-late Oct, mid-Dec-mid-Mar: S $75-$110; D $85-$125; each addl $10; MAP avail; wkly rates; lower rates rest of yr. Pool. Dining rm (public by res), 1 sitting 7 pm. Bar. Ck-out 11 am. Free bus depot transportation. Downhill/x-country ski 3 mi. Lawn games. Totally nonsmoking. Cr cds: MC, V.

★★★★ **THE GOVERNOR'S INN.** *86 Main St (05149). 802/228-8830; fax 802/228-2961; toll-free 800/468-3766. www.thegovernorsinn.com.* Govenor Stickney built this Victorian-style house for his bride in 1890. Slate fireplaces and antiques grace the guest rooms, making this quaint inn a lovely choice for a trip to Vermont. 8 rms, 1 suite, 3 story. MAP: S $105-$180; D $120-$195; suite $250-300; higher rates: ski season wkends, fall foliage. Adults only. Complimentary afternoon refreshments. Dining rm: bkfst 8-9:30 am sitting, dinner 7 pm sitting. Ck-out 11 am. No rm phones. Shuttle transportation avail during ski season. Local transportation avail. Downhill ski 1 mi; x-country ski 1½ mi. Golf. Sitting rm with fireplace. Some fireplaces. Totally nonsmoking. Cr cds: A, DS, MC, V.

Restaurants

★ **HARRY'S CAFE.** *RR 1, Box 179 (05758). 802/259-2996.* Varied menu. Specializes in Thai cuisine. Hrs: 5-10 pm. Closed Mon, Tues; Easter, Thanksgiving, Dec 24, 25; also last wk Apr-1st wk May. Res accepted. No A/C. Bar. Dinner $10.95-$16.95. Child's menu. Casual ambience. Totally nonsmoking. Cr cds: A, C, D, MC, V.

★★★ **NIKKI'S.** *44 Pond St (05149). 802/228-7797. www.nikkisrestaurant.com.* Specializes in steak au poivre, fresh seafood, black Angus beef. Hrs: 5-9:30 pm; Fri, Sat to 10 pm; summer hrs from 5:30 pm. Closed Thanksgiving. Bar. Wine cellar. A la carte entrees: dinner $9.95-$21.95. Child's menu. Cathedral ceiling. Totally nonsmoking. Cr cds: A, DS, MC, V.

D

Lyndonville

See also St. Johnsbury

Settled 1781 **Pop** 1,255 **Elev** 720 ft **Area code** 802 **Zip** 05851

Information Lyndon Area Chamber of Commerce, PO Box 886; 802/626-9696

Web www.lyndonvermont.com

Home of small industries and trading center for the surrounding dairy and stock raising farms, Lyndonville lies in the valley of the Passumpsic River. Five covered bridges, the earliest dating from 1795, are located within the town limits.

What to See and Do

Burke Mountain Ski Area. Area has two chairlifts, one Pomalift, J-bar; school, rentals; snowmaking. Two cafe terias, two bars; nursery. Forty-three runs, longest run approx 2¼ mi; vertical drop 2,000 ft. More than 57 mi of x-country trails. (Thanksgiving-early Apr, daily) 1 mi N on US 5, then 6 mi NE on VT 114, in Darling State Park. Phone 802/626-3322.

Lake Willoughby. Beaches, water sports, fishing; hiking trails to summit of Mt Pisgah at 2,741 ft. 18 mi N on VT 5A.

Motel/Motor Lodge

★ **COLONNADE INN.** *28 Back Center Rd (05851). 802/626-9316; fax 802/626-1023; toll-free 877/435-3688.* 40 rms, 2 story. S $42-$55; D $52-$70; each addl $5; under 12 free. TV; cable (premium). Complimentary continental bkfst. Restaurant nearby. Ck-out 11 am. Downhill/x-country ski 9 mi. Balconies. Cr cds: A, D, DS, MC, V.

B&Bs/Small Inns

★ **THE OLD CUTTER INN.** *143 Pinkham Rd, East Burke (05832). 802/626-5152; toll-free 800/295-1943. www..pbpub.com/cutter.htm.* 10 rms, 2 story. S $44-$56; D $54-$66; each addl $10-$12; kit. suite $120-$140; under 12 free; MAP avail. Closed Apr, Nov. Crib free. Pet accepted. TV in lobby. Pool. Dining rm (see also OLD CUTTER INN). Ck-out 11 am, ck-in 1 pm. Downhill/x-country ski ½ mi. Lawn games. Picnic tables. Sitting rm. In restored farmhouse (ca 1845) and renovated turn-of-the-century carriage house. Cr cds: MC, V.

D

★★ **THE WILDFLOWER INN.** *Darling Hill Rd (05851). 802/626-8310; fax 802/626-3039; toll-free 800/627-8310. www.wildflowerinn.com.* 22 rms in 4 bldgs, 2 share bath, 2 story, 9 kit. suites. No A/C. No rm phones. S $74-$84; D $89-$105; suites $120-$200; higher rates fall foliage. Closed 2 wks Apr and Nov. TV in sitting rm. Heated pool; wading pool, whirlpool, sauna. Free supervised children's activities (Memorial Day-Labor Day); ages 3-12. Complimentary full bkfst. Dining rm (public by res) 5-9 pm. Ck-out 11 am, ck-in 3 pm. Business servs avail. Gift shop. Art gallery. Free bus depot transportation. Tennis on site. Downhill ski 5 mi; x-country ski on site. Hay, sleigh rides. Game rm. Lawn games. Some balconies. Familyoriented inn on 500 acres; barns, farm animals; sledding slopes. Totally nonsmoking. Cr cds: MC, V.

D

Restaurant

★★ **OLD CUTTER INN.** *143 Pinkham Rd, East Burke (05851). 802/626-5152. www.pbpub.com/cutter.html.* Swiss, continental menu. Specialties: tournedos of beef, rack of lamb, Rahmschnitzel. Hrs: 5:30-9 pm; Sun brunch 11 am-1:30 pm. Closed Wed; also Apr, Nov. Res accepted. Bar. Dinner $13-$18.50. Sun brunch $10.50. Child's menu. Converted 1845 farmhouse. Cr cds: C, D, DS, ER, MC, V.

D

Manchester & Manchester Center

See also Arlington, Dorset, Londonderry, Peru, Stratton Mt

Settled 1764 **Pop** 3,622 **Elev** 899 & 753 ft **Area code** 802 **Zip** Manchester 05254; Manchester Center 05255

Information Manchester and the Mountains Regional Chamber of Commerce, 5046 Main St, Suite 1; 802/362-2100 or 800/362-4144

Web www.manchestervermont.net

These towns have been among Vermont's best-loved year-round resorts for 100 years. The surrounding mountains make them serenely attractive, and the ski business has added to their following. Bromley Mountain, Stratton Mountain, and other areas lure thousands each year. A Ranger District office of the Green Mountain National Forest (see) is located here.

What to See and Do

American Museum of Fly Fishing. Collection of fly-fishing memorabilia; tackle of many famous persons, incl Dwight D. Eisenhower, Ernest Hemingway, Andrew Carnegie, Winslow Homer, Bing Crosby, and others. (Apr-Nov, daily; Dec-Mar, Mon-Fri; closed hols) Corner of VT Historic Rte 7A and Seminary Ave. Phone 802/362-3300. ¢

Emerald Lake State Park. This 430-acre park has rich flora in a limestone-based bedrock. Swimming beach, bathhouse, fishing (also in nearby streams), boating (rentals); nature and hiking trails, picnicking, concession. Tent and trailer sites (dump station), lean-tos. (Memorial Day-Columbus Day) Standard fees. 6 mi N on US 7, in North Dorset. Phone 802/362-1655.

🌟 Equinox Sky Line Drive. A spectacular five-mi paved road that rises from 600 to 3,835 ft; parking and picnic areas along road; view from top of Mt Equinox. Fog or rain may make mountain road dangerous and travel inadvisable. (May-Oct, daily) No large camper vehicles. 5 mi S on VT Historic Rte 7A. Phone 802/362-1114. ¢¢¢

Factory outlet stores. Many outlet stores can be found in this area, mainly along VT 11/30 and at the intersection of VT 11/30 and VT 7A. Contact the Chamber of Commerce for a complete listing of stores. Phone 802/362-2100.

Historic Hildene. (1904) The 412-acre estate of Robert Todd Lincoln (Abraham Lincoln's son) incl a 24-rm Georgian manor house, held in the family until 1975; original furnishings; carriage barn; formal gardens; nature trails. Tours. (Mid-May-Oct, daily) 2 mi S via VT Historic Rte 7A, in Manchester Village. Phone 802/362-1788. ¢¢¢

Merck Forest & Farmland Center. Incl 3,100 acres of unspoiled upland forest, meadows, mountains, and ponds; 28 mi of roads and trails for hiking and x-country skiing. Fishing; picnicking, camping (res required). Educational programs. Fees for some activities. 8 mi NW on VT 30 to East Rupert, then 2½ mi W on VT 315. Phone 802/394-7836.

Southern Vermont Arts Center. Painting, sculpture, prints; concerts, music festivals; botany trail; cafe. Gift shop. (Late May-mid-Oct, Tues-Sun) 1 mi N off West Rd. Phone 802/362-1405. ¢¢¢

Vermont Wax Museum. Three Victorian buildings house 85 life-size wax figures from Mark Twain to JFK. Changing audio and video presentations. On-site wax casting studio. Fine art gallery features Vermont artists' work in various media. Museum store. (Daily; closed Jan 1, Easter, Thanksgiving, Dec 25) VT 11/30 between VT 7 & 7A. Phone 802/362-0609. ¢¢

Motels/Motor Lodges

★★ **ASPEN MOTEL.** *VT 7A N, Manchester Center (05255).* 802/362-2450; fax 802/362-1348. *www.thisisvermont.com/aspen.* 24 rms, 1 cottage (2-bedrm). Mid-June-Oct, mid-Dec-Mar: S, D $70-$90; each addl $10; cottage $150-$180; ski plan; July (2-day min); lower rates rest of yr. Crib $5. TV; cable. Pool. Complimentary coffee in rms. Ck-out 11 am. Free bus depot transportation. Tennis privileges. Golf privileges, greens fee, pro. Downhill ski 8 mi; x-country ski 3 mi. Lawn games. Refrigerators avail. Picnic tables. Cr cds: A, DS, MC, V.
[D] [🐾] [🔥] [🎿]

★ **THE BRITTANY INN MOTEL.** *Rte 7A S 1056 Main St, Manchester Center (05255).* 802/362-1033; fax 802/362-0551. *www.thisisvermont.com/brittany.* 12 rms. Jan-mid-Mar, mid-June-mid-Sept: S, D $59-$83; each addl $7; higher rates fall foliage; lower rates rest of yr. Crib free. TV; cable. Complimentary coffee in rms. Ck-out 11 am. Downhill ski 10 mi; x-country ski 2 mi. Refrigerators. Picnic tables, grill. Cr cds: A, MC, V.
[🐾] [🏄] [🎿] [🛶] [🔥]

★★ **EYRIE MOTEL.** *158 Bowen Hill Rd, East Dorset (05253).* 802/362-1208; fax 802/362-2948; res 802/362-1208. *www.thisisvermont.com/eyriemotel.* 12 rms. June-Oct, late Dec-mid-Mar (wkends): S, D $60-$87; each addl $10; wkday rates; lower rates rest of yr. TV. Pool. Complimentary continental bkfst. Ck-out 11 am. Downhill ski 10 mi; x-country ski on site. Hiking. Lawn games. Refrigerators. Picnic tables. Early Amer decor. On 23 acres; sweeping views. Cr cds: A, DS, MC, V.
[🐾] [🎿] [🛶] [🔥]

★★ **FOUR WINDS COUNTRY MOTEL.** *7379 Historic Rte 7A, Manchester Center (05255).* 802/362-1105; fax 802/362-0905; toll-free 877/456-7654. *www.fourwindscountrymotel.com.* 18 rms. Mid-June-mid-Oct: S $66-$115; D $78-$112; each addl $10; lower rates rest of yr. TV; cable. Pool. Coffee in rms. Complimentary continental bkfst. Ck-out 11 am. Meeting rm. Tennis privileges opp. 18-hole golf privileges opp, greens fee, pro. Downhill ski 6 mi; x-country ski 2 mi. Health club privileges. Rec rm. Refrigerators. Private patios. Colonial atmosphere; many antiques. Cr cds: A, MC, V.
[D] [🐾] [🏄] [🎿] [🍴] [🏃] [🏊] [🛶] [🔥] [SC]

★★★ **MANCHESTER VIEW.** *VT 7A & High Meadow Way, Manchester Center (05255).* 802/362-2739; fax 802/362-2199; toll-free 800/548-4141. *manchesterview.com.* 35 rms, 1-2 story. S, D $85-$90; each addl $10; suites $155-$190; wkly rates; ski plan; higher rates hols (3-day min). Crib $10. TV; cable, VCR avail. Heated pool. Restaurant 8-9:30 am. Ck-out 11 am. Meeting rm. Business servs avail. In-rm modem link. Tennis privileges. Golf privileges, greens fee, pro. Downhill ski 7 mi; x-country ski 3 mi. Exercise equipt. Refrigerators, fireplaces; some in-rm whirlpools. Private patios, balconies. Cr cds: A, C, D, DS, MC, V.
[D] [🏄] [🍴] [🏃] [🏊] [🛶] [🔥]

★★ **NORTH SHIRE MOTEL.** *Historic Route 7A, Manchester (05254). 802/362-2336; toll-free 888/339-2336. www.northshiremotel.com.* 14 rms. May-late Nov: S $65-$90; D $70-$110; each addl $5-$10. Closed rest of yr. Crib $3. TV; cable (premium). Pool. Continental bkfst (in season). Ck-out 11 am. Downhill ski 12 mi; x-country ski 2½ mi. Private patios. Extensive grounds. Cr cds: A, DS, MC, V.

★ **OLYMPIA MOTOR LODGE.** *7259 Main St, Manchester Center (05255). 802/362-1700; fax 802/362-1705. www.olympia-vt.com.* 24 rms, 2 story. Mid-June-Oct: S, D $70-$105; each addl $10; ski plan; lower rates rest of yr. TV; cable (premium). Heated pool. Bar noon-11 pm. Ck-out 11 am. Business servs avail. In-rm modem link. Tennis. Golf privileges, greens fee, pro. Downhill ski 7 mi; x-country ski 3½ mi. Private patios, balconies. Cr cds: A, DS, MC, V.

★ **STAMFORD MOTEL.** *6458 Main St, Manchester (05255). 802/362-2342; fax 802/362-1935. www.stamfordmotel.com.* 14 rms, 1-2 story. July-mid-Oct and winter wkends: S, D $56-$65; each addl $6; family, wkly rates; ski plan; lower rates rest of yr. Crib free. TV; cable. Heated pool. Coffee in rms. Ck-out 11 am. Tennis privileges. Golf privileges, greens fee, pro. Downhill ski 6 mi; x-country ski 2½ mi. Some refrigerators. Balconies. Picnic tables. Cr cds: A, DS, MC, V.

★★ **TOLL ROAD MOTOR INN.** *2220 Depot St, Manchester Center (05255). 802/362-1711; fax 802/362-1715.* 16 rms, 2 story. No rm phones. S $70-$95; D $75-$109; each addl $10; wkly rates in winter; ski, golf plans. TV. Pool. Complimentary coffee. Restaurant nearby. Ck-out 11 am. Tennis privileges. 18-hole golf privileges, greens fee, pro. Downhill ski 5 mi; x-country ski 3 mi. Refrigerators. Cr cds: A, DS, MC, V.

★★★ **WEATHERVANE HOTEL.** *2212 Main St, Rte 7A, Manchester (05254). 802/362-2444; fax 802/362-4616; res 802/362-2444.* 22 rms. Memorial Day-late Oct, Dec-late Mar: S, D $150; each addl $10; mid-wk rates (winter); higher rates: fall foliage, Washington's Birthday, wk of Dec 25; lower rates rest of yr. TV; cable (premium). Heated pool. Complimentary coffee in rms. Restaurant nearby. Ck-out 11 am. Business servs avail. In-rm modem link. Sundries. Tennis privileges. Golf privileges, greens fee, pro, putting green. Downhill ski 7 mi; x-country ski ¼ mi. Refrigerators avail. Private patios. Fireplace in lobby. Cr cds: A, JCB, MC, V.

★ **WEDGEWOOD MOTEL.** *5927 Main St, Manchester Center (05255). 802/362-2145; fax 802/362-0190; toll-free 800/254-2145.* 12 rms, 2 suites. June-Oct: S, D $68-$88, suites, $98-$118; TV; cable. Heated pool. Complimentary continental bkfst. Refrigerators. Picnic tables, grill. Cr cds: A, DS, MC, V.

Resorts

★★★ **THE EQUINOX.** *3567 Main St, Manchester Village (05254). 802/362-4700; fax 802/362-1595; toll-free 800/362-4747. www.equinoxresort.com.* 183 units, 3-4 story, 21 kits. EP: S $179; D $189; each addl $30; suites $369-$559, kit. units $359-$899; under 12 free; MAP avail; ski, golf plans. Crib $10. TV; cable (premium), VCR avail. 2 pools, 1 indoor. Restaurant 7 am-9:30 pm; Sun brunch 11 am-2:30 pm. Bar noon-midnight, wkends to 1 am; entertainment Fri-Sat. Ck-out 11 am. Meeting rms. Business servs avail. Concierge. Gift shop. Tennis, pro. 18-hole golf, greens fee $60-$65, pro, putting green. Downhill ski 6 mi; x-country ski on site. Exercise rm; sauna, steam rm. Private patios, balconies. Library. 1700s building; Green Mountain Boys met here. On 2,000 acres. Cr cds: A, C, D, DS, MC, V.

★★★ **PALMER HOUSE.** *VT 7A, Manchester Center (05255). 802/362-3600; toll-free 800/917-6245. www.palmerhouse.com.* 40 rms. Mid-May-Oct: S $60-$120; D $75-$150; each addl $10; lower rates rest of yr. TV; cable. Heated pool; whirlpool. Continental bkfst. Coffee in rms. Restaurant adj. Ck-out 11 am. Business servs avail. Tennis. Downhill ski 6 mi; x-country ski 2 mi. Refrigerators. Picnic tables. Grill. Surrounded by 22 acres of lawn and gardens; view of Green Mts. Lobby furnished with antiques; artwork. Antique doll collection. Cr cds: A, DS, MC, V.

B&Bs/Small Inns

★★★ **1811 HOUSE.** *Rte 7A, Manchester (05254). 802/362-1811; fax 802/362-2443; toll-free 800/432-1811. www.1811house.com.* 14 rms, 2 story. S $110-$210; D $120-$230; fall foliage (2-day min). Children over 16 yrs only. TV avail; cable. Complimentary full bkfst. Bar 5:30-8 pm. Ck-out 11 am, ck-in 2 pm. Tennis privileges. 18-hole golf privileges, pro. Downhill ski 8 mi; x-country ski ½ mi. Game rm. Some fireplaces. Library. Restored 1770 farmhouse; inn since 1811. Canopied beds; antiques; original artwork. Adj to golf course. Cr cds: A, DS, MC, V.

★ **BARNSTEAD INN.** *Bonnet St, Manchester Center (05255). 802/362-1619; fax 802/362-0688; toll-free 800/331-1619. www.barnsteadinn.com.* 14 rms, 1-3 story. S, D $65-$85; each addl $8; ski plan; higher rates special events. TV; cable. Heated pool. Complimentary coffee in rms. Restaurant nearby. Ck-out 11 am. Tennis privileges. Golf privileges, pro. Downhill ski 10 mi; x-country ski 7 mi. Converted barn (1830s). Fairgrounds opp. Totally non-smoking. Cr cds: A, DS, MC, V.

★★★ **INN AT MANCHESTER.** *VT 7A, Manchester (05254). 802/362-1793; fax 802/362-3218; toll-free 800/273-1793. www.innatmanchester.com.* 18 rms in 2 bldgs, 3 story. Mid-June-Labor Day, mid-Dec-late Mar: D $119-159; each addl $25; wkly rates; package plans; higher rates hols; lower rates rest of yr. Children over 8 yrs only. Serv charge 15%. TV in sitting rm; cable. Pool. Complimentary full bkfst;

afternoon refreshments. Dining rm 8-9:30 am. Ck-out 11 am, ck-in 2 pm. Downhill ski 7 mi; x-country ski 2 mi. Private patio. Picnic tables. Antique furnishings. Inn, carriage house (1880). Cr cds: A, DS, MC, V.

★★ **MANCHESTER HIGHLANDS INN.** *216 Highland Ave, Manchester Center (05255).* 802/362-4565; fax 802/362-4028; toll-free 800/743-4565. www.highlandsinn.com. 15 rms, 10 with shower only, 3 story. No rm phones. Mid-June-Oct: S, D $105-$165; each addl $20; under 6 free; ski plans; hols (2-day min). Crib free. TV in common rm. Pool. Complimentary full bkfst. Restaurant nearby. Ck-out 11 am, ck-in 2 pm. Luggage handling. Business servs avail. Downhill ski 6 mi; x-country ski 1 mi. Game rm. Picnic tables. Built in 1898. Totally nonsmoking. Cr cds: A, MC, V.

★★★ **RELUCTANT PANTHER INN AND RESTAURANT.** *39 West Rd, Manchester (05254).* 802/362-2568; toll-free 800/822-2331. www.reluctantpanther.com. 13 rms, 6 suites. MAP, mid-Sept-Oct: S, D $168-$450; wkends (2-day min), hols (3-day min); lower rates rest of yr. Adults only. TV; cable. Complimentary bkfst. Dining rm 6-9 pm; closed Tues, Wed. Ck-out 11 am, ck-in 3 pm. Downhill ski 15 mi; x-country ski 2 mi. Health club privileges. Many fireplaces; whirlpool in suites. Sitting rm. Built 1850. Cr cds: A, MC, V.

★★ **SILAS GRIFFITH INN.** *178 S Main St, Danby (05739).* 802/293-5567; fax 802/293-5559; res 800/545-1509. www.silasgriffith.com. 17 air-cooled rms, 1-3 story. No rm phones. S $119-$149; D $129-$159; each addl $20; under 10 free; wkly rates; ski plans. TV in sitting rm; cable. Pool. Complimentary full bkfst. Dining rm (public by res) 6-8:30 pm. Ck-out 11 am, ck-in 2 pm. Free bus depot transportation. Downhill ski 15 mi; x-country ski 16 mi. Game rm. Home of Vermont's 1st millionaire (1891); antiques. Library, sitting rm. Totally nonsmoking. Cr cds: MC, V.

★★★ **VILLAGE COUNTRY INN.** *3835 Main St, Historic Rte 7A, Manchester (05254).* 802/362-1792; fax 802/362-7238; res 800/370-0800. www.villagecountryinn.com. 33 rms, 3 story. No elvtr. MAP: S $119-$169; D $129-$179; each addl $65; suites $215-$350; ski, golf, fishing plans. Children over 12 yrs only. Serv charge 15%. Some TV. Pool. Complimentary full bkfst. Dining rm 8-9:30 am, 6-9 pm. Bar from 4 pm. Ck-out 11 am, ck-in 2 pm. Gift shop. Free bus depot transportation. Golf privileges, greens fee, pro. Downhill ski 6 mi; x-country ski ½ mi. Cr cds: A, DS, MC, V.

★★★ **WILBURTON INN.** *River Rd, Manchester Village (05254).* 802/362-2500; fax 802/362-1107; toll-free 800/648-4944. www.wilburton.com. 35 rms, 1-3 story. Aug-Oct: S, D $120-$215; suites $175; wkly, family rates; higher rates: hols; lower rates rest of yr. TV in most rms. Pool. Complimentary full bkfst. Dining rm (public by res) 8-10 am,

6-9 pm. Rm serv (in season). Bar from 5 pm. Ck-out 11 am, ck-in 1 pm. Business servs avail. Tennis. Golf privileges, greens fee. Downhill ski 6 mi; x-country ski ½ mi. Some refrigerators. Spacious grounds; sculptural displays. Early 1900s Victorian-style inn with mountain view. Cr cds: A, DS, MC, V.

Restaurants

★★★ **BLACK SWAN.** *VT 7A, Manchester (05254).* 802/362-3807. Continental menu. Specializes in fresh fish, pasta, veal. Own desserts. Hrs: 5:30-9 pm. Closed Dec 24, 25; 2 wks in Nov; also Tues, Wed Dec-May, Wed June-Oct. Res accepted. Bar. Dinner $11.75-$24. Parking. Converted farmhouse built in 1800s. Fireplaces. Cr cds: A, C, MC, V.

★★★ **CHANTICLEER.** *VT 7A, Manchester Center (05255).* 802/362-1616. Continental menu. Specializes in rack of lamb, sweetbreads, fresh seafood. Own desserts. Hrs: 6-10 pm. Closed Tues; Thanksgiving, Dec 25; Apr, mid-Nov-mid-Dec; also Mon in winter. Res accepted. Bar. Wine list. Dinner $19.95-$26. Parking. Tableside cooking. Former dairy barn. Fireplace. Cr cds: A, DS, MC, V.

★★ **GARLIC JOHN'S.** *VT 11, Manchester Center (05255).* 802/362-9843. Italian menu. Specializes in seafood, pasta, veal dishes. Hrs: 4:30-9:30 pm; Fri, Sat to 10 pm. Closed Thanksgiving, Dec 24. Bar. Dinner $7.95-$17.95. Child's menu. Parking. Totally nonsmoking. Cr cds: A, C, MC, V.

★★ **MARK ANTHONY'S YE OLDE TAVERN.** *5183 N Main St, Manchester (05255).* 802/362-0611. Specializes in poultry and veal dishes, fresh seafood. Hrs: 11:30 am-3 pm, 5-9 pm. Res accepted. Bar. Lunch $5.25-$12, dinner $12-$24.95. Parking. Historic 200-yr-old tavern. Cr cds: A, MC, V.

★★ **SIRLOIN SALOON.** *VT 11, Manchester Center (05255).* 802/362-2600. www.sirloinsaloon.com. Specializes in wood-grilled steak, chicken, seafood. Salad bar. Hrs: 5-10 pm; Fri, Sat to 11 pm. Closed Thanksgiving. Res accepted. Bar from 4 pm. Dinner $7.95-$19.95. Child's menu. Parking. Open hearth. Converted mill; antiques. Southwestern theme; Native American artwork, artifacts. Cr cds: A, D, DS, MC, V.

Marlboro

See also Brattleboro, Wilmington

Settled 1763 **Pop** 924 **Elev** 1,736 ft **Area code** 802 **Zip** 05344

What to See and Do

Marlboro College. (1946) 300 students. Arts and sciences, international studies. On campus is Drury Art Gallery (Mon-Fri; closed hols). 2½ mi S of VT 9. Phone 802/257-4333.

Special Event

Marlboro Music Festival. Marlboro College campus. Chamber music concerts. Phone 802/254-2394 or 215/569-4690. Mid-July-mid-Aug.

B&B/Small Inn

★ **WHETSTONE INN.** *550 South Rd (05344).* 802/254-2500; toll-free 877/254-2500. *www.whetstoneinn.com.* 11 rms, 3 share bath, 2 story, 3 kits. No A/C. S $35-$70; D $65-$85; each addl $15; kit. units $75-$90; wkly rates. Crib $2. Pet accepted. Restaurant 8-10 am, 7-8 pm (public by res). Ck-out 2 pm, ck-in after 2 pm. Some refrigerators. Picnic tables. 18th-century country inn was originally a stage-coach stop; fireplaces in public rms. Swimming pond. Cr cds: A, D, DS, MC, V.

🐾 🖼 🖐

Restaurant

★ **SKYLINE.** *VT 9 (05344).* 802/464-3536. Specializes in New England dishes. Hrs: 7:30 am-8 pm; Fri, Sat to 9 pm, Sun to 5 pm. Closed Thanksgiving, Dec 25. Serv bar. Bkfst $2.50-$7.95, lunch, dinner $5.25-$15.95. Child's menu. Early Amer decor; fireplace. On Hogback Mt; 100-mi view from dining rm. Cr cds: A, MC, V.

[D] [SC]

Middlebury

See also Brandon, Vergennes

Settled 1761 **Pop** 8,034 **Elev** 366 ft **Area code** 802 **Zip** 05753

Information Addison County Chamber of Commerce Information Center, 2 Court St; 802/388-7951 or 800/733-8376

Web www.midvermont.com

Benjamin Smalley built the first log house here just before the Revolution. In 1800 the town had a full-fledged college. By 1803 there was a flourishing marble quarry and a women's academy run by Emma Hart Willard, a pioneer in education for women; today, it is known as Middlebury College. A Ranger District office of the Green Mountain National Forest (see) is located here; map and guides for day hikes on Long Trail are available.

What to See and Do

Congregational Church. (1806-1809) Built after a plan in the *Country Builder's Assistant* and designed by architect Lavius Fillmore. Architecturally, one of finest in Vermont. (Mid-June-Aug, Fri and Sat) On the Common. Phone 802/388-7634.

Green Mountain National Forest. (see).

Historic Middlebury Village Walking Tour. Contact the Addison County Chamber of Commerce Information Center for map and information. Phone 802/388-7951.

Middlebury College. (1800) 1,950 students. Famous for the teaching of arts and sciences; summer language schools; Bread Loaf School of English and Writers' Conference. W of town on VT 125. Phone 802/443-5000. College includes

Bread Loaf. Site of nationally known Bread Loaf School of English in July and annual Writers' Conference in Aug. Also site of Robert Frost's cabin. In winter, it is the Carroll and Jane Rikert Ski Touring Center. 10 mi E on VT 125. Phone 802/388-7951.

Emma Willard House. Location of first women's seminary (1814), now admissions and financial aid offices. Phone 802/388-7951.

Middlebury College Museum of Art. (Tues-Sun; closed Jan 1, Thanksgiving, Dec 25) Phone 802/443-5007. **FREE**

Middlebury College Snow Bowl. Area has triple, two double chairlifts; patrol, school, rentals; snowmaking; cafeteria. Fourteen runs. (Early Dec-early Apr, daily; closed Dec 25) 13 mi E on VT 125, just E of Bread Loaf. Phone 802/388-4356. ¢¢¢¢

Old Stone Row. Incl Painter Hall (1815), oldest college building in state. Phone 802/388-7951.

⭐ **Starr Library.** Has collection of works by Robert Frost and other American writers. (Daily; closed hols) Phone 802/388-7951.

Henry Sheldon Museum. Comprehensive collection of 19th-century "Vermontiana" in brick house (1829) with black marble fireplaces. Authentic furnishings range from hand-forged kitchen utensils to country and high-style furniture. Museum also features oil portraits, pewter, Staffordshire, clocks, pianos, toys, dolls, and local relics. Guided & self-guided tours. (Daily, 10 am-5 pm) 1 Park St. Phone 802/388-2117. ¢¢

UVM Morgan Horse Farm. Breeding and training farm for internationally acclaimed Morgan horses; owned by the University of Vermont. Daily workouts and training can be viewed. Guided tours, slide presentations. (May-Oct, daily) 2½ mi NW off VT 23. Phone 802/388-2011. ¢¢

Vermont State Craft Center at Frog Hollow. Restored mill overlooking Otter Creek Falls houses an exhibition and sales gallery with works of more than 300 Vermont craftspeople. Special exhibitions, classes and workshops. (Spring-fall, daily; rest of yr, Mon-Sat; closed hols) 1 Mill St. Phone 802/388-3177. **FREE**

Special Events

Winter Carnival. Middlebury College Snow Bowl. Late Feb.

Addison County Home and Garden Show. Exhibits, demonstrations. Usually last wkend Mar.

Festival on the Green. Village green. Classical, modern, and traditional dance; chamber and folk music; theater and comedy presentations. Early July.

Motels/Motor Lodges

★ **BLUE SPRUCE MOTEL.** *2428 Rte 7 S (05753). 802/388-4091; fax 802/388-3003; toll-free 800/640-7671.* 22 rms, 6 cottages, 2 suites, 3 kits. S, D $58-$75; each addl $10; suites $95-$135; kit. units $10 addl; higher rates in fall. TV; cable. Ck-out 10 am. Downhill ski 8 mi; x-country ski 6 mi. Cr cds: A, C, D, DS, MC, V.
⊠ ⊠ 🔥

★ **GREYSTONE MOTEL.** *1395 Rte 7 S (05753). 802/388-4935; fax 802/388-7810. www.midvermont.com/lodging//greystone.htm.* 10 rms. Mid-May-Oct: S, D $70-$95; each addl $8; lower rates rest of yr. TV; cable. Restaurant nearby. Ck-out 10 am. Downhill ski 11 mi; x-country ski 9 mi. Picnic tables. Cr cds: MC, V.
🔥 ⊠

Hotel

★★ **MIDDLEBURY INN.** *14 Court House Sq (05753). 802/388-4961; fax 802/388-4563; toll-free 800/842-4666. www.middleburyinn.com.* 45 rms in inn, 20 motel rms, 2-3 story. S $100; D $165; each addl $8; suites $175-$365. Crib free. Pet accepted, some restrictions; $8. TV; cable. Complimentary continental bkfst; afternoon refreshments. Coffee in motel rms. Restaurants 7:30-10 am, 11:30 am-2 pm, 5:30-9 pm (winter to 8 pm); Sun brunch 10:30 am-2 pm. Bar. Ck-out 11 am, ck-in 3 pm. Meeting rms. Business servs avail. Bellhops. Gift shop. Downhill/x-country ski 13 mi. Bathrm phones. Antiques. Porch dining in summer. Established in 1827. Cr cds: A, D, DS, MC, V.
D 🔆 ⊠ ⊠ 🔥

B&Bs/Small Inns

★★★ **SWIFT HOUSE INN.** *25 Stewart Ln (05753). 802/388-9925; fax 802/388-9927. www.swifthouseinn.com* 21 rms in 3 bldgs, 2 story. S $110-$195; D $140-$235; each addl $20. Crib free. TV in some rms; cable. Complimentary continental bkfst. Restaurant. Rm serv. Ck-out 11 am, ck-in 3 pm. Meeting rms. Business servs avail. Downhill/x-country ski 10 mi. Sauna, steam rm. Some in-rm whirlpools, fireplaces. Built 1815; each rm individually decorated; four-poster beds, handmade quilts, antiques. Cr cds: A, C, D, DS, MC, V.
D 🔆 🔆 ⊠ ⊠ 🔥

★★ **WAYBURY INN.** *457 E Main Rte 125, East Middlebury (05743). 802/388-4015; fax 802/388-1248; toll-free 800/348-1810. www.wayburyinn.com.* 14 rms, 5 A/C. No rm phones. Jan-Feb, May-Oct: S, D $105-$195; each addl $10; lower rates rest of yr. TV in lobby; VCR. Complimentary full bkfst. Restaurant. Bar 4-11 pm. Ck-out 11 am, ck-in 3 pm. Meeting rms. Business servs avail. Downhill/x-country ski 10 mi. Hiking trails nearby. Constructed as a stagecoach stop; inn since 1810. Parlor, porch. Sun deck. Near Middlebury College. Cr cds: C, D, DS, MC, V.
🔆 🔆 ⊠ ⊠ 🔥

Restaurants

★★ **DOG TEAM TAVERN.** *1338 Dog Team Rd (05753). 802/388-7651. www.dogteamtavern.com.* Specializes in sticky buns, baked ham with fritters, fresh seafood. Hrs: 5-9 pm; Sat from 4 pm; Sun noon-9 pm. Closed Dec 24, 25. Bar. Dinner $11.95-$17.95. Child's menu. Parking. Country atmosphere. Totally nonsmoking. Cr cds: C, D, DS, ER, MC, V.
D

★★ **FIRE AND ICE.** *26 Seymour St (05753). 802/388-7166. www.fireandicerestaurant.com.* Specializes in steak, seafood. Salad bar. Hrs: 11:30 am-8:30 pm; Mon from 5 pm; Sat to 9 pm; Sun 1-8:30 pm. Closed Dec 25. Res accepted. Bar. Lunch $9.95-$13.95, dinner $14.95-$22.95. Child's menu. Parking. Eclectic decor, casual. Totally nonsmoking. Cr cds: A, C, D, DS, MC, V.
D

★ **MISTER UP'S.** *25 Bakery Ln (05753). 802/388-6724.* Continental menu. Specializes in fresh seafood. Salad bar. Hrs: 11:30 am-midnight; Sun brunch 11 am-2 pm. Closed Thanksgiving, Dec 24 eve, 25. Res accepted. Bar. A la carte entrees: lunch $5.25-$7.95, dinner $9.25-$13.95. Child's menu. Parking. Outdoor dining on river. Cr cds: A, D, DS, MC, V.
D

Montpelier

See also Barre, Waitsfield, Waterbury

Settled 1787 **Pop** 8,247 **Elev** 525 ft **Area code** 802

Information Central Vermont Chamber of Commerce, PO Box 336, Barre 05641; 802/229-5711

Web www.central-vt.com

The state capital, on the banks of the Winooski River, is also a life insurance center. Admiral Dewey, victor at Manila Bay, was born here. A popular summer vacation area, Montpelier absorbs the overflow from the nearby ski areas in winter.

What to See and Do

Hubbard Park. A 110-acre wooded area with picnic area (shelter, fireplaces, water). Stone observation tower (1932). 1 mi NW, on Hubbard Park Dr. Phone 802/223-5141. **FREE**

Morse Farm. Maple sugar and vegetable farm in rustic, wooded setting. Tour of sugar house; view sugarmaking process in season (Mar-Apr); slide show explains process off-season. Gift shop. (Daily; closed Easter, Dec 25) 3 mi N via County Rd (follow signs on Main St). Phone 802/223-2740. **FREE**

State House. (1859) Made of Vermont granite; dome covered with gold leaf. (Mon-Fri, also Sat late morning-early afternoon July-mid-Oct) State St. Phone 802/828-2228. **FREE**

Thomas Waterman Wood Art Gallery. Oils, watercolors, and etchings by Wood and other 19th-century American artists. Also American artists of the 1920s and '30s; changing monthly exhibits of works of contemporary local and regional artists. (Tues-Sun afternoons; closed hols) In Vermont College Arts Center, at College St. Phone 802/828-8743. ¢

Vermont Department of Libraries. Local and state history collections. (Mon-Fri; closed hols) Pavilion Office Building. 109 State St. Phone 802/828-3261. **FREE**

Vermont Historical Society Museum, Library. Historical exhibits. (Tues-Sun; closed hols) Pavilion Office Building, adj State House. Phone 802/479-8500. ¢¢

Motels/Motor Lodges

★ **COMFORT INN.** 213 Paine Turnpike N (05602). 802/229-2222; toll-free 800/228-5150. www.comfortinn.com 89 rms, 3 story, 19 kit. suites. No elvtr. S $95; D $115; each addl $10; kit. suites $99-$220; under 18 free; wkly rates; higher rates fall foliage. Crib free. TV; cable, VCR (movies). Complimentary continental bkfst. Restaurant adj 6 am-11 pm. Bar 5-10 pm. Ck-out 11 am. Coin lndry. Meeting rms. Business servs avail. In-rm modem link. Free airport transportation. Some refrigerators. Cr cds: A, D, DS, MC, V.
🅳 ✈ 🖼 🐾 SC

★★ **LAGUE INN.** 3472 Airport Rd; Box 573, Berlin (05602). 802/223-5766; fax 802/229-5766. www.lagueinns.com. 81 units, 2 story. S $65-$100; D $75-$120; each addl $10; under 6 free; wkly rates; higher rates: hols, fall foliage. Crib free. TV; cable (premium), VCR (movies $5). Indoor pool. Restaurant 6:30 am-9 pm. Bar. Ck-out 11 am. Meeting rms. Business servs avail. Free airport transportation. X-country ski 4 mi. Some refrigerators. Picnic tables. Cr cds: A, DS, MC, V.
🅳 🏊 🖼 ✈ 🐾 🖼 SC

Hotel

★★★ **CAPITOL PLAZA HOTEL AND CONFERENCE CENTER.** 100 State St (05602). 802/223-5252; fax 802/229-5427; toll-free 800/274-5252. www.capitolplaza.com. 56 rms, 3 with shower only, 4 story. S $69-$109; D $79-$119; each addl $10; under 16 free; higher rates: wkends, fall foliage. Crib free. TV; cable. Coffee in rms. Restaurant 7 am-9 pm; Sat, Sun from 8 am. Bar noon-11 pm. Ck-out 11 am. Meeting rms. Business servs avail. In-rm modem link. Gift shop. Barber, beauty shop. Health club privileges. Renovated 1930s hotel. Cr cds: A, DS, MC, V.
🅳 🖼 🐾 SC

B&Bs/Small Inns

★ **BETSY'S BED AND BREAKFAST.** 74 E State St (05602). 802/229-0466; fax 802/229-5412. www.centralvt.com/web/ /betsybb. 12 rms, 2 story, 5 kit. units. No A/C. S $60-$80; D $70-$100; kits. $110; higher rates May-Oct. Crib free. TV; cable. Complimentary full bkfst. Restaurant nearby. Ck-out 11 am, ck-in 5 pm. Exercise equipt. Built 1895; Victorian decor with many antiques. Cr cds: A, DS, MC, V.
🖼 🔥 🏃

★★★ **INN AT MONTPELIER.** 147 Main St (05602). 802/223-2727; fax 802/223-0722. www.innatmontpelier.com. 27 rms, 2 story. S $94-$167; D $104-$177; each addl $10; higher rates fall foliage. TV; cable. Complimentary continental bkfst. Ck-out 11 am, ck-in 3-10 pm. Business servs avail. In-rm modem link. Some fireplaces. Federal-style buildings with large front porch (1828); sitting rms; paintings. Cr cds: A, D, DS, MC, V.
🐾 🔥 🖼 SC

★★★ **THE INN ON THE COMMON.** 162 N Craftsbury Rd, Craftsbury Common (05827). 802/586-9619; fax 802/586-2249; toll-free 800/521-2233. www.innonthecommon.com. 16 rms in 3 bldgs, 2 story. No A/C. No rm phones. MAP: S $170-$195; D $250-$290; suites $270-$320; package plans; higher rates fall foliage. Serv charge 15%. Crib free. Pet accepted. TV in sitting rm; VCR. Heated pool. Afternoon refreshments. Dining rm 8-9:30 am, dinner (2 sittings) 6:30, 8 pm. Bar. Ck-out 11 am, ck-in 1 pm. Business servs avail. Tennis. Golf privileges. X-country ski on site. Bicycle rentals. Health club privileges. Lawn games. Antiques. Library. Some fireplaces. Restored Federal-period houses in scenic Vermont village; landscaped gardens. Extensive film collection. Cr cds: A, MC, V.
🐾 🔥 🏊 🎿 🚴 🖼

★★ **NORTHFIELD INN.** 228 Highland Ave, Northfield (05663). 802/485-8558; res 802/485-8558. www.vacationspot.com/northfieldinn1.htm. 28 rms, 3 story, 2 suites. No A/C. S $85; D $159; suites $130. Children over 15 yrs only. TV, VCR avail (free movies). Complimentary full bkfst; afternoon refreshments. Ck-out 11 am, ck-in 3 pm. Business servs avail. Game rm. Lawn games. Built 1901; furnished with period pieces. Totally nonsmoking. Cr cds: A, ER, MC, V.
🐾 🔥 🏊 🖼 🔥

Restaurants

★★ **CHEF'S TABLE.** 118 Main St (05602). 802/229-9202. Continental menu. Hrs: 6-9:30 pm. Closed Sun; most major hols. Res accepted. Bar 4-11 pm. A la carte entrees: dinner $13.50-$18.75. Prix fixe: $30, $45 with wines. Serv charge 15%. Owned and operated by New England Culinary Institute. Totally nonsmoking. Cr cds: A, DS, MC, V.
🅳 SC

★★ **MAIN STREET GRILL AND BAR.** 118 Main St (05602). 802/223-3188. Hrs: 7-10 am, 11:30 am-2 pm, 5:30-10 pm; Sat from 8 am. Sun brunch 10 am-2 pm. Closed major hols. Bar. Lunch $4.50-$6.50, dinner $6.95-$11.50 (serv charge 15%). Sun brunch $11.95. Outdoor dining. Training restaurant for 1st and 2nd year students of New England Culinary Institute. Totally nonsmoking. Cr cds: A, C, D, DS, ER, MC, V.
🅳 SC

Mount Mansfield State Forest

(See Stowe)

Newfane

See also Brattleboro

Settled 1774 **Pop** 1,555 **Elev** 536 ft **Area code** 802
Zip 05345
Information Town Clerk, PO Box 36; 802/365-7772
Web www.newfanevt.com

Originally settled high on Newfane Hill, this is a charming, sleepy town. American poet Eugene Field spent many summer holidays here.

What to See and Do

Jamaica State Park. On 758 acres. Old RR bed along West River serves as trail to Ball Mtn Dam. Fishing; hiking trails, picnicking, tent and trailer sites (dump station), lean-tos. Whitewater canoe on river. (May-Columbus Day) Standard fees. 13 mi W on VT 30, in Jamaica. Phone 802/874-4600. ¢¢

Scott Covered Bridge. (1870) Longest single span in state (166 ft), built with lattice-type trusses. Together, the three spans total 276 ft. Other two spans are of king post-type trusses. Over the West River in Townshend, 5 mi N via VT 30.

Townshend State Forest. A 1,690-acre area with foot trail to Bald Mtn (1,580 ft). Swimming at nearby Townshend Reservoir Recreation Area; hiking trails, picnic sites, tent and trailer sites. (May-Columbus Day) Standard fees. 6 mi N, off VT 30. Phone 802/365-7500.

Windham County Courthouse. (1825) On the green.

Windham County Historical Society Museum. Contains artifacts from the 21 towns of Windham County; exhibits on the Civil War and the Vermont Regiment. (Memorial Day-Columbus Day, Wed-Sun) Main St. Phone 802/365-4148. **Donation**

B&Bs/Small Inns

★★★ **FOUR COLUMNS INN.** *21 West St (05345). 802/365-7713; fax 802/365-0022; toll-free 800/787-6633. www.fourcolumnsinn.com.* 16 rms, 4 suites. S, D $120-$135; each addl $25; suites $140-$250. Pet accepted. TV in lounge; cable (premium). Pool. Complimentary full bkfst. Dining rm 6-9 pm, exc Tues (guests only) 8-9:30 am (see also FOUR COLUMNS). Bar from 4 pm. Ck-out 11 am, ck-in 2 pm. Business servs avail. Stately 19th-century house; Colonial furnishings. On 150 wooded acres; walking paths, gardens. Totally nonsmoking. Cr cds: A, DS, MC, V.

★★ **OLD NEWFANE INN.** *Rte 30 & Village Common (05345). 802/365-4427; toll-free 800/784-4427. www.oldnewfaneinn.com.* 10 rms, 9 baths, 3 story. No A/C. No elvtr. No rm phones. S $105; D $125; each addl $25; 2-day min wkends; 3-day min hols. Closed Mon; also Apr-late May, Nov-mid-Dec. Children over 10 yrs only. Complimentary continental bkfst. Restaurant (see also OLD NEWFANE). Bar. Ck-out 11 am, ck-in 4 pm. Downhill ski 2 mi; x-country ski 12 mi. Some fireplaces. Established in 1787; authentic Colonial furnishings. Cr cds: A, DS, MC, V.

★★★ **WINDHAM HILL INN.** *311 Lawrence Dr, West Townshend (05359). 802/874-4080; fax 802/874-4702; toll-free 800/944-4080. windhamhill.com.* 21 rms, 3 story. MAP: S $200-$240; D $250-$325; wkend, wkly rates; higher rates fall foliage. Closed Apr. Children over 12 yrs only. TV in sitting rm. Heated pool. Dining rm (public by res). Ck-out 11 am, ck-in 2 pm. Business servs avail. Tennis court. Downhill ski 15 mi; x-country ski on site. Some fireplaces. Sun deck. Built 1825; many antiques. Situated on 160-acre mountainside location; views. Totally nonsmoking. Cr cds: A, DS, MC, V.

Restaurants

★★★ **FOUR COLUMNS.** *21 West St (05345). 802/365-7713. www.fourcolumnsinn.com.* Mediterranean menu. Specializes in local lamb, fresh game, fresh fish. Own baking. Hrs: 6-9 pm. Closed Tues; Dec 24-25; also 2 wks Apr. Res accepted. Bar. Wine list. A la carte entrees: dinner $22-$30. Colonial decor. Totally nonsmoking. Cr cds: A, C, D, DS, ER, MC, V.

★★★ **OLD NEWFANE.** *VT 30 (05345). 802/365-4427. www.oldnewfaneinn.com.* Continental menu. Specialties: frogs' legs, wild game. Own baking. Hrs: 6-9 pm; Sun 5-8:30 pm. Closed Mon; Apr-late May, Nov-mid-Dec. Res accepted. Bar. Wine list. Dinner $18.95-$30. Historical landmark (1787); Colonial decor. Cr cds: A, DS, MC, V.

Newport

Settled 1793 **Pop** 4,434 **Elev** 723 ft **Area code** 802
Zip 05855
Information Chamber of Commerce, The Causeway; 802/334-7782

Just a few miles from the Canadian border, Newport lies at the southern end of Lake Memphremagog. Rugged Owl's Head (3,360 feet) guards the western shore of the lake. Recreational activities in the area include swimming, fishing, boating, camping, skiing, and snowmobiling.

What to See and Do

Goodrich Memorial Library. Artifacts of old Vermont in historic building; animal display. (Mon-Sat; closed hols) 202 Main St. Phone 802/334-7902. **FREE**

Haskell Opera House & Library. Historic turn-of-the-century building owned jointly by local Canadian and US residents. First floor houses library with reading rm in US, book stacks in Canada. Second floor is historic, turn-of-the-century opera house that preserves much of its antiquity (seats 400) with audience in US, stage in Canada. Summer concert series (fee). Tours (Tues-Sat, $2). 8 mi N via US 5, on Caswell Ave in Derby Line, VT, and Stanstead, QC, Canada. Phone 802/873-3022 or opera house 802/876-2020.

Newport's *Princess*. Cruise Lake Memphremagog in both US and Canadian waters aboard sternwheeler with turn-of-the-century decor. Cruises incl Sightseeing (90 min), Pizza (90 min, res required), Buffet Dinner (two hrs, res required), Moonlight (90 min), and Weekend Brunch (90 min, res required). (May-Oct, daily; departures vary) City Dock. Phone 802/334-6617.

Northeast Kingdom Tours. Escorted bus tours depart from Newport Municipal Building and local motels. Narrated trips (two and four hrs) explore international border region (Vermont/Canada); incl stops at dairy farm and Old Stone House museum. Cruises on Lake Memphremagog and trips to Montréal also avail. 3 Clough St. Phone 802/334-8687.

Old Stone House. (1836) Museum housed in four-story granite building with antique furniture; early farm, household, and military items; 19th-century schoolbooks. (July-Aug, daily; mid-May-June, Sept-mid-Oct, Mon, Tues, Fri-Sun) 11 mi SE via US 5S or I-91 S to Orleans, then 2 mi NE on unnumbered road to Brownington Village. Phone 802/754-2022. ¢¢

Motels/Motor Lodges

★★ **NEWPORT CITY MOTEL.** *444 E Main St (05855). 802/334-6558; fax 802/334-6557; toll-free 800/338-6558. www.vermonter.com/ncm.* 64 rms, 2 story. S, D $58-$75. Crib $6. TV; cable. Indoor pool; whirlpool. Coffee in rms. Restaurant opp 5:30 am-2 pm. Ck-out 11 am, ck-in 3 pm. Meeting rm. Business servs avail. In-rm modem link. Sundries. Downhill/x-country ski 15 mi. Exercise equipt. Some refrigerators. Balconies. Cr cds: A, D, DS, MC, V.

★ **SUPER 8.** *974 E Main St, Derby (05829). 802/334-1775; fax 802/334-1994; res 800/800-8000. www.super8.com.* 52 rms, 2 story. S $45.88; D $63.88; each addl $6; suites $111; under 12 free. Crib $6. TV; cable. Complimentary continental bkfst. Restaurant nearby. Ck-out 11 am. Business servs avail. Cr cds: A, D, DS, MC, V.

Restaurant

★★ **EAST SIDE RESTAURANT AND PUB.** *25 Landing St (05855). 802/334-2340.* Continental menu. Specializes in fresh seafood, steak, prime rib. Own desserts. Hrs: 7:30 am-10 pm; Sun from 7 am. Closed Mon (winter); Dec 25. Bar. Bkfst $3.25-$5.95, lunch $3.95-$6.95, dinner $7.50-$15. Outdoor dining. On lake; dockage. Cr cds: DS, MC, V.

North Hero

Pop 502 **Elev** 111 ft **Area code** 802 **Zip** 05474
Information Champlain Islands Chamber of Commerce, PO Box 213; 802/372-8400
Web www.champlainislands.com

What to See and Do

North Hero State Park. A 399-acre park located in the north part of the Champlain Islands; extensive shoreline on Lake Champlain. Swimming, fishing, boating (ramps); hiking trails, playground, tent and trailer sites (dump station), lean-tos. (Memorial Day-Labor Day) Standard fees. 6 mi N, off US 2 near South Alburg. Phone 802/372-8727.

Special Event

Royal Lippizan Stallions of Austria. Summer residence of the stallions. Performances Thurs and Fri eves, Sat and Sun afternoons. For ticket prices, contact Chamber of Commerce. July-Aug.

Motel/Motor Lodge

★★ **SHORE ACRES INN.** *237 Shore Acres Dr (05474). 802/372-8722. www.shoreacres.com.* 23 rms, 9 A/C. Mid-June-mid-Oct: S, D $89.50-$139.50; lower rates rest of yr; limited rms avail mid-Oct-May. Pet accepted. TV; cable. Restaurant 7:30-10 am, 5-9 pm. Bar. Ck-out 10:30 am. Driving range. Lawn games. Two tennis courts. Some refrigerators. 50 acres on Lake Champlain; panoramic view. Cr cds: DS, MC, V.

B&Bs/Small Inns

★★★ **NORTH HERO HOUSE INN.** *US 2 (05474). 802/372-4732; fax 802/372-3218; toll-free 888/525-3644. www.northherohouse.com.* 26 rms, 3 story. May-late Oct: S, D $95-$285; each addl $5-$45; MAP avail. TV. Complimentary continental bkfst. Restaurant (see also NORTH HERO HOUSE). Bar 5-11 pm. Ck-out 11 am, ck-in 2 pm. Tennis. Game rm. Lawn games. Some private patios, balconies. Rms vary in size, decor. Built in 1800; fireplace in lobby. On lake; beach, dockage. Cr cds: A, MC, V.

★ **RUTHCLIFFE LODGE & RESORT.** *1002 Quarry Rd, Isle La Motte (05463). 802/928-3200; toll-free 800/769-8162. www.virtualcities.com/~virtual.* 7 rms, shower only, 3 share bath, 2 story. No A/C. No rm phones. Mid-June-mid-Oct: S, D $87-$111.50; each addl $15; lower rates mid-May-mid-June. Closed rest of yr. Crib free. TV avail. Complimentary full bkfst. Complimentary coffee in rms. Restaurant 8:30-11 am, noon-2 pm, 5-9 pm. Ck-out 11:30 am. Bicycle rentals. Lawn games. Picnic tables, grills. On lake, dockage; boats, canoes avail. Totally nonsmoking. Cr cds: A, DS, MC, V.

★★ **THOMAS MOTT ALBURG HOMESTEAD B&B.** *63 Blue Rock Rd, Alburg (05440). 802/796-4402; fax 802/796-3736; toll-free 800/348-0843. www.thomas-mott-bb.com.* 4 rms, 2 story. No A/C. S, D $85-$150; each addl $10. Children over 6 yrs only. TV in sitting rm. Complimentary full bkfst; afternoon refreshments. Ck-out 11 am, ck-in 3 pm. X-country ski on site. Rec rm. Complimentary gourmet ice cream. Restored farmhouse (1838); overlooks lake. Totally nonsmoking. Cr cds: A, DS, MC, V.

CHAMPLAIN ISLANDS BICYCLE TOUR

A land chain composed of the Alburg peninsula and three islands—Isle La Motte, North Hero, and South Hero—straggles down the middle of Lake Champlain. The islands are connected by bridges to one another and by causeways to the mainland. Together they comprise Grand Isle County (population 4,000).

This is old farm and resort country. In the 19th century visitors arrived by lake steamer to stay at farms. Roads are flat, little trafficked once you are off VT 2 (the main road down the spine of the islands). Views are splendid: east across the lake to Vermont's Green Mountains and west to New York's Adirondacks. Isle La Motte, the smallest and quietest of the islands, is beloved by bicyclists.

The obvious place to begin a loop here is in the parking lot at St. Anne's Shrine on Route 129 in the northwestern corner of the island. Here an open-sided Victorian chapel on the shore marks the site of Vermont's first French settlement in 1666. There is a public beach, a picnic area in a large pine grove, and a large statue of Samuel de Champlain, who is credited with discovering New England's largest lake.

Pedal south from the shrine along the West Shore Road. Mountain bike rentals are available from Bike Shed Rentals, located a mile below the shrine. At 2.4 miles note the magnificent views west to the Adirondacks from the public boat access. At 3.7 miles the road turns to hard-packed dirt for 1.3 miles. Look for Fisk Farm (44 West Shore Road), a complex of buildings that includes an attractive bed-and-breakfast and gallery, also the ruins of a large old stone house that Vice President Theodore Roosevelt was visiting when he received the news that President McKinley had been shot. Beside the farm is the Fisk Quarry, the oldest in Vermont and part of a 480-million-year-old coral reef that underlies the southern third of the island. Open to the public, the quarry is studded with fossils that represent some of the most primitive life earth has known.

Keep to the main road as it curves to the east (pavement resumes), past Hall's Apple Orchards, which has been in the same family since the early 1800s. Its farmhouse is built of the island's distinctive "marble" (dark limestone). The road continues north, past the Isle La Motte Historical Society housed in an old school house; look for another reef (said to be 450 million years old) in a nearby field. At 7.4 miles you are at the four corners that mark the middle of Isle La Motte village with its country store and picnic benches by the pond. Another fine old stone building houses the public library. At nine miles turn onto Shrine Road and bear left at the "Y." Follow the paved road back to the shrine. The total loop is ten miles.

Restaurant

★★ **NORTH HERO HOUSE.** *VT 2 (05474). 802/372-4732. www.northherohouse.com.* Specializes in seasonal cuisine. Hrs: 8-10 am, 5:30-9 pm; Sun brunch 10:30 am-1:30 pm. Res accepted. Bar. dinner $11.95-$24.95. Bkfst buffet $6.95 (wkends). Sun brunch $14.95. Outdoor dining. Totally nonsmoking. MAP plan avail. Cr cds: A, MC, V.
D

Okemo State Forest

See also Ludlow, Weston

Mount Okemo (3,372 feet), almost a lone peak in south central Vermont near Ludlow, commands splendid views of the Adirondacks, the White Mountains, the Connecticut Valley, and Vermont's own Green Mountains. A road goes to within ½ mile of the mountain top (summer, fall; free); from there, it's an easy hike to the fire tower at the top. Surrounding Mount Okemo is the 4,527-acre state forest, which is primarily a skiing area. Area has seven quad, three triple chairlifts, two Pomalifts, J-bar; patrol, school, rentals; snowmaking; cafeteria, restaurants, bar; nursery; 83 runs, longest run 4½ miles; vertical drop 2,150 feet. (Early November-mid-April, daily) Phone 802/228-4041; snow conditions, 802/228-5222; for information about area lodging phone 800/78-OKEMO. ¢¢¢¢

Peru

See also Londonderry, Manchester & Manchester Center

Settled 1773 **Pop** 324 **Elev** 1,700 ft **Area code** 802 **Zip** 05152

This small mountain village has many fine examples of classic New England architecture, such as the Congregational Church (1846). Spectacular views of the Green Mountains surround this skiing center; also a popular area for fishing, hunting, and hiking.

What to See and Do

Bromley Mountain Ski Area. Area has two quad, five double chairlifts, two mitey-mites, J-bar; patrol, school, rentals; snowmaking; two cafeterias, restaurant, two lounges; nursery. Forty-two runs, longest run over two mi; vertical drop 1,334 ft. (Mid-Nov-mid-Apr, daily) 2 mi SW on VT 11. Phone 802/824-5522.

Bromley Alpine Slide. Speed-controlled sled ride and scenic chairlift; cafe, picnic area. Outdoor deck. Multistate view. (Late May-mid-Oct, daily, weather permitting) Phone 802/824-5522. ¢¢

Summer activities. Incl miniature golf, thrill sleds, children's theater. (Mid-June-mid-Oct)

Hapgood Pond Recreation Area. Swimming, fishing, boating; picnicking, camping. Fee for various activities. 2 mi NE on Hapgood Pond Rd, in Green Mtn National Forest (see). Phone 802/824-6456. ¢¢

J.J. Hapgood Store. (1827). General store featuring interesting old items; also penny candy, maple syrup, cheese. (Daily) Main St. Phone 802/824-5911.

Wild Wings Ski Touring Center. School, rentals; warming rm; concession. Twelve mi of groomed trails. 2½ mi N on North Rd. Phone 802/824-6793. ¢¢¢

Plymouth

See also Killington, Ludlow, Woodstock

Pop 440 **Elev** 1,406 ft **Area code** 802 **Zip** 05056
Information Town of Plymouth, HC 70, Box 39A; 802/672-3655

Seemingly unaware of the 20th century, this town hasn't changed much since July 4, 1872, when Calvin Coolidge was born in the back of the village store, still in business today. A country road leads to the cemetery where the former president and six generations of his family are buried. Nearby is the Coolidge Visitor's Center and Museum, which displays historical and presidential memorabilia.

What to See and Do

Calvin Coolidge State Forest. A 16,165-acre area. Hiking, snowmobile trails. Picnic facilities. Tent and trailer sites (dump station), primitive camping, lean-tos. (Memorial Day-Columbus Day) Standard fees. 1 mi N off VT 100A, Calvin Coolidge Memorial Hwy. Phone 802/672-3612.

Plymouth Cheese Corporation. Cheese, canned products, maple syrup, and honey. Cheese processed Mon-Wed. (Facility open late May-Nov, daily; rest of yr, Mon-Fri; closed Jan 1, Thanksgiving, Dec 25) Phone 802/672-3650. **FREE**

President Calvin Coolidge Homestead. Restored to its early 20th-century appearance, Calvin Coolidge was sworn in by his father in the sitting rm in 1923. The Plymouth Historic District also incl the General Store that was operated by the President's father, the house where the President was born, the village dance hall which served as the 1924 summer White House office, the Union Church with its Carpenter Gothic interior, the Wilder House (birthplace of Coolidge's mother), the Wilder Barn with 19th-century farming equipment, a restaurant, and a visitor center with museum. (Late May-mid-Oct, daily) 1 mi NE on VT 100A, in Plymouth Notch. Phone 802/672-3773. ¢¢

Motel/Motor Lodge

★ **FARMBROOK MOTEL.** *706 Rte 100A (05056). 802/672-3621.* 12 rms. No rm phones. S, D 55; each addl $7; kit. units $60-$69; wkly rates; higher rates fall foliage. TV. Complimentary coffee in rms. Ck-out 11 am. Picnic tables, grill. Stream, water wheel. Near birthplace of Calvin Coolidge. Cr cds: A, D, DS, MC, V.

⬛ ⬛ ⬛

Resort

★★★ **HAWK INN AND MOUNTAIN RESORT.** *HCR 70 Box 64 (05056). 802/672-3811; fax 802/672-5585; res 800/685-4295. www.hawkresort.com.* 150 houses, townhouses, 50 inn rms. Late Dec-Feb: 2-4 bedrm houses, townhouses $420-$765/house; inn rms (includes bkfst): S, D $310-$390; wkly, monthly rates; ski plans; MAP and EP avail; lower rates rest of yr. Crib free. Maid serv $25/hr (houses, townhouses). TV; cable (premium), VCR (movies $3.50). 2 pools; 1 indoor; whirlpool. Playground. Supervised children's activities (June-Aug); ages 5-12. Full bkfst. Coffee in rms. Dining rm 6-10 pm. Rm serv (inn rms). Box lunches, picnics. Chef for hire. Bar. Ck-out 11 am, ck-in 4 pm. Grocery 2 mi. Package store 8 mi. Meeting rms. Business servs avail. In-rm modem link. Valet serv. Airport, RR station, bus depot transportation. Tennis. Swimming in natural pond. Boats, rowboats, canoes, sailboats, paddleboats. Downhill ski 10 mi; x-country ski on site. Tobogganing, ice-skating. Horse-drawn sleigh rides. Hiking. Bicycles. Lawn games. Entertainment, movies. Exercise rm; sauna. Massage. Fishing guides. Refrigerators, minibars, fieldstone fireplaces. Private patios, balconies. Picnic tables, grills. Nature trails. Custom-designed vacation homes. Cr cds: A, DS, MC, V.

⬛ ⬛ ⬛ ⬛ ⬛ ⬛ ⬛ ⬛

Rutland

See also Brandon, Killington

Settled 1761 **Pop** 18,230 **Elev** 648 ft **Area code** 802
Information Chamber of Commerce, 256 N Main St; 802/773-2747
Web www.rutlandvermont.com

This is Vermont's second-largest city. Its oldest newspaper, the *Rutland Herald,* has been published continuously since 1794. The world's deepest marble quarry is in West Rutland. The office of the supervisor of the Green Mountain National Forest (see) is located here.

What to See and Do

Chaffee Center for the Visual Arts. Continuous exhibits of paintings, graphics, photography, crafts, sculpture. Print rm; gallery shop; annual art festivals (mid-Aug, Columbus Day wkend); other special events. (Mon, Wed-Sun; closed hols) 16 S Main St, on US 7, opp Main St Park. Phone 802/775-0356. **FREE**

Hubbardton Battlefield and Museum. On July 7, 1777, the Green Mountain Boys and Colonial troops from Massachusetts and New Hampshire stopped British forces pursuing the American Army from Fort Ticonderoga. This was the only battle of the Revolution fought on Vermont soil and the first in a series of engagements that led to the capitulation of Burgoyne at Saratoga. Visitor center with exhibits. Battle monument; trails; picnicking. (Memorial Day-Columbus Day, Wed-Sun) 7 mi W via US 4, exit 5. Phone 802/759-2412. ¢

Mountain Top Cross-Country Ski Resort. Patrol, school, rentals; snowmaking; concession area, restaurant at inn. Sixty-eight mi of x-country trails. Ice-skating, horse-drawn sleigh rides. (Nov-Mar, daily) N via US 7, then 10 mi NE on unnumbered road, follow signs. Phone 802/483-2311.

New England Maple Museum. One of largest collections of antique maple sugaring artifacts in the world; two large dioramas featuring more than 100 hand-carved figures; narrated slide show; demonstrations, samples of Vermont foodstuffs; craft and maple product gift shop. (Mid-Mar-Dec 24, daily; closed Thanksgiving) 7 mi N on US 7, in Pittsford. Phone 802/483-9414. ¢¢

Norman Rockwell Museum. More than 2,000 pictures and Rockwell memorabilia spanning 60 yrs of artist's career. Incl the *Four Freedoms,* Boy Scout series, many magazine covers, incl all 323 from the *Saturday Evening Post,* and nearly every illustration and advertisement. (Daily; closed hols) Gift shop. E on US 4. Phone 802/773-6095. ¢¢

★ **Vermont Marble Exhibit.** Exhibit explains how marble is formed and the process by which it is manufactured. Displays; sculptor at work; balcony view of factory; "Gallery of the Presidents"; movie on the marble industry; marble market, gift shop. (June-Oct, daily; rest of yr, Mon-Sat) 61 Main St, 2 mi W on US 4, then 4 mi N on VT 3 in Proctor, adj to Vermont Marble Company factory. Phone 802/459-3311. ¢¢

Wilson Castle. This 32-rm 19th-century mansion on a 115-acre estate features 19 open proscenium arches, 84 stained-glass windows, 13 imported tile fireplaces, a towering turret and parapet; European and Asian furnishings; art gallery; sculpture; 15 other buildings. Picnic area. Guided tours. (Late May-mid-Oct, daily) 2½ mi W on US 4, then 1 mi N on West Proctor Rd. Phone 802/773-3284. ¢¢¢

Special Events

Green Mountain International Rodeo. PRCA rodeo. Free pony rides, petting zoo. Bands, dancing. Phone 802/773-2747. Mid-June.

Vermont State Fair. Exhibits of arts and crafts, flowers, produce, home arts, pets, animals, maple sugaring. Daily special events. Late-Aug-early-Sept.

Motels/Motor Lodges

★★ **BEST WESTERN INN & SUITES.** *US 4 E (05702). 802/773-3200; res 800/528-1234. www.bestwestern.com.* 56 units, 2 story. S, D $89-$140; each addl $8; suites for 2-8, $119-$210; under 12 free; wkly rates; ski plan; higher rates: special events, fall foliage. Crib free. TV; cable, VCR avail (movies $6). Heated pool. Complimentary continen-

tal bkfst. Coffee in rms. Restaurant 7-11 am, 5-10 pm. Bar 4 pm-midnight. Ck-out 11 am. Coin lndry. Meeting rms. Business servs avail. In-rm modem link. Sundries. Exercise equipt. Tennis. Downhill/x-country ski 12 mi. Private patios, balconies. Fireplace in lobby. Cr cds: A, C, D, DS, MC, V.

★ **COMFORT INN TROLLEY SQUARE.** *19 Allen St (05701). 802/775-2200; fax 802/775-2694; res 800/228-5150. www.comfortinn.com.* 104 rms, 3 story. S, D $79-$170; each addl $10; under 18 free; higher rates: hols, fall foliage. Crib free. TV; cable. Indoor pool; whirlpool, sauna. Complimentary continental bkfst. Coffee in rms. Restaurant adj 11:30 am-10 pm. Ck-out 11 am. Meeting rms. Downhill/x-country ski 15 mi. Business servs avail. In-rm modem link. Refrigerators avail. Cr cds: A, C, D, DS, JCB, MC.

★ **HOWARD JOHNSON INN.** *401 S Main St (05701). 802/775-4303; fax 802/775-6840; res 800/446-4656. www.hojo.com.* 96 rms, 2 story. S, D $42-$100; each addl $8; under 18 free. Crib free. TV; cable (premium), VCR avail (movies $2). Indoor pool; sauna. Complimentary continental bkfst. Ck-out noon. Guest lndry. Meeting rms. Business servs avail. Downhill/x-country ski 16 mi. Health club privileges. Game rm. Private patios, balconies. Cr cds: A, DS, MC, V.

★ **RAMADA LIMITED.** *253 S Main St (05701). 802/773-3361; fax 802/773-4892; toll-free 888/818-3297.* 76 rms, 2 story, 3 kits. S, D $49-$89; each addl $6-$10; kit. units $89-$129; family rates; higher rates: hol wks. Crib free. TV; cable (premium). Indoor pool; sauna. Bkfst avail. Ck-out noon. Meeting rm. Downhill/x-country ski 16 mi. Health club privileges. Balconies. Cr cds: A, D, DS, MC, V.

Hotel

★★ **HOLIDAY INN RUTLAND-KILLINGTON.** *476 US Rte 7 S (05701). 802/775-1911; fax 802/775-0113; res 800/465-4329. www.holidayinn-vermont.com.* 151 rms. S, D $130-$279; MAP avail; ski plan; higher rates: wkends Jan-Mar, hols. Crib free. TV; cable (premium). Indoor pool; whirlpool, poolside serv. Coffee in rms. Restaurant 6:30 am-9 pm. Rm serv. Bar noon-1 am; entertainment. Ck-out noon. Coin lndry. Meeting rms. Business center. In-rm modem link. Bellhops. Sundries. Free airport, bus depot transportation. Downhill/x-country ski 10 mi. Exercise rm; sauna. Game rm. Lawn games. Fireplace in lobby. Cr cds: A, C, D, DS, MC, V.

Resort

★★★ **MOUNTAIN TOP INN.** *195 Mountain Top Rd, Chittenden (05737). 802/483-2311; fax 802/483-6373; toll-free 800/445-2100. www.mountaintopinn.com.* 60 units. EP: S, D $196-$226; each addl $60; cottages $210-$290; MAP avail. Closed Apr and 1st 3 wks Nov. Crib free. TV in lobby; VCR (free movies). Heated pool; sauna, poolside serv. Complimentary coffee in rms. Dining rm (public by res) 8-10 am, noon-2 pm, 6-8:30 pm; Fri, Sat 6-9 pm. Rm serv. Bar noon-11:30 pm. Business servs avail. Gift shop. Bus depot transportation. Tennis. Par-3 golf course, putting green, golf school. Boats, rowboats, canoes. Fly fishing instruction. Downhill ski 8 mi; x-country ski on site; lessons, rental, snow-making equipt. Sleigh rides. Hiking trails. Lawn games. Rec rm. Movie rm. Homemade maple syrup. On mountain top; 1,300 acres; scenic views. Cr cds: A, DS, MC, V.

B&Bs/Small Inns

★ **FINCH & CHUBB INN.** *82 N William St, Whitehall, NY (12887). 518/499-2049. www.visitwhitehall.com.* 8 rms, 1 shower only, 2 story. July-Aug: S $49; D $79-89; each addl $10; under 13 free; lower rates rest of yr. Crib free. TV; cable. Complimentary continental bkfst. Restaurant 11:30 am-2 pm, 4:30-9:30 pm. Ck-out 11:30 am, ck-in 3 pm. Pool. Built 1810 as an ammunition warehouse for US Navy during the War of 1812. Cr cds: A, C, D, DS, MC, V.

★★★ **INN AT RUTLAND BED AND BREAKFAST.** *70 N Main St (05701). 802/773-0575; fax 802/775-3506; toll-free 800/808-0575. www.innatrutland.com.* 11 rms, 4 with shower only, 3 story. Mid-Dec-Mar: S, D $135-$200; each addl $10; under 6 free; ski plans; hols; fall foliage (2-day min); lower rates rest of yr. TV; cable, VCR in common rm. Complimentary full bkfst. Restaurant nearby. Ck-out 11 am, ck-in 3 pm. Business servs avail. In-rm modem link. Downhill/x-country ski 10 mi. Health club privileges. Built in 1890; furnished with Victorian decor. Totally non-smoking. Cr cds: A, DS, MC, V.

★★★ **MAPLEWOOD INN.** *VT 22A S, Fair Haven (05743). 802/265-8039; fax 802/265-8210; toll-free 800/253-7729. www.maplewoodinn.net.* 5 rms, 2 story. Phones avail. S, D $95-$105; each addl $20; suites $115-$125. Children over 5 yrs only. TV; cable (premium). Complimentary continental bkfst. Setups. Ck-out 11 am, ck-in 3-9 pm. Business servs avail. Some fireplaces. Historic building (1843) part of dairy farm; antiques. Cr cds: A, MC, V.

Restaurants

★★★ **COUNTRYMAN'S PLEASURE.** *Townline Rd, Mendon (05701). 802/773-7141. www.countrymanspleasure.com.* German, Austrian menu. Specialties: roast duck with raspberry sauce, sauerbraten, wild game. Own baking. Hrs: 5-9 pm; Sat to 10 pm; early-bird dinner 5-6 pm. Closed Dec 24, 25. Res accepted. Bar. Dinner $14.95-$24.95. Child's menu. Restored farmhouse (1824). Sun porch dining. Cr cds: A, C, D, DS, ER, MC, V.

★★ **ROYAL'S 121 HEARTHSIDE.** *37 N Main St (05701). 802/775-0856.* Specializes in New England dishes, popovers, fresh seafood. Own desserts. Hrs: 11 am-10 pm; Sun noon-9 pm; early-bird dinner Mon-Fri 5-6:30 pm. Res accepted; required hols. Bar. Lunch $5.25-$10.95, dinner $11.95-$19.95. Open-hearth charcoal cooking. Fireplaces. Cr cds: A, MC, V.

★★ **SIRLOIN SALOON.** *200 S Main St (05701). 802/773-7900. www.sirloinsaloon.com.* Specializes in wood-grilled steak, chicken, seafood. Salad bar. Hrs: 5-10 pm; Fri, Sat to 11 pm. Closed Thanksgiving. Res accepted. Bar 4-10 pm; Fri, Sat to 11 pm. Dinner $8.95-$18.95. Child's menu. Native American artwork, artifacts. Cr cds: A, D, DS, MC, V.

St. Albans

See also Swanton

Settled 1785 **Pop** 7,339 **Elev** 429 ft **Area code** 802 **Zip** 05478

Information Chamber of Commerce, 2 N Main St, Suite 101, PO Box 327; 802/524-2444

Web www.stalbanschamber.com

This small city is a railroad town (Central Vermont Railway) and center of maple syrup and dairy interests. It was a stop on the Underground Railroad and has had a surprisingly violent history. Smugglers used the city as a base of operations during the War of 1812. On October 19, 1864, the northernmost engagement of the Civil War was fought here when a small group of Confederates raided the three banks in town and fled to Canada with $200,000. In 1866, the Fenians, an Irish organization pledged to capture Canada, had its headquarters here.

What to See and Do

Brainerd Monument. A father's revengeful commemoration of his son's death in Andersonville Prison. Greenwood Cemetery, S Main St. Phone 802/524-2444.

Burton Island State Park. This 253-acre park offers swimming beach, fishing, canoeing (rentals), boating (rentals), marina with electrical hookups); nature and hiking trails, picnicking, concession, tent sites, lean-tos. (Memorial Day-Labor Day) Standard fees. On island in Lake Champlain; 5 mi W on VT 36, then 3 mi SW on unnumbered road to Kamp Kill Kare State Park access area, where passenger ferry service (fee) is avail to island; visitors may use their own boats to reach the island. Phone 802/879-5674.

Chester A. Arthur Historic Site. Replica of second house of 21st president; nearby is brick church (1830) where Arthur's father was preacher. Exhibit of Chester A. Arthur's life and career. Rural setting; picnic area. (Mid June-mid Oct, Wed-Sun) 10 mi W via VT 36 to Fairfield, then unpaved road to site. Phone 802/828-3226.

Lake Carmi State Park. This 482-acre park features rolling farmland; two-mi lakefront, swimming beach, bathhouse, fishing, boating (ramps, rentals); nature trails, picnicking, concession, tent and trailer sites (dump station), lean-tos. (Memorial Day-Labor Day) Standard fees. 15 mi NE on VT 105 to North Sheldon, then 3 mi N on VT 236. Phone 802/879-5674.

St. Albans Historical Museum. Toys, dolls, clothing, RR memorabilia; farm implements; St. Albans Confederate Raid material, photographs; library and reference rm; re-created doctor's office with medical and X-ray collections; items and documents of local historical interest. (June-Sept, Tues-Sat, also by appt) Church St. Phone 802/527-7933.

Special Events

Maple Sugar Festival. A number of producers welcome visitors who join sugarhouse parties for sugar-on-snow, sour pickles, and raised doughnuts. Continuing events, arts and crafts, antiques, woodchopping contests. Usually last wkend Apr.

Bay Day. Family activity day. Great Race, one-legged running, family games; volleyball, canoeing, and bicycling. Concessions. Fireworks. July 4 wkend.

Civil War Days. Taylor Park. A three-day event depicting scenes of the Civil War in St. Albans, the northernmost point where the war was fought. Reenactment of major battle, entertainment, antiques. Mid-Oct.

Motels/Motor Lodges

★ **CADILLAC MOTEL.** *213 S Main St (05478). 802/524-2191; fax 802/527-1483. www.motel-cadillac.com.* 54 rms, S $55-$65; D $70-$80; each addl $7. Crib $7. TV; cable (premium). Heated pool. Restaurant 7 am-9 pm. Ck-out 11 am. Meeting rm. Sundries. Lawn games. Refrigerators. Picnic tables, grills. Cr cds: A, C, D, DS, MC, V.

★★ **COMFORT INN & SUITES.** *813 Fairfax Rd (05478). 802/524-3300; res 800/228-5150. www.vtcomfortinn.com.* 63 rms, 3 story, 17 suites. July-mid-Sept: S $69-$89; D $79-$99; each addl $5; suites $95-$114; under 18 free; higher rates fall foliage; lower rates rest of yr. Crib free. TV; cable (premium). Complimentary continental bkfst. Restaurant nearby. Ck-out noon. Meeting rms. Business servs avail. In-rm modem link. Coin lndry. Exercise equipt. Indoor pool. Game rm. Refrigerator, microwave in suites. Picnic tables. Cr cds: A, C, D, DS, JCB, MC, V.

St. Johnsbury

See also Lyndonville

Settled 1787 **Pop** 7,608 **Elev** 588 ft **Area code** 802 **Zip** 05819

Information Northeast Kingdom Chamber of Commerce, 357 Western Ave, Suite 2; 802/748-3678 or 800/639-6379

Web www.vermontnekchamber.org

This town was named for Ethan Allen's French friend, St. John de Crève Coeur, author of *Letters from an American Farmer.* The town gained fame and fortune when Thaddeus Fairbanks invented the platform scale in 1830. Fairbanks Scales, maple syrup, and manufacturing are among its major industries.

What to See and Do

Fairbanks Museum and Planetarium. Exhibits and programs on natural science, regional history, archeology, anthropology, astronomy and the arts. More than 4,500 mounted birds and mammals; antique toys; farm, village, and craft tools; Northern New England Weather Broadcasting Center; planetarium; Hall of Science; special exhibitions in Gallery Wing. (Mon-Sat, also Sun afternoons; closed Jan 1, Dec 25) Planetarium (July-Aug, daily; rest of yr, Sat and Sun only). Museum and planetarium closed some major hols. Main and Prospect Sts. Phone 802/748-2372. ¢¢

Maple Grove Farm of Vermont. Antique sugarhouse museum. Gift shop. Maple candy factory tours (Mon-Fri; closed hols). Res requested for tours. E edge of town on US 2; I-91, exit 20 or I-93, exit 1. Phone 802/748-5141. ¢

St. Johnsbury Athenaeum and Art Gallery. Works by Albert Bierstadt and artists of the Hudson River School. (Mon-Sat; closed hols) 30 Main St (public library and art gallery). Phone 802/748-8291. **Donation**

Special Event

St. Johnsbury Town Band. Courthouse Park. One of the oldest continuously performing bands (since 1830) in the country plays weekly outdoor evening concerts. Contact the Chamber of Commerce for further information. Mon, mid-June-late Aug.

Motels/Motor Lodges

★ **AIME'S MOTEL INC.** *46 VT Rte 18 (05819). 802/748-3194; toll-free 800/504-6663. www.virtualcities.com/vt/aimesmotel.htm.* 16 rms. S $37-$55; D $52-$70; each addl $5. Crib free. TV; cable. Ck-out noon. Screened porches. Near brook. Cr cds: A, DS, MC, V.

★★ **FAIRBANKS MOTOR INN.** *32 Western Ave (05819). 802/748-5666; fax 802/748-1242.* 46 rms, 3 story. S $55-$85; D $65-$95; each addl $10; package plans; higher rates fall foliage. TV; cable (premium). Heated pool. Complimentary continental bkfst. Ck-out 11 am. Business servs avail. In-rm modem link. Putting green. Downhill/x-country ski 15 mi. Health club privileges. Balconies. Picnic tables. On 2 acres along river. Cr cds: A, DS, MC, V.

★★ **HOLIDAY MOTEL.** *222 Hastings St (05819). 802/748-8192; fax 802/748-1244.* 34 rms. Mid-June-mid-Oct: S $48-$75; D $55-$89; each addl $5; higher rates: fall foliage, some hols; lower rates rest of yr. TV; cable. Heated pool. Coffee in lobby. Restaurant opp 7 am-9 pm. Ck-out 11 am. Picnic tables. Cr cds: A, DS, MC, V.

B&B/Small Inn

★★★★ **RABBIT HILL INN.** *48 Lower Waterford Rd, Lower Waterford (05848). 802/748-5168; fax 802/748-8342; toll-free 800/762-8669. www.rabbithillinn.com.* Guests can truly get away from it all at this 15-acre countryside property. Located in a tiny rural village and nestled between a river and the mountains, the white-pillared facade and American flag of this inn have charming New England style. Choose from the 19 guest rooms and suites in either the 1825 Main House or the 1795 Tavern Building. 21 rms, 2-3 story. 19 rms with A/C. No rm phones. MAP: S $210-$325; D $260-$375; each addl $75; higher rates July-Oct; fall foliage. Children over 13 yrs only. Complimentary refreshments 2-5:30 pm. Coffee in rms. Restaurant (see also RABBIT HILL). Bar. Ck-out 11 am, ck-in after 2 pm. Gift shop. Pond, canoes. Hiking. Golf privileges. Downhill ski 20 mi; x-country ski on site. Lawn games. Some in-rm whirlpools, fireplaces. Robes. Porches. Gazebo. Totally nonsmoking. Cr cds: A, MC, V.

🆔 🐾 ⚡ 🎿 🍴 🛒 🔥

Restaurants

★★ **CREAMERY.** *Hill St, Danville (05819). 802/684-3616.* Specializes in fresh seafood. Own baking, soups. Menu changes daily. Hrs: 11:30 am-2 pm, 5-8 pm; Sat from 5 pm. Closed Sun, Mon; Jan 1, Dec 24, 25. Res accepted. Bar from 4 pm. Lunch $5-$8, dinner $12-$17. Child's menu. Renovated creamery (1891); antiques, vintage photographs. Cr cds: A, MC, V.

🆔

★★★ **RABBIT HILL.** *48 Lower Waterford Rd (05848). 802/748-5168. www.rabbithillinn.com.* Contemporary Amer menu. Own baking. Menu changes seasonally. Hrs: 6-8:45 pm. Res required. Bar. Wine cellar. Complete meals: dinner $37. On grounds of historic inn. Totally nonsmoking. Cr cds: A, MC, V.

🆔

Shelburne

See also Burlington, Vergennes

Settled 1763 **Pop** 5,871 **Elev** 148 ft **Area code** 802 **Zip** 05482
Information Town Hall, 5420 Shelburne Rd, PO Box 88; 802/985-5110
Web www.shelburnevt.org

Shelburne is a small, friendly town bordering Lake Champlain. West of town are the Adirondack Mountains; to the east are the Green Mountains. The Shelburne Museum has one of the most comprehensive exhibits of early American life.

What to See and Do

Charlotte-Essex Ferry. Makes 20-min trips across Lake Champlain to Essex, NY (Apr-Jan, daily). 5 mi S on US 7 to Charlotte, then 2 mi W to dock. Phone 802/864-9804. One way, individual ¢ vehicle ¢¢

Mount Philo State Park. A 648-acre mountaintop park offering beautiful views of the Lake Champlain Valley. Picnicking, camping, lean-tos. Entrance and camp roads are steep; not recommended for trailers. (Memorial Day-Columbus Day) Standard fees. 5 mi S on US 7, then 1 mi E on local road. Phone 802/425-2390.

Shelburne Farms. Former estate of Dr. Seward Webb and his wife, Lila Vanderbilt, built at the turn of the 20th century; beautifully situated on the shores of Lake Champlain. The grounds, landscaped by Frederick Law Olmstead and forested by Gifford Pinchot, once totalled 3,800 acres. Structures incl the Webbs' mansion, Shelburne House, a 110-rm summer "cottage" built in the late 1800s on a bluff overlooking the lake; a five-story farm barn with a courtyard of more than two acres; and the coach barn, once the home of prize horses. Tours (Memorial Day-mid-Oct, daily; closed hols). Also hay rides; walking trail. Visitor center, phone 802/985-8442. Cheese shop (all yr, daily). Overnight stays avail. Harbor and Bay rds. Phone 802/985-8686. ¢¢¢

⭐ **Shelburne Museum.** Founded by Electra Webb, daughter of Sugar King H.O. Havemeyer, this stupendous collection of Americana is located on 45 acres of parklike setting with 37 historic buildings containing items such as historic circus posters, toys, weather vanes, trade signs, and an extensive collection of wildfowl decoys and dolls. American and European paintings and prints (incl works by Monet and Grandma Moses) are on display as well. Also here is the 220-ft sidewheel steamboat *Ticonderoga*, which carried passengers across Lake Champlain in the early part of the century and is now the last vertical beam passenger and freight sidewheel steamer intact in the US; a working carousel and a 5,000-piece hand-carved miniature traveling circus; a fully intact lighthouse; one-rm schoolhouse; the only two-lane covered bridge with footpath in Vermont; blacksmith shop; printing and weaving demonstrations; farm equipment and over 200 horse-drawn vehicles on display. Visitor orientation film; free jitney; cafeteria; museum stores; free parking. (Late May-late Oct, daily; rest of yr, limited hrs) On US 7, in center of town. Phone 802/985-3346. ¢¢¢¢

Vermont Teddy Bear Company. Guided tour of "bear" factory shows process of handcrafting these famous stuffed animals. Gift shop. (Mon-Sat, also Sun afternoons) 6655 Shelburne Rd (VT 7). Phone 802/985-3001. ¢

Vermont Wildflower Farm. Acres of wildflower gardens, flower fields, and woodlands; pond and brook. Changing slide/sound show (every ½ hr). Gift shop. (May-late Oct, daily) 5 mi S via US 7. Phone 802/425-3500. ¢¢

Motels/Motor Lodges

★ **DAYS INN.** *3229 Shelburne Rd (05482). 802/985-3334; fax 802/985-3419; res 800/329-7466. www.daysinn.com.* 58 rms, 2 story. July-mid-Sept: S, D $65-$75; each addl $7; higher rates: fall foliage season, Labor Day, Columbus Day; lower rates rest of yr. Crib free. TV; cable. Pool. Complimentary continental bkfst. Ck-out 11 am. Downhill ski 20 mi. Cr cds: A, D, DS, JCB, MC, V.

🆔 🎿 🛏 🔊 ♿

★ **ECONO LODGE AND SUITES.** *3164 Shelburne Rd (05482). 802/985-3377; res 800/553-2666. www.econolodge.com.* 51 rms, 1-2 story, 20 suites. S $39; D $45-$89; each addl $5; suites $84.95; under 17 free; higher rates fall foliage; lower rates rest of yr. Crib avail. Pet accepted; $100 deposit. TV; cable. Complimentary continental bkfst. Restaurant adj 4-9:30 pm. Ck-out 11 am. Meeting rms. Business servs avail. Coin lndry. Downhill/x-country ski 20 mi. Pool. Refrigerator, microwave in suites. Picnic tables, grills. Cr cds: A, C, D, DS, MC, V.

⬚ 🐾 🛗 ⛵ 🏊 ⛄ 🔥 SC

★★ **T-BIRD MOTOR INN.** *4405 Shelburne Rd (05482). 802/985-3663; toll-free 800/335-5029.* 24 rms. May-Oct: D $58-$140; each addl $10; higher rates: fall foliage, hol wkends, graduations. Closed Nov-mid May. Crib $5. TV; cable. Pool. Complimentary continental bkfst. Restaurant nearby. Ck-out 11 am. Lawn games. Some refrigerators. Picnic tables. Cr cds: A, MC, V.

⬚ 🏊 ⛄ 🔥 ⛵

B&B/Small Inn

★★★ **SHELBURNE FARMS.** *1611 Harbor Rd (05482). 802/985-8686; fax 802/985-8123. www.shelburnefarms.org.* 26 rms, 7 share bath, 3 story. No A/C. No elvtr. Sept-mid-Oct: S, D $195-$350; each addl $30; cottages $240-$365; wkends, hols (2-day min); lower rates rest of yr. Crib avail. Cable TV in common rm. Restaurant 7:30-11:30 am, 5:30-9:30 pm. Ck-out 11 am, ck-in 3 pm. Business servs avail. In-rm modem link. Luggage handling. Gift shop. Tennis. Downhill/x-country ski 20 mi. Rec rm. Lawn games. On lake. Built in 1887; still a working farm. Totally nonsmoking. Cr cds: A, DS, MC, V.

🛗 ⛵ 🎿 ⛄ 🔥 ⛵

Restaurants

★★★ **CAFE SHELBURNE.** *5573 Shelburne Rd (05482). 802/985-3939. www.cafeshelburne.com.* French, continental menu. Specializes in fillet of lamb, fresh seafood. Hrs: 5:30-9 pm. Closed Sun, Mon. Res accepted. Bar. Wine cellar. A la carte entrees: dinner $16-$21. Porch dining. Provençal bistro atmosphere. Chef-owned. Cr cds: A, D, MC, V.

★★ **SIRLOIN SALOON.** *1912 Shelburne Rd (05401). 802/985-2200. www.sirloinsaloon.com.* Specializes in woodgrilled steak, chicken, fresh seafood. Salad bar. Hrs: 4:30-10 pm; Fri to 11 pm; Sat 4-11 pm; Sun 4-10 pm. Closed Thanksgiving, Dec 25. Res accepted. Bar 4-10 pm; Fri, Sat to 11 pm. Dinner $9.95-$18.95. Child's menu. Parking. Greenhouse dining. Open hearth. Native American artwork, artifacts. Totally nonsmoking. Cr cds: A, C, D, DS, MC, V.

⬚

Springfield

See also Bellows Falls, Grafton

Settled 1761 **Pop** 9,579 **Elev** 410 ft **Area code** 802 **Zip** 05156

Information Chamber of Commerce, 14 Clinton St, Suite 6; 802/885-2779

Web www.springfieldvt.com

The cascades of the Black River once provided power for the machine tool plants that stretch along Springfield's banks. Lord Jeffrey Amherst started the Crown Point Military Road to Lake Champlain from here in 1759. Springfield has been the home of many New England inventors. It is also the headquarters of the Amateur Telescope Makers who meet at Stellafane, an observatory site west of VT 11.

What to See and Do

Eureka Schoolhouse. Oldest schoolhouse in the state; built in 1790 and recently restored. Nearby is a 100-yr-old lattice-truss covered bridge. (Memorial Day-Columbus Day, daily) On VT 11 (Charleston Rd). Phone 802/885-2779. ¢¢

Reverend Dan Foster House & Old Forge. Historic parsonage (1785) contains antique furniture, textiles, utensils, farm tools; old forge has working machinery and bellows. Guided tours. (Late June-Sept, Thurs-Mon or by appt) 6 mi N on Valley St to Weathersfield Center Rd in Weathersfield. For further information contact the Chamber of Commerce. Phone 802/885-2779.

Springfield Art and Historical Society. American art and artifacts. Collections incl Richard Lee pewter, Bennington pottery, 19th-century American paintings, costumes, dolls, toys; Springfield historical items. Changing exhibits. (May-Nov, Tues-Fri; closed hols) 9 Elm Hill. Phone 802/885-2415. **FREE**

Special Event

Vermont Apple Festival and Craft Show. Family activities, cider pressing, apple pie bake-off, entertainment, crafts. Phone 802/885-2779. Columbus Day wkend.

Motel/Motor Lodge

★★ **HOLIDAY INN EXPRESS.** *818 Charlestown Rd (05156). 802/885-4516; fax 802/885-4595; toll-free 800/465-4329. www.holiday-inn.com.* 88 rms, 4 suites, 2 story. July-mid-Oct: S, D $89-$125; each addl $5; suites $159-$179; under 19 free; higher rates graduation wk; lower rates rest of yr. Crib free. Pet accepted. TV; cable. Indoor pool. Complimentary continental bkfst. Restaurant 6 am-11 pm. Bar 4-11 pm. Ck-out noon. Meeting rms. Business servs avail. In-rm modem link. Valet serv. Downhill ski 20 mi; x-country ski 14 mi. Exercise equipt. Refrigerators, microwaves avail. Picnic tables. Cr cds: A, D, DS, MC, V.

⬚ 🐾 🛗 ⚡ ⛵ 🏊 🏃 ⛄ 🔥

Hotel

★★ **HARTNESS HOUSE.** *30 Orchard St (05156).* *802/885-2115; fax 802/885-2207; res 800/732-4789.* *www.hartnesshouse.com.* 41 rms in 2 bldgs, 3 story. S, D $99-$135; suites $150; under 14 free; wkly rates; package plans. Crib free. TV. Pool. Complimentary full bkfst. Restaurant (see also HARTNESS HOUSE INN). Rm serv. Ck-out 11 am. Business servs avail. Downhill ski 20 mi. Built 1903; an underground tunnel connects main house to a historic observatory with operational telescope. Cr cds: A, C, D, DS, MC, V.

D ≥ ⊴ ⊠ 🔥

B&Bs/Small Inns

★ **HUGGING BEAR INN.** *244 Main St, Chester (05143).* *802/875-2412; fax 802/875-3823; toll-free 800/325-0519.* *www.huggingbear.com.* 6 rms, 2 story. No A/C. No rm phones. S $65-$90; D $90-$135; each addl $10-$25; higher rates fall foliage. Closed Thanksgiving. Crib free. TV in sitting rm; VCR (free movies). Complimentary full bkfst. Restaurant opp 7 am-8 pm. Ck-out 11 am, ck-in 3 pm. Gift shop featuring extensive collection of teddy bears. Downhill ski 15 mi; x-country ski 7 mi. Victorian house (ca 1850) furnished with antiques and teddy bears. Totally nonsmoking. Cr cds: A, D, DS, MC, V.

🏃 ✈ ≥ ⊠ 🐾

★★★ **THE INN AT WEATHERSFIELD.** *Rte 106, Perkinsville (05151). 802/263-9217; fax 802/263-9219; toll-free 800/477-4828. www.weathersfieldinn.com.* 12 rms, 2 story, 3 suites. No A/C. MAP: S $78-$145; D $115-$350; each addl $75. Children over 8 yrs only. TV in game rm. Complimentary full bkfst; afternoon refreshments. Dining rm 6-9 pm. Ck-out 11 am, ck-in 1 pm. Downhill ski 20 mi. Game rm. Lawn games. Many fireplaces. On 21 acres at base of Hawks Mt. Original bldg dates back to 1795. Swimming pond. Cr cds: A, C, D, DS, MC, V.

🏃 ≥ ⊠ 🔥

★★ **STONE HEARTH INN.** *698 VT 11 W, Chester (05143).* *802/875-2525; fax 802/875-4688; toll-free 888/617-3656.* *www.virtualvermont.com/shinn.* 10 rms, 3 story. No A/C. No rm phones. S $59-$99; D $120-$150; each addl $12-$40; wkly rates; ski plans. MAP avail. Crib $6. TV in lounge. Complimentary full bkfst. Dining rm 7:30-9 am, 6-7:30 pm. Bar from 4 pm. Ck-out 11 am, ck-in 3 pm. Gift shop. Downhill ski 7 mi; x-country ski 6 mi. Whirlpool. Game rm. Lawn games. Some fireplaces. Picnic tables, grills. Restored farm house (1810); antiques. Cr cds: A, DS, MC.

D 🏃 ✈ ≥

Restaurant

★★ **HARTNESS HOUSE INN.** *30 Orchard St (05156).* *802/885-2115. www.hartnesshouse.com.* Continental menu. Specializes in fresh seafood. Hrs: 7-9 am, 11:30 am-2 pm, 5-9 pm; Sat, Sun 8-10 am. Res accepted. Bar from 5 pm; Fri, Sat to midnight. Bkfst $5.95, lunch $4.50-$8.95, dinner $16.95-$19.95. Outdoor dining. Historic building (1900). Tours. Totally nonsmoking. Cr cds: A, D, DS, MC, V.

D

Stowe

See also Waterbury

Settled 1794 **Pop** 3,433 **Elev** 723 ft **Area code** 802 **Zip** 05672

Information Stowe Area Association, Main St, PO Box 1320; 802/253-7321 or 877/467-8693

Web www.gostowe.com

Stowe is a year-round resort area, with more than half of its visitors coming during the summer. Mount Mansfield, Vermont's highest peak (4,393 feet), offers skiing, snowboarding, snowshoeing, and skating in the winter. Summer visitors enjoy outdoor concerts, hiking, biking, golf, tennis, and many events and attractions, including a Ben & Jerry's ice cream tour.

What to See and Do

Alpine Slide. Chairlift takes riders to 2,300-ft slide that runs through the woods and open field. Speed controlled by rider. (Memorial Day-mid-June, wkends and hols; mid-June-Labor Day, daily; after Labor Day-mid-Oct, wkends and hols) VT 108, N of Stowe Village. Phone 802/253-7321. ¢¢

Elmore State Park. This 709-acre park offers swimming beach, bathhouse, fishing, boating (rentals); hiking trails (one trail to Elmore Mtn fire tower), picnicking, concession, tent and trailer sites (dump station), lean-tos. Excellent views of Green Mt Range; fire tower. (Memorial Day-Columbus Day) Standard fees. N on VT 100, then S on VT 12, at Lake Elmore. Phone 802/888-2982.

Mount Mansfield State Forest. This 38,000-acre forest can be reached from Underhill Flats, off VT 15, or from Stowe, N on VT 108, through Smugglers Notch, a magnificent scenic drive. The Long Trail leads to the summit of Mt Mansfield from the north and south. There are three state recreation areas in the forest. **Smugglers Notch** (phone 802/253-4014 or 802/479-4280) and **Underhill** (phone 802/899-3022 or 802/879-5674) areas offer hiking, skiing, snowmobiling, picnicking, camping (dump station). **Little River Camping Area** (phone 802/244-7103 or 802/479-4280), NW of Waterbury, offers swimming, fishing, boating (rentals for campers only); hiking, camping. (Memorial Day-Columbus Day) Standard fees.

Stowe Mountain Auto Road. A 4½ mi drive to summit. (Mid-May-mid-Oct, daily) Approx 6 mi NW of Stowe off VT 108.

Stowe Mountain Resort. Resort has eight-passenger gondola, quad, triple, six double chairlifts; Mighty-mite handle tow; patrol, school, rentals; snowmaking; cafeterias, restaurants, bar, entertainment; nursery. Forty-seven runs, longest run over 3½ mi; vertical drop 2,360 ft. Night skiing. (Mid-Nov-mid-Apr, daily) Summer activities incl three outdoor swimming pools; alpine slide (mid-June-early Sept, daily), mountain biking (rentals); gondola rides, in-line skate park, fitness center, spa, recreation trail, tennis, golf. NW via VT 108 at 5781 Mountain Rd. Phone 802/253-3000. Nearby is

Mount Mansfield Gondola. An eight-passenger enclosed gondola ride to the summit of Vermont's highest peak. Spectacular view of the area. Restaurant and gift shop. (Late May-mid-June, wkends; mid-June-mid-Oct, daily) VT 108, N of Stowe Village.

Stowe Recreation Path. An approx five-mi riverside path designed for nature walks, bicycling, jogging, and in-line skating. Stowe Village. **FREE**

Special Events

Trapp Family Meadow Concerts. Classical concerts in the Trapp Family Lodge Meadow. Phone 802/253-7321. Sun eves, late June-mid-Aug.

Stoweflake Balloon Festival. Stoweflake Resort Field, Rte 108. Over 20 balloons launched continuously. Phone 802/253-7321. Second wkend July.

Motels/Motor Lodges

★★ **BUCCANEER COUNTRY LODGE.** *3214 Mountain Rd (05672). 802/253-4772; fax 802/253-9486; toll-free 800/543-1293. www.buccaneerlodge.com.* 12 rms, 2 story, 4 kit. suites. Mid-Dec-Mar, mid-Sept-mid-Oct: S, D $85-$109; each addl $10-$15; kit. suites $110; under 5 free; wkly rates; ski plans; wkends (2 day min); higher rates: hol wkends, wks of Washington's birthday, Dec 25; lower rates rest of yr. Crib free. TV; cable. Heated pool; whirlpool. Complimentary full bkfst (continental bkfst off-season). Restaurant nearby. Ck-out 11 am. Downhill ski 3 mi; x-country ski 1 mi. Rec rm. Refrigerators. Balconies. Picnic tables, grills. Fireplace. Library. Cr cds: MC, V.

★★ **HOB KNOB INN.** *2364 Mountain Rd (05672). 802/253-8549; fax 802/253-7621; toll-free 800/245-8540. www.hobknobinn.com.* 20 rms, 6 kits. Ski season: D $110-$145; each addl $15; kit. units $20 addl; MAP avail; wkly rates; golf, ski plans; higher rates: hols, special events; some lower rates off-season. Closed Nov. Crib free. TV. Pool. Complimentary full bkfst (winter), continental bkfst (summer). Restaurant 6-9 pm. Bar. Ck-out 11 am. Downhill ski 5 mi; x-country ski 1½ mi. Some refrigerators, fireplaces. Balconies. Cr cds: A, C, D, DS, MC, V.

★★ **HONEYWOOD COUNTRY LODGE.** *4527 Mountain Rd (05672). 802/253-4124; fax 802/253-7050; toll-free 800/659-6289. www.honeywoodinn.com.* 8 rms, 1 story, 2 suites. Feb, Sept-Oct, Dec: S, D $79-$149; suites $169-$199; each addl $20; ski plan; under 15 free; higher rates: hols, fall foliage; lower rates rest of yr. TV. Pool; whirlpool. Complimentary continental bkfst. Restaurant adj 8 am-10 pm. Ck-out 10 am. Downhill/x-country ski 1½ mi. Lawn games. Refrigerators; some wood stoves. Balconies. Picnic tables, grill. Fireplace in lounge. View of Mt Mansfield. Cr cds: A, DS, MC, V.

★★★ **INN AT THE MOUNTAIN.** *5781 Mountain Rd (05672). 802/253-3500; fax 802/253-3659; toll-free 800/253-4754. www.stowe.com.* 33 rms. MAP: Dec 25-mid-Apr: S, D $165-$190; suites $190-$250; under 12 free; condos $200-$600; learn-to-ski wk rates; golf plans; lower rates rest of yr. Crib $10. TV; cable. Heated pool; whirlpool. Restaurant 7:30-10 am, 5:30-9 pm. Rm serv. Bar 11-2 am. Ck-out 11 am. Meeting rm. Business servs avail. Bellhops. Tennis. Golf privileges. Downhill/x-country ski on site. Snowboarding; lessons, rentals. In-line skate park. Mountain bike center. Exercise equipt; sauna. Rec rm. Refrigerators, in-rm steam baths. Balconies. Sun deck. Ride attractions. Rms overlook ski slopes. Cr cds: A, D, DS, MC, V.

★★ **INNSBRUCK INN.** *4361 Mountain Rd (05672). 802/253-8582; fax 802/253-2260; toll-free 800/225-8582. www.innsbruckinn.com.* 25 rms, 2 suites, 2 story, 4 kits. Mid-Dec-mid-Apr: S $75-$89; D $89-$129; suites $139-$219; each addl $15; under 12 free; higher rates hol wks; lower rates rest of yr. Crib $10. Pet accepted, some restrictions; $8. TV; cable, VCR avail (movies). Heated pool; whirlpool. Coffee in rms. Restaurant 7:30-9:30 am. Bar (winter only) 3:30 pm-1 am. Ck-out 11 am. Business servs avail. Ski shuttle. Indoor tennis privileges. Downhill ski 2 mi; x-country ski adj. Exercise equipt; sauna. Game rm. Refrigerators. Balconies. Picnic tables. Cr cds: A, DS, MC, V.

★★ **STOWE MOTEL.** *2043 Mountain Rd (05672). 802/253-7629; fax 802/253-9971; toll-free 800/829-7629. www.stowemotel.com.* 59 units, 28 kit. units, 4 chalets. S, D $79-$99; kit. units $95-$115; each addl $8; chalets to 10, $1,000-$1,800/wk; under 6 free; higher rates: some hols, ski season; lower rates rest of yr. Crib $8. TV; cable. 2 heated pools; whirlpool. Restaurant nearby. Ck-out 11 am. Business servs avail. Tennis. Downhill ski 4½ mi; x-country ski 2½ mi. Lawn games. Bicycles; snowshoes. Refrigerators; some fireplaces. Picnic tables, grills. View of mountains; on 16 acres. Cr cds: A, DS, MC, V.

★★ **SUN AND SKI MOTOR INN.** *1613 Mountain Rd (05672). 802/253-7159; fax 802/253-7150; toll-free 800/448-5223. www.stowesunandski.com.* 25 rms. S $69-$127; D $69-$137; each addl $5-$16; suites $112-$171; ski plan; higher rates: hols, fall foliage, special events. Crib free. TV; cable. Heated pool; sauna. Complimentary continental bkfst 8-10 am. Coffee in rms. Restaurant opp 7:30 am-9:30 pm. Ck-out 11 am. Downhill ski 3 mi; x-country ski 2 mi. Lawn games. Bicycles. Trout stream. Refrigerators. Private patios. Picnic tables. Cr cds: A, DS, MC, V.

★★ **SUNSET MOTOR INN.** *160 VT Rte 15 W, Morrisville (05661). 802/888-4956; fax 802/888-3698; res 800/544-2347. www.sunsetmotorinn.com.* 55 rms. Mid-Sept-mid-Oct, mid-Dec-mid-Mar: S, D $78-$140; each addl $5-$10; under 12 free; higher rates hols; lower rates rest of yr. Crib $5. TV; cable (premium), VCR avail. Pool. Playground. Restaurant adj 6 am-10 pm. Ck-out 11 am. Free airport transportation. Downhill ski 9 mi; x-country ski 4 mi. Some in-rm whirlpools, refrigerators. Picnic tables, grills. Cr cds: A, D, DS, MC, V.

★★ **TOWN AND COUNTRY RESORT.** *876 Mountain Rd (05672). 802/253-7595; fax 802/253-4764; toll-free 800/323-0311. www.townandcountrystowe.com.* 45 rms, 1-2 story. Late June-Labor Day, late Dec-Mar: S, D $87-$120; each addl $8; under 13 free; MAP avail; ski plan; higher rates: winter hol wks, antique car rally; lower rates rest of yr. Crib $5. TV; cable. 2 pools, 1 indoor; wading pool, sauna. Restaurant 7:30-10 am, 5:30-9 pm. Bar 5 pm-1 am. Ck-out 11 am. Meeting rms. Business servs avail. Tennis. Downhill ski 5½ mi. Rec rm. Lawn games. Some refrigerators. Cr cds: A, C, D, DS, MC, V.

🖵⛱🏊🎿🛥🏊🔥

Resorts

★★ **COMMODORES INN.** *823 S Main St (05672). 802/253-7131; fax 802/253-2360; toll-free 800/447-8693. www.commodoresinn.com.* 50 rms, 2 story. Mid Sept-mid Oct, mid-Dec-mid-Mar: S $78-$98; D $98-$162; each addl $10-$34; under 12 free; wkend rates; higher rates wk of Dec 25; lower rates rest of yr. Crib free. Pet accepted; $10. TV; cable, VCR avail. 2 pools, heated, 1 indoor; wading pool, whirlpools. Complimentary continental bkfst off-season. Restaurant 7-10:30 am, 6-9:30 pm. Ck-out 11 am. Meeting rm. Business servs avail. In-rm modem link. Downhill ski 9 mi; x-country ski 6 mi. Exercise equipt; saunas. Game rm. Refrigerators avail. Cr cds: A, DS, MC, V.

🖵➤⛱🏊🛥🎿

★★★ **GOLDEN EAGLE RESORT.** *511 Mountain Rd (05672). 802/253-4811; fax 802/253-2561; toll-free 800/626-1010. www.stoweeagle.com.* 90 rms, 12 kits. Dec-Mar, late June-Oct: S $89-$114; D $99-$124; each addl $10; suites $129-$199; kit. units $139-$299; under 12 free; family rates; ski, golf, package plans; higher rates: hols, special event wkends; lower rates rest of yr. Crib $5. TV; cable (premium), VCR avail (movies $7). 3 heated pools, 1 indoor; whirlpool. Playground. Supervised children's activities (summer and winter); ages 4 and up. Complimentary coffee in rms. Restaurant 7-11 am, 5:30-9:30 pm. Rm serv 7-11 am. Bar 5-9:30 pm. Ck-out 11 am. Meeting rms. Business servs avail. Sundries. Free RR station, bus depot, ski slope transportation. Tennis. Downhill ski 5 mi; x-country ski 3 mi. Exercise rm; sauna. Massage. Rec rm. Lawn games. Refrigerators; some in-rm whirlpools, fireplaces; microwaves avail. Some balconies. Picnic tables, grills. Library, lounge. Stocked trout ponds on grounds; nature trails. Cr cds: A, C, D, DS, MC, V.

🖵⛱➤🎿🍴🎿🛥🏊✈🎿🔥

★★★ **GREEN MOUNTAIN INN.** *18 S Main St (05672). 802/253-7301; fax 802/253-5096; toll-free 800/253-7302. www.greenmountaininn.com.* 72 rms in inn, motel, 1-3 story, 1 carriage house. Dec-Mar: S $100-$140; D $110-$230; suites $125-$189; each addl $15; MAP avail; under 12 free; higher rates: hols, fall foliage. Crib free. Pet accepted. TV; cable, VCR (movies $3.50). Pool; whirlpool. Dining rm 7:30 am-9:30 pm. Rm serv. Bar noon-1 am. Ck-out 11 am, ck-in 2 pm. Meeting rm. Business servs avail. Downhill ski 6 mi; x-country ski 5 mi. Exercise equipt; sauna. Massage. Some fireplaces. Some balconies. Historic inn (1833); antiques, library, paintings by Vermont artist. Cr cds: A, D, DS, MC, V.

🖵➤🎿🛥🏊🎿🔥

★★★ **GREY FOX INN & RESORT.** *990 Mountain Rd (05672). 802/253-8921; fax 802/253-8344; toll-free 800/544-8454. www.stowegreyfoxinn.com.* 42 rms, 1-3 story, 7 kits. July-mid-Oct, ski season: S $75-$161; D $85-$171; each addl $5-$16; kits. $100-$275; under 3 free; MAP avail; wkly, golf, ski packages; higher rates: special events; lower rates rest of yr. Crib $5. TV; cable (premium), VCR avail (free movies). 2 pools, 1 indoor; whirlpool. Dining rm 8-10:30 am; dinner 5:30-8:30 pm. Ck-out 11 am, ck-in 2 pm. Coin lndry. Meeting rm. Business servs avail. In-rm modem link. Downhill ski 3 mi; x-country ski 1 mi. Game rm. Lawn games. Exercise equipt. Bicycle rental. Some microwaves, fireplaces. Picnic tables, grills. Late 19th-century farmhouse; library. Cr cds: A, DS, MC, V.

🖵➤🛥🍴🏊🔥

★★★ **THE MOUNTAIN RESORT AT STOWE.** *1007 Mountain Rd (05672). 802/253-4566; fax 802/253-7397; toll-free 800/367-6873.* 23 rms, 7 suites (some with kit.), 7 kit. units. June-Oct, late Dec-Mar: D $89-$175; each addl $8-$20; suites $185-$335; kits. $125-$199; MAP avail; family, wkly rates; golf, ski plans; higher rates: hols, special events; lower rates rest of yr. Crib $5. Pet accepted; $15. TV; cable (premium), VCR avail. 2 pools, 1 indoor; whirlpool. Playground. Coffee in rms. Restaurant opp 7 am-9 pm. Ck-out 11 am. Business servs avail. Coin lndry. Sundries. RR station, bus depot transportation. Tennis. Downhill ski 4 mi; x-country ski 2½ mi. Bicycles. Exercise equipt; saunas. Rec rm. Lawn games. Refrigerators; some in-rm whirlpools; microwaves avail. Some balconies. Picnic tables, grills. Cr cds: A, D, DS, MC, V.

🖵➤⛱🎿🛥🏊🎿🔥

★★★ **STOWEFLAKE MOUNTAIN RESORT & SPA.** *1746 Mountain Rd (05672). 802/253-7355; fax 802/253-6858; toll-free 800/253-2232. www.stoweflake.com.* 98 rms, 1-2 story, 24 townhouses. July-mid-Oct, late Dec-mid-Mar: S $70-$99; D $140-$180; each addl $10; suites, townhouses $195-$575; studio rms $175-$195; under 12 free; MAP avail; golf, tennis, ski plans; 2-day min hols; lower rates rest of yr. Crib free. TV; cable, VCR avail. 2 heated pools, 1 indoor; whirlpool, poolside serv. Restaurant 7:30-10:30 am, 4-10 pm. Summer lunch noon-3 pm. Rm serv. Bar 3 pm-1 am. Ck-out 11 am. Meeting rms. Business servs avail. In-rm modem link. Bellhops. Concierge. Gift shop. Tennis, pro. Golf privileges, putting green, driving range, lessons. Downhill ski 3½ mi; x-country ski 1½ mi. Exercise rm; sauna. Game rm. Lawn games. Sleigh and hay rides. Some refrigerators, microwave in suites; fireplace in townhouses. Library. Shopping mall adj. Cr cds: A, D, DS, MC, V.

🖵⛱🎿🎿🍴🎿🛥🏊🎿✈🎿🔥

★★★★ **TOPNOTCH AT STOWE.** *4000 Mountain Rd (05672). 802/253-8585; fax 802/253-9263; toll-free 800/451-8686. www.topnotch-resort.com.* Guests will enjoy the European country style at this 120-acre resort and spa in Vermont's Green Mountains. There are 90 rooms, suites, and townhouses, many with sundecks and views of Mount Mansfield. Dine at Maxwell's for seafood, prime aged meats, and game; get pampered at the 23,000-square-foot spa; or just choose something to read from one of the book-lined rooms. 92 rms in main bldg, 21 kit. townhouses.

A/C in townhouses, chalet. Late May-mid-Oct: S, D $240-$330; each addl $45; suites $375-$700; kit. townhouses $375-$700; tennis, golf, ski, spa plans; lower rates rest of yr. Crib free. TV; cable, VCR avail (movies). 2 heated pools, 1 indoor; whirlpool. Supervised children's activities (July-early Sept, wk of Dec 25); ages 5-12. Complimentary afternoon refreshments. Dining rm 7-10:30 am, 11:30 am-2:30 pm, 5:30-9:30 pm. Rm serv 7 am-9:30 pm. Box lunches. Bar noon-2 am; entertainment (seasonal). Ck-out 11 am, ck-in 3:30 pm. In-rm modem link. Business center. Meeting rms. Bellhops. Valet serv. Concierge. Gift shop. Beauty shop. 14 tennis courts, 4 indoor, pro. Golf privileges. Downhill ski 2 mi; x-country ski on site. Ski equipt, instruction. Trail rides, instruction. Mountain bike rentals. Hiking. Exercise rm; sauna, steam rm. Spa. Refrigerators. Some fireplaces. Bathrm phones. Microwaves avail. Some balconies. Libraries. Sun deck. Cr cds: A, C, D, DS, MC, V.

★★★ **TRAPP FAMILY LODGE.** *700 Trapp Hill Rd (05672). 802/253-8511; fax 802/253-5740; res 800/826-7000. www.trappfamily.com.* 73 rms in main lodge, 20 rms in lower lodge, 4 story, 100 guest houses. No A/C. Ski season: S, D $245-$375; each addl $25; guest houses $800-$2,200/wk; under 12 free (off-season and summer only); MAP avail; package plans; some higher rates hol wkends; lower rates rest of yr. Crib free. 3 pools, 1 indoor. Dining rm (public by res) 7:30-10:30 am, 5:30-9 pm; Austrian tea rm 10:30 am-5:30 pm. Bar 3:30-10 pm; entertainment, movies. Ck-out 11 am, ck-in 3 pm. Business servs avail. Bellhops. Gift shop. Tennis. Downhill ski 6 mi; x-country ski on site, equipt, instruction. Exercise equipt; sauna. Lawn games. Sleigh rides. Hiking trails; guided nature walks. Many balconies. Fireplaces in public rms. Library. Alpine lodge owned by Trapp family, whose lives were portrayed in "The Sound of Music." Cr cds: A, DS, MC, V.

B&Bs/Small Inns

★★ **BRASS LANTERN INN.** *717 Maple St (05672). 802/253-2229; fax 802/253-7425; toll-free 800/729-2980. www.brasslanterninn.com.* 9 rms, 2 story. No rm phones. Mid-Dec-early Apr, mid-June-mid-Oct: S, D $90-$160; each addl $25; ski, golf plans; higher rates Christmas wk; lower rates rest of yr. TV avail. Complimentary full bkfst; after-noon refreshments. Restaurant nearby. Ck-out 10:30 am, ck-in 3 pm. Gift shop. Downhill ski 7 mi; x-country ski 6½ mi. Health club privileges. Antiques. Library/sitting rm. Some in-rm whirlpools, fireplaces. Built 1810; operating farmhouse. Totally nonsmoking. Cr cds: A, MC, V.

★★ **BUTTERNUT INN AND COUNTRY GUEST HOUSE.** *2309 Mountain Rd (05672). 802/253-4277; fax 802/253-5263; toll-free 800/328-8837. www.butternutinnvt.com.* 18 rms, 3 story. July-Labor Day, mid-Sept-mid-Oct, mid-Dec-Mar: D $65-$95/person; ski plan; lower rates rest of yr. Adults only. TV, some B/W; cable. Heated pool. Complimentary bkfst; afternoon refreshments in sitting rm. Dining rm 8-10 am. Ck-out

11 am, ck-in 3 pm. Downhill ski 4 mi; x-country ski on site. Rec rm. Nature trail. Picnic table, grills. Fireplaces in public areas. Antique furnishings. Library. Totally non-smoking. Cr cds: A, DS, MC, V.

★★ **EDSON HILL MANOR.** *1500 Edson Hill Rd (05672). 802/253-7371; fax 802/253-4036; toll-free 800/621-0284. www.stowevt.com.* 9 rms in lodge, 16 carriage house units, 25 baths. A/C in lodge rms only. Mid-Dec-mid-Apr, MAP: D $139-$239; each addl $55; under 4 free; ski, riding and mid-wk plans; lower rates rest of yr. Serv charge 15%. Crib free. Pool. Complimentary full bkfst. Dining rm 8-10 am, 6-9:30 pm. Bar 4:30 pm-midnight; summer from 5 pm. Ck-out 11 am, ck-in 2 pm. Downhill ski 5 mi; x-country ski on site; marked trails, instruction, rentals. Sleigh rides. Carriage rides. Stocked trout pond. Lawn games. Many fireplaces. Varied accommodations. 225 acres on hillside; view of Green Mts. Cr cds: DS, MC, V.

★★ **SCANDINAVIA INN AND CHALETS.** *3576 Mountain Rd (05672). 802/253-8555; res 800/544-4229. www.scandinaviainn.com.* 18 rms, 12 A/C, 4 chalets, 2 story. Ski season: S $89; D $99-$129; chalets $225-$375; each addl $15; wkly rates; ski plans; lower rates rest of yr. Closed mid-Oct-late Nov. TV; cable (premium). Heated pool; whirlpool. Dining rm 7:30-10 am, wkends to 11 am. Setups. Ck-out 11 am, ck-in 2 pm. Coin lndry. Free ski shuttle. Downhill ski 2½ mi; x-country ski ⅛ mi. Exercise equipt; sauna. Game rm. Lawn games. Picnic tables, grills. Home of the trolls. Some refrigerators. Totally nonsmoking. Cr cds: A, DS, MC, V.

★★★ **STOWEHOF INN.** *434 Edson Hill Rd (05672). 802/253-9722; fax 802/253-7513; toll-free 800/932-7136. www.stowehofinn.com.* 44 rms, 3 story. Ski season, July-Oct: D $69-$120/person; each addl $35; MAP avail; higher rates: Christmas wk, fall season. Serv charge 15%. Crib free. TV; cable, VCR avail (free movies). Heated pool; indoor pool; whirlpool, poolside serv, sauna. Complimentary full bkfst. Dining rm 8-10 am, 6-9:30 pm; summer also noon-2 pm. Bar 4 pm-1 am. Ck-out noon, ck-in 3 pm. Meeting rm. Business servs avail. Luggage handling. Exercise equipt. Tennis, pro. Downhill ski 4 mi; x-country ski on site. Rec rm. Lawn games. Sleigh rides. Fireplaces. Private patios, balconies. Library. Trout pond. Cr cds: A, D, DS, MC, V.

★★ **STOWE INN AT LITTLE RIVER.** *123 Mountain Rd (05672). 802/253-4836; fax 802/253-7308; toll-free 800/227-1108. www.stoweinn.com.* 43 rms in motel, lodge, 4 kits., 8 condos (1-bedrm). Dec-Apr: D $65-$210; each addl $10; condos $150-$285; ski plan; higher rates special events; lower rates rest of yr. Crib $10. Pet accepted, some restrictions. TV; cable. Pool; whirlpool. Continental bkfst. Restaurant 11:30 am-9 pm. Bar. Ck-out 11 am. Business servs avail. Downhill ski 6 mi; x-country ski 4 mi. Rec rm. Some refrigerators. Cr cds: A, DS, MC, V.

★★ **THREE BEARS AT THE FOUNTAIN.** *1049 Pucker St (05672). 802/253-7671; fax 802/253-8804; toll-free 800/898-9634. www.threebearsbandb.com.* 5 rms, 4 with full bathrm, 2 story. No A/C. S, D $105-$225; each addl $25-$35; under 12 free; ski plans; fall foliage, hols 2-day min; higher rates: fall foliage, hols. Closed 1st 2 wks Nov. Crib avail. Premium cable TV in common rm. Complimentary full bkfst. Restaurant nearby. Ck-out 10:30 am, ck-in 3 pm. Downhill ski 7 mi; x-country ski 1 mi. Built in 1826; one of the oldest guesthouses in Stowe. Outdoor fountain. Totally nonsmoking. Cr cds: A, MC, V.

★ **WINDING BROOK...A CLASSIC MOUNTAIN LODGE.** *199 Edson Hill Rd (05672). 802/253-7354; fax 802/253-8429; toll-free 800/426-6697. www.windingbrooklodge.com.* 20 rms, 5 with shower only, 2 story. Mid-Dec-mid-Mar, mid-June-Labor Day: S $85-$95; D $95-$135; each addl $35; 3-bdrm townhouse $350; family, wkly, wkend rates; ski plans; higher rates hols (2-day min); lower rates rest of yr. Crib free. 5 TVs; cable (premium). Pool; whirlpool. Complimentary full bkfst. Restaurant 4-9 pm mid-June-Labor Day. Bar 4-1 am. Ck-out 11 am. Business servs avail. Tennis. Downhill ski 3 mi; x-country ski on site. Rec rm. Some balconies. Picnic tables. Totally nonsmoking. Cr cds: A, MC, V.

★★★ **YE OLDE ENGLAND INNE.** *433 Mountain Rd (05672). 802/253-7558; fax 802/253-8944; toll-free 800/643-1553. www.englandinn.com.* 30 rms, 3-5 story, 10 suites, 3 cottages. No elvtr. Mid-Sept-mid-Oct, ski season: S, D $179-$345; suites $345-$365; each addl $35; under 12 free; EP avail; wkly rates; ski, golf, gliding; higher rates late Dec-early Jan; lower rates rest of yr. Serv charge 10%, cottages 5%. Crib $5. Pet accepted, some restrictions. TV; cable (premium), VCR avail. Pool; whirlpool. Complimentary afternoon refreshments. Complimentary coffee in rms. Dining rm 8 am-10 pm in season. Bar 11:30-2 am; entertainment Wed-Sat (winter). Ck-out 11 am, ck-in 3 pm. Business servs avail. Tennis privileges. Downhill ski 5 mi; x-country ski 2 mi. Some in-rm whirlpools. Balconies. Picnic tables, grill. Built 1893. Totally nonsmoking. Cr cds: A, DS, MC, V.

Restaurants

★ **CLIFF HOUSE.** *5781 Mountain Rd (05672). 802/253-3000. www.stowe.com.* Eclectic menu. Specialties: Rock Cornish game hen, fresh seafood. Hrs: 11 am-3 pm, 5:30-9 pm; Sun, Wed to 2:30 pm. Closed Mon, Tues; Thanksgiving; also mid-Apr-late June, late Oct-mid-Dec. Res required dinner. No A/C. Serv bar. Buffet: lunch $12.10. Complete meals: dinner $42.50, includes gondola ride. Sun brunch $18.95. View of mountains. Totally nonsmoking. Cr cds: A, D, DS, MC, V.

★★★ **ISLE DE FRANCE.** *1899 Mountain Rd (05672). 802/253-7751. www.gostowe.com.* Hrs: 6-10 pm. Closed Mon. Res accepted. French menu. Bar. Wine list. A la carte entrees: dinner $19-$48. Specialties: lobster Newberg, Dover sole meuniere, châteaubriand. Own bread. Parking. French provincial decor; formal dining in elegant atmosphere. Cr cds: A, D, MC, V.

★★ **PARTRIDGE INN SEAFOOD RESTAURANT.** *504 Mountain Rd (05672). 802/253-8000. www.gostowe.com.* Specializes in Maine lobster, fresh Cape Cod seafood, pasta. Hrs: 5:30-9:30 pm. Closed first 3 wks Nov. Res accepted. Bar 5-11 pm. Dinner $16-$23. Child's menu. Parking. Fireplace. Totally nonsmoking. Cr cds: A, D, DS, MC, V.

★★ **THE SHED.** *1859 Mountain Rd (05672). 802/253-4364. www.gostowe.com.* Hrs: 11:30 am-10 pm; Sun brunch 10 am-2 pm. Res accepted. Bar. Lunch $4.95-$9.95, dinner $8.75-$18.95. Sun brunch $12.95. Child's menu. Specializes in baby back ribs, fresh seafood, calf liver. Parking. Outdoor dining. Brewery on premises. Family-owned. Totally nonsmoking. Cr cds: A, D, DS, MC, V.

★ **SWISSPOT.** *128 Main St (05672). 802/253-4622.* Swiss, Amer menu. Specializes in fondue, pasta, quiche. Hrs: 11:30 am-10 pm. Closed mid-Apr-mid-June, mid-Oct-mid-Dec. Res accepted. Bar. Lunch $4.95-$8.95, dinner $5.95-$17.95. Child's menu. Patio dining in summer. Built for 1967 Montreal Expo, then moved here. Totally nonsmoking. Cr cds: A, C, D, DS, MC, V.

★★ **WHISKERS.** *1652 Mountain Rd (05672). 802/253-8996. www.gostowe.com.* Continental menu. Specializes in fresh lobster, fresh seafood, prime rib. Salad bar (dinner). Own desserts. Hrs: 5-10 pm; summer 11:30 am-3:30 pm, 5-10 pm. Closed Mon-Fri during summer lunch hrs. Res accepted. Bar. Lunch $5.95-$12.95, dinner $10.95-$21.95. Child's menu. Parking. Outdoor and greenhouse dining. Old farmhouse, antiques. Lobster tanks. Flower garden. Totally nonsmoking. Cr cds: A, C, D, DS, MC, V.

Stratton Mountain

See also Londonderry, Manchester & Manchester Center, Peru

Area code 802 **Zip** 05155

What to See and Do

Skiing. Stratton Mountain. A high-speed gondola, two high-speed six-passenger, three quad, one triple, two double chairlifts, two surface lifts; patrol, school, rentals; snowmaking; cafeterias, restaurants, bars; nursery, sports center. Ninety runs, longest run 3 mi; vertical drop 2,003 ft. (Mid-Nov-mid-Apr, daily) Over 17 mi of cross-country trails (Dec-Mar, daily), rentals; snowboarding. Summer activities incl gondola ride; horseback riding, tennis, golf (school), festivals, concert series. On Stratton Mt access road, off VT 30. Phone 802/297-2200. ¢¢¢¢

Special Events

Labor Day Street Festival. Stratton Mtn. Festival with continuous entertainment, specialty foods, imported beer, activities for children. Phone 802/297-2200. Labor Day wkend.

Stratton Arts Festival. Stratton Mtn Base Lodge. Paintings, photography, sculpture, and crafts; special performing arts events, craft demonstrations. Phone 802/297-2200. Mid-Sept-mid-Oct. Phone 802/297-4000.

Resort

★ ★ ★ **STRATTON MOUNTAIN INN AND VILLAGE LODGE.** *RR 1 Box 145, Stratton (05155). 802/297-2200; fax 802/297-4084; toll-free 800/787-2886. www.stratton.com.* 110 condominiums (1-4 bedrm), 1-4 story. S, D $110-$490; family rates; ski-wk, tennis, golf plans; higher rates hols. TV; cable (premium), VCR (movies $3.50). 4 pools, 1 indoor; whirlpool. Supervised children's activities; ages 1-12. Box lunches. Snack bar. Ck-out 10 am, ck-in 5 pm. Lndry facilities. Package store 5 mi. Meeting rms. Business servs avail. Shopping arcade. Ski shuttle service. Sports dir. 15 tennis courts; indoor lighted tennis, clinic, pro. 27-hole golf, greens fee $49-$82, pro, putting green, driving range. Downhill/x-country ski on site. Racquetball/squash. Bicycles. Game rm. Rec rm. Exercise rm; sauna. Mountain bicycles (rentals). Refrigerators, fireplaces. Private patios, balconies. Picnic tables. Gondola rides (in season). Resort covers 4,000 acres. Cr cds: A, C, D, DS, MC, V.

ⓓ 🛇 👯 🏌 🎿 🐾 ⤢ ⛷ 🏃

Swanton

See also North Hero, St. Albans

Pop 2,360 **Elev** 119 ft **Area code** 802 **Zip** 05488
Information Chamber of Commerce, PO Box 210; 802/868-7200

The location of this town, just two miles east of Lake Champlain, makes it an attractive resort spot.

What to See and Do

Missisquoi National Wildlife Refuge. More than 6,400 acres, incl much of the Missisquoi River delta on Lake Champlain; primarily a waterfowl refuge (best in Apr, Sept, and Oct), but other wildlife and birds may be seen. Fishing; hunting, hiking and canoe trails. (Daily) 2½ mi W via VT 78. Phone 802/868-4781. **FREE**

Special Event

Swanton Summer Festival. On Village Green. Band concerts, square dancing, rides, children's events, parades, arts and crafts. Last wkend July.

Resort

★ ★ ★ **TYLER PLACE FAMILY RESORT.** *Old Dock Rd, Highgate Springs (05460). 802/868-3301; fax 802/868-5621; res 802/868-4000. www.tylerplace.com.* 12 suites in 1-2-story inn, 27 kit. cottages (3-6 rm). Late May-Labor Day, AP: $77-$264/person; children $41-$89. Closed rest of yr. Crib free. TV rm. 2 pools, 1 indoor pool; wading pool, lifeguard. Supervised children's activities (May-Sept); ages infant-16 yrs. Dining rm 7:30-10:30 am, 12:30-1:30 pm, 6:30-8 pm. Box lunches, buffets. Bar noon-midnight. Ck-out 10 am, ck-in 3 pm. Tennis. Sailing, canoeing, fishing boats, motors (fee). Waterskiing (fee), windsurfing. Nature trails. Soc dir. Rec rm. Exercise rm. Fireplace in cottages. Refrigerator in rms. On 165 acres; private lake shore. Cr cds: A, DS, MC, V.

🛇 🎿 ⤢ 🏌 🏃 🛇

Vergennes

See also Middlebury, Shelburne

Settled 1766 **Pop** 2,578 **Elev** 205 ft **Area code** 802 **Zip** 05491
Information Vergennes Chamber of Commerce, PO Box 335; 802/877-0080

Vergennes is one of the smallest incorporated cities in the nation (one square mile). It is also the oldest city in Vermont and the third oldest in New England.

What to See and Do

Button Bay State Park. This 236-acre park on a bluff overlooking Lake Champlain was named for the buttonlike formations in the clay banks; spectacular views of Adirondack Mtns. Swimming pool, fishing, boating (rentals); nature and hiking trails, picnicking, tent and trailer sites (dump station). Museum, naturalist. (Memorial Day-Columbus Day) Standard fees. 6 mi W on Button Bay Rd, just S of Basin Harbor. Phone 802/475-2377.

Chimney Point State Historic Site. (1700s) This 18th-century tavern was built on the site of a 17th-century French fort. Exhibits on the Native American and French settlement of Champlain Valley and Vermont. (Memorial Day-Columbus Day, Wed-Sun) 6 mi S via VT 22A, then 8 mi SW via VT 17, at the terminus of the Crown Point Military Rd on shoreline of Lake Champlain. Phone 802/759-2412. ¢

John Strong Mansion. (1795) Federalist house; restored and furnished in the period. (Mid-May-mid-Oct, Fri-Sun) 6 mi SW via VT 22A, on VT 17, in West Addison. Phone 802/759-2309. ¢¢

Kennedy Brothers Factory Marketplace. Renovated 1920s brick creamery building features gift, crafts, and antique shops. Deli, ice cream shop, picnic area. (Daily; closed Jan 1, Thanksgiving, Dec 25) 11 Main St. Phone 802/877-2975. **FREE**

Rokeby Museum. (ca 1785) Ancestral home of abolitionist Rowland T. Robinson was a station for the Underground Railroad. Artifacts and archives of four generations of the Robinson family. Set on 85 acres, farmstead incl an ice house, a creamery, and a stone smokehouse. Special events yr-round. Tours. (Mid-May-mid-Oct, Thurs-Sun) 2 mi N on US 7, 6 mi S of ferry route on US 7, Ferrisburg. Phone 802/877-3406. ¢¢

Motel/Motor Lodge

★ **SKYVIEW MOTEL.** *2956 US Rte 7, Ferrisburg (05456). 802/877-3410; toll-free 888/799-9090. www.vermontlodgers.com.* 15 rms, 3 kits. May-mid Sept: S $45-65; D $55-$90; each addl $5; kit. units $8 addl; family rates; higher rates fall foliage; lower rates rest of yr. Crib $10. TV; cable. Playground. Complimentary coffee in rms. Restaurant adj 6 am-8 pm. Ck-out 11 am. X-country ski 15 mi. Lawn games. Refrigerators. Picnic tables, grills. Cr cds: A, DS, MC, V.

⬛ 🖙 🛏 🔥

Resort

★★★ **BASIN HARBOR CLUB.** *Basin Harbor Rd (05491). 802/475-2311; fax 802/475-6545; toll-free 800/622-4000. www.basinharbor.com.* 40 rms in lodges, 77 cottages (1-3 bedrm). Mid-May-mid-Oct, AP: S $185; D $240-$425; each addl $5-$70; EP avail mid-May-mid-June, Sept-Oct; wkly rates. Closed rest of yr. Crib avail. Pet accepted, some restrictions. TV avail. Heated pool; poolside serv. Free supervised children's activities (July-Aug); ages 3-15. Dining rm 8 am-10 pm. Box lunches. Bar 11 am-midnight. Ck-out 11 am, ck-in 4 pm. Coin lndry. Business servs avail. Concierge. Gift shop. Airport, RR station, bus depot transportation. Rec dirs. Tennis. 18-hole golf, greens fee $42, putting green, driving range. Beach; motorboats, sailboats, canoes, kayaks, cruise boat; windsurfing, waterskiing. Exercise rm. Massage. Fitness, nature trails. Lawn games. Bicycles. Rec rm. Refrigerator in cottages. Family-owned since 1886; Colonial architecture. Located on 700 acres, on Lake Champlain; dockage. 3,200-ft airstrip avail. Cr cds: A, DS, MC, V.

⬛ 🐾 ⬛ 🏋 🖙 🏊 🎿 🛏 🔥

B&Bs/Small Inns

★ **EMERSON GUEST HOUSE.** *82 Main St (05491). 802/877-3293. www.emersonhouse.com.* 6 rms, 1 A/C, 1 with shower only, 4 rms share bath. No rm phones. S, D $65-$150; each addl $10-$15. Children over 8 yrs only. TV in common rm, VCR avail. Complimentary full bkfst. Restaurant nearby. Ck-out 10:30 am, ck-in 3 pm. Built in 1850; Victorian inn. Totally nonsmoking. Cr cds: MC, V.

⬛ 🔥

★★★ **STRONG HOUSE INN.** *94 W Main St (05491). 802/877-3337; fax 802/877-2599. www.stronghouseinn.com.* 8 rms, 2 story. Some rm phones. S $90-$175; D $135-$175; each addl $20; higher rates: fall foliage, hols. Children over 8 yrs only. TV in some rms. Complimentary full bkfst. Dining rm (guests only). Rm serv. Ck-out 11 am, ck-in 3 pm. Gift shop. Some fireplaces. Historic Federal-style house (1834); antiques, library. Views of the Green Mountains and Adirondack range. Totally nonsmoking. Cr cds: A, MC, V.

⬛ 🐾 ♿ 🔥

Waitsfield

See also Montpelier, Warren, Waterbury

Pop 1,422 **Elev** 698 ft **Area code** 802 **Zip** 05673
Information Sugarbush Chamber of Commerce, General Wait House - Rte 100, PO Box 173; 802/496-3409 or 800/828-4748
Web www.sugarbushchamber.org

This region, known as "the Valley," is a popular area in summer as well as in the winter ski season.

What to See and Do

Mad River Glen Ski Area. Area has three double, two single chairlifts; patrol, school, rentals; snowmaking; cafeterias, restaurant, bar; nursery. Forty-four runs, longest run 3 mi; vertical drop 2,000 ft. (Dec-Apr, daily) On VT 17, 5 mi W of VT 100. Phone 802/496-3551. ¢¢¢¢

Resort

★★ **TUCKER HILL INN.** *Rte 17 (05673). 802/496-3983; toll-free 800/543-7841. www.tuckerhill.com.* 22 rms, 16 baths. No A/C. Ski season, mid-June-late Oct, MAP: S $99-$169; D $169-$299; lower rates rest of yr. TV in sitting rm, bar. Pool. Restaurant (see also THE STEAK PLACE AT TUCKER HILL). Bar. Ck-out 11 am, ck-in 2 pm. Tennis; pro. Downhill ski 2 mi; x-country ski on site. Hiking trails. Handmade quilts. Cr cds: A, MC, V.

⬛ 🖙 🎿 🏊 🛏 🔥 SC

B&Bs/Small Inns

★★ **1824 HOUSE INN BED AND BREAKFAST.** *2150 Main st (05673). 802/496-7555; fax 802/496-7559; toll-free 800/426-3986. www.1824house.com.* 7 rms, 2 story. No rm phones. S, D $105-$135; each addl $35; higher rates: major hols, fall foliage. Complimentary full bkfst. Ck-out 11 am, ck-in 4 pm. Downhill ski 6 mi; x-country ski 5 mi. Whirlpool. Lawn games. Restored farmhouse (1824); feather beds, Oriental rugs, down quilts. Totally nonsmoking. Cr cds: A, DS, MC, V.

⬛ 🖙 🛏 🔥

★★★ THE INN AT THE ROUND BARN.
1661 E Warren Rd (05673). 802/496-2276; fax 802/496-8832.
www.theroundbarn.com. 12 rms, 4 A/C, 2 story. Some rm
phones. S $120-$215; D $130-$265; each addl $25. TV in
sitting rm. Indoor lap pool. Complimentary full bkfst.
Ck-out 11 am, ck-in 3 pm. Business servs avail. Gift shop.
Game rm. X-country ski on site, rentals. In restored farmhouse (ca 1810), named for its historic 12-sided barn (1910).
On 235 acres with perennial gardens and 5 ponds. Totally
nonsmoking. Cr cds: A, DS, MC, V.

D ⬡ ⬡ ⬡ ⬡ ⬡

★★ LAREAU FARM COUNTRY INN. *Rte 100 (05673).*
802/496-4949; fax 802/496-7979; toll-free 800/833-0766.
www.lareaufarminn.com. 13 rms, 11 with bath, 2 story. No
A/C. No rm phones. Ski and foliage season: S $90-$100; D
$100-$150; family, wkly rates; ski plan; lower rates rest of yr.
TV in living rm. Complimentary full bkfst. Ck-out 11 am,
ck-in 2 pm. Downhill ski 5 mi. Sleigh rides in winter. Picnic
tables. Farmhouse and barn built by area's first physician;
sitting rm; antiques. Cr cds: MC, V.

⬡ ⬡ ⬡ ⬡ ⬡

★★ THE WAITSFIELD INN. *5267 Main (05673).*
802/496-3979; fax 802/496-3970; toll-free 800/758-3801.
www.waitsfieldinn.com. 14 rms, 2 story. No rm phones. Fall
foliage season, mid-Dec-early Apr: S, D $120-$140; each
addl $15; family, wkly rates; ski plans; lower rates rest of yr.
Closed Apr, Nov. Ck-out 11 am, ck-in 3 pm. Meeting rms.
Downhill ski 6 mi; x-country ski 3 mi. Antiques, handmade
quilts.Totally nonsmoking.Cr cds: A, DS, MC, V.

⬡ ⬡ ⬡ ⬡ ⬡

★ WHITE HORSE INN. *999 German Flats Rd (05673).*
802/496-3260; fax 802/496-2476; toll-free 800/328-3260.
www.central-vt.com/web/whorse. 26 rms, 16 with shower
only, 2 story. No A/C. No rm phones. Dec-Mar: S $50-$65;
D $65-$95; each addl $15; ski plans; hols, wkends (2-day
min); lower rates rest of yr. Pet accepted. TV in some rms;
cable. Complimentary full bkfst. Ck-out noon, ck-in 3 pm.
Downhill ski ½ mi; x-country ski 2 mi. Picnic tables, grill.
Totally nonsmoking. Cr cds: A, DS, MC, V.

⬡ ⬡ ⬡ ⬡ ⬡

Restaurants

★ RESTAURANT DEN. *VT 100 (05673). 802/496-8880.*
Specializes in steak, fresh seafood. Salad bar. Hrs: 11:30
am-11 pm. Closed Thanksgiving, Dec 25. Bar to midnight.
Lunch $3.95-$6.95, dinner $8.95-$13.95. Outdoor dining.
Cr cds: A, MC, V.

D

★★ THE STEAK PLACE AT TUCKER HILL. *VT 17*
(05673). 802/496-3983. www.tuckerhill.com. Hrs: 5-9:30 pm.
Bar 5-11 pm. Dinner $8-$14.95. Child's menu. Outdoor
dining. Cr cds: A, MC, V.

Warren

See also Waitsfield, Waterbury

Pop 1,172 **Elev** 893 ft **Area code** 802 **Zip** 05674
Information Sugarbush Chamber of Commerce, PO Box 173,
Waitsfield 05673; 802/496-3409 or 800/828-4748
Web www.sugarbushchamber.org

What to See and Do

Sugarbush Golf Course. An 18-hole championship course
designed by Robert Trent Jones, Sr.; driving range; nine-hole
putting green; championship tees (6,524 yds). Restaurant.
(May-Oct, daily) Res recommended. 3 mi NW via VT 100.
Phone 802/583-2722. ¢¢¢¢

Sugarbush Resort. Area has seven quad, three triple, six
double chairlifts; four surface lifts; patrol, school, rentals;
concession area, cafeteria, restaurant, bar; nursery. One
hundred seven runs, longest run over 2 mi; vertical drop
2,650 ft. (Early Nov-early May, daily) 3 mi NW, off VT 100.
Phone 802/583-2381. ¢¢¢¢

Sugarbush Soaring Association. Soaring instruction, scenic
glider rides. Picnicking, restaurant. (May-Oct, daily) Res
preferred. 2 mi NE via VT 100, at Sugarbush Airport.
Phone 802/496-2290.

Sugarbush Sports Center. Complete sports and fitness
facility with pools and whirlpools, steam rm, saunas,
massage. Gym. Indoor/outdoor tennis courts, racquetball/
handball and squash courts. Sports instruction. Fee for
activities. (Daily) 3 mi NW via VT 100, in Sugarbush
Village. Phone 802/583-2391. ¢¢¢¢

Motel/Motor Lodge

★ GOLDEN LION RIVERSIDE INN. *731 VT 100 (05674).*
802/496-3084; fax 802/496-7438; toll-free 888/867-4491.
www.madriver.com/lodging/goldlion. 12 rms, 2 kit. units.
No A/C. Mid-Sept-mid-Apr: S, D $55-$125; each addl $10;
under 6 free; higher rates: wkends, hols; lower rates rest of
yr. Crib free. Pet accepted. TV; cable. Complimentary full
bkfst. Restaurant nearby. Ck-out 11 am. Downhill/x-country
ski 3 mi. Picnic table, grill. Cr cds: A, DS, MC, V.

⬡ ⬡ ⬡ ⬡ SC

Resort

★★ SUGARBUSH VILLAGE CONDOS. *RR 1, Box 68-12*
(05674). 802/583-3000; fax 802/583-2373; res 800/451-
4326. www.sugarbushvillage.com. 150 1-5 bedrm kit. condos, 1-5 story. No A/C. Ski season: 1-2 bedrm $105-$330;
3-5 bedrm $335-$520; wkly rates; ski-wk, sports plans;
lower rates rest of yr. Crib avail. TV; cable, VCR avail. Pool.
Ck-out 10 am. Coin lndry. Downhill ski adj; x-country ski
2 mi, Refrigerators; some microwaves, fireplaces or wood
stoves. Private patios, some balconies. Cr cds: A, DS,
MC, V.

⬡ ⬡ ⬡

B&Bs/Small Inns

★★★ **THE PITCHER INN.** 275 Main St (05674). 802/496-6350; toll-free 888/867-4824. www.pitcherinn.com. 9 rms, 3 story. S, D $300-$600. TV; cable (premium); VCR. Restaurant 6:30 am-10 pm. Bar to midnight. Ck-out noon, ck-in 4 pm. Meeting rms. In-rm modem link. Concierge. Exercise equipt. Some fireplaces. Cr cds: A, D, DS, MC, V.

★★★ **SUGARBUSH INN.** 2405 Sugarbush Access Rd (05674). 802/583-2301; fax 802/583-3209; toll-free 800/537-8427. www.sugarbush.com. 42 rms in inn, 196 kit. condos. No A/C in condos. Dec-Mar: S, D, suites $100-$200; each addl $20-$35; kit. condos $200-$450 (2-day min); ski, golf, tennis plans; higher rates hols; lower rates rest of yr. Crib $10. TV; cable (premium), VCR avail (movies $3.50). 2 pools, 1 indoor; whirlpool. Dining rm 7:30-10 am, 6-10 pm. Bar from 4:30 pm. Ck-out 11 am, ck-in 6 pm. Meeting rms. Business servs avail. Bellhops. Gift shop. Tennis, clinics, pro. 18-hole golf, putting green. Downhill ski ½ mi; x-country ski on site, rentals. Exercise equipt; sauna. Ice-skating. Rec rm. Lawn games. Some refrigerators. Some private patios, balconies. Cr cds: A, DS, MC, V.

★★ **SUGARTREE COUNTRY INN.** 2440 Sugarbush Access Rd (05674). 802/583-3211; fax 802/583-3203; toll-free 800/666-8907. www.sugartree.com. 9 rms, some A/C, 3 story. Late Dec-Mar: S $99-$115; D $109-$135; each addl $20-$30; ski plans; higher rates: hols, fall foliage; lower rates rest of yr. Closed 3 wks Apr. Children over 7 yrs only. Complimentary full bkfst. Restaurant adj 5:30-10 pm. Ck-out 11 am, ck-in 2 pm. Business servs avail. Downhill/x-country ski ¼ mi. Health club privileges. Antiques. Gazebo. Totally non-smoking. Cr cds: A, DS, MC, V.

Villas/Condos

★★ **BRIDGES FAMILY RESORT AND TENNIS CLUB.** 202 Bridges Cir (05674). 802/583-2922; fax 802/583-1018; toll-free 800/453-2922. www.bridgesresort.com. 100 kit. units (1-3 bedrm), 2-3 story. No A/C. No elvtr. Dec-Mar: S, D $175-$280; 3 bedrm $330-$585; under 12 free; wkly rates; tennis plan; wkends (2-day min); lower rates rest of yr. Crib $18. TV; cable (premium), VCR (movies $3). 3 pools, 1 indoor; poolside serv. Playground. Supervised children's activities (July-Aug); ages 4 and up. Restaurant nearby. Ck-out 11 am, ck-in 6 pm. Grocery nearby. Meeting rms. Business servs avail. Ski area transportation. Indoor and outdoor tennis; 12 courts. Downhill/x-country ski ¼ mi. Nature trail. Lawn games. Rec rm. Exercise equipt; sauna. Fireplaces. Private patios, balconies. Grills, picnic tables. Cr cds: A, MC, V.

★ **POWDER HOUND INN.** 203 Powderhound Rd (05674). 802/496-5100; fax 802/496-5163; toll-free 800/548-4022. www.powderhoundinn.com. 48 units, 44 kit. units, 1-2 story. No A/C. Dec-late Mar: S, D $75-$150; higher rates: wk of Washington's birthday, wk of Dec 25; lower rates rest of yr. Crib $5. Pet accepted; $5. TV; cable. Pool; whirlpool. Restaurant (in season only) 7:30-9:30 am. Ck-out 10 am.

Tennis. Downhill/x-country ski 3 mi. Balconies. Picnic tables, grills. Restored, 19th-century farmhouse. Cr cds: A, DS, MC, V.

Restaurants

★★ **BASS.** 527 Sugarbush Access Rd (05674). 802/583-3100. www.bassrestaurant.com. Specializes in prime rib, lobster, fresh seafood. Hrs: 5-10 pm; from 4 pm during ski season. Closed Wed June-Aug; also late Apr-mid-May. Bar. A la carte entrees: dinner $12-$24.50. Fireplace. Tri-level dining with view of mountains. Totally nonsmoking. Cr cds: A, DS, MC, V.

★★★ **THE COMMON MAN.** 3209 German Flats Rd (05674). 802/583-2800. www.commonmanrestaurant.com. Continental menu. Specialties: lapin mirabelle, carre d'agneau, escargot maison. Menu changes wkly. Hrs: 6:30-9 pm; Sat 6-10 pm; winter months from 5:30 pm. Closed Thanksgiving, Dec 25. Res accepted. Serv bar. A la carte entrees: dinner $14.50-$24.50. Child's menu. Casual dining in mid-1800s barn. Family-owned. Totally nonsmoking. Cr cds: A, D, MC, V.

Unrated Dining Spot

THE WARREN HOUSE RESTAURANT AND RUPERT'S BAR. 2585 Sugarbush Access Rd (05674). 802/583-2421. www.thewarrenhouse.com. Specializes in Amer, international cuisine. Own baking, desserts. Hrs: 6-9:30 pm; Fri, Sat to 10 pm. Closed Tues; also Easter, Dec 25. Res accepted. Bar. Wine list. Dinner $12-$23.95. Child's menu. Magician on wkends. Outdoor dining. Rustic, greenhouse atmosphere. Cr cds: A, MC, V.

Waterbury

See also Barre, Montpelier, Stowe, Waitsfield, Warren

Pop 4,589 **Elev** 428 ft **Area code** 802 **Zip** 05676
Information Central Vermont Chamber of Commerce, PO Box 336, Barre 05641; 802/229-5711

Centrally located near many outstanding ski resorts, including Stowe, Mad River Valley, and Bolton Valley, this area is also popular in summer for hiking, backpacking, and bicycling.

What to See and Do

Ben & Jerry's Ice Cream Factory. Half-hr guided tour, offered every 30 min, through ice cream factory incl slide show, free samples. Gift shop. (Daily; closed Jan 1, Thanksgiving, Dec 25) I-89 exit 10, then N on VT 100. Phone 802/244-TOUR. ¢

Camel's Hump Mountain. State's third-highest mountain. Trail is challenging. Weather permitting, Canada can be seen from the top. 8 mi SW of town on dirt road, then 3½-mi hike to summit.

Cold Hollow Cider Mill. One of the largest cider mills in New England features 43-inch rack-and-cloth press capable of producing 500 gallons of cider an hr; also jelly-making operations (fall). Samples are served. 3½ mi N on VT 100. Phone 802/244-8771 or 800/327-7537. **FREE**

Little River State Park. This 12,000-acre park offers swimming, fishing; nature and hiking trails, tent and trailer sites (dump station), lean-tos. (Memorial Day-Columbus Day) Standard fees. 2 mi W off, US 2. Phone 802/244-7103.

Long Trail. A 22-mi segment of backpacking trail connects Camel's Hump with Mt Mansfield (see STOWE), the state's highest peak. Primitive camping is allowed on both mountains. Recommended for the experienced hiker. Phone 802/229-5711.

Winter recreation. Area abounds in downhill, x-country, and ski touring facilities; also many snowmobile trails.

Hotel

★★ **HOLIDAY INN & SPA WATERBURY.** *45 Blush Hill Rd (05676).* 802/244-7822; fax 802/244-6395; res 800/465-4329. *www.holiday-inn.com.* 79 rms, 2 story. S, D $116-$150; each addl $10; under 12 free; higher rates fall foliage. Crib free. TV; cable. Indoor pool. Restaurant 7 am-2 pm, 5-9 pm. Rm serv. Bar. Ck-out noon. Coin lndry. Meeting rms. Business servs avail. In-rm modem link. Tennis. Downhill/x-country ski 12 mi. Exercise equipt; sauna. Game rm. Picnic tables. Covered bridge. Cr cds: A, DS, MC, V.

D 🛆 🏋 🏊 🚣 🛌 🏃

B&Bs/Small Inns

★★★ **BLACK LOCUST INN.** *5088 Waterbury-Stowe Rd, Waterbury Center (05677).* 802/244-7490; fax 802/244-8473; toll-free 800/366-5592. *www.blacklocustinn.com.* 6 rms, 2 story. No rm phones. S, D $125-$225; each addl $25. Children over 12 yrs only. TV in sitting rm. Complimentary full bkfst; afternoon refreshments. Ck-out 11 am, ck-in 2 pm. Downhill/x-country ski 7 mi. Restored 1832 farmhouse; individually decorated rms; antiques. Totally nonsmoking. Cr cds: DS, MC, V.

D 🛆 🏋 🏊 🖳 🔥

★ **GRUNBERG HAUS BED AND BREAKFAST.** *94 Pine St (05676).* 802/244-7726; toll-free 800/800-7760. *www.grunberghaus.com.* 11 rms, some share bath, 2 story, 2 cabins. No A/C. No rm phones. S, D $66-$175; each addl $7; wkly rates; ski plan; Complimentary full bkfst; afternoon refreshments. Ck-out 11 am, ck-in 3 pm. Tennis. Downhill ski 12 mi; x-country ski on site. Whirlpool, sauna. Game rm. Balconies. Tyrolean chalet; field stone fireplace, grand piano. On 14 acres; gardens, trails. Cr cds: DS, MC, V.

D 🛆 🏋 🏊 🖳 🔥

★ **INN AT BLUSH HILL.** *784 Blush Hill Rd (05676).* 802/244-7529; fax 802/244-7314; toll-free 800/736-7522. *www.blushhill.com.* 5 rms, 2 story. No A/C. No rm phones. S, D $99-$125; each addl $15; ski plans; higher rates: fall foliage, Christmas wk. TV in sitting rm; cable. Complimentary full bkfst; afternoon refreshments. Restaurant nearby. Ck-out 11 am, ck-in 3 pm. Downhill/x-country ski 10 mi. Picnic tables, grills. Library. Former stagecoach stop (1790); Colonial antiques; fireplaces.

Situated on five acres; gardens. 9-hole golf course opp. Cr cds: A, DS, MC, V.

🛆 🏋 🏊 🍴 🖳 🔥

★★ **THATCHER BROOK INN.** *Rte 100 (05676).* 802/244-5911; fax 802/244-1294; toll-free 800/292-5911. *www.thatcherbrook.com.* 24 rms, 3 with shower only, 2 story. No A/C. Sept-Mar: S, D $105-$195; each addl $20; under 12 free; ski plans; wkend rates; MAP avail; 2-day min hols; lower rates rest of yr. Crib free. TV; cable, VCR in common rm. Complimentary full bkfst. Restaurant (see also THATCHER BROOK). Ck-out 10:30 am, ck-in 3 pm. Business servs avail. Downhill ski 13 mi; x-country ski 10 mi. Rec rm. Built in 1899; twin gazebos with front porch. Cr cds: A, D, DS, MC, V.

D 🖳 🔥

Restaurants

★★★ **THATCHER BROOK.** *VT 100 N (05676).* 802/244-5911. *www.thatcherbrook.com.* French menu. Specialties: roasted rack of lamb, honey-glazed breast of duck, mushrooms a la Thatcher. Hrs: 5-9:30 pm. Res accepted. Bar. A la carte entrees: dinner $14.95-$24.95. Child's menu. Outdoor dining. Cr cds: A, D, DS, MC, V.

D

★★★ **VILLA TRAGARA.** *Rte 100 N, Waterbury Center (05677).* 802/244-5288. Northern Italian menu. Specializes in pasta, fish. Own baking, pasta. Hrs: 5:30-9:30 pm. Res accepted. Bar. Wine list. Dinner $12-$17.75. Converted 1820s farmhouse. Totally nonsmoking. Cr cds: A, MC, V.

D

Weathersfield

(see Springfield)

West Dover

See also Wilmington

Pop 250 **Elev** 1,674 ft **Area code** 802 **Zip** 05356
Information Mount Snow Valley Region Chamber of Commerce, VT 9, W Main St, PO Box 3, Wilmington 05363; 802/464-8092 or 877/887-6884
Web www.visitvermont.com

What to See and Do

Mt Snow Ski Area. Area has two quad, six triple, nine double chairlifts; patrol, school, rentals; snowmaking; cafeterias, restaurant, bars, entertainment; nursery. Over 100 trails spread over five interconnected mountain areas (also see WILMINGTON); shuttle bus. Longest run 2½ mi; vertical drop 1,700 ft. (Nov-early May, daily) Half-day rates. 9 mi N on VT 100, in Green Mtn National Forest. Phone 802/464-8501.

Special Events

Mountain Bike World Cup Race. Mt Snow. More than 1,500 cyclists from throughout the world compete in downhill, dual slalom, and circuit racing events. Phone 800/245-7669. Mid-June. Phone 802/464-3333.

Mount Snow Foliage Craft Fair. Mt Snow Ski Area (see). New England area artisans exhibit pottery, jewelry, glass, graphics, weaving, and other crafts; entertainment. Columbus Day wkend.

B&Bs/Small Inns

★ ★ ★ ★ **THE INN AT SAWMILL FARM.** *VT 100 and Crosstown Rd (05356). 802/464-8131; fax 802/464-1130; toll-free 800/493-1133. www.theinnatsawmillfarm.com.* The architecture and interior design backgrounds of innkeepers Rodney and Ione Williams, shine in this meticulously restored 18th-century farm. Weathered siding, exposed beams, stone fireplaces, and antique American furnishings create a taste of history at the 24-room property. With spectacular food and an unimaginable wine cellar of 36,000 bottles, it's no wonder guests visit just for the dinners. 21 rms, 2 story, 4 suites. No rm phones. MAP: S $350-$445; D $395-$500; each addl $85; suites $420-$750; higher rates: fall foliage, Thanksgiving, wk of Dec 25, Jan 1. Serv charge 15%. TV in library. Pool. Restaurant (see also INN AT SAW MILL FARM). Bar 4:30 pm-midnight. Ck-out noon, ck-in 3 pm. Business servs avail. Gift shop. Tennis. Fly-fishing. Downhill ski 5 mi; x-country ski on site. Fireplace in suites. Some whirlpools. Converted dairy farm (1790). Individually decorated rms. Two stocked trout ponds. Cr cds: A, D, DS, MC, V.

⬚ 🛇 🛇 🛇 🛇 🛇

★ **RED CRICKET INN.** *45 Rte 100 N (05356). 802/464-8817; fax 802/464-0508; toll-free 877/473-3274. www.redcricketinn.com.* 26 rms, 20 with shower only, 2 story. Mid-Dec-mid-Mar: S $60-$115; D $60-$125; each addl $5-$15; under 12 free midwk; wkly, hol rates (2-3-day min hols); ski plans; lower rates mid-Mar-mid-Apr, mid-May-mid-Dec. Closed rest of yr. Crib free. TV. Complimentary continental bkfst. Ck-out 11 am. Business servs avail. Downhill ski 3½ mi; x-country ski 3 mi. Picnic tables. Totally nonsmoking. Cr cds: A, DS, MC, V.

🛇 🛇 🛇 🛇

★ ★ **WEST DOVER INN.** *108 Rte 100, Box 1208 (05356). 802/464-5207; fax 802/464-2173. www.westdoverinn.com.* 12 rms, 2 story, 4 suites. No A/C. No rm phones. S, D $100-$145; each addl $25-$35; suites $145-$200; higher rates: fall foliage, hol wkends. Closed mid-Apr-Memorial Day. Children over 8 yrs only. TV; cable. Complimentary full bkfst. Dining rm 6-9:30 pm. Ck-out 11 am, ck-in 2 pm. Downhill ski 3½ mi; x-country ski 1 mi. Built 1846; was stagecoach stop and general store. Many antiques. Cr cds: A, DS, MC, V.

🛇 🛇 🛇

Restaurant

★ ★ ★ ★ **THE INN AT SAWMILL FARM.** *VT 100 and Crosstown Rd (05356). 802/464-8131. www.theinnatsawmillfarm.com.* Housed in an 18th-century barn, visitors travel from miles around just to dine at this historic inn. The menu is dotted with true continental classics, and the effect of its combination with faded walls, white exposed beams, and a cozy atmosphere is comfortably divine. You might even choose to stay for the night in one of 24 antique-filled rooms. Specializes in seafood, duck, rack of lamb. Own baking. Hrs: 6-9:30 pm. Res accepted. Bar. Wine list. A la carte entrees: dinner $27-$35. Cr cds: A, DS, MC, V.

⬚

Weston

See also Londonderry, Peru

Pop 620 **Elev** 1,295 ft **Area code** 802 **Zip** 05161

Once nearly a ghost town, Weston is now a serene village secluded in the beautiful hills of Vermont. Charming old houses are situated around a small common, and shops are scattered along Main Street. Weston is listed on the National Register of Historic Places.

What to See and Do

Farrar-Mansur House Museum. (1797) Restored house/tavern with nine rms. Period furnishings; paintings. Guided tours. (July-Aug, Mon-Fri; Memorial Day-Columbus Day, wkends) N side of Common. ¢¢

Greendale Camping Area. Picnicking, camping (fee). 2 mi N on VT 100, 2 mi W on Greendale Rd in Green Mtn National Forest (see).

Old Mill Museum. Museum of old time tools and industries; tinsmith in residence. Guided tours (July and Aug). (Memorial Day-Columbus Day, daily) On VT 100, in center of village. **Donation**

Vermont Country Store. Just like those Granddad used to patronize—rock candy and other old-fashioned foodstuffs. (Daily exc Sun; closed Thanksgiving, Dec 25) On VT 100, S of Village Green. Phone 802/824-3184.

Weston Bowl Mill. Wooden bowls, other wooden household products made on premises. Seconds avail. (Daily; closed Easter, Thanksgiving, Dec 25) Just N of Common on VT 100. Phone 802/824-6219. **FREE**

Weston Playhouse. One of the oldest professional theater companies in the state. Restaurant; cabaret. Village Green. Phone 802/824-5288.

B&Bs/Small Inns

★★ **THE COLONIAL HOUSE.** *287 Rte 100 (05161). 802/824-6286; fax 802/824-3934; toll-free 800/639-5033. www.cohoinn.com.* 6 rms in inn, 2 share bath, 9 rms in motel, 2 story. No A/C. No rm phones. Mid-Dec-Apr, fall foliage: S $40-$70; D $54-$100; each addl $15; family rates; golf, theater plans; lower rates rest of yr. Crib free. TV in lounge; cable. Complimentary bkfst. Restaurant 8-9:30 am, 6-7:30 pm (public by res exc Sun, Wed). Ck-out 11 am. Downhill ski 10 mi; x-country ski on site. Game rm. Lawn games. Sun rm. Cr cds: C, D, DS, MC, V.

⛵ ⚙ ⤢ 🔌 🔥

★★ **WILDER HOMESTEAD INN.** *25 Lawrence Hill Rd (05161). 802/824-8172; fax 802/824-5054; toll-free 877/838-9979. www.wilderhomestead.com.* 7 rms, 5 with bath, 3 story. No A/C. No rm phones. S, D $90-$135; each addl $30; higher rates: fall foliage, hol wks. Closed 2 wks Apr. Children over 12 yrs only. TV, cable in sitting rm; VCR (free movies). Complimentary full bkfst. Ck-out 11 am, ck-in 2 pm. Gift shop. Downhill ski 10 mi; x-country ski 3 mi. Federal-style country inn; built 1827. Player piano. Overlooks river. Totally nonsmoking. Cr cds: MC, V.

⛵ ⚙ ⤢ 🔌 🔥

White River Junction

See also Windsor, Woodstock; also see Hanover, NH

Settled 1764 **Pop** 2,521 **Elev** 368 ft **Area code** 802 **Zip** 05001

Appropriately named, this town is the meeting place of the Boston & Maine and Central Vermont railroads, the White and Connecticut rivers, and two interstate highways.

What to See and Do

Quechee Gorge. Often referred to as Vermont's "Little Grand Canyon," the Ottauquechee River has carved out a mi-long chasm that offers dramatic views of the landscape and neighboring towns. About 8 mi W on US 4.

Motels/Motor Lodges

★★ **BEST WESTERN AT THE JUNCTION.** *306 N. Hartland Rd (05001). 802/295-3015; fax 802/296-2581; toll-free 800/370-4656. www.bestwesternjunction.com.* 112 rms, 2 story. Mid-May-Mid-Sept: S $89-$139; D $99-$149; each addl $10; under 18 free; higher rates: fall foliage, special events; lower rates rest of yr. Crib free. Pet accepted; $10. TV; cable (premium). Indoor pool; wading pool, whirlpool. Playground. Complimentary continental bkfst. Restaurant adj 6 am-10 pm; Sat to 1 am. Bar 4 pm-1 am. Ck-out 11 am. Coin lndry. Meeting rms. Sundries. Downhill ski 20 mi; x-country ski 14 mi. Exercise equipt; sauna. Game rm. Refrigerators, microwaves avail. Private patios, balconies. Cr cds: A, DS, MC, V.

🅳 🐾 ⛵ ⚙ ⤢ 🔌 🔥

★ **COMFORT INN.** *8 Sykes Ave (05001). 802/295-3051; fax 802/295-5990; res 800/228-5150. www.comfortinn.com.* 70 rms, 4 story. S $89-$209; D $99-$219; each addl $5; under 18 free; higher rates fall foliage. Crib free. TV; cable. Heated pool. Complimentary continental bkfst. Restaurant nearby. Ck-out 11 am. Coin lndry. Meeting rms. Business servs avail. In-rm modem link. Health club privileges. Microwave in suites. Cr cds: A, C, D, DS, MC, V.

⤢ 🔌 🐾 **SC**

★ **RAMADA INN-WHITE RIVER JCT.** *259 Holiday Dr (05001). 802/295-3000; fax 802/295-3774; res 800/272-6232. www.ramada.com.* 136 rms, 2 story. S, D $85-$145; each addl $8; under 19 free; ski plan; wkend rates; higher rates fall foliage. Crib free. Pet accepted. TV; cable (premium). Indoor pool; whirlpool. Coffee in rms. Restaurants 7 am-10 pm. Rm serv. Bar 4 pm-1 am; entertainment. Ck-out noon. Meeting rms. Business servs avail. Sundries. Putting green. Downhill ski 15 mi. Exercise equipt; sauna. Game rm. Balconies. Cr cds: A, DS, MC, V.

🅳 🐾 ⤢ 🏊 🕴 🔌 🔥

B&B/Small Inn

★★ **STONCREST FARM BED AND BREAKFAST.** *1187 Christian St, Wilder (05088). 802/296-2425; fax 802/295-1135; toll-free 800/730-2425. www.stonecrestfarm.com.* 6 rms, 4 with shower only, 2 story. No A/C. No rm phones. Mid-May-mid-Nov: S $105-$115; D $125-$140; each addl $25; hols (2-day min); lower rates rest of yr. Closed wk of Dec 25. Children over 8 yrs only. Complimentary full bkfst. Ck-out 11 am, ck-in 3-7 pm. Business servs avail. Downhill ski 15 mi; x-country ski 3½ mi. Lawn games. Built in 1810; country Victorian atmosphere. Totally nonsmoking. Cr cds: A, MC, V.

⛵ ⚙ ⤢ 🔌 🔥

Restaurant

★★ **A.J.' S.** *40 Bowling Ln (05001). 802/295-3071.* Specializes in steak, prime rib, fresh seafood. Salad, soup bar. Hrs: 5-10 pm; Sun 4-9 pm. Res accepted. Lounge. Dinner $7.95-$16.95. Child's menu. Rustic decor; wood stoves, fireplace. Totally nonsmoking. Cr cds: A, D, DS, MC, V.

🅳

Wilmington

See also Bennington, Brattleboro, Marlboro, West Dover

Chartered 1751 and 1753 **Pop** 1,968 **Elev** 1,533 ft **Area code** 802 **Zip** 05363

Information Mount Snow Valley Region Chamber of Commerce, VT 9, W Main St, PO Box 3; 802/464-8092 or 877/887-6884

Web www.visitvermont.com

What to See and Do

Haystack Ski Area. Resort has double, three triple chairlifts; patrol, school, rentals, snowmaking; concession, cafeteria, bar, nursery, lodges. More than 100 trails spread over five interconnecting mountain areas (see WEST DOVER); shuttle bus. Longest run 1½ mi; vertical drop 1,400 ft. (Dec-Mar, daily) Golf, pro shop; restaurant, bar (early May-mid-Oct). Phone 802/464-8501. ¢¢¢¢

⊠ Molly Stark State Park. A 158-acre park named for wife of General John Stark, hero of Battle of Bennington (1777); on west slope of Mt Olga (2,438 ft). Fishing in nearby lake; hiking trails, tent and trailer sites (dump station), lean-tos. Fire tower with excellent views. (Memorial Day-Columbus Day) Standard fees. Approx 4 mi E on VT 9. Phone 802/464-5460.

Mount Snow Resort. Resort has three high-speed quads, quad, ten triple, four double chairlifts, two surface lifrs; patrol, school, rentals; snowmaking; concession, cafeteria, bar; nursery, lodges. More than 100 trails spread over five interconnecting mountain areas (also see WEST DOVER); shuttle bus. Longest run 1½ mi; vertical drop 1,700 ft. (Dec-Mar, daily) Golf, pro shop; restaurant, bar (early May-mid-Oct). 3 mi NW, off VT 100. Phone 802/464-8501. ¢¢¢¢

Special Events

Deerfield Valley Farmers Day Exhibition. Pony pull, midway rides; horse show, livestock judging, entertainment. Late Aug.

The Nights Before Christmas. Throughout Wilmington and West Dover (see). Celebrates holiday season with caroling, torchlight parade, fireworks, tree lighting. Festival of Light, living nativity, and children's hayrides. Phone 802/464-8092. Late Nov-late Dec.

Motel/Motor Lodge

★★ NORDIC HILLS LODGE. *34 Look Rd (05363). 802/464-5130; fax 802/464-8248; toll-free 800/326-5130. www.nordichillslodge.com.* 27 rms, 3 story. No A/C. No elvtr. S, D $69-$150; each addl $10-$45; higher rates: Presidents wkend, Christmas wk; winter wknds (2-day min). Closed Apr-mid-May. Crib free. TV. Heated pool; whirlpool, sauna. Complimentary full bkfst. Ck-out 11 am. Downhill/x-country ski 1½ mi. Game rm. Lawn games. Family-owned. Cr cds: A, DS, MC, V.

⚕ 🛌 ✈ ⚓ 🐕 🔥

Hotel

★★ HORIZON INN. *VT Rte 9 E (05363). 802/464-2131; fax 802/464-8302; toll-free 800/336-5513. www.horizoninn.com.* 27 rms, 2 story. Mid-Dec-mid-Apr: S $65-$115; D $80-$135; each addl $10; under 12 free; ski plans; wkend, hol rates (2-day min hols); lower rates rest of yr. Crib avail. TV; cable (premium). Indoor pool; whirlpool. Complimentary coffee in rms. Ck-out 11 am. Meeting rms. Business servs avail. Downhill ski 7 mi; x-country ski 2.5 mi. Exercise equipt; sauna. Game rm. Lawn games. Grills, picnic tables. Cr cds: A, DS, MC, V.

⚕ 🛌 ✈ ⚓ 🏃 🐕 🔥

B&Bs/Small Inns

★★ HERMITAGE INN. *Coldbrook Rd (05363). 802/464-3511; fax 802/464-2688. www.hermitageinn.com.* 29 air-cooled rms, 2 story. MAP: S $185- $210; D $225-$250; each addl $70; wkly rates; hunting packages. Serv charge 15%. TV; cable, VCR. Restaurant (see also HERMITAGE). Bar from 11 am. Ck-out 11 am, ck-in 2 pm. Meeting rm. Business servs avail. Tennis. Downhill ski ½ mi; x-country ski on site. Fireplaces. Private patios. Hunting preserve. Sporting clays. Art gallery. Cr cds: A, D, MC, V.

⚕ 🛌 🎿 ⚓ 🔥

★ THE INN AT QUAIL RUN. *106 Smith Rd (05363). 802/464-3362; fax 802/464-7784; toll-free 800/343-7227. www.bbonline.com/vt/quailrun.* 14 rms, 2 story. No A/C. No rm phones. S, D $90-$170; each addl $25; ski plans; higher rates: fall foliage, hols. Crib free. Pet accepted. TV in some rms; cable. Pool; sauna. Playground. Complimentary full bkfst. Ck-out 11 am, ck-in 3 pm. Business servs avail. Downhill ski 4½ mi; x-country ski on site. Rec rm. Lawn games. Picnic tables. On 12 acres in Green Mts, view of Deerfield Valley. Totally nonsmoking. Cr cds: A, DS, MC, V.

🐾 🛌 ⚓ 🔥

★★ TRAIL'S END - A COUNTRY INN. *5 Trail's End Ln (05363). 802/464-2727; fax 802/464-5532; toll-free 800/859-2585. www.trailsendvt.com.* 5 rms, 2 story. No A/C. No rm phones. S, D $110-$160; each addl $30; wkends (2-day min); hol wkends (3-day min); wkly rates. Crib avail. TV, VCR in some rms, sitting rm. Heated pool. Complimentary full bkfst; afternoon refreshments. Ck-out 11 am, ck-in 2 pm. Tennis. Downhill ski 4½mi; x-country ski ½ mi. Some fireplaces. On 10 acres; stocked trout pond. Cr cds: A, DS, MC, V.

⚕ 🎿 🛌 🎿 ⚓ 🐕 🔥

★★ WHITE HOUSE OF WILMINGTON. *178 VT 9 E (05363). 802/464-2135; fax 802/464-5222; toll-free 800/5412135. www.whitehouseinn.com.* 16 rms in inn, 7 rms in guest house. No A/C. No rm phones. S $98-$108; D $158-$178; higher rates: wk of Washington's Birthday, fall foliage, wk of Dec 25. Children over 10 yrs only. TV in sitting rm; cable, VCR. 2 pools, 1 indoor; whirlpool, sauna. Complimentary bkfst. Restaurant (see also WHITE HOUSE). Bar 3 pm-midnight. Ck-out 11 am, ck-in 1 pm. Downhill ski 8 mi; x-country ski on site. Rec rm. Lawn games. Balconies. Some fireplaces, in-rm whirlpools. View of valley. Built in 1915 as summer house for lumber baron Martin Brown. Cr cds: A, D, DS, MC, V.

🄳 ⚕ 🎿 ✈ ⚓ 🐕 🔥

Restaurants

★★★ HERMITAGE. *Coldbrook Rd (05363). 802/464-3511. www.hermitageinn.com.* Continental menu. Specializes in Wiener schnitzel, fresh trout, own game birds, home-raised venison. Own baking. Hrs: 5-11 pm; Sun brunch 11 am-2 pm. Res accepted. Bar 11-2 am. Wine cellar. Dinner $16-$27. Sun brunch $8-$16. Serv charge 15%. Wine collection spans over 2,000 varieties. Trout pond. Family-owned. Cr cds: A, D, MC, V.

★★ **WHITE HOUSE.** *178 VT 9 E (05363). 802/464-2135. www.whitehouseinn.com.* Continental menu. Specializes in boneless stuffed duck, veal dishes, fresh seafood. Own baking. Hrs: 8-9:30 am, 5:30-9 pm; Sun brunch 11 am-2:30 pm. Res accepted. No A/C. Bar 4 pm-midnight. Wine list. Bkfst $4.50-$12, dinner $18.95-$24.95. Sun brunch $14.95. Parking. Colonial Revival decor. Cr cds: C, D, DS, ER, MC, V.
🄳

Windsor

See also White River Junction

Settled 1764 **Pop** 3,714 **Elev** 354 ft **Area code** 802
Zip 05089
Information White River Area Chamber of Commerce, PO Box 697, White River Junction 05001; 802/295-6200

Situated on the Connecticut River in the shadow of Mount Ascutney, Windsor once was the political center of the Connecticut Valley towns. The name "Vermont" was adopted, and its constitution was drawn up here. Inventors and inventions flourished here in the 19th century; the hydraulic pump, a sewing machine, coffee percolator, and various refinements in firearms originated in Windsor.

What to See and Do

American Precision Museum. Exhibits incl hand and machine tools; illustrations of their uses and development. Housed in former Robbins and Lawrence Armory (1846). (Late May-Oct, daily; rest of yr, by appt) 196 Main St. Phone 802/674-5781. ¢¢

Constitution House. An 18th-century tavern where constitution of the Republic of Vermont was signed on July 8, 1777. Museum. (Mid-May-mid-Oct, Wed-Sun) 16 N Main St, on US 5. Phone 802/672-3773. ¢

Covered bridge. Crossing the Connecticut River; longest in US.

Mount Ascutney State Park. This 1,984-acre park has a paved road to summit of Mt Ascutney (3,144 ft). Hiking trails, picnicking, tent and trailer sites (dump station), lean-tos. (Memorial Day-Columbus Day) Standard fees. 3 mi S off US 5 on VT 44A; I-91 exit 8. Phone 802/674-2060.

Vermont State Craft Center at Windsor House. Restored building features works of more than 250 Vermont craftspeople. (June-Dec, daily; rest of yr, Mon-Sat) Main St. Phone 802/674-6729. **FREE**

Wilgus State Park. This 100-acre park overlooks the Connecticut River. Canoe launching. Hiking trails. Wooded picnic area. Tent and trailer sites (dump station), lean-tos. (Memorial Day-Columbus Day) Standard fees. 6 mi S on US 5. Phone 802/674-5422.

B&B/Small Inn

★★★ **JUNPIER HILL INN.** *153 Pembroke Rd (05089). 802/674-5273; fax 802/674-2041; toll-free 800/359-2541. www.juniperhillinn.com.* 16 rms, 2-3 story. No elvtr. No rm phones. S, D $130-$185; each addl $25; MAP avail; wkly rates; package plans. Children over 12 yrs only. TV in front rm. Pool. Complimentary full bkfst. Dining rm 8-9:30 am, 7 pm sitting (by res only). Bar 3:30-11 pm. Ck-out 11 am, ck-in 3 pm. Downhill/x-country ski 7 mi. Lawn games. Many fireplaces. Antique furnished mansion; library. Totally nonsmoking. Cr cds: DS, MC, V.
🄳 🐾 〽 🛇 🏊 🛇 🐾 🔥

Restaurant

★★ **WINDSOR STATION.** *27 Depot Ave (05089). 802/674-2052. www.windsorstation.com.* Continental menu. Specializes in seafood, veal, pasta. Own desserts. Hrs: 5:30-9:30 pm. Closed Jan 1, Dec 25. Bar from 4 pm. Dinner $16.95-$20.95. Child's menu. Restored RR depot (1900). Cr cds: A, D, DS, MC, V.
🄳

Woodstock

See also Killington, Plymouth, White River Junction

Settled 1768 **Pop** 3,212 **Elev** 705 ft **Area code** 802
Zip 05091
Information Chamber of Commerce, 18 Central St, PO Box 486; 802/457-3555
Web www.woodstockvt.com

The antique charm of Woodstock has been preserved, at least in part, by determination. Properties held for generations by descendants of original owners provided built-in zoning long before Historic District status was achieved. When the iron bridge that crosses the Ottauquechee River at Union Street was condemned in 1968, it was replaced by a covered wooden bridge.

What to See and Do

Billings Farm & Museum. Exhibits incl operating dairy farm and an 1890s farmhouse. (May-late Oct, daily) ½ mi N on VT 12. Phone 802/457-2355.

Covered bridge. (1968) First one built in Vermont since 1895. Two others cross the Ottauquechee River; one 3 mi W (1877), another 4 mi E, at Taftsville (1836). Center of village.

Kedron Valley Stables. Hayrides, sleigh rides, picnic trail rides; indoor ring; riding lessons by appt. About 5 mi S on VT 106, in S Woodstock. Phone 802/457-1480.

Marsh-Billings-Rockefeller National Historic Park. Incl Marsh-Billings-Rockefeller mansion, which contains extensive collection of American landscape paintings. Mansion is surrounded by 550-acre Mt Tom forest. Interpretive tours of the mansion, its grounds and gardens, and the Mt Tom forest are avail. Res recommended. Park also offers hiking, nature study, and x-country skiing. (June-Oct, daily) On Rte 12, ½ mi N of Woodstock Village Green. Phone 802/457-3368.

Silver Lake State Park. This 34-acre park offers swimming beach, bathhouse, fishing, boating (rentals); picnicking, concession, tent and trailer camping (dump station), lean-tos. Within walking distance of Barnard Village. (Memorial Day-Labor Day) Standard fees. 10 mi NW via VT 12 to Barnard, on Silver Lake. Phone 802/234-9451.

Suicide Six Ski Area. Area has two double chairlifts, J-Bar; patrol, PSIA school, rentals, snowmaking; cafeteria, wine and beer bar, lodge. Twenty-two runs, longest run 1 mi; vertical drop 650 ft. Site of first ski tow in US (1934). (Early Dec-late Mar, daily) 3 mi N on VT 12 (S Pomfret Rd). Phone 802/457-1666. ¢¢¢¢

Vermont Institute of Natural Science. Property incl a 75-acre preserve with trails (daily). Raptor Center, an outdoor museum, has 26 species of hawks, owls, and eagles (summer, daily; winter, Mon-Sat). Gift shop. 1½ mi SW on Church Hill Rd. Phone 802/457-2779. ¢

Walking Tours Around Woodstock. There are one-two-hr tours of Historic District, covering over one mi; depart from Chamber of Commerce information booth on the green. (Mid-June-mid-Oct, Mon, Wed, and Sat) Phone 802/457-2450. ¢¢

Woodstock Country Club. An 18-hole championship golf course, ten tennis courts, paddle tennis, x-country skiing center with more than 35 mi of trails; rentals, instruction, tours. Restaurant, lounge. (Daily; closed Apr and Nov) Fee for activities. S on VT 106. Phone 802/457-2112.

Woodstock Historical Society. Dana House (1807) has 11 rms spanning 1750-1900, incl a children's rm; also silver, glass, paintings, costumes, furniture; research library; Woodstock-related artifacts, photographs. Farm and textile equip. Gift shop. (Mid-May-late Oct, daily) 26 Elm St. Phone 802/457-1822.

Motels/Motor Lodges

★ **BRAESIDE MOTEL.** *432 Woodstock Rd (05091). 802/457-1366; fax 802/457-9892. www.braesidemotel.com.* 12 rms. S, D $68-$108. Crib free. TV; cable (premium), VCR avail. Pool. Restaurant nearby. Ck-out 11 am. Downhill ski 6 mi; x-country ski 2 mi. Picnic table. Cr cds: A, MC, V.

★ **OTTAUQUECHEE MOTEL.** *US 4 (05091). 802/672-3404; fax 802/672-3215. www.ottauquechee.com.* 15 rms, 14 A/C. S, D $46-$160; each addl $5-$10; higher rates: fall foliage, Christmas wk. TV; cable. Complimentary coffee in rms. Restaurant adj 6 am-9 pm. Ck-out 11 am. Downhill ski 10 mi; x-country ski 5 mi. Refrigerators. Cr cds: D, DS, MC, V.

★ **POND RIDGE MOTEL.** *US 4 (05091). 802/457-1667. www.vtliving.com/pondridgemotel.* 14 rms, 6 kits. S, D $39-$99; each addl $10; kit. units $99-$150; under 6 free; wkly rates; ski plans; higher rates fall foliage. Crib $10. TV; cable (premium). Complimentary coffee in rms. Ck-out 10 am. Downhill ski 8 mi; x-country ski 3 mi. Lawn games. Picnic tables, grills. On river; swimming. Cr cds: A, C, D, DS, ER, MC, V.

★★ **THE SHIRE MOTEL.** *46 Pleasant St (05091). 802/457-2211; fax 802/457-5836. www.shiremotel.com.* 33 rms. May-mid-Sept: S, D $88-$145; under 12 free; higher rates fall foliage. Crib $7. TV; cable. Coffee in lobby. Restaurant nearby. Ck-out 11 am. Business servs avail. Downhill ski 4 mi; x-country ski 1 mi. Refrigerators. Cr cds: A, DS, MC, V.

Resort

★★★ **WOODSTOCK INN & RESORT.** *14 The Green (05091). 802/457-1100; fax 802/457-6699; toll-free 800/448-7900. www.woodstockinn.com.* 144 rms, 3 story. S, D $195; each addl $30; suites $322-$589; under 14 free; MAP avail; ski, golf, tennis, fish, and other plans. Crib free. TV; cable. Dining rm (see also WOODSTOCK INN); nightly entertainment. Box lunches, picnics. Rm serv 7-9 pm. Bar noon-midnight. Ck-out 11 am, ck-in 3 pm. Grocery, package store 2 mi. In-room modem link. Meeting rms. Business servs avail. Bellhops. Concierge. Gift shop. Indoor/outdoor pool, whirlpool. Exercise rm; sauna, steam rm. Massage. Sports dir, raquetball, squash, paddle tennis. Indoor/outdoor tennis, pro. Lawn games; croquet. 18-hole golf, greens fee $58, pro, putting green, driving range. Downhill ski 4½ mi, 22 runs; x-country ski ½ mi, 60K of trails. Some refrigerators. Some fireplaces. Cr cds: A, JCB, MC, V.

B&Bs/Small Inns

★★ **APPLEBUTTER INN.** *Happy Valley Rd (05091). 802/457-4158.* 6 rms, 2 story. No rm phones. S, D $85-$185; each addl $15. TV in sitting rm; VCR (free movies). Complimentary full bkfst. Ck-out 10:30 am, ck-in 3 pm. Downhill ski 5 mi; x-country ski 3 mi. Restored Federal-style house (1850); period furnishings. Totally nonsmoking. Cr cds: A, DS, MC, V.

★★ **CANTERBURY HOUSE BED AND BREAKFAST.** *43 Pleasant St (05091). 802/457-3077; fax 802/457-4630; toll-free 800/390-3077. www.thecanterburyhouse.com.* 8 rms, 4 with shower only, 3 story. No rm phones. S, D $120-$175. Adults only. TV in sitting rm; VCR. Complimentary full bkfst; afternoon refreshments. Restaurant adj 5-10 pm. Ck-out 10:30 am, ck-in 2 pm. Victorian home built 1880; antiques. Totally nonsmoking. Cr cds: MC, V.

★★ **CHARLESTON HOUSE.** *21 Pleasant St (05091).* *802/457-3843; fax 802/457-2512; res 888/475-3800.* *www.charlestonhouse.com.* 9 rms, 2 story. No rm phones. S, D $110-$225; hol wkend (2-day min). Complimentary full bkfst. Restaurant nearby. Ck-out 11 am, ck-in 3 pm. Downhill ski 3 mi; x-country ski 1 mi. Greek Revival house built 1835; many antiques. Totally nonsmoking. Cr cds: A, MC, V.

★★ **FOUR PILLARS.** *Happy Valley Rd (05073).* *802/457-2797; fax 802/457-5138; toll-free 800/957-2797.* *www.fourpillarsbb.com.* 5 rms, 4 shower only, 2 story. No A/C. No rm phones. June-mid-Sept: S $78-$138; D $80-$150; each addl $15; higher rates fall foliage; lower rates rest of yr. Children over 10 yrs only. TV in common rm; VCR avail (movies). Complimentary full bkfst. Restaurant nearby. Ck-out 10:30 am, ck-in 3-6 pm. Business servs avail. Tennis privileges. 18-hole golf privileges, putting green. Downhill/x-country ski 3 mi. Built in 1836. Totally non-smoking. Cr cds: MC, V.

★★★ **KEDRON VALLEY INN.** *VT 106, South Woodstock (05071).* 802/457-1473; fax 802/457-4469; toll-free 800/836-1193. *www.kedronvalleyinn.com.* 26 inn rms, 1-3 story. 10 with A/C. No elvtr. No rm phones. S $125-154; D $183-$250; each addl $6.50; MAP avail; mid-wk rates; wknd riding plan; higher rates: fall foliage, Dec 25. Closed Apr. Crib free. Pet accepted. TV. Restaurant (see also KEDRON VALLEY). Bar 5-11 pm. Ck-out 11:30 am, ck-in 3:30 pm. Business servs avail. Downhill ski 7 mi; x-country ski 3 mi. Many fireplaces, wood stoves. Some private patios. Natural pond. Cr cds: A, DS, MC, V.

★★ **THE LINCOLN INN AT THE COVERED BRIDGE.** *530 Woodstock Rd (05091).* 802/457-3312; fax 802/457-5808. *www.lincolninn.com.* 6 rms, 5 with shower only, 4 A/C, 2 story. No rm phones. S $110-$145; D $125-$175; MAP avail; higher rates fall foliage. TV; cable, VCR in parlor. Complimentary full bkfst. Restaurant 6-9 pm; closed Mon. Ck-out 11 am, ck-in 3 pm. Business servs avail. Sundries. Downhill ski 4 mi; x-country ski 3 mi. Library. Renovated farmhouse (ca 1869). Property bordered by Ottauquechee River and covered bridge. Totally nonsmoking. Cr cds: DS, MC, V.

★★★ **MAPLE LEAF INN.** *VT 12, Barnard (05031).* 802/234-5342. *www.mapleleafinn.com.* 7 rms, 3 story. No A/C. S $170-$190; D $180-$355. TV; VCR (free movies). Complimentary full bkfst; afternoon refreshments. Restaurant nearby. Ck-out 11 am, ck-in 3-6 pm. Business servs avail. Gift shop. Tennis privileges. Downhill 5 mi; x-country ski on site. Many in-rm whirlpools, fireplaces. Replica of Victorian farmhouse with wraparound porch on 16 wooded acres; many antiques; library. Totally nonsmoking. Cr cds: A, C, D, DS, JCB, MC, V.

★★ **PARKER HOUSE INN.** *1792 Quechee Main St, Quechee (05059).* 802/295-6077; fax 802/296-6696. *www.theparkerhouseinn.com.* 7 rms, 3 A/C, 3 story. No rm phones. S, D $115-$165. TV in sitting rm. Complimentary full bkfst. Restaurant. Ck-out 11 am, ck-in 3 pm. Health club privileges. Antiques. Library. Victorian home (1857); former senator's residence. Cr cds: A, MC, V.

★★★ **QUECHEE INN AT MARSHLAND FARM.** *1619 Quechee Main St, Quechee (05059).* 802/295-3133; fax 802/295-6587; toll-free 800/235-3133. *www.quecheeinn.com.* 24 rms, 2 story. No rm phones. Aug-late Oct, hols, MAP: S $160-$210; D $200-$240; each addl $42; mid-wk rates; package plans; lower rates rest of yr. Crib $10. TV; cable. Swimming, sauna privileges. Complimentary full bkfst; afternoon refreshments. Restaurant 8-10 am, 6-9 pm (see also QUECHEE INN AT MARSHLAND FARM). Bar 5-11 pm. Ck-out 11 am, ck-in 3 pm. Meeting rms. Business servs avail. Tennis privileges. Golf privileges. Canoes. Fly fishing clinics. Downhill ski 2 mi; x-country ski on site; instructor, rentals. Bicycles. 1793 farmhouse. Cr cds: A, C, D, DS, MC, V.

★★★★★ **TWIN FARMS.** *Stage Rd, Barnard (05031).* 802/234-9999; fax 802/234-9990; toll-free 800/894-6327. *www.twinfarms.com.* This 1795 country inn, set on 300 acres of gardens, forests, and meadows, offers guests a restful retreat from their busy lives. Activities include canoeing, swimming, fishing, tennis, skiing, and biking. Guests will enjoy relaxing in the Furo after a workout at the fitness center. Rates are fully inclusive of all meals, wines, beverage, and recreation equipment. 9 cottages, 4 rms in 2-story inn. AP (advance payment required): S $900; D $1,000; cottages $1,050-$1,700; 2-day min wkends, 3-day min hols. Closed Apr. Adults only. TV. Complimentary afternoon refreshments. Dining rm for guests only. Ck-out 1 pm, ck-in 4 pm. Business servs avail. In-rm modem link. Tennis, pro. Downhill/x-country ski on site. Exercise rm; Japanese furo tubs. Massage. Hiking trails. Rec rm. Totally nonsmoking. Cr cds: A, D, DS, MC, V.

★★ **WINSLOW HOUSE.** *492 Woodstock Rd (05091).* 802/457-1820; fax 802/457-1820. *www.thewinslowhousevt.com.* 5 rms, 2 story. S, D $85-$165; each addl $30; Children over 8 yrs only; (2-day min hols, fall foliage). Pet accepted. TV; cable (premium). Complimentary full bkfst. Ck-out 11 am, ck-in 3 pm. Downhill ski 8 mi; x-country ski 3 mi. Refrigerators. Farmhouse built 1872; period furnishings. Totally nonsmoking. Cr cds: MC, V.

★★★ **WOODSTOCKER BED AND BREAKFAST.** *61 River St Rte 4 (05091).* 802/457-3896; fax 802/457-3897. *www.scenesofvermont.com/woodstocker.* 9 rms, 8 A/C, 2 story, 3 kits. No rm phones. S, D $85-$145; each addl $20; suites $115-$175; higher rates: fall foliage, wk of Dec 25. TV in sitting rm; cable, VCR (free movies). Whirlpool. Complimentary full bkfst; afternoon refreshments. Restaurant nearby. Ck-out 11 am, ck-in 3 pm. Downhill ski 3 mi; x-country ski ½ mi. Built in 1830; individually decorated rms, antiques. Cr cds: A, MC, V.

Restaurants

★★★ **BARNARD INN.** *VT 12, Barnard (05031). 802/234-9961.* French menu. Specialties: noisettes of lamb Green Mountain, roast crisp duck. Hrs: 6-11 pm. Closed Sun, Mon (winter), Mon (summer); Thanksgiving, Dec 25. Res accepted. Bar. Wine list. A la carte entrees: dinner $19-$25. Child's menu. Parking. Original brick structure of house built ca 1796. Totally nonsmoking. Cr cds: A, C, D, MC, V.

★★ **BENTLEY'S.** *3 Elm St (05091). 802/457-3232. www.bentleysrestaurant.com.* Specializes in gourmet hamburgers, steak, pasta. Hrs: 11:30 am-11 pm; Fri; Sun brunch 11 am-3 pm. Closed Thanksgiving, Dec 25. Res accepted. Bar to 2 am. Lunch $4.95-$12.95, dinner $9.95-$23.95. Child's menu. Totally nonsmoking. Cr cds: A, D, DS, MC, V.

★★★ **KEDRON VALLEY.** *VT 106, South Woodstock (05091). 802/457-1473. www.kedronvalleyinn.com.* Specialties: salmon in puff pastry, grilled loin of lamb, confit of duck. Own sorbet. Hrs: 8-10 am, 6-9 pm. Closed Wed exc fall foliage season and wk of Dec 25; also Apr. Res accepted. Bar 5-11 pm. Complete meals: bkfst $9. A la carte entrees: dinner $16-$26. Child's menu. Parking. Cr cds: D, MC, V.
[D]

★★★ **PRINCE AND THE PAUPER.** *24 Elm St (05091). 802/457-1818. www.princeandpauper.com.* Continental menu. Specialties: rack of lamb in puff pastry, crisp roast duck. Own baking. Hrs: 6-9 pm; Fri, Sat to 9:30 pm. Closed Thanksgiving, Dec 25. Res accepted. Bar from 5 pm. Wine list. A la carte entrees: dinner $21-$28. Prix fixe: dinner $40. Outdoor dining. French country atmosphere. Cr cds: D, MC, V.

★★★ **QUECHEE INN AT MARSHLAND FARM.** *1119 Quechee Main St, Quechee (05059). 802/295-3133. www.quecheeinn.com.* Continental menu. Specializes in duck, fresh seafood, lamb. Own baking. Hrs: 6-9 pm. Res accepted. Bar 5-11 pm. Wine list. Dinner $18-$26. Child's menu. Pianist Fri, Sat. Parking. View of garden and lake. 1793 farmhouse. Totally nonsmoking. Cr cds: A, C, D, DS, MC, V.

★★★ **SIMON PEARCE.** *Main St, Quechee (05059). 802/295-1470. www.simonpearce.com.* Continental menu. Specializes in duck, seafood, lamb. Own desserts. Hrs: 11:30 am-2:45 pm, 6-9 pm. Closed Thanksgiving, Dec 25. Serv bar. Wine cellar. A la carte entrees: lunch $9.50-$14.50, dinner $18.50-$28. Parking. Terrace dining. In renovated mill; overlooks river. Glassblowing, pottery shop. Totally nonsmoking. Cr cds: A, D, DS, MC, V.
[D]

★★★ **WOODSTOCK INN.** *14 The Green (05091). 802/457-1100. www.woodstockinn.com.* Specialties: jumbo lump crabmeat cake, roast rack of lamb. Changing menu. Hrs: 6-9 pm; Sun brunch 10 am-1 pm. Res accepted. Bar. Wine cellar. A la carte entrees: dinner $21-$28. Sun brunch $23.95. Child's menu. Parking. Limited outdoor dining in Eagle Cafe. Jacket suggested (Memorial Day-Labor Day). Totally nonsmoking. Cr cds: A, MC, V.
[D]

CANADA

Just north of the United States, with which it shares the world's longest undefended border, lies Canada, the world's largest country in terms of land area. Extending from the North Pole to the northern border of the United States and including all the islands from Greenland to Alaska, Canada's area encompasses nearly four million square miles (10.4 million square kilometers). The northern reaches of the country consist mainly of the Yukon and Northwest territories, which make up the vast, sparsely populated Canadian frontier.

Jacques Cartier erected a cross at Gaspé in 1534 and declared the establishment of New France. Samuel de Champlain founded Port Royal in Nova Scotia in 1604. Until 1759 Canada was under French rule. In that year, British General Wolfe defeated French General Montcalm at Québec and British possession followed. In 1867 the British North America Act established the Confederation of Canada, with four provinces: New Brunswick, Nova Scotia, Ontario, and Québec. The other provinces joined later. Canada was proclaimed a self-governing Dominion within the British Empire in 1931. The passage in 1981 of the Constitution Act severed Canada's final legislative link with Great Britain, which had until that time reserved the right to amend the Canadian Constitution.

Today, Canada is a sovereign nation—neither a colony nor a possession of Great Britain. Since Canada is a member of the Commonwealth of Nations, Queen Elizabeth II, through her representative, the Governor-General, is the nominal head of state. However, the Queen's functions are mostly ceremonial with no political power or authority. Instead, the nation's chief executive is the prime minister; the legislative branch consists of the Senate and the House of Commons.

Population: 31,006,347
Area: 6,181,778 square miles (9,970,610 square kilometers)
Peak: Mount Logan, Yukon Territory, 19,850 feet (5,951 meters)
Capital: Ottawa
Speed Limit: 50 or 60 mph (80 or 100 km/h), unless otherwise indicated

Visitor Information

Currency. The American dollar is accepted throughout Canada, but it is advisable to exchange your money into Canadian currency upon arrival. Banks and currency exchange firms typically give the best rate of exchange, but hotels and stores will also convert it for you with purchases. The Canadian monetary system is based on dollars and cents, and rates in *RoadMaster™ Drive USA Travel Guide* are given in Canadian currency. Generally, the credit cards you use at home are also honored in Canada.

Goods and Services Tax (GST). Most goods and services in Canada are subject to a 7% tax. Visitors to Canada may claim a rebate of the GST paid on *short-term accommodations* (hotel, motel, or similar lodging) and on *most consumer goods* purchased to take home. Rebates may be claimed for cash at participating Canadian Duty Free shops or by mail. For further information and a brochure detailing rebate procedures and restrictions contact Visitors' Rebate Program, Revenue Canada, Summerside Tax Center, Summerside, PE C1N 6C6; phone 613/991-3346 or 800/66-VISIT (in Canada).

Driving in Canada. Your American driver's license is valid in Canada; no special permit is required. In Canada the liter is the unit of measure for gasoline. One US gallon equals 3.78 liters. Traffic signs are clearly understood and in many cities are bilingual. All road speed limits and mileage signs have been posted in kilometers. A flashing green traffic light gives vehicles turning left the right-of-way, like a green left-turn arrow. The use of safety belts is generally mandatory in all provinces; consult the various provincial tourism bureaus for specific information.

Holidays. Canada observes the following holidays, and these are indicated in text: New Year's Day, Good Friday, Easter Monday, Victoria Day (usually 3rd Mon May), Canada Day (July 1), Labour Day, Thanksgiving (2nd Mon Oct), Remembrance Day (November 11), Christmas, and Boxing Day (December 26). See individual provinces for information on provincial holidays.

Liquor. The sale of liquor, wine, beer, and cider varies from province to province. Restaurants must be licensed to serve liquor, and in some cases liquor may not be sold unless it accompanies a meal. Generally there are no package sales on holidays. Minimum legal drinking age also varies by province. **Note:** It is illegal to take children into bars or cocktail lounges.

Daylight Saving Time. Canada observes Daylight Saving Time beginning the first Sunday in April through the last Sunday in October, except for most of the province of Saskatchewan, where Standard Time is observed year-round.

Tourist information is available from individual provincial and territorial tourism offices (see Border Crossing Regulations in MAKING THE MOST OF YOUR TRIP).

PROVINCE OF NEW BRUNSWICK

N ew Brunswick, discovered by Jacques Cartier in 1535, was one of the first areas in North America to be settled by Europeans. Established as a province in 1784, it became one of the original provinces of the Canadian Confederation (1867).

New Brunswick's rich historic past is reflected in major restorations such as the Acadian Historical Village near Caraquet, Kings Landing Historical Settlement near Fredericton, and MacDonald Historic Farm near Miramichi. The Acadian influence is found throughout the province, predominantly along the north and east coasts. Caraquet and Moncton are the major centers of Acadian culture.

But there is much more to New Brunswick than history—the Bay of Fundy to the south (featuring some of the highest tides in the world and a great variety of whales), the Reversing Falls in St. John, Magnetic Hill in Moncton, Hopewell Cape Rocks at Hopewell Cape—and always the sea. Some of the finest beaches in Atlantic Canada provide excellent recreational possibilities, exquisite seafood, and the warmest waters north of Virginia. The capital, Fredericton, offers a full range of big-city attractions. The weather is ideal for vacations, June through August being the warmest months. During September and October, the fall foliage is a spectacular sight, while the winter months attract many outdoor enthusiasts to ski over 600 miles (1,000 kilometers) of cross-country trails and snowmobile the 5,400 miles (9,000 kilometers) of groomed trails. Angling enthusiasts will be drawn to the world-famous Atlantic salmon river, Miramichi.

Visitor Information Centres are located throughout the province. It is important to note that reservations are not accepted at national parks and only at some provincial parks.

Safety belts are mandatory for all persons anywhere in vehicle. Children under five years or under 40 pounds in weight must be in an approved safety seat anywhere in vehicle.

Pop: 714,800
Land area: 28,354 sq mi (73,437 sq km)
Capital: Fredericton
Web: www.tourisnbcanada.com
Information: Tourism New Brunswick, PO Box 12345, Campbellton E3N 3T6; 800/561-0123

Edmundston

Also see Caribou, Fort Kent, and Presque Isle, ME

Pop 11,497 **Elev** 462 ft (141 m) **Area code** 506
Information Chamber of Commerce, 74 Canada Rd,
PO Box 338, E3V 1V5; 506/737-1866

The Madawaska County's origin revolves around a border
dispute between England and the United States. From
1785-1845 the areas around Edmundston, part of the state
of Maine, and part of the province of Quebec were left
without allegiance to any government. A large portion was
ceded to the United States in 1842 but the Canadian section
remained unattached, prompting residents to issue the
"proclamation of the Republic of Madawaska." Though
eventually becoming a part of New Brunswick and despite
never having been a reality, the mythical title has remained,
with the coat of arms registered in 1949.

Acadian culture predominates with almost all of the
population speaking French—but nearly all are bilingual.
The first families to arrive in Edmundston were Acadian
and French Canadian.

What to See and Do

Edmundston Golf Club. Challenging 18-hole course within
the city attracts people from a large area. (May-Sept, daily)
Victoria St. Phone 506/735-3086. ¢¢¢¢

Grand Falls. At 75 ft (23 m) high, one of largest cataracts
east of Niagara. Fascinating gorge and scenic lookouts
along trail; museum. Stairs to bottom of gorge (fee).
(Late May-Oct, daily) 40 mi (64 km) SE, in Grand Falls.
Phone 506/473-6013. ¢

Les Jardins de la République Provincial Park. (Gardens of
the Republic) Park of 107 acres (43 hectares) overlooking
the Madawaska River. Amphitheater, scene of music and
film performances; 20-acre (eight-hectare) botanical garden. Heated swimming pool, boat dock, launch; tennis,
volleyball, softball, horseshoes, bicycling, playground,
indoor game rm; snack bar. Various fees. 113 campsites
(most with electricity; fee). Park (June-Sept). 5 mi (8 km)
N via Trans-Canada Hwy 2. Phone 506/735-2525. In the
park is

> **Antique Auto Museum.** Impressive display of vintage
> vehicles and mechanical marvels of the past 70 yrs.
> (Mid-June-Labour Day, daily) Phone 506/735-2525. ¢¢

New Brunswick Botanical Garden. Conceived and designed
by a team from the prestigious Montreal Botanical Garden,
the garden covers over 17 acres. More than 30,000 annual
flowers and 80,000 plants are on display. (June-mid-Oct,
daily) exit 8, 4½ mi (7 km) N on Trans-Canada Hwy.
Phone 506/739-6335. ¢¢

New Denmark Memorial Museum. Museum building is
on site of original immigrant house built in 1872 to house
settlers. Household articles, documents, machinery belonging to original settlers from Denmark. (Mid-June-Labour
Day, daily; rest of yr, by appt) 45 mi (72 km) SE in farming
community of New Denmark, oldest Danish colony in
Canada (1872). Phone 506/553-6724. **FREE**

St. Basile Chapel Museum. Parish church; replica of first
chapel built in 1786. (July-Aug, daily) 321 Main St, 3 mi
(5 km) E in St Basile. Phone 506/263-5971.

Special Events

International Snowmobilers Festival. Phone 506/737-1866.
First wk Feb.

Jazz Festival. Phone 506/739-2104. Third wkend June.

Foire Brayonne. French heritage festival. Phone 506/739-
6608. Late July-early Aug.

Fredericton

Founded 1762 **Pop** 45,000 **Elev** 24 ft (7 m) **Area code** 506
Information Fredericton Tourism, 397 Queen St, PO Box 130,
E3B 4Y7; 506/460-2020
Web www.city.fredericton.nb.ca

Over the past 40 years the benefactions of the late Lord
Beaverbrook have raised Fredericton from a quiet provincial
capital to a major cultural center. Born in Ontario, this
British newspaper baron maintained a strong loyalty to New
Brunswick, the province of his youth. Wander the elm tree-
lined streets through the Green, a lovely park along the
St. John River, and admire examples of Beaverbrook's gen-
erosity that heighten the city's beauty. Nestled along the
tree-shaded Green sits Christ Church Cathedral, an 1853
example of decorated Gothic architecture.

What to See and Do

Beaverbrook Art Gallery. Collection incl 18th-20th-
century British paintings, 18th- and early 19th-century
English porcelains, historical and contemporary Canadian
and New Brunswick paintings, and Salvador Dali's *Santiago
el Grande;* Hosmer-Pillow-Vaughan Collection of European
fine and decorative arts from the 14th-20th centuries.
(Daily; closed Jan 1, Dec 25) 703 Queen St. Phone
506/458-8545. ¢¢

The Beaverbrook Playhouse. Home of professional company
Theatre New Brunswick. Contact PO Box 566, E3B 5A6.
686 Queen St. Phone 506/458-8345.

City Hall. (1876) Seat of municipal government. Guided
tours of council chambers, town history depicted in tapestry
form. Changing of the Guard (July-Labour Day, Tues-Sat).
Tourist Information Centre (May-Sept, daily; rest of yr,
Mon-Fri). Queen and York Sts. Phone 506/452-9616. **FREE**

Golf.

> **Fredericton.** Eighteen holes, very picturesque. Golf Club
> Rd, off Woodstock Rd. Phone 506/458-0003. ¢¢¢¢¢
>
> **Mactaquac.** Eighteen-hole championship course. In
> Mactaquac Provincial Park. Phone 506/363-3011. ¢¢¢¢

Kings Landing Historical Settlement. Settlement of 50
buildings, costumed staff of 100; recalls Loyalist lifestyle
of a century ago. Carpenter's shop, general store, school,
church, blacksmith shop, working sawmill and gristmill,

inn; replica of a 19th-century wood boat (river craft). All restoration and work is done with tools of the period. Settlement (June-early Oct, daily). Tours; children's programs. Restaurants, snack bar. 23 mi (37 km) W on Trans-Canada Hwy at exit 259. Phone 506/363-5805. ¢¢

Mactaquac Fish Hatchery. Sixty-seven rearing ponds with a potential annual production of 340,000 smolts (young salmon ready to migrate). Visitor center (mid-May-mid-Oct). (Daily) 10 mi (16 km) W on Rte 2/Trans-Canada Hwy. Phone 506/363-3021. **FREE**

Mactaquac Generating Station. Hydroelectric dam has powerhouse with turbines and generators; fish collection facilities at foot of dam. Free guided tours (mid-May-Aug, daily; rest of yr, by appt). 12 mi (19 km) W on Rte 2/Trans-Canada Hwy, exit 274. Phone 506/363-3093.

Mactaquac Provincial Park. Approx 1,400 acres (567 hectares) of farmland and forest overlooking headpond of Mactaquac Dam. Boating (launch, marinas), swimming beaches, fishing; hiking, camping (hookups, dump station), golf, picnicking, playgrounds, restaurant, store, lndry. Also in the vicinity are a historic village, fish culture station, and a generating plant. Some fees. On Rte 105, 15 mi (24 km) W. Phone 506/363-3011. Per vehicle (summer only) ¢¢

New Brunswick Legislative Assembly. Seat of provincial government; public galleries. Guided tour. Library (Mon-Fri) incl hand-colored engravings of Audubon *Birds of America.* (Mid-June-Labour Day, daily; rest of yr, Mon-Fri) Queen and St. John Sts. Phone 506/453-2527. **FREE**

Odell Park. Unique example of the primeval forest of New Brunswick; part of original land grant. Approx 400 acres (160 hectares) incl lodge, picnicking, play area, walking paths through woods; deer and other animals; ski trails; arboretum with 1¾ mi (2.8 km) trail. End of Rookwood Ave. Phone 506/458-8530. **FREE**

Officers' Square. Park with Lord Beaverbrook statue; changing of the guard ceremonies (July-Labour Day); band concerts Tues and Thurs eves (late June-Aug), theater in the park (July-Aug). Queen St. Phone 506/460-2129. On grounds are

Old Officers' Quarters. Typical architecture of Royal Engineers in the Colonial period; stone arches, iron handrails and stone staircase. Older part (1839-1840), near the river, has thicker walls of solid masonry and hand-hewn timbers; later end (1851) has thinner walls and sawn timbers. Phone 506/460-2129. ¢ Contains

York-Sunbury Historical Society Museum. Permanent and changing exhibits of military and domestic area history; seasonal exhibitions of history, New Brunswick crafts and fine arts; mounted 42-lb (16-kg) Coleman frog. (July-Aug, daily; May-June and Sept-mid-Oct, Mon-Sat; rest of yr, Mon, Wed, and Fri or by appt) Phone 506/455-6041. ¢¢

The Playhouse Theatre. Home of professional company Theatre New Brunswick. 686 Queen St. Contact PO Box 566, E3B 5A6. Phone 506/458-8345.

University of New Brunswick. (1785) 8,000 students. One of the oldest universities in North America. Tours (by appt). University Ave. Phone 506/453-4793.

Wilmot Park. Wading pool; lighted tennis, ball diamond, picnicking, playground, bowling green. Woodstock Rd. **FREE** Opp is

Old Government House. (1828) Former residence of Colonial governors; more recently headquarters of Royal Canadian Mounted Police. Not open to public. Woodstock Rd. Phone 506/453-2505.

Special Events

Canada Day Celebration. Phone 506/455-3866. Last wk June-early July.

Atlantic Crew Classic Rowing Regatta. Phone 506/453-9428. Early July.

NB Highland Games. Phone 888/368-8819. Last wkend July.

Fredericton Exhibition. Phone 506/458-8819. First wk Sept.

Harvest Jazz and Blues Festival. Phone 888/622-5837. Mid-Sept.

New Brunswick Summer Chamber Music Festival. Phone 506/453-4697. Late Aug.

Motels/Motor Lodges

★ ★ **FREDERICTON INN.** *1315 Regent St (E3C 1A1). 506/455-1430; fax 506/458-5448; toll-free 800/561-8777.* 199 rms, 1-3 story. July-Sept: S $65-$105; D $75-$105; each addl $10; suites $105; kit. unit $115; lower rates rest of yr. Crib $6. Pet accepted. TV; cable, VCR avail. Heated pool; wading pool, whirlpool, poolside serv. Restaurant 6:30 am-11 pm. Rm serv. Bar 4 pm-1 am. Ck-out 11 am. Meeting rms. Business servs avail. In-rm modem link. Bellhops. Sundries. Some in-rm whirlpools. Refrigerators avail. Balconies. Cr cds: A, D, DS, MC, V.

⊡ ⇗ ⬇ ⩩ ⩥ ⚲

★ **HOWARD JOHNSON.** *480 Riverside Dr (E3B 5E3). 506/460-5500; fax 506/472-0170; toll-free 800/596-4656. www.hojo.com.* 116 rms, 2 story. S $65-$76; D $74-$79; each addl $8; suites $136; under 18 free. Crib free. Pet accepted, some restrictions. TV; cable (premium), VCR avail. Heated pool; whirlpool, poolside serv. Restaurant 7 am-10 pm. Rm serv. Bar 4 pm-1 am. Ck-out noon. Coin lndry. Meeting rms. Business servs avail. In-rm modem link. Valet serv. Airport transportation. Indoor tennis. Downhill ski 10 mi; x-country ski 5 mi. Exercise equipt; sauna. Rec rm. Lawn games. Balconies. Cr cds: A, D, MC, V.

⊡ ⇗ ⚡ ⏃ ⩩ ⩥ 🎾 ⚲ ⩥

★ ★ **WANDLYN INN.** *958 Prospect St (E3B 4Y9). 506/462-4444; fax 506/452-7658; toll-free 800/561-0000. www.wandlyn.com.* 100 rms, 3 story. S, D $70-$99; studio rms $75-$100; each addl $10; suites $125-$199; under 18 free. Crib free. Pet accepted. TV; cable (premium), VCR avail. 2 pools, 1 indoor; whirlpool, poolside serv. Sauna. Restaurant 7 am-2 pm, 5-9:30 pm. Bar 11-1 am. Ck-out 11 am. Coin laundry. Meeting rms. Business servs avail. Valet serv. Sundries. Refrigerators avail. Cr cds: A, MC, V.

⇗ ⩥ ⚲

Hotels

★★★ **LORD BEAVERBROOK HOTEL.** *659 Queen St (E3B 5A6).* 506/455-3371; fax 506/455-1441; res 800/561-7666. www.lordbeaverbrookhotel.com. 168 rms, 7 story. S $139; D $149; each addl $10; suites $90-$150; under 19 free; package plans. Crib free. Pet accepted. TV; cable, VCR avail. Heated pool; wading pool, whirlpool, poolside serv. Sauna. Playground. Supervised children's activities. Restaurant 6 am-10 pm. Bar 11 am-2 am; entertainment, dancing; sun deck bar. Ck-out noon. Meeting rms. Business servs avail. In-rm modem link. Concierge. Gift shop. Airport transportation. Bicycle, boat, canoe rentals. Docking facilities. Rec rm. Game rm. Minibars. Picnic tables. Cr cds: A, D, DS, ER, MC, V.

⊡ 🐾 ⚡ ⛱ 🚫 🔥

★★★ **SHERATON FREDERICTON.** *225 Woodstock Rd (E3B 2H8).* 506/457-7000; fax 506/457-4000; toll-free 800/325-3535. www.sheraton.com. 223 rms, 7 story. S, D $144-$209; each addl $10; suites $155-$575; under 17 free. Crib free. TV; cable (premium), VCR avail. 2 pools, 1 indoor; wading pool, whirlpool, poolside serv, lifeguard. Complimentary coffee in rms. Restaurant 6:30 am-11 pm. Bar 11-2 am. Ck-out noon. Meeting rms. Business servs avail. Gift shop. In-rm modem link. Free airport transportation. Downhill ski 15 mi; x-country ski 2 mi. Exercise equipt; sauna. Minibars. On St. John River. Cr cds: A, D, ER, JCB, MC, V.

⊡ 🐾 ⛵ 🏊 🎿 🚫 🔥

Fundy National Park

See also Moncton, St. John

On the coast between St. John and Moncton (see both), the park's 80 square miles (207 square kilometers) of forested hills and valleys are crisscrossed by miles of hiking trails. Cliffs front much of the rugged coastline. Fish are found in its lakes and streams and the woods are filled with wildlife. The beaches at Herring Cove, Point Wolfe and Alma are exceptional for viewing the tides. Since the ocean water is frigid, swimming is enjoyed in the heated saltwater pool or one of the lakes; golf, tennis, lawn bowling, picnicking, camping (May-Oct), cross-country skiing. Programs in amphitheater. Some fees. Guided beach walks (June-Aug). The park and headquarters are open all year; visitor area (mid-May-Oct). Accommodations available in park.

Moncton

Pop 55,700 **Elev** 50 ft (15 m) **Area code** 506
Information Tourism Moncton, 655 Main St, E1C 1E8; 506/853-3590 or 800/363-4558
Web www.greater.moncton.nb.ca

This commercial and cultural center of the Atlantic provinces is located on the Petitcodiac River, which at low tide becomes a mud flat clustered with sea gulls. As the tide turns, a tidal bore (a small wave) runs upstream to herald the incoming waters. Just off the Trans-Canada Highway another phenomenon awaits the traveler—Magnetic Hill. The experience of sitting in your car, without power, seemingly rolling up the hill, is one remembered by many. There is nothing magnetic about the hill; it is just an optical illusion created by the contours of the countryside. Nearby are the Magnetic Hill Zoo with North American and exotic wildlife and Magic Mountain, a water theme park.

Existing as an Acadian center where English and French cultures have flourished for centuries, Moncton is an excellent beginning for a tour to the northeast along the coast to beautiful Kouchibouquac National Park. Visit the Acadian Museum at the University of Moncton, the Free Meeting House (1821), oldest building in Moncton, which has served nearly every faith, its pioneer cemetery with stones dating to 1816, and the adjacent Moncton Museum.

Nearby Shediac, lobster capital of the world, has a lobster festival in July. From here, northward along the coast of the Northumberland Strait, saltwater fishing and camping provide the visitor with a chance to relax and enjoy the French heritage of the area.

Stretching along the coast are little fishing villages where French-speaking people offer their hospitality. Each year for a few days in early August the village of Cocagne has a bazaar and international regatta—a curious mixture of Acadian and North American cultures. Hydroplane races attract thousands for two days; visitors remain to enjoy the Acadian festival with its special food, handcrafts, dancing, and singing.

What to See and Do

Crystal Palace Amusement Park. Indoor and outdoor attractions, incl rides, miniature golf, Science Center, video games, and go-carts. (Daily) 499 Paul St, E in Dieppe. Phone 506/859-4386.

Fort Beausejour National Historic Site. Approx 600 acres (225 hectares). Built by the French between 1751-1755 during their long struggle with England for possession of Acadia. Attacked in 1755, the fort was captured by the British under Colonel Monckton, who renamed it Fort Cumberland. Following its capture, the fort was strengthened and its defenses extended. During the American Revolution in 1776 it withstood an attack by revolutionaries under Jonathan Eddy. It was manned by a small garrison during the War of 1812. Three casemates and a massive stone curtain wall have been restored; displays on history and culture of Isthmus of Chignecto; outdoor paintings showing garrison as it existed in 18th century. Picnicking (shelters). Visitor center. Panoramic view of site and surrounding salt marshes. (June-mid-Oct, daily) Approx 37 mi (60 km) E on Hwy 2, exit 550. Contact Chief, Visitor Activities, Aulac E0A 3C0. Phone 506/536-0720.

Magnetic Hill Zoo. Wild animal park and petting zoo; many species represented, incl wildfowl. (May-Oct, daily) Near Magnetic Hill. Phone 506/384-0303. ¢¢

"The Rocks" Provincial Park. Unique cliffs, caves, and flowerpot-shaped pillars of conglomerate rock interspersed with shale and sandstone layers. Tourist information center has interpretive displays; tour guides avail. Visitors are advised to watch for caution signs, avoid loose cliff sections, not climb any flowerpot or cliff, and return from beach by the time posted at the stairs to avoid problems with rising tide. Picnicking, restaurant. (May-Oct, daily) Contact Parks Branch, Dept of Natural Resources, PO Box 6000, Fredericton E3B 5H1. Across Petitcodiac River, then 28 mi (45 km) SE on Hwy 114, "Rocks" exit, just S of Hopewell Cape. Phone 506/856-2940 or 800/561-0123 (US and Canada). ¢¢

Tidal bore. A small tidal wave running upstream to usher in the Bay of Fundy tides on the normally placid Petitcodiac River. Within one hr water level rises more than 25 ft. The bore arrives twice daily. Main St at Bore View Park. Phone 560/853-3590.

Motels/Motor Lodges

★★ **COLONIAL INN.** 42 Highfield St (E1C 8T6). 506/382-3395; fax 506/858-8991; toll-free 800/561-4667. www.colonial-inn.com. 61 rms, 1-2 story. S $62 D $68; each addl $5; studio rms $75; under 16 free. Crib $5. Pet accepted, some restrictions. TV; cable. Heated pool; whirlpool. Restaurant open 24 hrs. Rm serv. Bar 11 am-midnight. Ck-out noon-2 pm. Meeting rm. Business servs avail. Valet serv. Sundries. Sauna. Some refrigerators. Cr cds: A, D, ER, MC, V.
🐕 🏊 ⛵ 🔥 SC

★ **ECONO LODGE.** 1905 W Main St (E1E 1H9). 506/382-2587; fax 506/858-5998; res 800/553-2666. www.econolodge.com. 67 rms, 5 kit. units, 2 story. S $59; D $79; each addl $5; studio rms $79; kit. units $89; each addl $5; under 12 free; wkly rates. Pet accepted, some restrictions. TV; cable. Heated pool. Restaurant 7 am-9 pm; Sun to 2 pm. Bar. Ck-out 11 am. Business servs avail. Cr cds: A, C, D, DS, ER, MC, V.
D 🐕 ⛵ 🔧 🏊 ⛵ 🐾

★★ **RODD PARK HOUSE INN.** 434 Main St (E1C 1B9). 506/382-1664; fax 506/855-9494; res 800/565-7633. www.rodd-hotels.ca. 97 rms, 4 story. S $79; D $99; each addl $10; under 19 free. Crib free. Pet accepted, some restrictions. TV; cable (premium). Heated pool. Complimentary coffee in rms. Restaurant 7 am-2 pm, 5-10 pm. Bar. Ck-out noon. Meeting rms. Business servs avail. Valet serv. Cr cds: A, MC, V.
🐕 ⛵ 🔥

Hotel

★★★ **DELTA BEAUSEJOUR.** 750 Main St (E1C 1E6). 506/854-4344; fax 506/858-0957; res 800/268-1133. www.deltahotels.com. 310 rms, 9 story. S, D $109-$151; each addl $15; suites $240-$950; under 18 free; wkend rates. Crib free. Pet accepted. TV; cable (premium). Pool; poolside serv, lifeguard. Coffee in rms. Restaurants 6:30 am-11 pm. Rm serv 24 hrs. Bar 4:30 pm-1 am, wkends from 6 pm, closed Sun. Ck-out noon. Meeting rms. Business servs avail. In-rm modem link. Concierge. Gift shop. Barber. Exercise equipt. Minibars; many bathrm phones; some refrigerators. Cr cds: A, D, DS, ER, MC, V.
D 🐕 ⛵ 🏊 🏃 🐾

B&B/Small Inn

★ **BONACCORD HOUSE B&B.** 250 Bonaccord St (E1C 5M6). 506/388-1535; fax 506/853-7191. 5 rms, 2 share bath, 1 with shower only, 1 A/C, 3 story, 1 kit. suite. S $45; D $55; each addl $10. TV in sitting rm, suite; cable, VCR avail. Complimentary full bkfst. Restaurant nearby. Ck-out 10 am, ck-in 2 pm. Business servs avail. Some balconies. Victorian residence (1890) with columned wrap-around veranda. Totally nonsmoking. Cr cds: V.
🛫 🖼 🔥

St. Andrews

Also see Calais, ME

Pop 1,760 **Elev** 23 ft (7 m) **Area code** 506
Information Chamber of Commerce Tourist Information Centre, 46 Reed Ave, PO Box 89, EOG 2X0; 506/529-3555
Web www.townsearch.com/canada/nb/standrews

Explored by Champlain and later settled in 1783 by Loyalists from New England, this popular seaside resort is a beautiful village rich in history. On a peninsula projecting into Passamaquoddy Bay, fishing, swimming, sailing, and rockhounding are favorite pastimes. Feast on fresh lobster, watch the tides swirl in, visit the specialty shops, or wander down the streets past many buildings erected before 1800. The white-framed Greenock Church, begun in 1822, and the Court House (1840) and Gaol (1832) are worth special visits.

From the shore the Fundy Isles dot the bay, the most famous of which is Campobello. Here, Franklin Delano Roosevelt spent his summers from 1905-21 when he was stricken with infantile paralysis. Tours of Roosevelt's cottage in the International Park are available.

Northeast toward St. John, the road to Blacks Harbour affords views of lighthouses, lovely beaches, and covered bridges. From this village, a ferry leaves for Grand Manan Island, largest of the three islands. This is a popular vacation destination with picturesque lighthouses and tiny fishing villages nestled in the barren seaside cliffs.

What to See and Do

Algonquin Golf Courses. Opened in 1894, 18-hole championship course with wooded glades and breathtaking shoreline views (fee). Executive nine-hole woodland course (fee). (Late Apr-late Oct) Algonquin Hotel, Reed Ave.

Blockhouse Historic Site. Sole survivor of coastal defenses built during War of 1812; restored 1967. (Mid-May-mid-Oct, daily) In Centennial Park, Joe's Point Rd. Phone 506/529-4270. **FREE**

The Henry Phipps & Sarah Juliette Ross Memorial Museum. Private antique furniture and decorative art collection of the Rosses. (July-Aug, daily; May-June and Sept-early Oct, Tues-Sat) 188 Montague St. Phone 506/529-1824. **FREE**

Huntsman Marine Science Center/Aquarium-Museum.
Displays of coastal and marine environments with many
fish and invertebrates found in waters of Passamaquoddy
Region; "Touch Tank" allows visitors to handle marine life
found on local rocky beaches. Displays of live animals incl
local amphibians, reptiles, and a family of harbor seals.
Exhibits on local geology; seaweed collection. (May-early
Oct, daily) Brandy Cove Rd. Phone 506/529-1202. ¢¢

Motels/Motor Lodges

★ **BLUE MOON MOTEL.** *310 Mowat Dr (E5B 2P3).*
506/529-3245. 39 air-cooled rms, 2 kits. May-Oct: S $45-
$55; D $55-$75; each addl $7; kit. units $5 addl; under
6 free. Closed rest of yr. Crib free. Pet accepted, some
restrictions. TV; cable. Ck-out 11 am. Business servs avail.
18-hole golf privileges. Cr cds: A, D, DS, ER, MC, V.
🐟 🛎 🏃 🔅 🔥

★ **PICKET FENCE.** *102 Reed Ave (E0G 2X0). 506/529-*
8985. 17 rms. No A/C. May-Oct: S $55; D $75; each addl
$8; under 6 free. Closed rest of yr. Crib free. Pet accepted,
some restrictions. TV; cable. Restaurant nearby. Ck-out
11 am. Picnic tables. Cr cds: JCB, MC, V.
🐾 🐟 🔅 🔅 🔥

★ **ST STEPHEN INN.** *99 King St, St Stephen (E3L 2C6).*
506/466-1814; fax 506/466-6148; toll-free 800/565-3088.
52 rms, 2 story. July-Dec: S $65; D $80; each addl $8;
under 17 free; lower rates rest of yr. Crib free. Pet accepted.
TV; cable, VCR avail. Restaurant 7 am-10 pm. Meeting rms.
Business servs avail. Cr cds: A, MC, V.
🐟 🔥

★ **SEASIDE BEACH RESORT.** *339 Water St (E5B 2R2).*
506/529-3846; fax 506/529-4479; toll-free 800/506-8677.
www.seaside.nb.ca. 24 kit. units, 19 with shower only, 1-2
story, 4 cottages. No A/C. No rm phones. June-Labor Day:
S, D $65-$75; each addl $5; wkly rates; lower rates May,
early Sept-Oct. Closed rest of yr. Crib $5. Pet accepted.
TV; cable. Restaurant nearby. Ck-out 11 am. Coin lndry.
Microwaves avail. Balconies. Picnic tables, grills. Overlooks
bay. Cr cds: A, MC, V.
D 🐟 🐾 🔅 🔅 🔥

★ ★ ★ **TARA MANOR INN.** *559 Mowat Dr (E5B 2P2).*
506/529-3304; fax 506/529-4755. www.taramanor.com.
26 rms, 1-3 story, 15 suites. June-late Sept: S, D $98-$148;
each addl $10; under 13 free; lower rates May, mid-Sept-
mid-Oct. Closed rest of yr. Crib free. TV; cable. Heated
pool; whirlpool. Playground. Complimentary coffee in
library. Dining rm 7:30-10 am, 6-9 pm. Rm serv. Ck-out
11:30 am. Tennis. Golf privileges. Sauna. Refrigerator in
suites. Balconies. Former country estate (1871) of Sir Charles
Tupper; antiques. Situated on 16 acres of woods, lawns and
gardens. Cr cds: A, MC, V.
🏃 🎿 🔅 🔥

Hotel

★ ★ ★ ★ **KINGSBRAE ARMS.** *219 King St (E5B 1Y1).*
506/529-1897; fax 506/529-1197. www.kingsbrae.com.
≠Constructed in 1897, this country home property is
adjacent to the breathtaking Kingsbrae Horticultural
Garden and affords views of Passamaquoddy Bay. The inn,
located in an oceanside town where Maine and Canada
meet, has three suites and five guest rooms with oversized
cast iron or whirlpool tubs, feather and down comforters,
and period furnishings. Family-style dinners are creative
and highlight local produce and seafood. 8 rms, 3 story,
3 suites. Mid-Mar-mid-Oct: S, D $225; suites $250-$350;
package plans; wkends 2-day min; lower rates rest of yr.
Children over 9 yrs only. Pet accepted, some restrictions. TV;
cable, VCR avail (movies). Heated pool. Complimentary
full bkfst; afternoon refreshments. Rm serv 24 hrs. Bar.
Ck-out noon, ck-in 3 pm. Business center. In-rm modem
link. Valet serv. Concierge serv. Airport transportation.
Tennis privileges. Health club privileges. Lawn games.
Fireplaces; some in-rm whirlpools. Some balconies.
Totally nonsmoking. Cr cds: A, DS, MC, V.
🐟 🎿 🔅 🔅 🔅 🔥 🏃

Resorts

★ ★ ★ **THE FAIRMONT ALGONQUIN.** *184 Adolphus St*
(E5B 1T7). 506/529-8823; fax 506/529-7162; res 800/441-
1414. 250 rms, 54 A/C, 4 story, 42 kit. units. Mid-May-
mid-Oct: S, D $119-$219; each addl $20; suites $189-$369;
under 18 free. Crib free. Pet accepted. TV; cable, VCR avail.
Heated pool; whirlpool, lifeguard. Playground. Supervised
child's activities (mid-Jun-Aug); ages 12 and under. Coffee
in rms. Restaurant 7 am-10 pm. Rm serv. Bar; entertainment.
Ck-out noon, ck-in 4 pm. Coin lndry. Business servs avail.
Bellhops. Valet serv. Concierge. Gift shop. Free parking.
Tennis. 18-hole golf, greens fee $25-$39, pro, putting green.
Bicycle rentals. Exercise rm; sauna. Lawn games. Aerobics.
Some in-rm whirlpools, microwaves, fireplaces. On hill;
view of water from most rms. Cr cds: A, DS, MC, V.
🐟 🛎 🎿 🔅 🏃 🔥

★ ★ ★ **PANSY PATCH.** *59 Carleton St (EGB 1M8).*
506/529-3834; fax 506/529-9042; toll-free 888/726-7972.
www.pansypatch.com. 9 rms, 5 with shower only, 2-3 rms,
2 suites. No A/C. May-mid-Oct: S, D $120-$205; each addl
$15; suite $170. Closed rest of yr. Cable TV avail and in
common rm. Complimentary full bkfst; afternoon refreshments. Restaurant 11 am-3:30 pm, 5-9 pm. Ck-out 11 am,
ck-in 3 pm. Business servs avail. In-rm modem link. Luggage
handling. Gift shop. Tennis privileges. Exercise equipt.
Health club privileges. Lawn games. Refrigerator, microwave, fireplace in suite. Some balconies. Built in 1912.
Norman cottage architecture; extensive gardens. Totally
nonsmoking. Cr cds: A, MC, V.
🎿 🏃 🔅 🔥

Restaurant

★★ **ST. ANDREWS LIGHTHOUSE.** *1 Patrick St (E0G 2X0). 506/529-3082.* Continental menu. Specializes in fresh seafood, steak, chicken. Hrs: 5-9 pm; mid-June-mid-Sept 11:30 am-2 pm, 5-9 pm. Closed mid-Oct-mid-May. Res accepted. Lunch $3-$19.50, dinner $9.95-$26.50. Child's menu. Lighthouse (1833) on Passamaquoddy Bay. Cr cds: A, D, DS, MC, V.

D

St. John

Founded 1785 **Pop** 78,000 **Elev** 100 ft (31 m)
Area code 506
Information Visitor & Convention Bureau, City Hall, 11th floor, PO Box 1971, E2L 4L1; 506/658-2990 or 888/364-4444
Web www.tourismsaintjohn.com

The largest city in the province, this deep-sea port was founded by the United Empire Loyalists after the American Revolution. It is Canada's first incorporated city. The heart of the old town is King's Square, where many historic landmarks (including an ancient burial ground) are found.

The Reversing Falls, another of the phenomena caused by the 30-foot (9-meter) tides on the Bay of Fundy, are found near the eastern approach to the city center off Highway 1. Here, the high tidewater is forced back upstream into the St. John River, causing a whirling torrent. A deck, where the tourist bureau is located, overlooks the rapids.

What to See and Do

Barbour's General Store. Restored general store reflecting period 1840-1940; 2,000 artifacts and wide selection of old-fashioned grocery items, china, yard goods, farm implements, cooking tools; re-created post office; barbershop with wicker barber's chair, collection of shaving mugs; pharmacy with approx 300 samples of "cure-all or kill-alls"; potbellied stove; staff outfitted in period costumes. (Mid-May-mid-Oct, daily) In Market Slip area, Downtown. Phone 506/658-2939.

Carlton Martello Tower National Historic Park. Circular coastal forts built for War of 1812; used in WWII as fire command post for harbor defenses (when two-story superstructure was added); restored powder magazine of 1840s; barrack rm (ca 1865). Panoramic view of city, harbor, and surrounding landscape. Guided tours of tower (June-mid-Oct, daily). Grounds open all yr. Hwy 1, exit 107. Phone 506/636-4011. ¢¢

Ferry Service to Digby, NS. Car and passenger; 45 mi (72 km). (All yr) Res required. Contact Bay Ferries Ltd, Box 3427, Station B, E2M 4X9. Phone 506/636-4048 or 888/249-7245.

Irving Nature Park. Features winding coastal road and hiking trails. Harbor seals, porpoises, and many species of migrating birds can be viewed offshore. Picnicking. (Daily) Off of Sand Cove Rd on W side of city. Phone 506/653-7367. **FREE**

Loyalist House. (1810-1187) Built by David Daniel Merritt, a United Empire Loyalist from New York. Six generations have lived in the house; gracious Georgian mansion remains much as it was when built; excellent craftsmanship. (July-Aug, daily; June and Sept, Mon-Fri; also by appt) 120 Union St. Phone 506/652-3590. ¢¢

New Brunswick Museum. Intl fine art and decorative art objects; human and natural history of New Brunswick. Exhibits incl skeleton of Right Whale and Mastodon and geologic "trail through time." Also family discovery center. (Daily; closed Good Fri, Dec 25). 1 Market Sq. Phone 506/643-2300. The museum's archives and library (Mon-Fri, limited hrs; closed Good Fri, Dec 25) are at 277 Douglas Ave. 1 Market Sq. Phone 506/643-2300 or 506/643-2322 (library). ¢¢¢

Old City Market. Centralized market dating back to 1876 sells fresh meats and vegetables as well as indigenous baskets and handicrafts. Roof is wooden timbers, all wood pegs; fashioned like the hull of an old sailing ship. Magnificent iron gates of market designed in 1880 by local blacksmiths. Bell rung at opening, closing, and noon. (Mon-Sat; closed hols) 47 Charlotte St. Phone 506/658-2820. **FREE**

Rockwood Park. Municipal park with 2,200 acres of woodlands, lakes, and recreational areas, incl golf course, aquatic driving range, and campground. (Daily) Located off Mt Pleasant Ave in city center. Phone 506/658-2883 or 506/652-4050 (campground).

"Trinity Royal" Heritage Preservation Area. A 20-blk heritage area located in the city center; 19th-century residential and commercial architecture; handicrafts and specialty goods. Phone 506/693-8558.

Special Events

Loyalist Days' Heritage Celebration. Celebrates the arrival of the United Empire Loyalists in 1783 with reenactment of Loyalist landing; citizens in period costumes; parades, entertainment, sporting events. Phone 506/634-8123. Five days early July.

Festival by the Sea. Ten-day performing arts festival features Canadian entertainers. Phone 506/632-0086. Mid-Aug.

Motels/Motor Lodges

★★ **COLONIAL INN.** *175 City Rd (E2L 3T5). 506/652-3000; fax 506/658-1664; toll-free 800/561-4667.* 94 rms, 82 A/C, 2 story. S $65; D $71; each addl $6; suites $85; under 18 free. Crib free. Pet accepted. TV; cable. Heated pool; whirlpool. Sauna. Restaurant open 24 hrs. Rm serv. Bar 6 pm-2 am. Ck-out noon-2 pm. Meeting rms. Business servs avail. Valet serv. Cr cds: MC, V.

D 🐾 ⚓ ♨ ≈ ⇌ 🔉 📷

★★ **HOTEL COURTENAY BAY.** *350 Haymarket Sq (E2L 3P1). 506/657-3610; fax 506/633-1773; toll-free 800/563-2489.* 125 rms, 5 story. S $59-$69; D $69-$79; each addl $8; under 18 free. Pet accepted. TV; cable (premium). Heated pool. Restaurant 7 am-11 pm. Rm serv. Bar 11 am-11 pm. Ck-out 1 pm. Coin lndry. Meeting rms. Business servs avail. Bellhops. Valet serv. Sundries. Minibars. Some private patios, balconies. Cr cds: A, D, MC, V.

D 🐾 🛝 🏊 🚫 🔥

★ **HOWARD JOHNSON HOTEL.** *400 Main St (E2K 4N5). 506/642-2622; fax 506/658-1529; res 800/446-4656. www.hojo.com.* 96 rms, 7 story. S $95-$115; D $105-$125; each addl $10; suites $150; studio rms $79; under 12 free; wkend rates. Crib free. TV; cable, VCR avail (movies). Heated pool; whirlpool. Sauna. Complimentary coffee in rms. Restaurant 7 am-10 pm. Bar. Ck-out 1 pm. Business servs avail. Barber, beauty shop. Game rm. On Bay of Fundy. Cr cds: A, D, DS, ER, MC, V.

D 🏊 ✈ 🚫 🔥 SC

Hotels

★★ **DELTA BRUNSWICK.** *39 King St (E2L 4W3). 506/648-1981; fax 506/658-0914; res 800/268-1133. www.deltahotels.com.* 255 units, 5 story. May-mid-Oct: S, D $125-$135; each addl $10; suites $135-$500; studio rms $135-$145; under 18 free; lower rates rest of yr. Crib free. Pet accepted. Covered parking $8.50; valet $12. TV; cable. Indoor pool; whirlpool. Free supervised children's activities (wkends), over age 2. Restaurant 6:30 am-10 pm (June-Sept). Rm serv 24 hrs. Bar 11-1 am. Ck-out 1 pm. Convention facilities. Business servs avail. Shopping arcade. Exercise equipt; sauna, steam rm. Game rm. Rec rm. Minibars; refrigerators avail. Covered walkway to downtown offices, Market Sq. Cr cds: A, DS, MC, V.

🐾 🏊 🏋

★★★ **HILTON ST. JOHN.** *1 Market Sq (E2L 4Z6). 506/693-8484; fax 506/657-6610; res 800/445-8667. www.hilton.com.* 197 rms, 12 story. May-Sept: S, D $109-$149; each addl $15; suites $305-$439; lower rates rest of yr. Crib free. Pet accepted, some restrictions. Garage parking $11.44. TV; cable. Indoor pool; whirlpool. Complimentary coffee in rms. Restaurant 6:30 am-11 pm. Bar 11:30-1 am; entertainment. Ck-out noon. Meeting rms. Business center. Concierge. Shopping arcade. Barber, beauty shop. X-country ski 2 mi. Exercise equipt; sauna. Health club privileges. Game rm. Rec rm. Refrigerators, minibars. Harbor view. Underground access to Market Sq shopping mall. Cr cds: A, C, D, DS, MC, V.

🐾 🏊 🏊 🏋 🔥 🚶

PROVINCE OF NOVA SCOTIA

A fter a century of struggle between the British and French for control of North America, Nova Scotia became a British possession in 1710, with the seat of government in Halifax. In 1867 it joined with New Brunswick, Ontario, and Québec to form the Confederation of Canada.

Nova Scotia was settled by French, English, Irish, German, Scottish, and African peoples whose languages and traditions add to its flavor. Today a recreational wonderland awaits the tourist with fishing, boating, camping, golf, swimming, and charter cruising—since no part of Nova Scotia is more than 35 miles (56 kilometers) from the sea.

Major attractions include the Cabot Trail, often described as "the most spectacular drive in North America," the highlands of Cape Breton, the reconstructed Fortress of Louisbourg National Historic Site, and Lunenburg, a World Heritage Site renowned for its Colonial architecture and Fisheries Museum. The Greater Halifax area offers a variety of attractions including parks, noteworthy public gardens, art galleries, universities, theater, outdoor recreation, pubs, fine seafood dining, the world's second-largest harbor, and the Citadel Fortress—Canada's most visited historic site. Nearby is the rugged beauty of Peggy's Cove.

The weather is cool in the spring and late fall; warm in the summer and early fall. East Nova Scotia enjoys relatively mild winters due to the proximity of the Gulf Stream. Nova Scotia observes Atlantic Standard Time.

Safety belts are mandatory for all persons anywhere in vehicle. Children under 40 pounds in weight must be in an approved safety seat anywhere in vehicle. Compliance of passengers under age 16 is the responsibility of the driver. For further information phone 902/424-4256.

Pop: 874,100
Land area: 20,402 sq mi (52,841 sq km)
Capital: Halifax
Web: www.novascotia.com
Information: Nova Scotia Department of Tourism & Culture, PO Box 130, Halifax B3J 2M7; 902/425-5781 or 800/565-0000

Antigonish

See also Baddeck

Pop 5,205 **Elev** 15 ft (5 m) **Area code** 902
Information Provincial Tourist Bureau, 56 W Street, PO Box 1301, B2G 2L6; 902/863-4921

This harbor town, named for a Micmac word meaning "the place where branches were broken off the trees by bears gathering beechnuts," was settled by Highland Scottish immigrants and American Revolutionary War soldiers and their families. West of the Canso Causeway, Antigonish, intersected by rivers, is surrounded by hills from which may be seen the shores of Cape Breton.

What to See and Do

St. Ninian's Cathedral. (1874) Built in Roman Basilica style of blue limestone and granite from local quarries. Interior decorated by Ozias LeDuc, Paris-trained Québec artist. Gaelic words *Tigh Dhe* (House of God) appear inside and out, representing the large Scottish population in the diocese who are served by the cathedral. St. Ninian's St. Phone 902/863-2338.

Sherbrooke Village. Restored 1860s village reflects the area's former status as a prosperous river port. Historic buildings of that era are being restored and refurnished, incl family homes, a general store, drugstore, courthouse, jail, and post office; demonstrations of blacksmith forging, water-powered sawmill operation; horse-drawn wagon rides. Visitors can watch or try spinning, weaving, and quilting. Restaurant. (June-mid-Oct, daily) 40 mi S via Hwy 7, exit 32. Phone 902/522-2400. ¢¢

Special Event

Highland Games. Scottish festival; pipe bands, Highland dancing, traditional athletic events, concert, massed pipe band tattoo. Mid-July.

Motels/Motor Lodges

★★ **BEST WESTERN CLAYMORE INN.** *Church St (B2G 2M5). 902/863-1050; fax 902/863-1238; res 800/528-1234. www.bestwestern.com.* 76 rms, 3 story. July-mid-Oct: S $77-$85; D $99-$119; each addl $10; under 18 free; lower rates rest of yr. Crib free. Pet accepted. TV; cable. Indoor pool; whirlpool. Restaurant 7 am-2 pm; also 5:30-8 pm July-mid-Oct. Bar. Ck-out noon. Exercise equipt; sauna. Downhill/x-country ski 7 mi. Some minibars. Cr cds: A, D, ER, MC, V.
🔾 🏊 🖤 🏋 🖎 🐾 SC

★★ **MARITIME INN ANTIGONISH.** *158 Main St (B2G 2B7). 902/863-4001; fax 902/863-2672; toll-free 888/662-7484. www.maritimeinns.com.* 34 rms, 2 story. Mid-June-mid-Oct: S, D $103-$145; each addl $10; suites $124-$145; under 12 free; lower rates rest of yr. Crib free. Pet accepted. TV; cable. Restaurant 7 am-9 pm. Bar 4 pm-midnight. Ck-out 11 am. Sundries. Cr cds: A, D, DS, MC, V.
🔾 🐾

Hotel

★★ **HEATHER HOTEL AND CONVENTION CENTRE.** *Foord St, Stellarton (B0K 1S0). 902/752-8401; fax 902/755-4580; toll-free 800/565-4500. www.heatherhotel.com.* 77 rms, 2 story. S $64-$89; D $69-$99; each addl $10; under 12 free. Crib free. Pet accepted. TV; cable. Restaurant 7 am-10 pm. Rm serv. Bar 11 am-11 pm. Ck-out noon. Meeting rms. Business servs avail. X-country ski 5 mi. Refrigerators; minibars. Cr cds: A, D, ER, JCB, MC, V.
D 🐾 🖎 🐾 SC

Restaurant

★★ **LOBSTER TREAT.** *241 Post Rd (B2G 2K6). 902/863-5465.* Hrs: 11 am-10 pm. Closed Jan-Apr. Res accepted. Bar. Lunch $5.50-$10, dinner $7.95-$25. Child's menu. Specializes in fresh local seafood, steak, pasta. Former schoolhouse. Cr cds: A, ER, MC, V.
D

Baddeck

Pop 972 **Elev** 100 ft (30 m) **Area code** 902
Information Tourism Cape Breton, PO Box 1448, Sydney B1P 6R7; 902/563-4636 or 800/565-9464
Web www.cbisland.com

This tranquil scenic village, situated midway between Canso Causeway and Sydney, is a good headquarters community for viewing the many sights on the Cabot Trail and around the Bras d'Or lakes. Fishing, hiking, swimming, and picnicking are among favorite pastimes along the beautiful shoreline.

What to See and Do

Alexander Graham Bell National Historic Park. Three exhibition halls dealing with Bell's numerous fields of experimentation, incl displays on his work with the hearing impaired, the telephone, medicine, marine engineering, and aerodynamics. Expanded hrs, guide service June-Sept. (Daily) Chebucto St, E side of town. Phone 902/295-2069. ¢¢

The Gaelic College. Dedicated to preservation of Gaelic traditions; special summer and winter programs. 13 mi (22 km) E, at exit 11 off Trans-Canada Hwy 105 in St. Ann's. Phone 902/295-3411. On campus are

Craft Centre. Items of Scottish and Nova Scotian origins. Examples of handwoven blankets, ties, shopping bags, kilts, skirts. Phone 902/295-2101.

The Great Hall of the Clans. Colorful historic display of the Scot—origin, clans, tartans, and migrations. Genealogical and audiovisual section; life and times of Highland pioneers, relics of Cape Breton giant Angus MacAskill. Phone 902/295-3411. ¢¢

Motels/Motor Lodges

★ ★ ★ **AUBERGE GISELE'S INN.** *387 Shore Rd (B0E 1B0).*
902/295-2849; fax 902/295-2033; toll-free 800/304-0466.
www.giseles.com. 75 rms, 3 story. Late June-Dec: S, D $150-
$250; each addl $15; suites for 2, $125-$175; under 10 free;
lower rates rest of yr. Crib free. TV. Restaurant 7:30-9:30 am,
5:30-10 pm. Bar. Ck-out 10 am. Lndry facilities. Sauna.
Totally nonsmoking. Cr cds: A, DS, ER, MC, V.

★ ★ **SILVER DART LODGE.** *Shore Rd (B0E 1B0).*
902/295-2340; fax 902/295-2484; toll-free 888/662-7484.
www.silverdart.com. 88 rms, 20 A/C, 62 air-cooled, 2 story,
24 kits. Mid-June-mid-Oct: S $55-$85; D $59-$95; each
addl $8; under 16 free; suites $180-$225; cottages, kit.
units $85-$95; under 18 free; lower rates May-early June,
late Oct. Closed rest or yr. TV. Pool. Dining rm 7-9:30 am,
5:30-9 pm. Rm serv. Bar; entertainment. Ck-out 11 am.
Meeting rm. Gift shop. Tennis. Golf privileges. Lawn games.
Balconies. Private beach, dock; boat tours. Cr cds: A, ER,
MC, V.

★ ★ **TELEGRAPH HOUSE.** *479 Chebucto St*
(B0E 1B0). 902/295-1100; fax 902/295-1136.
www.baddeck.com/telegraph. 42 rms, 2-3 story. No elvtr.
July-Oct: S $57-$80; D $74-$95; each addl $8; under 6 free;
lower rates rest of yr. Crib free. TV; cable. Restaurant 7:30 am-
8:45 pm. Bar 11-2 am; entertainment. Ck-out 11 am.
Meeting rms. Golf privileges, greens fee $5. Miniature golf.
Some private patios, balconies. Family-operated since 1860.
Cr cds: A, MC, V.

Resort

★ ★ ★ **INVERARY RESORT.** *1/4 mi W on Hwy 205,*
PO Box 190 (B0E 1B6). 902/295-3500; fax 902/295-3527;
res 800/565-5660. www.inveraryresort.com. 124 rms in motel,
inn, 14 cottages, 4 kits. June-mid-Oct: S, D $95-$495; each
addl $10; kit. units $250; lower rates rest of yr. Crib $10.
TV; cable. Indoor pool; whirlpool. Playground. 2 dining
rms 7 am-3 pm, 5:30-8:30 pm; entertainment. Serv bar.
Ck-out 11 am, ck-in 3 pm. Grocery, coin lndry, package
store 2 blks. Convention facilities. Airport transportation.
Tennis. Fitness center. Exercise equipt. Private beach. Canoes,
paddleboats. Boat tours. Hiking tours. Lawn games. Sauna.
Gift shop. Some fireplaces. Balconies. Cr cds: A, DS, MC, V.

Cape Breton Highlands National Park

See also Baddeck

57 mi N on Cabot Tr.

In the northern part of Cape Breton Island, this park is
bounded on the west by the Gulf of St. Lawrence and on
the east by the Atlantic Ocean. The famous Cabot Trail,
a modern 184-mile (294-kilometer) paved highway loop
beginning at Baddeck, runs through the park, including
the scenic 66 miles (106 kilometers) between Ingonish
and Cheticamp offering visitors spectacular vistas.

Along the western shore steep hills, to a height of over
1,116 feet (335 meters), rise sharply from the gulf, affording magnificent views of the gulf and the broad plateau
covering most of the park interior. The eastern shore is
also rocky, indented with numerous coves at the mouths
of picturesque valleys. The interior, least seen by visitors,
is an area similar to subarctic regions.

Except for the interior, the 370-square-mile (950-
square-kilometer) park is covered with a typical Acadian
forest of mixed conifers and hardwoods. The interior is
covered with heath bogs, and along the seacoast headlands
the trees are stunted and twisted into grotesque shapes.

The park is home to many types of wildlife. Moose
are numerous and often seen along the highways. Other
animals native to the region range from black bear and
whitetail deer to smaller species such as lynx, red fox, and
snowshoe hare. Among the approximately 200 species of
birds to be seen are the red-tailed hawk and bald eagle.

The park is open all year but many facilities operate
only from mid-May-late October. Information centers are
maintained at Ingonish and Cheticamp, the main park
entrances along the Cabot Trail. Plan to stop at these
facilities, as the staff on duty can provide the latest information on what to see and do within the park. Roadside
picnic areas are provided and a variety of self-guiding trails
and interpretive events held during summer encourage
visitors to learn more about the park's significant areas
and features. All visitors must have a park entry permit,
which allows access to Cabot Trail, sightseeing facilities,
beaches, and trails. Permit ¢¢¢

One of the best ways to see the park is on foot. The
hiking trail system is large and diverse, providing access
to the area's remote interior as well as allowing you to
explore its rugged coastline. After a hike visitors can enjoy
a refreshing saltwater swim or just relax on one of the several developed natural sand beaches located within the park.

Golf is another popular sport in the park. The Highlands
Golf Links in Ingonish is one of the best 18-hole courses
in Canada.

Deep sea fishing is popular, with local fishermen providing transportation and equipment. For those interested in
freshwater fishing, a national park permit can be obtained
at park information centers; the season generally runs from
mid-April through September. There are fully equipped
campgrounds on the Cabot Trail as well as primitive
campsites on the coast.

Resort

★ ★ ★ **KELTIC LODGE.** *Middle Head Peninsula, Ingonish*
Beach (B0C 1L0). 902/285-2880; fax 902/285-2859; toll-free
800/565-0444. www.signatureresorts.com. 104 units, 32 in
lodge, 3 story, 2-, 4-bedrm cottages. MAP: S $221-$236;

D $301-$316; each addl $75; cottages $316; golf plans. Closed Jan-May, Nov-Dec. TV; cable. Heated pool. Dining rm 7-10 am, noon-2 pm, 6-9 pm. Bar. Ck-out 11 am, ck-in 3 pm. Package store 1 mi. Grocery, coin lndry 5 mi. Convention facilities. Business servs avail. Gift shop. Tennis privileges. Golf privileges, pro, greens fee $55, putting green. Exercise equipt. Lawn games. Some fireplaces. National park adj. Cr cds: A, D, DS, ER, MC, V.

⬛ 🏃 🏋️ 🏌️ 🏊 🔥 🛶

Dartmouth

See also Halifax

Founded 1750 **Pop** 62,277 **Elev** 75 ft (23 m) **Area code** 902
Information Halifax Regional Municipality Tourism Department, PO Box 1749, Halifax B3J 3A5; 902/490-5946
Web www.halifaxinfo.com

On the eastern side of Halifax Harbour, Dartmouth is Canada's "newest" city (incorporated in 1961) whose history extends back to the 18th century. The opening of the Angus L. MacDonald Bridge in 1955, a direct link to Halifax, and the Murray A. MacKay Bridge helped to make this an industrial city—with the largest naval bases in Canada, oil refineries, and the Bedford Institute of Oceanography. The 22 lakes within its borders make Dartmouth a swimmer's paradise.

What to See and Do

Black Cultural Centre. History and culture of African Americans in Nova Scotia. Library; exhibit rms; auditorium. (Daily) 1149 Main St, Rte 7 at Cherrybrook Rd. Phone 902/434-6223 or 800/465-0767. ¢¢

Quaker Whaler's House. Restored 1785 house. (July-Aug, daily) 59 Ochterloney St. Phone 902/464-2253. **Donation**

Shearwater Aviation Museum. Extensive collection of aircraft and exhibits on the history of Canadian Maritime Military Aviation. Art gallery; photo collection. (Apr-June and Sept-Nov, Tues, Wed, Fri, daily; July-Aug, Tues-Fri, Sat, Sun afternoons; rest of yr by appt) 13 Bonaventure Ave, at Shearwater Airport. Phone 902/460-1083. **Donation**

Swimming. Supervised beach, 12 mi (19 km) E on Marine Dr, Rte 207. Many others within city.

Special Event

Dartmouth Natal Day. Lake Banook. Parade, sports events, rowing and paddling regattas, entertainment, fireworks. First Mon Aug. Phone 800/565-0000.

Motels/Motor Lodges

★★ **BURNSIDE.** *739 Windmill Rd (Hwy 7) (B3B 1C1). 902/468-7117; fax 902/468-1770; res 800/830-4656.* 92 rms, 3 story. S $59; D, suites $79-$99; each addl $10; under 16 free. TV; cable (premium). Pool. Restaurant 8 am-11:30 pm. Ck-out noon. Meeting rms. Business center. Valet serv. Some minibars; microwaves avail. Cr cds: A, D, DS, ER, MC, V.

🏊 🏋️ 🔥 SC 🏃

★★ **PARK PLACE RAMADA PLAZA.** *240 Brownlow Ave (B3B 1X6). 902/468-8888; fax 902/468-8765; res 800/561-3733. www.ramada.com.* 178 rms, 5 story, 31 suites. May-Oct: S $150-$180; D $160-$190; each addl $10; suites $129; under 15 free; package plans; lower rates rest of yr. Crib $10. Pet accepted, some restrictions; $50 deposit. TV; cable. Indoor pool; wading pool, whirlpool, lifeguard. Complimentary coffee in rms. Restaurant 6:30 am-10 pm. Bar 11-1 am. Meeting rms. Business center. Gift shop. X-country ski 1 mi. Exercise equipt; sauna. Many minibars; microwaves avail. Cr cds: A, C, D, ER, JCB, MC, V.

⬛ 🏊 🏋️ 🏃 🔥 SC 🏃

★ **SEASONS MOTOR INN.** *40 Lakecrest Dr (B2X 1V1). 902/435-0060; fax 902/435-0804; toll-free 800/792-2497.* 42 rms, 2 story. June-mid-Oct: S, D $63-$68; each addl $10; under 13 free; wkly rates; lower rates rest of yr. TV; cable. Ck-out 11 am. Restaurant nearby. Business servs avail. Coin lndry. X-country ski 5 mi. Refrigerators avail. Cr cds: A, MC, V.

🏊 🔥 SC

Hotel

★★ **HOLIDAY INN HARBOURVIEW.** *101 Wyse Rd (B3A 1L9). 902/463-1100; fax 902/464-1227; res 888/434-0440. www.holiday-inn.com.* 196 rms, 7 story. May-Oct: S, D $129-$139; each addl $10; suites $195-$395; under 19 free; wkend rates; lower rates rest of yr. Crib free. Pet accepted, some restrictions. TV; cable. Heated pool. Restaurant 7 am-10:30 pm. Bar 11-1 am. Ck-out noon. Business servs avail. In-rm modem link. Airport transportation. X-country ski 15 mi. Health club privileges. Microwaves avail. Some balconies. Cr cds: A, D, DS, MC, V.

⬛ 🏊 🏊 🏃 🔥

Restaurant

★★ **ROCCO'S.** *300 Prince Albert Rd (B2Y 4J2). 902/461-0211.* Italian menu. Specializes in chicken, seafood, veal. Hrs: 11:30 am-2:30 pm, 5-10 pm; Sat 5-10 pm. Closed Sun; Jan 1, Dec 24, 25. Res accepted. Bar. A la carte entrees: lunch $8-$10, dinner $12-$25. Child's menu. View of lake. Cr cds: A, D, DS, ER, MC, V.

🏃

Digby

Pop 2,558 **Elev** 50 ft (15 m) **Area code** 902
Information Tourist Information Bureau, 110 Montague Row, PO Box 579, B0V 1A0; 902/245-5714 or 902/245-4769 (winter) or 888/463-4429

Best known for its delicious scallops and harbor sights, this summer resort has many historic landmarks which trace its founding in 1783 by Sir Robert Digby and 1500 Loyalists from New England and New York. This Annapolis Basin town is the ideal headquarters for a day drive southwest down the Digby Neck peninsula, whose shores are washed by the Bay of Fundy with the highest tides in the world.

Off Digby Neck are two islands which may be reached by ferry: Long Island and Brier Island, popular sites for rockhounding, whale watching, and bird-watching. Swimming along the sandy beaches and hiking the shores are favorite pastimes in this area of dashing spray, lighthouses, and wildflower-filled forests. A 35-mile (11-kilometer) drive to the northeast ends in Annapolis Royal and Port Royal, the first permanent European settlements in North America. Marking this is the restored fur trading fort, the Habitation of Port Royal, built by Samuel de Champlain. With high imposing cliffs, gently rolling farmland, and quiet woodland settings, this seacoast drive creates a study in contrasts.

What to See and Do

Ferry Service to St. John, NB. Car and passenger; all yr; summer, up to three times daily. Contact BAY Ferries, 94 Water St, PO Box 634, Charlottetown, PEI, C1A 7L3. Phone 888/249-7245.

Fishermen's Wharf. View one of the largest scallop fleets in the world. Phone 888/463-4429.

Fort Anne National Historic Site. Built between 1702-1708 in one of the central areas of conflict between the English and French for control of North America. Of the original site, only the 18th-century earthworks and a gunpowder magazine (1708) remain. Museum in restored officers' quarters. On grounds is Canada's oldest English graveyard, dating from 1720. (Mid-May-mid-Oct, daily; rest of yr, Mon-Fri; closed hols) 28 mi E on Hwy 1, Annapolis Royal exit. Phone 902/532-2397 or 902/532-2321. **FREE**

Pines Golf Course. An 18-hole championship golf course on provincially owned and operated resort (see RESORTS). Phone 902/245-2511.

Point Prim Lighthouse. Rocky promontory with view of Bay of Fundy. Lighthouse Rd. Phone 888/463-4429.

Port Royal National Historic Site. Reconstructed 17th-century fur trading post built by Sieur de Mons; follows plans, building techniques of that era. (Mid-May-mid-Oct, daily) 23 mi (38 km) NE via Rte 1, then 6 mi (10 km) W on Port Royal exit in Annapolis Royal. Phone 902/532-2898. ¢¢

Trinity Church. Only church in Canada built by shipwrights; church cemetery famous for inscriptions of pioneer settlers. (Mon-Fri) Queen St. Phone 888/463-4429.

Special Event

Scallop Days. Scallop-shucking contests; grand parade, pet show, entertainment; sporting, fishing, water events. Second wk Aug. Phone 902/245-4531.

Motels/Motor Lodges

★★ **ADMIRAL DIGBY INN.** *441 Shore Rd (B0V 1A0). 902/245-2531; fax 902/245-2533; toll-free 800/465-6262. www.digbyns.com.* 46 rms, 2 kit. cottages. Mid-June-mid-Sept: S, D $99-$110; each addl $10; kit. cottages $135; under 12 free; lower rates Apr-mid-June and mid-Sept-Oct. Closed rest of yr. Crib $6. Pet accepted. TV; cable. Heated pool. Restaurant 7:30-10:30 am, 5-9 pm. Bar 5-10 pm. Ck-out 11 am. Coin lndry. Business servs avail. Sundries. Gift shop. Overlooks Annapolis Basin. Cr cds: A, D, DS, MC, V.

⬛ 🐾 ⚓ 🛏

★★ **COASTAL INN KINGFISHER.** *111 Warwick St (B0V 1A0). 902/245-4747; fax 902/245-4866; toll-free 800/401-1155.* 36 rms. S $84; D $89; each addl $8; under 10 free; some lower rates. Crib free. Pet accepted. TV; cable. Playground. Restaurant 7 am-8:30 pm; Sat, Sun 8 am-8:30 pm. Ck-out 11 am. Coin lndry. Meeting rm. Business servs avail. Microwaves avail. Picnic tables. Beach 4 mi. Cr cds: A, D, ER, MC, V.

⬛ 🐾 ⚓ 🛏 🔥

Resorts

★★ **MOUNTAIN GAP RESORT.** *217 Hwy 1, Smith's Cove (B0V 1A0). 902/245-5841; fax 902/245-2277; toll-free 800/565-5020. www.mountaingap.ns.ca.* 96 rms, 12 cottages. No A/C. Mid-May-mid-Oct: S, D $90; each addl $10; kit. units, kit. cottages $159-$199; under 18 free; wkly rates. Closed rest of yr. Crib free. Pet accepted. TV; cable, VCR avail (movies). Heated pool. Playground. Dining rms 7:30-9:30 am, noon-2 pm, 5:30-9 pm. Bar 5:30 pm-midnight. Ck-out 11 am, ck-in 2 pm. Grocery store 1 mi. Business servs avail. Gift shop. Private beach. Tennis. 18-hole golf privileges. Lawn games. Bicycle rentals. Soc dir. Game rm. Private patios, grills. Rustic setting on 45 acres. Cr cds: A, D, DS, ER, MC, V.

⬛ 🐾 ⚓ 🍴 🎿 🏊 ✈ 🛏 🔥

★★★ **THE PINES RESORT.** *103 Shore Rd (B0V 1A0). 902/245-2511; fax 902/245-6133. www.signatureresorts.com.* 84 rms, 3 story, 30 cottages. May-mid Oct: S $162; D $189; each addl $20; suites $299; MAP: $45/person addl; family rates. Closed rest of yr. Crib free. TV; cable. Heated pool; poolside serv. Playground. Dining rm (public by res) 7-10 am, noon-2 pm, 6-9 pm. Limited rm serv. Bar 5-11 pm. Ck-out 11 am, ck-in 3 pm. Grocery store 2 mi. Gift shop. Meeting rms. Business servs avail. Bellhops. Lighted tennis. 18-hole golf, greens fee $55, pro, driving range. Exercise equipt; sauna. Lawn games. Nature trails. Bicycles (rentals). Soc dir. Fireplace in cottages. Balconies. Veranda. On 300 acres; overlooks Annapolis Basin of Bay of Fundy. Cr cds: A, D, DS, ER, MC, V.

⬛ 🐾 🍴 🎿 🏊 🛏 🔥

Restaurant

★★ **FUNDY.** *34 Water St (B0V 1A0). 902/245-4950. www.fundyrestaurant.com.* Specializes in seafood. Hrs: 7 am-10 pm; winter from 11 am. Closed Jan 1, Dec 25. Res accepted. Bar 11-2 am. A la carte entrees: bkfst $3.50-$8, lunch $4.95-$13.90, dinner $8.95-$24.95. Child's menu. Outdoor dining. Solarium dining area. On Annapolis basin. Cr cds: A, D, DS, ER, MC, V.

Fortress of Louisbourg National Historic Site

See also Baddeck

(On Cape Breton Island, 22 mi or 35 km south of Sydney via Highway 22)

This 11,860-acre (4,800-hectare) park includes the massive Fortress erected by the French between 1720-45 to defend their possessions in the New World. Under the terms of the Treaty of Utrecht (1713), France lost Newfoundland and Acadia but was permitted to keep Cape Breton Island (Isle Royale) and Prince Edward Island (Isle Saint-Jean). English Harbour, renamed Louisbourg, was then selected by the French as the most suitable point for an Atlantic stronghold. It served as headquarters for a large fishing fleet and became an important trading center. Later it was used as the base for French privateers preying on New England shipping.

In 1745, after a 47-day siege, Louisbourg was captured by a volunteer force from New England led by Colonel William Pepperrell and a British fleet under Commodore Warren. Three years later the colony was returned to France by the treaty of Aix-la-Chapelle. In the Seven Years' War Louisbourg, after being twice blockaded by British fleets, was finally captured in 1758. In 1760 its fortifications were demolished. Reconstruction of about ¼ of 18th-century Louisbourg is complete.

On the grounds and open are the Governor's apartment, the soldiers' barracks, the chapel, various guardhouses, the Dauphin Demi-Bastion, the King's storehouse, the Engineer's house, the residence of the commissaire-ordonnateur, several private dwellings and storehouses, and the royal bakery. At the Hôtel de la Marine, L'Epée Royale, and Grandchamps Inn visitors can sample food in the manner of the 18th-century, while period pastries may be enjoyed at the Destouches house and soldiers' bread purchased at the bakery. Costumed guides interpret the town as it was in 1744 with tours in English and French. Exhibits at various points inside and outside the reconstructed area; walking tours. Park (June-Sept, daily; May and Oct, limited tours). An average visit takes 4-5 hrs; comfortable shoes and warm clothes are advised. ¢¢- ¢¢¢

Restaurant

★★ **GRUBSTAKE.** *7499 Main St, Louisbourg (B0A 1M0). 902/733-2308. www.sealevel.ns.ca/grubstake/home.html.* Specializes in seafood, steak. Hrs: noon-9 pm. Closed Oct-mid-June. Lunch $5.95-$12, dinner $10.95-$43. Early 1800s building. Totally nonsmoking Cr cds: A, C, MC, V.
⊡

Grand Pre

Pop 305 **Elev** 125 ft (38 m) **Area code** 902

Information Nova Scotia Department of Tourism & Culture, PO Box 130, Halifax B3J 2M7; 902/490-5946 or 800/565-0000

Web www.explore.gov.ns

Site of one of the earliest French settlements in North America, this was the setting for Henry Wadsworth Longfellow's poem "Evangeline," which describes the tragic tale of the expulsion of the Acadians by the British in 1755. Its name refers to the extensively diked lands and means "the great meadow." Wolfville, nearby, is the center of the land of Evangeline and the starting point to memorable historic places.

What to See and Do

Grand Pré National Historic Site. Memorial to the Acadian people. Museum (mid-May-mid-Oct). Grounds and gardens (all yr). Phone 902/542-3631. On grounds is

  Acadian Memorial Church. Display commemorating Acadian settlement and expulsion. Old Acadian Forge; bust of Longfellow; "Evangeline" statue; formal landscaped gardens with original French willows. Guides avail. Phone 902/490-5946. **FREE**

Motels/Motor Lodges

★★ **GREENSBORO INN.** *9016 Commercial St, New Minas (B4N 3E2). 902/681-3201; fax 902/681-3399; res 800/561-3201. www.greensboroinn.com.* 26 rms. 1 kit. unit. Mid May-Oct: S $70; D $70-$90, kit. unit $110; under 18 free; each addl $6; lower rates rest of yr. Pet accepted. TV; cable. Indoor pool. Complimentary coffee in lobby. Restaurant adj 11 am-10 pm. Ck-out 11 am. Golf privileges. Downhill/x-country ski 20 mi. Picnic tables. Cr cds: A, D, ER, MC, V.
◐ ⊠ ⊠ ⊠ ⊠ SC

★ **SLUMBER INN-NEW MINAS.** *5534 Prospect Rd, New Minas (D4N 3K8). 902/681-5000; res 800/914-5005.* 79 rms, shower only, 2 story. No elvtr. S, D $75-$100; under 12 free. TV; cable (premium); VCR (movies). Restaurant opp. Ck-out 11 am. Business servs avail. Downhill/x-country ski 20 mi. Cr cds: A, D, ER, MC, V.
⊡ ⊠ ⊠ ⊠ SC

★★★ **WANDLYN INN.** *7270 Hwy 1, Kentville (B4R 1B9). 902/678-8311; fax 902/679-1253; res 800/561-0000. www.wandlyn.com.* 70 units, 3 story. Mid-June-Oct: S $85-$110; D $95-$120; each addl $10; suites $110-$125; under 18 free; lower rates rest of yr. Pet accepted, $10. TV; cable, VCR avail. Indoor pool. Restaurant 7 am-9 pm. Bar noon-2 am. Ck-out 11 am. Meeting rms. Business servs avail. Some refrigerators. Picnic tables. Cr cds: A, DS, MC, V.
◐ ⊠ ⊠

Resort

★★ **OLD ORCHARD INN.** *Hwy 101, exit 11, Wolfville (B0P 1X0).* 902/542-5751; fax 902/542-2276; toll-free 800/561-8090. www.oldorchardinn.com. 105 rms, 3 story, 29 cabins, 10 kits. May-Oct: S, D $115-$125; each addl $8; suites $150; cabins $59-$64 (with kit. $15 addl); family rates; ski plans. Crib free. TV; cable. Indoor pool. Sauna. Playground. Supervised children's activities (winter); ages 5-12. Dining rm 7 am-9 pm. Bar to 2 am. Ck-out 11 am. Coin lndry 3 mi. Meeting rms. Business center. Grocery, package store 3 mi. Lighted tennis. 18-hole golf privileges. Downhill ski 20 mi; x-country ski on site. Sleigh rides. Lawn games. Some private patios. Picnic tables. Cr cds: A, D, MC, V.

[icons]

B&Bs/Small Inns

★★★ **BLOMIDON.** *127 Main St, Wolfville (B0P 1X0).* 902/542-2291; fax 902/542-7461. www.blomidon.ns.ca. 28 rms, 3 story, 5 suites. May-Oct: S $79-$129; D $79-$139; each addl $12; suites $139; lower rates rest of yr. Crib $12. TV in sitting rm; cable, VCR avail. Complimentary continental bkfst; afternoon refreshments. Dining rm 11:30 am-2 pm, 5-9:30 pm. Ck-out 11 am, ck-in 3 pm. Meeting rms. Business servs avail. Tennis. Shuffleboard. Library, 2 parlors; antiques. Sea captain's mansion (1879) on 4 acres; period decor. Cr cds: A, D, MC, V.

[icons]

★★★ **TATTINGSTONE INN.** *434 Main St, Wolfville (B0P 1X0).* 902/542-7696; fax 902/542-4427; toll-free 800/565-7696. www.tattingstoneinn.com. 10 rms, 2 story. Apr-Oct: S, D $85-$158; lower rates rest of yr. TV; cable. Heated pool; steam rm, poolside serv. Dining rm 5-9 pm. Ck-out 11 am, ck-in 3 pm. Business servs avail. Lighted tennis. Some in-rm whirlpools. Former residence (1874), landscaped with many unusual trees. Victorian and Georgian period antiques. Totally nonsmoking. Cr cds: A, D, DS, MC, V.

[icons]

★★★ **VICTORIA'S HISTORIC INN.** *600 Main St, Wolfville (B0P 1X0).* 902/542-5744; fax 902/542-7794; toll-free 800/556-5744. www.victoriahistoricinn.com. 15 rms, 3 story. May-Oct: S, D $98-$225; each addl $20; suite $225; lower rates rest of yr. Complimentary full bkfst. Rm serv. Ck-out 11 am, ck-in 3 pm. Business servs avail. Some balconies. Historic inn built in 1893; period furnishings. Totally nonsmoking. Cr cds: A, MC, V.

Restaurant

★ **PADDY'S PUB AND BREWERY.** *42 Aberdeen St, Kentville (B4W 2N1).* 902/678-3199. www.paddysbrewpub.com. Irish, continental menu. Specializes in fish and chips, steak, seafood. Hrs: 11 am-midnight; Fri, Sat to 1 am; Sun to 11 pm; Sun brunch to 3 pm. Closed Dec 25, 26. Res accepted. Bar. Lunch $3-$7, dinner $5-$15. Sun brunch $4-$9. Child's menu. Entertainment Fri, Sat. Irish pub atmosphere. Cr cds: A, D, ER, JCB, MC, V.

[icons]

Halifax

See also Peggy's Cove

Founded 1749 **Pop** 340,000 **Elev** 25-225 ft (8-69 m)
Area code 902
Information International Visitors Centre, 1595 Barrington St, B3J 1Z9; 902/490-5946 or 800/565-0000
Web www.explorens.com

Capital of Nova Scotia, this largest city in the Atlantic provinces offers a delightful combination of old and new. Founded in 1749 to establish British strength in the North Atlantic, it is growing rapidly as a commercial, scientific, and educational center while continuing to preserve its natural heritage. Centrally situated in the province, it is perfectly suited as the starting point for the Evangeline and Glooscap Trails, the Lighthouse Route, and the Marine Drive with their scenic and historic sights. Located on Bedford Basin, the world's second-largest natural harbor, Halifax recently merged with the town of Dartmouth; this area lies across the harbor and is reached via the MacDonald and MacKay bridges.

What to See and Do

Art Gallery of Nova Scotia. More than 2,000 works on permanent display, incl folk art; changing exhibits. (Tues-Sat, also Sun afternoons; closed hols) Free admission Tues. 1741 Hollis-at-Cheapside. Phone 902/424-7542. ¢¢

Bluenose II. Exact replica of famed racing schooner depicted on Canadian dime; public cruises in Nova Scotia waters. At waterfront. Contact Bluenose Preservation Trust. Phone 800/565-0000.

Chapel of Our Lady of Sorrows. Built in one day by 2,000 men; altar carvings date from 1750. South & S Park Sts.

Churches.

St. George's Round Church. (1801) Anglican; Byzantine-style church built at the direction of Edward, Duke of Kent, father of Queen Victoria. Nearby is **St. Patrick's Roman Catholic Church**, a Victorian Gothic building still largely untouched by change. **St. Paul's Church** (1750). Barrington St. First church in Halifax and oldest Protestant church in Canada. "Explosion window" on Argyle St side; during 1917 explosion that destroyed a large portion of the city, the third window of the upper gallery shattered, leaving the silhouette of a human head. Tours (summer; free). (June-Sept, daily) Brunswick and Cornwallis Sts.

Halifax Citadel National Historic Park. Star-shaped hilltop fort built 1828-1856 on site of previous fortifications. Excellent view of city and harbor. Audiovisual presentation "Tides of History" (50 min). Restored signal masts, library, barrack rms, powder magazine, expense magazine, defense casemate, and garrison cell. Exhibits on communications, the four Citadels, and engineering and construction. Army Museum; orientation center. Coffee bar serving typical 19th-century soldiers' food; sales outlet; guided tours, military displays by uniformed students, bagpipe music, changing of the guard (summer). (Daily; closed Jan 1,

Good Friday, Dec 25) Entrances on Sackville St and Rainnie Dr. Phone 902/426-5080. Fee charged June 15-Labour Day ¢ On grounds are

Maritime Museum of the Atlantic. 1675 exhibits of nautical history incl *Titanic: The Unsinkable Ship* and *Halifax, Halifax Wrecked: The Story of the Halifax Explosion.* (Mid-May-mid-Oct, daily; rest of yr, Tues-Sun; closed hols) Lower Water St. Phone 902/424-7490. **Donation**

Town Clock. (1803) Halifax's most recognized landmark. Built under supervision of Prince Edward, Duke of Kent, father of Queen Victoria. Phone 902/426-5080.

Historic Properties (Privateers Wharf). Variety of clothing, specialty shops, restaurants, and pubs housed in several restored 18th-century buildings along the waterfront. (Daily) 1869-70 Upper Water St. Phone 902/429-0530.

Neptune Theatre. Home of internationally recognized theater company; presents five main stage plays per season. Small intimate theater with excellent acoustics. Res advised. Corner of Argyle and Sackville Sts. Phone 902/429-7070 or 902/429-7300.

Nova Scotia Museum of Natural History. Permanent exhibits on man and his environment in Nova Scotia; changing exhibits. (June-mid-Oct, daily; rest of yr, Tues-Sun; closed Jan 1, Good Friday, Dec 25) 1747 Summer St. Phone 902/424-7353. ¢¢

Pier 21. Canada's "Ellis Island"; between 1928-1971, more than a million immigrants and wartime evacuees took their first steps on Canadian soil at Pier 21. Now a National Historic Site, the Pier features traveling exhibits, live performances, Wall of Ships, Immigrant Testimonial Stations, and Wall of Honour. (Tues-Sun) 1055 Marginal Rd. Phone 902/425-7770. ¢¢

Point Pleasant Park. Remains of several forts. Nature trail, monuments, public beach, picnic areas; cross-country skiing. (Daily) Point Pleasant Dr. Phone 902/421-6519. **FREE** On grounds is

Prince of Wales Tower National Historic Park. (1796-1797) Built to protect British batteries; said to be first tower of its type in North America. Exhibits portray tower's history, architectural features, and significance as a defensive structure. (July-Labour Day, daily) Phone 902/426-5080. **FREE**

Province House. Oldest provincial Parliament building in Canada; office of Premier; legislative library. Guided tours (Mon-Fri; special summer hrs). Hollis St. Phone 902/424-8967. **FREE**

Public Archives of Nova Scotia. Provincial government records; private manuscripts; maps, photos, genealogies; film and sound archives; library. (Tues-Sat; closed hols) 6016 University Ave, S end of town. Phone 902/424-6060. **FREE**

Public Gardens. A 16¾ acre (seven-hectare) formal Victorian garden with trees, flower beds, fountains; bandstand; duck ponds; concession. (See SPECIAL EVENTS) (May-Nov, daily) Spring Garden Rd and S Park St. Phone 902/421-6550. **FREE**

Sightseeing tours.

Double Decker Tours. City tours on double-decker, English-style bus. Tours last approx 1½ hrs. Multiple departure points. (June-Oct, daily) Phone 902/420-1155. ¢¢¢¢

Gray Line bus tours. Phone 800/565-9662; **Cabana Tours**, PO Box 8683, Station A, B3K 5M4, phone 902/423-6066; **Markland Tours**, multilingual minivan tours, phone 902/499-2939

Harbour Hopper Tours. Narrated tours in amphibious vehicles styled after WWII landing craft. (May-Oct, daily) Phone 902/490-8687.

Murphy's on the Water. Three boats. Live narration and historical commentary; 2-hr tour. (May-mid-Oct, daily) Murphy's Pier next to Historic Properties. Phone 902/420-1015. ¢¢¢¢

York Redoubt National Historic Site. (1793) A 200-yr-old fortification on high bluff overlooking harbor entrance. Features muzzle-loading guns, photo display, picnic facilities, information service. Grounds (daily). (Mid-June-Labour Day, daily) 6 mi (9.7 km) SW via Purcell's Cove Rd. Phone 902/426-5050. **FREE**

Special Events

Winterfest. Feb.

Multicultural Festival. June. Phone 902/423-6534.

The Nova Scotia International Tattoo. Halifax Metro Centre. Ten-day event with military bands, pipes and drums, choirs, gymnasts, dancers, military displays and competitions. Phone 902/451-1221. Late June-early July.

Atlantic Jazz Festival. July. Phone 902/492-2225.

Highland games. July. Phone 902/469-2023.

Public Gardens Band Concerts. Sun afternoons. July-Aug. Phone 902/490-4895.

International Buskerfest. Aug. Phone 902/429-3910.

Nova Scotia Air Show. Sept.

Motels/Motor Lodges

★★ **BLUENOSE INN AND SUITES.** *636 Bedford Hwy (B3N 2L8).* 902/443-3171; fax 902/443-9368. 51 units, 1-2 story, 17 kit. suites. June-Oct: S, D $79-$89; each addl $7; kit. suites $89-$99; some wkly rates; lower rates rest of yr. Crib free. Pet accepted, $7. TV; cable. Playground. Restaurant 7-10 pm (off-season). Bar. Ck-out 11 am. Meeting rms. Balconies. Picnic tables. Cr cds: A, C, D, DS, ER, MC, V.

D 🐾 🖂 🐾

★ **GRAND VIEW.** *Black Point (B0J 1B0).* 902/857-9776; toll-free 881/591-5122. www.grandviewmotelandcottages.com. 13 rms, 10 kit. units, 2 cottages. No A/C. No rm phones. Mid-June-early Sept: S, D $55-$85; each addl $10; cottages $95-$110; under 5 free; wkly rates; lower rates rest of yr. Crib free. Pet accepted. TV; cable. Playground. Coffee in rms. Ck-out 10:30 am. Near swimming beach; all rms have view of St. Margaret's Bay. Cr cds: A, MC, V.

🐾 🌲 🖂 🐾

★ ★ **HOLIDAY INN SELECT HALIFAX CENTRE.** *1980 Robie St (B3H 3G5). 902/423-1161; fax 902/423-9069; res 888/810-7288. www.holiday-inn.com.* 232 rms, 14 story. S, D $125-$149.95; each addl $10; suites $195-$225; under 19 free; wkend rates. Crib free. Pet accepted. TV; cable. Indoor pool; wading pool, whirlpool, poolside serv. Complimentary coffee in rms. Restaurant 6:30 am-11 pm. Rm serv. Bars noon-1 am. Ck-out 1 pm. Meeting rms. Business center. In-rm modem link. Sundries. Indoor parking. Exercise equipt; sauna. Health club privileges. Microwaves avail. Cr cds: A, C, D, DS, ER, JCB, MC, V.

⬛ 🔧 🏊 🍽 ⬛ 🔥 ⬛ SC 🏃

★ **SEASONS MOTOR INN.** *4 Melrose Ave (B3N 2E2). 902/443-9341; fax 902/443-9344; toll-free 800/792-2498.* 37 rms, 20 air-cooled, 4 story. June-Oct: S $70; D $80; each addl $5; under 12 free; lower rates rest of yr. Pet accepted, some restrictions. TV; cable. Complimentary continental bkfst. Ck-out 11 am. Cr cds: A, MC, V.

🔧 ⬛ 🔥 ⬛

★ ★ **STARDUST.** *1791 St. Margarets Bay Rd (B3T 1B8). 902/876-2301.* 21 rms, 15 kit. units (no equipt.). June-Oct: S $89-$119; D $99-$129; each addl $10; suites $129-$169; under 12 free; wkly rates; lower rates rest of yr. TV; cable. Ck-out 11 am. Restaurant nearby. In-rm modem link. Picnic tables. On lake. Cr cds: A, D, ER, MC, V.

⬛ 🔧

★ ★ **STARDUST.** *1067 Bedford Hwy, Bedford (B4A 1B5). 902/835-3316; fax 902/835-4973.* 50 rms, 42 A/C, 3 story, 32 kits. June-Oct: S $69-$99; D $79-$109; each addl $10; family rms $89-$119; 2-bedrm apts $150-$200; under 12 free; lower rates rest of yr. Crib $5. Pet accepted. TV; cable. Restaurant 7 am-10 pm. Serv bar. Ck-out 11 am. Sundries. Some refrigerators. On Bedford Basin. Cr cds: A, ER, MC, V.

🔧 ⬛ 🔥 SC

★ ★ **WANDLYN INN HALIFAX.** *50 Bedford Hwy (B3M 2J2). 902/443-0416; fax 902/443-1353; res 800/561-0000. www.wandlyn.com.* 66 rms, 2 story. June-Sept: S $60-$85; D $65-$95; each addl $10; suites $95-$150; under 18 free; lower rates rest of yr. Pet accepted. TV, VCR avail (movies). Restaurant 7-11 am, 5-9 pm. Ck-out noon. Meeting rms. Business servs avail. Sundries. Exercise equipt. Microwaves avail. Ocean view from some rms. Cr cds: A, DS, MC, V.

⬛ 🔧 🏃 ⬛

Hotels

★ ★ ★ **AIRPORT HOTEL HALIFAX.** *60 Bell Blvd, Enfield (B2T 1K3). 902/873-3000; fax 902/873-3001; res 800/667-3333.* 151 rms, 3 story. No elvtr. May-Nov: S $124; D, kit. units $134; each addl $10; suites $160; under 18 free; lower rates rest of yr. Crib avail. Pet accepted. TV; cable. 2 pools, 1 indoor; whirlpool. Restaurant 5 am-10 pm. Rm serv. Bar. Ck-out noon. Meeting rms. Business servs avail. In-rm modem link. Free airport transportation. Exercise equipt; sauna. Some refrigerators, minibars; microwaves avail. Cr cds: A, D, DS, ER, MC, V.

🔧 🏊 🍽 ✈ ⬛ 🔥 ⬛

★ ★ ★ **CASINO NOVA SCOTIA HOTEL.** *1919 Upper Water St (B3J 3J5). 902/421-1700; fax 902/422-5805. www.casinonovascotia.com.* 352 rms, 6 story. S, D $94-$335; each addl $20; suites $335-$1,000; under 18 free. Crib free. Pet accepted. Parking $10. TV; cable. Indoor pool; whirlpool poolside serv. Complimentary coffee in rms. Restaurant 6:30 am-10 pm. Bars 4 pm-2 am; entertainment. Ck-out noon. Convention facilities. Business center. In-rm modem link. Concierge. Exercise equipt; sauna. Casino. Cr cds: A, C, D, DS, JCB, MC, V.

⬛ 🔧 🍽 🏊 🏃 ✈ 🏃

★ ★ ★ **CITADEL.** *1960 Brunswick St (B3J 2G7). 902/422-1391; fax 902/429-6672. www.citadelhalifax.com.* 264 rms, 7 and 11 story. S, D $139-$189; each addl $15; suites $250-$305; wkend rates; under 18 free. Crib free. Pet accepted, some restrictions. TV; cable. Indoor pool; whirlpool, poolside serv. Restaurant 7 am-3 pm, 5-11 pm. Bar 11 am-midnight. Ck-out 1 pm. Meeting rms. Business center. In-rm modem link. Exercise equipt; sauna. Minibars; some refrigerators. Private patios, balconies. Cr cds: A, D, ER, MC, V.

⬛ 🔧 🔧 🏊 🍽 ⬛ 🔧 🏃

★ ★ ★ **DELTA BARRINGTON.** *1875 Barrington St (B3J 3L6). 902/429-7410; fax 902/420-6524. www.deltahotels.com.* 202 rms, 4 story. S, D $189-$249; each addl $15; suites $289-$475; under 18 free; wkend rates; some lower rates. Crib free. Pet accepted, some restrictions. Parking $18.95. TV; cable. Indoor pool; whirlpool. Restaurant 6:30 am-2:30 pm, 5-9:30 pm. Rm serv to midnight. Bar. Ck-out 1 pm. Meeting rms. Business servs avail. In-rm modem link. Bellhops. Valet serv. Shopping arcade. Barber, beauty shop. Exercise equipt; sauna. Minibars; microwaves avail. Cr cds: A, D, DS, ER, MC, V.

⬛ 🔧 🔧 🍽 🏊 🍽 ⬛ 🔥 🏃

★ ★ ★ **DELTA HALIFAX.** *1990 Barrington St (B3J 1P2). 902/425-6700; fax 902/425-6214; res 800/268-1133. www.deltahotels.com.* 300 rms, 8 story. S, D $109-$389; each addl $20; suites $195-$400; under 18 free. Crib free. Pet accepted, some restrictions. Valet parking $12.95. TV; cable. Heated pool; whirlpool. Restaurant 6:30 am-10 pm. Bars 11-1 am. Ck-out noon. Meeting rms. Business center. Shopping arcade. Beauty shop. Exercise equipt; sauna. Minibars. On Halifax Harbour. Cr cds: A, DS, MC, V.

⬛ 🔧 🏊 🍽 🏃

★ ★ **HOWARD JOHNSON HOTEL HALIFAX.** *20 St. Margaret's Bay Rd (B3N 1J4). 902/477-5611; fax 902/479-2150; res 800/446-4656. www.hojo.com.* 135 rms, 9 story, 14 kits. S, D $79-$139; each addl $10; suites $109-$199; kit. units $57-$99; under 19 free; lower rates rest of yr. Crib free. Pet accepted. TV; cable, VCR avail (movies). Indoor pool. Complimentary continental bkfst. Restaurant 7 am-9 pm. Bar 11-1 am. Ck-out noon. Meeting rms. Business servs avail. In-rm modem link. Valet serv. Sauna. Cr cds: A, DS, MC, V.

🔧 🏊 🔥

★★ **INN ON THE LAKE.** *3009 Lake Thomas Dr, Waverly (B0N 2S0). 902/861-3480; fax 902/861-4883; toll-free 800/463-6465. www.innonthelake.com.* 41 rms, 3 story. May-Dec: S, D $110-$315; each addl $10; suites $235-$290; lower rates rest of yr. Crib free. TV; cable (premium), VCR avail (movies). Pool; poolside serv. Complimentary coffee in rms. Restaurant 7 am-10 pm. Bar 11-1 am. Ck-out 11 am. Meeting rms. Business servs avail. In-rm modem link. No bellhops. Gift shop. Free airport transportation. Tennis. Some refrigerators, microwaves. Some balconies. Picnic tables. Canoes. On lake. Cr cds: A, D, DS, MC, V.

★★ **LORD NELSON.** *1515 S Park St (B3J 2L2). 902/423-6331; fax 902/423-7148. www.lordnelsonhotel.com.* 243 rms, 9 story. S, D $79-$109; each addl $15; suites $199-$220; under 18 free. Crib free. TV; cable. Pets accepted, some restrictions. Ck-out 1 pm. Meeting rms. Business servs avail. Shopping arcade. Many microwaves. Cr cds: A, D, DS, ER, MC, V.

★★★ **PRINCE GEORGE.** *1725 Market St (B3J 3N9). 902/425-1986; fax 902/429-6048; res 902/425-6821. www.princegeorgehotel.com.* 203 rms, 6 story. S, D $149-$270; suites $250-$550; under 18 free. Crib free. Pet accepted, some restrictions. Garage $12.95/night. TV; cable (premium), VCR avail. Indoor pool; poolside serv. Restaurant 6:30 am-11 pm. Rm serv. Ck-out 1 pm. Convention facilities. Business center. Concierge. Gift shop. Exercise equipt. Minibars; microwaves avail. Directly connected to World Trade and Convention Centre and Metro Centre by shuttle elvtr and underground walkway. Cr cds: A, D, DS, JCB, MC, V.

★★★ **WESTIN NOVA SCOTIAN.** *1181 Hollis St (B3H 2P6). 902/421-1000; fax 902/422-9465; toll-free 888/679-3784. www.westin.ns.ca.* 297 rms, 11 story. S, D $195-$275; under 18 free. Crib free. TV; cable (premium). Indoor pool; whirlpool. Restaurant 6:30 am-10 pm. Bar to midnight. Ck-out noon, ck-in 3 pm. Meeting rms. Business center. In-rm modem link. Concierge. Exercise equipt. Refreshment center; many refrigerators in suites. Cr cds: A, D, DS, ER, MC, V.

Resort

★★★ **OAK ISLAND RESORT AND SPA.** *51 Vaughan Rd, Western Shore (B0J 3M0). 902/627-2600; fax 902/627-2020; toll-free 800/565-5075. www.oakislandinn.com.* 120 rms, 3 story. No elvtr. June-Sept: S, D $79-$89; each addl $15; suites $54-$209; under 16 free; wkend rates; lower rates rest of yr. Crib free. Pet accepted. TV; cable (premium), VCR avail. Indoor pool; whirlpool, poolside serv. Dining rm 7 am-2 pm, 5-9 pm. Rm serv. Bar. Ck-out noon, ck-in 3 pm. Convention facilities. Business center. Tennis. 18-hole golf privileges. Swimming beach. Sauna. X-country ski 1 mi. Hiking. Lawn games. Fishing guides, charter boats. Balconies. Oceanfront resort overlooking Oak Island. Cr cds: A, D, ER, MC, V.

B&Bs/Small Inns

★★ **DAUPHINEE INN.** *167 Shore Club Rd, Hubbards (B0J 1T0). 902/857-1790; fax 902/857-9555; toll-free 800/567-1790. www.dauphineeinn.com.* 6 air-cooled rms, 2 suites. No rm phones. S, D $95-$105; each addl $10; suites $149; under 5 free. Closed Nov-Apr. TV in common rm; cable (premium). Complimentary continental bkfst. Restaurant 5-9 pm. Ck-out 11 am, ck-in 2 pm. Gift shop. In-rm whirlpool in suites. On swimming beach. Built in 1900; panoramic views of Hubbards Cove. Totally nonsmoking. Cr cds: A, MC, V.

★ **FRESH START.** *2720 Gottingen St (B3K 3C7). 902/453-6616; fax 902/453-6617; toll-free 888/453-6616. www.bbcanada.com/2262.html.* 8 rms, 6 share baths, 2-3 story. No A/C. Rm phones avail. May-Oct: S $70-$100; D $80-$100; wkly rates; lower rates rest of yr. Pet accepted, some restrictions. TV in sitting rm; cable, VCR avail. Complimentary full bkfst. Ck-out 1 pm, ck-in 4 pm. Business servs avail. Microwaves avail. Victorian house (1880); antiques. Maritime Command Museum opp. Totally nonsmoking. Cr cds: A, D, ER, MC, V.

★★★ **HADDON HALL.** *67 Haddon Hill Rd, Chester (B0J 1J0). 902/275-3577; fax 902/275-5159. www.haddonhallinn.com.* 11 rms, 2 story. S $265-$440; D $333-$508; each addl $15; under 16 free; lower rates rest of yr. TV; cable, VCR avail. Complimentary continental bkfst. Restaurant 5:30-8:30 pm. Rm serv. Ck-out 10 am, ck-in 11 am. Business servs avail. Luggage handling. Valet serv. Tennis. Heated pool. Built in 1905; panoramic ocean view. Cr cds: D, MC, V.

★★ **WAVERLEY INN.** *1266 Barrington St (B3J 1Y5). 902/423-9346; fax 902/425-0167; toll-free 800/565-9346. www.waverleyinn.com.* 34 rms, 3 story. June-Oct: S, D $99-$244; each addl $15; under 12 free; lower rates rest of yr. Crib avail. TV; cable, VCR avail. Complimentary continental bkfst. Restaurant nearby. Ck-out noon, ck-in after 2 pm. Business servs avail. Some in-rm whirlpools; microwaves avail. Historic inn (1876); antiques. Near Halifax Harbour. Cr cds: ER, MC, V.

All Suite

★★★ **CAMBRIDGE SUITES HOTEL HALIFAX.** *1583 Brunswick St (B3J 3P5). 902/420-0555; fax 902/420-9379; toll-free 800/565-1263. www.cambridgesuiteshotel.com.* 200 suites, 6 story. S, D $149-$259; under 18 free. Crib free. Garage $10. TV; cable. Complimentary continental bkfst. Restaurant 7 am-10 pm. Ck-out 1 pm. Coin lndy. Meeting rms. In-rm modem link. Exercise equipt; sauna. Whirlpool. Rec rm. Sun deck. Refrigerators, microwaves, minibars. Cr cds: A, D, DS, ER, MC, V.

Restaurants

★ **ALFREDO, WEINSTEIN AND HO.** *1739 Grafton St (B3J 2C6). 902/421-1977. www.alfredoweinsteinho.com.* Hrs: 11 am-11 pm; Fri, Sat to 5 am. Closed Jan 1, Dec 24-26. Bar. Continental menu. Lunch $5.95-$9.95, dinner $9-$15. Child's menu. Specializes in Italian, Chinese, and delicatessen dishes. Sundae bar. Cr cds: A, D, ER, MC, V.
D

★★ **FIVE FISHERMEN.** *1740 Argyle St (B3J 2W1). 902/422-4421. www.fivefisherman.com.* Specializes in seafood, steak, and steamed mussels. Salad bar. Own desserts. Hrs: 5-11 pm; Sun to 10 pm. Closed Jan 1, Dec 22-25. Res accepted. Bar. Dinner $20-$28. Former school building (1816). Cr cds: A, D, ER, MC, V.

★★★ **SALTY'S ON THE WATERFRONT.** *1869 Upper Water St (B3J 1S9). 902/423-6818. www.energeticfoods.com.* Continental menu. Specializes in lobster, steak. Hrs: 11:30 am-10 pm. Res accepted. Bar to 10 pm. A la carte entrees: lunch $6.95-$10.95, dinner $15-$25. Child's menu. Nautical decor. Patio dining on harbor. Historic building (1800) on waterfront. Cr cds: A, D, DS, ER, MC, V.
D

Peggy's Cove

See also Halifax

Pop 54 **Elev** 25 ft (8 m) **Area code** 902
Information Tourism Nova Scotia, PO Box 130, Halifax B3J 2M7; 902/490-5946 or 800/565-0000

Twenty-seven miles (forty-four kilometers) southwest of Halifax, this tiny, picturesque village lies nestled in a snug harbor where lobster fishermen live and work. This area is surrounded by bold granite outcroppings where, during a storm, the sea dashes against the shoreline.

Within St. John's Anglican Church, two murals painted by the late William deGarthe, one of Canada's foremost artists, may be viewed. Additional works include carvings of villagers at work scribed into the rock cliff behind deGarthe's home, now a gallery. One of the many lighthouses dotting the Lighthouse Route extending southwest from Halifax to Yarmouth may be seen in this artist's haven.

What to See and Do

Fisheries Museum of the Atlantic. Restored schooner *Theresa E. Connor* and trawler *Cape Sable* serve as floating museum, situated in an old fish plant; *Bluenose* schooner exhibit; aquarium; working dory shop; hall of inshore fisheries, demonstrations rm, theatre, gift shop, gallery; restaurant. (Daily) Bluenose Dr, between Duke & Montague Sts in Lunenburg. Phone 902/634-4794. ¢¢

Town of Lunenburg. (Founded 1753) Walking tour of this historic town provides comprehensive information on its history and unique architectural character. The Tourist Bureau is located on Blockhouse Hill Rd, near Townsend St. Approx 50 mi (80 km) W on Hwy 103. Phone 800/565-0000.

Motel/Motor Lodge

★★ **WINDJAMMER.** *4070 Hwy 3, Chester (B0J 1J0). 902/275-3567.* 18 rms, 6 A/C. Mid-June-mid-Sept: S, D $50-$65; each addl $6; under 12 free; lower rates rest of yr. Crib $5. Pet accepted. TV; cable, VCR avail. Restaurant adj 8 am-9 pm. Ck-out 11 am. Refrigerators, microwaves avail. Picnic tables. On lake; swimming beach. Cr cds: A, C, D, DS, ER, MC, V.
D

Restaurant

★★ **SOU'WESTER.** *178 Peggys Cove, Peggys Cove (B0J 2N0). 902/823-2561. www.peggys-cove.com.* Specializes in seafood chowder, lobster, gingerbread. Own soups, sauces. Hrs: 8 am-10 pm; June-Oct from 10 am. Closed Dec 24, 25. No A/C. Serv bar. Bkfst $4.25-$7.25, lunch, dinner $3.25-$17.95. Child's menu. Gift shop. On oceanfront. View of lighthouse and cove. Family-owned. Cr cds: A, D, MC, V.
D

Truro

Settled 1703 **Pop** 12,885 **Elev** 15 ft (5 m) **Area code** 902
Information Chamber of Commerce, 577 Prince St, PO Box 54, B2N 1G2; 902/895-6328
Web www.trurochamber.com

After the expulsion of the Acadians following British acquisition of this territory, Truro was resettled in 1760 by 53 Loyalist families from New England. Other settlers followed, mainly from Northern Ireland and those fleeing the American Revolution. After the arrival of the railroad, Truro was incorporated as a town in 1875.

What to See and Do

Acres of the Golden Pheasant. Contains over 50 species of birds, incl pheasants, peacocks, parakeets, finches, and doves. (Daily) Queen St. Phone 902/893-2734. ¢

Colchester County Museum. Exhibits depict human and natural history of the county; changing exhibits. Archives, genealogy library. (June-Sept, Tues-Sun; rest of yr, Tues-Fri; closed hols) 29 Young St. Phone 902/895-6284. ¢

Little White Schoolhouse Museum. One-rm schoolhouse built in 1871, furnished with desks, artifacts, and textbooks from 1867-1952. (June-Aug, daily; rest of yr, by appt) Arthur St, on grounds of Nova Scotia Teachers College. Phone 902/895-5347. **FREE**

Tidal bore. A wave of water rushes *backward* up the Salmon River before high tide. Bores range in height from a ripple up to several ft. A timetable can be obtained from the Chamber of Commerce or by phoning "Dial-a-Tide." Viewing area on Tidal Bore Rd, just off Hwy 102, exit 14. Phone 902/426-5494.

Victoria Park. One thousand-acre national park with hiking trails, outdoor pool, playground, tennis courts, picnic grounds, and baseball field. (Daily) Brunswick St and Park Rd. Phone 902/895-6328. **FREE**

Special Event

International Tulip Festival. 577 Prince St. Over 250,000 tulips planted. Late May.

Motels/Motor Lodges

★★ **BEST WESTERN GLENGARRY.** *150 Willow St (B2N 4Z6).* 902/893-4311; fax 902/893-1759; toll-free 800/567-4276. www.bestwestern.com. 90 rms, 3 story. June-Oct: S $86.96-$97.39; D $97.39-$115; each addl $10; suites $180; under 18 free; lower rates rest of yr. Pet accepted. TV; cable. 2 pools, 1 indoor; wading pool, whirlpool, poolside serv. Restaurant 7 am-9 pm; Sun 8 am-8 pm. Rm serv. Bar 5 pm-1 am; entertainment. Ck-out 11 am. Meeting rms. Cr cds: A, C, D, DS, MC, V.

★ **PALLISER MOTEL.** *103/104 Tidal Bore Rd (B2N 5B3).* 902/893-8951. 42 rms. No A/C. No rm phones. Early May-late-Oct: S $45; D $53; each addl $7. Closed rest of yr. Crib $5. Pet accepted. TV; cable. Complimentary continental bkfst. Restaurant 7:30 am-8:30 pm. Bar from 11 am. Ck-out 11 am. Meeting rm. Business servs avail. Gift shop. Cr cds: A, DS, MC, V.

★ **STONE HOUSES MOTEL & REST.** *165 Willow St (B2N 4Z9).* 902/893-9413; fax 902/897-9937; res 877/660-6638. 39 rms. May-Oct: S $40-$60; D $60-$70; each addl $10; under 18 free; wkly rates; lower rates rest of yr. TV; cable. Restaurant 7 am-10 pm. Ck-out 11 am. Coin lndry. Meeting rm. Business servs avail. Sundries. Microwaves avail. Cr cds: A, MC, V.

★ **WILLOW BEND MOTEL.** *277 Willow St (B2N 5A3).* 902/895-5325; fax 902/893-8375; toll-free 800/594-5569. 27 rms, 9 kits. Mid-June-mid-Sept: S $55-$69; D $79; each addl $5; kits. $89; wkly rates; lower rates rest of yr. TV; cable (premium), VCR avail. Pool; poolside serv. Ck-out 11 am. Business servs avail. 18-hole golf privileges. Cr cds: A, DS, MC, V.

Yarmouth

Pop 7,475 **Elev** 140 ft (43 m) **Area code** 902
Information Yarmouth County Tourist Assn, PO Box 477, B5A 4B4; 902/742-5355
Web www.aboutyarmouth.com

This historic seaport is the largest town southwest of Halifax and the gateway to Nova Scotia from New England. While the town of Yarmouth was first settled by New Englanders in 1761, the Yarmouth County area was previously inhabited by the MicMac and French Acadians. Today it serves as the hub of the fishing, shipping, and transportation industries of western Nova Scotia.

During the days of sail in the 1800s, this was one of the major shipbuilding and ship owning ports in the world. There is much evidence of this "Golden Age of Sail" to be found in the architecture of many of its fine old homes as well as ship paintings and artifacts exhibited in museums. Travel north on the Evangeline Trail, which passes through French Acadian settlements, fishing centers and rich orchards and farmlands. South, follow the Lighthouse Route, which parallels the Atlantic coastline and passes near many picturesque lighthouses and fishing ports.

What to See and Do

Cape Forchu Lighthouse. Entrance to Bay of Fundy and Yarmouth Harbour. Route travels along rocky coastline and through colorful fishing villages. County park, picnicking. (Daily) On Cape Forchu Island, 7 mi (11 km) SW, linked by causeway to mainland. Phone 800/565-0000. **FREE**

Ferry services.

The CAT. Advance res required. Passenger and car ferry service to Bar Harbor, ME. (June-Oct) For res, rates, schedule, contact Bay Ferries. Phone 888/249-7245.

MS *Scotia Prince.* Advance res recommended. Passenger and car service between Yarmouth, NS and Portland, ME. (May-Oct, daily) For rates, res, schedule, contact Prince of Fundy Cruises, PO Box 4216, Portland, ME 04101. Phone 207/775-5616, 902/775-5611, 800/341-7540 (Canada and US exc ME), or 800/482-0955 (ME). ¢¢¢¢

Firefighters' Museum of Nova Scotia. Permanent display of history of firefighting service, incl hand pumps, steamers, horse-drawn apparatus. Gift shop. (July-Aug, daily; rest of yr, Mon-Sat) 451 Main St. Phone 902/742-5525. ¢ In the museum is

National Exhibit Centre. Traveling exhibits change every six wks. Contact museum for schedule.

Frost Park. First town cemetery. Gazebo, fountain. Picnicking. Overlooks Yarmouth Harbour, on Water St. Phone 800/565-0000.

Isaak Walton Killam Library. Unique memorial wall in park behind building. 405 Main St, between Parade and Grand Sts. Phone 902/742-5040.

Public wharves. Center of fishing fleet where herring seiners, inshore and offshore scallop draggers, Cape Island boats can be seen. On Yarmouth Harbour, on each side of BAY Ferry Terminal.

Yarmouth Arts Regional Centre. Center for visual and performing arts for southwestern Nova Scotia (356-seat capacity). Summer theatre, drama, musical comedy, concerts, art shows, courses, workshops, seminars. 76 Parade St. Phone 902/742-8150. ¢¢¢

Yarmouth County Museum. Displays history of county with emphasis on Victorian period. Features marine exhibits, period rms, blacksmith shop, stagecoach. Of special interest is a runic stone, found near Yarmouth Harbour in 1812, bearing clear inscription alleged to be left by Leif Ericson on voyage in 1007; Yarmouth Lighthouse lens. (June-Sept, daily; rest of yr, Tues-Sat; closed hols) 22 Collins St. Phone 902/742-5539. ¢

Special Events

Festival Acadien de Wedgeport. Parade, costumes. Talent show, concerts, music. During Canada Day wk.

Seafest. Sporting events, entertainment, cultural productions; parade, Queen's Pageant. Fish feast; dory races. Phone 902/742-7585. Mid-July.

Western Nova Scotia Exhibition. Exhibition grounds. Animal judging, equestrian events, agricultural displays, craft demonstrations and exhibits, midway and entertainment; Canada/US ox hauls. Early Aug.

Yarmouth Cup Races. International yacht race; dockside entertainment. Windsurfing races; small craft races. Labour Day wkend.

Motels/Motor Lodges

★★ **BEST WESTERN MERMAID.** *545 Main St (B5A 1J6). 902/742-7821; fax 902/742-2966; res 800/772-2774. www.bestwestern.com.* 45 rms, 2 story, 5 kits. No A/C. June-Oct: S, D $110-$170; each addl $8; kit. units $110-$135; under 18 free; lower rates rest of yr. Crib. Pet accepted, some restrictions. TV; cable. Heated pool. Restaurant nearby. Ck-out 11 am. Coin lndry. Business center. Some refrigerators. Cr cds: A, C, D, DS, ER, JCB, MC, V.

★★ **CAPRI MOTEL.** *8 Herbert St (B5A 1J6). 902/742-7168; fax 902/742-2966; toll-free 800/722-2774.* 35 rms, some A/C, 2 story. S, D $89-$99; each addl $8; suites $95-$135. Crib $6. TV; cable (premium). Pool privileges. Complimentary continental bkfst. Restaurant adj 11:30 am-10 pm. Bar to 2 am. Ck-out 11 am. Business servs avail. Refrigerators avail. Balconies. Cr cds: A, C, D, DS, ER, JCB, MC, V.

★ **LAKELAWN MOTEL.** *641 Main St (B5A 1K2). 902/742-3588; toll-free 877/664-0664.* 31 rms, 2 story. No rm phones. July-Sept: S, D $64-$79; each addl $5; under 12 free; lower rates May-June, Oct. Closed rest of yr. Crib free. Pet accepted, some restrictions. TV; cable. Full bkfst avail. Ck-out 11 am. Business servs avail. Free airport transportation. Cr cds: A, D, DS, MC, V.

★ **LA REINE MOTEL.** *RR 1 (B5A 4A5). 902/742-9154; fax 902/742-3262; res 902/742-7154.* 23 rms. No A/C. July-Aug: S $54, D $60-$64; each addl $6; under 12 free; lower rates June, Sept-mid-Oct. Closed rest of yr. Crib free. TV; cable (premium). Heated pool. Complimentary coffee in lobby. Restaurant adj 8 am-10 pm. Ck-out 11 am. Business servs avail. Picnic tables. On Doctors Lake. Cr cds: A, DS, MC, V.

★★ **RODD COLONY HARBOUR INN.** *6 Forest St (B5A 3K8). 902/742-9194; fax 902/742-6291; res 800/565-7633. www.rodd-hotels.ca.* 65 rms, 4 story, 8 suites. May-Sept: S $85; D $95; under 16 free; suites $101; lower rates rest of yr. Pet accepted. TV; cable, VCR avail (movies). Restaurant 7 am-11 pm. Rm serv. Bar noon-midnight. Meeting rms. Business servs avail. Valet serv. Airport transportation. Health club privileges. Microwaves avail. Cr cds: A, DS, MC, V.

★★ **VOYAGEUR.** *RR 1 (B5A 4A5). 902/742-7157; fax 902/742-1208.* 33 rms, 4 kits. Mid-June-mid-Sept: S, D $59-$86; each addl $10; kits. $85; family rates; lower rates rest of yr. Crib $6. TV; cable. Restaurant 7 am-10 pm. Ck-out 11 am. Whirlpool. Microwaves avail. Overlooks Doctors Lake. Cr cds: A, DS, MC, V.

Hotel

★★★ **RODD GRAND YARMOUTH.** *417 Main St (B5A 4B2). 902/742-2446; fax 902/742-4645; res 800/565-7633. www.rodd-hotels.ca.* 138 air-cooled rms, 7 story. June-Oct: S, D $95-$105; each addl $10; suites $120-$130; under 16 free; lower rates rest of yr. Crib free. Pet accepted. TV; cable. Indoor pool. Restaurants 6:30 am-9 pm. Bar 11-1 am. Ck-out 11 am. Meeting rms. Business center. In-rm modem link. Shopping arcade. Free airport, bus depot transportation. Exercise equipt. Microwaves avail. Cr cds: A, DS, MC, V.

B&B/Small Inn

★★★ **THE MANOR INN.** *417 Main St, Hebron (B0W 1X0). 902/742-2487; fax 902/742-8094; res 888/626-6746. www.manorinn.com.* 54 rms, 2 story. Mid-June-Sept: S, D $72-$145; lower rates rest of yr. Crib $12. TV; cable, VCR avail (movies). Heated pool. Dining rm 7-11 am, 5:30-9:30 pm. Ck-out 11 am, ck-in 2 pm. Business servs avail. Tennis. Lawn games. Microwaves avail. Some balconies. Picnic tables. Rms in Colonial-style inn (ca 1920), coach house and motel building; antiques. Nine landscaped acres on Doctor's Lake; private dock. Cr cds: A, C, D, ER, MC, V.

Restaurants

★★ **AUSTRIAN INN.** *Hwy 1 (B5A 4A5). 902/742-6202.* Continental menu. Specializes in seafood. Own desserts. Hrs: 11 am-10 pm; Mon, Tues, Sun to 9 pm; Sun brunch to 2 pm. Closed mid-Dec-Mar. Res accepted. No A/C. Bar. Lunch $5.35-$19.85, dinner $9.65-$19.85. Sun brunch $12.25. Child's menu. Cr cds: A, MC, V.

★ **CHINA COURT.** *67 Starrs Rd (B5A 2T6). 902/742-9128.* Chinese menu. Hrs: 11 am-10 pm; Fri, Sat to 10:30 pm; Sun 11:30 am-8 pm; Sun brunch to 2:30 pm. Closed major hols. Res accepted. Bar. Lunch $3.99-$8.25, dinner $5-$14. Sun brunch $5.95-$11.95. Child's menu. Chinese decor. Cr cds: A, MC, V.

★ **PRINCE ARTHUR STEAK AND SEAFOOD HOUSE.** *73 Starrs Rd (B5A 2T6). 902/742-1129. www.rknight.com.* Canadian menu. Specializes in T-bone steak, shrimp, lobster. Hrs: 11 am-9:30 pm; Sun 11 am-9 pm. Closed Dec 25. Res accepted. Bar to 2 am. Lunch $6.99, dinner $9.95-$24.95. Sun brunch $9.95-$13.95. Child's menu. Entertainment. Family-owned. Cr cds: A, D, ER, MC, V.

PROVINCE OF ONTARIO

Although first explored by Samuel de Champlain in the 17th century, the Ontario region was not heavily settled until the 18th century by Loyalist refugees from the American Revolution. British settled in what was to become Ontario while French populated Québec. Two territories were formed following the battle of 1759; in 1867 they became provinces in the Dominion of Canada.

This vast province can be divided into northern and southern Ontario; the far northern wilderness dominated by lakes, forests, and logging camps; the southern agricultural and industrial section inhabited by nine-tenths of the population. The province is easily accessible from many points across the United States, with each area offering exciting and beautiful sights for the traveler.

Pop: 9,101,690
Land area: 412,582 sq mi (1,068,175 sq km)
Capital: Toronto
Web: www.ontariotravel.net
Information: Ontario Travel, 5700 Explorers Dr, Mississauga L4W 5J3; 800/ONTARIO

Certainly one of the most spectacular sights is Niagara Falls. Cosmopolitan Toronto, the provincial capital, and Ottawa, the country's capital, offer the tourist a wide spectrum of experiences including theater, fine restaurants, galleries, museums, and recreational facilities. The Stratford Festival in Stratford, the Shaw Festival in Niagara-on-the-Lake, and Upper Canada Village in Morrisburg are not to be missed.

Ontario is also known for its many recreational areas, such as Algonquin and Quetico provincial parks and St. Lawrence Islands National Park. To the north lie Sudbury and Sault Ste. Marie; to the northwest, Thunder Bay, Fort Frances, and Kenora, offering a variety of wilderness activities including canoeing, fishing, and hunting. Perhaps more appealing than any one attraction is the vast, unspoiled nature of the province itself. More than 400,000 lakes and magnificent forests form a huge vacationland just a few miles from the US border, stretching all the way to Hudson Bay.

Ontario lies mostly within the Eastern Time Zone. Travelers should note that fees are charged at international bridges, tunnels, and ferries.

In addition to national holidays, Ontario observes Simcoe Day (first Monday in August).

Safety belts are mandatory for all persons anywhere in vehicle. Children under 40 pounds in weight must be in an approved safety seat anywhere in vehicle.

Brantford

See also Hamilton, Stratford

Founded 1784 **Pop** 81,290 **Elev** 815 ft (248 m)
Area code 519
Information Tourism Brantford, 1 Sherwood Dr, N3T 1N3;
519/751-9900 or 800/265-6299
Web www.city.brantford.on.ca

Brantford is located in the heart of southwestern Ontario along Grand River, a Canadian Heritage River. Captain Joseph Brant, leader of the Iroquois First Nations, crossed the river in 1784. It was through Native and European settlements that Brantford was born. Brantford is equally famous as the place where Alexander Graham Bell lived and invented the telephone.

What to See and Do

Bell Homestead. The house is furnished just as it was when Alexander Graham Bell lived here in the 1870s. Also located here are the first telephone office and artifacts housed in a display center (Tues-Sun; closed Jan 1, Thanksgiving, Dec 25). 57 Charlotte St. Phone 519/756-6220. ¢

Brant County Museum. Collection of Native American artifacts, life histories of Captain Joseph Brant and Pauline Johnson. Also displays of pioneer life in Brant County, incl Brant Square and Brant Corners, where former businesses are depicted. (Wed-Sat; also Sun June-Aug; closed Jan 1, Thanksgiving, Dec 25) 57 Charlotte St. Phone 519/752-2483. ¢

Glenhyrst Art Gallery of Brant. Gallery with changing exhibits of paintings, sculpture, photography, and crafts surrounded by 16-acre (seven-hectare) estate overlooking the Grand River. Beautiful grounds and nature trail. (Tues-Sun; closed hols) 20 Ava Rd. Phone 519/756-5932. **FREE**

Her Majesty's Royal Chapel of the Mohawks. (1785) The first Protestant church in Ontario, the "Mohawk Chapel" is the only Royal Native Chapel in the world belonging to Six Nations people. (May-June, Wed-Sun afternoons; July-Labour Day, daily; early Sept-mid-Oct, Sat and Sun afternoons) 190 Mohawk St. Phone 519/445-4528. ¢¢

Myrtleville House Museum. (1837) Georgian house is one of the oldest in Brant County; original furniture of the Good family, who lived here for more than 150 yrs. On 5½ acres (two hectares) of parkland. Picnicking. (Mid Apr-mid-Sept, Tues-Sun; closed hols) 34 Myrtleville Dr. Phone 519/752-3216. ¢

Riverboat Cruises. Big Creek Boat Farm. Dinner cruises on the Grand River. (Mid-May-Sept; res required) ON 54, 4 mi (6.4 km) W of Caledonia. Phone 905/765-4107. ¢¢¢¢

Sanderson Centre for the Performing Arts. This 1919 vaudeville house has been restored and transformed to a theater featuring music, dance, and dramatic performances. 88 Dalhousie St. Phone 519/758-8090 or 800/ 265-0710.

Woodland Cultural Centre. Preserves and promotes culture and heritage of First Nations of eastern woodland area. Education, research, and museum programs; art shows, festivals. (Daily; closed hols) 184 Mohawk St. Phone 519/759-2650. Museum ¢¢

Special Events

Riverfest. Three-day festival celebrates the Grand River. Entertainment, fireworks, crafts. Children's activities. Last wkend May. Phone 519/751-9900.

International Villages Festival. Ethnic villages celebrate with ethnic folk dancing, pageantry, and food. Early July. Phone 519/753-2350.

Six Nations Native Pageant. Forest Theatre, Sour Springs Rd, at Six Nations reserve. Six Nations people reenact their history and culture in natural forest amphitheater. First three wkends (Fri, Sat) Aug. Phone 519/445-4528.

Six Nations Native Fall Fair. Ohsweken Fairgrounds. Native dances, authentic craft and art exhibits. Phone 519/445-4528. Wkend after Labour Day.

Motels/Motor Lodges

★ ★ **BEST WESTERN BRANT PARK INN.** *19 Holiday Dr (N3T 5W5).* 519/753-8651; fax 519/753-2619; 800/258-1234 www.bestwestern.com. 116 rms, 2 story. June-Sept: S $94.95-$119.95; D $104.95-$129.95; each addl $10; under 12 free; lower rates rest of yr. Crib free. TV; cable. Indoor pool, whirlpool, lifeguard. Playground. Restaurant 6:30 am-9:30 pm. Rm serv. Ck-out 11 am. Meeting rms. Business servs avail. In-rm modem link. Bellhops. Valet serv. Exercise equipt; sauna. Private patios; some balconies. Cr cds: A, D, DS, ER, MC, V.

🄳 ⛱ 🛉 📵 🔥 SC

★ **DAYS INN.** *460 Fairview Dr (N3R 7A9).* 519/759-2700; fax 519/759-2089; 800/325-2525. www.daysinn.com. 75 rms, 2 story. Apr-Oct: S $91.95-$101.95; D $98.95-$101.95; each addl $7; under 12 free; wkly, wkend rates; lower rates rest of yr. Crib free. Pet accepted. TV; cable (premium). Pool privileges. Complimentary coffee in rms. Restaurant 7-1 am. Ck-out 11 am. Meeting rms. Business servs avail. In-rm modem link. Health club privileges. Cr cds: A, C, D, DS, JCB, MC, V.

🄳 🐾 📵 🔥 SC

★ ★ **HOLIDAY INN.** *664 Colborne St (N3S 3P8).* 519/758-9999; fax 519/758-1515; res 800/465-4329. www.holiday-inn.com. 98 rms, 2-3 story. No elvtr. May-Sept: S, D $89-$109; each addl $5; under 18 free; family rates; package plans; lower rates rest of yr. Crib free. TV; cable (premium), VCR avail. Complimentary coffee in rms. Restaurant 6:30 am-10 pm. Rm serv. Bar 11-2 am. Ck-out noon. Meeting rms. Business servs avail. In-rm modem link. Bellhops. Valet serv. Sundries. Coin lndry. Tennis privileges. Golf privileges. Downhill ski 6 mi; x-country ski 1 mi. Exercise equipt; sauna. Indoor pool; poolside serv. Game rm. Microwaves avail. Many balconies. Cr cds: A, D, ER, JCB, MC, V.

🏊 🎿 ⛱ 🛉 📵 🔥 SC

Restaurant

★★ **OLDE SCHOOL RESTAURANT.** *Hwy 2W and Powerline Rd W (N3T 5M1). 519/753-3131.* Canadian, European cuisine. Specializes in steak, seafood. Hrs: 11:30-1 am; Sat from 5 pm; Sun brunch 11 am-3 pm. Closed Dec 25. Res accepted; required Sat. Bar. Lunch $6.95-$14.95, dinner $18.95-$26.95. Complete meals: dinner (Mon-Fri) $16.95. Sun brunch $12.95. Piano lounge. Restored 1850s schoolhouse; antiques, pioneer and school memorabilia. Cr cds: A, D, DS, ER, MC, V.

D ⊛

Brockville

Settled 1784 **Pop** 21,000 **Elev** 300 ft (91 m) **Area code** 613
Information Tourism Office, 1 King St West, PO Box 5000, K6V 7A5; 613/342-8772, ext 430
Web www.brockville.com

Settled by United Empire Loyalists, the town was known as Elizabethtown until 1812 when it was named Brockville after Major General Sir Isaac Brock. It was incorporated as a town in 1832, the first in Ontario. Brockville is the eastern gateway to the Thousand Islands on the St. Lawrence River. It is home to the oldest railway tunnel in Canada which runs one-quarter of a mile under the city to the riverfront. The city features many Victorian homes along with a historic downtown business section with numerous buildings more than 100 years old.

What to See and Do

Brockville Museum. Devoted to history surrounding the city. Exhibits, workshops, afternoon teas. 5 Henry St. Phone 613/342-4397. ¢¢¢

Thousand Island Cruises. Aboard the *General Brock.* Shallow-draft boat makes trips (one hr) through heart of the region, incl Millionaires Row and many smaller channels inaccessible to larger boats. (May-late Oct, daily) 14 mi (23 km) W via Hwy 401 to 1000 Islands Pkwy. Phone 613/659-3402 or 800/563-8687. ¢¢¢¢

Special Events

Great Balloon Rodeo. Mid-June.

Riverfest. Waterfront. Mid-June-early July. Phone 613/342-8975.

Poker Run. Mid-Aug. Phone 613/382-8413.

Motels/Motor Lodges

★★ **BEST WESTERN WHITE HOUSE.** *1843 Hwy 2 E (K6V 5T1). 613/345-1622; fax 613/345-4284; 800/528-1234. www.bestwestern.com.* 56 rms. S $67; D $72-$77; each addl $5. Crib $5. Pet accepted. TV. Heated pool. Complimentary continental bkfst. Complimentary coffee in rms. Restaurant 6:30 am-2 pm, 5-9 pm. Ck-out 11 am. Meeting rms. Business servs avail. In-rm modem link. Sundries. Picnic tables. Cr cds: A, C, D, DS, ER, MC, V.

D 🐾 ⟲ ⊛ 🔥 SC

★ **DAYS INN.** *160 Stewart Blvd (K6V 4W6). 613/342-6613; fax 613/345-3811; 800/325-2525. www.daysinn.com.* 56 rms, 2 story. Mid-June-mid-Oct: S $57-$64; D $72-$74; each addl $7; under 17 free; lower rates rest of yr. Crib free. TV; cable (premium). Pool. Complimentary coffee in rms. Restaurant 11 am-2 pm, 4:30-9 pm. Bar noon-1 am. Ck-out 11 am. Meeting rms. Business servs avail. Picnic tables. Cr cds: A, C, D, DS, ER, JCB, MC, V.

⟲ ⊛ 🔥 SC

★★★ **QUALITY INN.** *100 Stewart Blvd (K6V 4W3). 613/345-1400; fax 613/345-5402; 800/228-5151. www.qualityinn.com.* 72 rms, 5 story. S $112-$128; D $124-$140; each addl $12; suites $235-$247; studio rms $121-$133; under 16 free. Crib free. TV; cable (premium). Indoor pool; whirlpool, poolside serv. Supervised children's activities. Restaurant 6:30 am-11 pm. Bar 11:30-2 am; entertainment exc Sun. Ck-out noon. Meeting rms. Business servs avail. In-rm modem link. Beauty shop. Tennis. Exercise rm; sauna, steam rm. Massage. Cr cds: A, C, D, DS, ER, JCB, MC, V.

🏋 ⟲ 🎾 ⊛ 🔥 SC

Cornwall

See also Morrisburg

Pop 46,144 **Elev** 200 ft (62 m) **Area code** 613
Information Cornwall and Seaway Valley Tourism, Gray's Creek, PO Box 36, K6H 5R9; 613/938-4748 or 800/937-4748
Web www.visit.cornwall.on.ca

Cornwall is a thriving community located on the banks of the St. Lawrence River. It is connected to Massena, New York (see) by the Seaway International Toll Bridge. The Robert H. Saunders Generating Station, one of the largest international generating stations in the world, is here.

What to See and Do

Inverarden Regency Cottage Museum. (1816) Retirement home of fur trader John McDonald of Garth. Collection of Canadian and English Georgian furniture; houses local picture archives. Tea rm (Sun in summer). (Apr-mid-Nov, daily; rest of yr by appt) Montreal and Boundary Rds. Phone 613/938-9585. **FREE**

Long Sault Parkway. 6½ mi (10 km) causeway loop connects 11 islands in the St. Lawrence River between Long Sault and Ingleside; 1,300 scenic acres (526 hectares) with beaches and campsites. Toll. 8 mi (13 km) W off ON 2.

United Counties Museum. Old stone house has displays showing early life of the United Empire Loyalists. (Apr-late Nov, daily) 731 Second St W. Phone 613/932-2381. **FREE**

Upper Canada Village. 25 mi (40 km) W on ON 2 in Morrisburg (see).

Special Events

Raisin River Canoe Races. On Raisin River. Mid-Apr.

Worldfest/Festimonde. Cornwall Civic Complex. International folk festival; ethnic music, dancing, displays, costumes. Six days early July.

Awesome August Festival. Balloon lift-off, Cornfest, performances. Mid-Aug. Phone 613/938-4748.

Williamstown Fair. Mid-Aug. Phone 613/938-4748.

Motel/Motor Lodge

★★ **BEST WESTERN PARKWAY INN.** *1515 Vincent Massey Dr (Hwy 2) (K6H 5R6).* 613/932-0451; fax 613/938-5479; 800/528-1234. 91 rms, 2 story. S $86; D $110-$145; each addl $6; suites $200; under 18 free. Crib free. Pet accepted. TV; cable (premium). Pool; whirlpool. Coffee in rms. Restaurant 6:30 am-10 pm; Sun to 9 pm. Bar 11-2 am. Ck-out noon. Meeting rms. Business servs avail. In-rm modem link. Valet serv. X-country ski 2 mi. Exercise equipt; sauna. Refrigerators, some fireplaces. Cr cds: A, C, D, ER, MC, V.

🖼️🖼️🖼️🖼️🖼️🖼️🖼️

Fort Frances

Pop 8,906 **Elev** 1,100 ft (335 m) **Area code** 807

Information Chamber of Commerce, 474 Scott St, P9A 1H2; 807/274-5773 or 800/820-3678

Web www.fortfranceschamber.com

Across the river from International Falls, Minnesota, Fort Frances is a prosperous paper town and an important border crossing point for visitors from the United States heading for northwestern Canadian destinations. "The Fort" is a popular summer resort town. It is also a major fly-in center for the vast wilderness areas to the north and east, a region of 40,000 lakes.

What to See and Do

Fort Frances Museum. This small museum has changing displays dealing with the indigenous era, the fur trade, and later settlement. (Mid-June-Labour Day, daily; rest of yr, Mon-Sat; closed hols) 259 Scott St. Phone 807/274-7891. Summer admission ¢

Industrial tour. Abitibi Consolidated. The paper manufacturing process is followed from debarking of the logs to the finished paper. (June-Aug, Mon-Fri, by res only) Ages 12 yrs and over only; flat, closed-toe shoes required. 145 3rd St W. Phone 807/274-5311. **FREE**

Noden Causeway. Excellent island views may be seen from this network of bridges. E on ON 11.

Pither's Point Park. This beautiful park has a reconstructed fort, logging tugboat, and a lookout tower with a pioneer logging museum at its base. Tower, fort, and boat (mid-June-Labour Day, daily). Campground (fee) with swimming beach, fishing, boating (rentals adj to park); playground, fitness trail, cafe. (Late June-Labour Day) On Rainy Lake. Phone 807/274-5087 or 807/274-5502. Museum ¢

Special Events

Culturama Festival. Early May. Phone 807/274-5773.

Fun in the Sun Festival. Late June. Phone 807/274-5773.

Motel/Motor Lodge

★★ **LA PLACE RENDEZ-VOUS.** *1201 Idylwild Dr (P9A 3M3).* 807/274-9811; fax 807/274-9553; toll-free 800/274-9811. www.rendezvoushotel.com. 54 units, 1-2 story. S $85-$90; D $92-$97; each addl $7; under 12 free. Crib free. TV; cable, VCR avail. Restaurant (see also LA PLACE RENDEZ-VOUS). Rm serv. Bar 11-1 am. Ck-out 11 am. Meeting rms. Business servs avail. In-rm modem link. Whirlpool. Sauna. Some balconies. Picnic tables. On Rainy Lake; swimming beach. Cr cds: A, MC, V.

🖼️🖼️🖼️🖼️

Restaurant

★★ **LA PLACE RENDEZ-VOUS.** *1201 Idylwild Dr (P9A 3M3).* 807/274-9811. www.rendezvoushotel.com. Specializes in prime rib, walleye. Hrs: 6 am-10 pm; Fri, Sat to 11 pm. Closed Dec 25. Res accepted. Bar 11-1 am. Bkfst $2.95-$9.95, lunch $4.95-$10.95, dinner $10.50-$19.95. Child's menu. Outdoor dining. Overlooks Rainy Lake. Family-owned. Cr cds: A, MC, V.

🖼️🖼️🖼️

Gananoque

See also Kingston

Pop 4,863 **Elev** 300 ft (91 m) **Area code** 613

Information 1000 Islands Gananoque Chamber of Commerce, 10 King St E, K7G 1E6; 613/382-3250 or 800/561-1595

Web www.1000islandsgananoque.com

What to See and Do

1000 Islands Camping Resort. Campground area with pool; tent and trailer sites (hookups, showers, dump station), playground, nature trails, miniature golf (fee). Store, snack bar. Coin lndry. (Mid-May-mid-Oct, daily) 1000 Islands Pkwy, 5 mi (8 km) E. Phone 613/659-3058. Within the park is

Giant Waterslide. A 175-ft (53-m) water slide. (Mid-June-Labour Day, daily) Per hr ¢¢

1000 Islands Skydeck. Atop 400-ft (146-m) tower; elevator to three observation decks. (Early May-late Oct, daily) Between spans of the Thousand Islands International Bridge, on Hill Island, Lansdowne. Phone 613/659-2335. ¢¢

Baskin Robbins Putt 'n Play. An 18-hole miniature golf course. (May-Oct, daily) 787 King St E. Phone 613/382-7888. ¢¢

Gananoque Boat Line. Three-hr tours through the 1000 Islands with a stop at Boldt Castle; snack bar. (Mid-May-mid-Oct; one-hr trips July-Aug) Water St. Phone 613/382-2146. ¢¢¢¢

Gananoque Historical Museum. Former Victoria Hotel (1863); parlour, dining rm, bedrm, kitchen furnished in Victorian style. Military and indigenous artifacts; china, glass, 19th- and 20th-century costumes. (June-Oct, daily) 10 King St E. Phone 613/382-4024. ¢

Motels/Motor Lodges

★★★ **GANANOQUE INN.** *550 Stone St S (K7G 2A8). 613/382-2165; fax 613/382-7912; res 800/465-3101. www.gananoqueinn.com.* 50 rms, 3 story. No elvtr. Early June-early Sept: S, D $99-$180; suites $275-$395; lower rates rest of yr. Crib free. TV; cable. Restaurant 7 am-11 pm. Rm serv. Bar 11:30-2 am, entertainment Thurs-Sat. Business servs avail. Ck-out 11 am. X-country ski 5 mi. Bicycle, boat rentals. Health club privileges. Some in-rm whirlpools. Balconies. Cr cds: A, ER, JCB, MC, V.

★★ **PROVINCIAL INN.** *846 King St E (Hwy 2) (K7G 1H3). 613/382-2038; fax 613/382-8663. www.provincialinn.com.* 78 rms. July-Labour Day: S $68-$120; D $72-$140; each addl $10; lower rates Mar-June, after Labour Day-Oct. Closed rest of yr. Crib $10. TV; cable. Heated pool. Restaurant 7 am-9:30 pm; off-season to 9 pm. Bar noon-10 pm. Ck-out 11 am. Sundries. Gift shop. Lighted tennis. Some in-rm whirlpools. Cr cds: A, C, D, DS, ER, MC, V.

★ **QUALITY INN & SUITES.** *650 King St E (K7G 1H3). 613/382-7292; fax 613/382-4387; 800/228-5151. www.qualityinn.com.* 34 rms, 2 story. Late June-Labour Day: S, D $89-$139; suites $149-$189; under 18 free; lower rates rest of yr. Crib free. TV; cable, VCR avail (movies). Heated pool. Complimentary coffee in rms. Restaurant 8 am-10 pm; off season 11 am-9 pm. Serv bar. Ck-out 11 am. Meeting rms. Business servs avail. Fireplace, in-rm whirlpool in suites. Cr cds: A, C, D, DS, ER, JCB, MC, V.

B&B/Small Inn

★★★ **TRINITY HOUSE.** *90 Stone St S (K7G 1Z8). 613/382-8383; fax 613/382-1599. www.trinityinn.com.* 8 rms, 3 story. No rm phones. S, D $75-$150; suites $135-$190; MAP avail. TV; cable, VCR avail. Complimentary continental bkfst. Dining rm (public by res) sittings from 5:30 pm; closed Mon. Rm serv. Bar. Ck-out 10 am, ck-in 2 pm. Business servs avail. Victorian mansion (1859) built with bricks imported from Scotland. Victorian gardens. Sun deck overlooking waterfalls. Cr cds: MC, V.

Restaurant

★★ **GOLDEN APPLE.** *45 King St W (K7G 2G1). 613/382-3300. www.gananoque.com/goldenapple.* Specializes in prime rib, roast lamb, seafood. Hrs: 11 am-9 pm; Sun brunch to 3 pm. Closed Jan-Mar. Res accepted. Serv bar. A la carte entrees: lunch $6.95-$13.95. Complete meals: dinner $16.95-$29.95. Sun brunch $12.95. Child's menu. Patio dining. Converted 1830 mansion; antiques. Exposed stone walls. Cr cds: A, MC, V.

Hamilton

See also Brantford, Mississauga, St. Catharines, Toronto

Pop 306,434 **Elev** 776 ft (237 m) **Area code** 905
Information Greater Hamilton Visitor and Convention Services, 1 James St S, 3rd Floor, L8P 4R5; 905/546-4222
Web www.hamilton-went.on.ca

Thriving both industrially and culturally, Hamilton is Canada's largest steel center. It is located on Hamilton Harbour, spanned by the majestic Skyway Bridge to Toronto, which offers excellent views of the city.

What to See and Do

African Lion Safari. Drive-through wildlife park; exotic animal and bird shows, demonstrations. Admission incl large game reserves, *African Queen* boat, shows, scenic railway; play areas. Camping (June-Sept, fee). Park (Apr-Oct, daily). W on Hwy 8 between Hamilton and Cambridge, on Safari Rd. Phone 519/623-2620. ¢¢¢¢

Andrés Wines. Escorted tours and tastings. (Apr-Dec, daily; rest of yr, by appt) Wine shop. 5 mi (8 km) W at Kelson Rd & S Service Rd, in Grimsby. Phone 905/643-TOUR.

Art Gallery of Hamilton. Collection of more than 8,000 photographs, sculptures, and photographs covering several centuries, by American, Canadian, British, and European artists. Impressive building; many international, national, and regional exhibitions. (Wed-Sun; closed hols) Fee may be higher for some shows. 123 King St W. Phone 905/527-6610. ¢

Battlefield House and Monument. Devoted to the "Battle of Stoney Creek," this 1795 settler's home and monument honors one of the most significant encounters of the War of 1812. Some rms furnished as a farm home of the 1830s. Guides in period costumes. (Open for tours; mid-May-June and early Sept-mid-Oct, Sun-Fri; July-Labour Day, daily; rest of yr, by appt) QEW exit at Centennial Pkwy, 77 King St in Stoney Creek. Phone 905/662-8458. ¢

Ben Veldhuis Limited. More than two acres (one hectare) of greenhouses; thousands of varieties of cacti, succulents, St. Paulias, and hibiscus; flowering tropical plants. Hibisci bloom all yr. (Daily; closed Jan 1, Dec 25) 154 King St E, off ON 8, W in Dundas. Phone 905/628-6307. **FREE**

Canadian Football Hall of Fame and Museum. Sports museum and national shrine tracing 120 yrs of history of Canadian football. (Daily; closed Sun in winter and spring) 58 Jackson St W. Phone 905/528-7566. ¢¢

Children's Museum. Participatory learning center where children ages 2-13 can expand sensory awareness of the world. "Hands-on" exhibits; changing theme exhibits. (Tues-Sun; closed Dec 25, 26, also Jan and Sept) 1072 Main St E. Phone 905/546-4848. Per child ¢¢

Dundurn Castle. Home of Sir Allan Napier MacNab, Prime Minister of the United Provinces of Canada (1854-1856). The 35-rm mansion is restored to its former splendor. Exhibits, programs, special events featured all yr. Castle (late May-Labour Day and Dec, daily; rest of yr, Tues-Sun; closed Jan 1, Dec 25). York Blvd. Phone 905/546-2872. ¢¢¢

Hamilton Military Museum. Displays Canadian uniforms, equipment, and weapons from ca 1800. (Late May-Labour Day and Dec, daily; rest of yr, Tues-Sun; closed Jan 1, Dec 25) Dundurn Park. Phone 905/546-4974. ¢

Flamboro Downs. Harness racing (all yr). Grandstand seats 3,000; restaurants, lounges. Confederation Cup race for top three-yr-old pacers in North America held here (Aug). 967 Hwy 5, W in Flamborough. Phone 905/627-3561. ¢¢

Hamilton Place. Live theater and concerts featuring international artists in a spectacular cultural center. (All yr) Main St. Phone 905/546-3050.

Hamilton's Farmers Market. Fresh produce, flowers, meat, poultry, fish, cheese, and baked goods are brought from all over the Niagara garden belt. (Tues, Thurs-Sat) 55 York Blvd. Phone 905/546-2096.

Museum of Steam and Technology. An 1859 pumping station contains unique examples of 19th-century steam technology; gallery features permanent and temporary exhibits on modern technology; also special events. Guided tours (daily; closed Jan 1, Dec 25). 900 Woodward Ave. Phone 905/546-4797. ¢¢

Ontario Workers Art & Heritage Centre. Canada's only museum dedicated to preserving the legacy of labor and working people. Incl public resource center, cafe, reading rm, and gift shop. (Wed-Sun) 51 Stuart St. Phone 905/522-3003. **Donation**

Royal Botanical Gardens. Colorful gardens, natural areas, and a wildlife sanctuary. Rock Garden with seasonal displays; Laking Garden (herbaceous perennials); Arboretum (world-famous lilacs in late May); Rose Garden; Teaching Garden; woodland, scented, and medicinal gardens. At Cootes Paradise Sanctuary trails wind around more than 1,200 acres (486 hectares) of water, marsh, and wooded ravines. Mediterranean Garden greenhouse wing has particularly interesting displays (fee). Guided tours (fee). Peak period for gardens: May-Sept. (All yr, daily) Information Centre. 680 Plains Rd W at ON 2, 6, and 403. Phone 905/527-1158. ¢¢¢

Whitehern. Former home of the McQuesten family; 19th-century Georgian mansion furnished with original family possessions. Landscaped gardens. (June-Labour Day, daily; rest of yr, Tues-Sun afternoons; closed Jan 1, Dec 25) Jackson St W and McNab St. Phone 905/522-2018. ¢¢

Special Events

Around the Bay Road Race. Canada's oldest footrace (1894). Phone 905/624-0046. Late Mar.

Hamilton International Air Show. Hamilton Civic Airport. Large international air show. Phone 905/528-4425. Mid-June.

Festival of Friends. Musicians, artists, craftsmen, puppets, dance, mime, theater. Phone 905/525-6644. Second wkend Aug.

FestItalia. Opera, concerts, bicycle race, fashion shows, ethnic foods. Phone 905/546-5300. Mid-Sept.

Hamilton Mum Show. Gage Park, in greenhouses. More than 6,000 blooms. Phone 905/546-2866 or 905/525-6644. First two wks Nov.

Motels/Motor Lodges

★ ★ **ADMIRAL INN.** *149 Dundurn St N (L8R 3E7). 905/529-2311; fax 905/529-9100; toll-free 866/236-4662. www.admiralinn.com.* 58 rms, 3 story. S $59.95; D $63.95; each addl $4; suites $79.95; under 12 free. Crib free. TV; cable (premium), VCR avail. Restaurant 7 am-11 pm. Rm serv. Ck-out 1 am. Meeting rms. Business servs avail. Valet serv. Downhill/x-country ski 10 mi. Microwaves avail. Cr cds: A, D, MC, V.
🐾 🖼 🔥 SC

★ ★ **ADMIRAL INN.** *3500 Billings Ct, Burlington (L7N 3N6). 905/639-4780; fax 905/639-1967; toll-free 866/236-4662. www.admiralinn.com.* 67 rms, 2 story. S $54.95; D $62.95; each addl $4; under 12 free. TV; cable (premium). Restaurant 7 am-11 pm. Bar 11 am-11 pm. Ck-out 11 am. Meeting rms. Business servs avail. Valet serv. Cr cds: A, D, ER, MC, V.
D 🖼 🔥 SC

★ **DAYS INN.** *1187 Upper James St (L9C 3B2). 905/575-9666; fax 905/575-1098; 800/325-2525. www.daysinn.com.* 30 rms, 2 story. Late May-late Sept: S $47-$69; D $55-$89; each addl $7; under 13 free; lower rates rest of yr. Crib free. TV; cable (premium), VCR avail. Complimentary coffee in lobby. Restaurant open 24 hrs. Bar. Ck-out 11 am. Meeting rms. Business servs avail. In-rm modem link. Downhill ski 7 mi. Health club privileges. Some refrigerators; microwaves avail. Cr cds: A, D, DS, ER, MC, V.
🐾 🖼 🔥 SC

★ **ECONO LODGE.** *175 Main St W (L8P 1J1). 905/528-0611; fax 905/528-1130; 800/446-6900. www.econolodge.com.* 57 rms, 2 story. Apr-Sept: S $54.95-$64.95; D $64.95-$74.95; each addl $8; suite $94.29; under 18 free; wkly, hol rates; higher rates wkends (2-day min); lower rates rest of yr. Crib free. TV. Restaurant 7 am-9 pm. Meeting rms. Business servs avail. In-rm modem link. Downhill/x-country ski 15 mi. Microwaves avail. Cr cds: A, C, D, ER, MC, V.
🐾 🖼 🔥 SC

★ **HOWARD JOHNSON.** *112 King St E (L8N 1A8). 905/546-8111; fax 905/546-8144; 800/446-4656. www.hojo.com.* 206 rms, 11 story. S $99; D $109; each addl $10; suites from $139; under 18 free; wknd rates. Crib free. Pet accepted. TV; cable (premium), VCR avail. Indoor pool; whirlpool. Coffee in rms. Restaurant open 24 hrs. Rm serv 24 hrs. Bars 11-2 am. Ck-out noon. Meeting rms. Business servs avail. Barber, beauty shop. Exercise equipt; sauna. Some refrigerators, minibars; microwaves avail. 124-ft (38-m) pool slide. Cr cds: A, C, D, DS, ER, MC, V.
D 🐾 🏊 🏋 🖼 🔥 SC

★ **RAMADA PLAZA HOTEL.** *150 King St E (L8N 1B2). 905/528-3451; fax 905/522-2281; 800/228-2825. www.ramada.com.* 215 rms, 12 story. S, D $69-$110; each addl $10; suites $187.50-$325; under 19 free. Crib free. Pet accepted. TV; cable, VCR avail. Heated pool; wading pool, whirlpool. Restaurant 7 am-9 pm. Bar Fri-Sat 5:30 pm-2 am. Ck-out 11 am. Meeting rms. Business servs avail. Shopping arcade. Barber, beauty shop. Exercise equipt; sauna. Health club privileges. Refrigerators, microwaves avail. Cr cds: A, C, D, DS, ER, MC, V.

D 🐾 ≈ 🏋 🛷 🔥 SC

★ **TRAVELODGE BURLINGTON ON THE LAKE.** *2020 Lakeshore Rd, Burlington (L7S 1Y2). 905/681-0762; fax 905/634-4398; 800/578-7878. www.travelodge.com.* 122 rms, 7 story. S $95; D $105; each addl $10; suites $159; under 18 free. Crib free. Pet accepted, some restrictions. Indoor pool; whirlpool. Continental bkfst. Restaurant adj 7-2 am; Sat, Sun 9 am-midnight. Bar; entertainment. Meeting rms. Business servs avail. Valet serv. Sauna. Sun deck. Picnic tables. Opp lake, beach. Cr cds: A, D, DS, ER, MC, V.

D 🐾 ⚓ ≈ 🛷 🔥 SC

Hotel

★★★ **SHERATON.** *116 King St W (L8P 4V3). 905/529-5515; fax 905/529-8266; 800/325-3535. www.sheraton.com.* 299 units, 18 story. S, D $185-$200; each addl $15; suites from $225; under 17 free; wknd rates. Crib free. Pet accepted. Parking $7.99. TV; cable (premium). Indoor pool; whirlpool. Complimentary coffee in rms. Restaurant 6:30 am-10.30 pm. Rm serv to 1 am. Bar 11-2 am; entertainment. Ck-out noon. Convention facilities. Business center. In-rm modem link. Shopping arcade. Barber, beauty shop. Downhill/x-country ski 4 mi. Exercise equipt; sauna. Health club privileges. Bathrm phones; microwaves avail. Direct access to Convention Centre and Hamilton Place Concert Hall Cr cds: A, C, D, DS, ER, JCB, MC, V.

D 🐾 ≈ ⚓ 🏋 🛷 🔥 SC 🏃

Restaurants

★★★ **ANCASTER OLD MILL INN.** *548 Old Dundas Rd, Ancaster (L9G 3J4). 905/648-1827. www.ancasteroldmill.com.* Continental menu. Specializes in steak, prime rib, fresh seafood. Own baking. Hrs: 11:30 am-2:30 pm, 4:30-8:30 pm; Fri, Sat to 11 pm; Sun to 8 pm; Sun brunch 9 am-2 pm. Res accepted. Bar. Wine list. A la carte entrees: lunch $9.47-$12.97, dinner $16.95-$24.95. Sun brunch $22.97. Child's menu. Pianist wkends. Outdoor dining. Originally a gristmill (1792); tour. Cr cds: A, D, ER, MC, V.

D

★★★ **SHAKESPEARE'S DINING LOUNGE.** *181 Main St E (L8N 1H2). 905/528-0689.* Continental menu. Specializes in steak, seafood, wild game. Hrs: noon-2:30 pm, 5-10:30 pm; Sat 5-11 pm. Closed Sun; Jan 1, Dec 25. Res accepted. Bar. A la carte entrees: lunch $6.50-$18.95, dinner $13.95-$38.95. Elizabethan decor; antique reproductions. Family-owned. Cr cds: A, D, ER, MC, V.

⊟

★★ **SIRLOIN CELLAR.** *14-1/2 James St N (L8R 2J9). 905/525-8620.* Specializes in steak, lobster, fresh seafood. Hrs: 11 am-2:30 pm, 4:30-10 pm; Sat, Sun from 4:30 pm. Closed most major hols. Res accepted. Bar. Lunch $7.95-$15.95, dinner $13.95-$33.95. Cr cds: A, ER, MC, V.

⊟

Kenora

Founded 1882 **Pop** 9,817 **Elev** 1,348 ft (411 m) **Area code** 807

Information Lake of the Woods Visitor Services, 1500 Hwy 17E, P9N 1M3; 807/467-4637 or 800/535-4549

Web www.lakeofthewoods.com

An attractive and prosperous pulp and paper town, Kenora is also a popular resort center and gateway to both the Lake of the Woods area to the south and the wilderness country to the north. Fishing, hunting, boating, sailing, and excellent resort accommodations may be found here, along with 14,500 islands and 65,000 miles (104,600 km) of shoreline on the lake. Winter activities include ice fishing, snowmobiling, downhill and cross-country skiing, curling, and hockey. The Harbourfront in downtown Kenora hosts weekend summer festivals. There are many indigenous pictographs in the area. As fly-in capital of the country, many visitors pass through Kenora on the way to the wilderness of the north.

What to See and Do

Lake cruises. Lake Navigation, Ltd. The MS *Kenora* makes three 18-mi (29-km) cruises through the many islands and channels of Lake of the Woods (daily). Incl is Devil's Gap, with its "spirit rock" painting. Lunch, mid-afternoon, and dinner cruises. Restaurant, bar. (Mid-May-early-Oct, daily) Harbourfront Wharf. Phone 807/468-9124. ¢¢¢

Lake of the Woods Museum. Houses more than 15,000 articles reflecting local, native, and pioneer history. (July-Aug, daily; Sept-June, Tues-Sat) 300 Main St. Phone 807/467-2105. ¢¢

Rushing River Provincial Park. Approx 400 acres (160 hectares). Beautiful natural setting with a long and photogenic cascade. Swimming, fishing, boating; nature and X-country skiing trails, picnicking, playground, camping (fee, res), museum (summer, daily). Park (all yr). 12 mi (20 km) E on Hwy 17 and 4 mi (6 km) S on Hwy 71. Per vehicle (summer) ¢¢

Stone Consolidated. Paper manufacturing process is followed from debarking of logs to the finished product. Ages 12 yrs and over only. Flat, closed-toe shoes required. (June-Sept, Mon and Wed-Fri, by res only) 504 9th St N. Phone 807/467-3000. **FREE**

Special Events

ESCAPE (Exciting, Scenic, Canadian/American Powerboat Excursion). Lake of the Woods. Four-day event for powerboats to explore the many channels, islands, and historic features of the lake. Canadian and US participants meet in vicinity of Flag Island, MN. Early July. Phone 807/467-4650.

Kenora International Bass Fishing Tournament. Three-day competition. Early Aug. Phone 807/467-4650.

Kenora Agricultural Fair. Kenora Recreation Centre Complex. Three days of competitions and cultural exhibitions incl a midway show. Mid-Aug. Phone 807/467-4650.

Motels/Motor Lodges

★★ **BEST WESTERN LAKESIDE INN.** *470 1st Ave S (P9N 1W5). 807/468-5521; fax 807/468-4734; toll-free 800/465-1120. www.bestwestern.com.* 94 rms, 11 story. S $96; D $106; each addl $10; suites $175-$225; under 12 free. TV; cable (premium). Indoor pool. Complimentary coffee in rms. Restaurant 7 am-10 pm. Bar 11:30 am-midnight. Ck-out 11 am. Meeting rms. Downhill/x-country ski 4 mi. Sauna. On lakeshore. Cr cds: A, C, D, ER, MC, V.

⊡ 🛍 ⊠ ⊠ 🐾 🖎 SC

★ **COMFORT INN.** *1230 Hwy 17E (P9N 1L9). 807/468-8845; fax 807/468-1588; toll-free 800/228-5150. www.comfortinn.com.* 77 rms, 2 story. Mid-June-mid-Sept: S $70-$90; D $75-$100; each addl $4; under 18 free; lower rates rest of yr. Crib free. Pet accepted. TV; cable. Restaurant nearby. Ck-out 11 am. Business servs avail. Cr cds: A, D, DS, ER, MC, V.

⊡ 🐾 ⊠ 🖎 SC

★ **TRAVELODGE.** *800 Sunset Strip (P9N 1L9). 807/468-3155; fax 807/468-4780; 800/578-7878. www.travelodge.com.* 42 rms, 1-2 story, 5 kits. Mid-June-mid-Sept: S $75-$80; D $75-$104; lower rates rest of yr. Crib $6. Pet accepted. TV; cable (premium). 2 pools, 1 indoor; whirlpool. Playground. Restaurant 6 am-11 pm. Rm serv. Bar 11-1 am. Ck-out noon. Meeting rms. Business servs avail. Valet serv. Downhill/x-country ski 6 mi. Exercise equipt; sauna. Health club privileges. Picnic tables. Cr cds: A, D, DS, ER, JCB, MC, V.

⊡ 🐾 ⊠ ⊠ 🕴 🖎 🔥 SC

Kingston

See also Gananoque

Founded 1673 **Pop** 55,051 **Elev** 305 ft (93 m)
Area code 613
Information Tourist Information Office, 209 Ontario St, K7L 2Z1; 613/548-4415 or 888/855-4555
Web www.kingstoncanada.com

Kingston is a city rich in tradition and Kingstonians are justly proud of their city's 300-year history. Since July 1673 when Count Frontenac, Governor of New France, erected a fort on the site of present-day Kingston, the city has played an important part in Canadian history. It was here that the United Empire Loyalists relocated to begin their new life. Kingston also had the honor of being the capital of the United Provinces from 1841-44. However, because Kingston was vulnerable to attack by water from the United States, the capital was moved to Montréal and later to Ottawa. Although Kingston did not retain its position as the capital city, its citizens can boast that it was a Kingstonian, Sir John A. MacDonald, who was the first Prime Minister of Canada and who later became known as the Father of Confederation.

Since Fort Frontenac was built in 1673, Kingston has grown and prospered to become a flourishing city. Yet over the years Kingston has not lost its unique charm and grace. In honor of the centennial year a beautiful waterfront area was created in front of City Hall with a new yacht basin.

Located at the eastern end of Lake Ontario where it empties into the St. Lawrence, Kingston is Canada's freshwater sailing capital.

What to See and Do

Bellevue House National Historic Site. Italianate villa (1840) was home of Sir John A. Macdonald, first Prime Minister of Canada. Restored and furnished with period pieces. Modern display and video presentation at Visitor Centre. (Apr-Oct, daily; rest of yr, by appt) 35 Centre St. Phone 613/545-8666. ¢

Boat trips.

Canadian Empress. This replica of a traditional steamship cruises St. Lawrence and Ottawa rivers on six different routes; trips span four or five nights, some reaching Montréal and Québec City. (Mid-May-Nov) Ages 12 and up. Departs from front of City Hall. Contact St. Lawrence Cruise Lines, 253 Ontario St, K7L 2Z4. Phone 613/549-8091. ¢¢¢¢

Island Queen. Showboat of the 1,000 Islands. Offers three-hr river cruises through the Islands. (May-Oct, daily) For information and res contact Kingston & The Islands Boatline, 6 Princess St, K7L 1A2. Departs from Kingston Harbour, Downtown. Phone 613/549-5544. ¢¢¢

City Hall. Built of limestone in 1843-1844 while Kingston was capital of the United Provinces of Canada. (Mon-Fri, daily) 216 Ontario St. Phone 613/546-4291. **FREE**

Confederation Tour Trolley. 50-min, 10-mi (16-km) narrated tour of Kingston. (Victoria Day-Labour Day, daily on the hr; charters avail) Leaves from Confederation Park, 209 Ontario St. Phone 613/548-4453. ¢¢

Correctional Service of Canada Museum. Displays a variety of artifacts and documents related to the early history of Canadian penitentiaries. Incl displays of contraband weapons and escape devices. 555 King St W. Phone 613/530-3122. **Donation**

Fort Henry. One of Ontario's most spectacular historic sites, the present fortification was built in the 1830s and restored during the 1930s. Guided tour; 19th-century British infantry and artillery drills; military pageantry; exhibits of military arms, uniforms, equipment; garrison life activities. Fort (mid-May-late Sept, daily). E at jct Hwys 2 & 15. Phone 613/542-7388. ¢¢

Grand Theatre. Century-old, renovated theater. Live theater, dance, symphonic, and children's performances by professional companies and local groups; summer theater (see SPECIAL EVENTS). (Daily) 218 Princess St. Phone 613/530-2050.

International Ice Hockey Federation Museum. Displays trace history of hockey from its beginning in Kingston in 1885-present. (Mid-June-Labour Day, daily; rest of yr, by appt) 303 York St. Phone 613/544-2355. ¢

MacLachlan Woodworking Museum. (ca 1850) "Wood in the service of humanity" is theme of museum; highlights life of the pioneer farmer in both the field and kitchen, as well as workshops of a cooper, blacksmith, cabinetmaker. (Victoria Day-Labour Day, daily; Mar-mid-May, early Sept-Oct, Wed-Sun) 2993 Hwy 2, 10 mi (16 km) E in Grass Creek Park. Phone 613/542-0543. ¢¢

Marine Museum of the Great Lakes at Kingston. Ships have been built in Kingston since 1678. This museum explores the tales, adventures, and enterprise of "Inland Seas" history. Ship Building Gallery, 1889 Engine Room, with dry dock engines and pumps; artifacts; changing exhibits. Library and archives. The **Museum Ship** *Alexander Henry,* a 3,000-ton icebreaker, is open for tours and bed & breakfast accommodations (Victoria Day-Thanksgiving). (May-Dec, daily; rest of yr, Mon-Fri; closed Dec 25) 55 Ontario St, on the waterfront. Phone 613/542-2261. Each museum ¢¢ One blk away is

   Pump House Steam Museum. Displays on steam technology, model trains, small engines. (June-Labour Day, daily) 23 Ontario St. Phone 613/542-2261. ¢¢

Murney Tower Museum. (1846) Martello tower is now a museum with exhibits of the area's military and social history. Changing exhibits. (Mid-May-Labour Day, daily) King St at Barrie. Phone 613/544-9925. ¢¢

Queen's University. (1841) 13,000 students. Between Barrie, Union, Collingwood, and King Sts. **FREE** On campus are

   Agnes Etherington Art Centre. Changing exhibitions of contemporary and historical art. (Tues-Sun; closed hols) University Ave and Queen's Crescent. Phone 613/545-2190. ¢

   Geology Museum. Collection of minerals from around the world. (Mon-Fri; closed hols) Miller Hall on Union St. Phone 613/545-6767.

Royal Military College of Canada. (1876) 800 students. Canada's first military college and first institution of its kind to achieve university status. E of Kingston Harbour on Hwy 2. On grounds is

   Fort Frederick & College Museum. Exhibits depict history of college and the earlier Royal Dockyard (1789-1853); Douglas Collection of small arms and weapons that once belonged to General Porfirio Diaz, president of Mexico from 1886-1912. (Late June-Labour Day, daily) In large Martello Tower. Phone 613/541-6000. **FREE**

Special Events

It's a Grand Summer. Grand Theatre. Late June-Labor Day. Phone 613/530-2050. **FREE**

Pittsburgh Sheepdog Trials. Grass Creek Park. Incl sheepshearing demonstrations and a variety of related activities. Phone 888/855-4555. Early Aug.

Motels/Motor Lodges

★★ **BEST WESTERN.** *1217 Princess St (K7M 3E1).* *613/549-2211; fax 613/549-4523; 800/528-1234.* *www.bestwestern.com.* 75 rms, 2 story. S, D $96.50-$139; each addl $10; under 17 free; suites $179-$429. Crib free. TV; cable (premium). Heated pool. Restaurant 7 am-11 pm. Rm serv. Bar 11:30-1 am. Ck-out noon. Meeting rms. Business servs avail. In-rm modem link. Valet serv. Sundries. Fireplaces; some in-rm whirlpools. Cr cds: A, C, D, DS, ER, MC, V.
⊠ 🔥 SC

★★ **FIRST CANADA INN.** *1 First Canada Ct (K7K 6W2).* *613/541-1111; fax 613/549-5735.* 74 rms, 2 story. June-Sept: S, D $61.95-$99.95; each addl $5; suites $85.95-$165.95; under 12 free; lower rates rest of yr. Crib free. Pet accepted. TV; cable, VCR avail (movies). Complimentary continental bkfst. Coin lndry. Meeting rms. Business servs avail. Refrigerators. Cr cds: A, D, ER, MC, V.
D 🔄 ⊠ 🔄 🐾 SC

★★ **GREEN ACRES.** *2480 Princess St (Hwy 2) (K7M 3G4).* *613/546-1796; fax 613/542-5521; toll-free 800/267-7889.* *www.greenacresinn.com.* 31 rms, 2 kits. July-Aug: S $74-$105; D $84-$185; each addl $6; kit. suites $175; lower rates rest of yr. Crib $6. TV; cable (premium), VCR. Heated pool. Playground. Continental bkfst. Coffee in rms. Ck-out 11 am. Coin lndry. Meeting rm. Valet serv. X-country ski 10 mi. Health club privileges. Lawn games. Refrigerators; fireplace, whirlpool in suites; some microwaves. Picnic tables, gas grill. Cr cds: A, MC, V.
🔄 ⊠ 🔄 🐾 SC

★ **HOWARD JOHNSON.** *237 Ontario St (K7L 2Z4).* *613/549-6300; fax 613/549-1508; 800/446-4656.* *www.hojo.com.* 94 rms, 6 story. May-late Sept: S, D $99-$160; each addl $10; suites $225-$250; under 18 free; higher rates special events; lower rates rest of yr. Crib free. Pet accepted. TV; cable. Heated pool; whirlpool, poolside serv. Restaurant 7 am-10 pm. Rm serv. Ck-out 11 am. Meeting rms. Business servs avail. Underground free parking. X-country ski 3 mi. Exercise equipt. Health club privileges. On waterfront. Cr cds: A, D, DS, ER, MC, V.
🐾 🔄 ⊠ 🧍 🔄 🐾 SC

★ **KINGSTON EAST.** *1488 Hwy 15 (K7L 5Y6).* *613/546-6674; fax 613/546-5896.* 22 rms. Mid-June-mid-Sept: S, D $60-$75; each addl $5; kit. units $10 addl; lower rates rest of yr. Crib $5. TV. Heated pool. Playground. Restaurant 7 am-7 pm. Ck-out 11 am. Sundries. Some refrigerators. Picnic tables, grills. Cr cds: MC, V.
⊠ 🔥

★ **KNIGHTS INN.** *2327 Princess St (Hwy 2) & Sybenham Rd (K7M 3G1).* *613/531-8929.* *www.knightsinn.com.* 32 rms, 8 kits. May-Labour Day: S $48; D $58-$78; each addl $7; kit. units $7 addl; lower rates rest of yr. Crib avail. Pet accepted; $12/day. TV; cable. Heated pool. Playground. Complimentary coffee in lobby. Restaurant adj 7 am-9 pm. Ck-out 11 am. Refrigerators. Picnic tables. Grills. Cr cds: A, C, D, ER, MC, V.
D 🐾 ⊠ 🔄 🐾 SC

★ **SEVEN OAKES.** *2331 Princess St (Hwy 2) (K7M 3G1). 613/546-3655; fax 613/546-0293.* 40 rms. June-Sept: S $64; D $68-$74; each addl $5; package plans; lower rates rest of yr. Crib free. Pet accepted. Heated pool; whirlpool. Sauna. Playground. Bar. Ck-out 11 am. Coin lndry. Sundries. Lighted tennis. Refrigerators; some in-rm whirlpools. Picnic tables, grills. Cr cds: A, D, DS, ER, MC, V.

★ **TRAVELODGE HOTEL LA SALLE.** *2360 Princess St (K7M 3G4). 613/546-4233; fax 613/546-0867; 800/578-7878. www.travelodge.com.* 69 rms, 4 story. May-mid Sept: S, D $72-$90; under 12 free; lower rates rest of yr. Crib free. TV; cable, VCR avail. Indoor pool; whirlpool. Restaurant 6 am-10 pm. Rm serv. Bar 11 am-11 pm. Ck-out noon. Meeting rms. Business servs avail. Sauna. Sundries. Balconies. Cr cds: A, D, DS, ER, JCB, MC, V.

Resort

★★★ **ISAIAH TUBBS RESORT.** *RR 1, W Lake Rd, Picton (K0K 2T0). 613/393-2090; fax 613/393-1291. www.someplacesdifferent.com.* 60 rms in lodge, inn, many A/C, 12 kit. cabins. No phone in cabins. July-Labour Day: S $95-$200; D $150-$220; each addl $10; kit. suites $219-$252; cabins $650-$900/wk; under 5 free; MAP, conference plan avail; lower rates rest of yr. Crib free. TV. 2 pools, 1 indoor; whirlpool. Playground. Free supervised children's activities (July-Aug); ages 4-12. Dining rm 8-1 am. Ck-out 11 am, ck-in 4 pm. Coin lndry. Meeting rms. Business servs avail. Tennis. Swimming beach. X-country ski 1 mi. Lawn games. Exercise equipt; sauna. Some refrigerators. Picnic tables, grills. On West Lake, adj Sandbanks Provincial Park. Cr cds: A, D, ER, MC, V.

B&Bs/Small Inns

★★★ **HOCHELAGA.** *24 S Sydenham St (K7L 3G9). 613/549-5534. www.someplacesdifferent.com.* 23 rms, 3 story. S, D $135-$185; each addl $10; under 5 free; lower rates rest of yr. Crib free. TV; cable (premium). Complimentary continental bkfst. Restaurant nearby. Ck-out 11 am, ck-in 3 pm. Business servs avail. Some balconies. Renovated house (1872); period antiques. Cr cds: A, D, ER, MC, V.

★★★ **MERRILL.** *343 Main St E, Picton (K0K 2T0). 613/476-7451; fax 613/476-8283. www.merrillinn.com.* 14 rms, 3 story, 2 suites. No elvtr. July-Sept: S, D $95-$185; each addl $10; suites $185; under 3 free; lower rates rest of yr. Crib free. TV; cable (premium). Complimentary continental bkfst. Restaurant 11 am-11 pm. Ck-out 11 am, ck-in 3 pm. Meeting rm. Lawn games. Rms individually decorated with period antiques. Brick Victorian house (ca 1878); built for Edwards Merrill, one of Canada's top barristers. Cr cds: A, D, ER, MC, V.

★★★ **ROSEMOUNT INN.** *46 Sydenham St S (K7L 3H1). 613/531-8844; fax 613/544-4895; toll-free 888/871-8844. www.rosemountinn.com.* 8 rms, 2 story, 1 cabin. No A/C. No rm phones. S, D $109-$159; each addl $30-$50; cabin $225; wkends, hols (2-day min). Closed Mid-Dec-early Jan. Children over 13 yrs only. Complimentary full bkfst; afternoon refreshments. Ck-out 11 am, ck-in 4 pm. Business servs avail. Luggage handling. Valet serv. Concierge serv. Gift shop. Some street parking. X-country ski 5 mi. Massage. Fireplace. Built in 1850. Victorian decor; antiques. Totally nonsmoking. Cr cds: A, MC, V.

Restaurant

★★ **AUNT LUCY'S.** *1399 Princess St (ON 2) (K7M 3E9). 613/542-2729.* Specializes in steak, seafood, pasta. Hrs: 11:30 am-11 pm. Bar. Lunch, dinner $5.95-$19.95. Sun brunch $10.99. Child's menu. Open-hearth grill. Family-owned. Cr cds: A, DS, MC, V.

Kitchener-Waterloo

Pop 139,734 **Elev** Kitchener, 1,100 ft (335 m); Waterloo, 1,075 ft (328 m) **Area code** 519

Information Visitor & Convention Bureau, 80 Queen St N, Kitchener N2H 6L4; 519/745-3536 or 800/265-6959

Web www.kw-visitor.on.ca

The twin cities of Kitchener-Waterloo were settled in the early 1800s by Mennonites, Amish, and Germans whose cultural heritage is still clearly visible. Not far to the north in Elmira is the heart of Ontario's Pennsylvania German country, with Maple Sugar Festival and tours of Mennonite country. Although Kitchener and Waterloo are separate cities, each takes pride in the achievements of the other. A vigorous spirit of youth and industry pervades both cities, making a visit to the Kitchener-Waterloo area a pleasure for any traveler.

What to See and Do

Bingeman Park. Recreation center on banks of Grand River; swimming (pool, wave pool), watersliding, bumper boats; go-cart track, arcade, roller skating, miniature golf, golf driving range, batting cages, X-country skiing; picnicking, restaurant; playground, camping. Park (summer, daily; also spring and fall, weather permitting). Campgrounds and restaurant (all yr, daily). Fee for some activities. 1380 Victoria St N, Kitchener. Phone 519/744-1555.

Doon Heritage Crossroads. Re-creation of early 20th-century village (ca 1915) incl museum, grocery store, post office/tailor shop, blacksmith, church, 2 farms, and several houses. (May-late Dec, daily; closed Dec 23) Hwy 401 exit 275, Homer Watson Blvd. Phone 519/748-1914 or 519/575-4530. ¢¢¢

Farmers Market. More than 100 vendors sell fresh produce, meat, cheese, and handicrafts. Mennonite specialties featured. (All yr, Sat; mid-May-mid-Oct, also Wed). Market Sq, Frederick and Duke Sts, downtown Kitchener. Phone 519/741-2287. **FREE**

Glockenspiel. Canada's first glockenspiel tells fairy tale of Snow White. Twenty-three bells form the carillon. Performance lasts 15 min (four times daily). King & Benton Sts.

Joseph Schneider Haus. Pennsylvania German Mennonite house (1820), one of area's oldest homesteads, restored and furnished; "living" museum with costumed interpreters; daily demonstrations. Adj Heritage Galleries, incl Germanic folk art; exhibits change every three months. (Victoria Day-Labour Day, daily; rest of yr, Tues-Sun; closed Jan 1, Dec 25, 26) 466 Queen St S, Kitchener. Phone 519/742-7752. ¢¢

Kitchener-Waterloo Art Gallery. Six exhibition areas cover all aspects of the visual arts. Gift shop. (Tues-Sun; closed hols) 101 Queen St N, at The Centre in the Square. Phone 519/579-5860. **FREE**

Laurel Creek Conservation Area. Approx 750 acres (305 hectares) of multipurpose area. Dam, swimming beach, boating (no motors); hiking, sports fields, camping (fee), picnicking, reforested areas, bird-watching. (May-mid-Oct) NW corner of Waterloo, bounded by Westmount Rd, Conservation Dr and Beaver Creek Rd. Phone 519/884-6620. ¢¢

Museum & Archive of Games. Collection incl over 3,500 games. Many "hands-on" exhibits drawn from collection ranging from Inuit bone games to computer games. Exhibits change every four months. Archive contains documents pertaining to games and game-playing. (Tues-Thurs and Sun; closed school hols) B.C. Matthews Hall, University of Waterloo. Phone 519/888-4424. **FREE**

The Seagram Museum. Complex is housed in century-old, renovated barrel warehouse and is devoted to history and technology of the wine and spirits industry; restaurant. (May-Dec, daily; rest of yr, Tues-Sun; closed Jan 1, Dec 25) 57 Erb St W, Waterloo. Phone 519/885-1857.

Waterloo Park. Log schoolhouse built 1820 surrounded by picnic area and lake; playground. Small zoo and band concerts in summer (Sun). Central St, Waterloo. Phone 519/747-8733. **FREE**

Waterloo-St. Jacobs Railway. Streamliner tourist train rolls into the heart of Mennonite farm country. Stops allow exploration of the quaint village of St. Jacobs and the St. Jacobs Farmers Market. Ninety min, round-trip. (May-Oct, daily; Nov-Apr, wkends) Departs Waterloo Station, 10 Father David Bauer Dr. Phone 519/746-1950. ¢¢¢

Woodside National Historic Site. Boyhood home of William Lyon Mackenzie King, Canada's 10th prime minister. 1890s Victorian restoration. Interpretive center has theater and display on King's early life and career. Picnicking. (May-Dec, daily; closed hols) 528 Wellington St N, Kitchener. Phone 519/742-5273. **FREE** Nearby is

Pioneer Memorial Tower. Tribute to industrious spirit of pioneers who first settled Waterloo County. Cemetery on grounds incl graves of several original founders. Excellent view of Grand River. (May-Oct) Phone 519/571-5684. **FREE**

Special Events

Waterloo County Quilt Festival. Quilt exhibits, displays, workshops, and demonstrations. Phone 800/265-6959 or 519/699-5628. Nine days mid-May.

Ale Trail. Showcases region's brewing industry and allows visitors to experience the craft of brewing at six different area breweries. Phone 800/334-4519. Mid-June.

Sounds of Summer Music Festival. Waterloo Park. Three days mid-June.

White Owl Culture Pow-Wow. Celebration of North American Aboriginal Culture in Waterloo Park. Phone 519/743-8635. Mid-June.

Kitchener-Waterloo Multicultural Festival. Victoria Park. Phone 519/745-2531. Late June.

Busker Carnival Festival. International showcase of street performers. Phone 519/747-8738. Late Aug.

Wellesley Apple Butter & Cheese Festival. Pancake breakfast, farmers market, free tours of farms, cider mill; horseshoe tournament, quilt auction, smorgasbord dinner, model boat regatta, antique cars and tractors. Phone 519/656-2222. Last Sat Sept.

Motels/Motor Lodges

★ **BEST WESTERN.** *730 Hespeler Rd, Cambridge (N3H 5L8). 519/623-4600; fax 519/623-2688; 800/528-1234. www.bestwestern.com.* 106 rms, 7 story, 11 suites. S $99.99; D $109; each addl $10; suites $119; under 12 free; wkly rates; higher rates Oktoberfest. Crib free. TV; cable (premium). Indoor pool; whirlpool. Sauna. Complimentary continental bkfst. Coffee in rms. Restaurant nearby. Ck-out 11 am. Coin lndry. Meeting rms. Business servs avail. In-rm modem link. Downhill/x-country ski 5 mi. Game rm. Refrigerators; microwaves avail. Cr cds: A, D, DS, ER, MC, V.
🅳 ⏷ ⌁ ⊠ 🌢 SC

★★ **COMFORT INN.** *220 Holiday Inn Dr, Cambridge (N3C 1Z4). 519/658-1100; fax 519/658-6979; 800/228-5150. www.comfortinn.com.* 84 rms, 2 story. S $59-$80; D $67-$95; each addl $4; under 18 free. Crib free. Pet accepted. TV; cable (premium). Complimentary coffee in lobby. Ck-out 11 am. Business servs avail. Sundries. Downhill/x-country ski 4 mi. Cr cds: A, C, D, DS, ER, JCB, MC, V.
🕐 ⏷ ⊠ 🌢 SC

★★★ **FOUR POINTS BY SHERATON.** *105 E King St, Kitchener (N2G 2K8). 519/744-4141; fax 519/578-6889; 800/325-3535. www.sheraton.com.* 201 rms, 9 story. S, D $119-$139; each addl $10; suites $130-$269; studio rms $79; under 18 free; wkend package. Crib free. Pet accepted, some restrictions. TV; cable. Pool; whirlpool, poolside serv. Complimentary coffee in rms. Restaurant 6:30 am-2 pm, 5:30-10:30 pm. Bar 5 pm-1 am. Ck-out noon. Meeting rms. Business center. In-rm modem link. Free covered parking. Downhill/x-country ski 4 mi. Exercise rm; sauna. Game rm. Miniature golf. Rec rm. Minibars; microwaves avail. Some balconies. Cr cds: A, C, D, ER, MC, V.
🅳 🕐 ⏷ ⌁ 🍴 ⊠ 🌢 SC 🏃

★★ **HOLIDAY INN.** *30 Fairway Rd S, Kitchener (N2A 2N2). 519/893-1211; fax 519/894-8518; 800/465-4329. www.holiday-inn.com.* 182 rms, 2-6 story. S $125.95-$145.95; D $136.95-$156.95; each addl $10; suites $205.95-$305.95; under 19 free. Crib free. Pet accepted. TV; cable (premium). Indoor/outdoor pool; poolside serv. Supervised children's activities (July-Aug). Complimentary coffee in rms. Restaurant 6:30 am-10 pm. Bar 11-1 am. Ck-out noon. Meeting rms. In-rm modem link. Valet serv. Downhill/x-country ski 2 mi. Exercise equipt. Microwaves avail. Private patios, balconies. Cr cds: A, C, D, DS, ER, JCB, MC, V.

D 🐾 ≈ 🏊 🏃 ⛷ 🔥 SC

★ **HOWARD JOHNSON CONESTOGA.** *1333 Weber St E, Kitchener (N2A 1C2). 519/893-1234; fax 519/893-2100; 800/446-4656. www.hojo.com.* 102 rms, 2-4 story. S $89-$109; D $99-$129; each addl $10; under 18 free; higher rates Oktoberfest. Crib free. Pet accepted, some restrictions; $50 refundable. TV; cable. Heated pool; whirlpool, poolside serv. Sauna. Complimentary coffee in rms. Restaurant 7 am-9 pm. Rm serv. Bar 11-1 am; entertainment Thurs-Sat. Ck-out 11:30 am. Meeting rms. Business center. Sundries. Some refrigerators; microwaves avail. Balconies. Cr cds: A, C, D, DS, ER, JCB, MC, V.

D 🐾 ≈ ⛷ 🔥 SC 🏃

★ **NEWBURG INN.** *Hwy 7 & 8 W, New Hamburg (N0B 2G0). 519/662-3990.* 12 rms. S $50; D $75; each addl $5; suite $75; monthly rates. TV; cable. Complimentary coffee in lobby. Restaurant nearby. Ck-out 11 am. Some refrigerators. Cr cds: A, MC, V.

🔥

★★★ **WATERLOO INN.** *475 King St N, Waterloo (N2J 2Z5). 519/884-0220; fax 519/884-0321; toll-free 800/361-4708. www.waterlooinn.com.* 155 rms, 4 story. S $93; D $103; each addl $12; suites from $125; under 16 free. Crib free. Pet accepted. TV; cable. Indoor pool; whirlpool, poolside serv. Complimentary coffee in rms. Restaurant 7 am-10 pm. Rm serv 24 hrs. Bar 11-1 am. Convention facilities. Business servs avail. In-rm modem link. Valet serv. Sundries. Downhill ski 10 mi; x-country ski ½ mi. Exercise equipt; sauna. Game rm. Balconies. Landscaped courtyard. Cr cds: A, D, DS, ER, JCB, MC, V.

D 🐾 ⛷ ≈ 🏃 ⛷ 🔥 SC

Hotels

★★★ **LANGDON HALL.** *RR 33, Cambridge (N3H 5R8). 519/740-2100; fax 519/740-8161. www.langdonhall.ca.* 43 rms, 3 story. 2-day min: S, D $229-$269; suites $369; under 10 free. Crib free. Pet accepted, some restrictions; $25. TV; cable (premium), VCR avail. Heated pool; whirlpool, poolside serv. Complimentary continental bkfst. Restaurant (see also LANGDON HALL). Rm serv 24 hrs. Bar. Ck-out noon. Meeting rms. Business servs avail. In-rm modem link. Gift shop. Tennis. Downhill ski 4 mi; x-country ski on site. Hiking trail. Exercise equipt; sauna, steam rm. Massage. Rec rm. Lawn games. Balconies. Antebellum-style building in rural setting. Cr cds: A, D, ER, MC, V.

D 🐾 ⛷ 🎿 ≈ 🏃 🏊 🔥

★★ **WALPER TERRACE.** *1 King St W, Kitchener (N2G 1A1). 519/745-4321; fax 519/745-3625; res 800/265-8749. www.walper.com.* 63 rms, 5 story, 22 suites. S, D $99; each addl $10; suites $110-$210; under 16 free; wkend rates. Crib free. TV; cable (premium), VCR avail. Complimentary coffee in rms. Restaurant 7:30-1 am. Bar from 11:30 am. Ck-out noon. Business servs avail. Barber, beauty shop. Free parking. Health club privileges. Restored landmark hotel in the heart of downtown; retains air of old-European elegance. Cr cds: A, D, DS, ER, MC, V.

🔀 🔥 SC

B&B/Small Inn

★★★ **ELORA MILL.** *77 Mill St W, Elora (N0B 1S0). 519/846-5356; fax 519/846-9180. www.eloramill.com.* 32 rms, 5 story. S, D $150-$170; each addl $50; suites $220; under 13, $25. TV; cable. Complimentary full bkfst. Restaurant (see also ELORA MILL). Bar 4:30 pm-1 am. Ck-out 11:30 am, ck-in 4 pm. Meeting rm. Business servs avail. Valet serv. X-country ski 1 mi. Health club privileges. Some refrigerators, fireplaces. Located in historic pre-Confederation village. Cr cds: A, ER, MC, V.

🔀 🔀

Restaurants

★★ **BENJAMIN'S.** *1430 King N, St. Jacobs (N0B 2N0). 519/664-3731. www.stjacobs.com/benjamins.* Contemporary menu. Specializes in beef, pasta, seafood. Hrs: 11:30 am-3 pm, 3-5 pm (tea), 5-9 pm; Thurs-Sat to 10 pm. Closed Jan 1, Dec 25, 26. Res accepted. Bar. A la carte entrees: lunch $6.95-$9.25, dinner $13.50-$21. Re-creation of 1850s country inn; fireplace, artifacts. Cr cds: A, C, D, DS, ER, MC, V.

D

★★★ **CHARCOAL STEAK HOUSE.** *2980 King St E, Kitchener (N2A 1A9). 519/893-6570.* Specializes in steak, spareribs, pigtails. Own baking. Hrs: 11:30-1 am; Sat from noon; Sun 10 am-11 pm. Res accepted. Bar. Wine list. A la carte entrees: lunch $7-$16, dinner $12-$44. Child's menu. Parking. Cr cds: A, D, ER, MC, V.

D

★★★ **ELORA MILL.** *77 Mill St W, Elora (N0B 1S0). 519/846-5356. www.eloramill.com.* Regional menu. Own baking. Hrs: 8-10 am, 11:30 am-2 pm, 5-8 pm; Fri, Sat to 9 pm. Res accepted. Bar. A la carte entrees: bkfst $7.95, lunch $8.95-$13.95, dinner $19.95-$29.95. Parking. Restored gristmill (1859). Cr cds: A, D, ER, MC, V.

D

★★★ **LANGDON HALL.** *RR 33, Cambridge (N3H 4R8). 519/740-2100. www.langdonhall.ca.* Specialties: goat cheese quenelle, roasted veal with tarragon, twice-cooked duck. Hrs: 7-10 am, noon-2 pm, 6-9 pm. Res required. Bar noon-1 am. Wine cellar. A la carte entrees: bkfst $4.75-$7.25, lunch $13.75-$19.75, dinner $54-$65. Parking. Outdoor dining. Elegant dining rm overlooking park. Gardens. Cr cds: A, D, ER, MC, V.

D

★★ **STONE CROCK.** *59 Church St W, Elmira (N3B 1M8).* *519/669-1521.* Specializes in spareribs, turkey, cabbage rolls. Salad bar. Hrs: 7 am-8:30 pm; Sun from 11 am. Closed Dec 25. Bkfst $1.75-$5.75, lunch $5-$9.50, dinner $8.50-$10.95. Buffet: dinner $13.25. Sat, Sun brunch $10.95. Child's menu. Parking. Country atmosphere. Gift shop. Cr cds: A, D, ER, MC, V.
D

★★★ **WATERLOT.** *17 Huron St, New Hamburg (N0B 2G0).* *519/662-2020. www3.sympatico.ca/waterlot.* French menu. Specializes in crab crepes, duckling. Own baking. Hrs: 11:30 am-2 pm, 5-8:30 pm; Sun 5-7:30 pm; Sun brunch (2 sittings) 11:30 am, 1:30 pm. Closed Mon; Good Friday, Dec 25. Res accepted. Bar. Wine list. A la carte entrees: lunch $7.95-$13.95, dinner $15.50-$28.50. Complete meals: dinner (Sun-Fri) $24. Sun brunch $16.95. Child's menu. Victorian house (1845); guest rms avail. Cr cds: A, D, MC, V.
D

London

Pop 300,000 **Elev** 912 ft (278 m) **Area code** 519
Information Tourism London, 300 Dufferin Ave, N6B 1Z2; 519/661-4500 or 800/265-2602
Web www.londontourism.ca

Called the "Forest City," London is a busy modern city with charming small-town atmosphere. Located on the Thames River, its street names are similar to those of the other London. A contrast of Victorian architecture and contemporary skyscrapers is prevalent here.

What to See and Do

Double-decker Bus Tour of London. Two-hr guided tour aboard authentic double-decker English bus with stop at Storybook Gardens in Springbank Park and Regional Art Museum. Departs City Hall (Wellington St and Dufferin Ave). (July-Labour Day, daily) Res suggested. Phone 519/661-5000 or 800/265-2602. ¢¢¢

Eldon House. (1834) Oldest house in town; occupied by same family until donated to the city. Furnished much as it was in the 19th century with many antiques from abroad. Spacious grounds, lawns, brick paths, gardens, conservatory-greenhouse. Guided tours (by appt). (Tues-Sun; closed Dec 25) 481 Ridout St N. Phone 519/661-5169. ¢¢

Fanshawe Pioneer Village. Living history museum of 24 buildings moved to this site to display artifacts and re-create the life of a typical 19th-century crossroads community in southwestern Ontario. Log cabin, barns, and stable; blacksmith, weaver, harness, gun, woodworking, and barber shops; general store, church, fire hall, school, and sawmill; costumed interpreters. (May-Oct, Wed-Sun; Nov-mid-Dec, daily) Also at Fanshawe Conservation Area

is Ontario's largest flood control structure; swimming, sailing, fishing (walleye); camping, various sports activities, and nature trails. NE edge of town; E end of Fanshawe Park Rd. Phone 519/457-1296. ¢¢

Grand Theatre. Contemporary facade houses 1901 theater, built by Colonel Whitney of Detroit and Ambrose Small of Toronto. Restored interior, proscenium arch, murals, and cast plasterwork. Professional stock theater (Oct-May). 471 Richmond St. Phone 519/672-8800.

Guy Lombardo Music Centre. Institution housing artifacts belonging to London-born musician. Exhibits on other big band era greats. (Mid-May-Labour Day, Thurs-Mon, daily; other times by appt) 205 Wonderland Rd S, in Springbank Park. Phone 519/473-9003. ¢

London Museum of Archaeology. Traces prehistory of southwestern Ontario; more than 40,000 artifacts show how indigenous people lived thousands of yrs before Columbus was born; archaeological and ethnographic exhibits from southwestern Ontario. Gallery, theater, and native gift shop. (May-Sept, daily; closed Good Friday, Dec 25) 1600 Attawandaron Rd. Phone 519/473-1360. ¢¢ Also here is

Indian Village. Ongoing excavation and reconstruction of authentic 500-yr-old Neutral village located on original site. (Admission included in Museum fee; May-Sept, daily)

London Regional Art and Historical Museums. Changing exhibits on art, history, and culture of the London area; regional, national, and intl art. (Tues-Sun; closed Dec 25) 421 Ridout St N. Phone 519/672-4580. **FREE**

London Regional Children's Museum. Hands-on galleries allow children to explore, touch, and discover. Artifacts to touch, costumes to put on, and crafts to make; also special events. (Sept-June, Tues-Sat; July-Aug, daily; closed Jan 1, Dec 25) 21 Wharncliffe Rd S. Phone 519/434-5726. ¢¢

The Royal Canadian Regiment Museum. Displays incl artifacts, battle scenes from 1883-present, weapons, and uniforms. (Tues-Sun; closed hols) Wolseley Hall, Canadian Forces Base. Phone 519/660-5173. **Donation**

Ska Nah Doht Indian Village. Re-created Iroquoian village depicting native culture in southwestern Ontario 800-1,000 yrs ago. Guided tours, slide shows, displays; nature trails, picnicking, group camping. Park (daily). Resource Centre & Village (Canada Day-Labour Day, daily; rest of yr, Mon-Fri). 20 mi (32 km) W via ON 2 in the Longwoods Rd Conservation Area. Phone 519/264-2420. Per vehicle ¢¢¢

Storybook Gardens. Family-oriented theme park, children's playworld and zoo, eight acres (three hectares) within London's largest park of 281 acres (114 hectares). (Early May-mid-Oct, daily) Springbank Park, Thames River Valley. Phone 519/661-5770. ¢¢

Special Events

The Air Ontario Air Show. Airport. Flying exhibitions (two-hr show); ground displays. First wkend June.

Royal Canadian Big Band Music Festival. Downtown and Wonderland gardens. Live and recorded big band music; part of Great Canadian Celebration. First wkend July.

Sunfest. Victoria Park. Features 25 music and dance ensembles from around the world, plus 70 food and craft vendors. Phone 519/661-5000 or 800/265-2602. Early July. Phone 519/663-9170.

Home County Folk Festival. Victoria Park. Three-day outdoor music fest. Mid-July.

Dragon Boat Festival. Fanshawe Conservation area. Mid-Aug. Phone 519/451-0760.

London Fringe Theatre Festival. Citywide theatrical event. Phone 519/433-3332. Mid-Aug.

Western Fair. Western Fairgrounds. Entertainment and educational extravaganza; horse shows, musicians, exhibits, livestock shows. Ten days early Sept.

Panorama Ethnic Festival. Throughout city. Open house of ethnic clubs; music, dance, food, crafts. Three days late Sept.

Motels/Motor Lodges

★★ **BEST WESTERN.** *591 Wellington Rd (N6C 4R3). 519/681-7151; fax 519/681-3271; toll-free 888/232-6747. www.bestwestern.com.* 126 rms, 2 story. S $79; D $109; each addl $8; suites $119-$209; under 12 free. Pet accepted, some restrictions. TV; cable. Pool. Complimentary coffee in rms. Restaurant 6:30 am-9 pm; Sun to 8 pm. Bar 4 pm-midnight. Ck-out 11 am. Meeting rms. Business servs avail. Some in-rm whirlpools. Private patios, balconies. Picnic tables. Cr cds: A, D, DS, ER, MC, V.

D 🍴 ⊜ ⊠ 🔥 SC

★ **RAMADA INN.** *817 Exeter Rd (N6E 1W1). 519/681-4900; fax 519/681-5065; 800/228-2828. www.ramada.com.* 124 rms, 2 story. S, D $99-$109; each addl $10; suites $175-$225; under 18 free. Crib free. TV; cable. Indoor pool; lifeguard (wkends). Complimentary coffee in rms. Restaurant 6:30 am-10 pm; Sat, Sun from 7 am. Rm serv. Bar 11-1 am. Ck-out 1 pm. Meeting rms. Business servs avail. Valet serv. Sundries. Sauna. Health club privileges. Microwaves avail. Cr cds: A, D, DS, ER, JCB, MC, V.

D ⊜ ⊠ 🔥 SC

★★ **TRAVELODGE.** *800 Exeter Rd (N6E 1L5). 519/681-1200; fax 519/681-6988; 800/578-7878. www.travelodge.com.* 125 rms, 2-3 story, 32 suites. S, D $84; each addl $7; under 19 free; suites $92-$96. Crib free. TV; cable (premium), VCR. Complimentary bkfst. Restaurant adj open 24 hrs. Ck-out 11 am. Meeting rms. Business servs avail. Microwaves avail. Cr cds: A, D, DS, ER, MC, V.

D ⊠ 🔥 SC

Hotels

★★ **DELTA LONDON ARMOURIES.** *325 Dundas St (N6B 1T9). 519/679-6111; fax 519/679-3957. www.deltahotels.com* 250 rms, 20 story. S $189; D $199; each addl $10; suites $250-$450; under 18 free; wkend rates. Crib free. Pet accepted. TV; cable (premium), VCR avail (movies). Indoor pool; wading pool, whirlpool. Supervised children's activities (July and Aug, daily; rest of yr, Fri-Sun); ages 5-12.

Coffee in rms. Restaurant 6:30 am-10 pm. Bar to 2 am. Ck-out noon. Meeting rms. Business center. Concierge. Valet parking. Putting green. Exercise equipt; sauna. Health club privileges. Rec rm. Minibars. Some balconies. Luxury level. Cr cds: A, C, D, DS, ER, MC, V.

D 🍴 ⊜ 🏋 ⊠ 🔥 SC 🏋

★★★ **HILTON HOTEL LONDON.** *300 King St (N6R 1S2). 519/439-1661; fax 519/439-9672; toll-free 800/210-9336. www.hilton.com.* 331 rms, 22 story. S, D $135-$155; suites $300; under 18 free; wkend rates. Crib free. Pet accepted. TV; cable, VCR avail. Heated pool; wading pool, whirlpool. Restaurant 7 am-11 pm. Bar 11:30-1 am; entertainment. Ck-out 1 pm. Convention facilities. Business servs avail. In-rm modem link. Concierge. Gift shop. Exercise equipt; sauna. Health club privileges. Minibars. Luxury level. Cr cds: A, C, D, DS, ER, JCB, MC, V.

D 🍴 ⊜ 🏋 ⊠ 🔥 SC

B&B/Small Inn

★★★ **IDLEWYLD.** *36 Grand Ave (N6C 1K8). 519/433-2891. www.someplacesdifferent.com.* 27 rms, 8 suites. S, D $125; each addl $10; suites $209; under 18 free; wkly rates. Crib free. TV; cable (premium). Complimentary continental bkfst. Ck-out noon, ck-in 3 pm. Business servs avail. In-rm modem link. X-country ski 3 mi. Some balconies. Picnic tables. Victorian mansion (1878); some original decor. Cr cds: A, D, ER, MC, V.

D ⊠ ⊠ 🔥 SC

Restaurants

★ **FELLINI KOOLINI'S.** *153 Albert St (N6A 1L9). 519/642-2300. www.fellinikoolinis.com.* Italian menu. Specializes in pizza, pasta. Hrs: 11 am-10 pm; Fri, Sat to midnight; Sun 4:30-10:30 pm. Closed Jan 1, Dec 25, 26. Bar to 1 am. Lunch, dinner $7.95-$16.95. Child's menu. Outdoor dining. Italian country inn decor. Cr cds: A, D, ER, MC, V.

🍽

★★ **MARIENBAD.** *122 Carling St (N6A 1H6). 519/679-9940.* Continental menu. Specialties: Wiener schnitzel, beef Tartare. Hrs: 11:30 am-midnight. Closed Jan 1, Dec 25. Res accepted. Bar 11:30-1 am. A la carte entrees: lunch $5.95-$10.75, dinner $8.95-$18.95. Child's menu. Atrium dining. Original and reproduction 19th-century furnishings. Murder mystery and dinner 3rd Fri each month. Cr cds: A, D, ER, MC, V.

D 🍽

★★ **MARLA JANE'S.** *460 King St E (N6B 1S9). 519/858-8669.* Specializes in Cajun dishes. Hrs: 11:30 am-11 pm; Sat 5-11 pm; Sun 5-10 pm. Closed Mon; Dec 25. Res accepted (dinner). A la carte entrees: lunch $7.25-$12.95, dinner $14.95-$24.95. Herb garden; terrace. Former embassy (ca 1900), Victorian architecture. Stained glass; changing art displays. Cr cds: A, D, DS, ER, MC, V.

🍽

★★ **MICHAEL'S-ON-THE-THAMES.** *1 York St (N6A 1A1). 519/672-0111. www.michaelsonthethames.com.* Continental menu. Specializes in tableside cooking, châteaubriand, fresh seafood. Hrs: 11:30 am-11 pm; Thurs, Fri to midnight; Sat 5 pm-midnight; Sun, hols 5-9 pm. Closed Jan 1, Labour Day, Dec 25. Res accepted. Bar. A la carte entrees: lunch $5.95-$9.95, dinner $9.95-$24.95. Child's menu. Pianist Sat, Sun. Cr cds: A, D, ER, MC, V.

Mississauga

See also Hamilton, Toronto

Pop 430,000 **Elev** 569 ft (173 m) **Area code** 905
Information City of Mississauga, 300 City Centre Dr, L5B 3C1; 905/896-5000

One of the fastest-growing areas in southern Ontario, Mississauga is a part of the greater Toronto area, bordering Lester B. Pearson International Airport.

Motels/Motor Lodges

★ **COMFORT INN.** *2420 Surveyor Rd (L5N 4E6). 905/858-8600; fax 905/858-8574; 800/228-5150. www.comfortinn.com.* 117 rms, 2 story. June-Sept: S $69-$74; D $74-$84; each addl $5; under 18 free; package plans; lower rates rest of yr. Crib free. Pet accepted, some restrictions. TV; cable (premium). Complimentary continental bkfst. Complimentary coffee in rms. Restaurant opp open 24 hrs. Ck-out 1 pm. Coin lndry. Meeting rms. Business servs avail. Downhill/x-country ski 15 mi. Game rm. Some refrigerators. Picnic tables.z Cr cds: A, D, DS, ER, MC, V.

★★ **DAYS HOTEL TORONTO AIRPORT.** *6257 Airport Rd (L4V 1E4). 905/678-1400; fax 905/678-9130; 800/325-2525. www.daysinn.com.* 202 rms, 7 story. S $159; D $178; each addl $10; suites $199; under 18 free; wkend rates. Crib free. TV; cable (premium). Indoor pool; whirlpool. Coffee in rms. Restaurant 7 am-midnight. Rm serv. Bar 11 am-1 am. Ck-out noon. Meeting rms. Business servs avail. Bellhops. Gift shop. Barber, beauty shop. Valet serv. Airport transportation. 18-hole golf privileges. Downhill/x-country ski 20 mi. Exercise equipt; sauna. Balconies. Cr cds: A, C, D, DS, ER, JCB, MC, V.

★ **DAYS INN.** *4635 Tomken Rd (L4W 1J9). 905/238-5480; fax 905/238-1031; 800/325-2525.* 61 rms, 3 story. No elvtr. S, D $60-$100; each addl $5; suites $150; under 18 free. Crib free. Pet accepted. TV; cable, VCR (movies). Complimentary continental bkfst. Complimentary coffee in rms. Restaurant opp 11:30 am- midnight. Ck-out 11:30 am. Business servs avail. Some refrigerators. Cr cds: A, C, D, DS, ER, JCB, MC, V.

★★ **FOUR POINTS BY SHERATON.** *5444 Dixie Rd (L4W 2L2). 905/624-1144; fax 905/624-9477; toll-free 800/737-3211. www.fourpoints.com/torontoairport.* 296 rms, 10 story. S, D $99-$209; each addl $15; suites $225-$395; under 18 free; package plans. Crib free. Pet accepted, some restrictions. TV; cable (premium), VCR avail. Heated pool. Supervised children's activities; ages 2-12. Complimentary coffee in rms. Restaurant 6:30 am-10 pm; Sat, Sun from 7 am. Bars 11:30-1 am. Ck-out 1 pm. Meeting rms. Business center. In-rm modem link. Gift shop. Beauty shop. Garage parking. Free airport transportation. Exercise equipt; sauna. Game rm. Refrigerators, minibars. Cr cds: A, C, D, DS, ER, JCB, MC, V.

★★ **HOLIDAY INN.** *2125 N Sheridan Way (L5K 1A3). 905/855-2000; fax 905/855-1433; 800/465-4329. www.holiday-inn.com.* 151 rms, 6 story, 80 suites. S, D, suites $140-$160; each addl $10; under 19 free. Crib free. TV; cable (premium), VCR avail. Heated pool; poolside serv. Coffee in rms. Restaurant 6:30 am-10 pm. Rm serv 7 am-midnight. Bar 11-1 am. Ck-out 1 pm. Meeting rms. Bellhops. Valet serv. Sundries. Airport transportation. Health club privileges. Wet bars; some in-rm whirlpools; refrigerators, microwaves avail. Cr cds: A, C, D, DS, ER, JCB, MC, V.

★★ **HOLIDAY INN TORONTO WEST.** *100 Britannia Rd (L4Z 2G1). 905/890-5700; fax 905/568-0868; 800/465-4329. www.holiday-inn.com.* 132 air-cooled rms, 6 story. S, D $145; each addl $8; under 20 free. Crib free. Pet accepted, some restrictions. TV; cable (premium), VCR avail. Coffee in rms. Restaurant from 6:30 am. Rm serv. Bar. Ck-out noon. Meeting rms. Business servs avail. In-rm modem link. Valet serv. Free airport transportation. Exercise equipt; sauna. Whirlpool. Refrigerators avail. Cr cds: A, D, DS, ER, JCB, MC, V.

★★ **NOVOTEL.** *3670 Hurontartio St (L5B 1P3). 905/896-1000; fax 905/896-2521; res 800/668-6835.* 325 air-cooled rms, 14 story. S, D $169-$189; each addl $15; suite $250; under 16 free; wkend rates. Crib free. Pet accepted. TV; cable (premium). Indoor pool. Restaurant 6 am-midnight. Bar 11-1 am. Ck-out 1 pm. Meeting rms. Business servs avail. In-rm modem link. Shopping arcade. Beauty shop. Covered parking. Free airport transportation. Exercise equipt. Health club privileges. Minibars; some bathrm phones. Shopping center opp. Cr cds: A, C, D, DS, ER, JCB, MC, V.

★ **QUALITY INN.** *50 Britannia Rd E (L4Z 2G2). 905/890-1200; fax 905/890-5183; 800/228-5151. www.qualityinn.com.* 108 rms, 2 story. S, D $78-$96; each addl $7; suites $123-$149; under 18 free; monthly rates. Crib free. TV; cable (premium). Restaurant 7 am-10 pm. Rm serv. Serv bar 11-1 am. Ck-out noon. Meeting rms. Business servs avail. Exercise equipt; sauna. Refrigerators avail. Cr cds: A, C, D, DS, ER, MC, V.

★ **RAMADA INN.** *5599 Ambler Dr (L4W 3Z1).* *905/624-9500; fax 905/624-1382; toll-free 866/247-6204. www.ramada.com.* 222 rms, 6 story. S $85; D $95; under 18 free; suites $115. Crib free. Pet accepted. TV; cable. Indoor pool; whirlpool. Complimentary bkfst, coffee in rms. Free airport transportation. Restaurant 7-1 am. Bar from noon. Ck-out noon. Guest lndry. Meeting rms. Business servs avail. Valet serv. Sundries. Cr cds: A, D, DS, ER, JCB, MC, V.

D ⬚ ⬚ ⬚ ⬚ ⬚ SC

★ **TRAVELODGE TORONTO SW/CARRIAGE INN.** *1767 Dundas St E (L4X 1L5).* 905/238-3400; *fax 905/238-9457; toll-free 800/578-7878. www.travelodge.com.* 85 rms, 2 story. June-Sept: S $70; D $75; each addl $5; suites $125-$150; under 12 free; wkly rates; lower rates rest of yr. Crib $5. TV; cable (premium). Complimentary continental bkfst. Coffee in rms. Restaurant nearby. Ck-out 11 am. Meeting rms. Health club privileges. Many refrigerators. Cr cds: A, D, DS, ER, MC, V.

D ⬚ ⬚ SC

Hotels

★★ **DELTA MEADOWVALE RESORT.** *6750 Mississauga Rd (L5N 2L3).* 905/821-1981; *fax 905/542-4036. www. deltahotels.com.* 374 rms, 15 story. S, D $190-$205; each addl $15; suites $150-$300; under 18 free. Crib free. Pet accepted. TV; cable (premium), VCR avail. 2 pools, 1 indoor; whirlpool, poolside serv. Supervised children's activities; ages 2-14. Restaurant 6:30 am-10 pm. Rm serv 24 hrs. Bar 11-1 am. Ck-out 1 pm. Meeting rms. Business servs avail. Barber, beauty shop. Airport transportation. Indoor tennis, pro shop. Golf privileges. Exercise rm. Minibars; some fireplaces. Microwaves avail. Balconies. Cr cds: A, D, DS, JCB, MC, V.

D ⬚ ⬚ ⬚ ⬚ ⬚ ⬚ SC

★★★ **HILTON INTERNATIONAL.** *5875 Airport Rd (L4V 1N1).* 905/677-9900; *fax 905/677-5073; 800/445-8667. www.hilton.com.* 413 rms, 11 story. S, D $165-$185; each addl $20; suites $185-$225; family rates; wkend packages. Crib free. Pet accepted, some restrictions. TV. Heated pool; poolside serv. Coffee in rms. Restaurant 6 am-midnight. Bars 11-2 am; entertainment. Ck-out noon. Meeting rms. Business center. Barber. Garage parking $6. Free airport transportation. Exercise equipt; sauna. Minibars; many bathrm phones. Cr cds: A, D, DS, ER, JCB, MC, V.

D ⬚ ⬚ ⬚ ⬚ ⬚ ⬚ SC ⬚

★★ **RADISSON.** *2501 Argentia Rd (L5N 4G8).* 905/858-2424; *fax 905/821-9821; 800/333-3333. www.radisson.com.* 207 rms, 8 story. S, D $155-$165; each addl $10; suites $185; under 18 free; wkend rates. Crib free. TV; cable (premium). Indoor pool; whirlpool. Coffee in rms. Restaurant. Rm serv. Bar 11-1 am. Ck-out noon. Coin lndry. Meeting rms. Business servs avail. In-rm modem link. Bellhops. Valet serv. Sundries. Gift shop. Free airport transportation. Exercise equipt; sauna. Refrigerators; bathrm phone in suites; microwaves avail. Picnic tables. Cr cds: A, D, DS, ER, JCB, MC, V.

D ⬚ ⬚ ⬚ ⬚ SC

★★★ **STAGE WEST HOTEL.** *5400 Dixie Rd (O4W 4T4).* 905/238-0159; *fax 905/238-9820; toll-free 800/668-9887. www.stagewest.com.* 224 suites, 16 story. Suites $175; family, wkly rates; package plans. Crib free. TV; cable (premium), VCR avail. Indoor pool; whirlpool, lifeguard, water slide. Supervised children's activities; ages 1-12. Restaurant 6:30 am-midnight. Bar 11-1 am. Ck-out 11 am. Meeting rms. Business center. In-rm modem link. Concierge. Shopping arcade. Barber, beauty shop. Valet parking $5/day. Free airport transportation. Downhill/x-country ski 20 mi. Exercise equipt. Microwaves avail. Complex includes Stage West Dinner Theatre. Cr cds: A, D, ER, MC, V.

D ⬚ ⬚ ⬚ ⬚ ⬚ ⬚ SC ⬚

B&B/Small Inn

★★★ **GLENERIN.** *1695 The Collegeway (L5L 3S7).* 905/828-6103; *res 800/267-0525.* 39 rms, 2½ story, 13 suites. S $125; D $165; each addl $10; suites $195-$375; under 18 free; wkly rates; wkend packages. Crib free. TV; cable (premium), VCR avail. Complimentary bkfst. Dining rm 7 am-11 pm. Rm serv. Ck-out 11 am, ck-in 4 pm. Meeting rms. Business servs avail. Downhill/x-country ski 10 mi. Health club privileges. Some fireplaces. English-style manor house (1927); antique and modern furnishings. Rms vary in size and style. Cr cds: A, D, ER, MC, V.

D ⬚ ⬚ ⬚ SC

Restaurants

★★ **CHERRINGTON'S.** *7355 Torbram Rd (L4T 3W3).* 905/672-0605. Continental menu. Specializes in fresh fish, steak, pasta. Hrs: 11:30 am-3 pm, 5-10:30 pm; Sat from 5 pm. Closed Sun; Easter, Dec 25. Res accepted. Bar to 1 am. Lunch $9.95-$14.95, dinner $15.95-$31.95. Child's menu. Entertainment Fri, Sat. Parking. Elegant dining rm divided by bar. Cr cds: A, D, ER, MC, V.

D ⬚

★★ **CHERRY HILL HOUSE.** *680 Silvercreek Blvd (L5A 3Z1).* 905/275-9300. French, continental menu. Specializes in rack of lamb, pasta with lobster. Hrs: 11:30 am-2:30 pm, 5:30-10 pm; Sat from 5:30 pm. Closed Sun; major hols. Res accepted. Bar. A la carte entrees: lunch $8.75-$13.25, dinner $13.50-$19.75. Converted house (ca 1850) is designated historic site. Cr cds: A, D, ER, MC, V.

D ⬚

★ **DECKER-TEN.** *1170 Burnhamthorpe Rd W (L5C 4E6).* 905/276-7419. Japanese menu. Specialties: sashimi, beef teriyaki. Sushi bar. Hrs: 11:45 am-2:30 pm, 5:30-10 pm; Sat, Sun 5:30-10 pm. Closed Jan 1, July 1, Dec 24, 25. Res accepted. Bar. A la carte entrees: lunch $8-$15, dinner $9-$20. Complete meal: dinner $14-$28. Child's menu. Japanese art. Cr cds: A, C, MC, V.

⬚

★★ **LA CASTILE.** *2179 Dundas St E (L4X 1M3).* 905/625-1137. Steak and seafood menu. Specialties: shrimp cocktail, prime rib, barbecued ribs. Hrs: 11:30 am-2:30 pm, 5 pm-midnight; Mon, Tues to 11 pm. Closed Sun; Dec 25. Res accepted. Bar to 2 am. Lunch $9.95-$18.95, dinner $16.95-$60. Pianist Wed-Sat. Parking. 16th-century castle decor; cathedral ceiling, tapestries, original oil painting. Cr cds: A, D, ER, MC, V.

[D] [⊟]

★ **MUSKY SUPPER HOUSE.** *261 Lakeshore Rd E (L5H 1G8).* 905/271-9727. Continental menu. Specialty: hickory-smoked pork with sour cherries. Hrs: 5:30-10 pm; Fri, Sat to 11 pm. Closed Sun, Mon; some major hols. Res accepted. Bar. A la carte entrees: dinner $15-$24. Original art and carvings. Totally nonsmoking. Cr cds: A, DS, MC, V.

[D]

★ ★ ★ **OLD BARBER HOUSE.** *5155 Mississauga Rd (L5M 2L9).* 905/858-7570. *www.oldbarberhouse.ca.* Specializes in veal, pasta, lamb. Own pastries. Hrs: 11:30 am-3 pm, 5-11 pm; Sat from 5 pm. Closed Sun; Jan 1, Dec 25. Res accepted. Bar 11-1 am. A la carte entrees: lunch $9.95-$13.95, dinner $11.95-$34.95. Parking. Victorian house (1862). Cr cds: A, MC, V.

[⊟]

★ ★ **OUTRIGGER STEAK AND SEAFOOD.** *2539 Dixie Rd (L4Y 2A1).* 905/275-7000. Specializes in steak, seafood. Salad bar. Own baking. Hrs: noon-11 pm; Sat, Sun from 4 pm. Closed Dec 25. Res accepted. Bar 4 pm-1 am. A la carte entrees: lunch $6.95-$12.95, dinner $10.95-$36.99. Child's menu. Cr cds: A, C, D, DS, MC, V.

[D] [⊟]

★ **SNUG HARBOUR.** *14 Stavebank Rd S (L5G 2T1).* 905/274-5000. *www.snugharbourrestaurant.com.* Continental menu. Specializes in fresh seafood, pasta. Hrs: 11:30 am-11 pm. Closed Jan 1, Dec 24-26. Res accepted. Bar. Lunch, dinner $6.95-$26.50. Child's menu. Jazz Fri, Sat. Outdoor dining. On Lake Ontario. Cr cds: A, MC, V.

[D] [⊟]

Morrisburg

See also Cornwall

Pop 2,308 **Elev** 250 ft (76 m) **Area code** 613
Information South Dundas Chamber of Commerce, PO Box 288, K0C 1X0; 613/543-3443
Web www.southdundaschamber.com

Rising waters of the St. Lawrence Seaway forced the removal of Morrisburg and many other towns to higher ground. This was one of the earliest settled parts of Canada, and homes, churches, and buildings of historic note were moved and reconstructed on the Crysler Farm located in Upper Canada Village, itself a historic spot.

What to See and Do

Crysler Farm Battlefield Park. Scene of a decisive battle of the War of 1812, where 800 British and Canadians defeated 4,000 American troops. Also here are Crysler Park Marina, Upper Canada Golf Course, Crysler Beach (fee), Battle of

Crysler's Farm Visitor Centre and Memorial Mound, Pioneer Memorial, Loyalist Memorial, Air Strip, and Queen Elizabeth Gardens. Varying fees. 7 mi (11 km) E on ON 2. Nearby is

Upper Canada Village. Authentic re-creation of rural 1860s riverfront village. Demonstrations by staff in period costumes. Historic buildings incl operating woolen mill, sawmill, gristmill; Willard's Hotel; blacksmith's, tinsmith's, dressmaker's, shoemaker's, and cabinetmaker's shops; tavern, churches, school, bakery, working farms, canal. May be seen on foot, by carryall, or *bateau.* (Mid-May-mid-Oct, daily; closed hols) Phone 613/543-3704. ¢¢¢

Fort Wellington National Historic Site. Original British fort first built in 1813, rebuilt in 1838 after Canadian Rebellions of 1837-1838. Restored blockhouse, officers' quarters, latrine; guides in period costume depict fort life ca 1846. Underground stone tunnel designed to defend the fort's flank. Large military pageant with mock battles (third wkend July). (Mid-May-Sept, daily; rest of yr, by appt) 33 mi (53 km) SW via Hwy 401, in Prescott. Phone 613/925-2896. **FREE**

Prehistoric World. Life-size reproductions of prehistoric animals along a ¾-mi (one-km) nature trail. More than 40 exhibits completed, incl Brontosaurus and Tyrannosaurus Rex; others in various stages of construction. (Late May-Labour Day, daily) 5 mi (7 km) E via Hwy 401, exit 758. Phone 613/543-2503. ¢

Niagara Falls

See also Niagara-on-the-Lake, St. Catharines

Pop 70,960 **Elev** 589 ft (180 m) **Area code** 905
Information Visitor & Convention Bureau, 5515 Stanley Ave, L2G 3X4; 905/356-6061 or 800/563-2557
Web www.discoverniagara.vom

The Canadian side of Niagara Falls offers viewpoints different from, and in many ways superior to, those on the American side. Center of a beautiful 35-mile (60-kilometer) stretch of parks and home of a tremendous range of man-made attractions, this area is popular all year with tourists from all over the world.

What to See and Do

Boat ride. *Maid of the Mist* leaves from foot of Clifton Hill on Niagara River Pkwy near Rainbow Bridge (see NIAGARA FALLS, NY). Phone 716/284-4233 (NY) or 905/358-5781 (Canada). ¢¢

Canada One Factory Outlets. Outlet Centre sells many national recognized brands of merchandise. 7500 Lundy's Ln. Phone 416/323-3977.

Great Gorge Adventure. Niagara River at its narrowest point. Elevator and 240-ft (73-m) tunnel takes visitors to the boardwalk at edge of whirlpool rapids. (Apr-Oct, daily) 2 mi (3 km) N at 4330 River Rd. Contact PO Box 150, L2E 6T2. Phone 905/356-2241. ¢¢

Guinness World of Records Museum. Based on the popular book of records; hundreds of original exhibits, artifacts; laser video galleries; re-creations of many of the world's greatest accomplishments. (Daily) 4943 Clifton Hill. Phone 905/356-2299. ¢¢

Historic Fort Erie. Site of some of the fiercest fighting of the War of 1812; restored to period. Guided tours by interpreters dressed in uniform of the Glengarry Light Infantry. (Mid-May-mid-Sept) 21 mi (34 km) S via QEW, at 4330 River Rd in Fort Erie. Phone 905/356-2241. ¢¢

Journey Behind the Falls. Elevator descends to point about 25 ft (8 m) above river, offering excellent view of Falls from below and behind; waterproof garments are supplied. (Daily; closed Dec 25) 1 mi S of Rainbow Bridge on Niagara Pkwy in Queen Victoria Park. Phone 905/354-1551. ¢¢ Also in park is

    Greenhouse. Tropical and native plants; animated fountain, garden shop. (Daily) Phone 905/354-1721. **FREE**

Louis Tussaud's Waxworks. Life-size, historically costumed wax figures of the past and present; Chamber of Horrors. (Daily; closed Dec 25) 4915 Clifton Hill. Phone 905/374-6601 or 905/374-4534. ¢¢

Lundy's Lane Historical Museum. (1874) On the site of the Battle of Lundy's Lane (1814). Interprets early settlement and tourism of Niagara Falls; 1812 war militaria; Victorian parlor, early kitchen, toys, dolls, photographs; galleries, and exhibits. (May-Nov, daily; rest of yr, Mon-Fri; closed Jan 1, Dec 25) 5810 Ferry St. Phone 905/358-5082. ¢

Marineland. Performing killer whales, dolphins, sea lions; wildlife displays with deer, bears, buffalo, and elk; thrill rides, incl one of the world's largest steel roller coasters; restaurants, picnic areas. Park (Mar-mid-Dec, daily); rides (mid-May-early Oct). 7657 Portage Rd. Phone 905/356-8250. ¢¢¢¢

Niagara Falls Museum. One of North America's oldest museums, founded in 1827. Twenty-six galleries of rare, worldwide artifacts, incl "Niagara's Original Daredevil Hall of Fame"; Egyptian mummy collection; dinosaur exhibit. (Summer, daily; winter, schedule varies) 5651 River Rd. Phone 416/598-9333. ¢¢

Niagara Parks Botanical Gardens. Nearly 100 acres of horticultural exhibits. Nature shop. (Daily) Niagara Pkwy N. Phone 905/356-8554. **FREE** On grounds is the

    Niagara Parks Butterfly Conservatory. Approx 2,000 butterflies make their home in this 11,000-square-ft (1,022-square-m), climate-controlled conservatory filled with exotic greenery and flowing water. Nearly 50 species of butterflies can be viewed from a 600-ft (180-m) network of walking paths. Outdoor butterfly garden (seasonal). Gift shop. (Daily) Phone 905/358-0025. ¢¢

Niagara Spanish Aero Car. The 1,800-ft (549-m) cables support a car that crosses the whirlpool and rapids of the Niagara River. Five-min trip each way. (Mid Apr-mid Oct, daily) 3½ mi (5 km) N on Niagara Pkwy. Phone 905/354-5711. ¢¢

Observation towers.

    IMAX Theatre and Daredevil Adventure. Six-story-high movie screen shows *Niagara: Miracles, Myths, and Magic,* a film highlighting the Falls. Daredevil Adventure has displays, exhibits, and some of the actual barrels used to traverse the Falls. (Daily; closed Dec 25) 6170 Buchanan Ave. Phone 905/358-3611. ¢¢

★ Minolta Tower Centre. This awesome 325-ft (99.06-m) tower offers a magnificent 360° view of the Falls and surrounding areas. Eight levels at top; specially designed glass for ideal photography; Minolta exhibit floor; "Waltzing Waters" water and light spectacle (free; seasonal); gift shops; incline railway to Falls (fee; free parking); "Top of the Rainbow" dining rms overlooking Falls (res suggested). (Daily; closed Dec 24, 25) 6732 Oakes Dr. Phone 905/356-1501. ¢¢

Skylon Tower. Stands 775 ft (236 m) above base of Falls. Three-level dome contains an indoor/outdoor observation deck and revolving and stationary dining rms served by three external, glass-enclosed "Yellow Bug" elevators. Specialty shops at base of tower. (Daily) 5200 Robinson St. Phone 905/356-2651. ¢¢

Typhoon Lagoon. Family water park featuring waterslides, pools, hot tubs; arcade, restaurant, gift shop. (June-mid-Sept, daily) 7430 Lundy's Ln. Phone 905/357-3380.

Special Event

Winter Festival of Lights. Queen Victoria Park. Phone 800/563-2557. Late Nov-late Jan.

Motels/Motor Lodges

★ ★ BEST WESTERN CAIRN CROFT. *6400 Lundy's Ln (L2G 1T6). 905/356-1161; fax 905/356-8664; toll-free 800/263-2551. www.bestwestern.com.* 165 rms, 5 story. Late June-Aug: S, D $99.50-$149.50; each addl $10; suites $150-$199; under 18 free; lower rates rest of yr. Crib free. TV. Playground. Indoor pool. Restaurant 7 am-2 pm, 5-8 pm. Rm serv. Bar 4 pm-1 am; entertainment Tues-Sat. Ck-out 11 am. Meeting rms. Business servs avail. Bellhops. Valet serv. X-country ski 3 mi. Health club privileges. Enclosed courtyard. Cr cds: A, C, D, DS, ER, MC, V.
🐾 ⛆ 🛏 🔥 SC

★ ★ BEST WESTERN FALLSVIEW. *5551 Murray St (L2G 2J4). 905/356-0551; fax 905/356-7773; toll-free 800/263-2580. www.bestwestern.com.* 244 rms, 4-6 story. June-Sept: S, D $79-$169; each addl $10; lower rates rest of yr. Crib $5. Pet accepted. TV; cable. Indoor pool; whirlpool. Sauna. Restaurant 6 am-10 pm. Bar 11-1 am. Ck-out 11 am. Coin lndry. Meeting rms. Business servs avail. Bellhops. Gift shop. Sundries. Game rm. Some in-rm whirlpools. Cr cds: A, C, D, DS, ER, JCB, MC, V.
D 🐾 ⛆ 🛏 🔥 SC

★ ★ CARRIAGE HOUSE. *8004 Lundy's Ln (On 20) (L2H 1H1). 905/356-7799; fax 905/358-6431; toll-free 800/267-9887.* 120 rms, 2 story. July-Aug: S, D $65-$105; each addl $10; suites $100-$150; family rates; higher rates special events; lower rates rest of yr. Crib free. TV. 2 pools, 1 indoor; whirlpool. Restaurant 7 am-noon. Ck-out 11 am. Business servs avail. Sundries. X-country ski 4 mi. Some in-rm whirlpools. Some balconies. Cr cds: A, C, D, DS, ER, MC, V.
D 🐾 ⛆ 🛏 🔥 SC

★ **CASCADE INN.** 5305 Murray St (L2G 2J3). 905/354-2796; fax 905/354-2797. www.cascade.on.ca. 65 rms, 3-6 story. Mid-June-Labour Day: D $139-$169; lower rates rest of yr. Crib free. TV. Pool. Restaurant 8 am-noon. Ck-out 11 am. Gift shop. X-country ski 2 mi. Near Skylon Tower. Cr cds: A, DS, MC, V.

⊠ ⚊ ⊠ 🔥 SC

★ **CAVALIER.** 5100 Centre St (L2G 3P2). 905/358-3288; fax 905/358-3289. 39 rms, 2 story. July-Aug: S, D $66-$94; under 5 free; lower rates rest of yr. Crib free. TV; cable (premium). Heated pool. Restaurant opp from 7 am. Ck-out 11 am. French Provincial decor. Cr cds: A, JCB, MC, V.

⚊ ⊠ 🔥 SC

★ **CRYSTAL MOTEL.** 4249 River Rd (Niagara River Pkwy) (L2E 3E7). 905/354-0460; fax 905/374-4972. 38 rms, 2 story. Mid-June-mid-Sept: S $69-$139; D $79-$149; each addl $10; lower rates rest of yr. Crib $4. TV; cable (premium). Heated pool. Restaurant nearby. Ck-out 11 am. Refrigerators; some in-rm whirlpools. Some balconies. 1 blk N of Whirlpool Rapids Bridge. Cr cds: A, DS, MC, V.

⚊ ⊠ 🔥 SC

★ **DAYS INN OVERLOOKING THE FALLS.** 6546 Fallsview Blvd (L2G 3W2). 905/356-4514; fax 905/356-3651; 800/325-2525. www.daysinn.com. 193 rms, 15 story. Late June-late Sept: S, D $99-$499; each addl $10; under 17 free; lower rates rest of yr. Crib free. TV. Indoor pool; whirlpool. Complimentary coffee in rms. Restaurant adj open 24 hrs. No rm serv. Bar. Ck-out 11 am. Meeting rms. Business servs avail. No bellhops. Gift shop. X-country ski 2 mi. Sauna. Game rm. Cr cds: A, D, DS, ER, MC, V.

⊠ ⚊ ⊠ 🔥 SC

★★ **FLAMINGO MOTOR INN.** 7701 Lundy's Ln (L2H 1H3). 905/356-4646; fax 905/356-9373; toll-free 800/738-7701. www.flamingomotorinn.com. 95 rms, 2 story. Mid-June-Labour Day: S, D $72-$104; each addl $10; whirlpool rm $104-$200; lower rates rest of yr. Crib free. Pet accepted, some restrictions. TV; cable. Heated pool. Restaurant adj 7 am-10 pm. Ck-out 11 am. Gift shop. Picnic tables. Cr cds: A, C, D, DS, MC, V.

🦩 ⚊ ⊠ 🔥 SC

★★ **FOUR POINTS BY SHERATON.** 6045 Stanley Ave (L2G 3Y3). 905/374-4142; fax 905/358-3430; 800/325-3535. www.fourpoints.com. 112 rms, 8 story. Late June-mid-Sept: S, D $129-$269; each addl $10; under 14 free; wkends (2-day min); higher rates hol wkends; lower rates rest of yr. Crib free. TV; cable. Indoor pool; whirlpool, poolside serv. Restaurant 7 am-2 pm, 5-10 pm. Bar from 5 pm. Ck-out 11 am. Meeting rms. Business center. Gift shop. X-country ski 2 mi. Cr cds: A, D, DS, ER, JCB, MC, V.

D ⊠ ⚊ ⊠ 🔥 🏃

★★ **HAMPTON INN AT THE FALLS.** 5591 Victoria Ave (L2G 3L4). 905/357-1626; fax 905/357-5869; 800/426-7866. www.hamptoninn.com. 127 units, 3-6 story. Mid June-Labour Day: S, D $89-$189; suites $139-$269; under 18 free; lower rates rest of yr. Crib free. TV; cable (premium). Indoor pool; whirlpool. Sauna. Complimentary continental bkfst. Complimentary coffee in rms. Bar 4 pm-1 am (in season). Ck-out 11 am. Meeting rms. Business servs avail. In-rm modem link. Sundries. Game rm. Balconies. Cr cds: A, D, DS, ER, MC, V.

D ⚊ ⊠ 🔥 SC

★★ **HOLIDAY INN BY THE FALLS.** 5339 Murray St (L2G 2J3). 905/356-1333; fax 905/356-7128; toll-free 800/263-9393. www.holiday-inn.com. 122 rms, 6 story. Mid-June-mid-Sept: S, D $95-$195; each addl $10; bridal suite $175-$225; lower rates rest of yr. Crib $5. Pet accepted. TV. 2 pools, 1 indoor; whirlpool. Restaurant 7 am-10 pm; winter from 8 am. Rm serv. Bar noon-2 am. Ck-out noon. Sundries. Sauna. Some in-rm whirlpools. Balconies. Cr cds: A, C, D, DS, ER, JCB, MC, V.

D 🐾 ⚊ ⊠ 🔥 SC

★ **HOWARD JOHNSON BY THE FALLS.** 5905 Victoria Ave (L2G 3L8). 905/357-4040; fax 905/357-6202; 800/446-4656. www.hojo.com. 199 rms, 6-7 story. S, D $59-$299; each addl $10; suites $69-$349; under 18 free. Crib free. TV; cable, VCR avail. Indoor/outdoor pool; whirlpool. Restaurant open 24 hrs. Ck-out noon. Meeting rms. Business servs avail. Gift shop. X-country ski 2 mi. Sauna. Game rm. Some in-rm whirlpools. Some balconies. Cr cds: A, C, D, DS, ER, JCB, MC, V.

D ⊠ ⚊ ⊠ 🔥 SC

★★ **IMPERIAL HOTEL AND SUITES.** 5851 Victoria St (L2G 3L6). 905/356-2648; fax 905/356-4068. www.imperialniagara.com. 104 suites, 10 story. July-Aug: S, D $129-$209; each addl $15; under 16 free; lower rates rest of yr. Crib $10. TV. Indoor pool; whirlpool. Restaurant adj 7-11 am. Ck-out noon. Coin lndry. Meeting rms. Business servs avail. Gift shop. X-country ski 2 mi. Game rm. Refrigerators; microwaves avail. Cr cds: A, D, DS, ER, MC, V.

D ⊠ ⚊ ⊠ 🔥 SC

★★★ **MICHAEL'S INN.** 5599 River Rd (L2E 3H3). 905/354-2727; fax 905/374-7706; toll-free 800/263-9390. www.michaelsinn.com. 130 rms, 4 story. May-Oct: S, D $59-$228; suites $125-$375; lower rates rest of yr. Crib $5. TV; cable (premium). Indoor pool; wading pool, whirlpool, lifeguard in season. Restaurant 7 am-11:30 pm. Rm serv. Bar. Ck-out 11 am. Meeting rms. Business servs avail. Bellhops. Valet serv. Sauna. Some refrigerators. Overlooks the falls. Cr cds: A, C, D, ER, JCB, MC, V.

D ⚊ ⊠ 🔥 SC

★★ **OLD STONE INN.** 5425 Robinson St (L2G 7L6). 905/357-1234; fax 905/357-9299. www.oldstoneinn.on.ca. 114 rms, 3 story. May-Oct: S, D $125-$225; each addl $10; suites $195-$349; under 12 free; wkend rates; higher rates hols; lower rates rest of yr. Crib free. TV; cable. 2 pools, 1 indoor; whirlpool, poolside serv. Restaurant (see also THE MILLERY). Rm serv. Bar 11-2 am. Ck-out 11 am. Meeting rms. Business servs avail. Bellhops. Gift shop. Valet serv. X-country ski 2 mi. Main bldg former flour mill built 1904. Cr cds: A, D, DS, ER, JCB, MC, V.

D ⊠ ⚊ ⊠ 🔥

★ **PILGRIM MOTOR INN.** *4955 Clifton Hill (L2G 3N5). 905/374-7777; fax 905/354-8086.* 40 rms, 3 story. Mid-June-mid-Sept: S, D $58-$149.50; each addl $10; higher rates: hols, wkends; lower rates rest of yr. Crib free. TV; cable. Ck-out noon. Balconies. Sun deck. Cr cds: A, MC, V.
🈳 🐾 SC

★ **QUALITY HOTEL.** *5257 Ferry St (L2G 1R6). 905/356-2842; fax 905/356-6629; toll-free 800/263-6917. www.hotelchoice.com.* 80 rms, 8 story. Mid-June-mid-Sept: S, D $89.99-$249.99; each addl $10-$50; lower rates rest of yr. Crib free. TV; cable. Indoor pool; whirlpool. Restaurant 7 am-noon. No rm serv. Ck-out noon. Meeting rms. Business servs avail. No bellhops. Gift shop. X-country ski 2 mi. Sauna. Cr cds: A, C, D, DS, ER, JCB, MC, V.
🏊 ≈ 🈳 🐾 SC

★ **RAMADA-CORAL INN RESORT.** *7429 Lundy's Ln (On 20) (L2H 1G9). 905/356-6116; fax 905/356-7204; 800/228-2828. www.ramada.com.* 130 units, 2-4 story. Mid June-early Sept: S, D $89-$139; each addl $10; suites, studio rms $129-$169; under 18 free; package plans; higher rates: Sat in season, hols, special events; lower rates rest of yr. Crib free. TV. 2 heated pools, 1 indoor; whirlpool. Restaurant 7 am-10 pm. Ck-out 11 am. Meeting rms. Business center. Valet serv. Gift shop. Exercise equipt; sauna. Health club privileges. Playground. Game rm. Refrigerators, in-rm whirlpools; fireplace in suites. Cr cds: A, C, D, DS, ER, JCB, MC, V.
≈ 🏋 🎿 🐾 SC 🚶

★★ **RAMADA SUITES NIAGARA.** *7389 Lundy's Ln (L2H 2W9). 905/356-6119; fax 905/356-7204; 800/228-2828. www.ramada.ca.* 73 suites, 7 story. Mid-June-early Sept: S, D $109-$159; each addl $10; under 18 free; suites $129-$169; family rates; higher rates: hol wkends, Sat in season; lower rates rest of yr. Crib free. TV. Indoor pool; whirlpool. Restaurant 7 am-11 pm. No rm serv. Bar 11:30 am-midnight. Ck-out 11 am. Meeting rms. Business center. In-rm modem link. Exercise equipt; sauna. Refrigerators; whirlpool in suites. Cr cds: A, C, D, DS, ER, JCB, MC, V.
D ≈ 🏋 🎿 🐾 SC 🚶

★ **SURFSIDE INN.** *3665 Macklem St (L2Q 6C8). 905/295-4354; fax 905/295-4374; toll-free 800/263-0713. www.falls.net/motel.* 31 rms. Mid-Apr-mid-Nov: D $55-$125; each addl $6; suites $99-$185; lower rates rest of yr. Crib free. TV. Pool. Coffee in rms. Restaurant nearby. Ck-out 11 am. Refrigerators; microwaves avail. Some whirlpools in suites. Bicycle trail. Cr cds: A, C, D, DS, ER, JCB, MC, V.
D ≈ 🈳 🐾 SC

★ **TRAVELODGE NEAR THE FALLS.** *5234 Ferry St (L2G 1R5). 905/374-7771; 800/578-7878. www.travelodge.com.* 81 rms, 4 story, 22 suites. July-Aug: S, D $99-$149; each addl $10; suites $129-$199; family, wkly rates; higher rates hol wkends, lower rates rest of yr. Crib free. TV; cable (premium). Indoor pool; whirlpool. Sauna. Complimentary coffee in lobby. Restaurant 7 am-3 pm. Ck-out 11 am. X-country ski 2 mi. Whirlpool in suites. Cr cds: A, D, MC, V.
D 🏊 ≈ 🈳 🐾 SC

Hotels

★★ **BROCK PLAZA.** *5685 Falls Ave (L2E 6W7). 905/374-4445; fax 905/357-4804.* 233 rms, 12 story. June-Sept: S, D $129-$369; each addl $10; suites $249-$429; under 18 free; lower rates rest of yr. Crib free. TV; cable. Parking $4-$6 (in season). Restaurant 7 am-10 pm. Bar in season 11-1 am. Ck-out 11 am. Meeting rms. Business servs avail. Health club privileges. Most rms overlook Falls. Cr cds: A, C, D, DS, ER, JCB, MC, V.
🈳 🐾 SC

★★★ **HILTON NIAGARA FALLS.** *6361 Fallsview Blvd (L2G 3V9). 905/354-7887; 800/445-8667. www.hilton.com.* 500 rms, 34 story. S, D $250-$375; under 18 free. Crib avail. TV; cable (premium). Indoor pool; whirlpool. Restaurant 6:30 am-10 pm. Bar to midnight. Ck-out noon. Meeting rms. Business center. In-rm modem link. Concierge. Exercise equipt. Minibars; many refrigerators in suites. Cr cds: A, D, DS, ER, MC, V
≈ 🏋 🚶

★★★ **MARRIOTT FALLSVIEW NIAGARA FALLS.** *6740 Fallsview Blvd (L2G 3W6). 905/357-7300; 800/228-9290. www.marriott.com.* 400 rms, 21 story. S, D $195-$350; under 18 free. Crib avail. TV; cable (premium). Indoor pool; whirlpool. Restaurant 6:30 am-10 pm. Bar to midnight. Ck-out noon, ck-in 4 pm. Meeting rms. Business center. In-rm modem link. Concierge. Exercise equipt. Minibars; many refrigerators in suites. Cr cds: A, C, D, DS, ER, JCB, MC, V.
≈ 🏋 🚶

★★★ **RENAISSANCE FALLSVIEW.** *6455 Buchanan Ave (L2G 3Z9). 905/357-5200; fax 905/357-3422. www.niagara.com/nf-renaissance.* 262 rms, 19 story. Mid-June-Sept: S, D $185-$309; each addl $20; under 18 free; lower rates rest of yr. Crib free. TV; cable. Indoor pool. Restaurants 7 am-11 pm. Bar 11-1 am. Ck-out 11 am. Meeting rms. Business servs avail. Exercise equipt; sauna. Cr cds: A, D, DS, ER, JCB, MC, V.
D ≈ 🏋 🈳 🐾 SC

★★★ **SHERATON FALLSVIEW HOTEL.** *6755 Fallsview Blvd (L2G 3W7). 905/374-1077; 800/325-3535. www.sheraton.com.* 402 rms, 31 story. S, D $250-$375; under 18 free. Crib avail. TV; cable (premium). Indoor pool; whirlpool. Restaurant 6:30 am-10 pm. Bar to midnight. Ck-out noon, ck-in 4 pm. Meeting rms. Business center. In-rm modem link. Concierge. Exercise equipt. Minibars; many refrigerators in suites. Cr cds: A, C, D, DS, ER, JCB, MC, V.
≈ 🏋 🚶

★★★ **SHERATON ON THE FALLS.** *5875 Falls Ave (L2E 6W7). 905/374-4444; fax 905/351-0157; res 800/263-7135. www.sheraton.com.* 399 rms, 14 story. June-Sept: S, D $119-$269; each addl $10; under 18 free; higher rates hol wkends; lower rates rest of yr. Crib free. Valet parking $12/day in season. TV; cable (premium). Pool. Restaurant 6:30 am-10 pm. Bar from 11 am. Ck-out 11 am. Meeting rms. Business center. Concierge. Shopping arcade.X-country ski 2 mi. Exercise equipt. Some balconies overlooking falls. Cr cds: A, C, D, DS, ER, JCB, MC, V.
D 🏊 ≈ 🏋 🎿 🐾 SC 🚶

Restaurants

★★ **CAPRI.** *5438 Ferry St (L2G 1S1). 905/354-7519.* Italian menu. Specializes in seafood, steak, pasta. Hrs: 11 am-11 pm. Closed Dec 24-26. Res accepted. Bar. A la carte entrees: lunch $5.75-$12.50, dinner $8.95-$34.95. Child's menu. Parking. Family-owned. Cr cds: A, C, D, ER, MC, V.
D ⊒

★ **FOUR BROTHERS.** *5383 Ferry St (L2G 1R6). 905/358-6951.* Italian menu. Specializes in steak, seafood, gourmet pasta dishes. Hrs: 11 am-11 pm; summer 7-1 am. Closed Dec 24, 25. Res accepted. Bar. A la carte entrees: bkfst $1.99-$5.50, lunch $1.95-$10.95, dinner $7.95-$19.95. Child's menu. Parking. Old World decor. Family-owned. Cr cds: A, C, D, DS, ER, MC, V.
D ⊒

★★ **THE MILLERY.** *5425 Robinson St (L2G 7LG). 905/357-1234.* Continental menu. Specialties: prime rib, rack of lamb. Hrs: 7 am-3 pm, 4:30-10 pm; early-bird dinner 4:30-6 pm. Res accepted (dinner). Bar 11-2 am. Bkfst $1.95-$8.95, lunch $4.95-$9.95, dinner $15.50-$40. Child's menu. Outdoor dining. In historic mill. Cr cds: A, D, DS, MC, V.
D ⊒

★★★ **QUEENSTON HEIGHTS.** *14184 Niagara Pkwy (L2E 6T2). 905/262-4274.* Specializes in prime rib, lamb, steak. Hrs: noon-3 pm, 5-9 pm; Sat to 10 pm; high tea 3-5 pm; mid-June-Labour Day to 9:30 pm; Sun brunch 11 am-3 pm. Closed Jan 5-wk before Easter. Res accepted. Bar. A la carte entrees: lunch $9.25-$11.95, dinner $15.95-$24.95. Sun brunch $17.95. Child's menu. Parking. Enclosed balcony dining overlooks river, orchards. Patio. War of 1812 battle site. Cr cds: A, D, MC, V.
D ⊒

★★ **VICTORIA PARK.** *6342 Niagara Pkwy. 905/356-2217.* Canadian, Amer menu. Specializes in prime rib. Menu changes seasonally. Hrs: 11:30 am-9 pm; early-bird dinner 4-6:30 pm; late June-Aug to 10 pm. Closed mid-Oct-Apr. Res accepted. No A/C. Bar. Lunch $8.29-$12.49, dinner $16.99-$21.99. Child's menu. Victorian decor. Parking. Outdoor patio with view of falls. Cr cds: A, C, D, ER, MC, V.
D

Niagara-on-the-Lake

See also Niagara Falls, St. Catharines

Settled 1776 **Pop** 12,186 **Elev** 262 ft (80 m) **Area code** 905

Information Chamber of Commerce, 26 Queen St, PO Box 1043, L0S 1J0; 905/468-4263

Web www.niagara-on-the-lake.com

Often called the loveliest in Ontario, this picturesque town has a long and distinguished history which parallels the growth of the province. Originally the Neutral village of Onghiara, it attracted Loyalist settlers after the American Revolution, many of whom were members of the feared Butler's Rangers. Pioneers followed from many European countries, and after a succession of names including Newark, the town finally received its present name. In 1792 it became the first capital of Upper Canada and remained so until 1796. Governor John Graves Simcoe, considering the proximity to the United States in case of war, moved the seat of government to York, near Toronto. The town played a significant role in the War of 1812, was occupied, and eventually burned along with Fort George in 1813.

Once a busy shipping, shipbuilding, and active commercial center, the beautiful old homes lining the tree-shaded streets testify to the area's prosperity. The town's attractions now include theater, historic sites, beautiful gardens, and Queen St with its shops, hotels, and restaurants. Delightful in any season, this is one of the best-preserved and prettiest remnants of the Georgian era.

What to See and Do

Brock's Monument. Massive, 185-ft (56-m) memorial to Sir Isaac Brock, who was felled by a sharpshooter while leading his troops against American forces at the Battle of Queenston Heights in Oct 1812. Narrow, winding staircase leads to tiny observation deck inside monument. Other memorial plaques in park; walking tour of important points on the Queenston Heights Battlefield begins at Brock Monument; brochure avail here. Brock and his aide-de-camp, Lieutenant-Colonel Macdonell, are buried here. (Mid-May-Labour Day, daily) 7 mi (11 km) S in Queenston Heights Park. Phone 905/468-4257. **FREE**

Court House. (1847) Built on site of original government house, three-story building is now the home of Court House Theatre. First home of the Shaw Festival (see SPECIAL EVENTS). Queen St. Opp

Clock Tower. (1921) Erected in memory of those who died in world wars. Set in center of road surrounded by floral displays.

Fort George National Historic Site. (1797) Once the principal British post on the frontier, this fort saw much action during the War of 1812. Eleven restored, refurnished bldgs and massive ramparts. (Mid-May-Oct, daily; rest of yr, by appt; living history mid-May-Labour Day) Guided tours by appt. On Niagara Pkwy. Phone 905/468-3938. ¢¢

Laura Secord Homestead. Restored home of Canadian heroine is furnished with early Upper Canada furniture. After overhearing the plans of Americans billetted in her home, Laura Secord made an exhausting and difficult 19 mi (30 km) walk to warn British troops, which resulted in a victory over the Americans at Beaverdams in 1813. (Victoria Day-Labour Day, daily) Partition St, 5 mi (8 km) S in Queenston. Phone 905/371-0254 or 877/642-7275. Tours ¢

McFarland House. (1800) Georgian brick home used as hospital in War of 1812; furnished in the Loyalist tradition, 1835-1845. (July-Labour Day, daily; mid-May-June and after Labour Day-Sept, wkends only) McFarland Point Park, Niagara Pkwy, 1 mi (1.6 km) S. Phone 905/356-2241. ¢

Niagara Apothecary. (ca 1820) Restoration of pharmacy which operated on the premises from 1866-1964. Has large golden mortar and pestle over door; original walnut and butternut fixtures, apothecary glass, and interesting remedies of the past. (May-Labour Day, daily) Queen and King Sts. Phone 905/468-3845. **FREE**

Niagara Historical Society Museum. Opened in 1907, the earliest museum building in Ontario. Items from the time of the United Empire Loyalists, War of 1812, early Upper Canada, and the Victorian era. (Mar-Dec, daily; rest of yr, wkends or by appt; closed hols) 43 Castlereagh St. Contact the Niagara Historical Society, PO Box 208, L0S 1J0. Phone 905/468-3912. ¢¢

St. Mark's Anglican Church. (1805, 1843) Original church damaged by fire after being used as a hospital and barracks during the War of 1812. Rebuilt in 1822 and enlarged in 1843. Unusual three-layer stained-glass window. Churchyard dates from earliest British settlement. (July-Aug, daily; rest of yr, by appt) 41 Byron St, opp Simcoe Park. Phone 905/468-3123.

St. Vincent de Paul Roman Catholic Church. (1835) First Roman Catholic parish in Upper Canada. Excellent example of Gothic Revival architecture; enlarged in 1965; older part largely preserved. Picton and Wellington Sts.

Special Events

Shaw Festival. Shaw Festival Theatre, specializing in works of George Bernard Shaw and his contemporaries, presents ten plays each yr in repertory. Housed in three theaters, incl Court House Theatre. Staged by internationally acclaimed ensemble company. Also lunchtime theater featuring one-act plays by Shaw. Queen's Parade and Wellington St. Contact PO Box 774, L0S 1J0; 800/724-2934 (US) or 800/267-4759 (Canada). Mid-Apr-Oct.

The Days of Wine and Roses. Phone 905/468-4263. Wkends during Feb.

Motel/Motor Lodge

★★★ **WHITE OAKS CONFERENCE RESORT AND SPA.** *253 Taylor Rd (L0F 1J0). 905/688-2550; fax 905/688-2220; toll-free 800/263-5766. www.whiteoaks.on.ca.* 150 rms, 3 story. S $115-$169; D $125-$189; each addl $10; suites $189-$279; under 13 free; wkend rates. TV; cable, VCR avail. Indoor pool; poolside serv. Playground. Supervised children's activities; to age 10. Complimentary coffee in rms. Restaurant 7 am-11 pm. Rm serv. Bar 11-1 am. Ck-out noon. Meeting rms. Business center. In-rm modem link. Concierge. Valet serv. Indoor, outdoor tennis, pro. Putting green. Exercise rm. Spa. Rec rm. Bathrm phones. Private patios, balconies. Cr cds: A, D, ER, MC, V.

D 🏌 ⛼ 🏋 🖺 🔥 SC 🏃

Hotels

★★★ **PRINCE OF WALES.** *6 Picton St (L0S 1J0). 905/468-3246; fax 905/468-5521; toll-free 888/669-5566. www.princeofwaleshotel.ca.* 101 rms. May-Oct: S, D $129-$225; each addl $20; suites $275; wkend rates (winter); lower rates rest of yr. Crib free. TV; cable (premium). Indoor pool; whirlpool. Restaurant 11 am-midnight (see also ESCABECHE). Bar 11:30-1 am. Ck-out 11 am. Meeting rms.

Business servs avail. In-rm modem link. Exercise equipt; sauna. Health club privileges. Sun deck. Victorian building (1864). Cr cds: A, D, DS, ER, MC, V.

D ⛼ 🏋 🖺 🔥 SC

B&Bs/Small Inns

★★★ **GATE HOUSE HOTEL.** *142 Queen St (L0S 1J0). 905/468-3263; fax 905/468-7400. www.gatehouse-niagara.com.* 10 rms, 2 story. June-Sept: S, D $195-$230; each addl $10; under 12 free; lower rates Mar-May, Oct-Dec. Closed rest of yr. Crib free. TV; cable (premium). Dining rm noon-2:30 pm, 5-10 pm. Bar 11:30-2 am. Ck-out 11 am. X-country ski 2 mi. Minibars. Modern decor. Cr cds: A, D, ER, JCB, MC, V.

D ⛼ 🖺 🔥 🖺

★★ **KIELY HOUSE HERITAGE INN.** *209 Queen St (L0S 1J0). 905/468-4588; fax 905/468-2194.* 12 rms, 2 story. Mid-Apr-Oct: S $130; D $200; under 12 $5; lower rates rest of yr. Crib free. Complimentary continental bkfst. Restaurant 11:30 am-9 pm. Ck-out 11 am, ck-in 2 pm. Balconies. Built 1832 as private summer residence; several screened porches. Cr cds: A, MC, V.

🖺 🖺

★★ **MOFFAT INN.** *60 Picton St (L0S 1J0). 905/468-4116; fax 905/468-4747. www.moffatinn.com.* 22 rms, 2 story. May-Oct: S, D $79-$125; each addl $10; lower rates rest of yr. TV. Complimentary coffee in rms. Dining rm 8 am-midnight. Bar. Ck-out 11 am, ck-in 2 pm. Business servs avail. In-rm modem link. Some private patios. Historic inn (1835); individually decorated rms, many with brass bed; some with fireplace. Totally nonsmoking. Cr cds: A, MC, V.

🖺 🖺

★★★ **PILLAR AND POST.** *48 John St (L0S 1J0). 905/468-2123; fax 905/468-3551; res 800/361-6788. www.vintageinns.com.* 123 rms. S, D $220; each addl $20; suites $225-$375; under 12 free; winter packages. TV; cable (premium). Heated pool; whirlpool. Restaurant (see also THE CARRIAGES). Rm serv. Bar 11-1 am. Ck-out 11 am, ck-in 3 pm. Meeting rm. Business center. In-rm modem link. Luggage handling. Gift shop. Bicycle rentals. Exercise rm; sauna. Spa. Minibars; some fireplaces. Turn-of-the-century fruit canning factory. Cr cds: A, D, DS, ER, MC, V.

D ⛼ 🏋 🖺 🔥 SC 🏃

Restaurants

★★ **BUTTERY THEATRE.** *19 Queen St (L0S 1J0). 905/468-2564.* Continental menu. Specialties: spareribs, roast leg of lamb, lobster Newburg. Hrs: 11-1 am. Closed Dec 25. Res accepted. Bar. A la carte entrees: lunch $7.50-$15.50, dinner $15-$23. Child's menu. Medieval feast Fri, Sat. Patio dining. Family-owned. Cr cds: A, D, DS, MC, V.

★★★ **THE CARRIAGES.** *48 John St (L0S 1J0). 905/468-2123. www.vintageinns.com.* Continental menu. Specializes in rack of lamb. Hrs: 7:30-10:30 am, noon-2 pm, 5-9 pm. Res required. Bar 11-1 am. Wine list. Bkfst $1.95-$7.25, lunch $9-$14.95, dinner $15.95-$26.95. Buffet: bkfst $11. Child's menu. Intimate dining. Cr cds: A, D, DS, MC, V.

D SC 🖺

★ ★ ★ **ESCABECHE.** *6 Picton St (L0S 1J0). 905/468-3246.* *www.vintageinns.com.* Continental menu. Specializes in rack of lamb, fresh salmon. Own pastries. Hrs: 7-11 am, noon-2 pm, 5-10 pm; Fri, Sat to 10 pm; Sun brunch noon-2:30 pm; winter hrs vary. Res accepted. Bar. A la carte entrees: bkfst $5.50-$12.95, lunch $11.50-$20, dinner $30-$45. Sun brunch $21.95. Child's menu. Greenhouse dining. Victorian decor. Built 1864. Cr cds: A, C, D, DS, MC, V.

[D]

★ **FANS COURT.** *135 Queen St (L0S 1J0). 905/468-4511.* Chinese menu. Hrs: noon-10 pm. Res accepted. Bar. A la carte entrees: lunch $5-$7.50, dinner $9-$15.80. Outdoor dining. Large display of antique Chinese vases, jade and figurines. Cr cds: A, MC, V.

[D]

Ottawa

Founded 1827 **Pop** 295,163 **Elev** 374 ft (114 m)
Area code 613
Information Tourism & Convention Authority, 130 Albert St, Suite 1800, K1P 5G4; 613/237-5150 or 800/363-4465
Web www.tourottawa.org

The capital city of Canada, Ottawa is situated at the confluence of the Ottawa, Gatineau, and Rideau rivers. A camp established by Champlain in 1615 served as headquarters for explorations from Québec to Lake Huron. For nearly two centuries fur traders and missionaries used the Ottawa River—their only transportation route—for travel to the interior.

The first European settlement in the area was Hull, Québec, founded across the Ottawa River in 1800. In 1823 the Earl of Dalhousie secured ground for the crown on what is now Parliament Hill. Shortly after, two settlements bordered this: Upper Town and Lower Town.

The area was named Bytown in 1827 after Colonel John By, an engineer in charge of construction of the Rideau Canal, which bisects the city and connects the Ottawa River to Lake Ontario. In 1854 Bytown was renamed Ottawa. About this time four cities were rivals for capital of the United Provinces of Upper and Lower Canada: Montréal, Québec City, Kingston, and Toronto. Queen Victoria, in anticipation of confederation, unexpectedly selected Ottawa as capital in 1857, because the city was a meeting point of French and English cultures. Ten years later confederation took place and Ottawa became capital of Canada.

Today Ottawa is an important cultural center with few heavy industries. With its parks full of flowers and its universities, museums, and diplomatic embassies, Ottawa is one of Canada's most beautiful cities.

What to See and Do

Bytown Museum. Artifacts, documents, and pictures relating to Colonel By, Bytown, and the history and social life of the region. Tours (by appt). (Early May-mid-Oct, daily; rest of yr, Mon-Fri or by appt) Commissariat Bldg, 50 Canal Ln, beside the Ottawa Locks, Rideau Canal. Phone 613/234-4570. ¢¢

By Ward Market. Traditional farmers market; building houses boutiques and art galleries; outdoor cafés. Exterior market (daily); interior market (Apr-Dec, daily; rest of yr, Tues-Sun). Bounded by Dalhousie and Sussex Dr, George and Clarence Sts. Phone 613/562-3325. **FREE**

✪ **Canadian Museum of Civilization.** This vast facility employs state-of-the-art exhibition technology to illustrate Canada's history and heritage over 1,000 yrs of settlement. Permanent attractions incl **The Children's Museum**, offering a variety of hands-on displays, workshops, and activities; **CINEPLUS**, the world's first convertible IMAX/Omnimax theater; **History Hall**, a setting for many life-size reconstructions of various buildings and environments in Canada's past; and **The Grand Hall**, an expansive space housing six Pacific Coast indigenous houses as well as demonstrations, native ceremonies, and participatory activities. Large galleries with changing exhibits; theater. Tours. (May-mid-Oct, daily; rest of yr, Tues-Sun; closed Jan 1, Dec 25) Free admission to museum Sun mornings. 100 Laurier St, Hull, PQ. Phone 819/776-7000. Museum ¢¢ CINEPLUS ¢¢¢

Canadian Museum of Contemporary Photography. Showcases the work of Canada's preeminent photographers. (Daily) 1 Rideau Canal. Phone 613/990-8527.

Canadian Parliament Buildings. Neo-Gothic architecture dominates this part of the city. House of Commons and Senate meet here; visitors may request tickets (free) to both chambers when Parliament is in session. Forty-five-min guided tour incl House of Commons, Senate Chamber, Parliamentary Library. (Daily; closed Jan 1, July 1, Dec 25) (See SPECIAL EVENTS) Also here are the **Centennial Flame**, lit in 1967 as a symbol of Canada's 100th birthday, and **Memorial Chapel**, dedicated to Canadian servicemen who lost their lives in the Boer War, WWI, WWII, and the Korean War. **Observation Deck** atop the Peace Tower. Wellington St on Parliament Hill. Phone 613/996-0896. **FREE**

Canadian Ski Museum. History of skiing; collection of old skis and ski equipment from Canada and around the world. (Daily; closed hols) 1960 Scott St. Phone 613/722-3584. ¢

Canadian War Museum. Exhibits tracing Canada's military history incl arms, aircraft, military vehicles, uniforms, and action displays. (May-mid-Oct, daily; rest of yr, Tues-Sun; closed Dec 25) 330 Sussex Dr. Phone 819/776-8600. ¢¢

Central Experimental Farm. Approx 1,200 acres (486 hectares) of field crops, ornamental gardens, arboretum; showcase herds of beef and dairy cattle, sheep, swine, horses. Tropical greenhouse (daily). Agricultural museum (daily; closed Dec 25). Clydesdale horse-drawn wagon or sleigh rides. Picnicking. (May-mid-Oct) Grounds (daily). Some fees. Prince of Wales Dr. Phone 613/991-3044.

City Hall. Situated on Green Island, on the Rideau River. View of city and surrounding area from 8th floor. Guided tours (Mon-Fri, by appt; closed hols). 111 Sussex Dr. Phone 613/244-5464. **FREE**

Currency Museum. Artifacts, maps, and exhibits tell the story of money and its use throughout the world. (May-Labour Day, daily; rest of yr, Tues-Sun) 245 Sparks St. Phone 613/782-8914. **FREE**

Laurier House. Former residence of two prime ministers: Sir Wilfrid Laurier and W.L. Mackenzie King. Re-created study of Prime Minister Lester B. Pearson. Books, furnishings, and memorabilia. (Tues-Sun; closed Jan 1, Good Friday, Dec 25) 335 Laurier Ave E. Phone 613/992-8142. ¢¢

Museum of Canadian Scouting. Depicts the history of Canadian Scouting; exhibits on the life of Lord R.S.S. Baden-Powell, founder of the Boy Scouts; pertinent documents, photographs, and artifacts. (Mon-Fri; closed hols) 1345 Base Line Rd, 8 mi (13 km) SW. Phone 613/224-5131. **FREE**

National Archives of Canada. Collections of all types of material relating to Canadian history. Changing exhibits. (Daily) Opp is **Garden of the Provinces.** Flags representing all Canadian provinces and territories; fountain illuminated at night. (May-Nov) 395 Wellington St. Phone 613/995-5183. **FREE**

National Arts Centre. Center for performing arts; houses a concert hall and two theaters for music, dance, variety, and drama; home of the National Arts Centre Orchestra; more than 800 performances each yr; canal-side cafe. Landscaped terraces with panoramic view of Ottawa. Guided tours (free). 53 Elgin St at Confederation Sq. Phone 613/996-5051.

✪ **National Gallery of Canada.** Permanent exhibits incl European paintings from 14th century-present; Canadian art from 17th century-present; contemporary and decorative arts, prints, drawings, photos, and Inuit art; video and film. Reconstructed 19th-century Rideau convent chapel with Neo-Gothic fan-vaulted ceiling, only known example of its kind in North America. Changing exhibits (fee), gallery talks, films; restaurants, bookstore. Guided tours (daily). (May-mid-Sept, daily; rest of yr, Wed-Sun; closed hols) 380 Sussex Dr, at St. Patrick St. Phone 613/990-1985. **FREE**

National Museum of Science and Technology. More than 400 exhibits with many do-it-yourself experiments; Canada's role in science and technology shown through displays on Canada in space, transportation, agriculture, computers, communications, physics, and astronomy. Unusual open restoration bay allows viewing of various stages of artifact repair and refurbishment. Cafeteria. (May-Labour Day, daily; rest of yr, Tues-Sun; closed Dec 25) 1867 St. Laurent Blvd. Phone 613/991-3044. ¢¢ The museum also maintains

National Aviation Museum. More than 100 historic aircraft, 49 on display in a "Walkway of Time." Displays demonstrate the development of aircraft in peace and war, emphasizing Canadian aviation. (Daily) Rockcliffe Airport, NE end of city. Phone 613/993-2010 or 800/463-2038. ¢¢

Nepean Point. Lovely view of the area; Astrolabe Theatre, a 700-seat amphitheater, is the scene of musical, variety, and dramatic shows in summer. Just W of Sussex Dr and St. Patrick. Phone 613/239-5000. **FREE**

Professional sports.

Ottawa Senators (NHL). Corel Centre. 1000 Palladium Dr. Kanata, Ontario. Phone 800/444-SENS.

Recreational facilities. For information on canoes, rowboats, docking and launching, swimming at outdoor beaches and pools, phone 613/239-5000. Gatineau Park, across the Ottawa River in Québec, offers swimming, fishing; bicycling, cross-country skiing, picnicking, and camping. There are more than 87 mi (140 km) of recreational trails and approx 50 golf courses in the area. Boats may be rented on the Rideau Canal at Dow's Lake, Queen Elizabeth Driveway and Preston St. Contact the National Capital Commission, 90 Wellington St, opp Parliament Hill, phone 613/239-5000. Fishing licenses (required in Québec for nonresidents) may be obtained at the Québec Dept of Tourism, Fish, and Game, 13 rue Buteau, J8Z 1V4 in Hull, PQ (wkdays, closed hols). Phone 613/771-4840.

✪ **Rideau Canal.** Constructed under the direction of Lieutenant-Colonel John By of the Royal Engineers between 1826-1832 as a safe supply route to Upper Canada. The purpose was to bypass the St. Lawrence River in case of an American attack. There are 24 lock stations where visitors can picnic, watch boats pass through the hand-operated locks, and see wooden lock gates, cut stone walls, and many historic structures. In summer there are interpretive programs and exhibits at various locations. Areas of special interest incl Kingston Mills Locks, Jones Falls Locks (off ON 15), Smith Falls Museum (off ON 15), Merrickville Locks (on ON 43), and Ottawa Locks. Boating is popular (mid-May-mid-Oct, daily) and ice-skating is avail (mid-Dec-late Feb, daily). Runs 125 mi (202 km) between Kingston and Ottawa. Phone 613/283-5170. **FREE**

Royal Canadian Mint. Production of coins; collection of coins and medals. Guided tours and film; detailed process of minting coins and printing bank notes is shown. (Daily; tours by appt) 320 Sussex Dr. Phone 613/993-8990. ¢

Sightseeing tours.

Double-Decker bus tours. Capital Trolley Tours. Buses seen in service in Britain visit various highlights of the city. (Apr-mid-Nov, daily) Phone 613/729-6888. ¢¢¢¢

Gray Line bus tours. (May-Oct, daily) Phone 613/725-1441.

Ottawa Riverboat Company. Two-hr cruises on Ottawa River. Boats depart from Hull and Ottawa docks (daily). Also eve dinner/dance cruises (Wed-Fri). Phone 613/562-4888. ¢¢¢

Paul's Boat Lines, Ltd. Rideau Canal sightseeing cruises depart from Conference Centre (mid-May-mid-Oct, daily). Ottawa River sightseeing cruises depart from foot of Rideau Canal Locks (mid-May-mid-Oct, daily). Phone 613/225-6781. ¢¢¢

Victoria Memorial Museum Building. Castlelike structure houses museum that interrelates man and his natural environment. Houses the **Canadian Museum of Nature.** Natural history exhibits from dinosaurs to present day plants and animals. Outstanding collection of minerals and gems. (Daily; closed Dec 25) Metcalfe & McLeod Sts. Phone 613/566-4700. ¢¢

Special Events

Winterlude. Extravaganza devoted to outdoor concerts, fireworks, skating contests, dances, music, ice sculptures. Phone 613/239-5000. Three wkends Feb.

Canadian Tulip Festival. Part of a two-wk celebration, culminated by the blooming of more than three million tulips presented to Ottawa by Queen Juliana of the Netherlands after she sought refuge here during WWII. Tours of flower beds; craft market and demonstrations, kite flying, boat parade. Phone 613/567-5757. May.

Sound & Light Show on Parliament Hill. Phone 613/239-5000. Mid-May-Labour Day.

Changing the Guard. Parliament Hill. Phone 613/239-5000. Late June-late Aug.

Canada Day. Celebration of Canada's birthday with many varied events throughout the city, incl canoe and sailing regattas, concerts, music and dance, art and craft demonstrations, children's entertainment, fireworks. Phone 613/239-5000. July 1.

Ottawa International Jazz Festival. Phone 613/594-3580. Ten days July.

Motels/Motor Lodges

★★ **BEST WESTERN HOTEL JACQUES CARTIER.** *131 Laurier St, Hull (J8X 3W3). 819/770-8550; fax 819/770-9705; res 800/265-8550. www.bestwestern.com.* 144 rms, 9 story. Mid-May-mid-Oct: S, D $86-$125; each addl $10; kit. units $100-$125; under 18 free; lower rates rest of yr. Crib $10. TV; cable. Indoor pool; lifeguard. Restaurant 7 am-2 pm, 5-10 pm; wkend hrs vary. Bar 11-3 am; entertainment. Ck-out noon. Meeting rms. Business servs avail. Many refrigerators. Some balconies. Opp Museum of Civilization. Cr cds: A, C, D, DS, ER, MC, V.
🌊 ⛷ 🐾 SC

★★ **BEST WESTERN VICTORIA PARK SUITES.** *377 O'Connor St, Ottawa (K2P 2M2). 613/567-7275; fax 613/567-1161; toll-free 800/465-7275. www.vpsuites.com.* 100 kit. units, 8 story. May-Oct: S, D $100-$145; wkend rates; lower rates rest of yr. Crib free. Garage parking $7. TV; cable. Complimentary continental bkfst. Restaurant nearby. Ck-out noon. Coin lndry. Meeting rms. Business servs avail. Exercise equipt. Microwaves. Cr cds: A, D, DS, ER, MC, V.
🏃 ⛷ 🐾 SC

Hotels

★★★ **ALBERT AT BAY.** *435 Albert St, Ottawa (K1R 7X4). 613/238-8858; fax 613/238-1433; toll-free 800/267-6644. www.albertatbay.com.* 195 kit. suites, 12 story. S, D $124-$144; under 16 free; wkend, monthly rates. Crib free. Garage $8.50. TV; cable. Restaurant 6:30 am-midnight; Sat, Sun from 11 am. Ck-out noon. Coin lndry. Meeting rms. Business servs avail. In-rm modem link. Downhill ski 8 mi; x-country ski 5 mi. Exercise equipt; sauna. Whirlpool. Microwaves. Balconies. Renovated apartment building. Rooftop garden with picnic tables, lawn chairs. Cr cds: A, C, D, DS, ER, JCB, MC, V.
D ⛷ 🏃 ⛷ 🐾 SC

★★★ **CROWNE PLAZA OTTAWA.** *101 Lyon St, Ottawa (K1R 5T9). 613/237-3600; fax 613/237-2351; toll-free 800/567-3600. www.crowneplaza.com.* 411 rms, 26 story. S, D $89-$155; each addl $12; suites $150-$450; under 18 free; package plans. Crib free. Garage (fee). TV; cable. Indoor pool. Restaurant 6:30 am-10 pm. Bar 11-1 am. Ck-out 1 pm. Meeting rms. Business center. Concierge. Gift shop. Downhill/x-country ski 12 mi. Exercise rm; sauna. Cr cds: A, C, D, DS, ER, MC, V.
D ⛷ 🌊 🏃 ⛷ 🐾 SC 🏃

★★ **DELTA HOTEL.** *361 Queen St, Ottawa (K1R 7F9). 613/238-6000; fax 613/238-2290. www.deltahotels.com.* 328 units, 18 story. May-June, Sept-Oct: S, D $155-$175; each addl $15; suites $180-$200; under 18 free; wkend rates; special summer rates; lower rates rest of yr. Crib free. Pet accepted. Garage $11.50. TV; cable. Indoor pool; whirlpool. Restaurant 6:30 am-10 pm. Rm serv 6 am-11 pm. Bars 11-2 am. Ck-out noon. Meeting rms. Business center. In-rm modem link. Barber, beauty shop. Downhill/x-country ski 12 mi. Exercise rm; saunas. Minibars. Some balconies. Luxury level. Cr cds: A, D, ER, JCB, MC, V.
D 🐾 ⛷ 🌊 🏃 ⛷ 🐾 SC 🏃

★★★ **FAIRMONT CHATEAU LAURIER.** *1 Rideau St, Ottawa (K1N 8S7). 613/241-1414; fax 613/562-7031. www.fairmont.com.* 426 rms, 8 story. S, D $149-$339; each addl $20; suites $339-$1,800. Under 18 free. Crib free. Garage parking (fee). TV; cable (premium), VCR avail. Indoor pool. Supervised children's activities (summer). Complimentary coffee in rms. Restaurant 6:30 am-10 pm; dining rm (mid-May-Labour Day) 11:30 am-10 pm. Rm serv 24 hrs. Bar 11:30-1 am. Ck-out noon. Convention facilities. Business center. In-rm modem link. Concierge. Shopping arcade. Downhill/x-country ski 12 mi. Exercise rm; sauna. Massage. Rec rm. Minibars. Luxury level. Cr cds: A, C, D, DS, ER, JCB, MC, V.
D ⛷ 🌊 🏃 ⛷ 🐾 🏃

★★★ **HILTON LAC LEAMY.** *3 Blvd Du Casino, Hull (J8Y 6X4). 819/790-6444; 800/445-8667. www.hilton.com.* 349 rms, 20 story. S, D $250-$375; under 18 free. Crib avail. TV; cable (premium). Indoor pool; whirlpool. Restaurant 6:30 am-10 pm. Bar to midnight. Ck-out noon. Meeting rms. Business center. In-rm modem link. Concierge. Exercise equipt. Minibars; many refrigerators in suites. Cr cds: A, D, DS, ER, MC, V.
🌊 🏃 🏃

★★ **LORD ELGIN.** *100 Elgin St, Ottawa (K1P 5K8). 613/235-3333; fax 613/235-3223; toll-free 800/267-4298. www.lordelginhotel.ca.* 311 rms, 11 story. S $115-$160; D $120-$170; each addl $5; suites $180-$200; under 18 free; wkend rates. Crib free. Pet accepted, some restrictions. Garage; valet, in/out $13.50. TV; cable. Coffee in rms. Restaurant 7 am-11 pm. Bar 11:30-1 am. Ck-out 1 pm. Meeting rms. Business servs avail. In-rm modem link. Gift shop. Downhill/x-country ski 12 mi. Exercise equipt. Originally opened 1941; completely renovated. Cr cds: A, C, D, ER, JCB, MC, V.
D 🐾 ⛷ 🏃 ⛷ 🐾 SC

★★★ **MARRIOTT OTTAWA.** *100 Kent St, Ottawa (K1P 5R7). 613/238-1122; fax 613/783-4229; 800/228-9290. www.marriott.com.* 478 rms, 26 story. S, D $125-$155; each addl $10; suites $300-$400; under 19 free; wkend rates. Crib free. Pet accepted. Garage (fee). TV; cable (premium). Indoor pool; whirlpool. Restaurant 6:30 am-11 pm; revolving rooftop dining rm 11:30 am-2:30 pm, 6-11 pm; Sat from 6 pm. Bar 11-1 am. Ck-out 1 pm. Meeting rms. Business servs avail. In-rm modem link. Downhill ski 15 mi. Exercise rm; sauna. Minibars. Many balconies. Adj underground shopping mall. Luxury level. Cr cds: A, C, D, DS, ER, JCB, MC, V.

⬛🐾🏊⛱🏃🏂🐾🆂🅒

★★★ **SHERATON.** *150 Albert St, Ottawa (K1P 5G2). 613/238-1500; fax 613/235-2723; toll-free 800/489-8333. www.sheraton.com.* 236 rms, 18 story. S $200; D $215; each addl $20; suites $280-$450; family rates; package plans. Crib free. Garage (fee). Pet accepted. TV; cable. Indoor pool; poolside serv. Coffee in rms. Restaurant 6:30 am-11 pm. Ck-out noon. Meeting rms. Business center. In-rm modem link. Gift shop. Downhill/x-country ski 12 mi. Exercise equipt; sauna. Minibars. Luxury level. Cr cds: A, D, DS, ER, JCB, MC, V.

⬛🐾🏊⛱🏃🏂🐾🆂🅒🏃

★★★ **THE WESTIN OTTAWA.** *11 Colonel By Dr, Ottawa (K1N 9H4). 613/560-7000; fax 613/234-5396; 800/937-8461. www.westin.com.* 484 rms, 24 story. Mid-Apr-June, mid-Sept-mid-Nov: S, D $190-$211; each addl $20; suites $265-$700; under 18 free; wkend rates; lower rates rest of yr. Crib free. Pet accepted, some restrictions. TV; cable. Indoor pool; whirlpool. Restaurants 6:30 am-11 pm. Rm serv 24 hrs. Bar 11:30-2 am. Ck-out 1 pm. Convention facilities. Business center. Concierge. Shopping arcade adj. Barber, beauty shop. Valet parking. Downhill/x-country ski 12 mi. Exercise rm; sauna. Massage. Minibars; some bathrm phones. Opp Rideau Canal; near Parliament Hill. Cr cds: A, C, D, DS, ER, JCB, MC, V.

⬛🐾🏊⛱🏃🏂🐾🆂🅒🏃

Resort

★★★ **FAIRMONT LE CHATEAU MONTEBELLO.** *392 rue Notre Dame, Montebello (J0V 1L0). 819/423-6341; fax 819/423-5283; toll-free 800/441-1414. www.fairmont.com.* 210 rms, 3 story. Mid-May-mid-Oct, MAP: S $186.50; D $238; each addl $71.50; under 4 free; lower rates rest of yr. Crib free. Pet accepted. TV; cable. 2 pools, 1 indoor; whirlpool; lifeguard. Playground. Supervised children's activities (mid-June-early Sept); ages 3-12. Dining rm (see also AUX CHANTIGNOLES). Rm serv 7 am-11 pm. Bar 11-1 am; entertainment Fri-Sat. Ck-out noon, ck-in 3 pm. Meeting rms. Business center. In-rm modem link. Bellhops. Valet serv. Gift shop. Sports dir. Indoor and outdoor tennis. 18-hole golf, greens fee (incl cart) $62, pro, putting green. X-country ski on site (rentals). Sleighing. Curling. Bicycles. Lawn games. Soc dir. Rec rm. Game rm. Squash courts. Exercise rm; sauna, steam rm. Massage. Fishing, hunting guides. Minibars. Marina. On 65,000 acres. Cr cds: A, DS, MC, V.

⛱🏃🎿🏃⛱

B&Bs/Small Inns

★★★ **GASTHAUS SWITZERLAND INN.** *89 Daly Ave, Ottawa (K1N 6E6). 613/237-0335; fax 613/594-3327; res 800/663-0000. www.gasthausswitzerlandinn.com.* 22 rms, 3 story. May-Oct: S, D $78-$128; each addl $20; suites $188; lower rates rest of yr. Children over 12 yrs only. TV; cable. Complimentary full bkfst. Restaurant nearby. Ck-out 11 am, ck-in 3 pm. In-rm modem link. Some in-rm whirlpools, fireplaces. Picnic tables. In restored 1872 house. Totally nonsmoking. Cr cds: A, D, ER, MC, V.

⬛

★ **VOYAGEUR'S GUEST HOUSE.** *95 Arlington Ave, Ottawa (K1R 5S4). 613/238-6445; fax 613/236-5551. www.bbcanada.com/1897.html.* 6 rms, 3 share bath, 2 story. No rm phones. S $39; D $49; each addl $10; higher rates Canada Day. TV; cable (premium). Complimentary full bkfst. Restaurant nearby. Ck-out 11 am, ck-in 11 am. Downhill ski 20 mi; x-country ski 3 mi. Totally nonsmoking. Cr cds: D, ER, MC, V.

⛱🏂🐾

Restaurants

★★★ **AUX CHANTIGNOLES.** *392 rue Notre Dame, Montebello (J0V 1L0). 819/423-6341. www.fairmont.com.* French, continental menu. Specializes in seafood, veal, game. Own baking. Hrs: 7 am-3 pm, 5:30-10 pm; Sun brunch 11 am-3 pm. Res accepted. Serv bar. Wine list. Buffet: bkfst $16.50. Complete meals: lunch $39.50. A la carte entrees: dinner $40-$85. Sun brunch $28.50. Child's menu. Parking. Outdoor dining. Rustic decor; fireplace. Cr cds: A, MC, V.

⬛⬛

★★ **BACO RESTAURANT AND WINE BAR.** *200 Beachwood Ave, Vanier (K1L 8A9). 613/747-0272.* Specializes in fresh fish, Canadian lamb. Hrs: 5-9 pm. Closed Sun, Mon. Res accepted. Wine list. Dinner $17-$32. Entertainment. Cr cds: A, C, D, DS, ER, JCB, MC, V.

⬛⬛

★★★ **DOMUS CAFI.** *87 Murray St, Ottawa (K2A OE7). 613/241-6007.* Canadian regional cuisine menu. Specializes in pan-seared Quebec foie gras, New Foundland Sea scallops. Hrs; 11:30 am-2:30 pm, 6-9 pm; Sun 11 am-2:30 pm. Closed Canada Day, Dec 25. Res accepted. Wine list. Lunch $6-$15; dinner $17-$35. Brunch $6-$15. Entertainment. Cr cds: A, D, DS, ER, MC, V.

⬛

★★ **LA GONDOLA.** *188 Bank St, Ottawa (K2P 1W8). 613/235-3733.* Continental, Italian menu. Specializes in veal, pasta. Hrs: 11:30 am-11:30 pm; Sun 10 am-10 pm; Sat, Sun brunch 10 am-3 pm. Closed Dec 25. Res accepted. Bar. A la carte entrees: lunch $5.95-$12.95, dinner $8.95-$22. Sat, Sun brunch $3.25-$7. Child's menu. Outdoor dining. Cr cds: A, D, ER, MC, V.

⬛⬛

★ **LAS PALMAS.** *111 Parent Ave, Ottawa (K1N 7B3).* *613/241-3738.* Mexican menu. Specializes in fajitas, enchiladas. Hrs: 11:30 am-11 pm. Bar. A la carte entrees: lunch, dinner $6-$15.95. Mexican village setting. Outdoor dining. Cr cds: A, D, DS, ER, MC, V.
[D] [⊟]

★★★ **LE BACCARA.** *1 Boul du Casino, Hull (J8Y 6W3).* *819/772-6210. www.casinos-quebec.com* . French menu. Specializes in regional French cuisine. Hrs: 5:30-11 pm. Res accepted. Wine list. Table d'hote $37-$45. Cr cds: A, MC, V.

★★ **LE CAFE.** *53 Elgin St, Ottawa (K1P 5W1). 613/594-5127.* Nouvelle Canadian menu. Own pastries. Hrs: noon-11 pm. Closed Jan 1, Dec 24, 25; also Sun Sept-May. Res accepted. Bar. A la carte entrees: lunch $7.95-$13.95, dinner $12.95-$22.95. Child's menu. Parking. Outdoor dining on terrace overlooking Rideau Canal. Totally nonsmoking. Cr cds: A, D, ER, MC, V.
[D]

★★ **MARBLE WORKS STEAKHOUSE.** *14 Waller St, Ottawa (K1N 9C4). 613/241-6764.* Specializes in steak. Hrs: 11:30 am-2 pm, 5-10 pm; Sat from 5 pm; Sun from 10:30 am. Closed Dec 25. Res accepted. Bar to 2 am. A la carte entrees: lunch $8-$16, dinner $12-$24. Sun brunch $11.95. Child's menu. Entertainment Sat . Parking. Outdoor dining. In renovated 1866 building. Cr cds: A, D, MC, V.
[⊟]

★★ **THE MILL.** *555 Ottawa River Pkwy, Ottawa (K1P 5R4). 613/237-1311. www.themilldininglounge.com.* Continental menu. Specializes in prime rib, fish, chicken. Hrs: 11:30 am-2:30 pm, 4:30-10 pm; wkends from 4:30 pm; Sun brunch 10:30 am-1:30 pm. Closed July 1. Bar. A la carte entrees: lunch $5.95-$9.95, dinner $9.95-$17.95. Sun brunch $4.95-$9.95. Child's menu. Parking. Outdoor dining. Former mill (1850); mill structure visible through glass wall. Cr cds: A, D, MC, V.
[D] [⊟]

★★ **SITAR.** *417A Rideau St, Ottawa (K1N 5Y6). 613/789-7979.* Indian menu. Specializes in tandoori-prepared dishes, vegetarian dishes. Own breads. Hrs: 11:45 am-2 pm, 5-10:30 pm; Sun 5-10:30 pm. Closed Jan 1, Dec 25. Complete meals: lunch $7.95, dinner $14.95-$18.75. Cr cds: A, D, ER, MC, V.
[D] [⊟]

Quetico Provincial Park

See also Fort Frances, Thunder Bay

27 mi W on ON 11/17.
Web www.hunterdon-chamber.org

Quetico is a wilderness park and as such is composed largely of rugged landscape. There are no roads in the park, but its vast network of connecting waterways allows for some of the best canoeing in North America. More than 900 miles (1,450 kilometers) of canoe routes are within Quetico's 1,832-square-mile (4,622-square-kilometer) area. Canoeing (no motor-powered craft allowed), fishing, and swimming are primary activities in the park. Appropriate fishing licenses are required.

Car camping is permitted at 107 sites in two areas of the Dawson Trail Campgrounds. Permits can be obtained at Park Ranger Stations. Payments may be made in Canadian or US currency (no personal checks). For reservations phone 807/597-2737 (Canadian residents) or 807/597-2735 (nonresidents).

Picnic facilities, trails, and a large assortment of pictographs may be enjoyed. In winter the vacationer can ice fish and cross-country ski, although there are no maintained facilities. Park (Victoria Day wkend-Thanksgiving wkend, daily).

St. Catharines

See also Hamilton, Niagara Falls, Niagara-on-the-Lake

Pop 124,018 **Elev** 321 ft (98 m) **Area code** 905
Information Tourism Marketing Coordinator, City Hall, 50 Church St, PO Box 3012, L2R 7C2; 905/688-5601
Web www.st.catharines.com

St. Catharines, "The Garden City of Canada," is located in the heart of the wine country and the Niagara fruit belt, which produces half of the province's entire output of fresh fruit. Originally a Loyalist settlement, it was also a depot of the Underground Railway. Located on the Welland Ship Canal, and the site of the first canal, St. Catharines was also the home of the first electric streetcar system in North America.

What to See and Do

Brock University. (1964) 6,000 students. A 540-acre (219-hectare) campus encompasses some of the finest woods and countryside in the Niagara region. Named in honor of General Sir Isaac Brock, commander of the British forces at the Battle of Queenston Heights in 1812. Tours (Mon-Fri, by appt). Glenridge Ave/Merrittville Hwy, at St. David's Rd. Phone 905/688-5550.

The Farmers Market. Large variety of fruit and vegetables from fruit belt farms of the surrounding area. (Tues, Thurs, Sat) Church and James Sts, behind City Hall. Phone 905/688-5601.

Happy Rolph Bird Sanctuary & Children's Farm. Feeding station for native fowl and farm animals; three ponds; nature trail, picnicking, playground. (Victoria Day-Thanksgiving, daily; ponds all yr) Queen Elizabeth Way, Lake St exit N to Lakeshore Rd E, cross ship canal, then N on Read Rd. Phone 905/937-7210. **FREE**

Morningstar Mill. Waterpowered, fine old mill containing rollers and millstones for grinding flour and feed. Picnic area. (Victoria Day wkend-Thanksgiving wkend, daily; rest of yr, Sat, Sun) De Cew Rd, at De Cew Falls. Phone 905/937-7210. **FREE**

Old Port Dalhousie. An 18th-century harborfront village, once the northern terminus of the first three Welland Ship Canals; now part of a larger recreation area with hand-crafted wooden carousel, restaurants, and shops. Ontario St, N of QEW to Lakeport Rd. Phone 905/935-7555.

Rodman Hall Arts Centre. Art exhibitions, films, concerts, children's theater. (Tues-Sun; closed hols) 109 St. Paul Crescent. Phone 905/684-2925. **FREE**

Welland Canal Viewing Complex at Lock III. Unique view of lock operations from an elevated platform. Ships from over 50 countries can be seen as they pass through the canal. Arrival times are posted. Large information center; picnicking, restaurant. Via Queen Elizabeth Way exit at Glendale Ave to Canal Rd then N. Phone 905/688-5601. Also here is

   St. Catharines Museum. Illustrates development, construction, and significance of Welland Canal; working scale model lock; displays on history of St. Catharines. Exhibitions on loan from major museums. (Daily; closed Jan 1, Dec 25-26) 1932 Government Rd. Phone 905/984-8880. ¢¢

Special Events

Royal Canadian Henley Regatta. Henley Rowing Course. Champion rowers from all parts of the world. Second in size only to the famous English regatta. Several nation- and continent-wide regattas take place on this world-famous course. Phone 905/935-9771. Apr-Oct.

Salmon Derby. Open season on Lake Ontario for coho and chinook salmon; rainbow, brown, and lake trout. Prizes for all categories. Phone 905/935-6700. Mid-Apr-mid-May.

Folk Arts Festival. Folk Art Multicultural Centre, 85 Church St. Open houses at ethnic clubs, concerts, ethnic dancing, and singing. Art and craft exhibits; big parade. Phone 905/685-6589. Two wks late May.

Can-Am Soapbox Derby. Jaycee Park, QEW N, exit Ontario St. More than 100 competitors from US and Canada. June.

Niagara Symphony Association. 73 Ontario St, Unit 104. Professional symphony orchestra; amateur chorus; summer music camp. Phone 905/687-4993. Sept-May.

Niagara Grape and Wine Festival. Wine and cheese parties, athletic events, grape stomping, arts and crafts, ethnic concerts, and parade with bands and floats to honor ripening of the grapes. Grand Parade last Sat of festival. Phone 905/688-2570. Ten days late Sept.

Motels/Motor Lodges

★★★ **FOUR POINTS BY SHERATON.** *3530 Schmon Pkwy, Thorold (L2V 4Y6). 905/984-8484; fax 905/984-6691. www.fourpoints.com.* 129 kit. suites, 4 story. S, D $94-$200; each addl $10; under 18 free. Crib free. Pet accepted. TV; cable, VCR avail. Indoor pool. Complimentary full bkfst. Coffee in rms. Restaurant 11 am-11 pm. Rm serv. Bar. Ck-out noon. Guest lndry. Meeting rms. Business center. In-rm modem link. Valet serv. Sundries. Exercise equipt; sauna. Lawn games. Microwaves. Cr cds: A, D, DS, ER, MC, V.

⊡ 🐾 ⩳ 🎿 ⩳ 🔥 SC 🎿

★★ **HOLIDAY INN.** *2 N Service Rd, St Catharines (L2N 4G9). 905/934-8000; fax 905/934-9117; 800/465-4329. www.holiday-inn.com.* 140 rms, 2 story. July-Sept: S $105-$135; D $115-$145; each addl $10; under 18 free; lower rates rest of yr. Crib free. Pet accepted. TV; cable (premium) VCR avail (movies). Indoor/outdoor pool; lifeguard. Playground. Complimentary coffee in rms. Restaurant 6:30 am-9 pm. Rm serv. Bar 11-1 am. Ck-out noon. Meeting rms. Business servs avail. In-rm modem link. Bellhops. Valet serv. Gift shop. Exercise rm; sauna. Balconies. Cr cds: A, C, D, DS, ER, JCB, MC, V.

⊡ 🐾 ⩳ 🎿 ⩳ 🔥 SC

★ **HOWARD JOHNSON.** *89 Meadowvale Dr (L2N 3Z8). 905/934-5400; fax 905/646-8700; 800/446-4656. www.hojo.com.* 96 rms, 5 story. S $69-$149; D $79-$159; each addl $10; under 18 free. Crib free. Pet accepted. TV. Indoor pool. Coffee in rms. Restaurant open 24 hrs. Bar 11-2 am. Ck-out noon. Coin lndry. Meeting rm. Business servs avail. In-rm modem link. X-country ski 10 mi. Exercise equipt; sauna. Microwaves avail. Cr cds: A, D, DS, ER, MC, V.

⊡ 🐾 ⩳ ⩳ 🎿 ⩳ 🔥 SC

★ **RAMADA PARKWAY INN.** *327 Ontario St (L2R 5L3). 905/688-2324; fax 905/684-6432; 800/228-2828. www.ramada.com.* 125 rms, 5 story. Late June-Labour Day: S $89.99; D $149.99; each addl $10; under 18 free; wkend plan off-season; lower rates rest of yr. Crib free. TV; cable. Indoor pool; whirlpool. Sauna. Coffee in rms. Restaurant 6:30 am-11 pm. Bar 11-2 am. Ck-out 11 am. Meeting rms. Business servs avail. Health club privileges. Bowling alley. Refrigerators; some in-rm whirlpools. Plaza adj. Cr cds: A, C, D, DS, ER, MC, V.

⊡ ⩳ ⩳ 🔥 SC

★★ **TRAVELODGE.** *420 Ontario St (L2R 5M1). 905/688-1646; 800/578-7878. www.travelodge.com.* 50 rms, 2 story. Mid-May-Sept: S $51.95; D $99.95; each addl $5; under 12 free; lower rates rest of yr. Crib $5. TV; cable (premium). Heated pool. Restaurant 7 am-2 pm. Ck-out noon. Meeting rms. Business servs avail. In-rm modem link. Valet serv. Sundries. Cr cds: A, C, D, DS, ER, MC, V.

⩳ ⩳ 🔥 SC

St. Lawrence Islands National Park

See also Gananoque, Kingston

14 mi (30 km) E.

Established in 1904, this park lies on a 50 mile (80 kilometer) stretch of the St. Lawrence River between Kingston and Brockville. It consists of 21 island areas and a mainland headquarters at Mallorytown Landing. The park offers boat launching facilities, beaches, natural and historic interpretive programs, island camping, picnicking, hiking, and boating. A visitor reception center and the remains of an 1817 British gunboat are at Mallorytown Landing (mid-May-mid-Oct, daily; rest of yr, by appt).

The islands can be accessed by water taxi or by boat rentals at numerous marinas along both the Canadian and American sides.

Sarnia

See also London

Founded 1856 **Pop** 50,892 **Elev** 610 ft (186 m)
Area code 519
Information Tourism Sarnia-Lambton, 556 N Christina St, N7T 5W6; 519/336-3232 or 800/265-0316

Sarnia was originally known as "The Rapids" and was renamed Port Sarnia in 1836. The town grew because of timber stands in the area, the discovery of oil, and the arrival of the Great Western Railway in 1858. Today it is Canada's most important petrochemical center.

Sarnia is located in the center of one of Canada's most popular recreation areas. Lake Huron offers beaches from Canatara Park to nearby Lambton County beaches; the St. Clair River flows south of Sarnia into Lake St. Clair. Facilities for water sports and boating are excellent. The city and surrounding area has many golf courses, camp-sites, and trailer parks. Easy access to the United States is provided by the International Blue Water Bridge (toll) spanning the St. Clair River between Sarnia and Port Huron, Michigan (see Border Crossing Regulations in MAKING THE MOST OF YOUR TRIP).

What to See and Do

Canatara Park. Information center housed in reconstructed 19th-century log cabin (Victoria Day wkend-Labour Day wkend, Mon-Fri afternoons; rest of yr, wkends). Facilities for swimming, beach, and bathhouse; picnicking, barbecu-ing, refreshments, lookout tower, fitness trail, natural area, toboggan hill, playground equipment, and ball diamond. (Daily) At Cathcart Blvd, off N Christina St. Phone 800/265-0316. **FREE** Also in the park are

Children's Animal Farm. Farm buildings; animals, poultry, and waterfowl. (Daily) **FREE**

Log Cabin. Two-floor cabin with natural wooden peg flooring, two fireplaces; interpretive programs featured in summer. Adj are carriage shed with farm implement artifacts from 1850, and a smokehouse. (Open for special events) **FREE**

The Gardens. Wide variety of plant life. The park also offers facilities for swimming (fee); tennis, lawn bowling, horseshoes, baseball, and soccer. Germain Park, East St. Phone 519/332-0330.

Lambton Heritage Museum. Features more than 400 Currier & Ives prints, Canada's largest collection of antique pressed-glass water pitchers; two farm machinery barns; slaughterhouse, chapel, and main exhibit center

with a chronological natural and human history of Lambton County. (Mar-Oct, daily; rest of yr, Mon-Fri; closed Dec 25-Jan 1) Picnicking. 45 mi (72 km) NE via ON 21, Grand Bend, opp Pinery Provincial Park. Phone 519/243-2600. ¢¢

Moore Museum. Country store, early switchboard, late-1800s church organ in main building; Victorian cottage; log cabin; farm implements; one-rm schoolhouse; 1890 lighthouse. (Mar-June, Wed-Sun; July and Aug, daily; Sept-mid Dec, Mon-Fri) 12 mi (19 km) S in Mooretown, 94 Moore Line, 2 blks E of St. Clair Pkwy (County Rd 33). Phone 519/867-2020. ¢

Oil Museum of Canada. On site of first commercialized oil well in North America; historic items and data regarding the discovery. Six acres (2½ hectares) of landscaped grounds with blacksmith shop, pioneer home, and post office; RR station, working oil field using 1860 methods; picnic pavilion. Guided tours. (May-Oct, daily; rest of yr, Mon-Fri) 30 mi SE in Oil Springs on Kelly Rd. Phone 519/834-2840. ¢¢

Sombra Township Museum. Pioneer home with displays of household goods, clothes, books, and deeds, marine artifacts, indigenous and military items, music boxes, photographic equipment, and farming tools. (June-Sept, afternoons; May, wkends; also by appt) 3470 St. Clair Pkwy, S in Sombra. Phone 519/892-3982. ¢

Special Events

Sarnia Waterfront Festival. Centennial Park. More than 80 events incl singers, dancers; children's shows. Phone 800/265-0316. Late Apr-Labour Day wkend.

Sarnia Highland Games. Centennial Park. Caber and hammer tossing; stone throwing; haggis-hurling; clan village, bands, dancers. Phone 519/336-5054. Mid-Aug.

Celebration of Lights. Seven-wk festive season featuring 60,000 lights in waterfront park. Residential, commercial displays. Phone 800/265-0316. Late Nov-Dec.

Motels/Motor Lodges

★★ **COMFORT INN.** *815 Mara St (N7V 1X4).* *519/383-6767; fax 519/383-8710; toll-free 800/228-5150.* *www.comfortinn.com.* 100 rms, 3 story. S $55-$75; D $65-$85; each addl $5; family rates. Crib free. TV; cable. Complimentary continental bkfst. Restaurant adj 6:30 am-midnight. Ck-out noon. Meeting rms. Business center. In-rm modem link. Exercise equipt. Refrigerators avail. Cr cds: A, D, DS, ER, MC, V.

🄳 🐾 ⛵ 🐾 **SC** 🏃

★★★ **DRAWBRIDGE INN.** *283 N Christina St (N7T 5V4).* *519/337-7571; fax 519/332-8181; toll-free 800/663-0376.* 97 rms, 3 story. S, D $82; each addl $9; suites $115-$135; under 12 free; wkend rates. Crib free. Pet accepted. TV; cable. Indoor pool. Sauna. Restaurant 7 am-2 pm, 5-9 pm; Fri-Sun 8 am-2 pm, 5-9 pm. Rm serv. Bar noon-11 pm. Ck-out noon. Meeting rms. Business center. In-rm modem link. Bellhops. Valet serv. Health club privileges. Cr cds: A, D, DS, ER, MC, V.

🐾 ⛵ 🐾 🐾 **SC** 🏃

★★ **HARBOURFRONT INN.** *505 Harbour Rd (N7T 5R8). 519/337-5434; fax 519/332-5882; toll-free 800/787-5010.* 102 rms, 2 story. S $51-$58; D $59-$67; each addl $4; under 16 free. Crib free. Pet accepted, some restrictions. TV; cable, VCR avail. Restaurant adj 11-1 am. Ck-out 11 am. Valet serv. Picnic tables. On river. Cr cds: A, D, ER, JCB, MC, V.

🄳 🐾 ⚓ ⊠ ▨ SC

★★ **HOLIDAY INN.** *1498 Venetian Blvd (N7T 7W6). 519/336-4130; fax 519/332-3326; 800/465-4329. www.holiday-inn.com.* 151 rms, 2 story. S, D $69-$89; suites $180-$240; under 19 free; wkend rates. Crib free. Pet accepted. TV; cable (premium). 2 pools, 1 indoor; whirlpool. Playground. Restaurant 6:30 am-10:30 pm. Rm serv. Bar 11-1 am. Ck-out 1 pm. Meeting rms. Bellhops. Valet serv. Golf privileges, greens fee $10, putting green. Exercise equipt; sauna. Lawn games. Balconies. Cr cds: A, C, D, DS, ER, JCB, MC, V.

🄳 🐾 ≋ 🏌 🏃 ⊠ ▨ SC

Sault Ste. Marie

Pop 83,300 **Elev** 580 ft (177 m) **Area code** 705
Information Chamber of Commerce, 334 Bay St, P6A 1X1; 705/949-7152
Web www.ssmcoc.com

Founded and built on steel, Sault Ste. Marie is separated from its sister city in Michigan by the St. Mary's River. Lake and ocean freighters traverse the river, which links Lake Huron and Lake Superior—locally known as "the Soo."

What to See and Do

Agawa Canyon Train Excursion. A scenic day trip by Algoma Central Railway through a wilderness of hills and fjordlike ravines. Two-hr stopover at the canyon. Dining car on train. (June-mid-Oct, daily; Jan-Mar, wkends only) Advance ticket orders avail by phone. Phone 705/946-7300 or 800/242-9287. ¢¢¢¢

Boat cruises. Two-hr boat cruises from Norgoma dock, next to Holiday Inn on MV *Chief Shingwauk* and MV *Bon Soo* through American locks; also three-hr dinner cruises. (June-mid-Oct) Contact Lock Tours Canada, PO Box 424, P6A 5M1. Phone 705/253-9850. ¢¢¢¢

Sault Ste. Marie Museum. Local and national exhibits in a structure originally built as a post office. Skylight Gallery traces history of the region dating back 9,000 yrs; incl prehistoric artifacts, displays of early industries, re-creation of 1912 Queen St house interiors. Durham Gallery displays traveling exhibits from the Royal Ontario Museum and locally curated displays. Discovery Gallery for children features hands-on exhibits. (Daily; closed hols) 690 Queen St E. Phone 705/759-7278.

Special Events

Ontario Winter Carnival Bon Soo. Features more than 100 events: fireworks, fiddle contest, winter sports, polar bear swim, winter playground sculptured from snow. Last wkend Jan-1st wkend Feb. Phone 705/759-3000.

Algoma Fall Festival. Visual and performing arts presentations by Canadian and intl artists. Late Sept-late Oct. Phone 705/949-0822.

Motels/Motor Lodges

★★★ **ALGOMA'S WATER TOWER INN.** *360 Great Northern Rd (P6A 5N3). 705/949-8111; fax 705/949-1912; toll-free 800/461-0800. www.watertowerinn.com.* 180 rms, 5 story. S, D $79-$99; each addl $7; suites $130-$290; under 18 free; ski plans. Crib free. Pet accepted. TV; cable (premium), VCR avail. Heated pool; whirlpool. Restaurant 7 am-11 pm. Rm serv 7-11 am, 5-10 pm. Bar noon-1 am. Ck-out noon. Meeting rms. Valet serv. Airport transportation. Sundries. X-country ski 5 mi. Exercise equipt. Some refrigerators, microwaves; whirlpool in suites. Cr cds: A, C, D, DS, ER, JCB, MC, V.

🄳 🐾 ≋ ≈ 🏃 ⊠ ▨ SC

★★ **HOLIDAY INN.** *208 St Mary's River Dr (P6A 5V4). 705/949-0611; fax 705/945-6972; res 888/713-8482. www.holiday-inn.com.* 195 rms, 9 story. June-mid-Oct: S, D $92-$139; each addl $10; suites $175-$275; under 12 free; lower rates rest of yr. Crib free. Pet accepted. TV; cable (premium). Indoor pool; whirlpool. Restaurant 6:30 am-10 pm. Rm serv. Bar 11-1 am. Ck-out 4 pm. Meeting rms. In-rm modem link. Bellhops. Valet serv. Sundries. Gift shop. Airport transportation. Exercise equipt; sauna. Game rm. Refrigerator in some suites. Cr cds: A, C, D, DS, ER, JCB, MC, V.

🄳 🐾 ≋ 🏃 ⊠ ▨ SC

★★ **QUALITY INN BAYFRONT.** *180 Bay St (P6A 6S2). 705/945-9264; fax 705/945-9766; 800/228-5151. www.qualityinn.com.* 109 rms, 7 story. Sept-mid-Oct: S $102-$165; D $112-$165; each addl $10; family rates; ski; package plans; lower rates rest of yr. Crib free. TV; cable (premium), VCR avail. Indoor pool; whirlpool. Coffee in rms. Restaurant 7 am-midnight. Rm serv. Bar from 11:30 am. Ck-out 1 pm. Meeting rms. Bellhops. Valet serv. Downhill/x-country ski 8 mi. Exercise equipt; sauna. Some refrigerators. Cr cds: A, C, D, DS, ER, JCB, MC, V.

🄳 ≋ ≈ 🏃 ⊠ ▨ SC

★ **RAMADA INN AND CONVENTION CENTRE.** *229 Great Northern Rd; Hwy 17N, Sault Ste Marie (P6B 4Z2). 705/942-2500; fax 705/942-2570; res 800/563-7262. www.ramada.com.* 211 units, 2-7 story. S $86-$109; D $96-$122; each addl $10; suites $150-$275; under 18 free; package plans. Crib free. Pet accepted. TV; cable, VCR avail. 2 pools, 1 indoor; whirlpool. Restaurant 7 am-11 pm. Rm serv. Bar to midnight. Ck-out noon. Meeting rms. Business servs avail. Bellhops. Valet serv (Mon-Fri). Sundries. Downhill ski 20 mi; x-country ski 3 mi. Exercise equipt. Miniature golf; water slide. Bowling. Game rms. Some refrigerators. Cr cds: A, C, D, DS, ER, JCB, MC, V.

🄳 🐾 ≋ ≈ 🏃 ⊠ ▨ SC

Restaurants

★ **GIOVANNI'S.** *516 Great Northern Rd (P6B 4Z9).* *705/942-3050.* Italian menu. Specializes in family-style dinners. Hrs: 11:30 am-midnight; Sun to 11 pm. Closed Jan 1, Labour Day, Dec 25. Res accepted. Bar. Lunch $5-$8, dinner $7-$15. Child's menu. Cr cds: A, MC, V.

D ⊟

★★ **NEW MARCONI.** *480 Albert St W (P6A 1C3).* *705/759-8250.* Italian, Amer menu. Specialties: barbecued ribs, steak, seafood. Own pasta. Hrs: noon-11 pm. Closed Sun; Jan 1, Dec 25. Res accepted. Serv bar. Lunch $4.25-$8.50, dinner $8-$50. Complete meals: dinner $16.95. Family-owned. Cr cds: A, D, ER, MC, V.

D ⊟

Stratford

See also Brantford, Kitchener-Waterloo

Pop 27,500 **Elev** 119 ft (36 m) **Area code** 519
Information Tourism Stratford, 47 Downey St, N5A 1W7; 519/271-5140 or 800/561-SWAN
Web www.city.stratford.on.ca

The names Stratford and Avon River can conjure up only one name in most travelers' minds—Shakespeare. And that is exactly what you will find in this lovely city. World-renowned, this festival of fine theater takes place here every year.

What to See and Do

The Gallery/Stratford. Public gallery in parkland setting; historical and contemporary works. Guided tours on request. (Daily) 54 Romeo St N. Phone 519/271-5271. ¢¢

◨ **Shakespearean Gardens.** Fragrant herbs, shrubs, and flowering plants common to William Shakespeare's time. Huron St. Phone 519/271-5140. **FREE**

Confederation Park. Features rock hill, waterfall, fountain, Japanese garden, and commemorative court. Phone 519/273-3352.

Special Events

Stratford Festival. Contemporary, classical, and Shakespearean dramas and modern musicals. Performances at Festival, Avon, and Tom Patterson theaters. Contact Box Office, Stratford Festival, PO Box 520, N5A 6V2. Phone 519/273-1600, 416/363-4471 (Toronto), or 800/567-1600. May-Nov, matinees and eves.

Kinsmen Antique Show. Stratford Arena. Late July-Aug. Phone 519/271-2161.

Motels/Motor Lodges

★★★ **FESTIVAL INN.** *1144 Ontario St (N5A 6W1).* *519/273-1150; fax 519/273-2111.* *www.festivalinnstratford.com.* 182 rms, 1-2 story. May-mid-Nov: S $74-$135; D $80-$139; each addl $10; suites $150; under 12 free; lower rates rest of yr. Crib free. TV; cable (premium), VCR avail. Indoor pool; whirlpool; poolside serv. Restaurant 7 am-9 pm; Sat from 7:30 am; Sun 7:30 am-9 pm. Bar 11:30-1 am. Ck-out 11 am. Meeting rms. Business servs avail. Exercise equipt; sauna. Lawn games. Many refrigerators. Cr cds: A, D, DS, ER, JCB, MC, V.

D ≈ 术 ⊠ ▨ SC

★ **MAJER'S.** *2970 Ontario St E (M5A 6S5).* *519/271-2010; fax 519/273-7951.* *www.majersmotel.com.* 31 rms. May-Oct: S $57-$65; D $70-$75; each addl $10; lower rates rest of yr. Crib free. TV; cable (premium). Heated pool. Playground. Complimentary coffee in lobby. Restaurant adj 11 am-11 pm. Ck-out 10:30 am. Refrigerators. Picnic tables. Cr cds: A, MC, V.

≈ ⊠ ▨

★★ **STRATFORD SUBURBAN.** *2808 Ontario St E (N5A 6S5).* *519/271-9650; fax 519/271-0193.* *www.suburbanmotel.com.* 25 rms. S $58-$67; D $68-$79; each addl $10. TV; cable. Heated pool. Restaurant nearby. Ck-out 11 am. Tennis. Refrigerators. Cr cds: MC, V.

⚲ ≈ ⊠ ▨

★★ **VICTORIAN INN.** *10 Romeo St N (N5A 5M7).* *519/271-4650; fax 519/271-2030; toll-free 800/741-2135.* *www.victorian-inn.on.ca.* 115 rms, 4 story. Mid-May-mid-Nov: S, D $79-$139; each addl $10; under 12 free; lower rates rest of yr. Crib $10. TV; cable (premium), VCR avail. Heated pool; poolside serv. Complimentary coffee in rms. Dining rm 7 am-11 am, 5-9 pm. Ck-out noon. Meeting rms. Business servs avail. In-rm modem link. Valet serv. Sundries. Exercise equipt. Game rm. Balconies. On Lake Victoria. Cr cds: A, D, DS, ER, JCB, MC, V.

D ≈ 术 ⊠ ▨

B&B/Small Inn

★★★ **QUEEN'S INN.** *161 Ontario St (N5A 3H3).* *519/271-1400; fax 519/271-7373; res 800/461-6450.* 32 rms, 3 story, 7 suites. May-Oct: S $75-$110; D $85-$120; each addl $25; suites $130-$200; kit. units $190-$200; under 12 free; ski plans; lower rates rest of yr. Crib free. Pet accepted, some restrictions. TV; cable, VCR avail (movies). Restaurant 7 am-10 pm. Rm serv. Ck-out 11 am, ck-in 2 pm. Business servs avail. Luggage handling. Valet serv. Concierge serv. Downhill ski 20 mi; x-country ski 10 mi. Exercise equipt. Microwaves avail. Built 1850. Cr cds: A, D, ER, MC, V.

D ⦿ ≍ 术 ⊠ ▨ SC

Restaurants

★★★ **THE CHURCH RESTAURANT AND THE BELFRY.** *70 Brunswick St (N5A 6V6).* *519/273-3424.* *www.chruch restaurant.com.* French menu. Specialties: salmon monette, filet mignon, loin of lamb. Own baking. Hrs: 11:30 am-2 pm, 5-9 pm; Tues from 5 pm; Fri, Sat 1 am. Closed Mon; Jan 1, Dec 25. Res accepted. Serv bar. Wine cellar. A la carte entrees: lunch $9.95-$16.25, dinner $26.50-$33.50. Complete meals: dinner $49.50-$58.50. Child's menu. Parking. In 1870 Gothic church. Cr cds: A, D, DS, MC, V.

⊟

★ **GENE'S.** *81 Ontario St (N5A 3H1). 519/271-9678.* Chinese menu. Specializes in Cantonese, Szechwan dishes. Own pies. Hrs: 11 am-midnight; Thurs to 11 pm; Fri, Sat to 2:30 am; Sun noon-9 pm. Closed Dec 25, 26. Res accepted. Bar. A la carte entrees: lunch $6-$7.50, dinner $8.25-$16.95. Child's menu. Oriental decor. Family-owned. Cr cds: A, C, D, DS, ER, MC, V.

[D⌐]

★★ **HOUSE OF GENE.** *108 Downie St (N5A 1X1). 519/271-3080.* Chinese menu. Specializes in Cantonese, Szechwan dishes. Hrs: 11:30 am-8 pm; Fri, Sat to 9 pm; Sun from noon. Closed Dec 25, 26. Bar. A la carte entrees: lunch $6.25-$7.95, dinner $6.25-$16.75. Buffet: lunch $6.95, dinner $8.95. Child's menu. Modern Asian decor. Cr cds: A, D, MC, V.

[D] [SC] [⌐]

★★ **KEYSTONE ALLEY CAFE.** *34 Brunswick St (N5A 3L8). 519/271-5645.* Continental menu. Specializes in pasta, fresh fish. Hrs: 11:30 am-3 pm, 5-9 pm; Mon to 3 pm. Closed Sun; most major hols. Res accepted. Bar. A la carte entrees: lunch $7.95-$9.95, dinner $15.95-$24.95. Child's menu. Open kitchen. Cr cds: A, D, MC, V.

[D] [⌐]

★ **MADELYN'S DINER.** *377 Huron St (N5A 5T6). 519/273-5296.* Specialties: English fish and chips, homemade pies. Hrs: 7 am-8 pm; Sun 8:30 am-1:30 pm. Closed Mon; Dec 25. Res accepted. Bar from 11 am. Bkfst $2.50-$7.95, lunch $2.75-$7.25, dinner $6.95-$10.95. Parking. Cr cds: A, MC, V.

[D] [⌐]

★★★ **OLD PRUNE.** *151 Albert St (N5A 3K5). 519/271-5052. www.cyg.net/~oldprune.* Specializes in seafood, lamb. Hrs: 11:30 am-1:30 pm, 5-10 pm; Tues from 5 pm. Closed Mon; also Nov-Apr. Res accepted. Bar. A la carte entrees: lunch $8.50-$14.95. Complete meals: dinner $53.50. Child's menu. Parking. Restored Edwardian residence; enclosed garden terrace. Cr cds: A, MC, V.

[D]

★★★ **RUNDLE'S.** *9 Cobourg St (N5A 3E4). 519/271-6442. www.rundlesrestaurant.com.* Continental menu. Specializes in regional wine country cuisine. Hrs: 11 am-11 pm; Mon to 9 pm; Fri, Sat to midnight; Sun 3-10 pm. Closed some major hols. Res accepted. Bar. A la carte entrees: lunch $6.50-$10.95, dinner $11.50-$17.95. Child's menu. Outdoor dining. Intimate atmosphere. Cr cds: D, DS, MC, V.

[D]

Thunder Bay

Pop 112,486 **Elev** 616 ft (188 m) **Area code** 807
Information Tourism Thunder Bay, 500 Donald St E, P7E 5V3; 800/667-8386 or 807/983-2041
Web www.city.thunder-bay.on.ca/tourism

Thunder Bay was formed with the joining of the twin cities of Fort William and Port Arthur. Located on Lake Superior, it is a major grain shipping port. The history of Thunder Bay is tied very closely to the fur trade in North America. In the early 19th century, the North West Company had acquired most of the fur trade. Fort William became the inland headquarters for the company, and today much of the activity and spirit of those days can be relived at the fort.

Thunder Bay offers the vacationer outdoor recreation including skiing, parks, and historical attractions and serves as a starting point for a drive around Lake Superior.

What to See and Do

Amethyst Centre. Full lapidary shop and gem cutting operation; retail, gift, and jewelry shop. Tours. (Mon-Sat; closed hols) 400 E Victoria Ave. Phone 807/622-6908. **FREE**

Amethyst Mine Panorama. Open-pit quarry adj to Elbow Lake. The quarrying operation, geological faults, Canadian Pre-Cambrian shield, and sample gem pockets are readily visible. Gem picking; tours. (Mid-May-mid-Oct, daily) 35 mi (56 km) NE, 5 mi (8 km) off Hwy 11/17 on E Loon Rd. Phone 807/622-6908. ¢

Centennial Conservatory. Wide variety of plant life incl banana plants, palm trees, cacti. (Daily; closed hols) Balmoral and Dease Sts. Phone 807/622-7036. **FREE**

Centennial Park. Summer features incl a reconstructed 1910 logging camp; logging camp museum. Playground. X-country skiing; sleigh rides (by appt; fee) in winter. (Daily) Near Boulevard Lake, at Centennial Park Rd. Phone 807/683-6511. **FREE**

✪ **International Friendship Gardens.** Park is composed of individual gardens designed and constructed by various ethnic groups incl Slovakian, Polish, German, Italian, Finnish, Danish, Ukranian, Hungarian, and Chinese. (Daily) 2000 Victoria Ave. Phone 807/625-3166. **FREE**

Kakabeka Falls Provincial Park. Spectacular waterfall on the historic Kaministiquia River, formerly a voyageur route from Montréal to the West. The 128-ft (39-km) high falls may be seen from highway stop. Waterflow is best in spring and on wkends—flow is reduced during the wk. Sand beach in the park; hiking and interpretive trails, camping (day-use, electrical hookups; fee), playground, visitor service center. 20 mi (32 km) W via ON 11/17. Per vehicle ¢¢

Old Fort William. Authentic reconstruction of the original Fort William as it was from 1803-1821. Visitors experience the adventure of the Nor'westers convergence for the Rendezvous (re-creation staged ten days mid-July). Costumed staff populate 42 buildings on the site, featuring trademen's shops, farm, apothecary, fur stores, warehouses, Great Hall, voyageur encampment, indigenous encampment; historic restaurant. Gift shop. Walking tours (exc winter). (May-Oct, daily) 1 King Rd, off Hwy 61S. Phone 807/577-8461. ¢¢

Thunder Bay Art Gallery. Changing exhibitions from major national and international museums; regional art; contemporary native art. Tours, films, lectures, concerts. Gift shop. (Tues-Sun; closed hols) On Confederation College Campus; use Harbour Expy from Hwy 11/17. Phone 807/577-6427. **FREE**

Motels/Motor Lodges

★★ **BEST WESTERN CROSSROADS.** *655 W Arthur St (P7E 5R6). 807/577-4241; fax 807/475-7059; 800/528-1234. www.bestwestern.com.* 60 rms, 2 story. May-Oct: S $73; D $78; under 12 free; lower rates rest of yr. Crib free. Pet accepted. TV; cable. Complimentary coffee. Restaurant opp 7 am-midnight. Ck-out 11 am. Business servs avail. In-rm modem link. Valet serv. Free airport transportation. Some refrigerators. Cr cds: A, C, D, DS, ER, MC, V.

★ **COMFORT INN.** *660 W Arthur St (P7E 5R8). 807/475-3155; fax 807/475-3816; 800/228-5150. www.comfortinn.com.* 80 rms, 2 story. S $70-$85; D $75-$93; each addl $8; under 19 free. Crib free. Pet accepted. TV; cable. Complimentary coffee in lobby. Restaurant adj 7 am-11 pm. Ck-out 11 am. Business servs avail. In-rm modem link. Cr cds: A, D, DS, ER, MC, V.

★★ **LANDMARK INN.** *1010 Dawson Rd (P7B 5J4). 807/767-1681; fax 807/767-1439.* 106 rms, 4 story. S $80; D $86; each addl $8; under 12 free. Crib free. Pet accepted; $50. TV; cable. Indoor pool; whirlpool, water slide, poolside serv. Sauna. Complimentary continental bkfst. Coffee in rms. Restaurant 7-1 am. Rm serv. Bar 11- 1 am. Ck-out 11 am. Meeting rms. Business servs avail. In-rm modem link. Valet serv. Sundries. Free airport transportation. Downhill ski 20 mi. Cr cds: A, D, DS, ER, MC, V.

★★ **PRINCE ARTHUR.** *17 N Cumberland (P7A 4K8). 807/345-5411; fax 807/345-8565. www.princearthur.on.ca.* 121 rms, 6 story. S $59-$77; D $67-$85; each addl $8; suites $115-$145; under 16 free. Crib free. Pet accepted. TV; cable. Indoor pool; wading pool, whirlpool. Saunas. Coffee in rms. Restaurant 6:30 am-10 pm. Bar 11-1 am. Rm serv. Ck-out noon. Meeting rms. Business servs avail. In-rm modem link. Valet serv. Sundries. Free airport transportation. Health club privileges. Some refrigerators; microwaves avail. Downhill ski 10 mi. Overlooks harbor. Shopping mall opp. Cr cds: A, C, D, ER, MC, V.

★ **TRAVELODGE AIRLANE HOTEL.** *698 W Arthur St (P7E 5R8). 807/577-1181; fax 807/475-4852; 800/578-7878. www.travelodge.com.* 160 rms, 2-3 story. S $79-$105; D $85-$110; each addl $5; wkend rates. Crib free. Pet accepted. TV; cable (premium), VCR avail. Indoor pool; whirlpool. Restaurants 7 am-11 pm. Rm serv. Bar 4 pm-1 am, closed Sun; entertainment. Ck-out 11 am. Meeting rms. Business center. In-rm modem link. Bellhops. Valet serv. Sundries. Free airport transportation. Exercise equipt; sauna. Minibars. Cr cds: A, C, D, ER, MC, V.

★ **TRAVELODGE THUNDER BAY.** *450 Memorial Ave (P7B 3Y7). 807/345-2343; fax 807/345-3246; 800-578-7878. www.travelodge.com.* 93 rms, 3 story. S $75; D $85; each addl $10; under 20 free. Crib free. Pet accepted. TV; cable. Indoor pool. Sauna. Complimentary continental bkfst. Restaurant adj 11-1 am. Ck-out 1 pm. Meeting rms. Business servs avail. In-rm modem link. Sun deck. Downhill ski 15 mi. Cr cds: A, C, D, DS, ER, MC, V.

★★★ **VALHALLA INN.** *1 Valhalla Inn Rd (P7E 6J1). 807/577-1121; fax 807/475-4723; res 800/964-1121. www.valhallainn.com.* 267 rms, 5 story. S $175-$190; D $185-$200; each addl $10; suites $295-$305; under 18 free; ski, wkend rates. Crib free. Pet accepted; $10. TV. Indoor pool; whirlpool. Complimentary coffee in rms. Restaurant 6:30 am-11:30 pm. Rm serv. Bar 4:30 pm-2 am. Ck-out 1 pm. Meeting rms. Business servs avail. In-rm modem link. Bellhops. Valet serv. Sundries. Free airport transportation. Downhill ski 3 mi; x-country ski 4 mi. Exercise equipt; sauna. Bicycle rentals. Game rm. Some bathrm phones, minibars; microwaves avail. Luxury level. Cr cds: A, C, D, DS, ER, MC, V.

★★★ **VICTORIA INN.** *555 W Arthur St (P7E 5R5). 807/577-8481; fax 807/475-8961; res 800/387-3331. www.tbaytel.net/vicinn.* 182 rms, 3 story. S $76.95-$155; D $86.95-$155; each addl $10; suites $179-$229; under 16 free. Crib free. Pet accepted; $5. Indoor pool; wading pool, whirlpool, poolside serv, lifeguard. TV; cable. Complimentary coffee in rms. Restaurant 7 am-11 pm. Rm serv. Bar 11:30-1 am. Ck-out noon. Meeting rms. Business servs avail. In-rm modem link. Valet serv. Sundries. Coin lndry. Free airport transportation. Downhill ski 8 mi; x-country ski 5 mi. Exercise equipt; sauna. Health club privileges. Some refrigerators. Cr cds: A, C, D, DS, ER, MC, V.

Restaurant

★★ **THE KEG.** *735 Hewitson Ave (P7B 6B5). 807/623-1960. www.kegsteakhouse.com.* Specializes in steak, seafood. Salad bar. Own cheesecake. Hrs: 4 pm-1 am. Closed Dec 24, 25. Bar. Dinner $15.99-$32.99. Child's menu. Pub atmosphere. Cr cds: A, D, MC, V.

Toronto

See also Hamilton, Mississauga

Founded 1793 **Pop** 3,400,000 **Elev** 569 ft (173 m)
Area code 416

Information Convention & Visitors Association, Queens Quay Terminal at Harbourfront, 207 Queens Quay W, M5J 1A7; 416/203-2500 or 800/363-1990

Web www.torontotourism.com

Toronto is one of Canada's leading industrial, commercial, and cultural centers. From its location on the shores of Lake Ontario, it has performed essential communications and transportation services throughout Canadian history. Its name derives from the native word for meeting place, as the area was called by the Hurons who led the first European, Etienne Brule, to the spot. In the mid-1800s the Grand Trunk and Great Western Railroad and the Northern Railway connected Toronto with the upper St. Lawrence, Portland, Maine and Chicago, Illinois.

After French fur traders from Québec established Fort Rouille in 1749, Toronto became a base for further Canadian settlement. Its population of Scottish, English, and United States emigrants was subject to frequent armed attacks, especially during the War of 1812 and immediately thereafter. From within the United States, the attackers aimed at annexation; from within Canada, they aimed at emancipation from England. One result of these unsuccessful threats was the protective confederation of Lower Canada, which later separated again as the province of Québec, and Upper Canada, which still later became the province of Ontario with Toronto as its capital.

Toronto today is a cosmopolitan city with many intriguing features. Once predominantly British, the population is now exceedingly multicultural—the United Nations deemed Toronto the world's most ethnically diverse city in 1989. A major theater center with many professional playhouses, including the Royal Alexandra Theatre, Toronto is also a major banking center, with several architecturally significant banks. Good shopping can be found throughout the city, but Torontonians are most proud of their "Underground City," a series of subterranean malls linking more than 300 shops and restaurants in the downtown area. For professional sports fans, Toronto offers the Maple Leafs (hockey), the Blue Jays (baseball), the Raptors (basketball), and the Argonauts (football). A visit to the Harbourfront, a boat tour to the islands or enjoying an evening on the town should round out your stay in Toronto.

Additional Visitor Information

For further information contact Tourism Toronto, Queens Quay Terminal at Harbourfront, 207 Queens Quay W, M5J 1A7; 416/203-2500 or 800/363-1990 (US and Canada). Toronto's public transportation system is extensive and includes buses, subways, streetcars, and trolley buses; for maps phone 416/393-4636.

What to See and Do

Art Gallery of Ontario. Changing exhibits of paintings, drawings, sculpture, and graphics from the 14th-20th centuries incl Henry Moore Collection; permanent Canadian Collection and Contemporary Galleries; films, lectures, concerts. (Tues-Sun; winter Wed-Sun; closed Jan 1, Dec 25) Free admission Wed eves. 317 Dundas St W. Phone 416/977-0414. ¢¢ Behind gallery is

The Grange. A Georgian house (ca 1817) restored and furnished in early Victorian style (1835-1840). (Same hrs as Art Gallery) **Free** with admission to Art Gallery.

Black Creek Pioneer Village. More than 30 buildings restored to re-create life in a rural Canadian village of mid-19th-century; incl general store, printing office, town hall, church, firehouse, blacksmith shop; special events wkends. Visitor reception centre has exhibit gallery, theater, restaurant. (Early Mar-Dec, variable schedule; closed Dec 25) 1000 Murray Ross Pkwy. Jane St and Steeles Ave, 2 mi (3 km) N on Hwy 400, E on Steeles, then ½ mi (1 km) to Jane St. Phone 416/736-1733. ¢¢

Casa Loma. A medieval-style castle built by Sir Henry Pellatt between 1911-1914. Furnished rms, secret passages, underground tunnel, and stables. Restored gardens (May-Oct). Gift shop; cafe. (Daily; closed Jan 1, Dec 25) One Austin Terr, 1½ mi (2 km) NW of downtown. Phone 416/923-1171. ¢¢ Adj is

Spadina. (ca 1865) Home of financier James Austin and his descendants; Victorian and Edwardian furnishings and fine art; restored gardens. (Tues-Sun, afternoons; closed hols) 285 Spadina Rd. Phone 416/392-6910. ¢¢

City Hall. (1965) Distinctive modern design features twin towers that appear to support round, elevated council chambers. Exhibits, concerts in Nathan Phillips Sq in front of building. Self-guided tours; guided tours (summer). (Mon-Fri) 100 Queen St W. Phone 416/392-7341. **FREE**

City parks. Listed below are some of Toronto's many parks. Contact the Department of Parks and Recreation. Phone 416/392-1111.

Allan Gardens. Indoor/outdoor botanical displays, wading pool, picnicking, concerts. (Daily) West side of Sherbourne St to Jarvis St between Carlton St and Gerrard St E. Phone 416/392-7288. **FREE**

Edwards Gardens. Civic garden center; rock gardens, pools, pond, rustic bridges. (Daily) NE of Downtown, at Leslie Ave E and Lawrence St. Phone 416/392-8186. **FREE**

Grange Park. Wading pool, playground. Natural ice rink (winter, weather permitting). (Daily) Dundas and Beverley Sts, located behind the Art Gallery of Ontario. **FREE**

High Park. The largest park in the city (399 acres or 161 hectares). Swimming, wading pool; tennis, playgrounds, picnicking, hiking, floral display and rock falls in Hillside Gardens, animal paddocks. Shakespeare performances at Dream Site outdoor theater. Restaurant, concessions; trackless tour train. Ice-skating. Also here is Colborne Lodge at south end of park. (Daily) Between Bloor St W and The Queensway at Parkside Dr, near lakeshore. Phone 416/392-1111. **FREE**

Queen's Park. Ontario Parliament Buildings are located in this park. (Daily) Queen's Park Crescent. Phone 416/325-7500. **FREE**

Riverdale Park. Summer: swimming, wading pools; tennis, playgrounds, picnicking, band concerts. Winter: skating; 19th-century farm. (Daily) W side of Broadview Ave, between Danforth Ave & Gerrard St E. Phone 416/392-1111.

Toronto Island Park. Accessible by ferry (fee; phone 416/392-8193) from foot of Bay St. Historic lighthouse, other buildings. Fishing, boating, swimming; bicycling, children's farmyard, scenic tram ride (free), amusement area (fee), mall with fountains and gardens, fine views of city and lake. (May-Oct, daily) S across Inner Harbour. Phone 416/392-8186. **FREE**

✪ **CN Tower.** World's tallest free-standing structure (1,815 ft/553 m). Three observation decks (daily), revolving restaurant (see 360 RESTAURANT), and nightclub. Also various activities incl SkyQuest Theatre, Maple Leaf Cinema, and four motion simulator rides (fees). 301 Front St W, just W of University Ave. Phone 416/360-8500 (information) or 416/362-5411 (dining res). ¢¢¢¢ Here is

Virtual World. Two virtual reality-based adventures, *Battletech* and *Red Planet,* allow users to navigate in a world of fantasy. (Daily) Phone 416/360-8500.

Colborne Lodge. (1837) Built by John G. Howard, architect and surveyor; restored to 1870 style; art gallery houses changing exhibits; artifacts of 1830s; artist's studio. (Tues-Sun; closed Good Friday, Dec 25-26) Colborne Lodge Dr and The Queensway in High Park. Phone 416/392-6916. ¢¢

Exhibition Place. Designed to accommodate the Canadian National Exhibition (see SPECIAL EVENTS), this 350-acre (141-hectare) park has events yr-round, as well as the Marine Museum of Upper Canada. (Aug-Sept, daily) S off Gardener Expy, on Lakeshore Blvd. Phone 416/393-6000.

George R. Gardiner Museum of Ceramic Art. One of the world's finest collections of Italian majolica, English Delftware, and 18th-century continental porcelain. (Daily; closed Jan 1, Dec 25) 111 Queen's Park, opp Royal Ontario Museum. Phone 416/586-8080. **Donation**

Gibson House. Home of land surveyor and local politician David Gibson; restored and furnished to 1850s style. Costumed interpreters conduct demonstrations. Tours. (Tues-Sun; closed hols) 5172 Yonge St (ON 11), in North York. Phone 416/395-7432. ¢

Harbourfront Centre. This ten-acre waterfront community is alive with theater, dance, films, art shows, music, crafts, and children's programs. Most events free. (Daily) 235 Queens Quay W at foot of York St. Phone 416/973-3000.

Historic Fort York. Restored War of 1812 fort and battle site. Costumed staff provide military demonstrations; eight original buildings house period environments and exhibits. Tours. (Daily; closed hols) Garrison Rd, SE near jct Bathurst and Fleet Sts by Strachan Ave. Phone 416/392-6907. ¢¢

Hummingbird Centre for the Performing Arts. Stage presentations of Broadway musicals, dramas, and concerts by intl artists. Home of the Canadian Opera Company and National Ballet of Canada. Pre-performance dining; gift shop. 1 Front St E at Yonge St. Phone 416/393-7469 or 416/812-2262 (tickets).

Huronia Historical Parks. Two living history sites animated by costumed interpreters. (Daily) 63 mi (101 km) N via Hwy 400, then 34 mi (55 km) N to Midland on Hwy 93. Phone 705/526-7838. ¢¢¢ Consists of

Discovery Harbour. Marine heritage center and reconstructed 19th-century British Naval dockyard. Established in 1817, site incl 19th-century military base. Now rebuilt, the site features eight furnished buildings and orientation center. Replica of 49-ft (15-m) British naval schooner HMS *Bee;* also HMS *Tecumseth* and *Perseverance.* Costumed interpreters bring base to life, ca 1830. Sail training and excursions (daily). Audiovisual display; free parking, docking, picnic facilities. Theater; gift shop, restaurant. (Victoria Day-Labour Day, Mon-Fri; after Labour Day-Sept, daily) Church St, Penetanguishene. ¢¢¢

Ste.-Marie among the Hurons. (1639-1649) Reconstruction of 17th-century Jesuit mission that was Ontario's first European community. Twenty-two furnished buildings incl native dwellings, workshops, barn, church, cookhouse, hospital. Candlelight tours, canoe excursions. Cafe features period-inspired meals and snacks. Orientation center, interpretive museum. Free parking and picnic facilities. (Victoria Day wkend-Oct, daily) E of Midland on Hwy 12. World-famous Martyrs' Shrine (site of papal visit) is located across the highway. Other area highlights incl pioneer museum, replica indigenous village, Wye Marsh Wildlife Centre. ¢¢¢

Kortright Centre for Conservation. Environmental center with trails, beehouse, maple syrup shack, wildlife pond, and plantings. Naturalist-guided hikes (daily). X-country skiing (no rentals); picnic area, cafe; indoor exhibits and theater. (Daily; closed Dec 24 and 25) 9550 Pine Valley Dr, Woodbridge; 12 mi (19.3 km) NW via Hwy 400, Major MacKenzie Dr exit, then 2 mi (3 km) W, then S on Pine Valley Dr. Phone 905/832-2289. ¢¢

Mackenzie House. Restored 19th-century home of William Lyon Mackenzie, first mayor of Toronto; furnishings and artifacts of the 1850s; 1840s print shop. Group tours (by appt). (Tues-Sun, afternoons; closed hols) 82 Bond St. Phone 416/392-6915. ¢¢

Marine Museum of Upper Canada. Contains exhibits depicting waterways of central Canada, the Great Lakes-St. Lawrence System; shipping memorabilia; marine artifacts; wireless rm; fur trade exhibit. Adj is 80-ft (24-m) steam tugboat preserved in dry berth; 12-ft (4-m) tall operating marine triple-expansion steam engine is also on display. (Tues-Sun; closed Jan 1, Good Fri, Dec 25, 26) Exhibition Place. Phone 416/392-1765.

The Market Gallery. Exhibition center for Toronto Archives; displays on city's historical, social, and cultural heritage; art, photographs, maps, documents, and artifacts. (Wed-Sat, also Sun afternoons; closed hols) 95 Front St E. Phone 416/392-7604. **FREE**

McMichael Canadian Art Collection. Works by Canada's most famous artists—the Group of Seven, Tom Thomson, Emily Carr, David Milne, Clarence Gagnon, and others. Also Inuit (Eskimo) and contemporary indigenous art and sculpture. Restaurant; book, gift shop. Constructed from hand-hewn timbers and native stone, the gallery stands in 100 acres (40 hectares) on the crest of Humber Valley; nature trail. (June-early Nov, daily; rest of yr, Tues-Sun; closed Dec 25) N via ON 400 or 427, 10365 Islington Ave in Kleinburg. Phone 905/893-1121. ¢¢

✪ **Metro Toronto Zoo.** Approx 710 acres (287 hectares) of native and exotic plants and animals in six geographic regions: Indo-Malaya, Africa, North and South America, Eurasia, and Australia. The North American Domain can be seen on a three-mi (five-km) A/C vehicle ride. The Zoomobile takes visitors on ½-hr drive through Eurasian, South American, and African areas. Parking fee. (Daily; closed Dec 25) 10 mi (16 km) E of Don Valley Pkwy on Hwy 401, then N on Meadowvale Rd, in Scarborough. Phone 416/392-5900. ¢¢¢

Ontario Parliament Buildings. Guided tours of the Legislature Building and walking tour of grounds. Gardens; art collection; historic displays. (Victoria Day-Labour Day, daily; rest of yr, Mon-Fri; closed hols) Queen's Park. Phone 416/325-7500. **FREE**

Ontario Place. A 96-acre (39-hectare) cultural, recreational, and entertainment complex on three artificial islands in Lake Ontario. Incl outdoor amphitheater for concerts, two pavilions with multimedia presentations, Cinesphere theater with IMAX films (yr-round; fee); children's village. Three villages of snack bars, restaurants, and pubs; miniature golf; lagoons, canals, two marinas; 370-ft (113-m) water slide, showboat, pedal and bumper boats; Wilderness Adventure Ride. (Mid-May-early Sept; daily) Parking fee. 955 Lakeshore Blvd W. Phone 416/314-9811. ¢¢¢¢

Ontario Science Centre. Hundreds of hands-on exhibits in the fields of space, technology, communications, food, chemistry, and earth science. Demonstrations on electricity, papermaking, metal casting, lasers, cryogenics. OmniMax theater (fee). Special exhibitions. (Daily; closed Dec 25) 770 Don Mills Rd, at Eglinton Ave E, 6 mi (10 km) NE via Don Valley Pkwy, in Don Mills. Per person ¢¢ Parking ¢¢

Paramount Canada's Wonderland. More than 125 attractions in eight themed areas offer 11 live stage shows and 50 rides, incl Vortex and Top Gun (suspended roller coasters). Splash Works, a ten-acre area offers 15 water-related rides and attractions (mid-June-Labour Day, weather permitting; free with Pay-One-Price admission). Special events, fireworks displays, top-name entertainment. (May and Sept, wkends; June-Aug, daily) 9580 Jane St, 18 mi (29 km) N on Hwy 400. Phone 905/832-7000. Pay-One-Price Passport ¢¢¢¢

The Pier: Toronto's Waterfront Museum. Original 1930s pier building on Toronto's celebrated waterfront incl two floors of hands-on interactive displays, rare historical artifacts, re-creations of marine history stories, art gallery, boat-building center, narrated walking excursions, children's programs. (Mar-Oct, daily) Central Harbourfront at 245 Queen's Quay W. Phone 416/597-0965. ¢

Professional sports.

Toronto Blue Jays (MLB). SkyDome. 1 Blue Jays Way. Phone 416/341-1000.

Toronto Maple Leafs (NHL). Air Canada Centre. 40 Bay St. Phone 416/815-5700.

Toronto Raptors (NBA). Air Canada Centre, 40 Bay St. Phone 416/366-DUNK.

Royal Ontario Museum. (ROM) Extensive permanent displays of fine and decorative art, archaeology, and earth and life sciences. The collection incl Chinese temple wall paintings; 12 dinosaur skeletons; the Ming Tomb Gallery; the hands-on Discovery Gallery; Greek, Etruscan, Chinese, European, and Egypt and Nubia galleries; special programs. (Daily; closed Jan 1, Dec 25) 100 Queen's Park. Phone 416/586-5549. ¢¢¢¢

St. Lawrence Centre for the Arts. Performing arts complex features theater, music, dance, films, and other public events. 27 Front St E.

Scarborough Civic Centre. Houses offices of municipal government. Guided tours (daily; closed Dec 25). Concert Sun afternoons. 150 Borough Dr in Scarborough. Phone 416/396-7216.

Sightseeing tours.

Gray Line bus tours. Contact 184 Front St E, Suite 601, M5A 4N3. Phone 416/594-3310.

Toronto Tours Ltd. Four different boat tours of Toronto Harbour. Phone 416/869-1372. ¢¢¢¢

SkyDome. State-of-the-art sports stadium with a fully retractable roof; contains a hotel (see HOTELS) and restaurants. Guided tours (one hr) begin with 15-min film *The Inside Story* and incl visits to a skybox, media center, locker rm, and playing field (all subject to availability). Tour (daily, schedule permitting). 1 Blue Jays Way, adj CN Tower. Phone 416/341-2770. ¢¢

Todmorden Mills Heritage Museum & Arts Centre. Restored historic houses; Parshall Terry House (1797) and William Helliwell House (1820). Also museum; restored 1899 train station. Picnicking. (May-Sept, Tues-Sun; Oct-Dec, Mon-Fri) 67 Pottery Rd, 2¼ mi (4 km) N, off Don Valley Pkwy in East York on Pottery Rd. between Broadview and Bayview Aves. Phone 416/396-2819. Tours ¢¢

Toronto Stock Exchange. Stock Market Place visitor center has multimedia displays, interactive games, and archival exhibits to aid visitors in understanding the market. The Exchange Tower, 2 First Canadian Pl (King and York Sts). Phone 416/947-4676. **FREE**

Toronto Symphony. Classical, pops and children's programs; Great Performers series. Wheelchair seating, audio enhancement for hearing-impaired. Roy Thomson Hall, 60 Simcoe St. Phone 416/593-4828.

University of Toronto. (1827) 55,000 students. Largest university in Canada. Guided walking tours of magnificent Gothic buildings begin at Hart House and incl account of campus ghost (June-Aug, Mon-Fri; free). Downtown, W of Queen's Park.

Woodbine Racetrack. Thoroughbred racing (late Apr-Oct, Wed-Sun afternoons; Queen's Plate race in mid-July). 15 mi (24 km) N via Hwy 427 in Etobicoke. Phone 416/675-RACE. ¢¢

Young People's Theatre. Professional productions for the entire family. (Sept-May, daily; Aug, wkends only) 165 Front St E. Phone 416/862-2222.

Special Events

International Caravan. Fifty pavilions scattered throughout the city present ethnic food, dancing, crafts. Phone 416/977-0466. Third wk June.

Chin International Picnic. At Paramount Canada's Wonderland. Contests, sports, picnicking. Phone 416/531-9991. First wkend July.

Outdoor Art Show. Nathan Phillips Sq. Phone 416/408-2754. Mid-July.

Caribana. Caribbean music, grand parade, floating nightclubs, dancing, costumes, food at various locations throughout city. Phone 416/465-4884. Late July-early Aug.

Canadian National Exhibition. Exhibition Place on the lakefront. This gala celebration originated in 1879 as the Toronto Industrial Exhibition for the encouragement of agriculture, industry, and the arts, although agricultural events dominated the show. Today sports, industry, labor, and the arts are of equal importance to CNE. The "Ex," as it is locally known, is so inclusive of the nation's activities that it is a condensed Canada. A special 350-acre (141-hectare) park has been built to accommodate the exhibition. Hundreds of events incl animal shows, parades, exhibits, a midway, water and air shows. Virtually every kind of sporting event is represented, from frisbee-throwing to the National Horse Show. Phone 416/393-6000. Mid-Aug-Labour Day.

Toronto International Film Festival. Celebration of world cinema in downtown theaters; Canadian and foreign films, international movie makers, and stars. Phone 416/967-7371. Early Sept.

Canadian International. Woodbine Racetrack. World-class thoroughbreds compete in one of Canada's most important races. Mid-late Oct. Phone 416/675-7223.

Royal Agricultural Winter Fair. Coliseum Building, Exhibition Place. World's largest indoor agricultural fair exhibits the finest livestock. Food shows; Royal Horse Show features international competitions in several categories. Phone 416/263-3400. Early Nov.

Motels/Motor Lodges

★★ **BEST WESTERN PRIMROSE.** *111 Carlton St (M5B 2G3).* 416/977-8000; fax 416/977-6323; 800/528-1234. *www.bestwestern.com.* 338 rms, 23 story. S, D $149; each addl $10; suites $275; under 16 free. Crib free. Garage $12.50. TV; cable. Pool. Complimentary coffee in rms. Restaurant 6:30 am-10 pm. Bar 11-1 am. Ck-out 11 am. Meeting rms. Business center. Exercise equipt; sauna. Cr cds: A, C, D, DS, ER, JCB, MC, V.

★★ **BEST WESTERN TORONTO AIRPORT-CARLTON PLACE.** *33 Carlson Ct (M9W 6H5).* 416/675-1234; fax 416/675-3436; 800/528-1234. *www.bestwestern.com.* 524 rms, 12 story. S $160-$175; D $175-$190; each addl $15; suites $250-$350; under 18 free; wkend, mid-wk rates. Crib free. Parking in/out $5/day. TV; cable (premium). Indoor pool; whirlpool. Complimentary coffee in rms. Restaurant 6:30-1 am. Rm serv 24 hrs. Bar 11-1 am. Ck-out 1 pm. Meeting rms. Business center. Gift shop. Airport transportation. Exercise equipt; sauna. Health club privileges. Minibars. Cr cds: A, D, DS, ER, JCB, MC, V.

★★ **COMFORT HOTEL DOWNTOWN.** *15 Charles St E (M4Y 1S1).* 416/924-1222; fax 416/927-1369; 800/228-5150. *www.comfortinn.com.* 108 rms, 10 story. S $109; D $119; each addl $10; suites $129-$139; under 18 free; wkend rates. Crib $10. Parking $9. TV; cable (premium), VCR avail. Restaurant noon-10 pm. Piano bar. Ck-out 11 am. Meeting rms. Business servs avail. Health club privileges. Refrigerators; microwaves avail. Cr cds: A, C, D, DS, ER, MC, V.

★ **DAYS INN DOWNTOWN.** *30 Carlton St (M5B 2E9).* 416/977-6655; fax 416/977-0502; toll-free 800/329-7466. *www.daysinn.com/daysinn.html.* 536 rms, 23 story. S, D $119-$135; each addl $15; under 16 free. Crib free. Pet accepted, some restrictions. Covered parking $15/day. TV; cable. Indoor pool. Restaurant 7 am-10 pm. Bar 11:30-2 am. Ck-out 11 am. Coin lndry. Meeting rms. Business servs avail. Sundries. Barber, beauty shop. Sauna. Some refrigerators. Sun deck. Cr cds: A, D, DS, ER, JCB, MC, V.

★★ **HOLIDAY INN - DON VALLEY.** *1100 Eglinton Ave E (M3C 1H8).* 416/446-3700; fax 416/446-3701; res 800/465-4329. *www.holiday-inn.com.* 298 rms, 14 story. S, D $115-$155; each addl $10; suites $175-$325; family, wkend, wkly rates. Crib free. Pet accepted, some restrictions. TV; cable (premium), VCR avail (movies). Complimentary coffee in lobby. Restaurant 6:30 am-11 pm. Rm serv. Bar 6 pm-2 am; entertainment Thurs-Sat. Ck-out noon. Convention facilities. Business center. In-rm modem link. Concierge. Shopping arcade. Barber, beauty shop. Free valet parking. Airport, RR station transportation. Indoor tennis, pro. X-country ski ¼ mi. Exercise equipt; sauna. Indoor/outdoor pool; whirlpool, poolside serv, lifeguard. Playground. Supervised children's activities (June-Sept); ages 5-12. Game rm. Lawn games. Bathrm phones, refrigerators. Many balconies. Cr cds: A, C, D, DS, ER, JCB, MC, V.

★★ **HOLIDAY INN EXPRESS.** *50 Estates Dr, Scarborough (M1H 2Z1).* 416/439-9666; fax 416/439-4295; 800/465-4329. *www.holiday-inn.com.* 138 rms, 2-3 story. No elvtrs. S $59; D $79; each addl $10; under 19 free; wkend rates. Crib free. TV; cable (premium). Complimentary continental bkfst. Restaurant adj 11:30-1 am, Sat, Sun from 4:30 pm. Ck-out 11 am. Meeting rms. Business servs avail. Health club privileges. Cr cds: A, C, D, DS, ER, JCB, MC, V.

★★ **HOLIDAY INN YORKDALE.** *3450 Dufferin St (M6A 2V1).* 416/789-5161; fax 416/785-6845; toll-free 800/465-4329. *www.holiday-inn.com.* 365 rms, 12 story. S $149.95; D $164.95; each addl $15; suites $350; under 12 free; wkend rates. Crib free. TV; cable (premium). Heated pool; whirlpool. Supervised children's activities. Complimentary coffee in rms. Restaurant 6 am-11 pm. Bar 11-1 am. Ck-out noon. Meeting rms. Business center. Exercise equipt; sauna. Rec rm. Minibars. Some balconies. Cr cds: A, C, D, DS, ER, JCB, MC, V.

★ **HOWARD JOHNSON EAST.** *940 Progress Ave, Scarborough (M1G 3T5).* 416/439-6200; fax 416/439-5689; 800/446-4656. *www.hojo.com.* 186 rms, 6 story. S $109; D $119; each addl $10; under 18 free; wkend rates; package plan. Crib free. Pet accepted. TV; cable (premium). Heated pool; whirlpool. Restaurant 6:30 am-2 pm, 5-10 pm. Rm serv. Bar 4:30 pm-1 am. Ck-out noon. Coin lndry. Meeting rms. Business servs avail. Valet serv. Sundries. Gift shop. Exercise equipt; sauna. Health club privileges. Microwaves avail. Cr cds: A, C, D, DS, ER, JCB, MC, V.

★ **HOWARD JOHNSON INN.** *89 Avenue Rd (M5R 2G3). 416/964-1220; fax 416/964-8692; 800/446-4656. www.hojo.com.* 71 rms, 8 story. S $124; D $134; each addl $10; under 19 free; wkend rates off-season. Crib free. Pet accepted, some restrictions. Parking $6.50/day. TV; cable (premium), VCR avail. Complimentary continental bkfst. Ck-out 1 pm. Meeting rms. Business servs avail. Health club privileges. Cr cds: A, D, DS, ER, MC, V.

★ **HOWARD JOHNSON PLAZA.** *2737 Keele St, North York (M3M 2E9). 416/636-4656; fax 416/633-5637; 800/446-4656. www.hojo.com.* 367 rms, most A/C, 10 story, 27 suites. S, D $129-$179; each addl $10; suites $175-$375; family rates; package plans. Crib free. Pet accepted. TV; cable (premium), VCR avail. Indoor pool. Supervised children's activities (June-Sept); ages 4-12. Complimentary coffee in rms. Restaurant 6:30 am-11 pm; Sun to 10 pm. Bar 11-1 am. Ck-out noon. Meeting rms. Business servs avail. Free garage parking. Downhill/x-country ski 10 mi. Exercise equipt; sauna. Game rm. Rec rm. Some minibars; microwaves avail. Cr cds: A, C, D, DS, ER, JCB, MC, V.

★ **QUALITY HOTEL.** *111 Lombard St (M5C 2T9). 416/367-5555; fax 416/367-3470; 800/228-5151. www.qualityinn.com.* 196 rms, 16 story. S $139; D $149; each addl $10; under 18 free. Crib free. Pet accepted. Garage $11.75/day. TV; cable. Ck-out 11 am. Business servs avail. Exercise equipt. Health club privileges. Cr cds: A, D, DS, ER, JCB, MC, V.

★ **QUALITY HOTEL.** *280 Bloor St W (M5S 1V8). 416/968-0010; fax 416/968-7765; 800/228-5151. www.qualityinn.com.* 210 rms, 14 story. Mid-Mar-Oct: S $120-$145; D $130-$155; under 18 free; wkend rates; higher rates special events; lower rates rest of yr. Crib free. Pet accepted, some restrictions. Garage in/out $11.50. TV; cable. Restaurant 7 am-11 pm. Ck-out 11 am. Meeting rms. Business servs avail. No bellhops. Health club privileges. Cr cds: A, D, DS, JCB, MC, V.

★ **QUALITY INN AIRPORT EAST.** *2180 Islington Ave (N9P 3P1). 416/240-9090; fax 416/240-9944; 800/228-5151. www.qualityinn.com.* 198 rms, 12 story. S, D $89-$139; each addl $10; under 18 free; package plans; higher rates special events. Crib free. Pet accepted. TV; cable (premium). Restaurant 6 am-midnight. Bar from 11 am. Ck-out 11 am. Meeting rms. In-rm modem link. Microwaves avail. Near airport. Cr cds: A, D, DS, ER, JCB, MC, V.

★ **QUALITY SUITES.** *262 Carlingview Dr, Etobicoke (M9W 5G1). 416/674-8442; fax 416/674-3088; toll-free 800/228-5151. www.qualityinn.com.* 254 suites, 12 story. S, D $120-$145; each addl $5; under 18 free; wkend, hol rates. Crib free. Pet accepted. TV; cable (premium). Complimentary coffee in rms. Restaurant 6:30-1 am. Bar. Ck-out 11 am. Meeting rms. Business servs avail. No bellhops. Gift shop. Downhill/x-country ski 15 mi. Exercise equipt. Health club privileges. Minibars; microwaves avail. Cr cds: A, D, DS, ER, JCB, MC, V.

★★ **RADISSON HOTEL TORONTO EAST.** *55 Hallcrown Pl, North York (M2J 4R1). 416/493-7000; fax 416/493-0681; 800/333-3333. www.radisson.com.* 228 rms, 9 story. S, D $98-$103; each addl $10; suites $225; under 17 free; wkend rates. Crib free. TV; cable (premium). Indoor pool; whirlpool. Complimentary coffee in rms. Restaurant 7 am-10 pm. Bar. Ck-out noon. Meeting rms. Business servs avail. Sauna. Cr cds: A, C, D, DS, ER, JCB, MC, V.

★ **RAMADA DON VALLEY.** *185 Yorkland Blvd (M2J 4R2). 416/493-9000; fax 416/493-5729; res 888/298-2054. www.ramada.com.* 285 rms, 10 story. S, D $105-$165; each addl $15; suites $175-$300; under 18 free; wkend rates. Crib free. TV; cable (premium). Indoor pool. Coffee in rms. Restaurant 6:30 am-10:30 pm; Sat from 7 am. Bar 11-2 am; Sun to 11 pm. Ck-out noon. Meeting rms. Business center. In-rm modem link. Exercise equipt; sauna. Health club privileges. Game rm. Rec rm. Some in-rm whirlpools. Luxury level. Cr cds: A, C, D, DS, ER, JCB, MC, V.

★ **RAMADA HOTEL TORONTO AIRPORT.** *2 Holiday Dr, Etobicoke (M9C 2Z7). 416/621-2121; fax 416/621-9840; 800/228-2828. www.ramada.com.* 179 rms, 2-6 story. June-Aug: S, D $150-$160; each addl $10; suites $250-$350; under 18 free; wkly, wkend rates; lower rates rest of yr. Crib free. Pet accepted. TV; cable (premium). Indoor/outdoor pool; whirlpool. Complimentary coffee in rms. Restaurant 6 am-11 pm. Rm serv. Bar 11:30-1 am. Ck-out noon. Business servs avail. In-rm modem link. Bellhops. Valet serv. Free airport transportation. Exercise equipt; sauna. Some minibars; microwaves avail. Cr cds: A, C, D, DS, ER, JCB, MC, V.

★ **RAMADA INN AND SUITES.** *300 Jarvis St (M5B 2C5). 416/977-4823; fax 416/977-4830; res 888/298-2054. www.ramada.com.* 102 rms, 10 story, 44 suites. S $155; D $170; each addl $15; suites $185-$265; under 18 free. Crib free. Garage parking $15. TV; cable (premium). Indoor pool; whirlpool. Complimentary coffee in rms. Restaurant 7 am-2 pm, 5-9 pm. Bar from 11 am. Ck-out 11 am. Meeting rms. Business servs avail. Concierge. Downhill/x-country ski 10 mi. Exercise equipt; sauna. Rec rm. Refrigerators. Cr cds: A, C, D, DS, ER, JCB, MC, V.

★ **SEA HORSE INN.** *2095 Lakeshore Blvd W (On 2) (M8V 1A1). 416/255-4433; fax 416/251-5121.* 74 rms, 1-3 story. S $57-$72; D $57-$89; each addl $5; suites $85-$170; under 18 free. TV; cable (premium). Pool; whirlpool. Playground. Complimentary continental bkfst. Ck-out 11 am. Meeting rms. Sauna. Refrigerators. Picnic tables, grills. On Lake Ontario. Cr cds: A, C, D, DS, ER, MC, V.

★ **TRAVELODGE - AIRPORT.** *925 Dixon Rd, Etobicoke (M9W 1J8). 416/674-2222; fax 416/674-5757; toll-free 888/483-6887. www.travelodge.com.* 283 rms, 17 story. S $120; D $140; each addl $10; suites $140-$275; under 18 free; wkend rates. Crib free. Pet accepted. TV, cable (premium). Indoor pool; whirlpool. Complimentary continental bkfst. Restaurant 11-2 am. Bar. Ck-out 1 pm. Convention facilities. Business servs avail. In-rm modem link. Airport transportation. Sauna. Health club privileges. Gift shop. Cr cds: A, D, DS, ER, MC, V.

⊡ ⬤ ⬛ ✈ ⬛ 🔥 SC

★ **TRAVELODGE EAST.** *20 Milner Business Ct, Scarborough (M1B 3C6).* 416/299-9500; fax 416/299-6172; 800/578-7878. www.travelodge.com. 156 rms, 6 story. S, D $71-$81; each addl $6; suites $85-$105; under 17 free. Pet accepted. TV; cable (premium). Indoor pool; whirlpool. Complimentary coffee in rms. Restaurant 11-2 am. Rm serv noon-11 pm. Ck-out 11 am. Meeting rms. Business servs avail. Sundries. Health club privileges. Microwaves avail. Cr cds: A, D, DS, ER, MC, V.

⊡ ⬤ ⬛ ⬛ SC

★ **TRAVELODGE NORTH.** *50 Norfinch Dr, North York (M3N 1X1).* 416/663-9500; fax 416/663-8480; 800/578-7878. www.travelodge.com. 184 rms, 6 story. S $89; D $97; each addl $8; under 17 free. Crib free. Pet accepted, some restrictions. TV; cable (premium). Indoor pool; whirlpool. Coffee in rms. Restaurant 7-1 am. Rm serv. Bar. Ck-out 11 am. Meeting rms. Business servs avail. Sundries. Cr cds: A, D, DS, ER, MC, V.

⊡ ⬤ ⬛ ⬛ 🔥 SC

★★★ **VALHALLA INN.** *1 Valhalla Inn Rd (M9B 1S9).* 416/239-2391; fax 416/239-8764. www.valhalla-inn.com. 240 rms, 2-12 story. S $160; D $170; each addl $10; suites $150-$275; under 18 free; wkend rates. Crib free. Pet accepted. TV; cable (premium). Heated pool. Coffee in rms. Restaurant 6 am-11 pm; dining rm noon-2:30 pm, 6-10 pm. Rm serv. Bars 11-2 am; entertainment. Ck-out 1 pm. Meeting rms. Business center. In-rm modem link. Bellhops. Valet serv. Sundries. Free airport transportation. Health club privileges. Some bathrm phones. Private patios, balconies. Grills. Cr cds: A, C, D, DS, ER, MC, V.

⬤ ⬛ ⬛ 🔥 SC 🏃

Hotels

★ **BOND PLACE.** *65 Dundas St E (N5B 2G8).* 416/362-6061; fax 416/360-6406. www.bondplacehoteltoronto.com. 286 rms, 18 story, 51 suites. May-Oct: S, D $89-$109; each addl $15; suites $104-$134; under 15 free; lower rates rest of yr. Crib free. Parking, in/out $11. TV; cable (premium), VCR avail. Restaurant 7 am-11 pm. Rm serv 11 am-10 pm. Bar 5 pm-1 am. Ck-out 11 am. Meeting rms. Business servs avail. Cr cds: A, C, D, DS, ER, MC, V.

⊡ ⬛ SC

★★★ **CROWNE PLAZA TORONTO CENTRE.** *225 Front St W (M5V 2X3).* 416/597-1400; fax 416/597-8128; toll-free 800/422-7969. www.crowneplaza.com. 587 rms, 25 story. S, D $239-$279; each addl $20; suites $375-$600; under 12 free; wkend rates. Crib free. TV; cable (premium), VCR avail. Indoor pool; wading pool, whirlpool, poolside serv. Coffee in rms. Restaurant (see also ACCOLADE). Bar 11:30-2 am;

Nightly entertainment. Ck-out noon. Meeting rms. Business center. In-rm modem link. Concierge. Valet parking. Exercise rm; sauna. Massage. Minibars; microwaves avail. Upscale and luxurious decor. Cr cds: A, C, D, DS, ER, JCB, MC, V.

⊡ ⬛ 🏛 ⬛ 🔥 SC 🏃

★★★ **DELTA CHELSEA INN.** *33 Gerrard St W (M5G 1Z4).* 416/595-1975; fax 416/585-4362. www.deltahotels.com. 1,590 rms, 26 story. S $245-$275; D $265-$295; each addl $15; suites, kit. units $255-$375; under 18 free; wkend rates. Crib free. Pet accepted, some restrictions. Valet parking $22 in/out. TV; cable, VCR avail. 2 heated pools; whirlpool. Supervised children's activities; ages 2-13. Restaurant 6:30-1 am. Rm serv 24 hrs. Bar 11-1 am; entertainment. Ck-out 11 am. Convention facilities. Business center. Gift shop. Exercise equipt; sauna. Health club privileges. Game rm. Refrigerator in some suites. Microwaves avail. Many balconies. Cr cds: A, C, D, DS, ER, JCB, MC, V.

⊡ ⬤ ⬛ 🏛 ⬛ 🔥 SC 🏃

★★ **DELTA TORONTO AIRPORT.** *801 Dixon Rd, Etobicoke (N9W 1J5).* 416/675-6100; fax 416/675-4022. www.deltahotels.com. 251 rms, 8 story. S, D $115-$165; each addl $15; suites $170-$220; under 18 free; package plans. Crib free. Pet accepted, some restrictions. TV; cable (premium). Indoor pool. Supervised children's activities (June-Aug). Restaurant 6 am-11 pm. Rm serv 24 hrs. Bar 11:30-2 am. Ck-out 1 pm. Convention facilities. Business center. Bellhops. Valet serv. Gift shops. Exercise equipt; sauna. Health club privileges. Minibars; microwaves avail. Cr cds: A, C, D, DS, ER, JCB, MC, V.

⊡ ⬤ ⬛ 🏛 ⬛ 🔥 SC 🏃

★★ **DELTA TORONTO EAST.** *2035 Kennedy Rd, Scarborough (M1T 3G2).* 416/299-1500; fax 416/299-8959. www.deltahotels.ca. 368 rms, 14 story. S, D $219; each addl $15; suites $365-$620; under 18 free; wkend rates. Crib free. Pet accepted. TV; cable. Indoor pool; wading pool; whirlpool. Free supervised children's activities (wkends, school hols); ages 3-15. Restaurants 6:30-2 am. Rm serv 24 hrs. Bar 11-2 am. Ck-out noon. Convention facilities. Business servs avail. In-rm modem link. Concierge. Gift shop. Barber, beauty shop. Covered valet parking. Putting green. Exercise rm; sauna. Game rm. Luxury level. Cr cds: A, D, DS, ER, JCB, MC, V.

⊡ ⬤ ⬛ 🏛 ⬛ ⬛ SC

★★★ **FAIRMONT ROYAL YORK.** *100 Front St W (M5J 1E3).* 416/368-2511; fax 416/368-2884; 800/527-4727. www.fairmont.com. 1,365 rms, 22 story. S, D $189-$289; each addl $20; suites $295-$1,750; under 18 free; package plans. Crib free. Pet accepted. Garage (fee). TV; cable. Pool; wading pool, whirlpool. Restaurant 6:30 am-10:30 pm. Rm serv 24 hrs. Bars noon-2 am; entertainment. Ck-out noon. Convention facilities. Business center. Concierge. Shopping arcade. Barber, beauty shop. Exercise rm; sauna. Massage. Health club privileges. Minibars; refrigerators, microwaves avail. Luxury level. Cr cds: A, D, DS, ER, JCB, MC, V.

⊡ ⬤ ⬛ 🏛 ⬛ 🔥 SC 🏃

★★★★ **FOUR SEASONS HOTEL TORONTO.** *21 Avenue Rd (M5R 2G1).* 416/964-0411; *fax* 416/964-2301; 800/819-5053. *www.fourseasons.com.* Visitors will enjoy all the expected luxuries at this 230-room, 150-suite hotel located in the heart of fashionable Yorkville, near the Royal Ontario Museum and Queen's Park. Business travelers can even reserve a complimentary limousine ride to the nearby financial district on weekday mornings. Several culinary experiences are available, including tasting the flavors of Provence at the renowned Truffles restaurant. 380 rms, 32 story. S $325-$485; D $365-$525; each addl $30; suites $755; under 18 free; wkend rates. Crib free. Pet accepted. Self-park $22/day, valet $24/day. TV; cable (premium), VCR avail (movies). Indoor/outdoor pool; whirlpool, poolside serv. Restaurants 6:30 am-11 pm; Sat, Sun from 7 am. Rm serv 24 hrs. Bar 11:30-2 am; entertainment Thurs-Sat. Ck-out noon, ck-in 3 pm. Convention facilities. Business center. In-rm modem link. Concierge. Exercise rm; sauna. Massage. Bathrm phones, minibars; microwaves avail. Some balconies. Cr cds: A, D, DS, JCB, MC, V.

D ⊠ ☎ ⛆ 🏃 ⊠ 🔥 SC 🏃

★★★ **HILTON.** *145 Richmond St W (M5H 2L2).* 416/869-3456; *fax* 416/869-3187; 800/445-8667. *www.hilton.com.* 601 rms, 32 story. Apr-Nov: S, D $239-$259; each addl $20; suites $249-$1,600; family rates; package plans; lower rates rest of yr. Crib free. Garage $17.50. TV; cable (premium). Indoor/outdoor pool; whirlpool, poolside serv in summer. Restaurant 6:30 am-11 pm. Rm serv 24 hrs. Bar 11:30-2 am. Ck-out noon. Convention facilities. Business center. Exercise equipt; sauna. Massage. Minibars. Luxury level. Cr cds: A, C, D, DS, ER, JCB, MC, V.

D ⊠ ☎ 🏃 ⊠ 🔥 🏃

★★ **HOLIDAY INN.** *970 Dixon Rd, Etobicoke (M9W 1J9).* 416/675-7611; *fax* 416/675-9162; *toll-free* 800/465-4329. *www.holiday-inn.com.* 445 rms, 12 story. S, D $160-$175; suites $230-$430; wkend rates. Crib free. Pet accepted. TV; cable (premium). 2 heated pools, 1 indoor; whirlpool. Playground. Coffee in rms. Restaurant 6 am-11 pm. Rm serv to 1 am. Bar 11-2 am; Sun noon-11 pm. Ck-out 1 pm. Meeting rms. Business center. Concierge. Barber, beauty shop. Free airport transportation. Exercise equipt; sauna. Rec rm. Minibars. Cr cds: A, C, D, DS, ER, JCB, MC, V.

D ⊠ ☎ ⛆ 🏃 ✈ ⊠ 🔥 SC 🏃

★★ **HOLIDAY INN.** *370 King St W (M5V 1J9).* 416/599-4000; *fax* 416/599-7394; *toll-free* 800/263-6364. *www.holiday-inn.com.* 425 rms, 20 story. S, D $189; each addl $15; suites $269; family rates; package plans. Crib free. Garage $16. TV; cable, VCR avail. Heated rooftop pool; poolside serv, lifeguard. Complimentary coffee in rms. Restaurant 6:30-2 am. Bar from 11 am. Ck-out noon. Convention facilities. Business center. Concierge. Gift shop. Exercise equipt; sauna. Massage. Wet bars. Cr cds: A, C, D, DS, ER, JCB, MC, V.

D ⊠ 🏃 ✈ ⊠ SC 🏃

★★ **HOLIDAY INN.** *600 Dixon Rd, Etobicoke (M9W 1J1).* 416/240-7511; *fax* 416/240-7519; *toll-free* 800/491-4656. *www.holiday-inn.com.* 186 rms, 2-5 story. S, D $89-$150; each addl $10; suites $129-$155; under 18 free. Crib free.

Pet accepted, some restrictions. TV; cable. Heated pool; wading pool, poolside serv. Coffee in rms. Restaurant open 24 hrs. Ck-out 1 pm. Meeting rms. Business servs avail. Airport transportation. Exercise equipt. Cr cds: A, C, D, DS, ER, JCB, MC, V.

D ☎ ⛆ 🏃 ⊠ 🔥 🖼 SC

★★★ **HOTEL INTER-CONTINENTAL TORONTO.** *220 Bloor St W (M5S 1T8).* 416/960-5200; *fax* 416/960-8269. *www.interconti.com.* 208 rms, 8 story. S, D $365-$405; suites $450-$2,000. Crib free. Valet parking $24. TV; cable (premium), VCR avail (movies). Indoor pool. Restaurants 7 am-11 pm. Rm serv 24 hrs. Bar noon-1 am. Ck-out 1 pm. Meeting rms. Business center. In-rm modem link. Concierge. Gift shop. Exercise equipt; sauna. Massage. Bathrm phones, minibars. Patios. Cr cds: A, C, D, ER, JCB, MC, V.

D ⛆ 🏃 ⊠ 🔥 SC 🏃

★ **INN ON THE PARK.** *1100 Eglinton Ave E (M3C 1H8).* 416/444-2561; *fax* 416/446-3308. *www.innonthepark.com.* 270 rms, 23 story. S, D $175-$235; each addl $20; suites $250-$800; under 18 free; wkend rates. Complimentary parking. Crib free. TV; cable (premium), VCR avail (movies). 2 heated pools, 1 indoor; whirlpool, lifeguards (summer season). Free supervised children's activities (June-Sept); ages 5-12. Restaurants 6:30 am-midnight. Bar 11:30-1 am; vocalist Fri-Sat. Ck-out noon. Meeting rms. Business center. In-rm modem link. Concierge. Barber, beauty shop. X-country ski opp hotel. Exercise equipt; sauna. Rec rm. Courtyard/playground games. Bathrm phones. Some minibars. Some private patios, balconies. Cr cds: A, C, D, DS, ER, JCB, MC, V.

D ⛆ ⛆ 🏃 ⊠ 🔥 SC 🏃

★★★ **INTERNATIONAL PLAZA.** *655 Dixon Rd (M9W 1J4).* 416/244-1711; *fax* 416/244-8031. *www.internationalplaza.com.* 415 rms, 12 story. S, D $170; each addl $10; suites $350-$500; under 18 free; wkend rates. Crib free. Pet accepted. Valet parking $6. TV; cable (premium). Indoor pool; wading pool, poolside serv, lifeguard. Supervised children's activities; ages 3-12. Restaurant 6:30 am-11 pm. Rm serv 24 hrs. Bar 11-2 am. Ck-out noon. Convention facilities. Business center. Concierge. Gift shop. Beauty, barber shop. Exercise equipt; sauna. Massages. Game rm. Refrigerators. Minibars in suites. Cr cds: A, D, DS, ER, MC, V.

D ☎ ⛆ 🏃 ⊠ 🔥 🏃

★★★ **LE ROYAL MERIDIEN KING EDWARD.** *37 King St E (M5C 1E9).* 416/863-9700; *fax* 416/367-5515. *www.lemeridien-kingedward.com.* 294 rms, 9 and 16 story. S $205-$360; D $230-$385; suites $435-$510; under 12 free; wkend rates. Crib free. Covered parking, valet $24. TV; cable (premium), VCR avail. Restaurants 6:30 am-2:30 pm, 5-11 pm (see also CHIARO'S). Rm serv 24 hrs. Bars 11:30-1 am. Ck-out noon. Convention facilities. Business center. In-rm modem link. Concierge. Shopping arcade. Beauty shop. Exercise equipt; sauna. Whirlpools. Massage. Health club privileges. Bathrm phones, minibars; microwaves avail. Cr cds: A, C, D, ER, JCB, MC, V.

D 🏃 ⊠ 🖼 SC 🏃

★ ★ ★ **MARRIOTT BLOOR YORKVILLE HOTEL TORONTO.** *90 Bloor St E (M4W 1A7). 416/961-8000; 800/228-9290. www.marriott.com.* 258 rms, 6 story. S, D $195-$325; under 18 free. Crib avail. TV; cable (premium). Restaurant 6:30 am-10 pm. Bar to midnight. Ck-out noon, ck-in 4 pm. Meeting rms. Business center. In-rm modem link. Concierge. Exercise equipt. Minibars; many refrigerators in suites. Cr cds: A, C, D, DS, ER, JCB, MC, V.

★ ★ ★ **MARRIOTT TORONTO AIRPORT.** *901 Dixon Rd, Etobicoke (M9W 1J5). 416/674-9400; fax 416/674-8292; toll-free 800/905-2811. www.marriott.com.* 424 rms, 9 story. S, D $240; suites $300-$1,200; under 18 free; wkend rates. Crib free. TV; cable (premium). Indoor pool; whirlpool. Restaurants 6 am-11 pm. Bar noon-2 am. Ck-out noon. Convention facilities. Business center. Gift shop. Covered parking. Free airport transportation. Exercise equipt; sauna. Luxury level. Cr cds: A, C, D, ER, JCB, MC, V.

★ ★ ★ **MARRIOTT TORONTO EATON CENTRE.** *525 Bay St (N5G 2L2). 416/597-9200; fax 416/597-9211; res 888/440-9300. www.marriott.com.* 459 rms, 18 story. May-Oct: S, D $350; suites $600-$1,800; family rates; package plans; higher rates special events; lower rates rest of yr. Crib free. Garage parking $14, valet $18. TV; cable (premium), VCR avail. Indoor pool; whirlpool, poolside serv. Restaurant 6:30 am-10 pm. Rm serv 24 hrs. Bar 11-1 am. Ck-out noon. Convention facilities. Business center. Concierge. Shopping arcade. Drug store. Barber, beauty shop. Exercise equipt; sauna. Cr cds: A, D, DS, ER, JCB, MC, V.

★ ★ ★ ★ **THE METROPOLITAN HOTEL.** *108 Chestnut St (M5G 1R3). 416/977-5000; fax 416/599-3317; res 800/668-6600. www.metropolitan.com.* The Metropolitan is a luxurious hotel in the heart of Toronto, close to internationally renowned art galleries and museums, and the world-class shops of Bloor Street. Well-appointed guest rooms feature deluxe European down duvets and Italian linens. The Metropolitan offers distinct accommodations for business and leisure travel, in addition to service and cuisine provided by their restaurants Hemispheres and Lai Wah Heen. 425 rms, 26 story. S, D $240-$380; each addl $30; suites $490-$1,800; wkend rates. Crib free. Parking, in/out $19/$24. Pet accepted, some restrictions. TV; cable (premium), VCR avail (free movies). Indoor pool; whirlpool. Restaurant 6:30 am-11:30 pm. Bar 11-1 am. Ck-out noon. Meeting rms. Business center. In-rm modem link. Concierge. Gift shop. Exercise equipt; sauna. Bathrm phones, minibars. Eaton Centre 2 blks. Cr cds: A, D, DS, ER, JCB, MC, V.

★ ★ **NOVOTEL TORONTO CENTRE.** *45 The Esplanade (M5E 1W2). 416/367-8900; fax 416/360-8285. www.novotel.com.* 262 rms, 9 story. S, D $205; each addl $20; suites $215; under 16 free; wkend rates. Crib free. Pet accepted. Garage, in/out $13.50. TV; cable (premium). Indoor pool; whirlpool. Restaurant 6 am-midnight. Bar 11-2 am. Ck-out 1 pm. Meeting rms. Business servs avail. Exercise equipt; sauna. Minibars. Cr cds: A, D, DS, ER, JCB, MC, V.

★ ★ ★ ★ **PARK HYATT TORONTO.** *4 Avenue Rd (M5R 2E8). 416/925-1234; fax 416/924-6693; res 800/233-1234. www.hyatt.com.* This hotel offers elegance and glamour in the heart of fashionable Yorkville. All 346 spacious guest rooms have opulent bathrooms, and the public spaces are filled with relaxing dark wood, gold tones, and rich, cream-colored couches. Visitors will enjoy getting pampered with warm and gracious service on either a business trip or a romantic getaway. 300 rms, 18 story, 46 suites. May-Sept: S, D $499; suites $559; each addl $40; under 17 free; lower rates rest of yr. Crib avail. Pet accepted. Valet parking. TV; cable, VCR avail. Complimentary newspaper. Restaurant 6 am-11 pm. Rm serv 24-hr. Bar. Ck-out noon, ck-in 3 pm. Conference center. Meeting rms. Business center. Concierge serv. Dry cleaning. Gift shop. Barber, beauty shop. Free airport transportation. Exercise equipt; sauna, steam rm. Golf, 18 holes. Cr cds: A, D, DS, JCB, MC, V.

★ ★ ★ **QUEEN'S LANDING.** *155 Byron St, Toronto (L0S 1J0). 905/468-2195; fax 905/468-2227; toll-free 888/669-5566. www.vintageinns.com.* 142 rms, 3 story. S, D $195-$255; each addl $20; suites $350-$450; under 18 free; some lower rates off-season. Crib free. TV; cable (premium), VCR avail. Indoor pool; whirlpool. Dining rm 7 am-10 pm. Rm serv to midnight. Bar 11-1 am. Ck-out 11 am, ck-in 3 pm. Meeting rms. Business servs avail. In-rm modem link. Bellhops. Valet serv. Concierge. Tennis privileges. 18-hole golf privileges. X-country ski 6 mi. Exercise equipt; sauna. Health club privileges. Minibars. Antique furnishings; distinctive appointments. Many in-rm whirlpools, fireplaces. Located at mouth of Niagara River, opp historic Fort Niagara. Bicycle rentals. Cr cds: A, D, DS, ER, MC, V.

★ ★ **RADISSON HOTEL TORONTO - MARKHAM.** *50 E Valhalla Dr, Markham (L3R 0A3). 905/477-2010; fax 905/477-2026; res 800/333-3333. www.radisson.com.* 204 rms, 15 story, 26 suites. S, D $220; each addl $15; suites $250; under 19 free; wkly, wkend rates; golf plans; higher rates Dec 31. Crib free. Indoor pool; whirlpool. Complimentary continental bkfst. Complimentary coffee in rms. Restaurant 6:30 am-11 pm. Bar 11-2 am. Ck-out noon. Meeting rms. Business servs avail. Gift shop. Tennis privileges. 18-hole golf privileges. Downhill/x-country ski 12 mi. Exercise equipt; sauna. Rec rm. Minibars; microwaves avail. Picnic tables. Cr cds: A, C, D, DS, ER, JCB, MC, V.

★ ★ **RADISSON PLAZA - HOTEL ADMIRAL.** *249 Queens Quay W (M5J 2N5). 416/203-3333; fax 416/203-3100; 800-333-3333. www.radisson.com.* 157 air-cooled rms, 8 story, 17 suites. Early-May-mid-Nov: S, D $265-$295; each addl $20; suites from $495; family, wkend rates. Crib free. Parking $15/day. TV; cable (premium). Heated pool; whirlpool, poolside serv. Complimentary coffee in rms. Restaurant 7 am-11 pm. Rm serv 24 hrs. Bar 11:30-1 am. Ck-out noon. Meeting rms. Business servs avail. Concierge. Gift shop. Health club privileges. Bathrm phones, minibars. On waterfront; nautical theme throughout. View of Harbour. Cr cds: A, C, D, DS, ER, JCB, MC, V.

★★ **RADISSON SUITE TORONTO AIRPORT.** *640 Dixon Rd, Etobicoke (M9W 1J1). 416/242-7400; fax 416/242-9888; res 800/333-3333. www.radisson.com.* 215 suites, 14 story. S, D $204-$216; under 18 free. Crib free. Pet accepted, some restrictions. TV; cable, VCR avail. Complimentary continental bkfst. Restaurant 6:30 am-11 pm. Bar 11-1 am. Ck-out noon. Meeting rms. Business center. In-rm modem link. Concierge. Gift shop. Free valet parking. Exercise equipt. Minibars, microwaves avail. Cr cds: A, C, D, DS, ER, JCB, MC, V.

★★★ **REGAL CONSTELLATION.** *900 Dixon Rd, Etobicoke (M9W 1J7). 416/675-1500; fax 416/675-1737. www.regal-hotels.com.* 710 rms, 8-16 story. S, D $95-$165; each addl $15; suites from $275; under 18 free; wkend package plan. Crib free. Pet accepted, some restrictions. Valet parking $9.25/day. TV; cable (premium), VCR avail. 2 heated pools, 1 indoor/outdoor; whirlpool, poolside serv in season. Restaurant 6:30 am-11 pm; dining rm 11 am-2 pm, 5:30-10 pm. Rm serv 24 hrs. Bar 11-1 am; entertainment Thurs-Sat. Ck-out noon. Concierge. Convention facilities. Business center. Gift shop. Beauty shop. Airport transportation. Exercise equipt; sauna. Some balconies. Cr cds: A, C, D, DS, ER, MC, V.

★★★ **RENAISSANCE AT SKYDOME.** *1 Blue Jays Way (M5V 1J4). 416/341-7100; fax 416/341-5091; toll-free 800/237-1512. www.renaissancehotels.com.* 348 rms, 11 story, 26 suites. May-Oct: S, D $169-$179; each addl $30; suites $299-$559; under 18 free; wkend rates; package plans; lower rates rest of yr. Crib avail. Pet accepted. Garage parking $16; valet $22. TV; cable, VCR avail. Indoor pool. Complimentary coffee in rms. Supervised children's activities (June-Sept). Restaurant 7-1 am. Rm serv 24 hrs. Bar. Ck-out 9:30 am-noon. Convention facilities. Business center. Concierge. Gift shop. Health club privileges. Massage. Minibars. Modern facility within SkyDome complex; lobby and some rms overlook playing field. Cr cds: A, C, D, DS, ER, JCB, MC, V.

★★★ **SHERATON CENTRE.** *123 Queen St W (M5H 2M9). 416/361-1000; fax 416/947-4854; 800/325-3535. www.sheraton.com.* 1,382 rms, 43 story. Late June-Dec: S $275; D $285; each addl $20; suites $450-$850; under 18 free; wkend rates; lower rates rest of yr. Covered parking, valet $22/day. TV; cable (premium), VCR avail. Indoor/outdoor pool; whirlpool, poolside serv (summer); lifeguard. Supervised children's activities (daily July-mid-Sept; wkends rest of yr). Complimentary coffee in rms. Restaurant 6 am-11 pm. Rm serv 24 hrs. Bars. Ck-out noon. Convention facilities. Business center. Concierge. Shopping arcade. Barber, beauty shop. Exercise equipt; sauna. Massage. Rec rm. Minibars; microwaves avail. Private patios, balconies. Waterfall in lobby; pond with live ducks. Cr cds: A, C, D, ER, JCB, MC, V.

★★★ **SHERATON GATEWAY.** *Toronto International Airport, Terminal 3 (L5P 1C4). 905/672-7000; fax 905/672-7100; 800/325-3535. www.sheraton.com.* 474 rms, 8 story. S, D $190-$240; each addl $15; suites $420-$800; under 18 free; wkly, wkend rates. Crib free. Pet accepted. Garage parking $9.50; valet $18. TV; cable (premium), VCR avail. Indoor pool; whirlpool. Restaurant 6 am-11 pm. Rm serv 24 hrs. Bar 11-1 am. Convention facilities. Business center. Concierge. Shopping arcade. Barber, beauty shop. Free airport transportation. Exercise equipt; sauna. Massage. Minibars. Modern facility connected by climate-controlled walkway to Terminal 3. Cr cds: A, C, D, DS, ER, JCB, MC, V.

★★★ **SHERATON PARKWAY HOTEL TORONTO NORTH.** *600 Hwy 7 E (L4B 1B2). 905/881-2121; 800/325-3535. www.sheraton.com.* 312 rms, 10 story. S, D $195-$325; under 18 free. Crib avail. TV; cable (premium). Indoor pool; whirlpool. Restaurant 6:30 am-10 pm. Bar to midnight. Ck-out noon, ck-in 4 pm. Meeting rms. Business center. In-rm modem link. Concierge. Exercise equipt. Minibars; many refrigerators in suites. Cr cds: A, C, D, DS, ER, JCB, MC, V.

★★★ **SUTTON PLACE.** *955 Bay St (M5S 2A2). 416/924-9221; fax 416/324-5617; res 800/268-3790. www.suttonplace.com.* 292 rms, 33 story, 62 suites. S, D $320; each addl $20; suites $390-$1,500; under 18 free; wkend rates. Crib free. Garage parking $18, valet $21. TV; cable (premium), VCR avail (movies). Indoor pool; poolside serv. Restaurant (see also ACCENTS). Rm serv 24 hrs. Bar 11-1:30 am; entertainment Thurs-Sat. Ck-out noon. Convention facilities. Business center. Concierge. Gift shop. Barber, beauty shop. Exercise equipt; sauna. Health club privileges. Massage. Minibars. Cr cds: A, C, D, ER, JCB, MC, V.

★★ **TOWN INN.** *620 Church St (M4Y 2G2). 416/964-3311; fax 416/924-9466. www.towninn.com.* 200 kit. units (1-2 bedrm), 26 story. June-Dec: S $95-$125; D $110-$135; each addl $15; under 12 free; monthly rates; lower rates rest of yr. Crib free. Pet accepted. Garage $14. TV; cable (premium). Heated pool. Complimentary continental bkfst. Restaurant 7-10 am. Ck-out 11 am. Meeting rms. Business servs avail. Tennis. Exercise equipt. Health club privileges; saunas. Refrigerators, microwaves. Balconies. Cr cds: A, C, D, ER, MC, V.

★★★ **WESTIN HARBOUR CASTLE.** *1 Harbour Sq (M5J 1A6). 416/869-1600; 800/937-8461. www.westin.com.* 980 rms, 20 story. S, D $250-$375; under 18 free. Crib avail. TV; cable (premium). Indoor pool; whirlpool. Restaurant 6:30 am-10 pm. Bar to midnight. Ck-out noon, ck-in 4 pm. Meeting rms. Business center. In-rm modem link. Concierge. Exercise equipt. Minibars; many refrigerators in suites. Cr cds: A, C, D, DS, ER, JCB, MC, V.

★★★ **WESTIN PRINCE.** *900 York Mills Rd, North York (M3B 3H2). 416/444-2511; fax 416/444-9597; 800/937-8461. www.westin.com.* 381 rms, 22 story. S $210-$245; D $230-$265; each addl $20; suites $340-$1,800; under 18 free; wkend rates. Crib free. TV; cable (premium), VCR avail (movies). Pool; whirlpool, poolside serv. Playground. Restaurant 6:30 am-10 pm. Rm serv 24 hrs. Bar 11:30-2 am; entertainment Mon-Sat. Ck-out 1 pm. Convention facilities. Business center. In-rm modem link. Concierge. Shopping arcade. Barber, beauty shop. Tennis. 18-hole golf privileges. Exercise equipt; sauna. Health club privileges. Game rm. Refrigerators. Balconies. Cr cds: A, C, D, DS, ER, JCB, MC, V.

⬚ 🍴 🥘 🏊 🚶 🦽 🏂 🚶

★★★★ **WINDSOR ARMS HOTEL.** *18 St. Thomas St (M5S 3E7). 416/971-9666; fax 416/921-9121. www.windsorarmshotel.com.* This hotel's century-old building, located in the uptown Yorkville shopping district, houses 28 luxurious suites. Public spaces are modern with a warm, countrylike aura, while rooms are urban sleek with a gray-toned color scheme. Guests can dine at the socially respected Courtyard Cafe, have tea by day and caviar by night in The Tea Room, or a drink at Club 22. 28 suites. Cribs. TV. Pool. Valet. Business center. Spa. Exercise rm. Restaurant. Cr cds: A, DS, MC, V.

🏊 🚶 🦽 🚶

★★★ **WYNDHAM BRISTOL PLACE.** *950 Dixon Rd, Etobicoke (M9W 5N4). 416/675-9444; fax 416/675-4426; 800/996-3426. www.wyndham.com.* 287 rms, 15 story. S, D $214-$350; each addl $10; suites from $625; under 18 free; wkend rates; package plans. Crib free. TV; cable (premium). Indoor/outdoor pool; poolside serv. Restaurant 6:30 am-10 pm (see also ZACHARY'S). Rm serv 24 hrs. Bars 11-2 am; entertainment Mon-Fri. Ck-out 1 pm. Convention facilities. Business center. In-rm modem link. Concierge. Valet parking. Free airport transportation. Exercise equipt; sauna. Minibars; bathrm phone, whirlpool in some suites. Some private patios. Coffee makers in room. Cr cds: A, C, D, DS, ER, JCB, MC, V.

⬚ 🥘 🚶 ✈ 🦽 🦽 SC 🚶

Resort

★★★ **INN AT MANITOU.** *Center Rd, McKellar (P0G 1C0). 705/389-2171. www.manitou-online.com.* 22 rms, 3 story. S, D $250-$400. TV; cable (premium). Restaurant 6:30 am-10 pm. Bar to midnight. Ck-out noon, ck-in 4 pm. Meeting rms. Business servs avail. In-rm modem link. Concierge. Exercise equipt. Golf. Tennis. Spa. Cr cds: A, ER, MC, V.

🚶 🏂 🚶

B&Bs/Small Inns

★★ **GUILD INN.** *201 Guildwood Pkwy, Scarborough (M1E 1T6). 416/261-3331; fax 416/261-5675.* 96 rms, 3-6 story. Apr-Dec: S, D $79; each addl $10; suites $140; under 18 free; AP, MAP avail; wkly rates; lower rates rest of yr. Crib free. TV; cable (premium). Pool. Restaurant (see also GUILD INN). Ck-out noon, ck-in 3 pm. Business servs

avail. Tennis. Balconies. Opened in 1923 as art community. On 90-acres overlooking Lake Ontario. Log cabin (1805) on grounds. Cr cds: A, C, D, DS, ER, MC, V.

⬚ 🚶 🥘 🦽 🦽 SC

★★★ **MILLCROFT.** *55 John St, Alton (L0N 1A0). 519/941-8111; fax 519/941-9192; res 800/383-3976. www.millcroft.com.* 52 rms, 2 story, 20 chalets. S, D $185-$275. Crib free. Heated pool; whirlpool, poolside serv. Complimentary continental bkfst. Restaurant (see also MILLCROFT INN). Bar. Ck-out noon, ck-in 4 pm. Guest lndry. Meeting rm. Business servs avail. Valet serv. Tennis. Golf privileges. X-country ski on site. Exercise equipt; sauna. Volleyball. Game rm. Some private patios. 100 acres on Credit River. Former knitting mill (1881). Cr cds: A, D, ER, MC, V.

⬚ 🚶 🍴 🥘 🦽 🚶 🦽 🦽

All Suite

★★★ **EMBASSY SUITES.** *8500 Warden Ave, Markham (L6G 1A5). 905/470-8500; fax 905/477-8611; 800/362-2779. www.embassysuites.com.* 332 suites, 10 story. S, D $160-$180; each addl $20; wkend rates; under 18 free. Crib free. Valet parking $3. TV; cable (premium). Indoor pool; whirlpool. Complimentary full bkfst. Coffee in rms. Restaurant 6:30 am-midnight. Bar 11-2 am. Ck-out noon. Convention facilities. Business center. Shopping arcade. Barber, beauty shop. Exercise rm; sauna, steam rm. Game rm. Minibars; microwaves avail. Extensive grounds; elaborate landscaping. Elegant atmosphere. Cr cds: A, C, D, ER, MC, V.

⬚ 🥘 🚶 ✈ 🦽 🦽 SC 🚶

Restaurants

★★★ **360.** *301 Front St W (M5V 2T6). 416/362-5411. www.cntower.ca.* Continental menu. Specializes in fresh rack of lamb, prime rib, corn-fed free-range chicken. Own baking. Hrs: 11 am-2:30 pm, 5-10:30 pm; Sun from 10:30 am. Res accepted. Bar. Wine cellar. A la carte entrees: lunch, dinner $19-$38. Sun brunch from $35. Revolving restaurant; view of harbor and city. Cr cds: A, C, D, DS, ER, MC, V.

⬚

★★★ **ACCENTS.** *955 Bay St (M5S 2A2). 416/324-5633. www.tasteoflife.com.* Continental menu. Specializes in market-fresh cuisine. Hrs: 6:30 am-11:30 pm. Res accepted. Bar. Wine cellar. A la carte entrees: bkfst $2.95-$10.50, lunch $11.50-$14.50, dinner $22-$36. Pianist Thurs-Sat. Parking. Continental atmosphere. Cr cds: A, D, ER, MC, V.

⬚ 🦽

★★★ **ACCOLADE.** *225 Front St W (M5V 2X3). 416/597-1400. www.crowneplaza.com.* Continental menu. Specialty: rack of lamb. Own baking. Hrs: 11:45 am-2 pm, 5:45-10 pm; Sat, Sun from 6 pm. Res accepted. Bar to 2 am. Wine list. Lunch $11.95-$21.95, dinner $26-$32. Complete meals: dinner $34.95. Valet parking. Cr cds: A, D, DS, MC, V.

⬚ 🦽

★★ **ARKADIA HOUSE.** *2007 Eglinton Ave E, Scarborough (M1L 2M9). 416/752-5685.* Greek menu. Specialties: roast lamb, souvlaki. Hrs: 11:30 am-3 pm, 4 pm-midnight. Closed Dec 24. Res accepted. Bar. Wine list. A la carte entrees: lunch $6.95-$12.95, dinner $10.95-$19.95. Child's menu. Parking. Garden cafe atmosphere. Cr cds: A, C, D, ER, MC, V.
SC 🖼

★★ **ARLEQUIN.** *134 Avenue Rd (M5R 2H6). 416/928-9521. www.tasteoflife.com.* French, Mediterranean menu. Hrs: 8:30 am-10 pm; Fri, Sat to 11 pm. Closed most major hols. Res accepted. Bar. A la carte entrees: lunch $7.95-$12.95, dinner $12.95-$18.95. Complete meals: dinner (Mon-Wed) $18.95, (Thurs-Sat) $22.95. Small bistro with harlequin motif. Cr cds: A, C, D, DS, ER, MC, V.
D 🖼

★★★ **AUBERGE DU POMMIER.** *4150 Yonge St (M2P 2C6). 416/222-2220. www.torontolife.com.* French-Amer cuisine with North Amer twist. Hrs: 11:30 am-2:30 pm, 5-10:30 pm; Sat from 5 pm. Closed Sun; some hols. Bar. Child's menu. Res required. Cr cds: A, D, MC, V.

★★★ **AVALON.** *270 Adelaide St W (M5H 1X6). 416/979-9918. www.torontolife.com.* Specialties: wood-roasted chicken, yellowfin tuna steak, grilled dry-aged rib steak. Hrs: noon-2:30 pm, 5:30-10 pm; Mon, Tues from 5:30 pm; Fri to 11 pm; Sat 5:30-11 pm. Closed Sun; most major hols. Res accepted. Bar. Wine list. A la carte entrees: lunch $13-$22, dinner $20-$30. Artwork by local artists. Cr cds: A, D, ER, MC, V.

★★ **BANGKOK GARDEN.** *18 Elm St (M5G 1G7). 416/977-6748. www.elmwoodcomplex.com.* Thai menu. Specializes in soup, curry dishes, seafood. Hrs: 11:30 am-2:30 pm, 5-10 pm; Sat, Sun from 5 pm. Res accepted. Bar. A la carte entrees: lunch $8.95-$10.95, dinner $14.95-$19.25. Complete meals: dinner $25.95-$39.95. Buffet (Mon, Fri): lunch $9.95. Child's menu. Thai decor; indoor garden. Cr cds: A, D, ER, MC, V.
D 🖼

★★ **BAROOTES.** *220 King St W (M5H 1K4). 416/979-7717.* International menu. Specialties: fresh stir-fry, Thai satay combination, grilled marinated lamb tenderloin. Hrs: 11:30 am-2:30 pm, 5-10:30 pm. Closed Sun; Jan 1, Dec 25. Res accepted. Bar. A la carte entrees: lunch $8.95-$12.95, dinner $11.50-$24.95. Traditional dining rm. Cr cds: A, D, MC, V.
D 🖼

★★★ **BIAGIO.** *155 King St E (M5C 1G9). 416/366-4040. www.torontolife.com.* Northern Italian cuisine. Specialties: risotto, veal. Hrs: noon-2:30 pm, 6-10 pm; Sat from 6 pm. Closed Sun. Lunch, dinner: $15-$33. Cr cds: D, MC, V.
D 🖼

★★ **BISTRO 990.** *990 Bay St (M5S 2A5). 416/921-9990. www.bistro990.com.* Specializes in lamb, fresh fish. Hrs: noon-10:30 pm; Sat from 5:30 pm. Closed Sun. Res accepted. Bar. A la carte entrees: lunch $13.50-$29, dinner $14-$32. Prix fixe: lunch, dinner $19.90. Outdoor dining. French bistro decor. Cr cds: A, C, D, DS, MC, V.
D 🖼

★★★ **BOBA.** *90 Avenue Rd (M5R 2H2). 416/961-2622. www.torontolife.com.* Contemporary Amer menu. Specializes in vegetarian dishes, desserts. Hrs: 5:30-10 pm. Closed Sun; Jan 1, Dec 25, 26. Res required. Bar. A la carte entrees: dinner $19.50-$29.95. Patio dining. Intimate dining rm; bistro atmosphere. Totally nonsmoking. Cr cds: A, C, D, DS, ER, MC, V.
D

★ **BUMPKINS.** *21 Gloucester St (M4Y 1L8). 416/922-8655.* French, Amer menu. Specialty: shrimp Bumpkins. Hrs: noon-2:30 pm, 5-11 pm; Sat from 5 pm. Closed Sun. A la carte entrees: lunch $3.95-$8.50, dinner $8.75-$20.95. Child's menu. Outdoor dining. Cr cds: A, D, ER, MC, V.
D 🖼

★★★★ **CANOE.** *66 Wellington St W (M5K 1H6). 416/364-0054. www.oliverbonacini.com.* The earthy, minimalist decor of sleek wood panels and muted colors at this modern dining room match its lofty location (54th floor of Toronto Dominion Bank Tower) and lofty crowd. But there's no refuting the excellent menu and impressive view. Inventive, Canadian dishes show a touch of the frontier such as caribou with wild mushroom tortiere and partridge berry jus. Specialties: Québec foie gras, Yukon caribou, Arctic char, sushi. Hrs: 11:30 am-2:30 pm, 5-10:30 pm. Closed Sat, Sun; hols. Res accepted. Bar to 11:30 pm. Wine cellar. Lunch $14-$23, dinner $25-$34. View of harbor and islands. Totally nonsmoking. Cr cds: A, C, D, ER, MC, V.
D

★★ **CARMAN'S CLUB.** *26 Alexander St (M8V 2K8). 416/924-8558. www.toronto.com/carmans.* Specialties: rack of lamb, Dover sole. Own pastries. Hrs: 5:30 pm-midnight. Closed Good Friday, Dec 25. Res accepted. Serv bar. Wine cellar. Complete meals: dinner $31.95-$35.95. Child's menu. In pre-1900 house; fireplaces. Family-owned. Cr cds: A, MC, V.
D 🖼

★★★ **CENTRO GRILL & WINE BAR.** *2472 Yonge St (M4P 2H5). 416/483-2211. www.centrorestaurant.com.* European, Continental menu. Specialty: rack of lamb in honey-mustard crust a la Provencal with rosemary and garlic jus. Own baking. Hrs: 5-11:30 pm. Closed Sun. Res accepted. A la carte entrees: dinner $25.95-$39.95. Bar with pianist (Mon-Wed), 4-piece band (Thurs-Sat). Valet parking. Cr cds: A, D, ER, MC, V.
D 🖼

★★★★ **CHIADO.** *864 College St (M6H 1A3). 416/538-1910. www.torontolife.com.* Guests will feel like they've dined at a small, authentic bistretto after experiencing this restaurant's warm decor, friendly service, and Mediterranean-influenced Portuguese menu. Named after Lisbon's oldest neighborhood, this restaurant is housed in a charming three-story home that is both beautifully sophisticated and comfortably Old World. The seasonal menu offers perfectly grilled fish. The Portuguese wine list is stellar. Portuguese classical cuisine. Hrs: noon-3 pm, 5-11 pm; Sun dinner only. Closed Dec 24-26. Res recommended. Wine cellar. A la carte entrees: lunch $14-$25, dinner $17.75-$30. Child's menu. Oil paintings. Cr cds: A, C, D, DS, ER, MC, V.
🖼

★★★ **CHIARO'S.** *37 King St E (M5C 1E9). 416/863-4126. www.toprestaurants.com/toronto/chiaros.htm.* Continental menu. Specialties: rack of lamb, Dover sole. Hrs: 5-10 pm. Closed Sun. Res accepted. Bar to 1 am. Wine cellar. Dinner $24-$43. Child's menu. Valet parking. Cr cds: A, D, ER, MC, V.

D 🔲

★★ **DAVID DUNCAN HOUSE.** *125 Moatfield Dr, North York (M3B 3L6). 416/391-1424. www.davidduncanhouse.com.* Specializes in steak, seafood, rack of lamb. Hrs: 11:30 am-3 pm, 5-11 pm; Sat, Sun from 5 pm. Res accepted. Bar. Wine list. Lunch $9.95-$14.95, dinner $17.95-$41.95. Valet parking. In restored, Gothic Revival house (1865) with elaborate gingerbread and millwork, antiques, stained-glass skylight. Jacket. Cr cds: A, D, MC, V.

D 🔲

★★★ **THE DOCTOR'S HOUSE.** *21 Nashville Rd, Kleinberg (L0J 1C0). 905/893-1615. www.toronto.com/thedoctorshouse.* Continental menu. Hrs: 11-1 am; Sun brunch 10:30 am-3 pm. Res accepted; required Sun brunch. Bar. Lunch $13-$16.50; dinner $16-$36.50. Sun brunch $29.50. Child's menu. Pianist Fri, Sat. Parking. Outdoor dining. Early Canadian atmosphere; antique cabinets with artifacts. Cr cds: A, MC, V.

D

★★ **DYNASTY CHINESE.** *131 Bloor St W (M5S 1R1). 416/923-3323. www.torontolife.com.* Cantonese menu. Specializes in Peking duck, dim sum. Hrs: 11 am-11 pm; Sat, Sun from 10 am. Res accepted. Wine, beer. Lunch, dinner $10.95-$20.95. Entertainment. Cr cds: A, JCB, MC, V.

D 🔲

★★ **ELLAS.** *702 Pape Ave (M4K 3S7). 416/463-0334. www.ellas.com.* Greek menu. Specializes in lamb, shish kebab, seafood. Own pastries. Hrs: 11-1 am; Sun to 11 pm. Closed Dec 25. Res accepted. Bar. Lunch $7.95-$9.95, dinner $9.95-$24.95. Ancient Athenian decor; sculptures. Family-owned. Cr cds: A, C, D, DS, MC, V.

D **SC** 🔲

★★★★ **THE FIFTH.** *225 Richmond St W (M5V 1W2). 416/979-3000. www.easyandthefifth.com.* This unique, highly coherent concept combines elegant cuisine and a candlelit atmosphere of rich sensory and social delights. It's a hidden gem, through the Easy nightclub and up a freight elevator to the fifth floor, which offers a limited prix fixe, classic French menu with state-of-the-art execution. Service is knowledgeable, friendly, and professional. Hrs: 6-10 pm. Closed Sun-Wed. Res required. Extensive wine list. Dinner prix fixe: $75. Entertainment: pianist, trio. Cr cds: A, D, ER, MC, V.

🔲

★ **GRANO.** *2035 Yonge St (M4S 2A2). 416/440-1986. www.grano.ca.* Italian menu. Specializes in pasta. Hrs: 10 am-11 pm. Closed Sun; major hols. Res accepted. Bar. Lunch $7.95-$13.95, dinner $8.95-$15.95. Outdoor dining. Italian street café ambience. Cr cds: A, D, DS, MC, V.

D 🔲

★★ **GRAZIE.** *2373 Yonge St (M4P 2C8). 416/488-0822. www.grazie.net.* Italian menu. Specializes in pizza, pasta. Hrs: noon-11 pm; Fri, Sat to midnight. Closed some major hols. Res accepted. Bar. A la carte entrees: lunch, dinner $7.50-$14. Child's menu. Bistro atmosphere. Cr cds: A, MC, V.

D 🔲

★ **GUILD INN.** *201 Guildwood Pkwy (M1E 1P6). 416/261-3331.* Continental menu. Specialties: rack of lamb, prime rib. Salad bar. Own baking. Hrs: 7 am-10 pm; Sun brunch 10:30 am-2:30 pm. Res accepted. Bar. Wine list. Bkfst $2.75-$8.50, lunch $6.50-$15.95, dinner $15.90-$29.50. Sun brunch $17.95. Child's menu. Garden setting in former artist's colony. Cr cds: A, MC, V.

D

★ **HAPPY SEVEN.** *358 Spadina Ave (M5T 2G4). 416/971-9820.* Chinese menu. Hrs: 11:30-5 am. Res accepted. Bar to 2 am. Wine, beer. Lunch, dinner $7.95-$8.95. A la carte entrees: lunch $4.75-$6.50, dinner $7.95-$14.99. Street parking. Fish, crab, lobster tanks. Cr cds: MC, V.

D 🔲

★★★★ **HEMISPHERES.** *110 Chestnut St (M5G 1R3). 416/599-8000. www.metropolitan.com.* Located in the Metropolitan Hotel, Hemispheres presents the freshest combinations of culinary styles and ingredients reflecting influences from around the world. The food, wine, and service appeals to a clientele that recognizes the subtleties that make a dining experience special. The secluded Chef's Table room is perfect for small groups wanting an intimate space to combine business or a social gathering with an unforgettable culinary experience. Mediterranean menu. Hrs: 6:30 am-10:30 pm. Closed Sun. Res accepted. Extensive wine list. Lunch $10.50-$23; dinner $12-$48. Child's menu. Cr cds: A, DS, ER, JCB, MC, V.

D

★★ **IL POSTO NUOVO.** *148 Yorkville Ave (M5R 1C2). 416/968-0469.* Northern Italian menu. Specializes in liver and veal chops, pasta with lobster, carpaccio. Hrs: noon-2:30 pm, 6-10:30 pm. Closed Sun; hols. Res accepted. A la carte entrees: $12-$18.50, dinner $14-$33. Outdoor dining. Cr cds: A, D, DS, MC, V.

D

★★ **JACQUES BISTRO DUPARC.** *126-A Cumberland St (M5R 1A6). 416/961-1893.* Specializes in sweet bread, rack of lamb. Hrs: 11:30 am-3 pm, 5-10:30 pm. Closed Sun. Res required. Wine, beer. Lunch $10.95-$18.50; dinner $10.95-$26.95. Entertainment. Cr cds: A, C, D, DS, ER, MC, V.

🔲

★★★ **JOSO'S.** *202 Davenport Rd (M5R 1J2). 416/925-1903.* Mediterranean menu. Specializes in Italian dishes, seafood. Hrs: 11:30 am-2:30 pm, 5:30-11 pm; Sat from 5:30 pm. Closed Sun; some major hols. Res accepted. A la carte entrees: lunch $7-$19, dinner $14-$27. Child's menu. Outdoor dining. Wine cellar. Cr cds: A, D, MC, V.

🔲

★ **KALLY'S.** *430 Nugget Ave (M1S 4A4). 416/293-9292.* Specializes in steak, ribs. Salad bar. Hrs: 11:30 am-10 pm; Sun 4-9 pm. Closed hols; also 1st Mon in Aug. Serv bar. A la carte entrees: lunch $4.45-$14.95, dinner $8.45-$14.95. Child's menu. Parking. Pyramid-shaped skylights. Cr cds: A, D, DS, ER, MC, V.

D SC ◳

★★★ **LA FENICE.** *319 King St W (M5V 1J5). 416/585-2377.* Italian menu. Specializes in fresh seafood, pasta. Hrs: 11:30 am-2:30 pm, 5:30-10:30 pm; Sat from 5:30 pm. Closed Sun; major hols. Res accepted. Bar to 1 am. Wine list. A la carte entrees: lunch $10.50-$24, dinner $16.50-$26. Sleek Milanese-style trattoria. Near theater district. Cr cds: A, D, DS, MC, V.

◳

★★★ **LAI WAH HEEN.** *108 Chestnut St (M5G 1R3). 416/977-9899. www.metropolitan.com/lwh.* Cantonese menu. Hrs: 11:30 am-3 pm, 5:30-10:30 pm. Res accepted. Wine cellar. A la carte entrees: lunch $16-$20, dinner $16-$48. Complete meal: lunch $16-$32, dinner $32-$42. Chinese decor. Cr cds: A, D, DS, ER, JCB, MC, V.

D

★ **LE PAPILLION.** *16 Church St (M5E 1M1). 416/363-0838.* French menu. Specialties: crepes Bretonne, French onion soup. Hrs: noon-2:30 pm, 5-10 pm; Fri, Sat to midnight; Sun brunch to 3 pm. Closed Mon. Res accepted. Bar. Lunch, dinner $7.75-$18.95. Sun brunch $18. Child's menu. French country kitchen decor. Braille menu. Cr cds: A, D, DS, ER, MC, V.

D ◳

★ **LE PARADIS.** *166 Bedford Rd (M5R 2K9). 416/921-0995. www.leparadis.com.* Hrs: noon-11 pm; Sat 5:30-11 pm; Mon, Sun 5:30-10 pm. Closed Jan 1, Dec 24, 25. Res required Fri, Sat (dinner). Bar. A la carte entrees: lunch $3.95-$14.95, dinner $8.50-$14.95. Specialties: steak frites, moules a la mariniere, cassoulet. Street parking. Outdoor dining. Dinner menu changes daily. Cr cds: A, D, MC, V.

◳

★ **MARCHE BCE PLACE.** *42 Yonge St (M5E 1T1). 416/366-8986.* Specializes in Caesar salad, crepes, waffles. Hrs: 7:30-2 am; Fri, Sat to 4 am. Res accepted. Wine list. Lunch $10-$15; dinner $15-$20. Child's menu. Entertainment: Latin band, clowns; Tues, Wed, Sun. Cr cds: A, C, D, DS, ER, MC, V.

D ◳

★ **MATIGNON.** *51 Ste Nicholas St (M4Y 1W6). 416/921-9226.* Specialties: rack of lamb, duck breast, la darne de saumon aux câpres. Hrs: 11:30 am-2:30 pm, 5-10 pm. Res accepted. Bar. A la carte entrees: lunch $8.25-$15.95, dinner $13.50-$17.95. French atmosphere. Cr cds: A, MC, V.

◳

★★ **MERCER STREET GRILL.** *36 Mercer St (M5V 1H3). 416/599-3399. www.mercerstreetgrill.com.* Specializes in lentil-crusted sea bass with jasmine rice papaya mint sambal and light green curry sauce, hand-rolled Belgian chocolate sushi. Hrs: 5-10 pm; Fri, Sat to 11 pm. Res accepted. Wine list. Dinner $24-$30. Entertainment. Exotic Japanese Garden. Cr cds: A, D, MC, V.

D ◳

★★ **MILLCROFT INN.** *55 John St, Alton (L0N 1A0). 519/941-8111. www.millcroft.com.* Continental menu. Specializes in game meat. Hrs: 7:30-10 am, noon-2 pm, 6-9 pm; Sat, Sun 8-10:30 am; Sun brunch noon-2:30 pm. Res accepted. Bar from 11 am. A la carte entrees: bkfst $6.95-$9.95, lunch $16.25-$18.50, dinner $23.50-$32. Sun brunch $27.95. Valet parking. Restored knitting mill (1881) on the Credit River. Cr cds: A, D, DS, ER, MC, V.

D

★ **MILLER'S COUNTRY FARE.** *5140 Dundas St W, Etobicoke (M9A 1C2). 416/234-5050.* Specializes in ribs, chicken, beef stew. Hrs: 11 am-10 pm; Fri to 11 pm; Sat 10 am-11 pm; Sat, Sun brunch to 2:30 pm. Closed Dec 25. Bar from 11 am. Lunch, dinner $6.25-$13.95. Sat, Sun brunch $3.95-$10.95. Child's menu. Parking. Country decor. Cr cds: A, D, ER, MC, V.

D ◳

★★★ **MISTURA.** *265 Davenport Rd (M5R 1J9). 416/515-0009.* Hrs: 5-11 pm. Closed Sun; major hols; also Victoria Day. Res accepted. Italian menu. A la carte entrees: dinner $18.50-$21.75. Specialties: beet risotto, veal chops, turkey breast. Parking. Cr cds: A, C, D, DS, ER, MC, V.

D ◳

★ **MOVENPICK OF SWITZERLAND.** *165 York St (M5H 3R8). 416/366-5234. www.movenpickcanada.com.* Continental menu. Specializes in Swiss dishes. Salad bar. Hrs: 7:30 am-midnight; Fri to 1 am; Sat 9-1 am; Sun 9 am-midnight. Res accepted. Bar. Bkfst $2.50-$13.80, lunch $6.50-$18.50, dinner $9.25-$22.50. Buffet: dinner (exc Sun) $16.80-$28.50. Sun brunch $27.80. Child's menu. Parking. Outdoor dining. European decor. Cr cds: A, D, DS, MC, V.

D ◳

★★★★ **NORTH 44 DEGREES.** *2537 Yonge St (M4P 2H9). 416/487-4897.* Chef Mark McEwan offers world-inspired, Continental cuisine in this chic, modern dining room. Although there are hints of exclusivity in the air, service is humble and the room's wood floors, soft lighting, and frosted-glass "compass" centerpiece create a sexy, comfortable environment. Creative presentations include squab "two ways": a roasted breast with preserved lemon, sea salt, and honey, and a foie gras-stuffed leg. Specializes in mixed appetizer platters, angel hair pasta, rack of lamb. Hrs: 5-11 pm. Closed Sun; hols. Res accepted. Bar. A la carte entrees: dinner $14.95-$39.95. Entertainment Wed-Sat. Valet parking. Cr cds: A, D, MC, V.

D ◳

★★ **OLD MILL.** *21 Old Mill Rd (M8X 1G5). 416/236-2641. www.oldmilltoronto.com.* Continental menu. Specializes in roast beef, prime rib. Own baking. Hrs: noon-2:30 pm, 3-5 pm, 5:30-10 pm; Sat 5:30-11 pm; Sun 5:30-9 pm; Sun brunch 10:30 am-2:30 pm. Closed Dec 24. Res accepted. Bar. A la carte entrees: lunch $10.95-$16.95, dinner $25.95-$34. Buffet: lunch (Mon-Fri) $19.95, dinner (Sun) $25.95. Sun brunch $23.95. Cover charge (Fri, Sat from 8 pm) $3.50. Child's menu. Entertainment exc Sun. Parking. Old English castle motif. Jacket (dinner). Cr cds: A, C, DS, ER, MC, V.

D ◳

★ **OLD SPAGHETTI FACTORY.** *54 The Esplanade (M5E 1A6).* 416/864-9761. *www.oldspaghettifactory.net.* Italian menu. Specialties: fettucine with seafood, chicken parmigiana. Hrs: 11:30 am-11 pm; Fri, Sat to midnight. Closed Dec 24. Bar. Lunch $5.99-$9.49, dinner $7.99-$14.50. Child's menu. Outdoor dining. Bright decor; carousel effect. Family-owned. Cr cds: A, C, D, DS, ER, MC, V.

⊡ ⊡

★★★ **OPUS.** *37 Prince Arthur Ave (M5R 1B2).* 416/921-3105. *www.opusrestaurant.com.* Continental menu. Own baking. Hrs: 5:30-11:30 pm. Res accepted. Bar to 2 am. Wine list of 850 vintages. Dinner $24-$32. Back patio dining. Cr cds: A, D, ER, MC, V.

⊡

★★★ **ORO.** *45 Elm St (M5G 1H1).* 416/597-0155. *www.ororestaurant.com.* Specializes in sea bass, rack of lamb. Hrs: noon-2 pm, 5-10 pm; Sat 5:30-10 pm. Closed Sun, hols. Res accepted. Beer, wine. Lunch $14-$27; dinner $16-$36. Entertainment. Cr cds: A, D, ER, MC, V.

⊡

★★★ **PANGAEA.** *1221 Bay St (M5R 3P5).* 416/920-2323. *www.pangaearestaurant.com.* Continental menu. Specialties: calamari, wild mushroom risotto, rack of lamb. Hrs: 11:30 am-11:30 pm. Closed Sun; hols. Res accepted. Bar. Wine list. A la carte entrees: lunch $12-$19, dinner $18-$29. Street parking. Skylight ceiling. Cr cds: A, D, MC, V.

⊡ ⊡

★★ **PASTIS.** *1158 Yonge St (M4W 2L9).* 416/928-2212. French cuisine. Hours: 5:30-11 pm. Closed Sun, Mon. Dinner: $18-$35. Res accepted. Cr cds: D, MC, V.

⊡ ⊡

★★ **PIER 4 STOREHOUSE.** *245 Queen's Quay W (M5J 2K9).* 416/203-1440. Specialties: pepper steak Peru, red snapper. Hrs: noon-2:30 pm; 4:30 pm-midnight; Sun 11:30-12:30 am. Closed Jan 1, Dec 25. Res accepted. Bar. Lunch $9.50-$14.95, dinner $16.50-$35.95. Child's menu. Patio dining. Located at water end of a quay on Toronto Bay. Cr cds: A, D, DS, MC, V.

⊡ ⊡

★★ **PREGO.** *15474 Yonge St, Aurora (L4G 1P2).* 905/727-5100. Italian menu. Specializes in baked rack of lamb, pasta. Hrs: 11:30 am-2:30 pm, 5:30-10:30 pm; Sat from 5:30 pm; Sun 5-9:30 pm. Closed Mon; Jan 1, Good Friday, Dec 25, 26. Res accepted. Bar. A la carte entrees: lunch $7.50-$11.95, dinner $9.50-$23.50. Parking. Casual atmosphere. Cr cds: A, ER, MC, V.

⊡ ⊡

★★★ **PRONTO.** *692 Mt Pleasant Rd (M4S 2N3).* 416/486-1111. Italian, continental menu. Hrs: 5-11:30 pm; Sun to 10:30 pm. Closed Jan 1, Dec 24, 25. Res accepted. Bar. A la carte entrees: dinner $12.95-$27.95. Valet parking. Elegant modern decor; local artwork. Cr cds: A, D, DS, MC, V.

⊡

★★★ **PROVENCE.** *12 Amelia St (M4X 1A1).* 416/924-9901. *www.provencerestaurant.com.* French menu. Specialties: rack of lamb, duck confit, steak. Hrs: noon-1 am; Sat, Sun brunch noon-2 pm. Closed Dec 25. Res accepted. Bar. Lunch, dinner $9.95-$32. Sat, Sun brunch $12.95. French country cottage decor; original artwork. Cr cds: A, ER, MC, V.

⊡ ⊡

★ **QUARTIER.** *2112 Yonge St (M4S 2A5).* 416/545-0505. Hrs: 11 am-2:30 pm, 5-10:30 pm; early-bird dinner 5-6 pm. Closed most major hols. Res required Sat (dinner). French menu. Bar. A la carte entrees: lunch $7.50-$12, dinner $13-$19. Specializes in fresh fish, lamb. Street parking. Outdoor dining. Cr cds: A, C, D, DS, ER, MC, V.

⊡

★ **RIVOLI CAFE.** *332 Queen St W (M5V 2A2).* 416/596-1908. Asian, Caribbean menu. Specialties: Sri Malay Bombay, Laotian spring rolls. Hrs: 11:30-2 am. Bar. A la carte entrees: lunch $6.50-$8.75, dinner $8.75-$14.95. Patio dining. Adj club offers comedy/variety shows evenings. Totally nonsmoking. Cr cds: A, MC, V.

⊡ ⊡

★★ **RODNEY'S OYSTER HOUSE.** *209 Adelaide St E (M5A 1M8).* 416/363-8105. *www.tasteoflife.com.* Specializes in oysters, mollusks. Hrs: 11:30-1 am. Closed Sun. Res required. Wine, beer. Lunch, dinner $6.50-$30. Entertainment. Cr cds: A, C, D, DS, ER, MC, V.

⊡

★ **THE ROSEDALE DINER.** *1164 Yonge St (M4W 2L9).* 416/923-3122. *www.zeygezunt.com.* Hrs: 11:30 am-midnight; Sat 11-1 am; Sun 11 am-11 pm; Sat, Sun brunch 11 am-3:30 pm. Closed Easter, Dec 25. Res accepted. Eclectic menu. Bar. A la carte entrees: lunch $9.50-$15, dinner $10-$28. Sat, Sun brunch $6.95-$15. Child's menu. Specialties: herb-crusted rack of lamb, fresh saffron spaghettini, slow-roasted chicken Dijonaise. Street parking. Outdoor dining. 1940s decor and music. Cr cds: A, D, DS, MC, V.

⊡

★★ **ROSEWATER SUPPER CLUB.** *19 Toronto St (M5C 2R1).* 416/214-5888. *www.libertygroup.com.* Continental menu. Own baking. Hrs: noon-2:30 pm, 5:30-11 pm; Sat from 5:30 pm. Closed Sun; major hols; also July 1, Dec 26. Res accepted. Bar 11:30-2 am. Wine cellar. A la carte entrees: lunch $9.95-$15.95, dinner $19-$32. Pianist. Early 20th-century atmosphere; elaborate Victorian crown moldings and cathedral-style windows. Totally nonsmoking. Cr cds: A, D, DS, MC, V.

⊡

★★ **SARKIS.** *67 Richmond St E (M5C 1N9).* 416/214-1337. Hrs: 5:30-10:30 pm; Fri, Sat to 11:30 pm. Closed Sun, hols. Res accepted. Wine list. Dinner $15-$25. Entertainment. Cr cds: A, D, ER, MC, V.

⊡

★★ **SASSAFRAZ.** *100 Cumberland St (M5R 1A6). 416/964-2222. www.toronto.com/sassafraz.* French menu. Specialty: Angus strip sirloin. Hrs: 11:30-2 am. Res accepted. Wine, beer. Lunch $11-$20; dinner $25-$35 Cr cds: A, ER, MC, V.

D ⊟

★★★★ **SCARAMOUCHE.** *1 Benvenuto Pl (M4V 2L1). 416/961-8011. www.toronto.com.* This restaurant and pasta bar has been attracting well-to-do regulars to its Benvenuto-location for years. What draws them? It could be the sparkling view of the Toronto skyline, one of the city's best wine lists, the superb French-influenced cuisine, or simply the comfortable chairs. Most likely, it's all of these things combined with a gentle atmosphere and divine creme brulee. Continental, French menu. Specialties: grilled Atlantic salmon, roasted rack of lamb. Own baking. Hrs: 5:30-10 pm; Sat to 11 pm. Closed Sun; hols. Res accepted. Bar to midnight. A la carte entrees: dinner $22.75-$36.75. Pasta bar $13.75-$22.75. Free valet parking. Cr cds: A, D, DS, MC, V.

D ⊟

★★ **SENATOR.** *249 Victoria St (M5B 1T8). 416/364-7517. www.toronto.com/senator.* Specializes in steak, seafood. Hrs: 11:30 am-2:30 pm, 5 pm-midnight. Closed Mon; some major hols. Res accepted. Bar. A la carte entrees: lunch $13.95-$19.95, dinner $20.95-$36.95. Parking. 1920s decor; in heart of theatre district. Cr cds: A, D, MC, V.

D ⊟

★★★ **SPLENDIDO.** *88 Harbord St (M5S 1G5). 416/929-7788.* Continental menu. Specialties: roast rack of veal, roast jumbo tiger shrimp Hrs: 5-11 pm. Closed Sun. Res accepted. Bar. Dinner $16.95-$35.95. Valet parking. Fashionable trattoria with inviting atmosphere. Cr cds: A, ER, MC, V.

D ⊟

★ **SPRING ROLL ON YONGE.** *693 Yonge St (M4Y 2B3). 416/972-7655.* Specializes in seafood. Hrs: 11 am-11 pm; Fri, Sat to midnight; Sun noon-11 pm. Res accepted. Wine, beer. Lunch $6.95-$8.95; dinner $6.95-$13.95. Entertainment. Cr cds: MC, V.

D ⊟

★ **SUSHI BISTRO.** *204 Queen St W (M5V 1Z2). 416/971-5315.* Japanese menu. Specialties: shrimp and mushrooms, sushi rolls, sashimi. Hrs: noon-2:45 pm, 5-10 pm; Fri, Sat noon-midnight. Closed Sun; major hols. Res accepted. Bar. A la carte entrees: lunch $7.25-$11, dinner $8.50-$18. Child's menu. Traditional Japanese food in modern setting. Cr cds: A, D, DS, MC, V.

D

★★ **TAKE SUSHI.** *22 Front St W (M5J 1N7). 416/862-1891.* Hrs: 11:45 am-2:30 pm, 5:30-10:30 pm; Sat 5:30-10:30 pm. Closed Sun; also major hols. Res accepted. Japanese menu. A la carte entrees: lunch, dinner $11-$29. Complete meal: lunch $9.50-$45, dinner $22-$30. Specialty: lobster sushi. Parking. Cr cds: A, D, MC, V.

D SC ⊟

★ **THAI FLAVOUR.** *1554 Avenue Rd (M5M 3X5). 416/782-3288.* Thai menu. Specialties: cashew nut chicken, pad Thai, basil shrimp. Hrs: 11 am-3 pm, 5-11 pm; Sun 5-10 pm. Closed Jan 1, Dec 25. Res accepted. Serv bar. A la carte entrees: lunch, dinner $7.45-$9.50. Cr cds: A, D, MC, V.

⊟

★ **TIGER LILY'S NOODLE HOUSE.** *257 Queen St W (M5V 1Z4). 416/977-5499.* Pan-Asian menu. Specializes in home-style egg roll. Hrs: 11:30 am-9 pm; Wed to 10 pm; Thurs-Sat to 11 pm. Closed most major hols. A la carte entrees: lunch, dinner $7.95-$12.95. Totally nonsmoking. Cr cds: A, MC, V.

D

★ **TOMMY COOKS.** *1911 Eglinton Ave E, Scarborough (M1L 2L6). 416/759-4448.* Specializes in steak, seafood. Salad bar. Hrs: 11 am-midnight; Sat from 4 pm; Sun 4-10 pm; Sun brunch 11 am-2:30 pm. Res accepted. Bar to 1 am. Lunch $7.95-$12.95, dinner $14.95-$29.95. Sun brunch $12.95. Child's menu. Parking. Mediterranean decor. Cr cds: A, D, ER, MC, V.

D ⊟

★ **TRAPPER'S.** *3479 Yonge St, North York (M4N 2N3). 416/482-6211.* Continental menu. Specializes in fresh fish, steak, pasta. Hrs: 11:30 am-2:30 pm, 5-10:30 pm; Sat from 5 pm; Sun 5-9:30 pm. Closed Dec 25. Res accepted. Bar. A la carte entrees: lunch $8.50-$11.50, dinner $13.95-$25.95. Child's menu. Casual dining. Cr cds: A, D, DS, MC, V.

D ⊟

★★★★ **TRUFFLES.** *21 Avenue Rd (M5R 2G1). 416/964-0411. www.fourseasons.com.* Housed in the Four Seasons Hotel, this dining room has received nationwide rave reviews. After walking past the entrance's boar sculptures, an elegant, well-spaced room awaits complete with vaulted ceilings and French garden murals. The menu, blending flavors of Provence with local ingredients, presents twists on the traditional, including a seafood and pearl pasta paella in a tomato-fennel broth. French cuisine. Specialties: pan-seared fillet of beef, foie gras, spaghettini with Périgord black gold. Hrs: 6-11 pm. Res required. Bar. A la carte entrees: $28-$40. Prix fixe: 5-course $62, 3-course $49. Valet. Cr cds: A, D, DS, MC, V.

D

★★ **VANIPHA LANNA.** *471 Eglinton Ave W (M5N 1A7). 416/484-0895.* Thai menu. Specializes in Northern Thai dishes. Hrs: noon-11 pm; Sat to midnight. Closed Sun; most major hols. Res accepted Fri, Sat. A la carte entrees: lunch $6.25-$9.95; dinner $8.25-$12.50. Thai decor. Totally nonsmoking. Cr cds: A, MC, V.

D

★★ **VILLA BORGHESE.** *2995 Bloor St W, Etobicoke (M8X 1C1). 416/239-1286.* Italian menu. Specializes in fresh fish, veal, pepper steak. Own pasta. Hrs: noon-midnight; Sat, Sun from 4 pm. Closed Mon; Easter, Dec 25. Res accepted. Bar. Lunch $8-$15, dinner $11.95-$23.95. Entertainment. Italian villa decor. Cr cds: A, D, DS, ER, MC, V.

D ⊟

★ **YAMASE.** *317 King St W (M5V 1J5). 416/598-1562.* Japanese menu. Specializes in sushi, teriyaki, tempura dishes. Hrs: noon-2:30 pm, 5:30-11 pm; Sat from 5 pm. Closed Sun; Jan 1. Res accepted. Bar. A la carte entrees: lunch $5.50-$14.50, dinner $7.50-$24.50. Complete meals: dinner $15-$50. Intimate atmosphere; Japanese decor, artwork. Cr cds: A, D, MC, V.

D ⟶

★★ **ZACHARY'S.** *950 Dixon Rd (M9W 5N4). 416/675-9444.* Continental menu. Specialty: rack of lamb. Own baking. Hrs: noon-2:30 pm, 6-10 pm; Sat from 6 pm; Sun brunch 11 am-2:30 pm. Res accepted. Bar 11-1 am. Wine list. A la carte entrees: lunch $12.50-$16.95, dinner $22.50-$31.95. Complete meals: lunch $19.75, dinner $29.50. Sun brunch $23.95. Valet parking. Modern decor with Chinese prints. Cr cds: A, D, DS, MC, V.

D SC ⟶

Unrated Dining Spots

PATACHOU. *1095 Yonge St (M4W 2L7). 416/927-1105.* French menu. Specialties: café au lait, croque Monsieur. Own baking. Hrs: 8:30 am-6 pm; Sun from 10:30 am. Closed some hols. Pastries, croissants, desserts, sandwiches, quiche $5-$10. Patio dining. Cr cds: V.

D

SHOPSY'S DELICATESSEN. *33 Yonge St (M5E 1G4). 416/365-3333.* Delicatessen, all-day bkfst menu. Hrs: 7-1 am. Bar 11-1 am. A la carte entrees: bkfst $2.10-$6.75, lunch $3.95-$8.95, dinner $3.75-$11.75. Outdoor dining. Cr cds: A, D, V.

D ⟶

UNITED BAKER'S DAIRY RESTAURANT. *506 Lawrence Ave W (M6A 1A1). 416/789-0519.* Jewish menu. Specializes in cheese blintzes, soups, gefilte fish. Hrs: 7 am-10 pm; Fri to 8 pm; Sat, Sun to 9 pm. A la carte entrees: lunch $5-$10, dinner to $12. Parking. Bakery on premises. Family-owned. Cr cds: MC, V.

Windsor

Pop 192,083 **Elev** 622 ft (190 m) **Area code** 519
Information Convention & Visitors Bureau of Windsor, Essex County and Pelee Island, 333 Riverside Dr W, City Centre Mall, Suite 103, N9A 5K4; 519/255-6530 or 800/265-3633
Web www.city.windsor.on.ca/cvb

Windsor is located at the tip of a peninsula and is linked to Detroit, Michigan by the Ambassador Bridge and the Detroit-Windsor Tunnel. Because of its proximity to the United States, it is often referred to as the Ambassador City. Windsor is also known as the City of Roses for its many beautiful parks. The Sunken Gardens and Rose Gardens in Jackson Park boast more than 500 varieties of roses. Coventry Garden & Peace Fountain has the only fountain floating in international waters. Whatever the nickname, for many people traveling from the United States, Canada begins here.

Windsor is a cosmopolitan city, designated a bilingual-bicultural area because of the French influence so much in evidence. Windsor also has a symphony orchestra, theaters, a light opera company, art galleries, nightlife, and all the amenities of a large city. Within its boundaries are 900 acres (364 hectares) of parks giving the city the charm of a rural environment. With easy access to lakes Erie and St. Clair and such pleasure troves as Pelee Island, it is also the major city in Canada's "Sun Parlor," Essex County. Mild climate and beautiful beaches make Windsor an excellent place to visit all year.

What to See and Do

Art Gallery of Windsor. Collections consist of Canadian art, incl Inuit prints and carvings, with emphasis on Canadian artists from the late 18th century to the present. Children's gallery; gift shop. (Tues-Sun; closed hols) 3100 Howard Ave. Phone 519/969-4494. **FREE**

Casino Windsor. The casino overlooks the Detroit skyline and is easily accessible from a number of hotels. (Daily) Riverside Dr in City Centre. Phone 800/991-7777.

Colasanti Farms, Ltd. Over 25 greenhouses with acres of exotic plants; large collection of cacti; farm animals, parrots, and tropical birds; crafts; mini-putt; restaurant. (Daily; closed Jan 1, Dec 25) 28 mi (45 km) SE, on Hwy 3 near Ruthven. Phone 519/322-2301. **FREE**

✪ **Coventry Gardens and Peace Fountain.** Riverfront park and floral gardens with 75-ft-high (23-m) floating fountain; a myriad of 3-D water displays with spectacular night illumination (May-Sept, daily). Concessions. (Daily) Riverside Dr E and Pillette Rd. Phone 519/253-2300. **FREE**

Fort Malden National Historic Park. Ten-acre (four-hectare) park with remains of fortification, original 1838 barracks, and 1851 pensioner's cottage; visitor and interpretation centers with exhibits. (Daily) Contact PO Box 38, 100 Laird Ave, N9V 2Z2. 18 mi (29 km) S via City Rd 20, in Amherstburg. Phone 519/736-5416. ¢¢

Heritage Village. Historical artifacts and structures on 54 acres (22 hectares). Log cabins (1826 and 1835), railway station (1854), house (1869), church (1885), schoolhouse (1907), barber shop (ca 1920), general store (1847); transportation museum. Special events. Picnic facilities. 20 mi (32 km) SE via ON 3, then 5 mi (8 km) S of Essex on County Rd 23. Phone 519/776-6909. ¢¢

Jack Miner Bird Sanctuary. Canada geese and other migratory waterfowl; ponds; picnicking; museum. Canada geese "air shows" during peak season (Mar and late Oct-Nov; daily). (Mon-Sat) 27 mi (44 km) SE via ON 3 and 29S, 2 mi (3 km) N of Kingsville. Phone 519/733-4034. **FREE**

John Freeman Walls Historic Site & Underground Railroad Museum. John Freeman Walls, a fugitive slave from North Carolina, built this log cabin in 1846. It subsequently served as a terminal of the Underground Railroad and the first meeting place of the Puce Baptist Church. It has remained in the possession of Walls's descendants. (May-Oct, by appt only) At Puce in Maidstone Township; Hwy 401 E from Windsor to Puce Rd exit N. Phone 519/258-6253.

North American Black Historical Museum. Chronicles achievements of black North Americans, many of whom fled the US for freedom in Canada. Permanent exhibits on Underground Railroad; artifacts, archives, genealogical library. (Apr-Nov, Wed-Fri, also Sat and Sun afternoons) 18 mi (29 km) S on City Rd 20, exit Richmond St E, at 227 King St in Amherstburg. Phone 519/736-5433. ¢¢

Park House Museum. Solid log, clapboard-sided house (ca 1795), considered to be oldest house in area. Built in Detroit, moved here in 1799. Restored and furnished as in the 1850s. Demonstrations of tinsmithing; pieces for sale. (June-Aug, daily; rest of yr, Tues-Fri and Sun) 219 Dalhousie St, 18 mi (29 km) S via City Rd 20, on the King's Naval Yard, near Fort Malden in Amherstburg. Phone 519/736-2511. ¢

Point Pelee National Park. The park is a six-sq-mi (16-sq-km) tip of the Point Pelee peninsula. Combination dry land and marshland, the park also has a deciduous forest and is situated on two major bird migration flyways. More than 350 species have been sighted in the park. A boardwalk winds through the 2,500 acres (1,011 hectares) of marshland. Fishing, swimming, canoeing; picnicking, trails, and interpretive center, biking (rentals), transit ride (free). (Daily) 30 mi (48 km) SE via ON 3, near Leamington. Contact Chief of Visitor Services, Rural Rte 1, Leamington, N8H 3V4. Phone 519/322-2365. Entrance fee ¢¢¢

University of Windsor. 16,000 students. On campus is Essex Hall Theatre, featuring seven productions/season (Sept-Mar, fee; box office phone 519/253-4565). 401 Sunset Ave. Phone 519/253-4232.

Willistead Manor. (1906) Restored English Tudor mansion built for Edward Chandler Walker, son of famous distiller Hiram Walker, on 15 acres (six hectares) of wooded parkland; elegant interiors with hand-carved woodwork; furnished in turn-of-the-century style. (July-Aug, Sun and Wed; Sept-June, first and third Sun of each month) 1899 Niagara St, at Kildare Rd. Phone 519/253-2365. ¢¢

Windsor's Community Museum. Exhibits and collections interpret the history of Windsor and southwestern Ontario. Located in the historic Francois Baby House. (Tues-Sat, also Sun afternoons; closed hols) 254 Pitt St W. Phone 519/253-1812. **FREE**

Wreck Exploration Tours. Exploration of a 130-yr-old wreck site. Shoreline cruise; artifact orientation. (May-Oct, res required) 303 Concession 5, Leamington, ON N8H 3V5. Phone 519/326-1566 or 888/229-7325.

Special Events

International Freedom Festival. Two-wk joint celebration by Detroit and Windsor with many events, culminating in fireworks display over the river. Phone 519/252-7264. Late June-1st wk July.

Leamington Tomato Festival. Leamington. Phone 519/326-2878. Mid-Aug.

Motels/Motor Lodges

★★ **BEST WESTERN CONTINENTAL INN.** *3345 Huron Church Rd (N9E 4H5). 519/966-5541; fax 519/972-3384; 800/528-1234. www.bestwestern.com.* 71 rms, 2 story. S $66-$76; D $70-$80; each addl $6-$10; under 12 free. TV; cable (premium), VCR avail. Heated pool. Restaurant 7 am-10 pm. Rm serv. Ck-out 11 am. Meeting rms. Cr cds: A, D, DS, MC, V.
⊠ ⊠ 🐾 SC

★★ **BEST WESTERN WHEELS INN.** *615 Richmond St, Chatham (N7M 1R2). 519/351-1100; fax 519/436-5541; 800/528-1234. www.wheelsinn.com.* 350 rms, 2-10 story. S, D $102.88-$154.88; each addl $5; suites $188.88-$208.88; under 18 free; lower rates mid-wk. Crib free. TV; cable. 2 pools, 1 indoor/outdoor; whirlpools, water slides. Restaurant 7-1 am. Rm serv 7-11 am, 5 pm-midnight. Bar noon-1 am; entertainment exc Sun. Ck-out 11:30 am. Convention facilities. Business center. Gift shop. Miniature golf. Exercise rm; sauna, steam rm. Bowling. Game rm. Rec rm. Some balconies. Resort atmosphere; more than 7 acres of indoor facilities. Atrium. Cr cds: A, C, D, DS, ER, JCB, MC, V.
D ⊠ 🏋 ⊠ 🐾 SC 🏋

★★ **COMFORT INN.** *1100 Richmond St, Chatham (N7M 5J5). 519/352-5500; fax 519/352-2520; 800/228-5150. www.comfortinn.com.* 81 rms, 2 story. May-Sept: S $57-$95; D $65-$105; each addl $4; under 19 free; wkend rates; lower rates rest of yr. Crib free. Pet accepted. TV; cable. Complimentary coffee in lobby. Restaurant adj 9 am-10 pm. Ck-out 11 am. Cr cds: A, C, D, DS, ER, JCB, MC, V.
D 🐾 ⊠ 🐾 SC

★★ **MARQUIS PLAZA.** *2530 Ouellette Ave (N8X 1L7). 519/966-1860; fax 519/966-6619. www.royalmarquis.com.* 97 rms, 2 story. S $48-$150; D $60; each addl $5; suites $90-$150. Crib $5. Pet accepted, some restrictions; $10. TV; cable (premium), VCR avail. Ck-out noon. Meeting rms. Cr cds: A, D, ER, MC, V.
D 🐾 ⊠ 🐾 SC

★★★ **ROYAL MARQUIS.** *590 Grand Marais E (N8X 3H4). 519/966-1900; fax 519/966-4689; toll-free 800/265-5032. www.royalmarquis.com.* 99 rms, 5 story, 14 suites. S $70; D $80; each addl $5; suites $90-$175; under 12 free; wkend rates; higher rates prom. Crib $5. Pet accepted, some restrictions; $10. TV; cable (premium), VCR avail. Indoor pool; whirlpool. Supervised children's activities; ages 5-10. Restaurant 6:30 am-10 pm. Rm serv. Bar; entertainment Thurs-Sun. Ck-out noon. Meeting rms. Valet serv. Concierge. Barber, beauty shop. X-country ski 5 mi. Exercise equipt; sauna. Luxurious furnishings, atmosphere. Cr cds: A, D, ER, MC, V.
D 🐾 ⊠ ⊠ 🏋 ⊠ 🐾

Hotels

★★★ **HILTON WINDSOR.** *277 Riverside Dr W (N9A 5K4).* *519/973-5555; 800/445-8667. www.hilton.com.* 305 rms, 25 story. S, D $275-$350; under 18 free. Crib avail. TV; cable (premium). Indoor pool; whirlpool. Restaurant 6:30 am-10 pm. Bar to midnight. Ck-out noon. Meeting rms. Business center. In-rm modem link. Concierge. Exercise equipt. Minibars; many refrigerators in suites. Cr cds: A, D, DS, ER, MC, V.

★★★ **RADISSON.** *333 Riverside Dr W (N9A 5K4).* *519/977-9777; fax 519/977-1411; res 800/333-3333.* *www.radisson.com.* 207 rms, 19 story. S, D $95; under 12 free. Crib free. Pet accepted, some restrictions. Garage avail. TV; cable (premium). Indoor pool; whirlpool. Complimentary full bkfst. Restaurant nearby. Ck-out noon. Meeting rms. In-rm modem link. Exercise equipt; saunas. Minibars. Cr cds: A, D, DS, ER, MC, V.

Restaurants

★★ **CHATHAM STREET GRILL.** *149 Chatham St W (N9A 5M7).* *519/256-2555.* Specializes in fresh seafood, certified Angus beef. Hrs: 11:30 am-midnight; Sat from noon; Sun 5-11 pm. Closed major hols; Good Friday. Res accepted. Bar. Lunch $5.95-$10, dinner $14.95-$24.95. Cr cds: A, C, D, ER, MC, V.

★★ **COOK SHOP.** *683 Ouellette Ave (N9A 4J4).* *519/254-3377.* Italian, continental menu. Specializes in pasta, steak, rack of lamb. Hrs: 5-10 pm; Fri, Sat to midnight. Closed Mon; Dec 24, 25; also Aug. Res required. Serv bar. Dinner $7.65-$16.85. Parking. Cr cds: A, MC, V.

★★ **PASTA SHOP.** *683 Ouellette Ave (N9A 4J4).* *519/254-1300.* Italian, continental menu. Specialties: steak Diane, veal scalloppini. Hrs: 5-10 pm; Fri, Sat to midnight. Closed Mon; Dec 24, 25; also Aug. Res required. Serv bar. Dinner $11.50-$16.85. Parking. Open kitchen; intimate dining. Cr cds: A, MC, V.

★★ **TOP HAT SUPPER CLUB.** *73 University Ave E (N9A 2Y6).* *519/253-4644.* Specializes in steak, seafood, baby-back ribs. Hrs: 11 am-midnight; Fri, Sat to 2 am. Res accepted. Bar. Lunch $4-$10, dinner $6.50-$25. Child's menu. Entertainment Fri, Sat. Parking. Fireplace. Family-owned. Cr cds: A, D, DS, MC, V.

★★ **TUNNEL BAR-B-Q.** *58 Park St E (N9A 3A7).* *519/258-3663. www.tunnel-bar-b-q.com.* Specializes in barbecued ribs, chicken, steak. Hrs: 8-2 am; Fri, Sat to 4 am. Closed Dec 25. Wine, beer. Bkfst $3.25-$5.95, lunch $4.25-$7.95, dinner $7.45-$18.95. Child's menu. Old English decor. Family-owned. Cr cds: D, MC, V.

★★ **YE OLDE STEAK HOUSE.** *46 Chatham St W (N9A 5M6).* *519/256-0222.* Specializes in soup, charcoal-broiled steak, fresh seafood. Hrs: 11:30 am-10 pm; Fri to 11 pm; Sat 4-11 pm: Sun from 4 pm. Closed Jan 1, Good Friday, Dec 25. Res accepted. Bar to 1 am. Lunch $3.75-$12, dinner $11-$24. Child's menu. Old English decor. Family-owned. Cr cds: A, D, MC, V.

PROVINCE OF PRINCE EDWARD ISLAND

Prince Edward Island is located in the Gulf of St. Lawrence on Canada's east coast, off the shores of Nova Scotia and New Brunswick. Although it is the smallest province, it is known as the "Birthplace of Canada" because Charlottetown hosted the Charlottetown Conference in 1864. This laid the foundation for the Confederation in 1867.

The island is 40 miles (64 kilometers) wide at its broadest point, narrowing to only four miles (six kilometers) wide near Summerside, and 140 miles (224 kilometers) long. Famous for its red soil, warm waters, fine white beaches, and deep-cut coves, it can be reached by air, ferry, and the Confederation Bridge, an eight-mile (12.9-kilometer) link between Borden-Carleton, PE and Cape Jourimain, New Brunswick.

Pop: 122,506
Land area: 2,186 sq mi (5,662 sq km)
Capital: Charlottetown
Web: www.peiplay.com
Information: Tourism PEI, PO Box 940, Charlottetown, C1A 7M5; 902/368-4444 or 888/734-7529

Prince Edward Island is divided into six daytour regions. The North by Northwest daytour region encompasses the northwestern parts of the province from North Cape to Cedar Dunes Provincial Park. It is an area of unspoiled beauty with secluded beaches, picturesque fishing and farming communities, and quaint churches. (Visitor Information Centre on Route 2 in Portage.)

The Ship to Shore daytour region covers the southwest. It introduces the visitor to the history of shipbuilding and fox farming, and the Malpeque oysters. Also here is the city of Summerside, located on the Bedeque Bay, which is gaining a reputation for hosting international sporting events. (Visitor Information Centre on Route 1A, east of Downtown.)

The Anne's Land daytour region features the central north shore of the province. It is home to many sites related to *Anne of Green Gables,* the children's story written by Lucy Maud Montgomery. The stunning white sand beaches of Prince Edward Island National Park (see) are also here. (Visitor Information Centre at jct Routes 6 and 13 in Cavendish and on Route 15 at Brackley Beach.)

The Charlotte's Shore daytour encompasses the south central region of Prince Edward Island. It is here that the visitor is introduced to Charlottetown, the provincial capital and birthplace of the Canadian Confederation. The scenic red cliffs and warm waters of the south shore beaches are also inviting. (Visitor Information Centre on Water Street in Charlottetown and at Gateway Village in Borden-Carleton.)

The Bays & Dunes daytour region covers the northeastern corner of the province. It offers the island's best coastline views, with miles of uncrowded white sand beaches and spectacular dunes bordering the scenic countryside. (Visitor Information Centre on Route 2 in Souris.)

The Hills & Harbours daytour details the southeastern region. It is home to some of the most pleasing vistas and peaceful fishing villages in the province. (Visitor Information Centre at the junction of Rtes 3 and 4 in Pooles Corner at the Wood Islands Ferry Terminal.)

Safety belts are mandatory for all persons anywhere in vehicle. Children under 40 pounds in weight must be in an approved safety seat anywhere in vehicle. Children 20-39 pounds may face forward in seat; however, children under 20 pounds must face backward in seat. For further information phone 902/368-5200.

Cavendish

See also Charlottetown

Pop 93 **Elev** 75 ft (23 m) **Area code** 902

Information Tourism PEI, PO Box 940; Charlottetown C1A 7M5; 800/463-4734

Web www.peiplay.com

Located near the western end of Prince Edward Island National Park (see), Cavendish encompasses more than 15 miles (24 kilometers) of beach area. World famous as the setting for *Anne of Green Gables,* the area also boasts excellent recreational facilities.

What to See and Do

Birthplace of Lucy Maud Montgomery. A replica of the "Blue Chest," the writer's personal scrapbooks, containing copies of her many stories and poems, and her wedding dress and veil are stored here. (May-Thanksgiving, daily) Jct Hwy 6, 20 in New London. Phone 902/436-7329 or 902/886-2099. ¢ Nearby is

Lucy Maud Montgomery's Cavendish Home. Site where Montgomery was raised by her grandparents from 1876-1911. Bookstore and museum houses the original desk, scales, and crown stamp used in post office. (June-Sept, daily) ¢

The Great Island Science & Adventure Park. Science centre; space shuttle replica; dinosaur museum; planetarium. (Mid-June-Labour Day, daily) 2.5 mi (4 km) W of Cavendish on Rte 6 at Stanley Bridge. Phone 902/886-2252. ¢¢

Green Gables. Famous as the setting for Lucy Maud Montgomery's *Anne of Green Gables.* Surroundings portray the Victorian setting described in the novel. Tours avail off-season (fee). (May-Oct, daily) Prince Edward Island National Park, on Hwy 6. ¢¢

Prince Edward Island National Park. (see).

Rainbow Valley Family Fun Park. Approx 40 acres of woodland, lakes and landscaped areas; children's farm with petting areas; playground, swan boats, flumes, water slides; entertainment; picnicking, cafe. Monorail ride. (June-Labour Day, daily) On Hwy 6 near Green Gables. Phone 902/963-2221. ¢¢

⊠ Woodleigh Replicas & Gardens. Extensive outdoor display of large-scale models of famous castles and buildings of legendary, historic, and literary interest. Incl are the Tower of London, Dunvegan Castle, and Anne Hathaway Cottage. Several models are large enough to enter and are furnished. Flower, shrub garden; children's playground; food service. (Early June-mid-Oct, daily) 14 mi (23 km) SW via Hwy 6, right on Hwy 20, left on Hwy 234 to Burlington. Phone 902/836-3401. ¢¢¢

Motels/Motor Lodges

★★ **CAVENDISH.** *Rte 6, Cavendish Beach (C0A 1M0). 902/963-2244; res 800/565-2243.* 38 rms, some A/C, 2 story, 3 kit. units, 8 kit. cottages. May-late Sept: S $72-$78; D $78-$88; each addl $3-$6; kit. units $88; cottages (1-4 persons) $81-$105. Closed rest of yr. TV; cable. Heated pool. Complimentary continental bkfst (June-Sept).

Restaurant adj 8 am-10 pm. Ck-out 10 am. Picnic tables, grills. Cr cds: A, MC, V.
🏊 🔥

★★ **SILVERWOOD MOTEL.** *Green Gables Post Office, Cavendish Beach (C0A 1M0). 902/963-2439; toll-free 800/565-4753. www.silverwoodmotel.com.* 50 rms, 35 A/C, 1-2 story, 23 kits. Mid-May-mid-Oct: S, D $82; each addl $8; kit. units $90-$120. Closed rest of yr. TV. Heated pool. Playground. Restaurant adj 7:30 am-9 pm. Ck-out 10 am. Meeting rms. Picnic tables, grills. Cr cds: A, MC, V.
🏊 ⊠ 🔥

Restaurants

★★ **IDLE OARS.** *North Rustico (C0A 1X0). 902/963-2534.* Specializes in seafood, steak, fried chicken. Hrs: 8 am-10:30 pm. Closed Apr; also Thanksgiving. Res accepted. Lunch $4.95-$12, dinner $5-$18.95. Child's menu. Rustic decor. Overlooks harbor. Cr cds: A, C, D, ER, MC, V.
Ⓓ ⊣

★★ **NEW GLASGOW LOBSTER SUPPER.** *Rt 258, New Glasgow (C0A 1N0). 902/964-2870.* Specializes in fresh fish chowder, mussels, lobster. Hrs: 4-8:30 pm. Closed Nov-May. Complete meals: dinner $15.95-$26.95. Child's menu. Lobster pound adj. View of river. Family-owned. Cr cds: A, C, D, ER, MC, V.
Ⓓ SC ⊣

Charlottetown

See also Cavendish

Pop 15,282 **Elev** 25 ft (8 m) **Area code** 902

Information Tourism PEI, PO Box 940, C1A 7M5; 902/368-4444 or 888/734-7529

Web www.peiplay.com

Named for Queen Charlotte, King George III's wife, Charlottetown was chosen in 1765 as the capital of Colonial St. John's Island, as it was then known. The name was changed to Prince Edward Island in 1799. The first settlement in the area was at Port la Joye across the harbour and was ruled by the French until ceded to Great Britain after the fall of Louisbourg. Known as the birthplace of Canada because the conference that led to confederation was held here in 1864, the city has many convention facilities, cultural and educational institutions, and attractions located within easy reach. Encircled by a scenic natural harbour, boating, yachting, swimming, golf, other sports, and a variety of seafood are all popular and readily available. Charlottetown is a main feature of the Charlotte's Shore daytour region; a Visitor Information Centre is here.

Prince Edward Island may be reached from the mainland at Caribou, NS, by car ferry to Wood Islands, PE, 38 mi (61 km) southeast of Charlottetown. Contact Northumberland Ferries, PO Box 634, Charlottetown, PE, C1A 7L3; 902/566-3838 or 888/249-7245. (Daily, May-mid-Dec; 1¼-hr crossing; fee) The island can also be reached from Cape Jourimain, New Brunswick, via the Confederation Bridge, an 8-mile bridge that leads to Borden-Carleton, PE (toll).

What to See and Do

Basin Head Fisheries Museum. Depicts history of fishing in the province. Fishing equipment, scale models showing methods; old photographs, fish charts, and other marine articles. Film and slide projections. (Mid-June-late Sept, daily) 58 mi (93 km) E via Rte 2 to Souris, then Rte 16 to Kingsboro. Phone 902/357-2966 or 902/368-6600. ¢¢

Beaconsfield. (1877) Mansard-style house built for ship-builder is architecturally intact; guided tours. Headquarters of Prince Edward Island Museum & Heritage Foundation; bookstore. Regular and annual events. (Mid-June-Labour Day, daily; after Labour Day, Sun and Tues-Fri afternoons) 2 Kent St. Phone 902/368-6600. Museum ¢¢

Confederation Centre of the Arts. (1964) Canada's National Memorial to the Fathers of Confederation; opened by Queen Elizabeth II to honor the centennial of the 1864 Confederation Conference. Contains provincial library, Confederation Centre Museum and Art Gallery, theatres, and the Robert Harris Collection of portraiture. Courtyard restaurant, gift shop. Home of the Charlottetown Festival (see SPECIAL EVENTS). Gallery and museum (Tues-Sat, also Sun afternoons). Centre (daily; closed hols). 145 Richmond St. Phone 902/628-1864 or 800/565-0278. ¢

Fort Amherst/Port La Joye National Historic Park. Only earthworks of the former French fort Port la Joye (built 1720) are still visible. Captured by British in 1758, abandoned in 1768. Cafe, boutique. Interpretive center. (Mid-June-Labour Day, daily) Near Rocky Point, on Hwy 19 across the harbour mouth. Phone 902/672-6350.

Green Park Shipbuilding Museum. Former estate of James Yeo, Jr. whose family members were leading shipbuilders of the 19th century. House (1865) restored to reflect life during the prosperous shipbuilding era. Photos of famous ships and artifacts in interpretive center; audiovisual presentation in museum theater. Lecture series and concerts. Annual events. Swimming; camping at Malpeque Bay. (Mid-June-Labour Day, daily) 63 mi (101 km) NW via Hwy 2 to Hwy 132 just past Richmond, right to jct with Hwy 12, left to Port Hill. Phone 902/831-7947 or 902/368-6600 (off-season). ¢¢

Orwell Corner Historic Village. Reconstructed rural cross-roads community of late 19th century. Combined store, post office, and farmhouse; school, church, cemetery, and barns. Farming activities as they were practiced 100 yrs ago. Annual events. Ceilidhs (Wed eves). (Late June-early Sept, daily; mid-May-late June, Mon-Fri; early Sept-late Oct, Tues-Sun) 18 mi (29 km) E via Trans Canada Hwy. Phone 902/651-2013. ¢¢

Prince Edward Island National Park. (see).

Province House. (1847) Birthplace of the Canadian nation and a national historic site. Confederation rm where delegates met in 1864 to discuss confederation. National memorial, seat of Provincial Legislature. Tours. (June-early Oct, daily; rest of yr, Mon-Fri; closed hols) Richmond St. Phone 902/566-7626.

St. Dunstan's Cathedral Basilica. Largest church on the island. Gothic cathedral with distinctive triple towers contains beautiful stained-glass windows and an impressive altar 37 ft (11 m) high made of many types of marble and crowned with a beautiful rose window. Audio loop for hearing impaired. Restoration in progress. (Daily) 45 Great George St. Phone 902/894-3486.

Sightseeing tour. Abegweit Tours. Charlottetown tours on authentic London double-decker buses; also north and south tours. Bilingual guide service avail. Contact 157 Nassau St, C1A 2X3. Phone 902/894-9966. ¢¢¢¢

Special Events

Charlottetown Festival. Confederation Centre of the Arts. Original Canadian musicals, incl *Anne of Green Gables* and other productions; special gallery presentations and theater. Box office 902/566-1267; information 902/628-1864. Late June-late Sept.

Festival of Lights. Charlottetown Waterfront. Buskers, children's concerts, Waterfront Magic, children's midway. Fireworks display over Charlottetown Harbour on July 1 (Canada Day). Late June-early July. Phone 902/629-1864.

Motels/Motor Lodges

★ ★ **BEST WESTERN CHARLOTTETOWN.** *238 Grafton St (C1A 1L5).* 902/892-2461; fax 902/566-2979; toll-free 800/ 528-1234. www.bestwestern.com. 143 rms, 2-3 story, 26 kits. June-mid-Oct: S $139-$149; D $149-$159; each addl $10; studio rms $149-$159; suites $169-$209; kit. units $149-$159; under 18 free; lower rates rest of yr. Pet accepted, some restrictions. TV; cable. Indoor pool; whirlpool. Complimentary coffee in rms. Restaurants 7 am-9 pm; Sun from 8 am. Ck-out noon. Meeting rms. Valet serv. Exercise equipt; sauna. Sundries. Microwaves avail. Cr cds: A, C, D, DS, ER, JCB, MC, V.
D ◀ ⌱ 🕏 ⊠ 🔥 SC

★ ★ **ISLANDER MOTOR LODGE.** *146-148 Pownal St (C1A 7N4).* 902/892-1217; fax 902/566-1623; toll-free 800/ 268-6261. www.islandermotorlodge.com. 49 rms, 2 story, 3 kits. Mid-May-mid-Oct: S, D $86-$96; each addl $8; suites, kit. units $96-$120; under 12 free; lower rates rest of yr. Crib $7. Pet accepted. TV; cable. Restaurant 7 am-8 pm. Ck-out 11 am. Meeting rms. Sundries. Microwaves avail. Cr cds: A, ER, MC, V.
D ◀ 🔥

★ **QUALITY INN ON THE HILL.** *150 Euston St (C1A 1W5).* 902/894-8572; fax 902/368-3556; 800/228-5151. www.qualityinn.com. 48 rms, 5 story. Late June-mid-Oct: S $116; D $127; each addl $9; studio rms $137-$142; suites $152-$174; under 16 free; lower rates rest of yr. Pet accepted. TV; cable. Coffee in rms. Restaurant 7 am-8 pm. Rm serv. Bar 11-1 am. Ck-out noon. Meeting rms. Bellhops. Health club privileges. Sundries. Cr cds: A, C, D, DS, ER, MC, V.
◀ ⊠ 🔥

★★★ **RODD CONFEDERATION INN & SUITES.**
Trans-Canada Hwy (C1A 7K7). 902/892-2481; fax 902/368-3247. www.rodd-hotels.ca. 62 rms, 2 story, 31 suites. Mid-June-Sept: S, D $85-$94; suites $99-$115; under 16 free; lower rates rest of yr. Crib free. Pet accepted. TV; cable. Heated pool. Restaurant 7-10 am, 5-9 pm. Bar 11-1 am; closed Sun. Ck-out 11 am. Health club privileges. Refrigerators, microwaves avail. Cr cds: A, C, D, DS, ER, JCB, MC, V.
🐾 ➰ ⊠ 🔥 **SC**

★★★ **RODD ROYALTY INN.** *Hwy 1 & Hwy 2 (C1A 8C2). 902/894-8566; fax 902/892-8488. www.rodd-hotels.ca.* 132 rms, 1-3 story, 6 kits. June-Oct: S $87; D $99; each addl $10; suites $125-$175; under 16 free; lower rates rest of yr. Crib free. TV; cable. Restaurant 7 am-10 pm. Rm serv. Bar 4:30 pm-1 am; closed Sun. Ck-out noon. Meeting rms. Bellhops. Sundries. Exercise equipt; sauna. Balconies. Indoor courtyard adj to pool area. Cr cds: A, C, D, ER, MC, V.
D ➰ 🏋 ⊠ 🔥

★★ **SUNNY KING.** *Hwy 1, Cavendish (C0A 1H0). 902/566-2209; fax 902/566-4209.* 37 rms, 1-2 story, 30 kits. No A/C. Late June-early Sept: S $54-$64; D $60-$70; each addl $8; suites, kit. units $68-$92; under 16 free; lower rates rest of yr. Crib $6. Pet accepted. TV; cable. Heated pool. Playground. Free supervised children's activities (May-mid-Nov). Restaurant adj 8 am-11 pm. Ck-out 11 am. Coin lndry. Business servs avail. Valet serv. Many microwaves. Picnic tables, grills. Cr cds: A, C, D, DS, ER, MC, V.
D 🐾 ➰ ⊠ 🔥 **SC**

Hotels

★★ **THE CHARLOTTETOWN.** *75 Kent St (C1A 7K4). 902/894-7371; fax 902/368-2178; toll-free 800/565-7633. www.rodd-hotels.ca.* 115 rms, 5 story. June-mid-Oct: S, D $135-$215; each addl $10; under 16 free; lower rates rest of yr. Crib free. Pet accepted. TV; cable. Indoor pool; whirlpool. Restaurant 7 am-2 pm, 5-10 pm. Bar 4 pm-1 am; closed Sun. Ck-out 11 am. Meeting rms. Exercise equipt; sauna. Cr cds: A, D, DS, ER, JCB, MC, V.
D 🐾 ➰ 🏋 ⊠ 🔥 **SC**

★★★ **THE DELTA PRINCE EDWARD.** *18 Queen St (C1A 8B9). 902/566-2222; fax 902/566-1745; toll-free 800/441-1414. www.deltahotels.com.* 211 rms, 10 story. May-mid-Oct: S $139-$229; D $159-$249; each addl $20; suites $299-$799; lower rates rest of yr. Crib avail. Pet accepted. TV; cable. Indoor pool; wading pool, whirlpool. Restaurants 6:30 am-11 pm. Bar; entertainment. Ck-out noon. Meeting rms. Business center. Exercise rm; sauna. Massage. On waterfront in Olde Charlottetown. Cr cds: A, D, DS, MC, V.
D 🐾 ➰ 🏋 ⊠ 🔥 **SC** 🚶

Prince Edward Island National Park

See also Cavendish, Charlottetown

Prince Edward Island National Park, 25 square miles (40 square kilometers), is one of eastern Canada's most popular vacation destinations. Warm salt waters and sandy beaches abound. There are several supervised beach areas for swimmers and miles of secluded shoreline to explore. In addition to golf, tennis, bicycling, and picnicking, the park offers an interpretation program highlighting the natural and cultural features and stories of the area; campfires; beach walks and more. Green Gables and its association with Lucy Maud Montgomery's *Anne of Green Gables* is a major attraction, with daily walks offered around the house and grounds (see CAVENDISH). Camping is also available (maximum stay 21 nights, reservations accepted). Dalvay-by-the-Sea offers hotel accommodations in a unique setting. Many private cabins, hotels, and campgrounds are available bordering the park.

Prince Edward Island may be reached by a car ferry. For further information, contact Marine Atlantic Reservation Bureau, PO Box 250, North Sydney, NS, B2A 3M3; 800/341-7981 (US). Another ferry crosses in 1¼ hours at Caribou, NS to Wood Islands, PEI (see CHARLOTTETOWN, PEI).

PROVINCE OF QUÉBEC

The Québécois, whose ancestors came from France more than 400 years ago, made their stronghold in the St. Lawrence River valley. These ancestors also gave this province its decidedly French character.

The geography of Québec is largely determined by the St. Lawrence River, the Laurentian mountains, lakes that are really inland seas, and streams that swell into broad rivers.

These magnificent natural settings provide the tourist with year-round vacation wonders. The Laurentians, only an hour's drive from Montréal, have some of the finest skiing, outdoor recreation, and restaurants in North America.

Combine the natural beauty of the area, the cosmopolitan yet historic ambience of Montréal and Québec City, and a tour of the unspoiled Gaspé Peninsula, and you will have a vacation destination nonpareil.

When dining in Québec, travelers should be aware that there is a 15.2 percent federal and provincial tax on food and alcohol added to all restaurant checks.

In addition to national holidays, Québec observes St. Jean Baptiste Day (June 24).

Safety belts are mandatory for all persons anywhere in vehicle. Children under five years or under 40 pounds in weight must be in an approved safety seat. Radar detectors are strictly forbidden. For further information phone 800/361-7620.

Pop: 6,438,403
Land area: 643,987 sq mi (1,667,926 sq km)
Capital: Québec
Web: www.bonjourquebec.com
Information: Tourisme/Québec, CP 979, Montréal H3C 2W3; 514/873-2015 or 800/363-7777

Drummondville

See also Montrèal, Sherbrooke

Pop 27,347 **Elev** 350 ft (107 m) **Area code** 819
Information Bureau du Tourisme et des Congrës,
1350 Michaud St, J2C 2Z5; 819/477-5529

Known as the "Center of Québec," this industrial and
commercial center is advantageously located on the
St. Francois River where the Trans-Canada and Trans-
Québec highways intersect.

What to See and Do

Le Village Québécois d'Antan. Historical village (1810-
1910) typical of the area. (June-Labour Day) N via Hwy 20,
exit 181 on rue Montplaisir. Phone 819/478-1441. ¢¢¢

Manoir et Domaine Trent. Period home (1836) restored
by artisans; restaurant. Camping (late June-Aug). Parc des
Voltigeurs. Phone 819/472-3662. **FREE**

Special Event

World Folklore Festival. One of the major folklore events
in North America. Intl singers, dancers, and musicians
participate at four different sites. Phone 819/472-1184.
Ten days July.

Motel/Motor Lodge

★★ **HOTEL UNIVERSEL.** *915 Hains St (J2C 3A1).
819/478-4971; fax 819/477-6604; toll-free 800/668-3521.
www.hoteluniversal.qc.ca.* 115 rms, 4 story. S $75.95;
D $85.95; each addl $10; suites $120-$150; under 15 free.
Crib free. Pet accepted. TV; cable. Indoor pool; poolside
serv. Restaurant 7 am-10 pm. Rm serv. Bar 11-3 am; entertainment Wed-Sat. Ck-out noon. Meeting rms. Business
servs avail. Cr cds: A, C, D, DS, ER, MC, V.

🄳 🐾 🏊 🖢 🔥

Restaurant

★★ **RESTAURANT DU BOIS-JOLI.** *505 St. Joseph Blvd W
(J2E 1K8). 819/472-4366.* French, continental menu.
Specialty: rôti de boeuf au jus. Hrs: 11 am-10 pm; Sun
brunch to 2 pm. Res accepted. Serv bar. A la carte entrees:
lunch, dinner $5.75-$15.50. Complete meals: lunch $5.50-
$9.75, dinner $9.95-$15.50. Buffet $6.50. Sun brunch $9.25.
Child's menu. Cr cds: A, C, D, MC, V.

🖢

Gaspé Peninsula

Jutting out into the Gulf of St.-Laurent, the Gaspé Peninsula
is a region of varying landforms including mountains,
plateaus, beaches, and cliffs. It is blessed with abundant
and rare wildlife and some unique flora, including 12-
foot-high (4-meter) centuries-old fir trees. Landscapes are
incredibly beautiful. The rivers, teeming with trout, flow
to meet the salmon coming from the sea. Called "Gespeg"
(meaning "land's end") by the aborigines, the area was
settled primarily by Basque, Breton, and Norman fishermen,
whose charming villages may be seen clinging to the shore
beneath the gigantic cliffs. The French influence is strong;
English is spoken in few villages.

For further information contact Association Touristique
du Bas St.-Laurent, 148 rue Froser, Rivière-du-Loup G5R
1C8; 418/867-3015 or 800/563-5268.

Granby

See also Montrèal, Sherbrooke

Pop 38,069 **Elev** 270 ft (82 m) **Area code** 450
Information Tourism Granby, 650 Principale St, J2G 8L4;
450/372-7273 or 800/567-7273
Web www.granby-bromont.com

Begun as a mission in 1824, with the first settlers arriving
in 1813, Granby was named for an English nobleman,
the Marquis of Granby. Only 45 miles (71 kilometers)
east of Montréal, the town is a favorite excursion spot for
Montréalers, with 18 beautiful parks containing a collection of old European fountains and its devotion to good
food. Located on the north bank of the Yamaska River,
Granby manufactures rubber products, candy, electrical
products, and cement. Because of the abundance of maple
groves, sugaring-off parties are a popular activity.

What to See and Do

Granby Zoological Garden. More than 1,000 animals of
225 species from every continent; education and African
pavillions, amusement park. (May-Sept, daily) 525 rue
Bourget. Phone 450/372-9113. ¢¢¢

Nature Interpretation Centre of Lake Boivin. Guided walking tours through woodland and marsh; concentrations of
waterfowl and nature exhibits. (Daily) 700 rue Drummond.
Phone 450/375-3861. **FREE**

Yamaska Provincial Park. Newly developed park with
swimming, fishing, boating (rentals); paths, hiking, cross-
country skiing (fee), picnicking, snack bar. Parking (fee).
3 mi (5 km) E. Phone 450/372-3204.

Special Event

Granby International. Antique car show. Phone 450/777-
1330. Last wkend July.

Resort

★★ **AUBERGE BROMONT.** *95 Rue Montmorency, Bromont
(G2H 2G1). 450/534-1199; fax 450/534-1700; toll-free
888/276-6668.* 50 rms, 3 story. No elvtr. S, D $98-$118;
MAP avail; family rates; ski, golf plans. Crib free. TV; cable
(premium). Pool; poolside serv, lifeguard. Dining rm
(public by res) 7 am-3 pm, 6-10 pm. Bar 11-3 am. Ck-out
noon, ck-in 4 pm. Business servs avail. Concierge. Lighted
tennis, pro. 18-hole golf, greens fee $26-$33. Downhill ski
1 mi; x-country ski on site (rentals). Exercise equipt. Some
minibars. Cr cds: C, D, ER, MC, V.

🄳 🐾 🏊 🎿 🏌 🏃 🖢 🔥

Hull

(see Ottawa, Ontario)

The Laurentians

The Laurentian region, just 45 miles from Montreal, is a rich tourist destination. Surrounded by forests, lakes, rivers, and the Laurentian Mountains, this area provides ample settings for open-air activities year-round. Water sports abound in summer, including canoeing, kayaking, swimming, rafting, scuba diving, and excellent fishing. Hunting, golfing, horseback riding, and mountain climbing are also popular in warmer months, as is bicycling along the 125-mile P'tit train du Nord trail. Brilliant fall colors lead into a winter ideal for snow lovers. The Laurentian region boasts a huge number of downhill ski centers, 600 miles of cross-country trails, and thousands of miles of snowmobiling trails. The territory of the Laurentian tourist zone is formed on the south by the Outaouais River, des Deux-Montagnes Lake, and the Milles-Iles River. On the east, its limits stretch from the limit of Terrebonne to Entrelacs. It is bounded on the north by Ste.-Anne du Lac and Baskatong Reservoir and on the west by the towns of Des Ruisseaux, Notre-Dame de Pontmain, and Notre Dame du Laus. Places listed are Mont Tremblant Provincial Park, St. Jérôme and Saint-Jovite.

Montrèal

Settled 1642 **Pop** 1,005,000 **Elev** 117 ft (36 m)
Area code 514
Information Tourisme-Quèbec, CP 979, H3C 2W3; 514/873-2015 or 800/363-7777
Web www.bonjourquebec.com

Blessed by its location on an island at the junction of the St. Lawrence and Ottawa rivers, Montrèal has served for more than three centuries as a gigantic trading post; its harbor can accommodate more than 100 oceangoing vessels. While it is a commercial, financial, and industrial center, Montrèal is also an internationally recognized patron of the fine arts, hosting several acclaimed festivals attended by enthusiasts world-wide.

A stockaded indigenous settlement called Hochelaga when it was discovered in 1535 by Jacques Cartier, the area contained a trading post by the early 1600s; but it was not settled as a missionary outpost until 1642 when the Frenchman Paul de Chomedey, Sieur de Maisonneuve, and a group of settlers, priests, and nuns founded Ville-Morie. This later grew as an important fur trading center and from here men such as Jolliet, Marquette, Duluth, and Father Hennepin set out on their western expeditions. Montrèal remained under French rule until 1763 when Canada was surrendered as a possession to the British under the Treaty of Paris. For seven months during the American Revolution, Montrèal was occupied by Americans, but it was later regained by the British.

Today Montrèal is an elegantly sophisticated city. Two-thirds of its people are French-speaking, and its French population is the largest outside of Europe. It is made up of two parts: the Old City, in the same area as the original Ville-Morie, which is a maze of narrow streets, restored buildings, and old houses, best seen on foot; and the modern Montrèal, with its many skyscrapers, museums, theaters, nearly 7,600 restaurants, and glittering nightlife.

There is an underground Montrèal also, with miles of shops, galleries, restaurants, and access to one of the most unique subway systems in the world. Each station has been decorated by a different architect in a different style, and visitors have called it "the largest underground art gallery in the world." Mont-Royal rises from the center of the island-city to a height of 764 feet (233 meters), affording a panoramic view. Calèches (horse-drawn carriages) provide tourists with a charming means of viewing the city and are, with the exception of bicycles, the only vehicles permitted in some areas of Mount Royal Park. Adjacent to the park is the Westmount area, a section of meandering roads and charming older homes of the early 1900s with delightful English-style gardens.

In 1967, Montrèal hosted Expo '67, celebrating Canada's centennial. The summer Olympic games were held here in 1976.

Additional Visitor Information

Quèbec Tourism, PO Box 979, Montrèal, H3C 2W3; phone 800/363-7777 or in person at Infotouriste, 1001 rue du Square-Dorchester (between Peel & Metcalfe Sts); also office at Old Montrèal, Place Jacques-Cartier, 174 Notre-Dame St E; all have helpful information for tourists. The Consulate General of the United States is located on 1155 rue St.-Alexandre, at Placé Felip-Martin, at the corner of René Levesque Blvd; phone 514/398-9695. Public transportation is provided by the Societé de Transport de la Communauté Urbaine de Montrèal (STCUM), phone 514/288-6287.

What to See and Do

Angrignon Park. On 262 acres (106 hectares) with more than 21,600 trees; lagoons, river; playground, picnicking, bicycling, ice-skating, X-country skiing. Park (daily). 3400 des Trinitaires Blvd. Phone 514/872-3816. Zoo ¢¢

Byzantine Museum. Gallery for icons and other works by Romanian-born artist Rosette Mociornitza, produced in the unique style of the Byzantine period using old wood, traditional techniques, materials from Europe. Works may be purchased. (Daily, by appt) 6780 Biarritz Ave, Brossard. Phone 450/656-0188. **FREE**

Casino Montrèal. The Casino de Montrèal offers guests a variety of games, with 112 gaming tables as well as 2,700 slot machines. (Open 24 hrs) 1 Ave du Casino, housed in Expo 67's famous French Pavilion. Phone 514/392-2746 or 800/665-2274.

Dorchester Square. In the center of Montrèal, this park is a popular meeting place. Also here is Mary Queen of the World Cathedral, a ⅓-scale replica of St. Peter's in Rome. Also information centre of Montrèal and Tourisme Quèbec. René-Lévesque Blvd O between Peel and Metcalfe Sts. **FREE**

Fort Lennox. 45 mi (72.4 km) SE. (See ROUSES POINT, NY) 45 mi (72.4 km) SE.

iSci Centre. Interactive science exhibits, IMAX, IMAX 3D, and the first immersion theater (interactive video game on giant screen) in Canada. Also boutiques, restaurants. (Daily) 2 de la Commune St. Phone 514/496-4724 or 877/496-4724. ¢¢¢¢

La Fontaine Park. Illuminated fountain, playground, monuments; two lakes, paddleboats; cycling trail. (Mid-May-Oct, daily) Winter activities incl ice-skating, X-country skiing; hockey rink. Sherbrooke St and Papineau St. Phone 514/872-2644. **FREE**

Maison St.-Gabriel. Built in late 17th century as a farm; also served as school for Marguerite Bourgeoys, founder of the Sisters of the Congrégatun de Notre-Dame, who looked after young French girls who were to marry the early colonists. Period furnishings; altar built in 1700s; items of French-Canadian heritage incl woodcuts from ancient churches and chapels. (Mid-Apr-mid-Dec, Tues-Sun) 2146 Dublin Pl. Phone 514/935-8136. ¢¢

McGill University. (1821) 31,000 students. The 80-acre main campus is set between the lower slopes of Mt Royal and the downtown commercial district. Guided tours by appt (free). Welcome Centre at 805 Sherbrooke St O. Phone 514/398-4455.

⭐ **Montréal Botanical Garden.** Within 180 acres (73 hectares) grow more than 26,000 species and varieties of plants; 30 specialized sections incl rose, perennial plant, heath gardens, flowery brook, bonsai, carnivorous plants, and arboretum; one of the world's largest orchid collections; seasonal flower shows. The bonsai and penjing collections are two of the most diversified in North America. Chinese and Japanese gardens; restaurant, tea rm. Parking (fee). (Daily) 4101 Sherbrooke St E. Phone 514/872-1400. ¢¢ Also here (and included in admission) is

Insectarium de Montreal. Collection of more than 350,000 insects in a building designed to resemble a stylized insect. Interactive and participatory concept takes visitors through aviaries and living displays in six geographically themed areas. Hands-on exhibits; Outside Gardens; butterfly aviary (summer); traveling exhibits; children's amusement center. (Daily)

The Montréal Museum of Fine Arts. (Musée des beaux-arts de Montréal) Canada's oldest art museum (founded 1860) has a wide variety of displays, ranging from Egyptian statues to 20th-century abstracts. Canadian section features old Québec furniture, silver, and paintings. (Tues-Sun; closed Jan 1, Dec 25) 1379-80 Sherbrooke St O. Phone 514/285-2000. ¢¢¢¢

Montréal Planetarium. Astronomy shows: projectors create all features of the night sky; special effects. (Tues-Sun) Phone 514/872-4530.

Mount Royal Park. On 430 acres (174 hectares) in center of city; lake, picnicking, bicycling, calèche tours, winter sports (skating, downhill/X-country skiing); observation point at chalet lookout. Permanent exhibits at Chalet de la Montagne, a nature-appreciation center (daily). Côte des Neiges & Remembrance Rds. Phone 514/843-8240. **FREE**

Museum of Decorative Arts. Historic mansion Chateau Dufresne (1918), partially restored and refurnished, now houses international exhibitions of glass, textiles, and ceramic art; changing exhibits. (Wed-Sun; closed Jan 1, Dec 25) 2200 rue Crescent. Phone 514/284-1252. ¢¢

⭐ **Old (Vieux) Montréal.** The city of Montréal evolved from the small settlement of Ville-Marie founded by de Maisonneuve in 1642. The largest concentration of 19th-century buildings in North America is found here; several original dwellings remain, while many other locations are marked by bronze plaques throughout the area. The expansion of this settlement led to what is now known as Old Montréal. The area roughly forms a 100-acre (40-hectare) quadrangle which corresponds approx to the area enclosed within the original fortifications. Bounded by McGill, Berri, Notre-Dame Sts, and the St. Lawrence River. Some major points of interest are

Place d'Armes. A square of great historical importance and center of Old Montréal. The founders of Ville-Marie encountered the Iroquois here in 1644 and rebuffed them. In the square's center is a statue of de Maisonneuve, first governor of Montréal, and at one end is the St. Sulpice seminary (1685) with an old wooden clock (1710), oldest building in Montréal. St. Sulpice & Notre-Dame Sts. At 119 St. Jacques St is the **Bank of Montréal.** This magnificent building contains a museum with collection of currency, mechanical savings banks, photographs, reproduction of old-fashioned teller's cage. (Mon-Fri; closed hols) Some of the most important financial houses of the city are grouped around the square. Phone 514/877-6810. **FREE** Across the square is

Notre-Dame Basilica. (1824) In 1672, a church described as "one of the most beautiful churches in North America" was erected on the present Notre-Dame St. When this became inadequate for the growing parish, a new church designed by New Yorker James O'Donnell was built. It was completed in 1829 and two towers and interior decorations were added later. *Le Gros Bourdon,* a bell cast in 1847 and weighing 24,780 lbs, is in Perseverance Tower; there is a ten-bell chime in Temperance Tower. Built of Montréal limestone, the basilica is Neo-Gothic in design with a beautiful main altar, pulpit, and numerous statues, paintings, and stained-glass windows. (Daily; concerts in summer) 110 Notre-Dame St O. **FREE**

Notre-Dame Basilica Museum. Works of religious and historical art; old furniture, statues; local folklore paintings. 424 St. Sulpice St. Phone 514/842-2925. ¢

St.-Paul St. Oldest street in Montréal. The mansions of Ville-Marie once stood here but they have been replaced by commercial houses and office buildings. Here is

Notre-Dame-de-Bonsecours Church. (1773) Founded in 1657 and rebuilt 115 yrs later, this is one of the oldest churches still standing in the city; tower has view of the river and city; museum (fee) has objects pertaining to early settlers. Miniature ships suspended from vault in church are votive offerings from sailors who worshiped here.

Château Ramezay. (1705) Historical museum, once the home of the governors of Montréal, the West Indies Company of France, and the Governors-General of British North America. Furniture, paintings, costumes, porcelain, manuscripts, art objects of the 17th-19th centuries. (Tues-Sun) 280 Notre-Dame E, in front of City Hall. Phone 514/861-3708.

Place Jacques-Cartier. Named for the discoverer of Canada, this was once a busy marketplace. Oldest monument in the city, the Nelson Column (1809) is in the square's upper section. Notre-Dame St.

Olympic Park. Stadium was site of 1976 Summer Olympic Games and is now home of Montréal Expos baseball team and les Alouettes de Montréal football team; observatory of world's tallest inclined tower. Cafeteria, souvenir shop. Tours (daily). 4141 Pierre de Coubertin St. Phone 514/252-8687. Tours (with tower) ¢¢ Adj stadium is

Biodôme de Montréal. Former Olympic Velodrome has been transformed into an environmental museum that combines elements of botanical garden, aquarium, zoo, and nature center. Four ecosystems—Laurentian Forest, Tropical Forest, Polar World, and St.-Laurent Marine—sustain thousands of plants and small animals. Also 500-m Nature Path with text panels and maps, interpreters; and discovery rm "Naturalia." (Daily; closed Jan 1, Dec 25) 4777 Pierre de Coubertin St. Phone 514/868-3000. ¢¢

Parc des Îles. Two islands in the middle of the St. Lawrence River; access via Jacques-Cartier Bridge or Metro subway. Île Ste.-Hélène (St. Helen's Island) was the main anchor site for Expo '67; now a 342-acre (138-hectare) multipurpose park with three swimming pools; picnicking; cross-country skiing, snowshoeing. Île Notre-Dame (Notre Dame Island), to the south, was partly built up from the river bed and was an important activity site for Expo '67. Here is Gilles-Villeneuve Formula 1 race track (see SPECIAL EVENTS); also beach, paddle boats, windsurfing, and sailing. Some fees. (Daily) Phone 514/872-6093. Located here are

The Old Fort. (1820-24) Oldest remaining fortification of Montréal, only the arsenal, powder magazine, and barracks bldg still stand. Two military companies dating from the 18th century, La Compagnie Franche de la Marine and the 78th Fraser Highlanders, perform colorful military drills and parades (late June-Aug, Wed-Sun). In the fort's arsenal is

David M. Stewart Museum. Artifacts trace Canadian history from the 15th century through maps, firearms, kitchen utensils, engravings, navigational and scientific instruments. (Wed-Mon; closed Jan 1, Dec 25) Phone 514/861-6701.

Floral Park. Site of Les Floralies Internationales 1980; now permanent, it displays collection of worldwide flowers and plants. Walking trails; pedal boats, canoeing; picnic area; snack bar and restaurant. Some fees. (Third wk June-mid-Sept, daily) Île Notre-Dame.

Théâtre des Lilas. Open-air theater with a variety of shows, incl music and dance. Île Notre-Dame.

La Ronde. A 135-acre amusement park with 35 rides, incl 132-ft (40-m) high wooden roller coaster; arcades, entertainment on a floating stage; waterskiing; live cartoon characters, children's village; circus, boutiques, and restaurants. (June-Labour Day, daily; May, wkends; closed four days late Aug) Île Ste.-Hélène. Phone 514/872-4537 or 800/797-4537.

Parc Safari. Features 750 animals, rides, and shows; children's theater and play area, swimming beach; drive-through wild animal reserve; picnicking, restaurants, boutiques. (Mid-May-mid-Sept, daily) 33 mi (56 km) S on Hwy 15 to exit 6, then follow zoo signs. Phone 800/465-8724. ¢¢¢¢

Place des Arts. This four-theater complex is the heart of Montréal's artistic life. L'Opéra de Montréal, the Montréal Symphony Orchestra, les Grands Ballets Canadiens, and La Compagnie Jean-Duceppe theatrical troupe have their permanent home here. Other entertainment incl chamber music, recitals, jazz, folk singers, variety shows, music hall, theater, musicals, and modern and classical dance. Corner of Ste.-Catherine and Jeonne-Mance. Phone 514/790-2787 (recording) or 514/842-2112 (tickets).

✪ **Pointe-à-Callière, the Montrèal Museum of Archaeology and History.** Deals with the founding and development of the City of Montréal. Built in 1992 over the actual site of the founding of Montréal, the main museum buildingg, the **Eperon**, actually rests on pillars built around ruins dating from the town's first cemetery and its earliest fortifications, which are now in its basement. Two balconies overlook this archaeological site and a 16-min multimedia show is presented using the actual remnants as a backdrop. From here visitors continue underground, amid still more remnants, to the **Archaeological Crypt**, a structure that allows access to many more artifacts and remains; architectural models beneath a transparent floor illustrate five different periods in the history of Place Royale. The **Old Customs House (Ancienne-Douane)** houses thematic exhibits on Montréal in the 19th and 20th centuries. Permanent and changing exhibits. Cafe; gift shop. (Tues-Sun; extended hrs summer) 350 Place Royale, corner of Place Youville in Old Montréal. Phone 514/872-9150. ¢¢

Professional sports.

Montréal Canadiens (NHL). Le Centre Molson, 1260 de La Gauchetiere St W. Phone 514/970-1245. Phone 514/790-1245.

Montréal Expos (MLB). Olympic Stadium. 549 Pierre de Coubertin St. Phone 514/253-3434.

Rafting Montréal. Rafting and hydro-jet trips on the Lachine Rapids of the St. Lawrence River. (May-Sept, daily; res required) Phone 514/767-2230. ¢¢¢¢

St. Joseph's Oratory. Chapel (1904), crypt church (1916); museum. Main church is a famous shrine attracting more than two million pilgrims yearly; basilica founded 1924; built in Italian Renaissance style; dome towers over city. Fifty-six-bell carillon made in France is outstanding. (Daily) 3800 Queen Mary Rd, on north slope of Mt Royal. Phone 514/733-8211.

Sightseeing tours.

Calèche tours. Horse-drawn carriages depart from Place d' Armes, Mt Royal Park, or Old Port of Montréal. ¢¢¢

Gray Line bus tours. Contact 1140 Wellington St, H3C 1V8. Phone 514/934-1222.

Montréal Harbour Cruises. Various guided cruises and dinner excursions (one-four hrs); bar service. Res advised. (May-mid-Oct, daily) Contact Croisières Vieure-Port de Montréal, Quai de l'Horlage, C.P. 1085, Succ. Place d'Armes, H2Y 3J6. Depart from Quai de L'Horloge in Old Montréal, at the foot of Berri St and from Quai Jacque Cartier. Phone 800/667-3131. ¢¢¢¢

Université de Montréal. (1920) 58,000 students. On N slope of Mt Royal. 2900 boul Èdouord-Montpetit. Phone 514/343-6111.

Special Events

Montréal Highlights Festival. Spotlights city's cultural and artistic diversity. Phone 800/363-7777. Mid-Feb-early Mar.

Montréal Bike Fest. An entire wk of events celebrating the bicycle, ending with Le Tour de l'Óle when 40,000 cyclists ride through the streets of Montréal. Incl a 16-mi outing for up to 10,000 children. Phone 514/521-8687. Late May-early June.

Canadian Grand Prix. Parc des Îles. Formula 1 racing at Gilles-Villeneuve track, Île Notre-Dame. Phone 514/350-0000. Early June.

Antiques Bonaventure. East Exhibition Hall, Place Bonaventure. Exhibits of private and public collections for sale; more than 100 dealers participate. Phone 514/397-2222. Mid-June.

Fíte Nationale. St.-Jean-Baptiste, patron saint of the French Canadians, is honored with three days of festivities surrounding provincial holiday. Celebration incl street festivals, bonfire, fireworks, musical events. Mid- June.

Montréal Jazz Festival. Downtown. More than 1,200 musicians and a million music lovers from around the world gather to celebrate jazz. Ten-day fest incl more than 500 indoor and outdoor concerts. Phone 514/871-1881 or 888/515-0515. Late June-early July.

Just for Laughs. International comedy festival. Phone 514/845-2322. Mid-July.

World Film Festival. Contact 1432 Bleury St. Phone 514/848-3883. Late Aug-early Sept.

Motels/Motor Lodges

★★ **AUBERGES WANDLYN.** 7200 Sherbrooke St E (H1N 1E7). 514/256-1613; fax 514/256-5150. www.wandlyn.com. 123 rms, 2 story. June-Oct: S $63-$89.50; D $63-$99.50; each addl $10; suites $99.50-$129.50; under 18 free; lower rates rest of yr. TV; cable. Heated pool; poolside serv; lifeguard. Restaurant 7 am-2 pm. Bar 4 pm-midnight. Ck-out noon. Meeting rms. Business servs avail. Balconies. Cr cds: A, C, D, DS, ER, MC, V.
🏊 ⊠ 🐾 SC

★ **COCONUT.** 7531 Rue Notre Dame, Trois-Rivieres-Ouest (G9B 1L7). 819/377-3221; fax 819/377-1344. 39 rms. Mid-June-Sept: S $42-$65; D $42-$70; each addl $5; suites $118; under 18 free; lower rates rest of yr. TV; cable (premium). Ck-out noon. Meeting rms. Refrigerator avail. Cr cds: A, C, D, ER, MC, V.
⊠ 🐾 SC

★ **DAYS INN MIDTOWN.** 1005 Guy St (H3H 2K4). 514/938-4611; fax 514/938-8718; toll-free 800/567-0880. www.daysinn.qc.ca. 205 rms, 7 story. May-Oct: S $129; D $139; each addl $10; under 12 free; wkend rates; lower rates rest of yr. Crib free. Parking (fee). TV; cable. Heated pool; lifeguard. Restaurant 7 am-10 pm; closed Nov-Apr. Ck-out noon. Meeting rms. Business servs avail. Gift shop. Cr cds: A, D, DS, ER, MC, V.
D ⬤ 🏊 ⊠ 🐾

★★ **FOUR POINTS BY SHERATON SUITES, MONTREAL CENTRE-VILLE.** 475 Sherbrooke St W (H3A 2L9). 514/842-3961; fax 514/844-0945; res 800/325-3535. www.fourpoints.com. 195 rms, 20 story, 89 suites, some kitchens. May-Oct: S, D $109-$149; each addl $15; suites $155; under 12 free; package plans; lower rates rest of yr. Crib $15. Pet accepted. Valet parking $15/day. TV; cable, VCR. Restaurant 7 am-10 pm. Bar. Rm serv. Ck-out noon. Meeting rms. Business center. In-rm modem link. Concierge. Exercise equipt; sauna. Valet lndry. Cr cds: A, C, D, ER, JCB, MC, V.
D 🐾 🏋 ⊠ 🐾 SC 🏃

★★★ **HOSTELLERIE LES TROIS TILLEULS.** 290 Richelieu St, St-Marc-Sur-Richelieu (G0L 2E0). 514/856-7787; fax 450/584-3146. www.lestroistilleuls.com. 41 rms, 3 story. S $95-$450; each addl $20; suites $250-$450. Crib free. TV; cable (premium), VCR. Heated pool. Restaurant (see also LES TROIS TILLEULS). Rm serv. Bar 11-2 am. Ck-out noon. Meeting rms. Business center. In-rm modem link. Lighted tennis. X-country ski 10 mi. Hunting trips. Private marina. Boat tours. Some in-rm whirlpools. Balconies. Golf nearby. In 1880 farmhouse. On Richelieu River. Cr cds: A, C, D, ER, JCB, MC, V.
🏊 🏋 ⊠ 🐾 🏃

★★★ **HOSTELLERIE RIVE GAUCHE.** 1810 Richelieu Blvd, Beloeil (J3G 4S4). 450/467-4477; fax 450/467-0525. 22 rms, 3 story. S $92-$110; D $125-$145; each addl $20; suites $225-$235. Crib free. TV; cable (premium). Pool. Restaurant 7:30 am-10:30 pm. Bar 11-midnight. Ck-out noon. Meeting rms. Business servs avail. Lighted tennis. X-country ski 8 mi. Balconies. View of Richelieu River and Mont Ste.-Hilaire. Cr cds: A, D, ER, MC, V.
🏊 🏋 ⊠ 🐾

★ **HOTEL LE SAINTE-ANDRE.** 1285 rue Ste.-Andre (H2L 3T1). 514/849-7070; fax 514/849-8167; toll-free 800/265-7071. 63 rms, 4 story. May-Oct: S $64.50; D $69.50; each addl $5; lower rates rest of yr. TV; cable. Complimentary continental bkfst. Restaurants nearby. Ck-out noon. Business servs avail. Located to main metro system Barrie-Uqam, walking distance to Old Montréal, Chinatown, and shopping district. Small, contemporary hotel. Cr cds: A, C, D, DS, ER, MC, V.
🐾

★ **QUALITY HOTEL DORVAL.** *7700 Cote de Liesse (H4T 1E7). 514/731-7821; fax 514/731-7267; toll-free 800/361-2643. www.qualityinn.com.* 159 rms, 4 story, 47 kit suites. S, D $145-$170; kit suites $185-$395. each addl $10; wkend rates. Parking. Crib free. Pet accepted, some restrictions. TV; cable (premium). Outdoor heated pool; 2 whirlpools. Restaurant 6:30 am-2 pm, 6-11 pm. Rm serv. Bar 5 pm-1 am. Ck-out noon. Coin lndry. Meeting rms. Business servs avail. Concierge. Valet serv. Free airport transportation. Exercise equipt; sauna. Health club privileges. Massage. Minibars. Cr cds: A, C, D, DS, ER, JCB, MC, V.

★ **QUALITY INN AND SUITES.** *6680 Taschereau Blvd, Brossard (J4W 1M8). 450/671-7213; fax 450/671-7041; res 800/267-3837. www.qualityinn.com.* 91 rms, 3 story, 9 suites. May-Oct: S, D $75-$85; each addl $10; suites $165; under 18 free; lower rates rest of yr. TV. Pool. Complimentary continental bkfst. Restaurant 11:30 am-10:30 pm. Bar. Ck-out noon. Meeting rms. Business servs avail. Health club privileges. Cr cds: A, ER, MC, V.

Hotels

★★ **CHATEAU ROYAL HOTEL SUITES.** *1420 Crescent St (H3G 2B7). 514/848-0999; fax 514/848-1891; toll-free 800/363-0335. www.chateauroyal.com.* 112 kit. suites, 21 story. May-Oct S, D $112-$214; each addl $20; under 14 free; wkend rates. Crib free. Garage parking $12; valet. TV; cable (premium). Complimentary coffee/tea in rms. Restaurant 7-1 am. Rm serv to 11 pm. Ck-out noon. Meeting rms. Business servs avail. Coin lndry. Some microwaves. Balconies. Walking distance to Museum of Fine Arts, Molson Centre, Casino, Plaza des Arts. Cr cds: A, C, D, DS, ER, MC, V.

★★★ **CHATEAU VAUDREUIL.** *21700 Trans-Canada Hwy, Vaudreuil (J7V 8P3). 450/455-0955; fax 450/455-6617. www.chateau-vaudreuil.com.* 117 rms, 6 story, 103 suites. May-Dec: S, D $165-$475; each addl $20; suites $350-$475; under 16 free; wkend rates; higher rates special events; lower rates rest of yr. Crib free. TV; cable, VCR (movies). Indoor pool; whirlpool. Complimentary coffee in rms. Restaurant 6:30 am-11 pm. Bar 11-2 am; entertainment Tues-Sun. Ck-out noon. Meeting rms. Business servs avail. In-rm modem link. Concierge. Tennis. Downhill/x-country ski 15 mi. Exercise equipt; sauna. Minibars. Some balconies. On lake. Cr cds: A, D, DS, ER, MC, V.

★★★ **CHATEAU VERSAILLES.** *1659 Sherbrooke St W (H3H 1E3). 514/933-3611; fax 514/933-6967; toll-free 800/361-3664.* 176 rms, 3-14 story, S, D $165-$250; each addl $15; suites $325-$350; under 16 free. Crib free. Heated garage; valet $12.50. TV; cable. Coffee in rms. Restaurant. Meeting rms. In-rm modem link. Some minibars. Comprised of 4 renovated Victorian houses and a 14-story tower. Cr cds: A, D, DS, ER, MC, V.

★★ **DELTA MONTREAL.** *475 President Kennedy Ave (H3A 1J4). 514/286-1986; fax 514/284-4342; toll-free 877/286-1986. www.deltahotels.com.* 446 rms, 7 suites, 23 story. S, D $205-$220; each addl $20; suites $450-$950; under 12 free; wkend packages. Crib free. Pet accepted, some restrictions; $20/day. Covered parking $12/day. TV; cable (premium). Complimentary coffee,tea in rms. Heated poolsindoor/ outdoor, whirlpool. Supervised children's activities; ages 4-12. Restaurant 7 am-9:30 pm. Rm serv 5 am-midnight. Bar 11 am-midnight. Ck-out noon. Meeting rooms. Business center. In-rm modem link. Concierge. Barber, beauty shop. Fitness center, exercise rm, sauna, spa. Massage. Minibars. Balconies. Located in the heart of downtown Montreal, near Cultural Arts Center, Place des Arts. Cr cds: A, C, D, DS, ER, JCB, MC, V.

★★★ **FAIRMONT QUEEN ELIZABETH.** *900 Rene Levesque Blvd W (H3B 4A5). 514/861-3511; fax 514/954-2255; toll-free 800/441-1414. www.fairmont.com.* 1,020 rms, 21 story. S, D $169-$279; each addl $30; suites $400-$2,000; under 18 free; wkend rates. Crib free. Garage $14. TV; cable (premium). Indoor pool; whirlpool. Coffee in rms. Restaurant (see also THE BEAVER CLUB). Rm serv 24 hrs. Bars from 11 am. Ck-out noon. Conference facilities. Business center. In-rm modem link. Shopping arcade. Beauty shop. Exercise rm. Massage. Minibars. Underground passage to Place Ville Marie. Luxury level. Cr cds: A, C, D, DS, ER, JCB, MC, V.

★★★ **HILTON MONTREAL AIRPORT.** *12505 Cote de Liesse (H9P 1B7). 514/631-2411; fax 514/631-0192; 800/445-8667. www.hilton.com.* 486 rms, 10 story. S, D $109-$279; under 18 free. Crib avail. TV; cable (premium). Indoor pool; whirlpool. Restaurant 6:30 am-10 pm. Bar to midnight. Ck-out noon. Meeting rms. Business center. In-rm modem link. Concierge. Exercise equipt. Minibars; many refrigerators in suites. Cr cds: A, D, DS, ER, MC, V.

★★★ **HILTON MONTREAL BONAVENTURE.** *1 Place Bonaventure (H5A 1E4). 514/878-2332; fax 514/878-3881; res 800/445-8667. www.hiltonmontreal.com.* 393 rms, 25 story. S, D $155-$425; under 18 free. Crib free. Pet accepted, some restrictions. TV; cable. Restaurant. Bar. Heated pool. Exercise rm. Concierge. Business center. Ck-out noon. Cr cds: A, C, D, DS, ER, MC, V.

★★★ **HILTON MONTREAL/LAVAL.** *2225, autoroute des Laurentides (H7S 1Z6). 450/682-2225; 800/445-8667. www.hilton.com.* 170 rms, 5 story. S, D $250-$375; under 18 free. Crib avail. TV; cable (premium). Indoor pool; whirlpool. Restaurant 6:30 am-10 pm. Bar to midnight. Ck-out noon. Meeting rms. Business center. In-rm modem link. Concierge. Exercise equipt. Minibars; many refrigerators in suites. Cr cds: A, D, DS, ER, MC, V.

★★ **HOLIDAY INN SELECT CENTRE VILLE.** *99 Viger Ave W (H2Z 1E9).* 514/878-9888; fax 514/878-6341; 800/465-4329. www.holiday-inn.com. 235 rms, 8 story. May-Oct: S $160-$185; D $170-$195; each addl $10; suites $399-$499; family, wkly, wkend rates; lower rates rest of yr. Crib free. Garage fee in/out. TV; cable. Indoor pool; whirlpool. Coffee in rms. Restaurant 6:30 am-11 pm. Bar 11-1 am. Ck-out noon. Meeting rms. Business center. In-rm modem link. Gift shop. Barber, beauty shop. Exercise equipt; saunas, steam rm. Massage. Some balconies. Pagoda-topped building in Chinatown area. Cr cds: A, C, D, DS, ER, JCB, MC, V.

D ⊷ 🏋 ⊠ 🔥 SC 🏌

★★ **HOTEL AUBERGE UNIVERSEL MONTREAL.** *5000 Sherbrooke St E (H1V 1A1).* 514/253-3365; fax 514/253-9958. www.auberge-universel.com. 229 rms, 7 story. S $97; D $107; each addl $12; under 16 free. TV; cable (premium), VCR avail. 2 pools, 1 indoor; whirlpool. Sauna. Restaurant 7 am-11 pm. Bar; entertainment Tues-Sat. Ck-out noon. Meeting rms. Business servs avail. Gift shop. Valet serv. Free covered parking. Refrigerator in suites. Microwaves avail. Across from Olympic stadium, biodome, botanical gardens. Cr cds: A, C, D, ER, MC, V.

⊠ ⊠ 🔥 SC

★★★ **HOTEL INTER-CONTINENTAL MONTREAL.** *360 Rue Ste Antoine W (H2Y 3X4).* 514/987-9900; fax 514/847-8550; toll-free 800/361-3600. www.interconti.com. 357 rms, 23 suites, 26 story. May-mid-Oct: S, D $189-$245; each addl $25; suites $360-$2,200; under 17 free; family, wkend rates; lower rates rest of yr. Crib free. Pet accepted, some restrictions. Valet parking $19/day. TV; cable (premium), VCR avail. Indoor heated pool. Restaurant 6:30 am-11:30 pm. Rm serv 24 hrs. Bar 11:30-1 am; entertainment. Ck-out 1 pm. Meeting rms. Convention facilities. Business center. In-rm modem link. Concierge. Barber, beauty shop. Exercise rm. Massage. Bathrm phones, minibars. Connected to shop and boutiques, metro system. Near Old Montréal. Next to Convention Center. Cr cds: A, DS, MC, V.

🏌 ⊷ ⊠ 🏋 🏌

★ **HOTEL LA RESIDENCE DU VOYAGEUR.** *847 Sherbrooke E (H2L 1K6).* 514/527-9515; fax 514/526-1070. www.hotelresidencevoyager.com. 28 units, 4 story. June-mid-Sept: S $50-$90; D $65-$105; each addl $5; under 12 free; wkly rates winter; lower rates rest of yr. TV; cable. Complimentary continental bkfst. Restaurants nearby. Ck-out noon. Business servs avail. Free parking. Airport transportation. Refrigerators, microwaves avail. Cr cds: A, DS, MC, V.

🏌 ⊠ 🔥 SC

★★★ **HOTEL L'EAU A LA BOUCHE.** *3003 Bd Ste-Adele, Sainte Adele (J8B 2N6).* 450/229-2991. 25 rms, 3 story. S, D $175-$315. TV; cable (premium). Restaurant 6:30 am-10 pm. Bar to midnight. Ck-out noon. Meeting rms. Business servs avail. In-rm modem link. Concierge. Exercise equipt. Spa. Cr cds: A, ER, MC, V.

🏌

★★★ **HOTEL LE GERMAIN.** *2050 Mansfield (H3A 1Y9).* 514/849-2050; fax 514/849-1437; toll-free 877/333-2050. www.hotelboutique.com. 100 rms, 16 story, 2 suites. July-Aug: S, D $210-$315; lower rates rest of yr. Crib avail. Pet accepted, some restrictions; fee. Valet parking. TV; cable (premium), VCR avail. Complimentary full bkfst, newspaper, toll-free calls. Restaurant nearby. Bar. Ck-out noon. Meeting rms. Business servs avail. Dry cleaning, coin lndry. Gift shop. Exercise privileges. Tennis. Downhill skiing. Bike rentals. Picnic facilities. Cr cds: A, D, ER, MC, V.

D ⊷ ⊠ 🏋 🏌 ⊠ 🔥

★★★ **HOTEL OMNI MONT-ROYAL.** *1050 Sherbrooke St W (H2A 2R6).* 514/284-1110; fax 514/845-3025; toll-free 800/842-6664. www.omnihotels.com. 271 rms, 29 suites, 31 story. May-Oct: S, D $149-$585; each addl $30; suites $250-$975; under 18 free; wkend rates; lower rates rest of yr. Crib free. Pet accepted, some restrictions. Valet parking $20/day. TV; cable (premium), VCR avail. Outdoor heated pool; whirlpool, poolside serv, lifeguard (summer only). Restaurants (see also ZEN). Rm serv 24 hrs. Bar noon-midnight. Ck-out 1 pm. Meeting rms. Business center. In-rm modem link. Concierge. Shopping boutiques. Barber, beauty shop. Fully-equipped fitness center, sauna, steam rm. Massage. Bathrm phones, minibars. Located at the foot of Mt. Royal, near all attractions and shopping. Cr cds: A, C, D, DS, MC, V.

⊷ 🏋 🔥 🏋 🏌 ⊠

★★★ **LA PINSONNIERE.** *124 rue St-Raphael, Cap a l'Aigle (G0T 1B0).* 418/665-4431. 25 rms, 3 story. S, D $160-$525. TV; cable (premium). Restaurant 6:30 am-10 pm. Bar to midnight. Ck-out noon. Meeting rms. Business servs avail. In-rm modem link. Concierge. Exercise equipt. Spa. Cr cds: A, ER, MC, V.

🏌

★★★ **LE CENTRE SHERATON.** *1201 Blvd Rene Levesque W (H3B 2L7).* 514/878-2000; fax 514/878-2305; res 800/325-3535. www.sheraton.com. 825 rms, 37 story, 42 suites. S, D $150-$290; each addl $25; suites $460-$1,200; under 17 free; wkend packages. Crib free. Valet parking $20/day. TV; cable (premium), VCR (suites). Indoor heated pool; whirlpool, lifeguard. Complimentary coffee in rms. Restaurant 6:30 am-2 pm, 5:30 pm-midnight. 2 bars 11:30-2 am. Ck-out noon. Meeting rms. Convention facilities. Business center. In-rm modem link. Some bathrm phones. Shopping arcade. Barber, beauty shop. Fitness center. Massage. Minibars avail. Club level avail. Across from the Molson Center. In the heart of downtown Montréal; minutes from Old Montréal. Cr cds: A, D, DS, ER, JCB, MC, V.

D ⊷ 🏋 ⊠ 🔥 🏌

★★ **LE NOUVEL HOTEL.** *1740 Rene Levesque Blvd W (H3H 1R3).* 514/931-8841; fax 514/931-3233; toll-free 800/363-6063. www.lenouveauhotel.com. 126 rms, 32 studios, 8 story. S, D $130-$150; each addl $10; studio $150-$170; under 12 free. Crib free. Indoor parking $9.50. TV; cable (premium). Pool; whirlpool. Restaurant 7 am-11 pm. Bar. Ck-out noon. Meeting rms. Business servs avail. In-rm modem link. Valet serv. Gift shop. Beauty shop. Game rm. Microwaves avail. Near Molson Centre. Cr cds: A, D, DS, ER, MC, V.

D ⊷ ⊠ 🔥

★★★★ **LOEWS HOTEL VOGUE.** *1425 rue de la Montagne (H3G 1Z3). 514/285-5555; fax 514/849-8903; res 800/465-6654. www.loewsvogue.com.* Located in the center of the city's golden square mile, this 126-room, 16-suite property has an intimate feel for such a central city location. Exclusive shops, museums, bars, and restaurants are within walking distance for those interested in exploring the city, while the needs of business travelers are also taken into account: personal fax machines, three boardrooms, and six executive boardroom suites. 126 rms, 9 story, 16 suites. Mid-May-mid-Oct: S, D $159-$599; each addl $20; suites $399-$2,200; under 18 free; wkend rates; lower rates rest of yr. Crib free. Pet accepted. Garage; valet parking $15. TV; cable, VCR (movies). Restaurant 7 am-11 pm. Rm serv 24 hrs. Bar 3 pm-1 am. Ck-out 1 pm. Meeting rms. Business servs avail. In-rm modem link. Gift shop. Exercise equipt. Massage. Health club privileges. Bathrm phones, TV. Some microwaves. In-rm whirlpools, minibars. Cr cds: A, C, D, ER, JCB, MC, V.

★★ **MARRIOTT CHATEAU CHAMPLAIN MONTREAL.** *1050 de la Gauchetiere (H3B 4C9). 514/878-9000; fax 514/878-6761; toll-free 800/200-5909. www.marriott.com.* 611 rms, 36 story. May-Dec: S, D $165-$200; suites $238-$1,350; under 18 free; wkend rates; lower rates rest of yr. Crib free. Parking (fee). TV; cable (premium), VCR avail. Indoor pool; whirlpool, poolside serv, lifeguard. Restaurant 7 am-2:30 pm, 5:30-10:30 pm. Rm serv 6:30-1 am. Bars. Ck-out noon. Meeting rms. Business center. In-rm modem link. Shopping arcade. Barber, beauty shop. Exercise rm; sauna. Massage. Minibars. Luxury level. Cr cds: A, C, D, DS, ER, JCB, MC, V.

★★★ **NOVOTEL MONTREAL CENTRE.** *1180 rue de la Montagne (H3G 1Z1). 514/861-6000; fax 514/861-6470; res 800/668-6835. www.novotel.com.* 226 rms, 9 story. May-Oct: S, D $129-$400; each addl $15; suites $500-$1,500; family, wkend and hol rates; higher rates during Grand Prix; lower rates rest of yr. Crib free. Pet accepted, some restrictions; $15. Parking garage $9.75. TV; cable (premium). Restaurant 6:30 am-10:30 pm. Bar noon-midnight. Ck-out 1 pm. Meeting rms. Business servs avail. In-rm modem link. Exercise equipt. Minibars. Cr cds: A, C, D, ER, JCB, MC, V.

★★★ **RENAISSANCE MONTREAL HOTEL.** *3625 Ave du Parc (H2X 3P8). 514/288-6666; fax 514/288-2469. www.renaissancehotels.com.* 459 rms, 16 story. May-Oct: S, D $109-$260; each addl $15; suites $250-$1,500; under 18 free; wkend rates; lower rates rest of yr. Crib free. Pet accepted, some restrictions. Garage (fee). TV; cable, VCR avail. Complimentary coffee in rms. Restaurant 6:30 am-10:30 pm. Bar from noon. Ck-out noon. Meeting rms. Business center. Shopping arcade. Barber, beauty shop. Exercise rm. Health club privileges. Luxury level. Cr cds: A, C, D, DS, ER, JCB, MC, V.

★★★ **THE RITZ-CARLTON, MONTREAL.** *1228 Sherbrooke St W (H3G 1H6). 514/842-4212; fax 514/842-3383; res 800/241-3333. www.ritzcarlton.com.* 230 rms, 9 story. May-Oct: S, D $235-$435; each addl $35; suites $425-$770; under 14 free; wkend rates; lower rates rest of yr. Crib free. TV; cable. Restaurants 6:30 am-10 pm (see also CAFE DE PARIS). Rm serv 24 hrs. Bar 11:30 am-midnight; pianist. Ck-out noon. Meeting rms. Business servs avail. In-rm modem link. Barber. Valet parking. Exercise equipt. Massage. Health club privileges. Minibars. Cr cds: A, D, DS, ER, MC, V.

★★★ **SHERATON LAVAL HOTEL.** *2440 Autoroute des Laurentides (H7T 1X5). 450/687-2440; fax 450/687-0655; res 800/325-3535. www.sheraton.com.* 241 rms, 6 story. S, D $119-$249; under 18 free. Crib avail. TV; cable (premium). Indoor pool; whirlpool. Restaurant 6:30 am-10 pm. Bar to midnight. Ck-out noon. Meeting rms. Business center. In-rm modem link. Concierge. Exercise equipt. Minibars; many refrigerators in suites. Cr cds: A, C, D, ER, MC, V.

★★ **WYNDHAM MONTREAL.** *1255 Jeanne Mance (H5B 1E5). 514/285-1450; fax 514/285-1243; toll-free 800/361-8234. www.wyndham.com.* 600 rms, 28 suites, 12 story. S, D $139-$189; each addl $20; suites $380-$950; under 18 free; wkend rates. Crib free. Valet parking $18. Pet accepted. TV; cable (premium), VCR avail. Complimentary coffee in rms. Indoor pool; whirlpool, poolside serv, lifeguard. Restaurant 7 am-midnight (see also LE CAFE FLEURI). Rm serv. Bar 11:30-1 am. Ck-out noon. Meeting rms. Business center. In-rm modem link. Concierge. 120 shops and boutiques. Exercise equipt, 2 saunas. Massage. Minibars. Located in the heart of Cultural District. Connected to Place des Arts, linked directly to Montreal Convention Center and metro system. Cr cds: A, C, D, DS, ER, JCB, MC, V.

Resorts

★★★ **FAIRMONT TREMBLANT.** *3045 Chemin Principale (J0T 1Z0). 819/681-7000. www.fairmont.com.* 316 rms, 10 story. S, D $250-$375; under 18 free. Crib avail. TV; cable (premium). Indoor pool; whirlpool. Restaurant 6:30 am-10 pm. Bar to midnight. Ck-out noon. Meeting rms. Business center. In-rm modem link. Concierge. Exercise equipt. Minibars; many refrigerators in suites. Cr cds: A, DS, ER, MC, V.

★★★ **WESTIN RESORT, TREMBLANT.** *One Chemin Kandahar (J0T 1Z0). 819/681-2000; fax 819/681-8001. www.westin.com.* 71 rms, 4 story. S, D $250-$325; under 18 free. Crib avail. TV; cable (premium). Indoor pool; whirlpool. Restaurant 6:30 am-10 pm. Bar to midnight. Ck-out noon. Meeting rms. Business center. In-rm modem link. Concierge. Exercise equipt. Minibars; many refrigerators in suites. Cr cds: A, C, D, DS, ER, JCB, MC, V.

B&Bs/Small Inns

★★★ **AUBERGE DE LA FONTAINE.** *1301 Rue Rachel E (H2J 2K1).* 514/597-0166; fax 514/597-0496. *www.auberge delafontaine.com.* 21 rms, 3 story, 3 suites. May-Nov: S $139-$163; D $154-$178; each addl $15; suites $221-$233; under 12 free. TV; cable, VCR avail. Complimentary bkfst buffet. Ck-out noon, ck-in 3 pm. Meeting rm. Business servs avail. In-rm modem link. Sun deck. Some in-rm whirlpools. Some balconies. Former residence; quiet setting in urban location; opp La Fontaine Parc. Cr cds: A, MC, V.

⊗

★★★ **AUBERGE HANDFIELD.** *555 Richelieu, St-Marc-Sur-Richelieu (J0L 2E0).* 450/584-2226; fax 450/584-3650. *www.aubergehandfield.com.* 53 rms, 2 story. S $70; D $80-$195; each addl $10; under 4 free; theatre, winter package plans. Crib free. TV; cable (premium). Outdoor pool; whirlpool, poolside serv. Restaurant (see also AUBERGE HANDFIELD). Bar 11 am-midnight. Ck-out noon, ck-in 3 pm. Meeting rms. Business servs avail. Golf privileges. Tennis privileges. Downhill/x-country ski 15 mi. Exercise rm; sauna. Bathrm phones. Theater boat (late June-early Sept). Marina. Sugar cabin (late Feb-late Apr). Built in 1880. Cr cds: A, C, D, DS, ER, MC, V.

⊗ ⊗ ⊗ ⊗ ⊗ ⊗ ⊗ ⊗ ⊗

★★★ **AUBERGE HATLEY.** *325 Virgin St, CP330, North Hatley (J0B 2C0).* 819/842-2451; fax 819/842-2907; toll-free 800/336-2451. *www.northhatley.com.* 25 rms, 3 story, 5 suites. MAP: D $245-$390; each addl $90; wkly, wkend rates; ski plans. Heated pool. Complimentary full bkfst. Dining rm 8-10 am, 6 pm-closing. Ck-out noon, ck-in 4 pm. Business servs avail. Downhill ski 1 mi; x-country ski on site. Many fireplaces; some in-rm whirlpools, balconies. Lake opp; swimming, boats avail for guest use. 1903 Victorian-style mansion. Cr cds: A, ER, MC, V.

⊗ ⊗ ⊗ ⊗ ⊗

★ **LE BRETON.** *1609 Rue St Hubert (H2L 3Z1).* 514/524-7273; fax 514/527-7016. 13 rms, 11 with private bath, 3 story. S $35-$55; D $45-$70; each addl $8. TV; cable. Complimentary continental bkfst. Restaurant nearby. Ck-out noon, ck-in 2 pm. Some rm phones. Business servs avail. Self-parking. Cr cds: MC, V.

⊗ ⊗

★ **MANOIR AMBROSE.** *3422 Stanley St (H3A 1R8).* 514/288-6922; fax 514/288-5757. *www.manoirambrose.com.* 21 rms, 16 with bath, 8 A/C, 3 story. May-Oct: S, D $60-$115; each addl $10; under 12 free; winter wkly rates; lower rates rest of yr. Crib free. Parking $5/day. TV; cable. Complimentary continental bkfst. Ck-out noon, ck-in 2:30 pm. Business servs avail. Near Peel metro station. Victorian mansion built 1883; large windows, high ceilings. Cr cds: MC, V.

⊗ ⊗

Conference Center

★★ **HOTEL CHERIBOURG.** *2603 Chemin du Parc, Orford (J1X 8C8).* 819/843-3308; fax 819/843-2639; toll-free 800/567-6132. *www.cheribourg.com.* 97 rms, 3 story. Mid-June-early Sept, late Jan-late Mar: S, D $84; each addl $44; suites $184-$192; under 12 free; lower rates rest of yr. Crib free. TV; cable (premium), VCR avail. 2 pools, 1 indoor; whirlpool, poolside serv, lifeguard. Playground. Restaurants 7:30 am-10 pm. Rm serv. Bar. Ck-out noon. Coin lndry. Meeting rms. Business servs avail. Concierge. Valet serv. Indoor tennis, pro. Downhill/x-country ski 2 mi. Exercise equipt; sauna. Massage. Game rm. Rec rm. Lawn games. Some balconies. Cr cds: A, C, D, DS, ER, MC, V.

⊗ ⊗ ⊗ ⊗ ⊗ ⊗ ⊗ ⊗

Restaurants

★★ **AUBERGE HANDFIELD.** *Richelieu, Saint-Marc-sur-Richelieu (J0L 2E0).* 450/584-2226. *www.aubergehandfield.com.* Canadian, French menu. Specialties: lapin saute, petit cochon de lait, ragout de pattes. Hrs: 8 am-midnight; Sun brunch 10 am-3 pm. Res accepted. Bar. A la carte entrees: lunch, dinner $15.50-$31. Sun brunch $19.50. Child's menu. Parking. In 1880 building. Indoor terrace with view of Richelieu River. Family-owned. Cr cds: A, C, D, DS, ER, MC, V.

⊗

★★ **AU PETIT EXTRA.** *1690 Rue Ontario E (H2L 1S7).* 514/527-5552. *www.aupetitextra.com.* Specializes in hot goat cheese, fish soup, homemade pate. Hrs: 11:30 am-10 pm; Fri, Sat to 10:30 pm. Res required. Wine, beer. Lunch $10.25-$13.50; dinner $14.50-$22. Entertainment. Cr cds: A, C, D, MC, V.

⊗ ⊗

★★★ **THE BEAVER CLUB.** *900 Rene Levesque Blvd W (H3B 4A5).* 514/861-3511. Continental menu. Specialties: chateaubriand, prime rib of beef. Hrs: noon-3 pm, 6-11 pm; Sat from 6 pm. Closed Sun, Mon eve; dinners only late June-mid-Sept. Res accepted. Bar. Wine cellar. A la carte entrees: dinner $33-$38. Child's menu. Valet parking. Jacket. Social dancing with live music Sat. Cr cds: A, D, DS, ER, JCB, MC, V.

⊗ ⊗ ⊗

★★★ **BICE RISTORANTE.** *1504 Rue Sherbrooke Ouest (H3G 1L3).* 514/937-6009. Hrs: noon-3 pm, 6-11 pm; Sat, Sun from 6 pm. Res accepted. Wine list. Lunch $20-$26; dinner $50-$75. Cr cds: A, C, D, DS, ER, JCB, MC, V.

⊗

★★★ **BISTRO A CHAMPLAIN.** *75 Chemin Masson, Ste. Marguerite (J0T1L0).450/2284988.www.bistroachamplain. com.* Cuisine eclectic. Hrs: 6-8:30 pm. Closed Mon, Tues. Dinner: $24-$36. Extensive wine cellar. Parking. Elegant restaurant in an 1864 old general store; located across from Lake Masson. Cr cds: A, C, D, ER, MC, V.

⊗ ⊗

★★ **CAFE DE PARIS.** *1228 Sherbrooke St W (H3G 1H6). 514/842-4212. www.ritzcarlton.com.* French menu. Specialties: feuillete de saumon, scallops. Own pastries. Hrs: 6:30-11:30 am, noon-2:30 pm, 3:30-5 pm, 6-10 pm; Sat, Sun brunch noon-2:30 pm. Res accepted; required for brunch. Bar. Wine list. A la carte entrees: bkfst $11.95-$21.95, dinner $30.50-$45. Sat brunch $28.95, Sun brunch $42.50. Child's menu. Entertainment Tues-Sat. Valet parking. Outdoor dining. Cr cds: A, C, D, DS, ER, JCB, MC, V.

D ⊟

★ **CAFE STE. ALEXANDRE.** *518 Duluth St E (H2L 1A7). 514/849-4251.* Greek menu. Specializes in steak, fish. Hrs: 11 am-midnight. Res accepted. Setups. A la carte entrees: lunch, dinner $10-$18.95. Table d'hôte: dinner $14.95-$17.95. Child's menu. Salad bar. Outdoor dining. Cr cds: A, MC, V.

D ⊟

★★★ **CAFI FERREIRA.** *1446 Rue Peel (H3A 1S8). 514/848-0988. www.ferreiracafe.com.* Mediterranean and Portuguese menu. Hrs: 11 am-11 pm; Sat 5-11 pm. Closed Sun. Res required. Wine list. Lunch $15-$40; dinner $22-$39. Jacket. Cr cds: A, D, DS, ER, MC, V.

D

★★★ **CHEZ GEORGE.** *1425 Rue de La Montagne. 514/285-5555.* Specializes in steak tartar, lobster crepes. Hrs: 7 am-10 pm. Res accepted. Wine list. Lunch $18-$28; dinner $22-$39. Sun brunch $25. Child's menu. Cr cds: A, D, ER, MC.

D ⊟

★★★ **CHEZ LA MERE MICHEL.** *1209 Guy St (H3H 2K5). 514/934-0473.* Classic French cuisine. Specialties: pintade au vinaigre de framboises, homard soufflé. Own pastries. Hrs: noon-2:30 pm, 5:30-10:30 pm; Sat, Mon from 5:30 pm. Closed Sun. Res required. Wine cellar. Table d'hôte: lunch $14.50-$17.50. A la carte entrees: dinner $24.50-$39. French provincial decor. Family-owned. Cr cds: A, ER, MC, V.

D ⊟

★★ **GLOBE.** *3455 St. Laurent (H2X 2V2). 514/284-3823. www.restaurantglobe.com.* Menu changes seasonally. Hrs: 6-11 pm; Thurs-Sat to midnight. Res required. Wine, beer. Dinner $22-$35. Entertainment. Cr cds: A, MC, V.

D ⊟

★★ **IL CORTILE.** *1442 Sherbrooke W (H3G 1K3). 514/843-8230.* Italian cuisine. Hrs: 11 am-11 pm. Lunch $15-$20, dinner $17.50-$35. Res required. Cr cds: A, MC, V.

⊟

★ **LA CAVERNE GREQUE.** *105 Prince Arthur E (H2X 1B6). 514/844-5114.* Greek menu. Specializes in seafood, steak. Hrs: 11 am-midnight; Fri, Sat to 1 am. Res accepted. Setups. Complete meals: lunch $5-$10. A la carte entrees: dinner $9-$19.95. Child's menu. Cr cds: A, D, DS, ER, MC, V.

⊟

★★ **LA GAUDRIOLE.** *825 Laurier E. 514/276-1580. www.lagaudriole.com.* French menu. Hrs: 11:30 am-2 pm, 5:30-9:30 pm; Sat 5:30-10:30 pm. Res accepted. Wine, beer. Lunch $9-$14; dinner $26-$29. Entertainment. Cr cds: A, D, ER, MC, V.

D ⊟

★ **LA LOUISIANE.** *5850 Rue Sherbrooke W (H4A 1X5). 514/369-3073.* Specializes in jambalaya, prime rib, shrimp magnolia. Hrs: 5:30-10:30 pm; Thurs, Fri 11:30 am-10:30 pm. Closed Mon. Wine, beer. Lunch $6.50-$13; dinner $9-$19. Entertainment. Cr cds: A, D, MC, V.

D ⊟

★★★ **LALOUX.** *250 Ave Des Pins Eastside (H2W 1P3). 514/287-9127.* Specializes in fish, shellfish. Hrs: 11:30 am-3 pm, 5:30-10:30 pm; Thurs, Fri to 11:30 pm; Sat 5:30-11:30 pm. Closed Jan 1, Dec 25. Res accepted. Wine list. Lunch $10-$16; dinner $20-$35. Entertainment: jazz music. Cr cds: A, D, ER, MC, V.

⊟

★★★ **LA MAREE.** *404 Place Jacques Cartier (H2Y 3B2). 514/861-8126.* French menu. Specialties: homard brunetiere, châteaubriand grille. Own pastries, sherbets. Hrs: noon-3 pm, 6-11 pm; Sat, Sun from 5:30 pm. Closed Jan 1, Dec 25. Res required. Serv bar. Wine cellar. Complete meals: lunch $14.50-$17.50. A la carte entrees: dinner $26.50-$45. Terrace dining avail May-Sept. Cr cds: A, D, DS, ER, JCB, MC, V.

⊟

★★★ **LA RAPIERE.** *1155 rue Metcalfe (H3B 2V6). 514/871-8920.* French menu. Specialties: le confit de canard au vinaigre de framboise, le cassoulet a la Toulousaine. Hrs: noon-3 pm, 5:30-10 pm; Sat from 5:30 pm. Closed Sun; major hols; also mid-July-mid-Aug. Res accepted. Bar. Wine list. A la carte entrees: lunch $17.75-$26.50, dinner $24.25-$38.75. French decor. Jacket. Cr cds: A, D, ER, MC, V.

D ⊟

★★★★ **L'EAU A LA BOUCHE.** *3003 Blvd Ste.-Adele (J8B 2N6). 450/229-2991. www.leaualabouche.com.* This hotel restaurant is tucked away just north of Montreal in what's called "cottage country" where charming Alpine houses dot the landscape. The name, meaning "mouth watering," is an apt description of chef Anne Desjardin's exquisite menu highlighting local ingredients. Lovely details of the original builder, a German cabinet-maker, are evident in the French-Canadian chalet's detailed paneling and wall carvings. French and original cuisine. Menu changes weekly. Hrs: 6-9 pm; Sat to 9:30 pm. Closed hols. 5-course $55, 7-course $65, 9-course $75. Bar. Cr cds: C, D, DS, ER, MC, V.

D

★★ **LE CAFE FLEURI.** *1255 Jeanne Mance (H5B 1E5). 514/285-1450. www.hoteldesjardins.com.* French, continental menu. Specialties: marinated Canadian salmon, casserole of scallops, puffed pastry shell stuffed with wild mushrooms. Salad bar. Own pastries. Hrs: 6:30 am-9:30 pm. Res accepted. Serv bar. A la carte entrees: bkfst $9.75-$12.75, lunch $13.75-$16.75, dinner $13.75-$18.75. Buffet: bkfst $14.75. Lunch $16.95. Child's menu. Parking. Terrace dining. Cr cds: A, DS, ER, MC, V.

D ⊟

★★ **LE CHRYSANTHEME.** *1208 Crescent (H3G 2A9). 514/397-1408.* Chinese, Szechuan menu. Specializes in won ton raviolis with sesame sauce, shrimp. Hrs: noon-2:30 pm, 6-10:30 pm; Fri, Sat 6-11:30 pm; Sun from 6 pm;

closed Mon; Jan 1, Dec 24, 25. Res accepted. Bar. A la carte entrees: lunch $10.80-$14. Complete meals: lunch $10-$13, dinner $12-$20. Chinese decor, artifacts. Cr cds: A, C, D, DS, MC, V.

[D] [symbol]

★ **LE JARDIN DE PANOS.** *521 Duluth St E (H2L 1A8). 514/521-4206.* Greek, French menu. Specialties: moussaka, dolmas, salade Grecque. Hrs: noon-midnight. Closed Dec 25. Complete meals: lunch $7-$15. A la carte entrees: dinner $9-$19. Outdoor dining. Mediterranean decor. Cr cds: A, MC, V.

[D] [symbol]

★ **LE KEG/BRANDY'S.** *25 St. Paul E (H2Y 1G2). 514/871-9093.* Specializes in steak, chicken, seafood. Hrs: 11:30 am-2:30 pm; 5-10 pm; Thurs, Fri to 11 pm; Sat 4:30-11 pm; summer hrs vary. Closed Dec 25. Res accepted. Bar 11:30-3 am. A la carte entrees: lunch $4.29-$14.99, dinner $13.99-$30. Child's menu. Cr cds: A, D, ER, MC, V.

[D] [symbol]

★★★ **LE LUTETIA.** *1430 rue de la Montagne (H3G 1Z5). 514/288-5656. www.hotellelamontagne.com.* Specializes in duck, squab, halibut, lobster. Hrs: 7 am-11 pm, noon-2:30 pm, 6-10 pm. Closed Sun, Mon. Res accepted. Wine list. Lunch $16-$20 a la carte; dinner $5-$24.50. Entertainment. Cr cds: A, D, ER, MC, V.

[D] [symbol]

★★ **LE MAISTRE.** *5700 Monkland (H4A 1E6). 514/481-2109.* Specializes in rack of lamb with thyme and honey sauce, duck confit with cremone mustard. Hrs: 5:30-9:30 pm; Thur, Fri from 11:30 am. Closed Sun, Mon. Res accepted. Wine, beer. Lunch $10.50-$16; dinner $24-$31. Entertainment. Cr cds: A, D, ER, MC, V.

★★★ **LE MAS DES OLIVIERS.** *1216 Rue Bishop (H3X 2R2). 514/861-6733.* Specializes in rack of lamb, blue tuna. Hrs: 10:30 am-11 pm, Sat 6-11 pm, Sun 6-10:30 pm. Res required. Wine list. Lunch $12-$22; dinner $21-$37. Cozy southern French house. Cr cds: A, D, ER, MC, V.

[symbol]

★★★ **LE MITOYEN.** *652 Place Publique Ste Dorothee Laval (H7X 1G1). 450/689-2977.* Nouvelle cuisine. Specialties: medaillons de caribou aux framboises, magrets de canard. Own pastries, baking. Hrs: 6-11 pm. Closed Mon. Res accepted. Wine list. A la carte entrees: dinner $20.50-$28.50. Complete meals: dinner $29.50-$58. Child's menu. Parking. Renovated 1870 house. Fireplace. Outdoor terrace. Cr cds: A, C, D, DS, ER, MC, V.

[D] [symbol]

★★ **LE MUSCADIN.** *639 Notre Dame W (H3C 1H8). 514/842-0588. www.muscadin.com.* Specializes in veal moscardino. Hrs: 11:30 am-2:30 pm, 6-10 pm. Closed Sun; most major hols. Res accepted. Wine list. Lunch $19-$23; dinner $23-$45. Entertainment. Cr cds: A, D, DS, ER, MC, V.

[D] [symbol]

★★ **LE PARCHEMIN.** *1333 rue University (H3A 2A4). 514/844-1619.* Specializes in beef Wellington, foie gras, Dover sole. Hrs: 11 am-3 pm, 5 pm-midnight. Closed Sun; Jan 1, Dec 25. Res accepted. Wine, beer. Lunch $10-$26; dinner $18-$35. Entertainment. Cr cds: A, C, D, ER, JCB, MC, V.

[D] [symbol]

★★ **LE PARIS.** *1812 Ste Catherine Ouest (H3H 1M1). 514/937-4898.* French menu. Specializes in fish, liver, steak. Hrs: noon-3 pm, 5-10 pm. Closed Sun; Dec 25. Res accepted. A la carte entrees: lunch, dinner $13-$20. Parisian atmosphere. Cr cds: A, D, MC, V.

[symbol]

★★★ **LE PASSE-PARTOUT.** *3857 Boul Decarie (H4A 3J6). 514/487-7750.* French menu. Specialties: smoked salmon, red snapper a la Provençal. Own baking. Hrs: 11:30 am-2 pm, 6:30-9:30 pm; Tues, Wed to 2 pm; Sat from 6:30 pm. Closed Sun, Mon; most major hols. Res accepted. Complete meals: lunch $18.50, dinner $40-$50. Classic French decor. Cr cds: A, D, DS, MC, V.

[D] [symbol]

★★★ **LE PIEMONTAIS.** *1145-A Rue de Bullion. 514/861-8122.* Hrs: Closed Sun. Res accepted. Wine list. Lunch $15-$20; dinner $22-$33. Cr cds: A, C, D, DS, ER, MC, V.

[D] [symbol]

★★★★ **LE PIMENT ROUGE .** *1170 Peel (H3B 4P2). 514/866-7816.* Proprietor Hazel Mah, who also owns Sherlock's and Boston's Ma Soba Pan Asian Noodles, oversees this dining room located in the renovated Windsor Hotel annex. It serves some of the city's best Chinese cuisine in a quiet and elegant setting, and with service that is refined and attentive. Specializes in General Tao's chicken. Hrs: 11:30 am-11 pm; Fri to midnight; Sat noon-midnight; Sun noon-11 pm. Res required. Wine, beer. Lunch $16.95-$21.95; dinner $24.95-$35.95. Entertainment. Cr cds: A, D, ER, MC, V.

[D] [symbol]

★★★ **LES CAPRICES DE NICOLAS.** *2072 rue Drummond (H3G 1W9). 514/282-9790. www.lescaprices.com.* French cuisine. Hrs: 6-10 pm. Specializes in fresh fish, foie gras. Dinner $28-$35. Res required. Bar. Cr cds: A, D, MC, V.

[symbol]

★★ **LES CONTINENTS.** *360 rue St-Antoine Ouest (H2Y 3X4). 514/987-9900. www.montreal.interconti.com.* Menu changes wkly. Hrs: 6:30 am-2:30 pm, 5-10:30 pm. Res accepted. Wine, beer. Lunch, dinner $19.25-$39.75. Child's menu. Entertainment: pianist. Cr cds: A, D, DS, ER, JCB, MC, V.

[D] [symbol]

★★★ **LES TROIS TILLEULS.** *290 Richelieu St (J0L 2E0). 514/856-7787. www.lestroistilleuls.com.* French menu. Specialties: ris de veau Trois Tilleuls, cuisse de canard confite et son aiguillette. Own baking. Hrs: 7:30 am-10 pm. Res accepted. Bar 11-2 am. Wine cellar. Complete meals: lunch $18.50-$22. A la carte entrees: dinner $37.50-$44.50. Child's menu. Parking. In 1880 farmhouse with garden, terrace; view of river. Cr cds: A, D, ER, JCB, MC, V.

[D]

★★★ **L'EXPRESS.** *3927 Ste. Denis (H2W 2M4). 514/845-5333.* French, continental menu. Specialties: steak tartare, fresh salmon, duck confit. Hrs: 8-2 am; Sat, Sun from 10 am. Closed Dec 25. Res accepted. Bar to 3 am. A la carte entrees: bkfst $2.45-$3.45, lunch, dinner $11-$22.80. Cr cds: A, C, D, DS, ER, MC, V.

D ⊒

★★★★ **MEDITERRANEO GRILL & WINE BAR.** *3500 Boul St, Laurent (H2X 2V1). 514/844-0027. www.medgrill.com.* Chef Claude Pelletier's Mediterranean cuisine is fresh, innovative in taste, and appealingly presented. The dining room atmosphere, including an impressive 63-foot-long bar, makes guests feel like they've stepped into the Mediterranean's warm sun, even in the cold Montreal winters. Service is friendly and professional, and despite the trendiness, the overall experience is genuinely first-rate. Californian with French influence menu. Hrs: 6-11:30 pm. Res accepted. Wine list. Dinner $35-$65. Child's menu. Cr cds: A, D, ER, MC, V.

D ⊒

★★ **MIKADO.** *368 Rue Laurier W. 514/279-4809.* Specializes in teriyaki plate, sushi. Hrs: 11:30 am-11 pm; Sun 5:30-10 pm. Res accepted. Wine, beer. Lunch $9-$14; dinner $12.50-$24. Entertainment. Cr cds: A, ER, MC, V.

⊒

★ **MOKUM.** *5795 rue Sherbrooke Ouest (H4A 1X2). 514/488-4827.* Frequently changing international menu. Hrs: 11:30 am-2:30 pm, 5:30-9:30 pm; Tues, Wed, Sat from 5:30 pm. Closed Sun, Mon; Jan 1, Dec 25. Res accepted. No A/C. Lunch $11.75-$15.50, dinner $20.75-$29.50. Outdoor dining. Casual dining. Cr cds: C, MC, V.

D ⊒

★★★★ **NUANCES.** *1 Ave de Casino (H3C 4W7). 514/392-2708. www.casinos-quebec.com.* Ten minutes from downtown, the Casino de Montreal may seem an unlikely place for this elegant restaurant. But this space rivals the most stunning dining rooms in all of Montreal and has a view to match. Although the interesting menu is not quite as mesmerizing as the room or service, which is warm, gracious, and unhurried, it is still fine and ambitious. French cuisine. Hrs: 5:30-10:30 pm. 5-course $62, 3-course $49. A la carte $33-$48. Bar. Valet. Res required. Cr cds: A, D, DS, ER, MC, V.

D ⊒

★★ **OPUS II.** *1050 Sherbooke St W (H3A 2R5). 514/849-6787.* French menu. Hrs: 6:30-11 am, noon-2:30 pm, 6-10 pm; Sun brunch 10:30 am-3 pm. Res accepted. Bar noon-11 pm. Wine cellar. A la carte entrees: lunch, dinner $19-$31. Complete meal: bkfst $12.75-$18.50. Buffet: bkfst $12. Sun brunch $24-$29. Child's menu. Specializes in seasonal menus with market freshness. Parking. Atrium; urban setting. Cr cds: A, C, D, ER, MC, V.

D ⊒

★★ **PRIMADONNA.** *3479 blvd St-laurent (H2X 2T6). 514/282-6644.* Italian menu. Hrs: 11:30 am-3 pm, 5:30-11 pm; Sat, Sun 5:30 pm-1 am. Res required. Extensive wine list. Lunch $20-$30; dinner $30-$40. Entertainment: musician. Cr cds: A, D, ER, MC, V.

⊒

★★ **QUELLI DELLA NOTTE.** *6834 Boulevard St-Laurent (H2S 3C7). 514/271-3929. www.quelli.com.* Specializes in sushi. Menu changes seasonally. Hrs: noon-3 pm, 5:30-11 pm; Fri 5:30 pm-midnight; Sat 5:30 pm-1 am. Res accepted. Wine, beer. Lunch $15-$22; dinner $13-$29. Entertainment. Cr cds: A, C, D, DS, JCB, MC, V.

⊒

★★★★ **QUEUE DE CHEVAL.** *1221 boul. Renè-Lèvesque W (H3G 1T1). 514/390-0090. www.queuedecheval.com.* Located in a renovated historic building in downtown Montreal, the restaurant is designed to evoke the city's financial roots. Framed by an arching staircase is the open grill, the walls are covered with Pierre Pivet and Ghislaine Cianciulli paintings. Specializes in steak. Hrs: 11:30 am-2:30 pm, 5:30-10:30 pm; Thurs-Sat to 11 pm. Res accepted. Bar. A la carte entrees: lunch, dinner. $23-$39. Cr cds: A, C, D, ER, MC, V.

D

★★ **RESTAURANT CHEZ LEVEQUE.** *1030 Rue Laurier Ouest (H2V 2K8). 514/279-7355.* French menu. Specializes in sea scallops over potato mousseline, torchon foie gras. Hrs: 8 am-midnight; Sat, Sun from 10 am. Res accepted. Wine, beer. Lunch $10-$32.50; dinner $15-$32.50. Entertainment. Chef-owned. Cr cds: A, D, DS, MC, V.

D

★★ **RESTAURANT LE LATINI.** *1130 Rue Jeanne Mance (H2Z 1L7). 514/861-3166.* Hrs: 11:30 am-3 pm, 5:30-11:45 pm; Sat 5-11:45 pm; Sun 4-10 pm. Wine list. Lunch $14-$28; dinner $24-$38. Entertainment. Cr cds: A, DS, MC, V.

⊒

★★★ **RISTORANTE DA VINCI.** *1180 Bishop (H3G 2E3). 514/874-2001. www.davinci.qc.ca/.* Specializes in osso bucco, meats, pasta. Hrs: noon-midnight, Sat 5 pm-midnight. Closed Sun. Res accepted. Wine, beer. Lunch $15-$20; dinner $20-$46. Cr cds: A, C, D, ER, MC, V.

⊒

★★ **SOTO RESTAURANT.** *3527 rue Ste. Laurent (H2X 2T6). 514/842-1150.* Japanese menu. Specializes in Omakase sushi, Maguro Yaki. Hrs: 5:30-10 pm; Thurs to 11 pm; Fri, Sat to 11:30 pm. Res accepted. Wine list. Dinner $20-$35. Entertainment. Cr cds: A, DS, MC, V.

⊒

★★ **SOUVENIRS D'INDOCHINE.** *243 Mont-Royal West. 514/848-0336.* Hrs: 11:30 am-2:30 pm, 5:30-10:30 pm. Res accepted. Wine, beer. Lunch $6.50-$10; dinner $20-$30. Entertainment. Cr cds: MC, V.

D ⊒

★★ **SZECHUAN.** *400 Notre Dame St W (H2Y 1V3). 514/844-4456.* Chinese menu. Specializes in General Tao's chicken, beef with orange, Szechuan shrimp. Hrs: 11:30 am-2:30 pm, 5:30-10:30 pm; Sat 5:30-11 pm. Closed Sun; Jan 1. Res accepted. Lunch $10.95-$15.95, dinner $15-$25.95. Cr cds: A, D, ER, JCB, MC, V.

D ⊒

★★ **TOKYO SUKIYAKI.** *7355 Mountain Sights Ave (H4P 2A7). 514/737-7245.* Japanese menu. Specialties: shabu shabu, sushi, sukiyaki. Hrs: 5:30-11:30 pm. Closed Mon; Jan 1, Dec 25. Res accepted. Japanese whiskey, wine, beer. Complete meals: dinner $27. Parking. Japanese decor; traditional Japanese seating. Family-owned. Cr cds: A, D, DS, M C , V.

★★★★ **TOQUE!.** *3842 rue Ste Denis (H2W 2M2). 514/499-2084.* It would not be a stretch to call this restaurant the best in Canada; it's certainly Montreal's finest. The food is always the star, and the kitchen, under the direction of chef Normand Laprise, is not afraid to take chances; how many others would dare to serve duck magret roasted with liquorice and caramelized kumquats? The service is without equal. French cuisine. Specializes in warm foie gras, fresh goat cheese. Hrs: 6-10:30 pm. Closed Sun, Mon; 2 wks late Dec-early Jan. Dinner $24-$34. Res required. Cr cds: A, D, MC, V.

[D] [⎍]

★★★ **TREEHOUSE.** *4120 St. Catherine St W (H3Z 1P4). 514/932-5654. www.kaizen-sushi-bar.com.* Specializes in new style sashimi, cobe cow steak. Hrs: 5:30-10:30 pm; Thurs-Sat to midnight. Closed Mon; Jan 1, Dec 25. Res accepted. Wine list. Dinner $45-$50. Entertainment: jazz Sun, Tues, Wed. Tatami rms. Cr cds: A, MC, V.

[D] [⎍]

★★ **ZEN.** *1050 Sherbrooke St W (H3A 2R6). 514/499-0801.* Asian menu. Specialties: Szechuan duck, General Tsao's chicken, sesame orange beef. Hrs: 11:30 am-2:30 pm, 5:30-10 pm. Closed Dec 25. Res required. A la carte entrees: lunch, dinner $10.50-$20. Complete meals: lunch $12-$25, dinner $29. Cr cds: A, C, D, DS, ER, MC, V.

[D] [⎍]

Unrated Dining Spots

AU TOURNANT DE LA RIVIERE. *5070 Salaberry, Carignan (J3L 3P9). 450/658-7372.* French cuisine. Hrs: 11 am-2 pm, 6:30-9:30 pm; Mon, Tues from 6:30 pm; Wed-Fri to 2 pm; Sun brunch 11 am-2 pm. Lunch, dinner: $28-$45. Prix fixe dinner $68. Cr cds: D, ER, MC, V.

[D]

BEN'S DELICATESSEN. *990 de Maisonneuve Blvd (H3A 1M5). 514/844-1001.* Specialties: pastrami, smoked meat, corned beef. Hrs: 7:30-3 am; Fri, Sat to 4 am; Dec 24 to 6 pm. Serv bar. Bkfst, lunch, dinner: $3.60-$9.95. Family-owned. Cr cds: MC, V.

[D] [⎍]

BIDDLE'S JAZZ AND RIBS. *2060 Aylmer (H3A 2E3). 514/842-8656.* Specializes in chicken, ribs, steak. Hrs: 11:30-2:30 am; Sun 6 pm-1 am. Res accepted. Bar. A la carte entrees: lunch, weekdays only $6.25-$11.95, dinner $7.95-$17.95. Jazz entertainment. Cr cds: A, C, D, ER, MC, V.

[⎍]

LA SAUVAGINE. *1592 Rte 329 Nord, Ste.-Agathe (J8C 2Z8). 819/326-7673. www.lasauvagine.com.* French cuisine. Hrs: 6:30-9:30 pm; closed Mon, Tues off season. Dinner $36-$50. Saloon. Res accepted. Cr cds: MC, V.

[D]

PIZZA MELLA. *107 Prince Arthur E (H2X 1B6). 514/849-4680.* Italian menu. Specializes in 30 types of pizza. Hrs: 11:30-1 am; wkends to 2 am. Closed Dec 25. Setups. Lunch, dinner $7.95-$10.95. Outdoor dining. Cooking on 3 wood-burning brick ovens; open kitchen. Cr cds: A, C, D, DS, ER, MC, V.

[D] [⎍]

RESTAURANT DAOU. *519 Faillon E (H2R 1L6). 514/276-8310.* Lebanese menu. Hrs: 11:30 am-10 pm; Sun to 9 pm. Closed Mon. Res required. Extensive wine list. Lunch, dinner $8-$22. Entertainment. Cr cds: A, D, DS, ER, MC, V.

[D] [SC] [⎍]

Mont Tremblant Provincial Park

(Approx 15 mi or 24 km N of Saint-Jovite on PQ 327)

In 1894 the provincial government of Québec established this 482-square-mile (1,248-square-kilometer) wilderness reserve as a park. A vast territory gifted with abundant wildlife and a large variety of plants, it is filled with 300 lakes, three rivers, three major hydrographical basins, innumerable streams, waterfalls, and mountains reaching as high as 3,120 feet (960 meters). Today it is a leisure haven for thousands of people interested in fishing, hiking, canoeing, biking, swimming, sailing, snowmobiling, snowshoeing, and cross-country and downhill skiing. Many come just to see the spectacular foliage in fall. Entrances are at St. Donat, on Hwy 125, St.-Faustin on Hwy 117 North, or St.-Côme on Hwy 343. Canoes and boats for rent. Reception areas, picnicking. Some facilities for the disabled; inquire for details.

Camping is available from mid-May to early October; some trailer hookups available (fee). Winter activities may be enjoyed mid-November-mid-March. Phone 819/688-2281 or 819/688-6176.

Hotel

★★★ **PINOTEAU VILLAGE.** *126 Pinoteau St, Mont Tremblant (J0T 1Z0). 819/425-2795; fax 819/425-9177.* 50 condos, 2 story. No A/C. Mid-June-mid-Sept and Nov-mid-Apr: 1-bedrm $125-$160; 2-bedrm $180-$210; 3-bedrm $260-$280; under 12 free; ski plans; lower rates rest of yr. TV; cable (premium). Heated pool. No rm serv. Ck-out noon. Tennis. Golf privileges. Downhill ski ¼ mi; x-country ski adj. Exercise equipt. Microwaves. Private patios. On lake, private beach; boat rentals. Ski shop; rentals. Cr cds: A, MC, V.

[⛷] [🏃] [≈] [🎿] [⛷] [🐾] [♨]

Resorts

★★★ **CLUB TREMBLANT.** *121 Cuttle St, Mont Tremblant (J1T 1Z0).* 819/425-8781; fax 819/425-5617; toll-free 800/567-8341. www.clubtremblant.com. 100 condos. No A/C. MAP, mid-July-mid-Aug: suites $250; wkly rates; ski plan; under 6 free; lower rates rest of yr. TV; cable. 2 pools, 1 indoor; whirlpool. Playground. Free supervised children's activities (July-Aug). Dining rm 7:30-9:30 am, 6-8:30 pm; wkends to 9 pm. Bar 4 pm-1 am. Ck-out noon, ck-in 4:30 pm. Meeting rms. Business servs avail. In-rm modem link. Tennis, pro. Canoes, rowboats, sailboats, kayaks. Downhill ski ¼mi; x-country ski adj. Ski shop; equipt rental. Rec dir. Rec rm. Exercise rm; sauna. Massage. Fireplaces. On Lake Tremblant; beach club. Cr cds: A, D, ER, JCB, MC, V.

★★★ **GRAY ROCKS RESORT AND CONVENTION CENTER.** *525 Chemin Principal, Mont Tremblant (J0T 1Z0).* 819/425-2771; fax 819/425-9156; res 800/567-6767. www.grayrocks.com. 56 rms in 5-story inn, 18 chalet suites, 39 deluxe rms, 2 cottages, 56 condos; 21 rms share bath, some A/C. AP: S $165-$230; D $125-$198/person; suites $198/person (4 min); condos $180-$420; family, wkly, wkend rates; ski, golf, tennis, package plans. Crib free. Pet accepted. TV; cable. Indoor pool; whirlpool, lifeguard. Playground. Supervised children's activities (late June-early Sept and late Nov-Mar). Dining rm (public by res) 7:30-9:30 am, noon-1:30 pm, 6:30-8:30 pm. Bar noon-1 am. Snack bar. Ck-out 1 pm; ck-in 3 pm. Coin lndry. Meeting rms. Business servs avail. Gift shop. Bellhops. Tennis. 18-hole golf, greens fee $25-$80, 2 putting greens, driving range. Private beach; beachside serv. Rowboats, canoes, sailboats, paddleboats, kayaks. Windsurfing lessons. Downhill/ x-country ski on site. Lawn games. Entertainment. Movies. Rec rm. Exercise equipt; sauna. Fireplace in some rms. Many private patios, balconies. Terrace. Sea plane base. Cr cds: A, D, DS, ER, MC, V.

Restaurants

★ **AUBERGE SAUVIGNON.** *2723 Chemin Principal, Village Mont-Tremblant (J0T 1Z0).* 819/425-5466. www.auberge sauvignon.qbc.net. French menu. Specializes in gradlax salmon, warm French goat cheese. Hrs: 6-11 pm. Res required. Wine list. Dinner $6.95-$8.95. Entertainment. Built in 1939 and in operation since 1957. Cr cds: A, D, DS, ER, JCB, MC, V.

★★★ **CAFE HENRY BURGER.** *69 rue Laurier (J8X 3V7).* 819/777-5646. Specializes in smoked salmon, venison, duck. Hrs: noon-3:30 pm, 6-10 pm. Res accepted. Extensive wine list. Lunch $3-$18; dinner $4-$44. Child's menu. Entertainment. Cr cds: A, D, DS, ER, JCB, MC, V.

★★ **LA FOURCHETTE FOLLE.** *2713 Chemin Principal, Village Mont-Tremblant (J0T 1Z0).* 819/425-7666. Specializes in pan-roasted salmon, duck, grain-fed chicken, risotto. Hrs: 6-10 pm; hrs vary per season. Res accepted. Wine, beer.

Dinner $16-$30. Child's menu. Entertainment. Name of restaurant means "Crazy Fork." Mountain terrace view. Cr cds: A, D, ER, MC, V.

★ **LE GASCON.** *Village Center, Mont Tremblant (J0T 1Z0).* 819/681-4606. www.tremblant.com. Specializes in pasta, seafood, steak. Hrs: 11 am-midnight. Res accepted. Wine, beer. Lunch $7-$15; dinner $10-$30. Child's menu. Entertainment: vocalist. Cr cds: A, D, ER, MC, V.

LE SHACK. *3035 Principal, Mont Tremblant (J0T 1Z0).* 819/681-4700. www.leshack.com. Menu changes seasonally. Hrs: 7-10 pm. Res required. Wine, beer. Lunch, dinner $8.95-$26.95. Child's menu. Entertainment. Cr cds: A, D, ER, MC, V.

★ **PIZZATERIA.** *Village Center, Mont Tremblant (G0T 1Z0).* 819/681-4522. Specializes in pizza. Hrs: 11 am-11 pm. Wine, beer. Lunch, dinner $6.75-$10.95. Child's menu. Entertainment. Cr cds: A, D, DS, MC, V.

Québec City

Founded 1608 **Pop** 166,474 **Elev** 239 ft (73 m) **Area code** 418

Information Greater Québec Area Tourism & Convention Bureau, 399 rue Saint-Joseph E, G1K 8E2; 418/522-3511

Web www.quebecregion.com

The city of Québec, one of the most beautiful in the Western Hemisphere, is 150 miles (240 kilometers) northeast of Montréal. Nestled on a historic rampart, Québec is antique, medieval, and lofty, a place of mellowed stone buildings and weathered cannon, horse-drawn calèches, ancient trees, and narrow, steeply angled streets. Here and there the 20th century has intruded, but Québec has preserved the ambience of the past.

Québec is a split-level city. Above is the sheer cliff and rock citadel that once made Québec the Gibraltar of the north. The Upper Town, built high on the cliff and surrounded by fortresslike walls, has one of the city's best-known landmarks, Le Château Frontenac, a hotel towering so high it is visible from ten miles (16 kilometers) away. The Lower Town is the region surrounding Cape Diamond and spreading up the valley of the St. Charles River, a tributary of the St. Lawrence. The two sections are divided by the Funicular, which affords magnificent views of the harbor, river, and hills beyond.

In soul and spirit Québec is French; the population is nine-tenths French. Although French is the official language, English is understood in many places. The city streets are perfect for a casual stroll and many of the things you'll want to see are convenient to one another. Winters here are quite brisk.

The first known visitor to what is now Québec was Jacques Cartier, who spent the winter of 1535 at what was then the local village of Stadacone. Undoubtedly, Cartier recognized the strategic significance of this site, but a European colony was not established until 1608 when Samuel de Champlain, a French nobleman acting in the name of the King of France, established Kebec (native for "the narrowing of the waters"). The French began to put down roots in 1617 when Louis Hebert, the first agricultural pioneer, arrived with his family. The first settlement was wiped out in 1629 by British seafarers, but was later ceded back to France. For more than a century, Québec thrived despite constant harassment and siege from both the English and the Iroquois.

The decisive date in Québec history—and in the history of the British colonies to the south—was September 13, 1759. After a heroic ascent up the towering cliffs, General James Wolfe led his British troops to the Plains of Abraham (named after an early settler) and engaged the forces of the brilliant French General, Louis Joseph, Marquis de Montcalm. In 15 minutes the battle was over, both generals were among the fatalities, and French dreams of an empire in America were shattered. (The last siege of Québec took place in 1775, when American troops under the command of Benedict Arnold attacked and were repelled.)

From its earliest days, Québec has been a center for military, administrative, religious, educational, and medical activities. Today the provincial capital, it still is a center for these endeavors and also for industry.

Additional Visitor Information

Information centers are located at Tourism Québec, 12 Ste.-Anne St, phone 800/363-7777 (US and Canada), (Mon-Fri); and at the Greater Québec Area Tourism & Convention Bureau, 835 Ave Wilfrid-Laurier, G1R 2L3; 418/649-2608 (daily). The US Consulate is located at 2 Terrasse Dufferin, phone 418/692-2095. Public transportation is operated throughout the city by the Québec Urban Community Transportation Commission.

What to See and Do

Artillery Park National Historic Site. A four-acre (two-hectare) site built by the French to defend the opening of the St. Charles River. By the end of the 17th century it was known as a strategic site, and military engineers began to build fortifications here. Until 1871 the park housed French and British soldiers, eventually becoming a large industrial complex. Dauphine Redoubt (1712-1748), gun carriage shed (1813-1815), officers' quarters (1818), and arsenal foundry (1903) have been restored. Interpretation center. (All yr; closed Jan 1, Easter, Dec 25) St. Jean and D'Auteuil Sts. Phone 418/648-4205. Admission (June 24-Labour Day) ¢¢

Basilica of Ste.-Anne-de-Beaupré. (1923) Noted as the oldest pilgrimage in North America. First chapel was built on this site in 1658; the present basilica, built of white Canadian granite, is a Romanesque masterpiece. Capitals tell story of Jesus' life in 88 scenes; vaults decorated with mosaics; unusual technique used for 240 stained-glass windows outlined in concrete. Fourteen life-size Stations of the Cross and *Scala Santa* (Holy Stairs) on hillside. (Daily) 22 mi (35 km) NE on Hwy 138. Phone 418/827-3781.

Cartier-Brébeuf National Historic Site. Commemorates Jacques Cartier, first European known to have wintered in mainland Canada (1535-1536) and Jean de Brébeuf, a martyred Jesuit priest. The *Grande Hermine,* a full-size replica of Cartier's 16th-century flagship, is in dry dock; the hold and between deck can be viewed. Interpretation center with videotaped material. Guided tours by res. Indigenous habitation on site is open to visitors. (Feb-Nov, daily; Dec-Jan by appt) 175 de l'Espinay St. Phone 418/648-4038.

Explore. High-tech sound and visual arts are used to illustrate the founding of Québec and the beginnings of New France during the Golden Age of Exploration, when Columbus, Cartier, Champlain, and others began to venture into the Americas. (Daily; closed Dec 1-26) 63 rue Dalhousie. Phone 418/692-1759.

Grand Théâtre. Ultramodern theater has giant mural by sculptor Jordi Bonet in lobby; home of the Québec Symphony Orchestra and Opera; theatrical performances, concerts. 269 Blvd René Levesque. Phone 418/643-4975.

Île d'Orléans. This 23-mi-long (37-km) island was visited by Champlain in 1608 and colonized in 1648. Old stone farmhouses and churches of the 18th century remain. Farms grow an abundance of fruits and vegetables, especially strawberries, for which the island is famous. Across bridge, in St. Lawrence River.

Jacques-Cartier Park. Beautiful views in boreal forest valley. Fishing, rafting, canoeing; mountain climbing, wilderness camping, x-country skiing, hiking, mountain biking, picnicking; magnificent nature trail; nature interpretation. (Late May-mid-Oct, mid-Dec-mid-Apr) 25 mi (40.2 km) N via Hwy 175. Phone 418/848-3169. **FREE**

✪ **La Citadelle.** Forming the eastern flank of the fortifications of Québec, La Citadelle was begun in 1820 and work continued on it until 1850. Vestiges of the French regime, such as the Cap Diamant Redoubt (1693) and a powder magazine (1750), can still be seen. Panoramic views; 50-min guided tours. Changing of the guard (mid-June-Labour Day, daily); Beating the Retreat, re-creation of a 16th-century ceremony (late June-Labour Day, Tues, Thurs, Sat, and Sun; fee). On Cap Diamant. Phone 418/648-5175. ¢¢ In La Citadelle is

Museum of the Royal 22e Régiment. Located in two buildings. Powder magazine (ca 1750), flanked on both sides by massive buttresses, contains replicas of old uniforms of French regiments, war trophies, 17th-20th-century weapons; diorama of historic battles under the French; old military prison contains insignias, rifle and bayonet collections, last cell left intact. (Mid-Mar-Oct, daily) Changing of the guard (mid-June-Labour Day, daily at 10 am). ¢

Laurentides Wildlife Reserve. Canoeing, fishing; camping, cottages, lodges, picnicking, small and big game hunting, x-country and backcountry skiing, snowshoeing. (Late May-Labour Day, mid-Dec-mid-Apr) Some fees. 35 mi (48 km) N via Hwy 175. **FREE**

Montmorency Park. Montmorency Falls; Wolfe's Redoubt, historic house (June-early Sept, by appt), artifacts. Picnicking. (May-Oct) 10 mi (16 km) E via Hwy 138. Phone 418/663-2877.

Mont-Ste.-Anne Park. Gondola travels to summit of mountain (2,625 ft or 800 m), affording beautiful view of St. Lawrence River (late June-early Sept, daily). Skiing (Nov-May): 12 lifts, 50 trails; 85% snowmaking; x-country, full service. Two 18-hole golf courses; bicycle trail. 166 campsites (phone 418/826-2323). The migration of 250,000 snow geese occurs in spring and fall at nearby wildlife reserve Cap Tourmente. Park (daily; closed May). Some fees. 23 mi (37 km) NE via ON 138, then N 3 mi (5 km) on Hwy 360. Phone 418/827-4561 or 800/463-1568 (lodging information).

Musée du Fort. Narrated historical re-creation of the six sieges of Québec between 1629-1775; sound and light show. (Daily; closed Dec 1-26) Place d'Armes, corner of Ste.-Anne and du Fort Sts. Phone 418/692-2175. ¢¢

Museum of Civilization (Musée de la Civilisation). At entrance is *La Débacle,* a massive sculpture representing ice breaking up in spring. Separate exhibition halls present four permanent and several changing exhibitions dealing with history of Québec and the French Canadian culture as well as cultures of other civilizations from around the world. All narrative panels and signs are in French; bilingual guides on duty in most exhibit areas and English guide books are avail (fee). Guided tours (1 hr; fee). (Late June-Labour Day, daily; rest of yr, Tues-Sun; closed Dec 25) 85 rue Dalhousie, near Place-Royale. Phone 418/643-2158. ¢¢

National Assembly of Québec. Guided tours (30 min) of century-old Parliament Building. Dufferin Ave. Phone 418/643-7239.

National Battlefields Park. Two hundred fifty acres (101 hectares) along edge of bluff overlooking St. Lawrence River from Citadel to Gilmour Hill. Also called the Plains of Abraham, park was site of 1759 battle between the armies of Wolfe and Montcalm and 1760 battle of Ste.-Foy between the armies of Murray and Lévis. Visitor reception and interpretation center presents history of the Plains of Abraham from the New France period to the present. Bus tour of the park. Entrances along Grand-Allée. Phone 418/648-4071. ¢ In the park are two Martello towers, part of the fortifications, a sunken garden, many statues and the

Jeanne d'Arc Garden. Floral jewel created in 1938 by landscape architect Louis Perron. Combines the French Classical style with British-style flower beds. More than 150 species of annuals, bulbs, and perennials. Phone 418/649-6159.

Musée du Québec. Collection of ancient, modern, and contemporary Québec paintings, sculpture, photography, drawings, decorative arts; changing exhibits. (Daily; closed Jan 1, Dec 25) Parc des Champs-de-Bataille. Phone 418/643-2150. ¢¢

Old Port of Québec Interpretation Centre. Located in an ancient cement works and integrated into harbor installations of Louise Basin. Permanent exhibit shows importance of city as a gateway to America in the mid-19th century; timber trade and shipbuilding displays; films, exhibits; guides. (Early May-early Sept, daily; rest of yr, Tues-Sun) 100 St.-André St. Phone 418/648-3300. ¢¢

Place-Royale. Encompasses earliest vestiges of French civilization in North America; ongoing restoration of 17th-19th-century buildings, which make this the greatest concentration of such structures in North America. Notre-Dame-des-Victoires Church (1688), exhibit, and several houses are open to the public; information center at 215 Marché Finlay, G1K 8R5. Lower Town along St. Lawrence Riverfront. One-hr guided tours by appt. Phone 418/643-6631.

Québec Aquarium. Extensive collection of tropical, fresh, and saltwater fish, marine mammals, and reptiles; overlooks St. Lawrence River. Seal feeding (morning and afternoon); films (mid-May-Aug; daily). Cafeteria, picnicking. (Daily) 1675 des Hôtels Ave in Ste.-Foy. Phone 418/659-5264. ¢¢

⭐ **Québec City Walls and Gates.** Encompassing Old Québec. Eighteenth-century fortifications encircle the only fortified city in North America; incl Governor's Promenade and provides scenic view of The Citadel, St. Lawrence River, and Lévis. (Daily exc Governor's Promenade) **FREE**

Québec Zoo. More than 270 species of native and exotic animals and birds in a setting of forests, fields, and streams; children's zoo, sea lion shows; gift shops; restaurant, picnicking. (Daily; closed Dec 25) 9300 Faune St, in Charlesbourg, 7 mi (11.3 km) NW on Hwy 73/175. Phone 418/622-0312. ¢¢

St. Andrew's Presbyterian Church. (1810) Serving the oldest English-speaking congregation of Scottish origin in Canada. Church interior is distinguished by a long front wall with a high center pulpit. Original petition to King George III asking for a "small plot of waste ground" on which to build a "Scotch" church; spiral stairway leading to century-old organ. Stained-glass windows, historic plaques. Guide service. (July-Aug, Mon-Fri) Ste.-Anne and Cook Sts. Phone 418/656-0625. **FREE**

St.-Jean-Port-Joli. Tradition of wood sculpture began in this town about 1936, initiated by the famed Bourgault family. Other craftsmen came and made this a premier handicraft center; sculptures, enamels, mosaics in copper and wood, fabrics, paintings. Golf club (May-Sept); tennis courts, mountain bike trails, marina. Guided tour. Approx 60 mi (96.6 km) NE on Hwy 132 halfway to the Gaspé Peninsula (see). Phone 418/598-3084. Also here are

Church. (1779) Designed and decorated by famous woodcarvers. Renowned for the beauty of its lines and interior decor; has not been altered since built. Sculpted wood vault, tabernacle, and reredos all by different artisans. **FREE**

Musée des Anciens Canadiens. Wood sculptures by St.-Jean artisans. Original carvings by Bourgault brothers. (Mid-May-Oct, daily) Phone 418/598-3392.

Sightseeing tours.

Baillairgé Cultural tours. Group tours lasting between three days and one wk. Specialized tours in art, cuisine, and education. (Late June-mid-Oct, daily) Phone 418/692-5737. ¢¢¢

Calèches. Horse-drawn carriages leave Esplanade parking lot on d'Auteuil St, next to Tourist Bureau.

Gray Line bus tours. Contact 1576 Ave des Hotels G1W 3Z5. Phone 418/523-9722.

Harbour Cruises. M/V *Louis Jolliet* offers daytime, eve dance, and dinner cruises on the St. Lawrence River. Bar service, entertainment. (May-Oct) Chouinard Pier, opp Place Royale. Contact Croisières AML, 124 rue St.-Pierre G1K 4A7. Phone 418/692-1159 or 800/563-4643. ¢¢¢¢

Université Laval. (1663) 35,900 students. Oldest French university on the continent, Laval evolved from Québec Seminary, which was founded in 1663 by Québec's first bishop, Msgr. de Laval. In 1950 the university moved from "Le Quartier Latin" in old Québec to a 470-acre (190-hectare) site in suburban Ste.-Foy, where it developed into the present, modern campus. Sir Wilfrid Laurier Blvd and Du Vallon Rte, in Ste.-Foy. Guided tours by appt. Phone 418/656-2571.

Special Events

Carnaval Québec Kellogg's. Internationally acclaimed French Canadian festival celebrated throughout the city. Main attraction is the Snow Palace, a two-story structure built of blocks of ice, open to visitors. Other highlights incl snow and ice sculptures, parades, canoe race on the St. Lawrence, fireworks, many special events. Contact Carnaval de Québec, Inc, 290 rue Joly, G1L 1N8. Phone 418/626-3716. Late Jan-mid Feb.

du Maurier Québec Summer Festival. Outdoor festival held at 15 locations throughout Old Québec. International event of the performing arts; more than 400 shows, most free. Contact 160 rue St.-Paul, CP 24, Succ B, G1K 7A1. Phone 418/692-4540. Eleven days beginning first Thurs July.

International Fireworks Competition. Montmorency Falls Park. Musical fireworks competition attracts master fireworks handlers from around the world. Phone 418/523-3389. Late July-early Aug.

New France Celebration. Family-oriented historical event that re-creates life of the colonists in New France and fills the streets with theatrical events, song and dance, and children's entertainment. Phone 418/694-3311. Early Aug.

Expo Québec. Exhibition Park. Agricultural, commercial, and industrial fair; shows, games. Phone 418/691-7110. Late Aug.

Motels/Motor Lodges

★★ **BEST WESTERN L'ARTISTOCRATE.** *3100 Chemin Ste. Louis, Ste. Foy (G1W 1R8). 418/653-2841; fax 418/653-8525; 800/528-1234. www.bestwestern.com.* 100 rms, 2 story. July-Aug: S, D $89-$119; each addl $5; under 18 free; wknd rates; lower rates rest of yr. Crib free. TV; cable, VCR avail. Pool; poolside serv, lifeguard. Restaurant 7 am-10 pm. Rm serv. Bar noon-10 pm. Ck-out noon. Meeting rms. Business servs avail. In-rm modem link. Valet serv. Health club privileges. Some refrigerators. Cr cds: A, C, D, DS, ER, MC, V.
🅓 ⊠ ➰ 🅰 SC

★★ **CHALETS MONTMORENCY.** *1768 Ave Royale, St Ferreol Les Neiges (G0A 3R0). 418/826-2600; fax 418/826-1123; toll-free 800/463-2612.* 35 rms, 3 story, 25 kit. suites. S $48-$51; D $64-$68; suites $79-$390; ski, golf

plans. Crib $5. TV; cable, VCR avail. 2 pools, 1 indoor; whirlpool. Sauna. Restaurant adj 8 am-11 pm. Ck-out noon. Business servs avail. Coin lndry. 18-hole golf. Downhill/x-country ski 1 mi. Rec rm. Microwaves. Balconies. Picnic tables. Cr cds: MC, V.
🅓 ✈ ➰ 🅰 SC 🍴

★ **DAYS INN.** *2250 Ste. Anne Blvd (Hwy 138) (G1J 1Y2). 418/661-7701; fax 418/661-5221; toll-free 800/463-5568. www.daysinn.com.* 62 rms, 2 story. Mid-June-mid-Sept: S $70; D $75; each addl $10; suites $130; under 12 free; wkly rates off-season; lower rates rest of yr. Crib free. TV; cable (premium). 2 pools, 1 indoor; poolside serv. Sauna. Coffee in rms. Restaurant 7-10 am; Sat, Sun to 11 am. Rm serv. Ck-out noon. Meeting rms. Business servs avail. Free parking. Some refrigerators. Balconies. Cr cds: A, D, ER, JCB, MC, V.
🅓 ➰ 🅰

★★ **HOTEL CHATEAU LAURIER.** *1220 Georges 5th W (G1R 5B8). 418/522-8108; fax 418/524-8768; toll-free 800/463-4453. www.old-quebec.com/laurier.* 57 rms, 4 story. May-Oct: S $79-$99; D $89-$109; each addl $10; under 12 free; lower rates rest of yr. Crib free. Pet accepted, some restrictions. TV; cable, VCR avail. Restaurant 7:30 am-3:30 pm. Bar 11-3 am. Ck-out noon. Business servs avail. Cr cds: A, D, DS, ER, MC, V.
🅓 ➰ 🅰 🅰 🐾

★ **MOTEL SPRING.** *8520 Blvd Ste. Anne, Ste. Anne (G0A 1N0). 418/824-4953; fax 418/824-4117; toll-free 888/824-4953.* 25 rms, 12 with shower only. No rm phones. July-early Sept: S, D $45; wkly rates; higher rates major hols; lower rates mid-May-June, early Sept-late Oct. Closed rest of yr. Crib free. Pet accepted. TV; cable. Restaurant 7 am-9 pm. Ck-out noon. Picnic tables. On river. Family-owned. Cr cds: MC, V.
✈ ➰ 🅰 🅰 🐾

★ **ONCLE SAM.** *7025 W Hamel Blvd, Ste. Foy (G2G 1V6). 418/872-1488; fax 418/871-5519; toll-free 800/414-1488.* 4 rms, 1-2 story. Mid-June-mid-Sept: S, D $59-$79; each addl $10; under 14 free; lower rates rest of yr. Pet accepted. TV; cable, VCR avail. Heated pool. Playground. Ck-out noon. Coin lndry. Business servs avail. X-country ski 5 mi. Picnic table. Cr cds: A, C, D, ER, MC, V.
🅓 🐾 ✈ ➰ 🅰 🅰 SC

★★ **SELECTOTEL ROND-POINT.** *53 Kennedy Blvd, Levis (J6W 6C7). 418/833-4920; fax 418/833-0634.* 124 rms, 2 story. July-mid-Sept: S $95-$105; D $119-$129; each addl $5; suites $150; each addl $10; lower rates rest of yr. Crib $5. TV; cable. Indoor heated pool. Restaurant 7 am-2 pm, 4:30-9:30 pm. Rm serv. Ck-out noon. Coin lndry. Meeting rms. Business servs avail. Barber. Downhill/x-country ski 30 mi. Massage. 18- and 9-hole golf nearby. Miniature golf. Some refrigerators. Some balconies. Ferry 5 min to Old Québec. Cr cds: A, C, D, DS, ER, MC, V.
✈ ➰ 🅰 🅰 SC 🍴

Hotels

★ **CHATEAU BELLVUE.** *16 Rue Laporte (G1R 4M9). 418/692-2573; fax 418/692-4876; toll-free 800/463-5256.* 58 rms, 3 story. May-Oct: S, D $129-$149; each addl $10; winter packages; under 12 free; lower rates rest of yr. Parking. A/C. Crib free. TV; cable. Complimentary continental bkfst (Mid-Oct-Apr). Restaurants nearby. No rm serv. Ck-out noon. In-rm modem link. Business servs avail. View of St Lawrence River. Cr cds: A, D, DS, ER, JCB, MC, V.

★★★ **CHATEAU BONNE ENTENTE.** *3400 Chemin Ste. Foy, Ste. Foy (G1X 1S6). 418/653-5221; fax 418/653-3098; toll-free 800/463-4390. www.chateaubonneentente.com.* 109 rms, 3 story. May-Oct: S $168-$188; D $174-$194; each addl $15; suites $298-$314; under 17 free; wkend rates; lower rates rest of yr. Crib free. TV; cable, VCR avail. Heated pool; poolside serv, lifeguard. Playground. Free supervised children's activities; ages 6 months and up. Complimentary coffee in lobby. Restaurant 6:30-11 am, noon-2 pm, 5-10 pm; Sat, Sun from 7 am (see also LE PAILLEUR). High tea service 2-4 pm. Rm serv. Bar 11-2 am. Ck-out 1 pm. Meeting rms. Business center. In-rm modem link. Valet serv. Sundries. Free airport, bus depot, RR station transportation. Tennis. X-country ski 5 mi. Exercise equipt. Massage. Rec rm. Lawn games. Whirlpool in suites. Picnic table. Stocked pond. Cr cds: A, DS, ER, MC, V.

★★ **CLARENDON.** *57 rue Ste Anne (G1R 3X4). 418/692-2480; fax 418/692-4652; res 888/554-6001. www.hotelclarendon.com.* 151 rms, 7 story. June-mid-Oct: S, D $99-$119; each addl $20; suites $189-$199; under 12 free; lower rates rest of yr. Crib free. Parking $6. TV; cable. Restaurant 7-10:30 am, noon-2 pm, 6-10 pm. Bar 11-3 am; entertainment. Ck-out noon. Meeting rms. Business servs avail. Historic hotel (1870), the oldest in Québec. Cr cds: A, MC, V.

★★★ **FAIRMONT LE CHATEAU FRONTENAC.** *1 Rue Des Carrieres (G1R 4P5). 418/692-3861; fax 418/692-1751; res 800/441-1414. www.fairmont.com.* 613 rms, 18 story. May-Oct: S, D $189-$359; each addl $25; suites $399-$1,000; under 18 free; lower rates rest of yr. Crib free. Garage parking $15.45. TV; cable, VCR avail. Indoor pool; whirlpool, wading pool, poolside serv. Restaurant 7 am-midnight (see also LE CHAMPLAIN). Bar 11-2 am; entertainment exc Sun. Ck-out noon. Meeting rms. Business center. In-rm modem link. Shopping arcade. Ice skating. Downhill ski 11 mi; x-country ski 3 mi. Exercise rm. Minibars. Landmark chateau-style hotel (1893); site of historic conferences during World War II. Cr cds: A, C, D, DS, ER, JCB, MC, V.

★★★ **GOUVERNEUR HOTEL SAINTE-FOY.** *3030 Laurier Blvd, Ste. Foy (G1V 2M5). 418/651-3030; fax 418/651-6797; toll-free 888/910-1111. www.gouverneur.com.* 320 rms. May-Sept: S $165; D $180; each addl $15; suites $200-$275; under 18 free; wkend rates; lower rates rest of yr. Self parking. Crib free. TV; cable (movies). Heated outdoor pool; poolside serv, lifeguard in summer. Restaurant 7 am-2 pm, 5-10 pm. Rm serv. Bar noon-midnight. Ck-out 1 pm. Meeting rms. Business servs avail. Bellhops. X-country ski 5 mi. Health club privileges. Some minibars. Many balconies. Cr cds: A, D, DS, ER, JCB, MC, V.

★★★ **HILTON.** *1100 Blvd Rene Levesque E (G1K 7M9). 418/647-2411; fax 418/647-3737; res 800/447-2411. www.hilton.com.* 571 rms, 23 story. Mid-May-mid-Oct: S $138-$187; D $160-$209; each addl $22; suites $355-$835; wkend rates. Crib free. Pet accepted, some restrictions. Parking $16. TV; cable. Pool; poolside serv, lifeguard. Coffee in rms. Restaurant 7 am-midnight. Bars 11 am-midnight. Ck-out noon. Meeting rms. Business center. Barber, beauty shop. Downhill ski 11 mi; x-country ski nearby. Exercise rm; sauna. Massage. Québec convention center opp. Luxury level. Cr cds: A, C, D, DS, ER, JCB, MC, V.

★★ **HOTEL CLASSIQUE.** *2815 Blvd Laurier, Ste. Foy (G1Z 4H3). 418/658-2793; fax 418/658-6816; res 888/463-0083.* 237 rms, 32 A/C, 12 story, 102 suites, 60 kit. units (no equipt). May-Sept: S $80-$110; D $110-$140; each addl $10; suites, kit. units $110-$180; under 12 free; wkly rates; lower rates rest of yr. Crib $10. TV; cable. 2 pools, 1 indoor; lifeguard. Restaurant open 24 hrs. Bar 11-3 am. Ck-out noon. Coin lndry. Meeting rms. Business servs avail. In-rm modem link. Free indoor parking. Gift shop. Health club privileges. Balconies. Cr cds: A, C, D, ER, MC, V.

★★★ **HOTEL GERMAIN-DES-PRES.** *1200 Ave Germain-Des-Pres, Ste. Foy (G1V 3M7). 418/658-1224; fax 418/658-8846; toll-free 800/463-5253. www.germaindespres.com.* 126 rms, 8 story. June-mid-Oct: S $130; D $140; each addl $15; wkend rates; lower rates rest of yr. Crib free. TV; cable, VCR avail. Coffee in rms. Restaurant (see also BISTANGO). Bar 5-11 pm. Ck-out noon. Business servs avail. In-rm modem link. Some free covered parking. Free airport, RR station, bus depot transportation. Health club privileges. Bathrm phones, minibars. Cactus garden in lobby. Cr cds: A, C, D, ER, MC, V.

★★ **HOTEL PLAZA QUEBEC.** *3031 Blvd Laurier, Ste. Foy (G1Z 2M2). 418/658-2727; fax 418/658-6587; toll-free 800/567-5276.* 233 rms, 7 story. May-Oct: S $105-$125; D $120-$140; each addl $10-$15; suites $150-$250; family, wkend rates; lower rates rest of yr. Crib free. Free garage parking. TV; cable. Indoor pool; lifeguard, whirlpool. Saunas. Restaurant 6 am-11 pm. Bar. Ck-out noon. Meeting rms. Business center. Gift shop. Refrigerator in suites. Some balconies. Indoor garden. Cr cds: A, D, DS, ER, MC, V.

★★ **HOTEL UNIVERSEL.** *2300 Chemin Ste. Foy (G1V 1S5). 418/653-5250; fax 418/653-4486; res 800/463-4495. www.hoteluniversel.qc.ca.* 127 rms, 3 story, 47 kits. S, D, suites $79; each addl $5; under 14 free. Crib free. TV; cable. Indoor pool. Sauna. Playground. Restaurant noon-11 pm. Rm serv. Bar 5 pm-1 am. Ck-out noon. Meeting rms. Business servs avail. Bellhops. X-country ski 3 mi. Some refrigerators. Balconies. Cr cds: A, DS, MC, V.

★★★ **LOEWS LE CONCORDE.** *1225 Cours du General De Montcalm (G1R 4W6).* 418/647-2222; fax 418/647-4710; toll-free 800/463-5256. www.loewshotels.com. 404 rms, 26 story. May-Oct: S, D $135-$290; each addl $25; suites $180-$750; wkend, ski plans; lower rates rest of yr. Crib free. Pet accepted. Garage $15; valet parking $18. TV; cable. Heated pool; whirlpool, poolside serv, lifeguard. Restaurant 6:45 am-midnight (see also L'ASTRAL). Bars 11-3 am. Ck-out 1 pm. Meeting rms. Business center. In-rm modem link. Concierge. Downhill ski 11 mi; x-country ski on site. Tennis privileges. Exercise rm; sauna. Health club privileges. Refrigerators, minibars; fireplace in 2 bilevel suites. Luxury level. Cr cds: A, C, D, DS, ER, JCB, MC, V.

[D] [symbols]

★ **QUEBEC INN.** *7175 W Hamel Blvd, Ste. Foy (G2G 1B6).* 418/872-9831; fax 418/872-1336; res 800/567-5276. 135 rms, 2 story. June-mid-Oct: S $76.95-$86.95; D $86.95-$96.95; each addl $10; family rates; package plans; lower rates rest of yr. TV; cable. Indoor pool; whirlpool, poolside serv. Restaurant 6:30 am-11 pm. Rm serv. Bar 11-3 am; entertainment Wed-Sun. Ck-out noon. Meeting rms. Business servs avail. In-rm modem link. Beauty, barber shop. X-country ski 5 mi. Exercise rm; sauna. Massage. Balconies. Indoor garden. Cr cds: A, D, ER, MC, V.

[symbols]

★★ **RADISSON HOTEL GOUVERNEUR QUEBEC.** *690 Blvd Rene-Levesque E (G1R 5A8).* 418/647-1717; fax 418/647-2146; res 800/333-3333. www.radisson.com. 377 rms, 12 story. May-Oct: S D $130-$245; each addl $15; suites $195-$275; under 18 free (max 2); wkend, ski plans; lower rates rest of yr. Crib free. Parking $11. TV; cable, VCR avail. Heated pool; whirlpool, poolside serv, lifeguard. Coffee in rms. Restaurant 7 am-10:30 pm. Bar 11 am-10 pm. Ck-out noon. Meeting rms. Business center. Shopping arcade. Barber, beauty shop. X-country ski ½ mi. Exercise rm; sauna. Some minibars. Parliament buildings, Québec convention center opp. Luxury level. Cr cds: A, C, D, DS, ER, MC, V.

[D] [symbols]

Resorts

★★★ **FAIRMONT LE MANOIR RICHELIEU.** *181 rue Richelieu, Charlevoix (G5A 1X7).* 418/665-3703; fax 418/665-7736; toll-free 800/441-1414. www.fairmont.com. 405 rms, 3 story. S, D $275-$425; under 18 free. Crib avail. TV; cable (premium). Indoor pool; whirlpool. Restaurant 6:30 am-10 pm. Bar to midnight. Ck-out noon, ck-in 4 pm. Meeting rms. Business center. In-rm modem link. Concierge. Exercise equipt. Minibars; many refrigerators in suites. Cr cds: A, D, ER, MC, V.

[symbols]

★★★ **MANOIR DU LAC DELAGE.** *40 Ave Du Lac, Ville Du Lac Delage (G0A 4P0).* 418/848-2551; fax 418/848-1352; toll-free 800/463-8841. www.lacdelage.com. 105 rms, 54 A/C, 1-3 story. MAP: S $119-$145; D $164-$190; each addl $60; EP avail. Crib free. TV; cable. 2 pools; 1 indoor, poolside serv. Playground. Dining rm 7-10 am, noon-2 pm, 6-9 pm. Bar 11-1 am; pianist. Ck-out noon, ck-in 3 pm. Meeting

rms. Business servs avail. Lighted tennis. Marina; canoes, paddleboats, sailboats, windsurfing. Downhill ski 2 mi; x-country ski on site. Snowshoe activities, sledding, skating. Bicycles. Lawn games. Exercise equipt; sauna. Massage. Some minibars. Balconies. On lake. Summer theater performances. Cr cds: A, D, MC, V.

[symbols]

B&Bs/Small Inns

★ **AU CHATEAU FLEUR DE LYS.** *15 Ste. Genevieve Ave (G1R 4A8).* 418/694-1884; fax 418/694-1666; toll-free 877/691-1884. 18 rms, 3 story. May-Oct: S, D $75-$120; each addl $10. Under 6 free, 12 yrs $6. Crib free. Parking $8/day. TV; cable. Continental bkfst. Restaurants nearby. Ck-out noon, ck-in 1 pm. Business servs avail. Refrigerators. Located in Old Québec in an 1873 greystone house. Panoramic view of gardens. Cr cds: A, DS, MC, V.

[symbol]

★★ **AU MANOIR STE.-GENEVIEVE.** *13 Ste. Genevieve Ave (G1R 4A7).* 418/694-1666; fax 418/694-1666; toll-free 877/694-1666. 9 rms, 3 story, 3 kit suites. No rm phones. May-Oct: S $87; D, kit. units $100; each addl $10; under 12 free; lower rates rest of yr. Crib free. Parking $6. TV; cable. Continental bkfst. Ck-out noon, ck-in 1 pm. Business servs avail. Greystone house (1895) with terrace on upper level. Cr cds: A, MC, V.

[symbol]

Restaurants

★ **AU CAFE SUISSE.** *32 Ste.-Anne St (G1R 3X3).* 418/694-1320. Hrs: 11 am-midnight. Summer 8 am-midnight. Res accepted. Swiss menu. Bar. A la carte entrees: bkfst $3.95-$9.95, lunch, dinner $7.95-$24.95. Complete meals: dinner $19.95-$24.95. Specializes in fondues, seafood, steak. Pianist Sat evenings. Parking. Sidewalk terrace dining in summer. Turn-of-the-century greystone house. Cr cds: A, MC, V.

[symbol]

★★ **AUX ANCIENS CANADIENS.** *34 rue Ste. Louis (G1R 4P3).* 418/692-1627. www.auxancienscanadiens.qc.ca. Hrs: noon-10 pm; summer to 11 pm. Res accepted. French-Canadian cuisine. Bar. Wine list. A la carte entrees: dinner $20-$29. Table d'hôte: dinner $24.50-$35. Specialties: country-style meat pie, small game. Own pastries. In building reputedly used as headquarters by General Montcalm; antiques. Family-owned. Cr cds: A, ER, MC, V.

[symbol]

★★ **BISTANGO.** *1200 Ave Germain des Pres, Ste. Foy (G1V 3M7).* 418/658-8780. www.lebistango.com. French menu. Specializes in light French and California-style cuisine. Hrs: 7-10 am, 11:30 am-2 pm, 5-11 pm; Sat 8-11 am, 5-11 pm; Sun 8 am-2 pm, 5-11 pm. Res accepted. Bar. A la carte entrees: lunch $9.95-$11.95. Complete meals: dinner $22-$25. Child's menu. Valet parking. French bistro decor. Cr cds: A, D, MC, V.

[D] [symbol]

★ **CAFE DE PARIS.** *66 rue Ste. Louis (G1R 3Z3). 418/694-9626.* Hrs: 11:30 am-11:30 pm. Closed Nov-Mar. Res accepted. French menu. A la carte: lunch $9.95-$14.95, dinner $19.95-$29.95. Child's menu. Specializes in seafood, veal. Entertainment. Free valet parking. Built in 1827. Rustic decor with many original oil paintings. Located in the heart of Québec, close to Le Château Frontenac Hotel. Cr cds: A, D, ER, MC, V.
[image]

★★★ **LA MAISON SERGE BRUYERE.** *1200 rue Ste. Jean (G1R 1S8). 418/694-0618.* French, Continental menu. Specialties: caribou (seasonal), grilled salmon. Own pastries. Hrs: 9 am-10:30 pm. Res accepted. Wine list. Prix fixe: dinner $8.95-$100. Valet parking. Fireplaces, original oil paintings. Family-owned. View of Ste. John's gate and city hall. Cr cds: A, D, ER, MC, V.
[image] [image]

★★ **LA RIPAILLE.** *9 rue de Buade (G1R 3Z9). 418/692-2450.* Hrs: 11:30 am-2:30 pm, 5-11 pm; Sun from 5 pm; early-bird dinner 5-7 pm. Res accepted. French menu. Serv bar. A la carte entrees: lunch $10-$15, dinner $17-$20.95. Complete meals: lunch $8.95-$13.50, dinner $25.95. Child's menu. Specializes in seafood, rack of lamb, veal tenderloin. Own pastries. Valet parking. In 1835 building. Cr cds: A, D, DS, ER, MC, V.
[image] [image]

★★★ **L'ASTRAL.** *1225 Place Montcalm (G1R 4W6). 418/647-2222.* Hrs: 11:45 am-3 pm, 6-11 pm; Sun brunch 10 am-3 pm. Res required. Bar to 12:30 am. Wine cellar. French, continental menu. A la carte entrees: lunch $9.50-$16.50, dinner $19.50-$35.50. Buffet: lunch $16.50, dinner $38.95. Sun brunch $23.75. Child's menu. Specialties: rack of lamb, filet of veal, duckling with maple syrup. Own pastries. Salad bar. Pianist nightly. Valet parking. Revolving rooftop restaurant. Cr cds: A, D, MC, V.
[image] [image]

★★★★ **LAURIE RAPHAEL.** *117 Dalhousie (G1K 9C8). 418/692-4555. www.laurieraphael.com.* Owner/chef Daniel Vezina and Suzanne Gagnon preside over this cheerful, Old Port district eatery with red-checked, upholstered chairs, red walls, and sparkling windows. The menu is adventurous "market cuisine," changing every two weeks to incorporate local ingredients and worldly spices. Try dishes such as Moroccan-style roast lamb with maple syrup and confit of leeks. Specializes in a mix of Asian and Quebecois cuisine. Hrs: 11:30 am-2 pm, 6-10 pm; Sat from 6 pm. Closed Sun, Mon. Dinner $19-$32. Res required. Cr cds: C, D, DS, ER, MC, V.
[image] [image]

★★ **LE BONAPARTE.** *680 E Grande-Allee (G1R 2K5). 418/647-4747.* Hrs: 11 am-11 pm. Closed Sat, Sun mornings in Nov-Mar. Res accepted. French, continental menu. Bar to 3 am. Complete meals: lunch $7.95-$14.95, dinner $22.95-$28.95. A la carte entrees: dinner $10.95-$28.95. Child's menu. Specializes in rack of lamb, steak, seafood. Own pastries. Patio dining. In 1823 building. French murder mystery dinner Fri nights. Cr cds: A, MC, V.
[image] [image]

★★★ **LE CHAMPLAIN.** *1 rue des Carrieres (G1R 4P5). 418/692-3861. www.cphotels.ca.* Hrs: 6-10 pm; Sun brunch 10 am-2 pm. Res accepted. Classic French menu. Serv bar. A la carte entrees: dinner $27-$66. Table d'hôte dinner $55-$59. Menu degustation $59-$65. Sun brunch $29.50-$30. Specialties: Québec smoked salmon, rack of lamb. Homemade pastries. Extensive wine list. Harpist Fri, Sat. Valet parking. Classic French atmosphere. Jacket required. Cr cds: A, C, D, DS, ER, MC, V.
[image] [image]

★★★ **LE CONTINENTAL.** *26 rue Ste Louis (G1R 3Y9). 418/694-9995. www.lecontinental.com.* Hrs: noon-11 pm; Sun from 5:30 pm. Closed Dec 24, 25. Res accepted. French, continental menu. Wine cellar. A la carte entrees: dinner $19-$31. Complete meals: lunch $9.75-$16.95, dinner $29-$35. Specialties: steak tartare, curried shrimp, orange duckling flambe. Own pastries. Near Château Frontenac. Tableside cooking. Family-owned. Valet parking. Cr cds: A, C, D, DS, ER, MC, V.
[image]

★ **LE MANOIR DU SPAGHETTI.** *3077 Chemin Ste. Louis, Ste.-Foy (G1W 1R6). 418/659-5628.* French, Italian menu. Specializes in pasta, veal. Hrs: 11 am-11 pm. Res accepted. Cafe bar. A la carte entrees: lunch, dinner $5.50-$16.99. Table d'hôte: lunch $5.49-$9.99, dinner $13-$24. Child's menu. Parking. Terrace dining in summer. Cr cds: A, D, MC, V.
[image] [image]

★★★ **LE PAILLEUR.** *3400 Chemin Ste Foy (G1X 1S6). 418/653-5221. www.chateaubonneentente.com.* Traditional and original Québec cooking, using local products. Specialties in grilled meats, seafood. Hrs: 6-10:30 am, 11:30 am-2 pm, 6-10 pm. Sun brunch 10 am-2 pm. Res accepted. Bar 11-1 am. Wine list. A la carte entrees: bkfst $4.95-$9.95. Buffet: bkfst $9.95, lunch $12.95. Table d'hôte: dinner $22-$33.95. Child's menu. Parking. Pianist Fri-Sun. Cr cds: A, C, D, DS, ER, MC, V.
[image] [image]

★★★ **LE SAINT-AMOUR.** *48 Ste Ursule (G1R 4E2). 418/694-0667. www.saint-amour.com.* Hrs: 11:30 am-2:30 pm, 6-11 pm; Mon, Sat, Sun 6-11 pm. Closed Dec 24. Res accepted. French menu. Serv bar. Wine cellar. A la carte entrees: lunch, dinner $19.50-$28.50. Child's menu. Specialties: foie gras, rack of lamb, royale chocolate. Valet parking. Outdoor dining. Family-owned since 1978. Cr cds: A, C, D, DS, ER, MC, V.
[image]

★★ **LE VENDOME.** *36 Cote de la Montagne (G1K 4E2). 418/692-0557.* Hrs: 11 am-11 pm. Closed Dec 24. Res accepted. French menu. Bar. A la carte entrees: lunch $7.50-$12.50, dinner $14.50-$23. Child's menu. Specializes in steaks, seafood, veal. Valet parking. Outdoor dining. Parisian decor; murals. Family-owned since 1951. Cr cds: A, C, D, DS, ER, MC, V.
[image]

★ **L'OMELETTE.** *64 rue Ste Louis (G1R 3Z3). 418/694-9626.* Hrs: 7 am-10:30 pm. Closed Nov-Mar. Res accepted. Specializies in omelets, eggs Benedict, seafood, beef. A la carte: bkfst $3.50-$5.25, lunch $3-$6.95, dinner $5-$13.75. Valet parking. Cr cds: A, D, ER, MC, V.

★★ **RESTAURANT AU PARMESAN.** *38 rue Ste Louis (G1R 3Z1). 418/692-0341.* Hrs: noon-midnight. Closed Dec 24, 25. Res accepted. Italian, French menu. Serv Bar. Wine cellar. A la carte entrees: lunch, dinner $9.95-$31. Complete meals: lunch $9.50-$13.50, dinner $17.75-$26.95. Menu gastronomique $59. Child's menu. Specializes in seafood, veal. Own pasta, pastries. Accordionist. Valet parking. 4,000 liqueur bottles displayed; many oil paintings. Chestnuts roasted in fireplaces in winter. Cr cds: A, D, DS, ER, MC, V.

St. Jerome

See also Montrèal, St. Jovite

Pop 25,123 **Elev** 362 ft (110 m) **Area code** 450
Information Laurentian Tourism Association, 14142, rue de Lachapelle, RR 1, J7Z 5T4; 450/436-8532 or 800/561-6673
Web www.laurentides.com

Founded in 1834 on the Rivière du Nord is the "Gateway to the Laurentians," St. Jérôme. In this resort area north of St. Jérôme amid the magnificent setting of mountains, forests, lakes and rivers, summer sports and recreation are unlimited, fall colors spectacular and winter sports and festivals delightful. Outfitters are available to help plan a wilderness vacation, but visitors may also choose from over 200 accommodations of every price and type.

Under the fierce leadership (1868-91) of Curé Labelle, a huge man and a near legendary figure, this area began to grow. Curé Labelle hoped to open the whole country, north and to the Pacific, which was nearly empty at that time. Making over 60 canoe and foot trips of exploration, he selected sites for new parishes and founded more than 20. By pen and pulpit he sought to stop the flow of labor to the United States, and in 1876, due to his inexhaustible efforts, the railroad came to St. Jérôme, bringing new prosperity. Curé Labelle became the Minister of Agriculture and Colonization in 1888. A bronze monument honoring him is in the park opposite the cathedral.

What to See and Do

Centre d'exposition du Vieux Palais. Exhibition centre of visual arts. 185 rue du Palais, Hwy 15 N, exit 43. Phone 514/432-7171.

St. Jovite

Pop 3,841 **Elev** 790 ft (241 m) **Area code** 819
Information Laurentian Tourism Association, 14142, rue de La Chapelle, RR 1, Saint-Jerôme, PQ, J7Z 5T4; 450/436-8532
Web www.laurentides.com

Nestled in the valley of the du Diable River and situated close to Mont Tremblant Provincial Park (see), this major all-year tourist area is one of the oldest in the Laurentians. Hunting, fishing, snowmobiling, and skiing are among the many available activities. Three public beaches around Lac des Sables in Ste.-Agathe make this a water sports paradise; international dogsled races on ice in nearby Ste.-Agathe-des-Monts add to the excitement. French summer theater, mountain climbing on Monts Condor and Césaire, antique shops, and a Santa Claus Village are other options in Val-David, to the southeast.

What to See and Do

Antiques, arts, and crafts. Interesting artisan's shops and galleries: **Le Coq Rouge,** an antique shop (phone 819/425-3205); **Alain Plourde, Artisan** (phone 819/425-7873).

Restaurant

★ **ANTIPASTO.** *855 Rue Ouimet, St-Jovite (J0T 2H0). 819/425-7580.* Specializes in pasta. Hrs: 11 am-11 pm. Wine list. Lunch, dinner $10-$29. Child's menu. Entertainment. Cr cds: A, MC, V.

Sherbrooke

See also Granby

Pop 85,000 **Elev** 600 ft (183 m) **Area code** 819
Information Office of Tourism, 3010 King W St, J1H 5G1; 819/821-1919 or 800/561-8331
Web www.sders.com/tourism

Nestled in a land of natural beauty at the confluence of the Magog and Saint-François rivers, Sherbrooke is a bilingual and bicultural community. Originally settled in 1791 by the French, an influx of Loyalist settlers and English colonists brought English influence to the city, which remains today despite the 95 percent French population. More than 150 types of industries, including pulp and paper, textile, and heavy machinery manufacturing, are carried on in this major railroad center. The principal city of Québec's Eastern Townships, Sherbrooke is the center of one of Canada's fastest developing winter sports areas. There are many beautiful open areas, such as the Howard Estate with its lovely pond and grounds and the Lake of Nations.

What to See and Do

Basilica of St. Michel. Center of archbishopric.

Beauvoir Sanctuary. Setting of natural splendor on a hill. Church built in 1920. Statue of the Sacred Heart here since 1916, making it a regional pilgrimage site. Gospel scenes in outdoor mountain setting. (May-Oct, daily; Nov-Apr, Sun) Summer: picnic tables, restaurant, gift shop. 4 mi (6 km) N, exit 146 off Hwy 10. On the east bank of the St.-François River. Phone 819/569-2535. **FREE**

Louis S. St. Laurent National Historic Site. Birthplace of Prime Minister Louis S. St. Laurent (1882-1973); landscaped grounds; general store and adj warehouse with sound and light show. (May-Oct, daily) S on Hwy 147, at 6 Main St in Compton. Phone 819/835-5448. **FREE**

Mena'Sen Place. Site of large illuminated cross. Many legends surround island and its original lone pine, destroyed in a storm in 1913 and replaced by the cross in 1934.

⭐ **Mount Orford.** Stands 2,800 ft (864 m) high with range stretching across the border into Vermont. Recreational park with swimming; campground, golf course, hiking, picnicking, lake, and wildlife. Downhill and x-country skiing in winter. Some fees. 22 mi (35 km) SW near Hwy 10, exit 118. Phone 819/843-6233. Here are

Orford Arts Centre. World renowned hall is one of the finest auditoriums anywhere. Pavilion with teaching and practice studios, 500-seat concert hall. Performances given by noted artists during Orford Summer Festival. Visual arts program. (May-Sept) Phone 819/843-3981.

Ski Mont Orford. Outstanding area and some of the best facilities in Québec. Thirty-nine runs, eight lifts; patrol, school, rentals; day care; cafeteria, restaurant, bar. Longest run 2½ mi (4 km). (Nov-Apr, daily) Twenty acres (8.09 hectares) of glade, 25 mi (40.2 km) of X-country skiing. Eighteen-hole golf (fee; rentals). Scenic chairlift (July-mid-Aug, daily; rest of summer, wkends only). 22 mi (36 km) SW. Phone 819/843-6548. ¢¢¢¢

Musée du Séminaire de Sherbrooke. More than 90,000 objects of natural history. (Tues-Sun afternoons) 195 rue Marquette. Phone 819/564-3200. ¢¢ Fee includes

Léon Marcotte Exhibition Centre. Presents traveling exhibitions from other museums and assembles others from the Seminary Museum. (Tues-Sun afternoons) 222 rue Frontenac. Phone 819/564-3200. ¢¢

Uplands Museum and Cultural Centre. This neo-Georgian home built in 1862 is located on four acres of beautifully wooded grounds. Changing exhibits interpret heritage of Lennoxville-Ascot and eastern townships. Museum contains period furniture. Red Barn, on grounds, is home to children's theater. Afternoon tea served all yr (res required in winter). (Tues-Sun; extended summer hrs) 50 Park St; S via Rte 143, W on Church to Park St in Lennoxville. Phone 819/564-0409.

Hotel

★★★ **HOTEL GOUVERNEUR SHERBROOKE.** *3131 King St W (J1L 1C8). 819/565-0464; fax 819/565-5505; res 888/910-1111. www.gouverneur.com.* 124 rms, 4 story. May-Sept: S, D $76-$79; each addl $10; suites $155; under 18 free; wkend rates; lower rates rest of yr. Crib $10. TV; cable (premium). Heated pool; lifeguard. Restaurant 7 am-9 pm. Bar; entertainment. Ck-out 1 pm. Lndry facilities. Bellhops. Cr cds: A, MC, V.

D ⊷ ⊠ ⚒

Trois-Rivières

Pop 50,466 **Elev** 120 ft (37 m) **Area code** 819
Information Tourism Information Bureau, 1457 Notre Dame St, G9A 4X4; 819/375-1122

Considered the second-oldest French city in North America, Trois-Rivières was founded in 1634. Many 17th- and 18th-century buildings remain, and the Old Town area is a favorite haunt for visitors. The St. Maurice River splits into three channels here as it joins the St. Lawrence, giving the name to this major commercial and industrial center and important inland seaport. Paper milling and shipment of cereals are some of the more important industries. Trois-Rivières is a cathedral and university (Université du Québec) center as well.

What to See and Do

The Cathedral. (1854) Built in Gothic Westminster style; contains huge stained-glass windows, brilliantly designed by Nincheri, considered the finest of their kind in North America. Renovated in 1967. 362 rue Bonaventure.

De Tonnancour Manor. (1723) Oldest house in city; housed soldiers in 1812; in 1852 became the bishop's home. Displays of painting, pottery, sculpture, engravings, serigraphy, and jewelry. (Tues-Sun) 864 rue des Ursulines, Place Pierre-Boucher. Phone 819/374-2355. **FREE**

Les Forges du St.-Maurice National Historic Site. Remains of the first ironworks industry in Canada (1729-1883). Blast furnace and Ironmaster's House interpretation centers; models, audiovisual displays. Guided tours. (Mid-May-Labour Day, daily; after Labour Day-late Oct, Wed-Sun) 8 mi (13 km) N at 10000 boul des Forges. Phone 819/378-5116. ¢¢

Notre Dame-du-Cap. Small stone church (1714) and large octagonal basilica renowned for its stained-glass windows. Important pilgrimage site. (May-Oct, daily) Across the river, at 626 rue Notre Dame in Cap-de-la-Madeleine. Phone 819/374-2441. **FREE**

Old Port. Magnificent view of the St. Lawrence River. Built over part of the old fortifications. Pulp and paper interpretation center; riverside park; monument to La Vérendrye, discoverer of the Rockies (1743). Off rue St.-Francois-Xavier, overlooking river. Phone 819/372-4633. Interpretation center ¢

St. James Anglican Church. (1699) Rebuilt in 1754; used at various times as a storehouse and court; rectory used as prison, hospital, and sheriff's office. In 1823 it became an Anglican church and is now shared with the United Church; carved woodwork added in 1917; cemetery dates from 1808. Still used for church services. 811 rue des Ursulines. Phone 819/374-6010.

Sightseeing tour. M/S *Jacques-Cartier.* Around Trois-Rivières Harbour and on the St. Lawrence River. Four-hundred-passenger ship. Orchestra on wkend eve cruises. Contact 1515 rue du Fleuve, CP 64, G9A 5E3. (Mid-May-mid-Sept) Wharf on des Forges St. Phone 819/375-3000. ¢¢¢

Ursuline Convent. (1700) Norman-style architecture; building has been enlarged and restored many times. Historic chapel; museum and art collection. (May-Aug, Tues-Sun; Oct-Apr, Wed-Sun) 734 rue des Ursulines. Phone 819/375-7922. ¢

Special Event

Trois-Rivières International Vocal Arts Festival. Downtown. A celebration of song. Religious, lyrical, popular, ethnic, traditional singing. Phone 819/372-4635. Late June-early July.

Hotels

★★ **DELTA.** *1620 Notre Dame St (G9A 6E5). 819/376-1991; fax 819/372-5975. www.deltahotels.com.* 159 rms, 12 story. S, D $72-$150; each addl $15; suites $150-$300; under 18 free; higher rates Formula Grand Prix (Aug). Crib free. Pet accepted. TV; cable. Indoor pool; whirlpool. Coffee in rms. Restaurant 7 am-9:30 pm. Bar 4 pm-midnight. Ck-out noon. Meeting rms. Business servs avail. In-rm modem link. Gift shop. Free garage parking. Downhill ski 15 mi; x-country ski 5 mi. Exercise equipt; sauna. Massage. Minibars; some bathrm phones. Cr cds: A, D, DS, ER, JCB, MC, V.
D ⬛ ⬛ ⬛ ⬛ ⬛ ⬛ SC

★★ **HOTEL GOUVERNEURTROIS RIVIERES.** *975 rue Hart (G9A 4S3). ; fax 819/379-3941; res 888/910-1111. www.gouverneur.com.* 127 rms, 1 suite, 5 story. S, D $52; each addl $10; suite $150; under 18 free; wkend rates. Ample parking. Crib free. TV; cable (premium). Outdoor pool. Complimentary continental bkfst. Ck-out 1 pm. Business servs avail. In-rm modem link. Some minibars. Located dowtown; walking distance to St Lawrence River, Trois-Rivières old district. Cr cds: A, D, DS, ER, MC, V.
D ⬛ ⬛

ATTRACTION LIST

Attraction names are listed in alphabetical order followed by a symbol identifying their classification and then city. The symbols for classification are: [S] for Special Events and [W] for What to See and Do.

1000 Islands Camping Resort [W] *Gananoque, ON*
1000 Islands Skydeck [W] *Gananoque, ON*
1627 Pilgrim Village [W] *Plymouth, MA*
1800 House [W] *Nantucket Island, MA*
Abbe Museum, The [W] *Bar Harbor, ME*
Abbot Hall [W] *Marblehead, MA*
Abigail Adams House [W] *Braintree, MA*
Academy of Performing Arts [W] *Orleans (Cape Cod), MA*
Acadia National Park [W] *Bar Harbor, ME*
Acadia National Park [W] *Cranberry Isles, ME*
Acadia National Park [W] *Northeast Harbor, ME*
Acadia National Park [W] *Southwest Harbor, ME*
Acadian Memorial Church [W] *Grand Pre, NS*
Accursed Tombstone [W] *Bucksport, ME*
Acres of the Golden Pheasant [W] *Truro, NS*
Adams Gristmill [W] *Bellows Falls, VT*
Adams National Historic Site, The [W] *Quincy, MA*
Adams National Historic Park [W] *Quincy, MA*
Addison County Home and Garden Show [S]
    Middlebury, VT
Addison Gallery of American Art [W] *Andover and
    North Andover, MA*
African Lion Safari [W] *Hamilton, ON*
Agawa Canyon Train Excursion [W] *Sault Ste. Marie, ON*
Agnes Etherington Art Centre [W] *Kingston, ON*
Air Ontario Air Show, The [S] *London, ON*
Aldrich Museum of Contemporary Art [W] *Ridgefield, CT*
Ale Trail [S] *Kitchener-Waterloo, ON*
Alexander Graham Bell National Historic Park [W]
    Baddeck, NS
Algoma Fall Festival [S] *Sault Ste. Marie, ON*
Algonquin Golf Courses [W] *St. Andrews, NB*
Allan Gardens [W] *Toronto, ON*
Allis-Bushnell House and Museum [W] *Madison, CT*
Alpine Slide [W] *Stowe, VT*
Altrusa Annual Antique Show and Sale [S] *Meredith, NH*
Amasa Day House [W] *East Haddam, CT*
American Antiquarian Society [W] *Worcester, MA*
American Clock and Watch Museum [W] *Bristol, CT*
American Independence Museum [W] *Exeter, NH*
American Museum of Fly Fishing [W] *Manchester &
    Manchester Center, VT*
American Precision Museum [W] *Windsor, VT*
American Stage Festival [S] *Nashua, NH*
American Textile History Museum [W] *Lowell, MA*
America's Hometown Thanksgiving Celebration [S]
    Plymouth, MA
America's Stonehenge [W] *Salem, NH*
Amesbury Sports Park [W] *Amesbury, MA*
Amethyst Centre [W] *Thunder Bay, ON*
Amethyst Mine Panorama [W] *Thunder Bay, ON*

Amherst College [W] *Amherst, MA*
Amherst History Museum [W] *Amherst, MA*
Amistad Memorial [W] *New Haven, CT*
Amos Blanchard House [W] *Andover and North Andover, MA*
Andrés Wines [W] *Hamilton, ON*
Androscoggin Historical Society Library and Museum [W]
    Auburn, ME
Angelique [W] *Camden, ME*
Angrignon Park [W] *Montréal, QC*
Anheuser-Busch, Inc [W] *Nashua, NH*
Annmary Brown Memorial [W] *Providence, RI*
Antique and Classic Car Show [S] *Bennington, VT*
Antique Auto Days [S] *Boothbay Harbor, ME*
Antique Auto Museum [W] *Edmundston, NB*
Antique Dealers Outdoor Show and Sale [S] *Westport, CT*
Antiques, arts, and crafts [W] *St. Jovite, QC*
Antiques Bonaventure [S] *Montréal, QC*
Appledore [W] *Camden, ME*
Apple Harvest Festival [S] *Meriden, CT*
Apple Squeeze Festival [S] *Lenox, MA*
Aptucxet Trading Post [W] *Bourne (Cape Cod), MA*
Aquaboggan Water Park [W] *Saco, ME*
Arcade, The [W] *Providence, RI*
Arcadia Nature Center and Wildlife Sanctuary,
    Massachusetts Audubon Society [W] *Northampton, MA*
Architectural Walking Tour [W] *Kennebunkport, ME*
Arethusa Falls [W] *Bretton Woods, NH*
Aroostook Farm—Maine Agricultural Experiment Station
    [W] *Presque Isle, ME*
Aroostook Historical and Art Museum [W] *Houlton, ME*
Aroostook State Park [W] *Presque Isle, ME*
Around the Bay Road Race [S] *Hamilton, ON*
Arrowhead [W] *Pittsfield, MA*
Art Exhibit [S] *Bar Harbor, ME*
Art Gallery of Hamilton [W] *Hamilton, ON*
Art Gallery of Nova Scotia [W] *Halifax, NS*
Art Gallery of Ontario [W] *Toronto, ON*
Art Gallery of Windsor [W] *Windsor, ON*
Artillery Company of Newport Military Museum [W]
    Newport, RI
Artillery Park National Historic Site [W] *Quebec City, QC*
Arts and Crafts Show [S] *Old Saybrook, CT*
Arts, Flowers, & All that Jazz [S] *Newburyport, MA*
Arts in the Park Performance Series [S] *Pawtucket, RI*
Ashumet Holly & Wildlife Sanctuary [W] *Falmouth
    (Cape Cod), MA*
Astors' Beechwood [W] *Newport, RI*
Atlantic Crew Classic Rowing Regatta [S] *Fredericton, NB*
Atlantic Jazz Festival [S] *Halifax, NS*
Atlantic Seal Cruises [W] *Freeport, ME*
Attitash Bear Peak Ski Resort [W] *Bartlett, NH*

Audubon Center in Greenwich [W] *Greenwich, CT*
August Meeting of the Narragansett Indian Tribe [S]
    Charlestown, RI
Auto ferry service [W] *Hyannis (Cape Cod), MA*
Auto road [W] *Mount Washington, NH*
Autumnal Feasting [S] *Plymouth, MA*
Autumn Celebration [S] *Auburn, ME*
Awesome August Festival [S] *Cornwall, ON*
Babcock-Smith House [W] *Westerly, RI*
Bailey Island Cribstone Bridge [W] *Bailey Island, ME*
Baillairgé Cultural tours [W] *Quebec City, QC*
Baker Memorial Library [W] *Hanover, NH*
Balch House [W] *Beverly, MA*
Ballard Institute and Museum of Puppetry [W] *Storrs, CT*
Balloons Over Bristol [S] *Bristol, CT*
Balmy Days [W] *Boothbay Harbor, ME*
Balsams/Wilderness Ski Area [W] *Dixville Notch, NH*
Band concerts [S] *Bangor, ME*
Band concerts [S] *Beverly, MA*
Band concerts [S] *Chatham (Cape Cod), MA*
Band concerts [S] *Hampton Beach, NH*
Bangor Fair [S] *Bangor, ME*
Bangor Historical Museum [W] *Bangor, ME*
Bapst Library [W] *Boston, MA*
Barbour's General Store [W] *St. John, NB*
Bar Harbor Historical Society Museum [W] *Bar Harbor, ME*
Bar Harbor Whale Watch Company [W] *Bar Harbor, ME*
Barn Playhouse [S] *New London, NH*
Barnstable County Fair [S] *Falmouth (Cape Cod), MA*
Barnum Festival [S] *Bridgeport, CT*
Barnum Museum, The [W] *Bridgeport, CT*
Barracks Museum [W] *Eastport, ME*
Barrett House "Forest Hall" [W] *Jaffrey, NH*
Barrett's Tours [W] *Nantucket Island, MA*
Bartlett Arboretum and Gardens [W] *Stamford, CT*
Bartlett Museum [W] *Amesbury, MA*
Baseball [S] *New Britain, CT*
Basilica of Ste.-Anne-de-Beaupré [W] *Quebec City, QC*
Basilica of St. Michel [W] *Sherbrooke, QC*
Basin, The [W] *Franconia Notch State Park, NH*
Basin Head Fisheries Museum [W] *Charlottetown, PE*
Basketball Hall of Fame [W] *Springfield, MA*
Baskin Robbins Putt 'n Play [W] *Gananoque, ON*
Bates College [W] *Lewiston, ME*
Battery Park [W] *Burlington, VT*
Battlefield House and Monument [W] *Hamilton, ON*
Battle Green [W] *Lexington, MA*
Battleship Cove [W] *Fall River, MA*
Baxter State Park [W] *Greenville, ME*
Baxter State Park [W] *Millinocket, ME*
Bay Chamber Concerts [W] *Camden, ME*
Bay Day [S] *St. Albans, VT*
Bay State Cruise Company [W] *Boston, MA*
Bay View Cruises [W] *Portland, ME*
Beaconsfield [W] *Charlottetown, PE*
Beardsley Zoological Gardens [W] *Bridgeport, CT*
Beartown State Forest [W] *Great Barrington, MA*
"Beauport," the Sleeper-McCann House [W] *Gloucester, MA*
Beauvoir Sanctuary [W] *Sherbrooke, QC*
Beaverbrook Art Gallery [W] *Fredericton, NB*
Beaver Brook Falls [W] *Colebrook, NH*

Beaverbrook Playhouse, The [W] *Fredericton, NB*
Beinecke Rare Book and Manuscript Library [W]
    New Haven, CT
Belcourt Castle [W] *Newport, RI*
Belfast Bay Festival [S] *Belfast, ME*
Bellevue House National Historic Site [W] *Kingston, ON*
Bell Homestead [W] *Brantford, ON*
Ben & Jerry's Ice Cream Factory [W] *Waterbury, VT*
Bennington Battle Monument [W] *Bennington, VT*
Bennington College [W] *Bennington, VT*
Bennington Museum [W] *Bennington, VT*
Ben Veldhuis Limited [W] *Hamilton, ON*
Berkshire Botanical Garden [W] *Stockbridge and*
    West Stockbridge, MA
Berkshire Craft Fair [S] *Great Barrington, MA*
Berkshire Museum [W] *Pittsfield, MA*
Berkshire Theatre Festival [S] *Stockbridge and*
    West Stockbridge, MA
Bible Exhibit, The [W] *Boston, MA*
Billings Farm & Museum [W] *Woodstock, VT*
Bingeman Park [W] *Kitchener-Waterloo, ON*
Biodôme de Montréal [W] *Montréal, QC*
Birds of Vermont Museum, The [W] *Burlington, VT*
Birthplace of Lucy Maud Montgomery [W] *Cavendish, PE*
Black Creek Pioneer Village [W] *Toronto, ON*
Black Cultural Centre [W] *Dartmouth, NS*
Black Heritage Trail [W] *Boston, MA*
Black Mountain [W] *Jackson, NH*
Blaine House [W] *Augusta, ME*
Blessing of the Fleet [S] *New Bedford, MA*
Blithewold Mansion and Gardens [W] *Bristol, RI*
Blithewold Mansion and Gardens [S] *Bristol, RI*
Blockhouse Historic Site [W] *St. Andrews, NB*
Block Island Ferry [W] *Narragansett, RI*
Block Island/Montauk, Long Island [W] *Block Island, RI*
Block Island/New London, CT [W] *Block Island, RI*
Block Island/Point Judith [W] *Block Island, RI*
Block Island/Providence, RI/Newport, RI [W]
    Block Island, RI
Bluegrass Festival [S] *Brunswick, ME*
Blue Grass Festival [S] *Norwich, CT*
Blue Hill Fair [S] *Blue Hill, ME*
Blue Hills Trailside Museum [W] *Boston, MA*
Bluenose II [W] *Halifax, NS*
Boat and ferry service [W] *Monhegan Island, ME*
Boat cruises [W] *Sault Ste. Marie, ON*
Boat ride [W] *Niagara Falls, ON*
Boat trips [W] *Boothbay Harbor, ME*
Boat trips [W] *Kingston, ON*
Boat trips [W] *New Bedford, MA*
Boat trips [W] *Portland, ME*
Boat trips. Hyannis-Nantucket Day Round Trip [W]
    Nantucket Island, MA
Bolton Valley Ski/Summer Resort [W] *Burlington, VT*
Boothbay Railway Village [W] *Boothbay Harbor, ME*
Boothbay Region Historical Society Museum [W]
    Boothbay Harbor, ME
Boothe Memorial Park [W] *Stratford, CT*
Boott Cotton Mills Museum [W] *Lowell, MA*
Boston African American National Historic Site [W]
    Boston, MA

Boston Bruins (NHL) [W] *Boston, MA*
Boston Celtics (NBA) [W] *Boston, MA*
Boston College [W] *Boston, MA*
Boston Common [W] *Boston, MA*
Boston Harbor Islands National Park Area [W] *Boston, MA*
Boston Marathon [S] *Boston, MA*
Boston Massacre Monument [W] *Boston, MA*
Boston Public Library [W] *Boston, MA*
Boston Red Sox (MLB) [W] *Boston, MA*
Boston Tea Party Ship and Museum [W] *Boston, MA*
Boston Tours from Suburban Hotels [W] *Boston, MA*
Boston University [W] *Boston, MA*
Bourne Scenic Park [W] *Bourne (Cape Cod), MA*
Bousquet [W] *Pittsfield, MA*
Bowdoin College [W] *Brunswick, ME*
Bowdoin Summer Music Festival and School [S]
        Brunswick, ME
Bradley House Museum [W] *Woods Hole, MA*
Brainerd Monument [W] *St. Albans, VT*
Branbury State Park [W] *Brandon, VT*
Brandeis University [W] *Waltham, MA*
Brant County Museum [W] *Brantford, ON*
Brass Mill Center [W] *Waterbury, CT*
Brattleboro Museum & Art Center [W] *Brattleboro, VT*
Bread Loaf [W] *Middlebury, VT*
Breakers, The [W] *Newport, RI*
Bretton Woods Ski Area [W] *Bretton Woods, NH*
Brick Market [W] *Newport, RI*
Brick Store Museum [W] *Kennebunk, ME*
Brimfield [W] *Springfield, MA*
Brock's Monument [W] *Niagara-on-the-Lake, ON*
Brockton Fair [S] *Brockton, MA*
Brockton Historical Society Museums [W] *Brockton, MA*
Brock University [W] *St. Catharines, ON*
Brockville Museum [W] *Brockville, ON*
Brodie Mountain [W] *Pittsfield, MA*
Bromley Alpine Slide [W] *Peru, VT*
Bromley Mountain Ski Area [W] *Peru, VT*
Brooks Free Library [W] *Harwich (Cape Cod), MA*
Brown & Hopkins Country Store [W] *Glocester, RI*
Brown University [W] *Providence, RI*
Bruce Museum [W] *Greenwich, CT*
Brush Hill Tours [W] *Boston, MA*
Buckman Tavern [W] *Lexington, MA*
Bullet Hill Schoolhouse [W] *Southbury, CT*
Bunker Hill Day [S] *Boston, MA*
Bunker Hill Monument [W] *Boston, MA*
Burial Hill [W] *Plymouth, MA*
Burke Mountain Ski Area [W] *Lyndonville, VT*
Burlingame State Park [W] *Charlestown, RI*
Burlington Ferry [W] *Burlington, VT*
Burlington Trout Hatchery [W] *Bristol, CT*
Burnham Tavern Museum [W] *Machias, ME*
Burton Island State Park [W] *St. Albans, VT*
Bush-Holley House [W] *Greenwich, CT*
Bushnell Park [W] *Hartford, CT*
Busker Carnival Festival [S] *Kitchener-Waterloo, ON*
Butler-McCook Homestead and Main Street History Center
        [W] *Hartford, CT*
Butterfly Zoo, The [W] *Portsmouth, RI*
Buttolph-Williams House [W] *Wethersfield, CT*

Button Bay State Park [W] *Vergennes, VT*
Buttonwood Park & Zoo [W] *New Bedford, MA*
Bytown Museum [W] *Ottawa, ON*
By Ward Market [W] *Ottawa, ON*
Byzantine Museum [W] *Montréal, QC*
Cabot House [W] *Beverly, MA*
Cadillac Shopping Outlet [W] *Warwick, RI*
Calèches [W] *Quebec City, QC*
Calèche tours [W] *Montréal, QC*
Calvin Coolidge Memorial Room [W] *Northampton, MA*
Calvin Coolidge State Forest [W] *Plymouth, VT*
Camden Hills State Park [W] *Camden, ME*
Camden Opera House [S] *Camden, ME*
Camelot Cruises, Inc [W] *East Haddam, CT*
Camel's Hump Mountain [W] *Waterbury, VT*
Campbell Falls [W] *Norfolk, CT*
Camping [W] *Rangeley, ME*
Canada Day [S] *Ottawa, ON*
Canada Day Celebration [S] *Fredericton, NB*
Canada One Factory Outlets [W] *Niagara Falls, ON*
Canadian Empress [W] *Kingston, ON*
Canadian Football Hall of Fame and Museum [W]
        Hamilton, ON
Canadian Grand Prix [S] *Montréal, QC*
Canadian International [S] *Toronto, ON*
Canadian Museum of Civilization [W] *Ottawa, ON*
Canadian Museum of Contemporary Photography [W]
        Ottawa, ON
Canadian National Exhibition [S] *Toronto, ON*
Canadian Parliament Buildings [W] *Ottawa , ON*
Canadian Ski Museum [W] *Ottawa, ON*
Canadian Tulip Festival [S] *Ottawa, ON*
Canadian War Museum [W] *Ottawa, ON*
Can Am Crown Sled Dog Races [S] *Fort Kent, ME*
Can-Am Soapbox Derby [S] *St. Catharines, ON*
Canatara Park [W] *Sarnia, ON*
Candle Mill Village [W] *Arlington, VT*
Candlewood Lake [W] *Danbury, CT*
Cannon Mt Ski Area [W] *Franconia Notch State Park, NH*
Canobie Lake Park [W] *Salem, NH*
Canoeing [W] *Fort Kent, ME*
Canoe Meadows Wildlife Sanctuary [W] *Pittsfield, MA*
Canterbury Shaker Village [W] *Concord, NH*
Cape Ann Historical Museum [W] *Gloucester, MA*
Cape Cod Art Association Gallery [W] *Barnstable
        (Cape Cod), MA*
Cape Cod Canal Cruises [W] *Buzzards Bay (Cape Cod), MA*
Cape Cod Melody Tent [S] *Hyannis (Cape Cod), MA*
Cape Cod Museum of Natural History [W] *Brewster
        (Cape Cod), MA*
Cape Forchu Lighthouse [W] *Yarmouth, NS*
Cape Playhouse [S] *Dennis (Cape Cod), MA*
Capitol Center for the Arts [W] *Concord, NH*
Cap'n Fish's Boat Trips and Deep Sea Fishing [W]
        Boothbay Harbor, ME
Caprilands Herb Farm [W] *Storrs, CT*
Captain Bangs Hallet House [W] *South Yarmouth
        (Cape Cod), MA*
Captain David Judson House [W] *Stratford, CT*
Captain's Cove Seaport [W] *Bridgeport, CT*
Cardinal Spellman Philatelic Museum [W] *Waltham, MA*

Caribana [S] *Toronto, ON*
Caribou Historical Center [W] *Caribou, ME*
Carlton Martello Tower National Historic Park [W]
    St. John, NB
Carnaval Québec Kellogg's [S] *Quebec City, QC*
Car/passenger boat trips [W] *Martha's Vineyard, MA*
Car/passenger boat trips [W] *Woods Hole, MA*
Carrabassett Valley Ski Touring Center [W] *Kingfield, ME*
Carter's X-C Ski Center [W] *Bethel, ME*
Cartier-Brébeuf National Historic Site [W] *Quebec City, QC*
Casa Loma [W] *Toronto, ON*
Casco Bay Lines [W] *Chebeague Islands, ME*
Casco Bay Lines [W] *Portland, ME*
Casey Farm [W] *North Kingstown, RI*
Casimir Pulaski State Park [W] *Glocester, RI*
Casino Montréal [W] *Montréal, QC*
Casino Windsor [W] *Windsor, ON*
Castle Craig Tower [W] *Meriden, CT*
The CAT [W] *Yarmouth, NS*
Catamount [W] *Great Barrington, MA*
Catharine B. Mitchell Museum [W] *Stratford, CT*
Cathedral, The [W] *Trois-Rivieres, QC*
Cathedral of St. John [W] *Providence, RI*
Cathedral of the Pines [W] *Jaffrey, NH*
CCInc Auto Tape Tours [W] *Newport, RI*
Celebrate Bar Harbor [S] *Bar Harbor, ME*
Celebration of Lights [S] *Sarnia, ON*
Centennial Conservatory [W] *Thunder Bay, ON*
Centennial Park [W] *Thunder Bay, ON*
Center Church and Ancient Burying Ground [W]
    Hartford, CT
Center for Maine History, The [W] *Portland, ME*
Centerville Historical Society Museum [W] *Centerville
    (Cape Cod), MA*
Central Burying Ground [W] *Boston, MA*
Central Connecticut State University [W] *New Britain, CT*
Central Experimental Farm [W] *Ottawa, ON*
Centre d'exposition du Vieux Palais [W] *St. Jerome, QC*
Chaffee Center for the Visual Arts [W] *Rutland, VT*
Chamard Vinyards [W] *Clinton, CT*
Chamber Arts & Crafts Festival [S] *Fairfield, CT*
Chamber Music Hall [W] *Lenox, MA*
Changing the Guard [S] *Ottawa, ON*
Chapel of Our Lady of Sorrows [W] *Halifax, NS*
Chapman-Hall House [W] *Damariscotta, ME*
Charles Hayden Planetarium [W] *Boston, MA*
Charles Ives Center for the Arts [S] *Danbury, CT*
Charles River Regatta [S] *Boston, MA*
Charlotte-Essex Ferry [W] *Shelburne, VT*
Charlottetown Festival [S] *Charlottetown, PE*
Charter fishing trips [W] *Groton, CT*
Charter fishing trips [W] *Norwalk, CT*
Chateau-sur-Mer [W] *Newport, RI*
Chatfield Hollow State Park [W] *Clinton, CT*
Chebeague Transportation [W] *Chebeague Islands, ME*
Chelsea Street Festival [S] *Norwich, CT*
Cheney Homestead [W] *Manchester, CT*
Cheshire Fair [S] *Keene, NH*
Chester A. Arthur Historic Site [W] *St. Albans, VT*
Chesterwood [W] *Stockbridge and West Stockbridge, MA*
Chestnut Street [W] *Salem, MA*

Chicken Barbecue [S] *Fairlee, VT*
Children's Animal Farm [W] *Sarnia, ON*
Children's Chimes Bell Tower [W] *Stockbridge and
    West Stockbridge, MA*
Children's Museum [W] *Hamilton, ON*
Children's Museum [W] *Holyoke, MA*
Children's Museum of Boston [W] *Boston, MA*
Children's Museum of Maine [W] *Portland, ME*
Children's Museum of Portsmouth [W] *Portsmouth, NH*
Chimney Point State Historic Site [W] *Vergennes, VT*
Chin International Picnic [S] *Toronto, ON*
Christa McAuliffe Planetarium [W] *Concord, NH*
Christ Church [W] *Cambridge, MA*
Christian Science Publishing Society [W] *Boston, MA*
Christmas by the Sea [S] *Camden, ME*
Christmas Crafts Expo I & II [S] *Hartford, CT*
Christmas in Newport [S] *Newport, RI*
Christmas Stroll [S] *Nantucket Island, MA*
Christmas Torchlight Parade [S] *Old Saybrook, CT*
Chronicle of Salem [W] *Salem, MA*
Chrysanthemum Festival [S] *Bristol, CT*
Château Ramezay [W] *Montréal, QC*
Church [W] *Quebec City, QC*
Churches [W] *Halifax, NS*
Church Street Marketplace [W] *Burlington, VT*
City Hall [W] *Fredericton, NB*
City Hall [W] *Kingston, ON*
City Hall [W] *Ottawa, ON*
City Hall [W] *Toronto, ON*
City parks [W] *Toronto, ON*
Civilian Conservation Corps Museum [W]
    Stafford Springs, CT
Civil War Days [S] *St. Albans, VT*
Clam Festival [S] *Yarmouth, ME*
Clark House [W] *Wolfeboro, NH*
Clark's Trading Post [W] *Lincoln/North Woodstock, NH*
Cliff Walk [W] *Newport, RI*
Clock Tower [W] *Niagara-on-the-Lake, ON*
Clydesdale Hamlet [W] *Nashua, NH*
CN Tower [W] *Toronto, ON*
Coasting schooners *Isaac H. Evans, American Eagle &
    Heritage* [W] *Rockland, ME*
Cobscook Bay [W] *Machias, ME*
Cocheco Arts Festival [S] *Dover, NH*
Codman House [W] *Concord, MA*
Coffin House [W] *Newburyport, MA*
Coggeshall Farm Museum [W] *Bristol, RI*
Cog railway [W] *Mount Washington, NH*
Colasanti Farms, Ltd [W] *Windsor, ON*
Colborne Lodge [W] *Toronto, ON*
Colby College [W] *Waterville, ME*
Colchester County Museum [W] *Truro, NS*
Cold Hollow Cider Mill [W] *Waterbury, VT*
Cole Land Transportation Museum [W] *Bangor, ME*
Coleman State Park [W] *Colebrook, NH*
Cole's Hill [W] *Plymouth, MA*
Collection of Musical Instruments [W] *New Haven, CT*
College Light Opera Company at Highfield Theatre [S]
    Falmouth (Cape Cod), MA
Colonel Ashley House [W] *Great Barrington, MA*
Colonial Pemaquid State Memorial [W] *Damariscotta, ME*

Colony Mill Marketplace [W] *Keene, NH*
Colt State Park [W] *Bristol, RI*
Colt State Park [S] *Bristol, RI*
Columbia Covered Bridge [W] *Colebrook, NH*
Concord Arts & Crafts [W] *Concord, NH*
Concord Free Public Library [W] *Concord, MA*
Concord Museum [W] *Concord, MA*
Confederation Centre of the Arts [W] *Charlottetown, PE*
Confederation Park [W] *Stratford, ON*
Confederation Tour Trolley [W] *Kingston, ON*
Congregational Christian Church [W] *Franklin, NH*
Congregational Church [W] *Middlebury, VT*
Connecticut Audubon Society Birdcraft Museum and
    Sanctuary [W] *Fairfield, CT*
Connecticut Audubon Society Fairfield Nature Center and
    Larsen Sanctuary [W] *Fairfield, CT*
Connecticut Audubon Society Holland Brook Nature
    Center [W] *Hartford, CT*
Connecticut Firemen's Historical Society Fire Museum [W]
    Manchester, CT
Connecticut Fire Museum [W] *Windsor Locks, CT*
Connecticut Historical Society [W] *Hartford, CT*
Connecticut Repertory Theatre [S] *Storrs, CT*
Connecticut River Cruise [W] *Hartford, CT*
Connecticut River Museum [W] *Essex, CT*
Connecticut State Museum of Natural History [W]
    Storrs, CT
Connecticut Storytelling Festival [S] *New London, CT*
Connecticut Trolley Museum [W] *Windsor, CT*
Constitution House [W] *Windsor, VT*
Conway Homestead-Cramer Museum [W] *Camden, ME*
Conway Scenic Railroad [W] *North Conway, NH*
Copp's Hill Burying Ground [W] *Boston, MA*
Correctional Service of Canada Museum [W] *Kingston, ON*
Court House [W] *Niagara-on-the-Lake, ON*
Coventry Gardens and Peace Fountain [W] *Windsor, ON*
Covered bridge [W] *Cornwall Bridge, CT*
Covered bridge [W] *Windsor, VT*
Covered bridge [W] *Woodstock, VT*
Covered bridges [W] *North Conway, NH*
Craft Centre [W] *Baddeck, NS*
Cranberry Cove Boating Company [W] *Southwest
    Harbor, ME*
Cranberry Harvest Festival [S] *Harwich (Cape Cod), MA*
Cranberry World [W] *Plymouth, MA*
Crane Beach [W] *Ipswich, MA*
Crawford Notch State Park [W] *Bretton Woods, NH*
Creamery Bridge [W] *Brattleboro, VT*
Crescent Beach [W] *Portland, ME*
Cross-country skiing [W] *Fort Kent, ME*
Crowley Cheese Factory [W] *Ludlow, VT*
Crowninshield-Bentley House [W] *Salem, MA*
Cruises on Lake Winnipesaukee [W] *Laconia, NH*
Crysler Farm Battlefield Park [W] *Morrisburg, ON*
Crystal Palace Amusement Park [W] *Moncton, NB*
Culinary Archives & Museum [W] *Providence, RI*
Culturama Festival [S] *Fort Frances, ON*
Currency Museum [W] *Ottawa , ON*
Currier Gallery of Art [W] *Manchester, NH*
Cushing House Museum [W] *Newburyport, MA*
Custom House [W] *Salem, MA*

Custom House Maritime Museum [W] *Newburyport, MA*
Daffodil Festival [S] *Meriden, CT*
Daffodil Festival [S] *Nantucket Island, MA*
Damon House [W] *Northampton, MA*
Danforth Museum of Art [W] *Framingham, MA*
Danvers Family Festival [S] *Danvers, MA*
Dartmouth College [W] *Hanover, NH*
Dartmouth Natal Day [S] *Dartmouth, NS*
Dartmouth Row [W] *Hanover, NH*
Dartmouth Skiway [W] *Hanover, NH*
David M. Stewart Museum [W] *Montréal, QC*
David Winton Bell Gallery [W] *Providence, RI*
Days of Wine and Roses, The [S] *Niagara-on-the-Lake, ON*
Deacon John Grave House [W] *Madison, CT*
DeCordova Museum & Sculpture Park [W] *Concord, MA*
Dedham Historical Society [W] *Dedham, MA*
Deep River Ancient Muster and Parade [S] *Essex, CT*
Deerfield Valley Farmers Day Exhibition [S] *Wilmington, VT*
Denison Homestead [W] *Mystic, CT*
Denison Pequotsepos Nature Center [W] *Mystic, CT*
Dennis Hill [W] *Norfolk, CT*
Derby House [W] *Salem, MA*
Derby Wharf [W] *Salem, MA*
Destination Plymouth Sprint Triathlon [S] *Plymouth, MA*
De Tonnancour Manor [W] *Trois-Rivieres, QC*
Dinosaur State Park [W] *Wethersfield, CT*
Discover Jazz Festival [S] *Burlington, VT*
Discovery Harbour [W] *Toronto, ON*
Discovery Museum [W] *Bridgeport, CT*
Discovery Museum [W] *Burlington, VT*
Dogwood Festival [S] *Fairfield, CT*
Dolly Copp Campground [W] *Gorham, NH*
Donald G. Trayser Memorial Museum [W] *Barnstable
    (Cape Cod), MA*
Doon Heritage Crossroads [W] *Kitchener-Waterloo, ON*
Dorchester Square [W] *Montréal, QC*
Dorset Theatre Festival [S] *Dorset, VT*
Double-decker Bus Tour of London [W] *London, ON*
Double-Decker bus tours. Capital Trolley Tours [W]
    Ottawa , ON
Double Decker Tours [W] *Halifax, NS*
Double Eagle II Launch Site Monument [W] *Presque Isle, ME*
Downeast Whitewater Rafting [W] *North Conway, NH*
Dozynki Polish Harvest Festival [S] *New Britain, CT*
Dragon Boat Festival [S] *London, ON*
Dr. Moses Mason House Museum [W] *Bethel, ME*
Drumlin Farm Education Center [W] *Concord, MA*
du Maurier Québec Summer Festival [S] *Quebec City, QC*
Dundurn Castle [W] *Hamilton, ON*
Durham Fair [S] *Middletown, CT*
Dyer Library & York Institute Museum [W] *Saco, ME*
Eagle Aviation [W] *East Haddam, CT*
Eagle Tours Inc [W] *Portland, ME*
Eartha [W] *Yarmouth, ME*
Eastern National Morgan Horse Show [S] *Northampton, MA*
Eastern Slope Playhouse [S] *North Conway, NH*
Eastern States Exposition (The Big E) [S] *Springfield, MA*
Eastham Historical Society [W] *Eastham (Cape Cod), MA*
Eastham Windmill [W] *Eastham (Cape Cod), MA*
Easton's Beach [W] *Newport, RI*
East Rock Park [W] *New Haven, CT*

Echo Lake State Park [W] *North Conway, NH*
EcoTarium [W] *Worcester, MA*
Edgartown [W] *Martha's Vineyard, MA*
Edith Wharton Restoration (The Mount) [W] *Lenox, MA*
Edmundston Golf Club [W] *Edmundston, NB*
Edward King House [W] *Newport, RI*
Edwards Gardens [W] *Toronto, ON*
Eldon House [W] *London, ON*
Eli Terry, Jr. Waterwheel [W] *Bristol, CT*
Elizabeth Park [W] *Hartford, CT*
Elizabeth Perkins House [W] *York, ME*
Elmore State Park [W] *Stowe, VT*
Elms, The [W] *Newport, RI*
Emerald Lake State Park [W] *Manchester & Manchester Center, VT*
Emerson-Wilcox House [W] *York, ME*
Emily Dickinson Homestead [W] *Amherst, MA*
Emma Willard House [W] *Middlebury, VT*
Enfield Shaker Museum [W] *Hanover, NH*
Equinox Sky Line Drive [W] *Manchester & Manchester Center, VT*
ESCAPE (Exciting, Scenic, Canadian/American Powerboat Excursion) [S] *Kenora, ON*
Esplanade Concerts [S] *Boston, MA*
Ethan Allen Homestead [W] *Burlington, VT*
Ethan Allen Park [W] *Burlington, VT*
Eugene O'Neill Theater Center [W] *New London, CT*
Eureka Schoolhouse [W] *Springfield, VT*
Excursion Cruises [W] *Burlington, VT*
Exhibition Place [W] *Toronto, ON*
Expedition Whydah's Sea Lab & Learning Center [W] *Provincetown (Cape Cod), MA*
Explore [W] *Quebec City, QC*
Expo Québec [S] *Quebec City, QC*
Factory Outlet District [W] *Fall River, MA*
Factory outlet stores [W] *Freeport, ME*
Factory Outlet Stores [W] *Kittery, ME*
Factory outlet stores [W] *Manchester & Manchester Center, VT*
Factory outlet stores [W] *North Conway, NH*
Fairbanks House [W] *Dedham, MA*
Fairbanks Museum and Planetarium [W] *St. Johnsbury, VT*
Fairfield Historical Society [W] *Fairfield, CT*
Fall Festival [S] *Kent, CT*
Fall Foliage Festival [S] *Boothbay Harbor, ME*
Fall Foliage Festival [S] *North Adams, MA*
Fall Harvest Festival [S] *Newburyport, MA*
Fall River Heritage State Park [W] *Fall River, MA*
Fall River Historical Society [W] *Fall River, MA*
Falmouth Historical Society Museums. Julia Wood House [W] *Falmouth (Cape Cod), MA*
Faneuil Hall Marketplace [W] *Boston, MA*
Fanshawe Pioneer Village [W] *London, ON*
Farmers Market [W] *Kitchener-Waterloo, ON*
Farmers Market, The [W] *St. Catharines, ON*
Farmington Antiques Weekend [S] *Farmington, CT*
Farmington Valley Arts Center [W] *Avon, CT*
Farnsworth Art Museum and Wyeth Center [W] *Rockland, ME*
Farnsworth Homestead [W] *Rockland, ME*
Farrar-Mansur House Museum [W] *Weston, VT*
Feast of the Blessed Sacrament [S] *New Bedford, MA*

Felix Neck Sanctuary [W] *Martha's Vineyard, MA*
Ferries [W] *New London, CT*
Ferry Beach State Park [W] *Saco, ME*
Ferry from Port Clyde [W] *Monhegan Island, ME*
Ferry service [W] *Block Island, RI*
Ferry service [W] *Cranberry Isles, ME*
Ferry Service [W] *Northeast Harbor, ME*
Ferry service from mainland [W] *Chebeague Islands, ME*
Ferry services [W] *Yarmouth, NS*
Ferry Service to Digby, NS [W] *St. John, NB*
Ferry Service to St. John, NB [W] *Digby, NS*
Ferry service to Yarmouth, Nova Scotia [W] *Bar Harbor, ME*
Ferry to Deer Island, New Brunswick [W] *Eastport, ME*
Ferry to Port Jefferson, Long Island [W] *Bridgeport, CT*
Ferry to Sheffield Island Lighthouse [W] *Norwalk, CT*
FestItalia [S] *Hamilton, ON*
Festival Acadien de Wedgeport [S] *Yarmouth, NS*
Festival by the Sea [S] *St. John, NB*
Festival de Joie [S] *Lewiston, ME*
Festival of Arts [S] *Stamford, CT*
Festival of Friends [S] *Hamilton, ON*
Festival of Lights [S] *Charlottetown, PE*
Festival of Lights [S] *North Kingstown, RI*
Festival on the Green [S] *Middlebury, VT*
Festival Week [S] *Dennis (Cape Cod), MA*
Fife & Drum Muster and Colonial Fair [S] *Sudbury Center, MA*
Fine Arts Center and Gallery [W] *Amherst, MA*
Firefighters' Museum of Nova Scotia [W] *Yarmouth, NS*
First Baptist Church in America [W] *Providence, RI*
First Church in Windsor, The [W] *Windsor, CT*
First Church of Christ, Congregational United Church of Christ [W] *Wethersfield, CT*
First Night Celebration [S] *Boston, MA*
First Night New Bedford [S] *New Bedford, MA*
First Presbyterian Church [W] *Stamford, CT*
First Unitarian Church [W] *Providence, RI*
Fisheries Museum of the Atlantic [W] *Peggy's Cove, NS*
Fisherman's Festival [S] *Boothbay Harbor, ME*
Fisherman's Memorial Pier and Chamber of Commerce [W] *Rockland, ME*
Fishermen's Wharf [W] *Digby, NS*
Fishing [W] *Arlington, VT*
Fishing [W] *Bar Harbor, ME*
Fishing [W] *Block Island, RI*
Fishing [W] *Boothbay Harbor, ME*
Fishing [W] *Eastport, ME*
Fishing [W] *Fort Kent, ME*
Fishing [W] *Hampton Beach, NH*
Fishing [W] *Jamestown, RI*
Fishing [W] *Narragansett, RI*
Fishing [W] *Rangeley, ME*
Fishing [W] *Truro and North Truro (Cape Cod), MA*
Fishing, boating on bay [W] *Searsport, ME*
Flamboro Downs [W] *Hamilton, ON*
Flanders Nature Center [W] *Woodbury, CT*
Floral Park [W] *Montréal, QC*
Florence Griswold Museum [W] *Old Lyme, CT*
Flume Cascade [W] *Bretton Woods, NH*
Flume Gorge & Park Information Center [W] *Franconia Notch State Park, NH*
Flying Horse Carousel [W] *Westerly, RI*

Fogg Art Museum [W] *Cambridge, MA*
Foire Brayonne [S] *Edmundston, NB*
Folger-Franklin Seat & Memorial Boulder [W]
    Nantucket Island, MA
Folk Arts Festival [S] *St. Catharines, ON*
Forest Park [W] *Springfield, MA*
Formal Gardens [W] *Lenox, MA*
Fort Adams State Park [W] *Newport, RI*
Fort Amherst/Port La Joye National Historic Park [W]
    Charlottetown, PE
Fort Anne National Historic Site [W] *Digby, NS*
Fort at No. 4 [W] *Newport, NH*
Fort Beausejour National Historic Site [W] *Moncton, NB*
Fort Constitution [W] *Portsmouth, NH*
Fort Foster Park [W] *Kittery, ME*
Fort Frances Museum [W] *Fort Frances, ON*
Fort Frederick & College Museum [W] *Kingston, ON*
Fort George National Historic Site [W]
    Niagara-on-the-Lake, ON
Fort Griswold Battlefield State Park [W] *Groton, CT*
Fort Henry [W] *Kingston, ON*
Fort Kent Block House [W] *Fort Kent, ME*
Fort Kent Historical Society Museum and Gardens [W]
    Fort Kent, ME
Fort Knox State Park [W] *Bucksport, ME*
Fort Lennox [W] *Montréal, QC*
Fort Malden National Historic Park [W] *Windsor, ON*
Fort McClary Memorial [W] *Kittery, ME*
Fort Nathan Hale Park and Black Rock Fort [W]
    New Haven, CT
Fort O'Brien State Historic Site [W] *Machias, ME*
Fort Phoenix Beach State Reservation [W] *New Bedford, MA*
Fort Point State Park [W] *Bucksport, ME*
Fort Popham Memorial [W] *Bath, ME*
Fort Saybrook Monument Park [W] *Old Saybrook, CT*
Fort Stark State Historic Site [W] *Portsmouth, NH*
Fort Wellington National Historic Site [W] *Morrisburg, ON*
Fort William Henry State Memorial [W] *Damariscotta, ME*
Foundation Headquarters [W] *Concord, NH*
Franconia Notch State Park [W] *Franconia, NH*
Franconia Notch State Park [W] *Lincoln/*
    North Woodstock, NH
Franklin County Fair [S] *Greenfield, MA*
Franklin Park Zoo [W] *Boston, MA*
Fred Benson Town Beach [W] *Block Island, RI*
Frederick Law Olmsted National Historic Site [W]
    Boston, MA
Fredericton [W] *Fredericton, NB*
Fredericton Exhibition [S] *Fredericton, NB*
Freedom Trail, The [W] *Boston, MA*
French Cable Station Museum [W] *Orleans (Cape Cod), MA*
Friends Meeting House [W] *Newport, RI*
Frost Park [W] *Yarmouth, NS*
Frost Place [W] *Franconia, NH*
Fruitlands Museums [W] *Concord, MA*
Fîte Nationale [S] *Montréal, QC*
Fuller Gardens [W] *Hampton Beach, NH*
Fuller Museum of Art [W] *Brockton, MA*
Fun in the Sun Festival [S] *Fort Frances, ON*
Funtown USA [W] *Saco, ME*
Gaelic College, The [W] *Baddeck, NS*

Gail's Tours [W] *Nantucket Island, MA*
Gallery/Stratford, The [W] *Stratford, ON*
Gananoque Boat Line [W] *Gananoque, ON*
Gananoque Historical Museum [W] *Gananoque, ON*
Garden Club Open House Day [S] *Camden, ME*
Garden in the Woods [W] *Framingham, MA*
Gardens, The [W] *Sarnia, ON*
Gardner-Pingree House [W] *Salem, MA*
Garlicfest [S] *Fairfield, CT*
Gaspee Days [S] *Warwick, RI*
General William Hart House [W] *Old Saybrook, CT*
Geology Museum [W] *Kingston, ON*
George Marshall Store [W] *York, ME*
George R. Gardiner Museum of Ceramic Art [W]
    Toronto, ON
George Washington State Campground [W] *Glocester, RI*
Giant Staircase [W] *Bailey Island, ME*
Giant Waterslide [W] *Gananoque, ON*
Gibbs Avenue Museum [W] *Bridgton, ME*
Gibson House [W] *Toronto, ON*
Gibson House Museum [W] *Boston, MA*
Gifford Woods State Park [W] *Killington, VT*
Gilbert Bean Museum [W] *Braintree, MA*
Gilbert Stuart Birthplace [W] *North Kingstown, RI*
Gillette Castle State Park [W] *East Haddam, CT*
Gilman Garrison House [W] *Exeter, NH*
Glebe House and Gertrude Jekyll Garden [W]
    Woodbury, CT
Glendi Greek Celebration [S] *Springfield, MA*
Glen Ellis Falls Scenic Area [W] *Pinkham Notch, NH*
Glenhyrst Art Gallery of Brant [W] *Brantford, ON*
Glen Magna Farms [W] *Danvers, MA*
Glockenspiel [W] *Kitchener-Waterloo, ON*
Gloucester Fisherman [W] *Gloucester, MA*
Goddard College [W] *Barre, VT*
Goddard Memorial State Park [W] *East Greenwich, RI*
Golf [W] *Fredericton, NB*
Goodrich Memorial Library [W] *Newport, VT*
Goodspeed Opera House [W] *East Haddam, CT*
Gore Place [W] *Waltham, MA*
Governor John Langdon House [W] *Portsmouth, NH*
Governor Stephen Hopkins House [W] *Providence, RI*
Grafton Notch State Park [W] *Bethel, ME*
Grafton Ponds Cross-Country Ski Center [W] *Grafton, VT*
Granary Burying Ground [W] *Boston, MA*
Granby International [S] *Granby, QC*
Granby Zoological Garden [W] *Granby, QC*
Grand Army of the Republic Museum [W] *Lynn, MA*
Grand Falls [W] *Edmundston, NB*
Grand Pré National Historic Site [W] *Grand Pre, NS*
Grand Prix at Lime Rock [S] *Lakeville, CT*
Grand Theatre [W] *Kingston, ON*
Grand Theatre [W] *London, ON*
Grand Théâtre [W] *Quebec City, QC*
Grange, The [W] *Toronto, ON*
Grange Park [W] *Toronto, ON*
Granite sculptures [W] *Barre, VT*
Granville [W] *Springfield, MA*
Gray Line bus tours [W] *Halifax, NS*
Gray Line bus tours [W] *Montréal, QC*
Gray Line bus tours [W] *Ottawa, ON*

Gray Line bus tours [W] *Quebec City, QC*
Gray Line bus tours [W] *Toronto, ON*
Gray's Store (1788) [W] *Little Compton, RI*
Great Balloon Rodeo [S] *Brockville, ON*
Great Glen Trails [W] *Mount Washington, NH*
Great Gorge Adventure [W] *Niagara Falls, ON*
Great Hall of the Clans, The [W] *Baddeck, NS*
Great Island Science & Adventure Park, The [W]
    Cavendish, PE
Great Meadows National Wildlife Refuge [W] *Concord, MA*
Great Meadows National Wildlife Refuge [W] *Sudbury
    Center, MA*
Great Rotary Fishing Derby [S] *Meredith, NH*
Great Whatever Family Festival Week [S] *Augusta, ME*
Green, The [W] *New Haven, CT*
Green Animals [W] *Portsmouth, RI*
Greendale Camping Area [W] *Weston, VT*
Greenfield State Park [W] *Peterborough, NH*
Green Gables [W] *Cavendish, PE*
Greenhouse [W] *Niagara Falls, ON*
Green Mountain Audubon Nature Center [W]
    Burlington, VT
Green Mountain International Rodeo [S] *Rutland, VT*
Green Mountain National Forest [W] *Brandon, VT*
Green Mountain National Forest [W] *Middlebury, VT*
Green Mountain Railroad [W] *Bellows Falls, VT*
Green Mountain Sugar House [W] *Ludlow, VT*
Green Park Shipbuilding Museum [W] *Charlottetown, PE*
Green River Music & Balloon Festival [S] *Greenfield, MA*
Gristmill [W] *Chatham (Cape Cod), MA*
Gristmill [W] *Sudbury Center, MA*
Gropius House [W] *Concord, MA*
Groton State Forest [W] *Barre, VT*
Grove Street Cemetery [W] *New Haven, CT*
Guided walking tours. Boston by Foot [W] *Boston, MA*
Guild of Boston Artists [W] *Boston, MA*
Guinness World of Records Museum [W] *Niagara Falls, ON*
Gunstock Recreation Area [W] *Laconia, NH*
Guy Lombardo Music Centre [W] *London, ON*
Hadley Farm Museum [W] *Amherst, MA*
Hadwen House [W] *Nantucket Island, MA*
Haffenreffer Museum of Anthropology [W] *Bristol, RI*
Haight Vineyard and Winery [W] *Litchfield, CT*
Hale House [W] *Beverly, MA*
Halifax Citadel National Historic Park [W] *Halifax, NS*
Hall of Fame Tip-off Classic [S] *Springfield, MA*
Hamilton House [W] *Kittery, ME*
Hamilton International Air Show [S] *Hamilton, ON*
Hamilton Military Museum [W] *Hamilton, ON*
Hamilton Mum Show [S] *Hamilton, ON*
Hamilton Place [W] *Hamilton, ON*
Hamilton's Farmers Market [W] *Hamilton, ON*
Hammersmith Farm [W] *Newport, RI*
Hammonasset Beach State Park [W] *Madison, CT*
Hammond Castle Museum [W] *Gloucester, MA*
Hampton Beach State Park [W] *Hampton Beach, NH*
Hampton Playhouse [S] *Hampton Beach, NH*
Hancock Barracks [W] *Houlton, ME*
Hancock-Clarke House [W] *Lexington, MA*
Hancock Shaker Village [W] *Pittsfield, MA*
Hapgood Pond Recreation Area [W] *Peru, VT*

Happy Rolph Bird Sanctuary & Children's Farm [W]
    St. Catharines, ON
Harbor Day [S] *Norwich, CT*
Harborfest [S] *Boston, MA*
Harborfest [S] *Nantucket Island, MA*
Harbor Lights Festival [S] *Boothbay Harbor, ME*
Harborwalk [W] *Boston, MA*
Harbour Cruises [W] *Quebec City, QC*
Harbourfront Centre [W] *Toronto, ON*
Harbour Hopper Tours [W] *Halifax, NS*
Harlow Old Fort House [W] *Plymouth, MA*
Harlow's Sugar House [W] *Brattleboro, VT*
Harness racing [S] *Scarborough, ME*
Harriet Beecher Stowe House [W] *Hartford, CT*
Harrison Gray Otis House [W] *Boston, MA*
Harrison House [W] *Branford, CT*
Hart Nautical Galleries [W] *Cambridge, MA*
Harvard Medical Area [W] *Boston, MA*
Harvard Museum of Natural History [W] *Cambridge, MA*
Harvard University [W] *Cambridge, MA*
Harvest Fair [S] *Bristol, RI*
Harvest Fest [S] *York, ME*
Harvest Festival [S] *Stockbridge and West Stockbridge, MA*
Harvest Jazz and Blues Festival [S] *Fredericton, NB*
Harwich Historical Society [W] *Harwich (Cape Cod), MA*
Harwich Junior Theatre [S] *Harwich (Cape Cod), MA*
Haskell Opera House & Library [W] *Newport, VT*
Hatstack Mountain [W] *Norfolk, CT*
Haunted Happenings [S] *Salem, MA*
Haverhill Historical Society [W] *Haverhill, MA*
Hawthorne Cottage [W] *Lenox, MA*
Haystack Ski Area [W] *Wilmington, VT*
H. C. Barnes Memorial Nature Center [W] *Bristol, CT*
Hedge House [W] *Plymouth, MA*
Helme House [W] *Kingston, RI*
Henry Phipps & Sarah Juliette Ross Memorial Museum,
    The [W] *St. Andrews, NB*
Henry Whitfield State Museum [W] *Guilford, CT*
Heritage Days Celebration [S] *Salem, MA*
Heritage-New Hampshire [W] *Jackson, NH*
Heritage Plantation [W] *Sandwich (Cape Cod), MA*
Heritage Trails Sightseeing [W] *Hartford, CT*
Heritage Village [W] *Windsor, ON*
Her Majesty's Royal Chapel of the Mohawks [W]
    Brantford, ON
Herreshoff Marine Museum [W] *Bristol, RI*
Higgins Armory Museum [W] *Worcester, MA*
Highland Games [S] *Antigonish, NS*
Highland games [S] *Halifax, NS*
High Park [W] *Toronto, ON*
Hiking trails [W] *Mount Washington, NH*
Hill-Stead Museum [W] *Farmington, CT*
Historical Museum [W] *Norfolk, CT*
Historical Museum of Gunn Memorial Library [W]
    New Preston, CT
Historical Society Museum [W] *Wellfleet, MA*
Historic areas [W] *Martha's Vineyard, MA*
Historic Deerfield, Inc [W] *Deerfield, MA*
Historic Fort Erie [W] *Niagara Falls, ON*
Historic Fort York [W] *Toronto, ON*
Historic Hildene [W] *Manchester & Manchester Center, VT*
Historic Mansions and Houses [W] *Newport, RI*

Historic Middlebury Village Walking Tour [W] *Middlebury, VT*
Historic Northampton Museum houses [W] *Northampton, MA*
Historic Norwichtown Days [S] *Norwich, CT*
Historic Pontiac Mills [W] *Warwick, RI*
Historic Properties (Privateers Wharf) [W] *Halifax, NS*
Historic Ship *Nautilus* and Submarine Force Museum [W] *Groton, CT*
Historic South Norwalk (SoNo) [W] *Norwalk, CT*
History House [W] *Skowhegan, ME*
Hitchcock Museum [W] *Riverton, CT*
Hobbamock's (Wampanoag) Homesite [W] *Plymouth, MA*
Hobo Railroad [W] *Lincoln/North Woodstock, NH*
Holley House [W] *Lakeville, CT*
Holt House [W] *Blue Hill, ME*
Holyoke Heritage State Park [W] *Holyoke, MA*
Home County Folk Festival [S] *London, ON*
Hood Museum and Hopkins Center for the Arts [W] *Hanover, NH*
Hope Cemetery [W] *Barre, VT*
Hope Street [W] *Bristol, RI*
Horatio Colony House Museum [W] *Keene, NH*
Hot-Air Balloon Festival [S] *Kingston, RI*
Houlton Fair [S] *Houlton, ME*
Houlton Potato Feast Days [S] *Houlton, ME*
Housatonic Meadows State Park [W] *Cornwall Bridge, CT*
House of Seven Gables [W] *Salem, MA*
Houses of Harvard-Radcliffe, The [W] *Cambridge, MA*
House Tours of Historic Lenox [S] *Lenox, MA*
Howland House [W] *Plymouth, MA*
Hoxie House & Dexter Gristmill [W] *Sandwich (Cape Cod), MA*
Hubbard Park [W] *Montpelier, VT*
Hubbardton Battlefield and Museum [W] *Rutland, VT*
Hudson Museum [W] *Orono, ME*
Hummingbird Centre for the Performing Arts [W] *Toronto, ON*
Hungerford Outdoor Education Center [W] *New Britain, CT*
Hunter House [W] *Newport, RI*
Huntsman Marine Science Center/Aquarium-Museum [W] *St. Andrews, NB*
Hurlburt-Dunham House [W] *Wethersfield, CT*
Huronia Historical Parks [W] *Toronto, ON*
Hyannis Harbor Festival [S] *Hyannis (Cape Cod), MA*
Hyannis-Martha's Vineyard Day Round Trip [W] *Martha's Vineyard, MA*
Hyannis-Nantucket or Martha's Vineyard Day Round Trip [W] *Hyannis (Cape Cod), MA*
Hyannis Whale Watcher Cruises [W] *Barnstable (Cape Cod), MA*
Hyland House [W] *Guilford, CT*
Île d'Orléans [W] *Quebec City, QC*
IMAX Theatre and Daredevil Adventure [W] *Niagara Falls, ON*
Indian Day [S] *Springfield, MA*
Indian Festival [S] *Eastport, ME*
Indian Leap [W] *Norwich, CT*
Indian Motocycle Museum [W] *Springfield, MA*
Indian Village [W] *London, ON*
Industrial tour. Abitibi Consolidated [W] *Fort Frances, ON*

Industrial Tour. Pairpoint Crystal Company [W] *Bourne (Cape Cod), MA*
Information Center [W] *Cambridge, MA*
Insectarium de Montreal [W] *Montréal, QC*
InSight Tours [W] *Portsmouth, NH*
Institute for American Indian Studies, The [W] *New Preston, CT*
Institute of Contemporary Art [W] *Boston, MA*
International Buskerfest [S] *Halifax, NS*
International Caravan [S] *Toronto, ON*
International Festival Week [S] *Calais, ME*
International Festival of Arts and Ideas [S] *New Haven, CT*
International Fireworks Competition [S] *Quebec City, QC*
International Freedom Festival [S] *Windsor, ON*
International Friendship Gardens [W] *Thunder Bay, ON*
International Ice Hockey Federation Museum [W] *Kingston, ON*
International In-water Boat Show [S] *Norwalk, CT*
International Snowmobilers Festival [S] *Edmundston, NB*
International Tennis Hall of Fame & Museum [W] *Newport, RI*
International Tulip Festival [S] *Truro, NS*
International Villages Festival [S] *Brantford, ON*
Inverarden Regency Cottage Museum [W] *Cornwall, ON*
Irving Nature Park [W] *St. John, NB*
Isaac Royall House [W] *Boston, MA*
Isaak Walton Killam Library [W] *Yarmouth, NS*
Isabella Stewart Gardner Museum [W] *Boston, MA*
iSci Centre [W] *Montréal, QC*
Island Queen [W] *Falmouth (Cape Cod), MA*
Island Queen [W] *Kingston, ON*
Isle au Haut [W] *Deer Isle, ME*
Isle au Haut Ferry Service [W] *Deer Isle, ME*
Islesford Historical Museum [W] *Cranberry Isles, ME*
It's a Grand Summer [S] *Kingston, ON*
Jack Miner Bird Sanctuary [W] *Windsor, ON*
Jackson Homestead Museum [W] *Newton, MA*
Jackson Laboratory, The [W] *Bar Harbor, ME*
Jackson Ski Touring Foundation [W] *Jackson, NH*
Jacob's Pillow Dance Festival [S] *Lee, MA*
Jacques-Cartier Park [W] *Quebec City, QC*
Jamaica State Park [W] *Newfane, VT*
Jamestown Museum [W] *Jamestown, RI*
Jazz Festival [S] *Edmundston, NB*
Jeanne d'Arc Garden [W] *Quebec City, QC*
Jefferds Tavern and Schoolhouse [W] *York, ME*
Jeremiah Lee Mansion [W] *Marblehead, MA*
Jericho House and Historical Center [W] *Dennis (Cape Cod), MA*
Jethro Coffin House [W] *Nantucket Island, MA*
Jiminy Peak [W] *Pittsfield, MA*
J.J. Hapgood Store [W] *Peru, VT*
John Adams and John Quincy Adams Birthplaces [W] *Quincy, MA*
John Brown House [W] *Providence, RI*
John Carter Brown Library [W] *Providence, RI*
John F. Kennedy Hyannis Museum [W] *Hyannis (Cape Cod), MA*
John F. Kennedy Memorial [W] *Hyannis (Cape Cod), MA*
John F. Kennedy National Historic Site [W] *Boston, MA*

John F. Kennedy School of Government [W] *Cambridge, MA*
John Freeman Walls Historic Site & Underground Railroad Museum [W] *Windsor, ON*
John Greenleaf Whittier Home [W] *Amesbury, MA*
John Greenleaf Whittier Birthplace [W] *Haverhill, MA*
John Hancock Observatory [W] *Boston, MA*
John Hancock Warehouse [W] *York, ME*
John Hay Library [W] *Providence, RI*
John H. Chaffy Blackstone River Valley National Heritage Corridor [W] *Worcester, MA*
John Heard House [W] *Ipswich, MA*
John Paul Jones House [W] *Portsmouth, NH*
John Paul Jones State Memorial [W] *Kittery, ME*
Johnson & Wales University [W] *Providence, RI*
John Strong Mansion [W] *Vergennes, VT*
John Ward House [W] *Salem, MA*
John Whipple House, The [W] *Ipswich, MA*
Jonathan Fisher House [W] *Blue Hill, ME*
Jones Library [W] *Amherst, MA*
Jones Museum of Glass and Ceramics, The [W] *Sebago Lake, ME*
Joseph Allen Skinner Museum [W] *South Hadley, MA*
Joseph Schneider Haus [W] *Kitchener-Waterloo, ON*
Joshua Hempsted House [W] *New London, CT*
Joshua L. Chamberlain Museum [W] *Brunswick, ME*
Josiah Dennis Manse [W] *Dennis (Cape Cod), MA*
Josiah Quincy House [W] *Quincy, MA*
Journey Behind the Falls [W] *Niagara Falls, ON*
Just for Laughs [S] *Montréal, QC*
JVC Jazz Festival [S] *Newport, RI*
Kakabeka Falls Provincial Park [W] *Thunder Bay, ON*
Kedron Valley Stables [W] *Woodstock, VT*
Keeler Tavern [W] *Ridgefield, CT*
Kelmscott Farm [W] *Camden, ME*
Kenduskeag Stream Canoe Race [S] *Bangor, ME*
Kennedy Brothers Factory Marketplace [W] *Vergennes, VT*
Kenora Agricultural Fair [S] *Kenora, ON*
Kenora International Bass Fishing Tournament [S] *Kenora, ON*
Kent Falls State Park [W] *Kent, CT*
Kentish Guards Armory [W] *East Greenwich, RI*
Kettletown [W] *Southbury, CT*
Kidspace [W] *North Adams, MA*
Kimball Wildlife Refuge [W] *Charlestown, RI*
King Hooper Mansion [W] *Marblehead, MA*
King Pine Ski Area [W] *Center Ossipee, NH*
King's Chapel [W] *Boston, MA*
Kingscote [W] *Newport, RI*
Kings Landing Historical Settlement [W] *Fredericton, NB*
Kingston Library [W] *Kingston, RI*
Kinsmen Antique Show [S] *Stratford, ON*
Kitchener-Waterloo Art Gallery [W] *Kitchener-Waterloo, ON*
Kitchener-Waterloo Multicultural Festival [S] *Kitchener-Waterloo, ON*
Kittery Historical and Naval Museum [W] *Kittery, ME*
Kortright Centre for Conservation [W] *Toronto, ON*
Koussevitzky Music Shed [W] *Lenox, MA*
Labor Day Street Festival [S] *Stratton Mt, VT*
La Citadelle [W] *Quebec City, QC*
Lafayette Campground [W] *Franconia Notch State Park, NH*
La Festa [S] *North Adams, MA*

La Fontaine Park [W] *Montréal, QC*
Lake Carmi State Park [W] *St. Albans, VT*
Lake Champlain Balloon and Craft Festival [S] *Burlington, VT*
Lake Champlain Chocolates [W] *Burlington, VT*
Lake Compounce Theme Park [W] *Bristol, CT*
Lake cruises [W] *Sunapee, NH*
Lake cruises. Lake Navigation, Ltd [W] *Kenora, ON*
Lake of the Woods Museum [W] *Kenora, ON*
Lakes Region Factory Stores [W] *Franklin, NH*
Lakes Region Fine Arts and Crafts Festival [S] *Meredith, NH*
Lake St. George State Park [W] *Belfast, ME*
Lake Waramaug State Park [W] *New Preston, CT*
Lake Willoughby [W] *Lyndonville, VT*
Lake Winnipesaukee cruises [W] *Wolfeboro, NH*
Lambton Heritage Museum [W] *Sarnia, ON*
Lamoine State Park [W] *Ellsworth, ME*
Lancaster Fair [S] *Jefferson, NH*
La Ronde [W] *Montréal, QC*
Laughing Brook Education Center and Wildlife Sanctuary [W] *Springfield, MA*
Laura Secord Homestead [W] *Niagara-on-the-Lake, ON*
Laurel Creek Conservation Area [W] *Kitchener-Waterloo, ON*
Laurentides Wildlife Reserve [W] *Quebec City, QC*
Laurier House [W] *Ottawa , ON*
Lawrence Heritage State Park [W] *Lawrence, MA*
League of New Hampshire Craftsmen [W] *Concord, NH*
League of New Hampshire Craftsmen/Exeter [W] *Exeter, NH*
League of New Hampshire Craftsmen [W] *Hanover, NH*
League of New Hampshire Craftsmen—Sandwich Home Industries [W] *Holderness, NH*
League of New Hampshire Craftsmen—Meredith/Laconia Arts & Crafts [W] *Meredith, NH*
League of New Hampshire Craftsmen [W] *North Conway, NH*
League of New Hampshire Craftsmen's Fair [S] *Sunapee, NH*
Leamington Tomato Festival [S] *Windsor, ON*
Leamington Tomato Festival [S] *Windsor, ON*
Leffingwell Inn [W] *Norwich, CT*
"Le Grand David and His Own Spectacular Magic Company" [W] *Beverly, MA*
Léon Marcotte Exhibition Centre [W] *Sherbrooke, QC*
Les Forges du St.-Maurice National Historic Site [W] *Trois-Rivières, QC*
Les Jardins de la République Provincial Park [W] *Edmundston, NB*
Le Village Québécois d'Antan [W] *Drummondville, QC*
Levitt Pavilion for the Performing Arts [S] *Westport, CT*
Lewiston-Auburn Garden Tour [S] *Lewiston, ME*
Lexington Historical Society [W] *Lexington, MA*
Libby Memorial Pool & Recreation Area [W] *Gorham, NH*
Library [W] *Providence, RI*
Library Gallery [W] *Salem, MA*
Lighthouse [W] *Westerly, RI*
Lighthouse Point Park [W] *New Haven, CT*
Lilac Time Festival [S] *Franconia, NH*
Lily Bay State Park [W] *Greenville, ME*
Lincoln County Museum and Old Jail [W] *Wiscasset, ME*
Lincoln Woods State Park [W] *Providence, RI*
List Visual Arts Center at MIT [W] *Cambridge, MA*
Litchfield History Museum [W] *Litchfield, CT*

Little River State Park [W] *Waterbury, VT*
Littleton Historical Museum [W] *Littleton, NH*
Little White Schoolhouse Museum [W] *Truro, NS*
Living Memorial Park [W] *Brattleboro, VT*
Lobsterfest [S] *Mystic, CT*
Lobster Hatchery [W] *Bar Harbor, ME*
Lock Museum of America [W] *Bristol, CT*
Lockwood-Mathews Mansion Museum [W] *Norwalk, CT*
Log Cabin [W] *Sarnia, ON*
Logging Museum Field Days [S] *Rangeley, ME*
London Fringe Theatre Festival [S] *London, ON*
London Museum of Archaeology [W] *London, ON*
London Regional Art and Historical Museums [W]
        London, ON
London Regional Children's Museum [W] *London, ON*
Longfellow National Historic Site [W] *Cambridge, MA*
Longfellow's Wayside Inn [W] *Sudbury Center, MA*
Long Sault Parkway [W] *Cornwall, ON*
Long Trail [W] *Bennington, VT*
Long Trail [W] *Waterbury, VT*
Long Wharf Theatre [S] *New Haven, CT*
Look Park [W] *Northampton, MA*
Lost River Gorge [W] *Lincoln/North Woodstock, NH*
Louisburg Square [W] *Boston, MA*
Louis S. St. Laurent National Historic Site [W]
        Sherbrooke, QC
Louis Tussaud's Waxworks [W] *Niagara Falls, ON*
Lowell Folk Festival [S] *Lowell, MA*
Lowell Heritage State Park [W] *Lowell, MA*
Lowell National Historical Park [W] *Lowell, MA*
Loyalist Days' Heritage Celebration [S] *St. John, NB*
Loyalist House [W] *St. John, NB*
Lucy Maud Montgomery's Cavendish Home [W]
        Cavendish, PE
Lundy's Lane Historical Museum [W] *Niagara Falls, ON*
Lutz Children's Museum [W] *Manchester, CT*
Lyman Allyn Art Museum [W] *New London, CT*
Lyman Estate "The Vale" [W] *Waltham, MA*
Lynn Heritage State Park [W] *Lynn, MA*
Lynn Woods Reservation [W] *Lynn, MA*
Macedonia Brook State Park [W] *Kent, CT*
Mackenzie House [W] *Toronto, ON*
MacLachlan Woodworking Museum [W] *Kingston, ON*
Mactaquac [W] *Fredericton, NB*
Mactaquac Fish Hatchery [W] *Fredericton, NB*
Mactaquac Generating Station [W] *Fredericton, NB*
Mactaquac Provincial Park [W] *Fredericton, NB*
Mad River Glen Ski Area [W] *Waitsfield, VT*
Magnetic Hill Zoo [W] *Moncton, NB*
Maine Art Gallery [W] *Wiscasset, ME*
Maine Historical Society [W] *Portland, ME*
Maine History Gallery [W] *Portland, ME*
Maine Lobster Festival [S] *Rockland, ME*
Maine Maritime Museum [W] *Bath, ME*
Maine State Ferry Service [W] *Camden, ME*
Maine State Ferry Service [W] *Rockland, ME*
Maine State Ferry Service [W] *Southwest Harbor, ME*
Maine State Museum [W] *Augusta, ME*
Maine State Music Theater [S] *Brunswick, ME*
Maine State Parade [S] *Lewiston, ME*
Maine Windjammer Cruises [W] *Camden, ME*

Main Gate Area [W] *Lenox, MA*
Main Stage Auditorium [W] *Salem, MA*
Main Street [W] *Nantucket Island, MA*
Main Street, USA [S] *New Britain, CT*
Main Street, Wickford Village [W] *North Kingstown, RI*
Maison St.-Gabriel [W] *Montréal, QC*
Manchester Historic Association [W] *Manchester, NH*
Manoir et Domaine Trent [W] *Drummondville, QC*
Maple Days [S] *Auburn, ME*
Maple Grove Farm of Vermont [W] *St. Johnsbury, VT*
Maple Sugar Festival [S] *St. Albans, VT*
Maple sugaring [S] *Amherst, MA*
Maple sugaring [S] *Northampton, MA*
Marble House [W] *Newport, RI*
Marginal Way [W] *Ogunquit, ME*
Marineland [W] *Niagara Falls, ON*
Marine Museum [W] *Fall River, MA*
Marine Museum of the Great Lakes at Kingston [W]
        Kingston, ON
Marine Museum of Upper Canada [W] *Toronto, ON*
Maritime Aquarium at Norwalk [W] *Norwalk, CT*
Maritime Museum of the Atlantic [W] *Halifax, NS*
Market Gallery, The [W] *Toronto, ON*
Market Square Days [S] *Portsmouth, NH*
Market Square Historic District [W] *Houlton, ME*
Mark Twain Days [S] *Hartford, CT*
Mark Twain House [W] *Hartford, CT*
Marlboro College [W] *Marlboro, VT*
Marlboro Music Festival [S] *Marlboro, VT*
Maron House [W] *Lenox, MA*
Marrett House and Garden [W] *Sebago Lake, ME*
Marsh-Billings-Rockefeller National Historic Park [W]
        Woodstock, VT
Martha A. Parsons House [W] *Enfield, CT*
Martha Mary Chapel [W] *Sudbury Center, MA*
Mary Baker Eddy Historical Home [W] *Lynn, MA*
Mary Baker Eddy Historic House [W] *Plymouth, NH*
Massachusetts Hall [W] *Cambridge, MA*
Massachusetts Institute of Technology [W] *Cambridge, MA*
MASS MoCA [W] *North Adams, MA*
Mast Landing Sanctuary [W] *Freeport, ME*
Mattatuck Museum [W] *Waterbury, CT*
Mayfest [S] *Bennington, VT*
Mayflower II [W] *Plymouth, MA*
Mayflower Society House Museum [W] *Plymouth, MA*
McFarland House [W] *Niagara-on-the-Lake, ON*
McGill University [W] *Montréal, QC*
McIntyre Ski Area [W] *Manchester, NH*
McMichael Canadian Art Collection [W] *Toronto, ON*
Mead Art Museum [W] *Amherst, MA*
Meduxnekeag River Canoe Race [S] *Houlton, ME*
Memorial Hall Museum [W] *Deerfield, MA*
Mena'Sen Place [W] *Sherbrooke, QC*
Merck Forest & Farmland Center [W] *Manchester &*
        Manchester Center, VT
Merwin House "Tranquility" [W] *Stockbridge and*
        West Stockbridge, MA
Metro Toronto Zoo [W] *Toronto, ON*
Middlebury College [W] *Middlebury, VT*
Middlebury College Museum of Art [W] *Middlebury, VT*
Middlebury College Snow Bowl [W] *Middlebury, VT*

Mid-winter New England Surfing Championship [S] *Narragansett, RI*

Milford Historical Society Wharf Lane Complex [W] *Milford, CT*

Miller State Park [W] *Peterborough, NH*

Mill Hill Historic Park [W] *Norwalk, CT*

Mineral Springs [W] *Stafford Springs, CT*

Minolta Tower Centre [W] *Niagara Falls, ON*

Minuteman National Historical Park [W] *Concord, MA*

Misquamicut State Beach [W] *Westerly, RI*

Mission House [W] *Stockbridge and West Stockbridge, MA*

Missisquoi National Wildlife Refuge [W] *Swanton, VT*

MIT Museum [W] *Cambridge, MA*

Moffatt-Ladd House [W] *Portsmouth, NH*

Mohawk Mountain Ski Area [W] *Cornwall Bridge, CT*

Mohawk Trail State Forest [W] *North Adams, MA*

Mohegan Park and Memorial Rose Garden [W] *Norwich, CT*

Molly Stark State Park [W] *Wilmington, VT*

Monadnock State Park [W] *Jaffrey, NH*

Monhegan Lighthouse [W] *Monhegan Island, ME*

Monomoy National Wildlife Refuge [W] *Chatham (Cape Cod), MA*

Monomoy Theatre [S] *Chatham (Cape Cod), MA*

Monte Cristo Cottage [W] *New London, CT*

Montmorency Park [W] *Quebec City, QC*

Montréal Bike Fest [S] *Montréal, QC*

Montréal Botanical Garden [W] *Montréal, QC*

Montréal Canadiens (NHL) [W] *Montréal, QC*

Montréal Expos (MLB) [W] *Montréal, QC*

Montréal Harbour Cruises [W] *Montréal, QC*

Montréal Highlights Festival [S] *Montréal, QC*

Montréal Jazz Festival [S] *Montréal, QC*

Montréal Museum of Fine Arts, The [W] *Montréal, QC*

Montréal Planetarium [W] *Montréal, QC*

Mont-Ste.-Anne Park [W] *Quebec City, QC*

Monument to Paul Bunyan [W] *Bangor, ME*

Moore Museum [W] *Sarnia, ON*

Moosalamoo Recreation Area [W] *Green Mountain National Forest, VT*

Moose Brook State Park [W] *Gorham, NH*

Moosehead Marine Museum [W] *Greenville, ME*

Moosehorn National Wildlife Refuge [W] *Calais, ME*

MooseMainea [S] *Greenville, ME*

Moose Tours [W] *Gorham, NH*

Morningstar Mill [W] *St. Catharines, ON*

Morse Farm [W] *Montpelier, VT*

Mother Church, the First Church of Christ, Scientist, The [W] *Boston, MA*

Mountain Bike World Cup Race [S] *West Dover, VT*

Mountain Top Cross-Country Ski Resort [W] *Rutland, VT*

Mount Ascutney State Park [W] *Windsor, VT*

Mount Blue State Park [W] *Rumford, ME*

Mount David [W] *Lewiston, ME*

Mount Desert Oceanarium [W] *Southwest Harbor, ME*

Mount Greylock State Reservation [W] *North Adams, MA*

Mount Holyoke College [W] *South Hadley, MA*

Mount Holyoke College Art Museum [W] *South Hadley, MA*

Mount Independence [W] *Brandon, VT*

Mount Mansfield Gondola [W] *Stowe, VT*

Mount Mansfield State Forest [W] *Stowe, VT*

Mount Orford [W] *Sherbrooke, QC*

Mount Philo State Park [W] *Shelburne, VT*

Mount Royal Park [W] *Montréal, QC*

M/S *Mount Washington* [W] *Laconia, NH*

Mount Snow Foliage Craft Fair [S] *West Dover, VT*

Mount Snow Resort [W] *Wilmington, VT*

Mt Snow Ski Area [W] *West Dover, VT*

M/S *Scotia Prince* [W] *Portland, ME*

Mt Sunapee State Park [W] *Sunapee, NH*

M/V *Kearsarge* Restaurant Ship [W] *Sunapee, NH*

M/V *Mt Sunapee II* Excursion Boat [W] *Sunapee, NH*

Mt Washington [W] *Gorham, NH*

Mt Washington [W] *Twin Mountain, NH*

Mt Washington Summit Museum [W] *Mount Washington, NH*

Mt Washington Valley Equine Classic [S] *North Conway, NH*

MS *Scotia Prince* [W] *Yarmouth, NS*

Mud Bowl [S] *North Conway, NH*

Multicultural Festival [S] *Halifax, NS*

Municipal Group [W] *Springfield, MA*

Munroe Tavern [W] *Lexington, MA*

Murney Tower Museum [W] *Kingston, ON*

Murphy's on the Water [W] *Halifax, NS*

Musée des Anciens Canadiens [W] *Quebec City, QC*

Musée du Fort [W] *Quebec City, QC*

Musée du Québec [W] *Quebec City, QC*

Musée du Séminaire de Sherbrooke [W] *Sherbrooke, QC*

Museum & Archive of Games [W] *Kitchener-Waterloo, ON*

Museum at Portland Headlight, The [W] *Portland, ME*

Museum at the John Fitzgerald Kennedy Library [W] *Boston, MA*

Museum of American Political Life [W] *Hartford, CT*

Museum of Art [W] *Brunswick, ME*

Museum of Art [W] *Northampton, MA*

Museum of Canadian Scouting [W] *Ottawa , ON*

Museum of Civilization (Musée de la Civilisation) [W] *Quebec City, QC*

Museum of Decorative Arts [W] *Montréal, QC*

Museum of Fine Arts [W] *Boston, MA*

Museum of Nantucket History (Macy Warehouse) [W] *Nantucket Island, MA*

Museum of Natural History and Cormack Planetarium [W] *Providence, RI*

Museum of New Hampshire History [W] *Concord, NH*

Museum of Primitive Art and Culture [W] *Kingston, RI*

Museum of Rhode Island History at Aldrich House [W] *Providence, RI*

Museum of Science [W] *Boston, MA*

Museum of Steam and Technology [W] *Hamilton, ON*

Museum of the Royal 22e Régiment [W] *Quebec City, QC*

Museum of Vintage Fashions [W] *Houlton, ME*

Musical Wonder House-Music Museum [W] *Wiscasset, ME*

Music Mountain Summer Music Festival [S] *Lakeville, CT*

Music on the Mall [S] *Brunswick, ME*

Myles Standish State Forest [W] *Plymouth, MA*

Myrtleville House Museum [W] *Brantford, ON*

Mystic Marinelife Aquarium [W] *Mystic, CT*

Mystic Seaport [W] *Mystic, CT*

Nantucket Maria Mitchell Association [W] *Nantucket Island, MA*

Narbonne House [W] *Salem, MA*

Nathan Hale Homestead [W] *Storrs, CT*

Nathan Hale Schoolhouse [W] *East Haddam, CT*
Nathaniel Bowditch [W] *Rockland, ME*
Nathaniel Hempsted House [W] *New London, CT*
National Archives of Canada [W] *Ottawa , ON*
National Arts Centre [W] *Ottawa , ON*
National Assembly of Québec [W] *Quebec City, QC*
National Aviation Museum [W] *Ottawa , ON*
National Battlefields Park [W] *Quebec City, QC*
National Exhibit Centre [W] *Yarmouth, NS*
National Gallery of Canada [W] *Ottawa , ON*
National Heritage Museum [W] *Lexington, MA*
National Monument to the Forefathers [W] *Plymouth, MA*
National Museum of Science and Technology [W]
    Ottawa, ON
National Yiddish Book Center [W] *Amherst, MA*
Native American Burial Grounds [W] *Norwich, CT*
Native American Petroglyphs [W] *Bellows Falls, VT*
Natural Bridge State Park [W] *North Adams, MA*
Natural formations. Mohegan Bluffs [W] *Block Island, RI*
Natural History Museum [W] *Bar Harbor, ME*
Nature Interpretation Centre of Lake Boivin [W]
    Granby, QC
Naumkeag [W] *Stockbridge and West Stockbridge, MA*
Nauset Beach [W] *Orleans (Cape Cod), MA*
NB Highland Games [S] *Fredericton, NB*
Nepean Point [W] *Ottawa, ON*
Neptune Theatre [W] *Halifax, NS*
New Bedford-Cuttyhunk Ferry [W] *New Bedford, MA*
New Bedford Whaling Museum [W] *New Bedford, MA*
New Britain Museum of American Art [W] *New Britain, CT*
New Britain Youth Museum [W] *New Britain, CT*
New Brunswick Botanical Garden [W] *Edmundston, NB*
New Brunswick Legislative Assembly [W] *Fredericton, NB*
New Brunswick Museum [W] *St. John, NB*
New Brunswick Summer Chamber Music Festival [S]
    Fredericton, NB
New Canaan Historical Society [W] *New Canaan, CT*
New Canaan Nature Center [W] *New Canaan, CT*
New Denmark Memorial Museum [W] *Edmundston, NB*
New England Airlines [W] *Block Island, RI*
New England Air Museum [W] *Windsor Locks, CT*
New England Aquarium [W] *Boston, MA*
New England Carousel Museum [W] *Bristol, CT*
New England Fire & History Museum [W] *Brewster
    (Cape Cod), MA*
New England Maple Museum [W] *Rutland, VT*
New England Marionette Opera [W] *Peterborough, NH*
New England Music Camp [S] *Waterville, ME*
New England Patriots (NFL) [W] *Foxboro, MA*
New England Quilt Museum [W] *Lowell, MA*
New England Revolution (MLS) [W] *Foxboro, MA*
New England Ski Museum [W] *Franconia, NH*
New England Thanksgiving [S] *Sturbridge, MA*
New France Celebration [S] *Quebec City, QC*
New Hampshire Highland Games [S] *Lincoln/North
    Woodstock, NH*
New Hampshire Music Festival [S] *Laconia, NH*
New Haven Colony Historical Society Museum [W]
    New Haven, CT
New Haven Symphony Orchestra [S] *New Haven, CT*
New London-Block Island, RI [W] *New London, CT*

New London-Fishers Island, NY [W] *New London, CT*
New London-Orient Point, NY [W] *New London, CT*
Newport Art Museum and Art Association [W] *Newport, RI*
Newport Historical Society Museum [W] *Newport, RI*
Newport Irish Heritage Month [S] *Newport, RI*
Newport Jai Alai [W] *Newport, RI*
Newport Music Festival [S] *Newport, RI*
Newport Navigation [W] *Newport, RI*
Newport's *Princess* [W] *Newport, VT*
Newport Winter Festival [S] *Newport, RI*
New Year's Eve Portland [S] *Portland, ME*
Niagara Apothecary [W] *Niagara-on-the-Lake, ON*
Niagara Falls Museum [W] *Niagara Falls, ON*
Niagara Grape and Wine Festival [S] *St. Catharines, ON*
Niagara Historical Society Museum [W]
    Niagara-on-the-Lake, ON
Niagara Parks Botanical Gardens [W] *Niagara Falls, ON*
Niagara Parks Butterfly Conservatory [W] *Niagara Falls, ON*
Niagara Spanish Aero Car [W] *Niagara Falls, ON*
Niagara Symphony Association [S] *St. Catharines, ON*
Nichols House Museum [W] *Boston, MA*
Nickels-Sortwell House [W] *Wiscasset, ME*
Nickerson State Park [W] *Brewster (Cape Cod), MA*
Night Heron Nature Cruises [W] *Kingston, MA*
Nights Before Christmas, The [S] *Wilmington, VT*
Noah Webster Foundation and Historical Society [W]
    Hartford, CT
Noden Causeway [W] *Fort Frances, ON*
Noden-Reed House & Barn [W] *Windsor Locks, CT*
Norfolk Chamber Music Festival [S] *Norfolk, CT*
Norlands Living History Center [W] *Auburn, ME*
Norman Rockwell Exhibition [W] *Arlington, VT*
Norman Rockwell Museum [W] *Rutland, VT*
Norman Rockwell Museum [W] *Stockbridge and
    West Stockbridge, MA*
North American Black Historical Museum [W] *Windsor, ON*
North Burial Ground [W] *Providence, RI*
Northeast Historic Film [W] *Bucksport, ME*
Northeast Kingdom Tours [W] *Newport, VT*
Northern Maine Fair [S] *Presque Isle, ME*
Northern Outdoors, Inc [W] *Rockwood, ME*
Northfield Mountain Recreation and Environmental
    Center [W] *Greenfield, MA*
North Hero State Park [W] *North Hero, VT*
North Light [W] *Block Island, RI*
North Shore Music Theatre [S] *Beverly, MA*
Norwalk Harbor Splash [S] *Norwalk, CT*
Notre-Dame Basilica [W] *Montréal, QC*
Notre-Dame Basilica Museum [W] *Montréal, QC*
Notre-Dame-de-Bonsecours Church [W] *Montréal, QC*
Notre Dame-du-Cap [W] *Trois-Rivieres, QC*
Nott House, The [W] *Kennebunkport, ME*
Nova Scotia Air Show [S] *Halifax, NS*
Nova Scotia International Tattoo, The [S] *Halifax, NS*
Nova Scotia Museum of Natural History [W] *Halifax, NS*
Novelty [W] *Boothbay Harbor, ME*
Nylander Museum [W] *Caribou, ME*
Oak Bluffs [W] *Martha's Vineyard, MA*
Oak Grove Nature Center [W] *Manchester, CT*
Observation towers [W] *Niagara Falls, ON*
Oceanarium-Bar Harbor [W] *Bar Harbor, ME*

Ocean Beach Park [W] *New London, CT*
Oceanographic cruise [W] *Groton, CT*
Octoberfest Parade and Craft Fair [S] *Pawtucket, RI*
October Mountain State Forest [W] *Lee, MA*
Odell Park [W] *Fredericton, NB*
Officers' Square [W] *Fredericton, NB*
Ogden House [W] *Fairfield, CT*
Ogunquit Museum of American Art [W] *Ogunquit, ME*
Ogunquit Playhouse [S] *Ogunquit, ME*
Oil Museum of Canada [W] *Sarnia, ON*
Okemo Mountain Ski Area [W] *Ludlow, VT*
Olad and *Northwind* [W] *Camden, ME*
Old Atwood House [W] *Chatham (Cape Cod), MA*
Old Burying Ground [W] *Bennington, VT*
Old Burying Ground, The [W] *Norwich, CT*
Old Campus, The [W] *New Haven, CT*
Old Castle [W] *Rockport, MA*
Old City Market [W] *St. John, NB*
Old Colony and Newport Railroad [W] *Newport, RI*
Olde Mistick Village [W] *Mystic, CT*
Olde Port Mariner Fleet, Inc [W] *Portland, ME*
Old Fire Hose Cart House [W] *Nantucket Island, MA*
Old Firehouse Museum [W] *South Hadley, MA*
Old First Church [W] *Bennington, VT*
Old Fort, The [W] *Montréal, QC*
Old Fort Halifax [W] *Waterville, ME*
Old Fort Western [W] *Augusta, ME*
Old Fort William [W] *Thunder Bay, ON*
Old Gaol [W] *Nantucket Island, MA*
Old Gaol [W] *York, ME*
Old Government House [W] *Fredericton, NB*
Old Harbour Area [W] *Portsmouth, NH*
The Old Homestead [S] *Keene, NH*
Old Ipswich Days [S] *Ipswich, MA*
Old Kent County Court House [W] *East Greenwich, RI*
Old Ledge School [W] *Yarmouth, ME*
Old Lighthouse Museum [W] *Stonington, CT*
Old Man of the Mountains [W] *Franconia Notch State Park, NH*
Old Manse, The [W] *Concord, MA*
Old Mill Museum [W] *Weston, VT*
Old Narragansett Church [W] *North Kingstown, RI*
Old New Gate Prison [W] *Windsor Locks, CT*
Old North Church [W] *Boston, MA*
Old Officers' Quarters [W] *Fredericton, NB*
Old Port [W] *Trois-Rivieres, QC*
Old Port Dalhousie [W] *St. Catharines, ON*
Old Port Exchange [W] *Portland, ME*
Old Port Festival [S] *Portland, ME*
Oldport Marine Harbor Tours [W] *Newport, RI*
Old Port of Québec Interpretation Centre [W] *Quebec City, QC*
Old South Meeting House [W] *Boston, MA*
Old Sow Whirlpool [W] *Eastport, ME*
Old State House [W] *Boston, MA*
Old State House [W] *Hartford, CT*
Old State House [W] *Providence, RI*
Old Stone House [W] *Newport, VT*
Old Stone Mill [W] *Newport, RI*
Old Stone Row [W] *Middlebury, VT*
Old Sturbridge Village [W] *Sturbridge, MA*
Old Tavern at Grafton, The [W] *Grafton, VT*

Old Time Fiddlers' Contest [S] *Barre, VT*
Old Town Hall (Purple Heart Museum) [W] *Enfield, CT*
Old (Vieux) Montréal [W] *Montréal, QC*
Old Whaling Church [W] *Martha's Vineyard, MA*
Old Windmill [W] *Jamestown, RI*
Old Windmill [W] *Nantucket Island, MA*
Old York Historical Society [W] *York, ME*
Olin Arts Center [W] *Lewiston, ME*
Oliver Ellsworth Homestead [W] *Windsor, CT*
Olympic Park [W] *Montréal, QC*
Ontario Parliament Buildings [W] *Toronto, ON*
Ontario Place [W] *Toronto, ON*
Ontario Science Centre [W] *Toronto, ON*
Ontario Winter Carnival Bon Soo [S] *Sault Ste. Marie, ON*
Ontario Workers Art & Heritage Centre [W] *Hamilton, ON*
Open House Tour [S] *Litchfield, CT*
Orchard House [W] *Concord, MA*
Orford Arts Centre [W] *Sherbrooke, QC*
Orwell Corner Historic Village [W] *Charlottetown, PE*
Osterville Historical Society Museum [W] *Centerville (Cape Cod), MA*
Otis Ridge [W] *Great Barrington, MA*
Ottawa International Jazz Festival [S] *Ottawa, ON*
Ottawa Riverboat Company [W] *Ottawa, ON*
Ottawa Senators (NHL) [W] *Ottawa, ON*
Outdoor Art Show [S] *Toronto, ON*
Outdoor summer concerts [S] *Portland, ME*
Owls Head Transportation Museum [W] *Rockland, ME*
Oyster Festival [S] *Milford, CT*
Oyster Festival [S] *Norwalk, CT*
Palace Playland [W] *Old Orchard Beach, ME*
Palace Theatre [W] *Manchester, NH*
Panorama Ethnic Festival [S] *London, ON*
Paper House, The [W] *Rockport, MA*
Paramount Canada's Wonderland [W] *Toronto, ON*
Parc des Îles [W] *Montréal, QC*
Parc Safari [W] *Montréal, QC*
Pardee-Morris House [W] *New Haven, CT*
Parker River National Wildlife Refuge [W] *Newburyport, MA*
Park House Museum [W] *Windsor, ON*
Park-McCullough House Museum [W] *Bennington, VT*
Park Street Church [W] *Boston, MA*
Parsons House [W] *Northampton, MA*
Passamaquoddy Indian Reservation [W] *Eastport, ME*
Patrick J. Mogan Cultural Center [W] *Lowell, MA*
Patriots Day Celebration [S] *Boston, MA*
Patriots Day Parade [S] *Concord, MA*
Pat's Peak Ski Area [W] *Concord, NH*
Paul Revere House [W] *Boston, MA*
Paul's Boat Lines, Ltd [W] *Ottawa, ON*
Pawtucket Red Sox [S] *Pawtucket, RI*
Peabody Museum [W] *Andover and North Andover, MA*
Peabody Museum & Essex Institute [W] *Salem, MA*
Peabody Museum of Natural History [W] *New Haven, CT*
Peary-MacMillan Arctic Museum [W] *Brunswick, ME*
Peirce-Nichols House [W] *Salem, MA*
Pejepscot Historical Society Museum [W] *Brunswick, ME*
Pemaquid Point Lighthouse Park [W] *Damariscotta, ME*
Pennesseewasee Lake [W] *Norway, ME*
Penobscot Marine Museum [W] *Searsport, ME*
Peterborough Historical Society [W] *Peterborough, NH*
Phelps Tavern Museum, The [W] *Simsbury, CT*

Phillips Academy [W] *Andover and North Andover, MA*
Phillips Exeter Academy [W] *Exeter, NH*
Pickering Wharf [W] *Salem, MA*
Picnicking [W] *Boothbay Harbor, ME*
Pico Alpine Slide and Scenic Chairlift [W] *Killington, VT*
Pier, The [W] *Old Orchard Beach, ME*
Pier 21 [W] *Halifax, NS*
Pierce Manse [W] *Concord, NH*
Pier: Toronto's Waterfront Museum, The [W] *Toronto, ON*
Pilgrim Hall Museum [W] *Plymouth, MA*
Pilgrim Heights Area [W] *Truro and North Truro
    (Cape Cod), MA*
Pilgrim Monument & Museum [W] *Provincetown
    (Cape Cod), MA*
Pilgrim's Progress [S] *Plymouth, MA*
Pilot Pen International Tennis Tournament [S]
    New Haven, CT
Pines Golf Course [W] *Digby, NS*
Pioneer Memorial Tower [W] *Kitchener-Waterloo, ON*
Pioneer Village: Salem In 1630 [W] *Salem, MA*
Pither's Point Park [W] *Fort Frances, ON*
Pittsburgh Sheepdog Trials [S] *Kingston, ON*
Place d'Armes [W] *Montréal, QC*
Place des Arts [W] *Montréal, QC*
Place Jacques-Cartier [W] *Montréal, QC*
Place-Royale [W] *Quebec City, QC*
Plainfield Greyhound Park [W] *Plainfield, CT*
Playhouse Theatre, The [W] *Fredericton, NB*
Pleasant Valley Wildlife Sanctuary [W] *Lenox, MA*
Plimoth Plantation [W] *Plymouth, MA*
Plymouth Cheese Corporation [W] *Plymouth, VT*
Plymouth Colony Winery [W] *Plymouth, MA*
Plymouth Harbor Cruises [W] *Plymouth, MA*
Plymouth National Wax Museum [W] *Plymouth, MA*
Plymouth Rock [W] *Plymouth, MA*
Plymouth State College [W] *Plymouth, NH*
Pointe-à-Callière, the Montréal Museum of Archaeology
    and History [W] *Montréal, QC*
Point Judith [W] *Narragansett, RI*
Point Pelee National Park [W] *Windsor, ON*
Point Pleasant Park [W] *Halifax, NS*
Point Prim Lighthouse [W] *Digby, NS*
Poker Run [S] *Brockville, ON*
Polar Caves Park [W] *Plymouth, NH*
Popham Beach [W] *Bath, ME*
Popham Colony [W] *Bath, ME*
Porter Thermometer Museum [W] *Buzzards Bay
    (Cape Cod), MA*
Portland Museum of Art [W] *Portland, ME*
Portland Observatory [W] *Portland, ME*
Port Royal National Historic Site [W] *Digby, NS*
Portsmouth Harbor Cruises [W] *Portsmouth, NH*
Portsmouth Historic Homes [W] *Portsmouth, NH*
Portsmouth Jazz Festival [S] *Portsmouth, NH*
Portuguese Festival [S] *Provincetown (Cape Cod), MA*
Portuguese Princess Whale Watch [W] *Provincetown
    (Cape Cod), MA*
Powder Ridge Ski Area [W] *Middletown, CT*
Pownalborough Courthouse [W] *Wiscasset, ME*
Pratt Museum of Geology [W] *Amherst, MA*
Prehistoric World [W] *Morrisburg, ON*

Prescott Farm and Windmill [W] *Portsmouth, RI*
President Calvin Coolidge Homestead [W] *Plymouth, VT*
Prince Edward Island National Park [W] *Cavendish, PE*
Prince Edward Island National Park [W] *Charlottetown, PE*
Prince of Wales Tower National Historic Park [W]
    Halifax, NS
Professional sports [W] *Boston, MA*
Professional sports [W] *Foxboro, MA*
Professional sports [W] *Montréal, QC*
Professional sports [W] *Ottawa, ON*
Professional sports [W] *Toronto, ON*
Providence Athenaeum Library [W] *Providence, RI*
Providence Children's Museum [W] *Providence, RI*
Providence Preservation Society [W] *Providence, RI*
Province House [W] *Charlottetown, PE*
Province House [W] *Halifax, NS*
Provincetown Art Association & Museum [W]
    Provincetown (Cape Cod), MA
Provincetown Ferry [W] *Plymouth, MA*
Provincetown Museum [W] *Provincetown (Cape Cod), MA*
Prudence Crandall House [W] *Plainfield, CT*
Prudence Island [W] *Bristol, RI*
Prudential Center [W] *Boston, MA*
Public Archives of Nova Scotia [W] *Halifax, NS*
Public Garden [W] *Boston, MA*
Public Gardens [W] *Halifax, NS*
Public Gardens Band Concerts [S] *Halifax, NS*
Public wharves [W] *Yarmouth, NS*
Pump House Steam Museum [W] *Kingston, ON*
Putnam Cottage/Knapp Tavern [W] *Greenwich, CT*
Quaker Whaler's House [W] *Dartmouth, NS*
Quassy Amusement Park [W] *Waterbury, CT*
Québec Aquarium [W] *Quebec City, QC*
Québec City Walls and Gates [W] *Quebec City, QC*
Québec Zoo [W] *Quebec City, QC*
Quechee Gorge [W] *White River Junction, VT*
Queen of Winnipesaukee [W] *Laconia, NH*
Queen's Park [W] *Toronto, ON*
Queen's University [W] *Kingston, ON*
Quilt Show [S] *Bridgton, ME*
Quincy Bay Race Week [S] *Quincy, MA*
Quincy Historical Society [W] *Quincy, MA*
Quincy Homestead [W] *Quincy, MA*
Quinebaug Valley Trout Hatchery [W] *Plainfield, CT*
Rachel Carson National Wildlife Refuge [W] *Wells, ME*
Rackliffe Pottery [W] *Blue Hill, ME*
Radcliffe Institute for Advanced Study, The [W]
    Cambridge, MA
Rafting Montréal [W] *Montréal, QC*
Raft trips [W] *Rockwood, ME*
Ragged Mountain [W] *New London, NH*
Railroad Museum [W] *Chatham (Cape Cod), MA*
Rainbow Valley Family Fun Park [W] *Cavendish, PE*
Raisin River Canoe Races [S] *Cornwall, ON*
Ralph Waldo Emerson House [W] *Concord, MA*
Rangeley Lake State Park [W] *Rangeley, ME*
Raymond E. Baldwin Museum of Connecticut History [W]
    Hartford, CT
Rebecca Nurse Homestead [W] *Danvers, MA*
Reconstructed 18th-Century Barn [W] *Braintree, MA*
Recreation [W] *Provincetown (Cape Cod), MA*

Recreational facilities [W] *Ottawa, ON*
Recreation. Swimming [W] *Martha's Vineyard, MA*
Recreation. The Weirs [W] *Laconia, NH*
Redington Museum [W] *Waterville, ME*
Red River Beach [W] *Harwich (Cape Cod), MA*
Redstone School [W] *Sudbury Center, MA*
Redwood Library and Athenaeum [W] *Newport, RI*
Reenactment of March of Sudbury Minutemen to Concord
       on April 19, 1775 [S] *Sudbury Center, MA*
Reenactment of the Battle of Lexington and Concord [S]
       Lexington, MA
Reid [W] *Bath, ME*
Research Center [W] *Nantucket Island, MA*
Research Library [W] *Portland, ME*
Reverend Dan Foster House & Old Forge [W]
       Springfield, VT
Rhode Island School of Design [W] *Providence, RI*
Rhode Island State House [W] *Providence, RI*
Richard Sparrow House [W] *Plymouth, MA*
Rideau Canal [W] *Ottawa, ON*
RISD Museum [W] *Providence, RI*
Riverboat Cruises. Big Creek Boat Farm [W] *Brantford, ON*
Riverdale Park [W] *Toronto, ON*
Riverfest [S] *Brantford, ON*
Riverfest [S] *Brockville, ON*
Riverfest [S] *Hartford, CT*
Riverfest [S] *Manchester, NH*
Riverton Fair [S] *Riverton, CT*
Roaring Brook Nature Center [W] *Avon, CT*
Robert Burns [W] *Barre, VT*
Robert Frost Farm [W] *Salem, NH*
Robert Hull Fleming Museum [W] *Burlington, VT*
Rockefeller Library [W] *Providence, RI*
Rockingham Meetinghouse [W] *Bellows Falls, VT*
Rockingham Old Home Days [S] *Bellows Falls, VT*
Rockingham Park [W] *Salem, NH*
Rock of Ages Quarry and Manufacturing Division [W]
       Barre, VT
Rockport Art Association [W] *Rockport, MA*
Rockport Chamber Music Festival [S] *Rockport, MA*
"The Rocks" Provincial Park [W] *Moncton, NB*
Rockwood Park [W] *St. John, NB*
Rocky Neck State Park [W] *Old Lyme, CT*
Rodman Hall Arts Centre [W] *St. Catharines, ON*
Roger Williams National Memorial [W] *Providence, RI*
Roger Williams Park [W] *Providence, RI*
Rokeby Museum [W] *Vergennes, VT*
Roosevelt Campobello International Park [W] *Lubec, ME*
Ropes Mansion and Garden [W] *Salem, MA*
Roque Bluffs [W] *Machias, ME*
Rose-Arts Festival [S] *Norwich, CT*
Rosecliff [W] *Newport, RI*
Roseland Cottage [W] *Putnam, CT*
Rosie O'Grady's Balloon of Peace Monument [W]
       Caribou, ME
Rotch-Jones-Duff House and Garden Museum [W]
       New Bedford, MA
Round Hill Highland Games [S] *Norwalk, CT*
Rowantrees Pottery [W] *Blue Hill, ME*
Royal Agricultural Winter Fair [S] *Toronto, ON*
Royal Botanical Gardens [W] *Hamilton, ON*
Royal Canadian Big Band Music Festival [S] *London, ON*

Royal Canadian Henley Regatta [S] *St. Catharines, ON*
Royal Canadian Mint [W] *Ottawa, ON*
Royal Canadian Regiment Museum, The [W] *London, ON*
Royal Lippizan Stallions of Austria [S] *North Hero, VT*
Royal Military College of Canada [W] *Kingston, ON*
Royal Ontario Museum [W] *Toronto, ON*
Ruggles House [W] *Machias, ME*
Rundlet-May House [W] *Portsmouth, NH*
Rushing River Provincial Park [W] *Kenora, ON*
Sailfest [S] *New London, CT*
Sailing [W] *Wellfleet, MA*
Sailing races [S] *Marblehead, MA*
Sailing trips [W] *Camden, ME*
Sailing trips [W] *Rockland, ME*
St. Albans Historical Museum [W] *St. Albans, VT*
St. Andrew's Presbyterian Church [W] *Quebec City, QC*
St. Anne's Church and Shrine [W] *Fall River, MA*
St. Basile Chapel Museum [W] *Edmundston, NB*
St. Catharines Museum [W] *St. Catharines, ON*
St. Croix Island International Historic Site [W] *Calais, ME*
St. Dunstan's Cathedral Basilica [W] *Charlottetown, PE*
Saint-Gaudens National Historic Site. [W] *Hanover, NH*
St. George's Round Church [W] *Halifax, NS*
St. James Anglican Church [W] *Trois-Rivieres, QC*
St.-Jean-Port-Joli [W] *Quebec City, QC*
St. Johnsbury Athenaeum and Art Gallery [W]
       St. Johnsbury, VT
St. Johnsbury Town Band [S] *St. Johnsbury, VT*
St. Joseph's Oratory [W] *Montréal, QC*
St. Lawrence Centre for the Arts [W] *Toronto, ON*
Ste.-Marie among the Hurons [W] *Toronto, ON*
St. Mark's Anglican Church [W] *Niagara-on-the-Lake, ON*
St. Michael's College [W] *Burlington, VT*
St. Michael's Playhouse [S] *Burlington, VT*
St. Ninian's Cathedral [W] *Antigonish, NS*
St. Patrick's Church [W] *Damariscotta, ME*
St. Patrick's Day Parade [S] *Pawtucket, RI*
St. Paul's-on-the-Green [W] *Norwalk, CT*
St.-Paul St [W] *Montréal, QC*
St. Peter's Fiesta [S] *Gloucester, MA*
St. Vincent de Paul Roman Catholic Church [W]
       Niagara-on-the-Lake, ON
Sakonnet Point [W] *Little Compton, RI*
Sakonnet Vineyards [W] *Little Compton, RI*
Salem Maritime National Historic Site [W] *Salem, MA*
Salem State College [W] *Salem, MA*
Salem Witch Museum [W] *Salem, MA*
Salisbury Cannon Museum [W] *Lakeville, CT*
Salisbury Mansion [W] *Worcester, MA*
Salmon Derby [S] *St. Catharines, ON*
Salmon Festival [S] *Eastport, ME*
Samuel C. Moore Station [W] *Littleton, NH*
Samuel Whitehorne House [W] *Newport, RI*
Sand Castle Contest [S] *Nantucket Island, MA*
Sanderson Centre for the Performing Arts [W]
       Brantford, ON
Sandwich Glass Museum [W] *Sandwich (Cape Cod), MA*
Sandy Bay Historical Society & Museums [W] *Rockport, MA*
Santarella Museum & Garden [W] *Lee, MA*
Santa's Land [W] *Brattleboro, VT*
Santa's Village [W] *Jefferson, NH*

Saquatucket Municipal Marina [W] *Harwich (Cape Cod), MA*
Sarah Orne Jewett House [W] *Kittery, ME*
Sargent House Museum [W] *Gloucester, MA*
Sarnia Highland Games [S] *Sarnia, ON*
Sarnia Waterfront Festival [S] *Sarnia, ON*
Saugus Iron Works National Historic Site [W] *Saugus, MA*
Sault Ste. Marie Museum [W] *Sault Ste. Marie, ON*
Savoy Mountain State Forest [W] *North Adams, MA*
Sayward-Wheeler House [W] *York, ME*
Scale House [W] *Salem, MA*
Scallop Days [S] *Digby, NS*
Scarborough Civic Centre [W] *Toronto, ON*
Scarborough Marsh Nature Center [W] *Scarborough, ME*
School House [W] *Kennebunkport, ME*
Schooner Days & North Atlantic Blues Festival [S] *Rockland, ME*
Schooner Festival [S] *Gloucester, MA*
Schooner *J. & E. Riggin* [W] *Rockland, ME*
Schooner *Lewis R. French* [W] *Camden, ME*
Schooner *Mary Day* [W] *Camden, ME*
Schooner *Roseway* [W] *Camden, ME*
Schooner *Stephen Taber* & Motor Yacht *Pauline* [W] *Rockland, ME*
Schooner *Surprise* [W] *Camden, ME*
Schooner *Timberwind* [W] *Camden, ME*
Schooner Yacht *Wendameen* [W] *Camden, ME*
Science Center of Connecticut [W] *Hartford, CT*
Science Center of Eastern Connecticut [W] *New London, CT*
Science Center of New Hampshire [W] *Holderness, NH*
Science Enrichment Encounters Museum [W] *Manchester, NH*
Scott Covered Bridge [W] *Newfane, VT*
Scott-Fanton Museum [W] *Danbury, CT*
Scusset Beach [W] *Sandwich (Cape Cod), MA*
Seafest [S] *Yarmouth, NS*
Seafood Festival [S] *Charlestown, RI*
Seagram Museum, The [W] *Kitchener-Waterloo, ON*
Seamen's Bethel [W] *New Bedford, MA*
Seashore Trolley Museum [W] *Kennebunkport, ME*
Sebago Lake State Park [W] *Sebago Lake, ME*
Seiji Ozawa Concert Hall [W] *Lenox, MA*
Seventh Day Baptist Meeting House [W] *Newport, RI*
Shaftsbury State Park [W] *Bennington, VT*
Shaker Museum [W] *Poland Spring, ME*
Shakespeare & Company [S] *Lenox, MA*
Shakespearean Gardens [W] *Stratford, ON*
Sharon Arts Center [W] *Peterborough, NH*
Sharon Audubon Center [W] *Cornwall Bridge, CT*
Shaw Festival [S] *Niagara-on-the-Lake, ON*
Shawme-Crowell State Forest [W] *Sandwich (Cape Cod), MA*
Shaw Perkins Mansion [W] *New London, CT*
Shearwater Aviation Museum [W] *Dartmouth, NS*
Shelburne Farms [W] *Shelburne, VT*
Shelburne Museum [W] *Shelburne, VT*
Sheldon Museum [W] *Middlebury, VT*
Shepherd House [W] *Northampton, MA*
Sherbrooke Village [W] *Antigonish, NS*
Sherman Hollow Cross-Country Skiing Center [W] *Burlington, VT*
Shirley-Eustis House [W] *Boston, MA*

Shopping [W] *Boston, MA*
Shopping [W] *Warwick, RI*
Shore Line Trolley Museum [W] *New Haven, CT*
Shore Village Museum [W] *Rockland, ME*
Shrine of Our Lady of Grace [W] *Colebrook, NH*
Shubert Performing Arts Center [W] *New Haven, CT*
Sidewalk Art Show [S] *Portland, ME*
Sightseeing [W] *East Haddam, CT*
Sightseeing cruises on Penobscot Bay [W] *Camden, ME*
Sightseeing tour. Abegweit Tours [W] *Charlottetown, PE*
Sightseeing tour. M/S *Jacques-Cartier* [W] *Trois-Rivières, QC*
Sightseeing tours [W] *Boston, MA*
Sightseeing tours [W] *Halifax, NS*
Sightseeing tours [W] *Hartford, CT*
Sightseeing tours [W] *Montréal, QC*
Sightseeing tours [W] *Nantucket Island, MA*
Sightseeing tours [W] *Ottawa , ON*
Sightseeing tours [W] *Quebec City, QC*
Sightseeing tours [W] *Toronto, ON*
Sightseeing tours and boat cruises [W] *Rockport, MA*
Silver Cascade [W] *Bretton Woods, NH*
Silver Lake State Park [W] *Nashua, NH*
Silver Lake State Park [W] *Woodstock, VT*
Silvermine Guild Arts Center [W] *New Canaan, CT*
Simsbury Farms [W] *Simsbury, CT*
Site of First Houses [W] *Plymouth, MA*
Site of the Boston Massacre [W] *Boston, MA*
Site of the first US free public school [W] *Boston, MA*
Six Flags New England [W] *Springfield, MA*
Six Gun City [W] *Jefferson, NH*
Six Nations Native Fall Fair [S] *Brantford, ON*
Six Nations Native Pageant [S] *Brantford, ON*
Ska Nah Doht Indian Village [W] *London, ON*
Ski areas [W] *Bethel, ME*
Ski areas [W] *Great Barrington, MA*
Ski areas [W] *Pittsfield, MA*
Ski Butternut [W] *Great Barrington, MA*
Skiing [W] *Hanover, NH*
Skiing [W] *Jackson, NH*
Skiing [W] *New London, NH*
Skiing [W] *Pinkham Notch, NH*
Skiing. Camden Snow Bowl [W] *Camden, ME*
Skiing. Killington Resort [W] *Killington, VT*
Skiing. Lonesome Pine Trails [W] *Fort Kent, ME*
Skiing. Loon Mountain Recreation Area [W] *Lincoln/North Woodstock, ME*
Skiing. Lost Valley Ski Area [W] *Auburn, ME*
Skiing. Moosehead Resort on Big Squaw Mountain [W] *Greenville, ME*
Skiing. Mount Cranmore [W] *North Conway, NH*
Skiing. Mount Jefferson Ski Area [W] *Lincoln, ME*
Skiing. Mount Southington Ski Area [W] *Meriden, CT*
Skiing. Saddleback Ski & Summer Lake Preserve [W] *Rangeley, ME*
Skiing. Shawnee Peak Ski Area [W] *Bridgton, ME*
Skiing. Ski Sundown [W] *Avon, CT*
Skiing. Stratton Mountain [W] *Stratton Mt, VT*
Ski Mont Orford [W] *Sherbrooke, QC*
Skolfield-Whittier House [W] *Brunswick, ME*
Skowhegan Log Days [S] *Skowhegan, ME*
Skowhegan State Fair [S] *Skowhegan, ME*

SkyDome [W] *Toronto, ON*
Skylon Tower [W] *Niagara Falls, ON*
Slater Memorial Museum & Converse Art Gallery [W]
    Norwich, CT
Slater Memorial Park [W] *Pawtucket, RI*
Slater Mill National Historic Site [W] *Pawtucket, RI*
Sled Dog Race [S] *Rangeley, ME*
Sleepy Hollow Cemetery [W] *Concord, MA*
Sloane-Stanley Museum and Kent Furnace [W] *Kent, CT*
Smith College [W] *Northampton, MA*
Smith's Castle [W] *North Kingstown, RI*
Smugglers' Notch [W] *Jeffersonville, VT*
Snowhill at Eastman Ski Area [W] *Sunapee, NH*
Solomon Goffe House [W] *Meriden, CT*
Solomon Rockwell House [W] *Riverton, CT*
Sombra Township Museum [W] *Sarnia, ON*
SoNo Arts Celebration [S] *Norwalk, CT*
Sound & Light Show on Parliament Hill [S] *Ottawa , ON*
Sounds of Summer Music Festival [S]
    Kitchener-Waterloo, ON
South County Museum [W] *Narragansett, RI*
Southern Vermont Art Center [W] *Manchester &
    Manchester Center, VT*
Southford Falls [W] *Southbury, CT*
South Mountain Concerts [S] *Pittsfield, MA*
South Shore Christmas Festival [S] *Quincy, MA*
Southworth Planetarium [W] *Portland, ME*
Spadina [W] *Toronto, ON*
Splashdown Amphibious Tours [W] *Plymouth, MA*
Spooner House [W] *Plymouth, MA*
Sports car racing [S] *Lakeville, CT*
Spring Festival of Historic Houses [S] *Providence, RI*
Springfield Armory National Historic Site [W]
    Springfield, MA
Springfield Art and Historical Society [W] *Springfield, VT*
Springfield Museums at the Quadrangle [W] *Springfield, MA*
Springtime in Paradise [S] *Northampton, MA*
Spudland Open Amateur Golf Tournament [S]
    Presque Isle, ME
Squam Lake Tours [W] *Holderness, NH*
Squantz Pond State Park [W] *Danbury, CT*
Stafford Motor Speedway [S] *Stafford Springs, CT*
Stanley-Whitman House [W] *Farmington, CT*
Stanton House [W] *Clinton, CT*
Stanwood Sanctuary (Birdsacre) and Homestead Museum
    [W] *Ellsworth, ME*
Star Island and Isles of Shoals [W] *Portsmouth, NH*
Starr Library [W] *Middlebury, VT*
State Capitol [W] *Hartford, CT*
State forests [W] *Springfield, MA*
State House [W] *Augusta, ME*
State House [W] *Boston, MA*
State House [W] *Concord, NH*
State House [W] *Montpelier, VT*
State parks [W] *Bath, ME*
State parks [W] *Machias, ME*
State parks [W] *Norfolk, CT*
State parks [W] *Portland, ME*
State parks [W] *Sandwich (Cape Cod), MA*
State parks [W] *Southbury, CT*
Statue of Benjamin Franklin [W] *Boston, MA*
Statue of Tom Thumb [W] *Bridgeport, CT*

Steamship Authority [W] *Martha's Vineyard, MA*
Steamship Authority [W] *Martha's Vineyard, MA*
Steamship Authority [W] *New Bedford, MA*
Stephen A. Douglas Birthplace [W] *Brandon, VT*
Stephen Phillips Memorial Trust House [W] *Salem, MA*
Sterling and Francine Clark Art Institute [W]
    Williamstown, MA
Stevens-Coolidge Place [W] *Andover and North Andover, MA*
Stockbridge Main Street at Christmas [S] *Stockbridge and
    West Stockbridge, MA*
Stone Consolidated [W] *Kenora, ON*
Stoney Brook Mill [W] *Brewster (Cape Cod), MA*
Storrowton Village [W] *Springfield, MA*
Storybook Gardens [W] *London, ON*
Story Land [W] *Jackson, NH*
Stoweflake Balloon Festival [S] *Stowe, VT*
Stowe Mountain Auto Road [W] *Stowe, VT*
Stowe Mountain Resort [W] *Stowe, VT*
Stowe Recreation Path [W] *Stowe, VT*
Stratford Festival [S] *Stratford, ON*
Stratton Arts Festival [S] *Stratton Mt, VT*
Strawbery Banke Museum [W] *Portsmouth, NH*
Striped Bass & Bluefish Derby [S] *Martha's Vineyard, MA*
Sturgis Library [W] *Barnstable (Cape Cod), MA*
Sugarbush Golf Course [W] *Warren, VT*
Sugarbush Resort [W] *Warren, VT*
Sugarbush Soaring Association [W] *Warren, VT*
Sugarbush Sports Center [W] *Warren, VT*
Sugarloaf/USA Ski Area [W] *Kingfield, ME*
Suicide Six Ski Area [W] *Woodstock, VT*
Summer [W] *Laconia, NH*
Summer [W] *Sunapee, NH*
Summer activities [W] *Killington, VT*
Summer activities [W] *Peru, VT*
Summerfest [S] *Quincy, MA*
Sunbeam Fleet Nature Cruises [W] *New London, CT*
Sunday River Ski Resort [W] *Bethel, ME*
Sunfest [S] *London, ON*
Supersports Family Fun Park [W] *Plymouth, MA*
Surf Coaster [W] *Laconia, NH*
Swanton Summer Festival [S] *Swanton, VT*
Swift-Daley House [W] *Eastham (Cape Cod), MA*
Swimming [W] *Center Ossipee, NH*
Swimming [W] *Damariscotta, ME*
Swimming [W] *Dartmouth, NS*
Swimming [W] *Kennebunkport, ME*
Swimming [W] *Narragansett, RI*
Swimming [W] *Newport, RI*
Swimming [W] *Plymouth, MA*
Swimming [W] *South Yarmouth (Cape Cod), MA*
Swimming [W] *Wellfleet, MA*
Swimming, boating [W] *Rangeley, ME*
Swimming. Craigville Beach [W] *Hyannis (Cape Cod), MA*
Swimming, fishing [W] *Charlestown, RI*
Swimming. Head of the Meadow [W] *Truro and North Truro
    (Cape Cod), MA*
Swimming, picnicking, camping, boating, fishing [W]
    Bethel, ME
Sydney L. Wright Museum [W] *Jamestown, RI*
Symphony Hall [W] *Boston, MA*
Table Rock [W] *Dixville Notch, NH*
Talcott Arboretum [W] *South Hadley, MA*

Talcott Mountain State Park [W] *Hartford, CT*
Tanglewood [W] *Lenox, MA*
Tanglewood Music Festival [S] *Lenox, MA*
Tantaquidgeon Indian Museum [W] *Norwich, CT*
Tapping Reeve House [W] *Litchfield, CT*
Taste O' Danbury [S] *Danbury, CT*
Taste of Hartford [S] *Hartford, CT*
Taste of Springfield [S] *Springfield, MA*
Tate House [W] *Portland, ME*
Taylor-Barry House [W] *Kennebunk, ME*
Theatre-by-the-Sea [S] *Charlestown, RI*
Théâtre des Lilas [W] *Montréal, QC*
Thimble Islands Cruise [W] *Branford, CT*
Thomas Griswold House Museum [W] *Guilford, CT*
Thomas Point Beach [W] *Brunswick, ME*
Thomas Waterman Wood Art Gallery [W] *Montpelier, VT*
Thousand Island Cruises [W] *Brockville, ON*
Three-County Fair [S] *Northampton, MA*
Thunder Bay Art Gallery [W] *Thunder Bay, ON*
Tidal bore [W] *Moncton, NB*
Tidal bore [W] *Truro, NS*
Todmorden Mills Heritage Museum & Arts Centre [W] *Toronto, ON*
Topsham Fair [S] *Brunswick, ME*
Topsmead State Forest [W] *Litchfield, CT*
Toronto Blue Jays (MLB) [W] *Toronto, ON*
Toronto International Film Festival [S] *Toronto, ON*
Toronto Island Park [W] *Toronto, ON*
Toronto Maple Leafs (NHL) [W] *Toronto, ON*
Toronto Raptors (NBA) [W] *Toronto, ON*
Toronto Stock Exchange [W] *Toronto, ON*
Toronto Symphony [W] *Toronto, ON*
Toronto Tours Ltd [W] *Toronto, ON*
Touro Synagogue National Historic Site [W] *Newport, RI*
Tours [W] *Newport, RI*
Towers, The [W] *Narragansett, RI*
Town Clock [W] *Halifax, NS*
Town of Lunenburg [W] *Peggy's Cove, NS*
Townshend State Forest [W] *Newfane, VT*
Town Wharf (MacMillan Wharf) [W] *Provincetown (Cape Cod), MA*
Trapp Family Meadow Concerts [S] *Stowe, VT*
Trinity Church [W] *Boston, MA*
Trinity Church [W] *Digby, NS*
Trinity Church [W] *Newport, RI*
"Trinity Royal" Heritage Preservation Area [W] *St. John, NB*
Trips from Boothbay Harbor [W] *Monhegan Island, ME*
Trois-Rivières International Vocal Arts Festival [S] *Trois-Rivières, QC*
Trolley Museum [W] *Windsor Locks, CT*
Truro Historical Society Museum [W] *Truro and North Truro (Cape Cod), MA*
Tuck Memorial Museum [W] *Hampton Beach, NH*
Two-Cent Footbridge [W] *Waterville, ME*
Two Lights [W] *Portland, ME*
Typhoon Lagoon [W] *Niagara Falls, ON*
United Counties Museum [W] *Cornwall, ON*
United First Parish Church [W] *Quincy, MA*
Université de Montréal [W] *Montréal, QC*
Université Laval [W] *Quebec City, QC*
University Hall [W] *Cambridge, MA*

University Hall [W] *Providence, RI*
University of Connecticut [W] *Storrs, CT*
University of Hartford [W] *Hartford, CT*
University of Maine at Presque Isle [W] *Presque Isle, ME*
University of Maine-Orono [W] *Orono, ME*
University of MA-Lowell [W] *Lowell, MA*
University of Massachusetts [W] *Amherst, MA*
University of New Brunswick [W] *Fredericton, NB*
University of Southern Maine [W] *Portland, ME*
University of Toronto [W] *Toronto, ON*
University of Vermont [W] *Burlington, VT*
University of Windsor [W] *Windsor, ON*
Uplands Museum and Cultural Centre [W] *Sherbrooke, QC*
Upper Canada Village [W] *Cornwall, ON*
Upper Canada Village [W] *Morrisburg, ON*
Ursuline Convent [W] *Trois-Rivieres, QC*
US Coast Guard Academy [W] *New London, CT*
USS *Constitution* [W] *Boston, MA*
UVM Morgan Horse Farm [W] *Middlebury, VT*
Valley Railroad [W] *Essex, CT*
Valley View Horses & Tack Shop, Inc [W] *Bennington, VT*
Varnum House Museum [W] *East Greenwich, RI*
Varnum Memorial Armory and Military Museum [W] *East Greenwich, RI*
Vermont Apple Festival and Craft Show [S] *Springfield, VT*
Vermont Country Store [W] *Weston, VT*
Vermont Department of Libraries [W] *Montpelier, VT*
Vermont Historical Society Museum, Library [W] *Montpelier, VT*
Vermont Institute of Natural Science [W] *Woodstock, VT*
Vermont Marble Exhibit [W] *Rutland, VT*
Vermont Mozart Festival [S] *Burlington, VT*
Vermont State Craft Center at Frog Hollow [W] *Middlebury, VT*
Vermont State Craft Center at Windsor House [W] *Windsor, VT*
Vermont State Fair [S] *Rutland, VT*
Vermont State Open Golf Tournament [S] *Fairlee, VT*
Vermont Teddy Bear Company [W] *Shelburne, VT*
Vermont Wax Museum [W] *Manchester & Manchester Center, VT*
Vermont Wildflower Farm [W] *Shelburne, VT*
Victoria Mansion [W] *Portland, ME*
Victoria Memorial Museum Building [W] *Ottawa , ON*
Victoria Park [W] *Truro, NS*
Victory Chimes [W] *Rockland, ME*
Viking Boat Tour [W] *Newport, RI*
Viking Bus Tour [W] *Newport, RI*
Village Landing Marketplace [W] *Plymouth, MA*
Vincent House [W] *Martha's Vineyard, MA*
Virtual World [W] *Toronto, ON*
Visitor Center [W] *Plymouth, MA*
Visitor Information [W] *Salem, MA*
Wadsworth Atheneum Museum of Art [W] *Hartford, CT*
Wadsworth Falls State Park [W] *Middletown, CT*
Wadsworth-Longfellow House [W] *Portland, ME*
Walden Pond State Reservation [W] *Concord, MA*
Walking Tour of Historic Apponaug Village [W] *Warwick, RI*
Walking Tours Around Woodstock [W] *Woodstock, VT*
Wanton-Lyman-Hazard House [W] *Newport, RI*

Warner House [W] *Portsmouth, NH*
Warwick Heritage Festival [S] *Warwick, RI*
Warwick Mall [W] *Warwick, RI*
Watch Hill [W] *Westerly, RI*
WaterFire [S] *Providence, RI*
Waterfront Festival [S] *Gloucester, MA*
Waterloo County Quilt Festival [S] *Kitchener-Waterloo, ON*
Waterloo Park [W] *Kitchener-Waterloo, ON*
Waterloo-St. Jacobs Railway [W] *Kitchener-Waterloo, ON*
Waterville Valley Ski Area [W] *Waterville Valley, NH*
Watson Farm [W] *Jamestown, RI*
Wayside, The [W] *Concord, MA*
Webb-Deane-Stevens Museum [W] *Wethersfield, CT*
Webster Cottage [W] *Hanover, NH*
Welland Canal Viewing Complex at Lock III [W]
     St. Catharines, ON
Wellesley Apple Butter & Cheese Festival [S]
     Kitchener-Waterloo, ON
Wellesley College [W] *Wellesley, MA*
Wellfleet Bay Wildlife Sanctuary [W] *Wellfleet, MA*
Wells Auto Museum [W] *Wells, ME*
Wells Natural Estuarine Research Reserve [W] *Wells, ME*
Wendell Gilley Museum [W] *Southwest Harbor, ME*
Wenham Museum [W] *Beverly, MA*
Wentworth-Gardner House [W] *Portsmouth, NH*
Wentworth State Park [W] *Wolfeboro, NH*
Western Fair [S] *London, ON*
Western Gateway Heritage State Park [W] *North Adams, MA*
Western Nova Scotia Exhibition [S] *Yarmouth, NS*
West India Goods Store [W] *Salem, MA*
Weston Bowl Mill [W] *Weston, VT*
Weston Playhouse [W] *Weston, VT*
West Parish Meetinghouse [W] *Barnstable (Cape Cod), MA*
Westport Country Playhouse [S] *Westport, CT*
Westport Handcrafts Fair [S] *Westport, CT*
West Rock Nature Center [W] *New Haven, CT*
Wethersfield Museum [W] *Wethersfield, CT*
Whale's Tale Water Park [W] *Lincoln/North Woodstock, NH*
Whale Watching [S] *Gloucester, MA*
Whale watching [W] *Plymouth, MA*
Whale Watching [W] *Provincetown (Cape Cod), MA*
Whale-watching trips [W] *Eastport, ME*
Whaling Museum [W] *Nantucket Island, MA*
Whistler House Museum of Art [W] *Lowell, MA*
Whitehall Museum House [W] *Newport, RI*
Whitehern [W] *Hamilton, ON*
White Horse Tavern [W] *Newport, RI*
White Lake State Park [W] *Center Ossipee, NH*
White Memorial Foundation, Inc [W] *Litchfield, CT*
White Mountain National Forest [W] *Bartlett, NH*
White Mountain National Forest [W] *Bethel, ME*
White Mountain National Forest [W] *Franconia, NH*
White Mountain National Forest [W] *Jackson, NH*
White Mountain National Forest [W] *Lincoln/North
     Woodstock, NH*
White Mountain National Forest [W] *North Conway, NH*
White Mountain National Forest [W] *Twin Mountain, NH*
White Owl Culture Pow-Wow [S] *Kitchener-Waterloo, ON*
"Whites of Their Eyes" [W] *Boston, MA*
Wickford Art Festival [S] *North Kingstown, RI*
Wickham Park [W] *Manchester, CT*
Widener Library [W] *Cambridge, MA*

Wilbor House [W] *Little Compton, RI*
Wild Blueberry Festival [S] *Machias, ME*
Wildcat Ski & Recreation Area [W] *Pinkham Notch, NH*
Wilderness Expeditions [W] *Bingham, ME*
Wilderness Expeditions, Inc [W] *Rockwood, ME*
Wild Wings Ski Touring Center [W] *Peru, VT*
Wilgus State Park [W] *Windsor, VT*
Wilhelm Reich Museum [W] *Rangeley, ME*
William Benton Museum of Art [W] *Storrs, CT*
Williams College [W] *Williamstown, MA*
Williams College Museum of Art [W] *Williamstown, MA*
Williamstown Fair [S] *Cornwall, ON*
Willistead Manor [W] *Windsor, ON*
Wilmot Park [W] *Fredericton, NB*
Wilson Castle [W] *Rutland, VT*
Wilson Museum [W] *Bucksport, ME*
Windham County Courthouse [W] *Newfane, VT*
Windham County Historical Society Museum [W]
     Newfane, VT
Windjammer Days [S] *Boothbay Harbor, ME*
Windjammers [W] *Rockland, ME*
Windjammer Weekend [S] *Camden, ME*
Windsor Historical Society [W] *Windsor, CT*
Windsor's Community Museum [W] *Windsor, ON*
Winfisky Art Gallery [W] *Salem, MA*
Winnipesaukee Railroad [W] *Laconia, NH*
Winnipesaukee Scenic Railroad [W] *Meredith, NH*
Winslow Crocker House [W] *South Yarmouth
     (Cape Cod), MA*
Winslow Memorial Park [W] *Freeport, ME*
Winter [W] *Laconia, NH*
Winter [W] *Sunapee, NH*
Winter Carnival [S] *Brattleboro, VT*
Winter Carnival [S] *Caribou, ME*
Winter Carnival [S] *Kennebunk, ME*
Winter Carnival [S] *Middlebury, VT*
Winterfest [S] *Halifax, NS*
Winter Festival of Lights [S] *Niagara Falls, ON*
Winterlude [S] *Ottawa , ON*
Winter recreation [W] *Waterbury, VT*
Wistariahurst Museum [W] *Holyoke, MA*
Witchcraft Victims Memorial [W] *Danvers, MA*
Witch Dungeon Museum [W] *Salem, MA*
Witch House [W] *Salem, MA*
Women's Regatta [S] *South Hadley, MA*
Woodbine Racetrack [W] *Toronto, ON*
Wooden Boat School [W] *Blue Hill, ME*
Woodford State Park [W] *Bennington, VT*
Woodland Cultural Centre [W] *Brantford, ON*
Woodlawn Museum (The Black House) [W] *Ellsworth, ME*
Woodleigh Replicas & Gardens [W] *Cavendish, PE*
Woodman Institute [W] *Dover, NH*
Woods-Gerry Gallery [W] *Providence, RI*
Woods Hole, Martha's Vineyard & Nantucket Steamship
     Authority [W] *Martha's Vineyard, MA*
Woodside National Historic Site [W] *Kitchener-Waterloo, ON*
Woodstock Country Club [W] *Woodstock, VT*
Woodstock Historical Society [W] *Woodstock, VT*
Worcester Art Museum [W] *Worcester, MA*
Worcester Common Outlets [W] *Worcester, MA*
Worcester Music Festival of the Worcester County Music
     Association [S] *Worcester, MA*

Words and Pictures Museum of Fine Sequential Art [W]
    Northampton, MA
Worldfest/Festimonde [S] *Cornwall, ON*
World Film Festival [S] *Montréal, QC*
World Folklore Festival [S] *Drummondville, QC*
World's Largest Pancake Breakfast [S] *Springfield, MA*
WPA Murals [W] *Norwalk, CT*
Wreck Exploration Tours [W] *Windsor, ON*
Wright Museum [W] *Wolfeboro, NH*
Wriston Quadrangle [W] *Providence, RI*
Wyman Tavern [W] *Keene, NH*
Yale Art Gallery [W] *New Haven, CT*
Yale Bowl [W] *New Haven, CT*
Yale Center for British Art [W] *New Haven, CT*
Yale Repertory Theater [S] *New Haven, CT*
Yale University [W] *New Haven, CT*
Yamaska Provincial Park [W] *Granby, QC*
Yankee Homecoming [S] *Newburyport, MA*
Yarmouth Arts Regional Centre [W] *Yarmouth, NS*
Yarmouth County Museum [W] *Yarmouth, NS*
Yarmouth Cup Races [S] *Yarmouth, NS*
Yarmouth Historical Society Museum [W] *Yarmouth, ME*
Ye Antientiest Burial Ground [W] *New London, CT*
Yellow Barn Music Festival [S] *Brattleboro, VT*
Ye Olde Towne Mill [W] *New London, CT*
York Redoubt National Historic Site [W] *Halifax, NS*
York-Sunbury Historical Society Museum [W]
    Fredericton, NB
Young People's Theatre [W] *Toronto, ON*
Youth Triumphant [W] *Barre, VT*
Zoo [W] *Providence, RI*

LODGING LIST

Establishment names are listed in alphabetical order followed by a symbol identifying their classification and then city and state. The symbols for classification are: [AS] for All Suites, [BB] for B&Bs/Small Inns, [CAS] for Casinos, [CC] for Cottage Colonies, [CON] for Villas/Condos, [CONF] for Conference Centers, [EX] for Extended Stays, [HOT] for Hotels, [MOT] for Motels/Motor Lodges, [RAN] for Guest Ranches, and [RST] for Resorts

1661 INN & GUEST HOUSE, THE [BB] *Block Island, RI*
1785 INN [BB] *North Conway, NH*
1811 HOUSE [BB] *Manchester & Manchester Center, VT*
181 MAIN STREET BED & BREAKFAST [BB] *Freeport, ME*
1824 HOUSE INN BED AND BREAKFAST [BB] *Waitsfield, VT*
1830 ADMIRAL'S QUARTERS INN [BB] *Boothbay Harbor, ME*
1896 HOUSE [MOT] *Williamstown, MA*
ABOVE TIDE INN [BB] *Ogunquit, ME*
ACADIA CABINS [CC] *Southwest Harbor, ME*
ACADIA INN [HOT] *Bar Harbor, ME*
A CAMBRIDGE HOUSE BED AND BREAKFAST INN [BB]
      Cambridge, MA
ACWORTH INN [BB] *Barnstable (Cape Cod), MA*
ADAIR COUNTRY INN [BB] *Littleton, NH*
ADAMS MOTEL AND RESTAURANT, THE [CC] *Brandon, VT*
ADAM'S TERRACE GARDENS INN [BB] *Centerville*
      (Cape Cod), MA
ADDISON CHOATE INN [BB] *Rockport, MA*
ADMIRAL DIGBY INN [MOT] *Digby, NS*
ADMIRAL INN [MOT] *Hamilton, ON*
ADMIRAL INN [MOT] *Hamilton, ON*
ADMIRAL PEARY HOUSE [BB] *Center Lovell, ME*
ADMIRALTY INN [MOT] *Falmouth (Cape Cod), MA*
AIME'S MOTEL INC [MOT] *St. Johnsbury, VT*
AIRPORT HOTEL HALIFAX [HOT] *Halifax, NS*
ALBERT AT BAY [HOT] *Ottawa , ON*
ALDEN COUNTRY INN [BB] *Hanover, NH*
ALGOMA'S WATER TOWER INN [MOT] *Sault Ste. Marie, ON*
ALLEN HOUSE VICTORIAN INN [BB] *Amherst, MA*
ALL SEASON MOTOR INN [MOT] *South Yarmouth*
      (Cape Cod), MA
AMERICANA HOLIDAY MOTEL [MOT] *South Yarmouth*
      (Cape Cod), MA
AMERICAN MOTOR LODGE [MOT] *Waterbury, CT*
ANCHORAGE BY THE SEA [RST] *Ogunquit, ME*
ANCHORAGE MOTOR INN [RST] *York, ME*
ANCHOR WATCH BED & BREAKFAST [BB]
      Boothbay Harbor, ME
ANDOVER INN [BB] *Andover and North Andover, MA*
ANDRIE ROSE INN [BB] *Ludlow, VT*
APPLEBUTTER INN [BB] *Woodstock, VT*
APPLEGATE [BB] *Lee, MA*
APPLE TREE INN [BB] *Lenox, MA*
APPLEWOOD FARMS INN [BB] *Mystic, CT*
ARABIAN HORSE INN, THE [BB] *Sudbury Center, MA*
ARBOR INN, THE [BB] *Martha's Vineyard, MA*

ARLINGTON INN [BB] *Arlington, VT*
ARLINGTONS WEST MOUNTAIN INN [BB] *Arlington, VT*
ARUNDEL MEADOWS INN [BB] *Kennebunk, ME*
ASHLEY INN [BB] *Martha's Vineyard, MA*
ASHLEY MANOR [BB] *Barnstable (Cape Cod), MA*
ASHWORTH BY THE SEA [HOT] *Hampton Beach, NH*
ASPEN MOTEL [MOT] *Manchester & Manchester Center, VT*
ASTICOU INN [BB] *Northeast Harbor, ME*
ATLANTIC BIRCHES INN [BB] *Old Orchard Beach, ME*
ATLANTIC EYRIE LODGE [MOT] *Bar Harbor, ME*
ATLANTIC MOTOR INN [MOT] *Wells, ME*
ATLANTIS MOTOR INN [MOT] *Gloucester, MA*
ATRIUM TRAVELODGE [MOT] *Brunswick, ME*
ATTITASH MOUNTAIN VILLAGE [RST] *Bartlett, NH*
AUBERGE BROMONT [RST] *Granby, QC*
AUBERGE DE LA FONTAINE [BB] *Montréal, QC*
AUBERGE GISELE'S INN [BB] *Baddeck, NS*
AUBERGE HANDFIELD [BB] *Montréal, QC*
AUBERGE HATLEY [BB] *Montréal, QC*
AUBERGES WANDLYN [MOT] *Montréal, QC*
AU CHATEAU FLEUR DE LYS [BB] *Quebec City, QC*
AUGUSTUS SNOW HOUSE [BB] *Harwich (Cape Cod), MA*
AU MANOIR STE.-GENEVIEVE [BB] *Quebec City, QC*
AUSTINS INN TOWN HOTEL [HOT] *Kennebunkport, ME*
AUTUMN INN [MOT] *Northampton, MA*
AVON OLD FARMS HOTEL [HOT] *Avon, CT*
BAGLEY HOUSE, THE [BB] *Freeport, ME*
BAILEY ISLAND MOTEL [BB] *Bailey Island, ME*
BAR HARBOR HOTEL - BLUENOSE INN [MOT]
      Bar Harbor, ME
BAR HARBOR INN [HOT] *Bar Harbor, ME*
BAR HARBOR MOTEL [MOT] *Bar Harbor, ME*
BAR HARBOR QUALITY INN [MOT] *Bar Harbor, ME*
BAR HARBOR REGENCY [RST] *Bar Harbor, ME*
BARNSTEAD INN [BB] *Manchester & Manchester Center, VT*
BARROWS HOUSE INN [BB] *Dorset, VT*
BARTON'S MOTEL [MOT] *Laconia, NH*
BASIN HARBOR CLUB [RST] *Vergennes, VT*
BAY BEACH BED & BREAKFAST [BB] *Sandwich*
      (Cape Cod), MA
BAY MOTOR INN [MOT] *Buzzards Bay (Cape Cod), MA*
BAYVIEW, THE [HOT] *Bar Harbor, ME*
BAY VIEW INN & COTTAGES [CC] *Wiscasset, ME*
BAY VOYAGE, THE [BB] *Jamestown, RI*
BEACH HOUSE, THE [BB] *Kennebunk, ME*
BEACH HOUSE, THE [BB] *Martha's Vineyard, MA*

BEACH HOUSE AT FALMOUTH HEIGHTS [BB] *Falmouth (Cape Cod), MA*
BEACHMERE INN, THE [MOT] *Ogunquit, ME*
BEACH N TOWNE MOTEL [MOT] *South Yarmouth (Cape Cod), MA*
BEACH PLUM INN [BB] *Martha's Vineyard, MA*
BEACON RESORT [MOT] *Lincoln/North Woodstock, NH*
BEDFORD VILLAGE INN [BB] *Manchester, NH*
BEE AND THISTLE INN [BB] *Old Lyme, CT*
BEECHWOOD HOTEL [HOT] *Worcester, MA*
BEECHWOOD INN [BB] *Barnstable (Cape Cod), MA*
BELFAST BAY MEADOWS INN [BB] *Belfast, ME*
BELFAST HARBOR INN [MOT] *Belfast, ME*
BELFRY INN & BISTRO, THE [BB] *Sandwich (Cape Cod), MA*
BELMONT MOTEL [MOT] *Skowhegan, ME*
BENNINGTON MOTOR INN [MOT] *Bennington, VT*
BERKSHIRE HILLS MOTEL [MOT] *Williamstown, MA*
BERNERHOF INN & PRINCE PLACE RESTAURANT [BB] *Jackson, NH*
BEST INN [MOT] *Augusta, ME*
BEST INN [MOT] *Plymouth, NH*
BEST INN BANGOR [MOT] *Bangor, ME*
BEST WESTERN [MOT] *Boston, MA*
BEST WESTERN [MOT] *Brockton, MA*
BEST WESTERN [MOT] *Cambridge, MA*
BEST WESTERN [MOT] *Camden, ME*
BEST WESTERN [MOT] *Concord, MA*
BEST WESTERN [MOT] *Haverhill, MA*
BEST WESTERN [MOT] *Kingston, ON*
BEST WESTERN [MOT] *Kitchener-Waterloo, ON*
BEST WESTERN [MOT] *London, ON*
BEST WESTERN AT THE JUNCTION [MOT] *White River Junction, VT*
BEST WESTERN BASS ROCKS OCEAN INN [MOT] *Gloucester, MA*
BEST WESTERN BERKSHIRE INN [MOT] *Danbury, CT*
BEST WESTERN BLACK BEAR INN [MOT] *Orono, ME*
BEST WESTERN BLACK SWAN INN [MOT] *Lee, MA*
BEST WESTERN BLUE ROCK [MOT] *South Yarmouth (Cape Cod), MA*
BEST WESTERN BLUE WATER ON THE OCEAN [MOT] *South Yarmouth (Cape Cod), MA*
BEST WESTERN BRANT PARK INN [MOT] *Brantford, ON*
BEST WESTERN CAIRN CROFT [MOT] *Niagara Falls, ON*
BEST WESTERN CHARLOTTETOWN [MOT] *Charlottetown, PE*
BEST WESTERN CHATEAU MOTOR INN [MOT] *Provincetown (Cape Cod), MA*
BEST WESTERN CHELMSFORD INN [MOT] *Lowell, MA*
BEST WESTERN CLAYMORE INN [MOT] *Antigonish, NS*
BEST WESTERN CONTINENTAL INN [MOT] *Windsor, ON*
BEST WESTERN CROSSROADS [MOT] *Thunder Bay, ON*
BEST WESTERN FALLSVIEW [MOT] *Niagara Falls, ON*
BEST WESTERN FALMOUTH MARINA TRADEWINDS [MOT] *Falmouth (Cape Cod), MA*
BEST WESTERN GLENGARRY [MOT] *Truro, NS*
BEST WESTERN HERITAGE MOTOR INN [MOT] *Millinocket, ME*
BEST WESTERN HOTEL JACQUES CARTIER [MOT] *Ottawa, ON*
BEST WESTERN INN [MOT] *Bar Harbor, ME*

BEST WESTERN INN & SUITES [MOT] *Rutland, VT*
BEST WESTERN JED PROUTY MOTOR INN [MOT] *Bucksport, ME*
BEST WESTERN LAKESIDE INN [MOT] *Kenora, ON*
BEST WESTERN L'ARTISTOCRATE [MOT] *Quebec City, QC*
BEST WESTERN MAINSTAY INN [MOT] *Newport, RI*
BEST WESTERN MERMAID [MOT] *Yarmouth, NS*
BEST WESTERN MERRY MANOR INN [MOT] *Portland, ME*
BEST WESTERN NEW ENGLANDER MOTOR INN [MOT] *Bennington, VT*
BEST WESTERN NORTHAMPTON [MOT] *Northampton, MA*
BEST WESTERN PARKWAY INN [MOT] *Cornwall, ON*
BEST WESTERN PRIMROSE [MOT] *Toronto, ON*
BEST WESTERN ROYAL PLAZA [MOT] *Sudbury Center, MA*
BEST WESTERN SENATOR INN [MOT] *Augusta, ME*
BEST WESTERN SOVEREIGN [MOT] *Keene, NH*
BEST WESTERN SOVEREIGN HOTEL [MOT] *Mystic, CT*
BEST WESTERN STONY HILL INN [MOT] *Danbury, CT*
BEST WESTERN TIDES BEACHFRONT [RST] *Provincetown (Cape Cod), MA*
BEST WESTERN TLC HOTEL [MOT] *Waltham, MA*
BEST WESTERN TORONTO AIRPORT-CARLTON PLACE [MOT] *Toronto, ON*
BEST WESTERN VICTORIA PARK SUITES [MOT] *Ottawa, ON*
BEST WESTERN WATERVILLE [MOT] *Waterville, ME*
BEST WESTERN WHEELS INN [MOT] *Windsor, ON*
BEST WESTERN WHITE HOUSE INN [MOT] *Bangor, ME*
BEST WESTERN WHITE HOUSE [MOT] *Brockville, ON*
BEST WESTERN WINDJAMMER INN [MOT] *Burlington, VT*
BETHEL INN AND COUNTRY CLUB [RST] *Bethel, ME*
BETSY'S BED AND BREAKFAST [BB] *Montpelier, VT*
BINGHAM MOTOR INN & SPORTS COMPLEX [MOT] *Bingham, ME*
BIRCHES & CATERING, THE [CC] *Rockwood, ME*
BIRCH KNOLL [MOT] *Laconia, NH*
BIRCHWOOD INN [BB] *Lenox, MA*
BISHOPSGATE INN [BB] *East Haddam, CT*
BLACK BEAR LODGE [HOT] *Waterville Valley, NH*
BLACK FRIAR INN [BB] *Bar Harbor, ME*
BLACK HORSE INN [MOT] *Camden, ME*
BLACK LOCUST INN [BB] *Waterbury, VT*
BLACK POINT INN [RST] *Portland, ME*
BLANTYRE [HOT] *Lenox, MA*
BLOMIDON [BB] *Grand Pre, NS*
BLUEBIRD MOTEL [MOT] *Machias, ME*
BLUE DOLPHIN INN [MOT] *Eastham (Cape Cod), MA*
BLUE GENTIAN LODGE [BB] *Londonderry, VT*
BLUE HARBOR HOUSE, A VILLAGE INN [BB] *Camden, ME*
BLUE HILL INN [BB] *Blue Hill, ME*
BLUE IRIS MOTOR INN [MOT] *Rumford, ME*
BLUE MOON MOTEL [MOT] *St. Andrews, NB*
BLUENOSE INN AND SUITES [MOT] *Halifax, NS*
BLUE SEA MOTOR INN [MOT] *Provincetown (Cape Cod), MA*
BLUE SPRUCE MOTEL [MOT] *Middlebury, VT*
BLUE SPRUCE MOTEL & TOWNHOUSES [MOT] *Plymouth, MA*
B MAE'S RESORT INN & SUITES [MOT] *Laconia, NH*
BONACCORD HOUSE B&B [BB] *Moncton, NB*
BOND PLACE [HOT] *Toronto, ON*
BOSTON HARBOR HOTEL [HOT] *Boston, MA*

BOSTON PARK PLAZA HOTEL, THE [HOT] *Boston, MA*
BOULDERS INN [BB] *New Preston, CT*
BRADLEY INN, THE [BB] *Damariscotta, ME*
BRAESIDE MOTEL [MOT] *Woodstock, VT*
BRAMBLE INN [BB] *Brewster (Cape Cod), MA*
BRANDON INN, THE [BB] *Brandon, VT*
BRANDT HOUSE [HOT] *Greenfield, MA*
BRANNON-BUNKER INN [BB] *Damariscotta, ME*
BRASS LANTERN INN [BB] *Stowe, VT*
BRASS LANTERN INN BED & BREAKFAST [BB] *Searsport, ME*
BREAKERS MOTEL [MOT] *Dennis (Cape Cod), MA*
BREAKWATER INN AND RESTAURANT [BB]
        Kennebunkport, ME
BREEZEWAY RESORT [RST] *Westerly, RI*
BRETTON ARMS COUNTRY INN, THE [BB]
        Bretton Woods, NH
BREWSTER FARMHOUSE INN [BB] *Brewster (Cape Cod), MA*
BREWSTER HOUSE BED & BREAKFAST [BB] *Freeport, ME*
BREWSTER INN [BB] *Newport, ME*
BRIAR LEA INN & RESTAURANT [BB] *Bethel, ME*
BRIARWOOD MOTOR INN [MOT] *Lincoln, ME*
BRICK TOWER MOTOR INN [MOT] *Concord, NH*
BRIDGES FAMILY RESORT AND TENNIS CLUB [CON]
        Warren, VT
BRINELY VICTORIAN INN [BB] *Newport, RI*
BRITTANY INN MOTEL, THE [MOT] *Manchester &
        Manchester Center, VT*
BROCK PLAZA [HOT] *Niagara Falls, ON*
BROOK FARM INN [BB] *Lenox, MA*
BROWN'S WHARF MOTEL RESTAURANT & MARINA [RST]
        Boothbay Harbor, ME
BUCCANEER COUNTRY LODGE [MOT] *Stowe, VT*
BUCKSPORT MOTOR INN [MOT] *Bucksport, ME*
BUDGET HOST MOTEL [MOT] *Hyannis (Cape Cod), MA*
BUDGET TRAVELER MOTOR LODGE [MOT]
        Presque Isle, ME
BUFFLEHEAD COVE [BB] *Kennebunkport, ME*
BURKEHAVEN AT SUNAPEE [MOT] *Sunapee, NH*
BURNSIDE [MOT] *Dartmouth, NS*
BUTTERNUT INN AND COUNTRY GUEST HOUSE [BB]
        Stowe, VT
BUTTONWOOD INN [BB] *North Conway, NH*
BY THE SEA GUESTS [BB] *Dennis (Cape Cod), MA*
CADILLAC MOTEL [MOT] *St. Albans, VT*
CADILLAC MOTOR INN [MOT] *Bar Harbor, ME*
CAMBRIDGE SUITES HOTEL HALIFAX [AS] *Halifax, NS*
CAMDEN WINDWARD HOUSE [BB] *Camden, ME*
CANDLELIGHT INN AND RESTAURANT [BB] *Lenox, MA*
CANDLELIGHT MOTEL [MOT] *Arlington, VT*
CANDLELITE INN [BB] *Sunapee, NH*
CANTERBURY COTTAGE [BB] *Bar Harbor, ME*
CANTERBURY HOUSE BED AND BREAKFAST [BB]
        Woodstock, VT
CAPATAIN DEXTER HOUSE [BB] *Martha's Vineyard, MA*
CAPE ARUNDEL INN [MOT] *Kennebunkport, ME*
CAPE COD CLADDAGH INN [BB] *Harwich (Cape Cod), MA*
CAPE CODDER [MOT] *Hyannis (Cape Cod), MA*
CAPITOL PLAZA HOTEL AND CONFERENCE CENTER
        [HOT] *Montpelier, VT*
CAP'N FISH'S MOTEL & MARINA [MOT]
        Boothbay Harbor, ME
CAPRI MOTEL [MOT] *Yarmouth, NS*

CAPTAIN BOUNTY MOTOR INN [MOT] *Rockport, MA*
CAPTAIN DANIEL STONE INN [BB] *Brunswick, ME*
CAPTAIN DEXTER HOUSE OF VINEYARD HAVEN, THE
        [BB] *Martha's Vineyard, MA*
CAPTAIN EZRA NYE HOUSE BED & BREAKFAST [BB]
        Sandwich (Cape Cod), MA
CAPTAIN FAIRFIELD INN [BB] *Kennebunkport, ME*
CAPTAIN FARRIS HOUSE BED & BREAKFAST [BB]
        South Yarmouth (Cape Cod), MA
CAPTAIN FREEMAN INN [BB] *Brewster (Cape Cod), MA*
CAPTAIN GOSNOLD VILLAGE [MOT] *Hyannis
        (Cape Cod), MA*
CAPTAIN JEFFERDS INN, THE [BB] *Kennebunkport, ME*
CAPTAIN LINDSEY HOUSE INN [BB] *Rockland, ME*
CAPTAIN LORD MANSION, THE [BB] *Kennebunkport, ME*
CAPTAIN NICKERSON INN [BB] *Dennis (Cape Cod), MA*
CAPTAIN'S HOUSE INN [BB] *Chatham (Cape Cod), MA*
CAPTAINS LODGE MOTEL [MOT] *Gloucester, MA*
CAPTAIN'S QUARTERS [MOT] *Eastham (Cape Cod), MA*
CAPT. TOM LAWRENCE HOUSE [BB] *Falmouth
        (Cape Cod), MA*
CARIBOU INN & CONVENTION CENTER [MOT]
        Caribou, ME
CARLISLE HOUSE INN [BB] *Nantucket Island, MA*
CAROLINA MOTEL [MOT] *Old Orchard Beach, ME*
CARRIAGE HOUSE, THE [BB] *Nantucket Island, MA*
CARRIAGE HOUSE [MOT] *Niagara Falls, ON*
CASCADE INN [MOT] *Niagara Falls, ON*
CASCADES LODGE [HOT] *Killington, VT*
CASCO BAY INN [MOT] *Freeport, ME*
CASTELMAINE [BB] *Bar Harbor, ME*
CASTINE INN [BB] *Bucksport, ME*
CATAMOUNT MOTEL [MOT] *Bennington, VT*
CAVALIER [MOT] *Niagara Falls, ON*
CAVALIER MOTOR LODGE [MOT] *South Yarmouth
        (Cape Cod), MA*
CAVENDISH [MOT] *Cavendish, PE*
CEDAR CREST MOTEL [MOT] *Camden, ME*
CENTENNIAL INN [AS] *Farmington, CT*
CENTERBOARD GUEST HOUSE [BB] *Nantucket Island, MA*
CENTER OF NH HOLIDAY INN [HOT] *Manchester, NH*
CENTERVILLE CORNERS MOTOR LODGE [MOT]
        Centerville (Cape Cod), MA
CENTRAL INN AND CONFERENCE CENTER [MOT]
        New Britain, CT
CENTRE STREET INN [BB] *Nantucket Island, MA*
CHALET [MOT] *Lewiston, ME*
CHALET MOOSEHEAD LAKEFRONT MOTEL [MOT]
        Greenville, ME
CHALETS MONTMORENCY [MOT] *Quebec City, QC*
CHAMBERY INN [BB] *Lee, MA*
CHARLES, THE [HOT] *Cambridge, MA*
CHARLES STREET INN [BB] *Boston, MA*
CHARLESTON HOUSE [BB] *Woodstock, VT*
CHARLOTTE INN, THE [BB] *Martha's Vineyard, MA*
CHARLOTTETOWN, THE [HOT] *Charlottetown, PE*
CHATEAU BELLVUE [HOT] *Quebec City, QC*
CHATEAU BONNE ENTENTE [HOT] *Quebec City, QC*
CHATEAU ROYAL HOTEL SUITES [HOT] *Montréal, QC*
CHATEAU VAUDREUIL [HOT] *Montréal, QC*
CHATEAU VERSAILLES [HOT] *Montréal, QC*
CHATHAM BARS INN [RST] *Chatham (Cape Cod), MA*

CHATHAM HIGHLANDER [MOT] *Chatham (Cape Cod), MA*
CHATHAM MOTEL, THE [MOT] *Chatham (Cape Cod), MA*
CHATHAM SEAFARER [MOT] *Chatham (Cape Cod), MA*
CHATHAM TIDES WATERFRONT MOTEL [MOT]
   Chatham (Cape Cod), MA
CHATHAM TOWN HOUSE INN [BB] *Chatham
   (Cape Cod), MA*
CHIEFTAIN MOTOR INN [MOT] *Hanover, NH*
CHIMNEY CREST MANOR [BB] *Bristol, CT*
CITADEL [HOT] *Halifax, NS*
CLARENDON [HOT] *Quebec City, QC*
CLARION CARRIAGE HOUSE INN [MOT]
   Sudbury Center, MA
CLARION HOTEL & CONFERENCE CENTER [HOT]
   Burlington, VT
CLARION INN [MOT] *Groton, CT*
CLARION SUITES INN [AS] *Manchester, CT*
CLARK CURRIER INN [BB] *Newburyport, MA*
CLARK POINT INN, THE [BB] *Southwest Harbor, ME*
CLASSIC [MOT] *Saco, ME*
CLEARWATER LODGES [CC] *Wolfeboro, NH*
CLEFTSTONE MANOR [BB] *Bar Harbor, ME*
CLIFFSIDE INN [BB] *Newport, RI*
CLINTON MOTEL [MOT] *Clinton, CT*
CLUB TREMBLANT [RST] *Mont Tremblant
   Provincial Park, QC*
COACH HOUSE INN [BB] *Salem, MA*
COACHMAN INN [BB] *Kittery, ME*
COACHMAN MOTOR LODGE [MOT] *Harwich
   (Cape Cod), MA*
COASTAL INN KINGFISHER [MOT] *Digby, NS*
COASTLINE INN [MOT] *Freeport, ME*
COBBLESTONE INN [BB] *Nantucket Island, MA*
COCONUT [MOT] *Montréal, QC*
COD COVE INN [MOT] *Wiscasset, ME*
COLBY HILL INN [BB] *Concord, NH*
COLD SPRING MOTEL [MOT] *Plymouth, MA*
COLONEL EBENEZER CRAFTS INN [BB] *Sturbridge, MA*
COLONIAL HOUSE, THE [BB] *Weston, VT*
COLONIAL HOUSE INN & RESTAURANT [BB]
   South Yarmouth (Cape Cod), MA
COLONIAL INN [BB] *Concord, MA*
COLONIAL INN [MOT] *Moncton, NB*
COLONIAL INN [MOT] *St. John, NB*
COLONIAL INN OF MARTHA'S VINEYARD [BB]
   Martha's Vineyard, MA
COLONIAL TRAVELODGE [MOT] *Ellsworth, ME*
COLONIAL VILLAGE RESORT [MOT] *Dennis
   (Cape Cod), MA*
COLONIAL VILLAGE RESORT [RST] *Ogunquit, ME*
COLONNADE HOTEL, THE [HOT] *Boston, MA*
COLONNADE INN [MOT] *Lyndonville, VT*
COLONY, THE [HOT] *New Haven, CT*
COLONY HOTEL [RST] *Kennebunkport, ME*
COMBES FAMILY INN [BB] *Ludlow, VT*
COMFORT HOTEL DOWNTOWN [MOT] *Toronto, ON*
COMFORT INN [MOT] *Augusta, ME*
COMFORT INN [MOT] *Bangor, ME*
COMFORT INN [MOT] *Brunswick, ME*
COMFORT INN [MOT] *Burlington, VT*
COMFORT INN [MOT] *Concord, NH*

COMFORT INN [MOT] *Hyannis (Cape Cod), MA*
COMFORT INN [MOT] *Kenora, ON*
COMFORT INN [MOT] *Kitchener-Waterloo, ON*
COMFORT INN [MOT] *Manchester, NH*
COMFORT INN [MOT] *Middletown, CT*
COMFORT INN [MOT] *Mississauga, ON*
COMFORT INN [MOT] *Montpelier, VT*
COMFORT INN [MOT] *Mystic, CT*
COMFORT INN [MOT] *Nashua, NH*
COMFORT INN [MOT] *New Bedford, MA*
COMFORT INN [MOT] *Pawtucket, RI*
COMFORT INN [MOT] *Portland, ME*
COMFORT INN [MOT] *Portsmouth, NH*
COMFORT INN [MOT] *Sarnia, ON*
COMFORT INN [MOT] *Thunder Bay, ON*
COMFORT INN [MOT] *Warwick, RI*
COMFORT INN [MOT] *White River Junction, VT*
COMFORT INN [MOT] *Windsor, ON*
COMFORT INN [MOT] *Worcester, MA*
COMFORT INN & SUITES [MOT] *St. Albans, VT*
COMFORT INN & SUITES [MOT] *Sturbridge, MA*
COMFORT INN TROLLEY SQUARE [MOT] *Rutland, VT*
COMFORT SUITES [AS] *Haverhill, MA*
COMMODORES INN [RST] *Stowe, VT*
CONNECTICUT MOTOR LODGE [MOT] *Manchester, CT*
COOK'S ISLAND VIEW MOTEL [MOT] *Bailey Island, ME*
COPLEY INN [HOT] *Boston, MA*
COPLEY SQUARE [HOT] *Boston, MA*
COPPER BEECH INN, THE [BB] *Essex, CT*
CORNER HOUSE INN [BB] *Nantucket Island, MA*
CORNWALL INN AND RESTAURANT [BB]
   Cornwall Bridge, CT
CORSAIR OCEANFRONT MOTEL [MOT] *Dennis
   (Cape Cod), MA*
CORTINA INN AND RESORT [RST] *Killington, VT*
COUNTRY ACRES MOTEL [MOT] *Sandwich (Cape Cod), MA*
COUNTRY CLUB INN [MOT] *Rangeley, ME*
COUNTRY GARDEN INN & MOTEL [MOT] *Ipswich, MA*
COUNTRY INN [BB] *Harwich (Cape Cod), MA*
COURTYARD BY MARRIOTT [MOT] *Burlington, MA*
COURTYARD BY MARRIOTT [MOT] *Danvers, MA*
COURTYARD BY MARRIOTT [MOT] *Foxboro, MA*
COURTYARD BY MARRIOTT [MOT] *Lowell, MA*
COURTYARD BY MARRIOTT [MOT] *Newport, RI*
COURTYARD BY MARRIOTT [MOT] *Windsor, CT*
COVE, THE [MOT] *Orleans (Cape Cod), MA*
CRAIGNAIR INN [BB] *Rockland, ME*
CRANBERRY COTTAGES [CC] *Eastham (Cape Cod), MA*
CRANBERRY INN [BB] *Chatham (Cape Cod), MA*
CRANMORE INN [BB] *North Conway, NH*
CRANMORE MOUNTAIN LODGE [BB] *North Conway, NH*
CRANWELL RESORT AND GOLF CLUB [HOT] *Lenox, MA*
CROMWELL HARBOR MOTEL [MOT] *Bar Harbor, ME*
CROWNE PLAZA [HOT] *Hartford, CT*
CROWNE PLAZA [HOT] *Pittsfield, MA*
CROWNE PLAZA AT THE CROSSING [HOT] *Warwick, RI*
CROWNE PLAZA HOTEL [HOT] *Nashua, NH*
CROWNE PLAZA HOTEL BOSTON - NATICK [HOT]
   Natick, MA
CROWNE PLAZA OTTAWA [HOT] *Ottawa, ON*
CROWNE PLAZA TORONTO CENTRE [HOT] *Toronto, ON*

CROWNE PLAZA WORCESTER [HOT] *Worcester, MA*
CROWN PARK INN [MOT] *Caribou, ME*
CROW'S NEST MOTEL [MOT] *Truro and North Truro (Cape Cod), MA*
CRYSTAL MOTEL [MOT] *Niagara Falls, ON*
CURTIS HOUSE [BB] *Woodbury, CT*
DAGGETT HOUSE [BB] *Martha's Vineyard, MA*
DANA PLACE INN [BB] *Jackson, NH*
DAN'L WEBSTER INN [BB] *Sandwich (Cape Cod), MA*
DARBY FIELD COUNTRY INN [BB] *North Conway, NH*
DARK HARBOR HOUSE [BB] *Camden, ME*
DAUPHINEE INN [BB] *Halifax, NS*
DAYS HOTEL TORONTO AIRPORT [MOT] *Mississauga, ON*
DAYS INN [MOT] *Bangor, ME*
DAYS INN [MOT] *Branford, CT*
DAYS INN [MOT] *Brantford, ON*
DAYS INN [MOT] *Brockville, ON*
DAYS INN [MOT] *Burlington, VT*
DAYS INN [MOT] *Concord, NH*
DAYS INN [MOT] *Danvers, MA*
DAYS INN [MOT] *Dover, NH*
DAYS INN [MOT] *Hamilton, ON*
DAYS INN [MOT] *Hyannis (Cape Cod), MA*
DAYS INN [MOT] *Kittery, ME*
DAYS INN [MOT] *Mississauga, ON*
DAYS INN [MOT] *Mystic, CT*
DAYS INN [MOT] *New Bedford, MA*
DAYS INN [MOT] *Quebec City, QC*
DAYS INN [MOT] *Shelburne, VT*
DAYS INN [MOT] *Springfield, MA*
DAYS INN DOWNTOWN [MOT] *Toronto, ON*
DAYS INN FALLSVIEW DISTRICT [MOT] *Niagara Falls, ON*
DAYS INN MIDTOWN [MOT] *Montréal, QC*
DAYS INN NEAR THE FALLS [MOT] *Niagara Falls, ON*
DAYS INN OF BARRE [MOT] *Barre, VT*
DAYS INN OVERLOOKING THE FALLS [MOT] *Niagara Falls, ON*
DEERFIELD INN [BB] *Deerfield, MA*
DELTA [HOT] *Trois-Rivieres, QC*
DELTA BARRINGTON [HOT] *Halifax, NS*
DELTA BEAUSEJOUR [HOT] *Moncton, NB*
DELTA BRUNSWICK [HOT] *St. John, NB*
DELTA CHELSEA INN [HOT] *Toronto, ON*
DELTA HALIFAX [HOT] *Halifax, NS*
DELTA HOTEL [HOT] *Ottawa , ON*
DELTA LONDON ARMOURIES [HOT] *London, ON*
DELTA MEADOWVALE RESORT [HOT] *Mississauga, ON*
DELTA MONTREAL [HOT] *Montréal, QC*
DELTA PRINCE EDWARD, THE [HOT] *Charlottetown, PE*
DELTA TORONTO AIRPORT [HOT] *Toronto, ON*
DELTA TORONTO EAST [HOT] *Toronto, ON*
DEVONFIELD INN [BB] *Lee, MA*
DEXTERS INN & TENNIS CLUB [BB] *Sunapee, NH*
DIAMOND DISTRICT BREAKFAST INN [BB] *Lynn, MA*
DOCKSIDE GUEST QUARTERS [BB] *York, ME*
DOCKSIDE INN [BB] *Martha's Vineyard, MA*
DOLPHIN OF CHATHAM INN AND MOTEL [MOT] *Chatham (Cape Cod), MA*
DORSET INN [BB] *Dorset, VT*
DOSTAL'S RESORT LODGE [MOT] *Londonderry, VT*
DOUBLETREE [HOT] *Lowell, MA*

DOUBLETREE CLUB HOTEL - NORWALK [HOT] *Norwalk, CT*
DOUBLETREE GUEST SUITES BOSTON/WALTHAM [AS] *Waltham, MA*
DOUBLETREE HOTEL [HOT] *Windsor Locks, CT*
DOUBLETREE SUITES [AS] *Boston, MA*
DOWD'S COUNTRY INN [BB] *Hanover, NH*
DOWN EASTER INN [BB] *Damariscotta, ME*
DRAWBRIDGE INN [MOT] *Sarnia, ON*
DREAMWOOD PINES MOTEL [MOT] *Bar Harbor, ME*
DRUMMER BOY MOTOR INN [MOT] *Lincoln/North Woodstock, NH*
DUNSCROFT BY THE SEA [BB] *Harwich (Cape Cod), MA*
D.W.'S OCEANSIDE INN [BB] *Hampton Beach, NH*
EAGLE HOUSE MOTEL [MOT] *Rockport, MA*
EAGLE MOUNTAIN HOUSE [RST] *Jackson, NH*
EAGLE WING GUEST MOTEL [MOT] *Eastham (Cape Cod), MA*
EARL OF SANDWICH MOTEL [MOT] *Sandwich (Cape Cod), MA*
EASTERN SLOPE INN RESORT [MOT] *North Conway, NH*
EASTGATE MOTOR INN [MOT] *Littleton, NH*
EASTHAM OCEAN VIEW MOTEL [MOT] *Eastham (Cape Cod), MA*
EAST HARBOUR MOTEL & COTTAGES [MOT] *Truro and North Truro (Cape Cod), MA*
EASTLAND [MOT] *Lubec, ME*
EASTLAND PARK HOTEL [HOT] *Portland, ME*
EASTMAN INN [BB] *North Conway, NH*
EASTVIEW [MOT] *Saco, ME*
ECHO LAKE INN [BB] *Ludlow, VT*
ECONO LODGE [MOT] *Bangor, ME*
ECONO LODGE [MOT] *Brunswick, ME*
ECONO LODGE [MOT] *Hamilton, ON*
ECONO LODGE [MOT] *Manchester, NH*
ECONO LODGE [MOT] *Moncton, NB*
ECONO LODGE [MOT] *Sturbridge, MA*
ECONO LODGE AND SUITES [MOT] *Shelburne, VT*
ECONO LODGE BY THE FALLS [MOT] *Niagara Falls, ON*
ECONO LODGE LUNDY'S LANE [MOT] *Niagara Falls, ON*
ECONO LODGE MANCHESTER [MOT] *Manchester, CT*
ECONO LODGE SPRING'S INN [MOT] *Pittsfield, MA*
EDENBROOK MOTEL [MOT] *Bar Harbor, ME*
EDGARTOWN INN, THE [BB] *Martha's Vineyard, MA*
EDGEWATER, THE [MOT] *Old Orchard Beach, ME*
EDGEWATER BEACH RESORT [RST] *Dennis (Cape Cod), MA*
EDGEWATER COTTAGES AND MOTEL [MOT] *Bar Harbor, ME*
EDSON HILL MANOR [BB] *Stowe, VT*
EDWARDS HARBORSIDE INN [BB] *York, ME*
EGREMONT INN, THE [BB] *Great Barrington, MA*
ELIOT HOTEL, THE [HOT] *Boston, MA*
ELLIS RIVER HOUSE [HOT] *Jackson, NH*
ELLSWORTH MOTEL [MOT] *Ellsworth, ME*
ELM ARCH INN [BB] *Falmouth (Cape Cod), MA*
ELMS BED & BREAKFAST [BB] *Camden, ME*
ELMS INN, THE [BB] *Ridgefield, CT*
ELORA MILL [BB] *Kitchener-Waterloo, ON*
EMBASSY SUITES [AS] *Portland, ME*
EMBASSY SUITES [AS] *Toronto, ON*
EMERSON GUEST HOUSE [BB] *Vergennes, VT*
EMERSON INN BY THE SEA [BB] *Rockport, MA*

EMERY'S COTTAGES ON THE SHORE [CC] *Bar Harbor, ME*
ENGLISH MEADOWS INN [BB] *Kennebunkport, ME*
EQUINOX, THE [RST] *Manchester & Manchester Center, VT*
ESSEX STREET INN [BB] *Newburyport, MA*
EVEN'TIDE MOTEL & COTTAGES [MOT] *Wellfleet, MA*
EVERGREEN MOTEL [MOT] *Jefferson, NH*
EYRIE MOTEL [MOT] *Manchester & Manchester Center, VT*
FAIRBANKS INN [BB] *Provincetown (Cape Cod), MA*
FAIRBANKS MOTOR INN [MOT] *St. Johnsbury, VT*
FAIRFIELD INN [MOT] *Amesbury, MA*
FAIRFIELD INN [MOT] *Bangor, ME*
FAIRFIELD INN [MOT] *Manchester, NH*
FAIRFIELD INN [MOT] *Nashua, NH*
FAIRFIELD INN [MOT] *Portsmouth, NH*
FAIRFIELD INN [MOT] *Salem, NH*
FAIRFIELD INN [MOT] *Scarborough, ME*
FAIRFIELD INN [MOT] *Warwick, RI*
FAIRFIELD INN AND RESTAURANT [MOT] *Fairfield, CT*
FAIRHAVEN INN [BB] *Bath, ME*
FAIRMONT ALGONQUIN, THE [RST] *St. Andrews, NB*
FAIRMONT CHATEAU LAURIER [HOT] *Ottawa , ON*
FAIRMONT COPLEY PLAZA BOSTON, THE [HOT]
    Boston, MA
FAIRMONT LE CHATEAU FRONTENAC [HOT]
    Quebec City, QC
FAIRMONT LE CHATEAU MONTEBELLO [RST] *Ottawa, ON*
FAIRMONT LE MANOIR RICHELIEU [RST] *Quebec City, QC*
FAIRMONT QUEEN ELIZABETH [HOT] *Montréal, QC*
FAIRMONT ROYAL YORK [HOT] *Toronto, ON*
FAIRMONT TREMBLANT [RST] *Montréal, QC*
FAIRWAY MOTEL [MOT] *New London, NH*
FARMBROOK MOTEL [MOT] *Plymouth, VT*
FARMINGTON INN OF GREATER HARTFORD [HOT]
    Farmington, CT
FEDERAL HOUSE INN [BB] *Lee, MA*
FESTIVAL INN [MOT] *Stratford, ON*
FIFE 'N DRUM [MOT] *Bennington, VT*
FIFE N DRUM RESTAURANT & INN [BB] *Kent, CT*
FINCH & CHUBB INN [BB] *Rutland, VT*
FIRST CANADA INN [MOT] *Kingston, ON*
FISHERMAN'S WHARF INN [HOT] *Boothbay Harbor, ME*
FIVE GABLES INN [BB] *Boothbay Harbor, ME*
FLAGSHIP MOTEL [MOT] *Old Orchard Beach, ME*
FLAGSHIP MOTOR INN [MOT] *Boothbay Harbor, ME*
FLAMINGO MOTOR INN [MOT] *Niagara Falls, ON*
FOLLANSBEE INN [BB] *New London, NH*
FOREST, A COUNTRY INN, THE [BB] *North Conway, NH*
FOUNDER'S BROOK MOTEL & SUITES [MOT]
    Portsmouth, RI
FOUR ACRES MOTEL [MOT] *Williamstown, MA*
FOUR CHIMNEYS INN [BB] *Bennington, VT*
FOUR CHIMNEYS INN [BB] *Dennis (Cape Cod), MA*
FOUR COLUMNS INN [BB] *Newfane, VT*
FOUR PILLARS [BB] *Woodstock, VT*
FOUR POINTS BY SHERATON [MOT] *Bangor, ME*
FOUR POINTS BY SHERATON [MOT] *Eastham
    (Cape Cod), MA*
FOUR POINTS BY SHERATON [MOT]
    Kitchener-Waterloo, ON
FOUR POINTS BY SHERATON LEOMINSTER [MOT]
    Leominster, MA

FOUR POINTS BY SHERATON [MOT] *Manchester, NH*
FOUR POINTS BY SHERATON [MOT] *Mississauga, ON*
FOUR POINTS BY SHERATON SUITES, MONTREAL
    CENTRE-VILLE [MOT] *Montréal, QC*
FOUR POINTS BY SHERATON [MOT] *Niagara Falls, ON*
FOUR POINTS BY SHERATON [MOT] *Norwalk, CT*
FOUR POINTS BY SHERATON [MOT] *St. Catharines, ON*
FOUR SEASONS HOTEL BOSTON [HOT] *Boston, MA*
FOUR SEASONS HOTEL TORONTO [HOT] *Toronto, ON*
FOUR SEASONS MOTOR INN [MOT] *Twin Mountain, NH*
FOUR WINDS COUNTRY MOTEL [MOT] *Manchester &
    Manchester Center, VT*
FOX RIDGE, THE [RST] *North Conway, NH*
FOXWOODS RESORT CASINO [CAS] *Mystic, CT*
FRANCIS MALBONE HOUSE [BB] *Newport, RI*
FRANCONIA INN [BB] *Franconia, NH*
FREDERICTON INN [MOT] *Fredericton, NB*
FREEPORT INN [HOT] *Freeport, ME*
FRESH START [BB] *Halifax, NS*
FRIENDSHIP MOTOR INN [MOT] *Old Orchard Beach, ME*
FROG'S LEAP INN [BB] *Londonderry, VT*
GABLES INN, THE [BB] *Lenox, MA*
GALEN C. MOSES HOUSE [BB] *Bath, ME*
GALE RIVER [MOT] *Franconia, NH*
GANANOQUE INN [MOT] *Gananoque, ON*
GARDEN GABLES INN [BB] *Lenox, MA*
GARLANDS, THE [MOT] *Dennis (Cape Cod), MA*
GARRISON INN [HOT] *Newburyport, MA*
GARRISON SUITES [RST] *Wells, ME*
GASTHAUS SWITZERLAND INN [BB] *Ottawa , ON*
GATE HOUSE HOTEL [BB] *Niagara-on-the-Lake, ON*
GATEWAYS INN [BB] *Lenox, MA*
GLEN COVE MOTEL [MOT] *Rockland, ME*
GLENERIN [BB] *Mississauga, ON*
GLENMOOR BY THE SEA [MOT] *Camden, ME*
GLYNN HOUSE INN [BB] *Holderness, NH*
GOLDEN ANCHOR INN [MOT] *Bar Harbor, ME*
GOLDEN EAGLE RESORT [RST] *Stowe, VT*
GOLDEN GABLES INN [MOT] *North Conway, NH*
GOLDEN LION RIVERSIDE INN [MOT] *Warren, VT*
GOLDEN STAGE INN [BB] *Ludlow, VT*
GOODWIN HOTEL [HOT] *Hartford, CT*
GOODWIN'S MOTOR INN [MOT] *Norway, ME*
GOOSE COVE LODGE [RST] *Deer Isle, ME*
GORGES GRANT HOTEL [HOT] *Ogunquit, ME*
GORHAM MOTOR INN [MOT] *Gorham, NH*
GOUVERNEUR HOTEL SAINTE-FOY [HOT] *Quebec City, QC*
GOVERNOR BRADFORD ON THE HARBOUR [MOT]
    Plymouth, MA
GOVERNOR'S INN, THE [BB] *Ludlow, VT*
GOVERNORS ROCK [MOT] *Bennington, VT*
GRAFTON INN [BB] *Falmouth (Cape Cod), MA*
GRAND BEACH INN [MOT] *Old Orchard Beach, ME*
GRAND HOTEL, THE [HOT] *Ogunquit, ME*
GRAND SUMMIT [RST] *Bethel, ME*
GRAND SUMMIT HOTEL [RST] *Kingfield, ME*
GRAND VIEW [MOT] *Halifax, NS*
GRAYCOTE INN [BB] *Bar Harbor, ME*
GRAY ROCKS RESORT AND CONVENTION CENTER [RST]
    Mont Tremblant Provincial Park, QC
GREEN ACRES [MOT] *Kingston, ON*

GREENFIELD INN [BB] *Peterborough, NH*
GREEN GRANITE INN [RST] *North Conway, NH*
GREEN MOUNTAIN INN [RST] *Stowe, VT*
GREENSBORO INN [MOT] *Grand Pre, NS*
GREEN TRAILS INN [BB] *Barre, VT*
GREENVILLE INN [BB] *Greenville, ME*
GREENWOOD [HOT] *Greenville, ME*
GREENWOOD HOUSE [BB] *Martha's Vineyard, MA*
GREY BONNET INN [MOT] *Killington, VT*
GREY FOX INN & RESORT [RST] *Stowe, VT*
GREYSTONE MOTEL [MOT] *Middlebury, VT*
GRISWOLD INN [BB] *Essex, CT*
GRUNBERG HAUS BED AND BREAKFAST [BB]
    Waterbury, VT
GUILD INN [BB] *Toronto, ON*
GULL MOTEL [MOT] *Belfast, ME*
GULL MOTEL INN & COTTAGES, THE [MOT] *Old Orchard
    Beach, ME*
GULL WING SUITES [MOT] *South Yarmouth (Cape Cod), MA*
HADDON HALL [BB] *Halifax, NS*
HAMMETT HOUSE INN [BB] *Newport, RI*
HAMPSHIRE INN [HOT] *Hampton Beach, NH*
HAMPTON FALLS INN [HOT] *Hampton Beach, NH*
HAMPTON INN [MOT] *Burlington, MA*
HAMPTON INN [MOT] *Burlington, VT*
HAMPTON INN [MOT] *Concord, NH*
HAMPTON INN [MOT] *Lawrence, MA*
HAMPTON INN [MOT] *Meriden, CT*
HAMPTON INN [MOT] *Milford, CT*
HAMPTON INN [MOT] *Natick, MA*
HAMPTON INN [MOT] *Portland, ME*
HAMPTON INN [MOT] *Springfield, MA*
HAMPTON INN [MOT] *Worcester, MA*
HAMPTON INN AT THE FALLS [MOT] *Niagara Falls, ON*
HAMPTON INN WESTPORT [MOT] *Fall River, MA*
HANCOCK INN [BB] *Peterborough, NH*
HANOVER HOUSE, THE [BB] *Martha's Vineyard, MA*
HANOVER INN [MOT] *Hanover, NH*
HARBOR HOUSE HOTEL [MOT] *Nantucket Island, MA*
HARBOR HOUSE INN [BB] *Greenwich, CT*
HARBOR LIGHT INN [BB] *Marblehead, MA*
HARBORSIDE INN [HOT] *Boston, MA*
HARBOR VIEW HOTEL OF MARTHA'S VINEYARD [HOT]
    Martha's Vineyard, MA
HARBOR VIEW VILLAGE [MOT] *Truro and North Truro
    (Cape Cod), MA*
HARBOURFRONT INN [MOT] *Sarnia, ON*
HARBOUR TOWNE INN ON WATERFRONT [BB]
    Boothbay Harbor, ME
HARRASEEKET INN [BB] *Freeport, ME*
HARRISON HOUSE [BB] *Lenox, MA*
HARTNESS HOUSE [HOT] *Springfield, VT*
HARTWELL HOUSE [BB] *Ogunquit, ME*
HARVARD SQUARE HOTEL [MOT] *Cambridge, MA*
HATFIELD BED & BREAKFAST [BB] *Bar Harbor, ME*
HAWK INN AND MOUNTAIN RESORT [RST] *Plymouth, VT*
HAWTHORNE, THE [MOT] *Chatham (Cape Cod), MA*
HAWTHORNE HOTEL [HOT] *Salem, MA*
HAWTHORNE INN [BB] *Concord, MA*
HAWTHORN INN [BB] *Camden, ME*
HEARTHSIDE BED & BREAKFAST [BB] *Bar Harbor, ME*

HEATHER HOTEL AND CONVENTION CENTRE [HOT]
    Antigonish, NS
HERBERT HOTEL, THE [HOT] *Kingfield, ME*
HERITAGE HOUSE HOTEL [MOT] *Hyannis (Cape Cod), MA*
HERITAGE INN [MOT] *Blue Hill, ME*
HERITAGE MOTOR INN [MOT] *Old Saybrook, CT*
HERMITAGE INN [BB] *Wilmington, VT*
HESLIN'S MOTEL DINIG ROOM [MOT] *Calais, ME*
HIGGINS HOLIDAY HOTEL [MOT] *Bar Harbor, ME*
HIGHLANDER MOTEL [MOT] *Jeffersonville, VT*
HIGH SEAS [MOT] *Bar Harbor, ME*
HILL FARM INN [BB] *Arlington, VT*
HILLSIDE ACRES CABINS & MOTEL [CC]
    Boothbay Harbor, ME
HILLTOP INN [BB] *Franconia, NH*
HILTON [HOT] *Hartford, CT*
HILTON [HOT] *Mystic, CT*
HILTON [HOT] *Quebec City, QC*
HILTON [HOT] *Toronto, ON*
HILTON AT DEDHAM PLACE [HOT] *Dedham, MA*
HILTON BACK BAY [HOT] *Boston, MA*
HILTON HOTEL LONDON [HOT] *London, ON*
HILTON INTERNATIONAL [HOT] *Mississauga, ON*
HILTON LAC LEAMY [HOT] *Ottawa , ON*
HILTON LOGAN AIRPORT [HOT] *Boston, MA*
HILTON MONTREAL AIRPORT [HOT] *Montréal, QC*
HILTON MONTREAL BONAVENTURE [HOT] *Montréal, QC*
HILTON MONTREAL/LAVAL [HOT] *Montréal, QC*
HILTON NIAGARA FALLS [HOT] *Niagara Falls, ON*
HILTON SOUTHBURY HOTEL [HOT] *Southbury, CT*
HILTON ST. JOHN [HOT] *St. John, NB*
HILTON WINDSOR [HOT] *Windsor, ON*
HISTORIC MERRELL INN [BB] *Lee, MA*
HOB KNOB INN [BB] *Martha's Vineyard, MA*
HOB KNOB INN [MOT] *Stowe, VT*
HOCHELAGA [BB] *Kingston, ON*
HO-HUM MOTEL [MOT] *Burlington, VT*
HOLDEN INN, THE [BB] *Wellfleet, MA*
HOLIDAY HOUSE INN & MOTEL [MOT] *Scarborough, ME*
HOLIDAY INN [MOT] *Andover and North Andover, MA*
HOLIDAY INN [HOT] *Bangor, ME*
HOLIDAY INN [HOT] *Bangor, ME*
HOLIDAY INN [MOT] *Brantford, ON*
HOLIDAY INN [MOT] *Bridgeport, CT*
HOLIDAY INN [MOT] *Burlington, VT*
HOLIDAY INN [HOT] *Cambridge, MA*
HOLIDAY INN [MOT] *Danbury, CT*
HOLIDAY INN [MOT] *Ellsworth, ME*
HOLIDAY INN [MOT] *Foxboro, MA*
HOLIDAY INN [MOT] *Hartford, CT*
HOLIDAY INN [MOT] *Holyoke, MA*
HOLIDAY INN [MOT] *Kingston, RI*
HOLIDAY INN [MOT] *Kitchener-Waterloo, ON*
HOLIDAY INN [MOT] *Middletown, CT*
HOLIDAY INN [MOT] *Mississauga, ON*
HOLIDAY INN [MOT] *Nashua, NH*
HOLIDAY INN [MOT] *Portland, ME*
HOLIDAY INN [MOT] *Portsmouth, NH*
HOLIDAY INN [MOT] *Salem, NH*
HOLIDAY INN [MOT] *Sarnia, ON*
HOLIDAY INN [MOT] *Sault Ste. Marie, ON*
HOLIDAY INN [MOT] *Springfield, MA*

HOLIDAY INN [MOT] *St. Catharines, ON*
HOLIDAY INN [HOT] *Toronto, ON*
HOLIDAY INN [HOT] *Toronto, ON*
HOLIDAY INN [HOT] *Toronto, ON*
HOLIDAY INN [MOT] *Waterville, ME*
HOLIDAY INN & SPA WATERBURY [HOT] *Waterbury, VT*
HOLIDAY INN AT LOGAN [MOT] *Boston, MA*
HOLIDAY INN AT YALE UNIVERSITY [MOT]
   New Haven, CT
HOLIDAY INN BATH [MOT] *Bath, ME*
HOLIDAY INN BOSTON-DEDHAM [MOT] *Dedham, MA*
HOLIDAY INN BOSTON METRO SOUTH [HOT]
   Brockton, MA
HOLIDAY INN BOXBOROUGH WOODS [MOT]
   Concord, MA
HOLIDAY INN BY THE BAY [MOT] *Portland, ME*
HOLIDAY INN BY THE FALLS [MOT] *Niagara Falls, ON*
HOLIDAY INN - DON VALLEY [MOT] *Toronto, ON*
HOLIDAY INN EXPRESS [MOT] *Braintree, MA*
HOLIDAY INN EXPRESS [MOT] *Lexington, MA*
HOLIDAY INN EXPRESS [MOT] *Meriden, CT*
HOLIDAY INN EXPRESS [MOT] *Springfield, VT*
HOLIDAY INN EXPRESS [MOT] *Toronto, ON*
HOLIDAY INN EXPRESS HOTEL & SUITES [AS]
   Burlington, VT
HOLIDAY INN HARBOURVIEW [HOT] *Dartmouth, NS*
HOLIDAY INN NEWTON-BOSTON [HOT] *Newton, MA*
HOLIDAY INN RANDOLPH [MOT] *Braintree, MA*
HOLIDAY INN RUTLAND-KILLINGTON [HOT] *Rutland, VT*
HOLIDAY INN SELECT [MOT] *Stamford, CT*
HOLIDAY INN SELECT BOSTON [MOT] *Boston, MA*
HOLIDAY INN SELECT CENTRE VILLE [HOT] *Montréal, QC*
HOLIDAY INN SELECT HALIFAX CENTRE [MOT]
   Halifax, NS
HOLIDAY INN TORONTO WEST [MOT] *Mississauga, ON*
HOLIDAY INN YORKDALE [MOT] *Toronto, ON*
HOLIDAY MOTEL [MOT] *St. Johnsbury, VT*
HOLLOW INN AND HOTEL [MOT] *Barre, VT*
HOME PORT INN [BB] *Lubec, ME*
HOMESTEAD INN, THE [BB] *Danbury, CT*
HOMESTEAD INN [BB] *Greenwich, CT*
HOMESTEAD INN BED AND BREAKFAST [BB] *York, ME*
HOMESTEAD MOTEL [MOT] *Ellsworth, ME*
HOME SUITES INN [MOT] *Waltham, MA*
HOMEWOOD SUITES BY HILTON [AS] *Windsor Locks, CT*
HONEYSPOT LODGE [MOT] *Stratford, CT*
HONEYSUCKLE HILL B&B [BB] *Barnstable (Cape Cod), MA*
HONEYWOOD COUNTRY LODGE [MOT] *Stowe, VT*
HOPKINS INN [BB] *New Preston, CT*
HORIZON [AS] *Old Orchard Beach, ME*
HORIZON INN [HOT] *Wilmington, VT*
HORSE & HOUND INN, THE [BB] *Franconia, NH*
HOSTELLERIE LES TROIS TILLEULS [MOT] *Montréal, QC*
HOSTELLERIE RIVE GAUCHE [MOT] *Montréal, QC*
HOTEL AUBERGE UNIVERSEL MONTREAL [HOT]
   Montréal, QC
HOTEL CHATEAU LAURIER [MOT] *Quebec City, QC*
HOTEL CHERIBOURG [CONF] *Montréal, QC*
HOTEL CLASSIQUE [HOT] *Quebec City, QC*
HOTEL COURTENAY BAY [MOT] *St. John, NB*
HOTEL GERMAIN-DES-PRES [HOT] *Quebec City, QC*

HOTEL GOUVERNEUR SHERBROOKE [HOT]
   Sherbrooke, QC
HOTEL GOUVERNEURTROIS RIVIERES [HOT]
   Trois-Rivières, QC
HOTEL INTER-CONTINENTAL MONTREAL [HOT]
   Montréal, QC
HOTEL INTER-CONTINENTAL TORONTO [HOT]
   Toronto, ON
HOTEL LA RESIDENCE DU VOYAGEUR [HOT]
   Montréal, QC
HOTEL L'EAU A LA BOUCHE [HOT] *Montréal, QC*
HOTEL LE GERMAIN [HOT] *Montréal, QC*
HOTEL LE SAINTE-ANDRE [MOT] *Montréal, QC*
HOTEL NORTHAMPTON [HOT] *Northampton, MA*
HOTEL OMNI MONT-ROYAL [HOT] *Montréal, QC*
HOTEL PLAZA QUEBEC [HOT] *Quebec City, QC*
HOTEL UNIVERSEL [MOT] *Drummondville, QC*
HOTEL UNIVERSEL [HOT] *Quebec City, QC*
HOTEL VIKING, THE [HOT] *Newport, RI*
HOUSE ON THE HILL BED & BREAKFAST [BB]
   Waterbury, CT
HOWARD HOUSE LODGE [BB] *Boothbay Harbor, ME*
HOWARD JOHNSON [MOT] *Fredericton, NB*
HOWARD JOHNSON [MOT] *Hamilton, ON*
HOWARD JOHNSON [MOT] *Kingston, ON*
HOWARD JOHNSON [MOT] *St. Catharines, ON*
HOWARD JOHNSON BY THE FALLS [MOT]
   Niagara Falls, ON
HOWARD JOHNSON CONESTOGA [MOT]
   Kitchener-Waterloo, ON
HOWARD JOHNSON EAST [MOT] *Toronto, ON*
HOWARD JOHNSON EXPRESS INN [MOT] *Lenox, MA*
HOWARD JOHNSON HOTEL [MOT] *Burlington, VT*
HOWARD JOHNSON HOTEL [MOT] *Portland, ME*
HOWARD JOHNSON HOTEL [MOT] *St. John, NB*
HOWARD JOHNSON HOTEL HALIFAX [HOT] *Halifax, NS*
HOWARD JOHNSON INN [MOT] *Amherst, MA*
HOWARD JOHNSON INN [MOT] *Rutland, VT*
HOWARD JOHNSON INN [MOT] *Toronto, ON*
HOWARD JOHNSON INN NEWPORT [MOT] *Newport, RI*
HOWARD JOHNSON LODGE [MOT] *Greenfield, MA*
HOWARD JOHNSON PLAZA [MOT] *Toronto, ON*
HUGGING BEAR INN [BB] *Springfield, VT*
HUNTERS GREEN MOTEL [MOT] *South Yarmouth*
   (Cape Cod), MA
HUNTSMAN MOTOR LODGE [MOT] *Dennis*
   (Cape Cod), MA
HYATT HARBORSIDE CONFERENCE CENTER AND HOTEL
   [HOT] *Boston, MA*
HYATT REGENCY [HOT] *Cambridge, MA*
HYATT REGENCY GREENWICH [HOT] *Greenwich, CT*
HYATT REGENCY NEWPORT [HOT] *Newport, RI*
IDLEWYLD [BB] *London, ON*
IMPERIAL HOTEL AND SUITES [MOT] *Niagara Falls, ON*
INDIAN HEAD RESORT [RST] *Lincoln/North Woodstock, NH*
INDIAN HILL [MOT] *Greenville, ME*
INN AT BAY LEDGE [BB] *Bar Harbor, ME*
INN AT BAY POINT, THE [BB] *Meredith, NH*
INN AT BLUSH HILL [BB] *Waterbury, VT*
INN AT CASTLE HILL, THE [BB] *Newport, RI*
INN AT CHRISTIAN SHORE, THE [BB] *Portsmouth, NH*

INN AT DUCK CREEK [BB] *Wellfleet, MA*
INN AT ESSEX [HOT] *Burlington, VT*
INN AT ETHAN ALLEN, THE [HOT] *Danbury, CT*
INN AT FOREST HILLS [BB] *Franconia, NH*
INN AT HARBOR HEAD, THE [BB] *Kennebunkport, ME*
INN AT HARVARD, THE [MOT] *Cambridge, MA*
INN AT IRON MASTERS [MOT] *Lakeville, CT*
INN AT LEWIS BAY [BB] *South Yarmouth (Cape Cod), MA*
INN AT LONG LAKE, THE [BB] *Bridgton, ME*
INN AT LONGSHORE, THE [BB] *Westport, CT*
INN AT MANCHESTER [BB] *Manchester & Manchester
    Center, VT*
INN AT MANITOU [RST] *Toronto, ON*
INN AT MILL FALLS, THE [BB] *Meredith, NH*
INN AT MONTPELIER [BB] *Montpelier, VT*
INN AT MYSTIC [MOT] *Mystic, CT*
INN AT NATIONAL HALL, THE [HOT] *Westport, CT*
INN AT NORTHAMPTON, THE [HOT] *Northampton, MA*
INN AT OCEAN'S EDGE [HOT] *Camden, ME*
INN AT PLEASANT LAKE [BB] *New London, NH*
INN AT QUAIL RUN, THE [BB] *Wilmington, VT*
INN AT RUTLAND BED AND BREAKFAST [BB] *Rutland, VT*
INN AT SAW MILL FARM, THE [BB] *West Dover, VT*
INN AT ST. JOHN [BB] *Portland, ME*
INN AT STOCKBRIDGE, THE [BB] *Stockbridge and
    West Stockbridge, MA*
INN AT SUNRISE POINT [BB] *Camden, ME*
INN AT THE MOUNTAIN [MOT] *Stowe, VT*
INN AT THE ROSTAY [MOT] *Bethel, ME*
INN AT THE ROUND BARN, THE [BB] *Waitsfield, VT*
INN AT THORN HILL [BB] *Jackson, NH*
INN AT WEATHERSFIELD, THE [BB] *Springfield, VT*
INN AT WEST VIEW FARM [BB] *Dorset, VT*
INN AT WOODCHUCK HILL FARM [BB] *Grafton, VT*
INN AT WOODSTOCK HILL [BB] *Putnam, CT*
INN BY THE SEA [RST] *Portland, ME*
INN OF HAMPTON [HOT] *Hampton Beach, NH*
INN OF THE SIX MOUNTAINS [RST] *Killington, VT*
INN ON CARLETON [BB] *Portland, ME*
INN ON COVE HILL, THE [BB] *Rockport, MA*
INN ON GOLDEN POND [BB] *Holderness, NH*
INN ON LONG WHARF [MOT] *Newport, RI*
INN ON THE COMMON, THE [BB] *Montpelier, VT*
INN ON THE HARBOR [MOT] *Newport, RI*
INN ON THE LAKE [HOT] *Halifax, NS*
INN ON THE PARK [HOT] *Toronto, ON*
INN ON THE SOUND [BB] *Falmouth (Cape Cod), MA*
INNSBRUCK INN [MOT] *Stowe, VT*
INTERLAKEN INN [RST] *Lakeville, CT*
INTERNATIONAL INN [HOT] *Hyannis (Cape Cod), MA*
INTERNATIONAL MOTEL [MOT] *Calais, ME*
INTERNATIONAL PLAZA [HOT] *Toronto, ON*
INVERARY RESORT [RST] *Baddeck, NS*
IRON HORSE INN [MOT] *Simsbury, CT*
IRON KETTLE [MOT] *Bennington, VT*
ISAIAH CLARK HOUSE [BB] *Brewster (Cape Cod), MA*
ISAIAH HALL BED AND BREAKFAST INN [BB] *Dennis
    (Cape Cod), MA*
ISAIAH JONES HOMESTEAD [BB] *Sandwich (Cape Cod), MA*
ISAIAH TUBBS RESORT [RST] *Kingston, ON*
ISLANDER MOTOR LODGE [MOT] *Charlottetown, PE*
ISLAND INN [RST] *Martha's Vineyard, MA*

ISLAND VIEW MOTEL [MOT] *Old Orchard Beach, ME*
IVEYS MOTOR LODGE [MOT] *Houlton, ME*
IVY LODGE [BB] *Newport, RI*
JACK DANIELS MOTOR INN [MOT] *Peterborough, NH*
JACK O'LANTERN RESORT [RST] *Lincoln/
    North Woodstock, NH*
JARED COFFIN HOUSE [BB] *Nantucket Island, MA*
JEFFERSON INN [BB] *Jefferson, NH*
JIMINY PEAK MOUNTAIN RESORT [RST] *Pittsfield, MA*
JOHN CARVER INN [BB] *Plymouth, MA*
JOHNSON & WALES INN [HOT] *Providence, RI*
JUNGE'S MOTEL [MOT] *North Conway, NH*
JUNIPER HILL INN [MOT] *Ogunquit, ME*
JUNPIER HILL INN [BB] *Windsor, VT*
KALMAR VILLAGE [CC] *Truro and North Truro
    (Cape Cod), MA*
KANCAMAGUS MOTOR LODGE [MOT] *Lincoln/North
    Woodstock, NH*
KATAHDIN INN [MOT] *Millinocket, ME*
KEDRON VALLEY INN [BB] *Woodstock, VT*
KELLEY HOUSE [HOT] *Martha's Vineyard, MA*
KELTIC LODGE [RST] *Cape Breton Highlands
    National Park, NS*
KEMBLE INN [BB] *Lenox, MA*
KENDALL TAVERN B&B [BB] *Freeport, ME*
KENNEBUNK INN, THE [BB] *Kennebunk, ME*
KENNEBUNKPORT INN [HOT] *Kennebunkport, ME*
KENNISTON HILL INN [BB] *Boothbay Harbor, ME*
KIELY HOUSE HERITAGE INN [BB] *Niagara-on-the-Lake, ON*
KILLINGTON PICO MOTOR INN [MOT] *Killington, VT*
KIMBALL TERRACE INN [MOT] *Northeast Harbor, ME*
KINEO VIEW MOTOR LODGE [MOT] *Greenville, ME*
KING PHILIP INN [MOT] *Bristol, RI*
KINGSBRAE ARMS [HOT] *St. Andrews, NB*
KINGS INN [MOT] *Putnam, CT*
KINGSLEIGH INN 1904 [BB] *Southwest Harbor, ME*
KINGSTON EAST [MOT] *Kingston, ON*
KNIGHTS INN [MOT] *Kingston, ON*
KNOTTY PINE [MOT] *Bennington, VT*
LAFAYETTES OCEANFRONT RESORT [MOT] *Wells, ME*
LAGUE INN [MOT] *Montpelier, VT*
LAKELAWN MOTEL [MOT] *Yarmouth, NS*
LAKE MOREY RESORT [RST] *Fairlee, VT*
LAKE MOTEL [MOT] *Wolfeboro, NH*
LAKESHORE INN BED & BREAKFAST, THE [BB]
    Rockland, ME
LAKEVIEW INN & MOTOR LODGE [MOT] *Wolfeboro, NH*
LAMAISON CAPPELLARI AT MOSTLY HALL [BB]
    Falmouth (Cape Cod), MA
LAMBERT'S COVE COUNTRY INN [BB]
    Martha's Vineyard, MA
LAMIE'S INN & TAVERN [BB] *Hampton Beach, NH*
LAMPLIGHTER MOTOR INN [MOT] *New London, NH*
LANDMARK INN [MOT] *Thunder Bay, ON*
LANGDON HALL [HOT] *Kitchener-Waterloo, ON*
LANTERN RESORT MOTEL & CAMPGROUND [MOT]
    Jefferson, NH
LA PINSONNIERE [HOT] *Montréal, QC*
LA PLACE RENDEZ-VOUS [MOT] *Fort Frances, ON*
LARCHWOOD INN [BB] *Kingston, RI*
LAREAU FARM COUNTRY INN [BB] *Waitsfield, VT*
LA REINE MOTEL [MOT] *Yarmouth, NS*

LATCHIS HOTEL [HOT] *Brattleboro, VT*
LAWNMEER INN [MOT] *Boothbay Harbor, ME*
LE BRETON [BB] *Montréal, QC*
LE CENTRE SHERATON [HOT] *Montréal, QC*
LE MERIDIEN BOSTON [HOT] *Boston, MA*
LE NOUVEL HOTEL [HOT] *Montréal, QC*
LENOX [HOT] *Boston, MA*
LE ROYAL MERIDIEN KING EDWARD [HOT] *Toronto, ON*
LEWIS BAY LODGE [MOT] *South Yarmouth (Cape Cod), MA*
LIBERTY HILL INN [BB] *South Yarmouth (Cape Cod), MA*
LIGHTHOUSE INN [RST] *Dennis (Cape Cod), MA*
LIGHTHOUSE MOTOR INN [MOT] *Scarborough, ME*
LILAC INN [BB] *Brandon, VT*
LINCOLN INN AT THE COVERED BRIDGE, THE [BB] *Woodstock, VT*
LINDEN TREE INN [BB] *Rockport, MA*
LINNELL MOTEL & RESTINN CONFERENCE CENTER [MOT] *Rumford, ME*
LITCHFIELD INN [BB] *Litchfield, CT*
LOCH LYME LODGE [RST] *Hanover, NH*
LODGE AT CAMDEN HILLS, THE [BB] *Camden, ME*
LODGE AT JACKSON VILLAGE [MOT] *Jackson, NH*
LODGE AT MOOSEHEAD LAKE, THE [BB] *Greenville, ME*
LOEWS HOTEL VOGUE [HOT] *Montréal, QC*
LOEWS LE CONCORDE [HOT] *Quebec City, QC*
LOG CABIN ISLAND INN [BB] *Bailey Island, ME*
LONDONDERRY INN [BB] *Londonderry, VT*
LONGFELLOWS WAYSIDE INN [BB] *Sudbury Center, MA*
LORD BEAVERBROOK HOTEL [HOT] *Fredericton, NB*
LORD ELGIN [HOT] *Ottawa , ON*
LORD HAMPSHIRE MOTEL & COTTAGES [RST] *Laconia, NH*
LORD JEFFREY INN [BB] *Amherst, MA*
LORD NELSON [HOT] *Halifax, NS*
LOVETTS INN [BB] *Franconia, NH*
LOVLEY'S MOTEL [MOT] *Newport, ME*
LUCERNE INN, THE [BB] *Bangor, ME*
MABBETT HOUSE, THE [BB] *Plymouth, MA*
MADISON BEACH HOTEL [BB] *Madison, CT*
MADISON RESORT INN [MOT] *Rumford, ME*
MAINE STAY BED & BREAKFAST [BB] *Camden, ME*
MAINE STAY INN & COTTAGES [BB] *Kennebunkport, ME*
MAINE STREET MOTEL [MOT] *Bar Harbor, ME*
MAISON SUISSE INN [BB] *Northeast Harbor, ME*
MAJER'S [MOT] *Stratford, ON*
MANCHESTER HIGHLANDS INN [BB] *Manchester & Manchester Center, VT*
MANCHESTER VIEW [MOT] *Manchester & Manchester Center, VT*
MANOIR AMBROSE [BB] *Montréal, QC*
MANOIR DU LAC DELAGE [RST] *Quebec City, QC*
MANOR HOUSE INN [BB] *Bar Harbor, ME*
MANOR INN, THE [MOT] *Gloucester, MA*
MANOR INN, THE [BB] *Yarmouth, NS*
MANOR ON GOLDEN POND [BB] *Holderness, NH*
MAPLE LEAF INN [BB] *Woodstock, VT*
MAPLES INN [BB] *Bar Harbor, ME*
MAPLEWOOD INN [BB] *Rutland, VT*
MARBLEHEAD INN [BB] *Marblehead, MA*
MARIA ATWOOD INN [BB] *Franklin, NH*
MARINER MOTEL [MOT] *Falmouth (Cape Cod), MA*

MARINER MOTOR LODGE [MOT] *South Yarmouth (Cape Cod), MA*
MARITIME INN ANTIGONISH [MOT] *Antigonish, NS*
MARQUIS PLAZA [MOT] *Windsor, ON*
MARRIOTT [HOT] *Newton, MA*
MARRIOTT BLOOR YORKVILLE HOTEL TORONTO [HOT] *Toronto, ON*
MARRIOTT BOSTON QUINCY [HOT] *Quincy, MA*
MARRIOTT BURLINGTON BOSTON [HOT] *Burlington, MA*
MARRIOTT CAMBRIDGE BOSTON [HOT] *Cambridge, MA*
MARRIOTT CHATEAU CHAMPLAIN MONTREAL [HOT] *Montréal, QC*
MARRIOTT COPLEY PLACE BOSTON [HOT] *Boston, MA*
MARRIOTT FALLSVIEW NIAGARA FALLS [HOT] *Niagara Falls, ON*
MARRIOTT FARMINGTON HARTFORD [HOT] *Farmington, CT*
MARRIOTT LONG WHARF BOSTON [HOT] *Boston, MA*
MARRIOTT MERRITT PARKWAY TRUMBULL [HOT] *Bridgeport, CT*
MARRIOTT MYSTIC HOTEL AND SPA [HOT] *Groton, CT*
MARRIOTT NASHUA [HOT] *Nashua, NH*
MARRIOTT NEWPORT [HOT] *Newport, RI*
MARRIOTT OTTAWA [HOT] *Ottawa , ON*
MARRIOTT PEABODY BOSTON [HOT] *Boston, MA*
MARRIOTT PROVIDENCE [HOT] *Providence, RI*
MARRIOTT ROCKY HILL [HOT] *Hartford, CT*
MARRIOTT SABLE OAKS PORTLAND [HOT] *Portland, ME*
MARRIOTT SPRINGFIELD [HOT] *Springfield, MA*
MARRIOTT STAMFORD [HOT] *Stamford, CT*
MARRIOTT TORONTO AIRPORT [HOT] *Toronto, ON*
MARRIOTT TORONTO EATON CENTRE [HOT] *Toronto, ON*
MARTHA'S PLACE B&B [BB] *Martha's Vineyard, MA*
MARTIN HOUSE INN [BB] *Nantucket Island, MA*
MASTHEAD RESORT, THE [RST] *Provincetown (Cape Cod), MA*
MATTERHORN MOTOR LODGE [MOT] *Meredith, NH*
MAYFLOWER INN, THE [BB] *Washington, CT*
MEADOWMERE [MOT] *Ogunquit, ME*
MEADOWS LAKESIDE LODGING [MOT] *Meredith, NH*
MELVILLE HOUSE [BB] *Newport, RI*
MERRILL [BB] *Kingston, ON*
MERRILL FARM RESORT [BB] *North Conway, NH*
METROPOLITAN HOTEL, THE [HOT] *Toronto, ON*
MICHAEL'S INN [MOT] *Niagara Falls, ON*
MIDDLEBURY INN [HOT] *Middlebury, VT*
MIDWAY MOTEL & COTTAGES [MOT] *Eastham (Cape Cod), MA*
MIGIS LODGE [RST] *Sebago Lake, ME*
MILES RIVER COUNTRY INN B&B [BB] *Ipswich, MA*
MILESTONE, THE [MOT] *Ogunquit, ME*
MILFORD MOTEL ON THE RIVER [MOT] *Orono, ME*
MILLBROOK [MOT] *Scarborough, ME*
MILLCROFT [BB] *Toronto, ON*
MILLENNIUM BOSTONIAN HOTEL [HOT] *Boston, MA*
MILL HOUSE INN [MOT] *Lincoln/North Woodstock, NH*
MILL STREET INN [BB] *Newport, RI*
MIRA MONTE INN & SUITES [BB] *Bar Harbor, ME*
MOFFAT INN [BB] *Niagara-on-the-Lake, ON*
MOFFETT HOUSE B & B [BB] *Brandon, VT*

MONUMENT MOUNTAIN MOTEL [MOT]
    Great Barrington, MA
MOORINGS INN, THE [BB] *Southwest Harbor, ME*
MOOSEHEAD MOTEL [MOT] *Rockwood, ME*
MOOSE MOUNTAIN LODGE [BB] *Hanover, NH*
MORGAN HOUSE [BB] *Lee, MA*
MORRILL PLACE [BB] *Newburyport, MA*
MOSES NICKERSON HOUSE INN [BB] *Chatham
    (Cape Cod), MA*
MOTEL 6 [MOT] *Augusta, ME*
MOTEL EAST, THE [MOT] *Eastport, ME*
MOTEL PEG LEG [MOT] *Rockport, MA*
MOTEL SPRING [MOT] *Quebec City, QC*
MOUNTAIN CLUB ON LOON [RST] *Lincoln/
    North Woodstock, NH*
MOUNTAIN GAP RESORT [RST] *Digby, NS*
MOUNTAIN RESORT AT STOWE, THE [RST] *Stowe, VT*
MOUNTAIN TOP INN [RST] *Rutland, VT*
MOUNTAIN VIEW INN [BB] *Norfolk, CT*
MOUNT BATTIE MOTEL [MOT] *Camden, ME*
MOUNT COOLIDGE MOTEL [MOT] *Lincoln/
    North Woodstock, NH*
MT. MADISON MOTEL [MOT] *Gorham, NH*
MOUNT WASHINGTON HOTEL [RST] *Bretton Woods, NH*
MULBURN [BB] *Littleton, NH*
NANTUCKET INN [RST] *Nantucket Island, MA*
NAUSET KNOLL MOTOR LODGE [MOT] *Orleans
    (Cape Cod), MA*
NAUTILUS MOTOR INN [MOT] *Woods Hole, MA*
NAVIGATOR MOTOR INN [MOT] *Rockland, ME*
NEPTUNE MOTEL [MOT] *Old Orchard Beach, ME*
NER BEACH MOTEL [MOT] *Wells, ME*
NESTLENOOK FARM RESORT [BB] *Jackson, NH*
NEWBURG INN [MOT] *Kitchener-Waterloo, ON*
NEWBURY GUEST HOUSE [BB] *Boston, MA*
NEWCASTLE INN [BB] *Damariscotta, ME*
NEW ENGLAND CENTER HOTEL [MOT] *Dover, NH*
NEW LONDON INN [BB] *New London, NH*
NEWPORT CITY MOTEL [MOT] *Newport, VT*
NEWPORT HARBOR HOTEL & MARINA [HOT] *Newport, RI*
NEWPORT MOTEL [BB] *Newport, NH*
NEWPORT RAMADA INN & CONFERENCE CENTER [MOT]
    Newport, RI
NEW SEABURY RESORT AND CONFERENCE CENTER
    [CONF] *Falmouth (Cape Cod), MA*
NIANTIC INN [MOT] *New London, CT*
NONANTUM RESORT [RST] *Kennebunkport, ME*
NORDIC HILLS LODGE [MOT] *Wilmington, VT*
NORSEMAN INN [MOT] *Bethel, ME*
NORSEMAN MOTOR INN [MOT] *Ogunquit, ME*
NORTH CONWAY GRAND HOTEL [HOT]
    North Conway, NH
NORTH CONWAY MOUNTAIN INN [HOT]
    North Conway, NH
NORTHERN COMFORT MOTEL [MOT] *Colebrook, NH*
NORTHERN LIGHTS [MOT] *Presque Isle, ME*
NORTHERN ZERMATT INN & MOTEL [BB]
    Twin Mountain, NH
NORTHFIELD INN [BB] *Montpelier, VT*
NORTH HERO HOUSE INN [BB] *North Hero, VT*
NORTH SHIRE MOTEL [MOT] *Manchester &
    Manchester Center, VT*

NORUMBEGA INN [BB] *Camden, ME*
NOVOTEL [MOT] *Mississauga, ON*
NOVOTEL MONTREAL CENTRE [HOT] *Montréal, QC*
NOVOTEL TORONTO CENTRE [HOT] *Toronto, ON*
OAK HOUSE, THE [BB] *Martha's Vineyard, MA*
OAK ISLAND RESORT AND SPA [RST] *Halifax, NS*
OCEAN EDGE RESORT AND GOLF CLUB [RST]
    Brewster (Cape Cod), MA
OCEAN GATE INN [MOT] *Boothbay Harbor, ME*
OCEAN POINT INN [BB] *Boothbay Harbor, ME*
OCEAN VIEW INN AND RESORT [RST] *Gloucester, MA*
OLD COLONY MOTEL [MOT] *Sandwich (Cape Cod), MA*
OLD COURT BED & BREAKFAST [BB] *Providence, RI*
OLD CUTTER INN, THE [BB] *Lyndonville, VT*
OLDE ORCHARD INN [BB] *Meredith, NH*
OLDE TAVERN MOTEL AND INN [MOT] *Orleans
    (Cape Cod), MA*
OLD FORT INN [BB] *Kennebunkport, ME*
OLD HARBOR INN [BB] *Chatham (Cape Cod), MA*
OLD LYME INN [BB] *Old Lyme, CT*
OLD MYSTIC INN, THE [BB] *Mystic, CT*
OLD NEWFANE INN [BB] *Newfane, VT*
OLD ORCHARD INN [RST] *Grand Pre, NS*
OLD SEA PINES INN [BB] *Brewster (Cape Cod), MA*
OLD STONE INN [MOT] *Niagara Falls, ON*
OLD STURBRIDGE VILLAGE LODGES [MOT] *Sturbridge, MA*
OLD TAVERN AT GRAFTON [BB] *Grafton, VT*
OLYMPIA MOTOR LODGE [MOT] *Manchester &
    Manchester Center, VT*
OMNI NEW HAVEN HOTEL AT YALE [HOT] *New Haven, CT*
OMNI PARKER HOUSE [HOT] *Boston, MA*
ONCLE SAM [MOT] *Quebec City, QC*
ORCHARDS HOTEL, THE [HOT] *Williamstown, MA*
OTTAUQUECHEE MOTEL [MOT] *Woodstock, VT*
OUTERMOST INN [BB] *Martha's Vineyard, MA*
OVERLOOK INN OF CAPE COD [BB] *Eastham
    (Cape Cod), MA*
OWEN HOUSE [BB] *Lubec, ME*
OXFORD HOUSE INN [BB] *Center Lovell, ME*
OYSTER SHELL MOTEL [MOT] *Damariscotta, ME*
PALLISER MOTEL [MOT] *Truro, NS*
PALMER HOUSE [RST] *Manchester & Manchester Center, VT*
PALMER HOUSE INN, THE [BB] *Falmouth (Cape Cod), MA*
PAMOLA MOTOR LODGE [MOT] *Millinocket, ME*
PANSY PATCH [RST] *St. Andrews, NB*
PARK ENTRANCE OCEANFRONT MOTEL [MOT]
    Bar Harbor, ME
PARKER HOUSE INN [BB] *Woodstock, VT*
PARK HYATT TORONTO [HOT] *Toronto, ON*
PARK PLACE RAMADA PLAZA [MOT] *Dartmouth, NS*
PARKVIEW INN [MOT] *Salem, NH*
PARSONAGE INN, THE [BB] *Orleans (Cape Cod), MA*
PEGLEG RESTAURANT AND INN [BB] *Rockport, MA*
PENNY HOUSE INN [BB] *Eastham (Cape Cod), MA*
PENTAGOET INN [BB] *Bucksport, ME*
PEQUOT HOTEL [BB] *Martha's Vineyard, MA*
PHENIX INN AT WEST MARKET SQUARE, THE [BB]
    Bangor, ME
PHILBROOK FARM INN [BB] *Gorham, NH*
PICKET FENCE [MOT] *St. Andrews, NB*
PILGRIM HOUSE [BB] *Newport, RI*
PILGRIM MOTOR INN [MOT] *Niagara Falls, ON*

PILGRIM SANDS [MOT] *Plymouth, MA*
PILGRIMS INN [BB] *Deer Isle, ME*
PILLAR AND POST [BB] *Niagara-on-the-Lake, ON*
PINE HAVEN MOTEL [MOT] *Portsmouth, NH*
PINE HILL INN, THE [BB] *Ogunquit, ME*
PINE LODGE, THE [CC] *Westerly, RI*
PINES MOTEL [MOT] *Boothbay Harbor, ME*
PINES RESORT, THE [RST] *Digby, NS*
PINE VIEW LODGE [MOT] *Wolfeboro, NH*
PINK BLOSSOMS FAMILY RESORT [RST] *Ogunquit, ME*
PINOTEAU VILLAGE [HOT] *Mont Tremblant*
    Provincial Park, QC
PITCHER INN, THE [HOT] *Warren, VT*
PLAINFIELD MOTEL [MOT] *Plainfield, CT*
PLAINFIELD YANKEE MOTOR INN [MOT] *Plainfield, CT*
PLEASANT BAY VILLAGE RESORT [RST] *Chatham*
    (Cape Cod), MA
POINT WAY INN [BB] *Martha's Vineyard, MA*
POMEGRANATE INN [BB] *Portland, ME*
POND RIDGE MOTEL [MOT] *Woodstock, VT*
POORE HOUSE INN [BB] *Brewster (Cape Cod), MA*
PORT FORTUNE INN [BB] *Chatham (Cape Cod), MA*
PORTLAND REGENCY HOTEL [HOT] *Portland, ME*
PORT MOTOR INN [MOT] *Portsmouth, NH*
POWDER HOUND INN [CON] *Warren, VT*
PRINCE ARTHUR [MOT] *Thunder Bay, ON*
PRINCE GEORGE [HOT] *Halifax, NS*
PRINCE OF WALES [HOT] *Niagara-on-the-Lake, ON*
PROFILE DELUXE MOTEL [MOT] *Twin Mountain, NH*
PROVIDENCE BILTMORE, THE [HOT] *Providence, RI*
PROVINCETOWN INN [RST] *Provincetown (Cape Cod), MA*
PROVINCIAL INN [MOT] *Gananoque, ON*
PUBLICK HOUSE HISTORIC INN [MOT] *Sturbridge, MA*
PURITY SPRING RESORT [RST] *North Conway, NH*
QUALITY HOTEL [MOT] *Niagara Falls, ON*
QUALITY HOTEL [MOT] *Toronto, ON*
QUALITY HOTEL [MOT] *Toronto, ON*
QUALITY HOTEL DORVAL [MOT] *Montréal, QC*
QUALITY INN [MOT] *Brockville, ON*
QUALITY INN [MOT] *Danvers, MA*
QUALITY INN [MOT] *Groton, CT*
QUALITY INN [MOT] *Mississauga, ON*
QUALITY INN AIRPORT EAST [MOT] *Toronto, ON*
QUALITY INN AND CONFERENCE CENTER [MOT]
    Vernon, CT
QUALITY INN AND SUITES [MOT] *Brattleboro, VT*
QUALITY INN & SUITES [MOT] *Gananoque, ON*
QUALITY INN AND SUITES [MOT] *Montréal, QC*
QUALITY INN BAYFRONT [MOT] *Sault Ste. Marie, ON*
QUALITY INN FALL [MOT] *Fall River, MA*
QUALITY INN ON THE HILL [MOT] *Charlottetown, PE*
QUALITY SUITES [MOT] *Toronto, ON*
QUEBEC INN [HOT] *Quebec City, QC*
QUECHEE INN AT MARSHLAND FARM [BB] *Woodstock, VT*
QUEEN ANNE INN [BB] *Chatham (Cape Cod), MA*
QUEEN ANNE INN [BB] *New London, CT*
QUEEN'S INN [BB] *Stratford, ON*
QUEEN'S LANDING [HOT] *Niagara-on-the-Lake, ON*
QUISISANA LODGE [RST] *Center Lovell, ME*
RABBIT HILL INN [BB] *St. Johnsbury, VT*
RACE BROOK LODGE [BB] *Great Barrington, MA*

RADISSON [HOT] *Boston, MA*
RADISSON [HOT] *Burlington, VT*
RADISSON [HOT] *Mississauga, ON*
RADISSON [HOT] *New London, CT*
RADISSON [HOT] *Windsor, ON*
RADISSON AIRPORT HOTEL [HOT] *Warwick, RI*
RADISSON HOTEL [HOT] *Lowell, MA*
RADISSON HOTEL AND CONFERENCE CENTER [HOT]
    Middletown, CT
RADISSON HOTEL CAMBRIDGE [MOT] *Cambridge, MA*
RADISSON HOTEL GOUVERNEUR QUEBEC [HOT]
    Quebec City, QC
RADISSON HOTEL PROVIDENCE HARBOR [HOT]
    Providence, RI
RADISSON HOTEL SPRINGFIELD [HOT] *Enfield, CT*
RADISSON HOTEL TORONTO EAST [MOT] *Toronto, ON*
RADISSON HOTEL TORONTO - MARKHAM [HOT]
    Toronto, ON
RADISSON INN [HOT] *Sudbury Center, MA*
RADISSON PLAZA - HOTEL ADMIRAL [HOT] *Toronto, ON*
RADISSON SUITE TORONTO AIRPORT [HOT] *Toronto, ON*
RAMADA-CORAL INN RESORT [MOT] *Niagara Falls, ON*
RAMADA DON VALLEY [MOT] *Toronto, ON*
RAMADA HOTEL [MOT] *Andover and North Andover, MA*
RAMADA HOTEL TORONTO AIRPORT [MOT] *Toronto, ON*
RAMADA INN [MOT] *Bedford, MA*
RAMADA INN [MOT] *Boston, MA*
RAMADA INN [MOT] *Danbury, CT*
RAMADA INN [MOT] *London, ON*
RAMADA INN [MOT] *Mississauga, ON*
RAMADA INN [MOT] *New London, CT*
RAMADA INN [MOT] *Norwich, CT*
RAMADA INN [MOT] *Providence, RI*
RAMADA INN [MOT] *Wethersfield, CT*
RAMADA INN AND CONVENTION CENTRE [MOT]
    Sault Ste. Marie, ON
RAMADA INN AND SUITES [MOT] *Toronto, ON*
RAMADA INN CAPITOL HILL [MOT] *Hartford, CT*
RAMADA INN CONFERENCE CENTER [MOT] *Lewiston, ME*
RAMADA INN REGENCY [MOT] *Hyannis (Cape Cod), MA*
RAMADA INN STRATFORD [MOT] *Stratford, CT*
RAMADA INN-WHITE RIVER JCT [MOT]
    White River Junction, VT
RAMADA LIMITED [MOT] *Rutland, VT*
RAMADA ON THE SQUARE [MOT] *Falmouth*
    (Cape Cod), MA
RAMADA PARKWAY INN [MOT] *St. Catharines, ON*
RAMADA PLAZA HOTEL [MOT] *Hamilton, ON*
RAMADA PLAZA INN [MOT] *Meriden, CT*
RAMADA SUITES NIAGARA [MOT] *Niagara Falls, ON*
RANDALL'S ORDINARY [BB] *Stonington, CT*
RANGELEY INN [RST] *Rangeley, ME*
RED APPLE INN [MOT] *Jackson, NH*
RED BROOK INN [BB] *Mystic, CT*
RED CLOVER INN [BB] *Killington, VT*
REDCLYFFE SHORE MOTOR INN [MOT] *Calais, ME*
RED CRICKET INN [BB] *West Dover, VT*
RED DOORS MOTEL [MOT] *Lincoln/North Woodstock, NH*
RED HORSE INN [MOT] *Falmouth (Cape Cod), MA*
RED JACKET BEACH MOTOR INN [MOT] *South Yarmouth*
    (Cape Cod), MA

RED JACKET MOUNTAIN VIEW [RST] *North Conway, NH*
RED LION INN [BB] *Stockbridge and West Stockbridge, MA*
RED ROOF INN [MOT] *Enfield, CT*
RED ROOF INN [MOT] *Nashua, NH*
RED ROOF INN [MOT] *New London, CT*
REGAL CONSTELLATION [HOT] *Toronto, ON*
REGAL INN OF HAMPTON BEACH [MOT]
   Hampton Beach, NH
RELUCTANT PANTHER INN AND RESTAURANT [BB]
   Manchester & Manchester Center, VT
RENAISSANCE AT SKYDOME [HOT] *Toronto, ON*
RENAISSANCE BEDFORD HOTEL [HOT] *Bedford, MA*
RENAISSANCE FALLSVIEW [HOT] *Niagara Falls, ON*
RENAISSANCE MONTREAL HOTEL [HOT] *Montréal, QC*
RESIDENCE INN BY MARRIOTT [EX] *Burlington, VT*
RESIDENCE INN BY MARRIOTT [EX] *Danvers, MA*
RESIDENCE INN BY MARRIOTT [EX] *Nashua, NH*
RESIDENCE INN BY MARRIOTT [EX] *New Haven, CT*
RESIDENCE INN BY MARRIOTT [EX] *Warwick, RI*
RESIDENCE INN BY MARRIOTT [EX] *Windsor, CT*
RHUMB LINE MOTOR LODGE [MOT] *Kennebunkport, ME*
RIDGEWAY INN, THE [BB] *Bar Harbor, ME*
RIDGEWOOD MOTEL AND COTTAGES [MOT]
   Orleans (Cape Cod), MA
RITZ-CARLTON, BOSTON, THE [HOT] *Boston, MA*
RITZ-CARLTON, MONTREAL, THE [HOT] *Montréal, QC*
RIVERSIDE [MOT] *Ogunquit, ME*
RIVER VIEW [MOT] *Bethel, ME*
RIVIERA BEACH RESORT [RST] *South Yarmouth
   (Cape Cod), MA*
ROBERTS HOUSE INN [BB] *Nantucket Island, MA*
ROCKWELL HOUSE INN [BB] *Bristol, RI*
ROCKY SHORES INN & COTTAGES [BB] *Rockport, MA*
RODD COLONY HARBOUR INN [MOT] *Yarmouth, NS*
RODD CONFEDERATION INN & SUITES [MOT]
   Charlottetown, PE
RODD GRAND YARMOUTH [HOT] *Yarmouth, NS*
RODD PARK HOUSE INN [MOT] *Moncton, NB*
RODD ROYALTY INN [MOT] *Charlottetown, PE*
ROGER SHERMAN INN [BB] *New Canaan, CT*
ROOKWOOD INN [BB] *Lenox, MA*
ROSEMOUNT INN [BB] *Kingston, ON*
ROYAL ANCHOR RESORT [MOT] *Old Orchard Beach, ME*
ROYAL MARQUIS [MOT] *Windsor, ON*
ROYAL PLAZA HOTEL [MOT] *Newport, RI*
ROYAL SONESTA [HOT] *Cambridge, MA*
ROYALTY INN [MOT] *Gorham, NH*
RUDDY TURNSTONE [BB] *Brewster (Cape Cod), MA*
RUTHCLIFFE LODGE & RESORT [BB] *North Hero, VT*
ST STEPHEN INN [MOT] *St. Andrews, NB*
SALEM INN [BB] *Salem, MA*
SAMOSET RESORT [RST] *Rockland, ME*
SAND PIPER BEACHFRONT MOTEL [MOT] *Old Orchard
   Beach, ME*
SANDPIPER MOTOR INN [MOT] *Old Saybrook, CT*
SANDY BAY MOTOR INN [MOT] *Rockport, MA*
SANDY NECK MOTEL [MOT] *Sandwich (Cape Cod), MA*
SAYBROOK POINT INN AND SPA [RST] *Old Saybrook, CT*
SCANDINAVIA INN AND CHALETS [BB] *Stowe, VT*
SCHOONERS INN, THE [HOT] *Kennebunkport, ME*
SCOTTISH INN [MOT] *Houlton, ME*
SEA BREEZE INN [BB] *Hyannis (Cape Cod), MA*

SEA CHAMBERS MOTOR LODGE [MOT] *Ogunquit, ME*
SEA CLIFF HOUSE & MOTEL [MOT] *Old Orchard Beach, ME*
SEACREST MANOR [BB] *Rockport, MA*
SEA CREST RESORT AND CONFERENCE CENTER [RST]
   Falmouth (Cape Cod), MA
SEADAR INN [MOT] *Harwich (Cape Cod), MA*
SEAFARER INN [BB] *Rockport, MA*
SEAGATE [MOT] *Boothbay Harbor, ME*
SEAGULL INN [BB] *Marblehead, MA*
SEAGULL MOTOR INN [MOT] *Wells, ME*
SEA HEATHER INN [BB] *Harwich (Cape Cod), MA*
SEA HORSE INN [MOT] *Toronto, ON*
SEA LORD RESORT MOTEL [MOT] *Dennis (Cape Cod), MA*
SEA MIST RESORT MOTEL [MOT] *Wells, ME*
SEAPORT HOTEL [HOT] *Boston, MA*
SEA SHELL MOTEL [MOT] *Dennis (Cape Cod), MA*
SEASHORE PARK MOTOR INN [MOT] *Orleans
   (Cape Cod), MA*
SEASIDE BEACH RESORT [MOT] *St. Andrews, NB*
SEASIDE HOUSE & COTTAGES [HOT] *Kennebunkport, ME*
SEASONS INN OF THE KENNEBUNK, THE [MOT]
   Kennebunk, ME
SEASONS MOTOR INN [MOT] *Dartmouth, NS*
SEASONS MOTOR INN [MOT] *Halifax, NS*
SEAVIEW CAMPGROUND [CC] *Eastport, ME*
SEA VIEW MOTEL [MOT] *Ogunquit, ME*
SEAWARD INN & COTTAGES [BB] *Rockport, MA*
SELECTOTEL ROND-POINT [MOT] *Quebec City, QC*
SERENITY MOTEL [CC] *Bennington, VT*
SESUIT HARBOR [MOT] *Dennis (Cape Cod), MA*
SEVEN OAKES [MOT] *Kingston, ON*
SEVEN SEA STREET INN [BB] *Nantucket Island, MA*
SHADY NOOK INN & MOTEL [MOT] *Sandwich
   (Cape Cod), MA*
SHAKER INN AT THE GREAT STONE DWELLING, THE [BB]
   Hanover, NH
SHAKESPEARE'S INN [MOT] *Twin Mountain, NH*
SHARON MOTOR LODGE [MOT] *Lakeville, CT*
SHELBURNE FARMS [BB] *Shelburne, VT*
SHELTER HARBOR INN [BB] *Westerly, RI*
SHERATON [HOT] *Hamilton, ON*
SHERATON [HOT] *Ottawa , ON*
SHERATON [HOT] *Portsmouth, NH*
SHERATON [HOT] *Warwick, RI*
SHERATON BOSTON HOTEL [HOT] *Boston, MA*
SHERATON BRADLEY [HOT] *Windsor Locks, CT*
SHERATON BRAINTREE HOTEL [HOT] *Braintree, MA*
SHERATON CENTRE [HOT] *Toronto, ON*
SHERATON COLONIAL HOTEL AND GOLF CLUB [HOT]
   Lynnfield, MA
SHERATON COMMANDER HOTEL [HOT] *Cambridge, MA*
SHERATON DANBURY AND TOWERS [HOT] *Danbury, CT*
SHERATON FALLSVIEW HOTEL [HOT] *Niagara Falls, ON*
SHERATON FERNCROFT RESORT [HOT] *Danvers, MA*
SHERATON FRAMINGHAM HOTEL [HOT] *Framingham, MA*
SHERATON FREDERICTON [HOT] *Fredericton, NB*
SHERATON GATEWAY [HOT] *Toronto, ON*
SHERATON HALIFAX HOTEL [HOT] *Halifax, NS*
SHERATON HARTFORD HOTEL [HOT] *Hartford, CT*
SHERATON HOTEL [HOT] *Newton, MA*
SHERATON HOTEL AND CONFERENCE CENTER [HOT]
   Burlington, VT

SHERATON HYANNIS RESORT [RST] *Hyannis
    (Cape Cod), MA*
SHERATON INN [HOT] *Plymouth, MA*
SHERATON LAVAL HOTEL [HOT] *Montréal, QC*
SHERATON LEXINGTON INN [HOT] *Lexington, MA*
SHERATON NASHUA HOTEL [HOT] *Nashua, NH*
SHERATON NEEDHAM HOTEL [HOT] *Wellesley, MA*
SHERATON NEWTON HOTEL [HOT] *Newton, MA*
SHERATON ON THE FALLS [HOT] *Niagara Falls, ON*
SHERATON PARKWAY HOTEL TORONTO NORTH [HOT]
    Toronto, ON
SHERATON SOUTH PORTLAND HOTEL [HOT]
    Portland, ME
SHERATON SPRINGFIELD AT MONARCH PLAZA [HOT]
    Springfield, MA
SHERATON STAMFORD HOTEL [HOT] *Stamford, CT*
SHERATON WATERBURY [HOT] *Waterbury, CT*
SHERBORN INN [HOT] *Natick, MA*
SHERBURNE INN [BB] *Nantucket Island, MA*
SHERBURNE-KILLINGTON MOTEL [MOT] *Killington, VT*
SHIPS INN [BB] *Nantucket Island, MA*
SHIPS KNEES INN [BB] *Orleans (Cape Cod), MA*
SHIRE INN [BB] *Barre, VT*
SHIRE MOTEL, THE [MOT] *Woodstock, VT*
SHIRETOWN INN [BB] *Martha's Vineyard, MA*
SHIRETOWN MOTOR INN [MOT] *Houlton, ME*
SHORE ACRES INN [MOT] *North Hero, VT*
SILAS GRIFFITH INN [BB] *Manchester & Manchester
    Center, VT*
SILVER DART LODGE [MOT] *Baddeck, NS*
SILVER MAPLE LODGE & COTTAGES [BB] *Fairlee, VT*
SILVERMINE TAVERN, THE [BB] *Norwalk, CT*
SILVER STREET INN [BB] *Dover, NH*
SILVERWOOD MOTEL [MOT] *Cavendish, PE*
SIMMONS HOMESTEAD INN [BB] *Hyannis (Cape Cod), MA*
SIMSBURY 1820 HOUSE [BB] *Simsbury, CT*
SIMSBURY INN [HOT] *Simsbury, CT*
SINCLAIR INN BED & BREAKFAST [BB] *Jeffersonville, VT*
SISE INN [HOT] *Portsmouth, NH*
SKAKET BEACH MOTEL [MOT] *Orleans (Cape Cod), MA*
SKYLARK MOTEL [MOT] *Old Orchard Beach, ME*
SKYVIEW MOTEL [MOT] *Vergennes, VT*
SLUMBER INN-NEW MINAS [MOT] *Grand Pre, NS*
SMUGGLER'S COVE MOTOR INN [MOT]
    Boothbay Harbor, ME
SMUGGLER'S NOTCH INN AND RESTAURANT [BB]
    Jeffersonville, VT
SMUGGLER'S NOTCH RESORT [RST] *Jeffersonville, VT*
SNOWDON MOTEL BED & BREAKFAST [BB]
    Londonderry, VT
SNOW HILL LODGE [MOT] *Camden, ME*
SNOWVILLAGE INN [BB] *North Conway, NH*
SNOWY OWL INN [RST] *Waterville Valley, NH*
SNUG COTTAGE [BB] *Provincetown (Cape Cod), MA*
SOMERSET HOUSE [BB] *Provincetown (Cape Cod), MA*
SOUDINGS SEASIDE RESORT [MOT] *Dennis (Cape Cod), MA*
SOUTHFLEET MOTOR INN [MOT] *Wellfleet, MA*
SOUTH SHIRE INN [BB] *Bennington, VT*
SPA AT NORWICH INN, THE [RST] *Norwich, CT*
SPARHAWK RESORT MOTEL [MOT] *Ogunquit, ME*

SPOUTER WHALE MOTOR INN [MOT] *Dennis
    (Cape Cod), MA*
SPRAY CLIFF ON THE OCEAN [BB] *Marblehead, MA*
SPRING HILL MOTOR LODGE [MOT] *Sandwich
    (Cape Cod), MA*
SPRING HOUSE [HOT] *Block Island, RI*
SPRUCE POINT INN [RST] *Boothbay Harbor, ME*
SQUIRE TARBOX INN [BB] *Wiscasset, ME*
STAGE NECK INN [RST] *York, ME*
STAGE RUN MOTEL [MOT] *Ogunquit, ME*
STAGE WEST HOTEL [HOT] *Mississauga, ON*
STAMFORD MOTEL [MOT] *Manchester & Manchester
    Center, VT*
STAMFORD SUITES [AS] *Stamford, CT*
STANTON HOUSE INN [BB] *Greenwich, CT*
STARDUST [MOT] *Halifax, NS*
STARDUST [MOT] *Halifax, NS*
STARDUST [MOT] *Houlton, ME*
STARLIGHT MOTOR INN [MOT] *New London, CT*
STATE HOUSE INN [BB] *Providence, RI*
STERLING RIDGE INN & CABINS [CC] *Jeffersonville, VT*
STONCREST FARM BED AND BREAKFAST [BB] *White River
    Junction, VT*
STONE HEARTH INN [BB] *Springfield, VT*
STONEHEDGE INN [RST] *Lowell, MA*
STONEHENGE INN [BB] *Ridgefield, CT*
STONE HOUSES MOTEL & REST [MOT] *Truro, NS*
STONYBROOK MOTEL & LODGE [MOT] *Franconia, NH*
STORYBOOK RESORT INN [RST] *Jackson, NH*
STOWEFLAKE MOUNTAIN RESORT & SPA [RST] *Stowe, VT*
STOWEHOF INN [BB] *Stowe, VT*
STOWE INN AT LITTLE RIVER [BB] *Stowe, VT*
STOWE MOTEL [MOT] *Stowe, VT*
STRATFORD HOUSE INN [BB] *Bar Harbor, ME*
STRATFORD SUBURBAN [MOT] *Stratford, ON*
STRATTON MOUNTAIN INN AND VILLAGE LODGE [RST]
    Stratton Mt, VT
STRONG HOUSE INN [BB] *Vergennes, VT*
STURBRIDGE COACH MOTOR LODGE [MOT]
    Sturbridge, MA
STURBRIDGE HOST HOTEL & CONFERENCE CENTER
    [CONF] *Sturbridge, MA*
SUBURBAN PINES [MOT] *Sebago Lake, ME*
SUGARBUSH INN [BB] *Warren, VT*
SUGARBUSH VILLAGE CONDOS [RST] *Warren, VT*
SUGAR HILL INN [BB] *Franconia, NH*
SUGARLOAF INN [HOT] *Kingfield, ME*
SUGARTREE COUNTRY INN [BB] *Warren, VT*
SUMMER WHITE HOUSE, THE [BB] *Lenox, MA*
SUMMIT LODGE [HOT] *Killington, VT*
SUN AND SKI MOTOR INN [MOT] *Stowe, VT*
SUNNY KING [MOT] *Charlottetown, PE*
SUNRISE MOTEL [MOT] *Saco, ME*
SUNSET HILL HOUSE — A GRAND INN [BB] *Franconia, NH*
SUNSET MOTOR INN [MOT] *Stowe, VT*
SUPER 8 [MOT] *Brattleboro, VT*
SUPER 8 [MOT] *Danvers, MA*
SUPER 8 [MOT] *Franklin, NH*
SUPER 8 [MOT] *Lewiston, ME*
SUPER 8 [MOT] *Manchester, NH*
SUPER 8 [MOT] *Newport, VT*

SUPER 8 [MOT] *Stamford, CT*
SUPER 8 [MOT] *Wells, ME*
SUPER 8 MOTEL [MOT] *Brunswick, ME*
SURF MOTEL [MOT] *Block Island, RI*
SURFSIDE INN [MOT] *Niagara Falls, ON*
SUSSE CHALET LODGE [MOT] *Portland, ME*
SUTTON PLACE [HOT] *Toronto, ON*
SWIFT HOUSE INN [BB] *Middlebury, VT*
SWISS CHALETS VILLAGE INN [MOT] *North Conway, NH*
SWISS INN [BB] *Londonderry, VT*
SWISSOTEL BOSTON [HOT] *Boston, MA*
TAGE INN-ANDOVER [HOT] *Andover and
    North Andover, MA*
TAGGART HOUSE, THE [BB] *Stockbridge and
    West Stockbridge, MA*
TARA MANOR INN [MOT] *St. Andrews, NB*
TATTINGSTONE INN [BB] *Grand Pre, NS*
T-BIRD MOTOR INN [MOT] *Shelburne, VT*
TELEGRAPH HOUSE [MOT] *Baddeck, NS*
TERRACE BY THE SEA, THE [RST] *Ogunquit, ME*
THATCHER BROOK INN [BB] *Waterbury, VT*
THAYER'S INN [BB] *Littleton, NH*
THOMAS MOTT ALBURG HOMESTEAD B&B [BB]
    North Hero, VT
THORNCROFT INN [BB] *Martha's Vineyard, MA*
THORNEWOOD INN & RESTAURANT [BB]
    Great Barrington, MA
THORNHEDGE INN [BB] *Bar Harbor, ME*
THREE BEARS AT THE FOUNTAIN [BB] *Stowe, VT*
THREE CHIMNEYS [BB] *New Haven, CT*
THREE SEASONS MOTOR LODGE [MOT] *Dennis
    (Cape Cod), MA*
TIDES INN BY THE SEA [BB] *Kennebunkport, ME*
TIDEWATER MOTOR LODGE [MOT] *South Yarmouth
    (Cape Cod), MA*
TODD HOUSE [BB] *Eastport, ME*
TOLLAND INN [BB] *Vernon, CT*
TOLL ROAD MOTOR INN [MOT] *Manchester &
    Manchester Center, VT*
TOPNOTCH AT STOWE [RST] *Stowe, VT*
TOPSIDE MOTEL [MOT] *Boothbay Harbor, ME*
TOWER SUITES MOTEL [AS] *Guilford, CT*
TOWN AND COUNTRY RESORT [MOT] *Stowe, VT*
TOWN CRIER MOTEL [MOT] *Eastham (Cape Cod), MA*
TOWNE LYNE MOTEL [MOT] *Ogunquit, ME*
TOWNE MOTEL, THE [MOT] *Skowhegan, ME*
TOWN INN [HOT] *Toronto, ON*
TRADE WINDS INN [MOT] *Centerville (Cape Cod), MA*
TRAIL'S END - A COUNTRY INN [BB] *Wilmington, VT*
TRAPP FAMILY LODGE [RST] *Stowe, VT*
TRAVELODGE [MOT] *Bedford, MA*
TRAVELODGE [MOT] *Kenora, ON*
TRAVELODGE [MOT] *London, ON*
TRAVELODGE [MOT] *Natick, MA*
TRAVELODGE [MOT] *Pittsfield, MA*
TRAVELODGE [MOT] *St. Catharines, ON*
TRAVELODGE AIRLANE HOTEL [MOT] *Thunder Bay, ON*
TRAVELODGE - AIRPORT [MOT] *Toronto, ON*
TRAVELODGE BONAVENTURE [MOT] *Niagara Falls, ON*
TRAVELODGE BURLINGTON ON THE LAKE [MOT]
    Hamilton, ON
TRAVELODGE CLIFTON HILL [MOT] *Niagara Falls, ON*

TRAVELODGE EAST [MOT] *Toronto, ON*
TRAVELODGE HOTEL [MOT] *Augusta, ME*
TRAVELODGE HOTEL LA SALLE [MOT] *Kingston, ON*
TRAVELODGE NEAR THE FALLS [MOT] *Niagara Falls, ON*
TRAVELODGE NORTH [MOT] *Toronto, ON*
TRAVELODGE THUNDER BAY [MOT] *Thunder Bay, ON*
TRAVELODGE TORONTO SW/CARRIAGE INN [MOT]
    Mississauga, ON
TREMONT BOSTON- A WYNDHAM HISTORIC HOTEL,
    THE [HOT] *Boston, MA*
TRINITY HOUSE [BB] *Gananoque, ON*
TUCKER HILL INN [RST] *Waitsfield, VT*
TUCKERNUCK INN [BB] *Nantucket Island, MA*
TUCK INN B&B, THE [BB] *Rockport, MA*
TUGBOAT INN [HOT] *Boothbay Harbor, ME*
TURK'S HEAD MOTOR INN [MOT] *Rockport, MA*
TURNPIKE MOTEL [MOT] *Kennebunk, ME*
TWILITE MOTEL [MOT] *Ellsworth, ME*
TWIN FARMS [BB] *Woodstock, VT*
TWO TREES INN [MOT] *Mystic, CT*
TYLER PLACE FAMILY RESORT [RST] *Swanton, VT*
UNIVERSITY MOTOR INN [MOT] *Orono, ME*
VALHALLA INN [MOT] *Thunder Bay, ON*
VALHALLA INN [MOT] *Toronto, ON*
VALLEY INN & TAVERN [RST] *Waterville Valley, NH*
VAL ROC MOTEL [MOT] *Killington, VT*
VERMONTER MOTOR LODGE [MOT] *Bennington, VT*
VERMONT INN [BB] *Killington, VT*
VICTORIA INN [MOT] *Thunder Bay, ON*
VICTORIAN BY THE SEA, THE [BB] *Camden, ME*
VICTORIAN INN [MOT] *Stratford, ON*
VICTORIAN LADIES INN [BB] *Newport, RI*
VICTORIA'S HISTORIC INN [BB] *Grand Pre, NS*
VIKING MOTOR INN [MOT] *Brunswick, ME*
VIKING SHORES RESORT [MOT] *Eastham (Cape Cod), MA*
VILLA BED & BREAKFAST [BB] *Westerly, RI*
VILLAGE BY THE SEA [AS] *Wells, ME*
VILLAGE COUNTRY INN [BB] *Manchester &
    Manchester Center, VT*
VILLAGE COVE INN [MOT] *Kennebunkport, ME*
VILLAGE GREEN MOTEL & COTTAGES [MOT] *Wells, ME*
VILLAGE INN, THE [BB] *Lenox, MA*
VILLAGE INN [MOT] *Narragansett, RI*
VILLAGE INN [BB] *Sandwich (Cape Cod), MA*
VILLAGER MOTEL [MOT] *Bar Harbor, ME*
VISTA MOTEL [MOT] *Gloucester, MA*
VOYAGEUR [MOT] *Yarmouth, NS*
VOYAGEUR'S GUEST HOUSE [BB] *Ottawa , ON*
WACHUSETT VILLAGE INN [CONF] *Leominster, MA*
WAITSFIELD INN, THE [BB] *Waitsfield, VT*
WAKE ROBIN INN [BB] *Lakeville, CT*
WALKER HOUSE [BB] *Lenox, MA*
WALPER TERRACE [HOT] *Kitchener-Waterloo, ON*
WANDLYN INN [MOT] *Fredericton, NB*
WANDLYN INN [MOT] *Grand Pre, NS*
WANDLYN INN HALIFAX [MOT] *Halifax, NS*
WATERCREST COTTAGES & MOTEL [CC] *Wells, ME*
WATERFORD INN [BB] *Norway, ME*
WATERLOO INN [MOT] *Kitchener-Waterloo, ON*
WATERMARK INN [AS] *Provincetown (Cape Cod), MA*
WATER'S EDGE MOTEL, THE [MOT] *Boothbay Harbor, ME*

WATER'S EDGE RESORT AND CONFERENCE CENTER [RST] *Old Saybrook, CT*
WATERSHIP INN [BB] *Provincetown (Cape Cod), MA*
WAUWINET, THE [BB] *Nantucket Island, MA*
WAVERLEY INN [BB] *Halifax, NS*
WAYBURY INN [BB] *Middlebury, VT*
WAYFARER INN [MOT] *Manchester, NH*
WAYSIDE [BB] *Littleton, NH*
WEATHERVANE HOTEL [MOT] *Manchester & Manchester Center, VT*
WEDGEWOOD MOTEL [MOT] *Manchester & Manchester Center, VT*
WELLESLEY INN ON THE SQUARE [MOT] *Wellesley, MA*
WELLFLEET MOTEL & LODGE [MOT] *Wellfleet, MA*
WELLS-MOODY MOTEL [MOT] *Wells, ME*
WENTWORTH RESORT HOTEL [HOT] *Jackson, NH*
WEQUASSETT INN [RST] *Chatham (Cape Cod), MA*
WEST DENNIS MOTOR LODGE [MOT] *Dennis (Cape Cod), MA*
WEST DOVER INN [BB] *West Dover, VT*
WESTFORD REGENCY INN [HOT] *Lowell, MA*
WESTIN [HOT] *Providence, RI*
WESTIN [HOT] *Waltham, MA*
WESTIN COPLEY PLACE HOTEL [HOT] *Boston, MA*
WESTIN HARBOR CASTLE [HOT] *Toronto, ON*
WESTIN NOVA SCOTIAN [HOT] *Halifax, NS*
WESTIN OTTAWA, THE [HOT] *Ottawa, ON*
WESTIN PRINCE [HOT] *Toronto, ON*
WESTIN RESORT, TREMBLANT [RST] *Montréal, QC*
WESTIN STAMFORD, THE [HOT] *Stamford, CT*
WEST LANE INN [BB] *Ridgefield, CT*
WEST MAIN LODGE [MOT] *Newport, RI*
WESTON HOUSE BED & BREAKFAST [BB] *Eastport, ME*
WESTPORT INN [HOT] *Westport, CT*
WHALER'S INN [BB] *Mystic, CT*
WHARF COTTAGES [MOT] *Nantucket Island, MA*
WHEATLEIGH HOTEL [HOT] *Lenox, MA*
WHETSTONE INN [BB] *Marlboro, VT*
WHISTLER'S INN [BB] *Lenox, MA*
WHITE BARN INN, THE [BB] *Kennebunkport, ME*
WHITE CEDAR INN [BB] *Freeport, ME*
WHITE ELEPHANT RESORT [HOT] *Nantucket Island, MA*
WHITE GATES INN [MOT] *Rockland, ME*
WHITE GOOSE INN [BB] *Hanover, NH*
WHITEHALL INN [BB] *Camden, ME*
WHITE HORSE INN [BB] *Waitsfield, VT*
WHITE HOUSE OF WILMINGTON [BB] *Wilmington, VT*
WHITE MOUNTAIN HOTEL & RESORT [RST] *North Conway, NH*
WHITE OAKS CONFERENCE RESORT AND SPA [MOT] *Niagara-on-the-Lake, ON*
WHITE TRELLIS MOTEL [MOT] *North Conway, NH*
WHITE WIND INN [BB] *Provincetown (Cape Cod), MA*
WILBURTON INN [BB] *Manchester & Manchester Center, VT*
WILDER HOMESTEAD INN [BB] *Weston, VT*
WILDERNESS INN BED & BREAKFAST [BB] *Lincoln/North Woodstock, NH*
WILDFLOWER INN [BB] *Falmouth (Cape Cod), MA*
WILDFLOWER INN, THE [BB] *Lyndonville, VT*
WILLIAMS GRANT INN [BB] *Bristol, RI*
WILLIAMS INN [HOT] *Williamstown, MA*

WILLIAMSVILLE INN [BB] *Stockbridge and West Stockbridge, MA*
WILLOW BEND MOTEL [MOT] *Truro, NS*
WILLOW OF NEWPORT ROMANTIC INN, THE [BB] *Newport, RI*
WILSON INN [AS] *Burlington, VT*
WINDFLOWER INN [BB] *Great Barrington, MA*
WINDHAM HILL INN [BB] *Newfane, VT*
WINDING BROOK...A CLASSIC MOUNTAIN LODGE [BB] *Stowe, VT*
WINDJAMMER [MOT] *Peggy's Cove, NS*
WINDSOR ARMS HOTEL [HOT] *Toronto, ON*
WINDSOR HOUSE [BB] *Newburyport, MA*
WINGS HILL INN [BB] *Augusta, ME*
WINNAPAUG INN [RST] *Westerly, RI*
WINSLOW HOUSE [BB] *Woodstock, VT*
WISCASSET MOTOR LODGE [MOT] *Wiscasset, ME*
WOLFEBORO INN, THE [BB] *Wolfeboro, NH*
WONDERVIEW COTTAGES [MOT] *Belfast, ME*
WONDER VIEW INN [MOT] *Bar Harbor, ME*
WOODSTOCKER BED AND BREAKFAST [BB] *Woodstock, VT*
WOODSTOCK INN [BB] *Lincoln/North Woodstock, NH*
WOODSTOCK INN & RESORT [RST] *Woodstock, VT*
WOODWARD RESORT [RST] *Lincoln/North Woodstock, NH*
WYCHMERE VILLAGE [MOT] *Harwich (Cape Cod), MA*
WYNDHAM [HOT] *Andover and North Andover, MA*
WYNDHAM BILLERICA [HOT] *Bedford, MA*
WYNDHAM BRISTOL PLACE [HOT] *Toronto, ON*
WYNDHAM CHELSEA [HOT] *Boston, MA*
WYNDHAM MONTREAL [HOT] *Montréal, QC*
WYNDHAM WESTBOROUGH [HOT] *Framingham, MA*
XV BEACON [HOT] *Boston, MA*
YACHTSMAN LODGE & MARINA [MOT] *Kennebunkport, ME*
YANKEE CLIPPER INN [BB] *Rockport, MA*
YANKEE HOME COMFORT, THE [MOT] *Lenox, MA*
YANKEE PEDLAR INN [BB] *Holyoke, MA*
YARDARM MOTEL [MOT] *Searsport, ME*
YARMOUTH RESORT [RST] *South Yarmouth (Cape Cod), MA*
YE OLDE ENGLAND INNE [BB] *Stowe, VT*
YORK COMMONS INN [MOT] *York, ME*
YORK HARBOR INN [BB] *York, ME*

RESTAURANT LIST

Establishment names are listed in alphabetical order followed by a symbol identifying their classification and then city and state. The symbols for classification are: [RES] for Restaurants and [URD] for Unrated Dining Spots.

124 COTTAGE STREET [RES] *Bar Harbor, ME*
1640 HART HOUSE [RES] *Ipswich, MA*
176 MAIN [RES] *Keene, NH*
1785 INN [RES] *North Conway, NH*
1896 HOUSE [RES] *Williamstown, MA*
21 FEDERAL [RES] *Nantucket Island, MA*
360 [RES] *Toronto, ON*
500 BLAKE ST [RES] *New Haven, CT*
ABBICCI [RES] *South Yarmouth (Cape Cod), MA*
ACCENTS [RES] *Toronto, ON*
ACCOLADE [RES] *Toronto, ON*
ADESSO [RES] *Providence, RI*
ADRIAN'S [RES] *Truro and North Truro (Cape Cod), MA*
AESOP'S TABLES [RES] *Wellfleet, MA*
A.J.'S [RES] *White River Junction, VT*
ALDARIO'S [RES] *Milford, CT*
ALEIA'S [RES] *Old Saybrook, CT*
AL FORNO [RES] *Providence, RI*
ALFREDO, WEINSTEIN AND HO [RES] *Halifax, NS*
ALISSON'S [RES] *Kennebunkport, ME*
AMBROSIA ON HUNTINGTON [RES] *Boston, MA*
AMERICAN SEASONS [RES] *Nantucket Island, MA*
ANAGO [RES] *Boston, MA*
ANCASTER OLD MILL INN [RES] *Hamilton, ON*
ANDIAMO [RES] *Greenfield, MA*
ANDREW'S HARBORSIDE [RES] *Boothbay Harbor, ME*
ANTHONY'S PIER 4 [RES] *Boston, MA*
ANTIPASTO [RES] *St. Jovite, QC*
APPLE TREE [RES] *Lenox, MA*
APRICOT'S [RES] *Farmington, CT*
AQUITAINE [RES] *Boston, MA*
ARKADIA HOUSE [RES] *Toronto, ON*
ARLEQUIN [RES] *Toronto, ON*
ARLINGTON INN [RES] *Arlington, VT*
ARMANDO'S [RES] *Ellsworth, ME*
ARROW'S [RES] *Ogunquit, ME*
ARUNDEL WHARF [RES] *Kennebunkport, ME*
ATLANTIC CAFE [RES] *Nantucket Island, MA*
AUBERGE DU POMMIER [RES] *Toronto, ON*
AUBERGE HANDFIELD [RES] *Montréal, QC*
AUBERGE SAUVIGNON [RES] *Mont Tremblant Provincial Park, QC*
AU CAFE SUISSE [RES] *Quebec City, QC*
AUJOURD'HUI [RES] *Boston, MA*
AUNT LUCY'S [RES] *Kingston, ON*
AU PETIT EXTRA [RES] *Montréal, QC*
AUSTRIAN INN [RES] *Yarmouth, NS*
AU TOURNANT DE LA RIVIERE [URD] *Montréal, QC*
AUX ANCIENS CANADIENS [RES] *Quebec City, QC*
AUX CHANTIGNOLES [RES] *Ottawa, ON*
AVALON [RES] *Toronto, ON*

AVON OLD FARMS INN [RES] *Avon, CT*
BACK BAY GRILL [RES] *Portland, ME*
BACKSTREET LANDING [RES] *Damariscotta, ME*
BACO RESTAURANT AND WINE BAR [RES] *Ottawa, ON*
BANGKOK GARDEN [RES] *Toronto, ON*
BARJO [RES] *Norway, ME*
BARLEY NECK INN [RES] *Orleans (Cape Cod), MA*
BARNACLE BILLY'S [RES] *Ogunquit, ME*
BARNARD INN [RES] *Woodstock, VT*
BARNHOUSE TAVERN RESTAURANT [RES] *Sebago Lake, ME*
BARNSTABLE TAVERN AND GRILLE [RES] *Barnstable (Cape Cod), MA*
BAROOTES [RES] *Toronto, ON*
BARROWS HOUSE INN [RES] *Dorset, VT*
BARTLEY'S DOCKSIDE DINING [RES] *Kennebunkport, ME*
BASS [RES] *Warren, VT*
BAY TOWER [RES] *Boston, MA*
BEAL'S LOBSTER PIER [URD] *Southwest Harbor, ME*
BEAVER CLUB, THE [RES] *Montréal, QC*
BEDFORD VILLAGE INN [RES] *Manchester, NH*
BEE AND THISTLE INN [RES] *Old Lyme, CT*
BELLINI'S [RES] *North Conway, NH*
BELVEDERE ROOM, THE [RES] *Kennebunkport, ME*
BENJAMIN'S [RES] *Kitchener-Waterloo, ON*
BENNINGTON STATION [RES] *Bennington, VT*
BEN'S DELICATESSEN [URD] *Montréal, QC*
BENTLEY'S [RES] *Woodstock, VT*
BEVERLY DEPOT [RES] *Beverly, MA*
BIAGIO [RES] *Toronto, ON*
BIBA [RES] *Boston, MA*
BICE RISTORANTE [RES] *Montréal, QC*
BIDDLE'S JAZZ AND RIBS [URD] *Montréal, QC*
BIG G'S DELI [URD] *Waterville, ME*
BILLY'S ETC [RES] *Ogunquit, ME*
BISHOP'S [RES] *Lawrence, MA*
BISHOP'S TERRACE [RES] *Harwich (Cape Cod), MA*
BISTANGO [RES] *Quebec City, QC*
BISTRO 990 [RES] *Toronto, ON*
BISTRO A CHAMPLAIN [RES] *Montréal, QC*
BLACK HORSE TAVERN [RES] *Bridgton, ME*
BLACK ROCK CASTLE [RES] *Bridgeport, CT*
BLACKSMITH SHOP RESTAURANT [RES] *Truro and North Truro (Cape Cod), MA*
BLACK SWAN [RES] *Manchester & Manchester Center, VT*
BLANTYRE [RES] *Lenox, MA*
BLUE GINGER [RES] *Wellesley, MA*
BLUE ROOM [RES] *Cambridge, MA*
BOARDING HOUSE [RES] *Nantucket Island, MA*
BOBA [RES] *Toronto, ON*
BOBBY BYRNE'S PUB [RES] *Sandwich (Cape Cod), MA*
BOB THE CHEF'S [RES] *Boston, MA*

BOMBAY CLUB [RES] *Cambridge, MA*
BOONE'S [RES] *Portland, ME*
BOULDERS [RES] *New Preston, CT*
BRACKETT'S OCEANIEW [RES] *Rockport, MA*
BRAMBLE INN [RES] *Brewster (Cape Cod), MA*
BRANNIGAN'S [RES] *Meriden, CT*
BRASSERIE JO [RES] *Boston, MA*
BRAVO BRAVO [RES] *Mystic, CT*
BREAKWATER INN [RES] *Kennebunkport, ME*
BRIDGE RESTAURANT [RES] *Sandwich (Cape Cod), MA*
BRISTOL LOUNGE [RES] *Boston, MA*
BROWN SUGAR CAFE [RES] *Boston, MA*
BUMPKINS [RES] *Toronto, ON*
BUTTERFLY [RES] *Hartford, CT*
BUTTERY THEATRE [RES] *Niagara-on-the-Lake, ON*
CAFE ALLEGRE [RES] *Madison, CT*
CAFE DE PARIS [RES] *Montréal, QC*
CAFE DE PARIS [RES] *Quebec City, QC*
CAFE EDWIGE [RES] *Provincetown (Cape Cod), MA*
CAFE FLEURI [RES] *Boston, MA*
CAFE HENRY BURGER [RES] *Mont Tremblant
    Provincial Park, QC*
CAFE LOUIS [RES] *Boston, MA*
CAFE LUCIA [RES] *Lenox, MA*
CAFE MARLIAVE [RES] *Boston, MA*
CAFE SHELBURNE [RES] *Shelburne, VT*
CAFE STE. ALEXANDRE [RES] *Montréal, QC*
CAFFE BELLA [RES] *Braintree, MA*
CAFI FERREIRA [RES] *Montréal, QC*
CAMERON'S [RES] *Gloucester, MA*
CANDLELIGHT [RES] *Skowhegan, ME*
CANFIELD HOUSE [RES] *Newport, RI*
CANNERY [RES] *Yarmouth, ME*
CANOE [RES] *Toronto, ON*
CAPE NEDDICK INN [RES] *York, ME*
CAPITAL GRILLE, THE [RES] *Boston, MA*
CAP'N TOBEY'S CHOWDER HOUSE [RES]
    Nantucket Island, MA
CAPRI [RES] *Niagara Falls, ON*
CAPTAIN LINNELL HOUSE [RES] *Orleans (Cape Cod), MA*
CAPTAIN NICK'S SEAFOOD HOUSE [RES] *Bangor, ME*
CAPTAIN SIMON'S GALLEY [RES] *Kittery, ME*
CAPTAIN WILLIAM'S HOUSE [RES] *Dennis (Cape Cod), MA*
CARBONE'S [RES] *Hartford, CT*
CARBUR'S [RES] *Burlington, VT*
CARMAN'S CLUB [RES] *Toronto, ON*
CAROLE PECK'S GOOD NEWS CAFE [RES] *Woodbury, CT*
CAROL'S [RES] *Lenox, MA*
CARRIAGES, THE [RES] *Niagara-on-the-Lake, ON*
CASA ROMERO [RES] *Boston, MA*
CASCADE INN [RES] *Saco, ME*
CASCADES LODGE [RES] *Killington, VT*
CASTLE [RES] *Worcester, MA*
CASTLE STREET CAFE [RES] *Great Barrington, MA*
CAVEY'S FRENCH RESTAURANT [RES] *Manchester, CT*
CAVEY'S ITALIAN RESTAURANT [RES] *Manchester, CT*
CENTRO GRILL & WINE BAR [RES] *Toronto, ON*
CHANTICLEER [RES] *Manchester & Manchester Center, VT*
CHANTICLEER [RES] *Nantucket Island, MA*
CHARCOAL STEAK HOUSE [RES] *Kitchener-Waterloo, ON*
CHARLEY'S [RES] *Boston, MA*

CHART HOUSE [RES] *Simsbury, CT*
CHATHAM SQUIRE [RES] *Chatham (Cape Cod), MA*
CHATHAM STREET GRILL [RES] *Windsor, ON*
CHEF'S TABLE [RES] *Montpelier, VT*
CHERRINGTON'S [RES] *Mississauga, ON*
CHERRY HILL HOUSE [RES] *Mississauga, ON*
CHEZ GEORGE [RES] *Montréal, QC*
CHEZ HENRI [RES] *Cambridge, MA*
CHEZ LA MERE MICHEL [RES] *Montréal, QC*
CHIADO [RES] *Toronto, ON*
CHIARO'S [RES] *Toronto, ON*
CHILE PEPPERS [RES] *Waterville Valley, NH*
CHILLINGSWORTH [RES] *Brewster (Cape Cod), MA*
CHINA BLOSSOM [RES] *Andover and North Andover, MA*
CHINA BY THE SEA [RES] *Boothbay Harbor, ME*
CHINA COURT [RES] *Yarmouth, NS*
CHRISTIAN'S [RES] *Chatham (Cape Cod), MA*
CHRISTIE'S OF NEWPORT [RES] *Newport, RI*
CHRISTINE'S [RES] *Dennis (Cape Cod), MA*
CHRISTMAS FARM INN [RES] *Jackson, NH*
CHRISTOS [RES] *Brockton, MA*
CHURCH RESTAURANT AND THE BELFRY, THE [RES]
    Stratford, ON
CHURCH STREET CAFE [RES] *Lenox, MA*
CIAO BELLA [RES] *Boston, MA*
CIAO CAFE AND WINE BAR [RES] *Danbury, CT*
CIOPPINO'S [RES] *Nantucket Island, MA*
CLAM SHELL [RES] *Littleton, NH*
CLAREMONT CAFE [RES] *Boston, MA*
CLAY HILL FARM [RES] *Ogunquit, ME*
CLIFF HOUSE [RES] *Stowe, VT*
CLIO [RES] *Boston, MA*
CLUB CAR [RES] *Nantucket Island, MA*
COACH HOUSE [RES] *Martha's Vineyard, MA*
COAST GUARD HOUSE [RES] *Narragansett, RI*
COBBLESTONES [RES] *Lowell, MA*
COBB'S MILL INN [RES] *Westport, CT*
COLBY HILL INN [RES] *Concord, NH*
COLONIAL INN [RES] *Concord, MA*
COMMON MAN [RES] *Holderness, NH*
COMMON MAN [RES] *Lincoln/North Woodstock, NH*
COMMON MAN, THE [RES] *Warren, VT*
COMPANY OF THE CAULDRON [RES] *Nantucket Island, MA*
CONNOLLY'S [RES] *Westport, CT*
CONSTANTINE'S [RES] *New London, CT*
COOK SHOP [RES] *Windsor, ON*
COOK'S LOBSTER HOUSE [RES] *Bailey Island, ME*
COONAMESSETT INN [RES] *Falmouth (Cape Cod), MA*
COPPER BEECH INN [RES] *Essex, CT*
CORK N' HEARTH [RES] *Lee, MA*
CORK RESTAURANT [RES] *Camden, ME*
CORNER HOUSE INN [RES] *Holderness, NH*
CORSICAN [RES] *Freeport, ME*
COUNTRY GOURMET [RES] *Nashua, NH*
COUNTRYMAN'S PLEASURE [RES] *Rutland, VT*
CRAB SHELL [RES] *Stamford, CT*
CREAMERY [RES] *St. Johnsbury, VT*
CURTIS HOUSE [RES] *Woodbury, CT*
DAILY PLANET [RES] *Burlington, VT*
DAKOTA [RES] *Avon, CT*
DAKOTA [RES] *Pittsfield, MA*

DALI [RES] *Cambridge, MA*
DANCING LOBSTER CAFE [RES] *Provincetown (Cape Cod), MA*
DANDELION INN [RES] *Burlington, MA*
DAN'L WEBSTER INN [RES] *Sandwich (Cape Cod), MA*
DARBY'S [RES] *Belfast, ME*
DAVID DUNCAN HOUSE [RES] *Toronto, ON*
DAVIDE [RES] *Boston, MA*
DAVID'S [RES] *Newburyport, MA*
DAVIO'S [RES] *Boston, MA*
DECKER-TEN [RES] *Mississauga, ON*
DEERFIELD INN [RES] *Deerfield, MA*
DELANY HOUSE [RES] *Holyoke, MA*
DI MILLO'S FLOATING RESTAURANT [RES] *Portland, ME*
DINING ROOM, THE [RES] *Boston, MA*
DOCK AND DINE [RES] *Old Saybrook, CT*
DOCKSIDE [RES] *York, ME*
DOCKSIDER [RES] *Northeast Harbor, ME*
DOCTOR'S HOUSE, THE [RES] *Toronto, ON*
DOG TEAM TAVERN [RES] *Middlebury, VT*
DOMUS CAFI [RES] *Ottawa, ON*
DONATELLO [RES] *Saugus, MA*
DORSET INN [RES] *Dorset, VT*
DOUBLE DRAGON INN [RES] *Orleans (Cape Cod), MA*
DRAGON LITE [RES] *Hyannis (Cape Cod), MA*
DUCK CREEKE TAVERN ROOM [RES] *Wellfleet, MA*
DURGIN PARK [RES] *Boston, MA*
DYNASTY CHINESE [RES] *Toronto, ON*
EAST COAST GRILL [RES] *Cambridge, MA*
EASTGATE [RES] *Littleton, NH*
EAST SIDE [RES] *New Britain, CT*
EASTSIDE GRILL [RES] *Northampton, MA*
EAST SIDE RESTAURANT AND PUB [RES] *Newport, VT*
EBB TIDE [RES] *Boothbay Harbor, ME*
EGG & I [RES] *Hyannis (Cape Cod), MA*
ELLAS [RES] *Toronto, ON*
ELMS, THE [RES] *Ridgefield, CT*
ELORA MILL [RES] *Kitchener-Waterloo, ON*
ESCABECHE [RES] *Niagara-on-the-Lake, ON*
FABYAN'S STATION [RES] *Bretton Woods, NH*
FAMOUS BILL'S [RES] *Greenfield, MA*
FANS COURT [RES] *Niagara-on-the-Lake, ON*
FAZIO'S ITALIAN [RES] *York, ME*
FEDERALIST, THE [RES] *Boston, MA*
FELLINI KOOLINI'S [RES] *London, ON*
FIFE'N DRUM [RES] *Kent, CT*
FIFTH, THE [RES] *Toronto, ON*
FILIPPO [RES] *Boston, MA*
FINN'S SEAFOOD [RES] *Block Island, RI*
FIRE AND ICE [RES] *Middlebury, VT*
FIREHOUSE ONE [RES] *Dover, NH*
FISHERMAN'S LANDING [URD] *Bar Harbor, ME*
FISHERMAN'S WHARF INN [RES] *Boothbay Harbor, ME*
FIVE FISHERMEN [RES] *Halifax, NS*
FLOOD TIDE [RES] *Mystic, CT*
FLYING BRIGE [RES] *Falmouth (Cape Cod), MA*
FORE STREET [RES] *Portland, ME*
FOUR BROTHERS [RES] *Niagara Falls, ON*
FOUR CHIMNEYS [RES] *Bennington, VT*
FOUR COLUMNS [RES] *Newfane, VT*
F. PARKER REIDY'S [RES] *Portland, ME*
FRANCONIA INN, THE [RES] *Franconia, NH*

FREDDIE'S ROUTE 66 [RES] *Bar Harbor, ME*
FREESTONE'S CITY GRILL [RES] *New Bedford, MA*
FRIENDS AND COMPANY [RES] *Madison, CT*
FRONT STREET [RES] *Provincetown (Cape Cod), MA*
FUNDY [RES] *Digby, NS*
GARLIC JOHN'S [RES] *Manchester & Manchester Center, VT*
GATEWAYS INN [RES] *Lenox, MA*
GATHERING, THE [RES] *Milford, CT*
GENE'S [RES] *Stratford, ON*
GEORGE'S [RES] *Bar Harbor, ME*
GINZA [RES] *Boston, MA*
GIOVANNI'S [RES] *Sault Ste. Marie, ON*
GIOVANNI'S [RES] *Stamford, CT*
GLENN'S GALLEY [RES] *Newburyport, MA*
GLOBE [RES] *Montréal, QC*
GLOUCESTER HOUSE RESTAURANT [RES] *Gloucester, MA*
GO FISH [RES] *Mystic, CT*
GOLDEN APPLE [RES] *Gananoque, ON*
GOLDEN SAILS CHINESE [RES] *Falmouth (Cape Cod), MA*
GORDI'S FISH & STEAK HOUSE [RES] *Lincoln/North Woodstock, NH*
GOVONI'S ITALIAN [RES] *Lincoln/North Woodstock, NH*
GRAND CHAU-CHOWS [RES] *Boston, MA*
GRANO [RES] *Toronto, ON*
GRAPE VINE [RES] *Salem, MA*
GRAZIE [RES] *Toronto, ON*
GREAT IMPASTA [RES] *Brunswick, ME*
GRENDEL'S DEN [RES] *Cambridge, MA*
GREY GULL [RES] *Wells, ME*
GRILL 23 & BAR [RES] *Boston, MA*
GRILL AT HOBBS BROOK [RES] *Waltham, MA*
GRISSINI [RES] *Kennebunk, ME*
GRISWOLD INN [RES] *Essex, CT*
GRITTY MCDUFF'S [RES] *Freeport, ME*
GROG, THE [RES] *Newburyport, MA*
GRUBSTAKE [RES] *Fortress of Louisbourg National Historic Site, NS*
GUILD INN [RES] *Toronto, ON*
GYPSY SWEETHEARTS [RES] *Ogunquit, ME*
HAMERSLEY'S BISTRO [RES] *Boston, MA*
HANCOCK INN [RES] *Peterborough, NH*
HANNAH JACK TAVERN [RES] *Nashua, NH*
HAPPY SEVEN [RES] *Toronto, ON*
HARBOR POINT [RES] *Barnstable (Cape Cod), MA*
HARBOR VIEW [RES] *Rockland, ME*
HARDCOVER, THE [RES] *Danvers, MA*
HARRY'S CAFE [RES] *Ludlow, VT*
HARTNESS HOUSE INN [RES] *Springfield, VT*
HART'S TURKEY FARM [RES] *Meredith, NH*
HARVEST [RES] *Cambridge, MA*
HAYLOFT [RES] *Wells, ME*
HEARTH, THE [RES] *Danbury, CT*
HEARTH AND KETTLE [RES] *Plymouth, MA*
HELM, THE [RES] *Camden, ME*
HELMAND [RES] *Cambridge, MA*
HEMENWAY'S SEAFOOD GRILL [RES] *Providence, RI*
HEMINGWAY'S [RES] *Killington, VT*
HEMISPHERES [RES] *Toronto, ON*
HENRIETTA'S TABLE [RES] *Cambridge, MA*
HERITAGE HOUSE [RES] *Skowhegan, ME*
HERMITAGE [RES] *Wilmington, VT*
HERM'S [RES] *Greenfield, MA*

HICKORY STICK FARM [RES] *Laconia, NH*
HILLTOP HOUSE [RES] *Ellsworth, ME*
HILLTOP STEAK HOUSE [RES] *Saugus, MA*
HOFBRAUHAUS [RES] *Springfield, MA*
HOME PORT [RES] *Martha's Vineyard, MA*
HOME PORT INN [RES] *Lubec, ME*
HOPKINS INN [RES] *New Preston, CT*
HORIZON'S [RES] *Sandwich (Cape Cod), MA*
HORSE & HOUND [RES] *Franconia, NH*
HORSEFEATHERS [RES] *North Conway, NH*
HOTEL MANISSES DINING ROOM [RES] *Block Island, RI*
HOT TOMATOES [RES] *Hartford, CT*
HOUSE OF GENE [RES] *Stratford, ON*
HOWE'S COTTAGE [RES] *South Yarmouth (Cape Cod), MA*
HUNGRY I, THE [RES] *Boston, MA*
HURRICANE [RES] *Ogunquit, ME*
ICARUS [RES] *Boston, MA*
ICE HOUSE [RES] *Burlington, VT*
IDLE OARS [RES] *Cavendish, PE*
IL CAPRICCIO [RES] *Waltham, MA*
IL CORTILE [RES] *Montréal, QC*
IL FALCO [RES] *Stamford, CT*
IL POSTO NUOVO [RES] *Toronto, ON*
IMPUDENT OYSTER [RES] *Chatham (Cape Cod), MA*
INAHO-JAPANESE RESTAURANT [RES] *South Yarmouth (Cape Cod), MA*
INDIA HOUSE [RES] *Nantucket Island, MA*
INDOCHINE PAVILLION [RES] *New Haven, CT*
INN AT SAW MILL FARM , THE [RES] *West Dover, VT*
INN AT THORN HILL [RES] *Jackson, NH*
INN AT WESTVIEW FARM [RES] *Dorset, VT*
ISLAND CHOWDER HOUSE [RES] *Bar Harbor, ME*
ISLE DE FRANCE [RES] *Stowe, VT*
ITALIAN OASIS [RES] *Littleton, NH*
IVANHOE [RES] *Springfield, MA*
JACOB MARLEY'S [RES] *Newburyport, MA*
JACQUES BISTRO DUPARC [RES] *Toronto, ON*
JADE PALACE [RES] *Caribou, ME*
JAE'S CAFE AND GRILL [RES] *Boston, MA*
JAMESON TAVERN [RES] *Freeport, ME*
JAMIE KENNEDY AT THE ROME [RES] *Toronto, ON*
JARED'S [RES] *Nantucket Island, MA*
JEAN-LOUIS [RES] *Greenwich, CT*
JESSE'S [RES] *Hanover, NH*
JIGGER JOHNSON'S [RES] *Plymouth, NH*
JIMMY'S HARBORSIDE [RES] *Boston, MA*
JODI'S COUNTRY CAFE [RES] *Great Barrington, MA*
JOHN ANDREW'S RESTAURANT [RES] *Great Barrington, MA*
JOHN MARTIN'S MANOR [RES] *Waterville, ME*
JOLLY BUTCHER'S [RES] *Brattleboro, VT*
JONATHAN'S [RES] *Blue Hill, ME*
JONATHAN'S [RES] *Ogunquit, ME*
JORDAN POND HOUSE [RES] *Northeast Harbor, ME*
JOSO'S [RES] *Toronto, ON*
J. P. DANIELS [RES] *Mystic, CT*
JULIEN [RES] *Boston, MA*
KALLY'S [RES] *Toronto, ON*
KASHMIR [RES] *Boston, MA*
KATSURA MONTREAL [RES] *Montréal, QC*
KEDRON VALLEY [RES] *Woodstock, VT*
KEG, THE [RES] *Thunder Bay, ON*

KENNEBUNK INN, THE [RES] *Kennebunk, ME*
KENSINGTON [RES] *Norwich, CT*
KERNWOOD [RES] *Lynnfield, MA*
KEYSTONE ALLEY CAFE [RES] *Stratford, ON*
KING'S ROOK [RES] *Marblehead, MA*
KRISTINA'S [RES] *Bath, ME*
LA BONICHE [RES] *Lowell, MA*
LA BRETAGNE [RES] *Stamford, CT*
LA CASTILE [RES] *Mississauga, ON*
LA CAVERNE GREQUE [RES] *Montréal, QC*
LAFAYETTE HOUSE [RES] *Foxboro, MA*
LA FENICE [RES] *Toronto, ON*
LA FORGE CASINO [RES] *Newport, RI*
LA FOURCHETTE FOLLE [RES] *Mont Tremblant Provincial Park, QC*
LA GAUDRIOLE [RES] *Montréal, QC*
LA GONDOLA [RES] *Ottawa, ON*
LA GROCERIA [RES] *Cambridge, MA*
LA HACIENDA [RES] *Stamford, CT*
LAI WAH HEEN [RES] *Toronto, ON*
LALA ROKH [RES] *Boston, MA*
L'ALOUETTE [RES] *Harwich (Cape Cod), MA*
LA LOUISIANE [RES] *Montréal, QC*
LALOUX [RES] *Montréal, QC*
LA MAISON SERGE BRUYERE [RES] *Quebec City, QC*
LA MAREE [RES] *Montréal, QC*
LA MIRAGE [RES] *New Haven, CT*
LANDFALL [RES] *Woods Hole, MA*
LANGDON HALL [RES] *Kitchener-Waterloo, ON*
LA PETITE AUBERGE [RES] *Newport, RI*
LA PLACE RENDEZ-VOUS [RES] *Fort Frances, ON*
LA RAPIERE [RES] *Montréal, QC*
LARCHWOOD INN [RES] *Kingston, RI*
LA RIPAILLE [RES] *Quebec City, QC*
LA SAUVAGINE [URD] *Montréal, QC*
LAS PALMAS [RES] *Ottawa, ON*
L'ASTRAL [RES] *Quebec City, QC*
LAURIE RAPHAEL [RES] *Quebec City, QC*
L'EAU A LA BOUCHE [RES] *Montréal, QC*
LE BACCARA [RES] *Ottawa, ON*
LE BISTRO [RES] *Newport, RI*
LE BONAPARTE [RES] *Quebec City, QC*
LE BON COIN [RES] *New Preston, CT*
LE CAFE [RES] *Ottawa, ON*
LE CAFE FLEURI [RES] *Montréal, QC*
LE CHAMPLAIN [RES] *Quebec City, QC*
LE CHRYSANTHEME [RES] *Montréal, QC*
LE CONTINENTAL [RES] *Quebec City, QC*
LEESIDE [RES] *Woods Hole, MA*
LEGAL SEAFOODS [RES] *Danvers, MA*
LEGAL SEAFOODS [RES] *Newton, MA*
LEGAL SEAFOODS [RES] *Warwick, RI*
LE GARAGE [RES] *Wiscasset, ME*
LE GASCON [RES] *Mont Tremblant Provincial Park, QC*
LE GRENIER FRENCH RESTAURANT [RES] *Martha's Vineyard, MA*
LE JARDIN [RES] *Williamstown, MA*
LE JARDIN DE PANOS [RES] *Montréal, QC*
LE KEG/BRANDY'S [RES] *Montréal, QC*
LE LANGUEDOC [RES] *Nantucket Island, MA*
LE LUTETIA [RES] *Montréal, QC*

LE MAISTRE [RES] *Montréal, QC*
LE MANOIR DU SPAGHETTI [RES] *Quebec City, QC*
LE MAS DES OLIVIERS [RES] *Montréal, QC*
LE MITOYEN [RES] *Montréal, QC*
LE MUSCADIN [RES] *Montréal, QC*
LENOX 218 RESTAURANT [RES] *Lenox, MA*
LENOX HOUSE [RES] *Lenox, MA*
LE PAILLEUR [RES] *Quebec City, QC*
LE PAPILLION [RES] *Toronto, ON*
LE PARADIS [RES] *Toronto, ON*
LE PARCHEMIN [RES] *Montréal, QC*
LE PARIS [RES] *Montréal, QC*
LE PASSE-PARTOUT [RES] *Montréal, QC*
LE PIEMONTAIS [RES] *Montréal, QC*
LE PIMENT ROUGE [RES] *Montréal, QC*
L'ERMITAGE [RES] *Bucksport, ME*
LE SAINT-AMOUR [RES] *Quebec City, QC*
LES CAPRICES DE NICOLAS [RES] *Montréal, QC*
LES CONTINENTS [RES] *Montréal, QC*
LE SHACK [RES] *Mont Tremblant Provincial Park, QC*
LES HALLES [RES] *Montréal, QC*
L'ESPALIER [RES] *Boston, MA*
LES REMPARTS [RES] *Montréal, QC*
LE STE AMABLE [RES] *Montréal, QC*
LES TROIS TILLEULS [RES] *Montréal, QC*
LES ZYGOMATES [RES] *Boston, MA*
LE VENDOME [RES] *Quebec City, QC*
L'EXPRESS [RES] *Montréal, QC*
LILAC INN [RES] *Brandon, VT*
LITCHFIELD'S [RES] *Wells, ME*
LOBSTER CLAW [RES] *Orleans (Cape Cod), MA*
LOBSTER COOKER [RES] *Freeport, ME*
LOBSTER POT [RES] *Barre, VT*
LOBSTER POT [RES] *Bristol, RI*
LOBSTER POT [RES] *Provincetown (Cape Cod), MA*
LOBSTER POUND [RES] *Camden, ME*
LOBSTER TREAT [RES] *Antigonish, NS*
LOCKE OBER [RES] *Boston, MA*
LOG CABIN DINER [RES] *Newport, ME*
LOG CABIN RESTAURANT AND LOUNGE [RES] *Clinton, CT*
L'OMELETTE [RES] *Quebec City, QC*
LONGFELLOW'S [RES] *Kingfield, ME*
LONGFELLOW'S WAYSIDE INN [RES] *Sudbury Center, MA*
L'ORCHIDEE DE CHINE [RES] *Montréal, QC*
LORD'S HARBORSIDE [RES] *Wells, ME*
LOUIS' TISBURY CAFE [RES] *Martha's Vineyard, MA*
LOVETT'S INN BY LAFAYETTE BROOK [RES] *Franconia, NH*
LUCIA [RES] *Boston, MA*
LUMIERE [RES] *Newton, MA*
LYCEUM [RES] *Salem, MA*
MABEL'S LOBSTER CLAW [RES] *Kennebunkport, ME*
MADELYN'S DINER [RES] *Stratford, ON*
MAGGIE'S CLASSIC SCALES [RES] *Bar Harbor, ME*
MAINE DINER [RES] *Wells, ME*
MAINE DINING ROOM, THE [RES] *Freeport, ME*
MAIN STREET GRILL AND BAR [RES] *Montpelier, VT*
MAISON ROBERT [RES] *Boston, MA*
MAME'S [RES] *Meredith, NH*
MAMMA MARIA [RES] *Boston, MA*
MANOR ON GOLDEN POND [RES] *Holderness, NH*
MAPLES [RES] *Dover, NH*
MARBLEHEAD LANDING [RES] *Marblehead, MA*

MARBLE WORKS STEAKHOUSE [RES] *Ottawa, ON*
MARCHE BCE PLACE [RES] *Toronto, ON*
MARCUCCIO'S [RES] *Boston, MA*
MARGARITA'S [RES] *Orono, ME*
MARIENBAD [RES] *London, ON*
MARINA [RES] *Brattleboro, VT*
MARK ANTHONY'S YE OLDE TAVERN [RES] *Manchester & Manchester Center, VT*
MARLA JANE'S [RES] *London, ON*
MARSHSIDE [RES] *Dennis (Cape Cod), MA*
MATIGNON [RES] *Toronto, ON*
MATTAKEESE WHARF [RES] *Barnstable (Cape Cod), MA*
MAURICE RESTAURANT FRANCAIS [RES] *Norway, ME*
MAX DOWNTOWN [RES] *Hartford, CT*
MEDITERRANEO GRILL & WINE BAR [RES] *Montréal, QC*
MEERA INDIAN CUISINE [RES] *Stamford, CT*
MERCER STREET GRILL [RES] *Toronto, ON*
MESON GALICIA [RES] *Norwalk, CT*
METRO [RES] *Portsmouth, NH*
METROPOLIS CAFE [RES] *Boston, MA*
MICHAEL'S [RES] *Stockbridge and West Stockbridge, MA*
MICHAEL'S HARBORSIDE [RES] *Newburyport, MA*
MICHAEL'S-ON-THE-THAMES [RES] *London, ON*
MIGUEL'S MEXICAN [RES] *Bar Harbor, ME*
MIKADO [RES] *Montréal, QC*
MILL, THE [RES] *Ottawa, ON*
MILLCROFT INN [RES] *Toronto, ON*
MILLER'S [RES] *Bangor, ME*
MILLER'S COUNTRY FARE [RES] *Toronto, ON*
MILLERY, THE [RES] *Niagara Falls, ON*
MILLSTONE [RES] *New London, NH*
MIRAMAR [RES] *Westport, CT*
MISTER UP'S [RES] *Middlebury, VT*
MISTRAL [RES] *Boston, MA*
MISTURA [RES] *Toronto, ON*
MODERN [RES] *Nashua, NH*
MOHEGAN CAFE [RES] *Block Island, RI*
MOKUM [RES] *Montréal, QC*
MOLLY'S [RES] *Hanover, NH*
MONTANO'S [RES] *Truro and North Truro (Cape Cod), MA*
MONTE CARLO [RES] *Springfield, MA*
MOORING, THE [RES] *Newport, RI*
MORTON'S OF CHICAGO [RES] *Boston, MA*
MOTHER'S [RES] *Bethel, ME*
MOVENPICK OF SWITZERLAND [RES] *Toronto, ON*
MR D'S [RES] *Franklin, NH*
MUSKY SUPPER HOUSE [RES] *Mississauga, ON*
MYSTIC PIZZA [RES] *Mystic, CT*
NAPI'S [RES] *Provincetown (Cape Cod), MA*
NATHANIEL PORTER INN [RES] *Bristol, RI*
NAUSET BEACH CLUB [RES] *Orleans (Cape Cod), MA*
NAVIGATOR, THE [RES] *Martha's Vineyard, MA*
NEW GLASGOW LOBSTER SUPPER [RES] *Cavendish, PE*
NEWICK'S [RES] *Nashua, NH*
NEWICK'S FISHERMAN'S LANDING [RES] *Hampton Beach, NH*
NEWICK'S SEAFOOD [RES] *Dover, NH*
NEWICK'S SEAFOOD [RES] *Portland, ME*
NEW LONDON INN [RES] *New London, NH*
NEW MARCONI [RES] *Sault Ste. Marie, ON*
NIKKI'S [RES] *Ludlow, VT*
NISTICO'S RED BARN [RES] *Westport, CT*

NO. 9 PARK [RES] *Boston, MA*
NORTH 44 DEGREES [RES] *Toronto, ON*
NORTH HERO HOUSE [RES] *North Hero, VT*
NUANCES [RES] *Montréal, QC*
OAK ROOM, THE [RES] *Boston, MA*
OARWEED COVE [RES] *Ogunquit, ME*
OGUNQUIT LOBSTER POUND [RES] *Ogunquit, ME*
OLD BARBER HOUSE [RES] *Mississauga, ON*
OLD CUTTER INN [RES] *Lyndonville, VT*
OLDE HOUSE [RES] *Sebago Lake, ME*
OLDE SCHOOL RESTAURANT [RES] *Brantford, ON*
OLD GRIST MILL TAVERN [RES] *Providence, RI*
OLD JAILHOUSE TAVERN [RES] *Orleans (Cape Cod), MA*
OLD LYME INN [RES] *Old Lyme, CT*
OLD MANSE INN AND RESTAURANT [RES] *Brewster
       (Cape Cod), MA*
OLD MILL, THE [RES] *Great Barrington, MA*
OLD MILL [RES] *Toronto, ON*
OLD NEWFANE [RES] *Newfane, VT*
OLD PRUNE [RES] *Stratford, ON*
OLD SPAGHETTI FACTORY [RES] *Toronto, ON*
OLD STORROWTON TAVERN [RES] *Springfield, MA*
OLD TIMBERMILL PUB & RESTAURANT [RES]
       Lincoln/North Woodstock, NH
OLD VILLAGE INN [RES] *Ogunquit, ME*
OLIVER'S RESTAURANT & PUB [RES] *Franklin, NH*
OLIVES [RES] *Boston, MA*
ONE-WAY FARE [RES] *Simsbury, CT*
OPUS [RES] *Toronto, ON*
OPUS II [RES] *Montréal, QC*
ORCHARDS, THE [RES] *Williamstown, MA*
ORIGINAL GOURMET BRUNCH [RES] *Hyannis
       (Cape Cod), MA*
ORO [RES] *Toronto, ON*
OUTRIGGER STEAK AND SEAFOOD [RES] *Mississauga, ON*
OXFORD HOUSE INN [RES] *Center Lovell, ME*
PADDOCK [RES] *Hyannis (Cape Cod), MA*
PADDY'S PUB AND BREWERY [RES] *Grand Pre, NS*
PAINTED LADY [RES] *Great Barrington, MA*
PALM [RES] *Boston, MA*
PANDA HOUSE CHINESE RESTAURANT [RES] *Lenox, MA*
PANGAEA [RES] *Toronto, ON*
PAPARAZZI [RES] *Truro and North Truro (Cape Cod), MA*
PARKER'S [RES] *Boston, MA*
PARTRIDGE INN SEAFOOD RESTAURANT [RES] *Stowe, VT*
PASTA NOSTRA [RES] *Norwalk, CT*
PASTA SHOP [RES] *Windsor, ON*
PASTIS [RES] *Hartford, CT*
PASTIS [RES] *Toronto, ON*
PATACHOU [URD] *Toronto, ON*
PAULINE'S [RES] *Burlington, VT*
PEACH'S [URD] *North Conway, NH*
PELLINO'S [RES] *Marblehead, MA*
PENGUINS SEA GRILL [RES] *Hyannis (Cape Cod), MA*
PEOPLE'S CHOICE [RES] *Rangeley, ME*
PEPPERCORN'S GRILL [RES] *Hartford, CT*
PERRY'S FISH HOUSE [RES] *Burlington, VT*
PETER OTT'S [RES] *Camden, ME*
PIER [RES] *Newport, RI*
PIER 4 STOREHOUSE [RES] *Toronto, ON*
PIER II [RES] *Portsmouth, NH*

PIGNOLI [RES] *Boston, MA*
PILOTS GRILL [RES] *Bangor, ME*
PIZZA MELLA [URD] *Montréal, QC*
PIZZATERIA [RES] *Mont Tremblant Provincial Park, QC*
PLAZA III KANSAS CITY STEAK [RES] *Boston, MA*
POLLY'S PANCAKE PARLOR [RES] *Franconia, NH*
POOR RICHARD'S TAVERN [RES] *Ogunquit, ME*
POT AU FEU [RES] *Providence, RI*
POTTER PLACE INN [RES] *New London, NH*
PREGO [RES] *Toronto, ON*
PRIMADONNA [RES] *Montréal, QC*
PRIMO [RES] *Rockland, ME*
PRINCE AND THE PAUPER [RES] *Woodstock, VT*
PRINCE ARTHUR STEAK AND SEAFOOD HOUSE [RES]
       Yarmouth, NS
PRINCE PLACE [RES] *Jackson, NH*
PRONTO [RES] *Toronto, ON*
PROVENCE [RES] *Ogunquit, ME*
PROVENCE [RES] *Toronto, ON*
PUB, THE [RES] *Keene, NH*
PUBLICK HOUSE [RES] *Sturbridge, MA*
PUBLYK HOUSE [RES] *Bennington, VT*
PURITAN BACKROOM [RES] *Manchester, NH*
PUTNEY INN, THE [RES] *Brattleboro, VT*
QUARTER DECK [RES] *Bar Harbor, ME*
QUARTIER [RES] *Toronto, ON*
QUECHEE INN AT MARSHLAND FARM [RES]
       Woodstock, VT
QUEENSTON HEIGHTS [RES] *Niagara Falls, ON*
QUELLI DELLA NOTTE [RES] *Montréal, QC*
QUEUE DE CHEVAL [RES] *Montréal, QC*
RABBIT HILL [RES] *St. Johnsbury, VT*
RADIUS [RES] *Boston, MA*
RANGELEY INN [RES] *Rangeley, ME*
READING ROOM [RES] *Bar Harbor, ME*
REDBONES [RES] *Cambridge, MA*
RED CLOVER [RES] *Killington, VT*
RED INN RESTAURANT [RES] *Provincetown (Cape Cod), MA*
RED LION, THE [RES] *Stockbridge and West Stockbridge, MA*
RED PARKA PUB [RES] *Jackson, NH*
RED PHEASANT INN [RES] *Dennis (Cape Cod), MA*
RED RAVEN'S LIMP NOODLE [RES] *Salem, MA*
REGATTA OF COTUIT [RES] *Centerville (Cape Cod), MA*
REIN'S NEW YORK-STYLE DELI [RES] *Vernon, CT*
RENO'S [RES] *Caribou, ME*
RESTAURANT AU PARMESAN [RES] *Quebec City, QC*
RESTAURANT BRICCO [URD] *Hartford, CT*
RESTAURANT CHEZ LEVEQUE [RES] *Montréal, QC*
RESTAURANT DAOU [URD] *Montréal, QC*
RESTAURANT DEN [RES] *Waitsfield, VT*
RESTAURANT DU BOIS-JOLI [RES] *Drummondville, QC*
RESTAURANT LE LATINI [RES] *Montréal, QC*
RESTAURANT SHO-DAN [RES] *Montréal, QC*
RHODE ISLAND QUAHOG COMPANY [RES] *Newport, RI*
RIALTO [RES] *Cambridge, MA*
RIBOLITA [RES] *Portland, ME*
RINEHART DINING PAVILLION [RES] *Bar Harbor, ME*
RISTORANTE BAROLO [RES] *Hyannis (Cape Cod), MA*
RISTORANTE DA VINCI [RES] *Montréal, QC*
RISTORANTE TOSCANO [RES] *Boston, MA*

RIVERWAY LOBSTER HOUSE [RES] *South Yarmouth (Cape Cod), MA*
RIVOLI CAFE [RES] *Toronto, ON*
ROADHOUSE CAFE [RES] *Hyannis (Cape Cod), MA*
ROCCO'S [RES] *Dartmouth, NS*
RODNEY'S OYSTER HOUSE [RES] *Toronto, ON*
ROMA, THE [RES] *Portland, ME*
ROM'S RESTAURANT [RES] *Sturbridge, MA*
ROPE WALK [RES] *Nantucket Island, MA*
ROSA FLAMINGOS [RES] *Littleton, NH*
ROSEDALE DINER, THE [RES] *Toronto, ON*
ROSEWATER SUPPER CLUB [RES] *Toronto, ON*
ROWES WHARF RESTAURANT [RES] *Boston, MA*
ROYAL PALACE [RES] *Dennis (Cape Cod), MA*
ROYAL'S 121 HEARTHSIDE [RES] *Rutland, VT*
R PLACE [RES] *Waltham, MA*
RUBIN'S KOSHER DELICATESSEN [URD] *Boston, MA*
RUNDLE'S [RES] *Stratford, ON*
SACHEM COUNTRY HOUSE [RES] *Guilford, CT*
SAGE [RES] *Boston, MA*
SAGE AMERICAN BAR & GRILL [RES] *Essex, CT*
ST. ANDREWS LIGHTHOUSE [RES] *St. Andrews, NB*
SAL'S PLACE [RES] *Provincetown (Cape Cod), MA*
SALTS [RES] *Cambridge, MA*
SALTY'S ON THE WATERFRONT [RES] *Halifax, NS*
SAM DIEGO'S [RES] *Hyannis (Cape Cod), MA*
SANDRINE'S [RES] *Cambridge, MA*
SARKIS [RES] *Toronto, ON*
SASSAFRAZ [RES] *Toronto, ON*
SAYBROOK FISH HOUSE [RES] *Old Saybrook, CT*
SCANDIA [RES] *Newburyport, MA*
SCARAMOUCHE [RES] *Toronto, ON*
SCARGO CAFE [RES] *Dennis (Cape Cod), MA*
SCRIBNER'S [RES] *Milford, CT*
SEAFARE INN [RES] *Portsmouth, RI*
SEAMEN'S INNE [RES] *Mystic, CT*
SEASCAPES [RES] *Kennebunkport, ME*
SEASONINGS [RES] *Jefferson, NH*
SEASONS [RES] *Boston, MA*
SEAWALL DINING ROOM [RES] *Southwest Harbor, ME*
SENATOR [RES] *Toronto, ON*
SENSES [RES] *Toronto, ON*
SHAKESPEARE'S DINING LOUNGE [RES] *Hamilton, ON*
SHED, THE [RES] *Stowe, VT*
SHERBORN INN [RES] *Natick, MA*
SHOPSY'S DELICATESSEN [URD] *Toronto, ON*
SIENNA [RES] *Deerfield, MA*
SILKS [RES] *Lowell, MA*
SILVERMINE TAVERN [RES] *Norwalk, CT*
SIMON PEARCE [RES] *Woodstock, VT*
SIRLOIN CELLAR [RES] *Hamilton, ON*
SIRLOIN SALOON [RES] *Manchester & Manchester Center, VT*
SIRLOIN SALOON [RES] *Rutland, VT*
SIRLOIN SALOON [RES] *Shelburne, VT*
SITAR [RES] *Ottawa , ON*
SKIPPER RESTAURANT [RES] *South Yarmouth (Cape Cod), MA*
SKYLINE [RES] *Marlboro, VT*
SNUG HARBOUR [RES] *Mississauga, ON*
SOTO RESTAURANT [RES] *Montréal, QC*
SOUVENIRS D'INDOCHINE [RES] *Montréal, QC*
SOU'WESTER [RES] *Peggy's Cove, NS*

SPENCER'S [RES] *Great Barrington, MA*
SPLENDIDO [RES] *Toronto, ON*
SPRING ROLL ON YONGE [RES] *Toronto, ON*
SQUARE RIGGER [RES] *Martha's Vineyard, MA*
STARBUCKS [RES] *Hyannis (Cape Cod), MA*
STEAKHOUSE [RES] *Wells, ME*
STEAK LOFT [RES] *Mystic, CT*
STEAK PLACE AT TUCKER HILL, THE [RES] *Waitsfield, VT*
STEVE CENTERBROOK CAFE [RES] *Essex, CT*
STONE CROCK [RES] *Kitchener-Waterloo, ON*
STONEHENGE [RES] *Ridgefield, CT*
STONEWELL [RES] *Farmington, CT*
STREET & CO [RES] *Portland, ME*
STUDENT PRINCE & FORT [RES] *Springfield, MA*
SULLIVAN STATION RESTAURANT [RES] *Lee, MA*
SUSHI BISTRO [RES] *Toronto, ON*
SWAN RIVER [RES] *Dennis (Cape Cod), MA*
SWEETWATERS [RES] *Burlington, VT*
SWISSPOT [RES] *Stowe, VT*
SZECHUAN [RES] *Montréal, QC*
TAKE SUSHI [RES] *Toronto, ON*
TAPEO [RES] *Boston, MA*
TARTUFO [RES] *Southbury, CT*
TASTE OF MAINE [RES] *Bath, ME*
TATSUKICHI [RES] *Boston, MA*
TAVERN AT HARBOR SQUARE [RES] *Nantucket Island, MA*
TEN CENTER STREET [RES] *Newburyport, MA*
TERRAMIA [RES] *Boston, MA*
TERRA RISTORANTE ITALIANO [RES] *Greenwich, CT*
THAI FLAVOUR [RES] *Toronto, ON*
THATCHER BROOK [RES] *Waterbury, VT*
THOMAS HENKELMANN [RES] *Greenwich, CT*
TIGER LILY'S NOODLE HOUSE [RES] *Toronto, ON*
TOKYO SUKIYAKI [RES] *Montréal, QC*
TOMMY COOKS [RES] *Toronto, ON*
TOP HAT SUPPER CLUB [RES] *Windsor, ON*
TOP OF THE HUB [RES] *Boston, MA*
TOPPER'S [RES] *Nantucket Island, MA*
TOQUE! [RES] *Montréal, QC*
TORCH [RES] *Boston, MA*
TRAPPER'S [RES] *Toronto, ON*
TRATTORIA IL PANINO [RES] *Boston, MA*
TREEHOUSE [RES] *Montréal, QC*
TREE HOUSE [RES] *Plymouth, NH*
TRUANTS TAVERNE [RES] *Lincoln/North Woodstock, NH*
TRUC [RES] *Boston, MA*
TRUC ORIENT EXPRESS [RES] *Stockbridge and West Stockbridge, MA*
TRUFFLES [RES] *Toronto, ON*
TUNNEL BAR-B-Q [RES] *Windsor, ON*
TURNER FISHERIES [RES] *Boston, MA*
TUSCAN GRILL [RES] *Waltham, MA*
TWO STEPS DOWNTOWN GRILLE [RES] *Danbury, CT*
UNITED BAKER'S DAIRY RESTAURANT [URD] *Toronto, ON*
UPSTAIRS AT THE PUDDING [RES] *Cambridge, MA*
VANIPHA LANNA [RES] *Toronto, ON*
VANRENSSELAER'S [RES] *Wellfleet, MA*
VAULT, THE [RES] *Boston, MA*
VERANDA AT THE YANKEE CLIPPER [RES] *Rockport, MA*
VERMONT INN [RES] *Killington, VT*
VICTORIA PARK [RES] *Niagara Falls, ON*
VICTORIA STATION [RES] *Salem, MA*

VILLA BORGHESE [RES] *Toronto, ON*
VILLAGE CAFE [RES] *Portland, ME*
VILLAGE RESTAURANT [RES] *Litchfield, CT*
VILLA TRAGARA [RES] *Waterbury, VT*
VILLA TROMBINO [RES] *Westerly, RI*
WALTER'S CAFE [RES] *Portland, ME*
WARREN HOUSE RESTAURANT AND RUPERT'S BAR, THE
    [URD] *Warren, VT*
WARREN'S LOBSTER HOUSE [RES] *Kittery, ME*
WATERFRONT [RES] *Camden, ME*
WATERLOT [RES] *Kitchener-Waterloo, ON*
WATER STREET GRILL [RES] *Williamstown, MA*
WEATHERVANE [RES] *Waterville, ME*
WEST CREEK CAFE [RES] *Nantucket Island, MA*
WEST STREET GRILL [RES] *Litchfield, CT*
WHARF & WHARF PUB [RES] *Martha's Vineyard, MA*
WHEATLEIGH [RES] *Lenox, MA*
WHISKERS [RES] *Stowe, VT*
WHISTLING SWAN [RES] *Sturbridge, MA*
WHITE BARN RESTAURANT, THE [RES] *Kennebunkport, ME*
WHITEHALL DINING ROOM [RES] *Camden, ME*
WHITE HORSE TAVERN [RES] *Newport, RI*
WHITE HOUSE [RES] *Wilmington, VT*
WHITE RAINBOW [RES] *Gloucester, MA*
WHITE'S OF WESTPORT [RES] *Fall River, MA*
WHITE STAR TAVERN [RES] *Boston, MA*
WICKACHEE [RES] *Calais, ME*
WILDCAT TAVERN [RES] *Jackson, NH*
WILLIAMSVILLE INN [RES] *Stockbridge and
    West Stockbridge, MA*
WILLIAM TELL [RES] *Waterville Valley, NH*
WINDOWS ON THE WATER [RES] *Kennebunk, ME*
WINDRIDGE INN [URD] *Jeffersonville, VT*
WINDSOR STATION [RES] *Windsor, VT*
WOODSTOCK INN [RES] *Woodstock, VT*
WYNDHURST RESTAURANT, THE [RES] *Lenox, MA*
YAMASE [RES] *Toronto, ON*
YANKEE PEDLAR [RES] *Holyoke, MA*
YARMOUTH HOUSE [RES] *South Yarmouth (Cape Cod), MA*
YE OLDE STEAK HOUSE [RES] *Windsor, ON*
YE OLDE UNION OYSTER HOUSE [RES] *Boston, MA*
YOKEN'S THAR SHE BLOWS [RES] *Portsmouth, NH*
YOKOHAMA [RES] *Gorham, NH*
YORK HARBOR INN [RES] *York, ME*
ZACHARY'S [RES] *Toronto, ON*
ZEN [RES] *Montréal, QC*
ZOLA'S GRILLE [RES] *Killington, VT*
ZUMA'S TEX-MEX CAFE [RES] *Boston, MA*

CITY INDEX

Notes

Notes

Notes

Notes

Notes